RATIFICATION OF THE TWENTY-FIRST AMENDMENT TO THE CONSTITUTION OF THE UNITED STATES

State Convention Records and Laws

COMPILED BY

EVERETT SOMERVILLE BROWN

Professor of Political Science
University of Michigan

THE LAWBOOK EXCHANGE, LTD.
Clark, New Jersey

ISBN 978-1-58477-278-1

Lawbook Exchange edition 2003, 2025

The quality of this reprint is equivalent to the quality of the original work.

THE LAWBOOK EXCHANGE, LTD.
33 Terminal Avenue
Clark, New Jersey 07066-1321

Please see our website for a selection of our other publications and fine facsimile reprints of classic works of legal history:
www.lawbookexchange.com

Library of Congress Cataloging-in-Publication Data

Ratification of the Twenty-first Amendment to the Constitution of the United States: state convention records and laws / compiled by Everett Somerville Brown.
p. cm.
Originally published: Ann Arbor: University of Michigan Press, 1938.
Includes index.
ISBN 1-58477-278-6 (cloth : alk. paper)
1. Liquor laws—United States. 2. United States. Constitution. 21st amendment. 3. United States. Constitution. 18th amendment. I. Title: Ratification of the 21st Amendment to the Constitution of the United States. II. Brown, Everett Somerville, 1886-1964.

KF3919 .R38 2002
344.73'0541—dc21 2002072857

Printed in the United States of America on acid-free paper

RATIFICATION OF THE TWENTY-FIRST AMENDMENT TO THE CONSTITUTION OF THE UNITED STATES

State Convention Records and Laws

COMPILED BY

EVERETT SOMERVILLE BROWN

Professor of Political Science
University of Michigan

ANN ARBOR

UNIVERSITY OF MICHIGAN PRESS

1938

Set up and printed, January, 1938

Printed in the United States of America

By R. R. Donnelley & Sons Company, Crawfordsville, Indiana

FOREWORD

THE Constitution of the United States provides as alternative methods for the ratification of amendments action by the state legislatures or by conventions called for that purpose in the several states; but no directions are given as to how such conventions shall be called and constituted, or how they shall proceed. As the method of ratification by conventions had never been resorted to prior to the proposal by the Congress of a repeal of the Eighteenth Amendment, there were neither authoritative directions nor precedents of any kind for the calling, organization, or functioning of the state conventions. Therefore the entire scheme for the consideration and ratification of the Twenty-first Amendment should be studied comprehensively and intensively. It relates to a fundamental feature of our organic law, the wise and successful operation of which is essential to the beneficial continuance of our present form of government, if not indeed to the substantial permanence of our national life.

By indefatigable efforts Professor Brown, with the aid of the library staff of the University of Michigan Law School, has secured copies of all available proceedings of the several state conventions, and the laws of the states relevant to the adoption of the amendment, and has carefully edited them for this volume. The faculty of the Law School believe this work to be of the utmost importance. The conditions of the period in which we live make it certain that there will be more frequent resort to constitutional amendment in the future than in the past, and in this volume there has been gathered in convenient form material indispensable for a study of the amending process. The publication of the book falls well within the terms and conditions of the great gift of the late William W. Cook, which, as he declared, he hoped would be used in aid of the preservation of American institutions. The book appears, moreover, as a most appropriate and timely contribution to the sesquicentennial celebration of the adoption of our Constitution.

HENRY M. BATES
Professor of Constitutional Law
and Dean of the Law School

PREFACE

THE collection of copies of the records of the state conventions which ratified the Twenty-first Amendment was begun shortly after ratification had been completed in 1933. The task was not an easy one. In some instances the records had been printed and copies were available in that form. In the greater number of states, however, only typewritten records were deposited in the state archives. After considerable correspondence with state officials copies of these were obtained. Several states apparently failed to preserve detailed records of the proceedings of their conventions.

The year 1937 marks the beginning of the sesquicentennial celebration of the adoption of the Constitution of the United States. By act of Congress a national commission was established to provide for suitable observance of the occasion, and a large sum of money was appropriated in support of the commission's activities. State officials and members of patriotic societies throughout the country have given the celebration their hearty support. The preservation of all records which can throw any light on the origin and development of the Constitution should be the concern of every student of American government. It seems peculiarly fitting at this time, therefore, to publish the documents contained in this volume.

For invaluable assistance in collecting these records, I am indebted to Professor Hobart R. Coffey, Law Librarian, Miss Esther Betz, Assistant Law Librarian, and Miss Rebecca Wilson, Head of the Order Department, of the University of Michigan Law Library. Reference ought also to be made to "A Check List of Records of State Conventions Held to Ratify the 21st Amendment to the Constitution of the United States," compiled by Joseph L. Andrews and Lewis W. Piacenza, and published in 29 *Law Library Journal,* No. 2 (April, 1936), 19-23.

The state laws which provided for the conventions have been compiled from the session laws of forty-three states and have been reprinted in this volume in order to make them more readily accessible. They form an indispensable part of the documentary history of the ratification of the Twenty-first Amendment.

The publication of documents so diversified inevitably raised some editorial problems. Entire consistency in arrangement and presentation of material seemed neither feasible nor desirable. A few liberties have been taken, however, in matters of form and style, but in no case do they affect the reading of the text. For example, more columns have been used in listing names of officers and delegates (although faulty alphabetizing has been kept) ; the length and the position of the dashes after the word "article" used as a center head have been standardized; a fair degree of uniformity has been striven for in the arrangement of date lines and signatures; some confusing or wrong uses of quotation marks have been simplified or corrected; and commas and periods after signatures and titles have been deleted, but no attempt has been made to introduce consistency in punctuation. The numerous inconsistencies of various kinds that still remain will make it clear to the reader that the unifying process has not been carried very far.

It seems hardly necessary to state that mistakes in English have not been corrected. Even trivial blemishes have been preserved. Fidelity to the original is shown, for example, by the retention of hyphens in "safe-guard" and "boot-legging" (pp. 175, 176). Errors in names spelled in two or more ways have been rectified when the correct spelling was known, but two spellings of one baptismal name have been kept. In the case of the Tennessee law, in the publication of which glaring misprints passed unnoticed, corrections have been tacitly made.

Several omissions of irrelevant material have been made. They are indicated at the proper places.

A small grant from the Faculty Research Fund of the University of Michigan helped to cover the cost of copying the convention records. As noted elsewhere, the volume has been published with funds derived from gifts made to the University of Michigan by the late William W. Cook. In this connection I wish to express my appreciation of the interested support and aid given me by Dean Henry M. Bates of the Law School.

The index was prepared by Alfred V. Boerner, Jr. I owe a very great debt of gratitude to Dr. Eugene S. McCartney and to his assistant, Miss Grace E. Potter, for editorial supervision and guidance of the volume through the press.

EVERETT SOMERVILLE BROWN

ANN ARBOR, MICHIGAN
September 1, 1937

CONTENTS

II. STATE LAWS PROVIDING FOR THE CONVENTIONS

I. CONVENTION RECORDS

INTRODUCTION

THE proposal by Congress that the question of the repeal of the Eighteenth Amendment should be submitted to conventions in the states, instead of to state legislatures, as in all previous instances, marked an important innovation in American Government. Americans are quite familiar with the convention idea, for it has played a large part in their political and social life. A convention drafted the Constitution itself, and conventions in the states, called for the express purpose, ratified it. Conventions have drafted state constitutions and have met to revise them. Every four years nominating conventions are called to name the presidential candidates of the respective political parties. Yet almost one hundred and fifty years elapsed between the calling of conventions in the states to ratify the Federal Constitution and the first use of the convention method in amending that document. Attempts to do so were made at various times, but to no avail.[1] The Corwin amendment of 1861, which provided that "no amendment shall be made to the Constitution which will authorize or give to Congress the power to abolish or to interfere, within any state, with the domestic institutions thereof, including that of persons held to labor or service by the laws of said State," although submitted to the legislatures of the several states, was "ratified" by a constitutional convention in Illinois,[2] an action which probably would have been held null and void if tested in the Supreme Court.[3] There was much contemporaneous criticism of the action of Illinois on two grounds: that the proposed amendment had not been submitted to conventions and that the convention in Illinois had been called, not to pass upon an amendment to the Federal Constitution, but to revise the constitution of the state.[4] Since the proposed amendment was not ratified the direct issue was never raised.

Much of the criticism of the Eighteenth Amendment was based on the claim that its ratification had not properly reflected the opinion of the people of the country. The point was constantly emphasized that no change in the Constitution vitally affecting the habits or the morals of the individual citizens ought to be made without recourse to conventions called for that specific purpose. The platforms of the two major parties in the presidential campaign of 1932 recommended that a repeal amendment be submitted to conventions. The Republican plank on this subject read: "Such an amendment should be promptly submitted to the States by Congress, to be acted upon by State conventions called for that sole purpose . . . and adequately safeguarded so as to be truly representative." The Democratic plank differed little from the Republican, so far as procedure is concerned. It was as follows: "We advocate the repeal of the Eighteenth Amendment. To effect such repeal we demand that Congress immedi-

[1] See Herman V. Ames, *The Proposed Amendments to the Constitution of the United States*, pp. 286–287; *Proposed Amendments to the Constitution*, 69th Congress, 1st Session, *Sen. Doc.*, No. 93, and 70th Congress, 2d Session, *House Doc.*, No. 551, p. 199. Also 71st Congress, 2d Session, *Sen. Doc.*, No. 78, wherein is given a compilation of applications to the Senate by the legislatures of various states for the calling of a constitutional convention for the purpose of proposing amendments. The classic treatise on the general subject is John A. Jameson, *Constitutional Conventions*. See also Everett S. Brown, "The Procedure of Ratification," 185, *Annals of the Academy of Political and Social Science*, 1936, pp. 85–91.

[2] Ames, *op. cit.*, pp. 196, 286; *Documentary History of the Constitution*, 518–519.

[3] Cf. *Hawke v. Smith*, 253 U. S. 221, 64 L. Ed. 871. *United States v. Sprague et al.*, 282 U. S. 716, 75 L. Ed. 640.

[4] See the remarks of Senator Ashurst, *Congressional Record*, 72d Congress, 2d Session, 4151.

ately propose a constitutional amendment to truly representative conventions in the States called to act solely on that subject."

In accordance with this latter pledge Senate Joint Resolution 211 was introduced by Senator Blaine of Wisconsin on December 6, 1932. It proposed submitting the question of repeal of the Eighteenth Amendment to conventions in the states.[5] The report of the Committee on the Judiciary, to which the resolution had been referred, was printed in the *Congressional Record* on January 12. The resolution had been amended by the committee to provide for the submission of the proposal of repeal to legislatures of the states, instead of to conventions.[6] This proposed change in procedure immediately aroused the criticism of officers of associations which had fought for years to persuade members of Congress to submit a repeal amendment to conventions in the states. Charles S. Rackemann, president of the Constitutional Liberty League, in a letter of January 9, 1933, to Senator Walsh of Massachusetts, wrote: "The proposal that the amendment should be referred to State legislatures comes as a complete surprise. We had supposed that the plan of referring this question, so important in its relations to the fundamental principles of the Constitution, to conventions of the people meeting in the several States had received practically unanimous support."[7] Jouett Shouse, president of the Association against the Prohibition Amendment, protested in similar vein. After referring to the platform pledges of the two major parties, he continued: "It would seem, therefore, wholly improbable that Congress in submitting the resolution would flaunt these specific platform promises and would refer it for action to legislatures instead of to conventions. . . . Moreover, it is obvious that the only method whereby popular expression on this proposition, which deals so intimately with the life and habits of the people, could be had is through the convention method of ratification."[8] Similarly, R. H. Anderson, coauthor of the repeal plank in the Democratic Party platform, pointed out that the proposed ratification by conventions was the "one phase of the prohibition question upon which sentiment was unanimous in both Republican and Democratic conventions," and declared: "In this way the question would be divorced from all others and an expression of popular sentiment obtained upon one of the most controversial issues which has ever faced this country."[9]

In explanation of the amendment of the proposal by the Committee on the Judiciary, Senator Blaine said that at the moment there were over forty state legislatures in session. If the joint resolution should be acted upon by the then session of Congress it could go to these legislatures immediately for action; if the convention method should be agreed upon as the mode of ratification it was obvious, according to Senator Blaine, that ratification would be deferred about four years, or even more.[10] He also emphasized the fact that the convention method would be an expensive one, involving large campaign expenses, as well as the cost of election of delegates and the holding of the convention. Time and expense could be saved by submitting the question to legislatures. So far as public debate was concerned, Blaine contended that the matter had been thoroughly discussed throughout the country. Replying to the suggestion that the Federal Government might pay the cost of holding an election for the purpose of electing delegates to the conventions in the respective states, Blaine said that it was the consensus of opinion of the Committee on the Judiciary that there was no constitutional authority for the Federal Government to set up machinery throughout the country for the conduct of such an election.[11]

[5] *Congressional Record,* 72d Congress, 2d Session, 64–65. [6] *Ibid.,* 1621.
[7] *Ibid.,* 1622. [8] *Ibid.,* 1622. [9] *Ibid.,* 4001. [10] *Ibid.,* 4005. [11] *Ibid.,* 4140.

Despite the opinion of the Committee and Blaine's argument in support of it, Senator Robinson of Arkansas, on February 15, 1933, offered an amendment to the resolution to change the method of ratification from state legislatures to conventions in the states.[12] In the debate which followed, much of the discussion was concerned with the power of Congress to provide by law for the election of delegates to the conventions in the states. Senator Walsh of Montana declared that such a suggestion was "contrary to the most fundamental principles upon which our dual system of government is founded."[13] In this contention he was supported by such prominent senators as Robinson of Arkansas, Borah, Ashurst, and Glass. Senator Robinson expressed the opinion that, even if the power of Congress were conceded, any attempt of Congress to exercise it would result in the defeat of ratification in a large number of states.[14] The Robinson amendment was then passed by a vote of 45 yeas to 15 nays,[15] and the proposed amendment in its final form by 63 to 23.[16]

There was little debate in the House on the method of ratification. The most pertinent remark on the subject was that of Representative Celler of New York, who stated that in his belief the word "convention" as used in Article V of the Constitution precluded and repelled the idea that the conventions in the states could be governed by congressional fiat. Each state must set up its own procedure. There might be forty-eight types of machinery, which was unfortunate, Mr. Celler said, but it could not be helped.[17] The joint resolution passed the House on February 20, 1933, by a vote of 289 to 121.[18]

The enrolled joint resolution was delivered on February 20, 1933, to the Secretary of State, Henry L. Stimson, who on the next day sent certified copies of it to the respective governors of the forty-eight states. During 1933 laws were passed in forty-three states (Georgia, Kansas, Louisiana, Mississippi, and North Dakota being the exceptions) providing for action upon the proposed amendment. During that same year conventions were held in thirty-eight states, and all except one, South Carolina, ratified the amendment. In North Carolina the electorate voted for convention delegates, but also voted against holding a convention. Montana, Nebraska, Oklahoma, and South Dakota made provision for the selection of convention delegates in 1934, but Montana alone elected delegates and held a convention in that year. Ratification of the amendment was completed on December 5, 1933, and a certificate to that effect, as required by law, was signed at 6:37 P.M. by Acting Secretary of State, William Phillips.[19]

Perhaps the most outstanding feature of the repeal conventions is their lack of a truly deliberative character. The fundamental nature of a constitutional convention was placed squarely before the justices of the supreme judicial court of Maine in the request of the Senate of that state for an advisory opinion on the question: "Must a convention assembling in a state to pass upon an amendment to the Constitution of the United States and submitted by vote of the Congress to the action of conventions in the several states be a deliberative convention?" The justices replied: "A conven-

---

[12] *Congressional Record,* 72d Congress, 2d Session, 4148–4149. [13] *Ibid.,* 4148–4149.

[14] *Ibid.,* 4154. [15] *Ibid.,* 4169. [16] *Ibid.,* 4231.

[17] *Ibid.,* 4515. [18] *Ibid.,* 4516.

[19] See *Ratification of the Twenty-first Amendment to the Constitution of the United States,* Publication No. 573, Department of State (1934). Also, Everett S. Brown, "The Ratification of the Twenty-first Amendment," *American Political Science Review,* XXIX (Dec., 1935), 1005 1017.

tion is a body or assembly representative of all the people of the state. The convention must be free to exercise the essential and characteristic function of rational deliberation. This question is, therefore, answered in the affirmative."[20]

A contrary view was expressed by the justices of the supreme court of Alabama. Replying to the question of whether the binding of delegates to abide by the result of the state referendum, as provided in the Alabama law, prevented the proposed convention from being a convention as intended by Article 5 of the Constitution of the United States, the justices advised in the negative. They held that a convention was more truly representative when expressing the known will of the people, and they were "unable to see in the federal Constitution any purpose to prohibit a direct and binding instruction to the members of the convention voicing the consent of the governed."[21]

The lack of deliberation in the conventions followed as a matter of course from the nature of the elections at which delegates were chosen. As a rule, the choice of the voters was between delegates pledged for or against repeal, although in some states provision was made for unpledged delegates. Aside from the South Carolina convention, which was composed of delegates opposed to repeal, who voted against the ratification of the proposed amendment, the delegates favoring repeal were overwhelmingly in the majority. In only six of the thirty-eight states which ratified the Twenty-first Amendment were votes registered in the conventions against repeal, and in five of these the vote was almost negligible: Oregon, 5; Montana, 4; Washington, 4; New Jersey, 2; and Michigan, 1. Indiana was the exception. There the vote stood 246 to 83, and, moreover, in the Indiana convention a definite attempt was made by the opponents of repeal to elect their slate of officers to preside over the convention. Speeches were delivered in opposition to repeal. Indiana more than any other state adhered to the idea of a deliberative convention, although even in Indiana the law required from each delegate a pledge that he would, if elected, vote in accordance with the declaration made in his petition of candidacy.[22] At the opposite extreme was Arizona, where the law providing for election of delegates to the convention declared that a delegate failing to carry out a previous pledge to vote for or against ratification would be "guilty of a misdemeanor, his vote not considered, and his office deemed vacant."[23] In Arkansas, in addition to the election of delegates to the convention, a popular referendum was held on the question of repeal. The law providing for the convention required the Secretary of State to tabulate the result of this referendum and to certify it to the chairman of the convention. The convention, in turn, was required to cast its vote for whichever side of the question had received a majority of the total number of votes cast in the entire state and immediately to adjourn.[24] In the Arkansas convention the amendment was adopted by a vote of 42 to 15, following which the unanimous vote of the convention was cast for repeal.[25] Even where there was no definite pledge the delegates were expected to

[20] *Maine Legislative Record,* 1933, pp. 598, 804; 167 *Atlantic Reporter,* 178, 180.

[21] 148 *Southern Reporter,* 107–111. See comments on these cases in 47 *Harvard Law Rev.,* 130; 18 *Minnesota Law Rev.,* 70–71; 37 *Law Notes,* 121–122. The comments in the latter two articles differ as widely as the opinions of the justices in the two cases cited.

[22] *Indiana Acts of the 78th Session, 1933,* p. 853.

[23] *Laws of Arizona, 1933,* p. 407.

[24] *Arkansas Acts of the 49th Assembly, 1933,* pp. 457–469.

[25] *Arkansas Gazette,* August 2, 1933.

follow the election returns. Their position was clearly stated by Delegate W. W. Montgomery, Jr., of Pennsylvania, in the following words:

"Men and women of this Convention, we are here under a solemn oath to do our duty. We are free agents to exercise our discretion; we are not pledged to any action. We must use our own conscience and our own judgment, as the Constitution of the United States requires that we shall do, in taking this most important action which we today are called upon to take; but in forming our judgment, irrespective of our former or present personal ideas, it seems to me proper to bear in mind that we, all of us, who are elected as delegates to this convention, asked and received the votes of the vast majority of the voters of Pennsylvania upon our representation that we favored the repeal of the Eighteenth Amendment, and that while we are free and are in duty bound to vote on this question as our conscience and our judgment dictate, we would I think be false if we fail to recognize as a very important influence in forming our conclusion, that position we took and upon which we individually invited the votes of the people, who elected us and sent us here."

President Goolrick of the Virginia convention summed the matter up tersely: "Conventions ordinarily are deliberative bodies but no deliberation is necessary where the people have spoken in plain and decisive manner on a public question, fully understood by every intelligent voter."

Because of the lack of deliberation the sessions of the conventions were correspondingly brief. New Hampshire required only seventeen minutes for her favorable action on repeal, and in no instance did the sessions of a convention extend beyond the space of a single day. Organization routine and roll calls consumed considerable time, but in this respect there were wide variations in practice. While some conventions were quite punctilious concerning the selection of committees, others regarded them as utterly unnecessary and a waste of time. So, too, did the conventions differ with respect to speeches. In some conventions there was little oratory; in others, brief extemporaneous talks were made; while still others were made the occasion of lengthy prepared addresses, principally on the history of the repeal movement.

In the speeches which were delivered certain points were commonly emphasized. One was the novelty and historical significance of the event. Governor Wilbur L. Cross of Connecticut, for example, in addressing the delegates in that state, said: "You may have been told that this is an historic occasion. Never before has this State ratified a proposed Amendment to the Constitution of the United States by means of a Convention." Similarly, attention was repeatedly called to the fact that for the first time an amendment was being repealed. Speaker after speaker in the various conventions stressed the theme of our federal form of government and deplored the granting to the National Government by the Eighteenth Amendment of a police power which ought never to have been taken from the states. For example, Henry Marshall, vice-president of the Indiana convention, declared: "So it is that we go forward, an impressive parade of the sovereign states, to bring about the orderly and inevitable repeal of a prohibition law which does not fit into the American scheme of ordered liberty; which is not in accord with the fundamentals of human rights as enunciated by the fathers. . . ." In like vein, Delegate Stricker in the Ohio convention decried "the error of writing into the Constitution a police regulation originally reserved to the states and placing same under federal control, without regard to the wishes, habits and temperament of the people of the several states, and imposing upon a large majority of the people the tyranny of a small minority with all its attendant evils."

Considerable space in the speeches was devoted to the problem confronting the states incident to their responsibility for the control of the liquor traffic. Opposition to the return of the open saloon was uniformly voiced.

Many of the conventions opened their sessions with prayer. The high note of Americanism was sounded by the Reverend Mr. Noll of the Indiana convention when he thanked God "for America, Our Flag and form of American Government, with the feeling that we should rather live in our beloved land in the most isolated district in a log house on a hillside, burn a tallow candle and draw our drinking water with an old fashioned well sweep than to live with every convenience in the most densely populated districts with all modern conveniences in any other nation on the earth."

Only a few of the conventions followed the example of Indiana in preparing a special set of rules to govern procedure. Florida did so, but also stipulated that Robert's Rules of Order should govern parliamentary practice where applicable and not inconsistent with the standing rules. Robert's Rules of Order were used in the conventions in a number of states. Others adopted the rules of their legislative bodies. Impatience with parliamentary rules of procedure and a desire to push the resolution of ratification with as little delay as possible were evident in some of the conventions. In Massachusetts Delegate Charles F. Ely moved the suspension of the rules. When President Young pointed out that as yet there were no rules, Mr. Ely moved the adoption of the rules of the House of Representatives, which was done.

Here and there delegates showed an ignorance of the niceties of parliamentary procedure. In the Washington convention when Delegate Robert Alexander moved that the convention adjourn *sine die,* Delegate W. W. Conner moved a substitute, explaining it as follows: "A great many of the States of the Union holding conventions, instead of adjourning *sine die,* have adjourned without day and that fixes it so if there is anything that might happen or that might be incorrect in our records, the chairman could call us back into session, therefore, I move you as a substitute that this convention do now adjourn without day. The only difference is when we adjourn *sine die* we absolutely cannot come back and the other is if we adjourn without day and we find anything wrong with our record the president can again call us into session." Whereupon Delegate Alexander withdrew his motion in favor of the substitute, which was then carried unanimously and the Washington convention adjourned *without day* instead of *sine die!*

When one considers that these conventions met in the year following a presidential election it is noteworthy how little political partisanship crept into their proceedings. It is true that here and there vocal tributes were paid to President Roosevelt and in one instance, in the Alabama convention, the delegates went so far as to adopt a resolution approving and endorsing the plans for relief of the administration in Washington and extending to President Roosevelt their best wishes for continued success. Yet on the whole the movement for repeal cut across party lines, as is reflected by the remark of James W. Wadsworth to Alfred E. Smith in the New York convention: "Think of you and me on the same ticket!"

A modern note was introduced by the broadcasting over the radio of the proceedings of several of the conventions, and in the New York convention popular stars of the radio world were called upon to sing the Star Spangled Banner.

In the action of these conventions was written another chapter in the history of the Constitution. They accomplished the purpose for which they were called and truly registered the will of the American people on a great national issue. Their detailed journals record the result of a popular referendum and will serve as a guide to future action in similar cases. But they also raise the important issue: Did these conventions justify the time and the expense incurred by them? Would it not be preferable to amend Article V of the Constitution and to permit the voters in the respective states to register their decision directly at the polls? A good argument for the latter alternative can be found in the journals of the repeal conventions.[26]

[26] On this point see Charles S. Lobinger, "Some Obsolete Features of Our Federal Constitution," 72d Congress, 2d Session, *Sen. Doc.*, No. 100, pp. 26–28.

ALABAMA*

PROCEEDINGS

OF

CONVENTION TO PASS UPON RATIFICATION OR REJECTION OF PROPOSED TWENTY-FIRST AMENDMENT TO THE CONSTITUTION OF THE UNITED STATES

JOURNAL

OF THE

CONVENTION TO PASS UPON

RATIFICATION OR REJECTION OF PROPOSED 21ST AMENDMENT

TO THE

CONSTITUTION OF THE UNITED STATES

Complying with the provisions and terms of "An Act to provide for holding a convention to pass upon the question of ratification or rejection of the proposed 21st amendment to the Constitution of the United States; to provide the date on which the members thereof shall be elected and the number thereof; the date on which the convention shall assemble; to provide for the holding of the election for delegates, the mode and manner thereof, and that each candidate shall pledge himself to abide by the results of the election in the State, and to provide that each voter shall cast his ballot for or against repeal of the 18th amendment and for or against ratification of the proposed 21st amendment," which was passed, the Governor's veto to the contrary notwithstanding, on March 28, 1933, there assembled in the Hall of the House of Representatives in the Capitol in the City of Montgomery on this August 8th, 1933, at 12 o'clock noon meridian, a Convention, composed of duly elected and accredited representatives of the people of Alabama, for the purpose indicated in said Act.

CONVENTION CALLED TO ORDER

The Convention was called to order by Hon. A. M. Tunstall.

PRAYER

Prayer was offered by Rev. Richard Wilkinson of the City.

---

* From a mimeographed copy. The vote by counties for and against the repeal of the Eighteenth Amendment is published in the *Alabama Official and Statistical Register 1935*, pp. 730–732.

NOMINATION AND ELECTION OF TEMPORARY CHAIRMAN

Mr. Wellborn, of Calhoun, placed in nomination Hon. Hugh D. Merrill for Temporary Chairman of the Convention and, there being no other nomination, Mr. Merrill was elected by a unanimous vote.

APPOINTMENT OF TEMPORARY OFFICERS

The Temporary Chairman then appointed as temporary officers of the Convention Mrs. Solon Jacobs, Secretary, J. E. Speight, Assistant Secretary, Thomas E. Martin, Reading Clerk, E. F. Taylor, Sergeant at Arms, E. L. Wampold, J. H. Weir and C. B. Smith, Doorkeepers.

ROLL CALL

Upon a call of the Roll the following delegates answered to their names:

Alexander
Allison
Atkins
Baldwin
Barnes
Bartlett
Benson
Bird
Boswell
Buckalew
Burke
Burr
Campbell
Carlton
Cater
Cook
Cope
Curry (Montgomery)
Curry (Pickens)
Dark
Davis
Dawkins
Deason
DeBardelaben
Dent
Dixon
Dorsey
Downing
Dozier
Duggan
Enslen
Farmer
Fletcher
Gerhardt (Miss)
Gibbs
Giddens
Gilmore
Goodwyn
Gordon
Griffin
Gullage
Hagood
Hansbrough
Haralson
Heine
Hicks
Holmes
Jackson (Jefferson)
Jackson (Lauderdale)
Jacobs (Mrs.)
Jones (Dale)
Jones (Fayette)
Jones (Limestone)
Jordan
Krudop
Lay
Legg
Lloyd
McCalman
McEachin
McGraw
McKinney
McQueen
Martin
May
Merrill
Mixon
Moore
Morgan
Morrisette
Mosely
Mullins
Norman
Oliver
Powe
Powell
Price
Pruet
Ramsey
Reynolds
Robinson
Russell
Sanders
Scarbrough
Scott (Montgomery)
Scott (Shelby)
Scott (Washington)
Sossaman
Sowell
Spragins
Springer
Stallworth
Tayloe
Thompson (Elmore)
Thompson (Jackson)
Tompkins
Toomer
Wallace
Wellborn
White
Wideman (Mrs.)
Winn
Wood (Houston)
Wood (Talladega)
Yerby
Young

(106)

CERTIFICATE OF ELECTION

I, Pete B. Jarman, Jr., Secretary of State of the State of Alabama, do hereby certify that in the election held on July 18, 1933, to pass upon the question of ratification or rejection of the proposed Twenty-first Amendment to the Constitution of the

United States, and for the election of delegates to a State convention, the vote was 100,269 for ratification and 70,631 against ratification.

I further certify that in that election the following were elected as delegates to the convention to be held in Montgomery, Alabama, on August 8, 1933:

FROM STATE AT LARGE

Evan F. Allison
S. H. Dent
Frank M. Dixon
L. A. Farmer
Shelby S. Fletcher
Mrs. Solon Jacobs
Hugh D. Merrill
J. Sanford Mullins
W. W. Ramsey
George A. Sossaman

FROM THE COUNTY

AUTAUGA COUNTY
C. E. Alexander

BALDWIN COUNTY
J. A. Baldwin

BARBOUR COUNTY
Jas. M. Springer
Guy W. Winn

BIBB COUNTY
C. C. McGraw

BLOUNT COUNTY
E. G. Hagood

BULLOCK COUNTY
R. E. L. Cope, Jr.
Hugh B. Tompkins

BUTLER COUNTY
H. P. Martin
Dr. R. H. Watson

CALHOUN COUNTY
F. D. Norman
Maximilian B. Wellborn

CHAMBERS COUNTY
E. R. Cook, Sr.
Sam H. Oliver

CHEROKEE COUNTY
E. L. McCalman

CHILTON COUNTY
Dr. V. J. Gragg

CHOCTAW COUNTY
D. D. Powe

CLARKE COUNTY
J. A. Gilmore
Richard Krudop

CLAY COUNTY
C. M. Pruet

CLEBURNE COUNTY
J. H. Gibbs

COFFEE COUNTY
Charles Dozier

COLBERT COUNTY
Allen J. Roulhac

CONECUH COUNTY
J. J. Sanders

COOSA COUNTY
D. M. White

COVINGTON COUNTY
F. B. Lloyd

CRENSHAW COUNTY
Dr. S. E. Jordan

CULIMAN COUNTY
G. C. Burke

DALE COUNTY
S. T. Jones

DALLAS COUNTY
V. B. Atkins
S. A. Reynolds
H. C. Stallworth

DEKALB COUNTY
John T. Bartlett

ELMORE COUNTY
P. J. Enslen
Dick Thompson

ESCAMBIA COUNTY
Adrian P. Downing

ETOWAH COUNTY
Carl Lay
W. R. Scarbrough

FAYETTE COUNTY
Ben E. Jones

FRANKLIN COUNTY
M. S. Hansbrough

GENEVA COUNTY
E. C. Boswell

GREENE COUNTY
W. J. Barnes, Jr.

HALE COUNTY
Cullen Morgan
Wm. E. W. Yerby

HENRY COUNTY
W. W. Dawkins
Lloyd Griffin

HOUSTON COUNTY
Alex D. Wood

JACKSON COUNTY
J. S. Benson
J. K. Thompson

JEFFERSON COUNTY
Wm. H. Burr
Cecil M. Deason
J. K. Jackson
A. D. McKinney
A. B. Powell
Lucy J. Wideman
J. S. Winters, M. C.

LAMAR COUNTY
O. E. Young

LAUDERDALE COUNTY
Alex Jackson
Henry J. Moore

LAWRENCE COUNTY
J. Kirk Howell

LEE COUNTY
I. J. Dorsey
S. L. Toomer

LIMESTONE COUNTY
Charles R. Jones

LOWNDES COUNTY
J. E. Holmes
W. P. Russell

MACON COUNTY
Wm. P. Campbell

MADISON COUNTY
John E. McEachin
Robert E. Spragins

MARENGO COUNTY
J. B. Cox
D. C. Mosely

MARION COUNTY
W. B. Mixon

MARSHALL COUNTY
L. S. Kirby

MOBILE COUNTY
W. D. DeBardelaben
James E. Duggan
Rosa Gerhardt

MONROE COUNTY
E. R. Morrisette

MONTGOMERY COUNTY
Silas D. Cater
L. C. Curry
Robert T. Goodwyn
John B. Scott

MORGAN COUNTY
B. P. Collier
E. L. Hays

PERRY COUNTY
S. A. Gordon
W. H. Tayloe

PICKENS COUNTY
M. B. Curry

PIKE COUNTY
J. F. Giddens
W. W. Haralson

RANDOLPH COUNTY
M. R. Buckalew

RUSSELL COUNTY
J. E. Bird
J. B. Hicks

SHELBY COUNTY
George Scott, Jr.

ST. CLAIR COUNTY
John R. Robinson

SUMTER COUNTY
C. H. May
Geo. A. Price

TALLADEGA COUNTY
R. Heine
T. D. Wood

TALLAPOOSA COUNTY
G. O. Dark
James Gullage

TUSCALOOSA COUNTY
Pete J. Davis
John D. McQueen, Jr.

WALKER COUNTY
A. B. Legg
J. L. Sewell

WASHINGTON COUNTY
Howard G. Scott

WILCOX COUNTY
A. C. Carlton
P. E. Wallace

WINSTON COUNTY
T. C. Burns

as shown by the returns on file and of record in this office.

In testimony whereof, I have hereunto set my hand and affixed the Great Seal of the State, at the Capitol, in the City of Montgomery, this the 8th day of August, 1933.

(*Signed*) PETE B. JARMAN, JR.
Secretary of State

OATH

Judge Leon McCord, of Montgomery, then administered the following oath to the delegates present:

"I solemnly swear that I will support the Constitution of the United States and the Constitution of the State of Alabama so long as I continue a citizen thereof, and that I will faithfully and honestly discharge the duties of the office upon which I am about to enter to the best of my ability so help me God."

On motion of Mr. Cope, which was unanimously adopted, the delegates as certified to the Convention by the Secretary of State as those duly elected be recognized as the regular and qualified delegates.

ELECTION OF PERMANENT CHAIRMAN

Mr. Scott, of Montgomery, placed in nomination Hon. S. H. Dent for Permanent Chairman.

Mr. Benson placed in nomination Hon. J. K. Thompson for Permanent Chairman.

Upon request of Mr. Thompson, Mr. Benson withdrew the name of Mr. Thompson from the nominations and Mr. Thompson then seconded the nomination of Mr. Dent.

There being no further nomination, upon a call of the roll by the Secretary, the following delegates cast their vote for Mr. Dent:

Alexander	Gilmore	Mullins
Allison	Goodwyn	Norman
Atkins	Gordon	Powe
Baldwin	Griffin	Price
Barnes	Gullage	Pruet
Bartlett	Hansbrough	Ramsey
Bird	Haralson	Reynolds
Boswell	Heine	Robinson
Buckalew	Hicks	Russell
Burke	Holmes	Scarbrough
Burr	Jackson (Jefferson)	Scott (Montgomery)
Campbell	Jackson (Lauderdale)	Scott (Shelby)
Cater	Jacobs (Mrs.)	Scott (Washington)
Cook	Jones (Limestone)	Sossaman
Cope	Jordan	Sowell
Curry (Montgomery)	Krudop	Spragins
Davis	Lay	Springer
Dawkins	Legg	Stallworth
Deason	Lloyd	Tayloe
DeBardelaben	McEachin	Thompson (Elmore)
Dixon	McGraw	Thompson (Jackson)
Dorsey	McKinney	Tompkins
Downing	McQueen	Toomer
Dozier	Martin	Wallace
Duggan	May	Wellborn
Farmer	Merrill	Winn
Fletcher	Mixon	Wood (Houston)
Gerhardt (Miss)	Moore	Wood (Talladega)
Gibbs	Morgan	Yerby
Giddens	Morrisette	Young

(90)

Mr. Dent, having received the entire vote cast, was declared duly elected as Permanent Chairman of the Convention.

The Temporary Chairman then appointed Messrs. Mullins Scott, of Montgomery, and Sossaman to escort Mr. Dent to the Chair, whereupon the Temporary Chairman, Mr. Merrill, introduced Mr. Dent to the Convention as its Permanent Chairman.

RULES

Upon motion of Mr. Goodwyn, the Rules of the House of Representatives of the Legislature of Alabama were unanimously adopted as the Rules to govern the Convention.

ELECTION OF PERMANENT SECRETARY

Mrs. Wideman placed in nomination Mrs. Solon Jacobs for Permanent Secretary.

Mr. Gullage placed in nomination Hon. John T. Bartlett for Permanent Secretary.

At the request of Mr. Bartlett, Mr. Gullage withdrew the name of Mr. Bartlett and Mr. Bartlett then seconded the nomination of Mrs. Jacobs for Permanent Secretary.

There being no further nomination Mrs. Jacobs was unanimously elected Secretary to the Convention.

COMMITTEE APPOINTED

Upon motion of Mr. Wellborn, which was unanimously adopted, the Chairman appointed one delegate from each Congressional District to compose a Committee on Resolutions as follows:

1st District—Mr. Sossaman
2nd District—Dr. Jordan
3rd District—Mr. Boswell
4th District—Mr. Wellborn (Chairman)
5th District—Mr. Mullins
6th District—Mr. McQueen
7th District—Mr. Hansbrough
8th District—Mr. Spragins
9th District—Mr. Dixon

RESOLUTION

Mr. Mosely offering the following Resolution:

Resolution 1.

WHEREAS, the Congress of the United States of America has proposed an amendment to the Constitution of the United States of America in words and figures as follows:

"That the following article is hereby proposed as an amendment to the Constitution of the United States, which shall be valid to all intents and purposes as part of the Constitution when ratified by Conventions in three-fourths of the several states:

ARTICLE ___ ___

Section 1. The 18th Article of amendment to the Constitution of the United States is hereby repealed.

Section 2. The transportation or importation into any state, territory or possession of the United States for delivery or use therein of intoxicating liquor, in violation of the laws thereof, is hereby prohibited.

Section 3. This article shall be inoperative unless it shall have been ratified as an amendment to the Constitution by Conventions in the several States, as provided in the Constitution, within seven years from the date of the submission to the states by Congress";

and

WHEREAS, said Amendment was submitted to Conventions to be called by the States either for ratification or rejection solely for that purpose; and

WHEREAS, the Legislature of Alabama in pursuance thereof did pass an Act on March 28th, 1933, entitled:

"An Act to provide for holding a convention to pass upon the question of ratification or rejection of the proposed 21st amendment to the Constitution of the United States; to provide the date on which the members thereof shall be elected and the number thereof; the date on which the convention shall assemble; to provide for the holding of the election for delegates, the mode and manner thereof, and that each candidate shall pledge himself to abide by the results of the election in the State, and to provide that each voter shall cast his ballot for or against repeal of the 18th amendment and for or against ratification of the proposed 21st amendment";

and

WHEREAS, an election was duly held on July 18th, 1933, in accordance with said Act; and

WHEREAS, this convention composed of the delegates duly elected at said election was organized in full accord with said Act of the Legislature of Alabama, and duly assembled in the House of Representatives of the State of Alabama;

Now therefore, be it resolved by the Convention of the State of Alabama duly organized and now assembled for the purpose, that said proposed amendment to the Constitution of the United States of America which is in words and figures as follows, to-wit:

"That the following article is hereby proposed as an amendment to the Constitution of the United States, which shall be valid to all intents and purposes as part of the Constitution when ratified by Conventions in three-fourths of the several states:

ARTICLE ___ ___

Section 1. The 18th article of Amendment to the Constitution of the United States is hereby repealed.

Section 2. The transportation or importation into any state, territory or possession of the United States for delivery or use therein of intoxicating liquor, in violation of the laws thereof, is hereby prohibited.

Section 3. This article shall be inoperative unless it shall have been ratified as an amendment to the Constitution by Convention in the several States, as provided in the Constitution, within seven years from the date of the submission to the states by Congress,"

be and the same is hereby approved and ratified.

Be it further resolved that a copy of said resolution duly attested by S. H. Dent, as President of said Convention, and Mrs. Solon Jacobs, as Secretary thereof, be certified to the Secretary of State of the State of Alabama for certification by him to the Secretary of State of the United States as the Act of the State of Alabama duly ratifying said Amendment to the Constitution of the United States of America.

And said Resolution was read and referred to the Committee on Resolutions.

COMMITTEE REPORT

Mr. Wellborn, Chairman of the Committee on Resolutions, reported Resolution No. 1, set out at length above, with the following notation thereon:

"The within Resolution having been referred to the Committee on Resolutions, the same has been carefully considered by said Committee, in session, unanimously approved and reported to the Convention with the recommendation that it be adopted.

"This Aug. 8, 1933

"M. B. Wellborn, Chairman"

The said Resolution No. 1 was then read again at length and put upon adoption. Those who voted in favor of the Resolution were:

Alexander	Burke	Dawkins
Allison	Burr	Deason
Atkins	Campbell	DeBardelaben
Baldwin	Cater	Dent
Barnes	Cook	Dixon
Bartlett	Cope	Dorsey
Benson	Curry (Montgomery)	Downing
Bird	Curry (Pickens)	Dozier
Boswell	Dark	Duggan
Buckalew	Davis	Enslen

Farmer
Fletcher
Gerhardt (Miss)
Gibbs
Giddens
Gilmore
Goodwyn
Gordon
Griffin
Gullage
Hagood
Hansbrough
Haralson
Hays
Heine
Hicks
Holmes
Jackson (Jefferson)
Jackson (Lauderdale)
Jacobs (Mrs.)
Jones (Fayette)
Jones (Limestone)
Jordan
Krudop
Lay
Legg
Lloyd
McCalman
McEachin
McGraw
McKinney
McQueen
Martin
May
Merrill
Mixon
Morgan
Morrisette
Mosely
Mullins
Norman
Oliver
Powe
Powell
Price
Pruet
Ramsey
Reynolds
Robinson
Russell
Scarbrough
Scott (Montgomery)
Scott (Shelby)
Scott (Washington)
Sossaman
Sowell
Spragins
Springer
Stallworth
Tayloe
Thompson (Elmore)
Thompson (Jackson)
Tompkins
Toomer
Wallace
Wellborn
White
Wideman (Mrs.)
Winn
Wood (Houston)
Wood (Talladega)
Yerby
Young

and the said Resolution having received the entire vote cast, 103 yeas, it was adopted.

RESOLUTION

The Chairman then called Hon. J. Sanford Mullins to the Chair and Mr. Dent, the Chairman, offered the following Resolution from the floor:

Resolution 2.

WHEREAS, the present administration at Washington came into power when the country was in dire distress; and

WHEREAS, Franklin D. Roosevelt immediately undertook radical measures of relief; and

WHEREAS, He is still pursuing a strenuous course of recovery for all the people;

Now therefore, be it resolved by this Convention of delegates from all parts of the State of Alabama duly assembled for the ratification of a proposed amendment repealing the 18th that we earnestly approve and endorse the plans of relief proposed by the present administration at Washington and extend to Franklin D. Roosevelt, President of the United States, our best wishes for continued success.

Resolved further, that the Secretary of this Convention be and she is hereby requested to send a copy of this Resolution to Hon. Franklin D. Roosevelt, President of the United States of America, with the compliments of this Convention."

And upon motion of Mr. Dent, the rules were suspended and the Resolution unanimously adopted.

RESOLUTION

Mr. McQueen offered the following Resolution:

Resolution 3.

"*Be it resolved* by this Convention that we hereby tender to Hon. A. M. Tunstall and his associates our sincere thanks for the successful conduct of the Campaign for the

Repeal of the 18th Amendment. The Campaign was conducted without bitterness or personalities and upon a splendid plane. We extend to Colonel Tunstall our very best wishes for continued health and happiness."
which was, on a suspension of the rules, unanimously adopted.

ADJOURNMENT

At 1 : 30 P.M., on motion of Mr. Merrill, the Convention adjourned *sine die*.

(*Signed*) S. H. DENT
Chairman

Attest:
Mrs. Solon Jacobs (*Signed*)
Secretary

ARIZONA*

JOURNAL

OF THE

PROCEEDINGS OF THE ARIZONA REPEAL CONVENTION

HELD UNDER THE PROVISIONS OF "AN ACT TO ASSEMBLE A CONVENTION

TO RATIFY OR REFUSE TO RATIFY A PROPOSED AMENDMENT

TO THE

CONSTITUTION OF THE UNITED STATES,"

APPROVED JUNE 14, 1933, IN FORCE JUNE 14, 1933

Pursuant to an act of the First Special Session of the Eleventh Legislature of the State of Arizona, entitled "House Bill No. 1," a convention of delegates elected for the purpose of ratifying or refusing to ratify the 21st Amendment to the Constitution of the United States, was called to order by His Excellency, The Governor, Honorable B. B. Mouer, at 10:00 A.M. Tuesday, September 5, 1933.

The Governor stated this was a convention called for the purpose of ratifying the 21st amendment to the Constitution of the United States, repealing the 18th amendment, and stated that he would entertain a motion for nominations for the presiding officer.

Delegate Greaber of Pima County, seconded by Delegate Flynn of Cochise County, placed in nomination the name of M. J. Hannon of Greenlee County for President.

Motion by Delegate Crothers, seconded by Delegate Flynn, that nominations be closed. Carried and Delegate Hannon was unanimously elected President.

Delegate Flynn escorted President Hannon to the chair.

The President called for nominations for the office of Secretary and stated that the secretary must be a member of the Convention.

Delegate Greaber, seconded by Delegate Flynn, placed in nomination the name of James V. Robins of Santa Cruz County, for secretary.

Motion by Delegate Flynn, seconded by Delegate Greaber, that the nominations be closed. Carried and Delegate Robins was unanimously elected Secretary.

Motion by Delegate Flynn, seconded by Delegate Crothers, that the President appoint a committee on credentials. Carried by unanimous vote and Mr. President appointed Joseph W. Berg of Yavapai County, Chester B. Campbell of Navajo County, and Thomas N. Wills of Pinal County, as Committee on Credentials.

Without objection the Convention stood at recess awaiting the report of the Committee on Credentials.

The President called the Convention to order.

The Credentials Committee submitted the following list of delegates and the Secretary of State certified that it was a true and correct list of all persons elected on August

* From a mimeographed copy.

8, 1933, as delegates to the Convention to be held in the City of Phoenix, September 5, 1933, which Convention was called for the purpose of ratifying or refusing to ratify the proposed 21st amendment to the Constitution of the United States:

Joe Crothers	Globe	Gila County
James P. Greaber	Tucson	Pima County
J. G. Flynn	Bisbee	Cochise County
Wm. P. Carr	Kingman	Mohave County
Lloyd E. Newton	Phoenix	Maricopa County
M. J. Hannon	Morenci	Greenlee County
James V. Robins	Nogales	Santa Cruz
Joseph W. Berg	Prescott	Yavapai County
T. Colter Phelps	Springerville	Apache County
Chester B. Campbell	Holbrook	Navajo County
Charles M. Proctor	Williams	Coconino County
Thos. N. Wills	Oracle	Pinal County
Frank S. Ming	Yuma	Yuma County
S. I. Allred	Safford	Graham County

Motion by Delegate Greaber, seconded by Delegate Flynn, that the report of the Credentials Committee be accepted. Carried by unanimous vote and the oath of office of each delegate was filed with the Secretary of State.

Motion by Delegate Flynn, seconded by Delegate Greaber, that a Committee on Resolutions be appointed. Carried by unanimous vote.

Mr. President appointed the following: James P. Greaber of Pima County, Joseph Berg of Yavapai County, and Lloyd E. Newton of Maricopa County, as a Committee on Resolutions.

Mr. President then stated that without objection the Convention would stand at recess awaiting report of the Committee on Resolutions.

After a recess of thirty minutes the Convention was again called to order by the President.

Delegate Greaber, Chairman of the Committee on Resolutions, presented the following resolution:

RESOLUTION NO. 1

WHEREAS, Both Houses of the Seventy-second Congress of the United States of America, by a constitutional majority of two-thirds thereof, proposed an amendment to the Constitution of the United States of America, which should be valid to all intents and purposes as a part of the Constitution of the United States when ratified by conventions in three-fourths of the states, which resolution is in words and figures following, to wit:

JOINT RESOLUTION

Proposing an amendment to the Constitution of the United States.

Resolved, by the Senate and House of Representatives of the United States of America in Congress assembled (two-thirds of each House concurring therein), That the following article is hereby proposed as an amendment to the Constitution of the United States, which shall be valid to all intents and purposes as part of the Constitution when ratified by conventions in three-fourths of the several states:

ARTICLE ___ ___

Section 1. The Eighteenth Article of Amendment to the Constitution of the United States is hereby repealed.

Section 2. The transportation or importation into any State, Territory or possession of the United States for delivery or use therein of intoxicating liquor, in violation of the laws thereof, is hereby prohibited.

Section 3. This article shall be inoperative unless it shall have been ratified as an amendment to the Constitution by conventions in the several states, as provided in the Constitution, within seven years from the date of the submission hereof to the states by the Congress.

Now, therefore, be it resolved, by the Convention, assembled pursuant to the authority of Chapter 2, Session Laws, 1933, First Special Session, entitled,

"AN ACT

To provide for conventions to pass on amendments to the Constitution of the United States proposed by the Congress of the United States for ratification by conventions in the several states, repealing Chapter 94 (House Bill 245), laws of the Eleventh Legislature, Regular Session, 1933, and declaring an emergency."

approved June 14, 1933, that said proposed Twenty-first Amendment to the Constitution of the United States of America be and the same is hereby ratified.

CERTIFICATE OF RATIFICATION

We, the undersigned, President and Secretary of the Convention, assembled pursuant to the authority of the provisions of Chapter 2, Session Laws, 1933, First Special Session, do hereby certify that the foregoing resolution ratifying the proposed Twenty-first Amendment to the Constitution of the United States of America was adopted by said Convention by the affirmative vote of all delegates present, being fourteen in number, on the 5th day of September, A.D., 1933.

(*Signed*) M. J. HANNON
President

(*Signed*) JAMES V. ROBINS
Secretary

Subscribed and sworn to before me this 5th day of September, A.D., 1933.

RUBY COULTER
Notary Public

My Commission Expires March 28, 1937.

Motion by Delegate Greaber, seconded by Delegate Flynn, that the resolution be adopted as read. Carried by the following vote:

Ayes: Crothers, Greaber, Flynn, Carr, Newton, Hannon, Robins, Berg, Phelps, Campbell, Proctor, Wills, Ming, and Allred—14.
Nays: 0

Delegate Greaber, Chairman of the Committee on Resolutions, presented the following Resolution:

RESOLUTION NO. 2

WHEREAS, Section 9 of Chapter 2, Session Laws 1933, First Special Session, provides as follows:

Section 9. The convention shall keep a journal of its proceedings in which shall be recorded the vote of each delegate on the question of ratification of the proposed amendment. Upon final adjournment the journal shall be filed with the secretary of state.

AND WHEREAS, it is necessary that this convention employ four attaches for the purpose of preparing the journal of the proceedings of the convention, as provided by the provisions of Section 9, Chapter 2, aforementioned,

Now therefore be it resolved, that the President of this convention appoint two journal clerks, one minute clerk, and one stenographer, each of whom shall receive the sum of $10.00 per day, for not exceeding three days, as compensation for their services in preparing the journal of this convention.

Motion by Delegate Greaber, seconded by Delegate Flynn, that the resolution be adopted as read. Carried by the following vote:

Ayes: Crothers, Greaber, Flynn, Carr, Newton, Hannon, Robins, Berg, Phelps, Campbell, Proctor, Wills, Ming, and Allred—14.
Nays: 0

Delegate Greaber, Chairman of the Committee on Resolutions, presented the following resolution:

RESOLUTION NO. 3

Resolved, that Secretary of this Convention, held pursuant to the provisions of Chapter 2, Session Laws 1933, First Special Session, be and is hereby authorized to have properly typed and bound the journal of the proceedings of this convention, and that the President and Secretary of this convention certify to said journal and transmit and file the same with the Secretary of State of Arizona.

Motion by Delegate Greaber, seconded by Delegate Flynn, that the resolution be adopted as read. Carried by the following vote:

Ayes: Crothers, Greaber, Flynn, Carr, Newton, Hannon, Robins, Berg, Phelps, Campbell, Proctor, Wills, Ming, and Allred—14.
Nays: 0

Pursuant to Resolution No. 2 the President appointed O. S French and W. L. Rigney, Journal Clerks, H. L. Hilbers, Minute Clerk, and Gertrude Miller, Stenographer.

The President announced that there being no further business before this Convention a motion to adjourn was in order.

Motion by Delegate Proctor, seconded by Delegate Phelps, that the Convention be adjourned *sine die.* Carried and at 1:40 P.M. Tuesday, September 5, 1933 the Convention so adjourned.

ATTEST:

We the undersigned, M. J. Hannon, President, and James V. Robins, Secretary of the Convention, do hereby certify that we have examined the above and foregoing record and minutes of the proceedings of said Convention and we and each of us certify that the said record and minutes are a true and correct report of the proceedings of said Convention.

(*Signed*) M. J. HANNON
President
(*Signed*) JAMES V. ROBINS
Secretary

Subscribed and sworn to before me this 12th day of September, 1933.
My Commission Expires March 28, 1937.

RUBY COULTER
Notary Public

Filed in the Office of the Secretary of the State of Arizona this 18th day of September, A.D. 1933 at 1:10 P.M.

JAMES H. KERBY
Secretary of State

ARKANSAS*

State of Arkansas

SEAL

ED. F. McDONALD
Secretary of State

DEPARTMENT OF STATE

LITTLE ROCK

CERTIFICATE

TO THE SECRETARY OF STATE OF THE UNITED STATES:

STATE OF ARKANSAS }
COUNTY OF PULASKI }

We, R. J. WILSON (*signed*) Chairman and

J. O. GOFF (*signed*) Secretary of a Convention called to meet in the Hall of the House of Representatives in the State Capitol in Little Rock, Arkansas on the First day of August, 1933 at ten o'clock in the forenoon, to reject or ratify the proposed Twenty-first Amendment to the Constitution of the United States, same being an amendment to repeal the Eighteenth Amendment to said Constitution did by their votes consent to and ratify the said Twenty-first Amendment to the Constitution of the United States of America.

Given under our hands as said Chairman and Secretary of said convention this the 1st day of August, 1933.

Attest:

(*Signed*) R. J. WILSON
Chairman

J. O. GOFF
Secretary

From *The Arkansas Gazette,* Little Rock, Wednesday, August 2, 1933

ARKANSAS RATIFIES WET AMENDMENT

CONVENTION CASTS STATE'S VOTE

IN FAVOR OF PROHIBITION REPEAL

Arkansas officially ratified the Twenty-first amendment to the federal constitution, repealing the Eighteenth amendment, yesterday, when the vote of delegates elected to a state convention in the special election July 18 was cast for repeal and Secretary of State

* Correspondence with Mr. Ed. F. McDonald, Secretary of State of Arkansas, disclosed the fact that the proceedings of the Arkansas convention were never filed in his office. Mr. R. J. Wilson, the president of the convention, stated that he was unable to find a copy of such record. A direct appeal to the secretary of the convention, Mr. J. O. Goff, also failed to get results. The newspaper account of the convention here presented was obtained through the courtesy of Mr. J. N. Heiskell, editor of the *Arkansas Gazette.*

Ed F. McDonald sent to the secretary of state at Washington, D. C., a certificate of the vote.

The vote in Arkansas July 18 was 67,622 for and 46,091 against repeal, and the delegates to the convention yesterday were bound by the law which called the election and convention to cast the state's vote in accordance with the majority poll on the prohibition question.

The convention was called to order by Mr. McDonald, who read the act of the 1933 legislature which called the convention, and then read the list of delegates elected July 18. The roll was called and delegates from 17 counties were marked absent. The counties which were not represented were: Boone, Calhoun, Clark, Craighead, Izard, Lafayette, Lee, Logan, Marion, Monroe, Montgomery, Ouachita, Poinsett, Searcy, Stone, Van Buren and White.

R. J. Wilson of Fayetteville, former senator from Washington county, a repeal delegate, was elected chairman and J. O. Goff of Newport, secretary. The certificate of the state's vote on repeal was read and a roll call vote was taken. The amendment was adopted by a vote of 42 to 15, and then the unanimous vote of the convention was cast for repeal.

Counties whose delegates voted against repeal in the first roll call were: Faulkner, Franklin, Fulton, Grant, Hempstead, Hot Spring, Howard, Independence, Johnson, Nevada, Pike, Polk, Randolph, Scott and Sharp.

M. L. Sigman of Monticello, president of the Roosevelt New Deal Repeal Club, and Miss Eleanor Neill, executive secretary of the United Forces for Prohibition in Arkansas, addressed the convention.

Frank McAnear of Johnson county attempted to introduce a resolution urging the legislature, in event of a special session to legalize beer, to provide for local option, but Chairman Wilson ruled him out of order.

The convention was adjourned shortly after noon.

CALIFORNIA*

PROCEEDINGS

OF THE

CONVENTION HELD IN THE STATE OF CALIFORNIA

to pass on the Amendment to the Constitution of the United States for the *Repeal of the Eighteenth Amendment thereof* and for the Prohibition of the Transportation and Importation of Intoxicating Liquor into the States and Territories in Violation of the Laws thereof.

Proposed by the Congress for Ratification by Conventions in the Several States
July Twenty-fourth 1933

We, JAMES ROLPH, JR., Governor of the State of California, and FRANK C. JORDAN, Secretary of State of said State, do hereby certify that at a Convention held in the City of Sacramento, State aforesaid, on the 24th day of July, 1933, at which twenty-two (22) duly elected delegates thereto were in attendance, the amendment to the Constitution of the United States proposed by the Congress and reading as follows:

JOINT RESOLUTION

proposing an amendment to the Constitution
of the United States

Resolved by the Senate and House of Representatives of the United States of America in Congress assembled (two-thirds of each house concurring therein), That the following article is hereby proposed as an amendment to the Constitution of the United States, which shall be valid to all intents and purposes as part of the Constitution when ratified by conventions in three-fourths of the several states:

ARTICLE ___

Section 1. The eighteenth article of amendment to the Constitution of the United States is hereby repealed.

Section 2. The transportation or importation into any State, Territory, or possession of the United States for delivery or use therein of intoxicating liquors, in violation of the laws thereof, is hereby prohibited.

Section 3. This article shall be inoperative unless it shall have been ratified as an amendment to the Constitution by conventions in the several States, as provided in the Constitution, within seven years from the date of submission hereof to the States by the Congress.

was ratified by the following vote:

For Ratification.................................Twenty-two (22)
Against Ratification..None

* From a printed form, with typed inserts.

We further certify that attached hereto is a counterpart of the record of the proceedings of said Convention on file in our respective offices.

In Witness Whereof, We have hereunto set our hands and have caused the Great Seal of the State of California to be affixed hereto this 24th day of July, 1933.

SEAL

James Rolph, Jr.
Governor of California
Frank C. Jordan
Secretary of State of California

PROCEEDINGS

Proceedings of the Convention Held in the State of California to Pass on the Amendment to the Constitution of the United States for the Repeal of the Eighteenth Amendment Thereof and for the Prohibition of the Transportation and Importation of Intoxicating Liquor Into the States and Territories in Violation of the Laws Thereof, Proposed by the Congress for Ratification by Conventions in the several States.

The Convention in the State of California to pass on the amendment to the Constitution of the United States for the repeal of the Eighteenth Amendment thereof and for the prohibition of the transportation and importation of intoxicating liquor into the states and territories in violation of the laws thereof, proposed by the Congress for ratification by conventions in the several states, was held, and the delegates thereto met, this twenty-fourth day of July, 1933, at the hour of eleven o'clock in the forenoon of said day, at the Senate Chamber in the State Capitol at Sacramento in said State, pursuant to an act of the Legislature of said State, Chapter 149 of the Statutes of 1933, and pursuant to a notice issued and given by the Secretary of State of said State selecting and appointing said time and place for the holding of said Convention and meeting of said delegates thereto, all pursuant to and in accordance with said act of the Legislature.

Honorable Frank C. Jordan, Secretary of State of the State of California, took the chair and presented and read to the Convention, and delegates thereto assembled, a Certificate under his hand and the Seal of said State, a copy whereof is as follows:

State of California
DEPARTMENT OF STATE

I, Frank C. Jordan, Secretary of State of the State of California, do hereby certify that at the special election held in said State on the twenty-seventh day of June, 1933,

H. H. Cotton
S. F. B. Morse
Sheridan Peterson
Roy M. Hardy
James M. Murphy
Felton Taylor
William B. Hornblower
Henry E. Harwood
Grace Montgomery
R. L. Hughes
B. W. Gearhart
John A. Parma
Dr. Patrick M. Walker
Eleanor Banning MacFarland
Earle C. Anthony
Gurney E. Newlin
Byron C. Hanna
Asa V. Call
John T. Gaffey
Roland G. Swaffield
Mrs. Imogene G. Hook
Edward J. Kelly

were elected delegates to the Convention in the State of California to pass on the amendment to the Constitution of the United States for the repeal of the Eighteenth Amendment thereof and for the prohibition of the transportation and importation of intoxicating liquor into the States and Territories in violation of the laws thereof, proposed by the Congress for ratification by conventions in the several states, as appears by the official returns of said election and statement thereof on file in my office.

SEAL

Witness my hand and official seal this 17th day of July, 1933.

FRANK C. JORDAN
Secretary of State

On motion of James M. Murphy duly seconded and carried, William B. Hornblower was chosen Temporary President of said Convention by the delegates assembled, and thereupon took the chair and called said Convention to order.

Thereupon on motion of Gurney E. Newlin duly seconded and carried, Grace Montgomery was chosen Temporary Secretary of said Convention and assumed his position as such Temporary Secretary.

Thereupon the Temporary President appointed a committee consisting of the following three delegates: Mrs. Imogene G. Hook, Roy M. Hardy, and Byron C. Hanna as a committee on credentials; and thereupon said committee reported to the Temporary President that they had examined the credentials as issued by said Secretary of State and they reported the following named twenty-two persons as those persons who had been certified by the said Secretary of State as the delegates regularly elected to said Convention:

H. H. Cotton
S. F. B. Morse
Sheridan Peterson
Roy M. Hardy
James M. Murphy
Felton Taylor
William B. Hornblower
Henry E. Harwood
Grace Montgomery
R. L. Hughes
B. W. Gearhart
John A. Parma
Dr. Patrick M. Walker
Eleanor Banning MacFarland
Earle C. Anthony
Gurney E. Newlin
Byron C. Hanna
Asa V. Call
John T. Gaffey
Roland G. Swaffield
Mrs. Imogene G. Hook
Edward J. Kelly

Thereupon on order of the Temporary President the Temporary Secretary called the roll of delegates to said Convention as certified by the Secretary of State of said State; and all of the foregoing twenty-two delegates answered to their names except Eleanor Banning MacFarland.

Thereupon, by nomination duly made and seconded, Wm. Moseley Jones was duly elected a delegate in place of Eleanor Banning MacFarland.

Thereupon the oath of office was administered to said delegates and each thereof by Honorable John F. Pullen, Presiding Justice of the District Court of Appeal, Third Appellate District of the State of California.

The Convention then proceeded to the election of a Permanent President.

Delegate S. F. B. Morse nominated H. H. Cotton for President of the Convention.

On motion of Delegate Edward J. Kelly, Delegate H. H. Cotton was declared elected President of the Convention.

Delegate William B. Hornblower nominated Grace Montgomery for Secretary of the Convention.

On motion of Delegate Henry E. Harwood, Delegate Grace Montgomery was declared elected Secretary of the Convention.

The President named the following committees:

Committee on Rules: Edward J. Kelly, Gurney E. Newlin, and S. F. B. Morse.

Committee on Credentials: Mrs. Imogene G. Hook, Roy M. Hardy, and Byron C. Hanna.

Committee on Resolutions: Felton Taylor, John A. Parma, and Earle C. Anthony.

Honorable William H. Metson of San Francisco, California, was, on motion duly made, seconded and unanimously carried, elected Honorary President of the Convention.

Delegate Edward J. Kelly, Chairman of the Committee on Rules, moved that Robert's Rules of Order be adopted as the Rules of this Convention. Said motion was duly adopted.

Delegate Mrs. Imogene G. Hook, Chairman of the Committee on Credentials, reported that all delegates present had been duly certified by the Secretary of State as elected delegates to this Convention, and that there were no contests.

Delegate Felton Taylor, Chairman of the Committee on Resolutions, offered the following Resolution and moved its approval, which motion was duly seconded:

WHEREAS, The Senate and House of Representatives of the United States of America in Congress assembled (two-thirds of each House concurring therein) did resolve that the following article is hereby proposed as an amendment to the Constitution of the United States, which shall be valid to all intents and purposes as a part of the Constitution when ratified by conventions in three-fourths of the several states; and

WHEREAS, The said proposed amendment reads as follows:

JOINT RESOLUTION

proposing an amendment to the Constitution
of the United States

Resolved by the Senate and House of Representatives of the United States of America in Congress assembled (two-thirds of each house concurring therein), That the following article is hereby proposed as an amendment to the Constitution of the United States, which shall be valid to all intents and purposes as part of the Constitution when ratified by conventions in three-fourths of the several states:

ARTICLE ___ ___

Section 1. The eighteenth article of amendment to the Constitution of the United States is hereby repealed.

Section 2. The transportation or importation into any State, Territory, or possession of the United States for delivery or use therein of intoxicating liquors, in violation of the laws thereof, is hereby prohibited.

Section 3. This article shall be inoperative unless it shall have been ratified as an amendment to the Constitution by conventions in the several States, as provided in the Constitution, within seven years from the date of submission hereof to the States by the Congress.

JNO. N. GARNER
Speaker of the House of Representatives

CHARLES CURTIS
Vice-President of the United States and President of the Senate

and

WHEREAS, There was duly transmitted to the Legislature of this State the said article of amendment proposed by the Congress to the Constitution of the United States; and

WHEREAS, The Legislature of this State, pursuant to law, did enact a Statute entitled,

"An act to provide for a Convention in the State of California to pass on the amendment to the Constitution of the United States for the repeal of the Eighteenth Amendment thereof and for the prohibition of the transportation and importation of intoxicating liquor into the states and territories in violation of the laws thereof, proposed by the Congress for ratification by conventions in the several States, and to call a special election for the purpose of filling the offices of delegates to such Convention in this State, and to provide that this act shall take effect immediately," which said act, having passed both Houses of the Legislature, was signed by the Governor of this State on April 21, 1933, and constitutes Chapter 149 of the Statutes of 1933 of the State of California; and said Legislature did also, pursuant to law, enact a Statute which constitutes Chapter 279 of the Statutes of 1933 of the State of California; and

WHEREAS, Pursuant to the provisions of said acts of the Legislature an election of delegates to said Convention was held in the State of California on the 27th day of June, 1933, at which said election delegates were chosen in accordance with the provisions of said Statutes; and

WHEREAS, on the 17th day of July, 1933, the Secretary of State of the State of California, pursuant to the provisions of said acts of the Legislature, issued a notice of the time and place when such Convention should meet, which notice reads as follows:

STATE OF CALIFORNIA

DEPARTMENT OF STATE

Notice of time when Convention shall meet

(Section 7, Chapter 149, Statutes of 1933)

OFFICE OF SECRETARY OF STATE
SACRAMENTO, CALIFORNIA

I, FRANK C. JORDAN, Secretary of State of the State of California, do hereby certify that:

WHEREAS, Pursuant to Chapters 149 and 279 of the Statutes of 1933 an election was held throughout the State of California on the 27th day of June, 1933, for the election of delegates to a Convention in said State to pass on the amendment to the Constitution of the United States for the repeal of the Eighteenth Amendment thereof and for the prohibition of the transportation and importation of intoxicating liquor into the states and territories in violation of the laws thereof, proposed by the Congress for ratification by conventions in the several states; and

WHEREAS, Section 7 of said Chapter 149 requires that on the fortieth day after the day of said election or as soon as the returns have been received from all counties in the State (if received within that time) the Secretary of State of said State shall compare and estimate the vote and file in his office a statement thereof and make out and deliver or transmit by mail to each person elected a certificate of election, and on the same date as the delivery or transmission by mail of such certificates of election shall deliver or transmit by mail to each person elected a delegate a notice of the time when such Convention shall meet, which time shall be on a date selected by said Secretary of State and shall be not less than five days nor more than ten days after the delivery or transmission of such notice; and

WHEREAS, The returns of said election have been received from all the counties of said State within said forty days after the date of said election, and said Secretary of State has compared and estimated the vote at said election as shown by said returns, and has determined therefrom that twenty-two delegates were elected to said Convention, and has filed in his office a statement thereof and made out and delivered or transmitted by mail on this date to each person elected a certificate of election; now, therefore,

I, FRANK C. JORDAN, Secretary of State of the State of California, pursuant to the power and authority vested in me by said act of the Legislature, do hereby select and appoint Monday, the 24th day of July, 1933, at the hour of eleven o'clock in the forenoon of said day, as the time when such Convention shall meet at the Senate Chamber at the State Capitol at Sacramento in said State.

SEAL

In Witness Whereof, I have hereunto set my hand and have caused the Great Seal of the State of California to be affixed hereto this 17th day of July, 1933.

FRANK C. JORDAN
Secretary of State of the State of California

WHEREAS, Pursuant to said notice of said Secretary of State, said Convention did meet at the time and place therein fixed, and having organized by the election of a President and Secretary, and having adopted rules governing its deliberations did proceed to consider the proposed articles of amendment; *now, therefore, be it*

Resolved, By this Convention of delegates representing the People of the State of California, duly assembled pursuant to law, that we do approve and ratify said proposed article of amendment to the Constitution of the United States for the repeal of the Eighteenth Amendment thereof and for the prohibition of the transportation and importation of intoxicating liquor into the states and territories in violation of the laws thereof, proposed by the Congress for ratification by Conventions in the several States; *and be it further*

Resolved, That the President and Secretary of this Convention shall certify the result of the votes of the delegates upon this motion and Resolution to the Governor and to the Secretary of State of the State of California, to be certified by them as directed by Section 11 of Chapter 149 of the Statutes of California for the year 1933.

Upon the direction of the President, the Secretary called the roll of delegates, and there were recorded 22 votes in the affirmative and no votes in the negative, and the Resolution was thereupon declared adopted.

On motion of Delegate S. F. B. Morse this Convention adjourned *sine die.*

H. H. COTTON
President

Attest:

GRACE MONTGOMERY
Secretary

COLORADO*

PROCEEDINGS

OF

CONVENTION CALLED IN ACCORDANCE WITH THE PROVISIONS OF CHAPTER 7 OF THE LAWS PASSED AT THE EXTRAORDINARY SESSION OF THE

TWENTY-NINTH GENERAL ASSEMBLY OF THE STATE OF COLORADO

WHICH CONVENED AUGUST 2ND, 1933

Held in the Senate Chamber, State Capitol, Denver, Colorado, Tuesday, September 26, 1933, at ten o'clock A.M.

To consider and act upon the ratification of the Proposed Amendment to the Constitution of the United States of America, providing for the repeal of the Eighteenth Amendment thereto.

HON. EDWIN C. JOHNSON, Governor of the State of Colorado, called the Convention to order at 10:00 o'clock A.M.

GOVERNOR JOHNSON: The Convention will come to order. The Very Rev. Benjamin D. Dagwell, Dean of St. John's Episcopal Cathedral, will lead us in prayer.

THE VERY REVEREND DAGWELL: Let us pray: Almighty God, Thou hast given us this good land for our heritage; we humbly beseech thee that we may always prove ourselves a people mindful of thy favors and glad to do thy will. Bless our land with honourable industry, sound learning and pure manners. Save us from violence, discord, and confusion; from pride and arrogancy, and from every evil way. Defend our liberties, and fashion into one united people the multitudes brought hither out of many kindreds and tongues. Endue with the spirit of wisdom those to whom in thy Name we entrust the authority of government, that there may be justice and peace at home, and that through obedience to thy law, we may show forth thy praise among the nations of the earth. In the time of prosperity, fill our hearts with thankfulness, and in the day of trouble, suffer not our trust in thee to fail; all which we ask through Jesus Christ our Lord. Amen.

GOVERNOR JOHNSON: This is the first time that the Federal Constitution has ever been in process of amendment by the Convention method. It is an honor to be a delegate to such a Convention.

Walter W. Lear, representative of the Secretary of State, will now read the Call for the Convention.

MR. LEAR: "A convention, the delegates to which shall be elected in the manner as herein provided, shall be held in the Senate Chamber at the Capitol, in the City and County of Denver, Colorado, on Tuesday, September 26, 1933, at the hour of ten o'clock A.M., to consider and act upon the ratification of the following amendment to

* From a photostat of the typewritten original.

the Constitution of the United States, proposed by the Congress of the United States to the several states:

Section 1. The eighteenth article of amendment to the Constitution of the United States is hereby repealed.

Section 2. The transportation or importation into any State, Territory, or possession of the United States for delivery or use therein of intoxicating liquors, in violation of the laws thereof is hereby prohibited.

Section 3. This Article shall be inoperative unless it shall have been ratified as an amendment to the Constitution by conventions in the several States, as provided in the Constitution, within seven years from the date of the submission hereof to the States by the Congress.

GOVERNOR JOHNSON: The representative of the Secretary of State will now read the Secretary of State's certifications of the delegates elected.

MR. LEAR: The following certificate which in identical terms, except as to names and specific number of votes in each case, has been officially issued by the Secretary of State to each of the following delegates who constitute the fifteen (15) delegates receiving the highest votes at the special election held September 12th, 1933, viz:

Earl Barker	Harry Lubers	Spencer Penrose
Anna Lou P. Boettcher	R. I. Lyles	Mike Rinn
Norma Wason Dodge	C. B. Moore	Charles E. Sabin
Delavan W. Gee	Edward D. Nicholson	Ray L. Sauter
W. W. Grant, Jr.	Jay M. Osborn	Sherman Williams

STATE OF COLORADO

OFFICE OF THE SECRETARY OF STATE

UNITED STATES OF AMERICA, }
STATE OF COLORADO } SS

CERTIFICATE OF ELECTION

I, CHAS. M. ARMSTRONG, Secretary of State of the State of Colorado, do hereby certify that at a meeting held at this office in the City of Denver, on the 25th day of September, A.D. 1933,

Ed C. Johnson, *Governor*

Chas. M. Armstrong, *Secretary of State* Benj. F. Stapleton, *Auditor*
Homer F. Bedford, *Treasurer* Paul P. Prosser, *Attorney General*

the State Board of Canvassers of the State of Colorado, proceeded to examine and make statements of the whole number of votes given at a special Election held on the 12th day of September, A.D. 1933, for delegates mentioned in Chapter 7, Extra Session Laws, 1933, that were voted for at said election; which statements certified to be correct, and subscribed by the members of said State Board of Canvassers, with a certificate of their determination as what persons were duly elected as Delegates, endorsed and subscribed thereon, were filed in my office.

I FURTHER CERTIFY, That by said statements and certificates of determination it appears that

____

having received the ________ highest number of votes cast at said election for any persons for the office of DELEGATE to a convention to consider and act upon the ratification of the Amendment to repeal the Eighteenth Amendment, said number being __________ votes, was by said State Board of Canvassers declared duly elected to said office.

SEAL

In testimony whereof, I have hereunto set my hand and affixed the Great Seal of the State of Colorado, at the City of Denver, this 25th day of September, A.D. 1933.

(Signed) CHAS. M. ARMSTRONG
Secretary of State
By A. G. SNEDEKER
Deputy

GOVERNOR JOHNSON: The representative of the Secretary of State will now call the roll.

MR. LEAR:

Earl Barker
Anna Lou P. Boettcher
Norma Wason Dodge
Delavan W. Gee
W. W. Grant, Jr.
Harry Lubers
R. I. Lyles
C. B. Moore
Edward D. Nicholson
Jay M. Osborn
Spencer Penrose
Mike Rinn
Charles E. Sabin
Ray L. Sauter
Sherman Williams

Mr. Lear then reported that thirteen (13) delegates had answered the roll call, and that the following delegates were absent:

Delavan W. Gee of Delta
C. B. Moore of La Jara

GOVERNOR JOHNSON: The chair recognizes W. W. Grant, Jr.

W. W. GRANT, JR.: I offer the following resolution and move its adoption:

Resolved, That the following substitutions be made for delegates who are absent and unable to be present: Mrs. M. M. Rinn of Boulder in place of Delavan W. Gee; Stuart P. Dodge of Colorado Springs in place of C. B. Moore.

The chair recognized Harry Lubers who seconded the resolution, which was put to vote and declared by the Chair to have been unanimously adopted.

Thereupon Mrs. M. M. Rinn and Stuart P. Dodge signed the following acceptances:

Denver, Colorado
September 26, 1933

TO THE PRESIDENT OF THE CONVENTION:

I do hereby accept this appointment as a delegate to the Convention being held this 26th day of September, 1933, to fill an existing vacancy, and I do agree to vote for ratification of repeal of the Eighteenth Amendment.

(*Signed*) MRS. M. M. RINN

DENVER, COLORADO
September 26, 1933

TO THE PRESIDENT OF THE CONVENTION:

I do hereby accept this appointment as a delegate to the Convention being held this

26th day of September, 1933, to fill an existing vacancy, and I do agree to vote for ratification of repeal of the Eighteenth Amendment.

(*Signed*) STUART P. DODGE

GOVERNOR JOHNSON: The election of a temporary secretary is now in order.

MRS. NORMA WASON DODGE: I nominate Mrs. Anna Lou P. Boettcher.

EDWARD D. NICHOLSON: I second the nomination.

There being no further nominations a roll call was had, the result of which disclosed Mrs. Boettcher's election as temporary secretary by the unanimous vote of all the delegates.

GOVERNOR JOHNSON: The election of a temporary chairman is now in order.

EDWARD D. NICHOLSON: I nominate Governor Johnson as temporary President.

W. W. GRANT, JR.: I second the nomination.

There being no further nominations a roll call was had, the result of which disclosed Governor Johnson's election as temporary President by unanimous vote of all the delegates.

A Committee on Credentials was thereupon dispensed with on motion by M. M. Rinn, seconded by Jay M. Osborn, and unanimously adopted, for the reason that the proper delegates and their credentials had been sufficiently established by the certification of the Secretary of State.

GOVERNOR JOHNSON: Mr. Justice E. V. Holland of the Supreme Court of Colorado will now administer the oath of office.

MR. JUSTICE HOLLAND: Delegates will raise their right hands.

MR. JUSTICE HOLLAND (continuing): Do you solemnly swear by the ever living God that you will support the Constitution of the United States and of the State of Colorado, and that you will in all things faithfully discharge the duties of the Office of Delegate to the Convention to act upon the amendment to the Constitution of the United States providing for the repeal of the Eighteenth Amendment, according to the best of your understanding and ability?

ALL THE DELEGATES: We do.

MR. JUSTICE HOLLAND: Please sign the oath.

(The Delegates sign.)

STATE OF COLORADO
CITY AND COUNTY OF DENVER } ss. Oath

I do solemnly swear by the ever living God that I will support the Constitution of the United States and of the State of Colorado, and that I will in all things faithfully discharge the duties of the Office of Delegate to the Convention to act upon the amendment to the Constitution of the United States providing for the repeal of the Eighteenth Amendment, according to the best of my understanding and ability.

(*Signed*)

Earl Barker	Harry Lubers	Spencer Penrose
Anna Lou P. Boettcher	R. I. Lyles	Mike Rinn
Norma Wason Dodge	M. M. Rinn	Charles E. Sabin
Stuart P. Dodge	Edward D. Nicholson	Ray L. Sauter
W. W. Grant, Jr.	Jay M. Osborn	Sherman Williams

GOVERNOR JOHNSON: A quorum being present, the Convention is in order for business. The first order is the election of a permanent President.

Edward D. Nicholson: I nominate Spencer Penrose of Colorado Springs as permanent President of this Convention.

Nomination seconded by Dr. Sherman Williams.

Dr. Williams: Mr. President, I move the nominations be closed, and that the Secretary be instructed to cast the unanimous ballot of this Convention for Spencer Penrose as permanent President.

Motion seconded by Harry Lubers.

Thereupon the Secretary reported that she had cast the ballot as directed, the temporary President declared Spencer Penrose to have been duly elected permanent President of the Convention and he thereupon took the chair.

President Penrose: Ladies and Gentlemen of the Convention, I am very pleased and grateful that you should have elected me as permanent President of this Convention. For seventeen years in El Paso County and in Colorado Springs I have fought the battle of repeal, practically single-handed. During much of that time there was very little encouragement to go ahead, but I felt so strongly that the principle of the Eighteenth Amendment was fundamentally wrong that in spite of unpromising prospects I could do nothing but continue.

The tyrannical efforts to enforce the Eighteenth Amendment had much to do with its present status in the eyes of the American people, although its basic fallacy would sooner or later have brought about its repeal in any event. Representatives of Colorado Springs and El Paso County in the Legislature no more truly represented that portion of the State than did members of the General Assembly from any other parts of the State. The hypocrisy to which the whole movement gave rise is now most fortunately at an end. For the future, may all attempts to tyrannize over the American people and to regulate their personal habits in a manner never intended by the fundamental law of the country break down as the Eighteenth Amendment has broken down, and end as it has ended.

President Penrose: I recognize Mrs. Dodge.

Mrs. Dodge: I nominate W. W. Grant, Jr., for Vice-President of the Convention.

The nomination was seconded by Jay M. Osborn, who also moved that the nominations be closed and that the Secretary be instructed to cast the unanimous ballot of the Convention for W. W. Grant, Jr., for Vice-President of the Convention. The Secretary reported that she had done so, and thereupon the President declared W. W. Grant, Jr., to have been duly elected Vice-President of the Convention.

President Penrose: I recognize Mr. Rinn.

Mr. Rinn: Mr. Chairman:

In the eternal fight for human rights and liberty as against fanaticism, un-Americanism and witch-burning, it is both refreshing and gratifying to observe the advancement of Colorado womanhood.

There was a time in the history of this country when the general idea was to make other people happy instead of merely "good" according to some pet formula or creed of one's own manufacturing. It was the thought of our forefathers that a reasonably happy people would be reasonably good. Unfortunately, this fundamental American doctrine was later overturned by an organized minority exercising control over cheap politicians, and as a consequence a continuing effort has been made to legislate citizens into some unique and inappropriate heaven, hypocrisy and oppression have ruled the land for years, and with the natural result that Americans came to hate and distrust one another to the extent that a breakdown in national progress and prosperity was inevitable. These evils have heretofore been tolerated by our people and despite the fact that the remedy is exceedingly simple, for as the late Ella Wheeler Wilcox truly said,

> "So many Gods, so many creeds,
> So many paths that wind and wind,
> When all this sad world needs,
> Is just the art of being kind."

The officers and members of the Colorado branch of the Women's Organization for National Prohibition Reform, co-operating with the Colorado Repeal League, have accomplished wonders in educating Colorado women who have heretofore been misled by false and hypocritical propaganda. The Women's Organization has been exceptionally fortunate in recent educational and liberal campaigns in having as its Vice-President and Denver Chairman a talented woman, whose loyalty, efficiency and untiring efforts in our progressive cause is the source of deep appreciation of all of us who have had the pleasure of being associated with her. This little lady has been constantly on the job for over a year, and although possessing exceptional intellectual faculties, she has not confined her services to executive matters only but has been untiring in office work and general effort in behalf of our cause. I have the great honor and pride of nominating as Secretary of this Convention, Mrs. Boettcher of Denver.

The nomination was seconded by Mrs. Norma Wason Dodge.

Thereupon it was moved by Dr. Sherman Williams, and seconded by Ray L. Sauter, that the nominations be closed and that the Vice-President be instructed to cast the unanimous ballot of the Convention for Mrs. Anna Lou P. Boettcher as Permanent Secretary. The Vice-President reported that he had cast the ballot as instructed, and the President declared Mrs. Anna Lou P. Boettcher to be the duly elected Secretary of the Convention.

PRESIDENT PENROSE: I recognize W. W. Grant, Jr.

W. W. GRANT, JR.: I move that the Rules' Committee be dispensed with and this Convention adopt Roberts' Rules of Order for its guidance.

The motion was seconded by Dr. Sherman Williams and unanimously carried.

PRESIDENT PENROSE: I recognize W. W. Grant, Jr.

W. W. GRANT, JR.: I nominate the following as a Resolutions' Committee;

Harry Lubers, *Chairman*
Edward D. Nicholson
Mrs. Norma Wason Dodge

Seconded by Jay M. Osborn.

Edward D. Nicholson nominated W. W. Grant, Jr.

Seconded by M. M. Rinn.

There being no further nominations, a vote was taken, and the following were declared by the President to constitute the duly elected Resolutions' Committee:

Harry L. Lubers, *Chairman*
Edward D. Nicholson, Denver
Mrs. Norma Wason Dodge, Colorado Springs
W. W. Grant, Jr., Denver

PRESIDENT PENROSE: I recognize Mr. Lubers.

MR. LUBERS: Mr. President, I offer a resolution entitled as follows:

"Resolution ratifying the Proposed Amendment to the Constitution of the United States of America, providing for the repeal of the Eighteenth Amendment thereto."

PRESIDENT PENROSE: The resolution will be referred to the Resolutions' Committee, and a recess will now be taken to permit that Committee to consider the resolution in question.

(*Recess*)

After the recess, the Convention reconvened.

PRESIDENT PENROSE: The chair recognizes Mr. Lubers.

MR. LUBERS: Mr. President, the Resolutions' Committee reports as follows:

We have considered the question of adoption of the amendment providing for the repeal of the Eighteenth Amendment to the Constitution of the United States, and we recommend the adoption of the following resolution:

RESOLUTION RATIFYING THE PROPOSED AMENDMENT TO THE CONSTITUTION OF THE UNITED STATES OF AMERICA, PROVIDING FOR THE REPEAL OF THE EIGHTEENTH AMENDMENT THERETO

WHEREAS, The Seventy-Second Congress of the United States of America, at the second session, begun and held at the City of Washington, on Monday, the 5th day of December, 1932, did pass the following resolution proposing an amendment to the Constitution of the United States, to-wit:

Joint Resolution Proposing an Amendment to the Constitution of the United States

Resolved by the Senate and House of Representatives of the United States of America in Congress assembled (two thirds of each House concurring therein), That the following article is hereby proposed as an amendment to the Constitution of the United States, which shall be valid to all intents and purposes as part of the Constitution when ratified by conventions in three fourths of the several States:

ARTICLE ——

Section 1. The eighteenth article of amendment to the Constitution of the United States is hereby repealed.

Section 2. The transportation or importation into any State, Territory, or possession of the United States for delivery or use therein of intoxicating liquors, in violation of the laws thereof is hereby prohibited.

Section 3. This article shall be inoperative unless it shall have been ratified as an amendment to the Constitution by conventions in the several States, as provided in the Constitution, within seven years from the date of the submission hereof to the States by the Congress.

JNO. N. GARNER
Speaker of the House of Representatives

CHARLES CURTIS
Vice President of the United States and President of the Senate

And

WHEREAS, There was duly transmitted to the General Assembly of this State the Said article of amendment proposed by the Congress to the Constitution of the United States; and

WHEREAS, The General Assembly of this State, pursuant to law, did enact an act entitled: "An act to provide for a convention to act upon the amendment to the Constitution of the United States, providing for the repeal of the Eighteenth Amendment," which said act, having passed both houses of the General Assembly, was approved by the Governor of this State on August 10, 1933, and constitutes Chapter 7 of the Session Laws of Colorado, Extraordinary Session, 1933; and

WHEREAS, Pursuant to the provisions of said act of the General Assembly, an election for the selection of delegates to the said convention was duly held on September 12, 1933, at which said election delegates were chosen in accordance with the provisions of said Act;

Now, therefore, be it resolved, By the convention of delegates duly elected and assembled, this 26th day of September, 1933, in the Senate Chamber at the State Capitol, in the City and County of Denver, State of Colorado, and duly organized pursuant to law: That said proposed article of amendment to the Constitution of the United States of America be and the same is hereby ratified by this convention; and

Be it further resolved, That the president and secretary of this convention shall certify the result of the votes of the delegates to the Secretary of State of this State; and

Be it further resolved, That the Secretary of State of this State shall certify the result of this vote to the Secretary of State of the United States in the manner in which amendments to the Constitution of the United States submitted to the legislature for ratification are certified.

HARRY LUBERS, *Chairman*
NORMA WASON DODGE
EDWARD D. NICHOLSON
W. W. GRANT, JR.
Constituting
The Resolutions' Committee

MR. LUBERS (*continuing*): I move the adoption of the report of the Resolutions' Committee and of the Proposed Resolution providing for the Repeal of the Eighteenth Amendment to the Constitution of the United States.

MRS. DODGE: It is a privilege to second the resolution ratifying this Amendment. It is also a responsibility. Repeal is almost won; the hour of victory is at hand. How long that hour will last depends upon whether we can take our victory with level heads.

We have an obligation to the voters who have expressed their confidence in the repeal cause by electing us as delegates to this convention. To fulfill that obligation, four responsibilities rest on us as repealists.

First, we must continue to face the liquor question, as we have done, honestly and courageously, wherever we meet it, in social life or in politics.

Second, we must work for decent legislation, realizing that after a decade and a half of social upheaval, whatever we do at the outset will be in the nature of legal experimentation; and remembering always that every law must adhere to the unchanging principles of democracy, justice for all, responsiveness to the will of the people, and economy in administration. If the Eighteenth Amendment has taught us anything, it is that legislation not founded upon these principles cannot endure.

Third, we must enact legislation which will be both an inspiration and a challenge to youth, who in the next ten years will be either the lawmakers or the law breakers of the country.

Fourth, we must work for a new form of temperance, not one which selfishly preaches the consequences of drink upon the individual, but one which emphasizes the effects upon the entire social panorama, and one which will be paralleled by a crusade to alleviate the conditions in society which drive men to drinking.

With a full knowledge of the responsibility involved in doing so, and a full confidence that the sincere repealists are equal to finishing the job, I am proud to second this resolution.

President Penrose: The Secretary will call the roll on the adoption of the report of the Resolutions' Committee.

(The Secretary calls the roll of delegates).

President Penrose: The Secretary will announce the result.

The Secretary: The result of the vote is 15 Ayes and no Nays.

President Penrose: The report of the Resolutions' Committee, embodying the passage of the resolution to repeal the Eighteenth Amendment to the Constitution of the United States has been unanimously adopted.

President Penrose (*continuing*): I now recognize Mr. Sabin.

Mr. Sabin: Mr. President, I offer the following resolution and move its adoption:

"*Resolved,* That the President and Secretary of the Convention execute and file the certificates and other papers required to be executed and filed by the law calling the Convention."

Motion seconded by Jay M. Osborn.

The roll was called and the Secretary reported the following result: 15 Ayes and no Nays.

President Penrose: The resolution is adopted. I now recognize Mrs. Boettcher.

Mrs. Boettcher: I offer the following resolution and move its adoption:

"*Resolved,* That the members of the Convention express their gratitude to Justice Holland, to Governor Johnson, to Dean Dagwell, to the Secretary of State, to the Hon. Allen Moore, to Mr. Norris Bakke, Mr. Walter Lear, Mr. William Hanrahan, and Mrs. Mary Brewster, for their courtesy in lending their services to make this Convention a success; and,

"*Be it further resolved,* That the Convention offer a special note of thanks to one whose unflagging loyalty to the repeal cause, and whose splendid cooperation and intelligent direction has contributed immeasurably to the attainment of our goal—Edward D. Nicholson."

Motion seconded by Dr. Sherman Williams and unanimously carried.

President Penrose: I now present to the Convention the Very Rev. Benjamin D. Dagwell of St. John's Cathedral, who will pronounce the Benediction.

Dean Dagwell thereupon pronounced the Benediction.

Mrs. Dodge: I move that the Convention do now adjourn.

The motion was duly seconded and unanimously carried.

President Penrose: The chair now declares the Convention adjourned *sine die.*

(Whereupon at 11:35 o'clock A.M., of September 26th, 1933, the Convention adjourned).

Approved:
Spencer Penrose (*Signed*)
President

Anna Lou P. Boettcher (*Signed*)
Secretary

CONNECTICUT*

PROCEEDINGS OF CONVENTION

CALLED IN ACCORDANCE WITH THE

PROCLAMATION OF THE GOVERNOR OF THE

STATE OF CONNECTICUT

To Consider and Act Upon the Ratification of the Amendment
to the United States Constitution Providing for
the Repeal of the Eighteenth Amendment

HELD AT

HALL OF THE HOUSE OF REPRESENTATIVES

HARTFORD, CONNECTICUT, THE 11TH DAY OF

JULY, 1933, AT 10:00 O'CLOCK A.M.

HONORABLE JOHN A. DANAHER, called the Convention to order;
HONORABLE LEONARD J. NICKERSON, Temporary Chairman
and HONORABLE LUCIUS F. ROBINSON, Chairman

SPECIAL ELECTION CONCERNING REPEAL OF EIGHTEENTH AMENDMENT

On June 20th, 1933, the Electors of the State of Connecticut in a Special Election voted on the question of whether or not the proposed amendment repealing the Eighteenth Article of Amendment of the Constitution of the United States be adopted. Those voting "For Ratification" chose the fifty delegates to a State Convention held in Hartford, July 11th, 1933. Of the fifty there were fifteen delegates at large and one elected from each of the Thirty-five Senatorial Districts in the State. The total vote "For Ratification" was Two Hundred Thirty-six Thousand Seven Hundred Forty-two. The Total vote "Against Ratification" was Thirty-four Thousand Eight Hundred Sixteen; the whole number of names on registry lists in the State was 672,728.

SEVENTY-SECOND CONGRESS OF THE UNITED STATES OF AMERICA
AT THE SECOND SESSION

Begun and held at the City of Washington on Monday, the fifth day
of December, one thousand nine hundred and thirty-two

---

* Printed.

JOINT RESOLUTION

Proposing an amendment to the Constitution of the United States

Resolved by the Senate and House of Representatives of the United States of America in Congress assembled (two-thirds of each House concurring therein), That the following article is hereby proposed as an amendment to the Constitution of the United States, which shall be valid to all intents and purposes as part of the Constitution when ratified by conventions in three-fourth of the several States:

ARTICLE __ __

Section I. The eighteenth article of amendment to the Constitution of the United States is hereby repealed.

Section 2. The transportation or importation into any State, Territory, or possession of the United States for delivery or use therein of intoxicating liquors, in violation of the laws thereof, is hereby prohibited.

Section 3. This article shall be inoperative unless it shall have been ratified as an amendment to the Constitution by conventions in the several States, as provided in the Constitution, within seven years from the date of the submission hereof to the States by the Congress.

JNO. N. GARNER
Speaker of the House of Representatives

CHARLES CURTIS
Vice-President of the United States and President of the Senate

UNITED STATES OF AMERICA

SEAL

DEPARTMENT OF STATE

To all to whom these presents shall come, GREETING:

I *Certify* That the copy hereto attached is a true copy of a Resolution of Congress entitled "JOINT RESOLUTION Proposing an Amendment to the Constitution of the United States" the original of which is on file in this Department.

In testimony whereof, I, HENRY L. STIMSON, *Secretary of State, have hereunto caused the Seal of the Department of State to be affixed and my name subscribed by the Acting Chief Clerk of the said Department, at the City of Washington, in the District of Columbia, this 21st day of February, 1933.*

HENRY L. STIMSON
Secretary of State

by P. F. ALLEN
Acting Chief Clerk

STATE OF CONNECTICUT
By His Excellency
WILBUR L. CROSS
Governor

A PROCLAMATION

WHEREAS, Special Act No. 137 of the January 1933 Session of the General Assembly of the State of Connecticut entitled "An act providing for a convention to consider the question of the adoption or rejection of an amendment repealing the Eighteenth Amendment submitted to this State by the Congress of the United States," has been duly passed and is now law, and

WHEREAS, it is provided by said Special Act that a convention for the sole purpose of ratifying or rejecting the proposed amendment to the Constitution of the United States, recited in the preamble of said Act, shall be held in the Hall of the House of Representatives in the State Capitol at Hartford on such date as shall be fixed by the Governor by proclamation, and

WHEREAS, said proposed amendment to the Constitution of the United States provides as follows:

Section 1. The 18th article of the Amendment to the Constitution of the United States is hereby repealed.

Section 2. The transportation or importation into any State, territory or possession of the United States for delivery or use therein of intoxicating liquors in violation of the laws thereof is hereby prohibited.

Section 3. This article shall be inoperative unless it shall have been ratified as an amendment to the Constitution by conventions in the several states as provided in the Constitution within seven years from the date of a submission hereof to the States by the Congress.

Now, Therefore, I, Wilbur L. Cross, Governor of the State of Connecticut, acting herein by virtue of the authority vested in me by said Special Act No. 137 of the January 1933 Session of the General Assembly, do hereby proclaim and designate Tuesday, July 11th next at ten o'clock in the forenoon Standard Time as the date and hour, and the Hall of the House of Representatives in the State Capitol at Hartford as the place for the convening and holding of such convention for the purpose of ratifying or rejecting said proposed amendment to the Constitution of the United States.

SEAL

In testimony whereof, I have caused the seal of the State to be hereunto affixed, and have hereunto set my hand, at Hartford, on this 21st day of June in the year of our Lord one thousand nine hundred and thirty-three and of the independence of the United States the one hundred and fifty-seventh.

WILBUR L. CROSS
Governor

By His Excellency's Command:
JOHN A. DANAHER
Secretary

STATE OF CONNECTICUT
SECRETARY'S OFFICE
STATE CAPITOL

JOHN A. DANAHER
Secretary of State

HARTFORD

THE HONORABLE
THE CONVENTION OF THE PEOPLE OF THE STATE OF CONNECTICUT
State Capitol
Hartford, Connecticut

Attention: THE PRESIDENT

HONORABLE SIR:

I have the honor to transmit herewith a certified copy of a Resolution passed during the second session of the 72nd Congress of the United States and entitled: "Joint Resolution proposing an Amendment to the Constitution of the United States."

This Resolution is to be submitted to the Convention called pursuant to Special Acts of the General Assembly, 1933, No. 137, approved April 10, 1933 and No. 247, approved May 5, 1933, for such action as the Convention may deem appropriate.

Faithfully yours,
JOHN A. DANAHER
Secretary

July 11, 1933

Proceedings of the Convention held in the Hall of the House of Representatives, State Capitol, Hartford, Connecticut, on Tuesday, July 11th, 1933, pursuant to the Proclamation of the Governor of the State, for the purpose of ratifying or rejecting a proposed amendment to the Constitution of the United States, repealing the Eighteenth Amendment thereto.

(10:07 A.M.)

SECRETARY OF THE STATE JOHN A. DANAHER:
The delegates will please be in order.

As the roll is called will you please answer to your names.

ROLL OF DELEGATES AT LARGE

Carol S. Chappell
Annie B. Jennings
Josephine H. Maxim
Augusta McLane Robinson
Caroline Ruutz-Rees
William Brosmith
Terrence F. Carmody
Frederick D. Grave
Charles D. Lockwood
Leonard J. Nickerson
Seldom B. Overlock
Lucius F. Robinson
Isaac D. Russell
Isaac Wolfe
William Francis Verdi

ROLL OF DISTRICT DELEGATES

District No. 1	William R. C. Corson	District No. 6	Henry Martin
District No. 2	Francis W. Cole	District No. 7	Samuel R. Spencer
District No. 3	James P. O'Brien	District No. 8	Margaret B. Clement
District No. 4	Frank D. Glazier	District No. 9	Philip Pond
District No. 5	John H. Trumbull	District No. 10	Frank S. Bergin

District No. 11	M. Frank Hope	District No. 24	Seth Low Pierrepont
District No. 12	May A. Moriarty	District No. 25	Albert E. Lavery
District No. 13	Fritz Weber	District No. 26	J. Brookes Spencer
District No. 14	Harris Whittemore, Jr.	District No. 27	Samuel F. Pryor, Jr.
District No. 15	Rowley W. Phillips	District No. 28	John Otis Fox, Jr.
District No. 16	Edward P. Egan	District No. 29	Harry S. Gaucher
District No. 17	Ralph H. Clark	District No. 30	John N. Brooks
District No. 18	Tracy Farnam	District No. 31	Donald J. Warner
District No. 19	Lee R. Robbins	District No. 32	John S. Addis
District No. 20	L. Horatio Biglow, Jr.	District No. 33	Clarence S. Wadsworth
District No. 21	William Conley	District No. 34	Peter Larsen
District No. 22	John J. Egan	District No. 35	Charles B. Pinney
District No. 23	John F. Hart		

(All delegates except May A. Moriarty responded.)

SECRETARY OF THE STATE DANAHER: Of the delegates at large fifteen have answered to their names. Of the roll of district delegates thirty-four have answered to their names.

May A. Moriarty?

(No response.)

SECRETARY OF THE STATE DANAHER: I will call upon the delegates to rise and attend upon the oath to be administered by the Chief Justice.

CHIEF JUSTICE WILLIAM M. MALTBIE OF THE SUPREME COURT: You, being chosen delegates to this Convention, for the purpose of casting your ballots upon a proposed article of amendment to the Constitution of the United States of America, do each solemnly swear that you will faithfully discharge, according to law, the duties devolving upon you to the best of your abilities, so help you God.

SECRETARY OF THE STATE DANAHER: The next order of business is the selection of a temporary clerk.

The Chair recognizes Mr. Robinson.

DELEGATE LUCIUS F. ROBINSON: May I nominate for the position of Temporary Clerk a man whose work for the repeal movement has been invaluable—Mr. J. Frederick Baker of New Haven.

SECRETARY OF THE STATE DANAHER: The name of J. Frederick Baker of New Haven is in nomination for the position of Temporary Clerk.

DELEGATE WILLIAM BROSMITH: I second the nomination.

SECRETARY OF THE STATE DANAHER: The nomination of Mr. Baker is seconded. Are there any further nominations?

(No response.)

SECRETARY OF THE STATE DANAHER: If not, the Chair will declare the nominations closed.

All those in favor of the nomination of J. Frederick Baker for the position of Temporary Clerk for this Convention will answer in the usual manner.

(Chorus of Ayes.)

SECRETARY OF THE STATE DANAHER: Contrary minds?

(No response.)

SECRETARY OF THE STATE DANAHER: Mr. Baker is declared elected.

We will next have the call of the Convention, Mr. Clerk.

Proclamation of the Governor read by Temporary Clerk Baker:

STATE OF CONNECTICUT

By His Excellency

Wilbur L. Cross

Governor

A PROCLAMATION

Whereas, Special Act No. 137 of the January 1933 Session of the General Assembly of the State of Connecticut entitled "An Act Providing for a Convention to Consider the Question of the Adoption or Rejection of an Amendment Repealing the Eighteenth Amendment Submitted to This State by the Congress of the United States," has been duly passed and is now law, and

Whereas, It is provided by said Special Act that a convention for the sole purpose of ratifying or rejecting the proposed amendment to the Constitution of the United States, recited in the preamble of said Act, shall be held in the Hall of the House of Representatives in the State Capitol at Hartford on such date as shall be fixed by the Governor by proclamation, and

Whereas, said proposed amendment to the Constitution of the United States provides as follows:

Section 1. The 18th article of the Amendment to the Constitution of the United States is hereby repealed.

Section 2. The transportation or importation into any State, territory or possession of the United States for delivery or use therein of intoxicating liquors in violation of the laws thereof is hereby prohibited.

Section 3. This article shall be inoperative unless it shall have been ratified as an amendment to the Constitution by convention in the several states as provided in the Constitution within seven years from the date of a submission hereof to the States by the Congress.

Now, therefore, I, Wilbur L. Cross, Governor of the State of Connecticut, acting herein by virtue of the authority vested in me by said Special Act No. 137 of the January 1933 Session of the General Assembly, do hereby proclaim and designate Tuesday, July 11th next at ten o'clock in the forenoon Standard Time as the date and hour, and the Hall of the House of Representatives in the State Capitol at Hartford as the place for the convening and holding of such convention for the purpose of ratifying or rejecting said proposed amendment to the Constitution of the United States.

SEAL

In testimony whereof, I have caused the seal of the State to be hereunto affixed, and have hereunto set my hand, at Hartford, on this 21st day of June in the year of our Lord one thousand nine hundred and thirty-three and of the independence of the United States the one hundred and fifty-seventh.

Wilbur L. Cross

By His Excellency's Command:

John A. Danaher

Secretary

Secretary of the State Danaher: The next order of business is the selection of a temporary chairman.

The Chair recognizes Mr. Brosmith.

Delegate William Brosmith: May I offer the following resolution—

Resolved by this Convention: That Honorable Leonard J. Nickerson, of Cornwall, a delegate at large, be and he hereby is elected Temporary Chairman of this Convention.

Delegate John N. Brooks: I second the nomination.

Secretary of the State Danaher: A resolution is offered that Leonard J. Nickerson be and is hereby elected Temporary Chairman of this Convention.

Delegate John N. Brooks: I second the nomination.

Secretary of the State Danaher: Are there any further nominations?

(No response.)

Secretary of the State Danaher: If not, the Chair declares the nominations closed.

All those in favor of the resolution will signify in the usual manner.

(Chorus of Ayes.)

Secretary of the State Danaher: Contrary minds?

(No response.)

Secretary of the State Danaher: It is so ordered—Leonard J. Nickerson is elected Temporary Chairman of the Convention.

(Temporary Chairman Leonard J. Nickerson ascends the rostrum.)

Temporary Chairman Nickerson: Ladies and Gentlemen of the Convention: It is needless for me to say to you that I am very deeply grateful for the honor you have conferred upon me in choosing me to preside over your temporary deliberations.

My duties here will be short. We are met here to carry out the mandate of the people. Speeches are not necessary.

We will now proceed to the permanent organization of the Convention.

The first business in order is the selection of a president of the Convention.

The Chair recognizes the gentleman from Plainville.

Delegate John H. Trumbull: Mr. Chairman and Members of the Convention: I desire at this time to place in nomination for President of this Convention the name of a man who has been outstanding in his opposition to the Eighteenth Amendment ever since its enactment; a man who has been fearless and courageous in his leadership in opposing it; a man who believes in the Constitution of Connecticut, and believes that Connecticut is capable of handling its own affairs in matters of prohibition without interference from the Federal government. His courage and leadership have been an inspiration to the people of the State in working for the repeal of what I think we all believe has been rather an ignoble experiment. An eminent member of the legal fraternity, and the oldest member of the Hartford County Bar, by virtue of his leadership and his activity it seems to me fitting at this time that he should be honored by being elected President of this Convention by the delegates.

It therefore gives me great pleasure, and I also consider it a great honor, to place in nomination for President of this Convention Lucius F. Robinson of Hartford.

Temporary Chairman Nickerson: You have heard the nomination made by the gentleman from Plainville. Will you remark?

(No response.)

Temporary Chairman Nickerson: Are there further nominations?

(No response.)

TEMPORARY CHAIRMAN NICKERSON: The Chair hears none.

The question is upon the motion of the gentleman from Plainville that we elect Lucius F. Robinson of Hartford as President of this Convention. Those in favor say Aye.

(Chorus of Ayes.)

TEMPORARY CHAIRMAN NICKERSON: Those opposed—No.

(No response.)

TEMPORARY CHAIRMAN NICKERSON: The Ayes have it. Mr. Robinson is unanimously elected President of this Convention. The Chair will appoint the gentleman from Plainville and Mr. Brosmith to escort President Robinson to the Chair.

(President Robinson escorted to the rostrum by Delegates John H. Trumbull and William Brosmith.)

TEMPORARY CHAIRMAN NICKERSON: Ladies and Gentlemen, it affords me great pleasure to present to you the President of this Convention—the Honorable Lucius F. Robinson of Hartford.

PRESIDENT ROBINSON: My fellow delegates—the honor which you confer by choosing me President of this history-making Convention is deeply appreciated. Perhaps the occasion justifies a few personal remarks.

From the time back in 1917 and 1918 when the nation's drift towards prohibition was ominous I perhaps more than many of you was deeply fearful that the perversion of the fundamental principles of our union of states involved in the noble experiment carried the seeds of disunion; and the tragic blunder, once committed, seemed for years irrevocable. But the night is passing and the day is breaking; and my hope, flickering dimly for years, that I might live long enough to see the dawn, is fast resolving into assurance of its realization.

While fundamentally our fight has been against the tyranny inherent in an attempt to put a free people into straight jacket, release from which might forever be denied by a paltry minority, and for the return to the peoples of the several states of their constitutional right to govern themselves in their internal affairs, our army, recruited by the tens of thousands from patriotic men and women, has become imbued with a spirit of reform militant, charging upon the ugly entanglements of a modern pharisaism with its hypocrisy and intolerance, to regain the citadels of honor and temperance and self respect. The governmental issue upon which the repeal movement is predicated has turned into a great moral issue. Soon the whole nation will be joining in the chorus of our Hymn of Victory, "Our God Is Marching On."

The injuries suffered by the nation from this grave and foolish blunder may some of them be irrevocable; but I am hopeful that there are large compensations—compensations through the education of the people both in the principles of government and in the essentials of morality; and again, compensations in a revival in the peoples of the several states, as here in our own Connecticut under the guidance of our honored Governor, of a state consciousness, and a sense of the responsibilities of citizenship.

We are met today in convention in the mode proposed by the Congress to take action upon the ratification of an amendment to the Constitution of the United States, which each House of the Congress, in the language of the Constitution, has "deemed it necessary to propose"; and which amendment in substance repeals the prohibition amendment. It is the first time in our history, I believe, of a convention so convened. It may be, as has been argued, that the framers of the Federal Constitution, in drafting this Article 5, did contemplate the election of such a convention of delegates to whose judgment, recorded after debate and due deliberation, the people would delegate the momentous decision involved in an amendment to the fundamental law. Upon this question we, the chosen delegates, have been debating and deliberating for more than twelve years, and we come into this hall prepared to record our deliberate judgment in full accord with the mandate of the electors.

In your behalf I have invited the Right Reverend E. Campion Acheson, Bishop of the Protestant Episcopal Church, to invoke upon this gathering the divine blessing.

BISHOP E. CAMPION ACHESON: O Lord, our governor, whose glory is in all the world, we commend this nation to Thy merciful care that, being guided by Thy providence, we may dwell secure in Thy peace. Grant to the President of the United States, the Governor of this State, and to all in authority, wisdom and strength to know and to do Thy will. Fill them with the love of truth, liberty and righteousness and make them ever mindful of their calling to serve this people in Thy fear. Bless our land with honorable industry, sound learning and pure manners. Save us from violence, discord and confusion, from pride and arrogance, and from every evil way. Incline our hearts ever to defend our rights and liberties and to be worthy of them. Fashion into one united people the multitudes brought hither out of many kindreds and tongues. Make justice and peace to prevail amongst us. Put Thy law into our hearts that we may show forth Thy praise among the nations of the earth.

We ask these things in His name, our Saviour, Jesus Christ. Amen.

PRESIDENT ROBINSON: The order of business has been carefully prepared by the Honorable Secretary of the State. That order of business I hold in my hand and will attempt to be guided by it.

The next suggested action is the appointment of a permanent clerk.

DELEGATE DONALD J. WARNER: I offer the following resolution—Resolved by this Convention: That J. Frederick Baker be and hereby is elected Clerk of said Convention.

PRESIDENT ROBINSON: You have heard the resolution. Is it seconded?

VOICES: I second the resolution.

PRESIDENT ROBINSON: Are you ready for the question? The question is on the adoption of the resolution presented by Delegate Warner. All in favor say Aye.

(Chorus of Ayes.)

PRESIDENT ROBINSON: Those opposed—No.

(No response.)

PRESIDENT ROBINSON: The resolution is adopted. Mr. Baker is our Permanent Clerk.

The permanent organization of this Convention will perhaps require some action dealing with the roll call. The Convention is, under the act of its creation, the judge of the election and qualifications of its own members. The Secretary of the State has presented his report of his canvass with the roll of the delegates elected.

Does the Convention desire to take any action?

DELEGATE LEONARD J. NICKERSON: I beg leave to present a resolution.

PRESIDENT ROBINSON: The clerk will read the resolution.

Clerk Baker read the following resolution:

Resolved by this Convention: That the roll of the delegates as read by the Secretary of the State be adopted as the permanent roll of the elected and qualified delegates to the Convention.

PRESIDENT ROBINSON: You have heard the resolution. Is it seconded?

DELEGATE JOHN H. TRUMBULL: I second it.

PRESIDENT ROBINSON: Will you debate it?

(No response.)

PRESIDENT ROBINSON: The question is on its adoption. Those in favor will say Aye.

(Chorus of Ayes.)

PRESIDENT ROBINSON: Those opposed—No.

(No response.)

PRESIDENT ROBINSON: The resolution is adopted.

DELEGATE LEE R. ROBBINS: I understand, Mr. President, that May Moriarty is now present attending this Convention. I move as an amendment that her name be placed upon this roll, and the same be adopted with her being present.

PRESIDENT ROBINSON: May the Chair suggest that her name is on the roll, and the only action that should be taken is the administration of the oath to Delegate Moriarty. If Delegate May Moriarty will please raise her right hand the Chief Justice will administer the oath.

(Oath administered by Chief Justice Maltbie to Delegate May A. Moriarty, in the form hereinbefore given.)

PRESIDENT ROBINSON: I think no further action is necessary as Mrs. Moriarty was on the original roll and is on the roll adopted for record by this Convention.

The act under which we are convened provides further that this Convention may adopt its own rules.

The Chair recognizes Delegate Cole from the 2nd District.

DELEGATE FRANCIS W. COLE: I offer a resolution concerning rules.

PRESIDENT ROBINSON: The Clerk will read the resolution.

Clerk Baker read the following resolution:

Resolved by this Convention: That the rules of parliamentary practice shall be the rules of this Convention insofar as the same shall be applicable.

PRESIDENT ROBINSON: You have heard the resolution. Is it seconded?

DELEGATE JOHN N. BROOKS: I second the resolution.

PRESIDENT ROBINSON: Will you debate it?

(No response.)

PRESIDENT ROBINSON: If not the question is on the adoption of this resolution. All those in favor say Aye.

(Chorus of Ayes.)

PRESIDENT ROBINSON: Those opposed—No.

(No response.)

PRESIDENT ROBINSON: The resolution is adopted.

The act provides that this Convention may elect its own president, secretary and other officers. You have elected your president and your clerk; and we are prepared to proceed with other elections if the Convention so determines.

Delegate Robbins of the 19th district.

DELEGATE LEE R. ROBBINS: I have a resolution to present.

PRESIDENT ROBINSON: The Clerk will read the resolution.

Clerk Baker read resolution as follows:

Resolved by this Convention: That William Brosmith, delegate at large from Haddam be and he hereby is elected Vice-President of this Convention.

PRESIDENT ROBINSON: You have heard the resolution. Is it seconded?

DELEGATE JOHN H. TRUMBULL: I second it.

President Robinson: The Chair will ask if there are any further nominations?

(No response.)

President Robinson: If not, the question is upon the adoption of the resolution appointing William Brosmith as Vice-President of the Convention. Those in favor will say Aye.

(Chorus of Ayes.)

President Robinson: Those opposed—No.

(No response.)

President Robinson: The Ayes have it. Mr. Brosmith is unanimously elected. It is open to him to make a speech if he wants to.

Will you take any further action in the matter of officers?

Delegate Albert E. Lavery: I present a resolution.

President Robinson: The Clerk will read the resolution.

Clerk Baker read the following resolution:

Resolved by this Convention: That Annie B. Jennings, delegate at large from Fairfield be and she hereby is elected Vice-President of this Convention.

Delegate Albert E. Lavery: I move the adoption of the resolution.

President Robinson: It is moved that the resolution be adopted.

Is the resolution seconded?

Voices: I second the resolution.

President Robinson: It is moved and seconded. Are there further nominations?

(No response.)

President Robinson: The Chair hears none. All those in favor of the adoption of the resolution say Aye.

(Chorus of Ayes.)

President Robinson: Those opposed—No.

(No response.)

President Robinson: It is a unanimous vote. Miss Jennings is elected Vice-President of the Convention.

President Robinson: Your Convention should elect a secretary.

Delegate Terrence F. Carmody: I present a resolution and move its adoption.

President Robinson: The Clerk will read the resolution.

Clerk Baker read the following resolution:

Resolved by this Convention: That Caroline Ruutz-Rees be and she hereby is elected Secretary of this Convention.

President Robinson: Is the motion seconded?

Voices: I second the resolution.

President Robinson: Will you discuss the resolution?

(No response.)

President Robinson: Are there any further nominations?

(No response.)

President Robinson: The Chair hears none. All those in favor of the passage of the resolution will say Aye.

(Chorus of Ayes.)

President Robinson: Those opposed—No.

(No response.)

President Robinson: The resolution is adopted and Miss Caroline Ruutz-Rees is Secretary of the Convention.

Will you take further action in regard to officers of the Convention?

DELEGATE JOHN J. EGAN: I have a resolution to offer pertaining of the official reporter.

Clerk Baker read the following resolution:

Resolved by this Convention: That Robert A. Winslow, Jr., be and he hereby is selected as Official Reporter of this Convention.

VOICE: I second the resolution.

PRESIDENT ROBINSON: All those in favor of the adoption of the resolution will say Aye.

(Chorus of Ayes.)

PRESIDENT ROBINSON: Those opposed—No.

(No response.)

PRESIDENT ROBINSON: The resolution is adopted; and Mr. Winslow, who has been taking notes for some time, will continue to do so.

Are there any further motions in connection with our organization?

DELEGATE JOHN J. EGAN: I offer a resolution.

PRESIDENT ROBINSON: The Clerk will read it.

Clerk Baker read the following resolution:

Resolved by this Convention: That Eugene P. Golden be and he hereby is selected as Official Messenger of this Convention.

DELEGATE JOHN J. EGAN: I move the adoption of the resolution.

A VOICE: I second the motion.

PRESIDENT ROBINSON: The question is on the adoption of the resolution. Those in favor say Aye.

(Chorus of Ayes.)

PRESIDENT ROBINSON: Those opposed—No.

(No response.)

PRESIDENT ROBINSON: It is a unanimous vote. The resolution is adopted.

Delegate Pond of the 9th District.

DELEGATE PHILIP POND: I move you, Sir, that a committee on resolutions be appointed, to consist of seven, appointed by the Chair, and that the President name the chairman of the committee.

PRESIDENT ROBINSON: Is the motion seconded?

VOICES: I second it.

PRESIDENT ROBINSON: Will you discuss the motion?

(No response.)

PRESIDENT ROBINSON: Are you ready for the question?

(No response.)

PRESIDENT ROBINSON: The Chair will put the question on Delegate Pond's motion—that the Chair appoint a Committee on Resolutions consisting of seven, and name the Chairman of the Resolution's Committee.

All those in favor of the passage of the resolution say Aye.

(Chorus of Ayes.)

PRESIDENT ROBINSON: Those opposed—No.

(No response.)

PRESIDENT ROBINSON: The Ayes have it. The motion is passed and the Chair will appoint upon the Committee on Resolutions delegate at large Isaac Wolfe as Chairman of the Committee.

Delegate at large, Charles D. Lockwood.

Delegate at large, Terrence F. Carmody.
Delegate from the 19th district, Lee R. Robbins.
Delegate from the 8th district, Margaret B. Clement.
Delegate at large, Josephine H. Maxim.
Delegate at large, Carol S. Chappell.

PRESIDENT ROBINSON: A communication from Honorable the Secretary of the State. The Convention will listen to the reading of this communication.

Clerk Baker read the following communication—

STATE OF CONNECTICUT
SECRETARY'S OFFICE
STATE CAPITOL

HARTFORD

THE HONORABLE
THE CONVENTION OF THE PEOPLE OF THE STATE OF CONNECTICUT
State Capitol
Hartford, Connecticut

Attention: The President.

HONORABLE SIR:

I have the honor to transmit herewith a certified copy of a Resolution passed during the second session of the 72nd Congress of the United States and entitled: "Joint Resolution Proposing an Amendment to the Constitution of the United States."

This Resolution is to be submitted to the Convention called pursuant to Special Acts of the General Assembly, 1933, No. 137, approved April 10, 1933 and No. 247, approved May 5, 1933, for such action as the Convention may deem appropriate.

Faithfully yours
JOHN A. DANAHER
Secretary

July 11, 1933

No. 691

UNITED STATES OF AMERICA

Department of State

To all to whom these presents shall come, GREETING:

I certify that the copy hereto attached is a true copy of a Resolution of Congress entitled, "JOINT RESOLUTION Proposing an Amendment to the Constitution of the United States," the original of which is on file in this Department.

In testimony whereof, I, Henry L. Stimson, Secretary of State, have hereunto caused the Seal of the Department of State to be affixed and my name subscribed by the Acting Chief Clerk of the said Department, at the City of Washington, in the District of Columbia, this 21st day of February, 1933.

SEAL

HENRY L. STIMSON
Secretary of State
By P. F. ALLEN
Acting Chief Clerk

SEVENTY-SECOND CONGRESS OF THE UNITED STATES

OF AMERICA

AT THE SECOND SESSION

Begun and held at the City of Washington on Monday, the fifth day of December, one thousand nine hundred and thirty-two.

JOINT RESOLUTION

Proposing an amendment to the Constitution of the United States.

Resolved by the Senate and House of Representatives of the United States of America in Congress assembled (two-thirds of each House concurring therein), That the following article is hereby proposed as an amendment to the Constitution of the United States, which shall be valid to all intents and purposes as part of the Constitution when ratified by conventions in three-fourths of the several States:

ARTICLE ___ ___

Section 1. The eighteenth article of amendment to the Constitution of the United States is hereby repealed.

Section 2. The transportation or importation into any State, Territory, or possession of the United States for delivery or use therein of intoxicating liquors, in violation of the laws thereof, is hereby prohibited.

Section 3. This article shall be inoperative unless it shall have been ratified as an amendment to the Constitution by conventions in the several States, as provided in the Constitution, within seven years from the date of the submission hereof to the States by the Congress.

JNO. N. GARNER
Speaker of the House of Representatives

CHARLES CURTIS
Vice-President of the United States and President of the Senate

PRESIDENT ROBINSON: If there is no objection the communication will be referred to the Committee on Resolutions.

The Chair hearing none, the communication is so referred.

Will the Committee on Resolutions confer and make its report at its early convenience?

CHAIRMAN WOLFE of the Committee on Resolutions: The Committee on Resolutions is ready to report, and submits the following for the consideration of the Convention.

PRESIDENT ROBINSON: The Clerk will read the report of the Committee on Resolutions.

Clerk Baker read the following Resolutions:

RESOLUTIONS

Ratifying the Proposed Amendment to the Constitution of the United States, entitled—*"Joint Resolution proposing an amendment to the Constitution of the United States."*

WHEREAS, the Seventy-second Congress of the United States of America at the second session begun and held at the City of Washington on Monday, the 5th day of December, 1932, by a constitutional majority of two-thirds thereof, has made the following proposition to amend the Constitution of the United States in the following words, to wit:

JOINT RESOLUTION

Proposing an amendment to the Constitution of the United States.

Resolved by the Senate and House of Representatives of the United States of America in Congress assembled (two-thirds of each House concurring therein),

That the following article is hereby proposed as an amendment to the Constitution of the United States, which shall be valid to all intents and purposes as part of the Constitution when ratified by conventions in three-fourths of the several States:

ARTICLE ___ ___

Section 1. The eighteenth article of amendment to the Constitution of the United States is hereby repealed.

Section 2. The transportation or importation into any State, Territory, or possession of the United States for delivery or use therein of intoxicating liquors, in violation of the laws thereof, is hereby prohibited.

Section 3. This article shall be inoperative unless it shall have been ratified as an amendment to the Constitution by conventions in the several States, as provided in the Constitution, within seven years from the date of the submission hereof to the States by the Congress.

JNO. N. GARNER
Speaker of the House of Representatives

CHARLES CURTIS
Vice-President of the United States and President of the Senate

and—

WHEREAS, Pursuant to the 3rd Section of said Joint Resolution and the provisions of Special Acts Nos. 137 and 247 of the January 1933 session of the General Assembly of the State of Connecticut, this Convention has assembled in response to the proclamation of His Excellency, The Governor of the State of Connecticut, issued under the provisions of said Special Act No. 137.

Therefore, be it resolved by this Convention that said Proposed Amendment to the Constitution of the United States of America, reading in words as follows:

Section 1. The eighteenth article of amendment to the Constitution of the United States is hereby repealed.

Section 2. The transportation or importation into any State, Territory or possession of the United States for delivery or use therein of intoxicating liquors, in violation of the laws thereof, is hereby prohibited.

Section 3. This article shall be inoperative unless it shall have been ratified as an amendment to the Constitution by conventions in the several States, as provided in the

Constitution, within seven years from the date of the submission hereof to the States by the Congress.

be and the same is hereby ratified.

Be it further resolved, That a certificate stating that this Convention has ratified the proposed amendment be executed by the President and Secretary of the Convention and transmitted to the Secretary of the State of Connecticut with the request that, pursuant to said Special Act No. 137, the Secretary of the State shall attach thereto the great seal of the State of Connecticut and transmit said certificate so sealed to the Secretary of State of the United States.

Be it further resolved, That certified copies of the foregoing preamble and this Resolution be forwarded by the Secretary of the State of Connecticut to the President of the United States, the Secretary of State of the United States, the President of the Senate of the United States and the Speaker of the House of Representatives of the United States.

Be it further resolved, That a copy of this Resolution be transmitted to the Secretary of the State of Connecticut.

PRESIDENT ROBINSON: You have heard the report of the Committee on Resolutions presented by the Committee.

The first action is on the acceptance of the report of the Committee, action upon the resolution to be taken later. Those in favor of accepting the report of the Committee, which the Chair understands to be a unanimous report, will say Aye.

(Chorus of Ayes.)

PRESIDENT ROBINSON: Those opposed—No.

(No response.)

PRESIDENT ROBINSON: The report is accepted.

The question now is upon the adoption of the resolutions. That vote, in the opinion of the Chair, should be on a roll call vote; and unless there is objection to that method of recording the votes of the delegates, which the act requires shall be noted, the Convention will proceed, after discussion of the resolutions, to vote on a roll call.

The question now on the adoption of the resolutions is before the house for its consideration and debate. Our rules adopted are merely the rules of parliamentary practice, and the Chair does not understand that they put any time limit upon oratory nor prescribe any order as between the affirmative and the negative upon this question. The Chairman of the Committee on Resolutions has precedence, I think, should he desire to speak; but the discussion is open to the delegates at this time; and it is fair for the Chair to say that after action upon these resolutions there will be no further opportunity for oratory.

Are you ready for the question?

VOICES: Question.

PRESIDENT ROBINSON: The Clerk will call the roll, and each delegate will answer to his name as called. The question is upon the adoption of the resolutions presented by the Committee on Resolutions and read by the Clerk.

DELEGATE CHARLES D. LOCKWOOD: It seems to me there ought to be a motion to adopt the resolutions; and I would so move.

DELEGATE LEONARD J. NICKERSON: Isn't the question before us on the resolutions prepared by the Committee on Resolutions? Isn't that the one now submitted to be passed upon by roll call vote?

PRESIDENT ROBINSON: Does the delegate from Cornwall raise the point of order?

DELEGATE NICKERSON: Oh, I would not like to do that.

PRESIDENT ROBINSON: The Chair thinks the point well taken.

DELEGATE LOCKWOOD: Mr. President——

PRESIDENT ROBINSON: In the opinion of the Chair, as expressed by Judge Nickerson, where the report of a committee accompanied by a resolution is before the house, it requires no specific motion by any delegate.

DELEGATE LOCKWOOD: In view of Judge Nickerson's opinion and the opinion of the learned Chairman I will withdraw the motion.

PRESIDENT ROBINSON: Then the question is upon the passage of the resolutions which you have heard read; and which, in effect and substance, ratify the proposed amendment to the Constitution of the United States, which in substance repeals the Prohibition amendment.

The Clerk will call the roll and the delegates will answer as their names are called.

Clerk Baker called the names of the delegates as follows:

DELEGATES AT LARGE

Carol S. Chappell	William Brosmith	Seldom B. Overlock
Annie B. Jennings	Terrence F. Carmody	Lucius F. Robinson
Josephine H. Maxim	Frederick D. Grave	Isaac D. Russell
Augusta McLane Robinson	Charles D. Lockwood	Isaac Wolfe
Caroline Ruutz-Rees	Leonard J. Nickerson	William Francis Verdi

DISTRICT DELEGATES

District No. 1	William R. C. Corson	District No. 19	Lee R. Robbins
District No. 2	Francis W. Cole	District No. 20	L. Horatio Biglow, Jr.
District No. 3	James P. O'Brien	District No. 21	William Conley
District No. 4	Frank D. Glazier	District No. 22	John J. Egan
District No. 5	John H. Trumbull	District No. 23	John F. Hart
District No. 6	Henry Martin	District No. 24	Seth Low Pierrepont
District No. 7	Samuel R. Spencer	District No. 25	Albert E. Lavery
District No. 8	Margaret B. Clement	District No. 26	J. Brookes Spencer
District No. 9	Philip Pond	District No. 27	Samuel F. Pryor, Jr.
District No. 10	Frank S. Bergin	District No. 28	John Otis Fox, Jr.
District No. 11	M. Frank Hope	District No. 29	Harry S. Gaucher
District No. 12	May A. Moriarty	District No. 30	John N. Brooks
District No. 13	Fritz Weber	District No. 31	Donald J. Warner
District No. 14	Harris Whittemore, Jr.	District No. 32	John S. Addis
District No. 15	Rowley W. Phillips	District No. 33	Clarence S. Wadsworth
District No. 16	Edward P. Egan	District No. 34	Peter Larsen
District No. 17	Ralph H. Clark	District No. 35	Charles B. Pinney
District No. 18	Tracy Farnam		

PRESIDENT ROBINSON: The vote is unanimous in the affirmative for the adoption of the resolutions; the fifteen delegates at large and the thirty-five district delegates all having voted. The resolutions are declared adopted.

DELEGATE FRANK S. BERGIN: I move you, Mr. President, that the Journal of the Convention be filed by the Clerk with the Secretary of the State.

PRESIDENT ROBINSON: Is the motion seconded?

DELEGATE JOHN H. TRUMBULL: I second the motion.

PRESIDENT ROBINSON: Will you discuss it?

(No response.)

PRESIDENT ROBINSON: All those in favor of the motion will say Aye.

(Chorus of Ayes.)

PRESIDENT ROBINSON: Those opposed—No.

(No response.)

PRESIDENT ROBINSON: The motion is carried.

Is there any other formal or informal business before the Convention? The Chair knows of no formal business.

DELEGATE W. R. C. CORSON: I move you, Sir, for the appointment of a committee by the President to wait upon His Excellency the Governor to advise him of the action of the Convention and to invite his appearance.

PRESIDENT ROBINSON: You have heard the motion of Delegate Corson. Is it seconded?

VOICES: I second the motion.

PRESIDENT ROBINSON: All those in favor of the motion will say Aye.

(Chorus of Ayes.)

PRESIDENT ROBINSON: Those opposed—No.

(No response.)

PRESIDENT ROBINSON: It is a vote. The Chair will appoint as the Committee to wait upon His Excellency——

John H. Trumbull.

Mrs. Augusta McLane Robinson.

Frank S. Bergin.

Will the Committee proceed to carry our invitation to His Excellency?

(Governor Cross escorted to the rostrum.)

PRESIDENT ROBINSON: Delegates of the Convention, His Excellency the Governor.

GOVERNOR WILBUR L. CROSS: Mr. President, and Members of the Convention:

The day has arrived and the event is passing into Connecticut History. A Committee of your honorable body has just informed me that following the deliberations of the morning you have ratified a proposed article of amendment to the Constitution of the United States, the first section of which would repeal the Eighteenth Article of Amendment to the fundamental law of the land, thus restoring to the several States of the Union full control within their borders of the manufacture and sale of alcoholic liquors. In so doing, you have acted as representatives of a large majority of the electors of this State who cast their ballots in the recent special election.

Your vote, I understand, was unanimous. The question at issue, which has been the football of political manipulation for more than a decade, you have come to regard as an issue transcending politics. Democrats and Republicans, you have sat side by side and voted the same way. In the light of my experience with the General Assembly this unanimity seems most extraordinary. You Democrats and Republicans have come together much as our forefathers came together in the fierce battle of 1860, when Abraham Lincoln was elected President of the United States on a platform which was based in its prime essentials on the political philosophy of Thomas Jefferson. Abraham Lincoln, whom you Republicans imagine that you vote for every four years; Thomas Jefferson whom we Democrats likewise imagine that we vote for as often as once in four years. It is a great political delusion which we think still helps us to win elections and keeps us in good humor like reading the fairy tale of Alice in Wonderland.

Once more it has been found that fundamental issues are never political in any narrow sense of that word. Irrespective of party affiliations, the people of Connecticut still hold, as Jefferson, and Lincoln after him held, "that the maintenance inviolate of the rights of the States, and especially the right of each State, to order and control its own domestic institutions according to its own judgment exclusively, is essential to that balance of power on which the perfection and endurance of our political fabric depend." These last words are not mine; they are taken from the Republican Platform of 1860, as quoted by Lincoln in his First Inaugural.

Not being present this morning, I am in danger of repeating what others have said here. You may have been told that this is an historic occasion. Never before has this State ratified a proposed Amendment to the Constitution of the United States by means of a Convention. In the Convention which framed the Federal Constitution under the guidance of Washington there was a difference of opinion on the best way of amending the Constitution. Eventually it was left to Congress to provide in any case either of two modes at its discretion. Ratification by State Legislatures may be the easier and simpler way, but in the election of members to a legislature there are, however, almost always involved a number of questions, so that there can rarely be a clean-cut decision on any one issue. Doubt generally remains. It was mainly for this reason that Lincoln expressed a preference for the convention mode of ratification as more nearly coming to the direct voice of the people. You recall his remark to the effect that God must love the common people else he would not have made so many of them. Had Lincoln lived, it is probable that his views on ratification would have prevailed during the Reconstruction Period and thereafter, down to the present day. Though there were many abstentions in the recent election, it undoubtedly shows nearly where Connecticut stands on the question of Prohibition. Many patriotic citizens would continue the experiment further, but a large majority of equally patriotic citizens are firmly convinced that the experiment has long since been an utter failure.

Both groups, however, are in full agreement on a most essential point. It is that the manufacture and sale of all alcoholic liquors in the State shall be, so far as is humanly possible, under strict control, free from sinister influences. The members of the Commission whom I appointed under the authority of the General Assembly, to submit a plan of control were representative men in law, business, social, and political science, and the two branches of the Church, Catholic and Protestant. Their recommendation of state-wide control, in distinction from the old-time county or town control, with which were associated many abuses, was adopted by the General Assembly to the satisfaction of the great body of our citizens. It is, I believe, the best liquor control law now on the statute books of any State in the Union. The commission of three members whom I afterwards appointed to administer the law under the courts comprises one Democrat and two Republicans. One is a former Lieutenant-Governor of the State, another is the United States District Attorney for Connecticut, and the third is the majority leader of the State Senate. If there are anywhere better men for the arduous work they have undertaken, I don't know where they are.

I assure you I account it a rare privilege to have been able as Governor of this State to play a role in an endeavor to free the people from the incubus of national Prohibition and its attendant evils. From the beginning it has been my conviction that the Eighteenth Amendment was a colossal mistake.

The Federal Constitution should never be amended except in cases of necessity, and then only within the sphere of the purposes for which it originated. The Federal Constitution is no place for the fixed embodiment of experimental legislation, which, at best, belongs to Congress or to State Governments, so that if it does not work, it may be quickly repealed instead of being nullified to the detriment of the enforcement of all law.

Militant advocates of Prohibition believed that if prohibition were once put into the Federal Constitution, it would remain there forever. Presumption was in their favor; for no Amendment to the Constitution has ever been repealed though some have been partially nullified. But contrary to expectation the Eighteenth Amendment seems to be going fast. I look forward to the time, not far off, when it shall be completely gone, leaving only the memory of it behind. When that time comes, you men and women who have fought the good fight in State and National organizations may furl your banners and lay them aside among memorabilia for the edification as well as the entertainment of your descendants. Those descendants, I trust, will have learned the lesson that experiments in social legislation, however noble they may be in intent, lie outside the realm of fundamental law.

In conclusion, I thank you for the service you have this day rendered to the people of the State. Connecticut has long been known as the land of steady habits. But too much reliance should not be placed upon tradition. The tradition can be maintained only by the earnest collective endeavor of us all, whether classed as wets or as drys, endeavor to promote temperance or abstinance as the case may be; for excess in the use of alcoholic liquors means moral and physical impairment and often human waste and human wreckage. A stupendous task awaits us. Our statutes for control must at all times represent the best public opinion in the existing mores. And these statutes must be enforced. It is expected that every good citizen will be vigilant and do his duty when he observes that the law is being disregarded. Only that way lies hopes of keeping this beautiful old State of Connecticut on her steady course.

And now, as we enter upon new times, I wish you, and the Commonwealth which we all love, prosperity and happy years. And again I thank you for the courtesy of the invitation to say a few words to you.

PRESIDENT ROBINSON: May I express to His Excellency our thanks and the deep appreciation of the Convention.

His Excellency wishes me to say that the delegates who have been invited by him—and that means all the delegates to the Convention—to luncheon at the Hartford Club are asked, after the adjournment of this Convention, to go over to the Club as speedily as possible, as the luncheon hour will be advanced to meet the convenience of the delegates. The program calls for luncheon at one o'clock, daylight saving time.

The Chair knows of no other business to come before the Convention; and if the Chair is not in error, a motion to adjourn without day is in order.

DELEGATE FRANCIS W. COLE: I move that we adjourn without day.

A VOICE: I second the motion.

PRESIDENT ROBINSON: It is moved and seconded that the Convention be now adjourned without day.

All those in favor say Aye.

(Chorus of Ayes.)

PRESIDENT ROBINSON: The Convention stands adjourned.

DELAWARE*

JOURNAL

OF THE

CONSTITUTIONAL CONVENTION

TO ACT UPON A PROPOSED AMENDMENT

TO THE

CONSTITUTION OF THE UNITED STATES

HELD AT

DOVER, DELAWARE, ON JUNE 24, 1933

Pursuant to the statutes of the State of Delaware, providing for conventions in the State of Delaware to take action upon amendments to the Constitution of the United States which may be proposed by the Congress for ratification by conventions in the several States, the said State Convention was convened on the twenty-fourth day of June, A.D. 1933, at twelve o'clock noon, in the Senate Chamber at the State Capitol in Dover, Delaware.

On motion of Dr. Wharton, and seconded, Mr. Pierre S. duPont and Mr. Eugene Ennalls Berl, of New Castle County, were elected temporary President and Secretary, respectively, of the convention.

The temporary Secretary read the Governor's proclamation providing for the election of delegates and the holding of the convention.

The Rt. Rev. Philip Cook, Bishop of the Diocese of Delaware of the Protestant Episcopal Church, then offered the invocation.

On motion of Mr. White, duly seconded by Mr. Cannon, both of Sussex County, a motion prevailed that the President should appoint a committee on credentials. The temporary President of the convention designated Dr. Wharton, of Kent County, and Mrs. Eliza N. Corbit Lea, of New Castle County, as the members of the committee on credentials. Without recess and during a slight interim in the proceedings, the delegates presented their credentials to the committee on credentials and shortly thereafter Dr. Wharton as chairman of the committee on credentials, submitted the following report:

"WE, the undersigned, being the members of the committee appointed by the President of the Convention to examine and report upon the credentials of the delegates present, do hereby report that we have examined the credentials of the following persons who are present at the said Convention and whose credentials we have found to be in order:

Eugene Ennalls Berl	Harry C. Darbee	Bankson T. Holcomb
Julia F. Burton	James L. Davis	Clarence E. Keyes
Harry L. Cannon	Pierre S. duPont	Eliza N. Corbit Lea
Charles Malcolm Cochran, Sr.	Charles Leland Harmonson	William P. Richardson

* From a mimeographed copy.

William G. Robelen	Jacob Reese White	Charles M. Wharton"
Thomas J. Virden	John Pilling Wright	
Charles M. Wharton	Eliza N. Corbit Lea	

On motion of Mr. Harmonson and seconded by Dr. Wharton, the report of the committee on credentials was approved and ordered to become a part of the record of the convention.

The temporary President then requested that Chief Justice Pennewill administer the oath to the members of the convention. The oath of office was administered to the delegates elected in a group, sworn and subscribed in the following form:

"STATE OF DELAWARE }
"KENT COUNTY } ss.

"I, ... do solemnly swear (or affirm) that I will support the Constitution of the United States, and the Constitution of the State of Delaware, and that I will faithfully discharge the duties of a Delegate to the Ratification Convention of an Amendment to the Constitution of the United States according to the best of my ability.

"And I do further solemnly swear (or affirm) that I have not directly or indirectly paid, offered, or promised to pay, contributed, or offered or promised to contribute, any money or other valuable thing as a consideration or reward for the giving or withholding a vote at the election at which I was elected to said office."

. . . .

Sworn to and subscribed before me this 24th day of June, in the year of our Lord one thousand nine hundred and thirty-three.

. . . .

Chief Justice

The convention then proceeded to the election of permanent officers. On motion made by Mr. White of Sussex County and seconded, the temporary officers of the convention were made the permanent officers.

The oath of office to the aforesaid officers of the convention was administered by Chief Justice Pennewill and is in the following form:

"STATE OF DELAWARE }
"KENT COUNTY } ss.

"I, Pierre S. duPont do solemnly swear (or affirm) that I will support the Constitution of the United States and the Constitution of the State of Delaware, and that I will faithfully discharge the duties of President to the Ratification Convention of an Amendment to the Constitution of the United States, according to the best of my ability.

"PIERRE S. DUPONT"

Sworn to and subscribed before me this 24th day of June, in the year of our Lord one thousand nine hundred and thirty-three.

JAMES PENNEWILL
Chief Justice

"STATE OF DELAWARE }
"KENT COUNTY } ss.

"I, Eugene Ennalls Berl, do solemnly swear (or affirm) that I will support the Constitution of the United States and the Constitution of the State of Delaware, and that I will faithfully discharge the duties of Secretary to the Ratification Convention of an Amendment to the Constitution of the United States, according to the best of my ability.

"EUGENE ENNALLS BERL"

Sworn to and subscribed before me this 24th day of June, in the year of our Lord one thousand nine hundred and thirty-three.

JAMES PENNEWILL
Chief Justice

The President announced that the Convention was properly constituted and ready for the business in order.

The first order of business was a resolution ratifying the proposed amendment to the Constitution of the United States. Mr. Holcomb, of New Castle County, presented the resolution and moved its adoption. The resolution was then read by the Secretary as follows:

The Constitutional Convention of the State of Delaware called to act upon a proposed amendment to the Constitution of the United States approves the following amendment to the Constitution of the United States:

ARTICLE ___ ___

Section 1. The eighteenth article of amendment to the Constitution of the United States is hereby repealed.

Section 2. The transportation or importation into any State, Territory or possession of the United States for delivery or use therein of intoxicating liquors, in violation of the laws thereof, is hereby prohibited.

Section 3. This article shall be inoperative unless it shall have been ratified as an amendment to the Constitution by conventions in the several States, as provided in the Constitution within seven years from the date of the submission hereof to the States by the Congress.

The motion of Mr. Holcomb was seconded by Mr. White.

The Secretary then proceeded with the roll call of the delegates present, who, answering to the call of the Secretary, voted as follows:

DELEGATES	*Yea*	*Nay*
Eugene Ennalls Berl	Yea	
Julia F. Burton	Yea	
Harry L. Cannon	Yea	
Charles Malcolm Cochran, Sr.	Yea	
Harry C. Darbee	Yea	
James L. Davis	Yea	
Pierre S. duPont	Yea	
Charles Leland Harmonson	Yea	
Bankson T. Holcomb	Yea	
Clarence E. Keyes	Yea	
Eliza N. Corbit Lea	Yea	
William P. Richardson	Yea	
William G. Robelen	Yea	
Thomas J. Virden	Yea	
Charles M. Wharton	Yea	
Jacob Reese White	Yea	
John Pilling Wright	Yea	

The President thereupon announced that the resolution had been unanimously adopted by the convention.

Mr. Keyes thereupon moved that the resolution be certified by the convention in accordance with the requirements of the statute. This motion was seconded by Mr. White and unanimously adopted. Thereupon each member of the convention signed the duplicate original resolution as provided by the statute, which was certified over the hand of the President and attested by the Secretary.

It was moved, seconded and carried that the Secretary of the Convention be directed to deliver the duplicate originals provided in the Statute to the Secretary of State of Delaware, together with a journal of the proceedings of the convention.

The adoption of the following resolution was made by Dr. Wharton, of Kent County, and seconded by Mr. White of Sussex County, and unanimously adopted. The resolution was then read by the Secretary, as follows:

WHEREAS, having performed the public office for which it was elected by the people of Delaware, by voting on behalf of the State to ratify the Resolution of Congress to Repeal the 18th Amendment, this Convention wishes to go on record as to the fundamental purpose and spirit of its action in so ratifying a resolution to abolish Federal Prohibition and return to the States their former power to control the manufacture, transportation and sale of alcoholic liquors within their own borders:

Be it resolved by this convention:

(1) The vote of this Convention has been cast to remove from the Federal Constitution, a provision wholly out of keeping with the constitutional principles of this Government, in that it attempts to control by force, through federal police power, the personal habits of the people;

(2) To restore conditions under which the evils fostered by Federal Prohibition may be so dealt with as to prevent their return, and to overcome their effects upon the American people in its Government and in its individual character;

(3) To enable the nation, and this State, to again take up, with hope of success, a program of education and character building among young and old, that will promote true temperance;

(4) To the foregoing ends the members of this convention assert that they do not ignore any of the evils associated with the abuse of liquor either under prohibition or under State control; that they know and abhor the evils which existed in connection with the old-time saloon, as well as with the prohibition speakeasy; and that they therefore pledge themselves to support such restrictions of the present Liquor Control Act as tend to promote seemliness and decency in those places where alcoholic beverages may legally be consumed by the glass, and to support especially those regulations and policies of the Liquor Control Commission which are intended to strike at the root of liquor abuses; and to consistently support and help to strengthen, as experience may dictate, the Liquor Control System of this State, to the end already stated: the development of true temperance among individuals and the promotion of honest and wise control, free from abuses in the conduct of the state's regulation.

Upon the announcement by the President that the delegates were entitled to present their application for mileage allowances, it was moved by Mr. Harmonson and seconded by Dr. Wharton that the delegates waive their right to mileage, which motion was thereupon carried.

Then followed a motion by Dr. Wharton, seconded by Mr. Harmonson, and carried, that the compensation of the delegates and officers be likewise waived.

Upon motion of Mr. White, seconded by Mr. Harmonson, and carried, the President was directed to forward to Congress of the United States for insertion in the Congressional Record, a copy of the record of the convention.

Thereupon, upon motion of Dr. Wharton, seconded by Mr. Holcomb, the convention adjourned.

Dated at Dover, Delaware, this twenty-fourth day of June, A.D. 1933.

PIERRE S. DUPONT, *President*
(*Signed*)

Attest:

EUGENE ENNALLS BERL, *Secretary*
(*Signed*)

The Constitutional Convention of the State of Delaware called to act upon a proposed amendment to the Constitution of the United States approves the following amendment to the Constitution of the United States:

ARTICLE ___

Section 1. The eighteenth article of amendment to the Constitution of the United States is hereby repealed.

Section 2. The transportation or importation into any State, Territory, or possession of the United States for delivery or use therein of intoxicating liquors, in violation of the laws thereof, is hereby prohibited.

Section 3. This article shall be inoperative unless it shall have been ratified as an amendment to the Constitution by conventions in the several States, as provided in the Constitution within seven years from the date of the submission hereof to the States by the Congress.

We, the delegates to the said Convention, attest that the foregoing is a true and correct copy of the resolution adopted unanimously at such Convention, on the 24th day of June, A.D. 1933.

Harry C. Darbee (*Signed*)
William G. Robelen (*Signed*)
James L. Davis (*Signed*)
Thos. J. Virden (*Signed*)
Jacob Reese White (*Signed*)
Harry L. Cannon (*Signed*)
Charles M. Wharton (*Signed*)
Bankson T. Holcomb (*Signed*)
Clarence E. Keyes (*Signed*)
Charles Leland Harmonson (*Signed*)
William P. Richardson (*Signed*)
Eliza N. Corbit Lea (*Signed*)
Julia F. Burton (*Signed*)
Charles Malcolm Cochran, Sr. (*Signed*)
John Pilling Wright (*Signed*)
Pierre S. duPont (*Signed*)
Eugene Ennalls Berl (*Signed*)

Certified to by

PIERRE S. DUPONT (*Signed*)
President of the Convention

Attest:

EUGENE ENNALLS BERL (*Signed*)
Secretary of the Convention

FLORIDA*

PROCEEDINGS OF A CONVENTION

HELD IN THE STATE OF FLORIDA, AT THE STATE HOUSE, IN TALLAHASSEE, ON NOVEMBER 14, 1933, TO RATIFY A PROPOSED AMENDMENT TO THE CONSTITUTION OF THE UNITED STATES TO REPEAL THE EIGHTEENTH AMENDMENT

HONORABLE R. A. GRAY (Secretary of State): The convention will come to order. The records of the office of the Secretary of State show that the following were duly elected as delegates to this convention. I will now call the roll of those delegates. You will answer present when your name is called.

Robert H. Anderson, present.
Henry Clay Armstrong, present.
George H. Asbell, present.
Clayton A. Avriett, present.
Claude H. Barnes, absent.
Fletcher A. Black, present.
John Lynn Blackswell, present.
Nathan A. Boswell, Sr., present.
James E. Calkins, present.
Rebecca A. Camp, present.
Guilford M. Cannon, III, absent.
Martin Caraballo, present.
Calvin D. Christ, M.D., present.
Val C. Cleary, present.
Alston Cockrell, present.
Clayton C. Codrington, present.
Harold Colee, present.
Henry Edmund Corry, present.
Hattie R. Crawford, present.
Jessie Currie, present.
Helen Glenn Dann, present.
Roy Dee, absent.
Otho Edwin Falls, Jr., absent.
Herbert U. Feibelman, present.
Asher Frank, present.
Edward V. Garcia, present.
Mrs. Joe Gill, present.
L. A. Grayson, present.
Beulah Hooks Hannah, present.
Mamie Sparkman Hart, present.
Wendell C. Heaton, present.
Raeburn C. Horne, present.
Sidney L. Kilgore, present.
Joseph Lee Kirby-Smith, present.
Gordon B. Knowles, present.
Erskine W. Landis, present.
Loomis C. Leedy, present.
C. D. Leffler, present.
Ben H. Lindsey, Jr., present.
William H. Malone, absent.
G. C. Martin, present.
Mrs. Hugh M. Matheson, present.
C. Parkhill Mays, present.
Baron de Hirsch Meyer, present.
Thomas Rogero Mickler, present.
W. H. Milton, present.
Albert Ives Pooser, present.
John O. Pugh, present.
Edwin H. Robinson, present.
Charles W. (Chuck) Ruckel, present.
James D. Russ, Sr., present.
Ray Selden, present.
Frank B. Stoneman, present.
H. Boyce Taylor, Jr., present.
Thomas S. Trantham, present.
L. E. Vause, present.
J. T. Vocelle, present.
Mrs. Harry M. Voorhis, present.
Nat G. Walker, absent.
Perry G. Wall, present.
J. V. Walton, present.
Charles H. Warwick, Jr., present.
R. H. Weaver, present.
W. E. Whitlock, present.
Errol S. Willes, present.
Herbert E. Wolfe, present.
R. Charlton Wright, absent.

* Printed.

A quorum is present. As the names of the delegates are now called they will please come forward and take the oath of office, which will be administered by Mr. Chief Justice Davis, of the Supreme Court of Florida.

The delegates present then took the oath of office, which was administered by Mr. Chief Justice Davis.

The delegates present having taken the oath of office, nominations are in order for President of this convention.

MR. ARMSTRONG: Mr. Chairman.

THE SECRETARY OF STATE: Mr. Armstrong.

MR. ARMSTRONG: Mr. Chairman, fellow delegates, we are all deeply conscious of the honor that is and will remain ours that we have aided in bringing this successful termination to the artfully, but, as events have shown, quite erroneously named "noble experiment." But the honor and joy of service permitted to me to experience must surpass that of the rest of you, as you will presently see.

As I think of the tragic error we are engaged in correcting, which came from a misconception of the very essence of the federal principle as that on which our national government was founded, as well as the yet more potent promptings of human nature, I am amazed and would be profoundly discouraged but for the manifest nation-wide evidence of a determination to correct a wrong, at the contemptuous but good natured indifference with which this national betrayal of liberty was generally regarded.

Hardly had the officials provided for the enforcement of the laws growing out of the Eighteenth Amendment been named than the question arose in the average American mind, "Have we not been stampeded, during a period of war-time hysteria by the zeal of an over fervent minority into writing into our fundamental national law a provision which at most might have a place in the local police regulation; and, not only so, but into making an observance of its provisions the shibboleth of good citizenship and personal morality?"

This question was more generally repeated each day, and with growing concern, as the consequences of the legislative monstrosity was unfolded for us to contemplate. And the worst of the consequences was the complacency with which the younger generation came to regard and, indeed, seem to justify law violations in general.

Those of us jealous of the blessings of local and personal liberty, as the principle has been handed down to us, would have felt easier concerning the safety of this household goddess, to whom, because of her blessings we all recognize our duty and reverent devotion and protection, had we seen none of the militant spirit of the colonists in their forcible resentment of the Four Intolerable Acts that brought on the revolution. It was not so much the practical enforcement and results of those Acts that made them odious to the point of exciting revolt, for they were as generally and successfully, if not so profitably evaded as has been our famous Volstead Law; but it was the outrage of having them made and their enforcement attempted by a distant tyranny with no regard to colonial interests or wishes. Such, too, has been the Eighteenth Amendment, with its legitimate children, the Volstead and the Jones Laws, to which the nation generally showed what should have been an alarming non-observance.

For national self-respect, as well as relief from increasing indications that the forces of lawlessness were in the way of becoming more powerful than law itself, we were brought to choosing between the frank recognition of this condition or the sham of a statutory national moral regulation.

To freely paraphrase a pronouncement of Abraham Lincoln, "We could no longer exist with three-fourths of the population of our country for Repeal and one-fourth for continuing to wear this moral high hat of prohibition, with the remaining complementary one-twentieth of that class known as the politicians, whose thoughts were made hideous by weighing what one side could do against what the minority he felt some would do; whose sole and constant principle was stated by the famous Vicar of Bray:

> "For this as law I will maintain
> Until my dying day, Sir;
> That whatsoever King shall reign,
> I'll be Vicar of Bray, Sir."

Such stalwart spirits still survive and obtain ample rewards.

I said a little while ago that I have more joy in my mission here than any of the rest of you will experience, for, with the satisfaction I share with you in belonging to this convention, I am privileged to put in nomination as President, if the subject of my remarks will permit me to say so, one of my own product.

It was my privilege to teach for several years the gentleman I am proposing that we choose to preside over our deliberations. My first acquaintance with him has been kept in my mind as a promise of the forth-rightness the boy gave to the man. He came to me a lad of some ten to eleven years, for such questioning for classification as seemed necessary. After the first few questions he thought he saw my object and to save time made a statement of what he had been studying and ended it by saying, "They (the teachers) said that I did pretty well, and the only trouble is that I am lazy."

After that gratuitous and honest report of his alleged short-comings I never expected and never found deception, concealment or indirection in his character. He has been, in all my knowledge since as straight-forward in asserting his views as he was in this report on himself; and, where principle is involved, as stubborn in maintaining them.

You can understand, then, that I have watched the career of this young man with great interest and pride. Were it not for some contradictory evidence I might liken myself, if not to his alma mater, at least to his *almus pater*.

But disregarding this nicety of distinction and my indulgence in a pardonable pride, remembering the persistent and very able handling of our campaign, with its most remarkable outcome, as a reward for service, I have the honor to place in nomination for President of this State Convention for the ratification of the Twenty-first Amendment to the Constitution of the United States, Robert H. Anderson, of Duval County.

Permit me to add, Mr. Chairman, that this colleague of ours is deeply conscious, as we all are, of the grave responsibility that rests upon us and other citizens of the State as we aid in destroying this veritable social octopus that was begotten of a nation-wide illicit traffic.

We are aware that our task is not done till we have rid our state constitution of the same absurdity that we are helping to erase from the National.

The thought of all of us is that we are fighting the battles of temperance and reason and social and political morality. I can think of no one among us who in his life more fully impersonates these ideas than does our colleague, President of the Florida Repeal Association—and my former pupil—Bob Anderson. (Applause.)

THE SECRETARY OF STATE: Are there other nominations?

A VOICE: I move that nominations be closed.

The motion was seconded, and on being put was carried.

THE SECRETARY OF STATE: I declare Mr. Robert H. Anderson unanimously chosen President of this convention. (Applause.)

A DELEGATE: Mr. President, I suggest that you appoint three delegates to escort the newly elected President to the rostrum.

THE SECRETARY OF STATE: I will ask delegates Val C. Cleary, of Miami Beach, Asher Frank, of Tampa, and H. Boyce Taylor, of Jacksonville, to act as a committee to escort the newly elected President to the rostrum.

Delegate Robert H. Anderson, of Jacksonville, was escorted to the rostrum amid loud applause.

MR. ANDERSON: Today marks the dawn of a new era. Hypocrisy has been unmasked; fanaticism has been dethroned; intolerance has been dealt a death blow.

The National revolt against the Eighteenth Amendment in the determination of the people of this country to have a free and democratic government, is the most important demonstration that has occurred since our forefathers threw the British tea overboard in Boston Harbor. Even as the yoke of British tyranny was cast off then, so now have we rid ourselves of the shackles of organized minorities, which have falsely claimed to represent public sentiment. It has been a long fight and a hard fight; but it has been won. Those who won it believe that "Nothing is ever settled until it is settled right." When a man knows deep down in his heart that he is right about a thing, and has the courage to speak out fearlessly about it, to bring the enemy out from under cover to fight him in the open, and has the determination to win, all the combined forces of fanaticism that have ever emerged from Hell cannot defeat him.

And it is this knowledge of being right that has won this fight. When right-thinking, God-fearing, patriotic men and women of this country said that they were tired of this farce, Prohibition's fate was sealed. The victory doesn't belong to the brewers, nor to the distillers. It belongs to temperate and sober men and women who abhor the despicable methods of the saloon-keeper as much as they abhor the contemptible methods of the Anti-Saloon League. It belongs to men and women who love temperance for its own sake and who are insistent that their children shall be raised in an atmosphere of sobriety—a sobriety that is free from the contaminating influences of hypocrisy in any form whatsoever.

The victory is a tribute also to the deep-rooted faith in the American ideals of our fathers concerning the Constitutional Government of the United States. It is a declaration that the people of the United States disapprove of Federal transgression of State's rights, and that it will oppose and resist that transgression. It is an expression of their resolution that they will not surrender their personal liberty and that it cannot be taken away from them.

And lastly, it is a warning to members of Congress that they cannot improve on the Federal Constitution. No amendment, since the twelfth, that Congress has proposed, has bettered the Constitution; on the contrary, every one that has been made has injured it. In the future, Congressmen will do well to confine their activities to the course that has been chartered for them and to let the Constitution alone.

Mindful, therefore, of the importance of our mission and the seriousness of our task, let me thank you for the honor, though undeserved, you have conferred upon me for the very small and insignificant part I have played in this program. Let me assure you of my deep and sincere appreciation. Let me say to you that you have made this great day one of the happiest of my life. (Loud applause.)

MR. CALKINS: Mr. President.

THE PRESIDENT: Mr. Calkins.

MR. CALKINS: Mr. President, I would like to interrupt our proceedings for the purpose of making a motion. I move that an invitation be extended to the Chief Executive of this State, the Honorable Dave Sholtz, to address this convention, and that a committee be appointed by the Chair for the purpose of extending that invitation.

The motion was seconded by Mr. Caraballo, of Tampa, and on being put was unanimously adopted.

THE PRESIDENT (Mr. Anderson): I shall appoint Mr. Colee, Mrs. Dann, Mrs. Matheson, Mr. Heaton and Mr. Ruckel to call on the Governor, and to announce to him that the convention is in session, and ask if he has any message for us.

MR. FEIBELMAN: Mr. President.

THE PRESIDENT: Mr. Feibelman.

MR. FEIBELMAN: Mr. President, at this juncture in the proceedings, I crave the indulgence of the Chair to express the wishes of a body of men and women in this state, who have undertaken responsibility for carrying forward the campaign for the adoption of the Twenty-first Amendment to the Constitution of the United States. Following the Governor's call for a popular election to select delegates to this Convention, it was the Florida Repeal Association which undertook to execute the mandate of the people of the United States and of this state, as rendered unmistakably in the presidential and congressional elections of November, 1932. That handful of zealous men and women, constituting the Florida Repeal Association, was determined to procure an expression of the unmistakable popular will for prohibition reform. Amongst its organizers was a prominent young member of the bar of this state, who had long labored for the restoration of states' rights in the management of the morals of the people. He was a delegate to the last Democratic National Convention and was placed on its committee on resolutions. When the question of the espousal of prohibition repeal was before the Convention, he was one of the speakers in its behalf. Millions of his countrymen heard him over the radio, as he decried "this orgy of crime and saturnalia of lawlessness," for which the Eighteenth Amendment was responsible. He fought a successful battle in the Convention, which accepted as one of its most important planks the forthright repeal of the Eighteenth Amendment by conventions of the people. He has consistently fought, at every opportunity, for the very privilege which is being accorded us today to express the popular will on this important question. After Congress had approved the Twenty-first Amendment, this leader was selected by the Voluntary Committee of Lawyers, Inc., a disinterested national organization of members of the bar, dedicated to the repeal of the Eighteenth Amendment, to draft an enabling act of the legislature. He drew the bill which was the basis of the very act by virtue of which the people recorded their votes on October last. He gave of his time and great talent to the end that the legislature should insure an expression of the majority will, and after the legislature had adopted a measure, embodying the principles of his bill, he gave his leadership to the selection of delegates to this Convention. He was in no small degree responsible for the outcome of the election.

The Florida Repeal Association wishes to recognize this leadership and foresight and has delegated me to present to him a gavel with which he can preside over this body. We trust it will be to him and his posterity an emblem of the ultimate authority of the people themselves.

Mr. Anderson, I therefore have the pleasure of presenting to you this gavel from your associates of the Florida Repeal Association.

(Applause.) Mr. Feibelman presents the gavel to Mr. Anderson.

THE PRESIDENT: I wish to thank you, my friends, for this expression of your confidence. I trust that I shall deserve it and I assure you that I will make every effort to do so.

MR. CALKINS: Mr. President.

THE PRESIDENT: Mr. Calkins.

MR. CALKINS: I move that we be at ease just a moment, until the Governor arrives.

THE PRESIDENT: There are several seats inside the rail. I shall be glad to have the members of the Supreme Court and the members of the cabinet, who are with us, occupy those seats.

Governor Sholtz was escorted to the platform, amid great applause.

THE PRESIDENT: Governor Sholtz, this convention is assembled pursuant to law, and it desires to ask you if you have any message to deliver.

GOVERNOR SHOLTZ: Mr. President and Ladies and Gentlemen of the Convention: I am very happy to have the privilege of being with you this morning. In fact, I postponed leaving Tallahassee for St. Petersburg, where I am scheduled to make a radio broadcast tonight on the school situation, in order to have the pleasure of welcoming you.

When I issued my proclamation calling the special election, at which you were elected as delegates to this convention, I did so in pursuance of a statute passed by the Legislature of this State and my own personal convictions that the people should have an opportunity of expressing themselves directly upon the question whether or not the Eighteenth Amendment should be retained in the Constitution of the United States. The people have spoken and in no uncertain terms, and I assure you that it is my wish to give effect to their expressed desires in every legitimate way. I welcome you, therefore, to this city and into this building, the Capitol of the State, and into these halls, where our lawmakers customarily sit, for the performance by you of your duties under the law and I take pleasure in extending to you the wholehearted assistance and support of my office for that purpose.

While I am in accord with the majority as to the failure of the Eighteenth Amendment to live up to what was expected of it, I am firm in my convictions, nevertheless, that the open saloon should not be permitted to return. The open saloon is the enemy of society and it has no place among the social institutions and as long as I am the Governor of this State I shall use every effort to prevent its becoming again a factor in our politics.

It is with regret that I am unable to remain with you for the reason which I have already stated, but before departing let me again place at your service the assistance of my office and reassure you of my best wishes in the performance of your work here today.

I thank you. (Loud applause.)

THE PRESIDENT: I recognize the President of the Senate in the gallery. I shall be pleased to have him come up and occupy this seat by me—Senator Futch.

The President of the Senate was thereupon escorted to a seat beside the President of the convention.

THE PRESIDENT: Nominations are now in order to fill the office of Secretary of the Convention.

MR. FEIBELMAN: Mr. President.

The President: Mr. Feibelman.

Mr. Feibelman: Mr. President, in placing in nomination the name of one to serve as secretary of this Convention, I have in mind the service which a great body of our people has rendered to the cause of prohibition reform and I think that proper recognition should be given to this body, the women of America. They were amongst the first to recognize the evils of national prohibition in its serious consequences upon the development of the youth of this country. When the folly of trying to regulate morals from Washington was brought to light, the women of this country, with a wisdom that surpassed all understanding, became convinced that the time was ripe for genuine prohibition reform. They rallied to the cause as they have ever been disposed to do, and with a patriotic fervor, such as the women have ever displayed during every period of stress in the Nation's history, they responded. With unstinted devotion they dignified the cause of national prohibition reform by their own presence and support. The Women's Organization for Prohibition Reform was organized and became a potent factor in the crystallization of public sentiment for repeal of the Eighteenth Amendment. In Florida, the brilliant daughter of a distinguished member of the bar was called to the chairmanship of the Women's Organization for Prohibition Reform. She gave of her fine talent, vision, and natural capacity for leadership, and with unswerving purpose she contributed in no small measure to the success of the election of October 10 last.

We compliment ourselves in recognizing the services of the women of America and particularly this leader of the women of Florida, by selecting as our Secretary, Mrs. Rebecca A. Camp, of Ocala. It gives me genuine pleasure and privilege to place her name in nomination for Secretary of this body. (Applause.)

The nomination was seconded by Dr. Calvin D. Christ.

Mr. Knowles moved that the nominations be closed and that the unanimous ballot of the convention be cast for Mrs. Camp, the Secretary thereof.

Which was agreed to by unanimous vote.

The President: By your unanimous vote you have elected Mrs. Rebecca A. Camp as Secretary of this convention. I shall appoint Mr. Feibelman and Mr. Calkins as a committee to escort her to the Secretary's seat.

Mr. Calkins: Mr. President.

The President: Mr. Calkins.

Mr. Calkins: We have now elected a President and Secretary of this convention, which completes the officers as prescribed by the statute. It seems to me proper we should have a set of rules for the government of the convention, and I move the President appoint a committee for the purpose of preparing and submitting to the convention at the earliest moment a set of rules for its government.

Which was agreed to by unanimous vote.

The President: I appoint on the Rules Committee Messrs. Calkins, Caraballo, Codrington, Mrs. Dann, Messrs. Heaton, Mickler and Taylor.

The President: The members of the committee will please meet Senator Calkins on the outside, for the purpose of preparing the report. In the meantime the convention will be at ease.

While we are at ease will you pardon me if I make one or two announcements? Mr. Feibelman has prepared this register of the delegates and we wish every member of this convention to sign his or her name to it at some convenient time. Please do not leave the assembly room until you have affixed your signatures to it.

Will you be good enough to permit me to read a telegram sent to delegate Knowles from Fort Myers:

Please present my regrets to Mr. Anderson and the convention. Owing to the sudden death of a close friend, I am unable to attend. (*Signed*) N. GAILLARD WALKER.

I am informed that delegate Roy Dee is unable to attend on account of illness; that is true also of delegate R. Charlton Wright.

The convention will come to order.

MR. CALKINS: Mr. President.

THE PRESIDENT: Mr. Calkins.

MR. CALKINS: Mr. President, your committee on rules has met and prepared a set of rules for the government of this convention and desires to present these rules.

THE PRESIDENT: Senator Calkins will read the rules.

MR. CALKINS: The following is the report of the committee on rules:

RULES FOR THE GOVERNMENT OF THE CONVENTION

OFFICERS OF THE CONVENTION

1. The Convention shall elect a President, five Vice-Presidents, a Secretary, a Reading Secretary, a Sergeant-at-Arms, and an Official Reporter.

DUTIES OF THE PRESIDENT

2. The President shall be the presiding officer of the Convention.

3. He shall preserve order and decorum.

4. He shall sign all resolutions passed by the Convention, and shall certify its minutes as required by statute.

5. He shall decide all questions of order subject to an appeal by any delegate, on which appeal no delegate shall speak more than once, nor for more than one minute.

6. He shall put questions in this form, to-wit: "As many as are in favor (state the question) say I" [Aye] and after the affirmative vote is expressed he shall put the negative, "as many as are opposed, say no"; if he doubts, or if a division is called for, the Convention shall divide, those in the affirmative of the question shall first arise to be counted by the Secretary, and then those in the negative.

7. He shall have the right to name any delegate to temporarily preside over the Convention.

8. He shall appoint all committees authorized by the rules, motions or resolutions of the Convention.

DUTIES OF THE VICE-PRESIDENTS

9. It shall be the duty of the Vice-Presidents, in the order their respective names appear on the roll call, to perform the duties of the President of the Convention in case of his illness, absence or other inability to discharge his duties.

DUTIES OF THE SECRETARY

10. The Secretary shall keep the record, or cause to be kept and recorded, the minutes of this Convention; and shall perform such other duties as are required by statute or order of the Presiding Officer.

11. The Secretary shall sign all resolutions passed by the Convention, and certify its minutes as required by statute.

DUTIES OF THE READING SECRETARY

12. The Reading Secretary shall read, under direction of the Presiding Officer, for the information of the Convention, all resolutions presented for consideration. The Reading Secretary shall perform such other duties as the Presiding Officer or Secretary may direct.

DUTIES OF THE SERGEANT-AT-ARMS

13. It shall be the duty of the Sergeant-at-Arms to attend the entrance to the Convention Chamber, and permit no person to enter within the bar of the Chamber except those authorized by the rules.

14. He shall carry into effect all orders of the Presiding Officer seeking to preserve decorum, and shall perform such other duties as the Presiding Officer or Secretary may direct.

DUTIES OF OFFICIAL REPORTER

15. It shall be the duty of the Official Reporter to take down and transcribe the minutes of the Convention, under the direction of the President.

THE DELEGATES

16. Every delegate shall be present within the Convention Chamber during the sitting of the Convention unless excused or necessarily prevented, and shall vote on each question unless excused from voting by the Convention.

QUORUM

17. A majority of the total number of delegates elected to the Convention shall constitute a quorum for the transaction of business.

ADMISSION TO THE FLOOR

18. No person not a delegate or officer of the Convention shall be allowed inside the bar of the Chamber while the Convention is in session, except the Governor, Cabinet Officers, Members of Congress, and Judges of the Supreme Court of Florida; provided, however, the President may admit to the floor of the Convention Chamber, under such regulations as he may prescribe, stenographers and reporters wishing to take down the debates and proceedings.

QUESTIONS OF PRIVILEGE

19. Questions of privilege shall be:

First. Those affecting the rights of the Convention, collectively, and the integrity of its proceedings.

Secondly. The rights, reputation and conduct of delegates, individually, in their respective capacity only, and shall have precedence of all other questions, except motions to adjourn or take a recess.

COMMITTEES

20. The President shall appoint, at the commencement of the session, the following standing committees, namely:

On Rules, to consist of 9 delegates.

On Resolutions, to consist of not more than 15 delegates.

On Engrossment and Enrollment of Resolutions, to consist of 9 delegates.

On Credentials, to consist of 9 delegates.

The first named member of the committee shall be the Chairman and, in his absence, the next named shall act as Chairman.

21. All committee reports on resolutions shall be made in writing and delivered to the Secretary and read to the Convention. Any resolution reported adversely shall automatically lie on the table, unless the Convention, by unanimous vote, decides to take such resolution from the table and consider it.

INTRODUCTION AND PASSAGE OF RESOLUTIONS

22. Each resolution, before final passage thereof, shall be read three times, the first time when it is introduced, the second time when it shall be open to amendment, and the third time when it is on final passage.

23. When a resolution is introduced, it shall be sent, endorsed with the name of the delegate introducing it, to the Secretary, and, after it has been read the first time, shall be, by the Presiding Officer, referred to the Resolution Committee for consideration and recommendation.

24. Each amended resolution shall be properly engrossed before being placed on final passage, and each resolution adopted shall be carefully enrolled under direction of the Enrolling Committee and deposited in the office of the Secretary of State of Florida.

DECORUM AND DEBATE

25. No delegate shall speak more than once, nor for more than 5 minutes, on any matter, subject or resolution, without the consent of the Convention.

26. When a delegate desires to speak he shall arise and address himself to "Mr. President," and shall not proceed until first being recognized by the Presiding Officer, and shall confine himself to the question under debate, avoiding all personalities. When two or more delegates arise at the same time, the Presiding Officer shall name the delegate who is first to speak.

27. If any delegate, in speaking or otherwise, disregards the rules, any delegate may call him to order, and the President shall decide whether he shall be permitted to proceed.

28. While the Presiding Officer is stating a question, or after a question is put to vote, no delegate shall speak to it, except by unanimous consent of the Convention.

CALLS OF THE ROLL

29. Upon every roll call the names of the delegates shall be called alphabetically by surname.

MOTIONS, THEIR PRECEDENCE, ETC.

30. When a motion has been made, the Presiding Officer shall state it, or, if it be in writing, cause it to be read aloud by the Reading Secretary before being debated. Such motion may be withdrawn by the maker thereof at any time before decision thereon.

31. When a question is pending no motion shall be received but

(*a*) To adjourn,

(*b*) To adjourn to a time certain,

(*c*) To take a recess,

(*d*) To lay on the table,

(*e*) To postpone to a date certain,

(*f*) To commit,
(*g*) To amend or to substitute,
(*h*) To postpone indefinitely,

which several motions shall have precedence as they stand arranged, and the motions relating to adjournment, to take a recess, or to lay on the table, shall be decided without debate.

32. Before a question is put, on demand of any delegate, the question shall be divided, if it includes two or more divisible propositions.

33. Pending a motion to suspend a rule, the Presiding Officer may entertain one motion, to-wit: that the Convention adjourn, or take a recess; but after the result thereof is announced he shall not entertain any other dilatory motion until a vote is taken on suspension.

34. A roll call shall be had upon the final passage of the resolution ratifying or rejecting the proposed amendment to the Constitution of the United States, and the "Aye" and "Nay" vote thereon shall be recorded in the minutes of the Convention.

35. All other matters, motions and resolutions coming before the Convention may be disposed of by a viva voce vote.

AMENDMENTS TO MOTIONS AND RESOLUTIONS

36. When a motion or resolution is under consideration, a motion to amend and a motion to amend that amendment shall be in order; and it shall also be in order to offer a further amendment by way of a substitute, to which one amendment may be offered, but which shall not be voted on until the original matter is perfected.

37. It shall not be in order to offer an amendment to a resolution on its third reading.

RECONSIDERATION

38. When a question has been decided by the Convention, any delegate voting with the prevailing side may move a reconsideration thereof, and if the Convention shall refuse to reconsider or, upon reconsideration, shall confirm its first decision, no further motion to reconsider shall be in order, except by unanimous consent.

AMENDMENT AND SUSPENSION OF RULES

39. No rule shall be suspended or amended except by a vote of two-thirds of the delegates voting, a quorum being present.

GENERAL PARLIAMENTARY RULES

40. The rules of Parliamentary Practice comprised in Roberts Rules of Order shall govern the Convention in all cases to which they are applicable and in which they are not inconsistent with the standing rules.

MR. CALKINS: Mr. President.

THE PRESIDENT: Mr. Calkins.

MR. CALKINS: Now, Mr. President, I move the adoption of the rules for the government of the convention as reported by the Committee on Rules.

The motion was seconded, and on being put was carried.

MR. LANDIS: Mr. President.

THE PRESIDENT: Mr. Landis.

MR. LANDIS: As I understand the rules which this convention has just adopted, there are certain officerships to be filled. In order that we may expedite the business of this convention, I now move you, sir, that the Chair appoint a nominating committee to nominate the officers provided for by the rules.

The motion was seconded by Mr. Caraballo and on being put was carried and Mr. Landis, Mrs. Gill, Mr. Kilgore, Mr. Pooser, Mr. Selden, Mr. Vocelle, Mr. Walton, Mr. Asbell and Mr. Cleary were appointed members of the Nominating Committee.

THE PRESIDENT: While the Nominating Committee is in retirement, I have a communication from delegate Stoneman, which I wish to read to the convention:

November 11, 1933

CHAIRMAN, STATE CONVENTION
Tallahassee, Florida

DEAR SIR:

Owing to the fact that I have very recently come out of the hospital after a serious operation, I find it impossible to be in Tallahassee on the fourteenth. I therefore regretfully submit my resignation as a member of the convention, to which I had the honor of being elected.

Respectfully,
(*Signed*) F. B. STONEMAN

Under the law it is proper for the convention to fill vacancies caused in this fashion. I shall entertain a motion to fill a vacancy caused by his resignation.

MR. FRANK: Mr. President.

THE PRESIDENT: Mr. Frank.

MR. FRANK: Mr. President, I should like to nominate Mr. E. Clay Lewis.

MR. LEFFLER: Mr. President.

THE PRESIDENT: Mr. Leffler.

MR. LEFFLER: I nominate Mrs. Frank B. Shutts.

THE PRESIDENT: Are there further nominations?

MR. KNOWLES: Mr. President.

THE PRESIDENT: Mr. Knowles.

MR. KNOWLES: I have a telegram that Mr. Cannon sent to me:

Impossible to get there stop if this can be used as proxy please cast my ballot as pledged (*Signed*) G. M. Cannon.

Will the President construe that as a resignation and fill that vacancy?

THE PRESIDENT: You are out of order. If you wish to nominate somebody to fill that vacancy, which I assume you do, you are out of order.

MR. FRANK: I understand Mr. Stoneman has made a request. I therefore withdraw the name of E. Clay Lewis.

THE PRESIDENT: In view of the withdrawal of Mr. E. Clay Lewis as many as favor the election of Mrs. Shutts to fill the vacancy will say "Aye," those opposed, "No." The "Ayes" have it, and Mrs. Shutts is declared elected as a delegate to the convention.

MR. CALKINS: Mr. President.

THE PRESIDENT: Mr. Calkins.

MR. CALKINS: I move the appointment of a committee of three to escort Mrs. Shutts into the Chamber to her proper seat.

THE PRESIDENT: I shall appoint on that committee, Mr. Leffler, Dr. Christ and Mr. Caraballo.

MRS. HANNAH: Mr. President.

THE PRESIDENT: Mrs. Hannah.

MRS. HANNAH: I move that a telegram be sent to Mr. Stoneman regretting his inability to be here, and expressing the appreciation of this body for the splendid work he has done for the repeal.

The motion was seconded by Mr. Frank, and on being put was carried.

THE PRESIDENT: The Chair construes the telegram addressed by delegate Cannon to delegate Knowles as a resignation, and I shall take it for such.

I next call your attention to the resignation of delegate William H. Malone, addressed to the Secretary of State, in the following words:

November 9, 1933

HON. R. A. GRAY
Secretary of State
Tallahassee, Florida

DEAR MR. SECRETARY:

Owing to official business detaining me in the City of Key West, on the 14th day of November, 1933, it will be impossible for me to attend the convention to be held in the City of Tallahassee on the 14th day of November, 1933, for the purpose of acting on a proposed Amendment to the Constitution of the United States, to which convention I was elected as a delegate on the 10th day of October, 1933.

I therefore respectfully tender to you my resignation as said delegate in order that the convention may fill the vacancy created by my inability to attend.

Very respectfully submitted,
W. H. MALONE

I shall therefore entertain a motion to fill these vacancies.

MR. BLACKWELL: Mr. President.

THE PRESIDENT: Mr. Blackwell.

MR. BLACKWELL: Mr. President, I nominate Honorable J. B. Hodges of Lake City to fill the vacancy caused by the resignation of delegate William H. Malone.

MR. FRANK: Mr. President.

THE PRESIDENT: Mr. Frank.

MR. FRANK: I move that nominations be closed.

The motion was seconded, and on being put was carried and Mr. Hodges was declared elected in place of William H. Malone.

DR. WHITLOCK: Mr. President.

THE PRESIDENT: Dr. Whitlock.

DR. WHITLOCK: I would like to place in nomination the name of Mrs. Gordon B. Knowles of Bradenton to fill the vacancy caused by the resignation of G. M. Cannon.

The motion was seconded and on being put was carried, and Mrs. Knowles was elected as a member of the convention.

THE PRESIDENT: Mrs. Knowles, will you and Mrs. Shutts and Mr. Hodges come up and be sworn in by the Chief Justice?

The oath of office was thereupon administered to Mrs. Knowles, Mrs. Shutts and Mr. Hodges, as members of the convention.

MR. LANDIS: Mr. President.

THE PRESIDENT: Mr. Landis.

MR. LANDIS: Mr. President, we have the report of the Nominating Committee. I have it with me. If it is now in order, may I read the report?

THE PRESIDENT: Read the report.

MR. LANDIS: The following is a report of the Nominating Committee:

TALLAHASSEE, FLORIDA
November 14, 1933

HONORABLE ROBERT H. ANDERSON
President, Constitutional Convention
Tallahassee, Florida

Your committee appointed to nominate the officers provided for in the rules of this Convention, except the statutory officers, beg leave to report that it has selected to fill the five offices of Vice-President, provided for by the rules, the following: Henry Clay Armstrong, W. H. Milton, Perry G. Wall, Dr. Joseph Lee Kirby-Smith, C. D. Leffler.

To fill the office of Reading Secretary, provided for by the rules: Frank Webb.

To fill the office of Official Reporter, provided for by the rules: R. C. Dowling.

To fill the office of Sergeant-at-Arms, provided for by the rules: Nathan H. Boswell.

Your Committee has found its task not an easy one. In deliberating and considering the entire membership of this Convention, your committee was impressed with the fact that all had given of their time, labor and efforts whole-heartedly and unstintingly and, were it possible the Committee feels that it would be splendid if all could be honored with an officership. As this, of course, is impossible, your Committee has endeavored to select not only those who have been outstanding in their efforts, but also those whom it believes will meet with the hearty accord and approval of this Convention, and it is a pleasure for the Committee to report that those nominated by it, as stated above, were nominated by the entire vote of the Committee, without dissent, and it is the hope of the Committee that this report will receive the unanimous approval of this Convention.

ERSKINE W. LANDIS
Chairman, Nominating Committee
MRS. JOE H. GILL
A. I. POOSER
VAL C. CLEARY
J. V. WALTON
RAY SELDEN
GEORGE H. ASBELL
SIDNEY S. KILGORE
JAMES T. VOCELLE
Members of Nominating Committee

MR. LANDIS: Mr. President.

THE PRESIDENT: Mr. Landis.

MR. LANDIS: Mr. President, we have now had the report of the Nominating Committee read. I now move the adoption of the report and the election of the officers named in the report.

The motion was seconded, and on being put, was carried, and the officers named therein were declared elected to the respective offices for which they were nominated.

THE PRESIDENT: To complete the committees provided in the rules, I shall make the following appointments:

The Rules Committee, I shall reappoint the same members.

The Resolutions Committee will be: Cockrell, Mrs. Hannah, Garcia, Hodges, Corry, Black, Frank, Horne, Warwick, Jr., Meyer, Wolfe, Blackwell, Knowles, Weaver, Vause.

Enrollment: Grayson, Mrs. Currie, Willes, Mays, Russ, Whitlock, Mrs. Crawford, Avriett, Robinson.

Credentials: Feibelman, Cannon, Lindsey, Mrs. Hart, Christ, Martin, Barnes, Falls, Pugh.

THE PRESIDENT: I shall ask Mrs. Gill to read the invocation and the delegates will please rise.

MRS. GILL: Almighty and All Merciful God: We, the delegates of the people of Florida, in convention assembled to do the will of a free and enlightened people, grateful for the blessings of liberty for ourselves and our posterity, humbly invoke divine guidance and earnestly pray for peace, prosperity and happiness for the people of Florida, and of the Country, and of the World.

THE PRESIDENT: That completes the organization of the convention. I shall entertain a motion to adjourn for the lunch hour. The Chairmen of the several committees will advise members of the committees where the committees meet.

MR. COCKRELL: Mr. President.

THE PRESIDENT: Mr. Cockrell.

MR. COCKRELL: Wouldn't it be well to get the resolution for the adoption of the amendment in before we go to lunch?

THE PRESIDENT: I think it will delay the proceedings.

MR. COCKRELL: Very well, I move you that we now recess until 2:30 o'clock.

The motion was seconded, and on being put was carried, and the convention was accordingly recessed until 2:30 o'clock in the afternoon.

AFTERNOON SESSION

At 2:30 o'clock P.M. the convention was called to order by the President, pursuant to the morning recess and the following further proceedings were had:

THE PRESIDENT: The convention will come to order. The Reading Secretary will call the roll to ascertain the presence of a quorum. Make a note of the names of the delegates who were elected to fill vacancies and add them to your roll call.

Thereupon the Reading Secretary called the roll and noted the presence and absence of the delegates as follows:

Robert H. Anderson, present.
Henry Clay Armstrong, present.
George H. Asbell, present.
Clayton A. Avriett, present.
Claude H. Barnes, absent.
Fletcher A. Black, present.
John Lynn Blackwell, present.
Nathan A. Boswell, Sr., present.
James E. Calkins, present.
Rebecca A. Camp, present.
Martin Caraballo, present.
Calvin D. Christ, M.D., present.
Val C. Cleary, present.
Alston Cockrell, present.
Clayton C. Codrington, present.
Harold Colee, present.

Henry Edmund Corry, present.
Hattie R. Crawford, present.
Jessie Currie, present.
Helen Glenn Dann, present.
Roy Dee, absent.
Otho Edwin Falls, Jr., absent.
Herbert U. Feibelman, present.
Asher Frank, present.
Edward V. Garcia, present.
Mrs. Joe Gill, present.
L. A. Grayson, present.
Beulah Hooks Hannah, present.
Mamie Sparkman Hart, present.
Wendell C. Heaton, present.
James B. Hodges, present.
Raeburn C. Horne, present.
Sidney L. Kilgore, present.
Joseph Lee Kirby-Smith, present.
Gordon B. Knowles, present.
Mrs. Gordon B. Knowles, present.
Erskine W. Landis, present.
Loomis C. Leedy, present.
C. D. Leffler, present.
Ben H. Lindsey, Jr., present.
G. C. Martin, present.
Mrs. Hugh M. Matheson, present.
C. Parkhill Mays, present.
Baron de Hirsch Meyer, present.
Thomas Rogero Mickler, present.
W. H. Milton, present.
Albert Ives Pooser, present.
John O. Pugh, present.
Edwin H. Robinson, present.
Charles W. (Chuck) Ruckel, present.
James D. Russ, Sr., present.
Ray Selden, present.
Mrs. Frank B. Shutts, present.
H. Boyce Taylor, Jr., present.
Thomas S. Trantham, present.
L. E. Vause, present.
J. T. Vocelle, present.
Mrs. Harry M. Voorhis, present.
Nat G. Walker, absent.
Perry H. Wall, present.
J. V. Walton, present.
Charles H. Warwick, Jr., present.
R. H. Weaver, present.
W. E. Whitlock, present.
Errol S. Willes, present.
Herbert E. Wolfe, present.
R. Charlton Wright, absent.

MR. HODGES: Mr. President.

THE PRESIDENT: Mr. Hodges.

MR. HODGES: Mr. President, I desire to read a telegram sent by one of our elected delegates. The telegram is addressed to Mrs. Hortense K. Wells, National Committeewoman and is as follows:

"Regret being unable attend Repeal Convention have been designated to deliver President Roosevelt's greetings over nationwide hookup tonight for and in connection with International Radio Club now in convention St. Petersburg also was necessary for me to be there last night to deliver Hon. James A. Farley's greetings to convention stop. Accept this as proxy to cast my ballot for ratification of Twenty-first Amendment also vote in my stead on any other matters.

(*Signed*) ROY DEE"

Now, Mr. President, this forenoon you held a like telegram was in effect a resignation, and I presume that this telegram will prove to be the resignation of Mr. Dee.

THE PRESIDENT: The Chair so considers it.

MR. HODGES: Mr. President.

THE PRESIDENT: Mr. Hodges.

MR. HODGES: Then I desire to place in nomination for the vacancy caused by this resignation, a woman of the State of Florida, whom the Democratic party has highly honored, and who has been selected to be the National Committeewoman of this party to represent this state, Mrs. Hortense K. Wells. (Applause.)

Mr. Frank seconded the nomination, and moved that nominations be closed, which motion on being put was carried, and Mrs. Wells was unanimously declared elected to fill the vacancy of Mr. Roy Dee. Mr. Hodges and Mrs. Gill were appointed as a committee to escort her to the Chair, and the Chief Justice administered the oath of office to her.

THE PRESIDENT: The next is a communication from the Secretary of State. The Reading Secretary will read communications from the Secretary of State:

The Reading Secretary read the communications as follows:

SEAL

OFFICE OF THE

SECRETARY OF STATE

STATE OF FLORIDA

Tallahassee

November 14th, 1933

HON. ROBERT H. ANDERSON, President
Repeal Convention
Capitol

MY DEAR SIR:

I have the honor to hand you herewith certified copy of the Certificate of the Secretary of State of the United States transmitting a Joint Resolution of Congress proposing an amendment to the Constitution of the United States and a certified copy of the proposed amendment submitted to the Conventions of the several States.

I have the honor to be
Very truly yours,
(*Signed*) R. A. GRAY
Secretary of State

UNITED STATES OF AMERICA

DEPARTMENT OF STATE

To all to whom these presents shall come, GREETING:

I Certify That the copy hereto attached is a true copy of a Resolution of Congress entitled "JOINT RESOLUTION Proposing an Amendment to the Constitution of the United States," the original of which is on file in this department.

SEAL

In testimony whereof, I, Henry L. Stimson, Secretary of State, have hereunto caused the seal of the Department of State to be affixed and my name subscribed by the Acting Chief Clerk of the said Department, at the City of Washington, in the District of Columbia, this 21st day of February, 1933.

HENRY L. STIMSON
Secretary of State

By: P. F. ALLEN
Acting Chief Clerk

SEVENTY-SECOND CONGRESS OF THE UNITED STATES OF AMERICA
AT THE SECOND SESSION

Begun and held at the City of Washington, on Monday, the fifth of December, one thousand nine hundred and thirty-two.

JOINT RESOLUTION

Proposing an amendment to the Constitution of the United States.

Resolved by the Senate and House of Representatives of the United States of America in Congress assembled (two thirds of each House concurring therein), that the following article is hereby proposed as an amendment to the Constitution of the United States, which shall be valid to all intents and purposes as part of the Constitution when ratified by conventions in three-fourths of the several States:

ARTICLE ___ ___

Section 1. The eighteenth article of amendment to the Constitution of the United States is hereby repealed.

Section 2. The transportation or importation into any State, Territory, or possession of the United States for delivery or use therein of intoxicating liquors, in violation of the laws thereof, is hereby prohibited.

Section 3. This article shall be inoperative unless it shall have been ratified as an amendment to the Constitution by conventions in the several states, as provided in the Constitution, within seven years from the date of the submission hereof to the States by the Congress.

JNO. N. GARNER
Speaker of the House of Representatives

CHARLES CURTIS
Vice-President of the United States and President of the Senate

I hereby certify that this Joint Resolution originated in the Senate.

EDWIN P. THAYER
Secretary

STATE OF FLORIDA

OFFICE OF SECRETARY OF STATE

I, R. A. GRAY, Secretary of State of the State of Florida, do hereby certify that the above and foregoing is a true and correct copy of Certificates on file in this office.

Given under my hand and the Great Seal of the State of Florida at Tallahassee, the Capital, this the fourteenth day of November, A.D., 1933.

SEAL

R. A. GRAY
Secretary of State.

THE PRESIDENT: The communication will be referred to the Committee on Resolutions.

MR. COCKRELL: Mr. President.

THE PRESIDENT: Mr. Cockrell.

MR. COCKRELL: Mr. President, as I understand the rules, a resolution is handed to the Secretary and read by the Reading Clerk on first reading? I offer this resolution:

THE PRESIDENT: The Reading Clerk will read the resolution.

The resolution was then read in full on first reading by the Reading Clerk as follows:

RESOLUTION RATIFYING A PROPOSED AMENDMENT TO THE CONSTITUTION OF THE UNITED STATES

WHEREAS, the Congress of the United States has proposed an Amendment to the Constitution of the United States, in substance and in effect as follows, to-wit:

Resolved by the Senate and House of Representatives of the United States of America in Congress assembled (two-thirds of each House concurring therein), That the following article is hereby proposed as an amendment to the Constitution of the United States, which shall be valid to all intents and purposes as part of the Constitution when ratified by conventions in three-fourths of the several states.

ARTICLE ___

Section 1. The eighteenth article of amendment to the Constitution of the United States is hereby repealed.

Section 2. The transportation or importation into any State, Territory, or possession of the United States for delivery or use therein of intoxicating liquors, in violation of the laws thereof, is hereby prohibited.

Section 3. This article shall be inoperative unless it shall have been ratified as an amendment to the Constitution by convention in the several states, as provided in the Constitution, within seven years from the date of the submission hereof to the States by the Congress and

WHEREAS, the Congress has proposed that the said proposed Amendment shall be valid to all intents and purposes, as part of the Constitution, when ratified by Conventions in three-fourths of the several States; and

WHEREAS, the people of Florida, at the election held in each County of the State, on October 10th, 1933, pursuant to the provisions of Chapter 16180, Acts 1933, Laws of Florida, regularly elected sixty-seven delegates from the State at Large, to constitute a convention to ratify or reject the said proposed Amendment; and

WHEREAS, the said delegates are now lawfully constituted into a Convention, sitting in the Capitol, and have considered the said proposed Amendment and are advised of the action they shall take therein;

Now, therefore,

Be it resolved that we, the delegates of the people of Florida, in convention regularly constituted, in the name, by the authority, and on behalf of the people of Florida, do ratify the said proposed Amendment to the Constitution of the United States.

Endorsed: Offered by Alston Cockrell.

THE PRESIDENT: The resolution will be referred to the Resolutions Committee. Are there other resolutions?

MR. LANDIS: Mr. President.

THE PRESIDENT: Mr. Landis.

MR. LANDIS: Mr. President, I have a resolution which I wish to offer at this time.

The Reading Clerk then read the resolution on first reading as follows:

Be it resolved by this Convention that the Secretary of State of the State of Florida be and he is hereby requested to have the minutes and proceedings of this Convention duly printed and bound in book form in a sufficient quantity to supply one copy of such book containing such minutes and proceedings to each of the delegates to this Convention, and with such additional copies as the Secretary of State may determine, to place in the archives of the State of Florida, and

Be it further resolved that the Secretary of State be and he is hereby requested, after the printing and binding of such minutes and proceedings, to duly send a copy of the same to each of the delegates to this Convention, and place the balance of the same in the archives of the State of Florida.

Endorsed: Offered by Erskine W. Landis.

MR. CARABALLO: Mr. President.

THE PRESIDENT: Mr. Caraballo.

MR. CARABELLO: May I ask if Mr. Landis will consider an amendment to that resolution by adding thereto—

THE PRESIDENT: The resolution is not open to amendment at this time. It goes to the Resolutions Committee, and you have an opportunity to appear before the Resolutions Committee and offer the amendment there, or after it is returned and read the second time, offer the amendment on the floor.

Are there any other resolutions? If not, the Resolutions Committee will retire and consider the resolutions that have been referred to it, and make its report with all due dispatch.

Has the Credentials Committee a report to make?

MR. FEIBELMAN: Mr. President, I have the report of the Committee on Credentials.

THE PRESIDENT: Send the report to the Reading Clerk, and have it read to the convention.

THE CAPITOL

TALLAHASSEE, FLORIDA

Tuesday, November 14, A.D. 1933

TO THE HONORABLE ROBERT H. ANDERSON,
The President, Florida State Constitutional Convention,
To Consider a Proposed Amendment to the Constitution
of the United States.

We, your Committee on Credentials, beg leave to report that we have examined the credentials of the delegates to this convention and have found that the following have been duly elected as delegates and are qualified to sit in this convention:

Robert H. Anderson
Henry Clay Armstrong
George H. Asbell
Clayton A. Avriett
Fletcher A. Black
John Lynn Blackwell
Nathan H. Boswell, Sr.
Clayton C. Codrington
Harold Colee
Henry Edmund Corry
Hattie R. Crawford
Jessie Currie
Helen Glenn Dann
Hortense Wells
Herbert U. Feibelman
Asher Frank
Edward V. Garcia
Mrs. Joe Gill
L. A. Grayson
Beulah Hooks Hannah
Mamie Sparkman Hart
Wendell E. Heaton
Raeburn C. Horne
Sidney L. Kilgore
Joseph Lee Kirby-Smith
Gordon B. Knowles
Erskine W. Landis
Loomis C. Leedy
C. D. Leffler
Ben H. Lindsey, Jr.
J. B. Hodges
G. C. Martin
James E. Calkins
Rebecca A. Camp
Mrs. Gordon E. Knowles
Martin Caraballo

Calvin D. Christ, M.D.
Val C. Cleary
Alston Cockrell
Mrs. Hugh M. Matheson
C. Parkhill Mays
Baron De Hirsch Meyer
Thomas Rogero Mickler
W. H. Milton
Albert Ives Pooser
John O. Pugh
Edwin H. Robinson
Chas. W. (Chuck) Ruckel
James D. Russ, Sr.
Ray Seldon
H. Boyce Taylor, Jr.
Thomas S. Trantham
L. E. Vause
J. T. Vocelle
Mrs. Harry M. Voorhis
Perry G. Wall
J. V. Walton
Chas. H. Warwick, Jr.
W. H. Weaver
W. E. Whitlock
Errol S. Willes
Herbert E. Wolfe
Mrs. Frank B. Shutts

Respectfully submitted,
HERBERT U. FEIBELMAN
Chairman Committee on Credentials
MAMIE SPARKMAN HART
C. O. CHRIST
W. H. MILTON
JOHN O. PUGH

MR. FEIBELMAN: Mr. President.

THE PRESIDENT: Mr. Feibelman.

MR. FEIBELMAN: I move you, Mr. President, the adoption of the report.

The motion was seconded by Mr. Avriett, and on being put was carried.

MR. COCKRELL: Mr. President.

THE PRESIDENT: Mr. Cockrell.

MR. COCKRELL: The Resolutions Committee is ready to report.

THE PRESIDENT: The convention will come to order. Before receiving the report, let me again call your attention to the fact that some of the delegates have not yet signed the register. I understand perhaps four have not signed it. Be good enough to sign it before getting away.

Let the report of the Resolutions Committee be read.

The Reading Clerk read the report of the Resolutions Committee as follows:

TALLAHASSEE, FLORIDA
November 14, 1933

HONORABLE ROBERT H. ANDERSON, PRESIDENT

Your Committee on Resolutions having considered the attached resolution and deliberated thereon, have unanimously voted that the said resolution be recommended for adoption by this Convention, and do report the same favorably for adoption.

BEULAH HOOKS HANNAH
ASHER FRANK
CHARLES H. WARWICK, JR.
R. H. WEAVER
L. E. VAUSE
HENRY EDMUND CORRY
BARON DE HIRSCH MEYER
JOHN LYNN BLACKWELL
EDWARD V. GARCIA
GORDON B. KNOWLES
J. B. HODGES
R. C. HORNE
F. A. BLACK
ALSTON COCKRELL

Attached to said report is the resolution hereinbefore appearing on pages 28-32.

MR. COCKRELL: Mr. President.

THE PRESIDENT: Mr. Cockrell.

MR. COCKRELL: Under the rules, I move that the resolution be placed on second reading.

THE PRESIDENT: Under the Rules Committee report goes on second reading. The Reading Clerk will read the resolution the second time.

The resolution was then read the second time in full.

THE PRESIDENT: Are there any amendments on second reading? If not, the resolution will be put on third reading and final passage. Read the resolution for the third time.

The resolution was then read in full by the Reading Clerk on third and final reading.

THE PRESIDENT: The resolution has been on the third and final reading. The question is on the adoption of the resolution. Is there any discussion?

MR. COCKRELL: Mr. President.

THE PRESIDENT: Mr. Cockrell.

MR. COCKRELL: Let me have the resolution, please, sir. There are a number of "Whereases" in the resolution, the first "Whereas" simply recites that the Congress has proposed the amendment, and then copies the proposed amendment in full. The second "Whereas" is that the people of Florida have elected us as delegates to this convention to pass upon the ratification or rejection of this amendment; and the third "Whereas" is that we are now lawfully constituted as a convention, and are deliberating on the amendment. The resolution then follows that we adopt this amendment, doing away with National Prohibition. I do not want to make a speech, Mr. President. The only thing I came here for was to vote "Aye" on that resolution. I do not think anything can be more eloquent than the "Ayes" which will be voted here today. (Applause.)

THE PRESIDENT: The question is on the adoption of the resolution. Is there further discussion?

MR. CARABALLO: Mr. President.

THE PRESIDENT: Mr. Caraballo.

MR. CARABALLO: I don't recall having heard a motion for its adoption. I make a motion now.

THE PRESIDENT: It was made automatically when the committee reported the resolution favorably, it went on second reading, and when it went on third reading, it was ready for adoption.

The Reading Clerk thereupon called the roll and the delegates answered thereunto as follows:

Robert H. Anderson, Aye
Henry Clay Armstrong, Aye
George H. Asbell, Aye
Clayton A. Avriett, Aye
Fletcher Black, Aye
John Lynn Blackwell, Aye
Nathan A. Boswell, Sr., Aye
James E. Calkins, Aye
Rebecca A. Camp, Aye
Martin Caraballo, Aye
Calvin D. Christ, M.D., Aye
Val C. Cleary, Aye
Alston Cockrell, Aye
Clayton C. Codrington, Aye
Harold Colee, Aye
Henry Edmund Corry, Aye
Hattie R. Crawford, Aye
Jessie Currie, Aye
Helen Glenn Dann, Aye
Herbert U. Feibelman, Aye
Asher Frank, Aye
Edward V. Garcia, Aye
Mrs. Joe Gill, Aye
L. A. Grayson, Aye
Beulah Hooks Hannah, Aye
Mamie Sparkman Hart, Aye
Wendell C. Heaton, Aye
James B. Hodges, Aye
Raeburn C. Horne, Aye
Sidney L. Kilgore, Aye
Joseph Lee Kirby-Smith, Aye
Gordon B. Knowles, Aye
Mrs. Gordon B. Knowles, Aye
Erskine W. Landis, Aye
Loomis C. Leedy, Aye
C. D. Leffler, Aye

Ben H. Lindsey, Jr., Aye
G. C. Martin, Aye
Mrs. Hugh M. Matheson, Aye
C. Parkhill Mays, Aye
Baron de Hirsch Meyer, Aye
Thomas Rogero Mickler, Aye
W. H. Milton, Aye
John O. Pugh, Aye
Albert Ives Pooser, Aye
Edwin H. Robinson, Aye
Charles W. (Chuck) Ruckel, Aye
James D. Russ, Sr., Aye
Ray Selden, Aye
Mrs. Frank B. Shutts, Aye
H. Boyce Taylor, Jr., Aye
Thomas S. Trantham, Aye
L. E. Vause, Aye
J. T. Vocelle, Aye
Mrs. Harry M. Voorhis, Aye
Perry G. Wall, Aye
J. V. Walton, Aye
Charles H. Warwick, Jr., Aye
R. H. Weaver, Aye
Mrs. Hortense K. Wells, Aye
W. E. Whitlock, Aye
Errol S. Willes, Aye
Herbert E. Wolfe, Aye

THE READING CLERK: "Ayes" 63; "Nays" none.

THE PRESIDENT: By your vote, you have adopted the resolution. (Loud applause.)

THE PRESIDENT: The resolution will be referred to the Enrollment Committee, who will take it and retire immediately and make its report, with all due speed. That Committee is Mr. Grayson, Mr. Mayes, Mrs. Crawford, Mrs. Currie, Mr. Russ, Mr. Avriett, Mr. Willes, Mr. Whitlock and Mr. Robinson.

MR. COCKRELL: Mr. President.

THE PRESIDENT: Mr. Cockrell.

MR. COCKRELL: There is another resolution that the Resolutions Committee reported favorably.

THE PRESIDENT: Let the report be read by the Reading Clerk.

TALLAHASSEE, FLORIDA
November 14th, 1933

HONORABLE ROBERT H. ANDERSON, PRESIDENT.

Your Committee on Resolutions having considered the attached resolution and deliberated thereon, have unanimously voted that the said resolution be recommended for adoption by this Convention and do report the same favorably for adoption.

ALSTON COCKRELL, *Chairman*

Attached to said report is the resolution offered by Mr. Landis appearing on page 32 hereof.

THE PRESIDENT: You have heard the Committee Report read. Are there any amendments?

MR. COCKRELL: Mr. President.

THE PRESIDENT: Mr. Cockrell.

MR. COCKRELL: If there are no amendments, I move that it be placed on the third and final reading.

The motion was seconded and on being put was carried and the resolution was read on its final reading, and was unanimously adopted, and it was ordered that it be transmitted to the Secretary of State.

MR. GRAYSON: Mr. President.

THE PRESIDENT: Mr. Grayson.

MR. GRAYSON: Mr. President, the Committee on Enrollment reports the resolution ratifying the proposed amendment to the Constitution, as having been properly enrolled and moves that its report be adopted.

THE PRESIDENT: The question is on the adoption of the Committee report. As many as favor the adoption of the report will say "Aye"; opposed will say "Nay." The "Ayes" have it and the report is adopted.

THE PRESIDENT: As President of this convention, I am now about to sign the resolution adopted by the Convention ratifying the proposal of the Congress of the United States to repeal the Eighteenth Amendment. (Loud Applause.)

Whereupon the President and the Secretary of the convention executed in conformity with the statute the following certificate:

CERTIFICATE OF ADOPTION OF RESOLUTION

WE, ROBERT H. ANDERSON, as President, and REBECCA A. CAMP, as Secretary, of the convention of delegates elected by the people of Florida, at the election held in each county of the State on October 10th, 1933, pursuant to the provisions of Chapter 16180, Laws of 1933, and consisting of sixty-seven (67) delegates regularly elected from the State at Large to constitute a convention to ratify or reject the following proposed amendment to the Constitution of the United States:

Resolved by the Senate and House of Representatives of the United States of America in Congress assembled (two-thirds of each House concurring therein), That the following article is hereby proposed as an amendment to the Constitution of the United States, which shall be valid to all intents and purposes as part of the Constitution when ratified by conventions in three-fourths of the several States:

ARTICLE ___ ___

Section 1. The eighteenth article of amendment to the Constitution of the United States is hereby repealed.

Section 2. The transportation or importation into any State, Territory, or possession of the United States for delivery or use therein of intoxicating liquors, in violation of the laws thereof, is hereby prohibited.

Section 3. This article shall be inoperative unless it shall have been ratified as an amendment to the Constitution by conventions in the several states, as provided in the Constitution, within seven years from the date of the submission hereof to the States by the Congress, hereby certify that said delegates regularly and lawfully convened at the place provided by the Secretary of State of Florida, at the State Capitol, at Tallahassee, at 12 o'clock noon, on the 14th day of November, 1933, that being the second Tuesday of the month following their election, and after due deliberation agreed, by "Yea" and "Nay" vote of a majority of the total number of delegates elected, to-wit: by 63 Yeas and 0 Nays, to the ratification of the said proposed amendment to the Constitution of the United States.

In testimony whereof, we have hereunto set our hands as President and Secretary, respectively, of said convention during the session thereof at the place and time aforesaid, this 14th day of November, A.D. 1933.

ROBERT H. ANDERSON
President
REBECCA A. CAMP
Secretary

MR. CALKINS: Mr. President.
THE PRESIDENT: Mr. Calkins.

MR. CALKINS: Inasmuch as this resolution has been properly authenticated as having been passed by this convention, I now move that it be filed in the office of the Secretary of State.

The motion was seconded, and on being put was carried.

THE PRESIDENT: The secretary of the convention is directed to transmit the Enrolled resolution to the Secretary of State to be filed, and report so doing to this convention. The Sergeant-At-Arms will accompany the Secretary of the Convention.

MR. COLEE: Mr. President.

THE PRESIDENT: Mr. Colee.

MR. COLEE: Mr. President, we have ratified that resolution, would it not be appropriate that a wire be immediately dispatched to the Federal Administration apprising them of the fact of what this convention has done?

THE PRESIDENT: I don't think so. They are charged with notice of it.

MR. LANDIS: Mr. President.

THE PRESIDENT: Mr. Landis.

MR. LANDIS: Mr. President, it has undoubtedly occurred to the members up here that someone is entitled to a great deal of thanks of this body for the detail work which has been done so carefully, in providing our quarters and various other details that have been thought of, and that work has been handled by our good friend the Secretary of State, Robert A. Gray. I think we would be derelict in our duty if we did not extend the thanks of our convention to Mr. Gray, and I so move.

MR. COCKRELL: Mr. President.

THE PRESIDENT: Mr. Cockrell.

MR. COCKRELL: Mr. President, in seconding that motion, I wish to express my thanks and appreciation to Mr. Gray.

THE PRESIDENT: The question is upon the adoption of the motion. Is there discussion? If not, as many as favor the motion will say "Aye"; those opposed will say "Nay." The "Ayes" have it. The motion is adopted by unanimous vote. Mr. Secretary of State, on behalf of this convention, I extend to you its thanks for the cooperation which you have given us in the performance of our work.

THE SECRETARY: Mr. President.

THE PRESIDENT: Madam Secretary.

THE SECRETARY: I wish to announce the resolution has been delivered to the Secretary of State.

THE PRESIDENT: The Secretary announces that the resolution ratifying the proposed repeal of the Eighteenth Amendment has been delivered to and filed with the Secretary of State.

MR. COCKRELL: Mr. President.

THE PRESIDENT: Mr. Cockrell.

MR. COCKRELL: Mr. President, I have another resolution. The resolution is in the following words and figures:

RESOLUTION

Be it resolved that we, the delegates of the people of Florida, in convention regularly constituted, in the name, by the authority, and on behalf of the people of Florida, have by resolution duly adopted, ratified the proposed amendment to the Constitution of the United States relating to prohibition; that said Resolution has been duly enrolled, has been signed by the President and the Secretary of this Convention in open session of this Convention in the presence of the Convention; and that said Resolution has been duly delivered by the Secretary of this Convention to the Secretary of State of the State of Florida, and has been filed by the Secretary of State of the State of Florida.

Endorsed: Offered by Alston Cockrell.

THE PRESIDENT: Under the rules, as I understand, that goes to the Resolutions Committee. The Resolutions Committee has already considered it.

MR. COCKRELL: I move that the rules be waived, and the resolution be placed on third reading and final passage.

THE PRESIDENT: The question is on waiving the rules and placing the resolution on final passage. As many as favor say "Aye"; those opposed say "No." The motion is carried by a two-thirds vote.

MR. COCKRELL: Mr. President.

THE PRESIDENT: Mr. Cockrell.

MR. COCKRELL: I move that the resolution be adopted.

THE PRESIDENT: Before putting the motion, I might state that this is a resolution that is required by statute. The law requires that the convention give affirmative evidence of its action, and the resolution is offered for the purpose of complying with the law.

The motion to adopt the resolution was put, and on being seconded, was unanimously adopted.

MR. AVRIETT: Mr. President.

THE PRESIDENT: Mr. Avriett.

MR. AVRIETT: I move that the thanks of this Convention be extended to the Chamber of Commerce of Tallahassee, the Junior Chamber of Commerce of this city and the Tallahassee Country Club and the several other organizations for the courtesies extended to us while in this city.

THE PRESIDENT: The question is on the adoption of the motion made by Mr. Avriett to extend the thanks of the Convention to the organizations named. Those in favor of the motion say "Aye"; those opposed "No." The "Ayes" have it; the motion is adopted, and the appreciation of this convention is expressed to the Tallahassee Chamber of Commerce, the Junior Chamber of Commerce, the Tallahassee Country Club and to each of the other organizations which has contributed to the entertainment of the delegates during this session.

MRS. HANNAH: Mr. President.

THE PRESIDENT: Mrs. Hannah.

MRS. HANNAH: This convention owes a real debt to those newspapers of the state and their editors, who long before repeal became popular, fought the good fight against the evils of prohibition.

It was the strong editorials by editors like Mr. Lambright of the Tampa Tribune and Mr. Stoneman, of the Miami Herald, which helped to open the eyes of the people and crystallize the sentiment that gave repeal its tremendous majority in this state, and I move that the thanks of this convention be extended to these newspapers for their efforts in this cause.

MR. COCKRELL: Mr. President.

THE PRESIDENT: Mr. Cockrell.

MR. COCKRELL: Mr. President, I am unwilling to let this opportunity pass without paying a tribute to the Jacksonville Journal for its constant and consistent fight in behalf of repeal, begun by it long before repeal was recognized as a popular move, to its editor, Gold V. Sanders, and to its city editor, a member of this Convention, H. Boyce Taylor.

THE PRESIDENT: The question is on the adoption of the motion. Those in favor of the motion say "Aye"; those opposed say "No." The "Ayes" have it. The motion is adopted and the appreciation of this convention is extended to the newspapers of this state whose efforts have contributed so much to the success of the repeal movement in Florida.

As far as the Chair can see, that completes the functions of this Convention in the performance of its duties under the law.

MR. CALKINS: Mr. President.

THE PRESIDENT: Mr. Calkins.

MR. CALKINS: I rise for the purpose of moving the adjournment *sine die* of this Convention, and if there is no other business coming before the Convention, I now move that this Convention stand adjourned, *sine die.*

The motion was seconded, and on being put was carried and the President thereupon declared that the Convention was adjourned, *sine die.*

We hereby certify that the foregoing is a true and correct transcript of the Minutes of the Convention, held pursuant to the provisions of Chapter 16180, Laws of Florida (1933), in the Chamber of the House of Representatives, in the State House, in Tallahassee, State of Florida, on November 14, 1933, to ratify a proposal to amend the Constitution of the United States by repealing Article Eighteen of the Amendments to the Constitution of the United States.

ROBERT H. ANDERSON
President

Attest:

REBECCA A. CAMP
Secretary

IDAHO*

JOURNAL

OF THE

IDAHO REPEAL CONVENTION

HELD UNDER THE PROVISIONS OF

Chapter 179 of the Idaho Session Laws of 1933 entitled the "CONSTITUTIONAL CONVENTION ACT," providing for conventions to pass on amendments to the Constitution of the United States which are now or may hereafter be proposed by the Congress of the United States for ratification by conventions in the several states

Approved March 11, 1933
In Force March 11, 1933

Held in the City of Boise, October 17, 1933 at 12:00 o'clock noon in THE CHAMBERS OF THE HOUSE OF REPRESENTATIVES

IN THE STATE CAPITOL

OFFICERS OF THE CONVENTION

President
Asher B. Wilson
Twin Falls

Secretary
Troy D. Smith
Mackay

Journal Clerk ....Dorothy Lonzwa
Minute Clerk ....Faye Stewart
Parliamentarian ....Frank Harris
Sergeant-at-Arms ....Duncan Johnston
Assistant Sergeant-at-Arms ....Dan J. Cavanagh
Doorkeeper ....Ben E. Thomas
Doorkeeper.............W. L. Korter
Doorkeeper ....Frank Williams
Doorkeeper ....B. G. Lane
Doorkeeper..........J. H. Fredrickson
Chaplain ....Dean Frank E. Rhea
Messenger ....James Galloway, Jr.
Page ....Arthur Riddle
Page ....Robert McDevitt

* Printed.

DELEGATES TO THE CONVENTION

Beecher Hitchcock ....Sandpoint
John P. Gray ....Coeur d'Alene
*Donald A. Callahan ....Wallace
M. Kenworthy ....Moscow
Robert S. Erb ....Lewiston
Frank Harris ....Weiser
Robert A. Davis, Jr. ....Nampa
William Healy ....Boise
D. S. Whitehead ....Boise
M. F. Cunningham ....Hailey
Robert Coulter ....Cascade
Asher B. Wilson ....Twin Falls
J. J. Boyd ....Buhl
Irel Gudmundsen ....Burley
Troy D. Smith ....Mackay
J. H. Peterson ....Pocatello
Frank E. DeKay ....Blackfoot
Harold R. Toomer ....Montpelier
Parley Rigby ....Idaho Falls
Earl D. Jones ....Roberts
Emmett Robins ....St. Anthony

STATE OF IDAHO

JOURNAL OF "REPEAL CONVENTION"

HALL OF THE HOUSE OF REPRESENTATIVES

BOISE, IDAHO

TUESDAY, OCTOBER 17, 1933

CONVENTION IN SESSION

Pursuant to an Act of the Twenty-second Legislature of the State of Idaho, entitled,

"AN ACT to provide for conventions to pass on amendments to the Constitution of the United States which are now or may hereafter be proposed by the Congress of the United States for ratification by conventions in the several states: providing that this Act may be inoperative if Congress shall prescribe the manner in which constitutional conventions shall be constituted: providing that if any part of the Act is adjudged unconstitutional or invalid, such adjudication shall not affect the validity of the remaining portions which can be given effect; providing that this Act may be referred to as the 'Constitutional Convention Act,' and declaring an emergency," approved March 11, 1933, the delegates-elect to the Convention were called to order by the Hon. Robert Coulter, Speaker of the House of Representatives of the Twenty-second Session, in the Hall of the House of Representatives in the Capitol, Boise, Idaho, at the hour of 12:00 o'clock M., October 17, 1933.

MR. COULTER: The hour has arrived for the calling of this Convention as provided by House Bill No. 337, recently enacted by the Twenty-second Session of the Idaho State Legislature, and approved on March 11, 1933. Pursuant to a statute enacted by the last general session of the Legislature, it is our duty at this time to organize as, and be, and constitute a Convention to pass upon the question of whether or not the proposed amendment to the Constitution of the United States of America be ratified so as to, in effect, repeal the Eighteenth Amendment.

The statute provides that this Convention shall be the judge of the election and qualification of its members, and shall have the power to elect a President, Secretary, and other officers and/or employees, and to adopt its own rules, and it is further provided that a Journal must be kept of our proceedings.

* Gladys Terhune Keel elected by convention to fill the vacancy caused by the absence of Donald A. Callahan.

Governor C. Ben Ross transmitted to the Convention a copy of Joint Resolution Proposing an Amendment to the Constitution of the United States, certified to by the Secretary of State, which is as follows:

I, FRANKLIN GIRARD, the duly elected, qualified and acting Secretary of State of the State of Idaho, hereby certify that the following is a true and correct copy of a Resolution of Congress, entitled "JOINT RESOLUTION Proposing an amendment to the Constitution of the United States," as the same has been sent and certified to the Governor of the State of Idaho by Henry L. Stimson, former Secretary of State of the United States, and filed in my office:

No. 587

UNITED STATES OF AMERICA

DEPARTMENT OF STATE

To all to whom these presents shall come, GREETING:

I certify that the copy hereto attached is a true copy of a Resolution of Congress entitled "JOINT RESOLUTION Proposing an Amendment to the Constitution of the United States," the original of which is on file in the Department.

In testimony whereof, I, Henry L. Stimson, Secretary of State, have hereunto caused the Seal of the Department of State to be affixed and my name subscribed by the Acting Chief Clerk of the said Department, at the City of Washington, in the District of Columbia, this 21st day of February, 1933.

HENRY L. STIMSON
Secretary of State

By P. F. ALLEN
Acting Chief Clerk

SEVENTY-SECOND CONGRESS OF THE UNITED STATES OF AMERICA

AT THE SECOND SESSION

Begun and held at the City of Washington on Monday, the fifth day of December, one thousand nine hundred and thirty-two

JOINT RESOLUTION

Proposing an amendment to the Constitution of the United States

Resolved by the Senate and House of Representatives of the United States of America in Congress assembled (two-thirds of each House concurring therein), That the following article is hereby proposed as an amendment to the Constitution of the United States, which shall be valid to all intents and purposes as part of the Constitution when ratified by conventions in three-fourths of the several States:

ARTICLE ___ ___

Section 1. The eighteenth article of amendment to the Constitution of the United States is hereby repealed.

Section 2. The transportation or importation into any State, Territory, or possession of the United States for delivery or use therein of intoxicating liquors, in violation of the laws thereof, is hereby prohibited.

Section 3. This article shall be inoperative unless it shall have been ratified as an amendment to the Constitution by convention in the several States, as provided in the Constitution, within seven years from the date of submission hereof to the States by the Congress.

JNO. N. GARNER
Speaker of the House of Representatives

CHARLES CURTIS
Vice President of the United States and
President of the Senate

In witness whereof, I have hereunto set my hand and caused the Great Seal of the State of Idaho to be affixed hereto, this 17th day of October, 1933.

FRANKLIN GIRARD
Secretary of State

Mr. Coulter then presented the Certificate of Election from the Secretary of State, which was read by Mr. John P. Mix, Assistant Secretary of State, and ordered it spread upon the pages of the Journal.

STATE OF IDAHO

DEPARTMENT OF STATE

I, FRANKLIN GIRARD, Secretary of State of the State of Idaho, do hereby certify that the annexed is a full, true and complete transcript of the names of the persons elected at the special election held on the 19th day of September, 1933, to the office of delegate to the Constitutional Convention to be held on the 17th day of October, 1933, as shown by the official records of the State Board of Canvassers on file in the office of the Secretary of State of the State of Idaho.

Beecher Hitchcock, Sandpoint
John P. Gray, Coeur d'Alene
Donald A. Callahan, Wallace
M. Kenworthy, Moscow
Robert S. Erb, Lewiston
Frank Harris, Weiser
Robert A. Davis, Jr., Nampa
William Healy, Boise
D. S. Whitehead, Boise
M. F. Cunningham, Hailey
Robert Coulter, Cascade
Asher B. Wilson, Twin Falls
J. J. Boyd, Buhl
Irel Gudmundsen, Burley
Troy D. Smith, Mackay
J. H. Peterson, Pocatello
Frank E. DeKay, Blackfoot
Harold R. Toomer, Montpelier
Parley Rigby, Idaho Falls
Earl D. Jones, Roberts
Emmett Robins, St. Anthony

In testimony whereof, I have hereunto set my hand and affixed the Great Seal of the State. Done at Boise City, the Capital of Idaho, this sixteenth day of October, in the year of our Lord one thousand nine hundred and thirty-three, and of the Independence of the United States of America the One Hundred and Fifty-eighth.

SEAL

FRANKLIN GIRARD
Secretary of State

Roll call showed all delegates present, except Donald Callahan, absent.

The presiding officer, Mr. Coulter, declared a quorum present.

Moved by Whitehead that the Rules of the House of Representatives of the Twenty-second Session of the Idaho Legislature, in so far as they apply, be adopted and used as the Rules of this Constitutional Convention.

Seconded by Mr. Smith.

Roll call resulted as follows:

Ayes: Boyd, Coulter, Cunningham, Davis, DeKay, Erb, Gray, Gudmundsen, Harris, Healy, Hitchcock, Jones, Kenworthy, Peterson, Rigby, Robins, Smith, Toomer, Whitehead, Wilson. Total, 20.

Nays: None.

Absent and not voting: Callahan. Total, 1.

Motion prevailed.

Mr. Coulter recognized the gentleman from Coeur d'Alene, Mr. Gray.

MR. GRAY: I nominate Mr. Asher B. Wilson as President of this convention. I think it is only a proper tribute to the service which he has rendered in presenting this matter of the people of the State.

MR. HITCHCOCK: I wish to second the nomination of Asher B. Wilson, in recognition of his effective work on behalf of the repeal of the Eighteenth Amendment.

The nominations being closed, the question was put.

Motion prevailed and the presiding officer, Mr. Coulter, declared Mr. Wilson unanimously elected President.

At this time Mr. Wilson took the Chair.

The President announced that the next item of business was the selection of Secretary.

MR. COULTER: It was my pleasure to preside over the Twenty-second Session of the Idaho Legislature as Speaker of the House. In that body we had a young man from Custer County, the man who introduced and fathered the passage of this bill, that provided for the election of delegates to a Constitutional Convention. I think it is only fitting that this man should be the Secretary of this Convention. I, therefore, take great pleasure in presenting the name of Troy D. Smith of Mackay as Secretary of the Convention.

Seconded by Peterson.

The nominations being closed, the question was put.

The motion prevailed and the President declared Mr. Smith unanimously elected Secretary.

The President appointed the following Committee to wait upon Chief Justice

Budge and request him to come to the House Chamber to administer the oath of office:

Frank Harris J. J. Boyd William Healy

At this time the Committee appeared and presented Justice Budge to the Chair. The Committee was discharged and Justice Budge administered the oath of office to all delegates-elect present.

The Secretary then read the following communication from Donald Callahan:

CHICAGO, October 13, 1933

MR. ASHER B. WILSON
Owyhee Hotel, Boise, Idaho

MY DEAR ASHER:

I received your wire in due time and wish to thank you for the information. I am very sorry that I shall be unable to attend the convention. I had looked forward to this meeting with the men who are interested, as I am, in the repeal of the Eighteenth Amendment and I did want to be put on record in the convention as having helped in the work.

Unfortunately the business of preparing and having approved the codes for the lead and zinc industry has kept me away from Idaho for the past seven weeks. It is quite imperative that I return to New York before Monday for a conference with N. R. A. representatives before the primary hearing upon the code which is tentatively set for October twenty-third.

I wish you would express to the members of the convention my extreme regret at my inability to be with them. I appreciate very much the honor that was given to me in being elected a delegate to this very important convention. I hope that you have a very pleasant time and I am certain that the seriousness of the step which you are to take has impressed itself upon you and all the other members of the convention.

I have a suggestion to make and that is that this convention provide for a commission to study the question of liquor control and in the event the Idaho constitutional amendment is repealed, have ready a sound piece of legislation along that line to offer the 1935 legislature. Only one-half of the battle has been won with the repeal of constitutional prohibition. No one who is right minded desires a return to old conditions before prohibition any more than they desire a continuance of the intolerable conditions which have existed under prohibition. It will be a test of the ability of our people to govern themselves when the time comes to write statutes that will minimize the evil effects of liquor traffic. In a state such as ours, without large industrial centers, it should be easy to adopt a policy which will have for its object true temperance and the removal of evils of unrestricted traffic in liquor.

I do not believe we should leave the preparation of such legislation to chance nor that we should do nothing until a legislature has been elected. You know that this legislature will not be chosen because of its particular fitness to handle questions of this kind. You know that very few of its members will have given serious thought to the problems which the repeal of prohibition legislation will bring about. You know, as I do, however, that a legislature elected in 1934 must be desirous of writing liquor laws conforming to the will of the people. Accordingly, it seems to me that between now and the time of the convening of the next legislature, a select group of men and women can be well engaged in a study of the various liquor laws now in effect throughout the world and those which have been proposed in other states and can select such a scheme as will best suit the conditions in Idaho.

It is my idea that such a commission will consist of men and women of those who have been classed as drys as well as those who have been classed as wets. In other words, a commission composed of earnest, intelligent, thoughtful citizens desirous only of presenting a scheme of liquor control which will promote true temperance, protect the weak and adolescent and above all provide a system which because of its reasonableness and conformity to the will of the great majority of our people will be possible of enforcement.

Again wishing you and my fellow delegates a pleasant meeting and congratulating you one and all upon this opportunity to serve your state, I am

Sincerely yours,
DONALD A. CALLAHAN

Moved by Jones that Gladys Terhune Keel be elected to take the place in this convention on account of absence of Donald Callahan.

Seconded by Coulter.

Motion prevailed and the President declared Gladys Terhune Keel of Jerome elected to fill the vacancy caused by the absence of Donald Callahan.

Whereupon, Chief Justice Budge administered the oath of office to Gladys Terhune Keel.

At this time invocation was given by Chaplain Rhea.

RESOLUTION

Be it resolved, that the President of this Convention appoint seven delegates to serve as a Committee on Resolutions; three delegates to serve as a Committee on Organization; four delegates to serve as a Committee on Mileage and Expense, the Chairman of which shall certify expense accounts of delegates, attachés and all other expense to the President of this Convention; and five delegates to serve as a Committee to wait upon the Secretary of State of Idaho and deliver to him such Resolutions as will be adopted by this Convention.

Moved by Coulter.

Seconded by DeKay.

Motion prevailed.

At this time the President made the following committee appointments:

Committee on Resolutions
Harris, *Chairman;* Gray; Peterson; Healy; Whitehead; Jones; Hitchcock.

Committee on Organization
Coulter, *Chairman;* DeKay; Robins.

Committee on Mileage and Expense
Keel, *Chairman;* Davis; Cunningham; Erb.

Committee to Wait on the Secretary of State and to Transmit Resolution to Said Secretary
Toomer, *Chairman;* Gudmundsen; Boyd; Rigby; Kenworthy.

The President declared the Convention at ease subject to the call of the Chair.

CONVENTION IN SESSION

Mr. Coulter read the following report of the Committee on Organization:

MR. PRESIDENT: *Be it resolved,* That the following offices be created for the performance of the necessary work connected with this convention.

One Chaplain
One Parliamentarian
One Sergeant-at-Arms
One Assistant Sergeant-at-Arms
One Journal Clerk
One Minute Clerk
Four Doorkeepers
One Messenger
Two Pages

Be it further resolved, That there be elected to such office above provided, the following named persons at the per diem named:

One Chaplain—Dean Frank E. Rhea at $3.00 per diem
Journal Clerk—Dorothy Lonzwa at $5.00 per diem

Minute Clerk—Faye Stewart at $5.00 per diem
Parliamentarian—Frank Harris, without compensation
Sergeant-at-Arms—Duncan Johnston at $5.00 per diem
Assistant Sergeant-at-Arms—Dan J. Cavanagh at $5.00 per diem
Doorkeeper—Ben E. Thomas at $5.00 per diem
Doorkeeper—W. L. Korter at $5.00 per diem
Doorkeeper—Frank Williams at $5.00 per diem
Doorkeeper—B. G. Lane at $5.00 per diem
Doorkeeper—J. H. Fredrickson, without compensation
Messenger—James Galloway, Jr. at $2.00 per diem
Page—Arthur Riddle at $2.00 per diem
Page—Robert McDevitt at $2.00 per diem

Moved by Coulter.

Seconded by Whitehead.

Roll call resulted as follows:

Ayes: Boyd, Coulter, Cunningham, Davis, DeKay, Erb, Gray, Gudmundsen, Harris, Healy, Hitchcock, Jones, Keel, Kenworthy, Peterson, Rigby, Robins, Smith, Toomer, Whitehead, Wilson. Total, 21.

Nays: None.

Whereupon the President declared the motion prevailed, the resolution adopted, and the above attaches elected.

The oath of office was administered to the following officers:

Dean Frank Rhea, Dorothy Lonzwa, Faye Stewart, Ben E. Thomas, Duncan Johnston, W. L. Korter, Frank Williams, B. G. Lane, J. H. Fredrickson, Dan J. Cavanagh, James Galloway, Jr., Arthur Riddle, Robert McDevitt.

Moved by Coulter that this Convention do now recess until the hour of 2:30 o'clock P.M., of this day.

Seconded by Rigby.

Whereupon the President declared the Convention recessed until 2:30 o'clock P.M., of this day.

(*Recess*)

(CONVENTION IN SESSION)

The hour of 2:30 o'clock P.M., having arrived, the delegates reconvened, pursuant to recess.

Roll call showed all members present.

The President recognized Mr. Harris of Weiser, who presented the following Resolution which was read by the Secretary:

REPORT OF COMMITTEE ON RESOLUTIONS

The Committee on Resolutions respectfully reports it has prepared a resolution which expresses the mandate and will of the people of the State of Idaho, said resolution is in words and figures as follows:

WHEREAS, Both Houses of the Seventy-second Congress of the United States of America, by a constitutional majority of two-thirds thereof, proposed an amendment to the Constitution of the United States of America, which should be valid to all intents and purposes as a part of the Constitution of the United States when ratified by conventions in three-fourths of the states, which resolution is in words and figures following, to-wit:

JOINT RESOLUTION

Proposing an amendment to the Constitution of the United States

Resolved, by the Senate and House of Representatives of the United States of America in Congress assembled (two-thirds of each House concurring therein). That the following article is hereby proposed as an amendment to the Constitution of the United States, which shall be valid to all intents and purposes as part of the Constitution when ratified by conventions in three-fourths of the several states:

ARTICLE ___

Section 1. The Eighteenth Article of Amendment to the Constitution of the United States is hereby repealed.

Section 2. The transportation and importation into any State, Territory or possession of the United States for delivery or use therein of intoxicating liquor, in violation of the laws thereof, is hereby prohibited.

Section 3. This article shall be inoperative unless it shall have been ratified as an amendment to the Constitution by conventions in the several states as provided in the Constitution, within seven years from the date of the submission thereof to the states by the Congress. Now, therefore, be it

Resolved, by the convention assembled pursuant to the authority of Chapter 179 of the General Laws of the State of Idaho passed at the Twenty-second Session of the State Legislature, entitled "An Act to Provide for Conventions to Pass on Amendments to the Constitution of the United States which are now or may hereafter be proposed by the Congress of the United States for ratification by Convention in the Several States," approved March 11, 1933, that said proposed amendment to the Constitution of the United States of America is hereby ratified.

Moved by Harris that the Resolution be adopted.

Seconded by Gray.

Roll call resulted as follows:

Ayes: Boyd, Coulter, Cunningham, Davis, DeKay, Erb, Gray, Gudmundsen, Harris, Healy, Hitchcock, Jones, Keel, Kenworthy, Peterson, Rigby, Robins, Smith, Toomer, Whitehead, Wilson. Total, 21.

Nays: None.

Whereupon the President declared the motion prevailed and the Resolution adopted.

Moved by Coulter that the Convention do recess subject to the call of the Chair.

Seconded by Whitehead.

Motion prevailed and the President declared the Convention recessed subject to the call of the Chair.

(*Recess*)

(CONVENTION IN SESSION)

The Convention reconvened at the call of the Chair.

Roll call showed all members present.

At this time the President, Mr. Wilson, addressed the Convention as follows:

GENTLEMEN OF THE CONVENTION: Repeal of the Eighteenth Amendment is now assured. This means that those who traffic in liquor across state lines which have dry laws may and will be prosecuted in the Federal courts as provision is made in the Twenty-first Amendment that "The transportation and importation into any State, Territory or possession of the United States for delivery or use therein of intoxicating liquor, in violation of the laws thereof, is hereby prohibited."

Although Idaho has declared for repeal of the Eighteenth Amendment, it is within the prohibited class so far as transportation and importation of liquor for delivery or use is concerned; and after ratification of the Twenty-first Amendment, which will be effective after December 5th next, it will be just as unlawful for liquor to be brought into the State of Idaho as it is now. For that reason the citizens of the State of Idaho must give further consideration to the distribution and use of intoxicating liquor, so far as possessing or using same is concerned, within the bounds of this great Commonwealth.

The Twenty-second Session of the Legislature of Idaho, of which three of the members of this convention—Senator Cunningham, Troy Smith, and Robert Coulter—were members, provided by resolution for submission to the voters of the State of Idaho an Amendment to Section Twenty-six of Article Three of the Constitution of the State of Idaho relating to prohibition of intoxicating liquor, said amendment, provided it is adopted, will read as follows:

"From and after the 31st day of December, 1934, the Legislature of the State of Idaho shall have full power and authority to permit, control and regulate or prohibit the manufacture, sale, keeping for sale, and transportation for sale, of intoxicating liquors for beverage purposes."

We have been delegated by the people of the State of Idaho to assemble as a Convention under the law and ratify the proposed amendment to the Constitution of the United States, which amendment when ratified by the requisite number of States will repeal the Eighteenth Amendment.

In view of the fact that provision has been made for submission of liquor regulation in our own State Constitution, it is well that the individual members of this body whose beliefs are that repeal is just, proper and necessary should dedicate their services to the cause of repeal in the State Constitution from this day until the closing of the polls at the next General Election when said question will be submitted to a vote.

Each delegate may, and hundreds of the other workers and voters undoubtedly will, disagree as to the method of control as and when liquor is available to the citizens of the State of Idaho. However, we may rely on the next legislature to provide sufficient just laws for proper regulation of sale, distribution and consumption of liquor within the State of Idaho. We may depend upon it that our Chief Executive will be such an officer as will not permit the passage of laws that will fail to properly regulate the liquor traffic. He will veto any proposed legislation which would permit return of the old-time saloon.

The present system of moonshining and bootlegging will vanish and I trust that those Prohibitionists who have heretofore fought the repeal movement will see the error of their judgment and will cease to support a cause which gives assistance to bootlegging and moonshining with its attendant forms of racketeering.

Moved by Coulter that the address of the President, Mr. Wilson, be spread upon the pages of the Journal.

Seconded by Smith.

The question was put by the Secretary, Mr. Smith.

Motion prevailed and it was so ordered.

RESOLUTION

Be it resolved, That the members of this Convention assembled do hereby extend their thanks and appreciation to the President, Asher B. Wilson, and the Secretary, Troy D. Smith, of this Convention, for the efficient and expeditious manner in which they have conducted the proceedings of this Convention.

Be it further resolved, That this resolution of appreciation be spread upon the pages of the Journal.

Moved by Coulter.

Seconded by Whitehead.

Motion prevailed and the Resolution adopted.

RESOLUTION

Be it resolved, That the President and the Secretary of this Convention be and hereby are directed and empowered to retain a sufficient number of employees of this Convention for a period of time after adjournment of said Convention to complete, transcribe, arrange, compare and file records of said Convention, and to make final disposition of any and all such files and records.

Be it further resolved, That the President and Secretary of this Convention assembled, be authorized to approve the written Journal of this Convention with the same force and effect as if the delegates of this Convention had approved the same.

Moved by Coulter.

Seconded by Whitehead.

Roll call resulted as follows:

Ayes: Boyd, Coulter, Cunningham, Davis, DeKay, Erb, Gudmundsen, Harris, Healy, Hitchcock, Jones, Keel, Kenworthy, Peterson, Robins, Smith, Toomer, Whitehead, Wilson. Total, 19.

Nays: None.

Absent and not voting: Gray, Rigby. Total, 2.

RESOLUTION

Be it resolved by this Convention assembled that 500 copies of Journal of Proceedings be printed. That the contract for the printing of said Journal be let by the Secretary of State to the lowest bidder.

Be it further resolved, That the Secretary of State is hereby instructed and authorized to mail one copy of said printed Journal to each member of the Twenty-second Legislature, two copies of said printed Journal to each member of this Convention, the remaining copies of said printed Journal to be distributed according to the discretion of the Secretary of State.

Moved by Coulter.

Seconded by Whitehead.

Roll call resulted as follows:

Ayes: Coulter, Erb, Harris, Smith, Whitehead, Wilson. Total, 6.

Nays: Boyd, Cunningham, Davis, DeKay, Gray, Gudmundsen, Healy, Hitchcock, Jones, Keel, Kenworthy, Peterson, Robins, Toomer. Total, 14.

Absent and not voting: Rigby. Total 1.

Whereupon the President declared the motion lost.

At this time the President and Secretary announced that they were signing the Resolution ratifying the proposed amendment to the Constitution of the United States repealing the Eighteenth Amendment. The certificate so signed and executed, is as follows:

We, the undersigned, President and Secretary of the Convention assembled pursuant to the authority of "An Act to assemble a convention to pass on amendments to the Constitution of the United States," approved March 11, 1933, do hereby certify that the foregoing resolution ratifying said proposed amendment to the Constitution of the United States was adopted by such Convention on the 17th day of October, A.D., 1933.

ASHER B. WILSON
President
TROY D. SMITH
Secretary

The Committee appointed for such purpose retired to wait upon the Secretary of State and transmit to him said Resolution. The Convention remained at ease until the return of the Committee, who reported delivery of the Resolution to the Secretary of State, and asked to be discharged.

REPORT OF MILEAGE AND EXPENSE COMMITTEE

BOISE, IDAHO, October 17, 1933

MR. PRESIDENT:

We, the Committee on Mileage and Expense for Members of this Convention assembled, beg leave to report that we find each member entitled to pay for mileage and necessary expense as set opposite his name.

Name and Town	*Amount*
Beecher Hitchcock, Sandpoint	$51.25
John P. Gray, Coeur d'Alene	36.10
M. Kenworthy, Moscow	35.60
Robert S. Erb, Lewiston	41.95
Frank Harris, Weiser	10.20
Robert A. Davis, Jr., Nampa	None
Wm. Healy, Boise	None
M. F. Cunningham, Hailey	23.74
Robert Coulter, Cascade	None
Asher B. Wilson, Twin Falls	32.36
Irel Gudmundsen, Burley	17.28
Troy D. Smith, Mackay	47.90
J. H. Peterson, Pocatello	19.05
F. E. DeKay, Blackfoot	31.68
Harold R. Toomer, Montpelier	31.52
Parley Rigby, Idaho Falls	34.98
Earl D. Jones, Roberts	13.00
Emmett Robins, St. Anthony	32.24
G. T. Keel, Jerome	21.96
J. J. Boyd, Buhl	24.02
Don S. Whitehead, Boise	None

GLADYS TERHUNE KEEL
Chairman

Moved by Coulter that the Mileage and Expense report be adopted.

Seconded by Whitehead.

Motion prevailed and the President declared the report adopted.

At this time the President, Mr. Wilson, and the Secretary, Mr. Smith, expressed their appreciation and thanks for the courtesy extended and co-operation given them by the members of the Convention.

Moved by Coulter that the Convention do now adjourn *sine die.*

Seconded by Whitehead.

Motion prevailed.

Whereupon the President declared the Convention adjourned *sine die.*

ASHER B. WILSON
President

Attest:

TROY D. SMITH
Secretary

CERTIFICATE

We, the undersigned, Asher B. Wilson, President, and Troy D. Smith, Secretary of the Convention, do hereby certify that we have examined the above and foregoing record and minutes of the proceedings of said Convention, and we, and each of us, certify that the said record and minutes are a true and correct report of the proceedings of said Convention.

ASHER B. WILSON
President

TROY D. SMITH
Secretary

ILLINOIS*

OFFICERS OF THE CONVENTION

Temporary Chairman
Governor Henry Horner

President
Bruce A. Campbell
Belleville

Secretary
Harold G. Ward
Chicago

Executive Assistant .... Belle P. White, Chicago
Parliamentarian .... Cornelius J. Harrington, Chicago
Sergeant-at-Arms .... George F. Ross, Chicago
Assistant Sergeant-at-Arms .... John H. Stelle, McLeansboro
Assistant Sergeant-at-Arms .... Stanley Watson, Mt. Vernon
Assistant Sergeant-at-Arms .... William J. Walsh, Chicago
Minute Clerk .... W. D. Forsythe, Champaign
Assistant Minute Clerk .... Marie Hess, Joliet

STATE OF ILLINOIS

THE HALL OF REPRESENTATIVES

OF THE GENERAL ASSEMBLY

IN THE CAPITOL BUILDING

IN THE CITY OF SPRINGFIELD

JULY 10, A.D. 1933

JOURNAL OF THE CONVENTION

12:00 o'clock M.

Pursuant to an Act of the General Assembly of the State of Illinois, entitled "An Act to assemble a convention to ratify or refuse to ratify a proposed amendment to the Constitution of the United States," approved April 28, 1933, the delegates-elect to the convention were called to order by His Excellency, the Governor, Honorable Henry Horner, in the Hall of Representatives of the General Assembly in the Capitol Building in the city of Springfield, at the hour of twelve o'clock noon, July 10, A.D. 1933.

GOVERNOR HORNER: Ladies and Gentlemen of the Convention, the hour has arrived for the calling of this Convention, as provided by House Bill No. 441, recently enacted by the Fifty-eighth General Assembly. It is to me a great privilege to call this

*Printed. The text of the act providing for the convention, which was printed as part of the convention record, has been omitted here.

Convention to order, pursuant to the statute enacted by the last General Assembly, and to preside over it until you shall, pursuant to your own act, elect one of your number as presiding officer, and the Convention will now be in order.

The Chair will appoint Senator Harold G. Ward, whose efforts in connection with the passage of the Act under which we meet are so well known it is unnecessary for me to enlarge upon them, to act as Provisional Secretary pending the organization of the Convention, and he will now call the roll of the delegates elected and compiled from the official returns on file in the office of the Secretary of State. As each name is called, the delegate will respond, if present.

Governor Horner then presented the following communication from the Secretary of State which was ordered placed in the Journal of today's proceedings:

SPRINGFIELD, ILLINOIS
July 10, 1933

STATE OF ILLINOIS
COUNTY OF SANGAMON } SS.

The following is a true and correct list of all persons elected at an election held on June 5, 1933, as delegates to a Convention to be held in the City of Springfield on July 10, 1933, which Convention was called for the purpose of ratifying or refusing to ratify a proposed amendment to the Federal Constitution, which proposed amendment is as follows:

JOINT RESOLUTION

Proposing an amendment to the Constitution of the United States.

Resolved, by the Senate and House of Representatives of the United States of America in Congress assembled (two-thirds of each House concurring therein), That the following article is hereby proposed as an amendment to the Constitution of the United States, which shall be valid to all intents and purposes as part of the Constitution when ratified by conventions in three-fourths of the several states:

ARTICLE ___ ___

Section 1. The Eighteenth Article of Amendment to the Constitution of the United States is hereby repealed.

Section 2. The transportation or importation into any State, Territory or possession of the United States for delivery or use therein of intoxicating liquor, in violation of the laws thereof, is hereby prohibited.

Section 3. This article shall be inoperative unless it shall have been ratified as an amendment to the Constitution by conventions in the several states, as provided in the Constitution, within seven years from the date of the submission thereof to the states by the Congress.

The said election and convention were called pursuant to the provisions of an Act passed by the Fifty-eighth General Assembly and approved by the Governor on April 28, 1933.

P. A. Nash,
3234 W. Washington Blvd., Chicago
George F. Harding,
4853 Lake Park Ave., Chicago
William L. O'Connell,
4418 Drexel Blvd., Chicago

Raymond J. Peacock,
3757 N. Keeler Ave., Chicago
Joseph C. Cerny,
1832 S. 50th Ct., Cicero
Ralph M. Shaw,
1427 N. State St., Chicago

Edward F. Moore,
4945 W. Washington Blvd., Chicago
Oscar F. Mayer,
5727 Sheridan Rd., Chicago
Jacob M. Arvey,
3716 Douglas Blvd., Chicago
John Toman,
4056 W. 21st Pl., Chicago
George F. Barrett,
1934 W. 22nd St., Chicago
Seymour Wheeler,
1291 N. Elm Tree Blvd., Lake Forest
Andrew C. Metzger,
7444 Blackstone Ave., Chicago
Louis Nettelhorst,
6107 Claremont Ave., Chicago
William H. Feigenbutz,
1521 Oakdale Ave., Chicago
Caswell W. Crews,
4431 Indiana Ave., Chicago
Joseph Z. Klenha,
1837 S. Austin Blvd., Cicero
Bruce A. Campbell,
Belleville
John G. Oglesby,
Elkhart
Leonard Condon,
Rockford
John W. Kapp, Jr.,
Springfield
Benjamin P. Alschuler,
Aurora
Edward R. Daly,
Joliet
Robert H. Green,
Streator
Orestes H. Wright
Freeport
Martin J. Gannon,
Dixon
Samuel R. Kenworthy,
Rock Island
L. P. Bonfoey,
Quincy
Elizabeth A. Conkey,
7420 Yates Ave., Chicago
William V. Pacelli,
767 W. Taylor St., Chicago
Charles W. Fry,
5959 S. Francisco Ave., Chicago
Bernard L. Majewski,
5459 Cullom Ave., Chicago
John J. Hoellen,
1842 Larchmont Ave., Chicago
Peter B. Carey,
9640 S. Winchester Ave., Chicago
Charles M. Postl,
8926 S. Hamilton Ave., Chicago
John P. Harding,
1050 Pratt Blvd., Chicago
Charles E. Sturtz,
Kewanee
John E. Cassidy,
Peoria
Arthur Lehman,
Peoria
Mary Bell Sloan,
Bloomington
Clint C. Tilton,
Danville
Harry Streetor,
Kankakee
James M. Allen
Decatur
Jessie Rink,
Beardstown
John A. Hogan,
Taylorville
William M. Sauvage,
Alton
A. B. Hammel,
Trenton
George H. Bauer,
Effingham
Loren Wasson,
Harrisburg
Reed Green,
Cairo

I, Edward J. Hughes, Secretary of State of the State of Illinois, do hereby certify that the above is a true and correct list of delegates elected as stated above, and shown by the abstracts of votes from the various county clerks of this State, and by the canvass sheets of the State Canvassing Board, the originals of which are now on file in my office.

(*Signed*) EDWARD J. HUGHES
Secretary of State

SEAL

The roll of the delegates as named in the foregoing communication of the Secretary of State was then called when the following answered to their names:

Allen	Condon	Harding, G. F.	Metzger	Sauvage
Alschuler	Conkey	Harding, J. P.	Moore	Shaw
Arvey	Crews	Hoellen	Nash	Sloan
Barrett	Daley	Hogan	Nettelhorst	Streetor
Bauer	Feigenbutz	Kapp	O'Connell	Sturtz
Bonfoey	Fry	Kenworthy	Oglesby	Tilton
Campbell	Gannon	Klenha	Pacelli	Toman
Carey	Green, R. H.	Lehman	Peacock	Wasson
Cassidy	Green, Reed	Majewski	Postl	Wheeler
Cerny	Hammel	Mayer	Rink	Wright

Governor Horner then announced that a quorum was present.

GOVERNOR HORNER: You are all familiar with the fact there was a disastrous fire in this wing of the Capitol Building last night, and it is apparent that this Chamber is unsafe as a location for the holding of this Convention, by reason of the damage resulting from fire and water and the danger from falling of plaster and fixtures. I recognize Delegate George F. Barrett, who has a resolution to present at this time.

Delegate George F. Barrett then offered the following resolution:

RESOLUTION NO. 1

WHEREAS, This convention is assembled pursuant to the authority of an Act of the Fifty-eighth General Assembly of the State of Illinois entitled, "An Act to Assemble a Convention to Ratify or Refuse to Ratify a Proposed Amendment to the Constitution of the United States," approved April 28, 1933; and

WHEREAS, Said Act provides that said convention shall meet in the Hall of Representatives of the General Assembly in the Capitol Building in the City of Springfield on this the 10th day of July, 1933, at the hour of 12 o'clock, M.; and

WHEREAS, Said Hall of Representatives of the General Assembly in the Capitol Building in the City of Springfield has been severely damaged by fire and water and the State Architect of the State of Illinois has declared the said Hall of Representatives to be in a dangerous and unsafe condition for the holding of this Convention and would jeopardize the lives of the delegates and the public in attendance; therefore, be it

Resolved, That this convention now assembled in the Hall of Representatives of the General Assembly in the Capitol Building in the City of Springfield do now recess to reconvene at once in the Senate Chamber of the General Assembly, in the Capitol Building, in the City of Springfield.

Delegate Barrett moved that the foregoing resolution be adopted and the roll being called, the motion was decided in the affirmative by the following vote: Yeas, 50; nays, none.

The following voted in the affirmative:

Allen	Condon	Harding, G. F.	Metzger	Sauvage
Alschuler	Conkey	Harding, J. P.	Moore	Shaw
Arvey	Crews	Hoellen	Nash	Sloan
Barrett	Daly	Hogan	Nettelhorst	Streetor
Bauer	Feigenbutz	Kapp	O'Connell	Sturtz
Bonfoey	Fry	Kenworthy	Oglesby	Tilton
Campbell	Gannon	Klenha	Pacelli	Toman
Carey	Green, R. H.	Lehman	Peacock	Wasson
Cassidy	Green, Reed	Majewski	Postl	Wheeler
Cerny	Hammel	Mayer	Rink	Wright

The convention, preceded by the Governor, then repaired to the Senate Chamber to continue its session.

At the request of the Governor the invocation was offered by Monsignor Wm. T. Sloan, president of the Catholic Welfare Council of Illinois.

GOVERNOR HORNER: This is a momentous occasion. Today the sovereign State of Illinois formally and officially declares itself for repeal of the Eighteenth Amendment to our National Constitution.

That, in itself, is of tremendous importance. But of even greater import is the fact that this convention, in casting its vote against the Amendment, is declaring the strong opposition of our people to any amendment of our National Constitution that denies to the several states the control of the habits, customs and privileges of its own citizens.

We, as law-abiding and loyal citizens of Illinois, rejoice in the fact that the will of the majority of our electors, as expressed at the polls not once but several times, no longer is to be ignored. It is to be recorded here in effective action through the votes of you who were chosen by popular vote as delegates to this Convention.

We rejoice in the realization that the voters of Illinois and the Nation have been given their long sought opportunity to regain rights that have been denied them for more than a dozen years.

Almost from the very beginning of national prohibition, the citizens of Illinois sought the right to express themselves directly upon the question of correcting the abuses that came with the enactment of the Volstead Act. Repeatedly, this was refused them except in a manner that left the issue clouded, and nullified their action at the polls.

This repeated refusal of the reactionary element in our national political life to heed the wishes of the people in this regard was effectively rebuffed in the experiences of last fall's election.

Upon his induction into office, President Roosevelt moved swiftly to give practical expression to the demands of the people. Sponsored and supported by him, legislation was enacted less than three weeks after his inauguration legalizing the sale of 3.2 beer and wine on April 7. From this single legislative act, business received more immediate impetus than had been its good fortune to have experienced for many months prior to that time. National recovery, now moving swiftly, may be said to date from the enactment of the federal beer and wine law.

Meanwhile, we in Illinois were fulfilling our pledges. One of the early acts of the Fifty-eighth General Assembly was to repeal the Illinois Prohibition Act, and then the Illinois Search and Seizure Act. This was followed with legislation regulating the sale of legalized beer and wine within our borders. This will produce seriously needed revenue and provide employment in this State.

When the Illinois Legislature first took under consideration the question of authorizing an election on the proposed repeal amendment, there was some disposition to delay the vote until 1934. The State administration opposed the delay with all the force at its command, and the General Assembly, to its everlasting credit, designated June 5 as the delegate election day, and fixed today as the date for the convention of delegates selected at that election.

You are gathered here, pledged to the people of the State who have elected you by overwhelming majorities, to express their view on the great issue upon which this convention is based.

It is needless for me to discuss with you at this time the evils that were brought about by the adoption of the Eighteenth Amendment to the National Constitution, and its basic wrong. You are of one mind on that subject. You have been chosen to act for the people of our State because they know that you believe as they do on this question. With them, you are firmly determined to restore the integrity of our form of government, and to show that Illinois stands, as it always has stood, for the basic theme of our constitutional government.

Before your adjournment, you will have fulfilled the trust that has been imposed in you by making our State one of the leaders in the hard fought battle which has been waged for several years to give the majority of the people of this Nation the right to express their opinion on legislation which was passed without their consent. You will have set an example which we hope and believe will be followed before the end of the present year by a sufficient number of states to crown our State success with National victory.

Millions are eagerly awaiting your action as a lesson which the adoption of the Eighteenth Amendment should have taught the people of the United States. That lesson is that political cowardice is the thing which is most dangerous to our institutions. Parties, officials or legislators who lack the courage to do what they believe is right because of the clamor of an organized minority are sufficiently warned by our experiences under the Eighteenth Amendment.

That lesson should have been learned long before the adoption of our Eighteenth Amendment. It was taught at the cost of the lives of thousands of Americans seventy years ago when Civil War was necessary to destroy the institution of human slavery. Political cowardice had permitted slavery to exist in the United States because there was a vociferous and active minority. Fearing to offend the minority, legislators of that era stifled their consciences. They permitted conditions which they knew were intolerable to exist because of what they were pleased to call expediency.

The history of national prohibition is much the same as that of slavery. At no time was a majority of the American people in favor of the Eighteenth Amendment and its accompanying legislation. That was demonstrated on every occasion on which there was anything like an opportunity for the free expression of the popular will by a referendum or otherwise.

A clamorous minority, well-meaning in the main, we will concede, was manipulated by men who found it to their own advantage to do so, so as to make it appear to members of Congress that it was dangerous to oppose the will of that minority. The majority of the people, engrossed at the time in the conduct of a great war, were too confident that the legislation proposed by the minority could never commend itself to thinking people. That majority was inactive while the minority was seizing every opportunity to exercise the balance of power in congressional and other elections.

In spite of the warnings of one of our greatest Presidents, Woodrow Wilson, a Congress was finally coerced into acting and the Eighteenth Amendment appeared as part of our National Constitution.

Its adoption seemed for a time to have paralyzed the Nation. There were, however, a few sturdy patriots who dared, from the very beginning, to raise their voice against the violence which had been done to American institutions. They were heartily supported by the forward-looking press of the country. Many of our citizens who have since taken an active part in the splendid fight were in the early days of the controversy unhappily silent. They feared the storm of criticism which they knew the men who had brought about the passage of the amendment would be able to arouse against them.

Fortunately, there were men and women who still possessed political courage. They kept the fires of liberty burning and held high the standards of repeal.

We all remember the difficulties which they had to encounter even among the members of their own party, before they could obtain a straightforward, wholesome endorsement of the cause of repeal.

The result in those states where the people have already had an opportunity to express their will is so far unanimous. State after state has hastened to give evidence that repeal is vigorously demanded by their people. As fast as the political machinery can be moved, the restoration of state responsibility is being brought about. No state has yet, in the present issue, declared against repeal.

As we meet today, there seems to be no question of the ultimate result. We can, I believe, rest assured that there will not be found enough states in the Union to defy the majority will so overwhelmingly expressed by the citizenship of the Nation.

The Eighteenth Amendment is doomed. Let us pray today that with it will go the political cowardice that made it possible.

July 10, 1933, becomes another date of great historical significance for our commonwealth.

From this day we shall reckon the restoration of State responsibility in Illinois. It fixes our undisputed right to hold our proper place in the forefront of those states that are progressive and forward-looking.

It is my hope, and I am certain it is yours, too, that memories of July 10, 1933, will serve forever as a warning and a deterrent to reactionaries in Illinois. In the future, even if they are again favored by tempting circumstances, they will hesitate to impose their will upon the majority, and to deprive our people of that freedom of local action which is our heritage from the framers of our Federal Constitution.

I hail you delegates as heralds of a great message entrusted to you by the people of Illinois. That message, when formally framed by you in the resolutions you will adopt, will be heard throughout the Nation and be welcomed wherever liberty is regarded as the birthright of American Citizenship.

Upon the conclusion of the address by Governor Horner, the Governor presented Mrs. William H. Mitchell, co-chairman, Women's Organization for National Prohibition Reform.

Mrs. Mitchell: As a member of the Women's Organization for National Prohibition Reform, I feel it is a great honor to be asked to address this Convention. You as delegates are also greatly blessed in being able to cast ballots for and therefore help in the repeal of this obnoxious Eighteenth Amendment. We wish to congratulate Governor Horner and our State Legislature in their prompt action in making possible this convention, and also in their appointment of the Liquor Commission. Our organization feels our work will not be accomplished, will not be finished until we have adequate State liquor laws. We feel that is the only way temperance can be achieved.

On motion of Delegate Conkey, the Convention proceeded to the election of a temporary presiding officer.

Delegate George F. Harding placed in nomination Honorable Bruce A. Campbell as Temporary Presiding Officer, and the roll being called, he was duly elected by the following vote: Yeas, 50; nays, none.

The following voted in the affirmative:

Allen	Condon	Harding, G. F.	Metzger	Sauvage
Alschuler	Conkey	Harding, J. P.	Moore	Shaw
Arvey	Crews	Hoellen	Nash	Sloan
Barrett	Daly	Hogan	Nettelhorst	Streetor
Bauer	Feigenbutz	Kapp	O'Connell	Sturtz
Bonfoey	Frey	Kenworthy	Oglesby	Tilton
Campbell	Gannon	Klenha	Pacelli	Toman
Carey	Green, R. H.	Lehman	Peacock	Wasson
Cassidy	Green, Reed	Majewski	Postl	Wheeler
Cerny	Hammel	Mayer	Rink	Wright

On motion of Delegate Oglesby, a committee of three was ordered appointed to wait upon the Temporary Presiding Officer and escort him to the chair.

Thereupon, Governor Horner appointed as such committee, Delegates Oglesby, Alschuler and Arvey who escorted Delegate Campbell at once to the chair.

DELEGATE JOHN G. OGLESBY: Governor Horner, your committee presents a loyal, outstanding Democrat, an able parliamentarian, a distinguished citizen of Illinois, as the Convention's choice for Temporary Chairman, Mr. Campbell.

GOVERNOR HORNER: The committee is discharged with the congratulations of the Chair upon the successful manner in which they completed their duty. Ladies and Gentlemen of the Convention, it is my pleasure to present to you your temporary presiding officer, Mr. Bruce A. Campbell.

At 12:30 o'clock Mr. Campbell assumed the duties of the chair.

TEMPORARY PRESIDING OFFICER CAMPBELL: Governor Horner, Ladies and Gentlemen of this Convention, I trust that the meaning of my words will be taken with inverse ratio to their triteness, when I say thank you for the distinguished honor you have conferred upon me in electing me the temporary presiding officer of this Convention.

There are a score of persuasive arguments I could advance in support of the action of this Convention. I shall refrain from advancing them or making any other observation upon this occasion, for two reasons: first, they are not needed to convince the delegates in this Convention; and secondly, I trust that the example of brevity set by your presiding officer will hasten the hour we have long sought and mourned because we found it not. I thank you for this honor.

The Temporary Presiding Officer recognizes Delegate John W. Kapp, Jr., Mayor of Springfield.

DELEGATE KAPP: Mr. Chairman, for Secretary of this Convention I have the high privilege to place in nomination Senator Harold G. Ward, of Chicago. Senator Ward for four years has represented not only the largest and most intelligent district of the State, but he has also endeared himself to us all by his efforts to champion the interests of the people of Illinois. Throughout the Legislature which recently adjourned it has been Senator Ward to whom the people have grown accustomed to turn for leadership when they wanted something actually accomplished.

Especially has Senator Ward distinguished himself for the relentless fight he has waged against prohibition. On the opening day of the last Legislature, on January 4, as soon as the Senate convened and before the inauguration of Governor Horner and the other State officers, Senator Ward introduced Senate Bills Nos. 1 and 2, to repeal the obnoxious Illinois Prohibition Act and the Search and Seizure Laws of the State of Illinois. With his customary energy, he pushed them to an early passage through both branches of the Legislature.

Senator Ward also drafted and introduced into the Legislature the present law regulating the sale of beer in Illinois, and provided much needed revenue for both the State and the local governments.

Not only has Senator Ward been of service to the people of the State of Illinois in these legislative halls, but he has also served his country in the last great war, and he is one of five brothers who made that great sacrifice of time. Two of his brothers are now resting on foreign soil, having made that supreme sacrifice that was necessary for the maintenance of good government.

Ladies and Gentlemen, it is now my privilege and high honor to present to this Convention for its consideration Senator Ward for Temporary Secretary of this Convention.

There being no other nomination, the roll was called and the Temporary Presiding Officer declared Harold G. Ward the Temporary Secretary of the Convention by the following vote: Yeas, 50; nays, none.

The following voted in the affirmative:

Allen	Condon	Harding, G. F.	Metzger	Sauvage
Alschuler	Conkey	Harding, J. P.	Moore	Shaw
Arvey	Crews	Hoellen	Nash	Sloan
Barrett	Daly	Hogan	Nettelhorst	Streetor
Bauer	Feigenbutz	Kapp	O'Connell	Sturtz
Bonfoey	Fry	Kenworthy	Oglesby	Tilton
Campbell	Gannon	Klenha	Pacelli	Toman
Carey	Green, R. H.	Lehman	Peacock	Wasson
Cassidy	Green, Reed	Majewski	Postl	Wheeler
Cerny	Hammel	Mayer	Rink	Wright

Delegate Barrett offered the following resolution, which was adopted:

RESOLUTION NO. 2

Be it resolved, That the Presiding Officer appoint a Committee on Credentials, consisting of seven delegates, to report the names of all delegates elected, qualified and entitled to seats in this Convention.

Whereupon, temporary Presiding Officer Campbell appointed as the committee provided for in the foregoing resolution, Delegates, Barrett, Chairman; Toman, Bonfoey, Klenha, Kapp, Alschuler and Pacelli.

Delegate Reed Green offered the following resolution and on his motion the same was adopted:

RESOLUTION NO. 3

Be it resolved, That the Presiding Officer appoint seven delegates to prepare and recommend rules for the control and conduct of the Convention.

Whereupon, temporary Presiding Officer Campbell appointed as the committee provided for in the foregoing resolution, Delegates Reed Green, Chairman; Bonfoey, Cerny, Majewski, Moore, Nettelhorst and Wright.

The Committee on Rules made the following report, which was adopted:

The Committee on Rules reports it is the recommendation of this Committee that Robert's Rules of Order govern the procedure of this Convention.

REED GREEN, *Chairman*

The Committee on Credentials made the following report:

REPORT OF COMMITTEE ON CREDENTIALS

The Committee on Credentials reports that they have examined the Credentials of the delegates to the State Convention to consider the proposed amendment to the Constitution of the United States for the repeal of the Eighteenth Amendment of the Constitution of the United States, and respectfully reports that the delegates present have been duly and properly elected and qualified in accordance with law and are entitled to seats in this Convention.

GEORGE F. BARRETT, *Chairman*
JOHN TOMAN
G. P. BONFOEY
JOSEPH Z. KLENHA
JOHN W. KAPP, JR.
B. P. ALSCHULER
WILLIAM V. PACELLI

On motion of Delegate Barrett, the foregoing report was adopted by the following vote: Yeas, 50; nays, none.

The following voted in the affirmative:

Allen	Condon	Harding, G. F.	Metzger	Sauvage
Alschuler	Conkey	Harding, J. P.	Moore	Shaw
Arvey	Crews	Hoellen	Nash	Sloan
Barrett	Daly	Hogan	Nettelhorst	Streetor
Bauer	Feigenbutz	Kapp	O'Connell	Sturtz
Bonfoey	Fry	Kenworthy	Oglesby	Tilton
Campbell	Gannon	Klenha	Pacelli	Toman
Carey	Green, R. H.	Lehman	Peacock	Wasson
Cassidy	Green, Reed	Majewski	Postl	Wheeler
Cerny	Hammel	Mayer	Rink	Wright

Temporary Presiding Officer Campbell appointed a committee of three members to wait upon the Honorable Norman L. Jones, Judge of the Supreme Court of the State of Illinois, and request his presence at the Convention to administer the oath of office to the members-elect, as certified to the Convention by the Secretary of State.

Mr. Cassidy offered the following resolution, which was adopted:

RESOLUTION NO. 4

Be it resolved, That the presiding officer of this Convention appoint seven delegates to serve as a Committee on Permanent Organization.

Whereupon, The Temporary Presiding Officer of the Convention appointed as a committee provided for by the foregoing resolution, Delegates Cassidy, Chairman; Bauer, Carey, Green, Robert H., Sauvage, Sloan, Wheeler.

The Committee on Permanent Organization thereupon reported as follows:

The Committee on Permanent Organization thereupon reports that they unanimously endorse and tender for election the name of Bruce A. Campbell, for President of this Convention.

Delegate Cassidy then moved the adoption of the report.

At the request of Presiding Officer Campbell, Delegate Cassidy put the motion to the Convention and directed the Secretary to call the roll on the motion to adopt the report. The motion was adopted unanimously by the following vote: Yeas, 50; nays, none.

The following voted in the affirmative:

Allen	Condon	Harding, G. F.	Metzger	Sauvage
Alschuler	Conkey	Harding, J. P.	Moore	Shaw
Arvey	Crews	Hoellen	Nash	Sloan
Barrett	Daly	Hogan	Nettelhorst	Streetor
Bauer	Feigenbutz	Kapp	O'Connell	Sturtz
Bonfoey	Fry	Kenworthy	Oglesby	Tilton
Campbell	Gannon	Klenha	Pacelli	Toman
Carey	Green, R. H.	Lehman	Peacock	Wasson
Cassidy	Green, Reed	Majewski	Postl	Wheeler
Cerny	Hammel	Mayer	Rink	Wright

Delegate Cassidy then declared Bruce A. Campbell unanimously elected President of the Convention.

The Committee on Permanent Organization further reports as follows:

The Committee on Permanent Organization reports that they unanimously recommend and endorse the name of Harold G. Ward for appointment as Permanent Secretary of the Convention, which report was adopted by the following vote: Yeas, 50; nays, none.

The following voted in the affirmative:

Allen	Condon	Harding, G. F.	Metzger	Sauvage
Alschuler	Conkey	Harding, J. P.	Moore	Shaw
Arvey	Crews	Hoellen	Nash	Sloan
Barrett	Daly	Hogan	Nettelhorst	Streetor
Bauer	Feigenbutz	Kapp	O'Connell	Sturtz
Bonfoey	Fry	Kenworthy	Oglesby	Tilton
Campbell	Gannon	Klenha	Pacelli	Toman
Carey	Green, R. H.	Lehman	Peacock	Wasson
Cassidy	Green, Reed	Majewski	Postl	Wheeler
Cerny	Hammel	Mayer	Rink	Wright

President Campbell then declared Harold G. Ward Permanent Secretary of the Convention.

The Committee on Permanent Organization made the further report as follows:

The Committee on Permanent Organization recommends the appointment by the President of the following officers and employes of the Convention at the per diem named:

1 Executive Assistant—(No compensation).
1 Minute Clerk—(No compensation).
1 Assistant Minute Clerk—(No compensation).
1 Sergeant-at-Arms—At a reasonable per diem.
3 Assistant Sergeant-at-Arms—(No compensation).
1 Chaplain—at $10.00
1 Journal Clerk—3 days at $10.00 per diem.
1 Honorary Doorkeeper—(No compensation).
7 Doorkeepers—At $8.00 per diem.
6 Pages—At $5.00 per diem.
2 Cloakroom Attendants—At $5.00 per diem.
Parliamentarian—Cornelius J. Harrington, of Chicago—(No compensation).

Sergeant-at-Arms—George F. Ross, Chicago.
Assistant Sergeant-at-Arms—John Stelle—(No compensation).
Stanley Watson—(No compensation).
Wm. J. Walsh—(No compensation).

On motion of Mr. Cassidy, the foregoing report was adopted by the following vote: Yeas, 50; nays, none.

The following voted in the affirmative:

Allen	Condon	Harding, G. F.	Metzger	Sauvage
Alschuler	Conkey	Harding, J. P.	Moore	Shaw
Arvey	Crews	Hoellen	Nash	Sloan
Barrett	Daly	Hogan	Nettelhorst	Streetor
Bauer	Feigenbutz	Kapp	O'Connell	Sturtz
Bonfoey	Fry	Kenworthy	Oglesby	Tilton
Campbell	Gannon	Klenha	Pacelli	Toman
Carey	Green, R. H.	Lehman	Peacock	Wasson
Cassidy	Green, Reed	Majewski	Postl	Wheeler
Cerny	Hammel	Mayer	Rink	Wright

The President of the Convention made the following announcement:

In accordance with the recommendations made in the report of the Committee on Permanent Organization, I announce the following appointments:

Executive Assistant—Belle P. White, Chicago.
Parliamentarian—Cornelius J. Harrington, Chicago.
Minute Clerk—W. D. Forsythe, Champaign.
Assistant Minute Clerk—Marie Hess, Joliet.
Sergeant-at-Arms—George F. Ross, Chicago.
Assistant Sergeant-at-Arms—John Stelle, McLeansboro; Stanley Watson, Mt. Vernon; William J. Walsh, Chicago.
Honorary Doorkeeper—Malden Jones, Springfield.
Chaplain—Monsignor Wm. T. Sloan, Springfield.
Journal Clerk—James H. Paddock, Springfield.
Doorkeepers—Hal Reading, Michael Walsh, Frank Leonard, Sherman Martin, Ned Peterson, R. K. Eden, William Hill.
Pages—James Sinnott, Howard Rachford, Paul Marrin, Roy Genus, Lloyd Owens.
Cloakroom Attendants—L. M. Magruder, Wm. Lynch.

Delegate Arvey offered the following resolution, which on his motion, was adopted:

RESOLUTION NO. 5

Be it resolved, That the President of this Convention appoint seven delegates to serve as a Committee on Resolutions.

The President of the Convention appointed the following as the committee: Delegates Nash, Chairman; Arvey, Daly, Hoellen, O'Connell, Shaw, Tilton.

Delegate Nash, Chairman of the Committee on Resolutions, made the following report:

REPORT OF COMMITTEE ON RESOLUTIONS

The Committee on Resolutions respectfully reports it has prepared a resolution which expresses the mandate and will of the people of the Sovereign State of Illinois. Said resolution is in words and figures as follows:

WHEREAS, Both Houses of the Seventy-second Congress of the United States of America, by a constitutional majority of two-thirds thereof, proposed an amendment to the Constitution of the United States, which should be valid to all intents and purposes as a part of the Constitution of the United States when ratified by conventions in three-fourths of the states, which resolution is in words and figures following, to-wit:

JOINT RESOLUTION

Proposing an amendment to the Constitution of the United States.

Resolved, by the Senate and House of Representatives of the United States of America in Congress assembled (two-thirds of each House concurring therein), That the following article is hereby proposed as an amendment to the Constitution of the United States, which shall be valid to all intents and purposes as part of the Constitution when ratified by conventions in three-fourths of the several states:

ARTICLE ____

Section 1. The Eighteenth Article of Amendment to the Constitution of the United States is hereby repealed.

Section 2. The transportation and importation into any State, Territory or possession of the United States for delivery or use therein of intoxicating liquor, in violation of the laws thereof, is hereby prohibited.

Section 3. This article shall be inoperative unless it shall have been ratified as an amendment to the Constitution by conventions in the several states, as provided in the Constitution, within seven years from the date of the submission thereof to the states by the Congress. Now, therefore, be it

Resolved, by the convention assembled pursuant to the authority of an Act of the General Assembly of the State of Illinois, entitled "An Act to assemble a convention to ratify or refuse to ratify a proposed amendment to the Constitution of the United States," approved April 28, 1933, That said proposed amendment to the Constitution of the United States of America is hereby ratified.

Delegate Nash moved that the foregoing report be concurred in and the above resolution be adopted by roll call, which motion was seconded by Delegate Toman, whereupon, the roll was called, and the resolution was adopted by the following vote: Yeas, 50; nays, none.

The following voted in the affirmative:

Allen
Alschuler
Arvey
Barrett
Bauer
Bonfoey
Campbell
Carey
Cassidy
Cerny
Condon
Conkey
Crews
Daly
Feigenbutz
Fry
Gannon
Green, R. H.
Green, Reed
Hammel
Harding, G. F.
Harding, J. P.
Hoellen
Hogan
Kapp
Kenworthy
Klenha
Lehman
Majewski
Mayer
Metzger
Moore
Nash
Nettelhorst
O'Connell
Oglesby
Pacelli
Peacock
Postl
Rink
Sauvage
Shaw
Sloan
Streetor
Sturtz
Tilton
Toman
Wasson
Wheeler
Wright

PRESIDENT CAMPBELL: On this roll call, the Chair with great pleasure that the yeas are fifty and the nays are none. Therefore, the Chair declares the motion carried and the resolution offered by the delegate from Cook County, Mr. Nash, is unanimously adopted by this Convention.

In the presence of the Convention, the President and Secretary executed and attached to the resolution, the following certificate to the Secretary of State for transmission to Washington, to declare the action of the State of Illinois:

We, the undersigned, President and Secretary of the Convention, assembled pursuant to the authority of "An Act to assemble a convention to ratify or refuse to ratify a proposed amendment to the Constitution of the United States," approved April 28, 1933, do hereby certify that the foregoing resolution ratifying said proposed amendment to the Constitution of the United States was adopted by such Convention, on the tenth day of July, A.D., 1933.

BRUCE A. CAMPBELL, *President*
HAROLD G. WARD, *Secretary*

Delegate Condon offered the following resolution, which was adopted:

RESOLUTION NO. 6

Be it resolved, That the President of this Convention appoint a committee of nine delegates to serve as a committee to examine and transmit, with the President and Secretary, to the Secretary of State of the State of Illinois, the executed resolution and certificate ratifying the proposed amendment to the Constitution of the United States repealing the Eighteenth Amendment.

Whereupon, President Campbell appointed as a committee provided for in the foregoing resolution the President and Secretary of the Convention, and Delegates Condon, Gannon, Hammel, Hogan, Kenworthy, Metzger, Postl, Rink and Wasson.

Delegate Moore offered the following resolution:

RESOLUTION NO. 7

Resolved, That the President and Secretary, in behalf of the Convention assembled, be authorized to approve the written minutes of this Convention with the same force and effect as if the delegates of this Convention had approved the same.

Which resolution was adopted by the following vote, on motion of Delegate Moore: Yeas, 50; nays, none.

The following voted in the affirmative:

Allen	Condon	Harding, G. F.	Metzger	Sauvage
Alschuler	Conkey	Harding, J. P.	Moore	Shaw
Arvey	Crews	Hoellen	Nash	Sloan
Barrett	Daly	Hogan	Nettelhorst	Streetor
Bauer	Feigenbutz	Kapp	O'Connell	Sturtz
Bonfoey	Fry	Kenworthy	Oglesby	Tilton
Campbell	Gannon	Klenha	Pacelli	Toman
Carey	Green, R. H.	Lehman	Peacock	Wasson
Cassidy	Green, Reed	Majewski	Postl	Wheeler
Cerny	Hammel	Mayer	Rink	Wright

Delegate Arvey offered the following resolution:

RESOLUTION NO. 8

Resolved, That the Secretary of the Convention be and is hereby authorized to have printed and bound fifteen hundred copies of the Journal of the Proceedings of this Convention, and that one copy be mailed to each delegate of the Convention, one copy to each member of the Legislature and such other persons as make request for the same, and be it further

Resolved, That twenty-five copies be furnished to the State Library, twenty-five copies to the State Law Library, two hundred and fifty copies to the Secretary of State to supply any requests made, one copy to each of the State Officers and Departments, and fifteen copies to the Clerk of the Supreme Court for the use of the Court.

Which resolution was adopted by the following vote, on motion of Mr. Arvey: Yeas, 50; nays, none.

The following voted in the affirmative:

Allen	Condon	Harding, G. F.	Metzger	Sauvage
Alschuler	Conkey	Harding, J. P.	Moore	Shaw
Arvey	Crews	Hoellen	Nash	Sloan
Barrett	Daly	Hogan	Nettelhorst	Streetor
Bauer	Feigenbutz	Kapp	O'Connell	Sturtz
Bonfoey	Fry	Kenworthy	Oglesby	Tilton
Campbell	Gannon	Klenha	Pacelli	Toman
Carey	Green, R. H.	Lehman	Peacock	Wasson
Cassidy	Green, Reed	Majewski	Postl	Wheeler
Cerny	Hammel	Mayer	Rink	Wright

Delegate Nash offered the following resolution, which was unanimously adopted:

RESOLUTION NO. 9

WHEREAS, The Honorable Edward J. Hughes, Secretary of State, under the Act providing for the assembling of this Convention was charged with the responsibility of preparing the Hall of Representatives for the holding of this Convention; and,

WHEREAS, After the Honorable Edward J. Hughes, Secretary of State, prepared said Hall of Representatives, it unfortunately was rendered unsafe for the holding of this Convention by damage caused by fire and water resulting from a fire which broke out in the Capitol Building upon the eve of this Convention; and,

WHEREAS, The Honorable Edward J. Hughes, Secretary of State, within a period of a few hours of the convening of this Convention, arranged and equipped the Senate Chamber in a most satisfactory manner for the use of the Convention; therefore, be it

Resolved, That this Convention assembled express to the Honorable Edward J. Hughes, Secretary of State, its deep appreciation and thanks for the expeditious manner in which he arranged and prepared this chamber for the meeting of this Convention.

At 12:55 o'clock P.M., on motion of Delegate Nash, the Convention adjourned *sine die.*

Attest:

HAROLD G. WARD

Secretary of the Convention

We, the undersigned, Bruce A. Campbell, President, and Harold G. Ward, Secretary of the Convention, do hereby certify that we have examined the above and foregoing record and minutes of the proceedings of said Convention and we and each of us certify that the said record and minutes are a true and correct report of the proceedings of said Convention.

BRUCE A. CAMPBELL, *President*

HAROLD G. WARD, *Secretary*

INDIANA*

JOURNAL

OF THE

CONVENTION OF THE PEOPLE

OF THE

STATE OF INDIANA

Begun and held in the Chambers of the House of Representatives, in the City of Indianapolis, on Monday, the twenty-sixth day of June, A.D. 1933, being the time and place fixed for it to meet by an Act of the General Assembly of the State of Indiana, entitled "An Act to provide for Conventions to pass on Amendments or Amendment to the Constitution of the United States, which has or have been or hereafter may be proffered by the Congress for ratification by Conventions in the several states, and declaring an emergency." Approved March 8, 1933.

INDIANAPOLIS, INDIANA
June 26, 1933

The Convention having been called to order at two o'clock P.M. Central Standard time, by the Lieutenant-Governor of the State of Indiana, the Hon. M. Clifford Townsend, who was in attendance in obedience to the aforesaid act for said purpose.

Chaplain Reverend Noll of Jay County gave the following invocation:

"God, our Heavenly Father, we approach Thee today with thanksgiving. Thanking Thee for America, Our Flag and form of American Government, with the feeling that we should rather live in our beloved land in the most isolated district in a log house on a hillside, burn a tallow candle and draw our drinking water with an old fashioned well sweep than to live with every convenience in the most densely populated districts with all modern conveniences in any other nation on the earth.

"We thank Thee that today God's command is being carried out here: 'In all they [Thy] ways acknowledge Him.' We thank Thee for the part the Church has in all questions that come before the American people through the representatives of the Church, the Ministers.

"We would therefore ask they [Thy] blessing upon every man of every creed; men in all walks and callings of life. Bless, we pray Thee, our rulers, state and national. We pray for men who make their living and livelihood by some honest effort to provide shelter, food, clothing and education for their children and comforts and luxuries for their families. We also pray for men irrespective of color, race, nationality, parties and straits.

"We recall that Thou has told us 'To pray without ceasing.' 'To sow by every water' and that men ought always to pray and not to feign. Therefore we continue to petition Thee, not only for men generally, but to us as individuals, that with the erring we may be more patient, to those who are weak we may seek to strengthen them, before

*Printed. A table of contents has been omitted here because it does not correspond with the pagination in this volume.

those who are haughty we may live lives of humility. To the destructive critic, we may give no heed. Help us to seek to comfort those who are downcast. Where men differ with us in our ideas, help us to be magnanimous. And make us to know that righteousness exalteth a nation, but that sin is a reproach to any people. Cause us to see that what has made America great will keep her grand.

"And beyond all this, may we each of us strive to help in every way we can to make men prosperous and happy and good. Instead of being obstinate to the powers that be, grant, Great God, that we shall endeavor to assist in every good work and word. Make us cooperative in every good work rather than negative. If we are wrong at any place, show us the way out. If right, give us Thy blessings and benediction. We acknowledge Thy wisdom and our ignorance; our weakness and Thy strength, Thy righteousness and our shortcomings. But before we close, we pray for every one here assembled; just what Thy blessings should be, we do not know, yet we are sure there is not one here but that needs the blessings of God to direct them. For each of us has some kind of burden to bear. All to the end that the Church of God throughout all the earth may prosper. That we may be law-abiding citizens; lovers of Home, State, and Nation, patriotic and loyal citizens. To study to know the will of God and practice it in all relationships of life. Help us to live so that our nation shall be sustained and perpetuated; that destructive forces shall not retard our progress. Yes, make us an example of right to all nations of the world in the Name of Him who died for us to Thy Glory, we ask it all. Amen."

Lieutenant-Governor gave the following address:

"Ladies and gentlemen, delegates of the Convention: Pursuant to the Provisions of Chapter 163 of the Acts of the General Assembly of 1933, this Convention, the delegates to which were elected at a special election held on June 6, 1933, has assembled for the purpose of passing upon the question of whether or not a proposed amendment for the repeal of the 18th Amendment of the Constitution of the United States, submitted by Congress to the several States, shall be ratified or rejected. And the delegates here assembled constitute a convention to pass upon that question.

"I shall ask the clerk to call the roll and you will answer Aye if you are present. Call the roll."

From the County of Adams: Jacob A. Long, Aye; Frank McConnell, Aye.

From the County of Allen: Helen Bruggeman, Aye; Ralph C. Dunkelberg, Aye; John W. Eggeman, Aye; Miller Ellingham, Aye; Oscar G. Foellinger, Aye; Herman F. Gerdon, Aye; Arthur F. Hall, Aye; Walter E. Helmke, Aye; Victor H. Hilgemann, Aye; Charles Solomon, Aye; Helen W. Sweet, Aye; Argo R. Vegalues, Aye; Fred Wehrenberg, Aye; John B. Wyss, Aye; Sam Wolf, Aye.

From the County of Bartholomew: Charles S. Kitzinger, Aye; Phillip R. Long, Aye.

From the County of Benton: Ernest L. Callaway, Aye.

From the County of Blackford: E. Floyd Willman, Aye.

From the County of Boone: Milton Hussey, Aye; Ben F. McKey, Aye.

From the County of Brown: Clarence Robertson, Aye.

From the County of Carroll: Joseph W. Eikenberry, Aye; Everett E. Flora, Aye.

From the County of Cass: James F. Digan, Aye; Oliver P. Erbaugh, Aye; Matthew Maroney, Sr., Aye.

From the County of Clark: Frank M. Fisher, Aye; Lunsford Jones, Aye; William Koetter, Aye.

From the County of Dekalb: Harry R. Bloom, Aye; Andrew Grube, Aye.

From the County of Clay: Harry A. Campbell, Aye; Cliff Lowe, Aye; Thomas Phillips, Aye.

From the County of Clinton: Effie C. Cochran, Aye; George H. Laughrey, Aye; Hiram V. Ransom, Aye.

From the County of Crawford: Claud A. Roberts, Aye.

From the County of Daviess: N. Maude Arthur, Aye; Frank Morgan, Aye; Peter R. Wadsworth, Aye.

From the County of Dearborn: Hubert Rullman, Aye; John Stahl, Aye.

From the County of Decatur: Robert W. Altizer, Aye; Henry L. Sefton, Aye.

From the County of Delaware: Edna Alexander, Aye; Clarke F. Johnson, Aye; Joseph W. Michael, Aye; Lillie Hannegan Mongrain, Aye; J. Byron Reed, Aye; John E. Schaubhut, Aye; Ralph Stout, Aye.

From the County of Dubois: Andrew B. Krempp, Aye; Leo H. Pfaff, Aye.

From the County of Elkhart: Floyd C. Best, Aye; Ira Eshelman, Aye; Harold B. Gray, Aye; Guy K. Keely, Aye; Charles L. Minser, Aye; John R. Swart, Aye; William A. Willhide, Aye.

From the County of Fayette: Jediah H. Clark, Aye; E. Ralph Himelick, Aye.

From the County of Floyd: R. W. Harris, Aye; Joseph Kahler, Aye; Gilbert E. Powell, Aye.

From the County of Fountain: Joseph W. Harrison, Aye; Carl Quigle, Aye.

From the County of Franklin: Simeon Colebank, Aye.

From the County of Fulton: Charles T. Jones, Aye; Erwin C. Mercer, Aye.

From the County of Gibson: Chester Braselton, Aye; Mrs. R. A. Cushman, Aye; W. P. Dearing, Aye.

From the County of Grant: Harry W. Cline, Aye; S. S. Condo, Aye; J. Harry Patterson, Aye; Paul G. Prail, Aye; John D. Williams, Aye.

From the County of Greene: John W. Brandon, Aye; Joseph H. Haseman, Aye; Charles V. Corbin, Aye.

From the County of Hamilton: Adam Kepner, Aye; Artemas H. Myers (sub. by Jesse Johnson), Aye.

From the County of Hancock: Charles F. Reeves, Aye; Anna McBane, Aye.

From the County of Harrison: Maurice Griffin, Aye; Clarence Quebbeman, Aye.

From the County of Hendricks: James E. Reitzel, Aye; Chester C. Bosstick, Aye.

From the County of Henry: Verl Byers, Aye; George N. Logan, Aye; Blanche White, Aye; Samuel E. Stout, Aye.

From the County of Howard: Cosmos J. Braun, Aye; Wesley E. Conway, Aye; Addison Jenkins, Aye; Chester F. McDaniel, Aye; Dan S. Troy, Aye.

From the County of Huntington: Levi A. Ertzinger, Aye; Thelma G. Foust, Aye; Eban Lesh, Aye.

From the County of Jackson: Thomas H. Branaman, Aye; Oscar H. Montgomery, Aye.

From the County of Jasper: I. H. Riley, Aye.

From the County of Jay: James Leonard Bickel, Aye; Sarah Margaret Murray, Aye.

From the County of Jefferson: Culver Dean Field, Aye; Daniel S. Mills, Aye.

From the County of Jennings: Edward E. Gudgel, Aye.

From the County of Johnson: Charles A. Brown, Aye; Robert H. Kent, Aye.

From the County of Knox: Anthony Hess, Aye; Charles Raymond Lenahan, Aye; Frank L. Oliphant, Aye; James Luther Phillippi, Aye.

From the County of Kosciusko: Hobart Creighton, Aye; Jesse E. Eschbach, Aye; Edson B. Sarber, Aye.

From the County of Lake: Garry J. August, Aye; Axel R. Carlson, Aye; Adwin A. Comstock, Aye; John A. Costello, Aye; Ladislaus J. Danieleski, Aye; James J. Farley, Aye; Bradford D. L. Glazebrook, Aye; Oscar Haney, Aye; Wilbur J. Hardway, Aye; George E. Hershman, Aye; William J. Huber, Aye; Joseph E. Klen, Aye; John S. McGuan, Aye; John L. Mears, Aye; Joseph E. Meyer, Aye; Fred C. Miller, Aye; Hugh P. Muckian, Aye; James J. Nejdl, Aye; Liquori A. O'Donnell, Aye; James A. Patterson, Aye; John L. Rohde, Aye; William J. Rossman, Aye; Walter E. Schrage, Aye; John W. Scott, Aye; John W. Werkowski, Aye; Helen R. White, Aye.

From the County of LaGrange: Lewis Price, Aye.

From the County of LaPorte: Gerhardt F. Decker, Aye; Francis G. Fedder, Aye; Frederick W. Flotow, Aye; Frederick W. Meissner, Aye; Caleb G. Stovall, Aye; Robert T. Wilson, Aye.

From the County of Lawrence: Earl Krausbeck, Aye; Warren A. Sanders, Aye; Hazel Fern Evans, Aye; W. O. Guthrie, Aye.

From the County of Madison: Benjamin J. Fettig, Aye; Cary Forkner, Aye; Robert H.

Louden, Aye; William B. Myers, Aye; Thomas McCullough, Aye; Jane G. McIlwraith, Aye; J. Ward Starr, Aye; Albert VanSlyke, Aye.

From the County of Marion: V. M. Armstrong, Aye; Wm. A. Atkins, Aye; Robert L. Bailey, Aye; Berthe Born, Aye; Silas J. Carr, Aye; Leora Chavers, Aye; Augustus Coburn, Aye; Helen V. Costello, Aye; Alvin H. Eickhoff, Aye; Mayme Fogarty, Aye; Robert C. Fox, Aye; Adolph F. Fritz, Aye; Sarah Wolf Goodman, Aye; Julius Hollander, Aye; Lotta K. Horst, Aye; Mary G. Johnson, Aye; Marie S. Kaiser, Aye; William C. Kern, Aye; John C. Kirch, Aye; Herman W. Kothe, Aye; Eldena Lauter, Aye; Robert V. Law, Aye; Ralph A. Lemcke, Aye; George J. Marott, Aye; Sirdastion D. Merriwether, Aye; Albert F. Meurer, Aye; Alice B. Mooney, Aye; Robert West Nicholson, Aye; Thomas B. Noble, Aye; Benjamin A. Osborne, Aye; Katherine F. Pantzer, Aye; Julian C. Ralston, Aye; Leo M. Rappaport, Aye; Otto G. Rassmann, Aye; William M. Rockwood, Aye; Adelaide G. Roemler, Aye; Thomas D. Sheerin, Aye; Theodore Stein, Jr., Aye; Genevieve Bassel Watson, Aye; Evans Woollen, Jr., Aye.

From the County of Marshall: Ferdinand F. Fribley, Aye; Daniel B. Mann, Aye; Alfred A. Thompson, Aye.

From the County of Martin: Simeon Hacker, Aye.

From the County of Miami: Chas. B. Ryder, Aye; Irven Swygert, Aye; Edwin F. Miller, Aye.

From the County of Monroe: William L. Bryan, Aye; Mary H. Neill, Aye; Fred J. Prow, Aye; Hiner J. Thompson, Aye.

From the County of Montgomery: John H. Binford, Aye; Claude C. Harshbarger, Aye; Frank D. Nolan, Aye.

From the County of Morgan: Gilbert R. Brown, Aye.

From the County of Newton: Charles R. Meyer, Aye.

From the County of Noble: Sol Henoch, Aye; Clement G. Routsong, Aye.

From the County of Ohio: Harry R. Clark, Aye.

From the County of Orange: Paul L. Coble, Aye; John W. McCullough, Aye.

From the County of Owen: Dillard M. Johnson, Aye.

From the County of Parke: Henrietta A. Adams, Aye; William J. Kerr, Aye.

From the County of Perry: William P. Birchler, Aye; Julius J. Wichser, Aye.

From the County of Pike: Harley E. Craig, Aye; William F. Traylor, Aye.

From the County of Porter: John M. Fabing, Sr., Aye; John W. Sieb, Aye.

From the County of Posey: Albert E. Heckmann, Aye; John H. Moeller, Aye.

From the County of Pulaski: Clarence Gilsinger, Aye.

From the County of Putnam: Francis C. Tilden, Aye; Maude M. Gough, Aye.

From the County of Randolph: Carmon J. Caplinger, Aye; Philip Kabel, Aye.

From the County of Ripley: George C. Bos, Aye; William H. Oatman, Aye.

From the County of Rush: John E. Booth, Aye; Walter Bitner, Aye.

From the County of Scott: Robert W. Blunt, Aye.

From the County of Shelby: J. Elmer Davison, Aye; William C. Groebl, Aye; Thomas Yates, Aye.

From the County of Spencer: Salem Parker, Aye; Margaret Sargent, Aye.

From the County of Starke: Charles Ruhl, Aye.

From the County of Steuben: Hercourt Sheets, Aye.

From the County of St. Joseph: William M. Stern, Aye; Rudolph Ackermann, Aye; William A. Thallmer, Aye; M. Edward Doran, Aye; Ivar Hennings, Aye; Nicholas Muszer, Aye; Casmir Lisek, Aye; Charles A. Gunn, Aye; James H. Greene, Aye; Joseph Duszynski, Aye; Anthony R. Gloyeski, Aye; Joseph P. Miller, Aye; Will G. Crabill, Aye; Alvin P. Kemper, Aye; W. H. Edwards, Aye; George Farage, Aye.

From the County of Sullivan: Ben F. Bolinger, Aye; Raymond A. Roberts, Aye; Enoch Stanley, Aye.

From the County of Switzerland: Elmer E. Hufford, Aye.

From the County of Tippecanoe: Henry W. Marshall, Sr., Aye; William T. Scanlon, Aye; Albert J. Krabbe, Aye; Mabel Vinton, Aye; Anna Mulherin, Aye.

From the County of Tipton: Clarence A. Smith, Aye; Franklin C. Suite, Aye.

From the County of Union: Cecil Leek, Aye.

From the County of Vanderburgh: William R. Etheridge, Aye; Arthur C. Folz, Aye; William D. Hardy, Aye; Charles M. LaFollette, Aye; Oscar Lanphar, Aye; George Schmadel, Aye; William G. Schnute, Aye; Charles Swoboda, Aye; George A. Theyson, Aye; Harold Van Orman, Aye; Mildred S. Wiggers, Aye.

From the County of Vermillion: Thomas H. Catlin, Aye; Louis M. Carli, Aye.

From the County of Vigo: Morton F. Hayman, Aye; John Hickey, Aye; Roy E. Hurt, Aye; William H. Johnson, Aye; Leonard B. Marshall, Aye; Albert L. Pfau, Aye; Samuel D. Royse, Aye; John F. Ryan, Aye; George A. Schaal, Aye; James H. Swango, Aye.

From the County of Wabash: Paul Brembeck, Aye; Will J. Guthrie, Aye; Robert C. Thompson, Aye.

From the County of Warren: Rev. Herman LeRoy Adams, Aye.

From the County of Warrick: Ernest Koch, Aye; Robert J. Derr, Aye.

From the County of Washington: Dennis Elrod, Aye; Rosco E. Hayes, Aye.

From the County of Wayne: William H. Bartel, Aye; John Hazelrigg, Aye; Henry U. Johnson, Aye; Oline C. Robinson, Aye; Anton Stolle, Sr., Aye.

From the County of Wells: Earl R. Deam, Aye; Walter F. Timbrook, Aye.

From the County of White: Nick H. Foltz, Aye; Bernie M. Pierce, Aye.

From the County of Whitley: Wm. C. Growcock, Aye; Robert H. Oliver, Aye.

Those absent were:

From the County of Hamilton: Artemas H. Myers.

From the County of Marion: Lilith H. Baur, Samuel E. Rauh, and Adelaide G. Roemler.

From the County of Morgan: Jap Miller.

CHAIRMAN TOWNSEND: 324 present and 5 absent. I think it is the desire of all that we have an entire delegation of 329. Under the law, the delegates present from the county where the absence occurs may fill a vacancy. If there are no delegates present from the county where there is an absentee, the Governor will fill the vacancy. So I am going to suggest that we be at ease for three or four minutes to allow the delegates from any county where there is an absentee to get together and decide on filling the vacancy. You understand the vacancy must be filled by a citizen of the county where the vacancy exists and it must be one who will vote as the representative was instructed to vote, the elected representative. If there be an absence where there is no other delegate and there are those from that county here that are interested, we suggest you go to the Governor's office where he will fill the delegation.

After the recess the following substitutions were reported:

From the County of Hamilton: Jesse Johnson (for Artemas H. Myers).

From the County of Marion: Catherine Atkins (for Lilith Baur), Mary McNutt (for Samuel F. Rauh).

From the County of Morgan: Ira Ogle (for Jap Miller).

CHAIRMAN TOWNSEND: The Chair recognizes a quorum. The delegates will now stand and receive the oath by acting Chief Justice Roll of the Supreme Court.

CHIEF JUSTICE ROLL: Raise your right hands.

Those of you who swear do solemnly swear; those of you who affirm, solemnly and sincerely affirm, that you will perform your duties as delegates of this Convention honestly and faithfully, to the best of your ability under the law. Those of you who swear [or affirm] will answer to God. Those of you who do so under the pain and penalty of perjury.

CLERK: Adelaide G. Roemler of Marion County is here.

CHAIRMAN TOWNSEND: The Chair recognizes the following Committee on Permanent Organization:

William D. Hardy, Evansville, Chairman.
John Stahl, Lawrenceburg.
J. Harry Patterson, Marion.
Robert C. Fox, Indianapolis.
Roberta West Nicholson, Indianapolis.
William Lowe Bryan, Bloomington.
Frank McConnell, Decatur.
Robert H. Kent, Franklin.
Joseph W. Harrison, Attica.
Daniel S. Mills, Madison.
Peter R. Wadsworth, Washington.
Edward N. Doran, South Bend.
George E. Hershman, Lake County.

The Chair recognized Mr. Harold Van Orman of Evansville.

MR. VAN ORMAN: I move, Mr. President, that we recess for five minutes.

MR. FOELLINGER: I second the motion.

CHAIRMAN TOWNSEND: The question is on the motion to recess. All in favor will say Aye. Contrary, No. The Ayes seem to have it. The House recessed.

The convention was called to order after a ten minute recess.

The following reports were presented by the Committee on Permanent Organization:

MAJORITY COMMITTEE REPORT

MR. PRESIDENT:

A majority of your Committee on Permanent Organization begs leave to make the following report and moves its adoption:

That John W. Eggeman of Fort Wayne, Allen County, Indiana, be the President of this convention,

That Henry W. Marshall, Sr., of Lafayette, Tippecanoe County, Indiana, be the Vice-President of this convention,

That Thomas McCullough, Anderson, Madison County, Indiana, be the Vice-President of this convention,

That Jacob Weiss of Indianapolis, Marion County, Indiana, be the Parliamentarian of this Convention,

That Rev. Noll of Jay County, Indiana, be the Chaplain of this Convention,

That Roberta West Nicholson of Indianapolis, Marion County, Indiana, be the Secretary of this Convention,

That James Morrissey of Peru, Miami County, Indiana, be the Sergeant-at-Arms of this Convention.

WILLIAM HARDY, *Chairman*
JOHN STAHL
ROBERTA WEST NICHOLSON
JOHN F. RYAN
EDWARD M. DORAN
ROBT. C. FOX
GEO. E. HERSHMAN
FRANK MCCONNELL
J. H. PATTERSON

MINORITY REPORT

MR. PRESIDENT:

A minority of your Committee on Permanent Organization begs leave to make the following report and move its adoption:

That Jesse Eschbach of Warsaw, Kosciusko County, Indiana, be the President of this Convention,

That Wm. Lowe Bryan, of Bloomington, Monroe County, Indiana, be the Vice-President of this Convention,

That Dr. W. P. Deering of Oakland City, Gibson County, Indiana, be the Vice-President of this Convention,

That F. C. Tilden of Greencastle, Putnam County, be the Secretary of this Convention.

Joseph W. Harrison
Daniel S. Mills
Wm. L. Bryan
Robert H. Kent
Peter R. Wadsworth

Chairman Townsend then recognized Delegate Rappaport, who made the motion that the minority report be tabled and the majority report be considered the report of the Committee.

This motion was seconded by Delegate McConnell.

Chairman Townsend stated that the question is: Shall the minority report be tabled and the majority report be considered the report of the Committee? And ordered a vote taken.

The vote resulted in the majority report being considered the report of the Committee.

The delegates concurred in the majority report.

The Chair now therefore declares John W. Eggeman as President of the Convention; Henry W. Marshall, Sr., as Vice-President; Thomas McCullough, Vice-President; Jacob Weiss, Parliamentarion [Parliamentarian]; Reverend Noll, Chaplain; Roberta West Nicholson as Secretary, and James Morrissey as Sergeant-at-Arms.

The delegates just named were requested to step forward in front and receive the oath.

Chief Justice Roll: You solemnly swear that you will perform your duties as officers honestly and faithfully, to the best of your ability, as you will answer to God.

Chairman Townsend: The Chair names John Ryan and Leo Rappaport and Oscar Foellinger as a Committee to escort the President to the rostrum.

Delegates to the Convention, I present to you Judge John W. Eggeman of Fort Wayne, your President.

President Eggeman: Happy days are here again. Some few years ago some newspaperman had the audacity to name the State of Indiana the State of "You Can't." Before the Convention has recessed or adjourned, I believe that she will again be put back in the galaxy of states known as the "Good Old State of Indiana."

It is not my purpose to make any talk. That statement I have made, I think, is sufficient. We want to get down to business, because it is warm and we want to finish up.

The President now announces the following Committees:

The Committee on Resolutions: Leo M. Rappaport, Marion County, Chairman; Senator James J. Nejdl of Lake County; Thomas H. Branaman of Jackson County; Charles R. Meyer of Newton County; William M. Stern of St. Joseph County; Miller Ellingham of Allen County; Sarah Margaret Murray of Jay County; John Hickey of Vigo County; and Harold Van Orman of Vanderburgh County.

The Committee on Rules: Mary G. Johnson of Marion County, Chairman; Bradford D. L. Glazebrook of Lake County; I. H. Riley of Jasper County; Rudolph Ackermann of St. Joseph County; Sam Wolf of Allen County; S. S. Condo of Grant County; Gilbert R. Brown of Morgan County; Evans Woollen, Jr., of Marion County.

The Committee on Inspection of the Journal: Julian C. Ralston, Marion County, Chairman; Berthe Born of Marion County; Anthony R. Gloyeski, St. Joseph County; Sol Henoch, Noble County; Robert H. Oliver of Whitley County; Clarence Robertson of Brown County; James H. Swango of Vigo County; Louis M. Carli, Vermillion County.

The Committee on Patronage: William C. Kern, Marion County, Chairman; Matthew Maroney, Sr., Cass County; Jacob A. Long, Adams County.

The Committee on Election and Credentials: Phillip R. Long, Bartholomew County, Chairman; John C. Kirch, Marion County; Mary R. Clark, Ohio County; William H. Bartel, Wayne County; Harry R. Bloom, DeKalb County; James Luther Phillippi, Knox County; Henrietta A. Adams, Parke County; Charles B. Ryder, Miami County.

The Committee on Phraseology: Helen Bruggeman, Allen County, Chairman; Sarah Wolf Goodman, Marion County; Clarence Gilsinger, Pulaski County; Ira Eshelman, Elkhart County; Claud A. Roberts, Crawford County; Thomas Phillips, Clay County; Andrew B. Krempp, Dubois County; Addison Jenkins, Howard County.

PRESIDENT EGGEMAN: I will recognize Delegate Helmke of Allen County.

MR. HELMKE: I move you that the Convention be recessed for ten minutes for the purpose of the Committees getting in their reports.

PRESIDENT EGGEMAN: All those in favor will say Aye. Opposed, No. It seems the Ayes have it.

The Committees will meet in the Lieutenant Governor's office immediately and make it as quick as you can so we may get at this business.

The Convention was called to order by President Eggeman.

The President recognized Mary G. Johnson, of Marion County, Chairman on Rules, who gave the following report:

COMMITTEE ON RULES REPORT

MR. PRESIDENT:

Your Committee on Rules respectfully submits the Rules of Order the Government of the Proceedings of the Convention her[e]to attached and moves their adoption.

MARY G. JOHNSON
Chairman

STANDING RULES AND ORDERS FOR THE GOVERNMENT OF THE CONVENTION

1. The President shall take the chair every week day precisely at 10 o'clock in the forenoon and 2 o'clock in the afternoon, unless the convention by motion shall have adjourned to some other hour appointed by such motion. He shall immediately call the delegates to order, and on the appearance of a majority, shall cause the Journal of the preceding day to be read.

2. One-third of the elected delegates, with the President, shall be authorized to call a convention, compel the attendance of absent delegates, make an order for their fine or censure and may adjourn.

3. The President shall preserve order and decorum, may speak to points of order in preference to delegates, rising for that purpose; and shall decide questions of order, subject to an appeal to the convention by any two delegates on which appeal no delegate shall speak more than once, unless by leave of the convention.

4. The President shall rise to put a question, but may state it sitting, and shall put questions in this form, to wit:

"As many as are in favor (as the question may be) say aye," And after the affirmative vote is expressed, "As many as are opposed say no." If he doubt, or division is called for, the convention shall divide; those in the affirmative of the question shall first arise from their seats and be counted, and afterward those in the negative.

5. The presiding officer shall have general direction of the convention chamber and of the officers and employees of the convention. In the absence of the President, a Vice-President shall preside over the convention, and in the absence of the President and either Vice-President, the convention shall select some delegate to preside.

6. The President, or other delegate then presiding, shall vote on each question, but the name of such person presiding shall be called last.

7. Six standing committees of not to exceed twelve members each, exclusive of the chairman, shall be selected and appointed by the President of the convention.

(1) Committee on Rules.
(2) Committee on Elections and Credentials.
(3) Committee on Resolutions.
(4) Committee on Phraseology of Resolutions.
(5) Committee on Supervision and Inspection of the Journal.
(6) Committee on Employing Assistants and Incurring Indebtedness.

8. The various committees shall perform such services, and take into consideration all subjects and matters required of them by the convention. The Committee on Elections and Credentials shall have leave to report at any time on the right of a delegate to his seat, by presenting its report to the convention or by filing with the Secretary thereof; and the report of such committee shall be a question of the highest privilege, and may be called up at any time by the Chairman of the Committee on Elections and Credentials or any member thereof; and when called up, the action of the convention, and all the proceedings thereon, shall be the same as if said report had been called up as provided in Rule 9.

9. As soon as the Journal shall have been read and approved, or the reading dispensed with, any delegate may call up for consideration any contest which may have been reported by the Committee on Elections and Credentials, or a majority thereof, and shall be entitled to address the convention thereon.

10. No committee, except the Committee on Rules, shall sit during the sitting of the convention without special leave, and that members of said committee leave with the Secretary of the convention the place where they are meeting, so that they may be called at any time when needed in the convention chamber.

11. All questions relating to the priority of business shall be decided without debate.

12. Every delegate shall be present at all sittings of the convention, unless excused or necessarily absent; and shall vote on each question put, unless he has a direct personal or pecuniary interest in the event of such question; and the question of excusing a delegate shall be decided without debate.

13. Upon a division and count of the convention on any question, no delegate without the bar shall be counted.

14. Each motion, except the motion to adjourn, to fix the time to which to adjourn, to lay on the table, for the previous question, to postpone indefinitely, to commit, or to suspend the further reading of the minutes, calling absentees, excusing absentees, shall be in writing, signed by the maker, and if demand be made, shall require a second. It shall be handed to the Secretary and read aloud before debate.

15. After a motion is read, and stated by the President, it shall be in the possession of the convention, but by consent of the convention may be withdrawn at any time before decision or amendment.

16. When a question is under debate no motion shall be in order except:

(1) To take up or receive the report of the Committee on Elections and Credentials.
(2) To adjourn.
(3) To lay on the table.
(4) For the previous question.
(5) To postpone to a certain day.
(6) To commit.
(7) To amend.
(8) To postpone indefinitely.

Which several motions shall have precedence in the foregoing order.

17. A motion to adjourn shall always be in order, except when the previous question is pending, and shall be decided without debate. The question pending on adjournment shall be resumed on reassembling unless otherwise ordered by the convention.

18. The previous question shall be put in this form: "Shall the main question be now put?" Until it is decided, it shall preclude all debate, and the introduction of all further amendments. The previous question having been ordered, the main question shall be the first question in order, and its effect shall be to put an end to all debate, and bring the convention to a direct vote on the subsidiary questions then pending, in their order, and then on the main question, there shall be no debate or explanation of votes.

19. Motions and reports may be committed at the pleasure of the convention.

20. Any delegate may call for the division of a question where the sense will admit of it.

21. No motion or proposition on a subject different from that under consideration shall be admitted under color of amendment.

22. When a motion has been once made and decided, it shall be in order for any delegate of the prevailing side to move a reconsideration thereof, but such motion shall not be in order unless made within three days following such action and shall be decided by a majority vote of the delegates elect.

23. Resolutions, petitions, memorials and other papers addressed to the convention may be presented by the President or by any delegate, but shall not then be read to the convention. The same, after presentation, shall be referred by the President to the Committee on Resolutions.

24. It shall be in order for the Committee on Phraseology of Resolutions to report at any time when no question is before the convention.

25. The committee, to which a resolution shall have been referred, may report thereon with or without amendments, or may report a substitute therefor. If no minority report be made, the question shall be upon concurring in the report of the committee without any motion therefor. If a minority report be made, the question shall be upon concurring in the minority report, and if not concurred in, the question shall then recur upon the majority report.

26. After commitment and report thereon to the convention, or at any time before its passage, a resolution may be recom[m]itted.

27. All questions, whether in committee or in the convention, shall be put in the order in which they are moved.

28. Each officer of the convention shall take an oath for the true and faithful discharge of the duties of his office, and shall be deemed to continue in office until his successor be chosen.

29. It shall be the duty of the Sergeant-at-Arms to attend the convention during its sittings, execute all commands and process to him given and directed, keep the chamber and furniture clean and in due order, and at all times keep the chamber properly heated and ventilated; when requested to call a delegate, he shall do so by name, and shall exclude from within the bar of the convention chamber all persons except the President and officers and employees of the convention, delegates, members of the legislature, officials of the executive and judicial departments and representatives of the press assigned to places on the floor of the convention and shall exclude from the convention chamber all persons except the President of the convention, officers, delegates, members of the legislature, or persons admitted by them and holding floor cards. Such persons shall be admitted only upon presentation to the Sergeant-at-Arms of a written pass or proper credential and such pass or credential shall be non-transferable.

30. When any matter is referred to a standing committee, the delegate introducing the same shall be a member of such committee during its deliberations thereon, but shall have no power to vote.

31. The order of transacting business shall be as follows, viz.:

(1) Reading and correcting the Journal of the preceding day.
(2) Report of Committee on Elections and Credentials.
(3) Reports of other standing committees.
(4) Introduction of petitions, memorials and remonstrances.
(5) Reports of select committees.
(6) Resolutions of the Convention.

This order of business may be suspended upon a majority vote of the delegates-elect.

If the above order of business be suspended by reason of adjournment or otherwise, upon reassembling or upon completion of the business which brought about such suspension, the regular order of business shall be resumed at the place where the same was suspended.

32. When a resolution shall have failed for want of a majority, but shall have received the vote of a majority of the delegates present, it may be called up in its order by any delegate, but when it shall have failed to receive the votes of a majority of the delegates present, it shall again be called up only by a motion to reconsider.

33. When the introduction of resolutions is in order, the list of delegates shall be called by counties, and each delegate shall be permitted to introduce only one resolution each time his county is so called; which resolution shall not be read at the time of its introduction, but shall be committed to the Committee on Resolutions.

34. All proposed amendments to the rules shall be referred to the Committee on Rules without debate, and said committee shall have the right to report at any time, and may at any time report any change in the rules, or in the order of business, and any such report shall be immediately disposed of, and such change in the rules or in the order of business shall be determined by a majority of the delegates-elect.

35. The Journal of the convention shall be kept in due form by the Assistant Secretary of the convention and his signature shall attest the same.

36. Any resolution not indorsed on the back thereof with the name of the delegate offering the same shall be regarded as out of order.

37. It shall be the duty of the Secretary to indorse, over his signature, the number, in its order, of each resolution, and the date when offered; and it shall be the further duty of the Secretary to keep all resolutions on file in regular order.

38. An Assistant Sergeant-at-Arms shall be stationed at the door of the enrolling

and engrossing room, and no person whosoever, except the President of the convention and delegates, and the clerks there employed, shall be allowed to enter such room at any time; and no one, except the Secretary of the Convention, or the chief of the clerks employed in such room, shall take from the room any enrolled or engrossed resolution, or any other resolution, amendment, memorandum or paper.

39. Decorum and debate.

First. When any delegate desires to speak or deliver any matter to the convention, he shall rise from his seat and respectfully address himself to the President, and, on being recognized, may address the convention from any place on the floor, or from the Secretary's desk, and shall confine himself to the question under debate, avoiding personalities. No delegate shall impeach the motives of any other delegate.

Second. When two or more delegates rise at once, the President shall name the delegate who is to speak first, and no delegate shall occupy more than five minutes in debate on any question in convention or in committee, except as further provided in this rule. The convention at any time, by resolution adopted by a majority of the delegates-elect, may further limit the time of debate.

Third. The delegate reporting from a committee a matter under consideration may open and close, where general debate is had thereon.

Fourth. If any delegate in speaking, or otherwise, transgress the rules of the convention, the President shall, or any delegate may, call him to order, in which case he shall immediately be seated, unless permitted, on motion of another delegate, to explain; and the convention shall, if appealed to, decide on the case without debate. If the decision be in favor of the delegate called to order, he shall be at liberty to proceed, but not otherwise; and, if the case requires it, he shall be liable to censure or such punishment as the convention may deem proper.

Fifth. If a delegate be called to order for words spoken in debate, the delegate calling him to order shall indicate the words objected to, and they shall be taken down in writing at the Secretary's desk and read aloud to the convention at the time, but he shall bot [not] be held to answer nor be subject to the censure of the convention therefor if further debate or other business has intervened.

Sixth. No delegate shall speak more than once to the same question without leave of the convention, unless he be the mover, proposer or introducer of the matter pending, in which case he shall be permitted to speak in reply, but not until every delegate choosing to speak shall have spoken.

Seventh. While the President is putting a question or addressing the convention, no delegate shall walk out of or across the chamber, nor, when a delegate is speaking, pass between him and the chair; and during the session of the convention, no delegate shall remain by the Secretary's desk during the call of the roll.

40. Jefferson's Manual shall apply to all points not covered by these rules.

41. Unless otherwise ordered by a majority vote of the delegates-elect of the convention, all committees and vacancies in committees shall be filled by the President of the convention. All resolutions shall be referred by the President of the convention to appropriate committees, unless the convention by motion, adopted by at least a majority vote of the delegates-elect of the convention, shall designate a particular committee to which such resolution be referred, in which event such resolution shall be referred to the committee so designated by the convention, unless said resolution is presented to the convention for its immediate consideration as provided for in Rule 23.

42. The Committee on Employing Assistants and Incurring Indebtedness shall order and have full charge of the purchase of all supplies for the convention, shall employ and discharge all assistants and employees of the convention other than the President, the two Vice-Presidents, Parliamentarian, Chaplain, Secretary, Assistant Secretary and Sergeant-at-Arms, and shall fix the compensation of all such assistants and employees at not to exceed, however, five dollars per day. The President, Parliamentarian, Chaplain, and Secretary shall receive eight dollars for each and every day that they shall serve; the Assistant Secretary and Sergeant-at-Arms shall each receive six dollars for each and every day that they shall serve. Said committee shall incur all indebtedness by and for the convention. At the time of the employment of any persons by said committee, it, through its chairman, shall file with the Assistant Secretary of the convention its written report, showing such employment and the compensation fixed therefor, and such report shall be sufficient authority to place such persons on the payroll of the convention. No warrant shall be drawn for any indebtedness not authorized by such committee, unless the same is ordered by resolution adopted by a majority vote of the delegates-elect of the convention.

All printing done for the convention and all supplies, including stationery purchased for the convention, shall be under the supervision of the Board of Public Printing and Stationery, and said printing shall be done and said supplies purchased only upon authorization of the Committee on Employing Assistants and Incurring Indebtedness.

43. After a committee has had a matter under consideration for six days (Sundays and the day of its introduction not included), the author of such matter or any delegate of the convention shall have the right to call the attention of the convention to such fact, and unless a majority of the convention shall grant such committee an extension of time or otherwise order, such matter on the next business day shall be returned to the convention by such committee, either with or without recommendation, and when so returned shall be before the convention for consideration the same as if such matter had been reported upon by such committee. If such matter is returned without recommendation, then it shall take the same course as if such matter had been favorably reported upon: Provided, That nothing in this rule shall prevent the majority of the convention from calling said matter from said committee at any time.

44. The author of a resolution shall have the right to a hearing before the committee to which it has been referred before an adverse or divided report shall be made upon it.

45. The vote of each delegate to the convention shall be recorded by the Secretary and counted for ratification or against ratification according to the declaration filed by said delegate with the clerk of the circuit court at the time that said delegate announced his or her intention to become a delegate to this convention.

46. The yeas and nays, on any question, shall, at the request of any two delegates, be granted by the Chair: Provided, That on a motion to adjourn, it shall require one-tenth of the delegates present to order the yeas and nays.

The Chair recognized Delegate Phillip R. Long, Chairman of the Committee on Elections and Credentials, who gave the following report:

Mr. President:

Your Committee on Elections and Credentials, having examined the certificates of election of the several delegates, hereby respectfully reports that the persons whose names are listed below were duly elected and are entitled to sit as delegates in this convention.

REPORT OF THE COMMITTEE ON ELECTIONS AND CREDENTIALS

From the County of Adams: Jacob A. Long, Frank McConnell.

From the County of Allen: Helen Bruggeman, Ralph C. Dunkelberg, John W. Eggeman, Miller Ellingham, Oscar G. Foellinger, Herman F. Gerdon, Arthur F. Hall, Walter E. Helmke, Victor H. Hilgeman, Charles Solomon, Helen W. Sweet, Argo R. Vegalues, Fred Wehrenberg, John B. Wyss, Sam Wolf.

From the County of Bartholomew: Charles S. Kitzinger, Phillip R. Long.

From the County of Benton: Ernest L. Callaway.

From the County of Blackford: E. Floyd Willman.

From the County of Boone: Milton Hussey, Ben F. McKey.

From the County of Brown: Clarence Robertson.

From the County of Carroll: Joseph W. Eikenberry, Everett E. Flora.

From the County of Cass: James F. Digan, Oliver P. Erbaugh, Matthew Maroney, Sr.

From the County of Clark: Frank M. Fisher, Lunsford Jones, William Koetter.

From the County of Dekalf [Dekalb]: Harry R. Bloom, Andrew Grube.

From the County of Clinton: Effie C. Cochran, George H. Laughrey, Hiram V. Ransom.

From the County of Crawford: Claud A. Roberts.

From the County of Daviess: N. Maude Arthur, Frank Morgan, Peter R. Wadsworth.

From the County of Dearborn: Hubert Rullman, John Stahl.

From the County of Decatur: Robert W. Altizer, Henry L. Sefton.

From the County of Delaware: Edna Alexander, Clarke F. Johnson, Joseph W. Michael, Lillie Hannegan Mongrain, J. Byron Reed, John E. Schaubhut, Ralph Stout.

From the County of Dubois: Andrew B. Krempp, Leo H. Pfaff.

From the County of Elkhart: Floyd C. Best, Ira Eshelman, Harold B. Gray, Guy K. Keely, Charles L. Minser, John R. Swart, William Willhide.

From the County of Fayette: Jediah H. Clark, E. Ralph Himelick.

From the County of Floyd: R. W. Harris, Joseph Kahler, Gilbert E. Powell.

From the County of Fountain: Joseph W. Harrison, Carl Quigle.

From the County of Franklin: Simeon Colebank.

From the County of Fulton: Charles T. Jones, Edwin C. Mercer.

From the County of Gibson: Chester Braselton, Mrs. R. A. Cushman, W. P. Dearing.

From the County of Grant: Harry W. Cline, S. S. Condo, J. Harry Patterson, Paul G. Prail, John D. Williams.

From the County of Greene: John W. Brandon, Joseph H. Haseman, Charles V. Corbin.

From the County of Hamilton: Jesse Johnson (sub. for Artemas H. Myers), Adam Kepner

From the County of Hancock: Charles F. Reeves, Anna McBane.

From the County of Harrison: Maurice Griffin, Clarence Quebbeman.

From the County of Hendricks: James E. Reitzel, Chester C. Bosstick.

From the County of Henry: Verl Byers, George N. Logan, Blanche White, Samuel E. Stout.

From the County of Howard: Cosmos J. Braun, Olin Holt (sub. for Wesley E. Conway), Addison Jenkins, Chester F. McDaniel, Dan S. Troy.

From the County of Huntington: Levi A. Ertzinger, Thelma G. Goust, Eban Lesh.

From the County of Jackson: Thomas H. Branaman, Oscar H. Montgomery.

From the County of Jasper: I. H. Riley.

From the County of Jay: James Leonard Bickel, Sarah Margaret Murray.

From the County of Jefferson: Culver Dean Field, Daniel S. Mills.

From the County of Jennings: Edward E. Gudgel.

From the County of Johnson: Charles A. Brown, Robert H. Kent.

From the County of Knox: Anthony Hess, Charles Raymond Lenahan, Frank L. Oliphant, James Luther Phillippi.

From the County of Kosciusko: Hobart Creighton, Jesse E. Eschbach, Edson B. Sarber.

From the County of Lake: E. J. Flannerey (sub. for Garry J. August), Joseph Mellon (sub. for Axel R. Carlson), Edwin A. Comstock, John A. Costello, Ladislaus J. Danielski, James J. Farley, Bradford D. L. Glazebrook, Oscar Haney, Wilbur J. Hardway, George E. Hershman,

William J. Huber, Joseph E. Klen, John S. McGuan, John L. Mears, Joseph E. Meyer, Fred C. Miller, Hugh P. Muckian, James J. Nejdl, Liquori A. O'Donnell, James A. Patterson, John L. Rohde, William J. Rossman, Walter E. Schrage, John W. Scott, John W. Werkowski, Helen R. White.

From the County of LaGrange: Lewis Price.

From the County of LaPorte: Gerhardt F. Decker, Francis G. Fedder, Frederick W. Flotow, Frederick W. Meissner, Caleb G. Stovall, Robert T. Wilson.

From the County of Lawrence: Earl Krausbeck, Warren A. Sanders, Hazel Fern Evans, W. O. Guthrie.

From the County of Madison: Benjamin J. Fettig, Cary Forkner, Robert H. Louden, William B. Myers, Thomas McCullough, Jane G. McIlwraith, J. Ward Starr, Albert VanSlyke.

From the County of Marion: V. M. Armstrong, Wm. A. Atkins, Robert L. Bailey, Katherine Atkins (sub. for Lilith M. Baur), Berthe Born, Silas J. Carr, Leora Chavers, Augustus Coburn, Helen V. Costello, Alvin H. Eickhoff, Mayme Fogarty, Robert C. Fox, Adolph F. Fritz, Sarah Wolf Goodman, Julius Hollander, Lotta K. Horst, Mary G. Johnson, Marie S. Kaiser, William C. Kern, John C. Kirch, Herman W. Kothe, Eldena Lauter, Robert V. Law, Ralph A. Lemcke, George J. Marott, Sirdastion D. Merriwether, Albert F. Meurer, Alice B. Mooney, Roberta West Nicholson, Thomas B. Noble, Benjamin A. Osborne, Katherine F. Pantzer, Julian C. Ralston, Leo M. Rappaport, Otto G. Rassmann, William M. Rockwood, Adelaide G. Roemler, Thomas D. Sheerin, Theodore Stein, Mary McNutt (sub. for Samuel F. Rauh), Genevieve Bassel Watson, Evans Woollen, Jr.

From the County of Marshall: Ferdinand F. Fribley, Daniel B. Mann, Alfred A. Thompson.

From the County of Martin: Simeon Hacker.

From the County of Miami: Chas. B. Ryder, Irven Swygert, Edwin P. Miller.

From the County of Monroe: William L. Bryan, Mary H. Neill, Fred J. Prow, Hiner J. Thompson.

From the County of Montgomery: John H. Binford, Claude C. Harshbarger, Frank D. Nolan.

From the County of Morgan: Gilbert R. Brown, Ora Ogle (sub. for Jap Miller).

From the County of Newton: Charles R. Meyer.

From the County of Noble: Sol Henoch, Clement G. Routsong.

From the County of Ohio: Harry R. Clark.

From the County of Orange: Paul L. Coble, John W. McCullough.

From the County of Owen: Dillard M. Johnson.

From the County of Parke: Henrietta A. Adams, William J. Kerr.

From the County of Perry: William P. Birchler, Julius J. Wichser.

From the County of Pike: Harley E. Craig, William F. Traylor.

From the County of Porter: John M. Fabing, Sr., John W. Sieb.

From the County of Posey: John H. Moeller, Albert E. Heckmann.

From the County of Pulaski: Clarence Gilsinger.

From the County of Putnam: Francis C. Tilden, Maude M. Gough.

From the County of Randolph: Garmon J. Caplinger, Philip Kabel.

From the County of Ripley: George C. Bos, William H. Oatman.

From the County of Rush: John E. Booth, Walter Bitner.

From the County of Scott: Robert W. Blunt.

From the County of Shelby: J. Elmer Davidson, William C. Groebel, Thomas Yates.

From the County of Spencer: Salem Parker, Margaret Sargent.

From the County of Starke: Charles Ruhl.

From the County of Steuben: Hercourt Sheets.

From the County of St. Joseph: William M. Stern, Rudolph Ackerman, William A. Thallmer, M. Edward Doran, Ivar Hennings, Nicholas Muszer, Casmir Lisek, Charles A. Gunn, James H. Greene, Joseph Dusznski, Anthony R. Gloyeski, Joseph P. Miller, Will G. Crabill, Alvin P. Kemper, W. H. Edwards, George Farage.

From the County of Sullivan: Ben F. Bolinger, Raymond A. Roberts, Enoch Stanley.

From the County of Switzerland: Elmer E. Hufford.

From the County of Tippecanoe: Henry W. Marshall, Sr., William T. Scanlon, Albert J. Krabbe, Mabel Vinton, Anna Mulherin.

From the County of Tipton: Clarence A. Smith, Franklin C. Suite.

From the County of Union: Cecil Leek.

From the County of Vanderburgh: William R. Etheridge, Arthur C. Folz, William D. Hardy, Charles M. LaFollette, Oscar Lanphar, George Schmadel, William G. Schnute, Charles Swoboda, George A. Theyson, Harold Van Orman, Mildred S. Wiggers.

From the County of Vermillion: Thomas H. Catlin, Louis M. Carli.

From the County of Vigo: Morton F. Hayman, John Hickey, Roy E. Hurt, William H. Johnson, Leonard B. Marshall, Albert L. Pfau, Samuel D. Royse, John F. Ryan, George A. Schaal, James H. Swango.

From the County of Wabash: Paul Brembeck, Will J. Guthrie, Robert C. Thompson.

From the County of Warren: Rev. Herman LeRoy Adams.

From the County of Warrick: Ernest Koch, Robert J. Derr.

From the County of Washington: Dennis Elrod, Rosco E. Hayes.

From the County of Wayne: William H. Bartel, John Hazelrigg, Henry U. Johnson, Sr., Oline C. Robinson, Anton Stolle, Sr.

From the County of Wells: Earl R. Deam, Walter F. Timbrook.

From the County of White: Nick H. Foltz, Bernie M. Pierce.

From the County of Whitley: Wm. C. Growcock, Robert H. Oliver.

The report of the committee was concurred in.

The President then recognized William C. Kern of Marion County, Chairman of the Committee on Incurring Expenses and Employing Assistants, who gave the following report:

COMMITTEE REPORT

MR. PRESIDENT:

Your Committee on Employing Assistants and Incurring Indebtedness respectfully reports the employment of certain assistants to discharge the duties devolved upon them in the transaction of the business of the Convention, and that the list of the persons so employed has been filed with the Secretary of the Convention.

WILLIAM C. KERN
Chairman

The delegates concurred in the Committee report.

The President then recognized Leo M. Rappaport of Marion County, Chairman of the Committee on Resolutions, who gave the following report:

CONVENTION RESOLUTION

MR. PRESIDENT:

Your Committee on Resolutions offers the following resolution and moves its adoption: That the Secretary of the Convention is hereby authorized and directed to edit the Journal of this Convention and to have not to exceed 1,000 copies thereof printed. The Journal, when ready, shall be distributed as follows:

One copy to each delegate;

One copy to each member of the General Assembly; and

The residue to be distributed in the same manner as the Journals of the General Assembly.

LEO M. RAPPAPORT
Chairman

The delegates concurred in the committee report.

The President then recognized Chairman Leo M. Rappaport, who gave the second report of the Committee, as follows;

CONVENTION RESOLUTION

MR. PRESIDENT:

Your Committee on Resolutions offers the following resolution and moves its adoption: That all expenses which may be incurred by the Convention or authorized by any resolution of the Convention shall be paid by warrant of the Auditor of State issued upon the Treasurer of State and shall be paid from the appropriation made by Section 14 of Chapter 163 of the Acts of the General Assembly of 1933, upon the certificate of the President, attested by the Secretary of the Convention.

LEO M. RAPPAPORT
Chairman

Report of the Committee was concurred in.

The President then asked the Reading Clerk to read the Convention report of the Committee on Resolutions.

CONVENTION REPORT

MR. PRESIDENT:

Your Committee on Resolutions respectfully submits a Resolution, hereto attached, for the ratification of an amendment to the Constitution of the United States relating to the liquor traffic, and moves its adoption.

LEO M. RAPPAPORT
Chairman
WILLIAM M. STERN
JAMES J. NEJDL
MILLER ELLINGHAM
CHAS. R. MEYER
CLARENCE GILSINGER
THOMAS H. BRANAMAN
F. HAROLD VAN ORMAN
JOHN HICKEY
SARAH MARGARET MURRAY

A Resolution ratifying a proposed amendment to the Constitution of the United States.

WHEREAS, The Seventy-second Congress of the United States, at its second session, begun and held at the City of Washington, in the District of Columbia, on Monday, the fifth day of December, 1932, passed a Joint Resolution proposing an amendment to the Constitution of the United States, which is as follows:

JOINT RESOLUTION

Proposing an amendment to the Constitution of the United States.

Resolved by the Senate and House of Representatives of the United States of America in Congress assembled (two-thirds of each House concurring therein), That the following Article is hereby proposed as an amendment to the Constitution of the United States, which shall be valid to all intents and purposes as part of the Constitution when ratified by conventions in three-fourths of the several States:

ARTICLE ___ ___

Section 1. The Eighteenth Article of Amendment to the Constitution of the United States is hereby repealed.

Section 2. The transportation or importation into any State, Territory, or Possession of the United States for delivery or use therein of intoxicating liquors, in violation of the laws thereof, is hereby prohibited.

Section 3. This article shall be inoperative unless it shall have been ratified as an amendment to the Constitution by conventions in the several States, as provided in the Constitution, within seven years from the date of the submission hereof to the States by the Congress.

WHEREAS, The Secretary of State of the United States certified a copy of this resolution to the Governor of the State of Indiana on the twenty-first day of February, 1933, and the copy so certified was received by the Governor of the State of Indiana on the twenty-second day of February, 1933; and

WHEREAS, The Secretary of State of the United States requested the Governor of the State of Indiana to cause the proposed amendment to be submitted to a convention for such action as might be had thereon; and

WHEREAS, The Indiana General Assembly, at its seventy-eighth regular session, was apprised of the passage of this Joint Resolution, and, in compliance with the request of the Governor and the Secretary of State of the United States, passed an act, which was approved and became effective on March 8, 1933, and which is designated as Chapter 163 of the Acts of the General Assembly of 1933, providing for the election of delegates to a convention to vote on the question of the ratification or rejection of the proposed amendment; and

WHEREAS, Pursuant to the provisions of Chapter 163 of the Acts of the General Assembly of 1933, the Governor of the State of Indiana did, by proclamation, issued on the eighth day of April, 1933, fix[ed] the sixth day of June, 1933, as the date for holding an election to elect delegates to a convention to vote on the question of the ratification or rejection of the proposed amendment to the Constitution of the United States; and

WHEREAS, The election so called was held on the sixth day of June, 1933, at which the delegates constituting this convention were elected; and

WHEREAS, This convention is assembled for the sole purpose of ratifying or rejecting the proposed amendment to the Constitution of the United States: Therefore

Section 1. *Be it Resolved by this Convention of the State of Indiana Assembled,* That the proposed amendment to the Constitution of the United States of America, as hereinbefore recited in the Preamble of this Resolution, be and the same is hereby ratified by this convention of the State of Indiana.

Section 2. The President and Secretary of this Convention are hereby authorized and directed to execute a certificate, certifying that this Convention, by vote of a majority of the total number of delegates elected thereto, has ratified the proposed amendment to the Constitution of the United States, set forth in the Preamble of this Resolution, and to transmit the certificate so executed to the Secretary of State of the State of Indiana and the Secretary of State of the State of Indiana shall transmit such certificate, under the great seal of the State of Indiana, to the Secretary of State of the United States.

The President stated that the question is on the adoption of the Resolution and he would recognize Mr. Henry Marshall of Tippecanoe County, Vice-President of the Convention.

Mr. President:

I rise to speak briefly in support of the resolution to ratify the Twenty-first Amendment to the constitution of the United States. This amendment repeals the Eighteenth or prohibition amendment to the constitution.

Prohibition is not a political issue in Indiana.

Early in June of 1932 the republican and democratic state platforms, in almost identical terms, recommended that the Congress of the United States immediately adopt a resolution for repeal of the prohibition amendment and its submission to conventions of the people in the several states for ratification or rejection.

These same platforms called for the repeal of the Wright "bone-dry" law in Indiana and for the enactment of legislation in accord with federal laws.

Indiana's call was heard and heeded at the National Capitol in Washington and the State Capitol at Indianapolis.

Through the adoption of the Twenty-first Amendment the Congress of the United States accepted Indiana's recommendation and our own state legislature has repealed the unwise Wright "bone-dry" law, putting Indiana in accord with recent federal legislation.

Both of the great political parties in the Hoosier State are for temperance, as a moral issue, and against prohibition as a political issue.

Experiment Fails

When prohibition was put in effect as a war measure, there were many of us who felt it might be made to work.

It was accepted as an experiment.

It was natural for all good citizens to expect and demand the betterments the prohibition advocates promised.

The evils of the saloon era called for correction.

It was our hope that prohibition might bring a better day. So, for years we experimented.

We saw prohibition fail. We saw enforcement collapse.

We began to realize that prohibition in the very nature of things was not workable.

We reached the point, when, in order to retain our own self respect, we had to acknowledge our mistake.

Against Human Nature

After more than 13 years of experimentation, impotence and wasted effort, we reached the inevitable decision that prohibition is against human nature.

As human society has to deal with human nature; as organized society must deal with free men and women, and not with serfs or slaves, we were compelled to take stock of our situation and make a new start.

We were forced to take into account the human element—the fundamental truth that no law can be imposed, inflicted or enforced unless it is upheld by majority opinion. We became convinced that majority opinion was against the prohibition amendment, just as we also became convinced, through sad experience over a period of prohibition years, that the evils of the prohibition era were so destructive, so serious and so all-pervading as to menace public safety and threaten government itself.

Not Temperance Measure

We were for temperance. We found that prohibition did not bring temperance to our people, but that it fostered scores of evils in addition to intemperance, outlawry and social demoralization.

When we were forced to admit that prohibition had failed to bring temperance to America we merely became a part of that vast army of good citizens who have seen the failure of other restrictive efforts which violated the rights and privileges of the individual inherent in himself.

The sacred nature of that inherent right of the individual to order his own life, respecting always the rights of his neighbors, is at the heart of the general movement for repeal of prohibition and for the abandonment of the costly folly which has afflicted the country for the last decade and more.

It is both foolish and intolerable to go on submitting to a fallacious system under which an illicit, outlaw liquor traffic annually draws hundreds of millions of dollars of profits out of the nation's capital, out of legitimate trade and commerce and employs those millions for the financing of crime syndicates, rackets, the demoralization of government, the destruction of business and the overthrow of our institutions. The American people refuse longer to countenance a system which breeds the gangster, the rum runner, the bootlegger, the hijacker, the racketeer and the corruptionist.

Outlaw Traffic

As matters stand today we have a vast liquor traffic, under an unworkable prohibition system, branded as an outlaw, yet defiantly reaping inordinate profits and identified closely with all the criminality known to the underworld. We have liquor traffic, but we get no revenue from that huge outlaw trade.

The effect has been to increase our taxes for law enforcement purposes; to swell the population of our jails and prisons inordinately, thus adding further to the tax load, and at the same time, the liquor traffic, outlawed, has been exempt from taxation.

Legitimate business, the law-abiding element, has been excessively burdened—the load has been shifted to a part of the population. We say the beverage business should be made to pay its share; that the outlaw should be regulated, controlled; that we should cease the foolish pretense that the liquor traffic has been eradicated, and use ordinary everyday horse sense in dealing with the liquor problem as it actually exists.

We have tried in vain to theorize the liquor problem out of existence. The conditions growing out of years of theory and unworkable schemes for making over human nature on a prohibition pattern are well known to all of us. We have got to make a new start. We can no longer spin our theories and dream rosy dreams.

Recovery Ahead

Nor do we have to consider only the tragedy and failure of the period of prohibition. We are in a position to contrast present improved conditions with those of the last three years and to show that modification of the rigors of the unreasonable Volstead act and repeal of the unwise Wright "bone-dry" law in Indiana have been real factors in the movement toward recovery and better times in nation and state. We are in a position to argue that the present promise of prohibition repeal is working powerfully to stimulate industry, to restore confidence and to offer hope of tax relief to the taxpayer.

A revived legal beverage business already has helped mightily to increase the prices of farm products. The regulation of the beverage industry already is bringing a definite measure of tax relief and as time goes on will become an important factor in solving the problems connected with the cost of government. This is as it should be. We now know that it was a mistake to outlaw the beverage business and turn the revenues over to the criminal forces of the underworld. We now know that we are bound to handle the problems of the saloon era on a modern basis suggested by the experience of other nations where the saloon evil as we used to know it has been abolished by constructive common sense.

Prices Improving

We do not have to theorize, for everybody knows there has been a considerable and progressive recovery of farm prices since the Volstead act was modified. The figures are not imaginary. The news of rising markets and enlivened industry in recent weeks is not only inspiring, it is convincing. The revival of a large industry, the beverage industry, has had and is having far-reaching economic effects. Those effects will continue to spread. They have given the new era of the new deal a hopeful tone; they have helped to put the fighting edge on a depressed people. We are seeing the difference between the liquor racket of prohibition and the legalized, regulated, tax-paying beverage industry that is to come in with prohibition repeal. We see plainly that prohibition repeal, beverage revenue and regulation are elements in business recovery.

Necessity of Repeal

Prohibition repeal is part and parcel of the great recovery movement which is now under way in all parts of the country. Not only in its job-making aspects, in its crop consumption field, but in its revenue paying, tax relief features, the beverage industry, now being revived and properly legalized, is an important recovery factor. Repeal is inevitable and not only because prohibition has failed to work, but because of the practical need of the revenues which the outlawed traffic of the prohibition regime has been turning over to anti-government uses. We are compelled to make the beverage business pay its way and help support the government just as we are compelled to get rid of the outlaw liquor traffic of the old prohibition period and to put an end to the underworld's system of financing the war against government.

Impressive Parade

So it is that we go forward, an impressive parade of the sovereign states, to bring about the orderly and inevitable repeal of a prohibition law which does not fit into the American scheme of ordered liberty; which is not in accord with the fundamentals of human rights as enunciated by the fathers, and which, by its unreason and unfairness in application, rouses our citizenry to revolt and demoralizes the oncoming generation. Indiana is well up in front in the repeal procession. Hoosier common sense and the Hoosier capacity to learn and profit from experience was strongly vindicated by the voters on June 6.

The handwriting upon the repeal wall is easily read.

Indiana, today, will formally add her illustrious name to the roster of repeal states.

The Hoosier state will demonstrate that her citizens have the courage to acknowledge error and to join sister states in righting the wrongs that have made the collapse of prohibition such a tragic and calamitous affliction.

The President recognized Delegate Jesse E. Eschbach of Kosciusko County.

To the Constitutional Convention:

The dry delegates to this Convention beg leave to submit the following statement:

The vote of Indiana for the Ratification of the Prohibition Repeal Amendment has been taken in a time of dire economic distress when the governments of state and nation have been searching for every possible revenue, when men and women have been trying to find relief from acute conditions of unemployment and from business and industrial stagnation, when a widespread breakdown of morale has been accompanied by much lawlessness and by the resort of many to the illicit traffic in liquor as a source of livelihood.

The proponents of prohibition repeal have urged it on the grounds that it would make possible the elimination of the illicit traffic; that it would make available to the government huge sums of revenue, and that it would afford jobs to great numbers of unemployed and would provide larger markets for certain farm products. With these promises, they have reiterated that the saloon and the old abuses associated with the liquor traffic would not be permitted to return.

In view of these facts the vote of the people of Indiana for Ratification of the Prohibition Repeal Amendment is not to be interpreted as sanctioning intensive promotion of the use of alcoholic beverages, but it is rather a vote of permission to the administration to demonstrate better methods of liquor control, to lead us back to a general condition of prosperity, and to lighten the burdens of taxation.

While the minority are greatly interested in lightening tax burdens, in bringing prosperity, in abolishing the corrupting influences of the illicit liquor traffic in alcoholic beverages, and in advancing the cause of genuine liberty, we must dissent from the adoption of the proposed Prohibition Repeal Amendment for the following reasons:

1. It provides absolutely no guaranty against the return of the saloon, nor against the return of the evils of the old liquor traffic. We hold that the promises of any official, however influential, or of any party platform, however positive, are quite inadequate protection of the people against this menacing traffic.

2. It relinquishes the right of the Federal Government to control the traffic at the very time when all other forms of industry are coming under national control.

3. It implies legalization of liquor advertising by press, bill-board, radio and screen. At the same time its advocates commonly recommend the promotion of temperance by "education." It is apparent even to the casual observer that it is the aim of the liquor interests to do everything in their power to increase the use of alcoholic beverages. The licensing of several of the most important educational media of our day to engage in false education in the interests of the liquor traffic is one of the most vicious attacks upon the well-being of the American people.

4. It does not give the economic panacea that its advocates promise. The economic aspects of the traffic in alcoholic liquors never can be adequately appraised merely in terms of revenue accruing to the government, nor in terms of the profits of a few businesses intimately associated with the traffic. The effects of the consumption of alcohol upon the total well-being of the people is the only adequate economic and social criterion. It re-legalizes a parasitic industry which derives its existence by sapping the life-blood from the legitimate industries of the nation. The liquor business creates no new value; it gives those who buy its product nothing except an unnatural desire for more of its product.

5. This business is recognized as so dangerous, even by its friends, that it must

be conducted under the most elaborate police regulations. Its product is known to be so deteriorating that it must not be sold except to adults. Certainly a business of such harmful tendencies should be under the supervision of local, state and federal powers. Certainly such a business should be tolerated only under laws that specifically provide a plan that is designed progressively to reduce the consumption of its products and ultimately to eliminate their use. The proposed Prohibition Repeal Amendment offers no such specific method.

The President then recognized Delegate Peter R. Wadsworth of Daviess County.

THE ELECTION ON JUNE 6, 1933

By

Peter R. Wadsworth
A Convention Delegate
In the State Convention
June 26, 1933

The public was told through newspapers a few days ago that the President of The Association Against the Eighteen.h Amendment was saying that eleven states had "already voted overwhelmingly for repeal." This is in keeping with advance and kept up noisy talk that has been and is being spread over our country by repeal leaders to the effect that just about all of our voters want to vote for repeal. An analysis of figures in our state of Indiana in this relation discloses the facts that make a showing quite different from this. By looking into the matter it is seen that an "overwhelming" number of our voters are not standing up and being counted for repeal.

We learn from official records in the office of our Secretary of State that 1,600,484 persons voted in the state at the November election in 1932, and we are informed through an unofficial press report, being either exactly or approximately correct, that 557,062 voted for repeal on June 6 and that 312,120 voted against repeal, the total for and against repeal being 869,182. By subtracting the number that voted for repeal, 557,062, from the number that did not vote at all, 731,302, it is shown that 174,240 more voters stayed away from the polls than the number that voted for repeal.

By adding together the number of votes against repeal, 312,120, and the number that did not vote at all, 731,302, and by considering the stated figures at the November and June elections, we get a total of 1,043,422, none of whom voted for repeal, and from this showing it is seen that 557,062 voters of the state have said, through the ballot, that they are in favor of repeal, and that 1,043,422 have not said so.

Looking further and counting all of the people, men, women, and children, according to the United States census for 1930, living in the counties of Adams, Bartholomew, Benton, Blackford, Boone, Brown, Carroll, Crawford, Daviess, Dearborn, Decatur, Dekalb, Dubois, Fayette, Fountain, Franklin, Fulton, Hamilton, Hancock, Harrison, Hendricks, Jackson, Jasper, Jay, Jefferson, Jennings, Johnson, LaGrange, Marshall, Martin, Morgan, Newton, Noble, Ohio, Orange, Owen, Parke, Perry, Pike, Porter, Posey, Pulaski, Steuben, Switzerland, Tipton, Union, Vermillion, Wabash, Warren, Warrick, Washington, Wells, White and Whitley, we see that the total number of persons in these 61 counties is 1,023,627. By adding to Vincennes, the first capital of our state, and then add a number, 2,009, being a number that shows how many people live in Corydon, the second capital of our state, we get 1,043,200, this total being 222 less than the 1,043,422, "none of whom voted for repeal."

Using this light that reveals the actual truth as to voting on June 6 our people can see that our voters refused "overwhelmingly" to say that they favor the repeal of the eighteenth amendment.

In addition to the foregoing a special point of significance to consider is the requirement for the ratification by our voters of proposed amendments to the Constitution of Indiana. The provision in our state constitution, as to this, is that "a majority of electors shall ratify the same." And it is held that the word "majority," in this use, means a majority of all of the voters of the state.

We voted on a proposed income tax amendment to our Indiana constitution at the general state election last November, and the result of the vote was 709,045 for the amendment and 209,076 against it, the majority being 491,060 in favor of the amendment. Yet it is held that the amendment was not ratified by the voters. The holding is that in order for it to be considered ratified that the number voting for ratification should be a majority of the 1,600,484 voters in the state at that time. If it should be held that this rule is controlling in the June 6 election, the conclusion must be that Indiana has not ratified the proposed amendment to repeal the eighteenth amendment.

Another look: As already stated the total number of votes in the state on the day of the election, November 8, last year, was 1,600,484. The one-half of this is 800,242. So to have carried a state constitutional amendment that day the smallest possible vote for ratification would had to have been 800,243 votes. From this number we subtract 557,062, this being the number of votes given on June 6 for ratification, and we have 243,181, this being the shortage of votes necessary to have a required majority under the state constitutional rule.

Why are we not proceeding throughout in this proposed ratification in the manner provided in our state constitution and court decisions under proposed federal constitutional amendment? But to this it can be answered that it is not the federal government that is acting here and now. It is the state of Indiana that is acting, separately, distinctly and alone.

Who is there that can say, truthfully, that Indiana has gone "overwhelmingly" for repeal of the eighteenth amendment? There is nothing more, at best, than an empty and hollow victory in favor of ratification.

The President recognized Delegate Van Orman from Evansville.

Mr. President, Delegates, Ladies and Gentlemen:

We have enjoyed with great avidity the long voluminous news report edited by Mr. Wadsworth and I know that we have been regaled. A portion of the law states that we have to have in our record both debates, for prohibition and against prohibition, but the mathematician of the prohibition party has confused the issue with figures and I move that the figures pertaining to the debate be stricken from the record. I thank you.

The President ruled the motion out of order.

The President recognized Senator Nejdl from Whiting.

Ladies and Gentlemen and Fellow Delegates:

I do not desire to waste your time nor do I aim to waste mine. If I am permitted, Mr. President, I move you that the report of the gentleman who has just rendered it from the platform be referred to the Committee on Credentials to ascertain whether the delegates on this floor are duly elected.

The President recognized Delegate Ryan who made the motion that the previous question be put.

The President stated to the Delegates that the previous question was being called for and asked all those in favor to signify by saying Aye. Contrary, No.

The President stated that the question is on the adoption of the Committee on Resolutions. All those in favor of the adoption of the report of the Committee will please signify when your name is called by saying "Aye." The clerk will call the roll.

Those voting in the affirmative were, Delegates:

From the County of Adams: Jacob A. Long, Frank McConnell.

From the County of Allen: Helen Bruggeman, Ralph C. Dunkelberg, John W. Eggeman, Miller Ellingham, Oscar G. Foellinger, Herman F. Gerdon, Arthur F. Hall, Walter E. Helmke, Victor H. Hilgemann, Charles Solomon, Helen W. Sweet, Argo R. Vegalues, Fred Wehrenberg, John B. Wyss, Sam Wolf.

From the County of Bartholomew: Charles S. Kitzinger, Phillip R. Long.

From the County of Benton: Ernest L. Callaway.

From the County of Blackford: E. Floyd Willman.

From the County of Brown: Clarence Robertson.

From the County of Cass: James F. Digan, Oliver P. Erbaugh, Matthew Maroney, Sr.

From the County of Clark: Frank M. Fisher, Lunsford Jones, William Koetter.

From the County of Clay: Harry A. Campbell, Cliff Lowe, Thomas Phillips.

From the County of Crawford: Claud A. Roberts.

From the County of Dearborn: Hubert Rullman, John Stahl.

From the County of Dekalb: Harry R. Bloom, Andrew Grube.

From the County of Delaware: Edna Alexander, Clarke F. Johnson, Joseph W. Michael, Lillie Hannegan Mongrain, J. Byron Reed, John E. Schaubhut, Ralph Stout.

From the County of Dubois: Andrew B. Krempp, Leo H. Pfaff.

From the County of Elkhart: Floyd C. Best, Ira Eshelman, Harold B. Gray, Guy K. Keely, John R. Swart, Charles L. Minser, William A. Willhide.

From the County of Fayette: Jediah H. Clark, E. Ralph Himelick.

From the County of Floyd: R. W. Harris, Joseph Kahler, Gilbert E. Powell.

From the County of Franklin: Simeon Colebank.

From the County of Grant: Harry W. Cline, S. S. Condo, J. Harry Patterson, Paul G. Prail, John D. Williams.

From the County of Howard: Cosmos J. Braun, Wesley E. Conway, Addison Jenkins, Chester F. McDaniel, Dan S. Troy.

From the County of Jackson: Thomas H. Branaman, Oscar H. Montgomery.

From the County of Jasper: I. H. Riley.

From the County of Jay: James Leonard Bickel, Sarah Margaret Murray.

From the County of Jennings: Edward E. Gudgel.

From the County of Knox: Anthony Hess, Charles Raymond Lenahan, Frank L. Oliphant, James Luther Phillippi.

From the County of Lake: Garry J. August (sub. by E. J. Flannery), Axel R. Carlson (sub. by Joseph Mellon), Edwin A. Comstock, John A. Costello, Ladislaus J. Danieleski, James J. Farley, Bradford D. L. Glazebrook, Oscar Haney, Wilbur J. Hardway, George E. Hershman, William J. Huber, Joseph E. Klen, John S. McGuan, John L. Mears, Joseph E. Meyer, Fred C. Miller, Hugh P. Muckian, James J. Nejdl, Liquori A. O'Donnell, James A. Patterson, John L. Rohde, William J. Rossman, Walter E. Schrage, John W. Scott, John W. Werkowski, Helen R. White.

From the County of LaPorte: Gerhardt F. Decker, Francis G. Fedder, Frederick W. Flotow, Frederick W. Meissner, Caleb G. Stovall, Robert T. Wilson.

From the County of Madison: Benjamin J. Fettig, Cary Forkner, Robert H. Louden, William B. Myers, Thomas McCullough, Jane G. McIlwraith, J. Ward Starr, Albert Van Slyke.

From the County of Marion: V. M. Armstrong, Wm. A. Atkins, Robert L. Bailey, Lilith M.

Baur (sub. by Katherine Atkins), Berthe Born, Silas J. Carr, Leora Chavers, Augustus Coburn, Helen V. Costello, Alvin H. Eickhoff, Mayme Fogarty, Robert C. Fox, Adolph J. Fritz, Sarah Wolf Goodman, Julius Hollander, Lotta K. Horst, Mary G. Johnson, Marie S. Kaiser, William C. Kern, John C. Kirch, Herman W. Kothe, Eldena Lauter, Robert V. Law, Ralph A. Lemcke, George J. Marott, Sirdastion D. Merriwether, Albert F. Meurer, Alice B. Mooney, Roberta West Nicholson, Thomas B. Noble, Benjamin A. Osborne, Katherine F. Pantzer, Julian C. Ralston, Leo M. Rappaport, Otto G. Rassmann, Samuel E. Rauh (sub. by Mary McNutt), William M. Rockwood, Adelaide G. Roemler, Thomas D. Sheerin, Theodore Stein, Jr., Genevieve Bassel Watson, Evans Woollen, Jr.

From the County of Martin: Simon Hacker.

From the County of Miami: Chas. B. Ryder, Irven Swygert, Edwin F. Miller.

From the County of Morgan: Gilbert R. Brown, Jap Miller (sub. by Ora Ogle).

From the County of Newton: Charles R. Meyer.

From the County of Noble: Sol Henoch, Clement G. Routsong.

From the County of Ohio: Harry R. Clark.

From the County of Parke: Henrietta A. Adams, William J. Kerr.

From the County of Perry: William P. Birchler, Julius J. Wichser.

From the County of Porter: John M. Fabing, Sr., John W. Sieb.

From the County of Posey: Albert E. Heckmann, John H. Moeller.

From the County of Pulaski: Clarence Gilsinger.

From the County of Ripley: George C. Bos, William H. Oatman.

From the County of St. Joseph: William M. Stern, Rudolph Ackermann, William A. Thallmer, M. Edward Doran, Ivar Hennings, Nicholas Muszer, Casmir Lisek, Charles A. Gunn, James H. Greene, Joseph Duszynski, Anthony R. Gloyeski, Joseph P. Miller, Will G. Crabill, Alvin P. Kemper, W. H. Edwards, George Farage.

From the County of Shelby: J. Elmer Davison, William C. Groebl, Thomas Yates.

From the County of Spencer: Salem Parker, Margaret Sargent.

From the County of Starke: Charles Ruhl.

From the County of Steuben: Harcourt Sheets.

From the County of Sullivan: Ben F. Bolinger, Raymond A. Roberts, Enoch Stanley.

From the County of Tippecanoe: Henry W. Marshall, Sr., William T. Scanlon, Albert J. Krabbe, Mabel Vinton, Anna Mulherin.

From the County of Vanderburgh: William R. Etheridge, Arthur C. Folz, William D. Hardy, Charles M. LaFollette, Oscar Lanphar, George Schmadel, William G. Schnute, Charles Swoboda, George A. Theyson, Harold Van Orman, Mildred S. Wiggers.

From the County of Vermillion: Thomas H. Catlin, Louis M. Carli.

From the County of Vigo: Morton F. Hayman, John Hickey, Roy E. Hurt, William H. Johnson, Leonard B. Marshall, Albert F. Pfau, Samuel D. Royse, John F. Ryan, George A. Schaal, James H. Swango.

From the County of Warrick: Ernest Koch, Robert J. Derr.

From the County of Wayne: William H. Bartel, John Hazelrigg, Henry U. Johnson, Sr., Oline C. Robinson, Anton Stolle, Sr.

From the County of White: Nick H. Foltz, Bernie M. Pierce.

From the County of Whitley: Wm. C. Growcock, Robert H. Oliver.

Those voting in the negative were, Delegates:

From the County of Boone: Milton Hussey, Ben F. McKey.

From the County of Carroll: Joseph W. Eikenberry, Everett E. Flora.

From the County of Clinton: Effie C. Cochran, George H. Laughrey, Hiram V. Ransom.

From the County of Daviess: N. Maude Arthur, Frank Morgan, Peter R. Wadsworth.

From the County of Decatur: Robert W. Altizer, Henry L. Sefton.

From the County of Fountain: Joseph W. Harrison, Carl Quigle.

From the County of Fulton: Charles T. Jones, Edwin C. Mercer.

From the County of Gibson: Chester Braselton, Mrs. R. A. Cushman, W. P. Dearing.

From the County of Greene: John W. Brandon, Joseph H. Haseman, Charles V. Corbin.

From the County of Hamilton: Artemas H. Myers (sub. by Jesse Johnson), Adam Kepner.

From the County of Hancock: Charles F. Reeves, Anna McBane.

From the County of Harrison: Maurice Griffin, Clarence Quebbeman.

From the County of Hendricks: James E. Reitzel, Chester C. Bosstick.
From the County of Henry: Verl Byers, George N. Logan, Blanche White, Samuel E. Stout.
From the County of Huntington: Levi A. Ertzinger, Thelma G. Foust, Eben Lesh.
From the County of Jefferson: Culver Dean Field, Daniel S. Mills.
From the County of Johnson: Charles A. Brown, Robert H. Kent.
From the County of Kosciusko: Hobart Creighton, Jesse E. Eschbach, Edson B. Sarber.
From the County of LaGrange: Lewis Price.
From the County of Lawrence: Earl Krausbeck, Warren A. Sanders, Hazel Fern Evans, W. O. Guthrie.
From the County of Marshall: Ferdinand F. Fribley, Daniel B. Mann, Alfred A. Thompson.
From the County of Montgomery: John H. Binford, Claude C. Harshbarger, Frank D. Nolan.
From the County of Orange: Paul L. Coble, John W. McCullough.
From the County of Owen: Dillard M. Johnson.
From the County of Pike: Harley E. Craig, William F. Traylor.
From the County of Putnam: Francis C. Tilden, Maude M. Gough.
From the County of Randolph: Carmon J. Caplinger, Philip Kabel.
From the County of Rush: John E. Booth, Walter Bitner.
From the County of Scott: Robert W. Blunt.
From the County of Switzerland: Elmer E. Hufford.
From the County of Tipton: Clarence A. Smith, Franklin C. Suite.
From the County of Union: Cecil Leek.
From the County of Wabash: Paul Brembeck, Will J. Guthrie, Robert C. Thompson.
From the County of Warren: Rev. Herman LeRoy Adams.
From the County of Washington: Dennis Elrod, Rosco E. Hayes.
From the County of Wells: Earl R. Deam, Walter F. Timbrook.

The roll call resulted in a total of 246 Ayes and 83 Noes.

The Resolution was adopted and the Delegates concurred in the Committee report.

The President announced to the Delegates that he was signing Enrolled Resolution and likewise the Resolution was signed by the Secretary of the Convention, Roberta West Nicholson.

The President announced to the Delegates that the same pen was used in signing the Resolution that Governor Paul V. McNutt used in signing the law repealing the Wright Bone Dry Law.

Delegate Lemcke made the motion that the Convention adjourn. Motion was seconded by Delegate Wolf.

The President asked that he have a moment before putting the motion and said the following:

I want to thank you all for the kindness you have given me in making me the Chairman of this great body of American delegates, of Indiana citizens. I want to thank you. I feel that way and I hope that I shall soon have the opportunity of meeting all of you again.

The Convention then adjourned, *sine die.*

John W. Eggeman
President of Convention

Roberta West Nicholson
Secretary of Convention

IOWA*

OFFICERS OF THE CONVENTION

Temporary President
Governor Clyde L. Herring

Temporary Secretary
Assistant Secretary of State

Permanent President
Senator Joseph R. Frailey
Fort Madison

Permanent Secretary
General Mat A. Tinley
Council Bluffs

Journal Clerk
Byron G. Allen, Pocahontas

Reading Clerk
Philip L. Shutt, Independence

Sergeant-at-Arms
Dan McEniry, Des Moines

Assistants—I. H. Wilson, L. S. Reinecke, E. A. Franquemont, Geo. T. Irwin, Wade Clark, G. A. Holland, H. N. Hay, Matt Theis, Ralph Lynch, A. B. Southworth, and Ronald Ryan, Des Moines.

JOURNAL

OF THE

STATE CONVENTION

ON REPEAL OF THE EIGHTEENTH AMENDMENT

HALL OF THE HOUSE OF REPRESENTATIVES
DES MOINES, Iowa, July 10, 1933

Pursuant to the law, as provided in Senate File No. 477, Chapter 1, acts of the Forty-fifth General Assembly, the state convention of delegates to determine whether a proposed Amendment to the Constitution of the United States, repealing the Eighteenth Amendment thereto, should be ratified by the State of Iowa, convened at 2:00 o'clock P.M. Monday, July 10, 1933.

The convention was called to order by Governor Clyde L. Herring as temporary president.

*** Printed. The text of the Joint Resolution of Congress and the facsimile of the certification of ratification, which preface the journal, are omitted here, as well as the text of the law providing for the convention and the result of the special election of the delegates.**

Governor Herring announced that James C. Green, Assistant Secretary of State, would act as temporary secretary.

Prayer was offered by Reverend Harry Longley, pastor of Saint Paul's Episcopal Church of Des Moines:

"O God, the Holy Spirit, we turn to Thee in prayer seeking Thy guidance and blessing in this convention.

"Appointed to repeal a social experiment which has failed, we have come with a conscientious purpose to do the bidding of a sovereign people. May this action be blessed with fruits which shall make for a law abiding citizenry, a temperate people, and an honest and sober commonwealth.

"May all things in this state and nation be so ordered and settled upon the best and surest foundations that peace and happiness, truth and justice, religion and piety may be established among us for all generations. All of which we ask in the name of Jesus Christ, the Prince of Peace, our Most Blessed Lord. Amen."

Governor Herring then addressed the convention as follows:

LADIES AND GENTLEMEN OF THE CONVENTION:

This Constitutional Convention has interesting and unusual significance.

It represents one of the steps by which the people of a great Democracy seek, in an orderly manner, to express their will in a matter of government.

Also, it provides the means for the people, by deliberate and thoughtful consideration, to express their decision on a matter which heretofore has not received independent consideration.

I venture to say that not in the memory of any delegate to this Convention has the question here involved been considered alone, divorced from all questions of personalities and politics.

Your presence here then, is evidence of advance in government and in public thought.

It is a wholesome sign that our people have the good sense to separate what has been so controversial a question from other considerations and then determine it solely upon its merits.

It is perhaps timely and appropriate that I, not alone as temporary chairman of this Convention, but also as Chief Executive of this state, should call to your attention some of the factors involved.

Conflicting reasons have been given for the original adoption of the Eighteenth Amendment.

All will agree, however, that its genesis may be found in the action of a great number of earnest and excellent people who believed that its passage and adoption would prohibit the sale of intoxicating liquors.

Their desire was to combat the evils of drunkenness.

They had tried moral persuasion, and the establishment of total abstinence and temperance societies.

The results seemed too slow, however, to satisfy the more ardent and enthusiastic of the reforming group.

Therefore, in their zeal to do good, they substituted a purpose,—that of forbidding the use of intoxicating liquors.

We forgot that character must be developed by moral means and we believed that we could develop character by making men stop drinking, and that we could make men stop drinking by the passage of a law.

We sought to accomplish by prohibition of the act, what we could not accomplish by pointing out its evil consequences.

As was said by former President Taft: "Drinking of liquor is a social practice."

We sought by the Eighteenth Amendment to make this social practice a crime.

It was believed that heavy penalties would prevent indulgence.

It was believed that mere enactment of the prohibitory law would stop drinking by ending manufacture and sale.

Many good citizens, opposed to drunkenness, although believing that the method might not accomplish its purpose, nevertheless thought it would do no harm, and supported prohibition.

It was found to the surprise of some, and to the dismay of others, that the prohibitory law, like other penal laws, would not execute itself and that the law of enforcement arm of the government must be set in motion to detect and prevent violation.

Former President Taft had said that he was opposed to prohibition because he believed that it would not prohibit throughout the country, especially in localities where the community did not favor prohibition.

His concern was well founded.

People, otherwise law-abiding, began privately to manufacture and to purchase prohibited liquors.

Law-abiding people refused to lend themselves to the enforcement of the law.

The profits from the illegitimate business became so great as to encourage those violating the law to organize into groups, nation-wide in extent, to furnish a constant source and means of corruption.

Those who believed that the evil consequences which arose were the effect of drinking rather than of the attempt to stop drinking by law, increased their efforts for its enforcement by securing larger appropriations for detection and heavier penalties for violation.

With thousands of other citizens I had mistakenly believed that the prohibitory law should be passed and could be enforced.

I believed so firmly in temperance and was so definitely against the saloon that I was slow to surrender my belief that the Eighteenth Amendment could be made effective.

However, it has been demonstrated beyond reasonable doubt that it does not bring temperance; that it is unenforcible and that its effect has been to increase crime and corruption beyond anything known in the history of our people by reason of the extent to which its ill-gotten profits have financed the underworld.

For many years the opinion has been growing that the evils which followed in the wake of the adoption of the Eighteenth Amendment were worse than the evil which it sought to cure.

Many of us who have been firm advocates of the cause of temperance believed that we saw that cause harmed by the events of the last few years.

These circumstances caused great numbers of people to change their view as to the wisdom of the Eighteenth Amendment.

So definite has that change become that last year the National Convention of the two major political parties recognized in their platforms the necessity for prompt and affirmative action.

As a result, Congress adopted the Amendment calling for repeal of the Eighteenth

Amendment to the Constitution and has submitted it to the several states for its ratification or rejection.

Our legislature made the necessary provision for the selection of delegates to this Convention and for the calling of the Convention to consider the question of ratification or rejection of the Amendment.

The campaign which preceded the county conventions and which preceded the state-wide selection of delegates, was an active one on the part both of those who favored retention and those who favored rejection of the Amendment.

The questions were fully discussed by radio, by newspaper, on the platform, from the pulpit and in all of our forums.

The question was considered by the people unobscured by any other issue.

A vote larger than that ever cast at any election, other than a presidential election, indicates the interest of the people and their determination definitely to settle this controversial matter.

Let us hope that throughout the nation it may receive as full, as complete, and as fair consideration as it has received by the people of Iowa.

It is a testimonial to the good sense of our citizens and to their interest in orderly government that they voted in such large numbers and that the delegates elected to this Convention are men and women of high standing in their various communities.

I am confident that your approach to the consideration of the question before this Convention will justify the confidence which the people of Iowa have reposed in you.

I believe that it is appropriate to say here and now that I construe the results of the June election as a vote for temperance as opposed to prohibition, and that I believe that the people of Iowa favor temperance rather than prohibition.

We are not unmindful that an honored and respected woman of this state has recently been elected head of one of the great national prohibition organizations.

There was a time before her organization adopted prohibition as the solution of the problem, when she battled courageously in the cause of temperance.

It is the hope of many of us who respect her earnestness of purpose and her ability, that she will recognize the expression of the will of the people of Iowa and will again ally herself with the cause of temperance.

In exchange for that support I will pledge to her and her organization my support in opposition to the saloon.

I believe that the people of Iowa are opposed to the return of the saloon and if and when the Eighteenth Amendment shall be repealed, we must adopt the necessary legislation to that end.

One of the matters appropriate to mention to you to aid in your consideration of the question before you today is what legislation may be adopted in the event of your vote to ratify the repeal of the Eighteenth Amendment.

I believe that the people of Iowa through its legislature will, in the event of repeal, adopt practical laws which will secure the enforcement of the declaration of the will of the people and will promote the cause of temperance.

That they may have the benefit of preliminary study to that end, I have considered the appropriateness, in the event of repeal, of appointing a committee of citizens of this state who may be willing, without compensation, to make some study of various manners of liquor control and to give to the legislature the results of their investigation.

The saloon as it was known of old is a thing of the past and this generation will not tolerate it.

Since the enactment of beer legislation in Iowa, our people have demonstrated that they may use the beverage in a sensible, practical manner under proper regulation.

It is my belief that should the Eighteenth Amendment be repealed, we must be prepared by appropriate legislation to take care of certain factors, which I firmly believe will best promote the cause of temperance.

First: The element of *unrestricted* private profit must be taken out of the sale of liquor.

Second: There must be limited sale under strict government regulation and control.

Third: There must be such license fees as will provide to the state the greatest revenue possible, without, however, being so high as to encourage the practice of bootlegging.

In the event of repeal, it will be well for our legislature to consider whether it may not profitably, both for the cause of temperance and the cause of revenue, center the matter of liquor control in the hands of a state agency and divert all license fees into the public treasury, the amount thereof to replace to that extent the state levy imposed on real estate and other tangible property.

In the event of repeal, our legislature might well consider the plans in operation in the Canadian Provinces and I am informed that those have operated most successfully where a maximum of authority has been conferred upon the licensing boards to issue regulations consistent with the purposes I have outlined above.

They have selected excellent men to administer and have given them broad discretionary powers.

The questions before the people at the time of the election of Governor Horace Boies in 1889 were in many respects identical with those with which we are confronted today.

In his inaugural speech in 1890, he told of the effects of prohibition and of intemperance.

He recognized the propriety of legislation to minimize the evils, and the difference of opinion as to what that legislation should be.

He said that of all the means ever employed to improve the morals of men, that of excessive punishment is the least effective and after discussion of the questions of that day, he said what I may well submit to you, the chosen representatives of the people of Iowa:

Governor Boies said in 1890: "What Iowa needs is practical legislation on this subject. Legislation that is broad enough to meet the views of more than a single class; that is liberal enough to command the respect of all her people; that is generous enough to invite to her borders every class of respectable persons; that is just enough to respect the person and property of every one of her citizens; and wise enough to exercise a practical control over traffic that today is unrestrained in most of her centers of population.

"He who strives for this is not a foe of temperance, is a friend of the state, too grand in its natural advantages, too broad in its diversity of interests, too widely at variance in the education, habits and customs of its people to be appropriated by any single class or sect."

On behalf of the people who have chosen you as their delegates to this Constitutional Convention, I bespeak your careful consideration of the question before you.

Delegate Diamond of O'Brien county moved that the temporary president name a committee of three to act as a Committee on Credentials.

The motion was seconded by Delegate Schaupp of Webster county.

The motion prevailed.

The temporary president appointed as a Committee on Credentials Delegates Diamond of O'Brien county, Shaw of Keokuk county, and Morganthaler of Carroll county.

The committee retired, and, upon returning, the chairman, Delegate Diamond of O'Brien county, presented the following report:

"MR. PRESIDENT: Your Committee on Credentials begs leave to report that they have examined the election returns and the records in the office of the Secretary of State which were kept in pursuance to the provisions of Senate File No. 477, Chapter 1, acts of the Forty-fifth General Assembly, and finds that the persons named in a communication from the Secretary of State and submitted herewith, were duly elected as Delegates to this convention, and are entitled to membership in this body.

"Your committee further recommends that counties which have unofficially designated alternates and from which the officially elected delegate is not present may be represented by the alternate as an honorary delegate without a vote."

The following communication from the Secretary of State, having been made a part of the report of the Committee on Credentials, was, at the order of the temporary president, read into the journal of the convention:

I, MRS. ALEX MILLER, Secretary of State of the state of Iowa, custodian of the files and records pertaining to elections in the state,

DO HEREBY CERTIFY that the attached instrument contains a true and correct list of Delegates elected at a Special Election held on June 20th, 1933, as provided for by an Act of the Forty-fifth General Assembly, known as Senate File 477.

I DO FURTHER CERTIFY that the Delegates herein named were duly elected in full compliance to the laws of the state of Iowa, and that said Special Election was held on June 20th, A.D. 1933 in full compliance to the laws of the state of Iowa.

Adair .... F. O. Welch
Adams .... Wm. E. Humbert
Allamakee .... John J. Dunlevy
Appanoose .... Dr. E. E. Bamford
Audubon .... Al Miller
Benton .... C. J. Snitkay
Black Hawk .... Saner C. Bell
Boone .... Mrs. Paul M. Seifert
Bremer .... Lee O. Peacock
Buchanan .... Philip Leslie Shutt
Buena Vista .... F. C. Foley
Butler .... C. E. Johnson
Calhoun .... Earl Stotts
Carroll .... Otis P. Morganthaler
Cass .... Hugh Reinig
Cedar .... L. E. Bees
Cerro Gordo .... R. F. Clough
Cherokee .... Wm. H. Smith
Chickasaw .... C. A. Upham
Clarke .... W. T. Cleghorn
Clay .... H. E. Jones
Clayton .... M. X. Geske
Clinton .... J. A. Lubbers
Crawford .... L. W. Powers
Dallas .... W. P. Kent
Davis .... O. D. Wray
Decatur .... J. P. Smith
Delaware .... E. E. Annis
Des Moines .... Max Conrad
Dickinson .... Ira F. Peacock
Dubuque .... A. E. Piekenbrock
Emmet .... J. O. Kasa
Fayette .... Fred H. Harms
Floyd .... Ed. Gayther
Franklin .... R. F. Schaefer
Fremont .... John F. Porterfield
Greene .... U. K. Willman
Grundy .... Herman B. Koolman
Guthrie .... Charles Owen
Hamilton .... Edward P. Prince
Hancock .... Walter T. Walfrom
Hardin .... Gilman H. Wisner
Harrison .... Howard A. Nelson
Henry .... Frank Price
Howard .... W. C. Sovereign
Humboldt .... D. F. Coyle
Ida .... C. W. Hoyer
Iowa .... Frank Owen
Jackson .... J. O. Ristine
Jasper .... Frank L. Smith

Jefferson .... John G. Barwise
Johnson .... Edwin B. Wilson
Jones .... C. M. Holst
Keokuk .... Robert J. Shaw
Kossuth .... Geo. D. Moulton
Lee .... Joe R. Frailey
Linn .... Ray J. Mills
Louisa .... John G. Keck
Lucas .... C. C. Pickerell
Lyon .... M. McLaughlin
Madison .... Elmer Orris
Mahaska .... B. J. Snyder
Marion .... Peter W. Visser
Marshall .... A. A. Moore
Mills .... Walter Breen
Mitchell .... Lloyd H. Koch
Monona .... Matt Riddle
Monroe .... T. E. Gutch
Montgomery .... Paul W. Richards
Muscatine .... Clarence A. Hahn
O'Brien .... T. E. Diamond
Osceola .... A. B. Callender
Page .... John P. Nye
Palo Alto .... Irving J. Weber
Plymouth .... R. J. Joynt
Pocahontas .... F. K. Hawley
Polk .... Wm. C. Harbach
Pottawattamie .... Mat A. Tinley
Poweshiek .... Lola G. Landes
Ringgold .... Geo. H. Bartels
Sac .... Frank Krejci
Scott .... Peter N. Jacobsen
Shelby .... John Buman
Sioux .... William Huisman, Sr.
Story .... M. McLaughlin
Tama .... F. E. Shortess
Taylor .... F. L. Marsh
Union .... L. E. Sternberg
Van Buren .... John G. Shott
Wapello .... C. S. Harper
Warren .... Mark J. Dolan
Washington .... T. A. Michels
Wayne .... C. W. Elson
Webster .... John M. Schaupp
Winnebago .... Grover Campbell
Winneshiek .... T. F. Schmitz
Woodbury .... Donald E. Tremaine
Worth .... F. L. Murphy
Wright .... John J. Henneberry

I DO FURTHER CERTIFY that such Delegates are entitled to sit in and vote in the Constitutional Amendment Convention called by the Governor to meet in the House Chamber, State Capitol, Des Moines, on July 10th for the purpose of ratifying or rejecting, in behalf of the state of Iowa, a proposed Article of Amendment to the Constitution of the United States, to-wit:

Section 1. The eighteenth article of amendment to the Constitution of the United States is hereby repealed.

Section 2. The transportation or importation into any State, Territory, or possession of the United States for delivery or use therein of intoxicating liquors, in violation of the laws thereof, is hereby prohibited.

Section 3. This article shall be inoperative unless it shall have been ratified as an amendment to the Constitution by conventions in the several states, as provided in the Constitution, within seven years from the date of the submission hereof to the States by the Congress.

SEAL

In testimony whereof, I have hereunto set my hand and affixed the official seal of the Secretary of State at the Capitol, Des Moines, this 10th day of July, A.D. 1933.

MRS. ALEX MILLER
Secretary of State
By JAMES C. GREEN, *Deputy*

Delegate Miss Landes of Poweshiek county moved that the report of the Credentials Committee be adopted, that the accredited list of delegates submitted by the Secretary of State be declared the duly elected delegates to this convention, and that a roll call be had to ascertain the delegates present.

The motion was seconded by Delegate Dunlevy of Allamakee county.

The motion prevailed, the report of the committee was adopted, and the committee was discharged.

The roll was called to ascertain the delegates present:

Those present were, 90.

Bamford of Appanoose
Bartels of Ringgold
Barwise of Jefferson
Bees of Cedar
Bell of Black Hawk
Breen of Mills
Buman of Shelby
Callender of Osceola
Campbell of Winnebago
Cleghorn of Clarke
Clough of Cerro Gordo
Conrad of Des Moines
Coyle of Humboldt
Diamond of O'Brien
Dolan of Warren
Dunlevy of Allamakee
Elson of Wayne
Foley of Buena Vista
Frailey of Lee
Gayther of Floyd
Geske of Clayton
Gutch of Monroe
Hahn of Muscatine
Harbach of Polk
Harms of Fayette
Harper of Wapello
Hawley of Pocahontas
Henneberry of Wright
Holst of Jones
Hoyer of Ida
Huisman of Sioux
Jacobsen of Scott
Johnson of Butler
Jones of Clay
Joynt of Plymouth
Kasa of Emmet
Kent of Dallas
Koch of Mitchell
Koolman of Grundy
Krejci of Sac
Landes of Poweshiek
McLaughlin of Lyon
McLaughlin of Story
Marsh of Taylor
Michels of Washington
Miller of Audubon
Mills of Linn
Moore of Marshall
Morganthaler of Carroll
Moulton of Kossuth
Murphy of Worth
Nelson of Harrison
Nye of Page
Orris of Madison
Owen of Guthrie
Owen of Iowa
Peacock of Bremer
Pickerell of Lucas
Piekenbrock of Dubuque
Porterfield of Fremont
Price of Henry
Prince of Hamilton
Reinig of Cass
Richards of Montgomery
Riddle of Monona
Ristine of Jackson
Schaefer of Franklin
Schaupp of Webster
Schmitz of Winneshiek
Seifert of Boone
Shaw of Keokuk
Shortess of Tama
Shott of Van Buren
Shutt of Buchanan
Smith of Cherokee
Smith of Decatur
Smith of Jasper
Snyder of Mahaska
Sovereign of Howard
Sternberg of Union
Stotts of Calhoun
Tinley of Pottawattamie
Tremaine of Woodbury
Upham of Chickasaw
Visser of Marion
Walfrom of Hancock
Weber of Palo Alto
Welch of Adair
Willman of Greene
Wilson of Johnson

Those absent were, 9.

Annis of Delaware
Humbert of Adams
Keck of Louisa
Lubbers of Clinton
Peacock of Dickinson
Powers of Crawford
Snitkay of Benton
Wisner of Hardin
Wray of Davis

Delegate Bamford of Appanoose county moved that all absent delegates, or those not answering the roll call, be excused.

The motion was seconded by Delegate Hahn of Muscatine county.

The motion prevailed.

The delegates present then took the oath of office in a body as follows:

"I do solemnly swear that I will support the Constitution of the United States and the Constitution of Iowa, that I will faithfully and impartially perform the duties of delegate in this convention called to consider a proposed Amendment to the Constitution of the United States, according to law and to the best of my ability, so help me God."

Delegate Harbach of Polk county moved that the Honorable Joseph R. Frailey, the delegate from Lee county, be chosen president of the convention.

The motion was seconded by Delegate Tinley, of Pottawattamie county.

Temporary President Herring put the motion, which motion prevailed, and the Hon. Joseph R. Frailey was declared the duly elected president of the convention. Delegates Harbach of Polk county, Tinley of Pottawattamie county, and Clough of Cerro Gordo county were named as a committee to escort the president to the chair.

Delegate Frailey took the following oath which was administered by the temporary secretary, Mr. Green:

"I do solemnly swear that I will support the Constitution of the United States and the Constitution of the State of Iowa, that I will faithfully and impartially perform the duties of the office of president of this convention according to law and to the best of my ability, so help me God."

Delegate Frailey assumed the duties of presiding officer and addressed the convention as follows:

YOUR EXCELLENCY, DELEGATES TO THE CONVENTION, AND LADIES AND GENTLEMEN:

First of all I want to thank you from the bottom of my heart for the great honor you have bestowed upon me in selecting me President of this Convention. And the honor is all the greater, and the obligation that I owe to you the more precious, when we stop to think that this is the first time, in the history of Iowa, that the people themselves have been the makers and reformers of their own Constitution and, indirectly, of the Constitution of the United States itself.

This is a non-partisan Convention. It represents no faction, no creed and no party. It is a meeting of the delegates of the people. And for that reason, as a citizen of this State, and one who has approved and admired the great things that our Governor has already accomplished and is about to accomplish in his administration, I want to take this opportunity to pay to him a tribute as one of the greatest and most effective administrators who has ever sat in the gubernatorial chair and guided the welfare of his people. It is well that the State of Iowa recognizes, as it does, Clyde L. Herring, as one of her most illustrious sons, who through all the years, in office and out, has been in the very forefront in rendering patriotic services to his fellow citizens.

In the year of grace, 1776, Liberty, for the first time, rang throughout this land of ours. Today, as we are about to solemnly record the mandate of more than a third of a million votes of the men and women of this State, Liberty again returns to the grand old Commonwealth of Iowa. It is hard to tell whether this is the Christmas Eve of a new Liberalism or a new Declaration of Independence of our people.

We meet here today to rewrite and rededicate, once more, the inexorable scroll of human rights and human liberties. It is the old, old story of the slow, the patient, but the inevitable march of mankind to ultimate freedom. For you may hang men on gibbets and on scaffolds, but you can't hang the truth. You may cast men into prisons and dungeons, but you can't imprison thought. You may crucify men upon a thousand hills of Golgotha, but you can't crucify the gospel of eternal right; and all the persecutions, all the bigotries, all the iniquities of red handed inquisition, yes, and all the whited sepulchres of hypocrisy, that have blighted the hopes and holy aspirations of mankind since first the sun of human history silvered the dawn of the world, can never and will never, place the hosts of wrong upon the everlasting throne of right.

It has indeed been a pathetic and a tragic era that we have just passed through; those sad years from nineteen hundred eighteen to nineteen hundred thirty-two—the Via

Dolorosa, the Road of Sorrows, of American rights, American liberties and American Constitutional Government.

In that era we have seen the Constitution of the United States spurned, trampled under foot and spit upon—all in the name of the "noble experiment."

We have seen the first ten amendments to that Constitution—The Magna Charta of America—the one Bill of Rights of the Common People of this Nation, raped, ruined and repudiated.

We have seen trial by jury denied.

We have seen American free men and free women placed twice, yea, thrice in jeopardy for the same offence.

We have seen the persons, houses, papers and effects of the people of America subjected to outrageous and unreasonable search and seizure by the Hessians and Cossacks of Volsteadism.

We have seen men and women sent to prison without indictment and without a jury trial.

We have seen a free press and free speech throttled by intimidation, blackmail and bigotry.

We have seen men and women shot down and murdered in cold blood and that murder condoned and justified by the smug Pharisees of a so-called "Free America."

If in that Tragic Era—the era of nineteen hundred eighteen to nineteen hundred thirty-two, George Washington and Thomas Jefferson, John Adams and James Madison, Benjamin Franklin, and all those other giant souls who dowered their country and the ages with the legacy of liberty in thought, and word and deed, had been with us here in this country of ours as they were in the days of our glorious past, it would have been impossible to elect them to a Constitutional Convention such as this that we are attending today. That great and good man, Bishop James Cannon, who is now under indictment in Washington, D.C., would immediately have sent out a questionnaire to George Washington and Thomas Jefferson, demanding to know at once if they, ever in their lives, had taken a drink, and the good Doctor Clarence True Wilson of the Blue Sunday League would have interrogated Benjamin Franklin as to whether or not he ever flew his experimental kite in Philadelphia on the Sabbath day. That era through which we have just passed was the age of the moral and political Lilliputians and the land of Lilliput instead of producing giants shackled them by the overwhelming numbers of its pigmies of mediocrity and hypocrisy.

That day and that era is done forever in this country. Its death knell has rung and we are here today at the outraged demand of the people to enact into fundamental law a safeguard for their future that will forever prevent in the days to come any other attempt or subterfuge to rob them of their constitutional heritage and birthright. There are thousands of good men and good women in this State, among them the very highest type of our citizenship, who believe, or have believed in the past, in the potency, effectiveness and idealism of prohibition as it was written into the Constitution of the United States some fifteen years ago. It is true that vast numbers of our citizens who so believed in 1918 do not hold that same belief today. Otherwise, we would not be meeting here today registering its repeal.

We have no quarrel with these good and sincere men and women. As American citizens we accord them the same right that we demand and treasure ourselves and that is the expression of a free and untrammeled opinion.

No matter what our convictions may have been or are now upon this perplexing problem we are all going to live here in the future of this State as neighbors and fellow citizens and we all believe, I love to think and hope, in the fundamental soundness of the doctrine of majority rule.

We are asking today, the aid and assistance of these good neighbors of ours, no matter whether we can see all things precisely alike, in the solution of the problems that lie before us.

Our quarrel is not with them, but with the professional "reformers" who for the purpose of private gain, personal aggrandizement, greed for power and political preferment have led honest and sincere men and women down the pathway of delusion and deceit, into the morass of disappointment in and destruction of all of the ideals in which those people trusted and believed.

Where railroads cross highways there are signs which read: "Stop, Look, Listen." It would be well for our people and their representatives in our government to follow that warning now. To stop and take account of our national strength and our national weaknesses. To look calmly and judicially, and without passion and prejudice, at the momentous changes that have arisen in our body politic, social, political and economic, fanned in this day to a fever heat by a world in turmoil and unrest, that must inevitably affect us and those who will come after us. To listen, not to the words of the traitorous, the querulous, the visionaries, the "reforming" racketeers, and the demagogues, but rather to those, the living and the dead, who through the exercise of patience, courage, loyalty, industry, thrift and devotion, have made this Republic; or, in other words, in listening now and at once, before it is too late, to the real voice of the great and patient American people.

It is time to call a halt. It is time to get back to the beginning of things, back to the real sources of our strength. Back to the Constitution of Washington, Jackson, John Adams, Benjamin Franklin, John Marshall, Andrew Jackson, Abraham Lincoln, Theodore Roosevelt and Woodrow Wilson.

It is time to impress upon our people the lesson that we have learned at so great a cost in this period through which we have just passed. That is, that American Constitutional Government, as our fathers framed that Constitution and as our great sons interpreted it in following in their footsteps, means a free government for all of the people and not a part of them. That means minority rule and the tyranny and inquisitions of minorities must forever cease in this country of ours. Closely knit and organized minorities, no matter under what high sounding names and titles they may exist, that seek nothing but their own selfish interests at the expense of the great mass and majority of our people have no place in our scheme of government and it has been their insistence and their plots and connivances, more than anything else in our history, that have brought this nation of ours perilously near to destruction. Today, let us hope, that danger is being met and defeated by an awakened people as represented in this Convention.

This has not been, and is not now, a question of bringing back the saloon to Iowa. Nobody wants to bring back the saloon to Iowa. It is not a question of drink and liquor. It is a reaffirmation upon the part of the people of Iowa of the fundamental constitutional principles upon which free government is founded.

We are standing in a new dawn of the second century of this Republic. The fixed stars are fading from the sky, and we grope in uncertain light. Strange shapes have come with the night. Established ways are lost—new roads perplex, and widening fields stretch beyond the vision. The unrest of dawn impels us to and fro—but doubt stalks amidst the confusion, and even on the beaten paths the shifting crowds are halted, and from the shadows the voices of the Nation's sentries cry, "Who comes there?"

In the obscurity of morning tremendous forces are at work. Nothing is steadfast, nothing approved, but amid it all beats the great American heart, unafraid and undismayed, and standing fast by the challenge of his conscience, the American citizen, tranquil and resolute, as were his fathers in the past, watches the drifting of the spectral currents and calmly awaits the full disclosures of the coming day.

The solemn purpose for which we are meeting here today and the action that we are about to take on the ratification of the Twenty-first Amendment to the Constitution of the United States is but the first flush of that new dawn. That new dawn, that we fervently and prayerfully believe, will usher in again the rule of the people themselves. The rule of the people themselves, that is the one and eternal cornerstone of American freedom and liberty. It was this vision and this dream that held up the hands of Washington at Valley Forge and for which Lincoln wandered down the Valley of the Shadow of Death to the deathlessness of martyrdom. And all the way from Plymouth Rock and Jamestown, down to our last far flung frontiers at San Francisco, Seattle and the Yukon, it was this same spirit of the rule of the people that established this Republic, carved it from the wilderness, conquered it from the Indians, wrested it from England, and at last, at last, stilling its own tumult, consecrated it forever on this American continent, as the ultimate theater of its transcendent achievement.

But throughout all of our history, in its dawns of promise and happiness and its dusks of darkness and despair—like a pillar of cloud by day—of fire by night—that one lodestar of our national might and national majesty has ever stood steadfast, constant and unchangeable—the God guided truth of the Rule of the People.

And the people of Iowa have spoken. What they have said no man or woman can mistake, and we, their delegated representatives, in a spirit of consecration to their voice, will now proceed, in this Constitutional Convention, to record their mandate.

Delegate Piekenbrock of Dubuque county moved that Delegate Tinley of Pottawattamie county be chosen permanent secretary of the convention.

The motion was seconded by Delegate Richards of Montgomery county.

The motion prevailed and Delegate Mat A. Tinley was declared duly elected secretary of the convention.

President Frailey named Delegates Piekenbrock of Dubuque county, Richards of Montgomery county and Bell of Black Hawk county to escort the secretary to the desk.

Delegate Tinley then took the following oath:

"I do solemnly swear that I will support the Constitution of the United States and the Constitution of the State of Iowa, that I will faithfully and impartially perform the duties of the office of secretary of this convention according to law and to the best of my ability, so help me God."

Delegate Joynt of Plymouth county moved that the president appoint a reading clerk and a journal clerk.

The motion was seconded by Delegate Henneberry of Wright county.

The motion prevailed.

The president appointed Delegates Shutt of Buchanan county and Byron G. Allen of Pocahontas county as reading clerk and journal clerk respectively, and they were sworn in by the president.

Delegate Diamond of O'Brien county, moved that Robert's rules of order be adopted as the rules of the convention.

The motion was seconded by Delegate Conrad of Des Moines county.

The motion prevailed.

At the order of the president there was read into the journal of the convention, as follows, a record of the enactment of Senate File No. 477, Chapter 1, acts of the Forty-fifth General Assembly together with the Governor's Proclamation calling a special election and the Constitutional Amendment Convention:

I, Mrs. Alex Miller, Secretary of State of the State of Iowa, and custodian of the records of the Forty-fifth General Assembly do hereby certify that the attached instrument is a true and correct copy of an Act of the Forty-fifth General Assembly known as Senate File No. 477 as passed and amended by the General Assembly and under which a special election was held on June 20th, A.D., 1933, for the selection of delegates to a State Convention to be convened for the purpose of ratifying or rejecting a proposed article of amendment to the Constitution of the United States.

I FURTHER CERTIFY that the attached instrument contains a true and correct copy of a proclamation issued on the 14th of April, A.D., 1933, calling said special election and the aforesaid State Convention.

SEAL

In testimony whereof, I have hereunto set my hand and affixed the official seal of the Secretary of State at the Capitol, in Des Moines, this 10th day of July, A.D. 1933.

Mrs. Alex Miller
Secretary of State
By James C. Green
Deputy

Delegate Geske of Clayton county introduced and offered the following resolution and moved its adoption:

RESOLUTION

Whereas, the Congress of the United States has submitted to the various states for ratification or rejection, a proposed Article of Amendment to the Constitution of the United States, to-wit:

Section 1. The eighteenth article of amendment to the Constitution of the United States is hereby repealed.

Section 2. The transportation or importation into any State, Territory, or possession of the United States for delivery or use therein of intoxicating liquors, in violation of the laws thereof, is hereby prohibited.

Section 3. This article shall be inoperative unless it shall have been ratified as an amendment to the Constitution by conventions in the several States, as provided in the Constitution, within seven years from the date of the submission hereof to the States by the Congress. And,

Whereas, the Congress directed by Resolution submitting the question of ratification or rejection to the States that such action be by state conventions called for that purpose, and

WHEREAS, the Forty-fifth General Assembly of Iowa, by an Act known as Senate File 477, provided for a special election for the election of delegates to such a convention, and

WHEREAS, such election was held on June 20th A.D. 1933, and

WHEREAS, HIS EXCELLENCY, the Governor of Iowa, pursuant to authority vested in him by Senate File 477, and in accordance with law, has called a convention of the delegates elected at said special election to meet in the House Chamber, State Capitol, Des Moines, on July 10th, A.D. 1933, and

WHEREAS, the duly accredited state convention delegates, elected at said special election, have convened in accordance with the call of the Governor of Iowa, and for the purpose set out in said call, therefore,

Be it resolved that the state of Iowa, through a convention duly called and organized for the purpose of ratifying or rejecting the aforesaid Article of Amendment to the Constitution of the United States, hereby declares its approval and ratification, in the name of the State of Iowa, of said proposed Amendment; and

Be it further resolved that the Governor of Iowa and the Secretary of State of the State of Iowa are directed to forthwith certify this action to the Secretary of State of the United States and to do such other acts as may be necessary or required fully to effectuate the action of this convention.

The motion was seconded by Delegate Coyle of Humboldt county.

On the question, "Shall the Resolution be adopted?" a roll call was demanded.

The ayes were, 90.

Bamford of Appanoose
Bartels of Ringgold
Barwise of Jefferson
Bees of Cedar
Bell of Black Hawk
Breen of Mills
Buman of Shelby
Callender of Osceola
Campbell of Winnebago
Cleghorn of Clarke
Clough of Cerro Gordo
Conrad of Des Moines
Coyle of Humboldt
Diamond of O'Brien
Dolan of Warren
Dunlevy of Allamakee
Elson of Wayne
Foley of Buena Vista
Frailey of Lee
Gayther of Floyd
Geske of Clayton
Gutch of Monroe
Hahn of Muscatine
Harbach of Polk
Harms of Fayette
Harper of Wapello
Hawley of Pocahontas
Henneberry of Wright
Holst of Jones
Hoyer of Ida
Huisman of Sioux
Jacobsen of Scott
Johnson of Butler
Jones of Clay
Joynt of Plymouth
Kasa of Emmet
Kent of Dallas
Koch of Mitchell
Koolman of Grundy
Krejci of Sac
Landes of Poweshiek
McLaughlin of Lyon
McLaughlin of Story
Marsh of Taylor
Michels of Washington
Miller of Audubon
Mills of Linn
Moore of Marshall
Morganthaler of Carroll
Moulton of Kossuth
Murphy of Worth
Nelson of Harrison
Nye of Page
Orris of Madison
Owen of Guthrie
Owen of Iowa
Peacock of Bremer
Pickerell of Lucas
Piekenbrock of Dubuque
Porterfield of Fremont
Price of Henry
Prince of Hamilton
Reinig of Cass
Richards of Montgomery
Riddle of Monona
Ristine of Jackson
Schaefer of Franklin
Schaupp of Webster
Schmitz of Winneshiek
Seifert of Boone
Shaw of Keokuk
Shortess of Tama
Shott of Van Buren
Shutt of Buchanan
Smith of Cherokee
Smith of Decatur
Smith of Jasper
Snyder of Mahaska
Sovereign of Howard
Sternberg of Union
Stotts of Calhoun
Tinley of Pottawattamie
Tremaine of Woodbury
Upham of Chickasaw
Visser of Marion
Walfrom of Hancock
Weber of Palo Alto
Welch of Adair
William of Greene
Wilson of Johnson

The nays were, none.

Absent, 9.

Annis of Delaware	Lubbers of Clinton	Snitkay of Benton
Humbert of Adams	Peacock of Dickinson	Wisner of Hardin
Keck of Louisa	Powers of Crawford	Wray of Davis

The Resolution having received a majority of the votes of the convention, it was declared to have been duly adopted.

The president and the secretary, in the presence of the convention, signed the certification to the adoption of the Resolution and the president proclaimed the proposed Amendment to the Constitution of the United States had been duly ratified by the State of Iowa.

The certification attached to the official document and resolution read as follows:

CERTIFICATION

WE, the undersigned President and Secretary, respectively, of the state convention duly called and assembled at Des Moines, Iowa, on July 10th A.D. 1933, for the purpose of ratification or rejection of the aforesaid proposed Amendment to the Constitution of the United States, hereby certify that the foregoing Resolution was adopted by said convention by a vote of 90 ayes, and no nays; 9 absent.

J. R. FRAILEY
President
MAT A. TINLEY
Secretary

Executed at Des Moines, Iowa, July 10th A.D. 1933.

I, Mat A. Tinley, Secretary of the Constitutional Amendment Convention held at Des Moines, Iowa, July 10th A.D. 1933, hereby certify that J. R. Frailey was the duly elected President of the aforesaid convention.

MAT A. TINLEY
Secretary

Executed at Des Moines, Iowa, July 10th A.D. 1933.

I, J. R. Frailey, President of the Constitutional Amendment Convention held at Des Moines, Iowa, July 10th A.D. 1933, hereby certify that Mat A. Tinley was the duly elected Secretary of the aforesaid convention.

J. R. FRAILEY
President

Executed at Des Moines, Iowa, July 10th A.D. 1933.

The delegate from Hancock county, Rev. Walfrom, moved that a committee be appointed to deposit the ratification resolution with the Secretary of State.

The motion was seconded by Delegate Jacobsen of Scott county.

The motion prevailed.

The president appointed Delegates Rev. Walfrom of Hancock county, Mrs. Seifert of Boone county and Jacobsen of Scott county, to deliver the official copy of the ratification resolution to the Secretary of State.

The committee retired, and upon returning, the chairman, Rev. Walfrom reported that the committee had officially deposited the ratification resolution with the Secretary of State.

The report was accepted and the committee discharged.

The president announced that the official business of the convention had been completed.

Delegate Hawley of Pocahontas county moved that the convention adjourn *sine die.*

The motion was seconded by Delegate Shott of Van Buren county.

The motion prevailed and President Frailey declared the convention adjourned *sine die.*

CERTIFICATION

WE, the undersigned President, Secretary and Journal Clerk of the Constitutional Amendment Convention, held at Des Moines, July 10, 1933, do hereby certify that the foregoing, to the best of our knowledge and belief, is a true and correct record of the proceedings of said convention.

J. R. FRAILEY
President
MAT A. TINLEY
Secretary
BYRON G. ALLEN
Journal Clerk

KENTUCKY*

PROCEEDINGS

OF A

CONVENTION HELD ON NOVEMBER 27, 1933

AT THE

STATE CAPITOL, FRANKFORT, KENTUCKY,

BY THE

DULY ELECTED DELEGATES OF THE COMMONWEALTH OF KENTUCKY

TO CONSIDER THE REPEAL OF THE EIGHTEENTH AMENDMENT

BY GOVERNOR RUBY LAFFOON: The Convention will come to order. I did not constitute myself the person to call this convention to order but it was suggested that I perform that function by parties interested.

This is a momentous occasion in Kentucky. This is a history making day in the old Commonwealth. For the first time in the history of this State, duly elected delegates have assembled for the purpose of amending or ratifying an amendment to the Constitution of the United States. That never happened before in the history of Kentucky. Depending upon the action of Kentucky and the other states of the Union, early in December, the Eighteenth Amendment to the Constitution of the United States will be repealed. By that action, the mode of handling the liquor industry of the country will be materially changed. It means, or will mean, an end to prohibition, and I sincerely hope that it will not be interpreted to mean an open saloon.

The action of Kentucky, and of the states of the nation in repealing the Eighteenth Amendment, will devolve upon the citizens of Kentucky, and of the whole country, a most gigantic task. It means that we will have to handle the great liquor question as it should always have been handled. We have before us the duty of teaching the people of our State and of our Nation temperance. We shall not say to them what they shall or shall not do, but we, as good citizens, ought to try to inculcate into the minds and lives of our citizens an overweening desire to be temperate in all things.

I am going to ask Captain Walker, the Clerk of the House of Representatives, to call the roll of delegates present.

As your names are called, you will please rise and remain standing until the oath can be administered by Judge Rees, Chief Justice of the Court of Appeals.

The clerk calls the following roll:

Mrs. Gaither	who	answered	Present	Miss Clay	who	answered	Present
Mr. Shelbourne	"	"	"	Mr. de Cognets	"	"	"
Mrs. Yeaman	"	"	"	Mr. Fitzpatrick	"	"	"
General Sibert	"	"	"	Dr. Smith	"	"	"
Mrs. Todd	"	"	"	Mr. Keenan	"	"	"
Mr. Haldeman	"	"	"	Mr. Fee	"	"	"
Mr. McLean	"	"	"	Mrs. Martin	"	"	"
Mr. Boldrick	"	"	"	Mr. Beecher Smith	"	"	"
Senator Simmons	"	"	"	Mr. Farnsley	"	"	"
Mr. Allington	"	"	"				

* From a typewritten copy.

By Governor Laffoon: Remain standing and Judge Rees, Chief Justice of the Court of Appeals, will administer the Oath:

By Judge Rees: Please raise your right hands.

You, and each of you, do solemnly swear that you will support the Constitution of the United States and the Constitution of this Commonwealth, and that you will be faithful and true to this Commonwealth and that you will faithfully execute to the best of your ability the office of delegate to a convention to consider and act upon the proposed Twenty-first Amendment to the Federal Constitution, according to law and you do further solemnly swear that since the adoption of the present Constitution you have not fought a duel with deadly weapons within this State or out of it, nor have you sent or accepted a challenge to fight a duel with deadly weapons, nor have you acted as second in carrying a challenge, nor have you aided or assisted anyone thus offending, so help you God.

By Governor Laffoon: Motions are in order for the election of a temporary chairman of this convention. Do I hear a motion for that purpose?

By Mr. Russell de Cognets: I would like to nominate Miss Laura Clay of Lexington as Temporary Chairman.

By Governor Laffoon: Do I hear a second?

By Mr. Bruce Haldeman: I second the motion.

By Governor Laffoon: All delegates who favor the election of Miss Clay will let it be known by saying "Aye."

(All delegates vote "Aye.")

By Governor Laffoon: If there are any opposed, let it be known by saying "No."

(No delegate voted "No.")

By Governor Laffoon: By your votes you have elected Miss Clay, and I will appoint Mrs. James Yeaman and Mr. McClain to escort Miss Clay to the chair.

(Miss Clay is escorted to chair.)

By Governor Laffoon (presenting Miss Clay with gavel): Miss Clay, it is with pleasure that I present you with this gavel.

To the Convention: I have the pleasure of introducing to you Miss Laura Clay, who is elected temporary chairman of this convention.

By Miss Clay: Friends, delegates and fellow citizens, I have the honor to extend greetings to you on this historic occasion. The people of Kentucky have voiced at the ballot box their mandate that the 18th Amendment of the Federal Constitution shall be repealed and the 21st Amendment adopted. Whatever their motives may have been in the giving of this mandate, it is evident that it expresses a widespread and deep rooted conviction among our people of the right of the states to govern their internal and local affairs, and it designates as one office of the Federal authority, government to uphold the states in their authority by providing punishment for all violation of our laws. With this renewed affirmation of the rights of the citizens, we may go forward with courage to solve the problems that meet us in the way to better and higher social conditions under our own state constitutional dry amendment. I will now proceed to the business of the convention by asking for motions for the nomination of a temporary secretary.

By Mrs. Todd: I nominate Mr. Boldrick.

By Miss Clay: Are there other nominations?

All in favor of Mr. Boldrick, make it known by voting "Aye" those opposed "No."

(All delegates vote "Aye.")

Mr. Boldrick is elected and I will ask him to come forward and take his seat as Temporary Secretary.

By Miss Clay: The next order of business is the nomination of an organizing and nominating committee for the office of Permanent Chairman and other offices.

By Mr. de Cognets: Madam Chairman, I move that the chair appoint the members of a committee on organization and nomination.

By Miss Clay: The chair will appoint Gen. Sibert, Chairman, Mr. Russell de Cognets, Mrs. Martin, Mr. McClain, Mr. Beecher Smith and Mr. Farnsley. I will ask that this committee retire for a few minutes and bring in a report immediately. In the meanwhile we will relax for a moment or two for recess.

(Committee retires.)

(Committee returns.)

By Mr. Sibert: Madam Chairman, your committee on nomination and organization recommends for president of the convention Mr. Bruce Haldeman, of Louisville. Your committee recommends for Secretary of the convention, Mr. C. C. Boldrick of Lebanon. The committee further recommends the appointment by the president of the convention the following committees:

Committee on Rules
Committee on Credentials
Committee on Resolutions
Committee on Inspection of Journal

The committee also recommends that any other needed officials or assistants shall be appointed by the President.

Madam Chairman: I move the adoption of the Committee's report.

By Miss Clay: We will not pass on the resolutions that have been offered. As I understand it, the Temporary Chairman's duty is only to receive the new officers, and after they have been received, that the further committees will be appointed by the Permanent Chairman. I believe I am correct in that impression. You have heard the nomination of officers. All those in favor of nominating the officers mentioned will say "Aye."

(All delegates vote "Aye.")

All opposed will make it known by saying "No."

(No delegate voted "No.")

I will request Mrs. Todd of Louisville, and Mr. Farnsley of Louisville, to escort the permanent chairman to the platform.

(Mrs. Todd and Mr. Farnsley escort Mr. Haldeman to chair.)

By Mr. Haldeman: Ladies and Gentlemen of the Convention: I believe it is in order for me to read to you the telegram sent to this convention by one whom you all honor, and a very distinguished man, who has worked hard for repeal and who has acquitted himself in a most brilliant manner, Mr. Jouett Shouse. He says:

"Washington, D.C. Permit me on behalf of the National Headquarters of the Association Against the Prohibition Amendment to send through you greetings and felicitations to the Kentucky Convention about to assemble to ratify the Twenty-first Amendment. This is an historic occasion. For the first time since our Government was created a provision placed in our Constitution is to be removed. The people themselves through direct elections, have passed upon the question and after fourteen years of trial, are repealing the

Eighteenth Amendment. The people have voted that control of the liquor problem shall be returned to the individual States. They will not tolerate any attempt to thwart this decision, no matter from what source it may originate. Kentucky is to be congratulated on its happy part in this constructive achievement, and I, as a Kentuckian, rejoice with you in it.

(*Signed*) JOUETT SHOUSE."

I believe the first thing in order is the election of a permanent secretary. Mr. Boldrick has been nominated by the nominating committee, and I will put the question of his election before you. All in favor of Mr. Boldrick's election as permanent secretary of this convention, let it be known by saying "Aye."

Convention votes "Aye."

All opposed let it be known by saying "No."

No member votes "No."

Mr. Boldrick is elected permanent secretary of this Convention.

Before calling for the reports of the committees, I believe it will be in order for me to make a brief statement. I am sure that I speak for the delegates when I thank Governor Laffoon and the Committee on Arrangements appointed by him for the kind forethought in preparing for the assembling of this convention.

It is hardly necessary for me to state that I deeply appreciate and thank you sincerely for the honor you bestow upon me by making me the President of this convention. During the past twelve years, or longer, if there was anything I considered more needed than the repeal of the 18th Amendment I fail to recall it. To have this hope fulfilled, and, moreover, to actually be the President of the convention whose delegates represent the sovereign commonwealth of Kentucky in registering the decision of its people as to prohibition is almost too good to be true.

We meet here to formally chronicle the verdict of Kentucky that she wishes the 18th Amendment repealed. Let me congratulate you fellow delegates that this verdict is spoken in no uncertain tones; spoken in a majority of over 140,000 votes with all the emphasis that that most decisive figure carries with it.

This is the first convention of its kind ever held in this state. It is one of a series of conventions already held and being held throughout the United States, by means of which our Constitution is being amended in a manner never before employed. I believe that all impartially minded people are convinced of the fairness of this method.

Let us also consider that in thus amending the Constitution we are not tearing down. We are doing a constructive work of restoration. Restoring not only the personal liberty of the American citizen, but elevating our organic law to the place of dignity it should occupy and which should command the respect and devotion of the people. We are eliminating a police regulation which should never have been placed in the Constitution.

While we rejoice at the happy result let us not forget the responsibilities which come with this changed situation. A person who would anticipate an immediate restoration of that respect for the law and immediate observance of the law desired by all good citizens after the deplorable conditions brought about by prohibition is, in my opinion, unduly optimistic. It will take time to correct these evils. I believe that the course of true temperance will be advanced in a manner which would have been impossible under prohibition.

If the individual states will adequately cooperate with the Federal Government under its present great leadership, I believe we can hopefully look forward to the future when crime will be minimized and law and order become supreme.

Next in order of business will be the report of the Committee on Nominations and Organization. That report is as follows:

Mr. President: The following delegates are suggested for appointment to the Committee on Resolutions:

Mrs. James Ross Todd, *Chairman*
Mr. D. E. Fee
Mr. Beecher Smith
Gen. William Luther Sibert
Mr. R. C. Simmons
Charles P. Farnsley
Russell de Cognets

The following delegates are suggested for appointment to the Committee on Rules:

Mr. Roy M. Shelbourne, *Chairman*
Mrs. James M. Yeaman
Mr. Henry D. Fitzpatrick
Mr. Dan S. Keenan
Mr. C. Lee McClain

The following delegates are suggested for appointment to the Committee on Credentials:

Mr. Harry J. Allington, *Chairman*
Mrs. J. G. Gaither
Dr. W. J. Smith
Miss Laura Clay

The following delegates are suggested for appointment to the Committee on Inspection of Journal:

Charles P. Farnsley, *Chairman*
C. C. Boldrick
Mrs. William M. Martin

BY MR. HALDEMAN: All these Committees will retire for a few minutes and prepare their reports and hand them to the Clerk. (Committees retire for a few minutes and return to Convention Hall.)

BY MR. HALDEMAN: I understand that the various committees are ready to report. We will hear the report of the Credentials Committee.

BY MR. WALKER: The Committee on Credentials reports that it has examined the certificates of election and finds that the following persons were duly elected as delegates to this convention:

Mrs. J. G. Gaither	Hopkinsville, Ky.	Harry J. Allington	Newport, Ky.
Roy M. Shelbourne	Paducah, Ky.	Miss Laura Clay	Lexington, Ky.
Mr. James M. Yeenan	Henderson, Ky.	Russell de Cognets	Lexington, Ky.
Gen. William Luther Sibert	Bowling Green, Ky.	Henry D. Fitzpatrick	Prestonsburg, Ky.
Mrs. James Ross Todd	Louisville, Ky.	Dr. W. J. Smith	Belfry, Ky.
Bruce Haldeman	Louisville, Ky.	Dan S. Keenan	Ashland, Ky.
G. Lee McClain	Bardstown, Ky.	Mrs. William M. Martin	Harlan, Ky.
C. C. Boldrick	Lebanon, Ky.	Beecher Smith	Somerset, Ky.
R. C. Simmons	Covington, Ky.	Charles P. Farnsley	Louisville, Ky.

By Mr. Haldeman: Ladies and Gentlemen, you have heard this report, is there any discussion? I will entertain a motion to adopt this report.

By Mr. Fee: Mr. President, I did not hear my name read on that report.

By Mr. Walker: Mr. Fee's name is not on there.

By Mr. de Cognets: Mr. President, I make a motion that Mr. Fee's name be added to the report.

By Mrs. James Ross Todd: I second the motion.

By Mr. Haldeman: It has been moved and seconded that Mr. Fee's name be added and placed with the names of the other delegates on this report. All in favor, let it be known by saying "Aye."

(Convention votes "Aye.")

All opposed, by saying "No."

(No delegate votes no.)

The next report is that of the Committee on Rules. The Chairman of that committee will please read this report.

By Mr. Shelbourne: Your Committee on Rules desires to report and recommend that until the committee has more opportunity to formulate any rules that may be considered necessary the convention will operate under the parliamentary rules which were those of the Legislature of the State of Kentucky in 1933.

Mr. President, I move the adoption of the committee's report.

By Mr. Haldeman: Do I hear a second?

By Mr. Keenan: I second the motion.

By Mr. Haldeman: It has been moved and seconded that this report be adopted. All in favor of the adoption of this report, let it be known by saying "Aye."

(Convention votes "Aye.")

All opposed, by saying "No."

(No delegate votes "No.")

The next report is the Committee on Inspection of the Journal.

By Mr. Farnsley: The Committee on Inspection of the Journal will report to the Chairman when the Journal has been received and signed by the officers of the Convention.

By Mr. Haldeman: You have heard the report of the Chairman. I suppose the formal adoption will be postponed until the Journal is finished.

The next report is a most important one, it is the report of the Committee on Resolutions. I think it not inappropriate for me to say at this time in connection with the report by the Chairman of that Committee that the friends of repeal owe to the Women's Organization an obligation that in my opinion can never be met. Their support was of inestimable value. No more prominent women in that movement aided Mrs. Sabin than our own Mrs. James Ross Todd of Louisville, who certainly conducted a great campaign in this State. We will hear from Mrs. Todd.

By Mrs. Todd: Mr. President: I am highly conscious of the honor bestowed upon me and I am also deeply imbued with the solemnity of the occasion. As Chairman of the Committee on Resolutions, it is my great privilege to present to this convention the document which expresses Kentucky's ratification of the proposed Twenty-first Amendment repealing the Eighteenth Amendment to the Constitution of the United States.

This is a triumphant victory; a victory for those who have worked for the purpose of including Kentucky's name among the thirty-six states necessary to repeal National Prohibition. In all probability the Eighteenth Amendment would have been repealed without Kentucky's assistance, but it is in keeping with this state's former traditions to share responsibility and assume an obligation for the betterment of the nation.

The seriousness of the action we are about to take cannot be minimized. It is marked with full knowledge that through repeal of the Eighteenth Amendment only the first essential step toward prohibition reform will have been accomplished.

Through the repeal of National Prohibition a basic American principle of local self-government will be rightfully restored to the several States. The very essence of Repeal is that the people of the States shall again be allowed to legislate for themselves in matters concerning control and regulation of alcoholic beverages.

It is my sincere hope that I am voicing the sentiment and determination of everyone in Kentucky who approves of law observance and temperance when I say that as individuals and through organized efforts, we will work unceasingly toward that goal by supporting only such laws which will promote true temperance.

Mr. President, with these thoughts in my mind and with the expectation that the State of Kentucky will gain full value from the mandate of its people, I now present the Resolution of Repeal.

WHEREAS, the Seventy-Second Congress of the United States of America, at the second session begun and held at the city of Washington on Monday the 5th day of December, 1932, did on the 20th day of February 1933, adopt a joint resolution proposing the following amendment to the Constitution of the United States, a copy of which is signed by the Speaker of the House of Representatives and by the Vice President of the United States and duly certified to the Governor of this Commonwealth and which is in words and figures to-wit:

Section I. The eighteenth article of amendment to the Constitution of the United States is hereby repealed.

Section II. the transportation or importation into any State, Territory, or possession of the United States for delivery or use therein of intoxicating liquors in violation of the laws thereof is hereby prohibited.

Section III. This article shall be inoperative unless it shall have been ratified as an amendment to the Constitution by convention in the several states, as provided in the Constitution, within seven years from the date of the submission hereof to the States by the Congress.

WHEREAS, Pursuant to the aforesaid joint resolution of Congress, the Governor of Kentucky called into Special Session on the 15th day of August, 1933, the General Assembly of Kentucky which enacted a law known as House Bill No. I, which was signed by the President of the Senate and by the Speaker of the House of Representatives, and approved by the Governor, providing for the selection of delegates, and providing for a Convention to be held in the Commonwealth of Kentucky, for the purpose of acting on the proposed amendment aforesaid, and

WHEREAS, pursuant to the aforesaid joint resolution of Congress and the aforesaid Act of the Special Session of the General Assembly of the Commonwealth of Kentucky, delegates were selected by the voters of the Commonwealth at the election held on the 7th day of November, 1933, and their election has been duly certified by the Board of Election Commissioners and the Secretary of State, and

WHEREAS, the aforesaid delegates so elected, have been duly assembled in convention at the Capital of the Commonwealth of Kentucky, in Frankfort, Kentucky, in pursuance of the Act of the Special Session of the General Assembly, now individually by their resolutions, declare that the foregoing recited amendment to the Constitution of the United States be, and the same is hereby ratified by said convention on behalf of the Commonwealth of Kentucky and its citizens, as a part of an amendment to the Constitution of the United States.

Wherefore be it resolved that this certification be executed by the President and Secretary of the Convention and delivered to the Secretary of State of the Commonwealth of Kentucky, who shall properly certify it under the great seal of the Commonwealth of Kentucky to the Secretary of State of the United States, Washington, District of Columbia.

Mr. President, I move the adoption of the resolution of repeal.

BY THE CHAIRMAN: Ladies and Gentlemen, you have heard the resolutions offered by Mrs. Todd. Is there a second to the motion to adopt them?

BY MR. R. C. SIMMONS: Mr. Chairman, Delegates, Ladies and Gentlemen: As has been stated by the temporary chairman and the permanent chairman and those who have preceded me, this session of the convention which is giving final expression to the expressed wishes of the people of this commonwealth to repeal the Eighteenth Amendment is of great importance, and in seconding the motion to adopt resolutions of Repeal, it seems to be that it will be well for me to express some of the reasons that actuated the people of Kentucky to come to this decision and at the same time it seems to me it would be well to say that we realize first the duties and responsibilities that are imposed upon us by the passage and going into effect of this law.

In view of the fact that what I may say may to some extent be interpreted as reflecting the views of the members of this convention, I have undertaken to write down briefly what I desire to say, and with your permission, I shall read what I have written to you:

The question of controlling the liquor traffic claimed the attention of law-makers in most of the States of the Union for many years before the World War. For at least 50 years the respective merits of prohibition, of high license or of local option, were discussed. The method of control adopted changed with the changing sentiment of each community. The public generally did not consider it a matter of supreme public moment, although eloquent temperance orators from time to time aroused the people to greater interest in the subject.

But at no time during that period did it become the leading and sometimes exclusive topic of conversation in homes, at clubs, at social gatherings, in railway cars, as has been the case since the passage of the Eighteenth Amendment.

The problem of control was always complicated in those days as now by local conditions. The cities where public sentiment did not wish to outlaw the traffic could not agree with the sparsely settled districts where supervision was more difficult and where it was felt absolute suppression was necessary. The population of some states by tradition and inherited habit felt that the use of beverages with a low alcoholic content was in the nature of an inalienable right. With such diversity of views, the problem of a regulation which would be effective and yet permit a reasonable use of liquor was never satisfactorily worked out. Those who felt there should be a regulated use of alcohol did not organize to remedy the abuses which existed. Those dealers who observed the law did not realize that others in the business who sold to minors, who violated state and municipal closing regulations, and otherwise flouted public opinion, were leading their trade toward a precipice. They refused to clean house. Others not interested in the business but who were in favor of the moderate and temperate use of alcohol, were indifferent.

Then the War came. The experiment of limiting the use of alcohol in the Army and Navy seemed to be justified by results. The exalted fervor which characterized our conduct of the War and promotion of war activities, found another field for the exercise of its altruistic zeal. It was believed that if once and for all time prohibition could be embodied in the Federal Constitution, all the difficulties which control or regulation presented would be solved. As a result of these and other causes, in this very chamber about fifteen years ago the Representatives of Kentucky in the lower house by an overhwelming majority approved the Eighteenth Amendment, and at about the same time in the Senate Chamber similar action was taken.

There were then, as there still are, many sincere and earnest citizens who felt that the only way to rid our country of the evils of intemperance was to blot out all traffic in liquor. Their argument was that if the youth of the land were brought up where liquor was banned by law, they would lose the ancient thirst for alcohol which seemed to inhere in human nature from the days of Noah. They sincerely felt that business would be better; that men would save their earnings; that wives would be happier and children better fed, clothed and educated, and the moral integrity of the rising generation assured.

There were many equally as good citizens and equally as sincere in the cause of temperance, who felt otherwise. Some felt that a general law of this sort in large communities where public sentiment did not favor the law, was destined to break down. Some believed that sumptuary laws of this sort were not a wise exercise of the power which the people unquestionably possessed. Others believed that the outlawing of mild beer and the wine hallowed for the use of mankind at Cana in Galilee was a tremendous blunder. Those who believed in supplementing precept by example, and those following the principle laid down by Saint Paul of abstaining even from harmless indulgences to avoid becoming a stumbling block to one's brother, felt that the moral force of example was weakened by compulsion. They believed that strength of character could not be acquired by freedom from all temptation, but by cultivating the will to resist it. And a large element of the American people did not want to be coerced into goodness, nor did they believe that real moral reform could thrive in a legal strait-jacket.

In addition to all these objections there were many thoughtful people who believed it was a violation of the fundamental spirit of the Constitution to incorporate in it the Eighteenth Amendment. The regulation of the sale of liquor is a state concern. Conditions varied, as I have said, in the different states. It was intolerable that a state like New York, for instance, should have its drinking habits regulated by another state, say Kansas, for example. The citizens of the latter state had no special personal interest in the administration of the laws of the former. Enforcement of any law depends on the sentiment of the community. When sentiment changes, or if a law doesn't work, the law of a state can be changed, and those citizens who do not approve of it are willing to accept it for the time being and wait for opinion to change. But the very difficulty of amending the Federal Constitution created in the hearts of the citizens, who did not approve of this amendment, a sullen resentment. As the amendment bade fair to be effective always, the hopelessness of those opposed to it found expression in lawlessness.

Not only was the principle of state rights thus violated, but many thought this amendment did not belong in the Federal Constitution for another reason. The Federal Constitution was designed to protect the rights of the individual. It did not define particular crimes. The only exception is the crime of treason, the definition of which is coupled with decided limitations for the protection of the individual who might be charged with that offense. But in the original constitution emphasis was always placed on liberty and individual freedom. It protected religious views; it guaranteed free speech; it sought to safe-guard life, liberty and property, and to protect the citizen from arbitrary searches and seizures.

But the enthusiastic believers in the successful enforcement of a law of this sort had their way, and a gradually increasing general prosperity for a while blinded many to the defects of law enforcement. Business prospered as never before; bank balances grew; wage earners reveled in unaccustomed luxuries. Yet the fact that prohibition did not actually prohibit was forced upon public attention. It was discovered that the enormous gains from illicit traffic were building up an underworld of unlimited financial power. The law was not violated occasionally but constantly. It was not an annual violation like that of the taxpayer under our former laws, who failed on assessment day to give in his intangible property for taxation, but the violation continued every day and every night, year in and year out. Control became weaker; convictions, padlocking, injunctions, confiscation of property, all were without result. Drastic laws under which a seller of a negligible quantity of whisky could be sent to the penitentiary for five years and fined $10,000, were ineffective. The youth of the land know more about liquor and its use than their elders. The law itself was flouted; a growing contempt for all laws developed; grosser forms of crime flourished, until gang murders, bank robberies, like the one which occurred the other day under the shadow of this building, and kidnappings, became a matter of every day occurrence.

Now, it might not be fair to charge all this disregard of law to prohibition, but it was the major cause. It permitted the financing of underworld activities, it placed huge sums at the disposal of gangdom, and the law itself became a dead letter. It cannot be successfully denied that before the passage of the prohibition amendment the drinking habits of our people had improved somewhat. It is true there were law violations; there were occasional furtive trips to the rear of a stable or behind a wood-shed on County Court day, but there is no comparison between the unorganized violation of the liquor laws of those days and the bold and organized defiance of this law since the advent of prohibition.

Stirred by this shocking condition of affairs, the public began gradually to question the validity of the claims made for prohibition. Many of the earnest advocates of prohibition studied the question anew, and moved by the discoveries they made, were forced, against their will, by the overwhelming evidence of the break-down of the law, to change their opinions. Philanthropists, teachers, industrialists, who had spoken, written and contributed money to spread propaganda in favor of prohibition, found they were in error, frankly admitted their mistake and joined the movement for Repeal.

You know the rest. In dry states, in wet states, in the cities, in the villages, in rural communities, the people have expressed themselves throughout the length and breadth of the land demanding a change. That change is about to take place. Prohibition will never again find a place in the Federal Constitution, and when I say "never" I realize that is a long time.

Kentucky is not going to take a step backward. It will take prohibition out of its

Constitution. We shall ally ourselves with the great movement for reform, almost unanimously adopted by our sister states. Kentucky cannot afford to retain for itself a discredited law, the enforcement of which will become daily more difficult. Every state adjoining us, Virginia, West Virginia, Ohio, Indiana, Illinois and Tennessee, has ratified the repeal amendment. Should we fail to do so we would be encircled by bootleg border-raiders on all our boundaries. We are told by credible authority that the nation, the states and cities have sustained an annual loss in income which could have been collected from the liquor sold under prohibition, of nearly a billion dollars. We know that Kentucky with thousands of home owners unable to pay their taxes; with the state itself unable to meet the reasonable demands of public relief, will not retain in its basic law a provision that will allow bootleggers to grow in riches and power. It may be that the time required to make repeal effective in Kentucky will not be wasted. For then we shall be able to profit by the experience of each of the other states. We shall be able to select the best and most approved methods of control, and thus inaugurate a more satisfactory system than if we were obliged to rely on our own experiments.

Today, as I have said, we as the chosen representatives to carry out the will of the people of our State, are meeting here to perform a solemn duty. But our duty does not end here. Because those who voted for this change, those who favored a repeal of prohibition have promised to put something better in its place, we and they are pledged to a wise and effective regulation of the liquor traffic. Conditions which will permit boot-legging to continue on a large and profitable scale, must not be imposed. But reasonable laws, those which can and must be obeyed, are to be passed. I have neither the time here, nor is this the place, nor have I the knowledge to suggest what these laws should be. It would be mere presumption for me to do so. But I can urge all who have sought to change the existing state of affairs, to make a mighty effort in co-operation with all lovers of our country and our State, to see that never again shall the abuses which brought about prohibition be permitted to re-appear.

Our State needs the help of those who have so emphatically placed Kentucky in the Repeal column, but it also needs the co-operation of those who voted to retain prohibition.

Let us start on common ground, the love of state and country. Let those who have contended for their respective views during the past years, forget their graphic vocabulary of recrimination and epithet, relegate to obscurity the cartoons of the bulbous-nosed John Barleycorn on the one side, and the equally overdrawn high-hatted and sour-faced embodiment of the spirit of prohibition on the other, and enter upon an era of co-operation in the stupendous task which lies before us.

And I believe that when we once strike from our Constitution this Prohibition Clause, we shall never again exchange the benefits of a properly controlled liquor traffic for the anarchy of inadequate prohibition enforcement.

The impressive minority vote here in Kentucky shows that a great many people are still unconvinced as to the benefits of Repeal. I believe the results of a regulated traffic in other states will convince them before we vote on state repeal that the Repealists are right, and then all true Kentuckians will unite in framing a law to control the selling of liquor which shall become a model for the entire Union.

Acting with this common purpose we shall recapture the unity of action, symbolized by the Great Seal of our State, that unity which has ever been the foundation-stone of Kentucky's greatness.

By Mr. Farnsley: Mr. Chairman, Ladies and Gentlemen, you have heard this second by Mr. Simmons, referring to the majority for repeal. I am requested to state that the majority for repeal shows, instead of 147,000, a majority of 152,000.

By the Chairman: Ladies and Gentlemen, I wish to say in introducing Mr. Farnsley, if I may be permitted to tell about Mr. Farnsley's record with the Crusader organization in Kentucky, that I don't know of any one during the long fight for repeal who was more active or indefatigable and more helpful in this work.

By Mr. Farnsley: Mr. Chairman, Delegates, Ladies and Gentlemen: I am especially pleased to second this motion because it is made by Mrs. Todd. I have such faith in Mrs. Todd whose work for the cause of temperance has been of such great help, that if she should bring into this convention a resolution asking for the continuance of the Eighteenth Amendment, I would be inclined to vote for it, because I would feel that it would be the right and proper course for the Repeal forces in Kentucky to follow. It seems to be that perhaps the most important part about this is that we must see that the next session of the General Assembly accepts the great mandate of the voters of Kentucky, of the tremendous majority given to repeal delegates, to submit to the voters the proposed amendment to our State Constitution in November, 1935. I know it takes a long time and a hard fight to struggle with the prohibition question in Kentucky, and for that reason it is up to everyone of us to keep at it. The question whether or not the Crusaders will continue has been asked. The answer is "Yes." We are organized to bring about true temperance and feel that repeal of the Eighteenth Amendment is merely the first step in that fight. We are glad to accept our share of responsibility, but we must have the aid of other repeal advocates. Over taxation can have but one effect, that is to bring about the same condition that prohibition had. I warn you to be on your guard against over taxation in the future.

I take great pleasure in seconding Mrs. Todd's resolution.

By the Chairman: Is there any further discussion of the resolution? If not, it will be in order to vote upon the adoption of this most important resolution of this convention. I believe that the roll must be called and each delegate vote individually. It cannot be put by ayes and nays, there must be a roll call of each individual delegate, and that must be of record. Please call the roll.

By the Clerk:

Mrs. Gaither, Aye
Mr. Shelbourne, Aye
Mrs. Yeaman, Aye
General Sibert, Aye
Mrs. Todd, Aye
Mr. Haldeman, Aye
Mr. McClain, Aye
Mr. Boldrick, Aye
Mr. Simmons, Aye
Mr. Allington, Aye
Miss Clay, Aye
Mr. De Cognets, Aye
Mr. Fitzpatrick, Aye
Dr. Smith, Aye
Mr. Keenan, Aye
Mrs. Martin, Aye
Mr. Beecher Smith, Aye
Mr. Farnsley, Aye
Mr. Fee, Aye

By the Chairman: The delegates vote nineteen "ayes" and no "nays." The State of Kentucky is registered in favor of repeal of the Eighteenth Amendment.

By the Secretary: The president of this convention is required to sign this in the presence of this convention, also the secretary of this convention. I understand that the delegates sign underneath the names of the chairman and secretary.

By the Chairman: It is suggested by the secretary of this convention that the delegates sign under the signatures of the president and secretary. I see no reason why that should not be done, and a good reason why it should be done is that this is the voice of the convention, and each delegate will sign under the signatures of the president and secretary.

By Mr. Keenan: Mr. Chairman, I move that Mr. Shouse be notified of the action of this convention at once.

By the Chairman: Is there a second?

By Mr. Fee: I second the motion.

By the Chairman: It is moved and seconded that Mr. Shouse be notified of the action of this convention. If there is no discussion, all in favor of that motion will signify by saying "Aye."

(The convention votes "Aye.")

By the Chairman: The "Ayes" have it.

By Mrs. Todd: Mr. Chairman, I would like to move that a telegram be sent to Mrs. Sabin, President of the Women's National Organization, notifying her of the action of this convention.

By Mr. Farnsley: Mr. Chairman, I second Mrs. Todd's motion that Mrs. Sabin, the president of the Women's National Organization for Prohibition Reform be also notified.

By the Chairman: Is there any discussion? If not, all in favor of that motion will signify it by saying "Aye."

The Convention votes "Aye."

By the Chairman: Is there anything further from the committee on resolutions?

By Mrs. Todd: No, Mr. Haldeman, that is everything.

By Mr. Fitzpatrick: Mr. President, I move that the secretary of this Convention be instructed to send a telegram to Bishop Cannon.

(Applause and laughter by whole Convention.)

By the Chairman: Mr. Fitzpatrick's motion will be accepted by the Convention in the spirit and humor in which it was made. I know I would not send a telegram to him, and I am pretty sure that the secretary would not.

The Governor wishes to make a statement I am sure you will be glad to hear.

By Governor Ruby Laffoon: I have two announcements to make. I have been requested by both drys and wets if we may classify them that way to name a committee upon liquor control to study the question and make recommendations to the incoming session of the Legislature. I shall name the committee today consisting of seven outstanding men. I have also been requested by some of the ladies who represented the repeal movement that they did not think a woman should have a place on that committee, although I would be delighted to name a lady on that committee, but acting on their request, I will not, but I will name a committee consisting of seven or possibly nine of the most outstanding men of Kentucky, if I am capable of selecting them to study the question. That committee will not be composed of men who have been unduly anxious about the outcome of the repeal of the Eighteenth Amendment in the State of Kentucky but will be men who have been rather neutral in their attitude, but nevertheless, outstanding men. That is one announcement that I wanted to make.

Another announcement is that on tomorrow night at 9:15 o'clock the combined broadcasting system has furnished to the State of Kentucky, a nation wide hook up that will be participated in by ninety-six stations in the United States in recognition and honor of the Kentucky Colonels. Of course, I have been criticised for appointing a number of Kentucky Colonels, but I have never appointed one that was not appointed upon the request of some outstanding citizen of this State, and I am glad to know that people throughout the country appreciate that as a great honor to be made a Kentucky Colonel. The radio broadcast will be in aid of N. R. A. and it will be participated in by such outstanding entertainers as Eddie Cantor, George Jessell, Jean Harlow, Jeannette McDonald, Gen. Hugh S. Johnson, and Mr. Howe, Secretary to the President of the United States, the Governor of this Commonwealth, and I don't know how many others, fifteen in all. All Kentucky Colonels will have charge of the program. The combined system assures me that that will be one of the best programs that they have ever put on. I hope you will tune in at that time and encourage your neighbors and friends to do likewise.

The invitation that I wanted to extend is that my wife has requested that you have one of these standing up lunches over at your house that is now occupied by me at one o'clock. That lunch is intended for the delegates to this convention and their friends who accompany them. I assure you that we will be greatly disappointed if we do not have the pleasure of welcoming you at the Mansion at one o'clock. I hope that all of you will be there. I thank you.

By the Chairman: I know that the delegates would wish me to acknowledge that most kind invitation and I am sure that we will all be delighted to accept the Governor's and Mrs. Laffoon's hospitality.

I know of no further business and I suppose that the motion to adjourn is now in order.

By Mrs. Keenan: Mr. Chairman, I would like to know if the Secretary of State has our certificates of election, or certified copies of each?

By Governor Laffoon: She has, and has certified the election of each of you.

By Mr. Farnsley: Mr. Chairman, I move that if there is no further business before the convention, that we adjourn.

By the Chairman: A motion to adjourn is in order.

By Mr. Farnsley: I move the convention be now adjourned.

By Mr. Smith: I second the motion.

By the Chairman: All in favor of adjourning, let it be known by saying "Aye."

All members of the Convention vote "Aye."

By the Chairman: The convention is now adjourned.

MAINE*

State of Maine

CONSTITUTIONAL CONVENTION

Hall of the House
Wednesday
December 6, 1933

Pursuant to an act of the Eighty-sixth Legislature entitled "An Act to provide for a Constitutional Convention to Pass on the Proposed Twenty-first Amendment to the Constitution of the United States" approved April 28th, 1933, the delegates-elect to the Constitutional Convention assembled in the Hall of the House in the State House, at Augusta, and were called to order by Royden V. Brown, Secretary of the Senate of the Eighty-sixth Legislature.

The chair read the following communication from the Secretary of State:

STATE OF MAINE

Office of the Secretary of State

To Royden V. Brown, Secretary of the Senate of the Eighty-sixth Legislature:

In compliance with Section 8, Chapter 83 of the Private and Special Laws of 1933, I hereby certify that the following are the names and residences of the delegates-elect to the Constitutional Convention, as appears by the report of the Governor and Council under date of September 29, 1933.

Androscoggin County—Waldo Deane of Livermore Falls, Wm. J. Fahey of Lewiston, Benjamin Jones of Auburn, Francois X. Marcotte of Lewiston, Hiram Ricker, Jr., of Poland, Charles L. Turgeon of Auburn, Wallace Edgar Webber of Lewiston.

Aroostook County—Winfield S. Brown of Mars Hill, Alfred G. Chambers of Haynesville, Della T. Conant of Fort Fairfield, Irenee Cyr of Fort Kent, Chas. H. Harmon of Caribou, Joseph A. Laliberte of Eagle Lake, Ray H. McGlauflin of Presque Isle, J. Wilfred Parent of Van Buren, Percy L. Rideout of Houlton.

Cumberland County—James P. Baxter, Jr., of Portland, Jacob H. Berman of Portland, Harold G. Braithwaite of Bridgton, Edward E. Chase of Cape Elizabeth, Mary d'Este Davis of Portland, Helen C. Donahue of Portland, Mary H. Eaton of Gray, Harold N. Hanold of Standish, William M. Ingraham of Portland, John J. Magee of Brunswick, John J. Maloney of South Portland, John Clark Scates of Westbrook, Robinson Verrill of Portland.

Franklin County—Walter D. Barker of Farmington, Nathan C. Burbank of Wilton.

Hancock County—Luere B. Deasy of Bar Harbor, Otis Littlefield of Bluehill, William E. Whiting of Ellsworth.

Kennebec County—Willard B. Arnold of Waterville, Ovide J. Cote of Augusta, Edmond Cyr of Waterville, Eleanor Emery of Gardiner, Lawrence B. Hill of Belgrade, Edward W. Paine of Winslow, Nathan S. Weston of Augusta.

Knox County—William T. Cobb of Rockland, Charles A. Creighton of Thomaston, Obadiah Gardner of Rockland.

Lincoln County—Enoch B. Robertson of Waldoboro, Cleveland B. Swett of Edgecomb.

Oxford County—Ezra W. Bosworth of Fryeburg, L. M. Carroll of Norway, Fred L. Edwards of Bethel, Oliver A. Pettengill of Rumford.

Penobscot County—Patrick J. Byrnes of Bangor, Sibyl Cram of Bangor, George R. Desjardin of Old Town, Hebron H. Hackett of Brewer, Percy A. Hasty of Dexter, Frank W. Rush of Millinocket, George F. Way of Lincoln, Frederick M. Woodman of Bangor, Fred York of Howland.

* From a typewritten copy.

Piscataquis County—John Ford of Brownville, Paul H. Knowlton of Guilford.

Sagadahoc County—Sumner Sewall of Bath, William F. Tate of Topsham.

Somerset County—James B. Daily of Pittsfield, F. Otis Gould of Madison, Frank A. MacKenzie of Jackman, Frank X. Oakes of Fairfield.

Waldo County—Ansel M. Lothrop of Belfast, Norman A. Read of Belfast.

Washington County—Leo J. Parant of Baileyville, John J. Pike of Eastport, Moses B. Pike of Lubec, Ernest A. White of Columbia Falls.

York County—William N. Campbell of Sanford, Charles W. Kinghorn of Kittery, Jere F. Shaw of Biddeford, Elvington P. Spinney of North Berwick, Thomas C. Wentworth of Cornish, Howard R. Whitehead of Saco, Arthur G. Wiley of Buxton.

SEAL

In Testimony Whereof, I have caused the Seal of the State to be herewith affixed at Augusta, this 6th day of December, A.D., 1933, of the Independence of the United States of America, the one hundred and Fifty-eighth.

(*Signed*) ROBINSON C. TOBY
Secretary of State

The Chair called the roll and the following delegates were noted absent: Aroostook County—Alfred G. Chambers of Haynesville; Cumberland County—James P. Baxter, Jr., of Portland; Jacob H. Berman of Portland; John Clark Scates of Westbrook; Hancock County—Otis Littlefield of Bluehill; Kennebec County—Edward Paine of Winslow; Penobscot County—Frank W. Rush of Millinocket; Somerset County—James B. Daily of Pittsfield.

THE CHAIR: A sufficient number having responded, I declare that a quorum is present and that the Convention is ready to transact the business for which it was called.

On motion by Mr. Deasy of Bar Harbor, it was voted that a committee be appointed to notify the Governor that a quorum of the delegates-elect are in convention assembled ready to take the oaths required to enable them to enter upon their official duties; and the Chair appointed Mr. Deasy of Bar Harbor as a committee of one to perform this duty.

Subsequently Mr. Deasy reported that he had attended to his duties and that the Governor would attend forthwith.

Whereupon, the Governor, the Honorable Louis J. Brann, accompanied by the Executive Council, entered, amid the applause of the Convention, the members rising.

The Governor then administered the required oaths to the assembled delegates-elect.

THE GOVERNOR: I think you will find at your seats the oaths to which you are asked to subscribe and leave for collection later. I wish you, of course, the best of luck and success in your deliberations and I wish to extend to each and every member of the Convention at this time a very cordial welcome to the capital city of the State. Thank you and Good Morning.

The Governor and Council withdrew amid the applause of the Convention, the members rising.

THE CHAIR: The first business to come before the Convention is the nomination and election of a President of the Convention.

MR. OBADIAH GARDNER of Rockland: Mr. Chairman, I rise to present to the Convention for its President the name of a man who needs no eulogy and no introduction from me. He has had a long series of successful public administrations and on the question that has called this Convention into existence he has always stood right.

I will not take the time of the Convention any further. Mr. Chairman, I present for President of this Convention the name of the Honorable William T. Cobb, ex-Governor of Maine.

MR. F. OTIS GOULD of Madison: Mr. Chairman, I rise to second the nomination of the William T. Cobb and move that it be made unanimous.

On motion by Mr. Ricker of Poland it was voted that a committee of four to collect and sort ballots for President of the Convention be appointed; and the Chair appointed as members of such committee, Mr. Hiram Ricker Jr. of Poland, Mr. Winfield S. Brown of Mars Hill, Mr. Lawrence B. Hill of Belgrade, Mr. Frank A. MacKenzie of Jackman.

THE CHAIR: Are there any further nominations?

Thereupon, on motion by Mr. Edmond Cyr of Waterville it was voted that nominations cease; and on further motion by the same gentleman the above committee were instructed to cast one ballot in favor of the Honorable William T. Cobb for President of the Convention.

Subsequently, Mr. Ricker for the Committee reported that it had attended to its duties. The Chair thereupon appointed Mr. Ricker of Poland to escort the President of the Convention to the chair.

Mr. Ricker escorted the President to the chair amid the applause of the Convention.

Prayer was offered by Reverend Herbert E. P. Pressey of Augusta.

THE PRESIDENT: Ladies and Gentlemen of the Convention, before proceeding to the further and necessary organization of the Convention may I express to its members my very deep appreciation of the honor they have conferred upon me by their action in electing me to preside over their deliberations and may I hope, in the transaction of all its business, to have their indulgence and their support.

As a matter of historical interest and one that is reflected to some extent in the dignity and importance of this occasion, it may be recalled that no body of a like nature, similar in power or authority has been called into existence in this state since 1819, when, pursuant to an act of the Commonwealth of Massachusetts relative to the separation of the District of Maine from Massachusetts proper, a convention was called for the purpose of forming a constitution for the State of Maine.

The convention of which we are duly elected members derives its authority from an act of the legislature passed in 1933 providing for a constitutional convention to pass upon the proposed Twenty-first Amendment to the Constitution of the United States; the second convention of its kind in Maine in more than one hundred years.

Following that Act a quorum has been declared to be present here. The Governor of the state has administered the oaths of office to the delegates-elect and with your permission we will now proceed to the election of a secretary and of such other subordinate officers as in the judgment of the Convention may be necessary for the proper conduct of its business. The Chair awaits your pleasure.

On nomination by Mr. John J. Magee of Brunswick, seconded by Mr. William M. Ingraham of Portland, the Honorable Royden V. Brown of Bingham, Secretary of the Senate, was unanimously elected Secretary of the Convention by viva voce vote.

The President appointed Mr. Magee to escort the Secretary-elect to the Council Chamber for the purpose of taking and subscribing to the necessary oaths of office to qualify him to enter upon the discharge of his official duties.

Subsequently Mr. Magee reported that he had attended to the duty assigned him and that Royden V. Brown had, before the Governor and Council, taken and subscribed to the oaths of office required to qualify him for the discharge of the duties of Secretary of the Convention.

On motion by Mr. Elvington P. Spinney of North Berwick, the Secretary of the Convention was authorized to appoint a parliamentarian, an official stenographer, a sergeant at arms, a typist, two pages, and two doorkeepers to act in connection with the deliberations of the Convention.

The President thereupon announced the following appointments by the Secretary: Harvey R. Pease of Wiscasset, Parliamentarian; Charles P. Lyford, of Augusta, Official Stenographer; Gladys T. Bradford of Augusta, Typist; Roy S. Humphrey of Augusta, Page; Chester T. Winslow of Raymond, Page; Waldo H. Clark, of Jefferson, Doorkeeper; Louis R. Fowler of Monmouth, Doorkeeper.

THE PRESIDENT: The question has been raised regarding the election of an honorary vice president. The Chair will state that there is nothing in the Act creating this Convention which provides for such an office, but of course a matter of that kind is entirely in the hands of the delegates themselves and if the Convention so wishes the Chair will be glad to receive nominations.

MR. GEORGE R. DESJARDINS of Old Town: Mr. President, I move you that three vice presidents of this Convention be nominated and elected.

THE PRESIDENT: How does the Convention wish these names to be nominated? The chair does not consider it his duty to do that. Those in favor of the motion will manifest it by saying "Aye." Those opposed, "No."

A viva voce vote being had, the motion did not prevail.

THE PRESIDENT: The Convention to which we are the duly elected delegates is confronted with but one issue and the views of every delegate here were publicly known to the State and its electorate when the election for such delegates took place. The Convention is now fully organized and the Chair awaits the pleasure of its members.

Thereupon Mrs. Mary d'Este Davis of Portland; presented the following resolution and moved its adoption:

RESOLUTION

WHEREAS, the Congress of the United States on February 20, 1933, submitted to the several states the following proposed Amendment to the Constitution of the United States:

Resolved by the Senate and House of Representatives of the United States of America in Congress assembled (two-thirds of each House concurring therein), that the following article is hereby proposed as an Amendment to the Constitution of the United States, which shall be valid to all intents and purposes as part of the Constitution when ratified by Conventions in three-fourths of the several states:

ARTICLE ____

Section 1. The eighteenth article of Amendment to the Constitution of the United States is hereby repealed.

Section 2. The transportation or importation into any State, Territory, or possession of the United States for delivery or use therein of intoxicating liquors, in violation of the laws thereof, is hereby prohibited.

Section 3. This article shall be inoperative unless it shall have been ratified as an Amendment to the Constitution by Conventions in the several States, as provided in

the Constitution, within seven years from the date of the submission hereof to the States by Congress.

Now, therefore, be it

Resolved, that this Convention assembled, pursuant to the authority of an Act of the Eighty-sixth Legislature of the State of Maine, entitled "An Act to provide for a Constitutional Convention to pass on the proposed twenty-first amendment to the Constitution of the United States" for the purpose of acting upon the proposal of amendment to the Constitution of the United States which is set forth in the aforesaid act, now ratifies and approves said proposed article as set forth in said Joint Resolution as an amendment to the Constitution of the United States.

MR. ROBINSON VERRILL of Portland: Mr. President, I second the motion that the resolution be adopted.

THE PRESIDENT: It will be necessary, under the provisions of the Act, to have a roll call. The Chair will suggest that as the Secretary calls the roll each delegate answer "Aye" if in favor of the resolution and "No" if opposed. The Secretary will please call the roll.

The Secretary called the roll.

THE PRESIDENT: There have seventy-two delegates voted, all voting, "Aye." Therefore, the resolution presented by Mrs. Davis providing for the repeal of the Eighteenth Amendment in fact, is declared unanimously passed. (Applause.)

THE PRESIDENT: Is there any further business to come before this Convention?

MR. VERRILL: Mr. President, I move that the President and Secretary of this Convention as required by Section 14 of said Chapter 83 make and execute the certificate for filing in the office of the Secretary of State of this State to the effect that this Convention has ratified the proposal of amendment to the Constitution of the United States passed by the Seventy-second Congress on February 20, 1933.

Thereupon the Secretary read the following certificate:

STATE OF MAINE

AUGUSTA

December 6, 1933

We, William T. Cobb, President, and Royden V. Brown, Secretary, respectively, of the Constitutional Convention of the State of Maine, duly elected by the electors of said State and held on the 6th day of December, 1933, in the Hall of the House of Representatives of said State at the State House, Augusta, Maine, in accordance with the provisions of Chapter 83 of the Private and Special Laws of 1933, to act upon that proposal of amendment to the Constitution of the United States which was set forth in a joint resolution passed on the 20th day of February, 1933, at the second session of the Seventy-second Congress of the United States:

DO HEREBY CERTIFY that the following proposed article of amendment to the Constitution of the United States which was set forth in said joint resolution was duly ratified by said Convention by the unanimous vote of all the delegates present, namely, seventy-two delegates, constituting more than a quorum:

ARTICLE ____

Section 1. The eighteenth article of amendment to the constitution of the United States is hereby repealed.

Section 2. The transportation or importation into any state, territory, or possession of the United States for delivery or use therein of intoxicating liquors, in violation of the law thereof, is hereby prohibited.

Section 3. This article shall be inoperative unless it shall have been ratified as an amendment in the constitution by conventions in the several states, as provided in the constitution, within seven years from the date of the submission hereof to the states by the Congress.

In testimony whereof, We have hereunto set our hands this sixth day of December, 1933.

_______________ *President*

_______________ *Secretary*

THE PRESIDENT: You have heard the certificate presented by Mr. Verrill read by the Secretary. Those in favor of the motion by Mr. Verrill that the President and Secretary execute the certificate for filing in the office of the Secretary of State will manifest by saying "Aye." Those opposed will say "No."

A viva voce vote being had, the motion prevailed.

Thereupon Mr. Magee of Brunswick presented the following and moved its adoption:

Resolved, That it is the sentiment of this Convention that the Controller of State pay the compensation set against the names of each, to the Secretary and subordinate officers of this Convention:

Royden V. Brown, Secretary	$25.00
Harvey R. Pease, Parliamentarian	20.00
Charles P. Lyford, Official Stenographer	15.00
Gladys T. Bradford, Typist	15.00
Roy S. Humphrey, Sergeant at Arms	5.00
Chester T. Winslow, Page	5.00
Waldo H. Clark, Doorkeeper	5.00
Louis R. Fowler, Doorkeeper	5.00

THE PRESIDENT: You have heard read the resolution presented by Mr. Magee. Those in favor of adopting this resolution will say "Aye." Those opposed will say "No."

A viva voce vote being had, the motion prevailed.

THE PRESIDENT: Is there any further business to come before the Convention? If not, the Chair will entertain a motion to adjourn.

Thereupon, on motion by Mr. Leo J. Parant of Baileyville, the Constitutional Convention adjourned without day.

I hereby certify that the foregoing is a true record of the proceedings of the Constitutional Convention of the State of Maine held in Augusta on Wednesday, December 6th, 1933.

Attest:

ROYDEN V. BROWN
Secretary

MARYLAND*

PROCEEDINGS

OF

CONSTITUTIONAL CONVENTION

HELD

OCTOBER 18, 1933

IN THE

SENATE CHAMBER, ANNAPOLIS, MARYLAND

MR. J. C. SHRIVER: Ladies and gentlemen of the Constitutional Convention, no greater honor could be conferred upon a citizen of the Maryland Free State than to call this convention to order, which I now do. I now call for nominations for Temporary Chairman.

(Colonel John Philip Hill was nominated as Temporary Chairman of the Convention, which nomination was duly seconded and upon being put to a vote, Colonel Hill was unanimously elected Temporary Chairman.)

MR. SHRIVER: All Delegates having voted in the affirmative, I will appoint a committee of two to escort Colonel Hill to the Chair. I appoint Mr. Klinefelter and Mr. Darnall.

THE CHAIRMAN: Your Excellency, Governor Ritchie, Delegates, Ladies and Gentlemen: We will ask the invocation of Divine Blessing upon the proceedings of this convention by Rev. Edward D. Johnson, Rector of St. Ann's Church, Annapolis.

(Divine blessing was then offered by Rev. Edward D. Johnson.)

THE CHAIRMAN: Your Excellency, and delegates, this historic building has witnessed many remarkable events in the career of the United States of America but it never has witnessed a more important event than the Convention of today, which at this City, will help in the return of the Constitution to the original doctrine of American freedom. I ask for nominations for temporary Secretary, and I recognize Mr. Klinefelter.

MR. KLINEFELTER: I take great pleasure in nominating Mr. Joseph P. McCurdy as Temporary Secretary.

(Which motion was duly seconded, and upon being put to a vote, was unanimously carried.)

THE CHAIRMAN: Mr. McCurdy is elected Temporary Secretary and will take his place at the Secretary's desk.

I now recognize the Secretary of State of the State of Maryland, who has a message for this Convention.

MR. DAVID C. WINEBRENNER, 3d: Mr. Chairman, here is the message.

THE CHAIRMAN: I receive this message and transmit it to the Secretary and he will read it. He need not read the enclosure which is the formal return of the election of Delegates.

* From a photostat of the typewritten original.

THE SECRETARY (reading):

EXECUTIVE DEPARTMENT
ANNAPOLIS, MARYLAND
October 18, 1933

HON. JOHN PHILIP HILL, Temporary Chairman
Maryland Constitutional Convention
State House, Annapolis, Maryland

MY DEAR MR. CHAIRMAN:

I have the honor to advise you that at a meeting of the State Board of Canvassers of Maryland, held in my office at Annapolis on September 26, 1933, for the purpose of canvassing the returns from Baltimore City and the several counties of the State of the special election held in Maryland on September 12, 1933, to elect delegates to attend a Constitutional Convention to assemble in Annapolis on October 18, 1933, for the purpose of ratifying or rejecting the Twenty-first Amendment to the Constitution of the United States, as provided by Chapter 253 of the Acts of 1933, the folowing persons were declared by said Board to be the duly elected delegates to the said Convention:

J. McFadden Dick, Salisbury, Maryland,
R. Bennett Darnall, Ruxton, Maryland,
Helen S. Athey, 100 S. Patterson Park Avenue, Baltimore, Maryland,
Ella T. Clotworthy, 4406 Greenway, Baltimore, Maryland,
Joseph P. McCurdy, 101 W. Clement Street, Baltimore, Maryland,
Elizabeth Lowndes, Cumberland, Maryland,
Edward J. Clarke, Pocomoke City, Maryland,
Henry Lloyd, Jr., Cambridge, Maryland,
Edward R. Buck, St. Michaels, Maryland,
William E. Conway, Westminster, Maryland,
Harry F. Klinefelter, Harvest Road, Baltimore, Md.
John A. Robinson, Bel Air, Maryland,
Peter M. Siewierski, 1706 Eastern Avenue, Baltimore, Maryland,
John Philip Hill, 3 W. Franklin Street, Baltimore, Maryland,
Thomas J. Flaherty, 2700 E. Preston Street, Baltimore, Maryland,
Leonard Weinberg, 943 Brooks Lane, Baltimore, Md.,
Robert W. Price, 1707 E. 31st Street, Baltimore, Maryland,
Harry O. Levin, 940 Brooks Lane, Baltimore, Md.,
Charles H. Heintzeman, 922 S. Charles Street, Baltimore, Maryland,
Hannah P. Lowndes, Ellicott City, Maryland,
James B. Berry, Seat Pleasant, Maryland,
Victor D. Miller, Hagerstown, Maryland,
James C. Shriver, Cumberland, Maryland,
Bernard O. Thomas, Frederick, Maryland.

With great respect, I am,
Sincerely yours,
DAVID C. WINEBRENNER, 3d
Secretary of State

THE STATE OF MARYLAND

EXECUTIVE DEPARTMENT

I, DAVID C. WINEBRENNER, 3d, Secretary of State, of the State of Maryland, under and by virtue of the authority vested in me by Section 59 of Article 35 of the Annotated Code of Maryland, do hereby certify that the attached is a true and correct copy of the DECLARATION OF THE RESULT OF THE SPECIAL ELECTION OF TUESDAY, SEPTEMBER 12th, 1933, as taken from the Minutes of the BOARD OF STATE CANVASSERS, of September 26th, 1933, and as the same is taken from and compared with the original DECLARATION, now on file in my office.

SEAL

In testimony whereof, I have hereunto set my hand and have caused to be affixed the official seal of the Secretary of State, at Annapolis, Maryland, this 18th day of October, in the year one thousand nine hundred and thirty-three.

DAVID C. WINEBRENNER, 3d
Secretary of State

THE CHAIRMAN: The message which has just been read by the Secretary of this Convention from the Secretary of State of Maryland will be spread upon the Minutes of this Convention, together with the official returns enclosed with the communication. The Secretary will now call the roll of Delegates.

THE SECRETARY: In order to facilitate matters, I will call the Delegates by their last names, and they will please answer. Dick – Present. Darnall – Present. Athey – (no response). Clotworthy – (no response). McCurdy – Present. Lowndes (Elizabeth) – Present. Clarke – Present. Lloyd – Present. Buck – Present. Conway – Present. Klinefelter – Present. Robinson – Present. Siewierski – Present. Hill – Present. Flaherty – Present. Weinberg – Present. Price – Present. Levin – Present. Heintzeman – Present. Lowndes (Hannah P.) – Present. Berry – Present. Miller – Present. Shriver – Present. Thomas – Present.

THE CHAIRMAN: The Secretary will report as to what absentees are disclosed by the call of the roll.

THE SECRETARY: There were two absentees, Mrs. Athey and Mrs. Clotworthy.

THE CHAIRMAN: The Chair recognizes Mr. John A. Robinson to nominate two delegates to fill the vacancies caused by the absence of Mrs. Athey and Mrs. Clotworthy; before the vacancies are filled, however, the Convention will ask his Excellency, the Honorable, Albert Cabel Ritchie, Governor of Maryland, to administer the oath to the Delegates here present.

GOVERNOR RITCHIE: Will the duly elected members to this Convention kindly rise?

(Governor Ritchie then administered the oath to the duly elected Delegates who answered the roll call, and requested that they step up to the desk of the Secretary of State and sign the Test Book, which was done.)

THE CHAIRMAN: The Secretary will repeat to the Convention the list of absentees.

THE SECRETARY: The list of absentees are Mrs. Athey and Mrs. Clotworthy.

THE CHAIRMAN: The Chair recognizes Delegate John A. Robinson to nominate two persons to fill the vacancies caused by the absence of Mrs. Athey and Mrs. Clotworthy.

MR. ROBINSON: I regret very much the absence of the two duly elected Delegates, and it gives me pleasure to place in nomination Mrs. Margaret Elizabeth Heller and Mrs. Jane L. West.

THE CHAIRMAN: Mrs. Margaret Elizabeth Heller and Mrs. Jane L. West have been nominated as Delegates in the place of Mrs. Athey and Mrs. Clotworthy, who are unavoidably absent.

(The nominations were duly seconded and upon being put to a vote by roll call, were unanimously elected.)

THE CHAIRMAN: I declare that Mrs. Margaret Elizabeth Heller and Mrs. Jane L. West are elected Delegates to this Convention, and I request his Excellency, the Governor of Maryland, to administer the oath to them.

(The Governor then administered the oath to the two newly elected Delegates, and requested them to sign the Test Book which was done.)

THE CHAIRMAN: Ladies and gentlemen of the Convention, the duly elected Delegates and substituted Delegates being present, it is now in order to provide for a Committee on Credentials and the Chair recognizes Mr. Flaherty to nominate a proper committee.

MR. FLAHERTY: Mr. Chairman, I want to offer this resolution (handing same to the Chairman).

THE CHAIRMAN: The Secretary will read the resolution offered by Mr. Flaherty.

THE SECRETARY (reading): "*Resolved,* That the temporary Chairman appoint a Committee on Credentials, consisting of five Delegates, to report the names of all Delegates elected, qualified and entitled to seats in this Convention."

(The motion was duly seconded and upon being put to a vote, was unanimously carried.)

THE CHAIRMAN: The Chair is ready and duly appoints the following committee, which the Secretary will read.

THE SECRETARY (reading): Dr. Edward J. Clarke, Chairman, John A. Robinson, Robert W. Price, Thomas J. Flaherty, and Mrs. Hannah P. Lowndes.

THE CHAIRMAN: The next business in order is a resolution, authorizing a Committee on Rules, and I recognize Mr. Siewierski.

MR. SIEWIERSKI: Mr. Chairman, I have a resolution and ask the Secretary to read same.

THE SECRETARY (reading): "*Resolved,* That the Temporary Chairman appoint a a Committee of five Delegates, to prepare and recommend rules for the control and conduct of the Convention."

(Which resolution was duly seconded and upon being put to a vote, was unanimously carried.)

THE CHAIRMAN: The Resolution is adopted and the Chair appoints the following committee, which the Secretary will read.

THE SECRETARY (reading): Peter M. Siewierski, Chairman, Edward R. Buck, William E. Conway, Dr. Bernard O. Thomas, and Henry Lloyd, Jr.

THE CHAIRMAN: The next order of business is a resolution authorizing the appointment of a Committee on Permanent Organization, and the Chair recognizes Mr. Heintzeman for the purpose of offering the resolution.

MR. HEINTZEMAN: I offer the following resolution and ask the Secretary to read same.

THE SECRETARY (reading): *Resolved,* That the Temporary Chairman appoint a Committee of five Delegates to serve as a Committee on Permanent Organization.

(Which resolution was duly seconded and upon being put to a vote, was unanimously adopted.)

THE CHAIRMAN: The Resolution is adopted, and the Chair announces the following Committee, which the Secretary will read.

THE SECRETARY (reading): Harry O. Levin, Chairman, Mrs. Mortimer W. West, Henry Lloyd, Jr., Charles H. Heintzeman, and Joseph B. Berry.

THE CHAIRMAN: Now, I will ask the Committees to retire to the chamber in the rear and prepare resolutions and submit same as soon as possible to the Convention. The remaining Delegates will simply remain in the Convention Hall until the reports are submitted. We will take a recess for a few minutes.

(*After Recess*)

THE CHAIRMAN: The Convention will come to order. The Convention will now receive the report of the Committee on Credentials, and the Chair recognizes the Chairman of the Committee.

DR. CLARKE: The Committee on Credentials submits its report and asks the Secretary of the Convention to read same.

THE SECRETARY (reading): The Committee on Credentials reports that they have examined the credentials of the Delegates to the State Convention to consider the proposed amendment to the Constitution of the United States, for the repeal of the Eighteenth Amendment to the Constitution of the United States, and that the following Delegates have been duly and properly elected, in accordance with law, and are entitled to seats in this Convention.

J. McFadden Dick
R. Bennett Darnall
Margaret Elizabeth Heller
Jane L. West
Joseph P. McCurdy
Elizabeth Lowndes
Edward J. Clarke
Henry Lloyd, Jr.
Edward R. Buck
William E. Conway
Harry F. Klinefelter
John A. Robinson
Peter H. Siewierski
John Philip Hill
Thomas J. Flaherty
Leonard Weinberg
Robert W. Price
Harry O. Levin
Charles H. Heintzeman
Hannah P. Lowndes
James B. Berry
Victor D. Miller
James C. Shriver
Bernard O. Thomas

(Motion made to adopt the committee's report, which was duly seconded, and upon being put to a vote was unanimously carried.)

THE CHAIRMAN: The report has been adopted. The Convention will now receive the report of the Committee on Rules.

MR. SIEWIERSKI: The Committee on Rules reports that it is the recommendation of this Committee that Robert's Rules of Order govern the procedure of this Convention.

(Motion made to adopt the Committee's report, which was duly seconded, and upon being put to a vote, was adopted.)

THE CHAIRMAN: The report has been adopted. The Convention will now receive the report of the Committee on Permanent Organization. The Chair recognizes Senator Levin.

MR. LEVIN: The Committee on Permanent Organization reports and recommends that the permanent officers of the Convention shall be a President, two Vice-Presidents, a Secretary, two Assistant Secretaries and a Sergeant-at-Arms.

The Committee further reports that they endorse and tender for election as permanent officers of the Convention, the following named persons: For President: R. Bennett Darnall. For Vice-President: Hannah P. Lowndes. For Vice-President: Leonard Weinberg. For Secretary: Joseph P. McCurdy. For Assistant Secretary: Elizabeth Lowndes. For Assistant Secretary: Dr. J. McFadden Dick. For Sergeant-at-Arms: Harry F. Klinefelter.

(Motion made to adopt the Committee's report, which was duly seconded, and on roll call, was unanimously carried.)

THE CHAIRMAN: You heard the unanimous vote of the eminent Delegates for Permanent Officers of the Convention, and the Chair declares them elected and the Officers of this Convention. The Chair asks Mrs. Heller and Mr. Berry to escort the President of this Convention to the Chair. (Applause.)

THE CHAIRMAN: The President of this Convention, Honorable R. Bennett Darnall, will now take charge of these proceedings.

MR. LEVIN: Mr. President, I think it would be in order at this point to thank Colonel Hill for the efficient manner in which he officiated as Chairman of this Convention.

(Which motion was duly seconded.)

THE PRESIDENT: I will be glad to recognize such a resolution.

(The motion was then put to a vote and carried.)

THE PRESIDENT: Colonel Hill, you are properly thanked

COLONEL HILL: Thank you very much.

THE PRESIDENT: As I did not leave the Rennert last night, where our caucus was held, until after midnight, I have had no time to prepare an address, but only a moment this morning to jot down a few facts with regard to our fight to which I thought it might be well to direct your attention.

I am exceedingly grateful for the honor which you have conferred upon me in electing me President of this Convention. It is, indeed, an honor to preside over the first and only Constitutional Convention ever held in this State for the passage or repeal of an amendment to the Federal Constitution.

All amendments heretofore proposed have been passed by the Legislatures of the States. There have been in all twenty amendments to the Constitution. Others have been submitted but have been rejected by the States. Never until now has Congress offered a proposal to repeal an amendment to the Constitution This proposal is unique in that it is the only opportunity ever presented for repeal of a part of the Constitution, and it is the only amendment to the Constitution which has ever been submitted to conventions in the States for ratification.

The Eighteenth Amendment, which the new amendment will repeal, is the first provision ever written into the Constitution which affects directly the life and habits of the people. It has no place in the Constitution. It brought about much suffering and corruption, and has made a nation of whiskey drinkers. Thousands of people who never drank before started immediately to drink as a protest against this infringement of their personal liberty. It has taken millions of dollars in revenue from the taxpayers of this country and has placed a tremendous burden upon them in a fruitless effort to enforce an unenforceable law, and put into the hands of a horde of bootleggers millions of dollars and given us also the racketeer and gangster.

We have been elected by the people of Maryland delegates to this Constitutional Convention for the purpose of ratifying an amendment repealing the Eighteenth Amendment to the Constitution of the United States. I am sure you feel, as I do, that it is a distinct privilege and a very great pleasure to represent the people of our State in ratifying their mandate in voting for the repeal of the Eighteenth Amendment.

We are happy in voting today to undo this wrong. I hope I may be pardoned if I suggest to you that while we represent the wet sentiment of our communities, otherwise we would not be here, we also represent the best sentiment in these communities. And we should do all in our power to bring about true temperance and advise and work for legislation which will bring sane and well regulated handling of the liquor so that the conditions which prevailed prior to prohibition and which may have been largely responsible for it, will not return.

I will not detain you longer for we have business before us, and you will presently hear from one who has been the real leader of the repeal fight—our splendid Governor—Albert C. Ritchie.

Now, ladies and gentlemen, a resolution authorizing a committee to notify the Governor that the Convention has been assembled and organized in accordance with law and inviting him to attend and submit the proposed amendment to the Constitution is in order, and I recognize Dr. Dick at this time.

DOCTOR DICK: I offer this resolution which I will ask the Secretary to read.

THE SECRETARY (reading): *Resolved,* That the President of the Convention appoint a Committee of five Delegates to notify the Governor that the Convention has been assembled and organized in accordance with law, and to invite him to address the Convention and to submit the proposed amendment to the Constitution of the United States.

(Which resolution was duly seconded and upon being put to a vote was unanimously carried.)

COLONEL HILL: I move that this Convention do stand in recess until such time as the Governor addresses the Convention.

(Which motion was duly seconded, and upon being put to a vote was carried.)

THE PRESIDENT: The Governor has asked me to invite all those present, the Delegates as well as those who are not Delegates, to lunch at the Executive mansion.

We will now retire to the front steps where a photographer will take a picture.

I have overlooked the appointment of a Committee to notify the Governor, and I appoint the following Committee:

Dr. J. McFadden Dick, *Chairman*
Mrs. Margaret Elizabeth Heller
Mrs. Hannah P. Lowndes
Thomas J. Flaherty
Charles H. Heintzeman

(At this point a recess was taken to attend the luncheon at the Governor's Mansion.)

(*After Recess*)

THE PRESIDENT: Will the Convention please come to order. Will the Committee appointed prior to recess escort the Governor to the rostrum.

Now, it is not necessary for me to introduce Governor Ritchie. You have the real leader of our fight in this Convention with you today.

GOVERNOR RITCHIE: Mr. President, members of the Constitutional Convention, Ladies and Gentlemen: Well, it is all over. We are all here and we are all happy in the duty which this Convention is about to discharge. I am very glad of the privilege of saying a word or two, although I have no prepared remarks. The fact is there is little more that can be said. The story has all been told during the last twelve or more years, and it is undoubtedly known to all the people of Maryland particularly. I don't know just why it is, but I think it is true, that the consummation of victory frequently is apt to be accompanied by a little let-down. The fight is over, the battle is through, any evidence of uncertainty which has existed has been removed, but I don't think feelings of that kind ought to make any of us forget or efface the fact that this is really a great and historic day in the history of Maryland, as well as in the history of the country.

Maryland is consummating a pledge and tradition which has always been hers of a free government and liberty-loving country. We have looked forward, I think to this day for many, many years, and I think that the people of Maryland asked for so many years, begged for and fought for so many years. When they were needed, the men and women of this State fought against the principles involved in the Eighteenth Amendment, and it has been the great fight that it has been because the cause has been a great cause. Maryland has fought for an issue which arose far above politics; it had no partisanship in it. It is true that originally the States' rights side on which we fought was the teachings and policies of Thomas Jefferson, but long years ago they really became a part of the American Government, and American policies, and so this case against these things for which the Eighteenth Amendment has stood has been better than parties and higher than partisanship; it has struck right at the heart of American institutions, and the question has been whether the sound principles of our Government were going to prevail, whether or not the safeguards of the liberties of the American people were going to be preserved and maintained, or whether they were going to be scrapped and destroyed, and we are happy in this State to know that in this great cause the men and women stood shoulder to shoulder, Republicans, Democrats and Independents stood shoulder to shoulder too.

I would like in the very brief remarks that I will make to pay my tribute, and in doing that I know I am simply voicing the tribute which the people of Maryland would pay to the part which the women of Maryland have undertaken in this great fight for repeal. I have heard it said that more than any other group the women of the country may have been responsible for the Eighteenth Amendment in the first place. I am not here to talk history; I am not here to express any opinion on it, but I am here to say whether that is true or is not true, there is no group to whom more credit is due for getting rid of the Eighteenth Amendment than the women of this country, and particularly the women of Maryland, and I feel that those of us who think as I do, all share that opinion and all express grateful appreciation and thanks to the fine women of this State for the part they played in the victory which has come from this great fight.

And I would like to express my own tribute also, and in doing so I know that I voice the feeling of those who belong to my party who were on the other side in this fight against the Eighteenth Amendment, my tribute to the part which the Republicans of this State of Maryland and of the country played in this fight too. We have been together regardless of party, we have been together regardless of sex, we have been together regardless of any denomination or discrimination of any kind. We have been in this fight one happy family, and I freely accord my appreciation for the work that the Republicans and the women of that party have done in this great struggle.

Of course, it is going to be a very serious question as to what we are going to do with this victory now that it has been won. This is not the place to discuss that, and it is not the time in any event. I am expecting early in November to convene the Maryland Legislature at special session in order to consider and decide that question, that is, what to do with the victory which we won, and what control or legislation should be adopted in this State; that is a controversial question—none more so. It is not going to be easy to gain what was lost since the Eighteenth Amendment was adopted, lost because that Amendment was adopted, and there is not going to be any magic escape or magic cure of the situation. I have an abiding faith that the Maryland people will do their best, the Maryland Legislature will do its best, and in the legislation that will be enacted, we will remember that the fight has been a great moral fight, a great moral victory. It is a fight and victory in the interest of temperance in the true sense, and broadest sense of temperance. It is a fight for the preservation of law, preservation of order, for respect of law, and respect for law and order, and fought to end the practices it brought about. The fight was one of high motives, and when the Legislature does meet, I am confident measures will come about which will recognize the great elements in this fight. In the meanwhile, my friends, I think we are all entitled to rejoice today, we are entitled to rejoice for knowing that this American nation of ours was big enough to realize it made a mistake, and big enough to realize when the mistake had been made, the thing to do was to retrace its steps and undoing that mistake. We are entitled to rejoice that Maryland was the pioneer from the beginning in this fight. We are entitled to look with satisfaction and gratification to the small group of men and women of both parties, who led that fight in Maryland, and whose work helped to spread it throughout the land. We are entitled to thank them today that they were determined to lead the fight for the undoing of the wrongs which the Eighteenth Amendment had done, even if it was going to take their lifetime to do it. So, I think today of all days the people of this State, the liberty-loving people, Constitution-loving people, freedom-loving people of Maryland, can take a just pride in the victory which has been won.

Now, it is my privilege and my honor to present to you for the purpose of laying it before this Convention, the duly certified copy which I have received from the Secretary of State of the United States, entitled "Joint Resolution Proposing an Amendment to the Constitution of the United States." This resolution embodies the Twenty-first Amendment to the Constitution of the United States, which, of course, repeals the Eighteenth Amendment, and I present this to you for such action as this Constitutional Convention may see fit to take upon it.

(Loud applause.)

THE SECRETARY (reading):

UNITED STATES OF AMERICA

Department of State

To all to whom these presents shall come, GREETING:

I certify that the copy hereto attached is a true copy of a Resolution of Congress entitled "JOINT RESOLUTION Proposing an Amendment to the Constitution of the United States" the original of which is on file in this Department.

SEAL

In testimony whereof, I, Henry L. Stimson, Secretary of State, have hereunto caused the Seal of the Department of State to be affixed and my name subscribed by the Acting Chief Clerk of the said Department, at the City of Washington, in the District of Columbia, this 21st day of February, 1933.

HENRY L. STIMSON
Secretary of State
By P. F. ALLEN
Acting Chief Clerk

SEVENTY-SECOND CONGRESS OF THE UNITED STATES OF AMERICA

AT THE SECOND SESSION

Begun and held at the City of Washington on Monday, the fifth day of December, one thousand nine hundred and thirty-two.

JOINT RESOLUTION

Proposing an amendment to the Constitution of the United States

Resolved by the Senate and House of Representatives of the United States of America in Congress assembled (two-thirds of each House concurring therein), That the following article is hereby proposed as an amendment to the Constitution of the United States, which shall be valid to all intents and purposes as part of the Constitution when ratified by conventions in three-fourths of the several States:

ARTICLE ___ ___

Section 1. The eighteenth article of amendment to the Constitution of the United States is hereby repealed.

Section 2. The transportation or importation into any State, Territory, or possession of the United States for delivery or use therein of intoxicating liquors, in violation of the laws thereof, is hereby prohibited.

Section 3. This article shall be inoperative unless it shall have been ratified as an amendment to the Constitution by conventions in the several States, as provided in the Constitution, within seven years from the date of the submission hereof to the States by the Congress.

JNO. N. GARNER
Speaker of the House of Representatives

CHARLES CURTIS
Vice-President of the United States and
President of the Senate

THE PRESIDENT: It is now proper to have a resolution to appoint a Committee on Resolutions, and I recognize Mr. Leonard Weinberg.

MR. WEINBERG: Mr. President, I wish to offer the following resolution:

Resolved, That the President of the Convention appoint a Committee of five Delegates to serve as a Committee on Resolutions, and that all Resolutions introduced in the Convention shall be referred to said Committee without debate.

(Which resolution was duly seconded and upon being put to a vote was carried.)

THE PRESIDENT: The Chair appoints as members of that Committee:

Leonard Weinberg, Chairman
Dr. J. McFadden Dick
Joseph R. Berry
John A. Robinson
Miss Elizabeth Lowndes

Will the Committee please retire and then submit their report?

(The Committee then retired.)

THE PRESIDENT: Now, has the Committee on Resolutions prepared a report, and if so, I would like to hear from Mr. Weinberg:

Mr. Weinberg: Mr. President, Ladies and Gentlemen of the Convention: The Committee on Resolutions respectfully reports that it has prepared a resolution which expresses the mind and will of the people of the State of Maryland, and said resolution I shall read in a moment. I rise to move the adoption of that resolution ratifying the Twenty-first Amendment to the Constitution of the United States and the repeal of the Eighteenth Amendment to the Constitution of the United States.

An occasion such as this must touch the sensibilities of every thoughtful person. It is not only, as has been pointed out by our presiding officer, unique, but it is momentous and it is historic. It is unique because it is the first time in the history of the United States that Constitutional Conventions have been called for the ratification of an Amendment to the Constitution of the United States. Heretofore, that has always been done by the Legislatures of the various States.

It is likewise unique because this is the first occasion that an Amendment has been adopted eliminating from the Constitution an Amendment to that Constitution.

But above all, this Convention is momentous and pregnant with meaning because in this day of Fascism and Sovietism and the subjugation of peoples to the domination of the State or of a man, this marks a rededication of the people of America to the principles of Democracy. It marks the return to that form of government, a pure democracy, which was the ideal on which this government was founded, where the people themselves express their will by their own votes.

Government, my friends, is really an interpretation of life. So this is an interpretation of our life in America, and particularly in this, the Free State of Maryland, where we have devoted ourselves to the maintenance and protection of those inalienable rights of the individual, ordered liberty, and the tolerance of the opinions of all men. The spirit of America and of Maryland is expressed in the determination that men's liberties shall remain as secure from the tyranny of the crowd as from the tyranny of a king. That is our contribution to civilization.

Let us, then, with that high hope, that splendid enthusiasm and determined purpose that are born of an appreciation of the inherent fineness of the institutions and traditions of America, and of the glory, dignity and responsibilities of citizenship in this land and State, consecrate this day and rededicate ourselves to the maintenance and perpetuation of those ideals.

It is in that spirit, my friends, that I move for your consideration and ratification this expression of the will and sentiment of the people of Maryland and of the United States.

Whereas, both Houses of the Seventy-Second Congress of the United States of America, by a constitutional majority of two-thirds thereof, proposed an amendment to the Constitution of the United States of America, which Resolution is in words and figures as follows:

JOINT RESOLUTION

Proposing an Amendment to the Constitution of the United States.

Resolved by the Senate and House of Representatives of the United States of America in Congress assembled (two-thirds of each House concurring therein), That the following article is hereby proposed as an amendment to the Constitution of the United States, which shall be valid to all intents and purposes as part of the Constitution when ratified by conventions in three-fourths of the several states:

ARTICLE ——

Section 1. The Eighteenth Article of Amendment to the Constitution of the United States is hereby repealed.

Section 2. The transportation or importation into any State, Territory or possession of the United States for delivery or use therein of intoxicating liquors, in violation of the laws thereof, is hereby prohibited.

Section 3. This article shall be inoperative unless it shall have been ratified as an amendment to the Constitution by conventions in the several states, as provided in the Constitution, within seven years from the date of the submission hereof to the states by the Congress.

Now, Therefore be it Resolved, by the Convention of the State of Maryland assembled pursuant to the authority of Chapter 253 of the Acts of the General Assembly of Maryland of 1933, entitled "AN ACT to provide for a Convention in the State of Maryland, for the ratification or rejection of the proposed amendment to the Constitution of the United States, repealing the Eighteenth Article of Amendment to said Constitution, and prohibiting the transportation or importation into any State, Territory or Possession of the United States for delivery or use therein of intoxicating liquors in violation of the laws thereof, which said amendment has been proposed by the Congress of the United States in accordance with Article V of the Constitution of the United States is hereby ratified.

THE PRESIDENT: You heard the Resolution offered to ratify the Twenty-first Amendment, repealing the Eighteenth Amendment. Do I hear a second?

MR. KLINEFELTER: I would like to second that, and I would like to address the Chair.

THE PRESIDENT: I will be glad to have you do so.

MR. KLINEFELTER: I am going to ask you to bear with me for a few seconds. I would like to read a paper that I have prepared—

THE PRESIDENT: Do I understand that you are now speaking on the Resolution to ratify the Twenty-first Amendment, repealing the Eighteenth Amendment? Do I understand you are speaking on that motion?

MR. KLINEFELTER: Yes, and I want to speak in favor of it. At this time, my friends, it seems fitting to try in some way to stress on the great importance of this momentous act, and to try, if possible, to impress on the minds of the American people that Democracy is alive, is not dead, and is not ready to be buried by a long shot, and with your permission I will read this paper:

The question "Has Democracy Failed?", is not new. It has been on the lips of many thoughtful people for years. The enemies of our government eagerly answer, yes, but many authorities still believe it to be the best form of government ever attempted on this globe, because they know that it is not the failure of democracy, but because we have never given democracy a fair trial.

Democracy has not failed. It has been betrayed by many of our politicians and pseudo statesmen. Instead of representing the people, who elect them, they selfishly look after their own interests, or are brow-beaten and intimidated by well-organized minorities, and bent to the will of the enemies of Democracy. Politics has become a business, and a means to livelihood, rather than a civic duty. This has caused the people to lose faith, because they feel it is a loss of valuable time even to go to the polls on election day, much less spend any time whatever in studying their government, only to be betrayed by so many of the men they elect to office.

The main trouble is, that the people of these United States never have had the right to vote directly on any national issues, nor on the application of any federal laws, except when the people are permitted to vote directly, as they are now doing, for members of State Conventions either to ratify or reject changes in the Constitution. Ours is now and has always been a representative form of government, hence it is only as good as the men we elect to office. Therefore, to re-kindle and re-establish interest in politics, which in fact is government, our very life itself, it seems logical that the American people should be allowed to vote directly by states on certain national issues, and on most changes in the Constitution. It, of course, goes without saying that the people should insist upon the right to vote directly on the more important State and local issues, instead of voting for the average Republican and Democratic politicians who are inoculated with the virus of self-aggrandizement. As the elder Vanderbilt said: "The people be damned," is now, always has, and will continue to be their motto.

The difference between voting directly on issues and voting for Democrats and Republicans, was demonstrated in April, 1932, when the people of Baltimore were given the right to vote directly on the open Sunday. It took over 100 years for Baltimoreans to secure this right. When they did, they voted overwhelmingly for the open Sunday, and if the issue had continued to be submerged in party politics, the advocates of the closed Sunday could and probably would have intimidated the politicians, and Baltimore would still be a graveyard over the week-ends.

Another illustration is what is now happening all over this country. We see state after state voting overwhelmingly wet. The deluded dry minority seems dumbfounded, but the professional drys knew that immediately the American people were given the opportunity to vote directly on prohibition that the 18th Amendment would be torn from the Constitution.

This is the first time since the Constitution was originally ratified by Conventions in 1788, that the American people have ever been permitted to vote directly on any national issue. The first ten Amendments to the Constitution, which composed the Bill of Rights, were ratified by Legislatures, away back in 1789, the last nine Amendments have all been ratified by Legislatures.

The prohibition issue is temporarily divorced from party politics while the people are voting for wet and dry delegates to State Conventions, because they are voting for wets and drys, and not for Democrats and Republicans, but immediately the Eighteenth Amendment is repealed the prohibition issue will again become the football of party politics in most States in the Union.

Regardless of what anyone might say to the contrary, the American people never voted for the Eighteenth Amendment. It was ratified by Legislatures, many of which were elected before the Amendment was submitted to the Congress. These Legislatures and the Congress itself were composed entirely of politicians, most of whom drank wet, but voted dry under the lash of the Anti-Saloon League and other dry organizations.

The people of these United States have been compelled, against their will, to wait impatiently for over thirteen years for the opportunity to vote directly against this usurpation of their personal rights and freedom, and they are proving themselves worthy of this trust.

The Constitution provides two methods by which amendments might be ratified or rejected. The Congress has the right to say whether it shall be done by Legislatures or by Conventions. See Article V of the Constitution. The lazy, cheap, cowardly way is by letting the Legislatures do it. This, probably, is why we have previously avoided the Convention method. But even the enemies of the direct vote, admit it is fortunate that repeal of the 18th Amendment is not now being submitted to Legislatures, because it would have been an easy matter for the advocates of national prohibition to have intimidated sufficient state Legislatures to prevent repeal, but they are powerless to influence much less threaten the people themselves. It is doubtful if any future Congresses would dare submit other liberty destroying amendments to State Legislatures for ratification.

The fathers in drafting the Constitution realized the danger of nationwide direct popular mass votes by the people, and, very wisely, guarded against them, because such votes would sweep aside and utterly destroy the rights of the minority, and annihilate absolutely "The Right of Local Self-Government," the keystone of our government arch. For example, in 1919 fifteen wringing wet states contained nearly 57% of all our people. Had a direct nationwide popular mass vote on national prohibition then been possible, the dry states would have been compelled to be wet against their will. This would have been unfair to them; and it was equally unfair, when the wet states were compelled, against their will, to be dry, due to the absence of the direct popular vote by States.

It is my belief, that had the fathers dreamed that anything like the 18th Amendment might have crept into the Constitution, they would, in all probability have worded the 10th Article to the Bill of Rights less ambiguously, or else have added another article to the Constitution which would have provided for the direct vote of the people by states on certain national issues, and on the application of certain federal laws. Therefore, in the light of what has happened the Constitution should be amended in this manner.

Of course, the direct vote, even by States and cities, has a great many enemies. They declare that the American people are still unfit to vote directly on any issues, because the masses will not give their government the study which is necessary to produce an intelligent direct popular vote. But I join with many authorities in the belief, that if the American people were given the direct vote, by States and cities, that very soon they would demonstrate that they were worthy of such a franchise.

The enemies of the direct vote claim that the people cannot be trusted to vote intelligently, because they would make too many mistakes. This sounds truer than it really is. The people can be depended upon to realize almost instantly when they have voted selfishly or thoughtlessly for bad laws, then they could and would change them promptly. This is exactly what occurred in Canada. The Canadians went overwhelmingly dry by the direct vote, entirely and absolutely divorced from party politics. This happened in 1919. But when they found that prohibition was as ghastly a failure there as it was here, they almost immediately began to vote wet by provinces, until now tiny Prince Edward Isle is the Lone Dry province in the whole of Canada. This demonstrates that if we had gone dry by the direct vote by States, that the people would not have been compelled to wait for thirteen years while a cowardly wet Congress continued to betray them by voting dry.

The Canadians must like their various liquor control laws. Evidently they are working most satisfactorily, otherwise the people themselves would change back to the dry states. Neither the Canadian politicians or the dry minority have anything whatever to do with the issue. The direct vote hangs, suspended like "The Sword of

Damocles" a menace alike to the lawless wets and tyrannical drys, and it will serve the same purpose right here in the United States. Not only would the direct vote of the people properly settle the liquor issue, as it has in Canada, but it would settle many other issues by divorcing them from party politics, because this is exactly what happens when the people vote directly.

Many also claim that the direct vote for Senators has not improved the calibre of the Senate. But it is neither logical nor fair to compare the direct vote for Republican, and Democratic Senators, who must come up each term for re-election, with the direct vote of all the people of all parties on a given issue. The party organizations can very easily control primary, and sometimes, even final elections, because the voters become confused, there being too many issues, but the politicians and the fanatical minorities are powerless to intimidate, seriously influence, or confuse the direct vote of the people of *all* the parties, when the people themselves vote directly on a single issue, instead of voting for Representatives, who become confused themselves, because they are confronted with many other issues, besides the one involved.

Which method properly reflected the real will of the people; the present direct vote to repeal the 18th Amendment, or its ratification by Legislatures, composed of Representatives, who wilfully misrepresented and frustrated the real will of a vast majority of the people?

There are many illustrations of the referenda. For example: In November 1928 Massachusetts gave wet Al Smith but 25,000 majority over dry Herbert Hoover, but simultaneously all the people of all the parties voting directly on the same ballot, gave a majority of nearly 400,000 against National Prohibition. The people usually vote very sanely on great issues. But as this referendum was only devised to ascertain how all the people felt, it had no immediate effect on National Prohibition.

The direct vote centralizes and fixes the attention of the voters on the issue involved. The voters are not asked to desert their parties to vote for candidates of the opposite parties. It has been next to impossible to induce wet Republicans and wet Democrats to cast aside party ties to vote for wets of the opposite parties.

The direct vote of the people by states and cities on certain issues, will blast them free from the influence and corruption of party politics, and organized minorities.

Instead of voting for Republicans and Democrats, who meet away off in Washington, and in the State Capitols, where they log roll, and often sell their votes to the highest bidders, or are bluffed or scared by well organized minorities, and thus betray the voters back home, we should be permitted to vote directly by States on the most important issues. No wonder the American people have lost faith. The wonder is, that we vote at all. This pleases the politicians. It is a political axiom, "that the smaller the vote the happier the politicians." The professional politicians have the small vote all counted and delivered, but the big vote generally disconcerts them. This especially applies to primary elections.

If the people in each separate state were permitted to vote directly on the soldier bonus, surely every deserving soldier would be more than fairly compensated for the sacrifice he had made for his country. Then it would be impossible for any organization of veterans to brow-beat the President, and both Houses of Congress. Politicians can be, and are intimidated, because they come up for re-election, but the American people are not running for office.

Our whole system of government was predicated upon the principle of The Right of Local Self-Government. This means:

1—That the Federal Government should keep hands off the States provided they do not interfere with the rights of other states, or with the true functions of the Federal Government, unless the people themselves wish to surrender their States Rights to the Federal authorities.

2—That the States should permit their cities to live their lives in their own way, so long as they do not interfere with the peace and tranquillity of the States, unless the city people care to surrender their rights to the State.

It was Thomas Jefferson who said: "Were not this great country already divided into States, the division must be made, that each State might do for itself directly what it can so much better do than a distant authority—were we directed from Washington when to sow and when to reap, we should want bread." And this was uttered when our country was tiny in comparison to what it is today as regards area, population and wealth. This fundamental applies yesterday; today and forever.

In 1832 De Toqueville, the famous Frenchman, after a long stay in this country, declared that we were headed straight toward paternalism. And Lord Brice, who knew us better than we knew ourselves, in his "American Commonwealth" published about 1893, advised us to "safeguard the Right of Local Self-Government."

Calvin Coolidge said: "Efficiency of Federal operation is diminished as their scope is unduly endangered, and efficiency of State governments is diminished as they relinquish and turn over to the Federal Government responsibilities which are rightfully theirs." And Chief Justice Charles Evans Hughes in his great speech before the American Bar Association, in Chicago, August 21, 1930, eloquently warned us not to interfere with the Right of Local Self-Government.

We Americans are Individualists not Socialists. The Right of Local Self-Government is so indelibly woven into the fabric of our government, and into our very lives, that if we were given the right directly to express ourselves, by States and Cities, we probably would vote as overwhelmingly against much of this centralization of power in Washington, and the various States Capitols, as we are now voting against national prohibition, the foulest blow Home Rule ever received. The Declaration of Independence and the Constitution, except for the Income Tax Amendment, and the Prohibition Amendment are fairly saturated with The Right of Local Self-Government, the very life blood of Democracy.

The keystone in our governmental arch is "The Right of Local Self-Government" —regardless what many of our present day politicians, counterfeit, statesmen, and the Enemies of Democracy say to the contrary. Entirely too much power has been concentrated in Washington, and the various State Capitols. The people have been ignored and robbed of their just rights, and have no direct voice in the conduct of our government. Therefore, the Federal Constitution should be amended in a manner that would produce a direct vote of the people by states on most changes in the Constitution, otherwise we will cease to have a Republican form of government even in name. We now seem about ready to apply many Socialistic theories. This is a disgrace for self-respecting citizens of the United States of America, whose ancestors fought to create and preserve but not obliterate The Right of Local Self-Government.

Instead of being an indissoluble union of indestructible and independent States, as envisioned by the fathers, who sought to guarantee our constitutional rights and liberties in the Bill of Rights, we have supinely permitted more power to be centralized in Washington than even Alexander Hamilton advocated.

The power to initiate changes in the Constitution now lies entirely with the Congress, or a national convention. The difficulty and danger which attends the latter, and the indifference and slowness of the Congress to initiate when influenced by party loyalty, self-interest, or intimidation by minorities, probably will lead to the initiative of the people by States on certain federal legislation and issues.

Our government structure is comparable to the delicate work of the most expert Swiss watchmakers, but it is being ruined by our Representatives composed largely of carpenters, cobblers, farmers, immature lawyers and others who know little and care less what happens to this great government, so long as their own selfish interests are served.

It should be the sense of this Convention that no future Amendments to the Constitution be tolerated which would put more power in the hands of the Congress than it now possesses. The proposed Child Labor Amendment, for example, which was defeated in forty States, has since been ratified by the Legislatures of several States despite the fact that it was overwhelmingly defeated over nine years ago. This Amendment now is unnecessary, because child labor has been outlawed by President Roosevelt, but if it ever is ratified, it would make the Congress more powerful than the Soviet. The future of our families, and their families' families, would be placed in the hands of a group of politicians, few of whom have the slightest semblance to statesmanship.

Therefore, it is hoped that the Congress will never again recommend such liberty-destroying legislation as the 18th Amendment or the Child Labor Amendment, but if it ever should be so misled, it is hoped that they will be submitted for ratification by State Conventions composed of Delegates chosen by the people themselves, elected for this single purpose, and not Legislatures composed of politicians who are confronted by many conflicting issues besides the one involved.

THE PRESIDENT: The resolution is now before you and the Delegates will answer the roll call as their names are called.

(The Secretary then called the roll, and upon the vote, the resolution was unanimously carried at 3:20 P.M.)

(Three copies of the resolution adopted were then signed by the President and Secretary of the Convention.)

THE PRESIDENT: The next in order is a resolution for the appointment of a Committee of five Delegates to examine and transmit to the Secretary of State three copies of the executed resolution and certificate ratifying said proposed Amendment to the Constitution of the United States. The Chair recognizes Dr. Miller.

DR. MILLER: Mr. President, I desire to offer the following resolution:

RESOLVED, That the President of the Convention appoint a Committee of five Delegates to examine and transmit to the Secretary of State of the State of Maryland, the three copies of the executed Resolution and certificate ratifying the proposed amendment to the Constitution of the United States.

THE PRESIDENT: The Chair appoints on that committee:

John A. Robinson, Chairman
James B. Berry
Mrs. George Heller
Dr. Victor D. Miller
Mrs. Mortimer W. West.

THE PRESIDENT: Is the Committee ready to report?

MR. ROBINSON: Yes, and we herewith submit the same.

THE PRESIDENT: The Committee has now delivered those copies to the Secretary of State.

The next order of business would be a resolution instructing the President and Secretary to prepare and certify a journal of the proceedings of this Convention to be filed in the office of the Secretary of State.

I recognize Dr. Dick.

DR. DICK: I offer the following resolution:

RESOLVED, That the President and Secretary of the Convention be authorized to prepare and approve the Journal of the proceedings of this Convention with the same force and effect as if the Delegates to this Convention had approved the same, and that they be requested to file the said Journal of Proceedings under their certificate with the Secretary of State of the State of Maryland.

(Which resolution was duly seconded and upon being put to a vote was carried.)

COLONEL HILL: I move that the thanks of this Convention be extended to his Honor, the Attorney-General of the State, for his assistance in this work, and particularly to the Deputy Attorney-General, Willis R. Jones, for the good work that he has done.

THE PRESIDENT: I think that is a very proper motion. I know some of the work that Mr. Jones has done and I do not know how the Convention could have gotten along without him.

(Which motion was duly seconded and upon being put to a vote was unanimously carried.)

COLONEL HILL: I move the thanks of this Convention to his Excellency, Governor Ritchie, for his hospitality to the Convention today.

(Which motion was duly seconded.)

THE PRESIDENT: You have heard the motion; all those in favor, please rise.

(A rising vote was then taken and unanimously carried.)

THE PRESIDENT: This concludes the order of business of the Convention.

MR. WEINBERG: In moving to adjourn the Convention, I do so with a motion that I know is concurred in by each of the ladies and gentlemen present, that we express to you our thanks for the splendid manner in which you presided, and we express to his Excellency, Governor Ritchie, the voice of the people of Maryland and of the United States for the consummation that we have just seen, and for the tremendous part in that consummation that he has so conspicuously played.

(Which motion was duly seconded, and upon being put to a vote, was carried.)

THE PRESIDENT: I now declare the thanks very heartily, and I declare this Convention adjourned.

(Whereupon at 3:30 P.M. the Convention adjourned.)

The undersigned President and Secretary of the Constitutional Convention of Maryland, held in the Senate Chamber of the State House at Annapolis, on the 18th day of October, 1933, do hereby certify that the aforegoing is a true and accurate copy of the Journal of proceedings of said Convention, and that this certificate is executed in accordance with a Resolution duly adopted at said Convention.

(*Signed*) R. BENNETT DARNALL
President

(*Signed*) JOSEPH P. MCCURDY
Secretary

MASSACHUSETTS*

PROCEEDINGS

OF THE

CONSTITUTIONAL CONVENTION

JUNE 26, 1933

The Delegates chosen at the election held on the thirteenth day of June, 1933, as Delegates to the Constitutional Convention called to ratify or reject the proposed amendment to the Constitution of the United States repealing the Eighteenth Amendment, met at the Gardner Auditorium at the State House, Boston, Massachusetts, at 12 o'clock noon on Monday, June 26, 1933, His Excellency the Governor, Joseph B. Ely, presiding, the Honorable Frederic W. Cook, Secretary of the Commonwealth, acting as Clerk pro tempore.

HIS EXCELLENCY THE GOVERNOR, JOSEPH B. ELY: The Convention will come to order. This Convention is held in pursuance of the Joint Resolution of the Congress of the United States, and Chapter 142 of the Acts of the Legislature of the Commonwealth of Massachusetts of the present year, for the purpose of acting upon the proposed amendment to the Constitution of the United States relative to the repeal of the Eighteenth Amendment.

In accordance with time honored custom of this nation, prayer will be offered by the Reverend Doctor Samuel A. Eliot.

Reverend Doctor SAMUEL A. ELIOT offered prayer:

"Let us pray. Almighty God, guide now and govern our thoughts and wills that we may honorably fulfill the task committed to us by our fellow-citizens. Animate us with a spirit of devotion to the common good. Quicken our desire to promote the welfare of the whole community. Exalt among us the covenants and tests and ideals of self-government. We pray not for immunity from risks but for courage and foresight and self-control wherewith to face risks and master life's conditions and dangers. Let the fear of thy judgment be the beginning of our wisdom and the end of all other fear. Amen."

HIS EXCELLENCY THE GOVERNOR, JOSEPH B. ELY: To facilitate the organization of this Convention, the section of the auditorium directly in front of the rostrum, on my right, is reserved for Delegates, and I wish that all the Delegates would take their seats in this section. Spectators and visitors will use some other portion of the auditorium. All Delegates will take chairs in the section reserved for the Delegates.

The Secretary of the Commonwealth will call the roll of the Delegates, and each Delegate as his name is called will answer "Present."

The roll of Delegates was called by the Secretary of the Commonwealth, and the several Delegates responded at the calling of their names, as indicated in the following list:

Thomas F. Bradley of Holyoke	Present	Sidney A. Bailey of Northampton	Present
Charles F. Ely of Westfield	Present	Samuel M. Green of Springfield	Present
James R. Savery of Pittsfield	Present	Sadie H. Mulrone of Springfield	Present

* Printed.

David E. Hobson of Southbridge	Present	Benjamin Loring Young of Weston	Present
J. Lovell Johnson of Fitchburg	Present	Elizabeth M. Lovett of Boston	Present
Albert J. Lamoureux of Gardner	Present	Arthur L. Stanek of Boston	Present
Charles F. Campbell of Worcester	Present	Jacob L. Wiseman of Boston	Present
Eben S. Draper of Hopedale	Present	Mary L. Bacigalupo of Boston	Present
T. Frank Hickey of Shrewsbury	Present	James H. Brennan of Boston	Present
J. Frank Facey of Cambridge	Present	James J. Mellen of Boston	Present
Judson Hannigan of Belmont	Present	Daniel J. Gallagher of Boston	Present
Elphege A. Phaneuf of Lowell	Present	Joseph J. Mulhern of Boston	Present
Robert B. Choate of Danvers	Present	Agnes K. Willey of Boston	Present
Raymond V. McNamara of Haverhill	Present	Frank A. Manning of Brockton	Present
Bayard Tuckerman, Jr., of Hamilton	Present	Neil A. McDonald of Quincy	Present
Rena M. Colson of Wakefield	Present	Mason Sears of Dedham	Present
Harold E. Russell of Lynn	Present	Spencer Borden of Fall River	Present
Michael F. Shaw of Revere	Present	Robert M. Leach of Taunton	Present
William F. Leahy of Medford	Present	John B. Morin of Attleboro	Present
Louis Newman of Malden	Present	Henry T. Geary of Plymouth	Present
George H. Norton of Somerville	Present	Gladys P. Swift of Barnstable	Present
Daniel H. Coakley, Jr., of Boston	Present	Ferdinand Sylvia of New Bedford	Present
James Roosevelt of Cambridge	Present		

THE SECRETARY OF THE COMMONWEALTH: Your Excellency, forty-five Delegates, being all of the Delegates elected, are present.

HIS EXCELLENCY THE GOVERNOR, JOSEPH B. ELY: Forty-five Delegates, more than the twenty-three required by the Act to constitute a quorum, have responded to the calling of the roll.

The oath of the Delegates will now be administered. Will you please rise and each raise your right hand and repeat after me the words of the oath, each Delegate filling in his or her own name at the proper places?

"I, ... do solemnly swear that I will bear true faith and allegiance to the Commonwealth of Massachusetts, and will support the Constitution thereof. So help me, God.

"I, ... do solemnly swear and affirm that I will faithfully and impartially discharge and perform all the duties incumbent on me as a Delegate to this Constitutional Convention, according to the best of my abilities and understanding, agreeably to the rules and regulations of the Constitution and Laws of the Commonwealth. So help me, God.

"I, ... do solemnly swear that I will support the Constitution of the United States."

It will now be necessary for each Delegate to sign the oath, and you may step forward to the table in front of the rostrum in order, and subscribe.

THE SECRETARY OF THE COMMONWEALTH: Your Excellency, all forty-five Delegates have subscribed to the oath of office.

HIS EXCELLENCY THE GOVERNOR, JOSEPH B. ELY: Having taken and subscribed the oaths required by the Constitution of the United States and this Commonwealth, you are now qualified to enter upon the discharge of your duties as Delegates to this Convention.

I believe you to be the first Convention of unanimous opinion ever assembled in this Commonwealth. (Laughter and applause.) You are here to ratify an Amendment repealing the Eighteenth Amendment. Your action is the result of years of agitation, to rid the Constitution of a provision which never should have been in it. It should not take you long. We are not unmindful, in the return of authority to the states for the regulation of the liquor traffic, of the responsibility which rests upon those charged with the duty of government here to so legislate and administer that the cause of temperance will be promoted, and whatever good may have resulted from the prohibition laws of the last years may be consolidated and the interest of the people in sane government and orderly living preserved.

The first business before the Convention will be the choice of a President. Nominations are now in order.

MR. MICHAEL F. SHAW: Mr. Chairman.

HIS EXCELLENCY THE GOVERNOR, JOSEPH B. ELY: The Chair recognizes the gentleman from Revere.

MR. MICHAEL F. SHAW: Mr. Chairman, and fellow Delegates to the Constitutional Convention, I rise, sir, to place in nomination for President of this Convention a man well and favorably known throughout the length and breadth of this Commonwealth, whose public record, whether elective or appointive, has been outstanding in the conduct of his duties.

From 1913 to 1915 he was a member of the Board of Parole of this Commonwealth, and today is chairman of the State Board of Probation.

In 1916 he came to the House of Representatives, and so conducted himself in the discharge of his duties that he was marked for further advancement.

In 1919, he was chosen Speaker of the House of Representatives, and from that time until 1924 he brought to that position a scholastic ability and great fundamental knowledge of parliamentary procedure which stamped him as an outstanding presiding officer and the peer of the most illustrious of his predecessors.

In 1925, at the conclusion of his elective public life, he was appointed by the District Judges of the United States District Court to be Referee in Bankruptcy in the Middlesex District, a position which he has held continuously since that date.

Mr. Chairman, I am not unmindful of the proud privilege which is mine, to bring before this Convention the Honorable B. Loring Young of Weston to be elected as its President, he a scholar and jurist. (Applause.)

HIS EXCELLENCY THE GOVERNOR, JOSEPH B. ELY: Are there other nominations?

MR. JUDSON HANNIGAN: Mr. Chairman.

HIS EXCELLENCY THE GOVERNOR, JOSEPH B. ELY: The Chair recognizes the gentleman from Belmont.

MR. JUDSON HANNIGAN: Your Excellency, I cannot draw a picture of a long career of varied public service, but I can draw a picture of a single-purposed public service from the benches of private life that has been rendered to effect the very purpose for which we meet here today, and she whom I am about to nominate has been not alone the leader in a cause; she has been the leader of the womanhood of Massachusetts, without whom this great day could not have been possible. And so, in tribute partially to her, for what she has done, but in greater measure in tribute to the women of Massachusetts for what they have accomplished for the good name of Massachusetts, I nominate Mrs. Elizabeth M. Lovett of Boston. (Applause.)

HIS EXCELLENCY THE GOVERNOR, JOSEPH B. ELY: Are there any further nominations?

MR. JAMES ROOSEVELT: Your Excellency, are seconding speeches in order?

His Excellency the Governor, Joseph B. Ely: The Chair will recognize the Delegate from Cambridge for the purpose of seconding a nomination.

Mr. James Roosevelt: Your Excellency, I wish to second the nomination made by the gentleman from Belmont [Mr. Hannigan] and to state that I feel that this great Convention is gathered here for the purpose of fulfilling the direction of the voters of Massachusetts, in repealing the Eighteenth Amendment.

I therefore feel that the outstanding Delegate who has done most towards securing that position from Massachusetts should be recognized at this time. I know her personally as a very dear friend, and I feel, having seen her preside on many occasions, I know she has all the qualities of a presiding officer, and therefore it is with honor and with pleasure that I second the nomination of Mrs. Elizabeth M. Lovett. (Applause.)

Mr. George H. Norton: Mr. Chairman.

His Excellency the Governor, Joseph B. Ely: The Chair recognizes the Delegate from Somerville.

Mr. George H. Norton: Your Excellency, I consider it an honor and a privilege to second the nomination of B. Loring Young of Weston for the President of this Convention. His qualifications and the reasons why the Delegates should give him their support have been fully expounded by the Delegate, Mr. Shaw, from Revere. I sincerely trust, and had hoped before coming into this Convention, that the President would be elected by acclamation, and I am very glad to state that Mr. Young, who has had the necessary experience, can certainly expedite the work of this Convention. And I sincerely hope that the Delegates will reconsider the other nomination and make the election by acclamation.

Mr. Daniel H. Coakley, Jr., of Boston: Your Excellency, and fellow Delegates, I wish to second the nomination, made by Mr. Shaw, of B. Loring Young for President of this Convention.

Mr. Eben S. Draper of Hopedale: Your Excellency, and fellow Delegates, I wish to second the nomination of Mrs. Lovett for the outstanding work which she has done in this cause, to which we are all here to testify today. (Applause.)

Mr. Spencer Borden of Fall River: Your Excellency, and fellow Delegates, I can add nothing to the eloquent words of the gentleman from Revere, but I wish also to second the nomination of the Honorable B. Loring Young.

Mr. Thomas F. Bradley of Holyoke: Mr. Chairman, I move that the nominations be closed.

Mr. James J. Mellen of Boston: I rise at this time to second the nomination of Benjamin Loring Young. Probably I knew him as well as any man living. I served with him for four years in the Legislature, and while I did not always agree with him, we were always very good friends. For one little incident I take advantage of this opportunity to second the nomination of Benjamin Loring Young.

His Excellency the Governor, Joseph B. Ely: If there are no other nominations, then the nominations are closed. I have received, as the presiding officer of this Convention, a list of the Delegates, and I will ask the Secretary of the Commonwealth to call the roll of Delegates. As the name of each Delegate is called he will rise and announce his choice for the office of President.

The roll of Delegates was called by the Secretary of the Commonwealth, and as each name was called the Delegate rose and announced his choice for the office of President of the Convention, as follows:

Thomas F. Bradley of Holyoke	B. Loring Young
Charles F. Ely of Westfield	Mrs. Elizabeth M. Lovett
James R. Savery of Pittsfield	Mrs. Elizabeth M. Lovett
Sidney A. Bailey of Northampton	Mrs. Elizabeth M. Lovett
Samuel M. Green of Springfield	B. Loring Young
Sadie H. Mulrone of Springfield	B. Loring Young
David E. Hobson of Southbridge	B. Loring Young
J. Lovell Johnson of Fitchburg	B. Loring Young
Albert J. Lamoureux of Gardner	B. Loring Young
Charles F. Campbell of Worcester	B. Loring Young
Eben S. Draper of Hopedale	Mrs. Elizabeth M. Lovett
T. Frank Hickey of Shrewsbury	B. Loring Young
J. Frank Facey of Cambridge	B. Loring Young
Judson Hannigan of Belmont	Mrs. Elizabeth M. Lovett
Elphege A. Phaneuf of Lowell	B. Loring Young
Robert B. Choate of Danvers	B. Loring Young
Raymond V. McNamara of Haverhill	B. Loring Young
Bayard Tuckerman, Jr., of Hamilton	Mrs. Elizabeth M. Lovett
Rena M. Colson of Wakefield	B. Loring Young
Harold E. Russell of Lynn	Mrs. Elizabeth M. Lovett
Michael F. Shaw of Revere	B. Loring Young
William F. Leahy of Medford	B. Loring Young
Louis Newman of Malden	B. Loring Young
George H. Norton of Somerville	B. Loring Young
Daniel H. Coakley, Jr., of Boston	B. Loring Young
James Roosevelt of Cambridge	Mrs. Elizabeth M. Lovett
Benjamin Loring Young of Weston	(Present)
Elizabeth M. Lovett of Boston	Mrs. Elizabeth M. Lovett
Arthur L. Stanek of Boston	B. Loring Young
Jacob L. Wiseman of Boston	B. Loring Young
Mary L. Bacigalupo of Boston	B. Loring Young
James H. Brennan of Boston	I desire to cast my vote for a man who has always been wet, and always been a Democrat, James Roosevelt of Cambridge.
James J. Mellen of Boston	B. Loring Young
Daniel J. Gallagher of Boston	Mrs. Elizabeth M. Lovett
Joseph J. Mulhern of Boston	B. Loring Young
Agnes K. Willey of Boston	Mrs. Elizabeth M. Lovett
Frank A. Manning of Brockton	B. Loring Young
Neil A. McDonald of Quincy	B. Loring Young
Mason Sears of Dedham	B. Loring Young
Spencer Borden of Fall River	B. Loring Young
Robert M. Leach of Taunton	B. Loring Young
John B. Morin of Attleboro	B. Loring Young
Henry T. Geary of Plymouth	B. Loring Young

MRS. ELIZABETH M. LOVETT: May I make a motion to make this unanimous?

HIS EXCELLENCY THE GOVERNOR, JOSEPH B. ELY: When the roll is completed.

The calling of the roll by the Secretary of the Commonwealth was resumed, as follows:

Gladys P. Swift of Barnstable	Mrs. Elizabeth M. Lovett
Ferdinand Sylvia of New Bedford	B. Loring Young

THE SECRETARY OF THE COMMONWEALTH: Your Excellency, the total number of votes cast is 44.

James Roosevelt has 1.
Elizabeth M. Lovett, 12.
Benjamin Loring Young, 31.

(Applause.)

MRS. ELIZABETH M. LOVETT: I make a motion to make it unanimous.

MR. JUDSON HANNIGAN: I second the motion.

HIS EXCELLENCY THE GOVERNOR, JOSEPH B. ELY: It is moved and seconded that the election of B. Loring Young as President of this Convention be made unanimous. Are there any remarks? (No response.) If not, then those in favor will say Aye. (Chorus of Ayes.) Opposed? (No response.) The Ayes have it, and I declare the election of B. Loring Young as President of this Convention to be unanimous. (Prolonged applause.) I appoint Mrs. Elizabeth M. Lovett and Mr. James Roosevelt to escort the President to the rostrum.

The President-Elect was thereupon conducted to the rostrum by the committee, amid applause.

HIS EXCELLENCY THE GOVERNOR, JOSEPH B. ELY: Mr. Young, I turn over to you the gavel of this Convention.

PRESIDENT B. LORING YOUNG: The Convention will be in order, and while the Governor retires the members will rise. (Applause, the members rising.)

Members of the Convention, it is my hope that the duty of this Convention may be performed with diligence, with dignity and with dispatch. It is for that reason that your President has prepared no formal address to be delivered upon what is, after all, a most historic occasion,—the first Constitutional Convention of the people of Massachusetts to consider a ratification or rejection of a proposed amendment to the Constitution of the United States.

I will therefore merely state my heartfelt gratitude to the Delegates of this Convention for selecting me for this great honor, and I assure them that my gratitude will last as long as life itself. And to the lady from Boston who so generously and kindly made the motion that the election be regarded as unanimous, I extend my most deep and sincere thanks.

Let us now proceed to the business of the Convention in order that we may terminate our duties today. The first duty will be the election of a Clerk of the Convention, and the Chair will recognize Mr. Hobson of Southbridge.

MR. DAVID E. HOBSON of Southbridge: Mr. President, I nominate for Clerk of this Convention Mrs. Rena M. Colson of Wakefield.

PRESIDENT YOUNG: You have heard the nomination. Is it seconded?

MR. CHARLES F. ELY of Westfield: Mr. President, I second the nomination and move that the nominations be closed, and that the Secretary of the Commonwealth be directed to cast one ballot for Mrs. Rena M. Colson.

PRESIDENT YOUNG: All those in favor will say Aye. (Chorus of Ayes.) Those opposed, No. (No response.) The Ayes have it, and the nominations are closed.

The Chair will rule that it is in order, to carry out the balance of the gentleman's motion, that the temporary clerk of the Convention, the Honorable the Secretary of the Commonwealth, cast one ballot for Mrs. Rena M. Colson of Wakefield to be clerk of this Convention.

THE SECRETARY OF THE COMMONWEALTH: The temporary clerk casts one ballot for Rena M. Colson of Wakefield as Clerk of this Convention.

PRESIDENT YOUNG: The Chair has received information that the Secretary of the Commonwealth, as the temporary clerk of this body, has cast one ballot for Mrs. Rena M. Colson of Wakefield for Clerk of the Convention. The Chair will appoint Mrs. Mary L. Bacigalupo of Boston and Mr. Albert J. Lamoureux of Gardner as a committee to conduct Mrs. Colson, the Clerk of the Convention, to the rostrum. (Applause.)

Mrs. Rena M. Colson of Wakefield is escorted to the rostrum and takes her seat as Clerk of the Convention.

PRESIDENT YOUNG: The Chair has received the following communication from the Secretary of the Commonwealth, which will be read by the Chair.

THE COMMONWEALTH OF MASSACHUSETTS

OFFICE OF THE SECRETARY, BOSTON, June 26, 1933

To the Constitutional Convention called to ratify or reject the Proposed Amendment to the Constitution of the United States repealing the Eighteenth Amendment.

I have the honor to lay before you the returns of votes cast at the election held in this Commonwealth on the thirteenth day of June, 1933, for delegates to the Constitutional Convention, together with schedules showing the number of ballots which appear to have been cast for each person voted for.

These returns have been duly canvassed by the Governor and Council, and are now transmitted for your examination as required by law.

Very truly yours,

F. W. COOK
Secretary of the Commonwealth

The Chair trusts that the Convention will permit its presiding officer to proceed with some informality because of the fact that we have no real precedent for the government and procedure of this Convention. As the Delegates know, this is the first time that the States have been called upon to ratify by Convention instead of by their respective State Legislatures an amendment to the Constitution of the United States.

We have received a partially complete record of the Convention in New Jersey. The convention held in New Jersey proceeded with commendable dispatch. It did, however, authorize the presiding officer, who was the President of the Senate of that State, to appoint a Committee on Elections, to make an examination as to whether the list of Delegates placed upon the temporary roll by the Secretary of the Commonwealth was the correct list of Delegates, and to determine any contests which might be presented; secondly, a Committee on Rules of the government of the Convention; and thirdly, a Committee on Resolutions to consider any resolutions which might be offered from the floor.

MR. JUDSON HANNIGAN: Mr. President.

PRESIDENT YOUNG: The Chair recognizes the gentleman from Belmont.

MR. JUDSON HANNIGAN: I move that the Chairman be authorized to appoint the three following committees: Committee on Rules, Committee on Elections, and a Committee on Resolutions.

PRESIDENT YOUNG: Is the motion seconded?

MR. MICHAEL F. SHAW of Revere: I second the motion.

PRESIDENT YOUNG: The motion, having been made and seconded, will now be put, to the effect that the Chair be authorized and directed to appoint a Committee on Elections, a Committee on Rules, and a Committee on Resolutions. Is there any debate? (No response.) If not, all those in favor——

MR. CHARLES F. ELY of Westfield: Mr. President, I am always wrong, but still

I know all that. We all know that we have been elected, and that we all have a vote.

PRESIDENT YOUNG: The Chair recognizes the gentleman from Westfield, Mr. Ely.

MR. CHARLES F. ELY (resuming): I do not see why we cannot simply vote, and call it a day. It is a long way from Westfield down here, and we had breakfast quite early. We all know for what we were elected, and I don't believe but what Mr. Cook can count the ballots correctly, and I don't see why we cannot vote without a lot of committees.

PRESIDENT YOUNG: The Chair will suggest that he is merely the servant of the Convention, to carry out the wishes of the Convention, and that if it be the desire of the Convention to proceed forthwith, not as a committee as a whole but in substance that, the Convention may dispense with committees and may upon motion adopt the temporary roll of the Convention as the permanent roll, without the appointment of a Committee on Elections. Preparatory to that, the Chair would ask if there are any contests or contesting Delegates present who desire to contest the election of any of the 45 men and women whose names appear upon the temporary roll? (No response.) The Chair hears no contestant, and the Chair will also suggest that a motion to adopt the rules of the House of Representatives to govern this Convention, and that a motion from the floor to ratify the proposed Amendment to the Constitution of the United States, would also be in order. The first proposal under consideration is that the temporary roll be made permanent,—that is, if the Convention desires to dispense with committees.

MR. CHARLES F. ELY of Westfield: Mr. Chairman.

MR. JUDSON HANNIGAN of Belmont: Mr. President, I withdraw my motion.

PRESIDENT YOUNG: The gentleman from Belmont withdraws his motion. Is there objection? (No response.) The Chair hears none and the motion is withdrawn.

MR. CHARLES F. ELY of Westfield: Mr. President, if it is in order, I move that, as the President has just stated, we suspend the rules—

PRESIDENT YOUNG: There are no rules at present.

MR. CHARLES F. ELY of Westfield: And that we adopt the rules of the House of Representatives.

PRESIDENT YOUNG: The Chair understands that the gentleman from Westfield, Mr. Ely, moves that this Convention adopt the rules of the House of Representatives of this Commonwealth for the current year as now in force, so far as applicable to these proceedings, as the rules of this Convention. Is that motion seconded?

The motion was seconded by several.

PRESIDENT YOUNG: All those in favor say Aye. (Chorus of Ayes.) Those opposed, No. (No response.) The motion is carried and the rules of the House of Representatives are the rules of the Convention.

MR. CHARLES F. ELY of Westfield: Mr. President, I move that the temporary list reported by the Secretary of the Commonwealth be made the permanent list of Delegates.

PRESIDENT YOUNG: Mr. Ely of Westfield now moves that the list of Delegates as read by the Secretary of the Commonwealth, being based upon the returns which have been duly approved by the Governor and Council and transmitted to this Convention, be adopted as the correct list of duly elected Delegates and accepted as the permanent roll of this Convention. Is that motion seconded?

The motion was seconded by several.

PRESIDENT YOUNG: The motion having been made and seconded, is there debate on the question? (No response.) If not, as many of the Delegates as favor that motion will say Aye. (Chorus of Ayes.) Opposed, No. (No response.) The Ayes have it, and the temporary roll read by the Secretary of the Commonwealth is the permanent roll of the Delegates to this Convention.

MR. JUDSON HANNIGAN of Belmont: Mr. President.

PRESIDENT YOUNG: The Chair recognizes the gentleman from Belmont, Mr. Hannigan.

MR. JUDSON HANNIGAN: The Convention having organized pursuant to the act providing for a Convention to act on the proposed amendment to the Constitution of the United States relative to the repeal of the Eighteenth Amendment, I move that this Convention now ratify the proposed Amendment to the Constitution of the United States, the text of said proposed amendment being as follows:

Section 1. The eighteenth article of amendment to the Constitution of the United States is hereby repealed.

Section 2. The transportation or importation into any State, Territory, or possession of the United States for delivery or use therein of intoxicating liquors, in violation of the laws thereof, is hereby prohibited.

Section 3. This article shall be inoperative unless it shall have been ratified as an amendment to the Constitution by conventions in the several States, as provided in the Constitution, within seven years from the date of the submission hereof to the States by the Congress.

MR. JAMES ROOSEVELT of Cambridge (and others at the same time): I second the motion.

PRESIDENT YOUNG: Is there debate on that question?

(Cries of "Question.")

PRESIDENT YOUNG: The previous question is moved.

MR. THOMAS F. BRADLEY of Holyoke: I second the motion.

PRESIDENT YOUNG: The question is, Shall the main question be now ordered? Those in favor will say Aye. (Cries of Aye.) Those opposed, No. (No response.) The main question is now ordered.

MR. JUDSON HANNIGAN of Belmont: Mr. President, in view of the importance of this vote I move that the vote on the main question be taken by a rising vote.

PRESIDENT YOUNG: The Chair will rule that that is a matter to be determined by the Chair, and the Chair will ask that it be determined by a call of the Yeas and Nays, in order that there may be a permanent record. The Clerk will call the roll, and each Delegate as his name is called will respond.

The Clerk of the Convention then called the name of each of the Delegates from the roll of Delegates, and the Delegates responded as stated in the following list:

Thomas F. Bradley of Holyoke	Yea	Eben S. Draper of Hopedale	Yea
Charles F. Ely of Westfield	Yea	T. Frank Hickey of Shrewsbury	Yea
James R. Savery of Pittsfield	Yea	J. Frank Facey of Cambridge	Yea
Sidney A. Bailey of Northampton	Yea	Judson Hannigan of Belmont	Yea
Samuel M. Green of Springfield	Yea	Elphege A. Phaneuf of Lowell	Yea
Sadie H. Mulrone of Springfield	Yea	Robert B. Choate of Danvers	Yea
David E. Hobson of Southbridge	Yea	Raymond V. McNamara of Haverhill	Yea
J. Lovell Johnson of Fitchburg	Yea	Bayard Tuckerman, Jr., of Hamilton	Yea
Albert J. Lamoureux of Gardner	Yea	Rena M. Colson of Wakefield	Yea
Charles F. Campbell of Worcester	Yea	Harold E. Russell of Lynn	Yea

Michael F. Shaw of Revere	Yea	Daniel J. Gallagher of Boston	Yea
William F. Leahy of Medford	Yea	Joseph J. Mulhern of Boston	Yea
Louis Newman of Malden	Yea	Agnes K. Willey of Boston	Yea
George H. Norton of Somerville	Yea	Frank A. Manning of Brockton	Yea
Daniel H. Coakley, Jr., of Boston	Yea	Neil A. McDonald of Quincy	Yea
James Roosevelt of Cambridge	Yea	Mason Sears of Dedham	Yea
Benjamin Loring Young of Weston	Yea	Spencer Borden of Fall River	Yea
Elizabeth M. Lovett of Boston	Yea	Robert M. Leach of Taunton	Yea
Arthur L. Stanek of Boston	Yea	John B. Morin of Attleboro	Yea
Jacob L. Wiseman of Boston	Yea	Henry T. Geary of Plymouth	Yea
Mary L. Bacigalupo of Boston	Yea	Gladys P. Swift of Barnstable	Yea
James H. Brennan of Boston	Yea	Ferdinand Sylvia of New Bedford	Yea
James J. Mellen of Boston	Yea		

THE CLERK OF THE CONVENTION: Mr. President, the roll having been called, I report that the 45 Delegates have all voted in the affirmative.

PRESIDENT YOUNG: You have heard the announcement made by the Clerk of the Convention, and the President will therefore state that by a vote of 45 to 0, a unanimous vote, this Convention has voted to ratify the proposed amendment to the Constitution of the United States submitted to this Convention for its consideration.

Is there any other business to come before the Convention?

MR. JUDSON HANNIGAN of Belmont: Mr. Chairman, I move that we adjourn without date.

MR. ARTHUR L. STANEK of Boston: Mr. President.

PRESIDENT YOUNG: For what purpose does the gentleman rise?

MR. ARTHUR L. STANEK: I believe this is an occasion when it is appropriate to pay our last respects to Mr. Prohibition, and if I am permitted I shall be very glad to perform the ceremony.

PRESIDENT YOUNG: There is a motion before the House.

(Cries of "Question.")

PRESIDENT YOUNG: The motion has been made that the Convention now adjourn without date, and upon that motion, under the rules of this Convention, no debate is in order. The Chair, with much regret, is therefore required to rule that the gentleman is out of order in speaking to the motion to adjourn. The question is on the motion that this Convention adjourn without date. All those in favor of the motion will say Aye. (Chorus of Ayes.) Those opposed, No. (No response.) The Ayes have it and the Convention is adjourned.

Thereupon, at 1 o'clock P.M., the Constitutional Convention was dissolved.

MICHIGAN*

CONVENTION RECORD

Lansing, Michigan

Monday, April 10, 1933

FIRST DAY

Monday, April 10, 1933

In pursuance of the provisions of Act No. 28 of the Public Acts of 1933, the delegates elected to ratify or reject the proposed amendments to the Constitution of the United States of America, as submitted by the Congress of the United States as follows:

Seventy-second Congress of the United States of America

AT THE SECOND SESSION

Begun and held at the City of Washington on Monday, the fifth day of December, one thousand nine hundred and thirty-two

JOINT RESOLUTION

Proposing an amendment to the Constitution of the United States

Resolved by the Senate and House of Representatives of the United States of America in Congress assembled (two-thirds of each House concurring therein), That the following article is hereby proposed as an amendment to the Constitution of the United States, which shall be valid to all intents and purposes as part of the Constitution when ratified by conventions in three-fourths of the several States:

ARTICLE ___

Section 1. The eighteenth article of amendment to the Constitution of the United States is hereby repealed.

Section 2. The transportation or importation into any State, Territory, or possession of the United States for delivery or use therein of intoxicating liquors, in violation of the laws thereof, is hereby prohibited.

Section 3. This article shall be inoperative unless it shall have been ratified as an amendment to the Constitution by conventions in the several States, as provided in the Constitution, within seven years from the date of the submission hereof to the States by the Congress.

Jno. N. Garner
Speaker of the House of Representatives

Charles Curtis
Vice-President of the United States and President of the Senate

* Printed. The act of the legislature providing for the convention is omitted here.

Met in Convention in the Hall of the House of Representatives in the Capitol in the city of Lansing, at 10:00 o'clock A.M., and were called to order by the Lieutenant Governor, Hon. Allen E. Stebbins, who was designated as President of the Convention by said Act No. 28.

The Rev. Father Clarence Kane, of Lansing, offered the following prayer:

"The Lord God of Wisdom set upon us thy divine light that we may know thy will. Give us, likewise, strength that we may always have the courage and the strength to follow what is right. Amen."

Myles F. Gray, Clerk of the House of Representatives, having been designated as Secretary of the Convention, and Fred B. Collins, Sergeant-at-Arms of the House of Representatives, having been designated as Sergeant-at-Arms of the Convention by said Act No. 28, took and subscribed the constitutional oath of office, which was administered by the President of the Convention.

DELEGATES-ELECT

The President directed the Secretary to read a communication from the Secretary of State, as follows:

DEPARTMENT OF STATE, LANSING, April 10, 1933

HONORABLE ALLEN E. STEBBINS
Lieutenant Governor
Lansing, Michigan

HONORABLE SIR:

I enclose herewith a certified list of delegates-elect to the convention called for the purpose of ratifying or rejecting the twenty-first amendment to the Constitution of the United States of America, as shown by the original returns as transmitted to this office.

Very respectfully,
FRANK D. FITZGERALD
Secretary of State

The following is the list of delegates-elect:

Alger District—L. B. Chittenden
Allegan County—Raymond Lee Anglemire
Alpena District—Arthur W. Wilcox
Antrim District—Guy H. Kane
Arenac District—Herman N. Butler
Barry County—Eugene Davenport
Bay County, First District—Adolph J. Rehmus
Bay County, Second District—Samuel H. Castanier
Berrien County, First District—Julius J. Krieger
Berrien County, Second District—Doric C. Hawks
Branch County—Mortimer W. Olds
Calhoun County, First District—Charles E. Gauss
Calhoun County, Second District—Howard W. Cavanaugh
Cass County—Earl B. Sill
Charlevoix District—Thomas C. Kroupa
Cheboygan District—John C. Rittenhouse
Chippewa County—Robert S. Moore
Clinton County—Herbert Armbrustmacher

Delta County—Cornelius Gallagher
Dickinson County—Earl M. Lafreniere
Eaton County—Albert M. Ewert
Emmet District—John B. Vallier
Genesee County, First District—
Carl Bonbright
James Martin
Genesee County, Second District—Frank J. Sawyer
Gogebic County—Thomas J. Landers
Grand Traverse County—Timothy R. Temple
Gratiot County—Edwin Rasor
Hillsdale County—George D. Schermerhorn
Houghton County, First District—William L. Stannard
Houghton County, Second District—James T. Healy
Huron County—William J. Riley
Ingham County, First District—Homer D. Parker
Ingham County, Second District—William J. Barber
Ionia County—Fred A. Chapman
Iron County—Martin S. McDonough
Isabella County—T. R. McNamara
Jackson County, First District—John W. Miner
Jackson County, Second District—Dean G. Kimball
Kalamazoo County, First District—Dean Halford
Kalamazoo County, Second District—William F. Montague
Kent County, First District—
Charles R. Bowman
Dorothy S. McAllister
John J. Smolenski
Kent County, Second District—John M. Dunham
Kent County, Third District—William S. Lamoreaux
Lapeer County—Loren H. Richards
Lenawee County—Bert D. Chandler
Livingston County—Bert S. Pate
Macomb County—Austin W. Heine
Manistee County—William D. Manchester
Marquette County—Connor Cowpland
Mason County—Fred J. Hermann
Mecosta District—Arnold C. Misteli
Menominee County—Hugh Bresnahan
Midland District—Frank I. Wixom
Monroe County—Henry F. R. Frincke
Montcalm County—Art Jensen
Muskegon County, First District—Fred J. Loewe
Muskegon County, Second District—Elliott D. Prescott
Newaygo District—Robert W. Mason
Oakland County, First District—Preston Allen
Oakland County, Second District—Clarence W. Seery
Ontonagon District—Edwin J. Evans
Osceola District—Floyd E. Doherty
Ottawa County—William A. Hanrahan
Presque Isle District—Edward A. Westrope
Saginaw County, First District—
Albert S. Harvey
Frank A. Picard
Saginaw County, Second District—Otto J. Conzelmann
Sanilac County—Robert A. Turrel
Shiawassee County—William J. McCullough
St. Clair County, First District—Charlotte H. McMorran

St. Clair County, Second District—John H. Schlinkert
St. Joseph County—Daniel J. Gerow
Tuscola County—Wilbert H. Cook
Van Buren County—Cecil A. Runyan
Washtenaw County—Nathan S. Potter
Wayne County, First District—
Mary E. Alger
Andrew C. Baird
Charles E. Bartlett
Robert H. Clancy
Helen R. Dean
Emil J. DeBaeke
William F. Dettling
Catherine D. Doran
Frank D. Eaman
Rex Humphrey
Roscoe B. Huston
Arthur J. Lacey
Sidney T. Miller
Geo. A. Ott
Charles A. Roxborough
Robert D. Wardell
John W. Woznak
Wayne County, Second District—Clyde Austin
Wayne County, Third District—Stephen S. Skrzycki
Wayne County, Fourth District—R. M. Ashley
Wayne County, Fifth District—Elton R. Eaton
Wexford District—Lundy J. Deming

STATE OF MICHIGAN—DEPARTMENT OF STATE

To all to whom these presents shall come:

I, FRANK D. FITZGERALD, Secretary of State of the State of Michigan and Custodian of the Great Seal thereof, DO HEREBY CERTIFY, That I have compared the annexed and foregoing list of all delegates-elect to the convention called for the purpose of ratifying or rejecting the twenty-first amendment to the Constitution of the United States of America, with the original returns as transmitted to this office, and that it is a true and correct list.

SEAL

In witness whereof, I have hereunto set my hand and affixed the Great Seal of the State at the Capitol, in the City of Lansing, this tenth day of April, A.D. 1933.

FRANK D. FITZGERALD
Secretary of State

The following communication from the Governor was read:

EXECUTIVE OFFICE, LANSING, April 10th, 1933

Because Charles E. Bartlett of Detroit, on account of a death in his family, cannot serve as a delegate to the Convention called for the purpose of acting upon the proposed Twenty-first Amendment to the Constitution of the United States, by virtue of authority vested in me I hereby appoint you, Robert J. Teagan, of 8100 Dexter Boulevard, Detroit, a delegate to said Convention in place of Charles E. Bartlett.

WILLIAM A. COMSTOCK
Governor

The roll of Delegates was called by the Secretary, who announced that a quorum was present.

Mr. DeBaeke was absent.

TAKING OATH OF OFFICE

The Secretary then called the names of the Delegates-elect, who came forward in groups of ten and took and subscribed the constitutional oath of office, which was administered by the President.

ADDRESS BY THE PRESIDENT

The President then addressed the convention as follows:

This is a historic gathering, the first of its kind in the United States, and the first in this state under the new law. By an extraordinary large majority the voters of America have unanimously demanded legislation legalizing the manufacture of intoxicating liquors, beer and wine, and due to the lengthy process necessary for the enactment of laws to that effect, have likewise demanded action for sale of light wines and beer. It would have cost this state $300,000.00 to have had a convention under the old law, but we had a Senator who saw a short route out, that would save this state that large amount of money in this time of stress, and at this time I want to introduce to this audience the Hon. Adolph Heidkamp of Houghton, Michigan.

ADDRESS BY SENATOR HEIDKAMP

MR. CHAIRMAN, DELEGATES TO THE CONVENTION, LADIES AND GENTLEMEN:

It was very kind of the presiding officer to ask me to come up here and be introduced to the members of this convention. As it is getting close to luncheon time, and you didn't come here to listen to speeches, I won't inflict one on you. As Lieutenant Governor Stebbins just said, you are making history. This is the first time that a convention of this nature has convened. The bill which I introduced, and which become law, paved the way and made it possible to have this convention today, and also made it possible for the State of Michigan to be the first state in the Union to vote for the repeal of the eighteenth amendment. My bill was meant to be fair to all. As the Governor mentioned, to call a special meeting or special election, would entail an expense of approximately $300,000.00 on the state. This way the total cost will be a little over $3,000.00. This is quite a saving, and we are here to economize, and this was a good way of doing it.

The voters at the election last Novermber expressed themselves in no uncertain way, showing they were not satisfied with the prohibition law, as we now have it, and this bill gave you delegates an opportunity to carry out the will of the people expressed at that election.

If conditions in the country were bad before the eighteenth amendment was placed on the books, every fair-minded and honest person must admit that it didn't improve since. I wish to congratulate the delegates to this convention who were elected from the various districts, and I hope that the action you will take here today, will be of benefit not only to the State of Michigan, but to the Union. After you cast your vote for repeal of the eighteenth amendment there is still a so-called Wiley Act, I believe, which prohibits the manufacture and sale of wines and beer, and unless that act is also repealed, it will be illegal to manufacture or sell wines or beers or liquors. There is a bill introduced in the legislature, and it may be passed within a few days, to regulate the manufacture and sale of intoxicating liquors. I warn the members of both Houses to be careful—take their time. The people waited for fifteen years for this convention and the repeal of the eighteenth amendment, and it will be a good deal better for all concerned, if they would wait another month or two if necessary, and have a bill passed that will better conditions, and if it will, I hope that everybody will obey that law. If it will not better conditions after giving it a fair trial, I would be the first one to say "repeal it." It is up to the people of the State to say what this should be and how it should work. I cannot say at this time, when it will be passed. It is in a committee of the Senate, and the same bill has been introduced in the House. The so-called prohibition committee, of which I am a member, has been working every day, and some changes have been suggested, and no doubt others will be made. As stated before, let us take our time, prepare a bill that is fair to everybody, then pass it, live up to it, and if we all do so, I know conditions will become better, and I hope you will help to make them so. I thank you.

The President announced that the convention would be governed by the Senate rules.

The President announced that the next order of business was the

NOMINATION AND ELECTION OF PRESIDENT PRO TEM

Mr. Clancy placed in nomination Mrs. Mary E. Alger of Detroit, as follows:

It was only a few years ago that one of the most terrible laws ever written on our statute books, "a pint for a life" law, was enacted, under which a woman with ten children was sent to prison for life for the sale of gin. The world got that news with great horror. Michigan got a black eye all over the United States. That law was the very essence of cruelty, brutality and barbarity, and so it is justice, and it is irony of history, that we meet in this very chamber where that law was put through and where it was supported and defended, to strike the death blow to the eighteenth amendment. That law, of course, was put through under the dictates of the Anti-Saloon League, and was defended and supported on the floor of the House of Congress by the congressmen of this district. Presidents, governors, legislators, practically every Senator and every Congressman was terrorized. Not only that, but the judiciary was under the yoke. Not only that, but the people lost in revenue close to four billion dollars. This system of tyranny supported and defended gangsters, gunmen and racketeers. A nation wondered who was going to deliver it. There arose in this country two groups, the Crusaders and the W. O. for N. P. R. Now the eighteenth amendment is on the way to its death. It was only a couple of months ago I had the honor of voting in Congress for repeal. This afternoon we are going to ratify the 21st amendment as the first state in the Union to have that honor. Michigan won by such a large majority that the United States will now say that Michigan has wiped from its standard the blood of that notorious "life for a pint" law.

From the various sections of the Women's Organizations for National Prohibition Reform one lady has stood out; a lady with a spirit as fine as silken strands, but with the strength of steel cables. This woman has gone night and day throughout the state, sometimes traveling all night, sometimes only speaking to a group of twenty or thirty persons, arousing them against this tyranny which threatened our representative government. The Alger family has always been known as a fine family. Colonel Alger, the father, discovered in the civil war a red-headed officer hidden in the middle west. He said, "this man has merit," and he became General Phil Sheridan. We in

Detroit, know how much Col. Alger and his good wife have done for our Commonwealth. It is unthinkable that we delegates should consider anybody else for this position of honor. I nominate as President pro tempore, as required in the law, Mrs. Mary E. Alger.

Delegate Robert D. Wardell was then recognized and spoke as follows:

MR. PRESIDENT, DELEGATES TO THE CONVENTION:

The nomination just made by Delegate Clancy, in my judgment, is a most fitting one because of the energy and the zeal that Mrs. Alger has put behind this work of prohibition reform.

I recall distinctly at the time of the adoption of the 19th amendment to the federal constitution that the professional prohibitionists caused to have broadcast throughout the length and breadth of the country this significant statement: "Now that the women have the vote in America, the 18th Amendment to the federal constitution is locked up forever."

As time went on, the women of the country commenced to realize the impractibility of prohibition as exemplified by the 18th amendment in the federal constitution. They commenced to realize that these iniquitous laws were not producing temperance, and this condition smoldered in the minds of the women and mothers in our country for many years, and particularly in this state.

It remained, however, without any concerted movement until the development of the Women's Organization, the Michigan Branch presided over by Mrs. Alger and her splendid associates. It was she and her organization that kindled the fires of patriotism and temperance in the prohibition reform movement in Michigan. It was through her untiring efforts and her zeal for prohibition reform that she was able to get into a functioning organization over 107,000 women, providing a phalanx of strength unheard of before.

It was largely through this organized effort of the associated groups for prohibition reform, but particularly the Women's Organization headed by Mrs. Alger, that we were able to drive from the legislative halls in this state such creatures as the Rev. R. N. Holsaple who cracked the whip over this legislature for many years.

To Mrs. Alger, more than to any other, is due this significant convention, and it is indeed a great, great pleasure and in fact a privilege for me to second the nomination of Mary E. Alger as president pro tempore of this convention, which has been called for the specific purpose of ratifying the 21st amendment to the federal constitution which repeals the 18th amendment.

MRS. MCALLISTER was recognized and spoke as follows:

I wish to second the nomination of Mrs. Mary E. Alger, as President pro tempore of this convention. Michigan is the first state of the entire United States in which women have ever had a chance to vote on the 18th amendment. Michigan is the first state to repeal the eighteenth amendment. Newspapers and the political leaders of the country said we would never repeal the eighteenth amendment. In order to achieve a victory over the dry forces and abolish prohibition it was necessary to have concerted plans and form battle lines for a militant campaign. Michigan was fortunate to have a fine group of disinterested young men to take up, under the banner of the Crusaders, the fight for repeal. It was doubly fortunate to have a woman of such splendid ability and untiring zeal to take the leadership of women in our state and transform into action the growing sentiment for repeal. Mrs. Alger was chairman of Women's Organization for National Prohibition Reform. Day by day she traveled over Michigan, attended countless meetings and marshalled the forces of every community for repeal. Without these organizations Michigan would today still be under the state prohibition law, which is even worse than the 18th amendment. But within six months we have had two great elections in our state. At one we repealed our state prohibition law and at the other we repealed the eighteenth amendment by a vote so overwhelmingly large we have given courage for repeal to every state in the nation. In this hour of success it is fitting we should reward with honor the distinguished woman who has led the fight for repeal. It is my honor to second the nomination of Mrs. Alger.

Mr. Anglemire was recognized and spoke as follows:

I come from a rural county, neighbor to Barry county, and in the same senatorial district, and I do not believe any man was insulted more because he took a stand for the repeal of the 18th amendment. Four years ago I was a candidate for Congress in the 4th district and at that time it was very unpopular. I just want to say: God made the country, man made the town, strange prophets made the prohibition law, which today we turn down. I also support the nomination of Mrs. Alger.

Mr. Wardell moved that the nominations be closed. There was no objection, and it was so ordered.

Mrs. McAllister moved that the Secretary cast a unanimous vote for Mrs. Alger. The motion prevailed. Ninety-seven votes were cast for the election of Mrs. Alger as President pro tempore, as follows:

FOR MARY E. ALGER

Allen	Dunham	Lamoreaux	Richards
Anglemire	Eaman	Landers	Riley
Armbrustmacher	Eaton	Loewe	Rittenhouse
Ashley	Evans	Manchester	Roxborough
Austin	Ewart	Martin	Runyan
Baird	Frincke	Mason	Sawyer
Barber	Gallagher	Miller	Schermerhorn
Bonbright	Gauss	Miner	Schlinkert
Bowman	Gerow	Misteli	Seery
Bresnahan	Halford	Montague	Sill
Butler	Hanrahan	Moore	Skrzycki
Castanier	Harvey	McAllister (Mrs.)	Smolenski
Cavanagh	Hawks	McCullough	Stannard
Chandler	Healy	McDonough	Teagan
Chapman	Heine	McMorran (Mrs.)	Temple
Chittenden	Hermann	McNamara	Turrel
Clancy	Humphrey	Olds	Vallier
Conzelman	Huston	Ott	Wardell
Cook	Jensen	Parker	Westrope
Cowpland	Kane	Pate	Wilcox
Dean (Mrs.)	Krieger	Picard	Wixom
Deming	Kimball	Potter	Woznak
Dettling	Kroupa	Prescott	
Doherty	Lacy	Rasor	
Doran (Miss)	Lafreniere	Rehmus	

Mr. Davenport, the dry delegate, asked that in deference to the community he represented, that he be excused from voting. He was excused.

Mr. DeBaeke not having answered to the roll call was not present to vote.

Mr. Wardell moved that a committee of three delegates be appointed by the President to escort the President pro tem to the chair.

The motion prevailed.

The President named as such committee, Messrs. Wardell, Martin and Gauss.

Mrs. Alger, escorted by the committee, was presented to the Convention by the President, and addressed the Convention as follows:

I fully realize that this honor is not conferred on me as an individual, but as Chairman of the Women's Organization for National Prohibition Reform, and so as representative of that organization I wish to express our grateful thanks and deep appreciation, and also wish to acknowledge the untiring help that was given by the citizens of Michigan, both men and women, in obtaining the goal of repeal of the 18th amendment. Today Michigan is the first state to ratify the 21st amendment. It is the first state to put its ideals into practical effect. Michigan leads the way in every way. The people of our state are a great people, but especially today they have just cause to take pride in their own action. We are proud of them, we are proud to belong to them, and we congratulate them.

RESOLUTIONS

Mr. Teagan offered the following resolution:

Convention Resolution No. 1.

Resolved, That a committee of nine delegates be appointed by the President to consider and recommend the compensation to be paid to employes of the convention.

The resolution was adopted.

The President named as such committee, Messrs. Teagan, Heine, Prescott, Seery, Wilcox, Roxborough, Healy, Conzelman and Madam McAllister.

Madam Dean offered the following resolution:

Convention Resolution No. 2.

Resolved, That the President appoint a committee of five delegates to audit and approve all incidental expense accounts incurred for the purpose of holding and conducting this convention.

The resolution was adopted.

The President named as such committee, Madam Dean and Messrs. Frincke, Westrope, Hanrahan and Wixom.

Mr. Lacy offered the following resolution:

Convention Resolution No. 3.

Resolved, That the President appoint a committee of five delegates to invite and escort the Justices of the Supreme Court to the convention.

The resolution was adopted.

The President named as such committee, Messrs. Lacy, Chandler, Cavanagh, McNamara and Madam Doran.

Mr. Sawyer offered the following resolution:

Convention Resolution No. 4.

Resolved, That the President appoint a committee of three delegates to invite and escort the state officers to the convention.

The resolution was adopted.

The President named as such committee, Messrs. Sawyer, Huston and Chapman.

Mr. Clancy offered the following resolution:

Convention Resolution No. 5.

Resolved, That the President appoint a committee of five delegates to invite and escort the Governor to the convention, and that the Governor be requested to address the Convention.

The resolution was adopted.

The President named as such committee, Messrs. Clancy, Miner, Picard, Schermerhorn and Manchester.

Mr. Miller offered the following resolution:

Convention Resolution No. 6.

Resolved, That the President appoint a committee of fifteen delegates to whom shall be submitted the record of this convention for approval before same shall be printed and bound.

The resolution was adopted.

The President named as such committee, Messrs. Miller, Chittenden, Bowman, Eaton, Butler, Temple, Rehmus, Davenport, Ewart, Parker, Halford, Dunham, Bresnahan, Allen and Madam McMorran.

Mr. Rittenhouse offered the following resolution:

Convention Resolution No. 7.

Resolved, That the Secretary of the convention be and he hereby is authorized and directed to execute voucher for all expenses of the convention and certify to the same when approved by the committee authorized for that purpose, and when so executed and certified shall be paid as other expenses of the state are paid out of the general fund of the state upon warrant of the auditor general.

The resolution was adopted.

Mr. Anglemire offered the following resolution:

Convention Resolution No. 8.

Resolved, That the Secretary of the convention be and he hereby is authorized and directed to have printed and bound 1,500 copies of the journal of proceedings of this convention, and that one copy be mailed to each delegate of the convention, one copy to each member of the legislature, and to such other parties as make request for the same. And be it further

Resolved, That twenty-five copies be furnished the State Library, twenty-five copies to the State Law Library, 250 copies to the Secretary of State to supply any requests made, and one copy to each of the state officers and department and fifteen copies to the clerk of the Supreme Court for use of the court.

The resolution was adopted.

Mrs. Alger offered the following resolution:

Convention Resolution No. 9.

A resolution ratifying the proposed amendment to the Constitution of the United States.

WHEREAS, On February twenty-eight, nineteen hundred thirty-three, William A. Comstock, Governor of the State of Michigan, submitted to the fifty-seventh Legislature of the State of Michigan a message, together with copy of a resolution of Congress, as follows:

EXECUTIVE OFFICE, LANSING, February 28, 1933

TO THE FIFTY-SEVENTH LEGISLATURE OF THE STATE OF MICHIGAN:

GENTLEMEN:—I have the honor to transmit herewith for your consideration a communication from the Secretary of State of the United States, together with copy referred to therein of a Resolution of Congress, entitled:

"JOINT RESOLUTION Proposing an amendment to the constitution of the United States."

Yours respectfully,

WILLIAM A. COMSTOCK
Governor

No. 677

UNITED STATES OF AMERICA

DEPARTMENT OF STATE

To all to whom these presents shall come, GREETING:

I Certify That the copy hereto attached is a true copy of a Resolution of Congress entitled "JOINT RESOLUTION Proposing an Amendment to the Constitution of the United States" the original of which is on file in this Department.

SEAL

In testimony whereof, I, Henry L. Stimson, Secretary of State, have hereunto caused the Seal of the Department of State to be affixed and my name subscribed by the Acting Chief Clerk of the said Department, at the City of Washington, in the District of Columbia, this 21st day of February, 1933.

HENRY L. STIMSON
Secretary of State
By P. F. ALLEN
Acting Chief Clerk

SEVENTY-SECOND CONGRESS OF THE UNITED STATES OF AMERICA

AT THE SECOND SESSION

Begun and held at the City of Washington on Monday, the fifth day of December, one thousand nine hundred and thirty-two

JOINT RESOLUTION

Proposing an amendment to the Constitution of the United States

Resolved by the Senate and House of Representatives of the United States of America in Congress assembled (two-thirds of each House concurring therein), That the following article is hereby proposed as an amendment to the Constitution of the United States, which shall be valid to all intents and purposes as part of the Constitution when ratified by conventions in three-fourths of the several States:

ARTICLE ___ ___

Section 1. The eighteenth article of amendment to the Constitution of the United States is hereby repealed.

Section 2. The transportation or importation into any State, Territory, or possession of the United States for delivery or use therein of intoxicating liquors, in violation of the laws thereof, is hereby prohibited.

Section 3. This article shall be inoperative unless it shall have been ratified as an amendment to the Constitution by conventions in the several States, as provided in the Constitution, within seven years from the date of submission hereof to the States by the Congress.

JNO. N. GARNER
Speaker of the House of Representatives
CHARLES CURTIS
Vice-President of the United States and President of the Senate

and

WHEREAS, The fifty-seventh Legislature of the State of Michigan did enact Senate Bill No. 63, file No. 71, (being Senate Enrolled Act No. 6, Public Act No. 28 of the Public Acts of the State of Michigan for the year nineteen hundred thirty-three), entitled:

"An act to provide for a convention for the purpose of ratifying or rejecting the twenty-first amendment to the constitution of the United States of America,"

in compliance with the Joint Resolution of the Congress of the United States as above stated, which said Public Act No. 28 was signed by the Governor of the State of Michigan on March eleventh, nineteen hundred thirty-three, and

WHEREAS, In accordance with the provisions of said Public Act No. 28, the people of the State of Michigan did elect delegates to a convention to be held on the tenth day of April, nineteen hundred thirty-three, for the purpose in said act set forth, viz: The ratification or rejection of said proposed amendment to the Constitution of the United States, and

WHEREAS, We, the delegates duly elected to said convention for the purpose above stated, are in convention assembled this tenth day of April, nineteen hundred thirty-three, now therefore be it

Resolved, By the delegates of the convention of the State of Michigan, that in the name of, and on behalf of the people of the State of Michigan, and by virtue of the authority vested in us, we do hereby ratify, approve and assent to the said proposed amendment to the Constitution of the United States; and be it further

Resolved, That certified copies of the foregoing preamble and resolution be transmitted to the Secretary of State of the State of Michigan, to be certified by him to the Secretary of State of the United States of America, in the manner provided by said Public Act No. 28 of the Public Acts of the State of Michigan for the year nineteen hundred thirty-three.

Mr. Clancy moved that the resolution be referred to a Special Committee of six to be appointed by the President.

The motion prevailed.

The President named as such committee: Messrs. Clancy, Eaman, Lacy, Baird, Cavanagh and Picard.

Mr. Chapman moved that the Convention take a recess until 2:00 o'clock P.M.

The motion prevailed, the time being 12:00 M.

The President announced that the Convention would be in recess until 2:00 o'clock P.M.

After Recess

2:00 o'clock P.M.

The Convention was called to order by the President pro tem.

The following communication from the Governor was read:

EXECUTIVE OFFICE, LANSING, April 10th, 1933

Because Emil J. DeBaeke of Detroit, on account of illness, cannot serve as a delegate to the convention called for the purpose of acting upon the proposed twenty-first amendment to the constitution of the United States, by virtue of the authority vested in me, I hereby appoint you, Victor H. DeBaeke, of Detroit, a delegate to said convention in place of Emil J. DeBaeke.

WILLIAM A. COMSTOCK
Governor of Michigan

Mr. DeBaeke then took and subscribed to the oath of office, which was administered by the President, and took his seat.

MR. EAMAN: The law under which this Convention is called, provides that the delegates adopt their own rules of order. It was stated this morning by the President, the rules of State Senate should obtain. However, it seems to several of us we should formally go on record adopting our own rules of order. Most of you are not familiar with the rules of either the House of Representatives or the Senate, but we are all generally familiar with Roberts' Rules of Order. I move that we adopt Roberts' Rules of Order under which the deliberations of this Convention shall be held.

The question being on the motion to adopt Roberts' Rules of Order.

The motion prevailed.

The Sergeant-at-Arms announced the committee with the State Officers. The State Officers, escorted by the committee, were conducted to seats.

The Sergeant-at-Arms announced the committee with the Justices of the Supreme Court. The Justices, escorted by the committee, were conducted to seats.

The Sergeant-at-Arms announced the committee with the Governor. The Governor, escorted by the committee, was conducted to the rostrum.

The President pro tempore introduced Captain Frank D. Picard, who presented the Governor to the Convention as follows:

Distinguished guests, delegates and friends: I am very happy that Mrs. Alger gave you my name, because I am supposed to introduce the Governor of the State, and I do not want to be in a position of a man who once introduced William Jennings Bryan. Mr. Bryan was supposed to speak and had 15 minutes between trains. The man spoke for 13 minutes of the 15, leaving Mr. Bryan only two minutes to speak and make the train. After the speech was over, an old fellow in the back of the room who could not hear very well was asked how he liked the speech of Mr. Bryan. He replied, "I didn't think so much of Bryan's speech, but the fellow who talked the last two minutes was a darby!" As has been said before, you delegates to this convention are making history, and you who are attending the convention are watching history in the making. If any one had predicted this scene ten years ago, they would have been hailed as fit candidates for the psychopathic ward, but even then the man who I am going to introduce, a courageous fellow, perhaps with more courage than political sense, who predicted just what would happen socially and politically in this country if the noble experiment continued being an experiment. Now we are here to start tearing down the house built upon the sands. We are here to lead the way for other states to follow, and for some reason or other I cannot understand why some persist that the end is not in sight, as is said in the morning paper by some extinguished leader of the dry cause, that they were going to keep up the fight. That reminds me of a story of a colored fellow who had gotten an opportunity to fight the champion. After the first round the manager asked the challenger how he was feeling, to which the fellow answered "He ain't doin' me no harm." After the second round the manager again asked how he felt, and the challenger again replied "He ain't doin' me no harm." After three more rounds, in which the colored fellow was looking in pretty bad shape, but still maintained he was being done no harm, the manager asked him how he was feeling by then. He replied "He ain't doin' me no harm, boss, an' he ain't doin' me no good." This convention ain't doin' the drys any good either. In this battle, there is no man who has taken a greater part than the present Governor of the State of Michigan. I might recall to you an incident that happened in Chicago at the national democratic convention. It was about 11 P.M., on the top floor of the Congress Hotel and a very tired man came out of the elevator and invited three or four friends to come into his room. He had just returned from a meeting of the platform committee of the democratic convention. He said to us: "You know, everybody on that committee feels the way we do about the 18th amendment, but I am afraid that for personal reasons it might not go through, as there is a great deal of pressure being brought to bear to stop the working of that plan, but I want to tell you and the rest of the delegation, so long as I am a member of the Michigan delegation on that platform committee, the words shall be written into that platform that "we favor repeal of the 18th amendment." As we look back at the deluge of votes against prohibition in the country, it does not seem such a courageous attitude, and on that night, with victory in your grasp, I think it took a lot of courage to do it. Other men might have had better press agents and been able to claim more than Governor Comstock, but I am here to tell you that "Bill" Comstock had more courage, because he came from a state that he didn't know at that time whether it was wet or dry, and had more to do with writing in that clause than any other man on that platform committee. You know personally that he is very charming, and there are those people who say he travels under false colors. They say he has a smile on his lips all the time, but back of that smile there is a seriousness that asserts itself when necessary. They say there is a twinkle in his eye, but that it is also very penetrating. They say he is easily approached, and that it really belies the dignity that is there, but they also say that there is no cloak about the friendship of this man, and after all, everybody admits that although there is the smile that can be a cloak for seriousness, and although there is the twinkle in his eyes, they can penetrate through spoken words, and the friendship that makes him easily accessible, all of that is a cloak for the human man, the friendly Governor. He has led us so far in this fight, and led us well. Some differ with him at this time, but his wisdom in refusing to permit any legislation on this matter to come before the people until after they had voiced their sentiments on the eighteenth amendment, has proven he looks into the future. As I say, he has led us well in the past. Let us have faith in him. I know you have democrats and republicans here today. This is no longer a political matter, and I say this for the benefit of the courteous gentleman who represents the dry cause. It is no longer a fight between them and us. It is a fight for this state. It is for the right, for principle and for country. May I now present the Governor of the State of Michigan, William A. Comstock.

ADDRESS BY GOVERNOR WILLIAM A. COMSTOCK

Members of the convention of Michigan and citizens of Michigan: It is a great privilege to be the Governor of the State of Michigan on this historic occasion. It is quite a chore to be the Governor of Michigan under present distressed conditions, and this occasion, which brings the fullfillment of one of the dreams of your Governor, makes up in part for some of the distress that comes to the Governor through the distressed conditions. As my flattering introducer has said, it has been many years that I have been in this fight to accomplish the repeal of the eighteenth amendment, and therefore the honor and distinction of coming before the Convention which finishes Michigan's part in the repeal of the eighteenth amendment, is something that I will always remember, and I know my descendants will also.

The last ten years when some of us discovered that after a short trial that prohibition didn't prohibit, that it only messed things up socially, these last ten years have been full of trials and tribulations, the first eight of them fighting an uphill fight in the interest of a principle, the last two of them fighting a fight to keep the rising tide of protest from sweeping everything before it and leaving chaos behind. I used to say that I spent the first few years of prohibition trying to keep the drys from getting the wets out of political life entirely, and I spent the last four years of my political life trying to keep the wets from "kicking" the drys out entirely. These great movements aren't won by the extremist. They carry the fight on and keep the principle alive, but the final decision lies in the great mass of people who want good government, and when they are sure they never fail in their verdict. So, we have decided to give up prohibition. We have decided to go back and try personal liberty once more, the personal liberty we had before prohibition. Now, personal liberty, my friends, doesn't mean license. That is what we people who have been in this fight for the sake of a principle, want to guard against. We want to be sure that in the reaction we don't go too far the other way again. That is why in the last ten days or two weeks I have asked my friends in the legislature, both republicans and democrats, to keep liquor legislation of all kinds from being discussed in these legislative halls. I wanted the people of the State of Michigan to vote on this question, shall we repeal the eighteenth amendment, and not get it messed up, whether we have 5c or 10c beer and drink it on the curbstone or in the top of a tree.

I want to congratulate the people of the State of Michigan on their good common sense and judgment, and for sending a convention here 99% pure, like Ivory soap. We are going to give the situation a good cleaning on that 99/100% pure soap. I am not saying a thing about the suds which will come later.

Now, I hope the next step in this matter will be that insofar as Michigan is concerned, will be the immediate consideration by this legislature of the beer bill, so-called, which really sets up the liquor control commission, as was contemplated in the amendment to the constitution last fall. It is going to be very simple to write into that bill, as presented to that legislature, the further legislation that is necessary to handle the whole liquor situation when the eighteenth amendment is repealed. Our present problem is to get the proper kind of a beer bill, because we are going to have by edict of congress, 3.2% beer, and it is going to be with us before the eighteenth amendment is repealed. Now, if we go too far, there is going to be a reaction which may prevent other states from taking the action we have taken here today We lead all the states of the Union in this action we are taking here today. We want to show the people of the United States of America and this State, that we can handle the beer situation and still be temperate, and we can do it, my friends, if the legislature, and I know they will, will give us the proper bill. We don't want the return of the old conditions—those conditions prior to 1918—any more than any one of those citizens who are dry on principle want the return of those conditions; nor do we want the conditions we have today to be maintained. We want a regulated traffic in liquor, one that makes for temperance and not for license. One of the things we have tried to guard against and want to guard against, all of us, is anything in a beer bill that will bring a return of the old barroom, so-called. We are all agreed on that. I think the bill the legislature is going to pass will prevent that.

Now, my friends, I trust we will all go away from here on this historic occasion with the resolve firmly in our hearts, that so far as we are able, we will bring these things that I have been discussing with you to pass, and if we do, we will return to Michigan, and to every state in the Union, that much to be desired personal liberty which we lost with the adoption of the eighteenth amendment in 1918. I thank you.

MRS. ALGER: We appreciate those very wise words and warning of the Governor.

Is the Special Committee appointed to consider the ratification resolution ready to report?

MR. EAMAN: Madam President, the committee is ready to report. The committee has carefully considered Convention Resolution No. 9, being the ratification resolution, and it was thought best, to amend the resolution along the line of the suggestion made by Mr. Picard this forenoon. It certainly can do no harm and might strengthen the resolution. We therefore recommend that the first resolving clause be amended so as to read as follows:

"*Resolved,* By the delegates of the convention of the State of Michigan, that in the name of, and on behalf of the people of the State of Michigan, and by virtue of the authority vested in us, we do hereby ratify, approve and assent to the said proposed amendment to the Constitution of the United States; and be it further"

And that as thus amended the resolution be adopted.

The question being on concurring in the report and recommendation of the committee,

The report and recommendation was adopted.

The question then being on the adoption of the ratification resolution, the roll was called and the Delegates voted as follows:

FOR RATIFICATION

Alger (Mrs.)	Armbrustmacher	Baird	Bowman
Allen	Ashley	Barber	Bresnahan
Anglemire	Austin	Bonbright	Butler

Castanier
Cavanagh
Chandler
Chapman
Chittenden
Clancy
Conzelman
Cook
Cowpland
Dean (Mrs.)
DeBaeke
Deming
Dettling
Doherty
Doran (Miss)
Dunham
Eaman
Eaton
Evans
Ewart
Fricke
Gallagher
Gauss
Gerow
Halford
Hanrahan
Harvey
Hawks
Healy
Heine
Hermann
Humphrey
Huston
Jensen
Kane
Krieger
Kimball
Kroupa
Lacy
Lafreniere
Lamoreaux
Landers
Loewe
Manchester
Martin
Mason
Miller
Miner
Misteli
Montague
Moore
McAllister (Mrs.)
McCullough
McDonough
McMorran (Mrs.)
McNamara
Olds
Ott
Parker
Pate
Picard
Potter
Prescott
Rasor
Rhemus
Riley
Richards
Rittenhouse
Roxborough
Runyan
Sawyer
Schermerhorn
Schlinkert
Seery
Sill
Skrzycki
Smolenski
Stannard
Teagan
Temple
Turrel
Vallier
Wardell
Westrope
Wilcox
Wixom
Woznak
99

AGAINST RATIFICATION 1

Davenport

THE PRESIDENT PRO TEM: A majority of all the delegates having voted therefore, the ratification resolution is adopted.

The president resumed the chair.

The Secretary then read the following telegram:

WASHINGTON, D.C., April 10, 1933

JUDGE B. D. CHANDLER

Lansing, Mich.

Extend my congratulations to Michigan Delegates on being first to ratify twenty-first amendment.

JOHN C. LEHR

Member of Congress, Second District

MR. LACY: I anticipate the main business of this Convention has been concluded, but I am unwilling to return home until I say something which will give us all an opportunity to reciprocate to one of the members of this Convention a very beautiful and courteous act which he performed this morning in explaining his vote on the question of election of our temporary president. I refer to the courteous and kindly manner in which our fellowmember of this Convention, Mr. Davenport, who acting under his commission from his district voted "no" on ratification, handled himself and his remarks to this Convention with respect to his vote. I want to personally acknowledge and I think every one of us wants him to know we all appreciate that very fine act which we would expect from a man of such culture and kindness. I rise to make the statement so that we may have an opportunity of paying to him our personal respects and admiration.

Mr. Davenport acknowledged the tribute, and thanked the delegates for their kind expressions.

Mr. Clancy: As has been said, our business is practically completed, but we should provide for the payment of the expenses of this convention. I therefore move that the compensation to be paid to the officers and employes of the convention be the same per diem as is paid officers and employes of the legislature.

The motion prevailed.

The President: As the Upper Peninsula has not been heard from, I want at this time to present the Honorable Martin S. McDonough of Iron River.

Mr. McDonough: Mr. Chairman, distinguished guests, fellow delegates: In behalf of those of us who come from the Northern Peninsula of Michigan, and personally, I point with a great deal of pride to the fact that the law, the Act which initiated the movement which brought us here, bore the name of a son of Houghton County, Senator Heidkamp, and having come this far, my fellow delegates from the Northern Peninsula feel as do I, that we should have our say before we leave. I take it that all who are here gathered believe and support that interpretation of government which promotes the genial and free spirit of our institution. Most of us here gathered feel that every person should have under the law the largest freedom consistent with the common good. For more than thirteen years many of us have with such eloquence as was possessed, expounded the virtue of this traditional American government and, my friends, we even continued so to do when for a long period of time such conduct was considered not quite respectable. We have, I maintain, today an unblemished, but all important element in man's self respect. With the coming of the prohibition era and in its wake came the Ku Klux Klan to impress upon us an intolerant will. Executives were so politically minded they did not oppose this, and we have seen all along the willingness during the past thirteen years, of this element in our political system to prostitute even the Christian religion to a political end. With these facts in mind we have proceeded to restore to all the people representative government. None of us are here to deny the evil of the old-time liquor traffic. Few are here but will admit that it is an evil only exceeded by the evil of the liquor traffic under the eighteenth amendment to the federal constitution, and it should be the sense of this convention that all the people should as far as possible, be protected against the abuse of a traffic which has always been vicious, but never more so than under the eighteenth amendment to the federal constitution. Now, my friends, through the ballot the people of Michigan have given us a mandate which we trust will dispose of this question. No controversy is admitted, and this comes at a time of grave national peril, when other and even greater matters of government await a national solution in order that our national life may be preserved, so in all sincerity, in closing, I urge the necessity of submission of all to the will of the great majority of our people on the question we have here considered, to do battle with and overcome the forces of indecision which threaten this country as a nation, and we as a people.

The Secretary: This morning a resolution was adopted providing for a committee of fifteen to approve of the journal of proceedings of this convention before the same is bound in printed form. After I have prepared the copy for printing, I will have it set up in type and submitted to the chairman (Mr. Miller), and copies will be mailed to each member of the committee, with a request that after he has read the journal he will return it to the chairman with any suggestions for corrections. The chairman will then send me the approved copy and the journal will be printed accordingly.

After debate as to the time to which the convention should adjourn, or whether it should be without day,

Mr. Rehmus moved that the convention adjourn without day.

The motion prevailed.

The Reverend Father William P. Schulte of Detroit offered the following benediction:

"We give Thee thanks, Almighty God, beneficent Father, and we ask that Thy blessing may descend upon all present who this day have convened in this historically important assembly by their deliberations and proceedings in restoration of that personal liberty on which it has been founded. We ask further that Thy blessing may descend most generously, upon those who gave their time and efforts in this cause. May the blessing of God, Father Almighty, Son and Holy Ghost descend upon you and remain with you forever, Amen."

The Governor, Justices of the Supreme Court and State Officers retired.

The President declared the convention adjourned *sine die,* the time being 3:25 o'clock P.M.

MYLES F. GRAY
Secretary of the Convention

CERTIFICATE

I, Myles F. Gray, Secretary of the convention called for the purpose of taking action on the proposed amendment to the constitution of the United States, hereby certify that the foregoing pages contain a correct record of the proceedings of said convention of the State of Michigan, held on the 10th day of April, 1933.

SEAL

In witness whereof, I have hereunto attached my official signature, at Lansing, this 11th day of April, 1933.

MYLES F. GRAY
Clerk of the House of Representatives
and Secretary of the Convention

ROSTER OF CONVENTION EMPLOYES

Myles F. Gray, Lansing, Clerk of the House, Secretary of Convention.
Don W. Canfield, Detroit, Secretary of Senate, Assistant Secretary.
Norman E. Philleo, Lansing, Journal Clerk.
Donna Miller, Cheboygan, Assistant Journal Clerk.
Rual H. Rice, Detroit, Official Stenographer.
Katherine Helmer, Lansing, Assistant Stenographer.
Isabel C. Nichols, Ann Arbor, Assistant Stenographer.
Catherine Heiler, Assistant Stenographer.
Fred B. Collins, Benton Harbor, Sergeant-at-Arms.
George B. McNally, Ionia, Chief Assistant Sergeant-at-Arms.
Carl McDonald, Menominee, Assistant Sergeant-at-Arms.
John R. Rowe, Benton Harbor, Assistant Sergeant-at-Arms.
James E. Holmes, Ferndale, Assistant Sergeant-at-Arms.
Louis D. Murphy, Edmore, Assistant Sergeant-at-Arms.
Armand Bergevin, Bay City, Assistant Sergeant-at-Arms.
H. W. Taft, Battle Creek, Assistant Sergeant-at-Arms.
Charles W. Stephenson, St. Joseph, Assistant Sergeant-at-Arms.

Theodore Goulait, St. Clair, Assistant Sergeant-at-Arms.
Ross W. Ross, Lansing, Financial Clerk.
Don Sigler, Battle Creek, Page.
Robert Harper, Lansing, Page.
Stanley Denek, Detroit, Page.
Dallard Murphy, Detroit, Page.
Arthur Jarrad, East Lansing, Page.
Chester McGee, Lansing, Cloak Room.
John H. Brown, Lansing, Cloak Room.
Hugh McLean, Sandusky, Janitor.
A. Lynn Barr, Shepherd, Janitor.
Con L. Pickott, Lansing, Janitor.
Richard Gleason, Lansing, Janitor.

RESOLUTION OF APPRECIATION

In view of the fact that none of the employes would accept any compensation for their services during the session of the Convention, the House of Representatives unanimously adopted the following resolution:

WHEREAS, Public Act No. 28 of the Public Acts of 1933 provided that the Clerk of the House of Representatives, Myles F. Gray, should act as secretary of the convention called for the purpose of taking action on the twenty-first amendment to the constitution of the United States, held at the Capitol in the city of Lansing on April 10th, 1933, and

WHEREAS, By virtue of said act the employes of the House also acted in their several capacities in assisting in the work of the convention, and

WHEREAS, The Clerk of the House devoted much time and effort in drafting the resolution providing for the repeal of the eighteenth amendment and the ratification of the twenty-first amendment, as well as all other resolutions and procedure for the holding of the convention, which was reflected in the orderly and successful conduct of said convention, and

WHEREAS, Each employe of the House and several employes of the Senate served in their several capacities in an efficient and satisfactory manner in helping to make the convention a success, and

WHEREAS, Neither the Clerk of the House nor any of the said employes expected or desired to receive any extra compensation for their services, and had requested that no allowance of compensation be made for such services; now, therefore, be it

Resolved, That we, the members of the House of Representatives, hereby give expression of our appreciation to the Clerk of the House and all employes for the services rendered, and commend the action of each one in declining to accept the compensation allowed by said convention by virtue of the provisions of said act.

MINNESOTA*

JOURNAL

OF THE

PROCEEDINGS OF THE CONVENTION

IN AND OF THE STATE OF MINNESOTA

HELD FOR THE PURPOSE OF CONSIDERING THE RATIFICATION

OF A CERTAIN PROPOSED AMENDMENT

TO THE

CONSTITUTION OF THE UNITED STATES OF AMERICA

PURSUANT TO CHAPTER 214 OF THE GENERAL LAWS OF 1933

On Tuesday, the 10th day of October, 1933, at twelve o'clock noon, at the Capitol in the City of St. Paul, Minnesota, all of the delegates to the convention provided for in Chapter 214 of the General Laws of Minnesota for the year 1933 met and proceeded to the transaction of business.

The Governor of the State of Minnesota called the meeting to order. Thereupon Fred A. Osanna, one of the delegates elected to said convention, nominated C. W. Bunn, also a delegate therein, to be president thereof and the nomination was seconded by A. C. Weiss, also a member of said convention. There being no other nominations for said office the said C. W. Bunn was thereupon duly elected president of said convention and took the chair and presided at the subsequent proceedings.

Following the election of president as aforesaid, Nate V. Keller, a delegate to said convention, nominated Margaret Culkin Banning, also a delegate therein, to be secretary of the said convention and the nomination was seconded by Mrs. Silas M. Bryan, also a delegate therein. There being no further nominations for said office the said Margaret Culkin Banning was thereupon duly elected as said secretary of said convention.

Thereupon the certificate of the Governor of Minnesota, certifying the names of all of the persons elected as delegates to this convention, was received and ordered to be placed on file, which was done.

It having been ascertained upon inspection of said certificate of the Governor that the following persons have been duly elected as members of this convention, to-wit:

Margaret Culkin Banning
C. W. Bunn
Victor E. Carlson
A. C. Welch
Edwin L. Lindell
A. C. Weiss
Harry J. O'Brien
Mrs. Silas M. Bryan
Laurence C. Hodgson
Thomas Gratzek
W. W. Nauth
Richard T. Daly
James F. Lynn
Fred Schilplin
Myrtle Harris
Fred A. Osanna
George W. Lawson
H. B. Hassenger
Nate V. Keller
W. E. Rowe
Jacob Ohlsen

* From a typewritten copy.

it was thereupon declared and ordered that said persons were the duly qualified and elected members of this convention. The oath of office of each of said delegates was then presented and having been found to be in proper form was received and ordered to be filed with the records of the convention.

Thereupon it was moved and seconded that the following resolution be adopted, to-wit:

WHEREAS, the Seventy-second Congress of the United States of America, at its second session, begun and held at the City of Washington on Monday, fifth day of December, One Thousand Nine Hundred and Thirty-two, did, by joint resolution duly adopted by each house of said Congress, propose as an amendment to the Constitution of the United States, which shall be valid to all intents and purposes as part of said Constitution when ratified by conventions in three-fourths of the several states, the following article, to-wit:

ARTICLE _____

Section 1. The eighteenth article of amendment to the Constitution of the United States is hereby repealed.

Section 2. The transportation or importation into any State, Territory, or possession of the United States for delivery or use therein of intoxicating liquors, in violation of the laws thereof, hereby is prohibited.

Section 3. This article shall be inoperative unless it shall have been ratified as an amendment to the Constitution by conventions in the several States, as provided in the Constitution, within seven years from the date of the submission hereof to the States by the Congress.

Now, therefore, be it resolved: That the said proposed amendment to the Constitution of the United States of America be and the same is hereby ratified by this Convention.

After due consideration the question was put upon the adoption of said resolution and the question being taken thereon.

And the roll of delegates being called, there were yeas 21 and nays none, as follows:

Those who voted in the affirmative were:

Margaret Culkin Banning
C. W. Bunn
Victor E. Carlson
A. C. Welch
Edwin L. Lindell
A. C. Weiss
Harry J. O'Brien
Mrs. Silas M. Bryan
Laurence C. Hodgson
Thomas Gratzek
W. W. Nauth
Richard T. Daly
James F. Lynn
Fred Schilplin
Myrtle Harris
Fred A. Osanna
George W. Lawson
H. B. Hassenger
Nate V. Keller
W. E. Rowe
Jacob Ohlsen

There were none voting in the negative.

So the resolution was unanimously adopted.

Thereupon it was ordered that the president and secretary of the convention should forthwith proceed to execute the certificate of the action of the convention in the adoption of the foregoing resolution pursuant to the provisions of Section 13, Chapter 214, General Laws of Minnesota of 1933, and report their action in executing such certificate to this convention.

Immediately thereupon the president and secretary, in the presence of the convention, executed a certificate of its said action in the adoption of the resolution above recited.

It was thereupon ordered that the president and secretary should transmit such certificate to the Secretary of State of Minnesota as provided by said statute.

A copy of said certificate was ordered to be attached to this Journal.

It was further ordered that the secretary of this convention, upon its final adjournment, should file with the Secretary of State of Minnesota the Journal of this convention, together with all other documents and papers received by this convention and referred to in this Journal.

It was further ordered that the secretary of the convention should certify to the proper state officers the record of each delegate in attending said convention and the number of miles necessarily traveled in going to and returning from St. Paul.

There being no further business before it the convention, upon motion duly made and seconded, then adjourned, *sine die.*

MARGARET CULKIN BANNING
Secretary

Attest:
C. W. BUNN
President

MISSOURI*

PROCEEDINGS OF CONVENTION

CALLED IN ACCORDANCE WITH THE PROCLAMATION

OF THE

GOVERNOR OF THE STATE OF MISSOURI

To consider and act upon the ratification of the
Amendment to the United States Constitution
providing for the repeal of the 18th Amendment

Held at

House Chamber, The Capitol
in the City of Jefferson
the 29th day of August
1933, at the hour of 10:00 o'clock A.M.

HONORABLE DWIGHT H. BROWN, called the Convention
to order; HONORABLE R. P. WEEKS, CHAIRMAN

JOURNAL OF A CONVENTION TO RATIFY THE 21st AMENDMENT TO THE CONSTITUTION OF THE UNITED STATES, HELD ON AUGUST THE 29th, 1933

Convention called to order by the Honorable Dwight H. Brown, Secretary of State, of the State of Missouri.

MR. DWIGHT H. BROWN: The hour of ten o'clock having arrived, by virtue of the proclamation of his Excellency, the Governor, this Convention will come to order. Will the delegates kindly stand while the Reverend E. W. Berlekamp, Pastor Central Evangelical Church, Jefferson City, invokes the divine blessing.

REV. E. W. BERLEKAMP: Adorable God, at the beginning of this Convention, we pause for a moment to invoke thy blessing upon the delegates to this Convention, upon the leaders and people of our beloved country, and thank thee for past blessings and benefits. We, as a people, are drawn from many people, yet under thy hand have we received your blessing. We are thankful for all those who were pioneers in the beginning of this Republic and we are grateful for the loyalty of those who gave the best they had of service and devotion for the common good to build a government that shall be based on justice and humanity. We are grateful for all these blessings, and help us, we beseech thee, to show our gratitude in ways which will leave to those who come after us as much of a blessing as we ourselves have received from those who have gone before us. Bless those who have been called to lead our people, and bless one who seeks to have thy will for himself and for the nation, whose

* Printed. The vote by counties on the election of delegates is omitted here.

servant he is. Continue to bless him as he brings his mind and heart to the solution of problems in our own and all nations.

We pray also for the Governor of this Commonwealth, for all others in positions of trust and responsibility. Give all men everywhere the will to bring us a new world in which all ungodly things shall have passed away, and in which righteousness and good will shall be eternally enthroned.

This we ask in the name of our common Lord—Amen.

MR. DWIGHT H. BROWN: At this time we will hear three communications directed to the delegates of this Convention. Mr. Warren D. Meng of the State Department, acting as reading clerk, will first read the message from the Second Session of the 72nd Congress.

MR. WARREN D. MENG (reads):

UNITED STATES OF AMERICA

DEPARTMENT OF STATE

To all to whom these presents shall come, GREETING:

I Certify That the copy hereto attached is a true copy of a Resolution of Congress entitled "JOINT RESOLUTION Proposing an Amendment to the Constitution of the United States," the original of which is on file in this department.

SEAL

In testimony whereof, I, Henry L. Stimson, Secretary of State, have hereunto caused the seal of the Department of State to be affixed and my name subscribed by the Acting Chief Clerk of the said Department, at the City of Washington, in the District of Columbia, this 21st day of February, 1933.

HENRY L. STIMSON
Secretary of State
By: P. F. ALLEN
Acting Chief Clerk

SEVENTY-SECOND CONGRESS OF THE UNITED STATES OF AMERICA

AT THE SECOND SESSION

Begun and held at the City of Washington on Monday, the fifth day of December, one thousand nine hundred and thirty-two

JOINT RESOLUTION

Proposing an amendment to the Constitution of the United States

Resolved by the Senate and House of Representatives of the United States of America in Congress assembled (two-thirds of each House concurring therein), that the following article is hereby proposed as an amendment to the Constitution of the United States, which shall be valid to all intents and purposes as part of the Constitution when ratified by conventions in three-fourths of the several States:

ARTICLE ___

Section 1. The eighteenth article of amendment to the Constitution of the United States is hereby repealed.

Section 2. The transportation or importation into any State, Territory, or possession of the United States for delivery or use therein of intoxicating liquors, in violation of the laws thereof, is hereby prohibited.

Section 3. This article shall be inoperative unless it shall have been ratified as an amendment to the Constitution by conventions in the several States, as provided in the Constitution, within seven years from the date of the submission hereof to the States by the Congress.

JNO. N. GARNER
Speaker of the House of Representatives

CHARLES CURTIS
Vice-President of the United States and President of the Senate

I certify that this Joint Resolution originated in the Senate.

EDWARD P. THAYER
Secretary

MR. DWIGHT H. BROWN: We will next hear a proclamation promulgated by his Excellency, Lieutenant-Governor Frank G. Harris, calling for elections in Missouri:

MR. WARREN D. MENG (reads):

STATE OF MISSOURI

DEPARTMENT OF STATE

To all to whom these presents shall come:

I, DWIGHT H. BROWN, Secretary of State of the State of Missouri, and keeper of the Great Seal thereof, hereby certify that the annexed pages contain a full, true and complete copy of the Proclamation of the Governor, dated July 25th, 1933, relating to the ratification by the State of Missouri of the 21st Amendment to the Constitution of the United States by Conventions and fixing the time and places for holding such Conventions.

As the same appears on file .... in this office.

SEAL

In testimony whereof, I hereunto set my hand and affix the GREAT SEAL of the State of Missouri. Done at the City of Jefferson, this Twenty-ninth day of August, A.D., Nineteen Hundred and Thirty-three.

DWIGHT H. BROWN
Secretary of State

J. R. HOLMAN
Chief Clerk

PROCLAMATION

I, FRANK G. HARRIS, Lieutenant-Governor and Acting Governor of the State of

Missouri, by virtue of the authority in me vested by law, do hereby make the following official Proclamation:

1. The Congress of the United States of America having proposed an amendment to the Constitution of the United States and having submitted such amendment to the several states by ratification by conventions, which said proposed amendment is as follows:

Section 1. The Eighteenth Article of Amendment to the Constitution of the United States is hereby repealed.

Section 2. The transportation or importation into any state, territory, or possession of the United States for delivery or use therein of intoxicating liquors, in violation of the laws there, is hereby prohibited.

Section 3. This Article shall be inoperative unless it shall have been ratified as an amendment to the Constitution by conventions in the several States, as provided in the Constitution, within seven years from the date of the submission hereof to the States by the Congress.

And House Bill No. 514 passed by the 57 General Assembly of Missouri, and which is now the law, authorizing the Governor by proclamation to call an election for the election of delegates to a State Convention, to be held for the purpose of voting upon the ratification of any amendment to the Constitution of the United States of America, proposed by the Congress thereof, and submitted to the several states for ratification by the convention method; and providing for the nomination of candidates for delegates to such conventions, and the manner of their election. Wherefore, pursuant to and under the authority of said Act this Proclamation is issued and the call for such an election and conventions is made.

2. I hereby fix Wednesday, July 26th, 1933, as the date and 3:00 o'clock P.M. of that day as the hour upon which the qualified electors of each precinct and voting district, of all counties and cities in the State having less than three hundred fifty thousand (350,000) inhabitants, shall meet in mass convention. Said mass conventions shall meet at places in such precinct or voting district as shall be designated by the County Court or board of election commissioners of such counties or cities, and elect four (4) delegates, qualified electors of such precinct or voting district, to attend a county convention to be held at the County Seat of such county on the date and hour fixed by me in this Proclamation; the qualified electors attending each such precinct or voting district convention shall divide into two (2) groups, one (1) favoring and one (1) opposing the proposed amendment, and each group shall elect two (2) delegates to said county convention.

3. I hereby fix Wednesday, July 26th, 1933, as the date and 3:00 o'clock P.M. as the hour upon which the qualified electors of each precinct and voting district, of all counties and cities in the State having three hundred fifty thousand (350,000) inhabitants or more, shall meet in mass conventions at places in such precinct or voting district to be designated by the board or boards of election commissioners of such counties and cities, and elect two (2) delegates, qualified electors of such precinct or voting district, to attend a senatorial district convention to be held on the date and hour and at the place in the senatorial district hereinafter fixed by me in this Proclamation; the qualified electors attending each such precinct or voting district convention in all counties and cities having three hundred fifty thousand (350,000) inhabitants, or more shall divide into two (2) groups, one (1) favoring and one (1) opposing the

proposed amendment, and each group shall elect one delegate to said senatorial district convention.

4. I hereby fix Thursday, July 27th, 1933, as the date and 11:00 o'clock A.M. of that day as the hour for the county conventions to be held at the County Seat of each county in this State having a population of less than three hundred fifty thousand (350,000) inhabitants. The delegates selected at the mass meetings in such counties shall assemble in such county conventions and divide into two (2) groups, one (1) favoring and one (1) opposing the proposed amendment, and each group shall elect four (4) delegates to a senatorial district convention to be held on the date and hour and at the place in such senatorial district fixed by me in this Proclamation.

5. I hereby fix Friday, July 28th, 1933, as the date and 3:00 o'clock P.M. of that day as the hour and the places designated at the end of this paragraph in each of the thirty-four (34) senatorial districts of this State as the place in such senatorial district for the holding of senatorial district conventions for the nomination of four (4) delegates (two (2) favoring and two (2) opposing the proposed amendment) to be voted upon at large, by the citizens qualified to vote, as delegates to the State Convention to be held as hereinafter provided. The places for the holding of senatorial district conventions are as follows:

DISTRICTS	NAME OF PLACE	CITY OR TOWN AND COUNTY IN MISSOURI
First	County Court House	Maryville, Mo., Nodaway Co.
Second	Division No. 3, County Court House	St. Joseph, Mo., Buchanan Co.
Third	County Court House	Plattsburg, Mo., Clinton Co.
Fourth	County Court House	Trenton, Mo., Grundy Co.
Fifth	Division No. 2, County Court House	Kansas City, Mo., Jackson Co.
Sixth	County Court House	Linneus, Mo., Linn Co.
Seventh	Assembly Hall of Southwest High Sch., 6521 Wornall Road	Kansas City, Mo., Jackson Co.
Eighth	County Court House	Kingston, Mo., Caldwell Co.
Ninth	County Court House	Macon, Mo., Macon Co.
Tenth	County Court House	Montgomery City, Mo., Montgomery Co.
Eleventh	County Court House	Bowling Green, Mo., Pike Co.
Twelfth	County Court House	Memphis, Mo., Scotland Co.
Thirteenth	County Court House	Paris, Mo., Monroe Co.
Fourteenth	County Court House	California, Mo., Moniteau Co.
Fifteenth	County Court House	Sedalia, Mo., Pettis Co.
Sixteenth	County Court House	Osceola, Mo., St. Clair Co.
Seventeenth	County Court House	Warrensburg, Mo., Johnson Co.
Eighteenth	County Court House	Neosho, Mo., Newton Co.
Nineteenth	County Court House	Marshfield, Mo., Webster Co.
Twentieth	County Court House	Greenfield, Mo., Dade Co.
Twenty-first	County Court House	Poplar Bluff, Mo., Butler Co.
Twenty-second	County Court House	Houston, Mo., Texas Co.
Twenty-third	County Court House	New Madrid, Mo., New Madrid Co.
Twenty-fourth	County Court House	Steelville, Mo., Crawford Co.
Twenty-fifth	Division No. 2, County Court House	Clayton, Mo., St Louis Co.
Twenty-sixth	County Court House	Farmington, Mo., St. Francois Co.
Twenty-seventh	County Court House	Vienna, Mo., Maries Co.

DISTRICTS	NAME OF PLACE	CITY OR TOWN AND COUNTY IN MISSOURI
Twenty-eighth	County Court House	Carthage, Mo., Jasper Co.
Twenty-ninth	Carpenter Branch Library, 3309 South Grand Ave.	City of St. Louis, Mo.
Thirtieth	Barr Branch Library, 1701 S. Jefferson Ave.	City of St. Louis, Mo.
Thirty-first	Public Library, 1301 Olive Street	City of St. Louis, Mo.
Thirty-second	Cabanne Branch Library, 1106 Union Blvd.	City of St. Louis, Mo.
Thirty-third	Howard School, 2333 Benton Street	City of St. Louis, Mo.
Thirty-fourth	Benton School, 2847 Kingshighway and Memorial Blvd.	City of St. Louis, Mo.

The delegates so elected to senatorial district conventions shall divide into two (2) groups, one (1) favoring and one (1) opposing the proposed amendment, and each group shall nominate two (2) candidates from such senatorial district to be voted upon at large by the qualified electors of this State as delegates to said State Convention.

6. I hereby fix Saturday, August 19, 1933, as the date and on that date between the hours fixed by law for the holding of General Elections in this State as the hours within and during which a Special Election shall be held in each voting precinct and district in the State of Missouri for the election in the State at large of the delegates to the State Convention aforesaid.

7. I hereby fix Tuesday, August 29th, 1933, as the date and 10:00 o'clock A.M. of that day as the hour and the State Capitol in the City of Jefferson as the place for the holding of a State Convention to be composed of the delegates elected thereto as aforesaid who shall proceed to organize by the election of a chairman and a secretary, and when so organized shall immediately vote upon the proposed amendment, whether to ratify or reject the same, and certify the result of such vote to the Secretary of State of the United States of America and Secretary of State of the State of Missouri.

8. The time intervening between the date of this Proclamation and the date herein fixed for the election of delegates to the Conventions in the State at large is limited. All state and county officers charged with the duties and responsibilities of carrying out the provisions of this Proclamation and of executing fully the law under which this Proclamation is issued are enjoined to special diligence for the orderly and effective holdings of the successive Conventions provided for hereunder and I request the chairmen and secretaries selected at all mass meetings and conventions held hereunder to make immediate report to proper authority of the actions had and taken at each such meeting and convention.

Done at the city of Jefferson on the 25th day of July, 1933.

FRANK G. HARRIS
Lieutenant-Governor and Acting Governor

Attest:

DWIGHT H. BROWN
Secretary of State

Mr. Dwight H. Brown: And now the proclamation promulgated by his Excellency, Honorable Guy B. Park, Governor of the State of Missouri, declaring the result of that election:

Mr. Warren D. Meng (reads):

PROCLAMATION

Whereas, by resolution of the Congress of the United States of America, duly assembled in regular session at the seat of government in Washington, an amendment was proposed to the states for the repeal of the 18th Amendment to the Constitution of the United States, and,

Whereas, by an act of the Congress it is provided that the people of the several states express their attitude through the medium of a convention called in each of the several states as to ratification or rejection of the proposed Amendment, and,

Whereas, the General Assembly of the State of Missouri, by an act approved April 13th, 1933, duly provided for calling of a special election at which the qualified electors of this state may choose delegates to meet in convention and ratify or reject said proposed Amendment in accordance with the expressed wish of the people, and,

Whereas, Frank G. Harris, Lieutenant Governor and Acting Governor, did on the 25th day of July, 1933, as Governor of the State of Missouri, officially proclaim that said special election be held on the 19th day of August, 1933, and

Whereas, on said date said election was held according to law and in conformity with the acts hereinbefore mentioned, and delegates to the state convention duly elected, and,

Whereas, the Honorable Dwight H. Brown, the duly elected and qualified Secretary of State of the State of Missouri, has officially certified to the election of delegates by the people of this state as follows, to-wit:—

LIST OF DELEGATES NOMINATED

1st District—
James F. Cook .... Maryville, Mo.
Wade Canaday .... Stanberry, Mo.

2nd District—
George D. Berry .... St. Joseph, Mo.
John D. McNeely.................................... St. Joseph, Mo.

3rd District—
K. D. Cross .... Savannah, Mo.
B. Waers .... Plattsburg, Mo.

4th District—
Randall Wilson .... Bethany, Mo.
John E. Powell .... Princeton, Mo.

5th District—
Sen. M. E. Casey, 423 Gladstone Blvd. .... Kansas City, Mo.
Sam B. Campbell, Coates House .... Kansas City, Mo.

6th District—
F. W. Hill .... Keytesville, Mo.
Thos. P. Burns .... Brockfield, Mo.

7th District—
James P. Aylward, 1312 E. 79th St. .... Kansas City, Mo.
James M. Pendergast, 2923 Victor .... Kansas City, Mo.

8th District—
Sam W. Vaughn .... Bogard, Mo.
C. W. James .... Elmira, Mo.

9th District—
W. F. Murrell .... Kirksville, Mo.
J. P. Gillaspie .... Leonard, Mo.

10th District—
Judge Jas. Ball .... Montgomery City, Mo.
Judge D. W. Herring .... Fulton, Mo.

11th District—
Sam D. Byrns .... Mexico, Mo.
Olin Bell .... Troy, Mo.

12th District—
S. S. Ball .... Kahoka, Mo.
Paul Gibbons .... Edina, Mo.

13th District—
Thomas V. Bodine .... Paris, Mo.
John W. Mahoney .... Hannibal, Mo.

14th District—
Harry F. Manion .... Boonville, Mo.
Carl Tising .... High Point, Mo.

15th District—
Wm. D. O'Bannon .... Sedalia, Mo.
Guy Abney .... Napton, Mo.

16th District—
Chas. W. McFarland .... Butler, Mo.
Henry E. Elder .... Lowry City, Mo.

17th District—
Judge S. N. Wilson .... Lexington, Mo.
Dr. J. I. Anderson .... Warrensburg, Mo.

18th District—
Fred Hubbert .... Neosho, Mo.
James Tatum .... Anderson, Mo.

19th District—
R. P. Weeks .... Brushyknob, Mo.
Mrs. T. S. Howard .... Marshfield, Mo.

20th District—
Mrs. Marie Deiterman .... Springfield, Mo.
J. B. Journey .... Nevada, Mo.

21st District—
Mrs. A. R. Zoelsmann .... Cape Girardeau, Mo.
Conley Grover .... Poplar Bluff, Mo.

22nd District—
W. C. McMillin .... West Plains, Mo.
W. Lewis Lindley .... Thayer, Mo.

23rd District—
Everett Reeves .... Caruthersville, Mo.
James V. Conran .... New Madrid, Mo.

24th District—
K. M. Lenox .... Rolla, Mo.
Eli P. Akes .... Ironton, Mo.

25th District—
J. E. Bryan .... Owensville, Mo.
Mrs. Clifford W. Gaylord .... Clayton, Mo.

26th District—
Jerry B. Burks ....Farmington, Mo.
Andrew E. Doerr ....Perryville, Mo.

27th District—
W. L. Zevely ....Linn, Mo.
W. M. Branson ....Dixon, Mo.

28th District—
Roy Coyne ....Joplin, Mo.
Westley Halliburton ....Carthage, Mo.

29th District—
Frank Harris, 4242 Louisiana Ave. ....St. Louis, Mo.
Sen. Wm. Doran, 3345 Oak Hill Ave. ....St. Louis, Mo.

30th District—
Joseph J. Mestres, 1104 S. 18th Street ....St. Louis, Mo.
Wm. Berberich, 2224 S. 13th Street ....St. Louis, Mo.

31st District—
William Sacks, Jefferson Hotel ....St. Louis, Mo.
Michael J. Kinney, 604 Chestnut Street ....St. Louis, Mo.

32nd District—
Daniel B. Johnston, 4483 Washington Ave. ....St. Louis, Mo.
Daniel G. Taylor, Greystone Apts. ....St. Louis, Mo.

33rd District—
James B. Quigley, 2529 University St. ....St. Louis, Mo.
Mrs. Sterling E. Edmunds, 33 Vandeventer Pl. ....St. Louis, Mo.

34th District—
B. J. Slattery, 5107 Wabada Ave. ....St. Louis, Mo.
Dr. N. J. Townsend, 1000 Bittner Street ....St. Louis, Mo.

WHEREAS, under and by virtue of the provisions of the act approved April 13, 1933, Frank G. Harris, Lieutenant-Governor and Acting Governor of the State of Missouri, did on the said 25th day of July, 1933, call the said convention to assemble on the 29th day of August, 1933.

Now, therefore, I, Guy B. Park, Governor of the State of Missouri, by virtue of the authority in me vested do hereby proclaim the result of said special election and the selection by the people of the delegates thereto, and of the calling of said convention to assemble on the 29th day of August, 1933, at the City of Jefferson in the State of Missouri.

SEAL

In witness whereof, I have hereunto set my hand and caused the seal of the State of Missouri to be affixed.

Done at the City of Jefferson, State of Missouri, this 28th day of August, in the year of our Lord, one thousand nine hundred thirty-three.

GUY B. PARK
Governor of the State of Missouri

Attest:

DWIGHT H. BROWN
Secretary of State

MR. DWIGHT H. BROWN: The next order of business is the election of a temporary chairman. What is the pleasure of the Convention?

DELEGATE KINNEY: Mr. Chairman.

MR. DWIGHT H. BROWN: Delegate Kinney of St. Louis.

DELEGATE KINNEY: At this time I place in nomination, Mrs. Clifford Gaylord as temporary chairman.

MR. DWIGHT H. BROWN: You have heard the nomination.

DELEGATE MCNEELY: Mr. Chairman.

MR. DWIGHT H. BROWN: Delegate McNeely.

DELEGATE MCNEELY: A great American statesman, one of the founders of this government has said, "eternal vigilance is the price of liberty." Since that day in every dark hour, the women of America have been the comrades and the inspiration of men who sought to preserve American liberty. In those dark years when we were in the throes of that fallacy some are pleased to call prohibition, a band of noble women in Missouri organized the Missouri Division of the Women's Organization for Prohibition Reform. At the head of that organization, Mrs. Clifford Gaylord has fought through to victory, so that now that organization numbers in its membership 53,000 of the women of Missouri, more than ten times the membership of any prohibition women's organization. It is fitting, Mr. President, that she should have the honor of being the Temporary Chairman of this Convention. It is with great pleasure that I second the nomination.

MR. DWIGHT H. BROWN: Are there any other nominations?

DELEGATE CONRAN: Mr. Chairman, I am from the 23rd district, down in the corner of Southeast Missouri, where we are grateful to all good ladies that have worked for prohibition reform, and to all of the ladies that have helped us in this cause. Since we can't vote for all of them, which we would like to do, it gives me great pleasure to second the nomination of one of the most charming ladies in the whole United States. I second the nomination of Mrs. Gaylord and move the nominations close.

MR. DWIGHT H. BROWN: You have heard the motion. Is there a second?

FROM THE FLOOR: Second the motion.

MR. DWIGHT H. BROWN: The motion is seconded. All in favor of the motion let it be known by saying aye.

FROM THE FLOOR: Aye.

MR. DWIGHT H. BROWN: Contrary, nay.

The motion carried.

MR. DWIGHT H. BROWN: All in favor of delegating the duties of temporary chairman to Mrs. Gaylord, let it be known by saying aye.

FROM THE FLOOR: Aye.

The motion carried.

MR. DWIGHT H. BROWN: I name a committee of Delegates Kinney, McNeely, Mrs. Edmunds and Judge Taylor to accompany the Madame Chairman to the platform.

Mrs. Gaylord accompanied to platform by committee.

MR. DWIGHT H. BROWN: I have the honor to present your chairman, Mrs. Clifford Gaylord, with the gavel of this convention.

DELEGATE MCNEELY: Ladies and Gentlemen. Is it too much to ask for you all to rise up in honor of the first woman who has ever presided at a Missouri Constitutional Convention?

Delegates all rise.

MADAME CHAIRMAN GAYLORD: I am simply overcome with the honor that you have conferred upon me in electing me temporary chairman of this Convention. I realize, however, that this honor which you have bestowed upon me is in reality only a tribute of respect to the members of the Women's Organization for National Prohibition Reform, which I have the honor to have been for the past two years chairman for the State of Missouri.

Three years ago when this organization was first formed in the State of Missouri, it took a lot of courage on the part of many of these women to come out as opposed to National Prohibition. Being a "dry" seemed to have such an overwhelming blanket of respectability and being a "wet" seemed to have quite the opposite. You know there are a lot of women who may be morally courageous and socially without courage. In other words, if Mrs. Perdoodle who stood for certain social standards will take a definite stand out in the open, all the Mrs. Dusenwackers will follow.

Whether the men like to admit it or not, I believe they look to women for moral leadership. Women have always been entrusted with the moral leadership of the home. It is my belief that the Women's Organization for National Prohibition Reform, functioning in 44 States in the Union, has made a major contribution toward the sentiment for the repeal of the 18th Amendment. So I repeat, it is my belief that it took a lot of courage on the part of many women to come out in the open against prohibition. All women believe in temperance, and insist upon temperance. Women of this organization do not minimize or overlook the evils that result from the abuse of alcoholic beverage, but they had the courage to face the facts. We are not facing the use of liquor, we are facing the abuse of liquor! They were not looking at the liquor problem as it existed 15 years ago; we are looking at it as it exists today.

There are many women who believed that National Prohibition would be the solution of the liquor problem. And they now realize that they have made a mistake. It takes another brand of courage to admit that one is in the wrong. I consider that these women have displayed that particular type of courage. We do not state that we encourage the use of alcoholic beverage; we have been fighting the abuse of alcoholic beverage. We believe that the cause of real temperance has been retarded 50 years by National Prohibition. Intoxicating beverage has been placed all out of proportion to its normal relationship in the daily lives of the rising generation. The program of the Women's Organization for National Prohibition Reform has been the repeal of the 18th Amendment, and the return to each state of its former right to regulate and control the manufacture, sale and transportation of intoxicating beverages within its own borders. We have never been in favor of a National Regulation to take the place of the 18th Amendment, because we believe that it was the attempt to enforce a National Regulation on the tastes and habits of the States, varying greatly in racial and traditional background, that brought us to the lamentable conditions that exist now under prohibition.

We believe that each state should work out sane and sensible liquor control measures, responsive to the sentiment of the people of each state, and therefore capable of enforcement. It would, for instance, ill behoove the citizens of Missouri to tell the citizens of Georgia what their liquor control measures should be, or for the citizens of Georgia to enact liquor control measures under which the State of New York should live by. There is too wide a variance in social custom, racial and traditional background.

I am sure none of us wish to see the open saloon return in our country. However, in making any regulations for liquor control, we must recognize first that anything that we do will be to a large degree experimental. The rising generation knows nothing of the conditions that existed before prohibition, except through hearsay. They have acquired certain habits, none of which are lamentable. There is a saying that you can't teach an old dog new tricks, but I believe this generation is sufficiently young and flexible that they can be taught the wisdom of temperance. The group of women, the W.C.T.U., have abandoned their splendid program of education for temperance as an attribute of character for one of total abstinence under the lash and the whip.

The women of the United States will continue to work for temperance as opposed to total abstinence. There are many women who resent having the stigma of criminality placed upon them and their homes because they indulge in the most temperate use of alcoholic beverage. Let us work out a law that will be sane and sensible as well as righteous.

MADAME CHAIRMAN GAYLORD: May I suggest that it would expedite the business of this convention if, when you address the chair, you will give your name and senatorial district. Although I have met a great many of the delegates, there are some I do not know. I believe the first order of business is the election of a Temporary Secretary. What is the pleasure of the convention?

DELEGATE HARRIS: Mrs. Chairman, Frank Harris, of St. Louis, 29th District. It gives me great pleasure to place in nomination the name of a delegate from the 13th district, the home of the immortal Mark Twain. Undoubtedly that soul of the immortal Mark Twain is looking down on this assemblage today, because of the fact that as history has it he was a strong believer in human liberty. So I take great pleasure in nominating Mr. John W. Mahoney of Hannibal for Temporary Secretary.

FROM THE FLOOR: I second the motion, Mrs. Chairman, of Mr. Mahoney.

MADAME CHAIRMAN GAYLORD: Are there any other nominations? If not, are you ready for the question?

FROM THE FLOOR: Question.

MADAME CHAIRMAN: You have heard the nomination of Mr. Mahoney as Temporary Secretary of this Convention. All in favor will signify by saying aye.

FROM THE FLOOR: Aye.

MADAME CHAIRMAN: Contrary, nay.

The motion carried.

MADAME CHAIRMAN: Will Mr. Mahoney come forward. I think the next order of business to be the appointment of a credentials committee to examine the credentials of all delegates present. On that Committee I appoint:—Mr. T. V. Bodine, Paris, from the 13th district as Chairman; Mr. Michael J. Kinney of St. Louis from the 31st district; Senator Casey, Kansas City, from the 5th district; Mr. Olin Bell of Troy, 11th district; Mrs. T. S. Howard, Marshfield, 19th district; Mr. James Ball, Montgomery City, 10th district; Mr. F. W. Hill, Keytesville, 6th district. The Credentials Committee will retire and come back with their resolutions.

DELEGATE TAYLOR: Madame Chairman.

MADAME CHAIRMAN: Mr. Taylor.

DELEGATE TAYLOR: I move that the Chair appoint a Committee of not less than five to wait upon the Governor of the State of Missouri to notify him that we are now in session, and we would be very happy if he could come and address us. I ask the Chair to appoint the Committee.

MADAME CHAIRMAN: Thank you. Is it necessary to have a second to that?

FROM THE FLOOR: I second the motion.

MADAME CHAIRMAN: Those in favor signify by saying aye.

FROM THE FLOOR: Aye.

MADAME CHAIRMAN: Contrary, nay.

The motion carried.

MADAME CHAIRMAN: The Chair appoints the following Committee to wait upon the Governor, inform him that the Convention is now in session, and ask him to come here:

Mr. James Aylward, Kansas City, from the 7th district;
Mr. W. L. Zevely, Linn, from the 27th district;
Mr. Sam D. Byrns, Mexico, from the 11th district;
Mrs. S. E. Edmunds, St. Louis, from the 33rd district;
Mr. Everett Reeves, Caruthersville, from the 23rd district;
Senator William Doran, St. Louis, from the 29th district;
Colonel John D. McNeely, St. Joseph, from the 2nd district;
Mr. J. B. Burks, Farmington, from the 26th district;
Mrs. Marie Deiterman, Springfield, from the 20th district;

Short interval before the Governor arrives.

The Governor, Honorable Guy B. Park, arrives and is greeted by applause.

MADAME CHAIRMAN: On behalf of the whole Convention, I wish to welcome you, Governor Park, to our Convention, and invite you to address us at this time.

HONORABLE GOVERNOR GUY B. PARK: Mrs. Chairman, you are gathered here to express the will of the people of Missouri, the 22nd State that has decided that prohibition has been a failure. I am proud on behalf of the people you represent to welcome you and to congratulate you and the people of the State on the wise action they have taken.

In a short time, probably before the first day of January next, the people of the United States, or at least more than thirty-six States of the Union, will have joined with Missouri and the other states in doing away with the evil of National Prohibition. (Applause.) By that I do not mean that the people of Missouri, or the people of the United States favor intemperance, but they are revolting because of an intolerable condition that comes out of the present situation. They are tired of bootlegging, they are tired with the gunmen and racketeers, they are tired of the failure of temperance in the United States. The people realize now that the progress made by the generations before prohibition went into effect, the progress towards temperance, has been checked and almost destroyed. The people realize that laws cannot make morals; they realize that in the home and in the church and in the school must be taught the principles that inculcate morals and temperance, and you cannot compel the people by law to do that which their own conscience and their own teachings, and their own ideas of right do not prompt them to do.

I mean this, that a law can, be enforced, this is the best illustration of it, only in so far as the masses of the people, desire it to be enforced. The only effective law is a law that is in the breast and hearts of the people of a State or a Nation.

It will be necessary and it will become my duty either to call the legislature together in special session, or the regular session, to see that when prohibition goes into effect that the rights of the people are protected, and that intemperance does not run rampant throughout their land. I take it that all of you believe in temperance, believe in good government, believe in morals in government, as I believe in them, and it will be necessary that strict regulation be had upon the sale of intoxicating liquors. Regulatory laws must be passed in Missouri that the people may be protected from the evils of hard liquor.

I have already appointed a Committee, headed by this distinguished chairman of this convention, or at least, a member of this Commission; headed by the President of the State University, to make an investigation as to what proper regulation should be had in Missouri; to study the different methods, and make such recommendations as they deem necessary that our Legislature may have the advantage of their investigations and recommendations.

I want to say this to you as delegates here, and to the people of Missouri, that when prohibition is repealed in the United States, as it will be, Missouri will not become a habitat of the lawless and the evils of strong drink will not be effective in the State of Missouri if I can prevent it. (Applause.)

Your stay here, of course, will be brief. It is a pleasure to welcome you, and I am delighted that such an intelligent, representative body of Missourians have been selected by those advocating the repeal of Prohibition.

I thank you for the honor of being permitted to thus briefly address you. (Applause.)

MADAME CHAIRMAN: Thank you, Governor Park. I think that was a very inspiring message, and the State of Missouri should be congratulated upon having a man as our Governor who has such great vision. I personally am very proud to be a Missourian.

MADAME CHAIRMAN: Is the Committee on Credentials ready to report?

Interval.

MADAME CHAIRMAN: Is the Committee on Credentials ready to report?

Interval.

MADAME CHAIRMAN: I have been informed that one of the delegates, Mr. William D. O'Bannon of Sedalia, Missouri, has been removed from the ranks by death. I think it is appropriate that we stand in silence for a few minutes in honor of his memory, and that this Convention send a message of sympathy to his widow, and that we ask the Resolutions Committee, when appointed, to draft a proper resolution, and if no objections, be it so ordered. Will someone put that in the form of a motion?

DELEGATE BURNS: I have a telegram announcing the sad and rather sudden death of brother O'Bannon. I would like to read it, or have it read.

MADAME CHAIRMAN: All right, will you please read it, or send it up.

READING CLERK: August 29th, 1933. James W. Byrnes, President Missouri Association against Prohibition, or someone concerned, Jefferson City, Missouri. Governor Guy B. Park, President Byrnes, and Delegates of the Convention assembled: It is with deep regret that I must inform you that my beloved husband, William D. O'Bannon, passed away Sunday night. His funeral is being held today. He was a delegate to the Repeal Convention from the 15th District and during his illness the election and Convention seemed constantly on his mind. Had his condition not remained serious, I intended to represent him, but God did not will that way. Accept my best wishes for a harmonious and successful Convention. Very sincerely, Mrs. W. D. O'Bannon. P.S. Will you please have this telegram read at the Convention.

MADAME CHAIRMAN: I entertain a motion that we send a resolution of sympathy to Mrs. O'Bannon. Will someone please make that motion.

FROM THE FLOOR: I will make that motion.

MADAME CHAIRMAN: Is it seconded?

FROM THE FLOOR: I second the motion.

MADAME CHAIRMAN: You have all heard the motion that we send a message of sympathy to Mrs. O'Bannon. Those in favor signify by saying aye. Contrary, nay.

FROM THE FLOOR: Aye.

The motion carried.

MADAME CHAIRMAN: It is so ordered. Is the Committee on Credentials ready to report?

Interval.

MADAME CHAIRMAN: Perhaps we could take a recess for ten minutes until the Credential Committee comes back.

Recess for ten minutes.

MADAME CHAIRMAN: Mr. Bodine, is the Chairman of the Credential Committee ready to report?

DELEGATE BODINE: Yes.

MADAME CHAIRMAN: Read the roll of delegates.

READING CLERK: "Your Committee recommends that the list of delegates as certified to the Convention by the Secretary of State act as the accredited delegates to the Convention. They follow:

1st District—
J. F. Cook, Maryville
Wade Canaday, Stanberry

2nd District—
J. D. McNeely, St. Joseph
George D. Berry, St. Joseph

3rd District—
K. D. Cross, Savannah
B. Waers, Plattsburg

4th District—
Randall Wilson, Bethany
J. E. Powell, Princeton

5th District—
M. E. Casey, Kansas City
S. B. Campbell, Kansas City

6th District—
F. W. Hill, Keytesville
T. P. Burns, Brookfield

7th District—
J. P. Aylward, Kansas City
J. M. Pendergast, Kansas City

8th District—
Sam W. Vaughn, Bogard
C. W. James, Elmira

9th District—
W. F. Murrell, Kirksville
J. P. Gillaspie, Leonard

10th District—
James Ball, Montgomery City
D. W. Herring, Fulton

11th District—
Sam D. Byrns, Mexico
Olin Bell, Troy

12th District—
S. S. Ball, Kahoka
Paul Gibbons, Edina

13th District—
T. V. Bodine, Paris
J. W. Mahoney, Hannibal

14th District—
H. F. Manion, Boonville
Carl Tising, High Point

15th District—
Guy Abnay, Napton
W. D. O'Bannon, Sedalia

16th District—
C. W. McFarland, Butler
H. E. Elder, Lowry City

17th District—
S. N. Wilson, Lexington
Dr. J. I. Anderson, Warrensburg

18th District—
Fred Hubbert, Neosho
James Tatum, Anderson

19th District—
R. P. Weeks, Brushyknob
Mrs. T. S. Howard, Marshfield

20th District—
Mrs. Marie Deiterman, Springfield
J. B. Journey, Nevada

21st District—
Mrs. A. R. Zoelsmann, Cape Girardeau
Conley Grover, Poplar Bluff

22nd District—
W. C. McMillin, West Plains
W. L. Lindley Thayer

23rd District—
Everett Reeves, Caruthersville
J. V. Conran, New Madrid

24th District—
K. M. Lenox, Rolla
Eli P. Akes, Ironton

25th District—
J. E. Bryan, Owensville
Mrs. Clifford W. Gaylord, Clayton

26th District—
J. B. Burks, Farmington
A. E. Doerr, Perryville

27th District—
W. L. Zevely, Linn
W. M. Branson, Dixon

28th District—
Roy Coyne, Joplin
Wesley Halliburton, Carthage

29th District—
Frank Harris, St. Louis
Wm. Doran, St. Louis

30th District—
J. J. Mestres, St. Louis
Wm. Berberich, St. Louis

31st District—
Wm. Sacks, St. Louis
Michael J. Kinney, St. Louis

32nd District—
D. G. Johnston, St. Louis
D. B. Taylor, St. Louis

33rd District—
J. B. Quigley, St. Louis
Mrs. S. E. Edmunds, St. Louis

34th District—
P. J. Slattery, St. Louis
Dr. N. J. Townsend, St. Louis

(*Signed*) THOMAS V. BODINE
Chairman of the Committee on Credentials"

MADAME CHAIRMAN: The Chair will entertain a motion that the report of the Credentials Committee be accepted.

FROM THE FLOOR: Madame Chairman, I move that the report be accepted.

MADAME CHAIRMAN: Is there a second to the motion?

FROM THE FLOOR: Seconded.

MADAME CHAIRMAN: Those in favor signify by saying aye.

FROM THE FLOOR: Aye.

MADAME CHAIRMAN: Contrary, nay.

The motion carried.

MADAME CHAIRMAN: It is so ordered. It is my understanding that Honorable Judge Tipton of the Missouri Supreme Court was to administer the oath to the delegates, and that the roll will then be reread and that each delegate will answer present when their names are called.

TEMPORARY SECRETARY MAHONEY: Madame Chairman, may I present Judge Tipton.

MADAME CHAIRMAN: As your names are called, will you come forward and we will have the delegates sworn in groups of 17. Answer present.

On roll call by the Reading Clerk the following Delegates from the first 17 Districts were present:

J. F. Cook	T. P. Burns	D. W. Herring	H. F. Manion
Wade Canaday	J. P. Aylward	Sam D. Byrns	Carl Tising
J. D. McNeely	Sam W. Vaughn	Olin Bell	Guy Abney
K. D. Cross	C. W. James	S. S. Ball	C. W. McFarland
B. Waers	W. F. Murrell	Paul Gibbons	H. E. Elder
J. E. Powell	J. P. Gillaspie	T. V. Bodine	S. N. Wilson
M. E. Casey	James Ball	J. W. Mahoney	Dr. J. I. Anderson
F. W. Hill			

ABSENT MEMBERS

George D. Berry	S. B. Campbell	J. M. Pendergast	W. D. O'Bannon
Randall Wilson			

The above were sworn in as follows:

HONORABLE JUDGE TIPTON: Do you, and each of you, solemnly swear that you will uphold the Constitution of the United States and the Constitution of the State of Missouri, and faithfully demean yourself as a delegate of this Convention?

THE DELEGATES: We do.

MADAME CHAIRMAN: Be seated. Mr. Clerk call the rest of the delegates.

On roll call by the Reading Clerk the following Delegates from the last 17 Districts were present:

Fred Hubbert	W. C. McMillin	J. B. Burks	Wm. Sacks
R. P. Weeks	W. L. Lindley	A. E. Doerr	Michael J. Kinney
Mrs. T. S. Howard	Everett Reeves	W. L. Zevely	D. B. Johnston
Mrs. Marie Deiterman	J. V. Conran	W. M. Branson	D. G. Taylor
J. B. Journey	K. M. Lenox	Roy Coyne	J. B. Quigley
Mrs. A. R. Zoelsmann	Eli P. Akes	Wesley Halliburton	Mrs. S. E. Edmunds
Conley Grover	J. E. Bryan	Frank Harris	P. J. Slattery
	Mrs. Clifford W. Gaylord	Wm. Doran	Dr. N. J. Townsend
		Wm. Berberich	

ABSENT

J. J. Mestres James Tatum

The above were sworn in as follows:

HONORABLE JUDGE TIPTON: Do you, and each of you, solemnly swear that you will uphold the Constitution of the United States and the Constitution of the State of Missouri, and faithfully demean yourself as a delegate of this Convention?

THE DELEGATES: We do.

MADAME CHAIRMAN: The next order of business is the nominations for Permanent Chairman and Permanent Secretary. The Chair recognizes Senator Casey.

SENATOR CASEY: Mrs. Chairman. I wish to place in nomination for Permanent Chairman of this Convention, Roger Prentiss Weeks of Douglas County, a member of this Convention. Mr. Weeks is a native Missourian, having been born and raised in Montgomery County previous to changing his home to Douglas County. Mr. Weeks was the author of the bill and labored diligently during the 57th General Assembly for the passage of that measure, calling for this Convention and the selection of delegates thereto. I feel that it is only fitting that the delegates to this Convention honor the distinguished member from Douglas County as Permanent Chairman of this Convention.

MADAME CHAIRMAN: The Chair recognizes Mr. James Ball, Montgomery County.

DELEGATE BALL: Mrs. Chairman, Ladies and Gentlemen of this Convention. I would be derelict to my duty if I did not second the nomination of Roger Prentiss Weeks, just nominated.

He was born and raised to manhood in one of the counties which I have the pleasure of representing. He comes from two of the strongest Democratic families in Montgomery and Callaway Counties, all high-class people. I cheerfully recommend the election as Chairman of this Convention of a man whom I have known from babyhood to manhood, and Montgomery County, of the 10th District, is glad to second the nomination of Roger Prentiss Weeks for Permanent Chairman of this Convention. I thank you.

MADAME CHAIRMAN: Are there any other nominations?

Delegate Reeves: I move that the nominations be now closed and that Mr. Weeks be elected by this Convention by acclamation.

Madame Chairman: Is there any second to that motion?

From the Floor: Second the motion.

Madame Chairman: It has been moved and seconded that nominations be closed and that Mr. Weeks be elected by acclamation as Permanent Chairman of this Convention. Are there any remarks? Those in favor will signify by saying aye.

From the Floor: Aye.

Madame Chairman: Contrary minded, no? Then it is so ordered. The Chair will now entertain a nomination for Permanent Secretary.

Delegate Burks: Ladies and Gentlemen of this Convention. I am just about to do something that I have never done before, and that is to present the name of a distinguished lady. I don't know her personally, but I have heard so many good things about her that I am taking the opportunity of presenting her name to this Convention as Permanent Secretary.

She comes from my "neck of the woods," and is just over the hill on the river side touching the great delta of Southeast Missouri. She comes from a splendid city and I am told a splendid family. Her name is Mrs. A. R. Zoelsmann of Cape Girardeau, and I take pleasure in presenting her in nomination.

Madame Chairman: Is there a second to the nomination of Mrs. Zoelsmann for the office of Permanent Secretary?

From the Floor: Mrs. Chairman, I take pleasure in seconding the nomination of Mrs. Zoelsmann. She comes from down in my country, Cape Girardeau. We all know her down in Southeast Missouri as the finest in her county. With pleasure I second her nomination.

Madame Chairman: Mrs. Zoelsmann has been nominated and the nomination seconded. Are there any other nominations?

From the Floor: Madame Chairman, I move that nominations be closed and that Mrs. Zoelsmann be elected by acclamation.

From the Floor: Second the motion.

Madame Chairman: Mrs. Zoelsmann of Cape Girardeau has been nominated as Permanent Secretary of this Convention and it has been moved and seconded that the nominations be closed and that Mrs. Zoelsmann be elected by acclamation. Those in favor signify by saying aye.

From the Floor: Aye.

Madame Chairman: Contrary minded, no? It is so ordered. Mrs. Zoelsmann, I want to welcome you and Mr. Weeks, and to say this, that we feel that in our organization that you have been a very strong friend of repeal and that you have been a great comfort to us in many ways in our organization, and I congratulate you, Mr. Weeks, on being selected the Permanent Chairman, which I think is an honor we feel is quite due you.

Madame Chairman: I want to present to you Mr. Carl Burdette, of Douglas County, who has a message, I believe, for the Permanent Chairman of this Convention. Mr. Carl Burdette.

Mr. Burdette: Mrs. Chairman, Mr. Chairman. Because of your great concern and your many and kind expressions of sympathy for the unfortunate youths of Missouri, the boys of the penitentiary and the intermediate reformatory of Algoa have asked me to present you with this beautiful gavel, which was hewn from the native walnut, and carried from your county, sir, which you so ably and fearlessly represented in the 57th General Assembly. They petition me to ask you to use this gavel in the further deliberations of this Convention, which is bound to go down in Missouri's history as a great stride in behalf of Morality, Christianity and good Citizenship. Please accept this gavel, Mr. Weeks.

PERMANENT CHAIRMAN WEEKS: Mr. Burdette, with pleasure I accept this tribute from the boys of Algoa reformatory, and express to them, sir, my message of understanding, and express to them my pleasure and gratification for this beautiful tribute of their interest in this Convention and my personal connection with same, and express to them, if you please, my belief that this Convention at this time will make a historic step toward the solving of many of our social problems. It is my wish, sir, too, that you will express to the officers and personnel of that institution my kindest regards.

Gentlemen of the Convention, and Ladies of the Convention, it is indeed a very great honor you have conferred upon me and one which I can scarcely deem myself fully worthy. It is truly an honor therefore to be coveted and to be appreciated; and at this time it is my desire to express to you as fellow delegates to this assemblage that we are now about to take our historic step in the progress of Missouri as a great State.

In our deliberations as to what course we should best proceed to improve the social, economic and moral conditions of this State, we are visited with grave problems of government and social control. The step taken by the people of the State of Missouri under the recent election has clearly proved which way the wind blows. The people of the State of Missouri are determined in their efforts to remove from their midst the racketeer, the gunman, the bootlegger and the speakeasy. It is our duty as sound thinking citizens of this State to approach these problems with intelligence and common old "horse sense," and understanding of the needs of our State.

It is indeed a pleasure and I shall ever cherish in my memory the kind sentiments of this Convention in which you have honored me with the office of Permanent Chairman. I thank you heartily. (Applause.)

The next order of business is the appointment of a Committee on Resolutions by the Chairman. I have the honor to present to you the names of the Committee on Resolutions:

The Honorable:
- James Aylward, Chairman of the Committee, 7th district;
- T. P. Burns of the 6th district;
- S. N. Wilson of the 17th district;
- Paul Gibbons of the 12th district;
- Dr. J. I. Anderson of the 17th district;
- James V. Conran of the 23rd district;
- W. L. Zevely of the 27th district;
- William Sacks of the 31st district;
- Judge D. B. Johnston of the 32nd district.

The Committee on Resolutions will please retire and present their report.

DELEGATE TAYLOR: Mr. Chairman.

CHAIRMAN WEEKS: Judge Taylor.

DELEGATE TAYLOR: During the absence of that Committee, while we are waiting for them, I suggest that we hear from a man who must administer the regulatory laws, who will have more to do in the next few years with the regulation of the liquor traffic than any other, that is our Attorney-General, Mr. Roy McKittrick. I suggest we hear from him. I am quite sure he is here. (Applause.)

CHAIRMAN WEEKS: The Chair recommends the suggestion of Judge Taylor and feels that it is most fitting and appropriate that we hear from the Attorney-General on this occasion. I have the pleasure to present our Attorney-General to this Convention, Mr. Roy McKittrick.

HONORABLE ATTORNEY-GENERAL MCKITTRICK: Mr. Chairman Weeks, delegates of this Convention, Ladies and Gentlemen, and members of the press. I am delighted and honored to have the opportunity to address a Convention of this kind and character. This is the first Convention of its kind in the history of Missouri. It is the first time that Congress has ever permitted the Sovereign States to pass upon a Federal Amendment, which was enacted at the recent Congress. Never before in the history of the American flag has a Constitutional Convention been authorized by Congress.

The delegates of this Convention are making history. The delegates of this Convention have had bestowed upon them an honor that no other citizen of the great Commonwealth has ever had. A new chapter in Missouri history and in the history of the United States is being written by my distinguished friends here today. Delegates, you are about to cast an official vote to carry out the wishes and the will of the people of Missouri, to repeal the 18th Amendment, which has denied for more than a decade the fundamental principles of government that were established and inaugurated in our country, in our land. As Cornwallis gave the sword to Washington, my friends, you are about to restore that principle, about to reaffirm that doctrine; that it isn't the function of government to tell the people what to wear, what to say, how to pray, what to eat, and what to drink. Again, the people of this country have been victorious in winning another battle, but by reason of the great precepts, by reason of the great ideals of our forefathers, we are more fortunate than they, because we have a method to exercise our rights in a passive and orderly manner, without resorting to opening the veins and arteries of the land.

I want to say to you that I realize and I appreciate that it is a presumption on my part to even suggest what should be done in the future with reference to control of what is ordinarily termed the liquor traffic, but I do believe that no Canadian Plan, that no Swedish Plan, that no Foreign Plan is applicable to Missourians, to Americans. I believe in a Missouri Plan, in an American Plan, because I believe that there are as many fertile brains, that there are as many noble men and women that can carry the standard of liberty in our country without going into some foreign field and undertaking to force upon the American people and upon Missourians especially, any plan but a Missouri Plan.

May I urge you, may I entreat you, that we forget about the plans under other flags and let us go back to our Constitution, let us go back to the principle of Thomas Jefferson, let us go back to the principle that we shall not be prohibited in exercising our inherent rights. When we establish again that doctrine, then we will have a principle that all true Americans, and all true Missourians, will help to enforce, will aid in carrying into effect, because whenever a citizen of our State will recognize it, whenever a citizen of our State will understand it, every citizen of our State will make an effort to see that Missouri's ideals shall lighten the pathway of the states in this nation and in this land.

The 18th Amendment is doomed, doomed; something must take its place. It has been a factor, it has shown to the people that the American citizen will not bear a yoke when it pinches and is burdensome, but don't forget that they have removed this yoke in order to put on another yoke.

My friends, the President of the United States promised the people something a short time ago. He promised us liberty, he promised us freedom, he promised to loosen the shackles that the American citizen has bowed down beneath under the Volstead Act, and the 18th Amendment. Swiftly as the wings of a bird, when he occupied the seat of power, he asked Congress to do something, and Congress did something, and that promise has been fulfilled. He has given you this opportunity, the first time since this government has been formed, that the American people have been given an opportunity to express their views independent of some machinery.

We have a modification of the Volstead Act, and in a short time a repeal of the 18th Amendment, but that isn't all. This man, with that alert and keen brain of his, perceived that it wasn't what came from the public mind that was dangerous, but he perceived that what remained in it was dangerous. He understood that something more must be done for the people of this nation. He understood that we were standing in the shadows, almost upon the brink that has sent other nations into oblivion, and then he brought forth another great doctrine. He stepped out upon the waves of distress and he has said unto them "Peace." I am confident, yes, I am more than that, I am certain, when the purposes of Franklin D. Roosevelt are carried out, then that day will be here when there will be to all classes of people an equal portion of prosperity, and then when that time comes, the property and the possessions of this country will not be exposed to unbridled power; then the people shall control the power.

The man is blind today who does not see the glimpses of that dawn of a golden age where we are being led, and where it is being brought to us nearer and nearer by the greatest Leader of All Times, of all time since the hand on the dial of the clock has been marking time.

It is the Missourians' duty, it is the Americans' duty, to follow his leadership in this hour of distress; follow him because he is the bulwark of safety, he will take us to the shores of prosperity; he will return to us the government; he will show to the poorest individual of this land the standard that was established for him by the leader of the Centuries gone by, Thomas Jefferson.

My countrymen, I say to you that the page of no history will shine as bright, will be embellished more, than when the historian writes that the leadership of Franklin D. Roosevelt has saved America and the World. (Applause.)

CHAIRMAN WEEKS: Is the Committee on Resolutions ready to report?

Interval.

DELEGATE BALL: Mr. Chairman.

CHAIRMAN WEEKS: Mr. Ball.

DELEGATE BALL: While the Committee on Resolutions is getting ready to report, I want to say to this Convention that the State of Missouri must control in the distribution of liquor when the 18th Amendment is repealed. It must be left to no local jurisdiction. (Applause.) It must be left to the entire State of Missouri. I want to suggest to you that I have had a good deal of experience in watching local option. I say it is ten times worse than prohibition in its present shape. I hope that the Committee that was appointed by the Governor to study liquor Control Laws, will recommend nothing in the world in favor of local option or any local distribution of liquor whatsoever. I want the liquor problem fixed so that it will be controlled, not by the prohibitionists, and not by the men who manufacture and sell liquor. I want it controlled by such men and such women as are here upon this occasion.

I am glad to say to you that I for one fully indorse the action of the Governor of

Missouri. I had prepared a resolution to introduce here requesting the Governor to do what he has done. That only illustrates how two great minds run together. I want to suggest another thing to this Convention, that we must one and all stand by the Governor of Missouri, and we must further stand up for the President of the United States. I think he is doing more for the return of prosperity than we ever expected that he should do. I want to say to you the happiest moment I ever felt in my life was when I was listening over the radio and heard Mr. Roosevelt after he had flown from New York to Chicago, when he uttered those words, that prohibition is doomed from now on.

I want to say to you that I have to some extent read the figures that prohibition has caused in our deficit. If it had not been for prohibition, we wouldn't have any deficit in our financial affairs today. I appeal to all of us to stand up loyally for Mr. Roosevelt and for Governor Park. I thank you.

CHAIRMAN WEEKS: Is the Committee on Resolutions ready to report? During the interim until the Committee on Resolutions reports, the Chair would be glad to hear from any other member of the Convention who feels that he has something worthwhile to contribute.

DELEGATE JOURNEY: Mr. Chairman. I want to second everything that Judge Ball has said about the matter of local option in the control of liquor. We people who live next to the Kansas line know what it is to have local option. We are going to get rid of the 18th Amendment and get rid of the bootlegger and all the forms of crime as far as we can. To continue local option in any one county would be to continue a condition that has existed for the last ten or twelve years. We are next to the Kansas line and there are other people here who are near the Kansas line and know something about the condition there. They make more brew there than any other people in the world who are close to us.

CHAIRMAN WEEKS: The remarks of Mr. Journey are most timely. Any further contributions to the discussion while we are waiting for the Committee on Resolutions?

DELEGATE MCFARLAND: I live in a county just about as close to that district referred to by Mr. Journey. I can support what he said. They make awful bad liquor there, and if the Committee on Resolutions shouldn't come in, it will be a hell of a long time between drinks.

CHAIRMAN WEEKS: The Committee on Resolutions will be ready to report in about five minutes. I feel that the assemblage would be both honored and cheered by having a few words from Judge Taylor of St. Louis, Missouri. Mr. Taylor.

JUDGE TAYLOR: Mr. Chairman, Ladies and Gentlemen of this Convention. I feel that it is entirely proper that I should be called upon, because of the absence of time, and having nothing else to do with it, I will be the best. This Convention has been referred to as a historic event. It is. Not only as Attorney-General McKittrick said a few minutes ago, it is the first time that the people of Missouri have been called upon to pass upon a Constitutional Amendment, that is, a Federal Constitutional Amendment by direct vote, but it marks, in my judgment, not only the passing of what President Hoover called a noble experiment, but it marks a point in Governmental education.

It teaches us that we Americans are capable of making experiments and when we find that they are a mistake, we can recall them. So this Convention now in Missouri is putting the finishing touch on what I would say has been a really great adventure.

During the past few years and half century, America has been spending billions and billions of dollars to educate its citizens, and establish our great public schools. We are getting our dividend now. There have always been many, many people who have opposed general education. During the past two or three years we have gone through one of the severest stresses that any people ever suffered from. We have seen men's souls tried; we have seen men's heads bowed with stress and fear, but we have had no disturbances to amount to anything that we have gone through.

And, so I say, we are getting our dividends now from this general scheme of education. This Convention, as I say, represents the capacity of the American people to try to do something, and adopt something; and when they find they can't do it, they are perfectly willing to take the back track.

I think there is no question that prohibition was a noble experiment. Its purpose was a glorious purpose, and if the people had done what was hoped for by the prohibition amendment, your country would have been vastly better off. Now, we failed. We are here today to turn, to take a back track, and say we tried, and we failed, and here we are. We are not ashamed to admit that we failed, that the prohibition amendment was a failure. We are here today to make the only amends we can, that is, to withdraw that glorious experiment.

You know, I, of course, was never in favor of the 18th Amendment; not because I wasn't in sympathy with its purpose, for I was, but I was opposed to it because I believed it would fail. Now it has failed, here we are, men and women of this country, forming what I regard as a great, courageous, noble truth, we are willing to back track and say we made a mistake and that we were wrong. I thank you all very much.

From the Floor: Mr. Chairman, your Committee on Resolutions is now ready to report. There are two resolutions which the Committee recommends for the consideration of the Convention and recommends their adoption.

Chairman Weeks: Before we read the report of the Committee on Resolutions, as the next order of business after consideration of resolutions will be a motion to adjourn; before that Resolution's Committee report is deliberated upon, it seems to the Chair that it would be a fitting occasion for a word from Colonel James W. Byrnes, State President of the Missouri Association Against Prohibition. Mr. Byrnes.

Mr. Byrnes: Mr. Chairman.

Chairman Weeks: Mr. Byrnes.

Mr. Byrnes: Delegates to the Convention. I did not come here to make a speech. I am not unmindful of the distinction of being asked to make a few remarks. It is a distinction, and I thank you for the honor.

Some thirteen years ago, with other men in Missouri, we started to organize, and at that time in certain borders let me remind you it was not respected, but today when I meet one of my old time dry friends, I say, "Take off your hat to me, I have become decent."

Oh, I don't want to make a speech, because for the last thirteen years I have been making speeches. The first address I made was in the Ball Park at Washington, Missouri, in September, 1921, and since that day, in season and out of season, morning, noon, and night, I have opposed the 18th Amendment, and I am very much in the position of her ladyship, who had been stripped of her wearing apparel. I quote you from Lady Godiva, "Thank God, I am coming to my clothes." I believe we have had too much talking already.

I opposed the 18th Amendment because it was not founded on right reasoning, and not in accord with the natural law. It was no law at all, merely a species of violence against free institutions, opposed to the intent and purpose of the Constitution of these United States. In its moral effect, with the speakeasies and beer flats, run by women, it has prostituted youth. It has financed crime until we are faced with the truth, in fact, that America is the most lawless Nation on God's Green Earth. Its economic effect, a catastrophe, taking capital out of agriculture and industry, and saddling them with unbearable taxes, with the consequent result of unemployment. It has cost the State $33,000,000 in the last ten years. It has cost the Nation $13,000,000,000 and it has accomplished no good, but a multitude of evil.

You men and women are here to register the voice expressed in no uncertain terms of the suffrage of Missouri. You are here for more than that. You are here to restore to its original purity, that sacred civil document, the Constitution of these United States, and saved by the blood of men who fought at Bunker Hill. By the blood of those men who held the ground at Gettysburg, I beg of you, by the blood of those men over whom now poppies grow, I beseech you, keep sacred those holy rights of America, all that liberty, let its fire shine out with a light as pure as the light from above, so that all the world, on bended knees, humbly in the depths of their souls, will thank God for America.

There is more than that. The Constitution of these United States rests upon the back of each and every one of us, the rights and privileges which we enjoy go echoing down the corridors of time. Yet more than that. They are the citizens with ideals so high, with purpose so pure, with character so strong, and with conduct so dignified that we respect the rights of others. So today, here, now, in this very hour, dedicate our lives and souls upon the altar of American liberty for the purity of the Constitution.

CHAIRMAN WEEKS: The Chair takes recognition of the fact that we have as a member of this Constitutional Convention, a very distinguished gentleman from St. Louis, who enjoys the honor of being the only Republican member of this assemblage from St. Louis, the Honorable William Sacks.

DELEGATE SACKS: Mr. Chairman.

CHAIRMAN WEEKS: Mr. Sacks.

DELEGATE SACKS: Fellow delegates: I would not have injected any word referring to either the Republican or Democratic Party, but since our worthy Chairman has referred to me as the only Republican delegate of St. Louis, I am going to take occasion to state that I feel in a sort of a strange atmosphere. In other words, when I look around me, and I have been accustomed to attending conventions for the last twenty years, Republican Conventions, where harmony such as I have witnessed here today hasn't prevailed all the time, I remarked to the worthy Chairman of our Resolutions Committee, that I never expected to see such a harmonious feeling in a Democratic Convention.

At the same time, it is a keen satisfaction that I am a delegate to this Convention and a party to the repeal of the Volstead Act, and I take particular pride in being present at its death in this State. This noble experiment has cost the American public very dearly. At the same time the Volstead Act itself has served a purpose, not the purpose for which it was enacted, but the purpose to stand out as a danger signal and mark a peril to all legislative bodies attempting to interfere with those rights that are purely personal. So I say, if the Volstead Act accomplishes that purpose, and I think it will, it has served some good.

To my mind, while we all, in a greater or lesser degree, have contributed to the repeal of this Volstead Act, one man, President Roosevelt, more than any other one man, stands out as having sensed the real sentiment of the American people against all sumptuary laws. He had the courage of his convictions against an intense, violent, and highly organized prohibition minority, and the wisdom to carry us through to moral freedom. I thank you, Mr. Chairman.

CHAIRMAN WEEKS: On behalf of this Convention, the Chair recognizes the contributions to this assemblage by the eminent gentlemen who have spoken to us, and on behalf of the Convention, the Chairman extends the thanks of this body to them.

CHAIRMAN WEEKS: The Committee on Resolutions has now reported and the report will be read by the Clerk; Mr. Clerk, read the report. It has been suggested to the Chair, and it is most opportune I believe, that if there is any delegate present who has not been sworn in, before the vote is cast, will he please rise to his feet? If there is any delegate present who has not been administered the oath, will he please rise; some of them were absent when the oath was administered, though probably they might have come in since. Evidently all were sworn in; read the Report Mr. Clerk.

READING CLERK: Mr. Chairman, in conformity with the resolution passed by this Convention, the Resolutions Committee has directed that a suitable memorial be prepared of the death of William D. O'Bannon, of Sedalia, Missouri. Our Chairman, Mr. J. P. Aylward, has kindly consented to arrange the details of composition and delivery to his widow, Mrs. William D. O'Bannon.

CHAIRMAN WEEKS: I believe there should be included in that resolution an order to have a copy of the resolution inserted in the records of this Convention. It would be a most fitting tribute. The Chair will entertain a motion to that effect.

FROM THE FLOOR: I make the motion.

CHAIRMAN WEEKS: Motion made that a copy of this resolution be included in the records of the Convention, do I hear a second?

FROM THE FLOOR: Seconded.

CHAIRMAN WEEKS: Duly made and seconded that a copy of this resolution be included in the records of this Convention. All in favor make it known by saying aye.

FROM THE FLOOR: Aye.

CHAIRMAN WEEKS: Contrary, nay. It is so ordered.

The motion carried.

READING CLERK—Continues.

RESOLUTION

WHEREAS the Congress of the United States on February 20, 1933, submitted to the several states the following proposed Amendment to the Constitution of the United States.

Resolved by the Senate and House of Representatives of the United States of America in Congress assembled (two-thirds of each House concurring therein), that the following article is hereby proposed as an amendment to the Constitution of the United States, which shall be valid to all intents and purposes as part of the Constitution when ratified by Conventions in three-fourths of the several States:

ARTICLE ___

Section 1. The eighteenth article of Amendment to the Constitution of the United States is hereby repealed.

Section 2. The transportation or importation into any State, Territory, or possession of the United States for delivery or use therein of intoxicating liquors, in violation of the laws thereof, is hereby prohibited.

Section 3. This article shall be inoperative unless it shall have been ratified as an Amendment to the Constitution by Conventions in the several States, as provided in the Constitution, within seven years from the date of the submission hereof to the States by the Congress.

AND WHEREAS the Fifty-seventh General Assembly of the State of Missouri enacted a law known as House Bill 514 providing for the selection of delegates and providing for a convention to be held in the State of Missouri for the purpose of acting upon the proposed Amendment aforesaid.

AND WHEREAS pursuant to the aforesaid resolution of Congress and the aforesaid Act of the Fifty-seventh General Assembly of the State of Missouri, the Honorable Frank G. Harris, Lieutenant-Governor and acting Governor of the State of Missouri, on the 25th day of July, 1933, issued the proclamation of the Governor to the people of the State of Missouri, calling upon them to select delegates and therein provided for the calling of a special election to be held on Saturday, August 19, 1933, for the purpose of electing delegates to a convention to be held at the capitol of the State of Missouri in Jefferson City, Missouri, on August 29, 1933.

AND WHEREAS said delegates as provided for in said proclamation of the Governor were duly selected by the voters in the several senatorial districts in the State of Missouri and that on August 19, 1933, "the delegates favoring the pending amendment to the Constitution of the United States" were duly elected as certified by the Secretary of State to the Governor and declared duly elected by the Governor of Missouri in his proclamation made and issued on August 25, 1933.

AND WHEREAS the aforesaid delegates so selected and elected have duly assembled in convention at the Capitol of the State of Missouri in Jefferson City, Missouri, in pursuance to the foregoing act of the Missouri Legislature and the proclamation of the Governor of Missouri.

Now therefore, be it resolved by the delegates in convention assembled as aforesaid that the amendment to the Constitution of the United States as proposed by Congress on February 20, 1933, which is as follows:

Resolved by the Senate and House of Representatives of the United States of America in Congress assembled (two-thirds of each House concurring therein), that the following article is hereby proposed as an Amendment to the Constitution of the United States, which shall be valid to all intents and purposes as part of the Constitution when ratified by Conventions in three-fourths of the several States:

ARTICLE ___

Section 1. The eighteenth article of Amendment to the Constitution of the United States is hereby repealed.

Section 2. The transportation or importation into any State, Territory, or possession of the United States for delivery or use therein of intoxicating liquors, in violation of the laws thereof, is hereby prohibited.

Section 3. This article shall be inoperative unless it shall have been ratified as an Amendment to the Constitution by Conventions in the several States, as provided in the Constitution, within seven years from the date of the submission thereof to the States by the Congress.

Be and the same is hereby ratified by this Convention on behalf of the State of Missouri and its citizens.

CHAIRMAN WEEKS: Any further reports, Mr. Clerk?

READING CLERK: No, that is all.

CHAIRMAN WEEKS: Ladies and Gentlemen of the Convention, you have heard read all reports; what is your pleasure?

JUDGE TAYLOR: Mr. Chairman.

CHAIRMAN WEEKS: Judge Taylor.

JUDGE TAYLOR: As I heard it, the date of the Governor's Proclamation was given as the 25th of the month. I think it should be the 28th.

READING CLERK: It is the 28th. I read the 25th, but it is the 28th; it is dim but really is the 28th.

JUDGE TAYLOR: May it be corrected before we go on?

CHAIRMAN WEEKS: That can be corrected before we go further.

READING CLERK: It is corrected.

CHAIRMAN WEEKS: It is corrected. What is your pleasure on the Resolution?

FROM THE FLOOR: Mr. Chairman, I move the adoption of the Resolution.

CHAIRMAN WEEKS: It is duly moved and seconded that the Resolution of the Committee be adopted as the voice of this Convention. All those in favor of the adoption of the motion will make it known by saying aye.

FROM THE FLOOR: Aye.

CHAIRMAN WEEKS: Contrary, nay. There being no dissenting voice, I declare the vote cast as unanimous.

JUDGE TAYLOR: Mr. Chairman, before the motion for adjournment is put, I have a question. In what manner will the proceedings of this Convention be preserved?

CHAIRMAN WEEKS: For your information and information of the Convention, Judge Taylor, I have been informed by the Honorable Dwight Brown that he and Governor Park propose to embody the deliberations of this Assemblage in printed form for preservation in the archives of the State of Missouri, and that a copy of the proceedings will be given each member of this Convention.

JUDGE TAYLOR: Now that will be in the archives of the State of Missouri?

CHAIRMAN WEEKS: Yes, sir. In the Secretary of State's office.

JUDGE TAYLOR: Is there any means of our communicating the action of this Convention to the Federal Government?

CHAIRMAN WEEKS: Under the terms of the Law, the very act of certification by the Secretary and the Chairman of this Convention is duly mailed to the Secretary of State of the United States, and the mailing thereof by the Secretary of the State of Missouri to the Secretary of State of the United States will complete the transaction. You have put your vote on record, the voice of the people of the State of Missouri, and there being no further deliberations before this Convention, a motion to adjourn is now in order.

FROM THE FLOOR: I move that we now adjourn.

CHAIRMAN WEEKS: Do I hear a second to the motion to adjourn?

FROM THE FLOOR: Seconded.

CHAIRMAN WEEKS: All in favor say aye.

FROM THE FLOOR: Aye.

CHAIRMAN WEEKS: Contrary, Nay. I now declare this Convention adjourned, *sine die*. (Applause.)

Whereupon at 1:08 o'clock P.M. on the 29th day of August, 1933, the Convention adjourned.

RESOLUTION OF RESPECT

To the Memory of Hon. William D. O'Bannon, of Sedalia, delegate to the Missouri Constitutional Convention from the Fifteenth Senatorial District, who died August 27, 1933.

(Adopted by the Convention, August 29, 1933.)

WHEREAS, Hon. William D. O'Bannon of Sedalia, Pettis County, Missouri, who was elected a delegate to this convention from the Fifteenth Senatorial District, departed this life on Sunday evening, August 27, 1933; and

WHEREAS, During his lifetime he was one of the best and most widely known lawyers in Missouri, a citizen of progressive and constructive views and constantly interested in the general welfare of the people of this state; he was also respected for his sincere and loving devotion to his family and friends, and his loyal and patriotic service to the State of Missouri; his professional and private life was marked by industry, integrity and courage;

Now, therefore, be it resolved that the State Ratification Convention, in convention assembled, stand in silence in honor of his memory, and extend its heartfelt sympathy to his bereaved family; and that a copy of this resolution be sent to them.

MONTANA*

PROCEEDINGS

OF THE

CONVENTION FOR THE RATIFICATION OR REJECTION

OF THE REPEAL OF THE EIGHTEENTH AMENDMENT

HELD AT

HELENA, MONTANA, AUGUST 6, 1934

The Convention was called to order by F. C. McWilliams of Cascade County. Nominations were called for Temporary President. James E. Fowler of Cascade County nominated R. A. O'Hara of Ravalli County, and the nomination was seconded by Thomas Hurley, Sr., of Cascade County. Thomas N. Bailey of Silver Bow County nominated John Rowe of Silver Bow County, and James J. Stafford of Silver Bow County, seconded the nomination of Mr. Rowe. Oliver Faribault of Deer Lodge County made a motion that the nominations be closed, and Thomas Hurley, Sr., of Cascade County, seconded the motion, which was duly passed.

Mrs. Margaret Marsh of Anaconda made a motion to recess for ten minutes. Thomas Hurley, Sr., of Cascade County, seconded the motion, which was duly passed.

The meeting was called to order after a ten minute recess, by the Chairman.

After recess, the Convention proceeded to the election of a Temporary President. There were forty-two (42) ballots cast, of which R. A. O'Hara received twenty-eight (28) and John Rowe fourteen (14).

Mr. O'Hara was declared elected Temporary President.

MR. O'HARA then took the Chair and addressed the Convention as follows: I don't think that I will take up time to make a speech. I want to thank you for the honor conferred upon me and say that I hope our labors will be pleasant and not strung out too long and that we are, for the first time, I believe, in the history of the country, at least for the last hundred years, met in a Constitutional Convention and we ought to be proud of the fact that we became delegates to the first Constitutional Convention for the purpose of amending the Constitution of the United States, even though our labor amounts to nothing further than putting Montana on record.

It was moved and seconded, and passed by unanimous vote, that a committee on credentials, consisting of five members, be appointed by the Chair. The President thereupon appointed:

James E. Fowler of Cascade County
John Rowe of Silver Bow County
C. A. Smithey of Ravalli County
Daniel Moltzau of Fergus County
L. D. Carver of Broadwater County.

The delegates were requested to present their credentials to Mr. Fowler, the Chair-

---

* From a typewritten copy.

man of the committee, and a recess of fifteen minutes was declared for that purpose.

The meeting was called to order by the President after recess.

The President thereupon called for nominations for Temporary Secretary. F. C. McWilliams of Cascade County nominated M. G. Carver of Chouteau County, and the nomination was seconded by Thomas Hurley, Sr., of Cascade County. James J. Stafford of Silver Bow County nominated Deane Jones of Missoula County. Oliver Faribault of Deer Lodge County nominated Mrs. Marsh of Deer Lodge County. The nomination was seconded by Fred Skalicky of Fergus County. John O. Peterson made a motion that the nominations be closed. The motion was seconded by James E. Fowler of Cascade County, and upon vote taken, carried.

The Convention then proceeded to the election of a Temporary Secretary by ballot.

There were forty-seven (47) ballots cast, of which Deane Jones received twenty-one (21); Mrs. Margaret Marsh fourteen (14) and W. G. Carver twelve (12).

A motion was made by Thomas Hurley, Sr., of Cascade County, that Mr. Carver's name be eliminated and that a vote be cast for the two receiving the highest vote. Motion was seconded by Oliver Faribault of Deer Lodge County, and carried.

The Convention then proceeded to ballot on Mr. Jones and Mrs. Marsh for Temporary Secretary.

There were forty-seven (47) votes cast as follows: Deane Jones received twenty-seven (27) votes; Mrs. Margaret Marsh nineteen (19) and W. G. Carver one (1).

A motion was made by Fred Skalicky of Fergus County, that Miss Anna Kain be elected stenographer to the Secretary, Mr. Jones. The motion was seconded by L. F. Greenup of Daniels County, and after unanimous vote Miss Kain was declared elected stenographer of the meeting.

F. C. McWilliams of Cascade made a motion that a committee of two be appointed to escort the Chief Justice in to swear in the delegates. The motion was seconded by James E. Fowler of Cascade County, and passed by unanimous vote.

On this committee President O'Hara appointed F. C. McWilliams and L. F. Greenup.

The committee on credentials reported that the credentials of the delegates were all found to be satisfactory.

John Rowe of Silver Bow made a motion, which was seconded by Mr. Emswiler of Carter County, that the report of the committee on credentials be adopted and that the committee be continued to consider any further credentials that may be presented. The motion was duly passed.

President O'Hara asked for a roll call of delegates. Forty-seven answered present.

Mr. Rowe made a motion that the Convention go on record as voting by acclamation the Temporary President and Temporary Secretary to be Permanent President and Permanent Secretary to the Convention. The motion was duly seconded and passed.

Chief Justice Callaway then appeared and administered the oath to the delegates present.

PRESIDENT O'HARA: The question now, gentlemen, is a method of procedure.

Oliver Faribault made a motion that E. K. Matson, Assistant Attorney General, who was present, give the delegates a line-up on the procedure of the Convention.

PRESIDENT O'HARA: The procedure is simply whether we proceed by a committee or resolution offered by the floor. In order to know what we are here for, I will read the proposed amendment to the Constitution of the United States.

Section 1. The Eighteenth Article of Amendment to the Constitution of the United States is hereby repealed.

Section 2. The transportation or importation into any State, Territory, or possession of the United States for delivery or use therein of intoxicating liquors, in violation of the laws thereof, is hereby prohibited.

Section 3. This article shall be inoperative unless it shall have been ratified as an amendment to the Constitution by Conventions in the several States, as provided in the Constitution, within seven years from the date of the submission hereof to the States by the Congress.

John Rowe of Silver Bow County made a motion for recess. Motion defeated.

L. F. GREENUP of Daniels County: It would facilitate matters greatly if we would appoint whatever committees are necessary and recess, giving the committees time to perform their duties.

PRESIDENT O'HARA: We are here on faith in the next legislature that they will pay our mileage and per diem and I think a committee should be appointed to look after that and that there should be a committee appointed to also see that everything is regular and that whatever is to be done will be done, and my suggestion would be that if these committees, or any other committees are agreeable to the Convention that they be appointed by the Chair, or selected by the Convention. I have no desire to run committees. And I suggest that we then adjourn, say until 1:30 or something like that, and have the committees ready to make their reports.

L. F. GREENUP of Daniels: I believe that we should have a committee to arrange mileage and per diem and I suggest that a committee of three be appointed to act on mileage and per diem and refer the matter to the State Board of Examiners.

M. G. CARVER of Chouteau County: I second the motion.

PRESIDENT O'HARA: It has been regularly moved and seconded that a committee of three be appointed to take care of the mileage and per diem. All those in favor signify by saying aye; contrary minded, no. The ayes have it. On this committee I appoint: L. F. Greenup, M. G. Carver and James Stafford.

JOHN ROWE of Silver Bow County: I make a motion that the Assistant Secretary receive the same pay as the delegates to the Convention.

THOMAS N. BAILEY of Silver Bow County: I wish to make an amendment to give her the same pay as the Secretary will receive. We are entitled to give the Secretary additional pay. We may pay any delegate of this Convention additional compensation if we so desire. It is up to the Convention to do so. That is why I make the amendment that she receive the same salary as the Secretary receives.

JOHN ROWE: I withdraw my motion, and ask that I may be allowed to read Section 8, Laws of 1933:

"Each delegate shall receive mileage and per diem as provided by law for members of the Legislative Assembly. The Secretary and other officers shall receive such compensation as may be fixed by the Convention."

I move that the regularly elected officers of this Convention, the President and Secretary be allowed $20.00 per day for their services and the same to include the Assistant Secretary.

PRESIDENT O'HARA: I rule the motion out of order. We are not going to accept any additional pay.

JOHN ROWE: I take an appeal from the decision of the Chair.

PRESIDENT O'HARA: All those in favor of the rule of the Chair will signify by saying aye; contrary minded, no. The ayes have it.

PRESIDENT O'HARA: I think that the Chair has been upheld. I rule that the committee on finances, mileage and per diem look after that and make whatever recommendations they want to.

We will now take up the proceedings for our resolution and platform. I suppose that we ought to have a committee to prepare a proper resolution and report it to the Convention, or someone can make a motion on the floor of the Convention—that is just a matter of procedure to be determined by you.

JOEL F. OVERHOLSER of Chouteau County: I move that we appoint a committee and make it a general discussion as to what the opinion of this Convention is as to the various phases of the Liquor Control Act.

THOMAS N. BAILEY of Silver Bow: If you obtain the standing of the delegates on a proposition of that kind, according to law, as I take it that would practically close the proposition because when we have received a vote a majority has agreed either for or against it and that practically ends the session.

OLIVER FARIBAULT of Deer Lodge County: I make a motion that you appoint a resolutions' committee.

The motion was duly seconded.

L. F. GREENUP of Daniels: I believe that a committee consisting of three members be appointed to draft resolutions with the aid of the Assistant Attorney General and that the resolution be in favor of ratifying the repeal of the Eighteenth Amendment. It will then come before the house and be discussed at length and either adopted or rejected.

PRESIDENT O'HARA: Do you accept the amendment, Mr. Faribault?

MR. FARIBAULT: I accept it.

F. C. MCWILLIAMS of Cascade County: I second the motion.

PRESIDENT O'HARA: It has been moved and seconded that a committee of three be appointed to prepare resolutions to present to the Convention on the subject of ratification or rejection of the proposed amendment. An amendment has been offered by Senator Greenup to the effect that the committee be directed to return a resolution favorable to repeal. The vote is on the amendment of Senator Greenup. Are you ready for the question?

The motion was put and carried.

PRESIDENT O'HARA: The vote now is on the original motion of Mr. Faribault of Deer Lodge—the appointment of a committee of three. All in favor signify by saying aye; contrary minded, no. The ayes have it. On this committee I appoint the following:

Faribault of Deer Lodge County
J. D. Walsh of Dawson County
James E. Fowler of Cascade County.

PRESIDENT O'HARA: When will these committees report? What is your pleasure with reference to recessing?

W. G. DUNLAP of Sanders: I make a motion that we recess until 2:00 P.M.

JAMES E. FOWLER of Cascade: I second the motion.

MR. O'HARA: You have heard the motion. Are you ready for the question?

The motion was then put and carried, and the Convention recessed until 2:00 P.M.

AUGUST 6, 1934—2:00 P.M.

Convention called to order, the President in the Chair.

The Secretary called the roll. Two additional delegates were present, making a total of forty-nine.

The resolution which was drafted by the committee on resolutions, was read by the Secretary, as follows:

A RESOLUTION RATIFYING THE AMENDMENT TO THE CONSTITUTION OF THE UNITED STATES RELATING TO INTOXICATING LIQUORS, AND REPEALING THE EIGHTEENTH ARTICLE OF AMENDMENT TO THE CONSTITUTION OF THE UNITED STATES

WHEREAS, at the second session of the Seventy-second Congress of the United States of America, it was resolved by the Senate and House of Representatives of the United States in Congress assembled, that the following amendment to the Constitution of the United States be made:

Section 1. The Eighteenth Article of Amendment to the Constitution of the United States is hereby repealed.

Section 2. The transportation or importation into any State, Territory, or possession of the United States for delivery or use therein of intoxicating liquors, in violation of the laws thereof, is hereby prohibited.

Section 3. This article shall be inoperative unless it shall have been ratified as an amendment to the Constitution by Conventions in the several States, as provided in the Constitution, within seven years from the date of the submission hereof to the States by the Congress.

AND, WHEREAS, this Convention has been duly called and held according to Chapter 188 of the Twenty-third Legislative Assembly of the State of Montana, and as provided by said Section 3 above;

Therefore, be it resolved by this Convention that the said proposed amendment to the Constitution of the United States of America be, and the same is hereby ratified by this Convention.

OLIVER FARIBAULT
JAMES E. FOWLER
J. D. WALSH
Resolutions Committee.

FARIBAULT of Deer Lodge County: I make a motion that the resolution be adopted.

FOWLER of Cascade County: I second the motion.

GREENUP of Daniels County: It seems to me that we are premature in offering this resolution at this time. There are other committees that should report prior to any action on the resolution.

PRESIDENT O'HARA: It doesn't make any difference about the way of matters.

The question was raised as to what constitutes a quorum, and discussed at length.

OVERHOLSER of Chouteau: It seems to me that before we take action on this resolution, this Convention should go on record in regard to the State Liquor Control situation in this: There have been a number of complaints regarding bootlegging that has gone on under the liquor system. We are not authorized to state whether we favor the ratification of this system, or its modification, or favor a change of the system and favor the adoption of a saloon system.

PRESIDENT O'HARA: I would rule any argument of that kind out of order. We are here to either ratify or reject the Eighteenth Amendment.

OVERHOLSER of Chouteau: The resolution that I recommend would give the state officials some kind of an idea how popular their liquor control system is.

PRESIDENT O'HARA: As far as the Chair is concerned, I think we should now consider the resolution.

James Stafford of Silver Bow read Section 7, Chapter 188, Laws of 1933:

"A majority of the total number of delegates to the convention shall constitute a quorum. The convention shall have power to choose a President and Secretary, and all other necessary officers, and to make rules governing the procedure of the convention. It shall be the judge of the qualifications and election of its own members."

MRS. MARSH: How many delegates voted this morning? I have heard rumors that forty-two were all that were qualified to sit in, and forty-seven votes were cast. It seems as if the ballot was padded.

JOHN ROWE of Silver Bow: The credentials' committee showed forty-two accredited delegates here. It deserves some explanation.

The Secretary's report showed forty-seven present.

PRESIDENT O'HARA: As the Chair understands the matter there were forty-seven delegates reported by the credentials' committee this morning and we are further advised that two delegates have since presented proper credentials. I will now ask the Chairman of the committee on credentials to report those two so there will be no misunderstanding as to who constitutes the Convention.

MR. FOWLER of Cascade: D. E. Daugherty of Fallon County and E. C. Harington of Granite County.

It was moved and seconded that the roll as originally reported by the credentials committee have added to it the names of D. E. Daugherty of Fallon County and E. C. Harington of Granite County.

The motion was put and carried.

SAM YOUNG of Golden Valley: As to the status of the delegates here, if I am not misinformed, each delegate is under instruction in his declaration to the voters that elected him, either for or against and it appears to me that in this motion that you offered and withdrew here that we come up with just one sweep and get it all over. It seems to me that this should be determined by a direct vote of each delegate to this Convention.

PRESIDENT O'HARA: It will be determined by a roll call. The motion has been made and seconded to adopt the resolution which has been read. Unless anyone wants it read again, we will proceed.

The vote on the resolution was as follows:

45 voting "yes"
4 voting "no"

PRESIDENT O'HARA: The resolution is adopted.

GREENUP of Daniels County: The committee on mileage and per diem has found many difficulties in performing their duties and so far we are not yet quite ready to report. We have not had sufficient time to write out a report though most of our work, I believe, is done. The Attorney General is drawing up some papers for us which are not yet complete. I might say our difficulty has been that the Attorney General's office has held for some time that each of you had to file an individual claim. It has taken some time to convince them that this committee could file a claim for the whole delegation. They finally came around to our point of view and the Attorney General is now drawing up a claim for all of us instead of the individual claims. It would be quite a task to fill out forty-nine of these individual claims and we figured that one would be sufficient and as soon as the Attorney General provides us with this claim we will be ready to report.

MR. MATSON, ASSISTANT ATTORNEY GENERAL: May I say a word in answer to what Mr. Greenup stated? I think there must be some misunderstanding as to what the Attorney General has ruled. The Attorney General simply ruled that there was no appropriation passed by the last legislature. Whether it shall be an individual claim or a joint claim—that question has never been submitted to the Attorney General's Office.

GROVER DOWEN of Blaine County: I move that we recess for half an hour in order to let this committee complete its work.

The motion was duly seconded.

PRESIDENT O'HARA: It has been regularly moved and seconded that we recess for half an hour in order to let this committee complete its work. Are you ready for the question?

The motion was put and carried.

PRESIDENT O'HARA: We will recess for half an hour.

The meeting was called to order by the President.

Motion was made by Harington of Granite County to adjourn until 10:00 o'clock Tuesday morning, August 7, 1934.

Motion defeated.

Motion was made by Emswiler of Carter County, and seconded by Skalicky of Fergus County, to send a committee to the State Board of Examiners to determine whether claims for the Convention could be paid from the Emergency Fund.

The motion was carried.

President O'Hara appointed the following committee:

Emswiler of Carter County
Howell of Richland County
Skalicky of Fergus County

Mr. Matson, Assistant Attorney General, reported on procedure for paying claims of delegates and suggested that in addition to report of Convention, as an extra precaution, individual claims be presented by delegates.

SECRETARY DEANE JONES read the report of the committee on mileage and per diem, which was as follows:

We, your Committee on Mileage and Per Diem having had under consideration the mileage and per diem of the various members of the Convention for the ratification or rejection of the repeal of the Eighteenth Amendment, beg leave to report.

That the mileage of the various members is as set forth in the accompanying sheet or sheets, and that up to and including August 6, the per diem will be only one day each in addition to the mileage as given.

We further recommend that the President and Secretary be allowed $5.00 per day additional and that the stenographer be entitled to $10.00 for her labors in transcribing the records and the minutes of the meeting.

L. F. Greenup
M. G. Carver
James J. Stafford
Committee on Mileage and Per Diem

We, your Committee on Mileage and Per Diem, beg leave to submit the following report indicating the number of miles traveled by the following elected delegates of State Convention for ratification or rejection of the Twenty-first amendment, and the sums due therefor:

NAMES OF DELEGATES	COUNTY	CITY	MILEAGE	AT 7c	PER DIEM
William J. Corkill	Meagher	White Sulphur Springs	240	$16.80	$10.00
Oliver Faribault	Deer Lodge	Anaconda	196	13.72	10.00
Alf Cullen	Hill	Havre	442	30.94	10.00
John O. Peterson	Hill	Havre	442	30.94	10.00
Deane S. Jones	Missoula	Missoula	238	16.65	15.00
Mrs. Chas. E. Behner	Yellowstone	Billings	478	33.46	10.00
R. A. O'Hara	Ravalli	Hamilton	350	24.50	15.00
J. D. Walsh	Dawson	Glendive	928	64.96	10.00
L. E. Lande	Liberty	Chester	520	36.40	10.00
J. E. Mallery	Park	Livingston	246	17.22	10.00
C. L. Krey	Park	Livingston	246	17.22	10.00
Chas. Glattly	Lake	Polson	390	27.30	10.00
I. E. Thomas	Prairie	Terry	848	59.36	10.00
Samuel Maloney	Madison	Alder	322	22.54	10.00
Joel F. Overholser	Chouteau	Fort Benton	284	19.88	10.00
Thomas N. Bailey	Silver Bow	Butte	144	10.08	10.00
Elmer H. Wolz	Lincoln	Libby	776	54.32	10.00
Fred Skalicky	Fergus	Lewistown	430	30.10	10.00
Ashton Jones	Powder River	Broadus	934	65.38	10.00
S. J. Emswiler	Garter	Ekalaka	1062	74.34	10.00
Margaret Marsh	Deer Lodge	Anaconda	196	13.72	10.00
James J. Stafford	Silver Bow	Butte	144	10.08	10.00
James E. Fowler	Cascade	Great Falls	196	13.72	10.00
Daniel Moltzau	Fergus	Fergus	500	35.00	10.00
C. A. Smithey	Ravalli	Hamilton	350	24.50	10.00
John Rowe	Silver Bow	Butte	144	10.08	10.00
L. D. Carver	Broadwater	Townsend	64	4.46	10.00
M. G. Carver	Chouteau	Fort Benton	284	19.88	10.00
W. F. Allison	Glacier	Cut Bank	428	29.96	10.00
Thomas Hurley, Sr.	Cascade	Great Falls	196	13.72	10.00
Edmund J. Blackwood	Yellowstone	Billings	478	33.40	10.00
F. J. Sherry	Sheridan	Redstone	1144	80.08	10.00
L. F. Greenup	Daniels	Peerless	1248	87.36	10.00
Fred C. Burgwald	Blaine	Chinook	486	34.02	10.00
Grover Dowen	Blaine	Chinook	486	34.02	10.00

NAMES OF DELEGATES	COUNTY	CITY	MILEAGE	AT 7c	PER DIEM
Terry F. C. Browning	Beaverhead	Dillon	274	19.18	10.00
Hans H. Larsen	Sheridan	Reserve	1068	74.76	10.00
W. S. Allen	McCone	Brockway	1056	73.92	10.00
George M. Howell	Richland	Lambert	1138	78.96	10.00
F. M. Poindexter	Beaverhead	Dillon	274	19.18	10.00
James D. Law	Wheatland	Harlowton	298	20.86	10.00
M. E. McConkey	Mineral	Alberton	306	21.42	10.00
Sam Young	Golden Valley	Ryegate	388	27.16	10.00
F. C. McWilliams	Cascade	Great Falls	196	13.72	10.00
J. L. Alexander	Petroleum	Winnett	540	37.80	10.00
Jack McCausland	Rosebud	Forsyth	740	51.80	10.00
W. G. Dunlap	Sanders	Thompson Falls	444	31.08	10.00
D. E. Daugherty	Fallon	Baker	938	65.66	10.00
E. C. Harington	Granite	Philipsburg	194	13.58	10.00
Anna A. Kain	Lewis and Clark	Helena	Stenographic services		10.00

We, the undersigned, hereby certify that the above and foregoing is a true and correct copy of the number of miles traveled by delegates of the convention as submitted by the Committee on Mileage and Per Diem.

L. F. GREENUP
M. G. CARVER
JAMES J. STAFFORD
Committee on Mileage and Per Diem

MR. GREENUP of Daniels: I move that the report of the committee be adopted.

The motion was duly seconded and carried.

PRESIDENT O'HARA: The committee's report is adopted.

MR. GREENUP of Daniels: I move that we give the Attorney General's Office, and Miss Kain a rising vote of thanks for their assistance.

The motion was seconded and carried by rising vote.

PRESIDENT O'HARA: Is the committee which was sent to interview the Board of Examiners, able to report any progress?

MR. EMSWILER: We found that we can't get any money.

PRESIDENT O'HARA: Our credentials should be filed with the Secretary and become a permanent record of the Convention. I am inclined to think that that is right and so rule that you all now file your credentials with the Secretary.

F. C. MCWILLIAMS of Cascade County: I move that the Convention adjourn *sine die.*

L. F. GREENUP of Daniels County: I second the motion.

PRESIDENT O'HARA: It has been moved and seconded that the Convention adjourn *sine die.* Those in favor of the motion will say aye; contrary minded, no.

The motion was declared carried.

PRESIDENT O'HARA: The Convention will adjourn *sine die.*

At 4:45 P.M. Monday, August 6th, 1934, the Convention of the State of Montana stood adjourned *sine die.*

Approved by
R. A. O'HARA
President

Attest:
DEANE S. JONES
Secretary

NEVADA*

CONVENTION RECORD

Ratifying the Proposed Amendment

Repealing the 18th Amendment

to the Constitution of the United States

September 5, 1933

LIST OF DELEGATES

Churchill County—
Mrs. A. D. Drumm, Sr.
E. J. Maupin, Jr.

Clark County—
A. C. Grant
Dave Holland
Harry C. Gravelle
Wm. J. Wallace, Jr.

Douglas County—
Grover L. Krick

Elko County—
John E. Robbins
Milton B. Badt
Mae McNamara
James Dysart

Esmeralda County—
John J. Noone

Eureka County—
Edgar Eather

Humboldt County—
J. A. Langwith
E. A. Smith

Lander County
D. F. Shovelin

Lincoln County—
A. L. Scott
Thos. E. Dixon

Lyon County—
George W. Friedhoff
William M. Penrose

Mineral County—
T. R. Pledge

Nye County—
Wm. Kennett
Don C. Lewers
George Greenwood

Ormsby County—
M. C. Kloskey

Pershing County—
J. P. Davin

Storey County—
J. W. Locklin

Washoe County—
W. R. Adams
Albert D. Ayres
Alfred Blundell
Lillie B. Clinedinst
F. M. Crosby
J. W. Dignan
James D. Finch
Morley Griswold
John S. Sinai

White Pine County—
F. E. Siegert
J. C. Wheeler
Joe Hopson
Neil A. McGill

CERTIFICATE

Of the Chairman and Secretary of the Nevada State Convention of Delegates, Duly Assembled in Compliance with Chapter 179 (page 252) of the Laws of Nevada, Thirty-Sixth Session (1933)

The undersigned, A. L. Scott, the duly elected Chairman, and Lillie B. Clinedinst,

* Printed. The act of the legislature and the governor's proclamation are omitted here.

the duly elected Secretary, of the State Convention of duly elected, accredited and qualified delegates, duly assembled at the Assembly Chamber of the State Capitol of the State of Nevada, at Carson City, Nevada, on September 5, 1933, at the hour of eleven o'clock A.M., in all respects in full compliance with the statutes in such case made and provided, for the ratification or rejection of a joint resolution of Congress entitled "Joint Resolution proposing an amendment to the Constitution when ratified by convention in three-fourths of the several States," hereby certify:

That at the time and place named above, a quorum, to-wit, thirty-nine (39) of the forty (40) elected delegates, were present, the credentials of each of whom were duly approved, and to each of whom the constitutional oath of office, as such delegate, was duly administered by Hon. J. A. Sanders, Chief Justice of the Supreme Court of the State of Nevada.

That the aforesaid joint resolution of Congress was duly transmitted to the said Convention in person by His Excellency, Fred B. Balzar, the Governor of the State of Nevada, and thereafter read and submitted to the Convention.

That thereupon, it was duly moved and seconded that said joint resolution of Congress be ratified forthwith; whereupon the roll of delegates was called by the Secretary of the Convention, and thirty-nine delegates responded "aye," signifying their desire to ratify the said joint resolution, and their votes were so recorded by the Secretary, whereupon the Chairman declared that said joint resolution had been duly ratified by a majority vote of the duly elected, accredited and qualified delegates, and by the unanimous vote of the delegates present and voting, and had thereby been duly ratified by the State of Nevada. It was thereupon moved, seconded, and unanimously carried that "the Chairman and Secretary of the Convention shall cause a certified copy of the action taken by the Convention on the question of the ratification of said joint resolution to be made, that they shall each affix their signatures thereto as such respective officers, and transmit same to the Secretary of State of Nevada, with the request that he certify to the same and deliver the certified copy, together with his certificate thereon, to His Excellency, the Governor of the State of Nevada, to be transmitted by the Governor, in compliance with the statute, to the Secretary of State of the United States."

In witness whereof we have hereunto subscribed our names at Carson City, Nevada, on this fifth day of September, A.D. 1933.

A. L. Scott
Chairman

Lillie B. Clinedinst
Secretary

ENDORSED

Certificate Relative to State Convention held September 5, 1933. Filed at the request of A. L. Scott, September 8, 1933.

W. G. Greathouse
Secretary of State

By Muriel M. Littlefield
Deputy Secretary of State

CERTIFICATE

STATE OF NEVADA, } ss.
DEPARTMENT OF STATE.

I, W. G. GREATHOUSE, Secretary of State of the State of Nevada, do hereby certify the foregoing is a full, true and correct copy of the original Senate Bill No. 208, Chapter 179, Statutes 1933.

I FURTHER CERTIFY that the foregoing Proclamation is a full, true and correct copy of the Proclamation of his Excellency, F. B. Balzar, Governor of Nevada, calling a convention to accept or reject the proposed amendment to the Constitution of the United States, which said Proclamation was filed in my office on April 18, 1933, and that said Proclamation was duly published as required by law.

I FURTHER CERTIFY that the number of members of the Assembly to which each county was entitled in the Assembly in the Thirty-sixth Session of the Nevada State Legislature totaled forty (40) and agreed in so far as each county was concerned with the number of delegates elected to the said Convention from each county, and that the foregoing list is a full, true and correct list of the delegates elected to attend the State Convention held at the State Capitol September 5, 1933.

I FURTHER CERTIFY that the Certificate of the Chairman and Secretary of the Nevada State Convention of Delegates, duly assembled in compliance with Chapter 179 (page 252) of the Laws of Nevada, Thirty-sixth Session (1933), herewith published, is a full, true and correct copy of the original Certificate filed in my office on September 8, 1933.

In witness whereof, I have hereunto set my hand and official seal the 8th day of September, 1933.

SEAL

W. G. GREATHOUSE
Secretary of State
By MURIEL M. LITTLEFIELD
Deputy Secretary of State

NEW HAMPSHIRE*

NEW HAMPSHIRE'S VOTE ON REPEAL

OF THE 18TH AMENDMENT

TO THE CONSTITUTION OF THE UNITED STATES

A communication dated February 21, 1933, was received by the Governor of this State, in which was enclosed a certified copy of the Resolution of Congress for the repeal of said Eighteenth Amendment, etc., with the request that this Joint Resolution be submitted to a convention in this State "for such action as may be had."

Accordingly "An Act providing for a Convention to pass on a proposed Amendment to the Constitution of the United States" was passed by our New Hampshire legislature, approved May 6, 1933, and became Chapter 110 of the Laws of 1933.

Among other things, this chapter provided for the choice of twenty candidates, ten of whom would be elected delegates to said Convention by the voters of the State, on June 20, 1933. Ten of these candidates assented to the placing of their names on the ballot as pledged to vote For Ratification and ten, Against Ratification of the Repeal of the Eighteenth Amendment.

The candidates for delegates were as follows:

FOR RATIFICATION	AGAINST RATIFICATION
Robert E. Gould, Newport	Charles E. Brackett, Greenland
Robert C. Murchie, Concord	Burt R. Cooper, Rochester
Norma R. T. Ordway, Berlin	John R. Goodnow, Keene
James P. Richardson, Hanover	John A. Hammond, Gilford
Ashton Rollins, Dover	Margaret E. Hunter, Tuftonboro
John L. Sullivan, Manchester	Gertrude W. Osborne, Weare
Harvey Clinton Taylor, Portsmouth	Alfred T. Pierce, Claremont
Virgil D. White, Ossipee	Charles B. Ross, Lebanon
Abby L. Wilder, Rindge	James S. Shaw, Franklin
Maurice G. Wiley, Laconia	Elbridge W. Snow, Whitefield

The ten favoring Ratification were the persons elected to attend the Convention the date of which was fixed by the Governor as July 11, 1933. At the Convention, *nine* of the ten delegates were present and voted in favor of the Repeal of the Eighteenth Amendment to the Constitution of the United States, there being *no* votes against Repeal.

July 12, 1933, a certificate to this effect was duly signed and attested by the proper officials and forwarded to the Secretary of State of the United States at Washington, D.C.

---

* From the *New Hampshire Manual for the General Court 1935*, pp. 84-85. A summary of the votes by counties is given on pages 86-94. A letter from Mr. James R. Wason of the Legislative Service of the New Hampshire State Library states that "a check with the Secretary of State's office leads us to believe that this is the only available printed record of this convention, the meeting of which was a purely nominal affair." For that reason the brief account of the convention as published in the *Concord Daily Monitor* is printed here.

THE CONCORD DAILY MONITOR

AND NEW HAMPSHIRE PATRIOT

July 11, 1933

Repeal Delegates Meet; Convention Ratifies Wet Vote

Ten delegates, representative of each county of the state but chosen at-large in last month's "referendum" on prohibition, met in convention at the State Senate Chamber this afternoon to formally ratify an amendment to the constitution which will, if ratified by 36 states, take national prohibition out of the constitution of the United States.

The first task of the convention was to organize, like every other legislative body, by election of a chairman. Its secretary will be Secretary of State Enoch D. Fuller, serving by virtue of his office and under arrangement fixed in the law providing machinery for New Hampshire's expression of opinion on the repeal of the amendment.

At 2 o'clock, standard time, the convention delegates were to be called together by Secretary Fuller for the election of the chairman.

The next business on the formal agenda was adoption of the resolution by which New Hampshire will ratify prohibition repeal. This resolution was prepared in advance for the convention of delegates by the secretary of state who was to transmit the action of the convention to the secretary of state at Washington.

New Hampshire's letter of transmittal certifying the state's action will report that the joint resolution adopted by Congress and submitted to the states for action was transmitted to the convention and that the members assembled in convention, duly elected for that purpose, "did cast their individual ballots at said convention."

The letter of transmittal will further report that the vote was unanimous for repeal of the 18th amendment.

This letter will carry the signatures of the chairman of the convention and of the secretary of the convention with their signatures attested by the secretary of state. It will carry the "great seal" of the state of New Hampshire.

July 12, 1933

Act on Repeal in 17 Minutes

Delegates Name Prof. J. P. Richardson, Hanover, as Chairman

Delegates to the New Hampshire convention elected for that purpose took just 17 minutes to formally record New Hampshire in favor of repeal of the 18th amendment at an assembly in the State House Senate Chamber yesterday. Professor James P. Richardson of Hanover, former member of the legislature, was elected chairman of the convention and he started the proceedings with a short statement in which he pointed out that there was no occasion for speeches.

The convention immediately proceeded to ballot with the nine attending members casting their votes according to their pledges for repeal of national prohibition.

Robert E. Gould of Newport was the only absent delegate and he sent word that only illness and the orders of a physician kept him away from the proceedings.

With the mailing of the certified record of the proceedings to Washington, New Hampshire's part in the repeal proceedings was completed.

Delegates elected to the convention were Robert E. Gould of Newport, Robert C. Murchie of Concord, Norma T. Ordway of Berlin, James P. Richardson of Hanover. Ashton Rollins of Dover, John L. Sullivan of Manchester, Harvey Clinton Taylor of Portsmouth, Virgil D. White of Ossipee, Abby L. Wilder of Rindge, and Maurice G. Wiley of Laconia.

To make way for the repeal convention, members of the state relief administration who have established their workshop in the Senate chamber were forced to move out while the convention proceedings were in process.

Today's convention marked the last phase of New Hampshire's participation in the repeal effort. It will now await with interest the subsequent repeal elections in other states as its own action will be of no avail unless 36 states take action similar to that taken by New Hampshire and the 16 other states which have so far acted on repeal.

NEW JERSEY*

CONVENTION

TO RATIFY THE TWENTY-FIRST AMENDMENT TO THE CONSTITUTION OF THE UNITED STATES

DESIGNED TO REPEAL THE EIGHTEENTH ARTICLE OF AMENDMENT

TO THE

CONSTITUTION OF THE UNITED STATES

HELD PURSUANT TO CHAPTER SEVENTY-THREE

OF THE

LAWS OF ONE THOUSAND NINE HUNDRED AND THIRTY-THREE

MEMORIAL BUILDING

STACY PARK

TRENTON, N. J.

In accordance with the proclamation of His Excellency, The Governor, A. Harry Moore, the Convention met in the Memorial Building, Stacy Park, City of Trenton, on Thursday, the first day of June, one thousand nine hundred and thirty-three, at eleven o'clock A.M. (Eastern Standard Time).

The Convention was called to order by His Excellency A. Harry Moore, Governor of the State of New Jersey.

The call of the Convention was read by the Honorable Thomas A. Mathis, Secretary of State, followed by the calling of the roll of delegates.

The Convention then proceeded to the election of a Permanent Chairman. The Honorable Emerson L. Richards, President of the Senate of the State of New Jersey was unanimously chosen Chairman of the Convention.

On taking the Chair Mr. Richards addressed the Convention as follows:

LADIES AND GENTLEMEN OF THE CONVENTION:

When we have made a mistake the American people are big enough to admit it. Today we meet to lend New Jersey's sanction to the repeal of the Eighteenth Amendment. After fifteen years of trial we have concluded almost unanimously that laws will not make us a temperate people. We are about to begin again.

It is significant that in righting a wrong that we have done to our government and ourselves we should return to this ancient form of popular expression—the convention. The structure of our government was wrought in the fires of debate

* From a photostat of the typewritten original.

in the colonial convention. We return to the convention to expunge from our Constitution a political and moral heresy.

Our Constitution is only a power of attorney, signed by the people, giving to their representatives limited powers. Laws governing the people have no place in such a document. If, for no other reason, the Eighteenth Amendment should never have been written into our Constitution. Today, not by revolution—not by bloody strife, but by a determined, clear-thinking and resolved citizenry we strike from that constitution the dangerous adventure which has so nearly wrecked our ship of state.

It is well that we act in the convention form. Representative councils by whatever name they are called—legislatures, congresses or Parliament—are unpopular in the eyes of the peoples of the world. Dictatorships, with their accompanying surrender of legislative power have momentarily captured the popular imagination. It is good, then, for us to remember that in the midst of a multitude of governmental experiments we still possess and exercise the greatest weapon for the correction of the evils of government—the constitutional convention.

It is a great honor to preside over this convention. The delegates here assembled represent the leadership, the intellect and the courage of two great political parties joined together in a common cause. The promotion of temperance and the sane regulation of the use of beverages containing alcohol is not a partisan question.

The recent action of our sister states indicates that within a very brief time the Eighteenth Amendment will have been repealed. We will then face an entirely new set of conditions.

The evils brought about by the Eighteenth Amendment were too many to recite here—its revival of intemperance—the spread of the use of liquor among people who had heretofore been abstainers—the change in the viewpoint of society toward the consumption of liquor—the rise of the racketeer—inevitable corruption of governmental functions—the loss of prestige of the Federal Government are but some of the grievious damages done to ourselves. Now, the course of destruction may be arrested, but there remains the greater task of reconstruction.

We have passed through a moral civil war. We have yet to reconcile the participants, bind up the wounds of the contestants, restore the damage to our institutions, and plan for a settled peace.

The experience of the past will be of slight advantage to us now. The world has moved forward in these fifteen years. The exterior of our civilization has been molded on modernistic lines. The change in transportation with the universal use of the automobile, the participation of women in those forms of social recreation formerly reserved for men, the changed viewpoint concerning the consumption of alcoholic beverages will all operate to surround the dispensation of such beverages with an entirely different atmosphere.

We have talked about the revival of the old-time saloon. After nearly two months of test we realize that beer did not bring back the saloon, but that it is on the other hand promoting temperance. The modern speak-easy is already deserted. It will not long survive. Undoubtedly, other unexpected and surprising changes in our preconceived notion of how to deal with the new condition awaits us. Careful planning and mutual counsel will be necessary for the adequate solution of the new problem. One mistake we will not make—the fanaticism of the drys must not be answered by a counter intolerance of the wets.

Temperance in thought and deed must be our watchword. Respect for the opinion and rights of the minority must be observed. The Eighteenth Amendment failed because it did not respect the principle that morality is not a matter of law, but a matter of eternal justice.

Before that seat of judgment we all stand to be judged by the way we have used this vindication of the right of the people to govern themselves.

The Convention then proceeded to the election of a Permanent Secretary.

Mr. Oliver F. Van Camp, Secretary of the Senate of New Jersey, was unanimously chosen Secretary.

The Chairman named the following committees:

Committee on rules

Mary T. Norton
Hamilton F. Kean
John J. Toohey, Jr.
Mary Sayles Moore
Charles V. Duffy
Aletta H. K. Stout
Alice R. Pickard
Grace Fanshaw Allen
Louis V. Aronson

Committee on credentials

Walter E. Edge
W. Warren Barbour
John D. Hinchliffe
David Wilentz
Daniel E. Pomeroy

Committee on resolutions

Arthur Foran
Thomas N. McCarter
William H. J. Ely
Joseph G. Wolber
Lewis Ballantyne
Edward M. Waldron
May M. Carty
George B. LaBarre
P. H. V. Frelinghuysen
F. A. McBride
Oscar L. Auf der Heide
Jesse Salmon

Honorable Mary T. Norton, Chairman of the Committee on Rules, moved that the rules of the House of Assembly of the State of New Jersey for 1933 be adopted as the rules of this convention.

Which motion was adopted.

Honorable Walter E. Edge, Chairman of the Committee on Credentials, reported all delegates duly elected and that there were no contests.

Arthur Foran, Chairman of the Committee on Resolutions, offered the following resolution and moved its adoption:

WHEREAS, the Senate and House of Representatives of the United States of America in Congress assembled (two-thirds of each House concurring therein) did resolve that the following article is hereby proposed as an amendment to the Constitution of the United States, which shall be valid to all intents and purposes as a part of the Constitution when ratified by convention in three-fourths of the several States; and,

WHEREAS, the said proposed amendment reads as follows:

Section 1. The eighteenth article of amendment to the Constitution of the United States is hereby repealed.

Section 2. The transportation or importation into any State, territory, or possession of the United States for delivery or use therein of intoxicating liquors, in violation of the laws thereof is hereby prohibited.

Section 3. This article shall be inoperative unless it shall have been ratified as an amendment to the Constitution by conventions in the several States, as provided in the Constitution, within seven years from the date of submission hereof to the States by the Congress; and,

WHEREAS, there was duly transmitted to the Legislature of this State the said article of amendment proposed by the Congress to the Constitution of the United States; and,

WHEREAS, the Legislature of this State, pursuant to law, did enact a statute entitled, "An Act providing for the election of delegates to a convention and providing for the holding of a convention to consider the article of amendment, proposed by the Congress, to the Constitution of the United States designed to repeal the eighteenth article of amendment," which said act having passed both Houses of the Legislature, was signed by the Governor of this State on March twenty-third, one thousand nine hundred and thirty-three and constitutes Chapter seventy-three of the Laws of New Jersey for the year one thousand nine hundred and thirty-three; and,

WHEREAS, pursuant to the provisions of said act of the Legislature an election for the selection of delegates to the said convention was held in this State on May sixteenth, one thousand nine hundred and thirty-three, at which said election delegates were chosen in accordance with the provisions of said statute; and,

WHEREAS, on May twenty-second, one thousand nine hundred and thirty-three, His Excellency, A. Harry Moore, Governor of the State of New Jersey, pursuant to the provisions of said act of the Legislature did issue his said proclamation for the holding of the said convention, which said proclamation reads as follows:

WHEREAS, pursuant to Chapter 73 of the Laws of 1933, an election was held on the sixteenth day of May, 1933, for the election of delegates to the Convention to consider the Article of Amendment proposed by the Congress to the Constitution of the United States, designed to repeal the Eighteenth Article of Amendment; and,

WHEREAS, Section 13 of said act requires the Governor of this State, within twenty days after the holding of said election, by proclamation, to convene the said convention,

Therefore, I, A. HARRY MOORE, Governor of the State of New Jersey, pursuant to the power and authority vested in me by said act of the Legislature do hereby convene the said convention to meet in the Memorial Building, Stacy Park, in the City of Trenton, on Thursday, the first day of June, next, at the hour of eleven o'clock in the forenoon of said day (Eastern Standard Time).

SEAL

Given under my hand and the Great Seal of the State of New Jersey, this twenty-second day of May, in the year one thousand nine hundred and thirty-three, and in the Independence of the United States the one hundred and fifty-seventh.

A. HARRY MOORE
Governor

THOMAS A. MATHIS,
Secretary of State

WHEREAS, pursuant to the said proclamation of His Excellency, the Governor, the said convention did meet at the time and place therein fixed and having organized by the election of a chairman and secretary and having adopted rules governing its deliberations did proceed to consider the proposed article of amendment; now, therefore,

Be it resolved, by this convention of delegates representing the people of the State of New Jersey, duly assembled pursuant to law, that we do approve and ratify the proposed article of amendment proposed by the Congress to the Constitution of the

United States designed to repeal the Eighteenth Article of Amendment, which said amendment reads as follows:

WHEREAS, The Senate and House of Representatives of the United States of America in Congress assembled (two-thirds of each House concurring therein) did resolve that the following article is hereby proposed as an amendment to the Constitution of the United States, which shall be valid to all intents and purposes as a part of the Constitution when ratified by conventions in three-fourths of the several States; and

WHEREAS, The said proposed amendment reads as follows:

Section 1. The eighteenth article of amendment to the Constitution of the United States is hereby repealed.

Section 2. The transportation or importation into any State, territory, or possession of the United States for delivery or use therein of intoxicating liquors, in violation of the laws thereof is hereby prohibited.

Section 3. This article shall be inoperative unless it shall have been ratified as an amendment to the Constitution by conventions in the several States, as provided in the Constitution, within seven years from the date of submission hereof to the States by the Congress;

And further the action of this convention in approving and ratifying the said proposed amendment is valid to all intents and purposes as representing the people of the State of New Jersey; and

Be it further resolved, That the Chairman and Secretary of this convention shall certify the result of the votes of the delegates to the Secretary of State of this State; and

Be it further resolved, That the Secretary of State of this State shall certify the result of this vote to the Secretary of State of the United States and to the Senate and House of Representatives of the United States.

(*Signed*) EMERSON RICHARDS
Chairman

Attest:

(*Signed*) OLIVER F. VAN CAMP
Secretary

Under the direction of the Chairman, the Secretary called the roll of delegates. There being recorded 202 in the affirmative and two in the negative, the resolution was declared adopted.

The Chairman presented His Excellency, A. Harry Moore, Governor of the State of New Jersey, who addressed the Convention.

The Chairman presented the Honorable Edward C. Stokes, former Governor of the State of New Jersey, who addressed the Convention.

The Chair also presented the Honorable Mary T. Norton, Congresswoman from New Jersey, the Honorable Warren Barbour, Junior United States Senator from New Jersey, the Honorable Hamilton F. Kean, Senior United States Senator from New Jersey, and the Honorable Walter E. Edge, former Governor of the State of New Jersey, former United States Senator from New Jersey, and former United States Ambassador to France, who addressed the Convention.

On motion of Arthur Foran, one of the delegates to the Convention, the Convention adjourned *sine die,*

OLIVER F. VAN CAMP
Secretary

ROLL CALL

Walter E. Edge	X	Louis V. Aronson	
Frank Hague		Pellegrino Pellecchia	X
Hamilton F. Kean	X	Alfred G. Cockefair	X
W. Warren Barbour	X	Frederic B. Kremer	
Emerson L. Richards	X	George V. McDonough	X
Joseph G. Wolber	X	Elizabeth F. Mateer	X
Daniel E. Pomeroy	X	William L. Fox	X
Mary T. Norton	X	William A. Rucki	X
Edward C. Stokes	X	Julia Blewitt	X
George W. Merck	X	John F. Monahan	X
Lewis Ballantyne	X	Edward D. Balentine, Jr.	X
Thomas N. McCarter	X	Helen E. Caldwell	
John J. Toohey, Jr.	X	William C. Fiedler	X
Lawrence H. Kingsford	X	Wm. Ricigliano	X
William H. J. Ely	X	Joseph Kraemer	X
Clarence E. F. Hetrick	X	Alice R. Pickard	X
Charles P. Gillen	X	Andrew C. Wittreich	X
Paul Moore	X	William B. Ross	X
William J. Egan		John Beier Theurer	X
Nathalie Pierrepont	X	Carl Bausewein	X
Charles I. Lafferty	X	John Preiss	X
Ruth W. Roebling	X	Warren G. Thompson	X
John V. Hinchliffe	X	Joseph Flynn	X
Theodore Boettger	X	William H. Butler	X
Mary Sayles Moore	X	Joseph M. Carson	X
J. Frank O'Donnell	X	Robert M. Fielder	X
George B. Post, Jr.	X	Albert F. Giese	X
Harry L. Maloney	X	W. Finley Jones	X
A. J. Cafiero	X	George B. LaBarre	X
Orville V. Mesler	X	Dayton D. McKean	X
Henry W. Peterson	X	Samuel J. Surtees	X
Edmund A. Hayes	X	Bernard J. Walsh	X
Arthur Foran	X	Frederic M. P. Pearse	X
Howard Height	X	Joseph A. Hermann	X
Oliver F. Van Camp	X	John P. Kirkpatrick	
Bernard N. McFeely	X	Henry Haywood	X
Joseph W. Mott	X	Elovine Carpender	X
Harvey J. Moynihan	X	Robert L. McKiernan	X
Charles S. Mackenzie	X	Mathilda H. Baldwin	X
Leo J. Rogers	X	William Hamilton	X
David T. Wilentz	X	Genevieve Tatum	X
Harry Hackney	X	Edward T. Rooney	X
Alfred J. Kurtz	X	John W. Flock	X
Walter Jeffries	X	William J. Ryan	X
Mamie R. Stone	X	Godfrey V. Baker	
Daniel H. V. Bell	X	J. Herbert Sickler	X
Irving I. Jacobs	X	Andrew J. Truckess	X
Ernest Alberque	X	Walter C. Wilkins Jr.	X
Gen'l Charles Burrows	X	Charles L. Munch	X
Charles Carella	X	Bert Daly	X
Charles V. Duffy	X	William J. McGovern	X

ROLL CALL

Jesse R. Salmon	X	Harry J. Thourot	X
Mary D. Meekins	X	Julius L. Reich	X
John McCutcheon	X	John W. Sweeney	X
Oscar L. Auf Der Heide	X	Daniel Herrmann	X
Mary Walsh Kobus	X	Frederick J. Cassert	X
Thomas Barber	X	Herman C. Lange	X
William H. Sutphin		May M. Carty	X
Frederick Richardson	X	Jerome J. Brady	X
Emma E. Hyland	X	Charles J. Murphy	X
Killam Bennett	X	Christian H. Ritter	X
Edward M. Waldron	X	Thomas F. Morgan	X
John A. Schlorer	X	Charles E. Stiles	X
J. Henry Harrison	X	John F. Streckfuss	X
William H. Fisher	X	George J. Tinney	X
Aletta H. K. Stout	X	Andrew Van Riper	
Erwin E. Marshall	X	Lawton W. Witt	X
Robert A. Alberts	X	Walter I. Bacon	X
John E. Toolan		Charles L. Smith	X
Emma Van Schoik	X	Harry H. Peacock	X
John J. Breslin, Jr.		Amory L. Haskell	X
Helen Haines Woodruff	X	William H. R. White	X
Edw. L. Whelan	X	Edwin G. Bruns, Sr.	X
Samuel A. Lanning	X	Peter H. B. Frelinghuysen	X
G. Fred Cronecker	X	Frank Waters	X
G. A. McKeen	X	Brace Fanshawe Allen	X
Emily Carleton		Frank C. Scerbo	
Margaret Hofener	X	Emil G. Kattermann	X
Lillian A. Mathis	X	William A. Hegarty	X
Doris M. Mehrhof	X	Anthony E. Wickham	X
Blanche Saffin	X	Morton Mencher	
Oliver B. Surpless		Arthur Gorman Gallagher	X
Bertha B. Van Stone	X	Caroline Johnson	X
Donald Waesche	X	Nicholas F. Cimmino	X
P. William Wiegers	X	Frank A. McBride	X
Richard P. Hughes	X	Dr. Lester F. Meloney	X
Elizabeth R. Cowperthwait	X	William A. Merz	X
Alma M. Evans	X	Manuel N. Mirsky	X
Walter S. Marter	X	John F. Wilkins	
C. Richard Allen	X	William A. Goddington	X
Gertrude Dugan	X	John Wyckoff Mettler	X
Samuel T. French	X	Milton S. Dillon	X
Anthony F. Gorham	X	Catesby L. Jones	X
C. Mae Marsh	X	William A. Dolan	
Albert S. Marvel, Jr.	X	Lewis Van Blarcom	X
Frank C. Stem		Samuel T. Munson	X
Joseph A. Varbalow	X	Alfred B. Littell	X
D. Miles Rigor	X	John F. Kensh	X
Charles T. Campbell		Wesley A. Stanger	X
James A. Templeton	X	Edward Nugent	X
Benjamin Zelinski	X	Virginia B. Stillman	X
George M. Eichler	X	Albert H. Atterbury	X
Jonathan W. Kirchhoff, Sr.	X	Jules Verner	X
J. Peter Davidow	X	Sarah V. Ackerman	X
Robert W. Kean	X	Allan B. Wallace	X
Mrs. Wm. A. Barstow	X	Francis J. Regula	X
Robert A. Drysdale	X	Harry I. Luftman	X
George M. Rogers	X	John H. Pursel	X

ROLL CALL

William H. Tobin, Jr.	X	Daniel B. McIntosh	X
Anastasia Royce	X	Charles A. Dahlke	X
James A. Whelan	X	Charles B. Brady	X
Mrs. Henry Young, Jr.	X	Samuel Iredell	X
William H. Seely	X	W. Egbert Thomas	X

TO ADOPT RESOLUTION

	Aye	*Nay*
Walter E. Edge	X	
Frank Hague		
Hamilton F. Kean	X	
J. Frank O'Donnell	X	
George B. Post, Jr.	X	
Harry L. Maloney	X	
W. Warren Barbour	X	
Emerson L. Richards	X	
Joseph G. Wolber	X	
Daniel E. Pomeroy	X	
Mary T. Norton	X	
Edward C. Stokes	X	
George W. Merck	X	
Lewis Ballantyne	X	
Thomas N. McCarter	X	
John J. Toohey, Jr.	X	
Lawrence H. Kingsford	X	
William H. J. Ely	X	
Clarence E. F. Hetrick	X	
Charles P. Gillen	X	
Paul Moore	X	
William J. Egan		
Nathalie Pierrepont	X	
Charles I. Lafferty	X	
Ruth W. Roebling	X	
John V. Hinchliffe	X	
Theodore Boettger	X	
Mary Sayles Moore	X	
Charles V. Duffy	X	
Jesse R. Salmon	X	
Mary D. Meekins	X	
John McCutcheon	X	
Oscar L. Auf Der Heide	X	
A. J. Cafiero	X	
Orville V. Meslar	X	
Henry W. Peterson	X	
Edmund A. Hayes	X	
Arthur Foran	X	
Howard Height	X	
Oliver F. Van Camp	X	
Bernard N. McFeely	X	
Joseph W. Mott	X	
Harvey J. Moynihan	X	
Charles S. Mackenzie	X	
Leo J. Rogers	X	
David T. Wilentz	X	
Harry Hackney	X	
Alfred J. Kurtz	X	

	Aye	*Nay*
John Beier Theurer		
Carl Bausewein	X	
John Preiss	X	
Anastasia Royce	X	
James A. Whelan	X	
Mrs. Henry Young, Jr.	X	
William H. Seely	X	
Louis V. Aronson		
Pellegrino Pellecchia	X	
Alfred G. Cockefair	X	
Frederic B. Kremer		
George V. McDonough	X	
Elizabeth F. Mateer	X	
William L. Fox	X	
William A. Ricki	X	
Julia Blewitt	X	
John F. Monahan	X	
Edward D. Balentine, Jr.	X	
Helen E. Caldwell	X	
William C. Fiedler	X	
Wm. Ricigliano	X	
Joseph Kraemer	X	
Alice R. Pickard	X	
William J. Ryan	X	
Godfrey V. Baker		
J. Herbert Sickler	X	
Andrew J. Trucksess	X	
Walter C. Wilkins, Jr.	X	
Warren G. Thompson	X	
Joseph Flynn	X	
William H. Butler	X	
Joseph M. Carson	X	
Robert M. Fielder	X	
Albert F. Giese	X	
W. Finley Jones	X	
George B. LaBarre	X	
Dayton D. McKean	X	
Samuel J. Surtees	X	
Bernard J. Walsh	X	
Frederic M. P. Pearse	X	
Joseph A. Hermann	X	
John P. Kirkpatrick		
Henry Haywood	X	
Elovine Carpender	X	
Robert L. McKiernan	X	
Mathilda H. Baldwin	X	
William Hamilton	X	
Genevieve Tatum	X	

TO ADOPT RESOLUTION

Name	Aye	Nay
Walter Jeffries	X	
Mamie R. Stone	X	
Daniel H. V. Bell	X	
Irving I. Jacobs	X	
Ernest Alberque	X	
Gen'l Charles Burrows	X	
Charles Carella	X	
Emily Carleton		
Margaret Hofener	X	
Lillian A. Mathis	X	
Doris M. Mehrhof	X	
Blanche Saffin	X	
Mary Walsh Kobus	X	
Thomas Barber	X	
William H. Sutphin		
Frederick Richardson	X	
Emma E. Hyland	X	
Killam Bennett	X	
Edward M. Waldron	X	
John A. Schlorer	X	
J. Henry Harrison	X	
William H. Fisher	X	
Aletta H. K. Stout	X	
Erwin E. Marshall	X	
Robert A. Alberts	X	
John E. Toolan		
Emma Van Schoik	X	
John J. Breslin, Jr.		
Helen Haines Woodruff	X	
Edw. L. Whelan	X	
Samuel A. Lanning	X	
G. Fred Cronecker	X	
G. A. McKeen	X	
Jonathan W. Kirchhoff, Sr.	X	
J. Peter Davidow	X	
Robert W. Kean	X	
Mrs. Wm. A. Barstow	X	
Robert A. Drysdale	X	
George M. Rogers	X	
Wm. H. Tobin, Jr.	X	
Oliver B. Surpless		
Bertha B. Van Stone	X	
Donald Waesche	X	
P. William Wiegers	X	
Richard P. Hughes	X	
Eliz. R. Cowperthwait	X	
Alma M. Evans	X	
Walter S. Marter	X	
C. Richard Allen	X	
Gertrude Dugan	X	
Samuel T. French	X	
Anthony F. Gorham	X	
G. Mae Marsh	X	
Albert S. Marvel, Jr.	X	
Frank O. Stem		
Joseph A. Varbalow	X	
Edward T. Rooney	X	
John W. Flock	X	
Amory L. Haskell	X	
William H. R. White	X	
Edwin G. Bruns, Sr.	X	
Charles L. Munch	X	
Bert Daly	X	
William J. McGovern	X	
Harry J. Thourot	X	
Julius L. Reich	X	
John W. Sweeney	X	
Daniel Herrmann	X	
Frederick J. Cassert	X	
Herman C. Lange	X	
May M. Carty	X	
Jerome J. Brady	X	
Charles J. Murphy	X	
Dr. Lester F. Meloney	X	
William A. Merz	X	
Manuel N. Mirsky	X	
Thomas F. Morgan	X	
Charles E. Stiles	X	
John F. Streckfuss		
George J. Tinney	X	
Andrew Van Riper		
Lawton W. Witt	X	
Walter I. Bacon	X	
Charles L. Smith	X	
Harry H. Peacock	X	
William A. Goddington	X	
John Wyckoff Mettler	X	
Milton S. Dillon	X	
Peter H. B. Frelinghuysen	X	
Frank Waters	X	
Grace Fanshawe Allen	X	
Frank C. Scerbo		
Emil G. Kattermann	X	
William A. Hegarty	X	
Anthony E. Wickham	X	
Morton Mencher		
Arthur Gorman Gallagher	X	
Caroline Johnson	X	
Nicholas F. Cimmino	X	
Frank A. McBride	X	
Catesby L. Jones	X	
William A. Dolan		
Lewis Van Blarcom	X	
Samuel T. Munson	X	
Alfred B. Littell	X	
John F. Kenah	X	
Wesley A. Stanger	X	
Edward Nugent	X	
Virginia B. Stillman	X	
Albert H. Atterbury	X	
Jules Verner	X	
Sarah V. Ackerman	X	

TO ADOPT RESOLUTION

	Aye	*Nay*		*Aye*	*Nay*
D. Miles Rigor	X		Allan B. Wallace	X	
Charles T. Campbell			Francis J. Regula	X	
Christian H. Ritter			Harry I. Luftman	X	
James A. Templeton	X		John H. Pursel	X	
Benjamin Zelinski	X		Daniel B. McIntosh	X	
George M. Eichler	X		Charles A. Dahlke	X	
Andrew O. Wittreich	X		Charles B. Brady	X	
William B. Ross	X		Samuel Iredell		X
John F. Wilkens			W. Egbert		X

NEW MEXICO*

JOURNAL

OF THE

MEETING OF THE CONVENTION OF DELEGATES

ELECTED TO VOTE ON RATIFICATION OF AMENDMENT

TO THE

CONSTITUTION OF THE UNITED STATES

Now on this day, pursuant to the laws of the State of New Mexico, the delegates, duly elected at the Special Election held on the nineteenth day of September, 1933, met at Santa Fe, New Mexico, at noon in the Chamber of the Senate of the State of New Mexico for the purpose of casting their vote to amend the Constitution of the United States, said proposal being in words and figures as follows, to-wit:

Resolved by the Senate and House of Representatives of the United States of America in Congress assembled (two-thirds of each House concurring therein), That the following article is hereby proposed as an amendment to the Constitution of the United States, which shall be valid to all intents and purposes as part of the Constitution when ratified by conventions in three-fourths of the several States:

ARTICLE ___

Section 1. The eighteenth article of amendment to the Constitution of the United States is hereby repealed.

Section 2. The transportation or importation into any State, Territory, or possession of the United States for delivery or use therein of intoxicating liquors, in violation of the laws thereof, is hereby prohibited.

Section 3. This article shall be inoperative unless it shall have been ratified as an amendment to the Constitution by conventions in the several States, as provided in the Constitution, within seven years from the date of the submission hereof to the States by the Congress.

JNO. N. GARNER
Speaker of the House of Representatives

CHARLES CURTIS
Vice President of the United States and President of the Senate

Present at said meeting:

Mrs. Franklin K. Lane
Prager Miller
Miguel A. Gonzales

All delegates being present the said delegates first organized by electing Mrs.

* From a typewritten copy.

Franklin K. Lane Chairman and Prager Miller Secretary. Thereupon the Convention recessed until two-thirty o'clock P.M., of said date.

Two-thirty o'clock, P.M., Nov. 2, 1933.

At the said hour of two-thirty o'clock P.M., the delegates met and proceeded to cast their votes upon the question of Ratification of the Proposed Amendment to the Constitution of the United States hereinabove set forth, with the following result, to-wit:

Ballots cast for ratification of the said proposed Amendment..........................Three
Ballots cast against the said proposed Amendment....................................None

In witness of the foregoing proceedings, the said delegates hereunto subscribe their names.

MRS. FRANKLIN K. LANE
Chairman

PRAGER MILLER
Secretary

MIGUEL A. GONZALES
Delegate

NEW YORK*

PROCEEDINGS

OF

CONVENTION CALLED IN ACCORDANCE WITH THE PROVISIONS
OF CHAPTER 143 OF THE LAWS OF 1933
OF THE
STATE OF NEW YORK

Held at Assembly Chamber, The Capitol,
Albany, New York, Tuesday, June 27, 1933, 11 A.M.

To consider and act upon the ratification of the Amendment to the United States Constitution providing for the repeal of the Eighteenth Amendment.

(Broadcast over National and Columbia Networks.)

HON. HERBERT H. LEHMAN called the Convention to order at
11:30 o'clock A.M.

HON. ALFRED E. SMITH, *President*

GOVERNOR LEHMAN: I am waiting for a gavel. Will you please be seated. The Convention will come to order. The Rev. William E. Sprenger, of Trinity Episcopal Church, will invoke the Divine Blessing.

REVEREND SPRENGER: Let us pray: O Heavenly Father who has filled the world with beauty open, we beseech Thee, our eyes to behold Thy gracious hand in all Thy works, that rejoicing in Thy whole creation we may learn to serve Thee with gladness. Endow us with the wisdom to bring about an order of society where there is no just cause for discontent or bitterness of spirit, and where every person may be enabled to come to the fulness of perfection for which he was made. Bless our State with honorable industry, sound learning, and pure manners that we may be fashioned into one united people ever ready to defend our liberties for the safety, honor and welfare of each citizen. This we ask in the name of the God of All Men. Amen.

GOVERNOR LEHMAN: The Misses Jane, Patty and Helen Pickens of Atlanta, Georgia, will now sing the Star Spangled Banner.

(Star Spangled Banner sung—applause)

The Chair designates the Honorable Vincent Dailey to act as Temporary Secretary of this Convention. Mr. Dailey.

We are met here today in the Capital City of the State and it is eminently fitting that the Chief Executive of the City of Albany address you.

I have great pleasure in introducing the Honorable John Boyd Thacher, Mayor of Albany, who will welcome the delegates. (Applause.)

* Printed.

HON. JOHN BOYD THACHER (Mayor of Albany): Mr. Chairman, Fellow Delegates, Ladies and Gentlemen, and Friends: I am very deeply privileged on this occasion to have the opportunity, by virtue of the office which I now hold as Chief Executive of the City of Albany, the capital city of the Empire State, to extend a very warm and cordial, but also a very long deferred, welcome to this distinguished gathering of men and women who have been delegated by an overwhelming expression of approval upon the part of the people of this State to express their will by the ratification of the Repeal Amendment.

It has been my pleasure upon very many occasions in the past to extend a welcome which carried with it the friendly hospitality of various conventions meeting here to further the very worthy purposes for which they had been organized, and always because those purposes have been worthy I have tried, to the best of my ability, to extend that welcome in such terms, in such words, and in such a way as to leave no doubt in their minds of the privilege which was ours to receive and entertain them.

However, I say to you today, with all sincerity, that many and as important as have been those prior occasions, no words of welcome that I have ever yet uttered have conferred upon me the same deep sense of honor and of privilege as those with which I now greet the members of this historic convention assembled to take that action, which if concurred in by the several states, will help not only to restore the economic balance of the nation, to promote temperance, but also to recreate the calm, well-ordered judgment, the understanding and respect for individual rights and the tolerance upon which these United States were founded.

I welcome you today not merely as the Mayor of a city, the City of Albany, but as the Mayor of the oldest chartered city in America, a city which has behind it centuries of contribution to the development of the state and of the nation, a city which through the first Colonial Congress held here in 1754, was the birthplace of that idea of union and of constitutional government which in the past century and a half has changed the political complexion of the entire world, a city at once conservative and progressive, a city which, however great may be its pride in its own accomplishments, places always first its duty to lend its aid and effort in helpful association and cooperation to advance the welfare and well-being of the people of other cities, towns and rural communities, which are the State itself, and which, with other states, help to build and preserve this union.

Therefore, when I say to you that this old and conservative City of Albany, on the 20th day of May last, elected delegates to this Convention, opposed to Prohibition by the overwhelming majority of 14 to 1, it means that such action was not the result of hasty judgment, but rather the result of a settled conviction, moulded by generations of belief in the inherent value and permanency of our form of constitutional government, a settled conviction, that no action ever taken by the American people has done more harm, morally and materially, than the enactment of the 18th Amendment.

May I also emphasize the fact that this convention is not one of recent origin. The people of the city acquired it years ago, when the lone voice crying in the wilderness, when about the only force and energy and intellect working to correct an abuse which was fast undermining the social and moral foundation of the nation, was the voice, the force, the energy and the intellect of that courageous leader, fighting in a then unpopular cause, a great leader whom you are about deservedly to honor by electing him Permanent Chairman of this Convention, the Honorable Alfred E. Smith. (Applause.)

As I once more assure you of the warmth of the welcome, which the people of the City of Albany now accord you, may I express the belief that it is the opinion of none of us who have been chosen delegates to this convention, that we are about to discharge a perfunctory duty merely because our course has been charted by mandate of the people of the State, themselves, but that we are here rather in the sense that out of the discharge of that duty we may not only abolish the evil of prohibition, but in its abolishment pledge ourselves, as this great state has already done, to the creation and operation of an effective method of control which will forever solve the question to the satisfaction of us all.

The happy omen, in my opinion, for ultimate repeal of the 18th Amendment, is not merely to be found in the overwhelming vote cast in favor by the fourteen states already voting, but the action which most of them have taken looking toward adequate, effective and satisfactory control, an action which should inspire elsewhere throughout the nation the confidence which will win final victory, and when that victory shall have been won, may our people realize in the future that there are certain cardinal principles in the Constitution of the United States that must not be violated, and with that realization may there be a final end to all experiments involving that great document.

I can not conclude without expressing the felicitations not only of the people of the City of Albany, but also of the Fellow Delegates to this convention and of the people of this entire nation to that distinguished statesman, the Honorable Elihu Root, whose long and noteworthy career of public service continues with undiminished lustre, and whose presence and ability once more grace a Constitutional Convention of the Empire State of New York; and of course I also include the same kindly acknowledgment, the same expression of good will for the Honorable Benjamin S. Dean, the only other member of this body who was a delegate to the New York State Constitutional Convention of 1894. Once more I welcome you, offer you our hospitality, and assure you of our deep regard and for the City of Albany I express the hope that the action of this convention, the proceedings here taken, may inspire in those states which have not yet voted, the determination to take prompt action in the disposition of this most urgent and important question, the ratification of the Repeal Amendment.

Governor Lehman: The Honorable Edward J. Flynn, Secretary of State, will now read the Call of the Convention issued to the Delegates thereunder.

Secretary of State Edward J. Flynn: "A State Convention, the delegates to which shall be elected in the manner herein provided, shall be held in the Assembly Chamber at the Capitol, in the City of Albany, in the State of New York, on Tuesday, June 27, 1933, at the hour of eleven antemeridian to consider an Act upon the ratification of the following amendment of the Constitution of the United States proposed by the Congress of the United States to the several States."

Governor Lehman: The Deputy Secretary of State will now call the roll.

(Deputy Secretary of State Miss Grace A. Reavy calls the roll certified by Edward J. Flynn, the Secretary of State, as follows):

William S. Andrews, Benjamin Antin, Warren B. Ashmead, David A. Avery, Selden Bacon, William R. Bayes, Peter C. Brashear, Thomas A. Brogan, Charles E. Buchner, John L. Buckley, Nathan Burkan, Nicholas Murray Butler, Martha Byrne, William M. Calder, Stephen Callaghan, Martin Cantine, Edward T. Carroll, Mary Chahoon, John E. Chapman, Joseph H. Choate, Jr., Robert E. Christie, Jr., Ashley T. Cole, Clarence F. Conroy, Ruth Mason Cook, Frederic R. Coudert, Jr., Dorothea Courten, John R. Crews, William Nelson Cromwell, Thomas H. Cullen, Henry H. Curran, John F. Curry, Robert F. Cutler, Louis A. Cuvillier, May Davie, Archie O.

Dawson, Benjamin S. Dean, William F. Delaney, Fred J. Douglas, James P. B. Duffy, John J. Dunnigan, James F. Dwyer, Keron F. Dwyer, Melvin C. Eaton, George Eilpern, Albert E. Fach, Livingston Farrand, Irene O'D. Ferrer, Ann Murray Flynn, Francis E. Fronczak, Kenneth Gardner, Abraham S. Gilbert, Harrison C. Glore, Alice Campbell Good, May M. Gooderson, Nisbet Grammer, Christiana M. Greene, Julia D. Hanson, James G. Harbord, Mary Stillman Harkness, Louis B. Hart, Robert W. Higbie, Jr., Charles D. Hilles, Katherine S. Hinckley, Thomas L. Holling, Bettie F. Holmes, Ferdinand R. Horn, Jr., Winfield H. Huppuch, Cornelius Huth, Joseph S. Israel, Aaron L. Jacoby, Ralph Jonas, Samuel J. Joseph, Frank V. Kelly, Warnick K. Kernan, John Hill Kitchen, Charles J. Knapp, Samuel S. Koenig, Frederick H. J. Kracke, Ernest Lappano, John E. Larney, Algernon Lee, David F. Lee, Leonard R. Lipowicz, Isabella R. Lovell, A. Augustus Low, Edward P. Lynch, John D. Lynn, James J. Lyons, John H. McCooey, Peter McGovern, William N. McIlravy, Joseph V. McKee, Terrence J. McManus, Harriet T. Mack, Dennis J. Mahon, George Z. Medalie, Chase Mellen, Jr., George J. Moore, Thomas E. Morrissey, Edward P. Mulrooney, Grayson M. P. Murphy, Vincent B. Murphy, Ione Nicoll, Godfrey Nurse, John J. O'Connor, Marion O'Connor, Albert Ottinger, Nathan D. Perlman, Rosalie S. Phillips, Generoso Pope, Ruth Baker Pratt, Nora Quinn, Elihu Root, Thomas G. Ryan, Pauline Morton Sabin, Joseph J. Sartori, John Godfrey Saxe, Helen Schaeffer, Edward Schoeneck, Elenore Sefton, James R. Sheffield, Jeanie Rumsey Sheppard, Mary C. Sinclaire, Alfred E. Smith, Homer P. Snyder, James Speyer, Bayard J. Stedman, Irwin Steingut, Samuel Strasbourger, John Sullivan, Arthur Sutherland, Herbert Bayard Swope, John Boyd Thacher, John Theofel, Hamilton Travis, Harold L. Turk, Charles H. Tuttle, James W. Wadsworth, Louis Waldman, Robert E. Whalen, Charles S. Whitman, Gustav W. M. Wieboldt, Russell Wiggins, Elizabeth C. Wing, Henry Rogers Winthrop, Frank L. Wiswall, Else C. Woodward, James A. Zickler, William Ziegler, Jr., Walter W. Zittel.

and Miss Reavy states that said delegates were, by the greatest number of votes cast at the Special Election held in said State on May 23rd, 1933, duly elected as delegates to the State Convention, to consider and act upon the ratification of the amendment to the Eighteenth Article of the Constitution of the United States.

(———— *Secretary of State.* Dated Albany, N. Y., June 15, 1933.)

Miss Reavy stated that 141 delegates had answered the roll call, and the following delegates were absent:

Nicholas Murray Butler, William M. Calder, Stephen Callaghan, Robert E. Christie, Jr., Livingston Farrand, Leonard R. Lipowicz, Joseph V. McKee, John Godfrey Saxe, and Herbert Bayard Swope.

GOVERNOR LEHMAN: The Chair recognizes the Honorable Harrison C. Glore of Brooklyn.

MR. HARRISON C. GLORE (of Brooklyn): I offer the following resolution and move its adoption:

Resolved, That the following substitutions be made for delegates who are absent and unable to be present:

Mrs. Jane Quintard Clark in place of Nicholas Murray Butler,
Charles F. Murphy in place of William M. Calder,
W. Kingsland Macy in place of Livingston Farrand,
William L. Marcy, Jr., in place of Leonard Lipowicz,
T. Frank Gorman in place of John G. Saxe,
James A. Farley in place of Herbert B. Swope,
Edward J. Flynn in place of Joseph V. McKee,
Donald A. Dailey in place of Robert E. Christie, Jr.,
Mrs. Rose M. Turk in place of Stephen Callaghan.

GOVERNOR LEHMAN: The Chair recognizes Isabella R. Lovell, of Elmira, who seconded the resolution.

GOVERNOR LEHMAN: The resolution has been read and the motion for its adoption has been seconded. If there is no objection by any delegate present, the substitutions will be made as carried in the resolution. The Chair requests that the men and women substituted for delegates who could not be present here today, proceed to the well of the house so that the constitutional oath may be administered to them, unless some have already done so. At the same time the Chair asks whether any delegate here has neglected to take the constitutional oath of office? If so, will he proceed to the well of the Chamber so that the oath may be administered to him or to her. Will the delegates please proceed to the well of the Chamber.

(Various delegates came down to the well of the Chamber.)

GOVERNOR LEHMAN: Miss Grace Reavy, Deputy Secretary of State, will now administer the oath of office.

(Miss Reavy repeats the oath to the delegates):

STATE OF NEW YORK }
COUNTY OF ALBANY } ss.

I do solemnly swear that I will support the Constitution of the United States and the Constitution of the State of New York, and that I will faithfully discharge the duties of the office of delegate to the Convention to consider and act upon the ratification of the amendment to the Constitution of the United States providing for the repeal of the Eighteenth Amendment, according to the best of my ability.

And I do further solemnly swear, that I have not directly or indirectly paid, offered or promised to pay, contributed, or offered or promised to contribute, any money or other valuable thing as a consideration or reward for the giving or withholding a vote at the election at which I was elected to said office, and have not made any promise to influence the giving or withholding any such vote.

MISS REAVY (continuing): Do you so swear?

(The delegates indicate that they so swear.)

MISS REAVY: Then you will please sign.

(The delegates sign the oath.)

GOVERNOR LEHMAN: The Secretary of State has an announcement to make.

SECRETARY OF STATE EDWARD J. FLYNN: A quorum being present, the convention is in order for business.

GOVERNOR LEHMAN: Delegates to the convention and friends: One of the great honors and pleasure of my public life is the privilege and duty given to me by statutory enactment of calling to order this convention. A truly historic event; on our participation in which we will look back with great satisfaction. It marks the end, so far as this state is concerned, of a 15-year old struggle carried on by thousands of devoted and patriotic men and women against sumptuary legislation which at no time represented the uncontrolled sentiment of a majority of the people of this country.

The adoption of the Eighteenth Amendment by the legislatures of the different states demonstrated the ruthless and almost unlimited power of militant minorities which, unfortunately, all too frequently have the means of influencing timid self-seeking legislators. The imminent repeal of the Eighteenth Amendment, on the other hand, shows the force of intelligent and well-considered public opinion, aroused by the abuses and failures of a statute that never commended itself to the reasoned judgment of the people.

Nothing, in my opinion, can now stop the movement for repeal which is sweeping all parts of the country. The fight against hypocrisy and racketeering and disrespect for the law is almost won, thanks to the force of public opinion, which can accomplish miracles if given the opportunity of becoming vocal. We here in New York today have the duty to give final effect to that overwhelming sentiment against prohibition expressed by the people of the state a month ago by a vote of more than seven to one.

It is fitting at this time, when victory is in sight, that we should pause and give credit to at least some of those who for years courageously led the fight to regain that balance between state and nation which is guaranteed by the Constitution of the United States, and to substitute temperance for hypocritical and unenforceable prohibition.

The army was a large one. Unfortunately, time will not permit me to call by name more than a very few of the scores of men and women who have rendered conspicuous service.

First of all, continuously in the front ranks, was one who always was a molder of thought and a leader of reform in the structure of government. Fearless in speech and in act, he more than anyone else in our generation has developed among our people an interest in government—a great Governor of this state, our beloved Alfred E. Smith.

It is recorded in an early edition of the Public Papers of Governor Smith that on the question of Prohibition he stated: "There is no committee or any other power that I know of that will at this time or at any other time prevent me from giving free expression to just what I think about any public question. I make as many mistakes as any other human being but I will never make the mistake of being afraid to talk out."

It is for us, assembled in convention today, to judge how much of a mistake he made in his espousal of the cause of temperance by the repeal of the Eighteenth Amendment. It was Governor Smith, outstanding leader and spokesman for that thought in America, who foresaw the inevitable coming of that repeal which we today are on the point of consummating, and which he with characteristic foresight so early envisioned.

Another great Governor of this state, now President of the United States, through his leadership on assuming the duties of Chief Executive of our country, insured the immediate adoption of legislation legalizing the sale of beer and the submission of the repeal resolution which has made possible the holding of this convention today. I know that all the delegates here assembled, as well as the people of the state generally, join me in an expression of appreciation to President Roosevelt for his leadership.

There is another man who I am happy to welcome here today. Long a leader in state and national councils, he devoted himself to prohibition reform courageously and without hesitation at a time when it was not popular to stand up and be counted on the side of repeal. I refer, of course, to Congressman James W. Wadsworth.

No recital of the events leading up to repeal would be complete without an expression of grateful appreciation to the untiring, devoted and constructive leadership of Dr. Nicholas Murray Butler. Few men in the country have been more forceful or, by his speech and writings, more soundly convincing than he. In the annals of this unfortunate episode of American life and American Democracy, some times referred to as "the noble experiment," the name of Nicholas Murray Butler will loom large among the captains of the crusading army.

There is another man who is here today that we are proud to honor. There have been few important civic activities or movements during the last fifty years to which he did not willingly bring the gift of his energy and genius. A leader in world affairs, as well as in those affecting his city, state and country, it was no mere coincidence that his interest in sound government compelled his militant participation in the fight against prohibition—a great American, a distinguished son of this state, Elihu Root.

It has been a hard fight, in which we men have played our part, but victory could not possibly have been achieved had it not been for the fact that throughout the struggle there always stood shoulder to shoulder with us countless thousands of devoted, unselfish women. I have long held the view that one of the outstanding factors in turning the tide of battle was the masterly manner in which a militant campaign, removed from politics or partisan considerations, was carried on by the women of this country.

Their educational campaign, based on sound moral grounds, created an influential public opinion which swept irresistibly from town to town, from county to county, throughout this state and nation. The interest and enthusiasm and judgment shown by the women of this country in the fight against prohibition is a guarantee of their profound interest in all sound and good government.

This convention, and the people of the state should rejoice, as I do, at the opportunity of expressing their appreciation to Mrs. Charles H. Sabin and her devoted army of women who have so valiantly fought towards our common goal.

I think of one other man—one who is not generally associated in the minds of people with the fight against prohibition, but who brought to it a reserve strength that was telling in the crucial hours of the struggle. I look upon the constructive and broad-visioned viewpoint publicly expressed last year at a psychological moment by John D. Rockefeller, Jr., as one of the outstanding factors that gave increased impetus to the movement for repeal.

There are, of course, countless other people throughout this state who deserve recognition and appreciation for the part which they have played in the struggle. I wish that time would permit me to mention them all by name. They and their comrades in this good fight will not be forgotten.

It is gratifying to me that this convention is composed of delegates elected on a state-wide basis. From the beginning I advocated this course, and I rejoice that the Legislature followed by suggestion. The vote that was cast on a state-wide basis on the simple question of "For or against repeal" was truly an expression of the sentiment of the state as a whole which no one can question. It left no doubt in the mind of anyone throughout the nation of the sentiment of the people of this state—a sentiment so overwhelming, so all-embracing, so deeply-rooted that it can not but be reflected in other sections of our country.

It is a source of particular satisfaction to me, too, that we in this state were able to set up machinery for the control of alcoholic beverages which must invoke the respect of all sections of the country. When I fought for the control legislation which was finally adopted I did not have in mind the problems arising out of the control of the traffic in beer alone. Had that been all, I would not have been so insistent that it be kept free from political influences, or so determined that we secure the best people available to administer it. I had in mind the far larger question of general repeal and the issue that will confront us when that comes into being. These were the questions that enlisted my interest and deep concern.

When repeal comes, as I am confident it will come within a comparatively short time, we will have already set up in this state machinery for liquor control that will require comparatively little amendment or change. The sale of beer in this state is proceeding in an orderly and sound manner. Temperance has been advanced beyond the hopes of even its most sincere advocates. The question of liquor control has been approached and considered on a high plane of citizenship. I rejoice in the confident feeling that we in this state will be able to handle the liquor question substantially free of politics, with due regard for the liberties and rights and natural desires of our people, yet on a level of high morals which will prevent the return of the evils of the old saloon. It is a development in the participation of which I frankly feel proud.

The fact that in this state and in other commonwealths there are being held conventions composed of delegates elected by the people for the sole and single purpose of acting on the question of the repeal of the 18th Amendment is to me one of the most encouraging recent developments in Democracy. The method pursued is unquestionably the right and fair one—the only means by which people can directly vote on and express their sentiments with regard to important constitutional issues.

For the first time it has substituted direct action by the people for what was frequently an unrepresentative decision of a handful of men controlled by sinister influences. It has proven conclusively, too, that our form of government is still sufficiently elastic and pliable to permit of the ready expression of the will of the people. There were many who felt that a constitutional amendment, once adopted, could not be repealed by constitutional procedure and that relief could be obtained only through nullification.

What is happening today in nearly all of the states of the Union justifies again our faith that public opinion and the will of the majority of the people of the nation are supreme. That assurance, that faith, are in my opinion, at least of equal importance to the victory which is in sight on the particular issue before us today.

The early repeal of the 18th Amendment will bring much needed revenues into the treasuries of the Federal and State governments. It will help in economic recovery. It would undoubtedly be justified on that basis alone. But the people of the country are actuated by far higher considerations than those of merely an economic character. They are fighting for repeal because they have been aroused and deeply moved by the abuses and evils of prohibition, and because they know that true and lasting temperance can be attained only through the casting out of the 18th Amendment from our basic law.

As Governor of the state, and as one deeply interested in and concerned with the purposes of this convention, I welcome you heartily to the Capitol and to this Chamber, which has been the scene of many previous conventions, but none of greater importance than this one.

You come with high purpose—may the result of your deliberations and the action you take here today be an inspiration to the people of this country now and hereafter.

The Chair recognizes the Honorable Edward J. Flynn to offer a resolution.

Secretary of State Edward J. Flynn: "Resolved that this convention now proceed to elect its President and the vote thereon to be taken by calling the Ayes and Nays."

GOVERNOR LEHMAN: The Chairman recognizes the Honorable Walter W. Zittel of Buffalo.

MR. WALTER W. ZITTEL (of Buffalo): I wish to second that resolution.

GOVERNOR LEHMAN: You have heard the resolution which has been duly seconded. Are you ready for the question, That the convention now proceed to elect its permanent president? All those in favor will signify by saying Aye; opposed, No. The resolution has been carried.

The Chair recognizes the Honorable James A. Farley, of New York.

MR. JAMES A. FARLEY: Governor Lehman, Governor Smith, Ladies and Gentlemen of the Convention: To use a simple but a true expression, I am glad to be here. I traveled in an automobile at the rate of 90 miles an hour to catch a train from Jackson, Michigan. I left the train at Buffalo this morning and I wondered if I would get here when I looked down occasionally and saw the shadow of the plane on a cloud.

I am very happy to be here at what is a most momentous occasion in the life not only of the people of this state, but of the nation. Millions of people are looking forward today to the action that is being taken at this convention.

This is a historic building. Many pieces of beneficial legislation have been passed in this Chamber, and undoubtedly many memories come back to many of the delegates who are assembled here today. I am satisfied, after looking around this Chamber, that many of the men assembled here today at one time or another, were members of either this body assembled here, or were members of the State Senate. This building means a lot to the gentleman whose name I shall present to you. For many years he was a member of this body. He sat, as I understand it, in the seat just back of where I am now standing.

He probably took the oath of office in this Chamber oftener than any other living person in the history of the state. For four times he was Governor of this state and made a record that will live as long as the memory of man. I do not know of anyone in the state more entitled to preside over the deliberations of this body, because there is no one in this country who gave more freely of his time and his efforts than he did to bring about the repeal of the 18th Amendment.

I know you are not desirous of listening to me at any length. So, without further remarks, I present to you as President of this convention the name of that former distinguished Governor, the Honorable Alfred E. Smith. (Applause.)

GOVERNOR LEHMAN: The Chair recognizes the Honorable W. Kingsland Macy. (Applause.)

MR. W. KINGSLAND MACY: Never in the history of this country, rarely in the history of any country, has a nation so completely changed its attitude on a subject of the importance of the 18th Amendment, and never before has there been a reversal by legal processes of an enactment so drastic.

In the vanguard of the army of men and women who have accomplished this astonishing result is the distinguished Democrat and statesman who has been nominated for presiding officer of this convention. With his unflinching courage, great steadiness of purpose and tireless application, he has made himself the national leader of the movement to repeal the 18th Amendment, and New York, by its action today, is the voice of the nation.

Interesting in this connection is the fact that the university of which I am a graduate recognized his leadership by adding one more to the honorable titles he already had.

During the past fourteen years many have come to feel that a visit to the Doctor was not necessarily unpleasant. It is therefore appropriate, and to me a great pleasure, to second the nomination of my fellow alumnus, Dr. Alfred E. Smith. (Applause.)

GOVERNOR LEHMAN: The Chair recognizes the Honorable James R. Sheffield, for the purpose of presenting a resolution.

MR. JAMES R. SHEFFIELD (of New York): I offer the following resolution: Resolved that the vote on the election of President of the Convention be an Aye and No vote.

GOVERNOR LEHMAN: The Chair recognizes Marion O'Connor for the purpose of presenting a resolution.

(Mrs. Marion O'Connor of Cortland, seconds the resolution presented.)

THE CLERK: Mr. James R. Sheffield of New York offers the following resolution: Resolved, that the vote on the election of President of the Convention be an Aye and No vote.

GOVERNOR LEHMAN: The question now is on the election of the Honorable Alfred E. Smith to serve as permanent president of this convention. All those in favor will signify by saying Aye. Opposed, No. The Honorable Alfred E. Smith has been unanimously elected as President of this Convention. (Applause.)

The Chair now presents the Honorable John F. Curry, the Honorable John H. McCooey and the Honorable Charles S. Whitman as a committee to escort President Smith to the Chair. (Applause.)

The Secretary of State will administer the oath.

SECRETARY OF STATE EDWARD J. FLYNN: I do solemnly swear—

MR. ALFRED E. SMITH: I do solemnly swear—

MR. FLYNN:—that I will support the Constitution of the United States—

MR. SMITH:—that I will support the Constitution of the United States—

MR. FLYNN:—the Constitution of the State of New York—

MR. SMITH:—the Constitution of the State of New York—

MR. FLYNN:—and I will faithfully discharge the duties of the office of President of the State Convention to consider and act upon the ratification of the amendment to the Constitution of the United States proposed by the Congress of the United States to the several states as set forth in Chapter 143 of the Laws of 1933 of the State of New York, according to the best of my ability.

MR. SMITH: I do solemnly swear that I will further conduct the office of the State Convention to consider and act upon the ratification of the amendment to the Constitution of the United States proposed by the Congress of the United States to the several states as set forth in Chapter 143 of the Laws of 1933 of the State of New York, according to the best of my ability.

GOVERNOR LEHMAN: Paragraph 23 of the Routine that has been handed to me says: "Governor introduces President Smith to the Convention." President Smith. (Applause.)

PRESIDENT SMITH: Well, (laughter) here we are. The distinguished State Chairman of the Republican Party spoke about my Doctorship; and just think of the hard luck that is coming to me to be made a doctor at a time when we are gathered here to do away with prescriptions. (Laughter, applause.)

I have had many honors conferred upon me in this building. I had the great honor to preside over the legislative body that meets in the Assembly Chamber. I was four times inaugurated for Governor in this Chamber. But no honor I more keenly appreciated in the past than I do the honor of presiding over this convention today; and I am deeply grateful to the delegates for their kindness to me in selecting me.

Of course, when we left our respective homes we knew exactly what was going to happen. The question of the repeal of the 18th Amendment has been settled, as far as the State of New York is concerned, by the people themselves. It was brought back to where it should have been originally acted on, at the end of thirteen years. But, however, the Convention has a great significance. It will have its place in history. It will stand out as a lesson and a warning for all time to come for the people of this and every other state to be very careful in the future and never allow anything like the 18th Amendment to get into our Federal Constitution. It has its lesson also for the people of our time, and that is, that ratification of constitutional amendments, taking anything away from the people, shall hereafter be decided by them and not by legislatures.

Right along we heard the statement that conventions were unworkable, it was difficult to do it, and that the convenient method was to refer it to the state and let the Legislature act upon it.

As I read our history, it was not the original intent of the framers of our Constitution that amendments like the 18th Amendment were to be passed upon by the Legislatures. The first ten amendments, which is really the Bill of Rights, under which there could not under any possible stretch of the human imagination, be any argument, it was all right to take them to the Legislatures; when it comes to an amendment like the 18th Amendment which seeks to regulate the ordinary, every day life of a citizen, or take away from him some privilege, or some liberty that he enjoyed, that is an entirely different question. For all time to come these conventions that are being held around the country should be a lesson and a warning not to permit submission by the National Congress through legislative branches, of such a matter.

Obviously, they are not organized to represent the popular will or the popular majority. I held back in 1919—I felt I was right then—that the Legislature of this state when it ratified the 18th Amendment did not express the popular will.

Now there may be some reason for acreage representation in legislative bodies as against square blocks of tenement houses in the city when it comes to the ordinary conduct of the business of government, but it is an entirely different thing when an unfair basis of representation can speak not the will of the people, not the desire of the majority, but what appears to be the politically expedient thing to do.

General Wickersham, in his report to the President of the United States, made the statement that state legislatures were not organized to pass upon amendments such as the 18th Amendment, and that there was a large volume, and a large body of people, that were not therein represented. We have another lesson to learn, and that is to keep our eye on organized minorities.

Of course, it must be to the delegates that I have seen struggling with this question for the last thirteen years, a great deal of satisfaction to be in this Chamber and to cast their votes after what they were compelled to go through during all of that thirteen years, to be referred to as Nullificationists, as enemies of the Constitution, as people that wanted to destroy organized and properly constituted government. However, the convention, and every other one that is held in any other part of the country, is a clear vindication of the fundamental theory of democratic government. All the ills of democracy can be cured by more democracy. Let the people speak. And we are here today to voice their sentiment as expressed at the special election, and without any further ceremony we will proceed to business.

The Chair recognizes the Honorable John F. Curry of New York, who offers a resolution which the Clerk will read.

THE CLERK: Resolved, that the Honorable Elihu Root be elected the Honorary President of the Convention. (Applause.)

PRESIDENT SMITH: The Chair recognizes the Honorable John H. McCooey of Kings, who offers a resolution. The Clerk will read.

THE CLERK: Mr. John H. McCooey, of Brooklyn, seconds the nomination of Elihu Root for Honorary President of the Convention. (Applause.)

PRESIDENT SMITH: You have heard the resolution. All in favor will rise. (Rising vote.) The resolution is adopted, and the Chair appoints the Honorable William S. Andrews, Mrs. Elsie C. Wadsworth, Mrs. Wood and Mrs. Rosalie Phillips to escort the Honorary President to the platform. It is just about eighteen years ago when in this Chamber the distinguished Senator, speaking from the middle aisle, in favor of a great reform in the government of the state, said he was looking forward to the day when he could go back to that humble town in the County of Oneida, on the banks of the Mohawk, where truth and honor dwelt in his youth. That truth and honor followed the Senator throughout all his long life. The only mistake was that he is not going back to Oneida, he is going to stay in New York. We claim him. We are going to keep him there, and I express, I am sure, here the sentiment of all citizens of the state that it is the hope in the providence of God Himself that he will be there with us a great many years.

I present to the convention your Honorary President, Honorable Elihu Root.

HONORARY PRESIDENT ELIHU ROOT: Mr. President two-thirds of the Senate of the United States, two-thirds of the House of Representatives of the United States, fourteen states, having a population of over 45,000,000 inhabitants, have all condemned the 18th Amendment.

There are those who say "Never mind, we will have thirteen states to prevent the repeal of that amendment." They are mistaken. This is not, this American people, a people inspired by hatred and dislike, it is a people with the same conception of justice and righteousness and honor, and there are no thirteen states, there will be no thirteen states that shall undertake to stand up against the overwhelming voice of the whole people of the United States. (Applause.)

We may fairly look forward to that, and we may hope, we are entitled to hope, that with the action of the thirty-six states, very soon the American people will have learned two vital lessons, and learned them forever. One is that our constitution government rests upon two bases, national strength and local self government, and that both are essential to the continuance of our free democracy.

The 18th Amendment was a departure from the great principle of local self-government in local affairs.

The other lesson is of higher and broader importance, that human progress, that advance along the long road of civilization from brutish animalism to the conceptions of justice and charity, of kindliness and beauty, of this latter century, every step has been made not by compulsion, but by the development of higher standards of conduct and nobler emotions among the people; a lesson that advance in all that is noble and good comes not from without, but from within. And if we have learned as a people those two great lessons, all the humiliations and the injuries that have elapsed since the 18th Amendment took effect will be but slight payment for a great and permanent reward. (Applause.)

President Smith: At this point the Chair desires to read a telegram into the record, dated Paris:

Alfred E. Smith, Chairman of Convention. Greatly regret that absence on most important work of the Carnegie Endowment for International Peace, deprives me of the pleasure and satisfaction of casting my vote for repeal of 18th Amendment. With repeal, the movement for true temperance will be resumed, and the liquor traffic regulated and made to pay its share of the cost of government. Hearty greetings. (*Signed*) Nicholas Murray Butler. (Applause.)

The next order of business is the election of a First Vice-President, which is now in order. The Chair recognizes the Honorable Edward H. Schoeneck, of Syracuse.

Mr. Edward H. Schoeneck (of Syracuse): Mr. President, the unanimous selection of the distinguished statesmen, the highly respected and admired former Governor of this State, with the enthusiastic approval of all those within this Chamber, and the selection by acclamation of Honorable Elihu Root, inspires me to propose with confidence for the position of First Vice-President of this Convention, a gentleman whom I will name.

Obviously, the standard set for the election of officers will take into consideration sincerity, courage and the spirit of devotion to that great issue which the people of the State of New York, through us today, will decide in a plain and decisive manner.

I am not unmindful that every one of the ladies and gentlemen who sit in this convention have contributed much of their time and talent to bring about the repeal of the 18th Amendment, and I regard their enthusiastic presence here as a renewed pledge of their loyalty to their cause and their determination to help in the fight to the very end. But my mind runs back to the days, the early days, when the pioneers were beginning the fight, beginning the battle, and in that sense this occasion revives memories of an outstanding figure that I see before me, a Senator who on all occasions, and at all times, stood shoulder to shoulder with the distinguished Honorary President and with the distinguished Presiding Officer of this convention and with the militant women headed by Mrs. Sabin and Mrs. Sheppard, fighting throughout the country on every available occasion and frequently raising his voice in the Congress of the United States to preach the doctrine and uphold the cause which motivates the presence of these delegates here today.

I can understand the great pride which Postmaster-General Farley has in sending to this convention his nominee for President. It was my pleasure many years ago, to spend four years in these halls as a colleague of his, and a colleague of the man whom I am now about to mention. My candidate also had the courage of his convictions. He had the vision of statesmanship and he had those qualifications which appeal to the mind and heart of every true American; and if I sense the sentiment of this convention correctly, I deem it not only a duty, but a pleasure to place in nomination for the office of Vice-President of this convention, the Honorable James W. Wadsworth, of Geneseo.

President Smith: The Chair recognizes the Honorable John D. Lynn.

Mr. John D. Lynn: I second the nomination.

President Smith: The Chair recognizes Mr. John Sullivan.

Mr. John Sullivan: Mr. President, I desire to offer the following resolution, and move its adoption:—

The Clerk: Mr. John Sullivan of New York offers the following resolution and moves its adoption: *Resolved,* That the vote on the election of the First Vice-President be an Aye and No vote.

PRESIDENT SMITH: The Chair recognizes Terrence J. McManus.

MR. TERRENCE J. MCMANUS: I second the resolution.

PRESIDENT SMITH: Gentlemen, you have heard the resolution. All in favor say Aye; contrary minded, No. It is carried.

The question occurs upon the original motion that the Honorable James W. Wadsworth be elected as Vice-President of the Convention. All in favor say Aye. Those opposed, No. It is carried.

The Chair appoints the Honorable Joseph H. Choate, Mrs. May M. Gooderson and Peter McGovern as a committee to escort the First Vice-President to the platform. (Applause.)

No further introduction needed, and no stranger to the rostrum.

FIRST VICE-PRESIDENT JAMES W. WADSWORTH: Governor—you need not fear, I shall not address you as "Doctor"—I am tempted to be reminiscent, and in that mood at least I shall refer to you once as Fellow Assemblyman. How times have changed! Think of you and me on the same ticket! (Laughter.)

Indeed, I am very grateful to the delegates in this convention for the honor they have conferred upon me. I do not expect to be bowed down with the weight of the duty of Vice-President, but I will confess to you, and I know you understand my feeling, that this is a happy hour.

Governor, it has been a long battle, but a battle well worth waging. (Applause.) Life is contention, and we are glad to be alive. Yes, a battle well worth waging, because it was waged for a fundamental principle of government; not merely a question as to how an individual should behave himself, not merely a question of how a particular law should be enforced, but a fundamental question of government itself.

We have listened with tremendous interest and great profit to ourselves to Governor Smith and Senator Root and to Governor Lehman, and we have had set before us by them very ably, some of the important elements in the decision which we, as representatives of the people of New York, are about to make here, or rather, the vote which we are about to cast.

It is not my purpose to detain this assembly with anything like a lengthy discussion of the constitutional questions with which we have been confronted in recent years. I am tempted to remind you, however, that something like 145 years ago, in the little City of Kingston, there met the first constitutional convention composed of delegates elected by the people of the State of New York, elected and called together for the purpose of considering the ratification of the original Constitution of the United States. Those delegates that met at Kingston under the leadership of Alexander Hamilton, came direct from the people. Approximately 145 years have gone by, and now once more a convention composed of delegates coming direct from the people is convened to express the will of the people upon a constitutional question.

Indeed, this is an historic moment. I think it is a healthy thing for the future of this country and the development of its government, that the repeal of the 18th Amendment was submitted by the Congress to conventions of the people in the several states. The original amendment should have been submitted direct to conventions of people in the several states, for it was a proposal which invited the states to surrender a very important part of their police power, and invited every citizen in the country to surrender over to the Federal Government, an important element in his personal liberty.

I can see that the founders of our government conceived that from time to time, as the years went along, amendments might be proposed to the Constitution of the United States having to do with the liberty of the individual, and the reserve power of the states, and that they intended that this alternative method of ratification by conventions of the people should be resorted to in all cases of that kind, and that ratification by Legislatures should be resorted to when the proposed amendments did nothing more than propose to change the mechanism of government, such as the recent amendment known as the Norris Amendment, changing the date of inauguration of the President of the United States, and the first meeting of the new Congress.

Clearly, the Legislatures of the states are competent to pass upon that, but the fathers of our government never intended that any group of legislators could vote away the liberties of a people. We are retracing our steps. We are correcting the error that was made. State by state the people have learned about the processes of constitutional law, about the fundamental principle involved in this question, and state by state delegates are coming direct from the people recording their view, as it should have been recorded fourteen years ago.

Is there any doubt as to the result? None whatsoever. We shall secure repeal quite possibly within the calendar year. If not, we will have it by the middle of next winter. (Applause.) And when that shall have been done, we shall have restored to the people of the states that power to govern their own affairs which was, unwisely, in a moment of hysteria, taken away from them back in 1918. With that restoration of power to the people where it belongs, there will dawn a better day for decency in government and soundness in constitutional procedure. (Applause.)

PRESIDENT SMITH: The next order of business is the election of a Second Vice-President, which I declare now to be in order, and the Chair recognizes Francis E. Fronczak, of Buffalo.

MR. FRANCIS E. FRONCZAK (of Buffalo): Mr. Chairman, I offer the following resolution:—

PRESIDENT SMITH: It is moved by Mr. Fronczak that Mrs. Norman E. Mack, of Buffalo, be elected Second Vice-President. The Chair recognizes Mrs. Nicoll—

MRS. IONE NICOLL: I second the motion.

PRESIDENT SMITH:—who seconds the nomination.

The Chair recognizes the Honorable Charles F. Murphy, of Brooklyn,—

MR. CHARLES F. MURPHY: Mr. President, I offer the following resolution, and upon being read I move its adoption.

PRESIDENT SMITH:—who offers a resolution. The Clerk will read.

THE CLERK: Mr. Charles Murphy of Brooklyn, offers the following resolution and moves its adoption: *Resolved,* That the vote on the election of the Second Vice-President be an Aye and No vote.

PRESIDENT SMITH: The Chair recognizes Joseph J. Sartori—

MR. JOSEPH J. SARTORI (of Brooklyn): I offer this resolution—

PRESIDENT SMITH:—who offers a resolution. The Clerk will read.

THE CLERK: Mr. Joseph Sartori of Brooklyn, seconds the resolution just presented.

PRESIDENT SMITH: You have heard the resolutions. All in favor say Aye. Contrary minded, No. They are carried.

The question occurs upon the election of Mrs. Mack. All in favor say Aye. Contrary, No. It is carried. (Applause.)

The Chair appoints the Honorable James F. Dwyer, Honorable Louis B. Hart and D. J. Mack, as a committee to escort the Second Vice-President to the platform.

MRS. NORMAN E. MACK (second vice-president): Well, as Governor Smith says, here I am, and I want to thank the people of the state for making it possible for me to take part in this wonderful historic occasion to speak for the women.

Mr. Chairman, your Excellency, Ladies and Gentlemen: As the Vice-Chairman of this splendid convention, it evolves upon me to say a few words in behalf of the glorious part which the women of America have played in bringing about the necessary steps of the repeal of the 18th Amendment. Their magnificent support of this cause, undoubtedly has hastened the arrival of the hour when our Constitution finally will be rid of the only blot ever placed upon its pages.

The greatest crime ever committed against the American people was the enactment of the 18th Amendment. It is not necessary for me to review the 13-year period of lawlessness. The whole story of that regrettable era is still fresh in our minds.

My desire is to give adequate expression to the debt of gratitude we all owe to outstanding American women like Mrs. Charles H. Sabin and others who, when they became convinced of the terrible evils of prohibition, had the courage to go forth and lead a militant intelligent campaign for repeal.

It was no easy task to muster the women of America on the side of repeal, until such organizations as that, headed by Mrs. Sabin, began to make themselves felt in all parts of the United States. They attacked prohibition in a dignified way. They assembled facts and figures that could not be ignored.

The women usually get what they want and when the women of America at last were fully aroused to the imperative necessity for repeal of the 18th Amendment, they welded themselves into an invincible force that disregarded all political and religious lines. The cause of repeal attracted to its ranks the finest of American womanhood and to me this constitutes the most notable moral victory in the entire history of our country.

This convention should serve as an inspiring symbol to all of us who are privileged to be a part of it. It proves once again that if you are convinced down deep in your heart that you are right about something and have the courage and tenacity to stand by your guns, you are bound ultimately to crown your efforts with victory. No one in America has waged a more relentless battle for repeal than has our own Happy Warrior, and to me along with millions of others, the name of Alfred E. Smith always will be a constant source of inspiration. I thank you.

PRESIDENT SMITH: Do you solemnly swear that you will support the Constitution of the United States and of the State of New York and that you will faithfully discharge the offices of First and Second Vice-Presidents of the State Convention to consider and act upon the ratification of the amendment to the Constitution proposed by the Congress of the United States to the several states as set forth in Chapter 143 of the Laws of 1933 of the State of New York, according to the best of your ability? (Oath administered.)

PRESIDENT SMITH: The next order of business is the election of the Secretary to the Convention. The Chair recognizes the Honorable William Nelson Cromwell.

MR. WILLIAM NELSON CROMWELL: I rise to present in nomination for Secretary, the name of Ruth Baker Pratt.

PRESIDENT SMITH: The Chair recognizes Miss Martha Byrne, of New York.

MISS MARTHA BYRNE (of New York): I second the nomination.

PRESIDENT SMITH: The Chair recognizes the Honorable Frank B. Kelly, who offers a resolution, which the Clerk will read.

THE CLERK: Resolution by Mr. Kelly: Resolved, that the vote for the Secretary of the Convention be an Aye and No vote.

PRESIDENT SMITH: The Chair recognizes James Speyer, of New York.

MR. JAMES SPEYER (of New York): I desire to offer a resolution.

PRESIDENT SMITH: Mr. Speyer offers a resolution which the Clerk will read.

THE CLERK: Resolution by Mr. Speyer seconds the resolution just presented.

PRESIDENT SMITH: You have heard the resolution. All in favor say Aye. Contrary, No. The resolution is adopted. The question recurs upon the election of Mrs. Pratt as Permanent Secretary of the Convention. All those in favor say Aye. Contrary minded, No. It is adopted.

The Chair appoints Chase Mellen, Jr., Mrs. Mary Chahoon and Cornelius Huth, as a committee to escort the Secretary to the platform.

(Secretary escorted to the platform. Oath administered.)

PRESIDENT SMITH: The Chair recognizes Ferdinand R. Horn, Jr.

MR. FERDINAND R. HORN, JR.: I offer the following resolution.

PRESIDENT SMITH: Mr. Horn offers a resolution which the Clerk will read.

THE CLERK: Mr. Horn offers a resolution and moves its adoption. Resolved, that the President of this Convention be authorized to appoint the following officers and employes:

4 assistant secretaries,
1 librarian,
1 assistant librarian,
2 stenographers,
1 parliamentarian,
1 assistant parliamentarian,
1 sergeant-at-arms,
3 assistant sergeants-at-arms,
1 reading clerk,
1 assistant reading clerk,
1 journal clerk,
1 assistant journal clerk,
1 financial clerk,
1 assistant financial clerk,
1 tally clerk,
1 assistant tally clerk,
1 president's clerk,
1 secretary's clerk,
1 clerk for the Committee on Rules,
1 Clerk for the Committee on Credentials,
1 Clerk for the Committee on Resolutions,
1 postmaster,
1 assistant postmaster,
8 doorkeepers,
8 messengers,
6 laborers,
10 pages.

PRESIDENT SMITH: The Chair recognizes Archie O. Dawson.

MR. ARCHIE O. DAWSON: I second the resolution.

PRESIDENT SMITH: You have heard the resolution; you have heard it seconded. All those in favor say Aye; contrary minded, No. It is adopted. The Chair hands to the Clerk a list of appointments for the record.

Are the stenographers here? And the sergeants-at-arms?

(Oaths administered to stenographers and sergeants-at-arms.)

PRESIDENT SMITH: The Chair recognizes Honorable Russell Wiggins of Middletown, who presents a resolution, which the Clerk will read.

THE CLERK: Resolved, that the Rules of the Assembly of the State of New York for 1933 be adopted as the temporary rules of this convention, and that the President appoint a Committee on Rules consisting of sixteen delegates.

PRESIDENT SMITH: The Chair recognizes Honorable Irwin Steingut.

MR. IRWIN STEINGUT: I second the resolution.

President Smith: The Chair recognizes Honorable Winfield A. Huppuch.

Mr. Huppuch: I offer a resolution and move its adoption.

President Smith: The resolution is offered and the Clerk will read.

The Clerk: Resolved, that the vote on the said resolution be an Aye and No vote.

President Smith: The Chair recognizes Mr. Generoso Pope, who offers a resolution which the Clerk will read.

The Clerk: Resolution by Mr. Pope, which seconds the resolution.

President Smith: The question recurs upon the original resolution by Mr. Wiggins. All in favor say Aye: contrary minded, No. It is adopted.

The Chair recognizes Mrs. Pauline Morton Sabin, of Suffolk.

Mrs. Pauline Morton Sabin (of Suffolk): I offer a resolution.

President Smith: The delegate offers a resolution which the Clerk will read.

The Clerk: Resolved, that the President be and is hereby authorized to appoint the Committee on Resolutions consisting of sixteen members, of which committee the President shall be an ex-officio member.

President Smith: The Chair recognizes Honorable Vincent B. Murphy, of Rochester.

Mr. Murphy: I second the resolution.

President Smith: The Chair recognizes the Honorable John L. Buckley.

Mr. John L. Buckley: I move that the vote on this resolution be an Aye and No vote.

President Smith: The Chair recognizes Honorable Selden Bacon.

Mr. Selden Bacon: I second the resolution.

President Smith: All those in favor say Aye. Contrary minded, No. They are adopted.

The question now recurs on the original resolution of Mrs. Sabin. All those in favor say Aye. Contrary minded, No. It is adopted.

The Chair recognizes Honorable Charles H. Tuttle, of New York.

Mr. Charles H. Tuttle (of New York): I desire to offer the following resolution.

President Smith: Mr. Tuttle offers a resolution which the Clerk will read.

The Clerk: Resolved, that the President be and he is hereby authorized to appoint a Committee on Credentials to consist of sixteen members to investigate and report to the convention if there is any contest for seats therein.

President Smith: The Chair recognizes Honorable David F. Lee.

Mr. David F. Lee: I second the resolution just presented.

President Smith: The Chair recognizes Mr. Ralph Jonas.

Mr. Ralph Jonas: I offer a resolution and move its adoption.

President Smith: The resolution is offered, which the Clerk will read.

The Clerk: Resolved, that the vote on the resolution be an Aye and No vote.

President Smith: You have heard the resolution. All in favor say Aye. Contrary minded, No. It is adopted.

The question recurs on the original resolution by Mr. Tuttle. All in favor say Aye; contrary minded, No. It is adopted.

The Chair recognizes Honorable John Theofel, of Queens, who offers a resolution, which the Clerk will read.

The Clerk: Resolved, that the convention take a recess to await reports from the Committees on Rules, Credentials and Resolutions.

PRESIDENT SMITH: The Chair recognizes Hamilton Travis of New York.

MR. HAMILTON TRAVIS (of New York): I second the resolution.

PRESIDENT SMITH: You have heard the resolution, and you have heard it seconded. All those in favor say Aye; contrary minded, No. It is adopted.

There will be a meeting of the Committees on Rules, Resolutions and Credentials, immediately. The Chair hands down the following appointments to various committees, which the Clerk will read.

THE CLERK (reads):

Committee on Credentials: Charles H. Tuttle, *Chairman;* Warren B. Ashmead, William R. Bayes, Peter C. Brashear, Martin Cantine, Ruth Mason Cook, James G. Harbord, Frank L. Wiswall, David A. Avery, Benjamin S. Dean, Nisbet Grammer, Warnick K. Kernan, John L. Buckley, Louis A. Cuvillier, Nora Quinn, Thomas G. Ryan.

Committee on Rules: Russell Wiggins, *Chairman;* Melvin C. Eaton, Christiana M. Greene, Samuel S. Koenig, George J. Moore, Albert Ottinger, Bayard J. Stedman, William Ziegler, Jr., Mary C. Sinclaire, Ellen Schaeffer, Edward P. Lynch, Charles J. Knapp, Ashley T. Cole, Dorothea Courten, Algernon Lee, Irwin Steingut.

Committee on Resolutions: Pauline Morton Sabin, *Chairman;* Donald A. Dailey, Fred J. Douglas, Julia D. Hanson, George Z. Medalie, Mary Stillman Harkness, John H. Kitchen, Fred J. H. Kracke, Henry Rogers Winthrop, Alfred E. Smith, *ex officio,* James P. B. Duffy, Irene O'D. Ferrer, Ann Murray Flynn, Kenneth Gardner, John J. Dunnigan, Dennis J. Mahon, Grayson M. P. Murphy.

PRESIDENT SMITH: The convention will stand in recess for fifteen minutes.

(*Recess*)

(AFTER RECESS. 2:10 P.M.)

PRESIDENT SMITH: The convention will be in order. The delegates will be seated.

The Chair desires to put the following telegram into the record. The Clerk will read.

THE CLERK (reading): "The Honorable Alfred E. Smith, President, Convention for the Repeal of the 18th Amendment, Albany, N. Y. In the Senate of the United States I voted against the adoption of the 18th Amendment and it is with keen regret that, due to illness, I will be unable to cast my vote in the convention for its repeal. Congratulations to you and other men and women of New York who have struggled during the years to rectify this deplorable blunder." (*Signed*). William M. Calder. (Applause.)

PRESIDENT SMITH: The Chair recognizes the Honorable Russell Wiggins.

MR. RUSSELL WIGGINS: Mr. President, the Committee on Rules begs leave to report that the committee has met and for its report recommends that the rules of the Assembly of the State of New York for the year 1933 be adopted as the rules of this convention, and I move you, Sir, the adoption of those rules.

(The Chair recognizes Mr. Godfrey Nurse.)

(The Chair recognizes Mrs. Elenore Sefton, of Auburn.)

THE CLERK: Mrs. Sefton moves that the vote on said resolution be an Aye and Nay vote.

(The Chair recognizes Delegate Keron F. Dwyer, who seconds the motion.)

PRESIDENT SMITH: You have heard both resolutions. Those in favor will say Aye; opposed, No. They are carried.

The question recurs on the original resolution which is the report of the Committee on Rules. All in favor of its adoption will say Aye; contrary minded, No. It is adopted.

The Chair recognizes the Honorable Charles H. Tuttle, Chairman of the Committee on Credentials.

MR. TUTTLE: The Committee has met, examined the roll of delegates as prepared by the Secretary of State, found the same to be correct, that the delegates on such roll had been duly elected and that there were no contests and recommended that this temporary roll as amended by the substitutions made by this convention be the permanent roll of the convention.

PRESIDENT SMITH: The Chair recognizes the Honorable William F. Delaney.

(William F. Delaney seconds resolution.)

PRESIDENT SMITH: The Chair recognizes the Honorable Henry H. Curran, who offers a resolution, which the Clerk will read.

THE CLERK: Mr. Curran offers a resolution that the vote on the resolution be adopted by an Aye and Nay vote.

PRESIDENT SMITH: The Chair recognizes the Honorable Edward T. Carroll, who seconds the motion.

PRESIDENT SMITH: The question occurs on the report of the Committee on Credentials submitted by Mr. Tuttle. Those in favor will say Aye; contrary-minded, No. It is adopted.

The Chair recognizes Mrs. Pauline Morton Sabin, Chairman of the Committee on Resolutions. (Applause.) Will Mrs. Sabin kindly come to the platform. (Applause.)

MRS. PAULINE MORTON SABIN: Mr. Chairman, the Committee on Resolutions reports:

We have carefully considered the question of acting upon the ratification of the amendment to the United States Constitution providing for the repeal of the 18th Amendment, and we recommend the adoption of the following resolution:

WHEREAS, The Senate and House of Representatives of the United States of America in Congress assembled (two-thirds of each House concurring therein) did resolve that the following article is hereby proposed as an amendment to the Constitution of the United States, which shall be valid to all intents and purposes as a part of the Constitution when ratified by convention in three-fourths of the several states; and,

WHEREAS, The said proposed amendment reads as follows:

Section 1. The eighteenth article of amendment to the Constitution of the United States is hereby repealed.

Section 2. The transportation or importation into any state, territory or possession of the United States for delivery or use therein of intoxicating liquors, in violation of the laws thereof is hereby prohibited.

Section 3. This article shall be inoperative unless it shall have been ratified as an amendment to the Constitution by conventions in the several states, as provided in the Constitution, within seven years from the date of submission hereof to the states by the Congress; and,

WHEREAS, There was duly transmitted to the Legislature of this State the said article of amendment proposed by the Congress to the Constitution of the United States, and

WHEREAS, The Legislature of this State pursuant to law, did enact a statute entitled, "An Act to provide for a Convention to consider and act upon the ratification of the amendment to the United States Constitution providing for the repeal of the eighteenth amendment," which said act having passed both houses of the Legislature was signed by the Governor of this State on April sixth, one thousand nine hundred and thirty-three and constitutes Chapter one hundred and forty-three of the laws of New York for the year one thousand nine hundred and thirty-three; and

WHEREAS, Pursuant to the provisions of said act of the Legislature an election for the selection of delegates to the said convention was held in this State on May twenty-third, one thousand nine hundred and thirty-three, at which said election one hundred and fifty delegates were chosen in accordance with the provisions of said statute; and,

WHEREAS, The Secretary of State has prepared a list of the delegates elected at said election and the same has been filed in the Department of State, and the Secretary of State has in accordance with the provisions of the said statute given notice of the time and place of holding the convention, which said notice reads as follows:

DEAR SIR OR MADAM:

You are hereby notified that the New York State Convention to act on the amendment to the eighteenth article of the Constitution of the United States, will convene in the Assembly Chamber, at the Capitol, Albany, on Tuesday, June 27th, 1933, at 11:00 A.M. Eastern Daylight Saving Time. It is expected the Convention will be in session approximately three hours.

If for any reason you find it impossible to attend, will you please notify me to that effect, so that the vacancy caused by your absence may be filled.

There is enclosed herewith a blank oath of office which you are requested to execute and return to this Department at the earliest possible moment.

Yours very truly,

EDWARD J. FLYNN
Secretary of State

and

WHEREAS, Pursuant to the said notice and as provided in said act, the said convention has met at the time and place therein fixed and has organized by the election of a President, First and Second Vice-Presidents, Secretary, and other officers, and has adopted rules governing its deliberations, and is ready to proceed to consider the proposed article of amendment; now, therefore,

Be it resolved, By this convention of the delegates representing the people of the State of New York duly assembled pursuant to law, that we do approve and ratify the proposed article of amendment proposed by the Congress to the Constitution of the United States designed to repeal the eighteenth article of the amendment, which said amendment reads as follows:

WHEREAS, The Senate and House of Representatives of the United States of America in Congress assembled (two-thirds of each House concurring therein) did resolve that the following article is hereby proposed as an amendment to the Constitution of the United States, which shall be valid to all intents and purposes as a part of the Constitution when ratified by conventions in three-fourths of the several states; and

WHEREAS, The said proposed amendment reads as follows:

Section 1. The eighteenth article of amendment to the Constitution of the United States is hereby repealed.

Section 2. The transportation or importation into any state, territory, or possession of the United States for delivery or use therein of intoxicating liquors, in violation of the laws thereof is hereby prohibited.

Section 3. This article shall be inoperative unless it shall have been ratified as amendment to the Constitution by conventions in the several States, as provided in the Constitution, within seven years from the date of submission hereof to the states by the Congress;

And further the action of this convention in approving and ratifying the said proposed amendment is valid to all intents and purposes as representing the people of the State of New York; and

Be it further resolved, That the Chairman and Secretary of this convention shall certify the result of the votes of the delegates to the ratification of said amendment in triplicate, each signed by the President and Secretary of the Convention to which there shall be attached a certificate certified by such officers of the record of the vote taken, showing the yeas and nays thereon, and that such certificates and certified copies of such record shall be deposited with the Secretary of State of the State of New York, and he shall transmit one such certificate and certified copy of such record to the Secretary of State of the United States, another certificate and certified copy of such record to the presiding officer of the Senate of the United States and another certificate and certified copy of such record to the speaker of the House of Representatives of the United States, which said certificates shall be accompanied by the certificate of the Secretary of State certifying that the persons signing the certificates so transmitted were the duly constituted President and Secretary of said Convention, and that their signatures are genuine, and that before transmitting the certificates and copies of records so deposited with the Secretary of State he shall make a copy of one of them, certifying it as such and record it as a permanent record of the Department of State; and

Be it further resolved, That the President, Secretary and any other officer of this convention and the delegates and Secretary of State or any or either of them are hereby authorized to comply with any act or resolution of Congress requiring other or further confirmation of such ratification of said proposed amendment.

MRS. SABIN (continuing): Mr. President, I move the acceptance of this report. (Applause.)

PRESIDENT SMITH: The Chair recognizes Congressman Cullen, of Kings County.

CONGRESSMAN CULLEN: Mr. Chairman, Ladies and Gentlemen of this historic convention: We are making history in our state today. It is going to redound to the credit of not only the people of the State but the delegates who are here representing them, and I don't know who, above anybody else, can get more complete satisfaction in what is about to happen here today than the present presiding officer of the Convention, the Honorable Alfred E. Smith. He has been one of the pioneers in behalf of this battle.

Dating away back into 1917, he started the battle for the repeal of the 18th Amendment, and followed along with it during his incumbency as Governor of this State, and still further, Ladies and Gentlemen, he pursued it when he became a presidential candidate of the great Democratic Party to the detriment and the sacrifice of the election of himself as President of the United States.

It is a great honor, indeed, for me to rise in my place and have the opportunity of seconding this resolution. I probably had something to do with the battle that was started years ago. I never could reconcile myself to the fact that the people of the State should not have a chance to determine whether the 18th Amendment should go into the organic law of our country, or not.

In fact, when I was a member of the State Senate in 1917, we absolutely refused to ratify the 18th Amendment. At the next session of the Legislature, however, they ratified it, and I always believed that we of the Senate of 1917, were right, because of the fact that there was never any intention by the Legislature of this State to ratify an amendment dealing with the lives and personal comfort and happiness of the people of the country generally.

So today we are assembled here to right that wrong, and it is a great honor indeed, for me to say that the men and women of this convention are writing history that will go down into the annals, not only of our State, but of the Federal Government itself. And in that connection I might say that the leaders and the pioneers in this fight include the men and the women you see on that platform and who were announced as President and Vice-Presidents of this Convention.

You have heard one of the foremost men in this state, the Honorable Elihu Root, speak to you about the rights of the people, and God love him, he has lived long enough to see constitutional law written by the people of the country itself.

He said, among other things today, that there were not thirteen states in the Union that would stop the repeal of the 18th Amendment, because the other states with the great population that they represent will just as sure as the sun rises and sets, by their example, cause them to vote for the repeal of this amendment when their elections come along within the next few months. There is Senator Wadsworth, with whom I have served in this Legislature, another pioneer in the fight, and one who took a defeat, if you please, because he would not surrender a principle for the price of votes.

I congratulate those pioneers in this fight because, after all, the people will remain supreme no matter what we may do or how we may do it. It is a great thing, Mr. President of this Convention, that the delegates and friends of the Convention assembled here on this very warm day in the summer, are doing their duty as they see it, and praying that it will give to the people not only of our State but of the country itself, an example of popular government.

I congratulate you and all those who have had the opportunity of fighting for the adoption of this resolution, thereby placing the great Empire State in the foreground of states that have repealed the 18th Amendment, thus placing her in the light, and in the position where she honestly and justly belongs.

President Smith: The Chair recognizes Congressman O'Connor of New York.

Congressman O'Connor: Mr. President, when I saw my distinguished colleague, Congressman Wadsworth, go to the rostrum, the thought occurred to me that we members of Congress are working overtime. We thought when we voted to submit this repeal amendment to the people of the country, that our job of many years was done. Now we find ourselves attending as delegates to Conventions to ratify the amendment. Daily we are asked to go out on the "huskings" in other states and speak in its behalf. But it will soon be all over, and, Mr. President, I doubt if one of the forty-eight states will vote against the ratification of this repeal amendment.

It is a great pleasure for me to rise here in support of this resolution. It is a day "devoutly wished" by your honored self and many of us here who have taken some part in the battle, not only in this historic Chamber, where we served, but in the House of Representatives. We rejoice to see this good day and hour come.

The fight we have waged for fourteen years has not always been pleasant or agreeable. At times we could have been discouraged, if we were not absolutely confident of the justice of our cause.

I recall one day in the House of Representatives—an occasion that I call "the zero hour"—when only three men stood up in favor of a wet proposition. Sometimes there were a bare dozen of us, sacrilegiously referred to at times by friends as "the twelve apostles." Because we were positive of our convictions in the matter, we developed thick skins. We withstood the shafts of ridicule. We had to "take it" and we did take it. We were constantly sneered at and our motives were impugned. We were called the representatives of "the rum sellers and the brewers." We were charged with catering to our own appetites. Jeers frequently occurred when we took the floor of the House of Representatives in behalf of Prohibition reform.

During all these years we have seen this battle go along, and we have watched it gradually come nearer to fruition day by day. Gladly are we here today to perform a duty.

Mr. President, this is a momentous day in the history of our State. What we do here today is founded on a firm conviction. Today we serve no interest. We serve no appetite. Today we, by our vote here, serve our conscience and our country. (Applause.)

President Smith: The Chair recognizes Mrs. Alice Campbell Good, of Kings County.

Mrs. Alice Campbell Good (of Kings County): I second the resolution.

President Smith: The Chair recognizes Hon. Aaron L. Jacoby, of Kings.

Mr. Aaron L. Jacoby (of Kings): I rejoice to be among those who have the honor to participate in the deliberations of this day. It affords me, as one who has never had the delight that those experience who imbibe the fluid, it affords me a distinct privilege and pleasure, as one who has not enjoyed that delight, to second the resolution which will vouchsafe once more to the people of this State, and, we hope, the country, the liberties which are rightly theirs. I second the resolution.

President Smith: The Chair recognizes the Honorable Louis Waldman.

Mr. Louis Waldman: Mr. Chairman, Governor Lehman, Ladies and Gentlemen of the Convention: I rise with particular pleasure to second the resolution for the repeal of the 18th Amendment for two reasons: First, because fourteen years ago, as a member of this House, I stood on this floor and in a debate that lasted two days helped to lead the fight—modesty prevents me saying anything else—against ratification of the 18th Amendment.

Our colleagues of the two major parties in this Chamber refused to place New York State in the minority. They are so accustomed to being in the majority, and we Socialists could not sway them. But there is some fun in being a minority. That fight was in 1918. We lost. It took us fourteen years, as it did our chairman, who I think caught up to the Socialists a year later, it took fourteen years for us to have the opportunity to win.

And here is the second reason why I am glad to second this resolution; for I am glad to find the Socialists on the winning side. You probably know fourteen years is a short time for the Socialists to win on any issue.

Now, Mr. Chairman, I am sorry that the debate on the resolution for the repeal of the 18th Amendment is going to be entirely one-sided. As a matter of fact, I should have liked to see a dozen or two dry delegates so that they might state their position, and then have the wets state theirs.

After all, the seconding speeches for the repeal of the 18th Amendment are being made to an audience that is already convinced. Yet I do want to add these remarks: This, of course, is not a party convention. Happily, it is a convention of the three major party delegates gathered to ratify an amendment to the Federal Constitution eliminating from the Constitution an amendment that should never have been in it.

But why was that amendment placed in it? I think that a realistic reading of history requires me to state,—and in what I am going to say I do not desire to retract one iota of the praise that was heaped upon the men and women who pioneered this movement,—that two world tragedies have written constitutional history in our country; referring, of course to the 18th Amendment particularly.

Our Constitution is being amended every day without convention and without formal amendment. But as far as the 18th Amendment is concerned, it was originally given to us as a result of the forces let loose by the World War, one of the greatest world tragedies known in modern times.

There was a natural predisposition to restrain liberty, to deny people their rights of their normal habits of free thinking and speaking, and it was easy for an organized minority to impose its will upon a nation that abandoned a balanced form of living under the Constitution. The 18th Amendment was an outgrowth of the war; it took a second great tragedy, the world crisis, to bring America back to the position where it wants to repeal the 18th Amendment.

And here is a point I want to impress upon this Convention: I think the amendment for the repeal of the 18th Amendment is going to be ratified by enough states to wipe that amendment off the books. But the lesson these two events—the bringing of the amendment and its elimination—which occurred in the short time of one generation, ought to teach our people that events of this kind are not the result of mere personal convictions of some. They are the result of great social forces sometimes producing effects which are not originally contemplated when those forces are let loose.

In ratifying this amendment today, we owe a duty not merely to the people of the State of New York,—that is plain enough—we owe a duty to the people of the other states, and under Section 2 of the Constitutional Amendment which we are ratifying, that duty is created directly by constitutional mandate which creates a new relationship between the states. We should not blindly sway from one position to the other, when we are dealing with the problem involved in the 18th Amendment.

I want to call your attention, Ladies and Gentlemen, that although the 18th Amendment was adopted at a time of great psychological stress, and the organized fanatical minority was able to take advantage of the situation, it was able to succeed only because the complaints of that organized minority had a real basis in the abuses of the saloon. And on this occasion, at this convention, our united delegates, representing as they do the three major parties of the state, should pledge themselves not only to the people of this State, but to the nation, that we shall see to it that the curse of intemperance and the abuse of alcoholism shall never visit our State or through us our neighboring states.

And one of the great ways of carrying out that pledge, is not merely by statutory enactment outlawing the saloon, but by going much farther into fundamental social conditions.

As those of us who come from the Greater City know, the outlawing of the saloon where the worst abuses of alcoholism take place, and where the people in the saloons find an outlet for their activities and life, is not enough. We have the saloon and its abuses not because the law permits them, but because we have poverty and slums in our cities. We do not give to those people the opportunities of living a life of security and decency.

I have not parted with my philosophy when I entered here with all of you. We are repealing the 18th Amendment, but that is not all. The great question is: How shall we observe and establish temperance? If we abolish the saloon, if we are to destroy the curse of alcoholism, we must alleviate the social condition in the lives of men and women which will make it unnecessary for them to use the saloons as the center of the social activity. I thank you, Mr. Chairman, Ladies and Gentlemen. (Applause.)

President Smith: The Chair recognizes Mrs. Jeanie Rumsey Sheppard, of New York.

Mrs. Jeanie Rumsey Sheppard: I am glad to have an opportunity to speak to this resolution. Hundreds of thousands of women in this state have fought long and valiantly for repeal. I wish that all of them could be here today to raise their voices in favor of this resolution. It is with deep emotion that I, as their Chairman, speak for them.

Our years of work throughout the State have shown us not only the evils of Prohibition, but have shown us the need for a sane, moderate law.

Today, when we are taking this great step to rid the State of Prohibition, let us remember one lesson which Prohibition has taught us,—it is a lesson which we must never forget—and that is, that no law can be effective unless it expresses the will of the majority.

For myself and the thousands of women whom I have the honor to represent, I favor this resolution which will ratify for our State the repeal of the 18th Amendment and clear the way for a sane system of liquor control.

President Smith: The Chair recognizes the Honorable Stephen Callaghan, of Brooklyn. The Chair is informed that he is absent, but if he was here he intended to move that the question now be put. (Laughter and applause.)

The Chair recognizes the Honorable Nathan Burkan, of New York, who seconds the resolution.

You have heard the resolution. It is moved and seconded. All in favor will say Aye; contrary minded, No. The resolution is carried.

The main question before the Convention now is the adoption of the report of the Committee on Resolutions.

The Secretary of the Convention will call the roll.

(The Secretary, Mrs. Ruth Pratt, calls roll of delegates.)

President Smith: The Chair calls for the absentees.

The Secretary: There are no absentees.

President Smith: The Clerk will announce the result.

The Secretary: The result of the vote by count is 150 Yeas and no Nays. (Applause.)

President Smith: The Chair declares the report of the committee adopted and the resolutions accompanying it, and the Chair recognizes Mr. Clarence F. Conroy.

Mr. Clarence F. Conroy (of Buffalo): Mr. Chairman, I offer the following resolution, and move its adoption.

Resolved, That the President and Secretary of the convention prepare, execute, acknowledge and file the certificates and other papers required to be executed and filed by Chapter 143 of the Laws of 1933.

President Smith: The Chair recognizes Mr. Ernest Lappano, of New York—

Mr. Ernest Lappano: I second the resolution.

President Smith:—who seconds the resolution.

You have heard the resolution. All in favor say Aye. Contrary minded, No. It is adopted. The President recognizes the Honorable Charles D. Hilles, of New York.

Mr. Charles D. Hilles: I offer the following resolution and move its adoption:

Resolved, that the delegates of this convention do hereby express to the Mayor and other officials of the City of Albany, their sincere thanks for the hospitality accorded to the delegates of the convention and to the members of the families of the delegates.

President Smith: The Chair recognizes the Honorable Albert Fach—

Mr. Albert E. Fach: I second the resolution.

President Smith:—who seconds the resolution. You have heard the resolution. All in favor say Aye. Contrary minded, No. The resolution is adopted.

The Chair recognizes the Honorable Edward P. Lynch.

Mr. Edward P. Lynch (of Ogdensburg): Mr. President, I offer the following resolution and move its adoption:

Resolved, That the thanks of the delegates of this convention be and they are hereby expressed to the Governor of the State of New York, the Secretary of the State, their assistants and to the other state officials for the courtesies extended to the delegates to this convention.

President Smith: The Chair recognizes Honorable Charles E. Buchner—

Mr. Charles E. Buchner: I second the resolution.

President Smith:—who seconds the resolution. You have heard the resolution. All in favor say Aye. Contrary minded, No. The resolution is adopted.

The Chair recognizes Mr. Gustav W. M. Wieboldt, of New York.

Mr. Gustav W. M. Wieboldt (Woodhaven, N. Y.): Mr. Chairman, I offer the following resolution, and move its adoption.

Resolved, That the delegates of this convention do hereby express to the officials of the Columbia and National Broadcasting Systems, their thanks for the generous and widespread publicity of the proceedings of this convention over their systems to the people of the state and of the nation.

President Smith: The Chair recognizes Honorable John Dunnigan, of the Bronx—

Mr. John J. Dunnigan (the Bronx, New York): I rise to second the resolution just read.

President Smith: You have heard the resolution. All in favor say Aye. Contrary, No. It is adopted.

The President recognizes the Honorable Benjamin Antin—

Mr. Benjamin Antin (of the Bronx, New York): This convention has concluded its deliberations, has acted wisely, expeditiously and harmoniously. I therefore offer the following resolution, and move its adoption.

President Smith:—who offers the resolution which the Clerk will read.

The Clerk: Mr. Benjamin Antin offers the following resolution:

Resolved, That the Convention do now adjourn *sine die.*

President Smith: The Chair recognizes the Honorable Robert F. Cutler,—

Mr. Robert F. Cutler: I second the resolution.

President Smith:—who seconds the resolution. One minute. Delegates will remain seated. All in favor of the resolution say Aye; contrary minded, No. The resolution is adopted.

The Chair desires to announce that the New York Central Railroad has added an extra train between Albany and New York leaving the Union Depot at 4:20 Daylight Saving Time.

The Chair now presents to the Convention the Reverend Edward J. Quinn, of St. Augustine's Church of Troy, who will pronounce the Benediction.

REV. EDWARD J. QUINN: In the name of the Father, the Son and the Holy Ghost, Amen: May the blessing of Almighty God, the Father, the Son and the Holy Ghost, descend upon the members of this Convention and remain with them always. May its benign influence extend throughout the State and the Nation so as to direct our people to the true idea of temperance and sobriety and thus give unto the world the real principles of morality founded on divine law and not human law. In the name of The Father, The Son and The Holy Ghost, Amen.

PRESIDENT SMITH: Pursuant to the resolution heretofore adopted, the Chair now declares the Convention adjourned *sine die*. (Applause.)

Proceedings stenographically reported in relay for immediate release by James Murray and John K. Marshall, official stenographers.

New York Office: 150 Nassau Street.

Telephone: Beekman 3-2764.

OHIO*

REPORT OF
OHIO CONSTITUTIONAL CONVENTION

Repeal of the Eighteenth Amendment

AND

Ratification of Twenty-First Amendment

State House

Columbus

December 5, 1933

DELEGATES ELECTED TO CONVENTION

Lockwood Thompson, Cleveland, Ohio
Laurence H. Norton, Cleveland, Ohio
Robert J. Bulkley, Bratenahl, Ohio
Genevieve G. Hoadley, Cincinnati, Ohio
†Harry McLaughlin, Cleveland, Ohio
Atlee Pomerene, Cleveland, Ohio
Sidney G. Stricker, Cincinnati, Ohio
†Josephine McGowan, Canton, Ohio
John E. Sater, Columbus, Ohio
Mira Steele Printz, Cleveland, Ohio
S. P. Bush, Columbus, Ohio
John Malick, Cincinnati, Ohio
Harold G. Mosier, Cleveland, Ohio
Keith Lawrence, Cleveland Heights, Ohio
John W. Pattison, Cincinnati, Ohio
Charles H. Gross, Norwalk, Ohio
Harry J. Gilligan, Cincinnati, Ohio
Arthur L. Limbach, New Philadelphia, Ohio
T. A. Conway, Elyria, Ohio
Hugh A. Galt, Akron, Ohio
T. R. Schoonover, Lima, Ohio
Wm. W. Wood, III, Piqua, Ohio
William Hunt Robbins, Springfield, Ohio
Willis D. Gradison, Cincinnati, Ohio
M. R. Denver, Wilmington, Ohio
Joseph N. Ackerman, Shaker Heights, Ohio
A. P. Rogge, Zanesville, Ohio
J. C. Heinlein, Bridgeport, Ohio
C V. Beatty, East Liverpool, Ohio
J. Farnley Bonnell, Youngstown, Ohio
James P. Wilson, Youngstown, Ohio
W. S. Whittaker, Dayton, Ohio
Joseph H. Dowling, Dayton, Ohio
W. H. Purcell, Alliance, Ohio
Paul B. Belden, Canton, Ohio
John M. Miller, Sandusky, Ohio
Philip R. Mather, Cleveland Heights, Ohio
Zora S. Cummings, Toledo, Ohio
Louis M. Hirshson, Maumee, Ohio
Frank F. Gentsch, Cleveland, Ohio
Wm. O'Neil, Akron, Ohio
Grace Chapman Rose, Lancaster, Ohio
E. H. Hanefeld, Ottawa, Ohio
Margaret C. Bannon, Portsmouth, Ohio
S. A. Cunningham, Marietta, Ohio
Charles F. Michael, Bucyrus, Ohio
Frank Detrick, Ada, Ohio
Carl F. Orth, Wauseon, Ohio
Maybel M. Huntington, Columbus, Ohio
Alexander B. Roe, Athens, Ohio
H. P. Carruth, Chillicothe, Ohio

† Died prior to Convention day.

OHIO CONSTITUTIONAL CONVENTION

In accordance with the provisions of Ohio Amended Senate Bill No. 204, the delegates elected to the Convention to consider ratification of the proposed Twenty-first

* Printed. The communication of Secretary of State Stimson and the text of the Joint Resolution of Congress are omitted here.

Amendment to the Constitution of the United States, convened and were called to order by Governor George White, in the hall of the House of Representatives, in the State House, Columbus, Ohio, at 1:11 P.M., the convention being known as the Fifth Constitutional Convention of Ohio.

The invocation was pronounced by Rev. John Malick, delegate from Hamilton County.

GOVERNOR WHITE: The Secretary of State, the Honorable George S. Myers will now give the call of the convention.

SECRETARY OF STATE MYERS (Reads):

GREETINGS:

Pursuant to a resolution of the Congress of the United States and in accordance with the provisions of Amended Senate Bill No. 204, enacted by the Ninetieth General Assembly of the State of Ohio, and pursuant to your election on the seventh day of November, 1933, as a delegate to the Ohio Constitutional Convention, you are hereby officially notified that such convention shall convene in the Chamber of the House of Representatives in the State House, at the seat of Government in Columbus, Ohio, at one o'clock P.M. on the fifth day of December, 1933.

You are hereby further notified that, by virtue of the authority vested in you as a duly elected delegate to the convention to be held in accordance with the mandate of the General Assembly of the State of Ohio, it shall become your solemn duty to act upon the proposed amendment to the Constitution of the United States, adopted at the second session of the Seventy-second Congress, which provides in part that "the Eighteenth Article of Amendment to the Constitution of the United States shall be repealed."

In witness whereof, I have hereunto subscribed my name and caused the Seal of the Secretary of the State of Ohio to be attached hereto on this twenty-fourth day of November, A.D. 1933.

GEORGE S. MYERS
Secretary of State

SECRETARY OF STATE MYERS: You have heard the official call to the convention and I will ask Mr. Neffner to read the roll call.

MR. NEFFNER (calls roll, to which the following delegates responded):

Mrs. Bannon
Mr. Beatty
Mr. Belden
Mr. Bonnell
Mr. Bulkley
Mr. Bush
Mr. Carruth
Mr. Conway
Mr. Cummings
Mr. Cunningham
Mr. Denver
Mr. O'Neil
Mr. Orth
Mr. Pattison
Mr. Pomerene
Mr. Purcell
Mrs. Printz
Mr. Robbins
Mr. Roe
Mr. Rogge
Mrs. Rose
Mr. Sater
Mr. Detrick
Mr. Dowling
Mr. Galt
Mr. Gentsch
Mr. Brunner
Mr. Gilligan
Mr. Gradison
Mr. Hanefeld
Mr. Hirshon
Mrs. Huntington
Mr. Limbach
Mr. Mather
Mr. Miller
Mr. Schoonover
Mr. Stricker
Mr. Thompson
Mr. Whittaker
Mr. Wilson
Mr. Wood
Mr. Gross
Mr. Heinlein
Mrs. Hoadley
Mr. Lawrence
Mr. Malick
Mr. Michael
Mr. Mosier
Mr. Norton

SECRETARY OF STATE MYERS: There being a quorum present the Convention will proceed. You will now hear Honorable Governor White.

GOVERNOR WHITE: Mr. Chairman, Ladies and Gentlemen of the Convention:

The fifth article of the Constitution of the United States provides means and methods for amendment. Acting under this article two-thirds of both houses of the Congress have proposed to the states for ratification an amendment to the Constitution which, if adopted, will effect the repeal of the Eighteenth Amendment thereof.

The fifth Article of the Federal Constitution likewise gives to Congress the authority to prescribe one of two modes; by action by the state legislatures, or, by state convention called for that purpose. Congress has prescribed that this amendment be passed upon by state conventions.

Under the authority of the Federal Constitution and pursuant to this action by Congress, the legislature of Ohio has enacted a measure providing for the election of delegates to this convention. You, who are assembled here, have been elected in accordance to the provisions of that measure.

Congress, undoubtedly, chose the convention method of ratification for this amendment rather than that of ratification by the state legislatures, in order that the choice of the people might be expressed upon this one question alone, freed from the complicating considerations of other problems. Legislators must be chosen for their fitness to represent constituencies upon a great variety of subjects. You have been chosen by the people of Ohio to voice their will upon one issue only: "Shall the Eighteenth Amendment be Repealed?"

In the election of delegates to this convention, the vote of every citizen counted equally with that of every other. Every voter in Ohio had the opportunity to express his choice, and a high percentage of the electorate availed itself of this opportunity. You, therefore, bear the mandate of the people to register the will of the state upon the question to come before you.

That the control of intoxicating liquors presents a problem of first magnitude was evidenced by the adoption of the Eighteenth Amendment. Trivial causes have never produced changes in our national Constitution. If, as now seems apparent, that amendment is about to be repealed, the volume of public sentiment which impels such action is ample evidence that the problem has grown no smaller. The solution of the problem will be returned to the several states.

What that solution may be in Ohio concerns you, officially, not at all. You are concerned only with the question whether the method of control, embodied in the Eighteenth Amendment, shall be continued or abolished.

But if, and when, that method shall be abolished, and you as citizens shall take your places once again in the ranks of your communities, the effort of the state to cope with this important responsibility should elicit your earnest consideration. The wisdom and unwisdom with which the problem is met will entail far-reaching consequences upon the people of this commonwealth. The solution of the liquor problem still remains to be effected.

In sending you as delegates to this convention the people of Ohio have conferred upon you a signal honor. To few among the millions of American citizens has it been given to frame or to alter the fundamental document of our federal government. That document is enshrined, like the ark of the covenant, in the hearts of our people, and none with impunity may stretch forth an impious hand to touch it. Like the chosen ministers of old, you may take it into your hands. Like them, you will do it with a full sense of your responsibility.

GOVERNOR WHITE: We will now have the election of the Honorable President of this Constitutional Convention, the chair recognizes Delegate Sidney G. Stricker of Cincinnati.

MR. STRICKER: Mr. President, Governor White, and Delegates of the Convention:

Ohio traditionally rich and prolific in statesmen, is fortunate in having present as delegates to this convention, not only Senator Bulkley, but also that peerless leader and statesman, former United States Senator Atlee Pomerene, who as you will remember, when a member of the Senate in 1917 voted against the Eighteenth Amendment. His wisdom and foresight in that respect is confirmed by the fact that we are here today to ratify the repeal of the Eighteenth Amendment.

Unwilling to sacrifice his convictions or yield to the prohibition forces, Senator Pomerene was defeated for reelection. Because of his well-known courage and ability as a lawyer, he was recalled to service by President Coolidge as counsel for the government with present Justice Roberts in the Teapot Dome Oil cases, in which he succeeded in recovering many millions of dollars and oil leases of inestimable value.

Later, because of his fine record in the Senate and unimpeachable character, he was again called to public service by President Hoover, who as you all know appointed him chairman of the Reconstruction Finance Corporation, a position of importance second only to that of Secretary of the Treasury. The manner in which Senator Pomerene discharged his high duties of public trust, testify more eloquently to his ability, character and integrity, than any words I might add.

That he was not re-nominated by President Roosevelt was due solely to that fact that the law under which the Reconstruction Finance Corporation was created, did not permit the appointment of more than four members of the same political party, as members of the committee. The law further makes the Secretary of the Treasury ex-officio a member of that committee. Upon change of the new administration, the then newly appointed Secretary of the Treasury thereby became a member of the committee, which made it necessary to make room for the newly appointed secretary.

With characteristic modesty and self-sacrifice, and in order to relieve President Roosevelt of the embarrassment of calling for the resignation of one of the Democratic members of that committee, Senator Pomerene declined re-nomination as chairman. Would that I were at liberty to read to you the letters in Senator Pomerene's possession from Presidents Hoover and Roosevelt, expressing their high appreciation of his service as chairman of the Reconstruction Finance Corporation and their regret of his inability to serve longer in that capacity. Senator Pomerene's modesty forbids me to read them to you.

Without taking the time of the convention to review the Senator's many fine qualities as a statesman, citizen and friend, it seems to me that this convention cannot do less than honor itself by electing Senator Pomerene as Honorary President of this Convention. I therefore move you, Mr. President, that Senator Pomerene be elected Honorary President of this Convention.

GOVERNOR WHITE: You have heard Hon. Atlee Pomerene nominated as Honorary President. Are there any other nominations? If not, I take the highest pleasure in naming as Honorary President of this Convention, Mr. Pomerene.

SENATOR ATLEE POMERENE: Governor White, and Ladies and Gentlemen of the Convention:

I deem myself happy to be chosen Temporary President of this Convention. It is a rare privilege to participate in the making of history, not only in Ohio, but in the nation.

As you have been told, while in the Senate in 1917, I voted against the Eighteenth Amendment. I did it partly because Ohio up to that time had always voted against Prohibition, but principally because I was convinced that with our cosmopolitan population state-wide Prohibition could never be enforced. If I were in the Senate again, and a similar resolution were to be presented, I would vote as I did in 1917.

I realized in 1917 that my vote would probably lead to my defeat for reelection. Please do not think that I have any regrets. I was firm in the conviction that the future would justify my course. The result of the submission of this question to the electors verifies my judgment. I am happy to be back in private life and in the practice of the law.

The delegates of this convention and its guests know the evils of the old saloon. After years of experience they know also the evils of nationwide Prohibition. I trust the repeal forces will avoid the mistakes of the past. As one citizen appealing to his fellow citizens, let this repeal be a warning to the radicals of the country. People of a great democracy will not for any length of time be led or controlled by the extremists on either side of any question.

The repeal of the Eighteenth Amendment here in Ohio received a majority of 850,000 votes. The vote throughout the entire country is about, if not more than, three to one in favor of the repeal.

When Prohibition was adopted we were told that it would empty the jails, workhouses and penitentiaries. These penal institutions have more inmates now than ever in the history of the state. A substantial portion of them have been committed for offenses traceable directly, or indirectly, to Prohibition. Radicalism on this subject has only emptied the churches.

Now that nation-wide and state-wide Prohibition have been repealed, let us be restrained. Let us be conscious of past evils and let us remember that the old saloon must not return. Let us have strict control with the principle of local option extended to municipalities, townships, counties and residential districts.

But, has the Eighteenth Amendment been repealed? Let me refer to the prophecies made by some of the leaders of the Anti-Saloon League in the recent past.

The public prints within perhaps the last year carried the report that my friend, Senator Sheppard, said there was no more chance of repealing the Eighteenth Amendment than there was for a humming bird to fly to the moon with the Washington monument tied to its tail.

Andrew W. Volstead, the author of the Volstead law, said: "Go out and tell your neighbor that you might as well try to climb over the moon as to repeal the prohibition amendment and the prohibition enforcement act. You can't repeal it! You can't weaken it! You can't get beer and light wines!"

Dr. F. Scott McBride of the Anti-Saloon League said: "There is no reaction against the prohibition amendment in this country and those who are awaiting such a reaction will be in their graves before it comes. As a political question, prohibition is a dead issue, and it always will be political suicide for any person to sponsor the wet cause . . . There will never be any modification of the law."

Dr. Clarence True Wilson said: "Prohibition has been a marvelous financial success and is slowly eliminating the memories and the tendencies of the old days. Prohibition can never be defeated."

Wayne B. Wheeler said: "The fight to repeal the amendment is just as hopeless as an attempt to bring back slavery."

Verily these leaders of a lost cause will not be honored as prophets.

I shall not take the time to discuss the details of the new legislation on this subject, whether by the General Assembly, or by the Congress of the United States. I shall leave that subject to those who are charged with the responsibility.

Ohio is fortunate in having present as a delegate to this convention my friend, the Honorable Robert J. Bulkley. He has only been in the Senate a short time, but he has made an enviable record. He is a member of some of its most important committees. So long as he remains in the Senate, Ohio and the nation will be well represented.

I have the honor of presenting your Permanent Chairman, Senator Bulkley.

SENATOR POMERENE: We will now have the selection of a temporary secretary—we recognize Mrs. Printz.

MRS. PRINTZ: I am very happy to nominate Mrs. Genevieve Hoadly of Cincinnati as temporary secretary of the convention.

SENATOR POMERENE: Are there any other nominations? If not, and without objection, I declare Mrs. Hoadly elected as temporary secretary.

SENATOR POMERENE: The next order of business is the election of a clerk of the convention.

MR. WOOD: I desire to nominate Mr. Dwight L. Matchette as clerk of this convention.

SENATOR POMERENE: Mr. Dwight L. Matchette has been nominated clerk; are there any other nominations? If not, and without objection, I declare him elected clerk of this convention.

SENATOR POMERENE: It seems that this convention has suffered two very serious losses among the delegates: One Harry McLaughlin, who represented the laboring interests, has passed to his reward. We will now nominate to fill that vacancy.

MR. BUSH: I nominate Thomas J. Donnelly to succeed Mr. McLaughlin.

SENATOR POMERENE: Are there any other nominations? If not, and without objection, I declare him elected to fill the vacancy.

SENATOR POMERENE: Then again we lost one who was a dear friend to all of us. We know of her active work politically, and we knew her as a wonderful worker both socially and charitably. I can say without any reservation that her very presence was an inspiration to all who had the honor of her acquaintance. I refer to Mrs. Josephine McGowan, whose death occurred only recently.

MR. BUSH: I take pleasure in nominating Mrs. Richard Rector of Columbus, to fill the vacancy.

SENATOR POMERENE: Are there any other nominations? If not, and without objection, I declare Mrs. Richard Rector to succeed Mrs. Josephine McGowan.

SENATOR POMERENE: And now I have a telegram which came this morning addressed to Senator Bulkley and myself jointly:

HONORABLE ATLEE POMERENE OR HONORABLE ROBERT J. BULKLEY, personal chairman, Ohio Prohibition Repeal Convention, House of Representatives, Columbus, Ohio.

Serious illness makes it impossible for me to attend and participate in this convention when Ohio will repeal the Eighteenth Amendment and ratify the Twenty-first amendment to the Federal Constitution. For thirteen years I have fought in the ranks to bring Ohio and our nation back to sanity and during all this time have dreamed and looked forward to participating in this history-making event. I cannot adequately express my disappointment in not being able to be with you. Please convey to the delegates assembled my regrets and my best wishes for the success of the convention.

(*Signed*) SENATOR JOSEPH N. ACKERMAN

SENATOR POMERENE: Do I hear any nominations to fill this vacancy?

MR. MOSIER: I nominate to fill the vacancy caused by the resignation of Senator Ackerman, Thomas E. Bateman, who is now clerk of the Ohio Senate.

MR. STRICKER: I second the nomination.

SENATOR POMERENE: The name of Thomas E. Bateman has been presented and seconded; are there any other nominations?

MR. LOCKWOOD THOMPSON: I desire to nominate Frank R. Uible, a member of the state legislature.

SENATOR POMERENE: There are two nominations: Thomas E. Bateman and Frank R. Uible; the clerk will call the roll.

MR. MATCHETTE (calls roll which shows the following voting for Mr. Bateman):

Mrs. Bannon
Mr. Beatty
Mr. Belden
Mr. Bonnell
Mr. Brunner
Mr. Bulkley
Mr. Bush
Mr. Carruth
Mr. Conway
Mr. Cummings
Mr. Denver
Mr. Detrick
Mr. Donnelly
Mr. Gradison
Mr. Gross
Mr. Hanefeld
Mr. Heinlein
Mr. Hirshon
Mrs. Hoadly
Mrs. Huntington
Mr. Lawrence
Mr. Limbach
Mr. Malick
Mr. Mather
Mr. Michael
Mr. Miller
Mr. Orth
Mr. Pattison
Mr. Pomerene
Mrs. Printz
Mr. Purcell
Mrs. Rector
Mr. Robbins
Mr. Roe
Mr. Rogge
Mrs. Rose
Mr. Sater
Mr. Schoonover
Mr. Stricker
Mr. Dowling
Mr. Galt
Mr. Gentsch
Mr. Gilligan
Mr. Mosier
Mr. Norton
Mr. O'Neil
Mr. Whittaker
Mr. Wilson
Mr. Wood

and for Mr. Uible:
Mr. Lockwood Thompson.

SENATOR POMERENE: The clerk has advised the result of the roll call to be Mr. Bateman, 50; Mr. Uible, 1. Mr. Bateman having received more than a majority, I declare him elected to succeed Mr. Joseph N. Ackerman, resigned.

SENATOR POMERENE: We now have a letter from the Ohio Legislative Correspondents Association which gives a list of the newspaper correspondents who are authorized to represent their respective newspapers. I will ask the clerk to read this letter.

MR. MATCHETTE: Following is a list of the legislative correspondents and the newspapers, news services, or legislative information services which they represent, whose credentials have been approved by the executive committee of the Legislative Correspondents Association.

We respectfully request that floor privileges be granted these correspondents during the meeting of this honorable constitutional convention:

William C. Howells, Cleveland Plain Dealer.
John W. Fisher, News League of Ohio.
Karl B. Pauly, Ohio State Journal.
Hal W. Conefry, Scripps-Howard Newspapers.
H. H. Daugherty, Associated Press.
Herbert R. Mengert, Cincinnati Enquirer.
George Smallsreed, Columbus Dispatch.
H. Preston Wolfe, Columbus Dispatch.
A. E. McKee, Ohio State Journal.
J. A. Meckstroth, Ohio State Journal.

Kenneth D. Tooill, Ohio State Journal.
James T. Keenan, Scripps-Howard Newspapers.
Carlton K. Matson, Scripps-Howard Newspapers.
George A. Snodgrass, Columbus Citizen.
John P. Biehn, Associated Press.
Joseph S. Deutschle, Associated Press.
Henry T. Gorrell, United Press.
Richard A. Forster, Cincinnati Times-Star.
I. L. Kenen, Cleveland News.
Carroll McCrea, Toledo Blade.
E. O. Fehlhaber, Cleveland News.
Earl Wilson, Akron Beacon-Journal.
Paul B. Mason, Cincinnati Enquirer.
Richard L. Maher, Cleveland Press.
James Johnson, The Gongwer Service.
Earl W. Baird, Hamilton Journal.
Ralph J. Donaldson, Cleveland Plain Dealer.
Charles S. Gongwer, The Gongwer Service.
G. Edward Hancock, Akron Beacon-Journal.
Carl Turner, International News Service.
Frank M. Heller, The Gongwer Service.

Respectfully,

(*Signed*) W. C. HOWELLS, *President*
(*Signed*) KARL B. PAULY, *Secretary*

SENATOR POMERENE: You have heard the names of the correspondents and I presume there is no objection.

SENATOR POMERENE: Chief Justice Weygandt has just come in and he will immediately administer the oath of office to the delegates of this convention.

(Delegates in standing position take oath of office administered by the Hon. Chief Justice Carl V. Weygandt.)

SENATOR POMERENE: The next order of business is the selection of a permanent president of the convention.

MR. MOSIER: I have the honor to nominate as permanent president of this convention the Hon. Robert J. Bulkley of Cleveland.

SENATOR POMERENE: You have heard the name of Hon. Robert J. Bulkley to be permanent president of this convention. Are there any other nominations? If not, and without objection, I hereby declare him to be unanimously elected as permanent president of this convention.

SENATOR BULKLEY: Fellow delegates of the convention:

I appreciate the honor of being chosen president of this convention and also appreciate Senator Pomerene's remarks concerning me.

This is a great day, to which many of us have long looked forward. We are taking out of the Federal Constitution that which never should have been put in, a sumptuary law, the only provision in the constitution intended to restrict the liberties of American citizens.

It is a coincidence that Ohio's convention should meet on the day when repeal will be accomplished. The Democratic party should be lauded for its stand on prohibition repeal, particularly the action taken at the national convention last June, but credit should likewise be given to many members of the Republican party who have aided greatly in accomplishing repeal.

The great majorities for repeal are not to be interpreted as votes for more and better liquor; they are votes for more orderly liquor control, and for more enforceable liquor legislation, to the end that Americans may again become as law-abiding as we would like to be.

I pause now to call attention to the untimely death of two members of this convention, Mrs. Josephine McGowan, a true friend, a loyal and tireless Democrat, who will long be remembered by her many friends in Ohio and throughout the nation for her efforts and accomplishments, politically, socially and charitably; Mr. Harry McLaughlin, who gave his very life in the interest of labor and its many problems.

Later on in the meeting we will appoint committees on memorials to both, to be made a part of the record of this convention.

I also cherish the memory of my friend, Charles L. Knight, who was chosen as a repeal candidate for delegate, but died before the election. He was always a fearless thinker and we always knew where he stood on all questions.

We are making history here in Ohio today for the entire nation. The 21st or Repeal Amendment, submitted to the states last February, is being ratified in the record time of nine months. We who have fought the fight for repeal approach the new day with some feeling of triumph, but still more with a feeling of responsibility for the future.

With Pennsylvania and Utah also voting this afternoon, we may have news of the final results before we adjourn. The Secretary of State of Ohio is ready here with a special wire to send our message to the President at the White House as soon as we shall have voted.

SENATOR BULKLEY: Next in order of business will be the election of a first vice-president of the convention.

MRS. HOADLY: I am happy to nominate Mrs. Margaret Bannon of Portsmouth as first vice president.

MR. BATEMAN: I second the nomination and ask that the nominations be closed.

SENATOR BULKLEY: You have heard Mrs. Bannon nominated, there being no objection, I declare her elected first vice-president of this convention.

SENATOR BULKLEY: Next, the nomination for second vice president.

MR. GENTSCH: It gives me great pleasure to nominate Mr. J. C. Heinlein.

MR. MOSIER: I second the nomination of Mr. Heinlein and move that the nominations be closed.

SENATOR BULKLEY: You have heard Mr. Heinlein nominated. If there are no objections, I declare him elected second vice president of this convention.

SENATOR BULKLEY: We now have the election of a permanent secretary.

MR. STRICKER: I move that Mrs. Hoadly, the temporary secretary, be made permanent secretary of the convention.

SENATOR BULKLEY: If there are no other nominations, I declare Mrs. Hoadly permanent secretary of the convention.

SENATOR BULKLEY: The following persons have been named for different duties this afternoon:

Sergeants-at-Arms—John W. Edwards and S. I. Gruner.
Convention Reporter—Lucille Brick.
Minute Clerk—Clifford E. Garwick.
Doorkeepers—William Hamilton, Val Stokley, W. T. Roberts, Jr., and Birch Scott.
Pages—Richard Shepard, Joseph Heyman, Frank Huttenmiller, Wilford Heaton, Lloyd Wonsettler, Fred Burgy, and Lucas Schockman.
Parliamentarian—E. W. Hughes.

SENATOR BULKLEY: The next order of business will be the appointment of committees:

RESOLUTIONS COMMITTEE

Delegates—Mr. Stricker, Mrs. Cummings, and Mr. O'Neil.

MEMORIAL COMMITTEE FOR MRS. McGOWAN

Delegates—Mrs. Rose, Mr. Belden, and Mrs. Huntington.

MEMORIAL FOR HARRY McLAUGHLIN

Delegates—Mr. Norton, Mr. Donnelly, and Mr. Gentsch.

(The convention unanimously adopted the rules of the House of Representatives to govern this convention.)

SENATOR BULKLEY: Now we have the question of mileage and convention expenditures: The chair recognizes Delegate Galt.

Mr. Galt presented the following resolution:

WHEREAS, The Delegates to this Constitutional Convention for ratification of the Twenty-first Amendment to the United States Constitution are highly honored in their selection as delegates by the voters of Ohio, therefore, be it

Resolved, That we waive the mileage allowance provided for us, and be it further

Resolved, That from the funds thus provided, as authorized by Senate Bill No. 204—Mr. Mosier, the actual expenses for stenographic labor, the preparation of the convention record and such other actual labor and other costs, be disbursed through the clerk of this convention.

SENATOR BULKLEY: In order that there will be no question regarding mileage and convention expenses, the chair will put the question—Is anyone against the adoption of the resolution of Mr. Galt? Is there objection? The chair hears none and the resolution is unanimously adopted.

SENATOR BULKLEY: The convention is now fully organized. The next order of business is the report of the committees. It is requested that we act on the principal resolution so that the delegates may have the opportunity of signing the resolution which is to be transmitted to the Secretary of State.

(*Recess; At 2:20* P.M. *for five minutes*
The convention met pursuant to recess, at 2:25 P.M.)

SENATOR BULKLEY: Delegate Stricker reports that the committee on resolutions is ready.

MR. STRICKER: Mr. President, Governor White, and Delegates of the Convention:

This is a historic day for Ohio and the nation. We have assembled here in convention to pass upon the ratification of a proposed amendment to the Constitution of the United States repealing the Eighteenth Amendment. No issue since the days of slavery has so engaged and absorbed the thoughts and wishes of the people as the question of prohibition.

After many years of agitation, while the country was engaged in war and the people were eager and ready to make any sacrifice thought necessary to promote social order and economy, the Eighteenth Amendment was adopted and ratified by every state in the union saving and excepting two. Self denial then the order of the day, was eagerly offered and practiced by a large majority of our people. Human impulses and desires were subordinated to what was deemed necessary for the general welfare. Personal liberty was surrendered for what was deemed public necessity.

The error of writing into the constitution a police regulation originally reserved to the states and placing same under federal control, without regard to the wishes, habits and temperament of the people of the several states, and imposing upon a large majority of the people the tyranny of a small minority with all of its attendant evils, soon became manifest. Nullification or revolt, which is the usual outlet of a suffering people against a bad law, soon asserted itself. Murmurings grew into indignation and open protest took the place of individual sacrifice.

Defiance and disrespect for law followed until protest became clamor and outcry throughout the nation. State after state repealed their enforcement laws, or openly refused to enforce the law. Crime and lawlessness followed. The bootlegger, the racketeer, the gunman and kidnaper each became the offspring of this unwise and iniquitous legislation. The youth who before never tasted liquor, was not considered smart or eligible to good society without the hip flask, and the morale of society soon became debased. Citizens of reputation, noted educators and persons high in public life, women of character, and the public press generally, became advocates of repeal. It was generally conceded that, as a temperance measure, Prohibition was a failure. The cure was worse than the disease.

With it all, the government and states were losing hundreds of millions of dollars each year in what theretofore was a source of necessary and legitimate revenue. Large deficiencies in the budget of the federal government and the states followed as the inevitable consequence, and new taxes had to be imposed.

Under these circumstances, it is not surprising that public sentiment changed quickly and with astounding force. Each of the great political parties yielded to the public will and pledged themselves for repeal of the Eighteenth Amendment in their last national platforms at the Chicago conventions. The Democratic party pleaded for unqualified repeal; the Republican party for modified repeal. In last analysis, however, both parties were for repeal.

Congress responsive to the sense and will of the people, in February, 1933, by more than the necessary two-thirds majority, adopted a joint resolution repealing the Eighteenth Amendment and submitted the same for ratification to the states by conventions. The latter method was invoked for the first time in our history covering a period of more than one hundred and forty-five years. Theretofore each amendment to the constitution was submitted for ratification to the legislatures of the several states. Owing to its importance and in order that there might be a more truly representative expression of the will of the people, Congress wisely submitted the proposed amendment for ratification by the several states in conventions.

No legislation having been previously provided by Congress or the legislatures of the several states for the election of delegates and holding the conventions, it became necessary for the legislatures of each state to provide the necessary machinery for the election of delegates and establishing the Conventions. Within the short space of less than nine months since the adoption of the joint resolution of Congress, thirty-five states had enacted the necessary legislation, and before the sun goes down today, thirty-six states in obedience to the will of the people, will have ratified the proposed amendment repealing the Eighteenth Amendment, thereby relieving the country from the greatest political blunder in our history.

Mr. President and Delegates of the Convention: It is a great privilege to be here today to voice the will of our people. It is a great privilege to record as the solemn and deliberate judgment of this convention, that tyranny and intolerance cannot survive in this state; that we are a law-abiding people, but will not consent that a small and unimportant minority shall rule a large and important majority with laws that affect the lives, habits and liberties of our people; that anarchy, lawlessness and crime have no place in our government; that ours is a government of free institutions responsive to the will of the people, actuated by the highest and best motives of human conduct.

I, therefore, propose, Mr. President, the adoption of the following resolution:

WHEREAS, The Senate and House of Representatives of the United States of America in Congress assembled (two-thirds of each House concurring therein) did resolve that the following article is hereby proposed as an amendment to the Constitution of the United States, which shall be valid to all intents and purposes as a part of the Constitution when ratified by conventions in three-fourths of the several states; and

WHEREAS, The said proposed amendment reads as follows:

Section 1. The Eighteenth Article of Amendment to the Constitution of the United States is hereby repealed.

Section 2. The transportation or importation into any state, territory or possession of the United States for delivery or use therein of intoxicating liquors, in violation of the laws thereof, is hereby prohibited.

Section 3. This article shall be inoperative unless it shall have been ratified as an amendment to the constitution by conventions in the several states, as provided in the constitution, within seven years from the date of submission hereof to the states by Congress; and

WHEREAS, There was duly transmitted to the Ninetieth General Assembly of the State of Ohio, in regular session assembled, the said proposed article of amendment to the Constitution of the United States; and

WHEREAS, The said General Assembly of the State of Ohio, pursuant to law, did enact Senate Bill No. 204, entitled "An Act to provide for a convention to pass on amendments to the constitution of the United States which may hereafter be proposed by the Congress for ratification by conventions in the several states," which act was passed on March 20, 1933, and signed by the Governor on March 23, 1933, and filed with the Secretary of State on March 24, 1933; and

WHEREAS, Pursuant to the provisions of said Amended Senate Bill No. 204, the Governor of Ohio did on June 22, 1933, issue a proclamation ordering that an election be held on November 7, 1933, for the election of delegates to a convention to be called to pass upon the ratification or rejection of the proposed repeal of the said Eighteenth Article of Amendment to the Constitution of the United States; and

WHEREAS, Fifty-two delegates were duly elected on the 7th day of November, 1933, as shown by the canvass of the returns of said elections by the Secretary of State, which canvass was conducted in the presence of the Governor of Ohio, the Auditor of State and the Attorney General; and

WHEREAS, Pursuant to the official call issued by the Secretary of State, a copy of which is herewith presented, the said fifty-two delegates elect, did meet and are now assembled at the time and place therein fixed, and having duly organized by the election of a president and a secretary, and having adopted rules with which to govern their deliberations, they do now constitute the official and legal Constitutional Convention of Ohio, officially called to consider the ratification of the Amendment to the Constitution of the United States proposing the repeal of the Eighteenth Article of Amendment thereto; now, therefore

After due deliberation and consideration by said delegates in convention so assembled, representing the people of the State of Ohio

Be it resolved, By this convention of the delegates representing the people of the State of Ohio, duly assembled pursuant to law that we do approve and ratify the proposed Article of Amendment proposed by the Congress to the Constitution of the

United States designed to repeal the Eighteenth Article of said Amendment.

Further be it resolved, That the president and the secretary of this convention forthwith execute and transmit a certificate of this resolution to the Secretary of State of the State of Ohio, Hon. George S. Myers, for transmission by the said Secretary of State, under the Great Seal of the State of Ohio to the Secretary of State of the United States of America.

MR. CONWAY: I second the adoption of the resolution.

SENATOR BULKLEY: Considering the circumstances under which the delegates of this convention were elected, it may be that we shall not need much discussion of the resolution. Remarks, however, are in order. (Pause.) If there are no further remarks we shall put the question:

Shall the Resolution Pass? The clerk will call the roll.

MR. MATCHETTE (begins roll call at 2:41 P.M.):

For the Amendment:

Mrs. Bannon
Mr. Bateman
Mr. Beatty
Mr. Belden
Mr. Bonnell
Mr. Brunner
Mr. Bulkley
Mr. Bush
Mr. Carruth
Mr. Conway
Mr. Cummings
Mr. Cunningham
Mr. Denver
Mr. Detrick
Mr. Donnelly
Mr. Dowling
Mr. Galt
Mr. Gentsch
Mr. Gilligan
Mr. Gradison
Mr. Gross
Mr. Hanefeld
Mr. Heinlein
Mr. Hirshon
Mrs. Hoadly
Mrs. Huntington
Mr. Lawrence
Mr. Limbach
Mr. Malick
Mr. Mather
Mr. Michael
Mr. Miller
Mr. Mosier
Mr. Norton
Mr. O'Neil
Mr. Orth
Mr. Pattison
Mr. Pomerene
Mrs. Printz
Mr. Purcell
Mrs. Rector
Mr. Robbins
Mr. Roe
Mr. Rogge
Mrs. Rose
Mr. Sater
Mr. Schoonover
Mr. Stricker
Mr. Whittaker
Mr. Wilson
Mr. Wood
Mr. Thompson

Against the Amendment:
None

SENATOR BULKLEY: The result of the roll call shows: Yeas, 52; Nays, none. (Roll call completed 2:44 P.M.)

SENATOR BULKLEY: The Amendment is ratified. Ohio repeals the Eighteenth Amendment.

SENATOR BULKLEY: The Secretary of State is here and we have wires direct into the White House to transmit to the President of the United States the information that Ohio has ratified the Twenty-first Amendment.

SECRETARY OF STATE MR. MYERS: This telegram will be sent (reads to telegrapher):

STATE HOUSE, COLUMBUS, OHIO
December 5, 1933, 2:50 P.M.

PRESIDENT FRANKLIN D. ROOSEVELT
WHITE HOUSE
WASHINGTON, D.C.

Ohio takes pleasure in sending you this official notification that on December 5, 1933, the Ohio Constitutional Convention assembled at the capitol at Columbus, ratified on behalf of said state the proposed amendment to the Constitution of the United States providing for the repeal of the Eighteenth Amendment.

(*Signed*) GEORGE S. MYERS
Secretary of State

SENATOR BULKLEY: The Secretary of State informs me that he will now wire Acting United States Secretary of State, Mr. William Phillips, to whom the signed certificate will be sent.

SECRETARY OF STATE MYERS (reads to telegrapher):

STATE HOUSE, COLUMBUS, OHIO
December 5, 1933

HON. WILLIAM PHILLIPS
Acting Secretary of State
Washington, D.C.

You are hereby officially notified that on December 5, 1933, a convention duly held in the State of Ohio ratified on behalf of the said state the proposed amendment to the Constitution of the United States providing for the repeal of the Eighteenth Amendment and the duly authenticated papers evidencing the action of said convention are being forwarded to you.

(*Signed*) GEORGE S. MYERS
Secretary of State

SENATOR BULKLEY: The chair recognizes Mrs. Rose, on the memorial resolution for Mrs. McGowan.

MRS. ROSE (reads resolution):

RESOLUTION

WHEREAS, Mrs. Josephine McGowan, a delegate to this convention, having been called in death

It is resolved, That this convention, in recognition of Mrs. McGowan's active work in connection with the Women's Organization for National Prohibition Reform, and as a citizen of splendid ability, known and loved throughout the state and nation for her political, religious, civic, and welfare activities, express its deep regret over her loss.

Be it further resolved, That the clerk be instructed to forward a copy of this resolution to the family of the deceased and that as a further mark of our high regard for the deceased this resolution be adopted by rising vote.

(*Signed*) GRACE CHAPMAN ROSE
JANE B. BELDEN
MAYBEL M. HUNTINGTON

SENATOR BULKLEY: You have heard the resolution. All those in favor please indicate by rising.

(Delegates all arise.)

SENATOR BULKLEY: The resolution is unanimously adopted.

SENATOR BULKLEY: Pending the receipt of the other committee report, the clerk will call the roll and the delegates will please come up to the clerk's desk to sign the certificate of the action of this convention.

(*This roll call was broadcast over the N. B. C. and C. B. S. networks.*)

(Delegates respond as called.)

SENATOR BULKLEY: While the delegates are coming up to sign the certification, we can proceed with the next order of business. The chair recognizes Mr. Donnelly, who presents the following resolution:

WHEREAS, This Constitutional Convention has learned with deep regret of the death of Harry McLaughlin, president of the Ohio State Federation of Labor and president of the Cleveland Federation of Labor, and an elected delegate to this convention; and

WHEREAS, In the death of this outstanding leader in the cause of union labor and strong advocate of the repeal of the Eighteenth Amendment, the state has suffered a great loss; therefore be it

Resolved, That this convention express its deep regrets and that the clerk be instructed to forward a copy of this resolution to the family of the deceased, and to the Cleveland Federation of Labor and the Ohio State Federation of Labor.

(*Signed*) LAWRENCE H. NORTON
THOS. J. DONNELLY
FRANK F. GENTSCH
Committee on Memorial to Delegate Harry McLaughlin.

SENATOR BULKLEY: You have heard the report of the committee. All those in favor, please indicate by rising.

(Delegates all arise.)

SENATOR BULKLEY: The resolution is unanimously adopted.

SENATOR BULKLEY: We are now advised that we are connected up on the national hook-up and we will take this opportunity to report to the listeners on this great hook-up that the Constitutional Convention of the State of Ohio, about twenty minutes ago, voted 52 to 0 to ratify the amendment proposed to the Constitution of the United States which shall repeal the Eighteenth Amendment. Wires direct to the department at Washington have already carried the news in the form of telegrams signed by the Secretary of State, the Hon. George S. Myers. The delegates to this convention are now coming up, one by one, to sign the certificate of the action of this convention, and when this has been completed the convention will have accomplished its purpose.

SENATOR BULKLEY: The Secretary of State reports that he has just had a telegraph message from the Acting Secretary of State the Hon. William P. Phillips (acting in the absence of the Hon. Cordell Hull) that he is in receipt of the telegram which was sent to him at the request of this convention and expresses best wishes of the Department of State at Washington.

(3:15 P.M.)

SENATOR BULKLEY: One more item of interest, we are advised that the constitutional convention of the State of Utah is now voting for ratification.

SENATOR BULKLEY: The action of the constitutional convention in the State of Pennsylvania reports the ratification of the Twenty-first Amendment to repeal the Eighteenth Amendment has been officially confirmed. Their action was about fifteen minutes before ours, so that makes Pennsylvania the thirty-fourth state to ratify, Ohio the thirty-fifth state.

SENATOR BULKLEY: For some few minutes the telegrapher has been making an effort to get in touch with Utah; it is my judgment that it would be worth while to wait a few minutes now and see if we can get an announcement.

SENATOR BULKLEY: There is now a flash that officials of the Pennsylvania Convention went to Washington by air to deliver their signed certificate.

SENATOR BULKLEY: I am sorry that the latest news from Utah is not so hopeful as we had. The report is that an address is being made by the Governor of Utah. *I am sure, however, that the result will be favorable.*

SENATOR BULKLEY: Is there any other business?

MR. HEINLEIN: I move that this Convention having completed the purpose for which it was called, adjourn.

MR. CARRUTH: I second the motion for adjournment.

SENATOR BULKLEY: The motion has been carried unanimously and we stand adjourned.

(Time 3:45 P.M.)

CERTIFICATION BY PRESIDENT AND SECRETARY

TO THE HONORABLE GEORGE S. MYERS
Secretary of State
State of Ohio

We, the undersigned, duly elected President and Secretary, respectively, of the Constitutional Convention of Ohio, hereby certify that the said Convention has, on the 5th day of December, 1933, ratified the Amendment proposing the repeal of the Eighteenth Article of Amendment to the Constitution of the United States, by a majority of the total number of delegates, fifty-two of said delegates voting in favor of the ratification and none of the said delegates voting against the ratification of the said proposed Amendment.

In testimony whereof, we have hereunto set our hands at the City of Columbus, Ohio, this 5th day of December, in the year of our Lord, One Thousand Nine Hundred and Thirty-Three.

(*Signed*) ROBERT J. BULKLEY
President
GENEVIEVE G. HOADLY
Secretary

Attest: DWIGHT L. MATCHETTE
Clerk

UNITED STATES OF AMERICA

STATE OF OHIO

TO THE HONORABLE CORDELL HULL
Secretary of State of the
United States of America

I, George S. Myers, Secretary of State of the State of Ohio, do hereby certify that Hon. Robert J. Bulkley and Mrs. Genevieve G. Hoadly, whose names appear subscribed to the attached certificate of ratification of the proposed amendment to the Constitution of the United States, relating to the repeal of the Eighteenth Article of

Amendment to the Constitution of the United States, were at the time of the signing of same, the duly elected, qualified and acting President and Secretary, respectively, of the Constitutional Convention of the State of Ohio, duly assembled and convened under the provisions of an Act of the General Assembly of said State entitled Amended Senate Bill No. 204.

I further certify that said Convention did meet on Tuesday, December 5, 1933, such date being the twenty-eighth day following the election of such delegates on November 7, 1933.

I further certify that the accompanying certificate does set forth the true and full action of the duly constituted Constitutional Convention of the State of Ohio.

In testimony whereof, I have hereunto set my hand and affixed the Great Seal of the State of Ohio at the Capitol in the City of Columbus, Ohio, on this fifth day of December, in the year of our Lord, 1933.

(*Signed*) GEORGE S. MYERS
Secretary of State

Attest: DWIGHT L. MATCHETTE
Clerk

THE WHITE HOUSE

WASHINGTON

December 7, 1933

MY DEAR MR. MYERS:

I appreciate your kindness in advising me so promptly of the action of the Ohio Constitutional Convention in ratifying the twenty-first amendment to the Federal Constitution.

Sincerely yours,
(*Signed*) FRANKLIN D. ROOSEVELT

HONORABLE GEORGE S. MYERS
Secretary of State
Columbus, Ohio

CERTIFICATION

I, Dwight L. Matchette, Clerk of the Fifth Constitutional Convention, held this date, December 5, 1933, hereby certify that the foregoing is a true and complete record of the business of said convention.

DWIGHT L. MATCHETTE

OREGON*

OREGON CONSTITUTIONAL CONVENTION

Repeal of 18th Amendment. 1933

REPORT OF COMMITTEE ON RULES

Your committee respectfully proposes for adoption by the convention the following rules:

I

This convention shall be permanently organized by the election of: (*a*) a president, and (*b*) a chief clerk, and the appointment by the president of (*c*) a sergeant-at-arms. The president and chief clerk shall be elected from among the delegates seated and in attendance; the sergeant at arms may be appointed by the president from among the delegates seated in the convention, or otherwise, at the discretion of the president.

II

Only delegates shall have the privilege of the floor, provided, that upon a majority vote of the convention assembled, the courtesy of the floor and of addressing the convention may be extended to other than delegates.

III

No delegate may speak more than five minutes on any motion or nomination and the Convention may, by a majority vote, limit debates at any time and upon any matter.

IV

A majority of the delegates seated shall decide all elections and motions.

V

All questions of procedure shall be decided by *Robert's Rules of Order,* Revised Edition of 1915.

VI

The temporary president (Nan Wood Honeyman) and the temporary Chief Clerk (Ben Litfin) shall, and the same are hereby declared to be the permanent president and chief clerk, respectively, of this convention.

Howard Waddell
Chairman
Lotta C. Smith
Thomas R. Mahoney

---

* From a typewritten copy.

REPORT OF COMMITTEE ON CREDENTIALS

SALEM, OREGON
August 7, 1933

MADAME TEMPORARY PRESIDENT:

We, your Committee on Credentials, have carefully examined the credentials presented to us, and find that there are one hundred and fourteen (114) accredited delegates present in person, in accordance with the list hereto attached. Two delegates as certified to by the Secretary of State are not present, or at least have not presented credentials, same being Mr. A. C. Nininger of Jackson County, and Mr. J. T. Woody of Lin County. If either of the gentlemen are present the committee will be glad to pass upon their credentials.

Respectfully submitted,
WALTER B. GLEASON
Chairman
C. E. HADLEY
C. J. VAN BLARICOM
Committee on Credentials

LIST OF DELEGATES ELECTED JULY 21, 1933, TO ATTEND STATE CONVENTION PROVIDED BY CHAPTER 447, OREGON LAWS, 1933

A. S. Grant, of Baker	Baker County
William Wendt, of Baker	Baker County
Claude Buchanan, of Corvallis	Benton County
H. L. Mack, of Corvallis	Benton County
A. L. Beatie, of Oregon City	Clackamas County
O. D. Eby, of Oregon City	Clackamas County
L. R. O'Neill, of Oregon City	Clackamas County
C. J. Van Blaricom, of Garthwick Addition, Portland	Clackamas County
Walter S. Wessling, of Oswego	Clackamas County
Geo. F. Mosteller, of Westport	Clatsop County
John E. Oates, of Seaside	Clatsop County
Fred Thiel, of Astoria	Clatsop County
N. N. Blumensaadt, of Rainier	Columbia County
John H. Flynn, of St. Helens	Columbia County
Emil L. Mueller, of Clatskanie	Columbia County
J. B. Bedingfield, of Marshfield	Coos County
Fred B. Hollister, of North Bend	Coos County
Chris Rasmussen, of Bandon	Coos County
Lyn Nichols, of Prineville	Crook County
Jesse Turner, of Gold Beach	Curry County
J. F. Nosch, of Bend	Deschutes County
Tom Quigley, of Redmond	Deschutes County
William O. Clinger, of Roseburg	Douglas County
S. J. Ely, of Reedsport	Douglas County
Howard Waddell, of Roseburg	Douglas County
C. L. Darnielle, of Arlington	Gilliam County
Louis Woldenberg, of Canyon City	Grant County
N. F. Reed, of Burns	Harney County
George T. Galligan, of Hood River	Hood River County
Edward C. Kelly, of Medford	Jackson County
Rawles Moore, of Medford	Jackson County
A. C. Ninkenger, of Ashland	Jackson County

George M. Roberts, of Medford	Jackson County
Lewis H. Irving, of Marras	Jefferson County
Rolla E. Stephenson, of Grants Pass	Josephine County
H. L. Wilson, of Grants Pass	Josephine County
Noble H. Canter, of Klamath Falls	Klamath County
G. B. Cozad, of Klamath Falls	Klamath County
Roy W. Hodges, of Merrill	Klamath County
J. C. Dineill, of Klamath Falls	Klamath County
Warner B. Snider, of Paisley	Lake County
Victor Chambers, of Cottage Grove	Lane County
Hugh H. Earle, of Eugene	Lane County
Mrs. Dorothy Hesse, of Eugene	Lane County
Van N. Kemery, of Eugene	Lane County
Geo. C. Stanley, of Eugene	Lane County
Welby Stevens, of Springfield	Lane County
Dean Johnson, of Toledo	Lincoln County
Lloyd Everett Gilson, of Lebanon	Linn County
Geo. C. Richards, of Albany	Linn County
J. T. Wooddy, of Brownsville	Linn County
J. R. Blackaby, of Ontario	Malheur County
C. L. McCoy, of Nyssa	Malheur County
Ray J. Glatt, of Woodburn	Marion County
Harry Humphreys, of Stayton	Marion County
T. A. Livesley, of Salem	Marion County
Warren Pohle, of Salem	Marion County
Edward Rostein, of Salem	Marion County
Lotta C. Smith, of Salem	Marion County
P. N. Smith, of Mt. Angel	Marion County
Hanson Hughes, of Heppner	Morrow County
Gust Anderson, of Portland	Multnomah County
George L. Baker, of Portland	Multnomah County
John J. Beckman, of Portland	Multnomah County
Hamilton F. Corbett, of Portland	Multnomah County
Harry B. Critchlow, of Portland	Multnomah County
Cully Crumpacker, of Portland	Multnomah County
F. H. Dammasch, of Portland	Multnomah County
Mike Murphy DeCicco, of Portland	Multnomah County
Arthur H. Devers, of Portland	Multnomah County
Seneca Fouts, of Portland	Multnomah County
Walters B. Gleason, of Portland	Multnomah County
John H. Hall, of Portland	Multnomah County
Clementine S. Hirsch, of Portland	Multnomah County
Sam E. Holcomb, of Portland	Multnomah County
Nanny Wood Honeyman, of Portland	Multnomah County
Maria C. Jackson, of Portland	Multnomah County
Edith Waldo Johnson, of Portland	Multnomah County
Howard F. Latourette, of Portland	Multnomah County
Barge E. Leonard, of Portland	Multnomah County
Donald E. Long, of Portland	Multnomah County
Paul M. Long, of Portland	Multnomah County
Thomas R. Mahoney, of Portland	Multnomah County
Dan J. Malarkey, of Portland	Multnomah County
Frank E. Manning, of Portland	Multnomah County
Roscoe E. Nelson, of Portland	Multnomah County
Ben T. Osborne, of Portland	Multnomah County
Agnes M. Quinn, of Portland	Multnomah County
Frank A. Spencer, of Portland	Multnomah County
Cameron Squires, of Portland	Multnomah County
Mrs. Eldon J. Steele, of Portland	Multnomah County

W. H. Treece, of Portland	Multnomah County
John C. Veatch, of Portland	Multnomah County
Mrs. Geo. F. Wilson, of Portland	Multnomah County
Joseph F. Wood, of Portland	Multnomah County
Oscar Hayter, of Dallas	Polk County
James Imlah, of West Salem	Polk County
E. Fred Pickett, of Moro	Sherman County
C. E. Hadley, of Tillamook	Tillamook County
J. H. Hennessy, of Garibaldi	Tillamook County
Jack E. Allen, of Pendleton	Umatilla County
E. C. Prestbye, of Athena	Umatilla County
D. T. Randall, of Freewater	Umatilla County
Vernon D. Bull, of La Grande	Union County
J. B. McLaughlin, of La Grande	Union County
A. W. Eggleson, of Enterprise	Wallowa County
Roscoe Krier, of The Dalles	Wasco County
Ben R. Litfin, of The Dalles	Wasco County
Jack Anderson, of Forest Grove	Washington County
J. W. Bailey, of Hillsboro	Washington County
E. L. Ross, of Hillsboro	Washington County
H. A. Stohler, of Banks	Washington County
Fred Misener, of Fossil	Wheeler County
Elijah Corbett, of McMinnville	Yamhill County
E. A. Ellis, of Newberg	Yamhill County
Carl S. Trullinger, of Yamhill	Yamhill County

August 8, 1933

WALTER B. GLEASON
C. E. HADLEY
C. J. VAN BLARICOM

CERTIFICATE OF PRESIDENT AND CHIEF CLERK OF THE STATE CONVENTION OF OREGON RELATIVE TO RATIFICATION OF REPEAL OF THE EIGHTEENTH AMENDMENT, HELD AUGUST 7, 1933, AT SALEM, OREGON

We, Nanny Wood Honeyman, of Portland, Multnomah County, Oregon, President, and Ben R. Litfin, of The Dalles, Wasco County, Oregon, Chief Clerk, of the State Convention of the State of Oregon, called to pass upon the question of whether or not the proposed amendment to the Constitution of the United States relating to the Repeal of the Eighteenth Amendment to be ratified, do

HEREBY CERTIFY that, pursuant to Chapter 447, Oregon Laws, 1933, said convention was duly called and held at the Capitol in the city of Salem, Marion County, Oregon, on the 7th day of August, 1933; that all the delegates, certified by the Secretary of State as duly elected, were present and answered the roll call with the exception of A. C. Nininger, of Ashland, Jackson County, Oregon; that the oath of office was administered to the delegates by Chief Justice John L. Rand, of the Supreme Court of Oregon; and that upon completion of its organization, by the election of the aforesaid President and Chief Clerk, the said convention did adopt a resolution of ratification of the proposed amendment to the Constitution of the United States repealing said Eighteenth Amendment. The said resolution was as follows:

A Resolution ratifying a proposed amendment to
the Constitution of the United States

Whereas, the 72nd Congress of the United States proposed to the several States an amendment to the Constitution of the United States as follows:

Section 1. The eighteenth article of amendment to the Constitution of the United States is hereby repealed.

Sec. 2. The transportation or importation into any State, Territory, or possession of the United States for delivery or use therein of intoxicating liquors, in violation of the laws thereof, is hereby prohibited.

Sec. 3. This article shall be inoperative unless it shall have been ratified as an amendment to the Constitution by conventions in the several states, as provided in the Constitution, within seven years from the date of the submission hereof to the States by the Congress.

and

Whereas, The 37th Legislative Assembly of the State of Oregon, by an Act designated as Chapter 447, Oregon Laws, 1933, approved by the Governor March 15, 1933, and filed in the office of the Secretary of State on the same day, provided for the election of delegates to a convention to determine whether the State of Oregon shall ratify or reject the proposed amendment hereinabove set forth; and

Whereas, An election was duly held throughout the State of Oregon on the 21st day of July, 1933, and at said election delegates to a State Convention, to act upon the said proposed amendment, were duly chosen as provided by said Act; and

Whereas, On the 27th day of July, 1933, the Governor of said State duly named and designated Monday, August 7, 1933, at 2:30 o'clock P.M., at the State House, in Salem, Oregon, as the time and place for the meeting of the delegates so elected; and

Whereas, A majority of said elected and qualified delegates have duly met at the time and place so appointed, and after taking their oaths of office have duly elected a president and a chief clerk of said convention;

Therefore, be it resolved by the said State Convention, as follows:

Section 1. The proposed amendment to the Constitution of the United States, copied in full in the preamble of this Resolution, is hereby ratified by the State of Oregon.

Adopted by affirmative vote of a majority of the elected and qualified members of said Convention, August 7, 1933.

(*Signed*) Nanny Wood Honeyman
President

Attest:

(*Signed*) Ben R. Litfin
Chief Clerk

A roll call having been ordered, those voting in the affirmative were: Grant and Wendt of Baker County; Beatie, Eby, O'Neill, Van Blaricom and Wessling of Clackamas County; Mosteller, Oates and Thiel of Clatsop County Blumensaadt, Flynn and Mueller of Columbia County; Bedingfield, Hollister and Rasmussen of Coos County; Nichols of Crook County; Turner of Curry County; Hosch and Quigley of Deschutes County; Clinger, Ely and Waddell of Douglas County; Darnielle of Gilliam County; Woldenberg of Grant County; Reed of Harney County; Galligan of Hood River County; Kelly, Moore and Roberts of Jackson County; Irving of Jefferson County; Stephenson and Wilson of Josephine County; Canter, Cozad,

Hodges and O'Neill of Klamath County; Snider of Lake County; Chambers, Earle, Hesse, Kemery, Stanley and Stevens of Lane County; Johnson of Lincoln County; Blackaby and McCoy of Malheur County; Glatt, Humphreys, Livesley, Pohle, Rostein, L. Smith and P. Smith of Marion County; Hughes of Morrow County; Anderson, Baker, Beckman, Corbett, Critchlow, Crumpacker, Dammasch, DeCicco, Devers, Fouts, Gleason, Hall, Hirsch, Holcomb, Honeyman, Jackson, Johnson, Latourette, Leonard, D. Long, P. Long, Mahoney, Malarkey, Manning, Nelson, Osborne, Quinn, Spencer, Squires, Steele, Treece, Veatch, Wilson, Wood, of Multnomah County; Hayter and Imlah of Polk County; Pickett of Sherman County; Hadley and Hennessy, of Tillamook County; Allen, Prestbye and Randall of Umatilla County; Bull and McLaughlin of Union County; Eggleson of Wallowa County; Krier and Litfin of Wasco County; Anderson, Bailey, Ross, and Stohler of Washington County; Misener of Wheeler County; Corbett, Ellis and Trullinger of Yamhill County. (110)

Those voting in the negative were: Buchanan and Mack of Benton County; Gilson, Richards and Wooddy of Linn County. (5)

Those absent were Nininger of Jackson County. (1)

We do therefore hereby further certify that the said convention has agreed by a majority vote of the total number of delegates to the ratification of the foregoing proposed amendment. One hundred and ten of said delegates voting in favor of ratification of the proposed amendment; five of said delegates voting against the ratification of the proposed amendment; one delegate being absent and not voting.

In testimony whereof we have hereunto set our hands, done at the City of Salem, County of Marion and State of Oregon, this 7th day of August, in the year of Our Lord, one thousand nine hundred and thirty-three.

NANNY WOOD HONEYMAN
President
BEN R. LITFIN
Chief Clerk

REPORT OF COMMITTEE ON REPEAL RESOLUTION

SALEM, OREGON
August 7, 1933

TO THE CONVENTION OF THE STATE OF OREGON
to act upon the proposed repeal of the Eighteenth Amendment to the Constitution of the United States:

We, your Committee, appointed to draft and submit a Resolution declaring and showing the action of the State of Oregon upon the proposed repeal of the Eighteenth Amendment to the Constitution of the United States, herewith submit such a Resolution and recommend its adoption by this Convention.

DAN J. MALARKEY
E. C. PRESTBYE
OSCAR HAYTER
Committee

A Resolution ratifying a proposed amendment to
the Constitution of the United States

WHEREAS, The 72nd Congress of the United States proposed to the several States an amendment to the Constitution of the United States as follows:

Section 1. The eighteenth article of amendment to the Constitution of the United States is hereby repealed.

Section 2. The transportation or importation into any State, Territory, or possession of the United States for delivery or use therein of intoxicating liquors, in violation of the laws thereof, is hereby prohibited.

Section 3. This article shall be inoperative unless it shall have been ratified as an amendment to the Constitution by conventions in the several States, as provided in the Constitution, within seven years from the date of the submission hereof to the States by the Congress.

and,

WHEREAS, The 37th Legislative Assembly of the State of Oregon, by an Act designated as Chapter 447, Oregon Laws, 1933, approved by the Governor March 15, 1933, and filed in the office of the Secretary of State on the same day, provided for the election of delegates to a convention to determine whether the State of Oregon shall ratify or reject the proposed amendment hereinabove set forth; and

WHEREAS, an election was duly held throughout the State of Oregon on the 21st day of July, 1933, and at said election delegates to a State Convention, to act upon the said proposed amendment, were duly chosen as provided by said Act; and

WHEREAS, On the 27th day of July, 1933, the Governor of said State duly named and designated Monday, August 7, 1933, at 2:30 o'clock P.M., at the State House, in Salem, Oregon, as the time and place for the meeting of the delegates so elected; and

WHEREAS, A majority of said elected and qualified delegates have duly met at the time and place so appointed, and after taking their oaths of office have duly elected a president and a chief clerk of said convention:

Therefore, be it resolved by the said State Convention, as follows:

Section 1. The proposed amendment to the Constitution of the United States, copied in full in the preamble of this Resolution, is hereby ratified by the State of Oregon.

Adopted by affirmative vote of a majority of the elected and qualified members of said Convention August 7, 1933.

NANNY WOOD HONEYMAN
President

Attest:

BEN R. LITFIN
Chief Clerk

Result of oral vote on repeal resolution was as follows:

[*In the record "No." appears before the names of those who voted against the resolution. Votes in the affirmative are indicated by check marks, which are not reproduced here.*]

A. S. Grant, of Baker	Baker County
William Wendt, of Baker	Baker County
Claude Buchanan, of Corvallis, *No*	Clackamas County
H. L. Mack, of Corvallis, *No*	Clackamas County

A. L. Beatie, of Oregon City	Clackamas County
O. D. Eby, of Oregon City	Clackamas County
L. R. O'Neill, of Oregon City	Clackamas County
C. J. Van Blaricom, of Garthwick Addition, Portland	Clackamas County
Walter S. Wessling, of Oswego	Clackamas County
Geo. F. Mosteller, of Westport	Clatsop County
John E. Oates, of Seaside	Clatsop County
Fred Thiel, of Astoria	Clatsop County
N. N. Blumensaadt, of Rainier	Columbia County
John H. Flynn, of St. Helens	Columbia County
Emil L. Mueller, of Clatskanie	Columbia County
J. B. Bedingfield, of Marshfield	Coos County
Fred B. Hollister, of North Bend	Coos County
Chris Rasmussen, of Bandon	Coos County
Lyn Nichols, of Prineville	Crook County
Jesse Turner, of Gold Beach	Curry County
J. F. Hosch, of Bend	Deschutes County
Tom Quigley, of Redmond	Deschutes County
William O. Clinger, of Roseburg	Douglas County
S. J. Ely, of Reedsport	Douglas County
Howard Waddell, of Roseburg	Douglas County
C. L. Darnielle, of Arlington	Gilliam County
Louis Woldenberg, of Canyon City	Grant County
N. F. Reed, of Burns	Harney County
George T. Galligan, of Hood River	Hood River County
Edward C. Kelly, of Medford	Jackson County
Rawles Moore, of Medford	Jackson County
A. C. Nininger, of Ashland, *Absent*	Jackson County
George M. Roberts, of Medford	Jackson County
Lewis H. Irving, of Madras	Jefferson County
Rolla E. Stephenson, of Grants Pass	Josephine County
H. L. Wilson, of Grants Pass	Josephine County
Noble H. Canter, of Klamath Falls	Klamath County
G. B. Cozad, of Klamath Falls	Klamath County
Roy W. Hodges, of Merrill	Klamath County
J. C. O'Neill, of Klamath Falls	Klamath County
Warner B. Snider, of Paisley	Lake County
Victor Chambers, of Cottage Grove	Lane County
Hugh H. Earle, of Eugene	Lane County
Mrs. Dorothy Hesse, of Eugene	Lane County
Van N. Kemery, of Eugene	Lane County
Geo. C. Stanley, of Eugene	Lane County
Welby Stevens, of Springfield	Lane County
Dean Johnson, of Toledo	Lincoln County
Lloyd Everett Gilson, of Lebanon, *No*	Linn County
Geo. C. Richards, of Albany, *No*	Linn County
J. T. Wooddy, of Brownsville, *No*	Linn County
J. R. Blackaby, of Ontario	Malheur County
C. L. McCoy, of Nyssa	Malheur County
Ray J. Glatt, of Woodburn	Marion County
Harry Humphreys, of Stayton	Marion County
T. A. Livesley, of Salem	Marion County
Warren Pohle, of Salem	Marion County
Edward Rostein, of Salem	Marion County
Lotta C. Smith, of Salem	Marion County
P. N. Smith, of Mt. Angel	Marion County
Hanson Hughes, of Heppner	Morrow County
Gust Anderson, of Portland	Multnomah County

George L. Baker, of Portland	Multnomah County
John J. Beckman, of Portland	Multnomah County
Hamilton F. Corbett, of Portland	Multnomah County
Harry B. Critchlow, of Portland	Multnomah County
Cully Crumpacker, of Portland	Multnomah County
F. H. Dammasch, of Portland	Multnomah County
Mike Murphy DeCicco, of Portland	Multnomah County
Arthur H. Devers, of Portland	Multnomah County
Seneca Fouts, of Portland	Multnomah County
Walter B. Gleason, of Portland	Multnomah County
John H. Hall, of Portland	Multnomah County
Clementine S. Hirsch, of Portland	Multnomah County
Sam E. Holcomb, of Portland	Multnomah County
Nanny Wood Honeyman, of Portland	Multnomah County
Maria C. Jackson, of Portland	Multnomah County
Edith Waldo Johnson, of Portland	Multnomah County
Howard F. Latourette, of Portland	Multnomah County
Barge E. Leonard, of Portland	Multnomah County
Donald E. Long, of Portland	Multnomah County
Paul M. Long, of Portland	Multnomah County
Thomas R. Mahoney, of Portland	Multnomah County
Dan J. Malarkey, of Portland	Multnomah County
Frank E. Manning, of Portland	Multnomah County
Roscoe C. Nelson, of Portland	Multnomah County
Ben T. Osborne, of Portland	Multnomah County
Agnes M. Quinn, of Portland	Multnomah County
Frank A. Spencer, of Portland	Multnomah County
Cameron Squires, of Portland	Multnomah County
Mrs. Eldon J. Steele, of Portland	Multnomah County
W. H. Treece, of Portland	Multnomah County
John C. Veatch, of Portland	Multnomah County
Mrs. Geo. F. Wilson, of Portland	Multnomah County
Joseph F. Wood, of Portland	Multnomah County
Oscar Hayter, of Dallas	Polk County
James Imlah, of West Salem	Polk County
E. Fred Pickett, of Moro	Sherman County
C. E. Hadley, of Tillamook	Tillamook County
J. H. Hennessy, of Garibaldi	Tillamook County
Jack E. Allen, of Pendleton	Umatilla County
E. C. Prestbye, of Athena	Umatilla County
D. T. Randall, of Freewater	Umatilla County
Vernon D. Bull, of La Grande	Union County
J. B. McLaughlin, of La Grande	Union County
A. W. Eggleson, of Enterprise	Wallowa County
Roscoe Krier, of The Dalles	Wasco County
Ben R. Litfin, of The Dalles	Wasco County
Jack Anderson, of Forest Grove	Washington County
J. W. Bailey, of Hillsboro	Washington County
E. L. Ross, of Hillsboro	Washington County
H. A. Stohler, of Banks	Washington County
Fred Misener, of Fossil	Wheeler County
Elijah Corbett, of McMinnville	Yamhill County
E. A. Ellis, of Newburg	Yamhill County
Carl S. Trullinger, of Yamhill	Yamhill County

110 ayes
5 nays
1 absent

PENNSYLVANIA*

OFFICERS OF THE CONVENTION

Chairman

General Edward C. Shannon, Lieutenant Governor, Columbia

Secretary

A. Boyd Hamilton, Harrisburg

Tellers

John E. McKirdy, Pittsburgh
M. K. Burgner, Chambersburg

Parliamentarian

John H. Fertig, Pottsville

Sergeant at Arms

Ellwood H. Bauman, Easton

Chaplain

The Rev. Dr. Oscar F. R. Treder, Harrisburg

Reporters

John Ruth, Lebanon
Eugene E. Moyer, Harrisburg

Clerks

Wilbur Morse, Philadelphia
Andrew E. Brice, Pittsburgh
Dennis J. Mulvihill, Pittsburgh
Mrs. Mary McFadden, Philadelphia
A. S. Cooper, Harrisburg

Page

Mrs. Claire Miller LaFitte, Ardmore

ROLL OF DELEGATES TO CONSTITUTIONAL CONVENTION

Elected, November 7, 1933

Robert K. Cassatt, Rosemont .... Banker
Samuel Harden Church, 4781 Wallingford Street, Pittsburgh .... Educator
Elizabeth Conway Clark, Bryn Mawr .... Housewife
Joseph S. Clark, Jr., St. Martin's Lane, Philadelphia .... Attorney-at-Law
Maria N. Dougherty, Wyncote .... Housewife
Thomas E. Durban, Chestnut Hill, R. D. 4, Erie .... Retired
William J. Fitzgerald, 1631 Madison Avenue, Dunmore .... Attorney-at-Law
John Hemphill, 210 East Biddle Street, West Chester .... Attorney-at-Law
Richard Henry Koch, 19th & Oak Road, Pottsville .... Retired Judge

* Printed. The act providing for the convention is omitted here.

Alvan Markle, Jr., 338 W. Green Street, Hazleton .... Banker
Emma Guffey Miller, 4 Von Lent Place, Pittsburgh .... Housewife
W. W. Montgomery, Jr., Radnor .... Attorney-at-Law
George Stuart Patterson, 1822 DeLancey St., Philadelphia .... Cotton Merchant
John A. Phillips, 1609 N. 18th Street, Philadelphia .... Labor Executive
Raymond Pitcairn, Bryn Athyn .... Attorney-at-Law

JOURNAL

OF THE

PENNSYLVANIA CONSTITUTIONAL CONVENTION

ON REPEAL OF THE 18TH ARTICLE OF AMENDMENT

TO THE

CONSTITUTION OF THE UNITED STATES

SENATE CHAMBER

STATE CAPITOL, HARRISBURG

TUESDAY, DECEMBER 5, 1933

LIEUTENANT-GOVERNOR EDWARD C. SHANNON, *Ex-Officio Chairman*

THE CHAIRMAN: This being the day, December 5, 1933, and hour, 12 o'clock noon, fixed by the Act of May 3, 1933, for the assembling of Delegates chosen at the election held on November 7, 1933, to constitute a convention to ratify or reject an amendment to the Constitution of the United States, the convention will be in order and will be opened with prayer by the Rev. Dr. Oscar F. R. Treder, Dean of St. Stephen's Cathedral.

PRAYER

The Rev. Dr. Oscar F. R. Treder, Dean, Saint Stephen's Cathedral, offered the following prayer:

"God, our Father, Preserver, and Disposer of all things Who waterest the hills from above and fillest the earth with the fruit of Thy works; Who bringest forth grass for the cattle, and green herb for the service of men, wine that maketh glad the heart of man, oil to make him a cheerful countenance, and bread to strengthen man's heart; to Thee only appertaineth Counsel, and Wisdom and Understanding.

"Send down of Thy Wisdom, to direct and guide this Convention, the people of this Commonwealth, and of our Nation. Let not us try to be wiser than Thou. Let the Spirit of Thy people, their understanding, will and conscience; their souls (the appetites, affections and passions) and their bodies, the tabernacles of their souls, be preserved blameless. As we rejoice in the insuperable courage of those who, loving liberty and knowledge, have pushed away the veil of mountains and seas, and have sought light and freedom for themselves and their children, give to us the same spirit, and make us worthy of these heroic ideals and traditions.

"Grant us, O Lord, such boldness in Thee that we may set our faces as a flint, and not be ashamed, but, contending valiantly for the truth in social righteousness, may out of weakness be made strong, and conquer in Thy might.

"And mayest Thou, God, Who are the Alpha and Omega, and Who worketh in us both to will and to do of Thy good pleasure, be Thyself the beginning and the end of our work. Amen."

THE CHAIRMAN: The Act of May 3, 1933, provides for the organization of this convention, the Lieutenant-Governor, Edward C. Shannon, being designated as Chairman; the Secretary of the Senate, A. Boyd Hamilton, as Secretary, and the Chief Clerk of the Senate, John E. McKirdy, and the Chief Clerk of the House of Representatives, M. K. Burgner, presently acting, as Tellers. The Secretary is directed therein to provide the various other officers and will announce his appointments.

APPOINTMENTS

The Secretary announced the following appointments:

Parliamentarian	—John H. Fertig, Schuylkill County.
Sergeant-at-Arms	—Ellwood Bauman, Northampton County.
Chaplain	—The Rev. Dr. Oscar F. R. Treder, Dauphin County.
Reporters	—John Ruth, Lebanon County.
	Eugene E. Moyer, Dauphin County.
Clerks	—Wilbur Morse, Philadelphia.
	Andrew E. Brice, Allegheny County.
	Dennis J. Mulcihill, Allegheny County.
	Mrs. Mary McFadden, Philadelphia.
	A. S. Cooper, Dauphin County.
Page	—Mrs. Claire Miller LaFitte, Montgomery County.

THE CHAIRMAN: The Chair recognizes the Sergeant-at-Arms.

THE SERGEANT-AT-ARMS: I have the honor to introduce the Secretary of the Commonwealth.

THE CHAIRMAN: The Secretary of the Commonwealth, the Honorable Richard J. Beamish.

THE SECRETARY OF THE COMMONWEALTH: Mr. Chairman, I have the honor to present to this honorable body the certificate of the Secretary of the Commonwealth, of the official returns received from the prothonotaries of the several counties for the several candidates for the offices of delegates to the Constitutional Convention to ratify or reject the proposal to repeal the Eighteenth Article of Amendment to the Constitution of the United States.

I now hand you the certificate of official returns from the several counties of the Commonwealth.

THE CHAIRMAN: The Secretary will open and read the certificate of official returns.

The Secretary then opened and read the certificate of official returns, as follows:

IN THE NAME AND BY AUTHORITY OF THE
COMMONWEALTH OF PENNSYLVANIA

SEAL

OFFICE OF THE SECRETARY OF THE COMMONWEALTH

I, RICHARD J. BEAMISH, Secretary of the Commonwealth, do hereby certify, that it appears from the returns of the Election held on Tuesday, the seventh day of November, A.D. 1933, as computed from the official returns received from the prothonotaries of the several counties, that the following is the number of votes cast for the several candidates for the office of Delegate to the Constitutional Convention to ratify or reject the proposal to repeal the Eighteenth Article of Amendment to the Constitution of the United States.

DELEGATES THAT FAVOR REPEAL

Robert K. Cassatt	had	1,864,411
Samuel Harden Church	had	1,855,797
Elizabeth Conway Clark	had	1,855,189
Joseph S. Clark, Jr.	had	1,854,361
Maria N. Dougherty	had	1,854,698
Thomas E. Durban	had	1,852,792
William J. Fitzgerald	had	1,854,014
John Hemphill	had	1,854,565
Richard Henry Koch	had	1,853,138
Alvan Markle, Jr.	had	1,852,343
Emma Guffey Miller	had	1,853,134
W. W. Montgomery, Jr.	had	1,852,871
George Stuart Patterson	had	1,853,279
John A. Phillips	had	1,853,150
Raymond Pitcairn	had	1,852,475

DELEGATES THAT OPPOSE REPEAL

John A. McSparran	had	583,513
Ella B. Black	had	579,087
Ralph E. Weeks	had	578,108
J. Horace McFarland	had	578,527
D. Glenn Moore	had	578,314
J. Audley Boak	had	577,650
E. H. Bonsall, Jr.	had	577,903
B. A. McGarvey	had	577,862
J. Henry Morgan	had	578,311
Francis Taylor	had	578,000
Minnie K. L. Karnell	had	577,819
Archie E. Driggers	had	577,061
Charles C. Ellis	had	577,455
Robert A. Hutchison	had	577,687
Henry K. Ober	had	577,773

SEAL

In testimony whereof, I have hereunto set my hand and caused the Seal of the Secretary's Office to be affixed this fourth day of December, A.D. 1933.

(*Signed*) RICHARD J. BEAMISH
Secretary of the Commonwealth

THE CHAIRMAN: The roll of Delegates elected to this convention as shown by the certificate of official returns will now be called by the Secretary and those present will answer to their names.

The roll of Delegates was called by the Secretary, and was as follows:

Robert K. Cassatt
Samuel Harden Church
Elizabeth Conway Clark
Joseph S. Clark, Jr.
Maria N. Dougherty
Thomas E. Durban
William J. Fitzgerald
John Hemphill
Richard Henry Koch
Alvan Markle, Jr.
Emma Guffey Miller
W. W. Montgomery, Jr.
George Stuart Patterson
John A. Phillips
Raymond Pitcairn

THE CHAIRMAN: All the Delegates elected have answered to their names. The Delegates are requested to come to the bar of the Senate where the Constitutional oath will be administered by the Honorable William M. Hargest, President Judge of the Court of Common Pleas of Dauphin County.

The constitutional oath was then administered to all the Delegates.

THE CHAIRMAN: The Constitutional oath will now be administered to the officers of the convention by Judge Hargest.

The Constitutional oath was then administered to the officers.

THE CHAIRMAN: The Secretary will read communications transmitted by the Secretary of the Commonwealth.

The communications transmitted were then read by the Secretary as follows:

SEAL

Received in
Governor's Office
Feb. 23, 1933
and referred to:
Governor

DEPARTMENT OF STATE, WASHINGTON, *February 21, 1933*

THE HONORABLE
THE GOVERNOR OF PENNSYLVANIA
Harrisburg

SIR:

I have the honor to enclose a certified copy of a Resolution of Congress, entitled *"Joint Resolution Proposing an Amendment to the Constitution of the United States"* passed during the second session of the Seventy-second Congress of the United States, "Begun and held at the City of Washington on Monday the fifth day of December, one thousand nine hundred and thirty-two." It is requested that you cause this Joint Resolution to be submitted to a convention in your State for such action as may be had and that a certified copy of such action be communicated to the Secretary of State, as required by Section 160, Title 5, United States Code. (See overleaf.)

An acknowledgment of the receipt of this communication is requested.

I have the honor to be, Sir,
Your obedient servant,
(*Signed*) HENRY L. STIMSON

Enclosure:
Joint Resolution
proposing the
repeal of the
18th Amendment,
et cetera.

SECTION 160, TITLE 5, UNITED STATES CODE

Whenever official notice is received at the Department of State that any amendment proposed to the Constitution of the United States has been adopted, according to the provisions of the Constitution, the Secretary of State shall forthwith cause the amendment to be published, with his certificate, specifying the States by which the same may have been adopted, and that the same has become valid, to all intents and purposes as a part of the Constitution of the United States.

No. 662

UNITED STATES OF AMERICA

SEAL

DEPARTMENT OF STATE

To all to whom these presents shall come, Greetings:

I certify that the copy hereto attached is a true copy of a Resolution of Congress entitled *"Joint Resolution Proposing an Amendment to the Constitution of the United States"* the original of which is on file in this Department.

SEAL

In testimony whereof, I, Henry L. Stimson, Secretary of State, have hereunto caused the Seal of the Department of State to be affixed and my name subscribed by the Acting Chief Clerk of the said Department, at the City of Washington, in the District.

(*Signed*) HENRY L. STIMSON
Secretary of State
By P. F. ALLEN
Acting Chief Clerk

SEVENTY-SECOND CONGRESS OF THE UNITED STATES OF AMERICA AT THE

SECOND SESSION

Begun and held at the City of Washington on Monday, the fifth day of December, one thousand nine hundred and thirty-two.

JOINT RESOLUTION

Proposing an amendment to the Constitution of the United States.

Resolved by the Senate and House of Representatives of the United States of America in Congress assembled (two-thirds of each House concurring therein), That the following article is hereby proposed as an amendment to the Constitution of the United States, which shall be valid to all intents and purposes as part of the Constitution when ratified by conventions in three-fourths of the several States:

ARTICLE ——

Section 1. The eighteenth article of amendment to the Constitution of the United States is hereby repealed.

Section 2. The transportation or importation into any State, Territory, or possession of the United States for delivery or use therein of intoxicating liquors, in violation of the laws thereof, is hereby prohibited.

Section 3. This article shall be inoperative unless it shall have been ratified as an amendment to the Constitution by conventions in the several States, as provided in the Constitution, within seven years from the date of submission hereof to the States by Congress.

JNO. N. GARNER
Speaker of the House of Representatives
CHARLES CURTIS
Vice-President of the United States and President of the Senate

Address Official Communications To
The Secretary of State,
Washington, D.C.

Received in Governor's Office,
Nov. 21, 1933,
and referred to: S of C
P. G.

in reply refer to
HA

November 20, 1933
Nov. 21, 1933
101

THE HONORABLE
THE GOVERNOR OF PENNSYLVANIA
Harrisburg

SIR:

The Department is informed that on December 5, 1933, a convention in the Commonwealth of Pennsylvania will meet for the purpose of ratfying the proposed amendment to the Constitution of the United States for the repeal of the Eighteenth Amendment, et cetera.

Because of the great importance of the proposed amendment and considering particularly the provisions of Section 217 (*a*) of the National Industrial Recovery Act approved June 16, 1933, it is requested that the authenticated act of the convention in the Commonwealth of Pennsylvania be prepared and forwarded to the Department as soon as may be found possible after the proceedings of the convention are had; and if, as is perhaps probable, the convention shall take action in the matter on December 5, 1933, it is hoped that it may be found feasible to have the appropriate instrument not only prepared and authenticated but also forwarded to the Department on that day so that in the ordinary course of the mail the instrument in question may reach the Department the following day, December 6, 1933.

Your obedient servant,
(*Signed*) WILLIAM PHILLIPS
Acting Secretary of State

OATH ADMINISTERED

THE CHAIRMAN: The oath book will now be presented to the Delegates for their signatures.

Whereupon the oath book was signed by all the Delegates.

THE CHAIRMAN: The Chair recognizes Mr. Markle.

RESOLUTION THANKING HONORABLE WILLIAM M. HARGEST

MR. MARKLE: Mr. Chairman, I desire to offer a resolution.

The resolution was twice read by the Secretary as follows:

HALL OF THE SENATE
December 5, 1933

Resolved, That the thanks of this Convention be extended to the Honorable William M. Hargest, President Judge of the Court of Common Pleas, of the Twelfth

Judicial District, for his presence and courtesy in administering the Constitutional oath of office to the delegates here assembled.

The resolution was unanimously adopted.

SENATE EXTENDS WELCOME TO CONVENTION

THE CHAIRMAN: The Chair recognizes the Sergeant-at-Arms.

THE SERGEANT-AT-ARMS: Mr. Chairman, I have the honor to introduce the Sergeant-at-Arms of the Senate of Pennsylvania.

THE SERGEANT-AT-ARMS OF THE SENATE: Mr. Chairman, The Chief Clerk of the Senate of Pennsylvania has directed me to present to this Convention a communication from the Senate of Pennsylvania.

THE CHAIRMAN: The Secretary will open and read the communication.

The communication was then opened and read by the Secretary as follows:

IN THE SENATE
December 4, 1933

WHEREAS, The Act of Assembly approved May 3, 1933, No. 81, provides that the Convention, called on behalf of the Commonwealth of Pennsylvania to ratify or reject the proposed amendment to the Constitution of the United States to repeal the eighteenth amendment, shall meet in the Hall of the Senate on December 5, 1933, at twelve o'clock noon, and shall be presided over by the Lieutenant-Governor, and that the Secretary of the Senate shall be the Secretary of said Convention; therefor be it

Resolved, That the Senate of Pennsylvania cordially welcomes the delegates of the Convention to the Hall of the Senate, and directs the officers and employes of the Senate to afford every convenience and facility possible to the Convention in order that the business of the Convention may be duly carried out;

Resolved, In order that the Convention may meet promptly at the time appointed by law, the Senate shall recess not later than 11:30 A.M. this date;

Resolved, That a copy of this resolution be transmitted to the Convention by the Chief Clerk.

The foregoing is a true and correct copy of a resolution adopted by the Senate of Pennsylvania, December four, one thousand nine hundred and thirty-three.

(*Signed*) JOHN E. MCKIRDY
Chief Clerk
Senate of Pennsylvania

CONVENTION RULES ADOPTED

THE CHAIRMAN: The Chair recognizes Mrs. Elizabeth Conway Clark.

MRS. CLARK: Mr. Chairman, I have the honor to offer a resolution.

The resolution was twice read by the Secretary as follows:

HALL OF THE SENATE
December 5, 1933

Resolved, That the standing rules of the Senate of Pennsylvania, in Extraordinary Session, be adopted, so far as applicable, as the rules of this Constitutional Convention.

The resolution was unanimously adopted.

THE CHAIRMAN: The Chair recognizes Mr. W. W. Montgomery.

MR. MONTGOMERY: Mr. Chairman, I have the honor to present a resolution for the consideration of this convention.

The resolution was twice read by the Secretary as follows:

HALL OF THE SENATE
December 5, 1933

Resolved, That the Chairman of this Convention be authorized to appoint a Committee on Resolutions, to be composed of five delegates to this Convention, whose duty it shall be to frame a proper resolution, for the consideration of this Convention, setting forth the action of this Convention on behalf of the Commonwealth of Pennsylvania, with respect to the proposed amendment to the Constitution of the United States to repeal the eighteenth amendment.

The resolution was adopted.

APPOINTMENT OF COMMITTEE ON RESOLUTIONS

THE CHAIRMAN: The Chair appoints as a Committee on Resolutions:

W. W. Montgomery, Jr.
George Stuart Patterson
Maria N. Dougherty
Emma Guffey Miller
William J. Fitzgerald

The Chair suggests that the Committee meet to the rear and to the right of the Senate Chamber in the office of the Lieutenant-Governor.

The Chair declares a recess of five minutes, during which time the Committee will meet.

(After Recess)

THE CHAIRMAN: The time of the recess having expired, the Convention will be in order.

REPORT OF COMMITTEE ON RESOLUTIONS

THE CHAIRMAN: The Chair recognizes Mr. W. W. Montgomery.

MR. MONTGOMERY: Mr. Chairman, the Committee on Resolutions reports and offers a resolution for the consideration of the Convention.

The resolution was twice read by the Secretary as follows:

RESOLUTION OF RATIFICATION

WHEREAS, The Congress of the United States has proposed an amendment to the Constitution of the United States, as follows:

JOINT RESOLUTION

Proposing an amendment to the Constitution of the United States.

Resolved by the Senate and House of Representatives of the United States of America in Congress assembled (two-thirds of each House concurring therein), That the following article is hereby proposed as an amendment to the Constitution of the United States, which shall be valid to all intents and purposes as part of the Constitution when ratified by conventions in three-fourths of the several States:

ARTICLE ___ ___

Section 1. The eighteenth article of amendment to the Constitution of the United States is hereby repealed.

Section 2. The transportation or importation into any State, territory, or possession of the United States, for delivery or use therein, of intoxicating liquors in violation of the laws thereof is hereby prohibited.

Section 3. This article shall be inoperative unless it shall have been ratified as an amendment to the Constitution by conventions in the several States, as provided in the Constitution, within seven years from the date of the submission hereof to the States by the Congress.

and

WHEREAS, By an act duly approved on the third day of May, 1933, the General Assembly of the Commonwealth of Pennsylvania made provision in accordance with said resolution of the Congress of the United States for the election at the same time as the municipal election in the year 1933, to wit, November 7, 1933, of fifteen delegates to a convention to be held on the twenty-eighth day after their election, to wit, December 5, 1933, at twelve o'clock noon, in the Hall of the Senate, for the purpose of ratifying or rejecting the proposed amendment to the Constitution of the United States recited in the foregoing preamble; now therefore be it

Resolved, In the name of the People of Pennsylvania, be it known to all men that we, the delegates of the people of the Commonwealth in Convention assembled, have assented to and ratified, and by these presents do in the name and by the authority of the same people, and for ourselves, assent to and ratify the foregoing proposed amendment to the Constitution of the United States of America.

Done in Convention in Harrisburg the fifth day of December, in the year of our Lord one thousand nine hundred thirty-three and of the Independence of the United States of America the one hundred and fifty-eighth.

THE CHAIRMAN: The resolution of ratification is before you. What is the pleasure of the Convention?

THE CHAIRMAN: The Chair recognizes Mr. Montgomery.

MR. MONTGOMERY: Mr. Chairman, I move the adoption of the resolution.

MR. PHILLIPS: Mr. Chairman, I second the motion.

On the question,

Will the Convention agree to the motion to adopt the resolution?

THE CHAIRMAN: The Chair recognizes Mr. Montgomery.

MR. MONTGOMERY: Mr. Chairman, this is a day for which many of us have long waited. It is just a few weeks short of fifteen years since I stood in this hall and pleaded with the Law and Order Committee of the Senate against the ratification of the Eighteenth Amendment. I did so because I believed then, as I believe now, that the Constitution of the United States was most wise in reserving to the several states the police power and in delegating or granting no police power to the Federal Government. The Legislature of this State, and of others, thought differently, and, I think, made a grave mistake in ratifying the Eighteenth Amendment.

For these fifteen long years I have lost no opportunity, in conjunction with many many others, to fight for the repeal of the Eighteenth Amendment, and the opportunity is now before us at this convention today. I personally feel that if I were a well known and prominent citizen of our Commonwealth to whom the people of the Commonwealth wanted to do honor, they could pay me no more welcome tribute than to send me here as a delegate to this Convention.

It has been a pleasure to have participated in this long fight. It has brought me in contact with many men whom I did not know before, and who have now become my close friends. I know they will agree with me when I assert that this fight has been kept on a high plane; that it has not been permitted to become a political wrangle; that it has not been permitted to become a question of whether or not we shall have something to drink; but it has been a question of whether the Constitution of the United States should be preserved as it is written in this essential respect of the reservation to the States of its police power. We have felt that that was essential; that without it America, as we have known it in the past, cannot exist, and now is our opportunity to reclaim for the Commonwealth of Pennsylvania the sovereignty which was originally its, and which was, I regret to say, abdicated in the early part of 1919.

Men and women of this Convention, we are here under a solemn oath to do our duty. We are free agents to exercise our discretion; we are not pledged to any action. We must use our own conscience and our own judgment, as the Constitution of the United States requires that we shall do, in taking this most important action which we today are called upon to take; but in forming our judgment, irrespective of our former or present personal ideas, it seems to me proper to bear in mind that we, all of us, who are elected as delegates to this convention, asked and received the votes of the vast majority of the voters of Pennsylvania upon our representation that we favored the repeal of the Eighteenth Amendment, and that while we are free and are in duty bound to vote on this question as our conscience and our judgment dictate, we would I think, be false if we fail to recognize as a very important influence in forming our conclusions, that position which we took and upon which we individually invited the votes of the people who elected us and sent us here.

In the name of the vast majority of the people of Pennsylvania and for the honor and dignity of this Commonwealth, for the preservation of those things in the fundamentals of our Government which we hold dear and which we hold essential to the continued existence of the America that we have known and loved, I ask the unanimous vote of the members of this Convention in support of the resolution of ratification which has been read and is now before you.

On the question recurring

Will the Convention agree to the motion to adopt the resolution?

The Chairman: The Secretary will call the roll, and the tellers will keep an accurate count.

The roll was called and was as follows:

AYES

Robert K. Cassatt
Samuel Harden Church
Elizabeth Conway Clark
Joseph S. Clark, Jr.
Maria N. Dougherty
Thomas E. Durban
William J. Fitzgerald
John Hemphill
Richard Henry Koch
Alvin Markle, Jr.
Emma Guffey Miller
W. W. Montgomery, Jr.
George Stuart Patterson
John A. Phillips
Raymond Pitcairn

NAYS

None

The Chairman: The report of the tellers is fifteen votes for the repeal of the Eighteenth Amendment and none against. The amendment is ratified and adopted by this Convention. The hour is 12:50 p.m., December 5, 1933.

RESOLUTION OF CERTIFICATION

THE CHAIRMAN: The Chair recognizes Judge Koch.

MR. KOCH: Mr. Chairman, since we have discharged the great work for which we have been elected, in order to relieve the people of the United States from the anxiety from which they may suffer, I submit and ask the adoption of a resolution.

The resolution was twice read by the Secretary as follows:

HALL OF THE SENATE
December 5, 1933

Resolved, That the Chairman and Secretary of this Convention, duly called and convened to determine the action to be taken by the Commonwealth of Pennsylvania with respect to the proposed amendment to the Constitution of the United States to repeal the eighteenth amendment, be directed to forthwith execute a certificate setting forth at length the resolution adopted by this convention ratifying said proposed amendment to the Constitution of the United States, and to transmit said certificate to the Secretary of the Commonwealth of this State, who shall transmit the said certificate under the Great Seal of the Commonwealth to the Secretary of State of the United States;

Resolved, That a copy of this resolution be transmitted to the Secretary of the Commonwealth by the Secretary of the Convention.

THE CHAIRMAN: The Chair recognizes Judge Koch.

MR. KOCH: Mr. Chairman, I move the adoption of the resolution.

MRS. MILLER: Mr. Chairman, I second the motion.

On the question,

Will the Convention agree to the motion to adopt the resolution?

THE CHAIRMAN: The Secretary will call the roll.

The roll was called and was as follows:

AYES

Robert K. Cassatt
Samuel Harden Church
Elizabeth Conway Clark
Joseph S. Clark, Jr.
Maria N. Dougherty
Thomas E. Durban
William J. Fitzgerald
John Hemphill
Richard Henry Koch
Alvan Markle, Jr.
Emma Guffey Miller
W. W. Montgomery, Jr.
George Stuart Patterson
John A. Phillips
Raymond Pitcairn

NAYS

None

THE CHAIRMAN: The result of the roll call is fifteen in favor of and none against, and the resolution of certification is adopted.

The resolution of ratification will be presented to the members whose signatures will be written on the certificate. The third original copy of the resolution will be presented to you, ladies and gentlemen, for your signature and will be deposited with the Journal of the proceedings of this Convention in the office of the Department of State in the State Capitol Building, where are preserved permanently the records of the Province and Commonwealth of Pennsylvania. That is why the additional copy is presented.

The Resolution of Ratification was then signed by the Delegates to the Convention.

THE CHAIRMAN: Secretary of the Commonwealth Beamish, I have the honor to hand you two official copies of the Resolution ratifying the proposed amendment to the

Constitution of the United States to repeal the Eighteenth Amendment, adopted by the Delegates here assembled representing the people of Pennsylvania. The Act of May 3, 1933, directs you to transmit a copy of this document under the Great Seal of the Commonwealth to the Secretary of State of the United States at Washington, which duty you will now perform.

THANKING CHAIRMAN OF THE CONVENTION

THE CHAIRMAN: The Chair recognizes Mr. Church.

MR. CHURCH: Mr. Chairman, I desire to offer a resolution.

The resolution was twice read by the Secretary as follows:

HALL OF THE SENATE
December 5, 1933

Resolved, That the members of this Convention express their appreciation and thanks for the consideration and courtesy extended to the delegates by the Chairman of the Convention, General Edward C. Shannon, Lieutenant Governor of the Common wealth of Pennsylvania.

THE CHAIRMAN: The Chair recognizes Mr. Church.

MR. CHURCH: Mr. Chairman, I move the adoption of the resolution.

MR. PATTERSON: Mr. Chairman, I second the motion.

The question was then put by the Secretary and the resolution was unanimously adopted.

THE CHAIRMAN: I thank you very much, ladies and gentlemen.

JOURNAL OF PROCEEDINGS TO BE FILED

THE CHAIRMAN: The Chair recognizes Mr. Durban.

MR. DURBAN: Mr. Chairman, I desire to offer a resolution.

The resolution was twice read by the Secretary as follows:

HALL OF THE SENATE
December 5, 1933

Resolved, That the Secretary of this Convention be directed to file the Journal of proceedings of this Convention in the office of the Secretary of the Commonwealth, there to be preserved as a permanent public record.

The resolution was unanimously adopted.

THE CHAIRMAN: Is there any further business? If not, the Chair awaits the pleasure of the Convention.

ADJOURNMENT SINE DIE

THE CHAIRMAN: The Chair recognizes Mrs. Dougherty.

MRS. DOUGHERTY: Mr. Chairman, I move that this Convention do now adjourn *sine die.*

The motion was agreed to and (at 1:04 P.M.) the Convention adjourned *sine die.*

ATTEST

We, the undersigned, Edward C. Shannon, Chairman, and A. Boyd Hamilton, Secretary of the Convention, do hereby certify that we have examined the above and foregoing record and find it to be a correct report of the proceedings.

(*Signed*) EDWARD C. SHANNON, *Chairman*
(*Signed*) A. BOYD HAMILTON, *Secretary*

RHODE ISLAND*

STATE OF RHODE ISLAND AND PROVIDENCE PLANTATIONS

Convention to pass on a proposal of amendment to the Constitution of the United States made on February 20, 1933, at the Second Session of the Seventy-Second Congress, held Monday, May 8, 1933, at one o'clock Eastern Standard Time in the House Chamber in the State House at Providence.

Convention called to order by Governor Theodore F. Green who, under the provisions of Chapter 2014 of the Public Laws, approved April 7, 1933, is the temporary chairman.

THE CHAIRMAN: The Secretary of State will call the temporary roll of delegates.

Roll of delegates called by the Secretary of State Louis W. Cappelli, as follows:

Susan Sharp Adams, present
John Nicholas Brown, present
John W. Burke, present
Luke H. Callan, present
Michael Cicerchia, present
Patrick P. Cullen, present
George A. Dolan, present
Ellen L. Donnelly, present
Marion Eppley, present
Frank E. Fitzsimmons, present
William S. Flynn, present
Peter G. Gerry, present
John E. Graham, present
Mary Colt Gross, present
Russell H. Handy, present
Eugene L. Jalbert, present
Howard Knight, present
Henry Lapan, present
Leopold L. Maynard, present
Daniel F. McLaughlin, present
Wilfred L. Paquin, present
Mabel H. S. Peirce, present
John F. Quinn, present
Maurice Robinson, present
Ellen W. Smith, present
Walter I. Sundlun, present
William H. Tolman, present
Charles T. Toomey, present
Lina Post Webster, present
Prescott J. Williams, present
Joseph Veneziale, present

THE CHAIRMAN: The Secretary of State reports the roll call shows that the thirty-one delegates authorized by law to be elected are present. The Chair, therefore, declares there is a quorum and the Convention is ready to transact the business for which it is called.

Is there any objection to the temporary roll being made the permanent roll of this Convention? The Chair hearing none, it is so made.

The members of the Convention will now qualify. The Secretary of State will administer the oath.

The oath was duly administered to the delegates as follows:

THE SECRETARY OF STATE: "You severally and solemnly swear to uphold the Constitution and the laws of this State and of the United States and to faithfully and impartially discharge the duties of your office to the best of your ability, so help you God."

The delegates severally: "I do."

THE CHAIRMAN: It is appropriate that a Convention such as this be opened with prayer. I will call upon the Right Reverend Peter E. Blessing to offer prayer.

MONSIGNOR BLESSING: In the name of the Father and of the Son and of the Holy Ghost, Amen. Almighty and eternal Father, we adore Thy infinite majesty and ac-

* Printed.

knowledge Thee to be the source and giver of all good gifts. Assembled here to exercise the mandate of a free people we humbly beg Thee endow us with sincere consciousness of our high duty to the people whom we represent.

We pray Thee, most merciful Father, to bless our work when it shall have been accomplished. In these troubled times guide in wisdom and justice the President of these United States, that his administration may be conducted with righteous fortitude and be eminently useful to the whole nation. Let the light of Thy divine wisdom direct the deliberations of the National Congress and shine forth in all the laws which it frames for our government, so that they may tend to the preservation of business, the promotion of national happiness, the increase of industry, sobriety, and useful knowledge, and perpetuate the blessings of equal liberty.

Bless, we beseech Thee, most merciful Father, his Excellency the Governor of this State, the members of the Assembly, all judges, magistrates, and other officers who are appointed to guard our political welfare, that they may be enabled by Thy powerful protection to discharge the duties of their respective stations with honesty and ability.

Grant to the citizens of this State and the whole nation fortitude in times of trial, sobriety in the enjoyment of prosperity, toleration that assures to us the perpetuation of Thy priceless gift of liberty and charity that makes for greater understanding, through Jesus Christ, our Lord, Amen. In the name of the Father and of the Son and of the Holy Ghost, Amen.

THE CHAIRMAN: Ladies and gentlemen of the Convention: this is the first time in the history of this State that a Constitutional convention has been held to pass upon an amendment to the Federal Constitution, and I am appreciative of the exceptional honor that I, as Governor, have of calling it to order. The amendment upon which you are to act is that proposed by the Seventy-Second Congress for the repeal of the Eighteenth Amendment to the Constitution, and although Rhode Island has never ratified this amendment, its action on its repeal is just as necessary as though it had done so.

From the beginning of our Federal Government, three ways were provided for amending the Constitution, but up to the present time, only one method has been used, namely, that of ratification by the legislatures of the several States. The Federal Constitution, however, emanated directly from the people. It was adopted by the several States by constitutional conventions similar to the one we are holding here today. Consequently there has always been a question as to whether our forefathers did not hold the opinion that the safest way to protect the Constitution was through this direct method of amendment. Our Constitutions, both Federal and State, are limitations upon the liberties of the people voluntarily imposed upon them by themselves. It seems both logical and just, therefore, that when other liberties are to be given up and other rights of the people are to be limited by the Constitutions, such limitations should be made in the same manner that the original Constitution was adopted, through the medium of conventions. It seems, therefore, strange that the only amendment to be so adopted is one not taking away but giving back to the people a portion of their liberties.

I personally believe that the method of amendment whereby proposals are referred to the legislatures of the several States for ratification was meant to apply only in the cases where the proposed changes deal with matters already contained in the Constitution and not with matters to be written into the Constitution for the first time and of a nature entirely new to that instrument.

The first ten amendments were in effect part of the original document and were proposed by the authors of the Constitution themselves. Article 10 of the amendments was the last and final word of its original authors. It provides expressly that "Powers not delegated to the United States by the Constitution, nor prohibited by it to the States are reserved to the States respectively or to the people." Was not this antitheses between States and people meant to reserve certain powers to the States and certain other powers to the people themselves? Continuing down to the passage of the Eighteenth Amendment we find that the articles of amendment related to matters previously dealt with in the Constitution. For example, Article 11 of the amendments dealt with the "Judicial Power" already provided in Article 3 of the original Constitution. Article 12 dealt with the "Elective Power" and merely changed a system that had been set up in Article 2 of the original Constitution. And so on down to the Eighteenth Amendment, with the possible exception of Article 13 which dealt with Slavery, no new subject matter was written into the Constitution by amendment.

The Eighteenth Amendment, however, affected the liberties of the people and was essentially new matter in the Constitution. Though its ratification was by the action of the State Legislatures, it is still a question whether State Legislatures are the agents of the people to the extent of being authorized to deprive them of rights and privileges which they enjoyed at the time of the adoption of the original Constitution, and which they reserved to themselves when they adopted the Constitution. Was it not such rights and powers as this which the founders had in mind when, in Article 10, they said, "Certain powers are reserved to the people"?

This theory of Constitutional law finds expression in our own State Constitution, Article 1, Section 1, which says:

"In the words of the father of his country we declare that the basis of our political systems is the right of the people to make and alter their constitutions of government."

This is not only an expression of approval of George Washington's words, but it is also the declaration of an unqualified absolute right in the people both of this nation and of this State respectively. This right exists even if it had not been stated. The same power which made our Constitution may unmake it. That is the power of the sovereign people. That right has remained in the people during the life of the Constitution, although that right has never been exercised until today. This Convention, therefore, has a significance to the people of this State far beyond the action it is to take on the repeal of the Eighteenth Amendment. The people of Rhode Island today in this Convention for the first time since the original Constitution was adopted by our State exactly one hundred and forty-three years ago this month reassert their sovereign power never since lost. As May 29, 1790, is a day ever to be remembered as the date when the people of Rhode Island through their Representatives in convention voted to adopt the Constitution of the United States, so May 8, 1933, will be remembered as the date when the people again through their Representatives in convention voted to repeal an amendment to that Constitution. These facts should impress upon us the solemn duty we are to perform and the importance of the historical event in which we are to take part today. You have received a mandate from the people of Rhode Island to add the vote of Rhode Island to that of two of its sister States, Michigan and Wisconsin, that have already voted to take from the Federal Constitution matter which I believe and you believe and probably the citizens of at least thirty-six states believe never should have found its way into the Constitution.

There is at least no question as far as the people of Rhode Island are concerned that your action here today will be an expression of their will. You meet with no doubts as to what is expected of you. It is unnecessary for me, who as Governor has been designated by the General Assembly to open this Convention, to discuss the merits or demerits of Prohibition, or to exhort you to favor its repeal. It is, however, appropriate for me to emphasize the importance of this occasion, because I feel it exemplifies the very spirit of Rhode Island throughout its history. As future generations look back upon the history of our time, they may gain inspiration as they realize that the same ideal of independence has been our guiding light since the day Roger Williams founded the Colony.

Though the facts leading up to this Convention are familiar to you, they should find some place in its records.

Rhode Island and its sister State, Connecticut, have alone during the past thirteen years of trial of this experiment "noble in purpose" steadfastly refused to give their sanction to the encroachment upon private rights which the Eighteenth Amendment perpetrated. This steadfastness stamps them as the sanest of our States and the ones having the clearest conception of the purpose and scope of the Federal Constitution.

Not content merely with withholding its ratification of the Eighteenth Amendment, Rhode Island appropriated money from its treasury and sent its Attorney-General to Washington to contest the legality of the amendment in the Federal Supreme Court. This was a bold step which started the onward march toward repeal.

Through thirteen years of trial, the people of Rhode Island have remained unchanged in their opinion on this question. However, the opinion of the people of many other States has been undergoing a great change. They have been coming to agree with Rhode Island in her original position. It is true that during a part of this period some influential politicians sought to obtain partisan advantage, holding themselves out as all things to all men. In this endeavor, they brought about the passage by the General Assembly in 1922 of a drastic State Enforcement Act. Under the authority of the Eighteenth Amendment, this Act gave concurrent power in enforcement to the State Government, but I feel justified in claiming that at no time was this in accordance with the will of the majority of the people of Rhode Island. It was not their will that State aid and the expenditure of a large amount of State revenue should be used for this purpose. The minority party fought unsuccessfully through several sessions of the General Assembly to bring about the repeal of this Act and thus keep Rhode Island's record entirely consistent on this question. As a result of that effort, ten years later this Enforcement Act was in effect repealed and a Nuisance Law enacted in its stead. The abuses connected with the administration of that Act were one of the effective voices in eventually bringing about its repeal. The people themselves had an opportunity to express their opinion in the General Election in 1930 and voted about three to one against the Eighteenth Amendment. At the special election held one week ago, at which you were chosen by the people as their Representatives, I am glad to note the vote against the Eighteenth Amendment was in excess of seven to one. You represent this overwhelming expression of public opinion. You may go forward in your work with the conviction that your State administration means to avoid the evils which existed prior to the adoption of the Eighteenth Amendment and helped to bring about its adoption. We have already made a reassuring start. From many different sources come expressions of approval of the recent action of the General Assembly in passing an act for the control of traffic in alcoholic beverages, which will regulate such control not only now but also when the Eighteenth Amendment is itself repealed.

In conclusion, may I thank the citizens of Rhode Island for responding as they did on May 1st to my call for a special election. A larger number voted than ever before at any special election held in this State. The overwhelming expression of their opinion is to be recorded by you at this Convention today.

The first business of this Convention is the nomination and election of a President. Under the law that must be by ballot. Nominations are in order.

MR. FITZSIMMONS: Mr. Chairman and fellow delegates: my purpose in rising is respectfully to present for your consideration the name of the Honorable William S. Flynn as a candidate for President of this Convention, and to urge upon you the propriety of his election to that most important office. As a former Governor of our State and as a consistent and persistent opponent of prohibition with all its evil works and pomps, he embodies the spirit and purpose behind the calling of this Convention by the General Assembly. To choose Governor Flynn for its presidency will emphasize as perhaps no other act possible to this gathering could emphasize the attitude of the sovereign citizens of Rhode Island toward the proposed amendment of repeal. His choice will reflect in unmistakable fashion the composite conviction of the electors that genuine temperance will best be served by doing away with the Eighteenth Amendment which has worked so much ill among many classes of our people.

THE CHAIRMAN: The name of William S. Flynn has been placed in nomination.

MRS. ADAMS: I second that nomination.

THE CHAIRMAN: Mrs. Adams has seconded the nomination.

MR. TOOMEY: Your Excellency and delegates to this Convention: for President of this historic Convention I nominate that sturdy champion of temperance and inveterate foe of the sumptuary legislation which has darkened this country for more than thirteen years, the Honorable Russell H. Handy of Lincoln.

In presenting his name, I am deeply conscious that all here in this assemblage have labored long and sincerely in the battle for the eradication of the Eighteenth Amendment from the Federal Constitution.

On this floor are the representatives of the liberal thought of this Commonwealth. The choice of every delegate here is a tribute to the intelligent discretion of the electorate of Rhode Island. Men and women of every walk of life sit in this chamber today as an expression of the will of the vast majority of the people of this State. To every organization and individual that aided in the triumph over fanaticism and hypocrisy, all of us are indebted. Much credit must be given to the National Association Against the Prohibition Amendment and the tireless activities of the Women's Organization for Prohibition Reform.

Rhode Island never ratified this iniquitous amendment, so it is therefore fitting that the tremendous vote for its removal from the Constitution should be unanimously given voice in this gathering. The victory has been non partisan in spirit. The presidency should be non partisan in selection.

Senator Handy's ten years of vigorous opposition to its retention in the Federal law should be rewarded by seating him as presiding officer in the deliberations of this body. I bespeak for him your united support.

THE CHAIRMAN: The name of Russell H. Handy has been placed in nomination.

MRS. GROSS: I deem it a great privilege to rise to second the nomination of the Honorable Russell H. Handy as President of this Convention. As Senator Toomey has already stated, Senator Handy has stood consistently for the repeal of the Eighteenth Amendment, and therefore it seems most fitting today that he should serve us as the President of this Convention. I therefore deem it a privilege to second his nomination.

THE CHAIRMAN: Mrs. Gross has seconded the nomination.

MR. JALBERT: We have gathered here today, Your Excellency and fellow delegates, in answer to the call to carry out the mandate of the people. Our purpose for the moment is the selection of the President of the permanent Convention. If I had to make my choice purely on the grounds of friendship, I frankly confess that I would be deeply embarrassed, because both candidates are men whose friendship I cherish with pride. However, there are other reasons that appear to me sufficient to relieve me of that personal embarrassment. When the list of candidates to appear before the people on this ticket to repeal the Eighteenth Amendment was made, the party leaders conceded an equal degree of merit in the work and in the struggle of the past for the expunging from the Constitution of that blot which has been known as the Eighteenth Amendment, so fifteen men from the Democratic side and fifteen men from the Republican side were selected, and there being an odd number to select, one was left to Fate. Today we are here elected on a non partisan ticket. The fact remains that the selection was made upon party lines and by that I mean as I have just stated, that fifteen Republicans were selected on the one side and fifteen Democrats on the other. We are here to perform our duties. We are here to restore to the people that portion of their liberty which, as the Governor has so well said, was taken away from them some thirteen years ago. It seems to me as I recall the past that of all the men who have worked consistently, who have fought most perseveringly, who have struggled most patiently for the restoration of this liberty as well as for all principles involving the rights of the common people, Senator Handy deserves a place in the front rank. We are here in a non partisan spirit, but we are not here devoid of our human intelligence, and we must admit the facts are here staring us in the face—that is, it has been the privilege of our good friends, the Democrats, to have the Governor open the Convention, to have the Secretary of State take the minutes of this Convention both during its temporary life and its official permanent existence. If they are willing to concede an equal degree of merit in the fights and in the struggles of the past, they ought to be willing to concede some degree of participation in the honors that go with the Convention. We are all legitimately entitled to aspire to this honor, but we are not all equally entitled to seek it. Our friends, the Democrats, have brought forward our good friend, former Governor Flynn—perfectly all right, legitimate in all respects, but it strikes me for one that the Democrats ought to be willing to let a Republican preside over the permanent Convention, and that is the reason why, forgetting my friendship for both, I second the nomination of Senator Handy for permanent President.

THE CHAIRMAN: Are there any further nominations? Hearing none, we will proceed to ballot. Under the law, this election must be by ballot, and under the law the Governor and the Secretary of State are to count the ballots, but I do not suppose there is anything to prevent me inviting the gentlemen who nominated the two candidates, to use a familiar phrase, to be official observers. I would like to ask those two gentlemen to come to the rostrum.

Mr. Fitzsimmons and Mr. Toomey went to the rostrum.

THE CHAIRMAN: Thirty-one ballots have been cast; of those sixteen have been cast for Senator Handy, fourteen for Governor Flynn and one for Senator Gerry. Sixteen are necessary for choice, and I declare Senator Handy elected President of the Convention.

Mr. Flynn: I move that the election of Senator Handy as permanent chairman be made unanimous.

Mr. Brown: I second Governor Flynn's motion.

The Chairman: The motion is made and seconded that the election of Senator Handy be made unanimous. All those in favor say aye; those opposed, no. The motion is carried.

Mr. Handy took the chair as President of the Convention.

The President: Ladies and gentlemen of the Convention, first of all I want to thank you most heartily for this honor you have conferred upon me here today, and I want to state that inasmuch as you are all familiar with my views in regard to prohibition, I will leave the remarks in regard to the repeal of the Eighteenth Amendment to the delegates.

Mr. Jalbert: I move that the Secretary be directed to keep the journal of the proceedings of this Convention as provided in Section 15 of Chapter 2014 of the Public Laws approved April 7, 1933.

Mr. Sundlun: I second the motion.

The President: The motion is made and seconded that the Secretary be directed to keep the journal of the proceedings of this Convention as provided in Section 15 of Chapter 2014 of the Public Laws approved April 7, 1933. All those in favor, say aye; those opposed, no. The motion is carried.

Mr. Flynn: I move that this Convention confirm the Honorable Louis W. Cappelli as Secretary of the Convention, and that as such he be authorized to appoint an official Stenographer, two pages and two doorkeepers to act in the deliberations of the Convention.

Mr. Callan: I second the motion made by Governor Flynn.

The President: The motion is made and seconded that this Convention confirm the Honorable Louis W. Cappelli as Secretary of the Convention, and that as such he be authorized to appoint an official Stenographer, two pages and two doorkeepers to act in the deliberations of the Convention. Those in favor, say aye; those opposed, no. The motion is carried.

The Secretary of State appointed Elizabeth O'Keefe as official Stenographer, Samuel Warnock and Stephen F. Rafferty as doorkeepers and Frank Del Sesto and George B. Tormey as pages.

Mr. Flynn: I offer this resolution and move its adoption.

The resolution moved by Mr. Flynn was handed to and read by the Secretary as follows: "Whereas the Congress of the United States on February 20, 1933, passed the following:

JOINT RESOLUTION

Proposing an amendment to the Constitution of the United States

Resolved by the Senate and House of Representatives of the United States of America in Congress assembled (two-thirds of each House concurring therein), That the following article is hereby proposed as an amendment to the Constitution of the United States, which shall be valid to all intents and purposes as part of the Constitution when ratified by conventions in three-fourths of the several States:

ARTICLE ___

Section 1. The eighteenth article of amendment to the Constitution of the United States is hereby repealed.

Section 2. The transportation or importation into any State, Territory, or possession of the United States for delivery or use therein of intoxicating liquors, in violation of the laws thereof, is hereby prohibited.

Section 3. This article shall be inoperative unless it shall have been ratified as an amendment to the Constitution by conventions in the several States, as provided in the Constitution, within seven years from the date of the submission hereof to the States by the Congress.

Now, THEREFORE, Be It Resolved that this Convention, duly elected by the electors of the State of Rhode Island and Providence Plantations and held in the city of Providence in said State to act upon that proposal of amendment to the Constitution of the United States which is set forth in the aforesaid Joint Resolution, now ratifies and approves said proposed Article as set forth in said Joint Resolution, as an amendment to the Constitution of the United States.

MR. FLYNN: I do not propose to intrude myself upon this Convention at any great length, but I have a particular source of pride in presenting this resolution, for back in the days when the Eighteenth Amendment was proposed as an amendment to the Constitution, by the designation of both Republicans and Democrats in this Assembly Hall on this very floor, I had the high honor of leading the fight against the Eighteenth Amendment in so far as it related to matters in the House.

May is a memorable month in the annals of our beloved State. It was on May 4, 1776, that Rhode Island became the first of all the colonies to declare its independence and renounce allegiance to the British Crown.

On May 29, 1790, the Constitution of the United States was adopted and ratified by a convention elected by the people of this State.

On May 2, 1843, our State Constitution became operative and the government under which we live organized thereunder.

It is, therefore, most fitting that this Convention, the first of its kind to be held in this State since the ratification of the Federal Constitution, should derive its sanction from the people and assemble in solemn meeting during this month of May.

It demanded the highest courage fostered and sustained by our people's passion for true liberty to lead all the other colonies in taking the momentous step of complete separation from Great Britain, thus defying the greatest world power of that day. In the same spirit our people refused to ratify the Federal Constitution until assured of the guarantees contained in the Bill of Rights.

True to her best traditions, Rhode Island rejected the Eighteenth Amendment when it was proposed for adoption. Not only did we remain steadfast in our opposition to the adoption of this amendment, but after the amendment was promulgated we alone of all the States carried the fight against it in defense of our sovereignty to the bar of the Supreme Court of the United States. Throughout the years during which this amendment has been operative, Rhode Island has spared no effort to encompass its repeal.

It is, therefore, a great source of pride and satisfaction for the delegates to assemble here today armed with the most decisive mandate ever given to their representatives by the people of Rhode Island to record as real servants of our people their unquestionable disapproval of the Eighteenth Amendment itself, the method of its introduction into the Constitution, and the demoralizing consequences which inevitably followed its adoption.

We hope that our action here today will be followed speedily by similar action in the other States to the end that the Eighteenth Amendment may be banished from the fundamental law of our beloved country, and that henceforth and forever the sovereign people of America will vigilantly guard the sacred charter of their liberties from the intrusion of like profane policies of government under whatever guise they may appear.

MR. GERRY: I take great pleasure in seconding the motion to adopt this resolution because, to my mind, it is the triumph of a fight waged many years to bring back personal liberty to the people. When this amendment came up in the Senate of the United States, I was a member of that body, and I voted against it. I was one I think, of twenty in the Senate of the United States, to vote against it, and it is indeed a satisfaction to me to see how well I then interpreted the sentiment of Rhode Island, and how now the people have come to realize the fundamental principle that you cannot make people good by law, and that sumptuary legislation has no place in the Constitution of the United States. It is indeed a source of great pride for Rhode Island that we are going to be the third State to vote for the repeal of the Eighteenth Amendment.

MR. SUNDLUN: Mr. President: We have gathered here today as duly constituted delegates of the Convention held in accordance with the mandate of the General Assembly of the State of Rhode Island and the Providence Plantations of the January Session, 1933, to act upon a proposed Amendment to the Constitution of the United States at the second session of the Seventy-Second Congress, and which provides that

"the eighteenth article of amendment to the Constitution of the United States shall be repealed";

(Sec. 2) that "the transportation or importation into any State, Territory or possession of the United States for delivery or use therein of intoxicating liquors in violation of the law thereof, shall be prohibited" and further that

(Sec. 3) "this article shall be inoperative unless it shall have been ratified as an amendment to the Constitution by Conventions in the several States, as provided in the Constitution, within seven years from the date of the submission thereof to the States by the Congress."

The State of Rhode Island and Providence Plantations has waited a long time for this eventful day, not only to give vent to its own feelings so often expressed, but also to contribute its strength, wisdom and power in bringing about an early termination of the harmful effects, which the Eighteenth Amendment has had upon the national life of our country.

In the formative days of our country, the colony of Rhode Island proclaimed its independence by an overwhelming vote of its General Assembly. Two months before the Declaration of Independence was pronounced at Philadelphia on July 4, 1776, Rhode Island, then a colony, adopted a militant attitude for its freedom, and proclaimed its independence from England. It thus became the first Republic in America. This action gave great encouragement to the delegates to the Congress held in Philadelphia, July 4, 1776, and largely contributed to the Declaration of Independence of our country upon that historic date.

Though Rhode Island was the first colony to declare its independence from England, it was the last of the members of the Old Confederation to ratify the Constitution, for there again Rhode Island steadfastly clung to its ideas of free government, and insisted that the Bill of Rights must be incorporated as part of the Federal Constitution. Rhode Island refused to ratify the Constitution until this great act was accomplished, and once again Rhode Island held up its Beacon Light and guided our nation to the path of security and freedom for its people, and the Bill of Rights was made part of the Constitution.

It was not until Rhode Island had ratified the Constitution that the bond of Union became complete.

Washington, in acknowledging a letter which was sent by the Governor of Rhode Island communicating the news of Rhode Island's ratification, replied,

"That the bond of Union was now complete."

Today, for the first time since that historic date, May 29, 1790, Rhode Island is holding its first Convention to ratify a proposed amendment to the Constitution. This is a historic date in the history of Rhode Island.

The proposed amendment is now before us because of the constant and persistent demand made by a vast number of citizens of our country covering a period of fourteen years.

Ever since the adoption of the Eighteenth Amendment to the Constitution, Rhode Island has raised its voice in protest against it. It was the only State that appropriated money and sent its Attorney General, the late Honorable Herbert Rice, to contest the constitutionality of the amendment, and though it had failed in this endeavor, it still refused to ratify the Eighteenth Amendment.

Why should our State be so insistent in its position? The answer is clear.

Rhode Island has always maintained that a constitutional provision of a sumptuary nature which is not self-enforceable cannot remain effective without the approval and support of citizens of this country.

Rhode Island has always had a clear understanding of human nature, a comprehension of our institutions and the purpose of our government, a recognition of the great basic principles that our government, in order to retain its character, must respond to the popular will, and always maintained that our government in order to remain a government "of the people, for the people and by the people" must recognize the principle that it derives its powers from the governed.

The Eighteenth Amendment struck a note of great discord in the Constitution.

During the years of Federal prohibition, there has been more law-breaking, more corruption in public offices, more intemperate use of intoxicating liquors than in all of our previous national history. Men and women who in every other respect are law abiding citizens of our great country have, during the years that prohibition has been in force, gradually adopted a philosophy that to conspire with and aid the bootlegger in his illegal sale of liquors was not contrary to good morals or ethical conduct. These same men and women, who represent the backbone of our nation, treated indeed lightly their constant interference with the enforcement of the Eighteenth Amendment.

In the homes of millions of citizens, who are indeed patriotic citizens, no social gathering took place unless the guests were first given as a repast a cocktail made of bootleg liquor.

The Eighteenth Amendment has caused more disrespect for other laws than any other single act or law.

When a people become lawless, corruption creeps into government. Only an innate sense of honor, honesty and loyalty can compel the governed to support the laws of our country, and when a law is of such a character that our citizens adopt a philosophy that it is not dishonorable, dishonest, or disloyal to violate it, there is then something fundamentally wrong with the law.

The Eighteenth Amendment has to a marked degree destroyed the teachings of the value of true temperance. Our nation is a temperate nation. During prohibition alcoholism greatly increased. The very benefits which it was hoped would be accomplished by prohibition, have been destroyed by prohibition itself.

There is no need at this time to recite in detail the great harm that has come to our country from prohibition, let alone the great waste of money expended in the mild and ineffective effort to enforce it.

The Eighteenth Amendment and its enforcement acts are radical departures from the legitimate functions of our Federal Government.

This amendment has greatly encroached upon State rights. Many of our citizens still hold to the belief that it is a serious invasion of the sovereign powers of the States. It is also still maintained by many that the Eighteenth Amendment has greatly lessened the protection intended for all citizens by the Bill of Rights.

It has been arduously argued that the Eighteenth Amendment has no place in the Constitution of the United States and the provision that,

> "The powers not delegated to the United States by the Constitution nor prohibited by it to the States, are reserved to the States respectively or to the people."

renders the Eighteenth Amendment as an illogical member of the family of amendments to the Constitution.

Countless other objections with far reaching effects have been offered. This amendment has caused much unrest in our country. It is not a partisan measure. Large numbers of citizens of both major political parties have strenuously opposed the retention of the Eighteenth Amendment.

The eyes of the nation are upon us today. By our act today we will be maintaining and continuing to foster the ideals which Rhode Island has entertained throughout its entire enriched and patriotic life as one of the States of this great Union.

Rhode Island again records its insistence that it be permitted to exercise its sovereign powers over its citizens and that every other State be granted the same right without Federal encroachment.

I am pleased to have the privilege and honor as a delegate of this historic Convention to second the adoption of the resolution ratifying the proposed amendment repealing the Eighteenth Amendment.

MR. CALLAN: Mr. President, as the so-called Independent Party, after holding a caucus, representing said party at the caucus, and as a total abstainer and as one of the five million men who were in the service of our country when this matter was started by an organized minority under the guise of benefiting those men who were in service—in fact, that is the basis upon which they started their activities that finally put the Eighteenth Amendment into the Constitution—as one of those men and as representing those men who were unable to record their vote in 1919 because of absence from the country, it gives me great pleasure to second the motion that this resolution prevail.

MR. JALBERT: I have no desire to prolong the deliberations of this Convention, nor have I any desire to prolong the agony of those who still believe in the Eighteenth Amendment. However, it seems to me that this is an occasion on which every one of us ought to be glad to express by voice his feelings about the proposition which is before the Convention for consideration. When this proposal came up in Congress, I did not have the privilege of voting against it for the plain reason that I was not there. When it came up here in this chamber, I did not have the privilege of voting against it, because I was not a member of the House. When the Legislature of this State failed to ratify the proposal, I was entirely in accord with its official act. As a matter of fact, it is now before us and it is the first opportunity that we, as representatives of the people, have had to express our will, and it is my first opportunity officially to express myself in the matter. I am not going to repeat the history which we heard through the happy expression and the happy reminiscences of former Governor Flynn. We all endorse what he said. To my mind, this is not so much an opportunity for us to grasp to vote for the repeal of the Eighteenth Amendment as it is an opportunity for us to meet publicly and draw a lesson from history. This Eighteenth Amendment was grafted upon the Federal Constitution by the machinations of a well organized minority. The majority was asleep, and it took thirteen years for this majority to wake up, and after all these thirteen years of hard struggle throughout the length and breadth of this country, we have the opportunity finally arising to right what has been wrong for so long, and the lesson that we want to draw is this: that for thirteen years this Eighteenth Amendment in our Constitution has been a living challenge to the will of the majority. It has been a challenge to the republican form of government of this great country. If we want this republican form of government to endure in this country, we must see to it that the majority continue to rule and not be ruled by a minority, organized or disorganized. That is the reason, Mr. President, that I am glad to be one of the delegates voting to ratify the present amendment which in effect will bring about the repeal of the Eighteenth Amendment.

Mr. Veneziale: When I came to this Convention, this afternoon, I did not intend to say anything at all, but after listening to the reasons given for the repeal of the Eighteenth Amendment, I think there is one thing that stands out prominently before me pertaining strictly and particularly to the State of Rhode Island, that has been omitted. We know that the State of Rhode Island has a cosmopolitan population. It is heterogeneous, not homogeneous at all. In the State of Rhode Island we have a large number of people who trace their ancestry to Europe, particularly to some of the countries in the southern part of Europe, and those people who were born there who are now American citizens and thousands of their children who were born here have registered themselves vociferously against the Eighteenth Amendment. At the election which was held here last Monday, the people of Rhode Island directly for the first time voted against the Eighteenth Amendment. I have reference to the Italo-Americans particularly in the Federal Hill district, where approximately five thousand people registered their votes against the Eighteenth Amendment, and only about a score of people registered their votes in favor of it. For this reason I say that the people of the State of Rhode Island no longer have to live in an atmosphere of hypocrisy. Hereafter when our sister States follow our example and trample upon the Eighteenth Amendment, the people of Rhode Island will live in a State where law and order will be respected and the people will respect this country more because of the just laws that are made and because they will no longer be dominated by a minority. For that reason, I want to second the motion that the resolution be adopted.

Mr. Flynn: I move that the vote on the resolution be by roll call and that if the resolution is adopted, the delegates proceed to the secretary's desk and sign the same in token of their approval.

Mr. Jalbert: I second that motion.

The President: If there is no objection, that procedure will be followed. The Secretary of State will call the roll.

The roll was called by the Secretary of State as follows:

Susan Sharp Adams, aye
John Nicholas Brown, aye
John W. Burke, aye
Luke H. Callan, aye
Michael Cicerchia, aye
Patrick P. Cullen, aye
George A. Dolan, aye
Ellen L. Donnelly, aye
Marion Eppley, aye
Frank E. Fitzsimmons, aye
William S. Flynn, aye
Peter G. Gerry, aye
John E. Graham, aye
Mary Colt Gross, aye
Russell H. Handy, aye
Eugene L. Jalbert, aye
Howard Knight, aye
Henry Lapan, aye
Leopold L. Maynard, aye
Daniel F. McLaughlin, aye
Wilfred L. Paquin, aye
Mabel H. S. Peirce, aye
John F. Quinn, aye
Maurice Robinson, aye
Ellen W. Smith, aye
Walter I. Sundlun, aye
William H. Tolman, aye
Charles T. Toomey, aye
Lina Post Webster, aye
Prescott J. Williams, aye
Joseph Veneziale, aye

THE PRESIDENT: The vote is unanimous. The resolution is carried and Rhode Island is wet again.

MR. TOOMEY: I move that this body of delegates meeting in Convention pursuant to Chapter 2014 of the Public Laws of the State of Rhode Island and Providence Plantations approved April 7, 1933, does hereby instruct its President and Secretary, as required by Section 16 of said Chapter 2014, to make and execute the certificate for filing in the office of the Secretary of State of this State, to the effect that this Convention has ratified the proposal of amendment to the Constitution of the United States passed by the Seventy-second Congress on February 20, 1933.

MR. SUNDLUN: I second that motion.

THE PRESIDENT: The motion has been made and seconded that this body of delegates meeting in Convention pursuant to Chapter 2014 of the Public Laws of the State of Rhode Island and Providence Plantations approved April 7, 1933, does hereby instruct its President and Secretary, as required by Section 16 of said Chapter 2014, to make and execute the certificate for filing in the office of the Secretary of State of this State, to the effect that this Convention has ratified the proposal of amendment to the Constitution of the United States passed by the Seventy-second Congress on February 20, 1933.

All in favor of the motion, say aye; those opposed, no. The ayes have it; the resolution is passed.

Is there any further business before the Convention? If not, and since none is proposed, I assume there is none, the Reverend Anthony L. Parshley will offer the Benediction.

DR. PARSHLEY: Almighty God, who hast given us this good land for our heritage; we humbly beseech Thee that we may always prove ourselves a people mindful of Thy favor and glad to do Thy will. Bless our land with honorable industry, sound learning, and pure manners. Save us from violence, discord, and confusion; from pride and arrogancy, and from every evil way. Defend our liberties, and fashion into one united people the multitudes brought hither out of many kindreds and tongues. Endue with the spirit of wisdom those to whom in Thy name we entrust the authority of government, that there may be justice and peace at home, and that through obedience to Thy law, we may show forth Thy praise among the nations of the earth. In the time of prosperity, fill our hearts with thankfulness, and in the day of trouble, suffer not our trust in Thee to fail; all which we ask through Jesus Christ our Lord, Amen.

MR. MCLAUGHLIN: I move that this Convention now adjourn, *sine die.*

MR. MAYNARD: I second the motion.

THE PRESIDENT: The motion has been made and seconded that the Convention adjourn *sine die.* All those in favor say aye; those opposed, no. The Convention voted aye unanimously.

I declare the Convention adjourned *sine die.*

WHEREAS, The Congress of the United States on February 20, 1933, passed the following:

JOINT RESOLUTION

Proposing an amendment to the Constitution of the United States

Resolved by the Senate and House of Representatives of the United States of America in Congress assembled (two-thirds of each House concurring therein), That the following article is hereby proposed as an amendment to the Constitution of the United States, which shall be valid to all intents and purposes as part of the Constitution when ratified by conventions in three-fourths of the several States:

ARTICLE ___ ___

Section 1. The eighteenth article of amendment to the Constitution of the United States is hereby repealed.

Section 2. The transportation or importation into any State, Territory, or possession of the United States for delivery or use therein of intoxicating liquors, in violation of the laws thereof, is hereby prohibited.

Section 3. This article shall be inoperative unless it shall have been ratified as an amendment to the Constitution by conventions in the several States, as provided in the Constitution, within seven years from the date of the submission hereof to the States by the Congress.

Now, therefore, be it resolved that this convention duly elected by the electors of the State of Rhode Island and Providence Plantations and held in the city of Providence in said State to act upon that proposal of amendment to the Constitution of the United States which is set forth in the aforesaid Joint Resolution, now ratifies and approves said proposed Article, as set forth in said Joint Resolution, as an amendment to the Constitution of the United States.

Adopted in convention, by the unanimous consent of the delegates present, the eighth day of May, in the year of our Lord one thousand nine hundred and thirty-three.

In witness whereof, we have hereunto subscribed our names

Russell H. Handy, Pres.
Susan Sharp Adams
John Nicholas Brown
John W. Burke
Luke H. Callan
Michael Cicerchia
Patrick P. Cullen
George H. Dolan
Ellen L. Donnelly
Marion Eppley
Frank E. Fitzsimmons
William S. Flynn
Peter G. Gerry
John E. Graham
Mary Colt Gross
Eugene L. Jalbert
Howard Knight
Henry Lapan
Leopold L. Maynard
Daniel F. McLaughlin
Wilfred J. Paquin
Mabel H. S. Peirce

John F. Quinn
Maurice Robinson
Ellen W. Smith
Walter I. Sundlun
William H. Tolman
Charles T. Toomey
Lina Post Webster
Prescott J. Williams
Joseph Veneziale

I HEREBY CERTIFY that the foregoing are the signatures of all the elected delegates to the above mentioned Convention.

LOUIS W. CAPPELLI
Secretary of State and Secretary of the Convention

(L. S.)

STATE OF RHODE ISLAND AND PROVIDENCE PLANTATIONS

PROVIDENCE, R. I.

May 9, 1933

We, Russell H. Handy and Louis W. Cappelli, President and Secretary, respectively, of the Convention of the State of Rhode Island and Providence Plantations, duly elected by the electors of said State and held on the eighth day of May, A.D. 1933, in the chamber of the house of representatives of said State at the state house, Providence, R. I., in accordance with the provision of Chapter 2014 of the Public Laws of said State, A.D. 1933, to act upon that proposal of Amendment to the Constitution of the United States which was set forth in a Joint Resolution passed on the twentieth day of February, A.D. 1933, at the Second Session of the Seventy-second Congress of the United States;

Do HEREBY CERTIFY that the following proposed Article of Amendment to the Constitution of the United States which was set forth in said Joint Resolution, was duly ratified by said Convention by the unanimous vote of all the delegates:

ARTICLE ___

Section 1. The eighteenth article of amendment to the constitution of the United States is hereby repealed.

Section 2. The transportation or importation into any state, territory, or possession of the United States for delivery or use therein of intoxicating liquors, in violation of the law thereof, is hereby prohibited.

Section 3. This article shall be inoperative unless it shall have been ratified as an amendment to the constitution by conventions in the several states, as provided in the constitution, within seven years from the date of the submission hereof to the states by the Congress.

In testimony whereof, We have hereunto set our hands and seals, this ninth day of May, in the year 1933.

(L. S.)

RUSSELL H. HANDY
President
LOUIS W. CAPPELLI
Secretary

STATE OF RHODE ISLAND AND PROVIDENCE PLANTATIONS

PROVIDENCE, R. I.

May 9, 1933

We, the undersigned, respectively the Governor and the Secretary of State of the State of Rhode Island and Providence Plantations, do hereby this ninth day of May, A.D. 1933, certify that the foregoing certificate is in all respects true and that the Convention therein referred to was duly elected, organized and held in accordance with Chapter 2014 of the Public Laws, A.D. 1933, of said State and the proclamation of the Governor of said State.

In testimony whereof, We have hereunto set our hands and affixed the seal of the State of Rhode Island, this ninth day of May, in the year 1933.

THEODORE FRANCIS GREEN
Governor
LOUISE W. CAPPELLI
Secretary of State

(L. S.)

SOUTH CAROLINA*

CERTIFICATE OF RATIFICATION AND A NEWSPAPER REPORT

CERTIFICATE OF RATIFICATION

Be it resolved by the Delegates duly elected and assembled in this Convention of South Carolina for the Purpose of ratifying or rejecting the proposed Twenty-first Amendment to the Constitution of the United States that the said Twenty-first Amendment be, and the same hereby is rejected.

Resolved, Further, that the original of this Resolution duly signed by the President of this Convention and attested by the Secretary be filed with the Secretary of State of the State of South Carolina, and a certified copy be filed with the Secretary of State of the United States at Washington, D. C.

Done in Convention in Columbia on the fourth day of December, in the year of our Lord one thousand nine hundred and thirty-three.

HENRY N. SNYDER
President of the Convention

Attest:

W. W. SMOAK
Secretary of the Convention

Copy of the original on file in this office.

(*Signed*) W. O. BLACKWELL
Secretary of State

A NEWSPAPER REPORT

THE STATE

Columbia, S. C.

December 5, 1933

STATE GOES OFFICIALLY
AGAINST DRY LAW REPEAL

Delegates Declare South Carolina
Opposed to Repeal of 18th Amendment in Convention
Termed "Historic" by President—Business is Dispatched in Short Period

South Carolina, in convention duly called, yesterday officially declared herself opposed to the ratification of the 21st amendment, repealing the 18th amendment to

* From a typewritten copy. Mr. W. F. Blackwell, Secretary of State, reported that there was no record of the proceedings of the convention in the Department of State. To offset lack of official information, the report of the convention as published in the Columbia *State* is printed here. Acknowledgment is duly made to Mr. William E. Gonzales, editor of the *State,* for his courtesy in supplying a copy of the issue of his paper containing this report.

the federal constitution and so notified Cordell Hull, secretary of state of the United States.

So well organized and smoothly working was the machinery of the "dry" convention, that it organized; elected officers; had a roll call; heard two or three short addresses and then adopted a resolution, all within 32 minutes. The convention was called to order promptly at noon—within less than 35 minutes thereafter, it had adjourned and some of the delegates were cashing their pay vouchers. A new record for brevity so far as state conventions go in South Carolina, was established.

The state was the first, through convention, to reject the 21st amendment. North Carolina, though she voted against repeal, having voted against holding a convention.

The vote of the convention against repeal of the 18th amendment was unanimous, pursuant to the anti-repeal vote cast November 7 at the special election. In that election the vote stood: against repeal, 35,845; for repeal, 33,074.

Utmost order and temperance, in word and action, prevailed yesterday throughout the convention termed "Historic" by the presiding officer, Dr. Henry Nelson Snyder, of Spartanburg, who declared he had "never felt prouder of his adopted state than he had in recent days" and who said that those who struggled through obstacles for the dry cause had "found an intelligence which refused not to see that as yesterday, today and forever the curse of any land is the use of alcohol."

RESOLUTION ADOPTED

The resolution, setting forth South Carolina's position on the 18th amendment, was introduced by John G. Richards, Liberty Hill, former governor of South Carolina, and was adopted by a vote of 41 to 0. Five of the delegates were absent.

The resolution was as follows:

"Be it resolved by the delegates duly elected and assembled in this convention of South Carolina for the purpose of ratifying or rejecting the proposed 21st amendment to the constitution of the United States, That the said 21st amendment be, and the same hereby is rejected.

"Resolved, further, That the original of this resolution duly signed by the president of this convention and attested by the secretary be filed with the secretary of state of the state of South Carolina, and a certified copy be filed with the secretary of state of the United States at Washington, D. C.

"Done in convention in Columbia on the fourth day of December, in the year of our Lord, one thousand, nine hundred and thirty-three."

Smoak in Chair

When the noon hour struck, W. W. Smoak mounted the stand in the hall of the house of representatives, and called the convention to order, asking for nominations for a temporary president. John G. Richards, Liberty Hill, was unanimously elected and was escorted to the stand by Dr. J. C. Roper, Greenville.

As he took the gavel, the former governor said he regarded it as "one of the greatest privileges of my life" to preside for a little while over a convention which "represents the moral forces" of the state.

Dr. E. O. Watson, Richland, then opened the convention with prayer, saying in its course, "Our hearts stir within us for love of the Father, our nation and the Carolinas" and expressing thanks for the spirit of those who would "maintain the sobriety, the welfare and the prosperity of the state and the nation."

A committee on credentials, composed of J. J. Lawton, chairman; Charlton DuRant and David A. Wamer, was appointed by the temporary president, and its report was presented at once by Mr. DuRant, it being adopted and the list of delegates elected being called, all but five responding.

Snyder Made Chairman

On motion of Doctor Roper, Dr. H. N. Snyder, Spartanburg, was elected permanent president. As he ascended the stand, the delegates arose and applauded, as they had done at the election of the temporary president.

Doctor Snyder, on taking the gavel as permanent president of the convention said, "You honor me beyond my deserts in naming me president of this historic convention. I say, historic convention. I never felt prouder of my adopted state than I have in recent days. She has had many high points in her long history in meeting emergencies which arose; it seems to me, though, that she never rose higher than on this occasion.

"When you go with the current, it is easy enough. Yet when there was great temptation to say, 'Oh, what's the use?' we found an intelligence which refused not to see that the curse of any land is the use of alcohol. In spite of the dust and cross currents, which blinded some and confused others, South Carolina stuck to her convictions to the last.

"We honor those who go to war. In the citations for bravery there is a phrase which I like, 'for gallantry above and beyond the requirements of actual duty.' And in the election of this convention there is shown a gallantry beyond the call of actual duty.

"It may be the last time for any of us to register our convictions legally in the matter of alcoholic liquors but we hand on to coming generations our record, and by and by in a better day it may be that we shall have a better way of doing than we have yet known."

Roper Speaks

After the applause following this address had subsided, Mr. Richards nominated Dr. J. C. Roper as permanent vice president, and in accepting the place to which he was elected unanimously, he said, "This may prove as historic a convention as any of the conventions our state has known.

"I lent myself," he said, "to serve a cause—a cause which I fought for through three years of dust and sometimes near dirt, to serve the best interests of religion and humanity, and on November 8, when I learned how the election had gone, I was never prouder of the state, which I love and in which rest the bones of my ancestors. We bless God we are able to do our part now."

W. W. Smoak, who had been serving as temporary secretary, was made permanent on motion of W. Stackhouse. "I am thankful for being allowed to play a part in this historic convention which our posterity will be pleased to remember. I am glad our state did not desert its adherence to an ideal. This convention represents people who voted their conviction without hope of reward or profit other than service to humanity," he said.

Mr. Richards, former governor, then presented the formal resolution which was adopted, after which the convention was adjourned.

DELEGATES ATTENDING

The accredited delegates to the convention were:

J. R. Power, Abbeville; John C. Whatley, Aiken; Otis Brabham, Allendale; Dr.

A. L. Smethers, Anderson; Dr. L. A. Hartzog, Bamberg; R. E. Woodward, Barnwell; W. G. Heyward, Beaufort; Mrs. Evelyn deM. Harvey, Berkeley; J. A. Merritt, Calhoun; John A. McCormick, Charleston; Dr. R. C. Granberry, Cherokee; R. B. Caldwell, Chester; W. T. McBride, Chesterfield; Carlton DuRant, Clarendon; W. W. Smoak, Colleton; J. J. Lawton, Darlington; Hugh C. Stanton, Dillon; D. A. Wamer, Dorchester; G. W. Scott, Edgefield; H. J. Surles, Fairfield; W. M. Waters, Florence; F. J. Tyson, Georgetown; the Rev. J. C. Roper, Greenville; Andrew E. Taylor, Greenwood; E. M. Peeples, Hampton; C. H. Snider, Horry; T. W. Malphrus, Jasper; John G. Richards, Kershaw; George M. Faile, Lancaster; the Rev. J. A. Martin, Laurens; Mrs. W. I. Herbert, Lee; B. E. Williams, Lexington; H. E. Freeland, McCormick; W. Stackhouse, Marion; Mrs. Eula Roper McColl, Marlboro; Dr. George B. Cromer, Newberry; W. A. Strickland, Oconee; Dr. James A. Fort, Orangeburg; C. T. Martin, Pickens; Dr. E. O. Watson, Richland; Mrs. James A. Satcher, Saluda; Dr. Henry N. Snyder, Spartanburg; E. B. Boyle, Sumter; John R. Mathis, Union; T. W. Boyle, Williamsburg, and Dr. J. H. Saye, York.

Delegates not attending the convention were: Mrs. Evelyn deM. Harvey, Berkeley; W. T. McBride, Chesterfield; R. W. Malphrus, Jasper; B. E. Williams, Lexington; Dr. George B. Cromer, Newberry.

The vouchers, 40 paid yesterday, totaled $400.50. Vouchers were not cashed during the day.

TENNESSEE*

CERTIFICATION OF RATIFICATION PROCEEDINGS

By the STATE OF TENNESSEE in a CONVENTION constituted and convened as provided by Chapter 38 of the Public Acts of the General Assembly of the State of Tennessee for the year 1933, passed March 29th, 1933, and approved by the Governor of Tennessee March 31st, 1933, entitled, "AN ACT to provide for a Convention to pass on an Amendment to the Constitution of the United States, relating to the repeal of the Eighteenth Article of Amendment to said Constitution, which has been heretofore proposed by the Congress for ratification by Conventions in the several States,"—said proposed Amendment having been duly submitted to the State of Tennessee by certification of the Secretary of State of the United States of America, in manner and form and in words and figures, as follows, to-wit:

SEVENTY-SECOND CONGRESS OF THE UNITED STATES OF AMERICA

AT THE SECOND SESSION

JOINT RESOLUTION

Proposing an Amendment to the Constitution of the United States.

Resolved by the Senate and House of Representatives of the United States of America in Congress assembled (two-thirds of each House concurring therein), That the following article is hereby proposed as an amendment to the Constitution of the United States, which shall be valid to all intents and purposes as part of the Constitution when ratified by conventions in three-fourths of the several states:

ARTICLE ___

Section 1. The eighteenth article of amendment to the Constitution of the United States is hereby repealed.

Section 2. The transportation or importation into any State, Territory or possession of the United States for delivery or use therein of intoxicating liquors, in violation of the laws thereof, is hereby prohibited.

Section 3. The article shall be inoperative unless it shall have been ratified as an amendment to the Constitution by conventions in the several states, as provided in the Constitution, within seven years from the date of the submission hereof to the States by Congress.

JOHN N. GARNER
Speaker of the House of Representatives

CHARLES CURTIS
Vice-President of the United States and
President of the Senate

---

* From a typewritten copy. The certified list of delegates, with the votes cast for each, and the certificate of the president and secretary of the convention are omitted. The latter duplicates in considerable detail the journal which is printed here.

(*On reverse side*)

I certify that the Joint Resolution originated in the Senate.

EDWIN P. THAYER
Secretary

No. 658

UNITED STATES OF AMERICA

DEPARTMENT OF STATE

To all to whom these presents shall come, GREETINGS:

I CERTIFY THAT THE copy hereto attached is a true copy of a resolution of Congress entitled "JOINT RESOLUTION proposing an Amendment to the Constitution of the United States," the original of which is on file in this Department.

SEAL

In testimony whereof, I, Henry L. Stimson, Secretary of State, have hereunto caused the seal of the Department of State to be affixed and my name subscribed by the Acting Chief Clerk of said Department, in the City of Washington, in District of Columbia, this 21st day of February, 1933.

(*Signed*) HENRY L. STIMSON
Secretary of State
(*Signed*) P. F. ALLEN
Acting Chief Clerk

We, the undersigned, E. L. McNeilly, Sr., President, and E. C. Anderson, Secretary, respectively, of the Convention in the STATE OF TENNESSEE, held (pursuant to Section 9 of the aforesaid Chapter 38 of the Acts of the General Assembly of Tennessee for 1933) to pass upon the ratification of the aforesaid proposed Amendment to the Constitution of the United States, do hereby CERTIFY as follows, to-wit:

1. That the delegates attending the Convention aforesaid met in the Chamber of the House of Representatives in the Capitol at Nashville, Tennessee, at ten o'clock, A.M., on the eleventh day of August, 1933; and, having been called to order, a communication from the Secretary of State of the State of Tennessee was thereupon made to the delegates then and there assembled, certifying from the official records of his office, that the following sixty-three persons, from the respective districts stated, received the highest number of votes cast at an election held within and throughout the State of Tennessee (as provided by the aforesaid Chapter 38 of the Acts of the General Assembly of Tennessee) on the Third Thursday in July (namely, July 20th), 1933, for the purpose of electing Delegates to a Convention in Tennessee to pass on the aforesaid proposed Amendment to the Constitution of the United States, and that said sixty-three persons were the duly and constitutionally elected Delegates to said Convention, legally entitled to membership therein as constituting the entire membership lawfully authorized to said Convention and have been furnished certificates of election as provided by law, to-wit:

FIRST DISTRICT

John I. Cox
John Heilman
J. R. Ketron
John R. King
John K. Shields
Mrs. Frank B. St. John
T. W. Stevens

SECOND DISTRICT

Chas. H. Bacon
Hamilton S. Burnett
Hal. H. Clements
Mrs. Bruce Kenner, Jr.
Mrs. Thomas P. Miller
John Toomey
Wm. Turnblazer

THIRD DISTRICT

Wm. L. Frierson
Malcolm C. Hill
Mrs. Richard H. Kimball
Paul J. Kruesi
W. M. Lowery
E. C. Norvell
B. M. Smoot

FOURTH DISTRICT

J. B. Dow
W. P. Cooper
W. T. Gerhardt
Mrs. R. M. Kirby-Smith
J. L. McCawley
Roy H. Parkes
W. P. Rains

FIFTH DISTRICT

W. E. Cheek
Henry E. Colton
A. O. Denning
Mrs. Guilford Dudley
Josiah Fort
Chas. S. McMurry
E. L. McNeilly, Sr.

SIXTH DISTRICT

W. E. Bratton
R. H. Crockett
Thos. Harris
J. F. Murff
Glen Nelson
Ray Stuart
William J. Towler

SEVENTH DISTRICT

E. C. Anderson
J. E. DeFord
Mrs. Lizzie Lea Miller Henderson
Flake Humphrey
R. M. Murray
J. R. Rison, Jr.
George L. Wortham

EIGHTH DISTRICT

Geo. M. Brooks
M. W. Darden
Fred Lowery
C. P. Moss
Rice A. Pierce
R. M. Prichard
Mrs. R. E. Ross

NINTH DISTRICT

Joseph Henkel
Mrs. Merrill P. Hudson
Mrs. Andrew H. Lawo
Courtney Lewis
R. G. Morrow
C. D. Smith
Roane Waring

The names of the foregoing Delegates having been called, each were present and, respectively, answered to his or her name, except the following, to-wit:

John K. Shields, of the First District.
Mrs. Thos. P. Miller, of the Second District.
William Turnblazer, of the Second District.
Malcolm C. Hill, of the Third District.
Mrs. Guilford Dudley, of the Fifth District.
William J. Towler, of the Sixth District.
Flake Humphrey, of the Seventh District.
J. R. Rison, Jr., of the Seventh District.
Courtney Lewis, of the Ninth District.
C. D. Smith, of the Ninth District.

2. The fact appearing, from the foregoing, that there was present a quorum of the Delegates elected to said Convention, there was duly administered to each of the Delegates constituting said quorum an oath by Honorable Arthur Crownover, Judge of the Court of Appeals of Tennessee, to faithfully perform the duties of his or her office as such Delegate; and, thereupon, the said quorum of Delegates so assembled proceeded with organizing said convention by electing, from their number, a President of the Convention, with the following result, to-wit:

Delegate Thos. Harris nominated Delegate E. L. McNeilly, Sr., as President of the Convention and there being no other nominations, upon motion made by Delegate Ray Stuart and seconded by Delegate Henry E. Colton and unanimously adopted, the nominations were closed and Delegate E. L. McNeilly, Sr., was, by acclamation elected President of the Convention.

Thereupon, E. L. McNeilly, Sr., accepted the office of President of the Convention and entered upon performing the duties thereof.

It was then moved and seconded and duly carried that the Convention proceed further by electing, from their number, a Secretary of the Convention, with the following result, to-wit:

Delegate Mrs. Andrew H. Lawo, of Memphis, nominated Delegate E. C. Anderson as Secretary of the Convention and there being no other nominations, upon motion made by Delegate Glen Nelson, seconded by Delegate Henry E. Colton and unanimously adopted, the nominations were closed and Delegate E. C. Anderson, by acclamation, was elected Secretary of the Convention.

E. C. Anderson was declared duly elected Secretary, accepted the office and entered upon performing the duties thereof.

Upon motion, duly made, seconded and passed, the President appointed the following as Sergeant-at-arms of the Convention, to-wit: C. C. Clark and W. M. Martin, Jr.

3. It was next resolved, upon motion of Wm. L. Frierson, seconded by Henry E. Colton, and adopted by the Convention, that, except when otherwise ordered upon motion, by a majority of the Convention all Resolutions presented to the Convention by any member thereof, be read to the Convention from the floor by such member and be considered immediately and passed upon by the Convention, as soon as reasonably practicable following a motion, by the member proposing any such Resolution or Resolutions, for an adoption thereof, without referring such Resolution or Resolutions, to a committee for a report to the Convention thereon.

4. It appearing to the satisfaction of the Convention that the following of the aforesaid duly elected Delegates to the Convention are not in attendance thereon because of disability and that the absence of each has created a vacancy in the office of each such Delegate, caused by the disability of such Delegate to attend the Convention, namely:

John K. Shields, of the First District.
Courtney Lewis, of the Ninth District.
C. D. Smith, of the Ninth District.

The following residents of the respective Congressional Districts, in which said absentee Delegates severally reside, were duly nominated and elected by the Convention to fill the said vacancies, to-wit:

George S. Barger, of the First District, in the place of John K. Shields; Bertrand W. Cohn, of the Ninth District, in the place of C. D. Smith and C. P. J. Mooney, of the Ninth District, in the place of Courtney Lewis.

Malcolm C. Hill, who was not present at the initial roll call, entered the Convention Hall and an oath of office, of similar nature to that administered to each of the Delegates, was thereupon administered by Honorable Arthur Crownover, Judge of the Court of Appeals of Tennessee, to said Delegate Malcolm C. Hill and to each of the aforesaid substituted Delegates, immediately following which the said Delegate Malcolm C. Hill and each of said substituted Delegates were admitted to the Convention as members thereof and seated as such.

5. Delegate John I. Cox, having been recognized by the President, presented the following resolution, which was read to the Convention by the Secretary, to-wit:

RESOLUTION

WHEREAS, The Seventy-second Congress of the United States of America, at the second session thereof, adopted for submission to the several states a Resolution proposing the following amendment to the Constitution of the United States, to-wit:

ARTICLE ___ ___

Section 1. The eighteenth article of amendment to the Constitution of the United States is hereby repealed.

Section 2. The transportation or importation into any state, Territory or possession of the United States for delivery or use therein of intoxicating liquors in violation of the laws thereof, is hereby prohibited.

Section 3. The Article shall be inoperative unless it shall have been ratified as an amendment to the constitution by Conventions in the several states, as provided in the Constitution, within seven years from the date of the submission hereof to the States by Congress.

And WHEREAS, by the express terms of the aforesaid Resolution of Congress, it is provided and declared, that the said proposed article, as an amendment to the constitution of the United States, "shall be valid to all intents and purposes as part of the constitution when ratified by conventions in three-fourths of the several states";

And WHEREAS, the aforesaid proposed Article of Amendment was transmitted to the State of Tennessee and duly received, during the regular session in the year of 1933 of the General Assembly of the State of Tennessee;

And WHEREAS, the said General Assembly, after being officially notified of the aforesaid Resolution of the Congress and the said proposed Article of Amendment embodied in said Resolution, enacted into law Chapter 38 of the Public Acts of the General Assembly of the State of Tennessee for the year 1933, entitled "AN ACT to provide for a Convention to pass on an Amendment to the Constitution of the United States, relating to the Repeal of the Eighteenth Article of Amendment to said Constitution, which has heretofore been proposed by the Congress for Ratification by Conventions in the several states";—which said Chapter 38 was duly passed by the General Assembly of Tennessee, on March 29th, 1933, and approved by the Governor of Tennessee on March 31st, 1933;

And WHEREAS, provision was made by the said Chapter 38 of the Public Acts of the General Assembly of Tennessee for the holding of a Convention in the State of Tennessee to pass on the aforesaid proposed Article amending the Constitution of the United States;

And WHEREAS, pursuant to the provisions of said Chapter 38 of the Public Acts of the General Assembly of Tennessee an election was duly and legally held, on the Third Thursday of July (namely, on July 20th), 1933, within and throughout the State of Tennessee for the purpose of electing sixty-three Delegates to constitute the aforesaid Convention in Tennessee; at which said election sixty-three such Delegates were duly and constitutionally elected;

And WHEREAS, pursuant to the provisions of the said Chapter 38 of the Public Acts of the General Assembly of Tennessee, more than a quorum of the sixty-three Delegates elected to the said Convention has assembled and convened in the Chamber of the House of Representatives at the Capitol at Nashville, Tennessee, at 10 o'clock, A.M., on the eleventh day of August, 1933, and are now (namely, on said August 11th) in Convention assembled, having duly organized and having elected E. L. McNeilly, Sr., President and E. C. Anderson Secretary of said Convention, and having elected substitute Delegates as members of said Convention in the place of each of the Delegates regularly elected at the aforesaid election of July 20th, 1933, whose offices became vacant because of their disability;

Now, therefore, be it resolved, by the Delegates of, in and to the Convention in the State of Tennessee, in Convention assembled in the House of Representatives at the Capitol in Nashville, Tennessee, on this eleventh day of August, 1933, as follows, to-wit:

1. That the aforesaid Article proposed by the Congress, amending the constitution of the United States, be and the same is hereby ratified, by the State of Tennessee and the people of said State acting by and through their Delegates constituting this Convention and lawfully authorized to pass upon said proposed Article of Amendment for and on behalf of the State of Tennessee.

2. That, in accordance with Section 10 of the aforesaid Chapter 38 of the Public Acts of the General Assembly of Tennessee, the President and Secretary of this Convention forthwith execute and transmit a certificate of this Resolution, to the Secretary of State of Tennessee, for transmission by the said Secretary of State, under the Great Seal of the State of Tennessee, to the Secretary of State of the United States of America.

The proponent of the foregoing Resolution, Delegate John I. Cox, moved the adoption of the said Resolution.

The motion for adoption was seconded by the following Delegates to-wit, Rice A. Pierce and Ray Stuart.

The motion for adoption of the Resolution, having been duly seconded and considered by the Convention and the President of the Convention having ordered a vote of the Convention thereon a vote was accordingly taken, upon a roll call of the Delegates, with the following result, to-wit:

DELEGATES	HOW VOTING	DELEGATES	HOW VOTING	DELEGATES	HOW VOTING
E. C. Anderson	Aye	Joseph Henkel	Aye	E. L. McNeilly, Sr.	Aye
Charles H. Bacon	Aye	Malcolm C. Hill	Aye	Glen Nelson	Aye
W. E. Bratton	Aye	Mrs. Merrill P. Hudson	Aye	E. C. Norvell	Aye
Geo. M. Brooks	Aye	Flake Humphrey	Aye	Roy H. Parkes	Aye
Hamilton S. Burnett	Aye	Mrs. Bruce Keener, Jr.	Aye	Rice A. Pierce	Aye
W. E. Cheek	Aye	J. R. Ketron	Aye	R. M. Prichard	Aye
Hal H. Clements	Aye	Mrs. Richard H. Kimball	Aye	W. P. Rains	Aye
Henry E. Colton	Aye	John R. King	Aye	Mrs. R. E. Ross	Aye
W. P. Cooper	Aye	Paul J. Kruesi	Aye	Mrs. R. M. Kirby-Smith	Aye
John I. Cox	Aye	Mrs. Andrew H. Lawo	Aye	B. M. Smoot	Aye
R. H. Crockett	Aye	W. M. Lowery	Aye	T. W. Stevens	Aye
M. W. Darden	Aye	Fred Lowery	Aye	Ray Stuart	Aye
J. E. DeFord	Aye	R. G. Morrow	Aye	Mrs. Frank B. St. John	Aye
A. O. Denning	Aye	C. P. Moss	Aye	John Toomey	Aye
J. B. Dow	Aye	R. M. Murray	Aye	Roane Waring	Aye
Josiah Fort	Aye	J. P. Murff	Aye	Geo. L. Wortham	Aye
Wm. L. Frierson	Aye	J. L. McCawley	Aye	George S. Barger	Aye
W. T. Gerhardt	Aye	Chas. C. McMurry	Aye	Bertrand W. Cohn	Aye
Thos. Harris	Aye			C. P. J. Mooney	Aye
John Heilman	Aye				
Mrs. Lizzie Lee Miller Henderson	Aye				

6. Upon motion made by Delegate Hal H. Clements, duly seconded by Delegate Henry E. Colton, and adopted by the Convention, it was ordered that the President and Secretary of the Convention certify, to the Secretary of State of Tennessee, for preservation in the archives of Tennessee, a copy hereof, as being a full, true and perfect journal of the proceedings of the Convention and to take any and all necessary steps to officially bring the action of the Convention to the attention of the necessary authorities.

7. The business for which the Convention was called having been transacted, and there being no other or further business before or to come before the Convention, the Convention, upon motion, duly seconded and adopted,

Adjourned *sine die,* on this August 11th, 1933.

Certified to the Secretary of State of Tennessee.

E. L. McNeilly, Sr.
President
E. C. Anderson
Secretary

TEXAS*

THE STATE OF TEXAS
SENATE CHAMBER
OF THE
LEGISLATURE
IN THE
CAPITOL BUILDING
IN THE
CITY OF AUSTIN

NOVEMBER 24TH, A.D., 1933

JOURNAL OF THE CONVENTION

10 O'CLOCK A.M.

Pursuant to an Act of the Legislature of the State of Texas entitled "An Act providing for conventions to pass on amendments to the Constitution of the United States," approved and becoming effective on the 16th day of May, 1933, the delegates elect to the convention, called for the purpose of ratifying or of refusing to ratify the Twenty-first Article of Amendment to the Constitution of the United States of America, were called to order by the Honorable W. W. Heath, Secretary of State of the State of Texas in the Senate Chamber of the Legislature in the Capitol Building in the City of Austin at the hour of 10 A.M., November 24th, A.D., 1933.

The Secretary of State explained to those gathered that only those who had been duly elected at an election held in the State of Texas on the 26th day of August, 1933, in pursuance to the above mentioned Act as delegates to the convention could take part in the proceedings, providing, however, that in case where a delegate failed to appear from death, sickness or other cause, that the alternate elected in his place should act in his stead. The Secretary of State then read a formal certificate issued by him and called the roll of those elected as delegates and alternates to the convention, the certificate of the Secretary of State as read to the convention being in words and figures as follows:

THE STATE OF TEXAS }
DEPARTMENT OF STATE }

I, W. W. Heath, Secretary of State of the State of Texas, duly qualified and acting as such, do hereby certify that the following is a true and correct list of all persons elected at an election held in the State of Texas on the 26th day of August, 1933, as delegates and alternates to a convention to be held in the City of Austin,

* From a photostat of the typewritten original. The act providing for the convention is omitted here.

Texas, on the ninetieth day after the said 26th day of August, 1933, which convention was called for the purpose of ratifying or refusing to ratify the proposed Twenty-first Article of Amendment to the Constitution of the United States of America, which proposed Article of Amendment is in words and figures as follows:

ARTICLE ___ ___

Section 1. The Eighteenth Article of Amendment to the Constitution of the United States is hereby repealed.

Section 2. The transportation or importation into any State, Territory or possession of the United States for delivery or use therein of intoxicating liquor, in violation of the laws thereof, is hereby prohibited.

Section 3. This article shall be inoperative unless it shall have been ratified as an amendment to the Constitution, within seven years from the date of the submission thereof to the States by the Congress.

The said election and convention were called pursuant to the provisions of an Act passed by the Forty-third Legislature of Texas at its regular session, and approved by the Governor of Texas.

DELEGATES

Name	*Senatorial District*	*Address*
Ward, J. A.	1	Mt. Pleasant
Foster, Tom E.	2	Kilgore
Mosley, E. M.	3	Rusk
Pickett, E. B.	4	Liberty
Barnes, L. A.	5	Huntsville
Cone, Adam	6	Palestine
Flynt, Alvin C. (Deceased)	7	Tyler
Munn, Paul	8	Sulphur Springs
Lipscomb, R. T.	9	Bonham
McMahon, B. M.	10	Greenville
Hughes, Maury	11	Dallas
Underwood, E. T.	12	Itasca
McDonnell, A. V.	13	Waco
Giddings, D. C. (Deceased)	14	Brenham
Sulak, John L.	15	La Grange
Kirby, John Henry	16	Houston
Hancock, R. H.	17	El Campo
Hartman, A. C.	18	Cuero
Coopwood, E. B.	19	Lockhart
Loving, Mrs. Jas. M.	20	Austin
Denison, F. L.	21	Temple
Pickett, Gus	22	Decatur
Harris, Harvey	23	Wichita Falls
McCarty, Milburn	24	Eastland
Baker, J. K.	25	Coleman
Boyle, John	26	San Antonio
Miller, Roy	27	Corpus Christi
Davis, W. D.	28	Fort Worth
Culwell, A. H.	29	El Paso
Robertson, E. H.	30	Lubbock
Simpson, E. A.	31	Amarillo

ALTERNATES

Name	*Senatorial District*	*Address*
McCartney, W. A., Sr.	1	Texarkana
Gray, John C.	2	Henderson
Kurth, Joe H.	3	Keltys
McFarland, A. C.	4	Orange
Bray, A. G.	5	Lovelady
Curington, John	6	Corsicana
Gentry, Nat, Sr.	7	Tyler
Pollard, W. J.	8	Paris
Reed, R. S.	9	Denison
Rosenberg, Leon	10	Greenville
Lancaster, John L.	11	Dallas
Chrisman, O. O.	12	Cleburne
Bartlett, Tom	13	Marlin
Hilliard, W. M.	14	Caldwell
Machamehl, L. A.	15	Bellville
Fisher, Lewis	16	Houston
Dew, Henry	17	De Walts
Smith, R. R.	18	Jourdanton
Dunning, W. T.	19	Gonzales
Burleson, A. S.	20	Austin
Bailey, Ralph	21	Gatesville
Harmonson, John	22	Justin
Stephens, J. A.	23	Benjamin
McCarty, Richard	24	Albany
Reiley, E. H.	25	Fredericksburg
Terrell, Dick O. (Deceased)	26	San Antonio
Martin, Mrs. R. F.	27	Crystal City
Walker, C. E.	28	Grapevine
Burell, L. W.	29	Hondo
Rogers, C. P.	30	Big Springs
Peck, Mrs. Josie Fay	31	Amarillo

In testimony whereof, I have hereunto signed my name officially and caused the Seal of State to be impressed hereon at Austin, this 18th day of November A.D., 1933.

(*Signed*) W. W. HEATH
Secretary of State

Following the call of the roll by the Secretary of State, the following delegates answered "Present":

Name	*Senatorial District*	*Address*
Foster, Tom E.	2	Kilgore
Mosley, E. M.	3	Rusk
Cone, Adam	6	Palestine
McMahon, B. M.	10	Greenville
Hughes, Maury	11	Dallas
Underwood, E. T.	12	Itasca
McDonnell, A. V.	13	Waco
Sulak, John L.	15	La Grange
Kirby, John Henry	16	Houston

Name	*Senatorial District*	*Address*
Hancock, R. H.	17	El Campo
Hartman, A. C.	18	Cuero
Coopwood, E. B.	19	Lockhart
Loving, Mrs. Jas. M.	20	Austin
Denison, F. L.	21	Temple
Pickett, Gus	22	Decatur
Harris, Harvey	23	Wichita Falls
Baker, J. K.	25	Coleman
Boyle, John	26	San Antonio
Miller, Roy	27	Corpus Christi
Davis, W. D.	28	Fort Worth
Culwell, A. H.	29	El Paso

The delegates elected from the 1st, 4th, 5th, 7th, 8th, 9th, 14th, 21st, 24th, 30th and 31st Senatorial Districts of Texas failed to answer roll call and were recorded as being absent. Whereupon the roll call was sounded by the Secretary of State for the alternate delegates elected from the above numbered Senatorial Districts, to which roll call, alternate delegates from five Senatorial Districts, to-wit: 4th, 7th, 8th, 9th and 30th answered "Present," and were substituted as delegates in the convention in the place and stead of the persons elected as delegates to the convention from the above numbered Senatorial Districts. The names of the persons so elected as alternate delegates and seated as delegates in the convention are as follows:

Name	*Senatorial District*	*Address*
McFarland, A. C.	4th	Orange
Gentry, Nat, Sr.	7th	Tyler
Pollard, W. J.	8th	Paris
Reed, R. S.	9th	Denison
Rogers, C. P.	30th	Big Springs

After the call of roll had been completed, the Secretary of State announced that the convention should proceed to the election of its temporary officials, and the Secretary of State acted as chairman for said purpose. The Honorable Roy Miller, delegate from the 27th Senatorial District, placed in nomination for the position of temporary chairman, the name of the Honorable John Henry Kirby of the city of Houston, Texas, delegate elected from the 16th Senatorial District. This nomination was then duly seconded by the Honorable Maury Hughes of Dallas, Texas, delegate from the 11th Senatorial District. The chairman asked for other nominations, and there being none, placed the name of John Henry Kirby before the convention as temporary chairman, and in response thereto, the convention voted unanimously to elect John Henry Kirby temporary chairman of the convention.

The Secretary of State appointed Honorable Maury Hughes, Honorable Roy Miller and Honorable John Boyle as a committee to wait upon the newly elected temporary chairman and escort him to the platform. The committee responded by escorting Judge Kirby to the platform and presented him to the Secretary of State. Thereupon the Secretary of State presented him, the Honorable John Henry Kirby, of Houston, Texas, to the convention as its temporary chairman.

The chair announced that nominations would be in order for a temporary secretary of the convention. Whereupon, Honorable Roy Miller nominated Mrs. Jas. M.

Loving of Austin, Texas, delegate from the 20th Senatorial District, which nomination was dully seconded by Honorable Maury Hughes of Dallas, Texas. The chair asked for other nominations, and there being none, submitted the name of Mrs. Jas. M. Loving to the convention. Whereupon a vote being taken, Mrs. Loving was unanimously elected temporary secretary of the convention.

The chair then appointed Honorable Roy Miller as a committee of one to escort the newly elected temporary secretary to take her seat upon the platform. Mr. Miller then presented Mrs. Loving to the chair, and the chair in turn presented her to the convention as its temporary secretary. Upon being presented to the convention, Mrs. Loving made the fact known that she greatly appreciated the honor of being the only woman in the State of Texas elected as a delegate to the convention called for the purpose of repealing the Eighteenth Amendment to the Constitution of the United States of America. Mrs. Loving then took her place as temporary secretary.

Motion was made by Honorable Roy Miller of Corpus Christi that a committee on Credentials, consisting of three be appointed by the chair. The motion being duly seconded by Honorable John Boyle of San Antonio, the chair submitted the same to the convention, which voted unanimously in favor of the motion.

The chairman announced the result of the vote on the motion and then proceeded to appoint the committee on Credentials as follows: Honorable Roy Miller, Honorable Adam Cone and Honorable Tom Foster. The committee on Credentials made the following report in words and figures as follows:

To the Honorable John Henry Kirby, Temporary Chairman of the Convention Meeting for the purpose of ratifying or refusing to ratify the Twenty-first Amendment to the Constitution of the United States of America:

We, your committee on Credentials beg to report that we have examined the credentials of all delegates and alternates present and presented to us, and find that the following delegates and alternates have proper credentials and are entitled to participate in this convention.

The alternates named are the alternates of delegates from their respective Senatorial Districts who are absent:

Delegate	*Senatorial District*	*Alternates*
Foster, Tom E.	2	
Mosley, E. M.	3	
	4	McFarland, A. C.
Cone, Adam	6	
	7	Gentry, Nat, Sr.
	8	Pollard, W. J.
	9	Reed, R. S.
McMahon, B. M.	10	
Hughes, Maury	11	
Underwood, E. T.	12	
McDonnell, A. V.	13	
Sulak, John L.	15	
Kirby, John Henry	16	
Hancock, R. H.	17	
Hartman, A. C.	18	
Coopwood, E. B.	19	
Loving, Mrs. Jas. M.	20	
Pickett, Gus	22	

Delegate	*Senatorial District*	*Alternates*
Harris, Harvey	23	
Baker, J. K.	25	
Boyle, John	26	
Miller, Roy	27	
Davis, W. D.	28	
Culwell, A. H.	29	
	30	Rogers, C. P.

We have also examined the credentials of the following alternates and find that same are correct and in proper form, but that on account of the presence of their delegates, they are not entitled to participate in this convention:

Alternates	*Senatorial District*
Rosenberg, Leon	10th
Chrisman, O. O.	12th
Bartlett, Tom	13th
Machamehl, L. A.	15th
Smith, R. R.	18th
Dunning, W. T.	19th
Harmonson, John	22nd
Martin, Mrs. R. F.	27th

Respectfully submitted,
(*Signed*)

ROY MILLER
ADAM CONE
TOM E. FOSTER

The report of the committee upon motion of Honorable Roy Miller was unanimously adopted by the convention.

The temporary chairman then appointed as Sergeant-at-Arms of the convention, the Honorable George Slater.

The Honorable Roy Miller of Corpus Christi moved that the temporary officers of the convention be made the permanent officers of the convention. The motion being duly seconded by the Honorable Maury Hughes of Dallas, the question was submitted by the Honorable W. W. Heath, Secretary of State, acting in the place and stead of the temporary chairman. Whereupon the motion was voted upon by the convention and unanimously adopted.

The Honorable John Boyle of San Antonio moved that the chair appoint a committee on Resolutions, composed of five members. The motion was duly seconded by Honorable Maury Hughes of Dallas. The question was submitted by the chair to the convention, which voted unanimously in favor of the adoption of the motion.

The chairman then appointed the following delegates as members of the committee on Resolutions: Honorable Maury Hughes of Dallas, Honorable Roy Miller of Corpus Christi, Honorable John Boyle of San Antonio, Honorable W. D. Davis of Fort Worth and Honorable A. H. Culwell of El Paso.

The committee upon Resolutions then reported in words and figures as follows:

The Committee on Resolutions respectfully reports it has prepared a resolution which expresses the mandate and will of the people of the Sovereign State of Texas.

Resolution No. 1: *Resolved* by this convention assembled pursuant to the authority of an Act of the Legislature of the State of Texas, entitled an Act providing for conventions to pass on amendments to the Constitution of the United States, approved May 16, 1933, and effective May 16, 1933, that the Twenty-first Amendment to the Constitution of the United States of America, proposed by the Seventy-second Congress, as follows:

Section 1. The Eighteenth Article of Amendment to the Constitution of the United States is hereby repealed.

Section 2. The transportation and importation into any State, Territory or possession of the United States for delivery or use therein of intoxicating liquor, in violation of the laws thereof, is hereby prohibited.

Section 3. This article shall be inoperative unless it shall have been ratified as an amendment to the Constitution by conventions in the several states, as provided in the Constitution, within seven years from the date of the submission thereof to the states by the Congress.

The Honorable Roy Miller of Corpus Christi then moved that the roll call of all qualified delegates to the convention be again sounded for the purpose of permitting each individual delegate to cast a recorded vote on said Resolution No. 1. This motion was duly seconded by the Honorable John Boyle of San Antonio. The question was presented to the convention by the chairman, and was carried unanimously. The call of roll of all persons qualified to sit as delegates in the convention was then made by the Secretary. Whereupon each and every delegate qualified to sit in said convention voted in favor of the adoption of Resolution No. 1 following the call of his or her respective name. The names and Senatorial Districts of the persons voting in favor of said Resolution No. 1 are as follows:

Name	*Senatorial District*	*Name*	*Senatorial District*	*Name*	*Senatorial District*	*Name*	*Senatorial District*
Foster, Tom E.	2nd	McMahon, B. M.	10th	Kirby, John Henry	16th	Pickett, Gus	22nd
Mosley, E. M.	3rd	Hughes, Maury	11th	Hancock, R. H.	17th	Harris, Harvey	23rd
Cone, Adam	4th	Underwood, E. T.	12th	Hartman, A. C.	18th	Baker, J. K.	25th
McFarland, A. C.	6th	McDonnell, A. V.	13th	Coopwood, E. B.	19th	Boyle, John	26th
Gentry, Nat, Sr.	7th	Sulak, John L.	15th	Loving, Mrs. Jas. M.	20th	Miller, Roy	27th
Pollard, W. J.	8th					Davis, W. D.	28th
Reed, R. S.	9th					Culwell, A. H.	29th
						Rogers, C. P.	30th

The chairman of the convention then announced that twenty-five delegates had voted in favor of the adoption by the convention of Resolution No. 1, which embodied the ratification by the Sovereign State of Texas of the Twenty-first Article of Amendment to the Constitution of the United States of America, and that no delegate had voted against the adoption of said Resolution.

The Honorable Roy Miller of Corpus Christi then announced that the Honorable Maury Hughes of Dallas present another Resolution in behalf of the committee on Resolutions to the convention. The Honorable Maury Hughes of Dallas then presented in behalf of the Committee on Resolutions Resolution No. 2 in words and figures as follows:

Resolution No. 2: WHEREAS, This convention here assembled missing from its ranks Honorable D. C. Giddings of Brenham, Honorable Dick O. Terrell of San Antonio, and Honorable Alvin C. Flynt of Mineola, who were on the 26th day of August, last, elected to cast a vote of their people on the momentous question now confronting this convention; and,

WHEREAS, These men in their lives and in their relations with their fellowmen, and by their honorable and upright lives, and as Democrats loyal to their party were instrumental in bringing about the achievement of our higher purposes; and,

WHEREAS, This convention desires to render homage to them and their memory, and that it extend its sympathy to their bereaved families:

Now, therefore, be it resolved by this convention assembled that it deplore the untimely passing of their comrades and as a token of our admiration for them and their lives, that a copy of this resolution be spread upon the minutes of this convention, copies be delivered to the press and forwarded to their respective families, and that when this convention adjourns today that it do so in their memory.

Mr. Hughes then made a motion that the Resolution be adopted. The motion was seconded by the Honorable C. P. Rogers of Big Springs. The question of the adoption of the motion was presented by the chairman to the convention, and was adopted unanimously by a standing vote.

The chairman of the convention then announced that Resolution No. 2 had been unanimously adopted and made a part of the proceedings of the convention.

Honorable Maury Hughes made a motion that the convention adjourn *sine die.* The question being presented by the chair, the motion was adopted unanimously.

Attest:

(*Signed*) MRS. JAS. M. LOVING
Secretary of the Convention

We, the undersigned, John Henry Kirby, Chairman, and Mrs. Jas. M. Loving, Secretary of the Convention, do hereby certify that we have examined the above and foregoing record and minutes of the proceedings of said Convention and we and each of us certify that the said record and minutes are a true and correct report of the proceedings of said Convention.

(*Signed*) JNO. H. KIRBY
Chairman
MRS. JAS. M. LOVING
Secretary

UTAH*

Salt Lake City, Utah

STATE CAPITOL

Tuesday, December 5, 1933

12:00 O'clock Noon

Proceedings of

CONSTITUTIONAL CONVENTION

Ratifying the 21st Amendment to the

Constitution of the United States

Governor Henry H. Blood: The Convention will be in order.

Ladies and gentlemen of the Convention, you are assembled here today for the purpose of putting into effect the mandate of the people of the State of Utah, who on November 7th voted for the 21st Amendment to the Federal Constitution.

What is the pleasure of the Convention?

Mr. Franklin Riter: Mr. President.

Governor Blood: Mr. Riter.

Mr. Riter: I move you that Mr. Edward M. Garnett be appointed official reporter of this Convention, and that the oath be administered by the Chief Justice of the Supreme Court of Utah.

Delegate George S. Ballif: I second the motion.

Governor Blood: The motion is seconded. The motion is that Mr. E. M. Garnett be appointed official reporter of this Convention. Those in favor of the motion will say "aye." (Contrary, "no.")

The "ayes" have it. Mr. Garnett is appointed official reporter, and the oath will be administered by Chief Justice Straup.

Chief Justice Straup: You do solemnly swear that you will support, obey and defend the Constitution of the United States and the Constitution of this state, and that you will discharge the duties of the office of official reporter of this convention to the best of your ability, and with fidelity?

Mr. Garnett: I do.

Governor Blood: If you will all rise, I shall call upon Dr. Elmer I. Goshen, Pastor of the First Congregational Church of Salt Lake City, to offer the invocation.

Dr. Goshen: Almighty God, surrounded by the wonders of Thy works and the glories of Thy universe, of which we have been made a part, may we have grateful hearts, a reverent attitude and understanding minds as representatives of a sovereign state engaged in the protection of our sister states.

May we come with determination to perform loyally, without fear, the duty that is before us.

---

* Printed.

May we have an opportunity fearlessly and courageously to protect our state and the sisterhood of states in a return to lawfulness, in a departure from lawlessness, in a return to temperance under the law, and away from debauchery outside the law.

May our officials be fearless and courageous in the administration of their duties. Because of their actions and their determinations may this state become better and cleaner. May law come into full and commanding respect and may our children and their children's children look back to this period and to what is done here as a step towards the permanence and the integrity of our great society.

May Thy blessing and Thy goodness rest upon us, upon all the peoples of the earth, upon all sects and creeds and beliefs and faiths, and upon all who profess no faith at all, remembering the eternal Fatherhood of Thy goodness and the eternal brotherhood of our responsibilities. Amen.

GOVERNOR BLOOD: Convention members, I have the honor to appoint as temporary secretary of the Convention Mrs. Paul Keyser, of Salt Lake City.

Will Mr. Olson conduct Mrs. Keyser to her position at the front? (Mrs. Keyser is conducted to the Secretary's desk.)

Honorable Milton H. Welling, Secretary of State, will now present the official certificates of election of the delegates to this convention.

SECRETARY OF STATE MILTON H. WELLING: Your Excellency, members of the Convention:

It is my duty as Secretary of State to transmit to the Convention the following certificates of election to a Constitutional Convention to consider an Article of Amendment to the Constitution of the United States of America, as representing the people of the State of Utah. (Reads.)

THE OFFICE OF THE SECRETARY OF STATE:

WHEREAS, The Seventy-second Congress of the United States of America, at the second session, proposed the following amendment to the Constitution of the United States:

Section One. The Eighteenth Article of Amendment to the Constitution of the United States is hereby repealed.

Section Two. The transportation or importation into any state, territory or possession of the United States for delivery or use therein of intoxicating liquors, in violation of the laws thereof, is hereby prohibited.

Section Three. This Article shall be inoperative unless it shall have been ratified as an amendment to the Constitution by conventions in the several states, as provided in the Constitution, within seven years from the date of the submission hereof to the states by the Congress; and

WHEREAS Chapter 22, Laws of Utah 1933, provided for the election of twenty-one delegates nominated by petition, to attend a Constitutional Convention to be held at Salt Lake City, December 5, 1933, to ratify or reject the above-proposed Amendment to the Constitution of the United States, and provided further for the holding of an election on the proclamation of the Governor of the State of Utah; and

WHEREAS, On October 10, 1933, Governor Henry H. Blood proclaimed said election to be held November 7, 1933; and

WHEREAS, Nominating petitions containing the required number of names were filed with the Secretary of State for twenty-one delegates to the aforesaid Constitutional Convention for ratification of the proposed Amendment to the Constitution of the United States; and

That nominating petitions containing the required number of names were filed with the Secretary of State for twenty-one delegates to the aforesaid Constitutional Convention against ratification of the proposed Amendment to the Constitution of the United States; and

WHEREAS, Pursuant to law, an election was held November 7, 1933, to determine the names of delegates to the aforesaid Constitutional Convention; and

WHEREAS, The Board of State Canvassers, meeting according to law in the office of the Secretary of State, at noon, November 27, 1933, did canvass the returns of the aforesaid election, and by their computation did find that the twenty-one delegates for ratification of the proposed Amendment to the Constitution of the United States, received a greater number of votes than the twenty-one delegates against ratification of the proposed Amendment to the Constitution of the United States:

Now, therefore, I, Milton H. Welling, Secretary of State of the State of Utah, certify that the following twenty-one delegates, pledged to vote for ratification of the proposed Amendment to the Constitution of the United States, each received the number of votes placed opposite his or her name, they are hereby declared to be the duly elected delegates to a Constitutional Convention which by law is called to convene at twelve o'clock, noon, Tuesday, December 5, 1933, at the Capitol in Salt Lake City, to ratify, as representing the people of the State of Utah, the proposed Amendment to the Constitution of the United States.

The names of these elected delegates are:

Glen O. Allred
George S. Ballif
Clarence Bamberger
John O. Beesley
Ephraim Bergeson
Sophus Bertelson
A. S. Brown
Lawrence Clayton
T. Earl Clements
Miah Day
A. C. Ellis, Jr.
Mat Gilmour
L. B. Hampton
Franklin Hansen
Mrs. John A. Hendricks
L. A. Hollenbeck
Mrs. L. B. McCornick
R. L. Olson
Mrs. S. Grover Rich
Franklin Riter
Sam D. Thurman

In witness whereof I have set my hand and affixed the Great Seal of the State of Utah, in Salt Lake City, this 28th day of November, A.D. 1933.

MILTON H. WELLING
Secretary of State

MR. WELLING: Governor Blood, I have the honor to file this certificate, which has already been presented personally to each of the twenty-one delegates to this Convention, with the secretary of the Convention.

GOVERNOR BLOOD: Thank you, Mr. Welling.

We shall now have roll call of the delegates to the Convention, by Honorable Milton H. Welling.

Thereupon, the roll was called. All delegates answered present, except Mrs. S. Grover Rich.

Mr. Welling: Governor Blood, twenty delegates have responded to their names. A quorum of the Convention is present.

Governor Blood: A vacancy in the list of delegates is observed, in that Mrs. S. Grover Rich did not respond to her name, the reason being that she is at present in Washington, D. C.

Delegate McCornick: Mr. President, I move that Mrs. Paul Keyser of Salt Lake City be designated and elected as delegate to this Convention in lieu of Mrs. S. Grover Rich, absent and unable to be present.

Delegate Hendricks: I second the motion.

Governor Blood: The motion is that Mrs. Paul Keyser be declared by the delegates of this Convention as a member of the Convention in place of Mrs. S. Grover Rich.

Those in favor of the motion will say "aye."

Contrary, "no." Motion unanimously carried.

Mrs. Paul Keyser is elected a delegate to this Convention.

Chief Justice Straup will administer the oath of office to the delegates of the Convention.

(The delegates stood.)

Chief Justice Straup: Raise your right hands.

You, and each of you, do solemnly swear that you will support, obey and defend the Constitution of the United States, and the Constitution of this state, and that you will discharge the duties of the office of delegate to the Convention to consider and act upon the ratification of the proposed Twenty-first Article of Amendment to the Constitution of the United States, to the best of your ability and with fidelity. So say you all.

Delegates: We do.

Chief Justice Straup: Be seated.

Governor Blood: We shall now proceed to the election of a president, a vice-president, and a secretary of the Convention.

Delegate A. C. Ellis, Jr.: I move you, sir, that the officers of this Convention be designated as a president, vice-president and a secretary, and that they shall be elected by an aye-and-nay vote, the nominee for such office receiving the highest vote shall be declared elected.

Delegate L. B. Hampton: Mr. Chairman, I second the motion.

Governor Blood: You have heard the motion that a president, vice-president and secretary be nominated and be voted upon by aye-and-nay votes. Are you ready for the question?

Those in favor of the motion will say "aye."

Contrary?

The "ayes" have it.

Delegate Lawrence Clayton: I desire to place in nomination for president of the Convention a man whom I believe is entitled to the honor, and who can fill it with ability and distinction; a man who was active in the initial stages, the middle stages and the final stages of the repeal campaign in this state, and who eventually became campaign director of the state for the allied forces of repeal.

I place in nomination for the president of this Convention, Mr. Ray L. Olson, of Ogden.

Governor Blood: Are there other nominations for president?

Delegate Keyser: I second the nomination.

Governor Blood: The nomination is seconded by Mrs. Keyser.

Any further nominations?

Delegate A. S. Brown: I move that the nominations be closed, and that the unanimous vote of the Convention be cast for Mr. Olson for president.

Governor Blood: The motion of Mr. Brown is before you. Any second?

Delegate George S. Ballif: Second the motion.

Governor Blood: Mr. Brown's motion is that the nominations close; that the nomination of Mr. Ray L. Olson for President be placed before the house and that the unanimous vote of the house be given in favor of Mr. Ray L. Olson. This will carry with it the election.

Those in favor of the motion will say "aye."

Contrary, if there are any.

The "ayes" have it. Mr. Olson is unanimously elected.

Will Mr. Olson please come to the front. The Chief Justice will administer the oath of office to Mr. Olson.

Chief Justice Straup: You do solemnly swear that you will support, obey and defend the Constitution of the United States, and the Constitution of Utah, and that you will discharge the duties of your office as president of this Convention, to which you have been just elected, to the best of your ability, and with fidelity?

Mr. Olson: I do.

Governor Blood: I now call for nominations for vice-president.

Delegate Franklin Riter: Mr. President, one of the pioneers in the movement for the emasculation of the Eighteenth Amendment from the organic law; one of the indefatigable workers in the cause, one who is worthy of the trust and the honor, I nominate for vice-president, Mr. Clarence Bamberger of Salt Lake City.

Delegate A. S. Brown: Mr. President, I wish to second the nomination of Mr. Bamberger. If activity in bringing about this Convention here today were to have its reward, Mr. Bamberger might well aspire to be president, vice-president, secretary and treasurer. I second the nomination.

Delegate Franklin Riter: Mr. President, I move that nominations close and the secretary of this Convention be directed to cast the unanimous vote of the delegates for Mr. Bamberger for the office of vice-president.

Delegate Lawrence Clayton: I second that motion.

Governor Blood: The motion is that nominations close and that the secretary of this Convention be authorized and instructed to cast the entire vote of the delegates for Mr. Clarence Bamberger as vice-president of the Convention.

Those in favor of the motion will say "aye."

Contrary, if there are any.

The "ayes" have it. Mr. Bamberger is unanimously elected vice-president.

Mr. Bamberger, will you please come forward and be sworn.

Chief Justice Straup: You do solemnly swear to support, obey and defend the Constitution of the United States, and the Constitution of this state, and that you will discharge the duties of your office as vice-president of this Convention to the best of your ability, and with fidelity?

Mr. Bamberger: I do.

Governor Blood: Nominations are in order for secretary of the Convention.

DELEGATE GEORGE S. BALLIF: Mr. President, the women of the State of Utah played no small part in the fight for repeal.

I have the honor to name as a candidate for the secretary of this Convention a leader among the women of this state in that fight, a woman who combines charm and dignity with a fearless and courageous leadership.

It is my pleasure to nominate Mrs. Paul Keyser of Salt Lake City as the secretary of this Convention.

GOVERNOR BLOOD: Mrs. Paul Keyser is nominated.

DELEGATE HENDRICKS: I take pleasure in seconding the nomination of Mrs. Keyser.

GOVERNOR BLOOD: Mrs. Hendricks seconds the nomination.

DELEGATE GEORGE S. BALLIF: Mr. President, if no further nominations, I move that the rules be suspended and that the unanimous vote of this Convention be cast for Mrs. Paul Keyser for the office of secretary.

DELEGATE FRANKLIN RITER: Second the motion.

GOVERNOR BLOOD: The motion is that the rules be suspended and that the entire vote of the delegates to this Convention be cast for Mrs. Paul Keyser as secretary of the Convention.

Those in favor of the motion will say "aye."

Contrary, if there are any.

The "ayes" have it.

Mrs. Keyser, you are unanimously elected secretary. I congratulate you. The Chief Justice will administer the oath.

CHIEF JUSTICE STRAUP: You do solemnly swear to support, obey and defend the Constitution of the United States and the Constitution of this state, and that you will perform the duties of your office as secretary of this Convention to the best of your ability, and with fidelity?

MRS. KEYSER: I do.

GOVERNOR BLOOD: Ladies and gentlemen of the Convention, and assembled friends and citizens of the State of Utah:

It is now my pleasure to turn over the Convention from this point forward to my friend Ray L. Olson, whom you have honored by election as president of this Convention.

You have chosen a man who always puts things over when he undertakes them, a man of energy and courage and devotion to the cause he espouses.

Mr. Olson, I need not introduce you,—I present you to the Convention.

PRESIDENT RAY L. OLSON: Your Excellency, the Governor, fellow delegates, ladies and gentlemen of the State of Utah:

With the eyes of the nation fixed upon us, we meet to enact, for and in behalf of the people of this sovereign state, a formality which will alter our fundamental law. Our duty is mandatory and rather perfunctory, but from this experience we are impressed with the righteousness and sacredness of our republican form of government in which the functions of government are by and with the consent of the governed.

The simplicity of our proceedings will be rivalled only by the great significance of this occasion and the distinction it will bring to the State of Utah. When this historic Convention will have completed its business, the Twenty-first Amendment to the Constitution of the United States will be a part of our basic law. This amendment, as you know, repeals the Eighteenth Amendment, being therefore the first time in the nation's history that an amendment has been erased from the Constitution of the United States.

I deem it fitting that we indulge for a moment in retrospection and review our Constitutional history.

It was on September 17, 1787, that the Federal Constitutional Convention adopted a resolution to the effect that the Constitution, which the Convention had written, should be laid before the Congress and that Congress should submit the proposed Constitution to each state for ratification. It is important to note that the great statesmen who framed the Constitution specified that it should be ratified by conventions of the several states made up of delegates chosen by the people of each state for that specific purpose.

In compliance with this resolution, the Congress, on September 28, 1787, transmitted the Constitution to the states, each of which called conventions of delegates chosen by the people. Ratification followed quickly, in the following order:

Delaware	December 7, 1787
Pennsylvania	December 12, 1787
New Jersey	December 18, 1787
Georgia	January 2, 1788
Connecticut	January 9, 1788
Massachusetts	February 6, 1788
Maryland	April 28, 1788
South Carolina	May 23, 1788
New Hampshire	June 21, 1788
Virginia	June 26, 1788
New York	July 26, 1788

It is interesting to observe that Rhode Island and North Carolina at first failed to ratify. With the seeds of rebellion and nullification planted so early in its people we can perhaps understand why the North Carolinians of 1933 refused to ratify the Twenty-first Amendment.

The first ten amendments to the Constitution were ratified in 1791 by the state legislatures. These amendments are familiarly referred to as the Bill of Rights. The Eleventh Amendment, exempting states from suits by citizens, was ratified in 1798. The Twelfth Amendment, prescribing the manner of electing the President, and Vice-president, was ratified in 1804. The Thirteenth Amendment, abolishing slavery and involuntary servitude, in 1865. The Fourteenth Amendment, with various new issues in government, was adopted in 1868 and the Fifteenth Amendment, dealing with the right of suffrage, was ratified in 1870.

We then jump down to our own time. Two Constitutional Amendments, the Sixteenth and Seventeenth, relating to the Income Tax and the popular election of senators, were ratified in 1913.

Next came the now unlamented Eighteenth Amendment, which was ratified in 1920 by an overwhelming vote of the states, including Utah.

In the same year the Woman Suffrage amendment was ratified.

The Twentieth Amendment, eliminating the lame duck sessions of Congress and changing the date of inauguration of our President, was ratified this year.

From this historical resume we can readily see that the Constitution is a stable and secure document of government. It was created, piece by piece, by patriots possessing foresight and wisdom. Considering the countless millions who have submitted to its authority during several generations of changing conditions, the amendments to it have been exceedingly few. Your action today, therefore, is one of great moment and historical importance in the panorama of fleeting events of time. I am sure the delegates to this Convention share with me the pride which we may properly assume in bringing such a great honor to our beloved state and her splendid citizenry.

The Eighteenth Amendment to the Constitution ventured into an entirely new field in constitutional government. It was actually a prohibition against the manufacture and use of intoxicating liquors. Its sponsors were sanguine that this piece of constitutional legislation would solve an age-old problem while the then minority loudly protested that the new amendment denied a certain element of personal liberty. The Eighteenth Amendment from its inception precipitated controversy and open defiance on the part of individual citizens developed an indifference toward prohibition.

I do not believe that this Convention is in a facetious mood with respect to the failure of prohibition, but I am free to remind you that a President of the United States termed it an experiment and clothed the experiment with nobility. It was truly an experiment. And whether noble or otherwise, it failed. The principal reason for its failure was that sufficient public and private sentiment would not respect and observe this law.

The devastating results of prohibition are not confined to the use of, or abstinence from the use of, intoxicating liquors. The by-products of prohibition have shocked the sensibilities of our national life. We have observed crime become as powerful in a sense as the government itself. Nullification, graft, corruption, racketeering, debauchery, murder and gang rule have become terms synonymous with prohibition. It would be absurd to charge the Eighteenth Amendment with responsibility for all of them, but we have a right to assume that they took root in the fertile soil of lawlessness afforded by prohibition. The American people have, in no uncertain terms, repudiated their own action by repealing the Eighteenth Amendment. And I point again to the desirability and righteousness of our system of government, which permits alterations from time to time in our constitutions, national and state, to meet changing conditions.

During the political campaign which preceded our glorious victory on November 7th, our opponents, in their desperation for want of sound issues, sought to give the impression that the fight was one of liquor versus no liquor, or saloons against no saloons. That assumption, accepted by the credulous, was entirely wrong. Those of us who assumed leadership in the repeal movement repeat now that we were as earnestly in favor of temperance in the use of intoxicating beverages as our opponents. We have discovered that governmental restrictions failed to regulate, or in the least bit influence, the appetites of men, hence our energies were in the direction of better government.

Today, perhaps within this hour, the Eighteenth Amendment will be repealed, but repeal alone will not correct our many national and local ills attributed to prohibition. We must find new ways for encouraging temperance. We must adjust the economic and social conditions to meet the change.

But above and beyond all else there should be aroused a new conscientiousness of respect for law. We have observed a demoralization in the moral fibre of the nation with reference to law and order, allegedly due to the conscientious scruples of a large percentage of our people against observance of this one law—prohibition. A shocking indifference has developed among all classes of citizens to the functions of law and government, which attitude played its part in precipitating economic chaos. The example of an aroused electorate in abandoning the Eighteenth Amendment must be followed in relation to all unenforceable and improper laws. Character and honesty, patriotism and loyalty must go hand in hand with capacity and ability for service in the administration of the people's rights under the Constitution and sumptuary laws.

This, ladies and gentlemen of America, is Utah's admonition and suggestion in ratifying the Twenty-first Amendment.

DELEGATE FRANKLIN RITER: Mr. President.

PRESIDENT OLSON: The Chair recognizes Delegate Riter.

DELEGATE RITER: I have information by United Press from Columbus, Ohio, that the commonwealth of Ohio ratified the Twenty-first Amendment at 12:44 P.M., Eastern Standard Time, today.

PRESIDENT OLSON: Thank you, Mr. Riter. The Convention will receive that information.

PRESIDENT OLSON: It affords me great pleasure to introduce to this convention His Excellency, Henry H. Blood, Governor of the State of Utah.

GOVERNOR BLOOD: Mr. Chairman, ladies and gentlemen of the Convention, and friends assembled:

The eyes of the nation are at this moment turned towards Utah. This commonwealth, situated high in the mountains, far removed from the populous centers of the east, and distant also from the golden western coast of the country, is suddenly placed in a position where it will make history.

Upon you who are delegates to this Convention devolves the duty of representing the expressed sentiment of a very large majority of the people of this state.

Utah, the thirty-sixth state to complete its vote for ratification of the Twenty-first Amendment of the Federal Constitution, today is accorded the privilege and the solemn responsibility of taking final action officially removing from the Constitution the Prohibition Amendment.

The proceedings to this end are being taken in a legal, orderly and dignified manner, wholly befitting the signal importance and unusual character of the event. Never before has an amendment to the Federal Constitution been repealed, and never before has the Constitution been amended through the medium of state conventions.

Nothing that I possibly can say will add to the impressiveness of this occasion. The privilege has already been accorded to me to preside during the preliminary exercises leading to the final, complete organization of this Convention. It will not be expected, therefore, that I occupy now much of your time. May I, however, take occasion to review what has led up to the present moment?

The past year has been marked by a pronounced shift of popular sentiment, countrywide, on the liquor question. The change of thought has swept the nation, from the Atlantic to the Pacific; and whenever the people have been given the opportunity of expressing themselves, the result has been almost universally toward abolishment of Constitutional restrictions. Once before I have taken occasion to say that there has appeared an almost irresistible mass-movement of such potency and force that everything in opposition to it has been swept aside.

With full recognition of the right of the people to vote directly or through duly elected representatives on any public question, it was my privilege during the second special session of the legislature of 1933 to place before that body the liquor question for its consideration and action.

Careful preparation had been made in advance of the session by the drafting of bills to be presented to the Legislature. The Legislature in regular session already had provided for a vote on the ratification of the Twenty-first Amendment to the Federal Constitution. By proper enactment provision was made by the second special session for a vote on the repeal of the Prohibition Section of the State Constitution.

There was a general desire, in which I heartily concurred, that the two questions, that of federal and state repeal, should be placed before the people at a single election. This was in the interest of economy, and in accord, as I viewed it, with sound judgment. Under another Act, November 7, 1933, was designated as the date for holding a general election for the purpose of such vote.

These bills I proudly approved, and in due time proclamation was made calling the election in accordance with the enactments.

The vote in this state, as in other states, gave evidence that a very large majority of the people had quite definitely decided that the time had come when some method other than National Constitutional prohibition should be adopted as a means of controlling the liquor traffic. After the recording of the vote of this Convention today this state, and the country at large, will be facing the serious and highly important problem of what shall be that new method of control.

I am convinced that there is wide-spread and perhaps almost universal desire to promote temperance. Such differences as have arisen have to do, in large part, with the manner of bringing about this important accomplishment. Surely there is wisdom enough available to meet the issue here presented.

It is to be hoped that such legislation as ultimately is deemed necessary will be enacted only after calm, sober, clear-minded and intelligent study has been given to the whole subject, and then by the exercise of wise judgment. To this task the entire citizenry should dedicate united efforts, not as winners or losers at the recent election, but as loyal citizens of the state and of our common country.

So far as our own state is concerned, I have already acted in line with the suggestion made herein by the appointment of a committee of leading citizens, later to be enlarged by the addition of men and women from all over the state, who will be charged with the duty of making exhaustive research in the line of control of the liquor traffic and of reporting its findings.

Ladies and gentlemen, this is a democracy. The will of the majority, expressed through duly constituted representatives, has binding force and effect, which must be respected. It therefore becomes a duty of prime importance that the change to be effected today shall be the first step in a purposeful plan to promote respect for and observance of the provisions of the Constitution and the laws based thereon.

It shall be my pleasure, as it is my duty, to support and sustain and defend the Constitution as amended by the will of the majority.

I thank you.

President Olson: Your Excellency, the convention is indebted to you for your splendid address.

The Chair is prepared to entertain a motion designating the type of proceedings for this Convention.

Delegate George S. Ballif: Mr. Chairman.

President Olson: The Chair recognizes Delegate George S. Ballif.

Delegate Ballif: May I present the following resolution, and move its adoption?

Resolved, That Roberts' Rules of Parliamentary Practice be, and the same is, hereby adopted as the rules of the procedure of this Convention.

President Olson: Is the resolution supported?

Delegate Franklin Riter: Second the motion for adoption.

PRESIDENT OLSON: Motion has been made that Roberts' Rules of Parliamentary Practice be used in guiding the proceedings of this Convention.

Is there further discussion?

All in favor of the motion will say "aye."

Opposed, "no."

The motion is carried.

Honorable Milton H. Welling, Secretary of State, will present the resolution of the Congress of the United States proposing the Twenty-first Amendment to the Constitution.

SECRETARY OF STATE WELLING: I hold in my hand the official certificate of the Secretary of State at Washington transmitting to the State of Utah the pending amendment to the Constitution of the United States, which certificate reads as follows:

UNITED STATES OF AMERICA

DEPARTMENT OF STATE

TO ALL TO WHOM THESE PRESENTS SHALL COME, GREETING:

I certify that the copy hereto attached is a true copy of a resolution of Congress entitled "JOINT RESOLUTION Proposing an Amendment to the Constitution of the United States," the original of which is on file in this Department.

In testimony whereof I, Henry L. Stimson, Secretary of State, have caused the seal of the Department of State to be affixed and my name subscribed.

Done at the Department in the City of Washington in the District of Columbia this 21st day of February, 1933.

HENRY L. STIMSON
Secretary of State

Accompanying the certificate of the Secretary of State I present the proposed Twenty-first Article of Amendment to the Constitution of the United States.

WHEREAS, The Senate and House of Representatives of the United States of America in Congress assembled (two-thirds of each House concurring therein), each resolved that the following article is hereby proposed as an amendment to the Constitution of the United States, which shall be valid to all intents and purposes as part of the Constitution when ratified by conventions in three-fourths of the several States;

Section 1. The eighteenth article of amendment to the Constitution of the United States is hereby repealed.

Section 2. The transportation or importation into any State, Territory, or possession of the United States for delivery or use therein of intoxicating liquors, in violation of the laws thereof, is hereby prohibited.

Section 3. This article shall be inoperative unless it shall have been ratified as an amendment to the Constitution by conventions in the several States, as provided in the Constitution, within seven years from the date of the submission hereof to the States by the Congress.

PRESIDENT OLSON: The resolution of the Congress of the United States will be received and made a part of the proceedings of this Convention.

The Chair is prepared to entertain a motion for the appointment of committees.

DELEGATE SAM D. THURMAN: Mr. Chairman.

PRESIDENT OLSON: The Chair recognizes Delegate Sam D. Thurman.

DELEGATE THURMAN: I move that the president now proceed to name the committees of this Convention, one committee, that on resolutions, to consist of ten members, and a committee on credentials, likewise to consist of ten members.

PRESIDENT OLSON: You have heard the motion. Is the motion supported?

DELEGATE FRANKLIN RITER: Second the motion.

PRESIDENT OLSON: The motion is that the president appoint a committee on resolutions consisting of ten members and a committee on credentials consisting of ten members. Is there any discussion?

All in favor of the motion will say "aye."

Opposed, "no."

The motion is carried.

The president announces the appointment of the following committee on resolutions:

Franklin Riter, Chairman
George S. Ballif
Clarence Bamberger
A. S. Brown
Lawrence Clayton
A. C. Ellis, Jr.
Mat Gilmour
L. B. Hampton
L. A. Hollenbeck
Mrs. Paul Keyser

The committee on credentials will consist of:

Sam D. Thurman, Chairman
Glen O. Allred
John O. Beesley
Sophus Bertelson
T. Earl Clements
Miah Day
Franklin Hansen
Mrs. John A. Hendricks
Mrs. L. B. McCornick
Ephraim Bergeson

What is the pleasure of the Convention?

DELEGATE FRANKLIN RITER: I move a recess of fifteen minutes be taken at this time.

PRESIDENT OLSON: You have heard the motion. Is there any second?

DELEGATE LAWRENCE CLAYTON: Second.

PRESIDENT OLSON: Motion has been made and seconded that a recess be taken for fifteen minutes. All in favor say "aye." The motion is carried.

DELEGATE RITER: Do you wish the delegates to assemble in the House Lounge?

PRESIDENT OLSON: The chair wishes to make an announcement in that respect. The president is very anxious to meet all of the delegates at once in the House Lounge, and Governor Blood is requested to meet with the delegation.

To the public, I would suggest that you entertain yourselves and be on hand, because we shall not be more than fifteen minutes. The reports of the committees have been prepared, and are ready for presentation.

The Convention will be adjourned for fifteen minutes.

(*Recess*)

The Convention reassembled after a 15 minute recess.

PRESIDENT OLSON: The delegates will please take their seats. The Convention will be in order. Let the record show that all delegates are present.

At this time the chair presumes to make an announcement which will be of considerable importance to the delegates and visitors at the Convention.

The Press has announced that this Convention would be recessed until tonight in order to permit our proceedings to be broadcast over the nation. Certain conditions and developments have made it necessary for us to immediately change our plans, so that our business will be as follows.

After the address which will be given within a few moments, the Convention will recess for one hour. Then we will reconvene and complete entirely the business of the Convention, which is the business of ratification. That, of course, is the most interesting part of the Convention, and the part which you people wish to witness. Therefore announcement will be made of the hour at which we convene after that recess at the commencement of the next recess.

It is now my pleasure, ladies and gentlemen of the Convention, to present an outstanding citizen of this state, one who has been a leader in the community life of the commonwealth ever since the state was created; in fact, he helped create the state of Utah by his participation in the Constitutional Convention of the State of Utah held in 1895.

The man I will introduce really needs no introduction, and it is therefore a distinct pleasure for me to present Honorable Anthony W. Ivins.

MR. IVINS: Members of the Convention, and others who may be present:

I suppose I have the distinction to occupy this position because I was—I was going to say a relic—a member, I will say, rather, of the Convention which framed the Constitution for the State of Utah under the Enabling Act that had been passed by Congress which finally resulted in the admission of Utah as a state of the Union.

I am not going to talk politics. I feel very much as Mark Antony did at the funeral services of Caesar. I am not going to talk about the Eighteenth Amendment or the Twenty-first Amendment. I leave you to discuss those matters—you younger men.

It is now nearly eighty years since the first Constitutional Convention met in the State of Utah. They drafted a Constitution and delineated the boundaries of the state that was to be. It took in, I think, all of Idaho, all of Nevada—I don't know whether it went over the California line—I guess hardly that—but the brethren were very ambitious, and if we had been admitted I suppose we would have been the largest state in the Union. But we were not admitted.

At various times efforts were made to persuade the Congress of the United States to admit Utah as a sovereign state, but they were never successful until Congress finally passed the Enabling Act which called together the body of men who framed the original accepted Constitution for the State of Utah.

They came in from the north and south, the east and west. There were merchants and bankers and lawyers and doctors, literary men, cattle and sheep men, men of all avocations, many of them who had never known one another before, and went to work on the great undertaking which had been allotted to them.

I have been thinking of these men, thinking of the past first, and later of the present, and a little of the future, since I have been here this morning. And I remembered these names—I have only done this from memory, consequently I may have omitted some part that I should have had here—but I thought of the men who were members of that Constitutional Convention who have passed away, and their accomplishments in it.

There was Thomas Kearns. We all know what he did for Utah, and particularly for this city. I first contacted with him upon that occasion. I learned to know him intimately, and I want to say right here that Thomas Kearns was always the friend of the people of Utah.

And then in education we had W. J. Kerr, now at the head of one of the largest colleges in the State of Oregon.

We had, in law, S. R. Thurman and Franklin S. Richards, both of whom are still living.

We had in music A. C. Lund, the present leader of the Tabernacle Choir.

We had in literature Noble Warrum, Jr., and Heber M. Wells, and other men in all of these different vocations perhaps equally competent, but these are the people that I thought directly of.

Among these men that are still living that I remember were George M. Cannon, Abel John Evans, Charles H. Hart, W. J. Kerr, A. C. Lund, Lars Peterson, F. S. Richards, Joseph E. Robinson, C. N. Strevell, I. C. Thoresen, S. R. Thurman, Noble Warrum, Jr., Heber M. Wells, Judge Corfman, who is present, William H. Gibbs.

These are men that I met and knew.

This one thing I learned in that Convention that I would like to impress upon the minds, not only of the members of this Convention, but of you who are present, that when you come into close contact with men, you come to know them as you never could have known them under other circumstances, and the more you know of men and women the more of good you find in them. That was one of the things that impressed me in my activities in that Convention. I was on committees with such men as C. S. Varian, C. C. Goodwin and other men. I found them without exception fair-minded, patriotic, loyal to the country and loyal to the state. I have never ceased to be grateful for the experiences of that Convention, and we made a Constitution that we thought was a good one. It was nearly forty years ago. If you stop and think for a moment of the changes that have come to the world during that period of time, the things which are adapted to our necessities, our requirements, would not be at all appropriate, many of them, at the present time. In development, in intelligence, in forward movement the past fifty years of the history of the world has made it the miracle period of the ages. Never has knowledge and intelligence so increased; and with it, of course, our necessities change.

I remember I came up to the Constitutional convention in a Miller buggy with a mighty good pair of horses on it—I always had good horses—and I was proud of it. It was the very best thing that could be had at that time. It took me about ten days to drive up here. And I do not need to tell you how we come now.

That one incident illustrates the changes that have come to us, and so, naturally, the Constitution which we built up and submitted to the people and which was accepted by the government was different to the Constitution that we have now.

I wanted to say that much in honor of these men that I was associated with at the time, both those who are living and those who have passed away. They were a splendid lot of men, the peers of any of you fellows that constitute this Convention today. I am going to venture to say that. They were not Democrats, but very few of them. That was a Convention made up of members of the Republican party. The mills of the gods had ground on and on, and the idea of rotary had prevailed until while at the first session of the legislature that I attended there was scarcely a Republican there, when the time of the Constitutional Convention came there was scarcely a Democrat.

These men in the corner (indicating surviving delegates to Utah State Constitutional Convention of 1895), are men living who were connected with it. Our methods have changed, conditions have changed, and there is one thing has greatly changed, too, and that is that the parties which you people represent—long the outs, long underneath—in this transformation, this wonderful evolution which has come to the country and to the world, has been brought again into prominence, and placed upon you responsibilities greater than you have ever had before.

I want to say here that the country is never going back again to the conditions of the last twenty years. I do not know where we are going to go in the future—the Lord help us—but we are never going back to where we have been during that period.

I thank you.

DELEGATE L. A. HOLLENBECK: Mr. Chairman.

PRESIDENT OLSON: The chair recognizes Mr. Hollenbeck.

DELEGATE HOLLENBECK: I move we take recess for one hour.

PRESIDENT OLSON: The motion is that the Convention recess for one hour. Is the motion supported?

DELEGATE BALLIF: I second the motion.

PRESIDENT OLSON: Is there any discussion? Before putting the motion the chair wishes to formally announce that the Convention will reconvene at 2:45 o'clock and we invite cordially all of the citizens who are here to join us again, and we request that others inform their friends to be here and witness the conclusion of our proceedings.

PRESIDENT OLSON: All in favor of the motion will say "aye." Opposed, "no." The motion is carried.

The convention is recessed until 2:45 o'clock.

(2:45 P.M.—*After Recess*)

PRESIDENT OLSON: The delegates will please take their seats. The Convention will be in order. The record will show that all delegates are in their seats.

The next order of business will be the report of the committee on credentials.

The chair recognizes Delegate Sam D. Thurman.

DELEGATE THURMAN: Your committee has examined the roll of delegates as prepared by the Secretary of State, and his certificate of election, and has found the same to be correct, and that the delegates named in said certificate of election have been duly elected, and that there were no contests, and recommend that the list of delegates as certified to the Convention by the Secretary of State, together with Mrs. Paul Keyser of Salt Lake City, who has been elected a delegate to this convention to fill the vacancy created by the absence of Mrs. S. Grover Rich, act as the accredited delegates of this Convention.

A list of the delegates has heretofore been presented to the Convention, and I move the adoption of the report of the committee on credentials.

PRESIDENT OLSON: You have heard the motion. Is it seconded?

DELEGATE BALLIF: I second the motion.

President Olson: All in favor of the motion to adopt the report of the committee on credentials will say "aye."

Opposed signify by saying "no." The motion is carried and the report of the credentials committee is adopted.

Ladies and gentlemen of the Convention, we now come to the chief purpose of this Convention. The next order of business will be the report of the committee on resolutions.

The chair recognizes Delegate Franklin Riter, chairman of the committee on resolutions.

Delegate Riter: Delegates of this Convention, His Excellency, Governor Blood, citizens of the State of Utah:

This is a momentous and history-making occasion. We, who have the honor of representing the citizens of the State of Utah in this Convention will always remember and recall with pride the events of today. There has never been a similar assemblage of representatives of a free people, because in the history of the Republic there has never been a combination of events like those which produced this Convocation.

We may well pause in our deliberations to consider the lessons in constitutional government which our unhappy experience with the Eighteenth article of Amendment to the Federal Constitution has taught. We find cause for great exultation in the fact that the operation of the tragic appendage to our fundamental law is about to end, but in the hour of triumph, solemn and serious thoughts must come if we rightly sense the responsibilities and duties of citizenship. This is no time for emotional flag-waving, nor for frivolous demonstrations. Great and serious problems confront our beloved land and its people. They must be met and solved with brave hearts and clear comprehension of our cultural and political inheritance. Correct and careful analysis of our experience with this ill-fated amendment during the past thirteen years may give us valuable guides for future conduct. There have been certain fundamentals of social organization involved in this experiment; certain definite violations of the principles upon which our government is founded and certain specific indications as to the future course we should follow.

The political mechanism which was put into operation to attach the Eighteenth Amendment to the Constitution played no small part in condemning the amendment to failure. Its proponents, forgetful of the American traditions and culture concerning individual freedom (I can not believe that they deliberately chose the method they followed with a desire to frustrate or defeat the inherited individualism of our people), cause the Congressional resolution to be submitted to the legislatures of the forty-eight states for consideration instead of providing for conventions of the type we hold today. A superficial study of our Constitutional history would seem to justify such action, but this conclusion is erroneous. Two arguments have been made to justify the method pursued: First, that submission to legislatures of the states of proposed articles of amendment to the Constitution had been the usual and ordinary method of modifying or adding to the organic document; and second, that the first ten amendments to the Constitution, which primarily concern the rights of the individual citizen, were ratified through legislative channels.

Consider the amendments, their nature and purposes and the answers to those arguments are obvious. The first ten amendments compose our "Bill of Rights"—an inheritance from the Magna Charta of Runnymede. They were intended as a guarantee of the individual, personal rights of the citizens, and a definite limitation upon the powers of the central government. They were a covenant of quiet enjoyment of political and civil rights made by the Federal government as covenantor in favor of the individual as covenantee. They did not seek to prohibit the individual from free action, but sustained him in his rights, personal and civil, which had been recognized as natural rights acquired by free men in their long struggle against tyranny and autocracy. We know now that the Constitution was adopted by the states only because the people were assured that these amendments would be speedily submitted by Congress to the states. The Eighteenth Amendment contradicted the principle of the first ten amendments as it sought to curb and limit human action; instead of sustaining an individual in his natural rights, it sought to deprive him of free action in a certain specified direction. Obviously it was a startling innovation in our theory of constitutional government. It has been termed an "experiment" even by its supporters.

The remaining amendments classify easily. The Eleventh Amendment operated on the judicial power of the Federal government. It stands alone. The twelfth, pertaining to the electoral college; the seventeenth providing for direct election of United States Senators; the twentieth eliminating the "Lame Duck" session of Congress and changing the date of inauguration of the President and Vice-President—are changes in the Constitution which are natural and sequential in the growth and development of the nation. They simply altered out-moded methods in the mechanical operation of the federal government. The thirteenth, fourteenth and fifteenth amendments were the product of the internecine strife and were peculiar to the period of reconstruction which followed. The sixteenth, or Income Tax, amendment was a change in paragraph four, Section IX of Article I of the Constitution and the nineteenth amendment was a further protection of the individual citizen—the guarantee of suffrage to women citizens.

Contrast the Eighteenth Amendment with the other amendments. Its anomalous position is self-evident even to the most casual student. It puzzles us to discover why its friends did not sense that it represented an attempted change in the individual's political philosophy. It may be surmised that had they comprehended that it would produce among great masses of the citizens an antagonistic reaction because of its departure from our established ideas of the individual's rights, they would have possessed sufficient political sagacity to have secured its adoption through a vote of the people. Therefore, they would have used the convention system of submission instead of the legislative. By the method followed the amendment was classed as the other amendments. It has been demonstrated how grossly erroneous such classification is. Time and experience has piled proof on proof of the error. During the past fifty years there has been throughout the world a steady enlargement of democratic doctrines, and political action and policy are increasingly determined by plebiscites. In the fact of this acknowledged tendency, the Eighteenth Amendment was not submitted to the citizens for direct consideration on a sharply created issue as to whether they were willing to surrender a certain degree of free action. Instead, it was submitted to legislatures which only the most liberal imagination will say had a direct and specific mandate from the people on this important question. The legislatures are elected—on cross currents of political motives and antagonisms. The question of federal prohibition had not been presented to the people as the sole basis for selecting the state legislators. It is doubtful whether or not the issue was ever directly raised except in a few isolated instances. Here, then, is found a fundamental defect in the prohibition structure which with other imperfections finally caused its destruction. Here also is the first great lesson to be learned. If at some future time there is contemplated a restriction on the free action of the individual citizen which requires a federal Constitutional Amendment, there can be no hope for success in its subsequent operation, if adopted, unless the people are given the opportunity to vote directly on the issue, within the sacred precinct of the election booth. There must be presented a definite issue not complicated by political cross currents. Then, and then only, will the average citizen yield his personal belief and action to the will of the majority. In matters involving the individual rights, powers and prerogatives, the convention system of amending the Constitution is the only sound and honest method, and is the only method consistent with our theory of government.

When we pass beyond a consideration of the mechanism employed to secure its ratification and reflect upon the intrinsic merits of the Eighteenth Amendment we find that it flagrantly opposed the established philosophy of our form of social organization, and was repugnant to one of our fundamental conceptions of the purposes and functions of the Federal Constitution. The United States of America, as a governmental agency, is and was intended to be one of granted powers, and its sphere of action is limited. "The powers not delegated to the United States by the Constitution, not prohibited by it to the States, are reserved to the States respectively, or to the people." "The enumeration in the Constitution of certain rights shall not be construed to deny or disparage others retained by the people." In these quotations we find the underlying doctrine of the Constitution and its adoption was made possible only when the people were assured that such was the major premise upon which the government was founded.

There remained in and was reserved to the States in particular that power known as the "police power." Without attempting a complete elucidation of its functions and limits it will suffice at this time simply to declare that it has always been a peculiarly distinctive function of the state government as opposed to the federal government, to exercise this "police power" with reference to the control of or limitations on the actions of the citizen. The basis of all organized society has been the idea that the greatest good for the greatest number must determine any specific course of social policy. Consequently, we must all surrender a certain degree of freedom of action in order to secure unity of action and an orderly mode of life. This is a consequence of our social compact. By it, no liberty has been sacrificed but in truth liberty is obtained and preserved. The opposite idea is that of a brutal barbarism where might controls, and the strong tyrannize over the weak.

Within the long acknowledged political sphere of the state was the control of the subject matter of the Eighteenth Amendment. Not only control, but prohibition was declared by our courts to be within the proper exercise of this "police power." Due to the fact that forty-eight sovereign powers exist within the federation which is sovereign within its own field of action, divergent policies in the matter of control or prohibition resulted. In the minds of the proponents of the Eighteenth Amendment this was a defect which must be eliminated, no matter what the cost or how radical or revolutionary the treatment. Here is the genesis of the Eighteenth Amendment, and it is here that the primary reason for its failure is found.

The amendment transferred from the states to the federal government police power in regard to control and prohibition of personal conduct of citizens in a matter which per se was not wrong. Only abuses and excesses produced the evil which it was sought to destroy by governmental action. Drastic dislocation of philosophic thought resulted, and following upon such displacement came tangible and visible anti-social acts.

Except within an extremely narrow limit, it was never intended that the federal government should exercise police control over the citizen; it is a function and duty of the state, but a penal code provision was inserted in the basic framework of government—the Federal Constitution. It was more than an irregular or anomalous proceeding; it was in direct opposition to the fundamental proposition in our conception and plan of government. No matter how desirable was the objective to be attained, the means adopted subjected the operation to positive failure. Opposition developed at once when accelerated into a terrific demonstration against this attempted annihilation of a cardinal principle of our social organization. The repeal of the Eighteenth Amendment is a positive declaration by the citizens that hereafter this foundation stone of their governmental structure must not be dislocated nor its position changed.

This experience in tampering with a fundamental principle of our political structure will be long remembered, and the reproof administered to the propagators of such plan of action is a dynamic warning that we will not tolerate any further attempt to change a basic principle in the balance of powers between state and federal government.

A discussion of the involvement of personal, individual rights of the citizen under the operation of the Eighteenth Amendment sequentially leads us to deliberate on our fundamental political philosophy concerning the individual. It is most fitting and proper at this time and on this occasion to re-examine our creed and re-announce our allegiance to the same. Of late it has been most popular to regard "individualism" as out-of-date and old-fashioned. Harsh language has been used and some people would lead us to believe that we have been dupes of a false idealism. Personally, I do not subscribe to any such doctrine, and it is to be doubted whether any of us regard the charge seriously. However, it has been repeated much of late and the time is propitious to restate this thesis of our political philosophy. I have sought a modern pronouncement, and one of the best is found in that memorable address delivered by the Honorable James M. Beck, former solicitor general of the United States, delivered by him in the House of Representatives on February 7, 1930. He said:

"And what is the meaning of this 'conception of natural rights classical in our polity' . . . To understand it, we must go back to the epic days of our Republic. In the Colonial period, the sturdy yeomen of America believed, as all their ancestors had before them, that the state was a thing separate and apart from the people, and that its authority to impose its will without restriction upon its subjects was only secondary to that of God. In the middle of the Eighteenth century, the new conception of the sovereignty of the people, and the reserved rights of the individual became the great ideal. It gave the burning significance to the great preamble of the Declaration of Independence, which has given not only to us, but to all mankind a definition of liberty which 'time cannot wither, nor custom stale.' Even the pathfinder of the Mayflower limited the power of government to the imposition of 'just and equal' laws, so there is in the hearts of all generations of Americans a profound instinct that, whether safe-guarded by constitutional limitations or not, there is a moral limit to the power of government to regulate private conduct."

The evolution of this philosophy of the rights of the individual as against those of the state since its beginning in the early 1700's, has been rapid and world-wide. It may be said that, except as to certain tenets of Christianity, there has been no doctrine that has had such profound influence upon the development and progress of man.

It represents the opposite of all of the political beliefs and dogma of the prior centuries, and its birth came only after man attained moral and mental stature. It blossomed in the "Age of Reason" and when the sun of intelligence pierced the miasma of ignorance, superstition and fear. It must remain forever glorified in the hearts of those who love liberty.

The Federal Constitution was a crystallization of these conceptions into a social mechanism—called government. Thereby the mental processes and beliefs became a living organism which has operated upon and constantly influenced the daily lives of all citizens. Under it, freedom of action became part of the "flesh and bone" of the individual, and we of today accept it as we do the air of heaven. The state exists for the benefit of the people and not the people for the benefit of the state. The state has no superhuman or sacred existence apart from the people. It is not sacrosanct nor untouchable and it must not become tyrannical or despotic.

It is curious that a democratic state, founded on the philosophy of individualism can become despotic or tyrannical, but the founders of our republic understood full well that such was a possibility, and they prepared against such contingency. They were no longer concerned with kings or princes, claiming to rule by Divine Right. They knew that doctrine had been exploded. The office of President created by them was circumscribed with very practical limitations upon its power. Congress, directly elected by the people for comparatively short durations, could not assert plenary authority of any lasting importance. Whence then came the fear of autocracy against which the Constitution protects the individual? The rule of the majority might well become despotic in the treatment of the minority. Our forefathers well knew that the "voice of the people was not always the voice of God." They adopted the rule of the majority because it was the practical method of government by the people, but they realized keenly that if true freedom was to be perpetuated in this land that the minority must be protected against the majority. Hence we find the specific limitations upon the power of the federal government and the precautionary checks and counter checks of the branches of government against each other. Here we recognize the importance of the "Bill of Rights" and its potency. History has proven that a majority led by demagogues and false prophets would in an hour of public hysteria or pressing need substitute itself for kings and autocrats and become cruel and merciless. The majority may become a mob, and mob rule at all times has no reason; no moral understanding; no tolerance with opposition. It rules as the barbaric emperors of old. It was against this contingency that founders of the republic erected the barriers and safeguards to shield the minority and the individual.

The Constitutional limitations and prohibitions placed upon the federal government and upon the states in the Constitution required something more than their enactment to make them effective. Otherwise they would remain mere declarations of principle. It was at this point that the ingenuity of the Constitutional craftsmen reached its greatest heights. The creation of the judicial branch with its power to declare parliamentary enactments void because of their violation of the Constitution has been characterized as the great contribution of America to civilization. It eliminates the doctrine of force and substitutes the power of intelligence and reason. At times some of us have become impatient at the functioning of the courts and the apparent reactionary tendency in dealing with problems of today, but in our impatience we forget that the alleged lack of progressiveness in the tribunals is one of their great virtues. They have refused to hearken to the cry of the hour or to the demands of a hysterical crowd. They stand as the defenders of the Constitution and as guardians of the political and civil rights of the individual.

We are having a wonderful experience today in reestablishing and reasserting one of the basic principles of our Constitution. Utah is proud of the distinction which has come to it. It greets the Nation on this auspicious occasion with felicitations and good will and declares before the world its belief in our institutions and political ideals; its determination to fulfill its responsibilities as a sovereign State of the Republic and its confidence that this government "of the people, by the people, for the people, shall not perish from the earth."

DELEGATE RITER: The committee on resolutions has met and has carefully considered the question of acting upon the ratification of the proposed Twenty-first Article of Amendment to the Constitution of the United States of America providing for the repeal of the Eighteenth Amendment to the Constitution of the United States, and we recommend the adoption of the following resolution:

(Reads.)

WHEREAS, the Senate and House of Representatives of the United States of America in Congress Assembled (two-thirds of each House concurring therein) did resolve that the following article is hereby proposed as an amendment to the Constitution of the United States, which shall be valid to all intents and purposes as part of the Constitution when ratified by conventions in three-fourths of the several States; and

WHEREAS the said proposed amendment reads as follows:

Section 1. The eighteenth article of amendment to the Constitution of the United States is hereby repealed.

Section 2. The transportation or importation into any state, Territory or possession of the United States for delivery or use therein of intoxicating liquors, in violation of the laws thereof, is hereby prohibited.

Section 3. This article shall be inoperative unless it shall have been ratified as an amendment to the Constitution by conventions in the several States, as provided in the Constitution, within seven years from the date of the submission hereof to the States by the Congress; and

WHEREAS, the Legislature of this State, pursuant to its constitutional authority, did enact a statute entitled "AN ACT to provide for conventions to pass on amendments to the Constitution of the United States which have or may hereafter be proposed by Congress for ratification by conventions of the several states," which said statute having passed both houses of the Legislature of this State, was signed by the Governor of this State on March 21, 1933, and constitutes Chapter 22, Laws of the State of Utah, twentieth Regular Session of the Legislature, 1933, and

WHEREAS, on August 10, 1933, Governor Henry H. Blood proclaimed that an election for the election of twenty-one delegates to attend a Constitutional Convention to be held at Salt Lake City, December 5, 1933, to ratify or reject the above proposed amendment to the Constitution of the United States, to be held November 7, 1933, and

WHEREAS, nominating petitions containing the required number of names were filed with the Secretary of State for twenty-one delegates to the aforesaid Constitutional convention for ratification of the proposed amendment to the Constitution of the United States, and

WHEREAS, nominating petitions containing the required number of names were filed with the Secretary of State for twenty-one delegates to the aforesaid Constitutional convention against ratification of the proposed amendment to the Constitution of the United States, and

WHEREAS, pursuant to the provisions of said statute of the Legislature, an election for the election of delegates to said convention was held in this State on November 7, 1933, at which said election twenty-one delegates were chosen, in accordance with the provisions of said statute, and

WHEREAS, the Board of State Canvassers, meeting according to law in the office of the Secretary of State at noon, November 27, 1933, did canvass the returns of the aforesaid election, and by their computation did find that the twenty-one delegates for ratification of the proposed amendment to the Constitution of the United States received a greater number of votes than the twenty-one delegates against ratification of the said proposed amendment to the Constitution of the United States, and

WHEREAS, Milton H. Welling, Secretary of State of the State of Utah, did, under his hand and the Great Seal of the State of Utah, at Salt Lake City, Utah, on the twenty-eighth day of November, 1933, certify that the following twenty-one delegates, pledged to vote for ratification of the proposed amendment to the Constitution of the United States, are the duly elected delegates to the Constitutional convention which, by law, is called to convene at twelve o'clock noon, December 5, 1933, at the Capitol in Salt Lake City:

Glen O. Allred	Price	Mat Gilmour	Price
George S. Ballif	Provo	L. B. Hampton	Salt Lake City
Clarence Bamberger	Salt Lake City	Franklin Hansen	Moroni
John O. Beesley	Provo	Mrs. John A. Hendricks	Ogden
Ephraim Bergeson	Cornish	L. A. Hollenbeck	Duchesne
Sophus Bertelson	Ephraim	Mrs. L. B. McCornick	Salt Lake City
A. S. Brown	Salt Lake City	R. L. Olson	Ogden
Lawrence Clayton	Ogden	Mrs. S. Grover Rich	Salt Lake City
T. Earl Clements	Park City	Franklin Riter	Salt Lake City
Miah Day	Fillmore	Sam D. Thurman	Salt Lake City
A. C. Ellis, Jr.	Salt Lake City		

AND WHEREAS, said certificate of election has been filed in the Department of State of the State of Utah, and

WHEREAS, pursuant to Section 8 of said statute, designated as Chapter 22, Laws of the State of Utah, passed at the Twentieth Session of the Legislature, 1933, the said convention has met at the time and place fixed by said statute to-wit: at twelve o'clock noon, December 5, 1933, and has organized by the election of a President, Vice-president, Secretary and other officers, and has adopted rules governing its deliberations, and is ready to proceed to consider the proposed article of amendment; and

WHEREAS, Mrs. S. Grover Rich of Salt Lake City, the regularly elected and qualified delegate to this convention, was and is absent from the State of Utah and is not present at the sessions of said convention, and pursuant to the authority vested in said convention by Section 7, Chapter 22, Laws of Utah, 1933 (regular session), Mrs. Paul Keyser of Salt Lake City has been elected and designated a delegate to said convention to fill the vacancy created by the absence of Mrs. S. Grover Rich.

Now, therefore, be it resolved that this convention of the delegates representing the people of the State of Utah, duly assembled pursuant to law, that we do approve and ratify the proposed article of amendment to the Constitution of the United States of America proposed by the Congress thereof and designed to repeal the Eighteenth

Article of amendment to said Constitution, which proposed article of amendment reads as follows:

WHEREAS, the Senate and House of Representatives of the United States of America in Congress assembled (two-thirds of each House concurring therein), each resolved that the following article is hereby proposed as an amendment to the Constitution of the United States, which shall be valid to all intents and purposes as part of the Constitution when ratified by conventions in three-fourths of the several States;

Section 1. The eighteenth article of amendment to the Constitution of the United States is hereby repealed.

Section 2. The transportation or importation into any State, Territory or possession of the United States for delivery or use therein of intoxicating liquors, in violation of the laws thereof, is hereby prohibited.

Section 3. This article shall be inoperative unless it shall have been ratified as an amendment to the Constitution by conventions in the several States, as provided in the Constitution, within seven years from the date of the submission hereof to the States by the Congress.

Be it further resolved, that the action of this convention in approving and ratifying the said proposed amendment is valid to all intents and purposes as representing the people of the State of Utah, and

Be it further resolved, that the President and Secretary of this convention shall certify the results of the votes of the delegates to the ratification of said amendment in triplicate, each signed by the President and Secretary of the convention to which there shall be attached a certificate certified by such officers of the record of the vote taken, showing the yeas and nays thereon, and that such certificates and certified copies of such record shall be deposited with the Secretary of State of the State of Utah, and he shall transmit one such certificate and certified copy of such record to the Secretary of State of the United States, another certificate and certified copy of such record to the presiding officer of the Senate of the United States and another certificate and certified copy of such record to the Speaker of the House of Representatives of the United States, which said certificates shall be accompanied by the certificate of the Secretary of State certifying that the persons signing the certificates so transmitted were the duly constituted President and Secretary of said Convention, and that their signatures are genuine, and that before transmitting the certificates and copies of records so deposited with the Secretary of State he shall make a copy of one of them, certifying it as such, and record it as a permanent record of the Secretary of State of the State of Utah; and

Be it further resolved, That the President, Secretary and any other officer of this convention and the delegates and Secretary of State or any or either of them are hereby authorized to comply with any act or resolution of the Congress of the United States requiring other or further confirmation of such ratification or rejection of said proposed amendment; and

Resolved further That in the event of the death, disability or absence of the President of this convention from the State of Utah, the Vice-president of this convention be, and he is hereby authorized to execute all instruments and documents intended or required to be executed by said President, and,

Resolved further That in the event of the death, disability or absence from the

State of Utah of the Secretary of this convention, that the signature of the Chairman of the committee on resolutions of this convention to said certificates and documents shall to all intents and purposes be of the same legal effect as the signature of said secretary.

(*Signed*) FRANKLIN RITER, *Chairman*
GEORGE S. BALLIF
A. S. BROWN
LAWRENCE CLAYTON
A. C. ELLIS, JR.
CLARENCE BAMBERGER
L. B. HAMPTON
L. A. HOLLENBECK
MRS. PAUL KEYSER

DELEGATE RITER: Mr. President, I move the adoption of the report of the committee on resolutions.

PRESIDENT OLSON: The convention has heard the motion to adopt the report of the committee on resolutions, which report embodies our action in ratifying the Twenty-first Amendment. What is your further pleasure?

DELEGATE CLAYTON: Mr. President, I rise to second this resolution and I crave the indulgence of the delegates for one moment to make some observations which are prompted by the presence here this afternoon of several of the delegates who ran in the election on the ticket against repeal.

I heartily concur, and I am sure all of us do, in the arguments of Mr. Riter which are founded upon considerations of political science. There is however, a practical viewpoint which I think this moment makes opportune to present in connection with our deliberations. I welcome the new order from this viewpoint. The proclamation by President Roosevelt, which we hope will take place within a few minutes now, of the adoption of the Twenty-first Amendment makes effective some important reductions in federal taxes and permits states, counties and cities to realize needed revenues hitherto unavailable.

And I disagree with those pessimists who cry that such revenues can not be realized except by this country of ours going on a permanent spree. If the total consumption per capita in this country of ours should never increase beyond the present consumption of home brews, bad liquors and smuggled good liquors—and happily now, good beer—I am confident that a very important revenue will accrue to both national and state units. And best of all, most of this revenue *can come* from the worst by-product of prohibition, namely, the bootlegger, the moonshiner, the racketeer. Whether it *will* come from him depends largely upon the wisdom of government in enacting taxes and control. A foolish policy of over-eagerness to exact the last cent may well make it possible for these criminals to resume their trade. The average citizen is willing to pay a reasonable premium to patronize a legitimate dealer, either private or public, but it is perfectly obvious that if legal beer, legal wine and legal spirits are made expensive through excessive taxation, such beverages, all of them, without exception, will again be the stock-in-trade of the bootlegger and racketeer. Prohibition created a millennium for crime, by providing high profits and small penalties. No, if we are wise in this country, repeal will create a Waterloo for crime, by providing small profit and heavy penalties.

Mr. President, we are not here to debate control, I realize. But I believe a principle is indicated in these thoughts, namely, that crime varies directly with the profit and indirectly with the penalty. And I conceive it to be the duty of all those who worked either for or against repeal, to work just as diligently for a wise and effective control. This resolution which is now before us, history-making as it is, can not of itself solve the problem. But most happily, it opens a gate, hitherto barred by a foolish law, through which all those who sincerely place temperance above bigotry and frankness above hypocrisy, may pass to the open road along which, I trust, this nation and this state may journey to better times and happier days.

Mr. President, I call for the question.

PRESIDENT OLSON: The question is upon the motion to adopt the report of the committee on resolutions, which report, as has been stated, is the ratifying action of this convention in ratifying the Twenty-first Amendment.

The Secretary will call the roll of delegates upon the resolution.

SECRETARY KEYSER: Allred.
DELEGATE ALLRED: Aye.
SECRETARY KEYSER: Ballif.
DELEGATE BALLIF: Aye.
SECRETARY KEYSER: Bamberger.
DELEGATE BAMBERGER: Aye.
SECRETARY KEYSER: Beesley.
DELEGATE BEESLEY: Aye.
SECRETARY KEYSER: Bergeson.
DELEGATE BERGESON: Aye.
SECRETARY KEYSER: Bertelson.
DELEGATE BERTELSON: Aye.
SECRETARY KEYSER: Brown.
DELEGATE BROWN: Aye.
SECRETARY KEYSER: Clayton.
DELEGATE CLAYTON: Aye.
SECRETARY KEYSER: Clements.
DELEGATE CLEMENTS: Aye.
SECRETARY KEYSER: Day.
DELEGATE DAY: Aye.
SECRETARY KEYSER: Ellis.
DELEGATE ELLIS: Aye.
SECRETARY KEYSER: Gilmour.
(Delegate Gilmour absent.)
SECRETARY KEYSER: Hampton.
DELEGATE HAMPTON: Aye.
SECRETARY KEYSER: Hansen.
DELEGATE HANSEN: Aye.
SECRETARY KEYSER: Hendricks.
DELEGATE HENDRICKS: Aye.
SECRETARY KEYSER: Hollenbeck.
SECRETARY KEYSER: McCornick.
DELEGATE MCCORNICK: Aye.
SECRETARY KEYSER: Olson.
DELEGATE OLSON: Aye.
SECRETARY KEYSER: Riter.
DELEGATE RITER: Aye.
SECRETARY KEYSER: Thurman.

DELEGATE THURMAN: Mr. President.

PRESIDENT OLSON: The chair recognizes Delegate Sam D. Thurman.

DELEGATE THURMAN: I have the unique honor of being the last delegate of the thirty-sixth state of the Union to record its vote, and, I might add, the deciding vote in favor of the ratification of the Twenty-first Amendment. When this vote is cast the Eighteenth Amendment to the Federal Constitution will stand repealed.

Mr. President, on the resolution I vote aye.

PRESIDENT OLSON: The vote upon the resolution is unanimous.

Ladies and gentlemen:

It is my pleasure to announce that at this moment, 3:32½ P.M., Mountain Standard Time, Tuesday, December 5, A.D. 1933, the Twenty-first Amendment to the Constitution of the United States, which repeals the Eighteenth Amendment, is in force and effect.

At this moment our Convention turns in thought to our great and courageous President in the White House.

It is my pleasure to recognize Delegate A. S. Brown, who will extend this Convention's greetings to President Franklin Delano Roosevelt.

Mr. Brown.

DELEGATE BROWN: Mr. President, fellow delegates to Utah's Constitutional Convention, distinguished guests and my fellow countrymen:

I am informed that our dearly beloved President, Franklin D. Roosevelt, is listening in on our deliberations here today.

If you are so honoring us, my dear President Roosevelt, on behalf of the delegates of this Convention and on behalf of every citizen of Utah I salute you. To you more than to any other human being we owe our presence here today.

You have said that the cause of temperance and the welfare of our country would be promoted by the repeal of the Eighteenth Amendment and we believed you because we had confidence in your wisdom and exalted leadership.

In a crisis greater even than that of the great war, a crisis which has enveloped us for four long years, which has laid its withering and devastating touch upon untold millions of men and women and little children, you came to us with your great heart and inspired leadership, sent, as many of us believe, by a Power from on high.

"Greater love hath no man than this, that a man lay down his life for his friend." We know that, night and day, you are working to remove this terrible burden from our shoulders—this blight from our lives. We know that you are literally giving your life that we and our children may live and work and be happy, as God ordained that we should do. We know that your heart is filled to overflowing with love for us and our fellowmen.

Is it strange that we should believe in you?

From the delegates to Utah's Constitutional Convention, from every man and woman and child in the State of Utah, I send you this message of love and confidence.

May the God of our fathers bless and guard you. May He help you and inspire you and give you strength to complete your task—the regeneration of your fellow-countrymen.

PRESIDENT OLSON: The President will now sign the resolution in the presence of the Convention.

At this time, ladies and gentlemen of the Convention, it is proper to recognize receipt of a large number of greetings from various parts of the country. In particular I wish to read a telegram received from Mrs. S. Grover Rich, who was elected a member of this Convention but who could not attend.

In a telegram addressed to his Excellency, Governor Blood, from Washington, D.C., Mrs. Rich says: (Reads.)

Greetings to you and to Delegates assembled in Convention. Utah is about to usher in a new order of law abiding liberty and temperance. My good wishes are with you.

MRS. S. GROVER RICH.

And to you, Mrs. Rich, this Convention sends its greetings, with regrets that you could not attend and be with us on this occasion.

The next order of business will be the presentation of several resolutions.

The chair recognizes Delegate Miah Day.

DELEGATE DAY: Fellow Delegates: I present the following resolution:

Resolved that we tender a vote of thanks to the Secretary of State, Milton H. Welling, and his staff, to the Salt Lake Chamber of Commerce, to radio station KSL of Salt Lake City and the Columbia Broadcasting Company, to the National Guard officers and to the press of Utah for their helpful cooperation and assistance.

I move the adoption of the resolution.

DELEGATE RITER: Second the motion.

PRESIDENT OLSON: You have heard the motion. Is there any discussion?

DELEGATE ALLRED: I wish to second that motion.

PRESIDENT OLSON: All in favor of the motion will say "Aye." Opposed, "No." The resolution is adopted unanimously.

At this time I wish to introduce Honorable Milton H. Welling, Secretary of State, who will read a telegram which will be simultaneously dispatched to the proper officers at Washington, D.C.

SECRETARY OF STATE WELLING: I have official communications in my hand from the Honorable William Phillips, Acting Secretary of State, Washington, D.C., and from John S. Hurley, Assistant Director Prohibition Unit, Washington, D.C., asking for an immediate report of the ratifying action of this Convention. I have sent identical telegrams to these gentlemen as follows:

You are hereby officially notified that, on December 5, 1933, a convention duly held in the state of Utah ratified on behalf of the said state the proposed amendment to the constitution of the United States providing for the repeal of the eighteenth amendment at 3:32½ P.M., and the duly authenticated papers evidencing the action of said convention will go forward to you by airmail at 1:15 A.M., Wednesday, December 6.

(*Signed*) MILTON H. WELLING
Secretary of State

PRESIDENT OLSON: That, ladies and gentlemen, was the official notification of the proper officer of the State of Utah that the Convention has ratified the Twenty-first Amendment.

What is the further pleasure of the Convention?

DELEGATE HENDRICKS: I move the adoption of the following resolution:

WHEREAS, Section 12 of Chapter 22, Laws of the State of Utah, passed at the Twentieth Regular Session of the Legislature of the State of Utah, 1933, reads as follows:

"Delegates to the convention shall receive a per diem of $4.00 per day while the convention is in session and mileage at the rate of ten cents per mile for the distance necessarily traveled in going to and returning from the place of meeting by the most usual route and they shall receive no other pay or prerequisite. Such per diem and mileage, together with the necessary expenses of such convention for printing and stenographic services shall be paid out of the state treasury."

Be it resolved that the President and Secretary of this convention shall certify to the state auditor the items of expense of this convention within the purview of the above quoted section for action by the State Auditor and State Treasurer, as required by law.

Resolved further that in the event of the death, disability or absence from the State of the President of this convention, that the Vice-President is vested with full authority to act under this resolution.

PRESIDENT OLSON: You have heard the motion. Is there a second?

DELEGATE MCCORNICK: I second the motion.

PRESIDENT OLSON: All those in favor of the adoption of the resolution will say "aye."

Opposed, "no."

The motion is carried. The resolution is adopted.

What is the further pleasure of the Convention?

DELEGATE RITER: I move that the Convention adjourn without day.

PRESIDENT OLSON: Motion for adjournment *sine die* is made.

DELEGATE BALLIF: I second the motion.

PRESIDENT OLSON: Is there any discussion? All in favor of the motion say "aye." Opposed, "no."

There is a unanimous vote in the affirmative. I hereby declare this Constitutional Convention adjourned *sine die.*

VERMONT*

RECORD

OF THE

PROCEEDINGS of convention called in accordance with the provisions of No. 6 of the Acts and Resolves of Vermont, entitled "An Act Providing for the Calling of Conventions for Adoption or Rejection of Proposed Amendments to the Constitution of the United States, Submitted by Congress to Conventions," held in the Senate Chamber of the Capitol at Montpelier, in the county of Washington, on Tuesday, the 26th day of September, A.D. 1933, at eleven o'clock in the forenoon for the purpose of acting upon proposal of amendment to the Constitution of the United States, proposed by the Seventy-Second Congress, at the Second Session thereof

At eleven o'clock in the forenoon the Convention held in the Senate Chamber of the Capitol at Montpelier, on Tuesday the 26th day of September, A.D. 1933, was called to order by Secretary of State, Rawson C. Myrick, ex officio Secretary of the Convention.

Prayer was offered by Rev. Frank J. Knapp of Montpelier:

"O, God, forasmuch as without Thee we are not able to please Thee, grant that Thy holy spirit may at all times direct and rule our hearts. Bless this nation of ours and may its laws be for the furtherance of Thy kingdom in harmony with Thy will. This we ask in the name of Him who taught us how to pray: Our Father who art in heaven, hallowed be Thy name. Thy kingdom come, Thy will be done on earth as it is in heaven. Give us this day our daily bread and forgive us our trespasses as we forgive those who trespass against us, and lead us not into temptation but deliver us from evil, for Thine is the kingdom, the power and the glory forever. Amen."

The Secretary of State directed the Convention to the election of a Temporary Chairman.

Mr. Fenton of Rutland City presented the name of Honorable Franklin S. Billings of Woodstock, as Temporary Chairman of the Convention, in the following words:

"It seems to me that it is altogether fitting at this first Constitutional Convention to be held in Vermont since 1791 that we should select as our presiding officer one who has had the experience of presiding over the House of Representatives as its Speaker, who has presided over the Senate as Lieutenant Governor and who has graced the Executive Chamber as Governor of Vermont. Therefore I have the honor to present the name, as Temporary Chairman of this Convention, of the Honorable Franklin S. Billings of Woodstock."

The nomination was seconded by Mr. Barber of Northfield.

No other nomination being made, Honorable Franklin S. Billings of Woodstock, was unanimously elected, viva voce, Temporary Chairman of the Convention. He assumed the Chair and spoke briefly, as follows:

"I thank you extremely for this honor, and I thank you, Mr. Fenton. It is so long since I have presided over a body so dignified as this body that it is to be expected that I may make some errors. I hope you will excuse me."

* From a typewritten copy.

The Temporary Chairman directed the Convention to the election of a Temporary Secretary, and on motion of Mr. Wilson of St. Albans City, seconded by Mr. Richardson of St. Johnsbury, Rawson C. Myrick of Montpelier was nominated for that office, with power to appoint an assistant Temporary Secretary.

No other nomination being made, Rawson C. Myrick of Montpelier was unanimously elected, viva voce, Temporary Secretary.

Mr. Myrick then announced the appointment of Miss Helen E. Burbank of Montpelier as Assistant Temporary Secretary.

The Temporary Chairman directed the attention of the Convention to the reading of the Proclamation of Governor Stanley C. Wilson calling the Convention and the Special Election of Delegates to said Convention, which was read by the Temporary Secretary, as follows:

STATE OF VERMONT

STANLEY C. WILSON, *Governor*

A PROCLAMATION

WHEREAS, the Seventy-second Congress of the United States, at the second session thereof, proposed an amendment to the Constitution of the United States by adopting a Joint Resolution which reads as follows, namely:

Resolved by the Senate and House of Representatives of the United States of America in Congress Assembled (two-thirds of each House concurring therein), That the following article is hereby proposed as an amendment to the Constitution of the United States, which shall be valid to all intents and purposes as part of the Constitution when ratified by conventions in three-fourths of the several States:

ARTICLE ___ ___

Section 1. The eighteenth article of amendment to the Constitution of the United States is hereby repealed.

Section 2. The transportation or importation into any State, Territory, or possession of the United States for delivery or use therein of intoxicating liquors, in violation of the laws thereof, is hereby prohibited.

Section 3. This article shall be inoperative unless it shall have been ratified as an amendment to the Constitution by conventions in the several States, as provided in the Constitution, within seven years from the date of the submission hereof to the States by the Congress.

AND, WHEREAS, Said proposal of amendment has been officially transmitted from the United States to this State;

Now, Therefore, I, STANLEY C. WILSON, Governor, by virtue of the authority vested in me by law, direct that a convention be held in the Senate Chamber of the Capitol at Montpelier, in the County of Washington, on Tuesday, the 26th day of September, A.D. 1933, at eleven o'clock in the forenoon, for the purpose of acting upon such proposal of amendment;

AND, I do further order that a

SPECIAL ELECTION

be held on Tuesday, the fifth day of September, A.D. 1933, from ten o'clock in the forenoon to eight o'clock in the afternoon, for the purpose of electing delegates to said convention. Said delegates shall be nominated and elected and said convention shall be held in accordance with the provisions of an Act of the General Assembly of the State of Vermont entitled "S. 41. An Act Providing for the Calling of Conventions for Adoption or Rejection or Proposed Amendments to the Constitution of the United States, submitted by Congress to Conventions," approved March 22, A.D. 1933.

SEAL

Given under my hand and the Great Seal of the State, at Montpelier, this 12th day of April, A.D. 1933.

STANLEY C. WILSON
Governor

By the Governor:
LUA B. EDSON
Secretary of Civil and Military Affairs

The Temporary Chairman directed the attention of the Convention to the reading of the Certificate of the Canvassing Board, which was read by the Assistant Temporary Secretary, as follows:

CERTIFICATE

Of the Lieutenant Governor, the Speaker of the House of Representatives and the Secretary of State of the canvass of votes cast for Delegates to the Convention to be held at Montpelier on Tuesday, September 26, A.D. 1933.

STATE OF VERMONT, SS:

Pursuant to the provisions of Section 9 of No. 6 of the Acts of 1933, we, CHARLES M. SMITH, Lieutenant Governor, GEORGE D. AIKEN, Speaker of the House of Representatives, and RAWSON C. MYRICK, Secretary of State, did meet at the State House in Montpelier, on Thursday, the 14th day of September, for the purpose of canvassing the votes cast at the Special Election held on Tuesday, the fifth day of September, A.D. 1933, for Delegates to the Convention to be held at Montpelier on Tuesday, the 26th day of September, A.D. 1933, to act on the proposal of amendment to the Constitution of the United States, proposed by the Seventy-second Congress of the United States at the second session thereof, and first having been duly sworn did then and there publicly canvass said votes and thereupon found that votes for Delegates to the Convention to be held in the Senate Chamber of the State Capitol at Montpelier on Tuesday, the 26th day of September, A.D. 1933, to act on said proposal of amendment to the Constitution of the United States, had been cast at said election for the following named persons to the number indicated against their respective names:

FOR RATIFICATION

Charles E. Pinney,	Middlebury	41,182
Pauline B. Campbell,	Manchester	41,092
Samuel E. Richardson,	St. Johnsbury	41,109
Thomas Magner,	Burlington	41,158
Karl E. Hayes,	Guildhall	41,064
Leo F. Willson,	St. Albans City	41,100

Charles Tudhope,	North Hero	41,069
Joseph C. Benson,	Stowe	41,078
Moses L. Brock,	Newbury	41,075
Hubert S. Pierce,	Newport	41,090
Walter S. Fenton,	Rutland City	41,162
Charles N. Barber,	Northfield	41,078
Harold W. Mason,	Woodstock	41,044
Franklin S. Billings,	Brattleboro	41,094
Scattering		10

AGAINST RATIFICATION

John E. Weeks,	Middlebury	20,714
Homer H. Webster,	Bennington	20,583
Arthur F. Stone,	St Johnsbury	20,584
Harry S. Howard,	Burlington	20,589
Rosella Thomas Morrison,	Lunenburg	20,563
Ernest W. Gilpin,	Richford	20,576
J. Byron Hoag,	Grand Isle	20,566
Thomas C. Cheney,	Morristown	20,573
Fred E. Doe,	Bradford	20,572
George R. Davis,	Greensboro	20,571
Clarence H. Murdick,	Rutland City	20,601
Ai. A. McCullough,	Fayston	20,570
Paul F. Swarthout,	Brattleboro	20,581
Olin D. Gay,	Cavendish	20,566
Scattering		1
	Scattering	7

and we did thereupon declare, and do hereby certify and declare the fourteen persons

Charles E. Pinney, Middlebury
Pauline B. Campbell, Manchester
Samuel E. Richardson, St. Johnsbury
Thomas Magner, Burlington
Karl E. Hayes, Guildhall
Leo F. Willson, St. Albans City
Charles Tudhope, North Hero
Joseph C. Benson, Stowe
Moses L. Brock, Newbury
Hubert S. Pierce, Newport
Walter S. Fenton, Rutland City
Charles N. Barber, Northfield
Harold W. Mason, Brattleboro
Franklin S. Billings, Woodstock

who received the greatest number of votes, duly elected Delegates to the Convention to be held on Tuesday, the 26th day of September A.D. 1933, to act upon the proposal of amendment to the Constitution of the United States, proposed by the Seventy-second Congress of the United States at the second session thereof, as follows:

ARTICLE ___ ___

Section 1. The eighteenth article of amendment to the Constitution of the United States is hereby repealed.

Section 2. The transportation or importation into any State, Territory, or possession of the United States for delivery or use there in of intoxicating liquors, in violation of the laws thereof, is hereby prohibited.

Section 3. This article shall be inoperative unless it shall have been ratified as an amendment to the Constitution by conventions in the several States, as provided in the Constitution, within seven years from the date of the submission hereof to the States by the Congress.

Done at the State House in Montpelier, Vermont, this 14th day of September, A.D. 1933.

CHAS M. SMITH
Lieutenant Governor

GEORGE D. AIKEN
Speaker of the House of Representatives

RAWSON C. MYRICK
Secretary of State

RAWSON C. MYRICK *Secretary of State*

At the direction of the Temporary Chairman, the roll was called by the Temporary Secretary, as follows:

Charles E. Pinney, Middlebury
Pauline B. Campbell, Manchester
Samuel E. Richardson, St. Johnsbury
Thomas Magner, Burlington
Karl E. Hayes, Guildhall
Leo F. Willson, St. Albans City
Charles Tudhope, North Hero
Joseph C. Benson, Stowe
Moses L. Brock, Newbury
Hubert S. Pierce, Newport
Walter S. Fenton, Rutland City
Charles N. Barber, Northfield
Harold W. Mason, Brattleboro
Franklin S. Billings, Woodstock

All of the Delegates were present except Karl E. Hayes of Guildhall.

The Temporary Chairman then directed attention to a communication from Governor Wilson to the Secretary of State, as ex officio Secretary of the Convention, dated September 22, 1933, transmitting a letter from Karl E. Hayes of Guildhall, a delegate elected to the Convention, and a certified copy of appointment of Joseph M. Pendrigh as a Delegate to said Convention to fill the vacancy caused by the disability of Mr. Hayes. Said letters and certified copy were read by the Temporary Secretary, as follows:

STATE OF VERMONT

EXECUTIVE DEPARTMENT

MONTPELIER

September 22, 1933

HON. RAWSON C. MYRICK
Secretary of State
Ex officio Secretary of Convention to act upon
Amendment to the Constitution of the United States
Montpelier, Vermont

Dear Mr. Myrick:

I am herewith transmitting to you the following:

Letter from Karl E. Hayes, a delegate elected to the Convention, to be held September 26th, to act upon an amendment to the Constitution of the United States, disclosing disability of said Karl E. Hayes preventing his serving as a delegate at said Convention;

Certified copy of appointment of Joseph M. Pendrigh as a delegate to said Convention to fill the vacancy caused by the disability of Mr. Hayes.

Yours very truly,
STANLEY C. WILSON
Governor

TOWN CLERK'S OFFICE
GUILDHALL, VERMONT
Sept. 20, 1933

HONORABLE STANLEY C. WILSON
Governor State of Vermont
DEAR GOVERNOR WILSON—

Having met with an accident of somewhat serious nature on Aug. 25, 1933 and being confined to the Hospital ever since, I am very sorry to inform you that I will not be able to attend the Convention of the 26th to which I was duly elected; however I had hopes that I might be able to attend this Convention but the Doctor said it was impossible. With best wishes to all the Delegates, and a successful and pleasant Convention,

I am, Yours truly,
KARL E. HAYES

THE FREEMEN OF THE

STATE OF VERMONT

By STANLEY C. WILSON, *Governor*

To JOSEPH M. PENDRIGH

of Guildhall

GREETING:

KNOW, by these presents, that under the authority of the State of Vermont, in the Governor vested, you are hereby appointed and constituted A Delegate to a Convention to be held in the Senate Chamber of the Capitol at Montpelier, in the County of Washington, on Tuesday, the 26th day of September, A.D. 1933, at eleven o'clock in the forenoon, for the purpose of acting upon the proposal of amendment to the Constitution of the United States, proposed by the Seventy-second Congress of the United States, at the second session thereof, to fill the vacancy caused by the disability of Karl E. Hayes and you are fully authorized and empowered to exercise the duties of said office.

You will, therefore, with care and faithfulness, execute the duties of your said office, for the term aforesaid, by doing and performing, all and singular, the matters and things thereto relating, without partiality or favor to any person or party, but with equal right and justice to all, according to law. And all persons concerned are required to take due notice hereof and govern themselves accordingly.

SEAL

In testimony whereof, I have hereunto subscribed my name and caused the Great Seal of this State to be hereunto affixed. Done in the Executive Chamber at Montpelier, this 22nd day of September, in the year of our Lord, one thousand nine hundred and thirty-three, and of the Independence of the United States, the one hundred and fifty-eighth.

STANLEY C. WILSON

By the Governor:
LUA B. EDSON
Secretary of Civil and Military Affairs

STATE OF VERMONT

EXECUTIVE DEPARTMENT

I hereby certify that the foregoing is a true copy of appointment by Stanley C. Wilson, Governor of the State of Vermont, of JOSEPH M. PENDRIGH of Guildhall as a Delegate to a Convention to be held in the Senate Chamber of the Capitol at Montpelier, in the County of Washington, on Tuesday, the 26th day of September, A.D. 1933, at eleven o'clock in the forenoon, for the purpose of acting upon the proposal of amendment to the Constitution of the United States, proposed by the Seventy-second Congress of the United States, at the second session thereof, to fill the vacancy caused by the disability of Karl E. Hayes.

SEAL

In testimony whereof, I have hereunto set my hand and affixed my Official Seal, at Montpelier, this 22nd day of September, A.D. 1933

LUA B. EDSON
Secretary of Civil and Military Affairs

The following oath of office was administered by Associate Justice Leighton P. Slack, to the delegates:

"You, each of you, solemnly swear that you will faithfully execute the office of delegate to this Convention which has been called pursuant to the provisions of Act No. 6 of the Acts and Resolves passed by the General Assembly at the biennial session 1933, and therein will do equal right and justice to all men, to the best of your judgment and ability, according to law. So help you God."

On motion of Mr. Mason, seconded by Mr. Pinney, the temporary organization was made permanent.

On motion of Mr. Magner, duly seconded, the Chairman appointed a committee of three, consisting of Mr. Fenton, Mr. Magner and Mrs. Campbell, to wait upon His Excellency, Governor Stanley G. Wilson, and inform him that the Convention had completed its organization and was ready to receive any communication from him.

The committee performed the duties assigned it and reported that the Governor had been notified.

A message was received from His Excellency, the Governor, by Mrs. Vivian A. Lang for Secretary of Civil and Military Affairs, as follows:

MR. CHAIRMAN:

I am directed by the Governor to deliver to the Convention a communication in writing.

The communication was read by the Secretary:

STATE OF VERMONT

EXECUTIVE DEPARTMENT

MONTPELIER

September 26, 1933

TO THE HONORABLE
THE CHAIRMAN of the Convention to be held
in Montpelier on the 26th day of September,
A.D. 1933, to act upon a proposal of amendment
to the Constitution of the United States.

SIR:

I hand you herewith, to be submitted to the Convention, a copy of a Resolution of Congress entitled "JOINT RESOLUTION Proposing an Amendment to the Constitution of the United States," duly certified to by Henry L. Stimson, Secretary of State.

Action should be taken upon this proposal of amendment at said Convention, and a certified copy of such action communicated to said Secretary of State at Washington, D. C., as required by Section 160, Title 5, United States Code.

Yours respectfully,
STANLEY C. WILSON
Governor

No. 655

UNITED STATES OF AMERICA

DEPARTMENT OF STATE

To all to whom these presents shall come, GREETING:

I Certify That the copy hereto attached is a true copy of a Resolution of Congress entitled "JOINT RESOLUTION Proposing an Amendment to the Constitution of the United States" the original of which is on file in this Department.

SEAL

In testimony whereof, I, Henry L. Stimson, Secretary of State, have hereunto caused the Seal of the Department of State to be affixed and my name subscribed by the Acting Chief Clerk of the said Department, at the City of Washington, in the District of Columbia, this 21st day of February, 1933.

HENRY L. STIMSON
Secretary of State

By P. F. ALLEN
Acting Chief Clerk

SEVENTY-SECOND CONGRESS OF THE UNITED STATES OF AMERICA

AT THE SECOND SESSION

Begun and held at the City of Washington on Monday, the fifth day of December one thousand nine hundred and thirty-two

JOINT RESOLUTION

Proposing and amendment to the Constitution of the United States

Resolved by the Senate and House of Representatives of the United States of America in Congress assembled (two-thirds of each House concurring therein), That the following article is hereby proposed as an amendment to the Constitution of the United States, which shall be valid to all intents and purposes as part of the Constitution when ratified by conventions in three-fourths of the several States:

ARTICLE ___ ___

Section 1. The eighteenth article of amendment to the Constitution of the United States is hereby repealed.

Section 2. The transportation or importation into any State, Territory, or possession of the United States for delivery or use therein of intoxicating liquors, in violation of the laws thereof, is hereby prohibited.

Section 3. This article shall be inoperative unless it shall have been ratified as an amendment to the Constitution by conventions in the several States, as provided in the Constitution, within seven years from the date of the submission hereof to the States by the Congress.

JNO. N. GARNER
Speaker of the House of Representatives

CHARLES CURTIS
Vice President of the United States and
President of the Senate

The following resolution ratifying the proposed amendment to the Constitution of the United States was offered by Mr. Pinney, who moved its adoption. His motion was seconded by Mr. Pierce and Mr. Richardson:

RESOLUTION

Ratifying the Proposed Amendment to the Constitution
of the United States

WHEREAS, The Seventy-second Congress of the United States at the second session thereof, proposed an amendment to the Constitution of the United States by adopting a joint resolution which reads as follows, namely:

Resolved by the Senate and House of Representatives of the United States of America in Congress assembled (two-thirds of each House concurring therein), That the following article is hereby proposed as an amendment to the Constitution of the United States, which shall be valid to all intents and purposes as part of the Constitution when ratified by conventions in three-fourths of the several States:

ARTICLE ___ ___

Section 1. The eighteenth article of amendment to the Constitution of the United States is hereby repealed.

Section 2. The transportation or importation into any State, Territory, or possession of the United States for delivery or use therein of intoxicating liquors, in violation of the laws thereof, is hereby prohibited.

Section 3. This article shall be inoperative unless it shall have been ratified as an amendment to the Constitution by conventions in the several States, as provided in the

Constitution, within seven years from the date of the submission hereof to the States by the Congress.

Now, therefore, be it resolved by this convention of delegates, representing the people of the State of Vermont, duly assembled pursuant to law in the Senate Chamber in the Capitol at Montpelier, in the County of Washington and State of Vermont, on this 26th day of September, A.D. 1933, as follows:

1. That the aforesaid article proposed by the Congress amending the Constitution of the United States be and the same is hereby ratified by the State of Vermont and the people of said State, acting by and through their delegates constituting this convention and lawfully authorized to pass upon said proposed article of amendment for and on behalf of the State of Vermont.

2. That the Secretary of State, and as he is such, Secretary ex officio of this convention, together with the Chairman of this convention be and they hereby are authorized, empowered and directed to certify and transmit the action and vote of this convention to the Secretary of State of the United States, all in accordance with the statutes and laws of the State of Vermont and of the United States of America.

Mr. Fenton then addressed the Convention, as follows:

"I hardly think that action of such important effect should be taken without at least some discussion of the subject matter, and for want of someone else to start it, I will be the victim. Some of us can remember back fourteen or fifteen years when there seemed to be a great hue and cry for the adoption of the eighteenth amendment. Some of us can remember back fourteen or fifteen years when the body sitting in this chamber, the Senate of that session, undertook action to adopt the eighteenth amendment before the proposal was ever transmitted, as a result of which, in due course of time and in proper orderly manner, they subsequently had the matter brought before them and did adopt it. It was my great privilege at that time to be a part of the official family of a great citizen of Vermont, Percival W. Clement, who had been nominated by the Republican party for the office of Governor upon a platform the first plank of which was opposition to the eighteenth amendment. I recall very vividly an occasion when that gentleman, with the courage which he always possessed, appeared before the committee on federal relations in the hall of the House of Representatives with the room as crowded with people as I had ever seen it, and in a very strong speech pointed out to the persons assembled there and to the people of Vermont, what would probably result if the eighteenth amendment was adopted. Somehow or other every one of the prophecies which he uttered at that time came true just as he said they would come true, but they went even further and conditions developed that no one thought possible or dreamed of under the operation of the eighteenth amendment, until the people of this country, disregarding the loud voice of the organized minority who too frequently mistook the echo of their own voice for the voice of the people, rose up in their might in protest against the continuance of such conditions and are now taking out of the Constitution of the United States an article which never should have been put there in the first place. It is a very great privilege to be a member of this convention representing the people of the State of Vermont and to vote in favor of this resolution and the only regret which I have on this auspicious and historic occasion is that the Honorable Percival W. Clement is not here to witness and participate in the repeal of the eighteenth amendment which he so vigorously opposed in his lifetime."

Whereupon, the roll of the delegates was called, and the resolution was adopted by the following vote:

Yeas, 14
Nays, 0

The following voted in the affirmative:

Charles E. Pinney	Joseph C. Benson
Pauline B. Campbell	Moses L. Brock
Samuel E. Richardson	Hubert S. Pierce
Thomas Magner	Walter S. Fenton
Joseph M. Pendrigh	Charles N. Barber
Leo F. Willson	Harold W. Mason
Charles Tudhope	Franklin S. Billings

On motion of Mr. Richardson, seconded by Mr. Pierce, an invitation was extended to His Excellency, the Governor, to address the Convention. Mr. Richardson and Mr. Barber were appointed a committee to escort the Governor into the presence of the Convention.

The committee performed the duty assigned it, and appeared within the Convention accompanied by His Excellency, the Governor, who was presented to the Convention.

Thereupon Governor Wilson addressed the Convention as follows:

"This invitation is rather unexpected to me as I thought I had performed all the duties pertaining to this function when I caused to be presented to you the certified copy of the resolution. I have not yet been informed as to what your action was upon that resolution, but I am assuming that so far as Vermont is concerned, it was ratified. I can truthfully say that I am glad to see you here. I can also say that as one of those who selected you as delegates to this Convention we had rather of a peculiar condition. It is not very often that you can select or nominate delegates to this sort of a convention and be sure that a majority of the people of the State will approve the delegates that you name. We selected two lists and of course we did not know which list would be elected, but we knew that a list of delegates we had selected would be elected. I congratulate you upon your election.

"I am not going to talk on the proposed twenty-first amendment. That is your business. If you have done any talking, why that is your business, too, to answer to your constituents for what you said. But I want to call your attention to one thing with reference to this convention. Your meeting here to-day is breaking new ground in the work of the constitutional law. This is the first time that an amendment to the Constitution of the United States has been acted upon by Vermonters after a popular vote which leaves without question the feelings of the people of the State with reference to that vote. While in some ways the machinery is a little cumbersome and you have to strain the bounds a little bit to say that you people are delegates to this Convention in the sense of delegates ordinarily going to a convention, yet it is a pretty good working way. I believe that the people of this country are to be congratulated upon finding a way by which the people themselves may determine whether they want an amendment to the Federal Constitution or whether they don't. There have been claims made that the eighteenth amendment was adopted at a time when the people would not have ratified it. We have no means of knowing whether that is so or not, but we do know that if this method is adopted of providing for an amendment to the Constitution, there can be no question about how the people feel as to the amendment. The Constitution of the United States should represent the ideas of the people of this country as to the frame of government under which they are to live. If the people want one kind of frame of government, they have a right to it. If they want a different one, they have a right to that, but they should not have anything put upon the Constitution that they do not want and they should not have anything taken away from the Constitution that they do want. I believe that in these times when it almost seems as though the constitutional rights of the people are being endangered, here is a salutary event that shows that the people of the country are going to use this great document which is the foundation of our political existence and that they are going to watch it in the future and protect it and that no matter what we may have for emergency measures, we are going to be guided by the Constitution in the end for permanent and lasting government. Thank you."

The Governor having concluded his address, was escorted to the Executive Chamber by the committee.

On motion of Mr. Benson, seconded by Mr. Pinney, the Convention adjourned.

Attest:
RAWSON C. MYRICK
Secretary of the Convention

VIRGINIA*

JOURNAL OF THE CONVENTION

Held in the Old Hall of the House of Delegates in the State Capitol at Richmond, Virginia, at 12 o'clock Noon on

Wednesday, October 25, 1933

in Pursuance of

AN ACT to provide for a convention to ratify or reject an amendment to the Constitution of the United States, proposed by the Congress of the United States, for repeal of the eighteenth article of amendment to the said Constitution, and for the prohibition of the transportation or importation into any State, territory or possession of the United States for delivery or use therein of intoxicating liquors in violation of the laws thereof; to provide for the nomination and election of delegates to such convention; and to make an appropriation therefor.

MR. WILLIAMS: As authorized and directed by the act approved August 28, 1933, I call this Convention to order.

I request the members of the Convention to arise and be led in prayer by Rev. Dr. George C. Bellingrath, pastor of Westminster Presbyterian Church, Richmond, Virginia.

DR. BELLINGRATH: Almighty God, our Father; we stand in Thy presence and worship Thee, and we bow before Thee, acknowledging that Thou art the ruler of all mankind. We thank Thee for Thy blessings upon this State; we thank Thee for Thy blessings upon each one of us. We are grateful to Thee that we live in a time when the will of the people may be so immediately known through their representatives. We pray for Thy continued blessing and guidance upon the affairs of our State and Nation. We pray for the President of these United States and the members of his cabinet and those that advise with him. We pray for the Governor of our own State and for all who are in positions of authority and responsibility; for the various local governments; and we pray Thee that the spirit of God may rest upon the citizens of our nation, that in righteousness we may obey Thee, that we may enjoy the blessings of prosperity and peace at Thy hands, and our petition we make in the name of Jesus Christ, our Saviour. Amen.

MR. WILLIAMS: I read the following communications, the first addressed to the Clerk of the House of Delegates by the Secretary of the Commonwealth in relation to the Convention called for today in accordance with the act of August 28, 1933:

---

* Printed. Photographs of the convention in session, the certificate to the governor with facsimiles of the signatures of the delegates, and the appendices containing the Joint Resolution of Congress, the communication of Secretary of State Stimson, the text of the act providing for the convention, the addresses of members of the convention, and a statement of votes cast for and against ratification of the amendment and on a plan for state liquor control are omitted here.

OFFICE OF

SECRETARY OF THE COMMONWEALTH

RICHMOND, VIRGINIA
October 18, 1933

To the Honorable the Clerk of the House of Delegates:

SIR:

As required by Chapter 2, Acts of the General Assembly, 1933, page 3, I herewith respectfully transmit a list of the Delegates to the State Convention to be held on the 25th day of October, 1933, to ratify or reject an Amendment to the Constitution of the United States, proposed by the Congress of the United States, for the repeal of the 18th Amendment to the said Constitution and for other purposes, as ascertained and determined by the Board of State Canvassers at a meeting held on the 10th day of October, 1933, the official record of which is on file in this office.

Very respectfully,
PETER SAUNDERS
Secretary of the Commonwealth

LIST OF DELEGATES

Mrs. Elizabeth C. Hull
C. O'Conor Goolrick
Larkin F. Bristow
James S. Barron
Elizabeth Gregory Hill
W. J. Sebrell
Jno. B. Minor
Mrs. Eleanor Parrish Barton
Cyrus W. Beale
Mrs. Lottie L. Hines
D. L. Elder
Robert K. Brock
Jas. S. Easley
J. M. Parsons
Kennon C. Whittle
Whitwell W. Coxe
Mrs. R. A. Owen
O. L. Stearnes
Bernard P. Chamberlain
Brantz M. Roszel
Mrs. Genevieve Y. Hitt
W. J. Strother
Charles Pickett
Mrs. Margaret N. Keith
Robert Lane Anderson
William Bane Snidow
Charles W. Crush
W. N. Breckinridge
Duncan Curry
S. D. Timberlake, Jr.

MR. WILLIAMS: A communication from the Secretary of the Commonwealth addressed to the Convention:

OFFICE OF

SECRETARY OF THE COMMONWEALTH

RICHMOND, VIRGINIA, OCTOBER 25, 1933

To the Convention Called to Ratify or Reject an Amendment to the Constitution of the United States, Proposed by the Congress of the United States, for the Repeal of the Eighteenth Amendment to the said Constitution and for Other Purposes:

GENTLEMEN:

As required by Chapter 2, Acts of the General Assembly, 1933, page 3, I herewith lay before you a list of the Delegates to the State Convention to be held on the 25th day of October, 1933, to ratify or reject an Amendment to the Constitution of the United States, proposed by the Congress of the United States, for the repeal of the Eighteenth Amendment to the said Constitution and for other purposes, as ascertained and determined by the Board of State Canvassers at a meeting held on the 10th day of October, 1933, the official record of which is on file in this office.

Very respectfully,
PETER SAUNDERS
Secretary of the Commonwealth

LIST OF DELEGATES

Mrs. Elizabeth C. Hull	Whitwell W. Coxe
C. O'Conor Goolrick	Mrs. R. A. Owen
Larkin F. Bristow	O. L. Stearnes
James S. Barron	Bernard P. Chamberlain
Elizabeth Gregory Hill	Brantz M. Roszel
W. J. Sebrell	Mrs. Genevieve Y. Hitt
Jno. B. Minor	W. J. Strother
Mrs. Eleanor Parrish Barton	Charles Pickett
Cyrus W. Beale	Mrs. Margaret N. Keith
Mrs. Lottie L. Hines	Robert Lane Anderson
D. L. Elder	William Bane Snidow
Robert K. Brock	Charles W. Crush
Jas. S. Easley	W. N. Breckinridge
J. M. Parsons	Duncan Curry
Kennon C. Whittle	S. D. Timberlake, Jr.

MR. WILLIAMS: Both of which will be included in the Journal of the Convention. I request the Assistant Secretary to call the roll of members.

The Assistant Secretary called the roll as certified by the Secretary of the Commonwealth, with the following members present:

Robert Lane Anderson	D. L. Elder
James S. Barron	C. O'Conor Goolrick
Mrs. Eleanor Parrish Barton	Miss Elizabeth Gregory Hill
Cyrus W. Beale	Mrs. Lottie L. Hines
W. N. Breckinridge	Mrs. Genevieve Y. Hitt
Larkin F. Bristow	Mrs. Elizabeth C. Hull
Robert K. Brock	Mrs. Margaret N. Keith
Bernard P. Chamberlain	Jno. B. Minor
Whitwell W. Coxe	Mrs. R. A. Owen
Charles W. Crush	J. M. Parsons
Duncan Curry	Charles Pickett
Jas. S. Easley	Brantz M. Roszel
W. J. Sebrell	William Bane Snidow
O. L. Stearnes	S. D. Timberlake, Jr.
W. J. Strother	Kennon C. Whittle

MR. WILLIAMS: The Assistant Secretary will verify the list.
THE ASSISTANT SECRETARY: Those members present are:

Robert Lane Anderson	Bernard P. Chamberlain
James S. Barron	Whitwell W. Coxe
Mrs. Eleanor Parrish Barton	Charles W. Crush
Cyrus W. Beale	Duncan Curry
W. N. Breckinridge	Jas. S. Easley
Larkin F. Bristow	D. L. Elder
Robert K. Brock	C. O'Conor Goolrick

Miss Elizabeth Gregory Hill	Charles Pickett
Mrs. Lottie L. Hines	Brantz M. Roszel
Mrs. Genevieve Y. Hitt	W. J. Sebrell
Mrs. Elizabeth C. Hull	O. L. Stearnes
Mrs. Margaret N. Keith	W. J. Strother
Jno. B. Minor	William Bane Snidow
Mrs. R. A. Owen	S. D. Timberlake, Jr.
J. M. Parsons	Kennon C. Whittle

MR. WILLIAMS: I declare a quorum of the Convention present and I request the members of the Convention to arise and take the oath of office prescribed by the Constitution.

The members arose and took the following oath, administered by Jno. W. Williams, Clerk of the House of Delegates: "I do solemnly swear (or affirm) that I will support the Constitution of the United States, and the Constitution of the State of Virginia, and that I will faithfully and impartially discharge and perform all the duties incumbent on me as a member of the Convention assembled under act approved August 28, 1933, according to the best of my ability; so help me God."

MR. WILLIAMS: The members will find upon their desks copies of this oath which they are requested to sign and send to the desk.

The first business before the Convention is the election of a President of the Convention. The Chair recognizes Mrs. Margaret N. Keith, the delegate from the county of Fauquier.

MRS. KEITH: Mr. Williams, Ladies and Gentlemen: It is a privilege to be present at all today in this historic room, where in the past great issues have been decided; it is doubly so to be one of those chosen by the people of our great Commonwealth to represent them and carry out their will on a matter of National importance. Personally, it is a cause for deep gratitude to be selected to nominate the President of this Convention.

There are present many who are worthy of that office, but there is one who, I am sure we all agree, is outstanding in his fitness for this honor; one so associated with the repeal movement that his name comes naturally to the mind with the mention of the word, for he has always opposed prohibition, believing it to be a weakening of the structure of the Constitution of the United States; a menace to our social fabric, perversive of law and inimical to our traditions.

In that fevered time when a man's political integrity was measured by his blind and slavish acceptance of this now discredited doctrine, he stood almost alone—to many, a Pariah—but fearlessly and tenaciously holding to the right, as he saw the right. And now, with the recent change in public sentiment, he is equally unmoved by popular plaudits, feeling he has but done his duty as God gave him to see that duty.

And, in speaking of courage, I would like to make a simile, which, if a little light for this very grave gathering, I crave your indulgence, remembering I have the precedent of our Government at the opening of the special session of the General Assembly when he told some stories that were amusing and clever, but not in the least legislative.

In speaking of courage I am reminded of the story of Murphy. When asked if his family had sprung from any great man he replied indignantly: "The Murphys never sprang from any man; they sprang at them!" (Laughter.)

Our country has produced many able politicians, but we are justly proud of Virginia for her Statesmen—illustrious leaders, among whom we number this man who, like the Chevalier Bayard of old, is without fear and without reproach. These are admirable qualities, but of greater import to most of us ordinary mortals is the fact that he is beloved by the people.

Fellow Delegates: I have the honor of presenting for your consideration the name of C. O'Conor Goolrick. (Applause.)

MR. WILLIAMS: The Chair recognizes the member from the city of Staunton—Mr. Duncan Curry.

MR. CURRY: Mr. Chairman and Ladies and Gentlemen: This is a unique Convention. All of us agree to the solution of the one problem before us. In Virginia, for nearly twenty years, it was a forlorn hope for any candidate for any office, high or low, publicly to oppose prohibition. His "wet" record was against him, if he was a candidate for Governor or mayor, for judge or justice of the peace. Politicians were never held in less esteem than in this period of prohibition when so many of them publicly approved what they were known not to be following privately.

Until 1932 C. O'Conor Goolrick almost alone among Virginia politicians, with more than a local reputation, stood for the repeal of the Eighteenth Amendment. He is recognized as the leader of repeal in Virginia.

I, therefore, take pleasure in seconding his nomination for President of this Convention. (Applause.)

MR. WILLIAMS: Are there any further nominations for President? If not, the Assistant Secretary will call the roll.

The roll was called and the following delegates answered in the affirmative:

Anderson	Coxe	Hitt	Roszel
Barron	Crush	Hull	Sebrell
Barton	Curry	Keith	Stearnes
Beale	Easley	Minor	Strother
Breckinridge	Elder	Owen	Snidow
Bristow	Hill	Parsons	Timberlake
Brock	Hines	Pickett	Whittle—29
Chamberlain			

MR. WILLIAMS: Twenty-nine delegates to the Convention voting for the Honorable C. O'Conor Goolrick, President of the Convention. The oath of office as President of the Convention will be administered by Justice Louis S. Epes of the Supreme Court of Appeals.

JUSTICE EPES: Do you solemnly swear that you will support the Constitution of the United States, and the Constitution of the State of Virginia, and that you will faithfully and impartially discharge and perform all the duties incumbent on you as President of the Convention assembled under act approved August 28, 1933, according to the best of your ability; so help you God.

PRESIDENT GOOLRICK: I do.

MR. WILLIAMS: I present the President of the Convention.

ADDRESS BY PRESIDENT OF THE CONVENTION

PRESIDENT GOOLRICK: Members of the Virginia Constitutional Convention:

I am deeply appreciative of the honor you have conferred in electing me your presiding officer. We have fought the repeal fight together and this tribute from you assures me that my contribution to the victory won has merited your approval.

If you will pardon a personal allusion I think it not out of place to say that as a member of the State Senate I spoke and voted against the ratification of the Eighteenth Amendment and I have never had cause to regret my action. Consistently since that time I have worked for its repeal and I am glad that the opportunity is now afforded me to preside over a convention which will add Virginia's voice to those of her sister States which have already declared for its repeal.

I think we should all take pride in the fact that we meet here today as the accredited representatives of the sovereign people of Virginia elected to fulfill a pleasant duty, but at the same time, one of great importance.

It may be said that this is an historic occasion because for the first time in the history of the Commonwealth delegates chosen by direct vote of the people assemble in convention to act on a proposed amendment to the Constitution of the United States. It is significant that such convention should be called to consider repeal of the only amendment to the Constitution which was designed to govern the habits and to restrict the privileges of citizens of the several States. It seems to me eminently fitting that the ultimate fate of such an amendment should have been sealed by the people themselves through the medium of the ballot box. We assemble here not to review but to confirm their judgment.

Conventions ordinarily are deliberative bodies but no deliberation is necessary where the people have spoken in plain and decisive manner on a public question, fully understood by every intelligent voter. No question in modern times has aroused so much interest throughout the Nation as that which we call "prohibition", none has been more fully discussed.

Despite assertions to the contrary, prohibition was given a fair trial. It failed tragically, notwithstanding the fact that it was buttressed by Federal and State statutory laws of the most extraordinary character. The ablest and shrewdest minds in the camp of its supporters, framed these measures and American legislative bodies unhesitatingly put them in effect. More than this, these legislative bodies appropriated unstintingly the public funds to enforce the laws and a vast and costly department of enforcement was set up and maintained. Never before in the history of the Nation was such an effort made to insure success of a Governmental experiment.

The dramatic failure of prohibition cannot be laid at the door of government, either National or State. The explanation of this failure may be found in the fact that it was violative of sound Constitutional principles; destructive of the balance of power which should exist between the Federal and State governments, and restrictive of the individual rights and privileges of the people.

If it be conceded that under impulse of great national emotion it rested for a time upon majority public sentiment it must be admitted that this support vanished in the calmer aftermath which followed the World War and once withdrawn its end was inevitable. If it be asked why was this support withdrawn, the answer is that prohibition retarded rather than promoted temperance; broke down rather than built up respect for law; gave birth to nation-wide racketeering, adding to rather than subtracting from the original element; provided a fertile source of official graft and corruption and was responsible for more humiliating political hypocrisy than any other public question in the history of the country. Its downfall had its origin in the people themselves. Substantial citizens in all ranks of life, both men and women, irrespective of party or creed, many of them its former supporters, determined that the time had come to end this ghastly experiment.

Politicians of both parties deserve little, if any, credit for the change in the attitude of the people towards prohibition. They, or most of them, contributed nothing to this end and actually impeded the repeal movement. It remained for a courageous leader, a statesman by all the tests which distinguished the latter from a politician, to bring final victory to the liberal forces in America. This leader is our President, Franklin Roosevelt. (Applause.)

It must be to you, as it is to me, a matter of pride that we are afforded the opportunity to register Virginia's recent verdict. It must rejoice you, as it does me, that the Commonwealth once more returns to sound governmental principles.

When we vote, as we will today, for the ratification of the Twenty-first Amendment, let us do so, conscious of the fact that upon us and those who think as we do, there rests an immediate and vital responsibility—that of replacing prohibition with a sound control system, so framed as to rid us of the evils which now encompass us and at the same time to avoid so far as humanly possible those which may spring up.

Let us not lose sight of the fact that in repudiating the Eighteenth Amendment, the people of this Commonwealth have likewise registered their opposition to a continuation of State prohibition. It is manifestly the duty of all of us who have contributed to these results to now help solve the immediate problem of control.

Virginia should, and I believe will, demand a system, liberal but at the same time divorced from the evil features of the old days; a system unattended by too many restrictions but guarded against license, one in short which, while supplying a popular demand for alcoholic beverages, will tend to promote temperance among our people. If the action we take here today should contribute to this end, we may in the future congratulate ourselves that we were privileged to sit in this Convention.

I again thank you for the distinguished honor you have done me and I declare the Convention ready to proceed with the business of the day. (Applause.)

PRESIDENT GOOLRICK: The act assembling this Convention provided that the Clerk of the House of Delegates shall act as temporary Chairman in the organization of the Convention and shall administer the oath of office to the delegates, after which he shall act as Secretary of the Convention. This authority seems sufficient and it is not deemed essential that the Secretary be elected by the Convention, but to complete the record and remove any doubt, the Chair suggests the formal election of the Secretary and recognizes the Hon. William Bane Snidow, delegate from the county of Giles.

MR. SNIDOW: Mr. President: In this historic hall, where have occurred so many historical events in the more than a century and a quarter of its existence, where the doctrine of States Rights has had a most prominent part, for here it was that the Virginia Resolutions of 1798 were adopted, which sprang from the brain of our Madison, the father of the Constitution—the best qualified to construe it, and to define its limitations; here it was that the immortal hero, to whose name new luster is added with the passing of the years, Jefferson Davis, President of our short-lived, but glorious republic, dedicated to the principle of States Rights, communicated his messages to the Congress of our vanished but not forgotten Confederacy.

The principles of States Rights have ever been a part of the political creed of Virginians. Virginia was one of the States which created the Union; many other States were created by the Union. We have a different viewpoint; we are yet loyal to those principles which have made our Commonwealth the land of glory and romance.

We are called here today by the suffrage of Virginians who still hold to the principles which were kindled in their hearts by our Henry, fanned into a living flame by our Madison, and kept alive by the hundred others whose voices have reverberated around these walls, to add Virginia's ordinance to the effort to return to the several States that which in an evil hour was given, or taken, away from them.

In the performance of our duty here we shall make history in lending the assent of Virginia to another Amendment to the Constitution of the United States, the effect of which is to erase from it that which ought never to have been in it.

It is meet and proper that a record should be kept of what we do here, and there is no one so fit, so capable, so deserving to keep it, as the gentleman whose name I shall suggest; a gentleman whose background is found in the memory of many of those men whose eloquence and devotion to Virginia here in this place have made it a shrine; a gentleman so long identified with this old capitol, years so many that should I name them you would exclaim: "It could not thus have been." The General Assembly, anticipating the will of this Convention, has suggested that which is, and in any event, would have been the pleasure of the Convention to have done; so that joining hands with inevitable destiny, and the decree of the gods, I take pleasure in nominating for Secretary of this Constitutional Convention of 1933 the veteran Clerk of the House of Delegates and Keeper of the Rolls of Virginia, Virginia's most popular Clerk, and Giles county's favorite son and most distinguished citizen, the Honorable John W. Williams.

President Goolrick: Are there any other nominations? The Chair hears none. The Secretary will call the roll.

The roll was called and the following delegates answered in the affirmative:

Anderson	Coxe	Hines	Pickett
Barron	Crush	Hitt	Roszel
Barton	Curry	Hull	Sebrell
Beale	Easley	Keith	Stearnes
Breckinridge	Elder	Minor	Strother
Bristow	Goolrick	Owen	Snidow
Brock	Hill	Parsons	Timberlake
Chamberlain			Whittle—30

President Goolrick: Thirty votes having been cast for Mr. Williams, the Chair declares him duly elected Secretary of the Convention and requests Justice Louis S. Epes of the Supreme Court of Appeals to administer the oath of office.

Justice Epes: Do you solemnly swear that you will support the Constitution of the United States, and the Constitution of the State of Virginia, and that you will faithfully and impartially discharge and perform all the duties incumbent on you as Secretary of the Convention assembled under act approved August 28, 1933, according to the best of your ability; so help you God?

Mr. Williams: I do.

President Goolrick: The Chair now recognizes Mrs. R. A. Owen, delegate from the city of Lynchburg.

Mrs. Owen: I beg leave to submit the following resolution:

Resolved, That the President of the Convention appoint an Assistant Secretary, a Sergeant-at-arms, an Assistant Sergeant-at-arms, a pay clerk, and two pages, to assist in the work of the Convention, and that the Secretary of the Convention certify to the Comptroller for payment out of the fund appropriated for the purpose the mileage allowed delegates for their attendance; and

Resolved, Further, that the President appoint an official Reporter whose compensation shall be fixed by the President and certified for payment by the Secretary as provided by law.

The resolution was duly adopted.

PRESIDENT GOOLRICK: Under the resolution the Chair appoints:

O. V. Hanger, *Assistant Secretary*
Wm. Bullitt Fitzhugh, *Sergeant-at-Arms*
A. B. Davies, *Assistant Sergeant-at-Arms*
Geo. O. Greene, *Pay Clerk*
A. C. Williams, *Reporter*
Walter Aubrey Page, *Page*
Robert F. Scott, *Page*

PRESIDENT GOOLRICK: The Chair now recognizes the Hon. Jno. B. Minor, delegate from the city of Richmond.

MR. MINOR: Mr. President, I move the adoption of the rules of the House of Delegates to control the action taken today by this Convention.

The motion was duly adopted.

PRESIDENT GOOLRICK: The Chair now recognizes the delegate from the county of Culpeper, Dr. W. J. Strother.

DR. STROTHER: I move the adoption of the following resolution:

Resolved, That the Convention invite His Excellency, the Governor of Virginia, to attend and address this session of the Convention, and that the President appoint a committee of three to extend this invitation to His Excellency and to escort him to this hall.

The resolution was duly adopted.

PRESIDENT GOOLRICK: The Chair designates Dr. Strother, Mr. Coxe and Mrs. Hull to extend the invitation to the Governor of Virginia to address this Convention.

The committee extended the invitation and, returning, escorted the Governor of Virginia into the hall.

PRESIDENT GOOLRICK: The Chair takes great pleasure in presenting to this Convention His Excellency, the Governor of Virginia. (Applause.)

ADDRESS BY GOVERNOR POLLARD

GOVERNOR POLLARD: Mr. President, Ladies and Gentlemen of the Convention: It was said of old that "the voice of the people is the voice of God." Whether or not we subscribe to this doctrine, there is something inspiring about a body like this met to register the will of a sovereign people.

In theory a constitutional convention is a gathering of all the people, as distinguished from a legislative body composed of their representatives. Hence we find the acts of constitutional conventions beginning with the sentence, "We, the people, do ordain. . . ."

Today we find additional inspiration in the very place in which we are gathered, for within these four walls the people of Virginia in the last 100 years have five times met in convention assembled to record their will.

In this very room have been heard the voices of James Madison, James Monroe, John Marshall and Robert E. Lee. As I come in yonder door, I frequently recall what my friend, John Stewart Bryan, once said here: "Loose thy shoe from off thy foot for the place whereon thou standest is holy." Jos. 5:15.

On May 6, 1776, our forefathers met in the city of Williamsburg and "framed the first written Constitution of a free State in the annals of the world."

On June 2, 1788, the people of Virginia met in convention to consider the ratification of the Constitution of the United States, framed by the Federal Convention which met in Philadelphia the preceding year. It was called to order in the temporary frame Capitol which had been erected in this city near the corner of 14th and Cary streets, and it is recorded that that building being inadequate, the convention adjourned to the new Academy building which was located near the present site of Monumental Church.

The first convention which met in this hall assembled October 5, 1829. It was a gathering of giants. Ex-President James Monroe was elected to preside. Ex-President James Madison, Chief Justice Marshall and John Randolph were also members of the body.

On October 14, 1850, another convention was assembled with John Y. Mason as its president.

On the 13th of February, 1861, the secession convention met in this hall. John Janney was elected president. It was during this convention that Robert E. Lee accepted the command of the armed forces of Virginia, standing on the very spot now occupied by his statue. Four years of bloodshed, sorrow and suffering followed and after Virginia was conquered, the sad days of reconstruction began.

Another convention assembled on December 3, 1867. Its membership was unique. It was composed of twenty-four ex-slaves, thirteen New Yorkers, two Englishmen, and one member each from Pennsylvania, Maine, Ohio, Connecticut, Vermont, South Carolina, Maryland, District of Columbia, Nova Scotia, Canada, Ireland and Scotland, and only fourteen native white Virginians. John C. Underwood of New York was elected president and the chaplain was from the State of Illinois. This convention gave us the Constitution under which we lived until the beginning of this century.

The last constitutional convention met on June 12, 1901. The venerable John Goode was elected president. More than forty years before he had as a member of the convention of 1861 offered the ordinance of secession. The body was composed of one hundred members. The twenty survivors of this Convention are to meet in reunion at the Executive Mansion on November 11th next. Among those members still in official position are United States Senator Carter Glass, Chief Justice Preston W. Campbell, R. Walton Moore, Assistant Secretary of State of the United States, and the present Governor of Virginia.

Each of these conventions mark new eras in the history of the Commonwealth, but this is not the time nor the occasion to recall the great problems they considered.

To the right of where I now stand you will observe portrayed in beautiful white marble the features of George Mason, who, as a member of the convention of 1776, wrote the immortal Declaration of Rights which has come down through each succeeding Constitution and appears with little change in the fundamental law under which we now live.

The principles embodied in that document had profound effect not only on the Constitution of the United States and the States of the American Union, but have been an inspiration to liberty loving people throughout the world. It has been declared by competent judges to be the most complete statement of the rights of mankind and the fundamental principles of government ever penned.

That declaration contains one statement especially applicable to this occasion. It proclaims that "a majority of the community hath an indubitable, inalienable and indefeasible right to reform, alter, or abolish its government in such manner as shall be judged most conducive to the public weal." This weighty sentence is remarkable because of the cogency of the three adjectives used to describe the right of the majority to rule. Note that this right is indubitable—it cannot be disputed. It is inalienable—it cannot be sold or given away. It is indefeasible, that is, it is incapable of being defeated, set aside or made void.

You are met today to express the will of the majority to abolish a measure which has been adjudged no longer conducive to the public weal. Many may doubt the soundness of that judgment, but no believer in popular government can deny the right of the people to rule.

You are here to vote for the repeal of national prohibition. Your function, while destructive in its nature, is none the less necessary because often we must tear down before we can rebuild. The condemned structure whose foundation of public sentiment has crumbled away must be removed and the ground cleared. But this is only the beginning of the task which now confronts us. It leaves the problem unsolved and serious-minded statesmen must now direct their attention to devising means to continue the fight against the evil of intemperance which since the dawn of history has brought mankind so much sorrow and suffering.

There is another provision in the Virginia Bill of Rights which we would do well to recall on this occasion. It reads: "that no free government or the blessing of liberty can be preserved to any people but by a firm adherence to justice, moderation, temperance, frugality and virtue, and by frequent recurrence to fundamental principles."

Now that prohibition is doomed the supreme question of the hour is: What new weapon shall we adopt to combat this age-old evil? Prohibition is gone, but the evil remains. In the effort to devise new means of fighting intemperance we shall find two classes of undesirable citizens: first, those drys who because of their devotion to prohibition are not interested in any other means of promoting temperance and second, those wets who having helped to destroy prohibition refuse to take part in the new movement to lessen the evils of strong drink.

In your capacity as members of this Convention and in obedience to overwhelming public sentiment, you are now to vote to repeal the Eighteenth Amendment. You will then adjourn and return to your homes, but when I remember the virtue and patriotism represented in the membership of this Convention I feel safe in saying that in your capacity as citizens you will, in the language of the platform of the party to which most of us owe allegiance, "urge the enactment of such measures by your State as will actually promote temperance; effectively prevent the return of the saloon, and bring the liquor traffic into the open under complete supervision and control by the State."

In pursuance of the act of the General Assembly of Virginia, the action of this Convention will be transmitted by the Governor to the Honorable Secretary of State of the United States, through the President and Secretary of this Convention whom I shall appoint for the purpose.

I thank you for the honor you have done me in inviting me to appear before this Convention. You have my hearty good will and best wishes. (Applause.)

President Goolrick: The Chair now presents the delegate from the city of Norfolk to offer a resolution for the adoption of the Twenty-first Amendment—Mr. James S. Barron.

Mr. Barron: Mr. President, I move the adoption of this resolution:

Whereas, The Congress of the United States has proposed an amendment to the Constitution of the United States in the following language:

Joint resolution proposing an amendment to the Constitution of the United States. Resolved by the Senate and House of Representatives of the United States of America in Congress assembled (two-thirds of each House concurring therein), That the following article is hereby proposed as an amendment to the Constitution of the United States, which shall be valid to all intents and purposes as part of the Constitution when ratified by conventions in three-fourths of the several States:

ARTICLE ___ ___

Section 1. The eighteenth article of amendment to the Constitution of the United States is hereby repealed.

Section 2. The transportation or importation into any State, territory or possession of the United States for delivery or use therein of intoxicating liquors, in violation of the laws thereof, is hereby prohibited.

Section 3. This article shall be inoperative unless it shall have been ratified as an amendment to the Constitution by conventions in the several States, as provided in the Constitution, within seven years from the date of the submission hereof to the States by the Congress. And

Whereas, This Convention chosen under authority of the Act of the General Assembly of Virginia approved August 28, 1933, is duly assembled and constituted and is met for the purposes named in the resolution of the Congress of the United States and in the said act of the General Assembly of Virginia now, therefore, be it

Resolved by this Convention that the said proposed amendment to the Constitution of the United States be, and the same is hereby, ratified by the Commonwealth of Virginia.

ADDRESS BY MR. BARRON

With the tender of this resolution let me pause to felicitate the members of the Convention, gathered here to record the mandate of the Commonwealth to sweep root and branch the Eighteenth Amendment from the Constitution of the Republic.

We who saw the rock and guessed the snare and swore that the mind and will of man should no longer be enslaved by the chains of this amendment, sense no personal victory, only the triumph of the enduring genius of our institutions. If we rejoice it is to see cast off this Chinese shoe of human conduct.

In our act is found no criticism of those who sought temperance amid the wilderness of desire and saw the promised land in the mirage of prohibition. Sir, they smote the rock but no sweet waters gushed forth.

We trust that out of this grim experiment will come a clearer vision; that intemperance will find its grave in the ruins of intolerance, and temperance find "a jewel in the toad head of defeat." Let the children of men shed their tears no more at the tomb of prohibition, for the spirit of temperance dwells not there but has gone forth to found a wiser world.

Sir, the history of man is a record of strange desires and a mind struggling to be free. Always are those who would crush the urge of man and cast him into a mould of their making. They made prohibition a religion and the Eighteenth Amendment a creed. We accept no such thing and tear down the rude hut of prohibition to build the temple of temperance.

The profound significance of this hour lies in setting free the will and mind of man from those who would enslave it. He does not grasp its full import who sees merely the ebb and flow of a social experiment. It means more than that. This day marks another escape from the embrace of the moral constrictor, another triumph in the long warfare of the human mind against its oppressor.

A wonderful thing is this which calls itself the human mind. It has discovered all that is known and the unknown it strives to pierce. Prometheus-like, it seizes the fires of the Gods to illumine its way. Yet there are those who would chain it to a rock and let the vulture of intolerance forever gnaw at its vitals.

Sir, the spirit of an unbound Prometheus ranges this hall. The hall where Wythe gave to man its Bill of Rights and the South to Lee its sword. The hall where Henry thundered and Jefferson wrought; one the Titian of liberty, the other its Michelangelo.

On this spot which marks their place we take the Jeffersonian oath: "I have sworn on the altar of God eternal enmity against every form of tyranny over the mind of man."

Mr. President, this is the spirit of the resolution now by us to be adopted. (Applause.)

President Goolrick: The Chair now recognizes the delegate from the county of Grayson—Hon. J. M. Parsons.

Mr. Parsons: Mr. President and Members of the Constitutional Convention:

At the election held October 3, 1933, to elect delegates to this Convention to ratify or reject an amendment to the Constitution of the United States proposed by the Congress of the United States for the repeal of the Eighteenth Amendment to the said Constitution and for other purposes, we were duly elected delegates with mandate from the voters to repeal said amendment to the said Constitution and it is our duty to cast our votes accordingly.

I was opposed to statewide prohibition in Virginia, when election was held many years ago, and I thought it was a mistake to have it, and I am now of the same opinion. The people were told in that election, if statewide prohibition carried it would empty the jails and county homes of the State, decrease the number in the State Penitentiary and would cut down the criminal expenses of the State considerably. This has proven to be erroneous. The criminals have increased at least three times and the number of men and women in the State Penitentiary, jails and county homes are today at least three times as many as there were at that time, and has caused disrespect for law and order. I forcibly recall at that time there were no prisoners in jail in Grayson county, three inmates in the county home and very few people calling for aid outside of the county home. Now, the average number of prisoners in jail in Grayson county is from fifteen to twenty and about the same number of paupers in the county home, and I am reliably informed this same condition practically exists in every other county in the State. Before the statewide prohibition election Grayson county received fifteen thousand dollars each year for schools from taxes imposed on ardent spirits in the State, and every other county and city in the State were paid prorata amounts.

The Governor of this State has selected an able body of men to make recommendations to the next General Assembly of Virginia relative to the control, manufacture and sale of ardent spirits, and I wish now to state that if the United States government and the State government undertake to make too great a profit from the manufacture and sale of ardent spirits, the bootlegger will continue to do a thriving business, and this should be carefully avoided.

Mr. President, I second the motion to ratify the Amendment to the Constitution of the United States, and I verily believe that it will be to the interest of temperance. (Applause.)

PRESIDENT GOOLRICK: Does any other delegate wish to address himself to this resolution? The Secretary will call the roll on the adoption of the resolution.

The roll was called and the following delegates answered in the affirmative:

Anderson	Coxe	Hines	Pickett
Barron	Crush	Hitt	Roszel
Barton	Curry	Hull	Sebrell
Beale	Easley	Keith	Stearnes
Breckinridge	Elder	Minor	Strother
Bristow	Goolrick	Owen	Snidow
Brock.	Hill	Parsons	Timberlake
Chamberlain			Whittle—30

PRESIDENT GOOLRICK: The Secretary will verify the roll call.

ASSISTANT SECRETARY: Those answering in the affirmative are:

Anderson	Coxe	Hines	Pickett
Barron	Crush	Hitt	Roszel
Barton	Curry	Hull	Sebrell
Beale	Easley	Keith	Stearnes
Breckinridge	Elder	Minor	Strother
Bristow	Goolrick	Owen	Snidow
Brock	Hill	Parsons	Timberlake
Chamberlain			Whittle—30

PRESIDENT GOOLRICK: Thirty delegates having voted for the resolution offered by the gentleman from Norfolk, seconded by the gentleman from Grayson, the Chair declares the resolution adopted and this Convention by that act has formally ratified the Twenty-first Amendment to the Constitution of the United States. (Applause.)

The Chair now recognizes the delegate from the city of Staunton—Mr. Timberlake.

MR. TIMBERLAKE: Mr. President, I offer and move the adoption of a resolution which I request the Secretary to read to the Convention.

THE SECRETARY (reading):

Resolved, That the President and Secretary of the Convention execute a certificate, in duplicate, of the ratification of the proposed amendment to the Constitution of the United States, and transmit the same to the Governor of this Commonwealth.

The resolution was duly adopted.

PRESIDENT GOOLRICK: The Chair now recognizes the delegate from the town of Farmville—Mr. Brock.

MR. BROCK: Mr. President, as has been observed, this is a sacred occasion. It represents the return of Virginia from her temporary apostasy to the temple of liberty to right her wrongs. I, therefore, offer this resolution for adoption:

Resolved, That the Journal of this Convention be filed with the Secretary of the Commonwealth as provided by law and that three hundred (300) copies thereof be printed for distribution to the members of the Convention, its officers, libraries and departments of government, and such further distribution as the President and Secretary may deem necessary.

The resolution was duly adopted.

PRESIDENT GOOLRICK: The Chair now recognizes the delegate from the county of Halifax—Mr. Easley.

MR. EASLEY: I offer a resolution in regard to the expenses of this Convention.

Resolved, That the Secretary of the Convention be authorized to certify to the Comptroller for payment of mileage and such actual expenses of the Convention as may be incurred, the same to be payable out of the appropriation made therefor.

The resolution was duly adopted.

PRESIDENT GOOLRICK: The Chair now recognizes the delegate from the city of Hopewell—Dr. Elder.

DR. ELDER: Mr. President, I wish to offer a resolution thanking WRVA for broadcasting this Convention.

The Richmond, Virginia, broadcasting station, WRVA, has patriotically provided a complete broadcast of this Convention without charge or expense to the Commonwealth; and this Convention desires to acknowledge this courtesy so generously shown. Now, therefore,

Resolved, That the President and Secretary of this Convention certify a copy of this resolution and deliver it to WRVA as an evidence of the Convention's appreciation.

The resolution was duly adopted.

THE PRESIDENT: Does any other member of the Convention wish to address the Convention on any subject? The Chair recognizes the gentleman from the city of Charlottesville—Mr. Chamberlain.

MR. CHAMBERLAIN: Mr. President, I know that I express the sentiment of the Convention in mentioning our appreciation of the gracious hospitality extended to us by the Governor and Mrs. Pollard, and our congratulations to Colonel Williams for his efforts in holding this Convention in this historic Hall.

I believe that subsequent events following repeal will cause us to have increasing pride in what we have done this day and I should like to move that the Secretary of this Convention will preserve a permanent roster of the members to the end that in some future time on a fitting occasion we may have a reunion informally to renew again what we have done this day.

PRESIDENT GOOLRICK: The Chair now recognizes the gentleman from Salem—Mr. Stearnes.

MR. STEARNES: Mr. Chairman and members of the Convention, I wish to call your attention to one statement of Section 8 of the act under which we are operating here today: "If because of sickness or for any other reason the Clerk of the House of Delegates cannot perform the duties herein imposed upon him, the Governor shall designate some other person."

Now we have elected our Assistant Secretary who, in the event of the illness or for any other reason that the Clerk couldn't act in this hiatus between now and the preparation of our minutes and the proper certification of our resolution adopting the 21st Amendment shall act. Now in the matter of the Secretary and of his Assistant that is provided for. However, it is going to take some little time to prepare this Journal and have the certificate ready, and it does seem to me that these things are not probable, but possible, and when we adjourn we will have adjourned, as I take it, *sine die.* It seems to me under the circumstances that it would be a wise and proper thing for us to elect a Vice-President of this Convention to meet this situation, and if you will allow me and the Convention is disposed to consider it, I would like to make a nomination for Vice-President of the Convention.

President Goolrick: The Chair sees no objection to that procedure. If the gentleman wishes to nominate a Vice-President, it can be done.

Mr. Stearnes: Mr. President and members of the Convention, in the contest that Virginia has just won in the successful election of October 3rd there were three men who stood out conspicuously as our leaders in that fight. There was an association of the public-spirited and patriotically-minded men and women in this State in several organizations who banded themselves together to get rid of this ignoble experiment, the Eighteenth Amendment, and in the final homestretch of our contest three men were named as an executive committee to look after the details of that contest; one of them our honored President—and how fitting it has been that we should recognize him in every way and from every point of view at this time. But there is also another man, that big-hearted, broad-minded, level-headed citizen of Norfolk—Colonel James S. Barron. There is also that outstanding public servant and citizen of Richmond—Hon. Jno. B. Minor. These two men in my mind should be recognized and I would like to see one named as our First Vice-President and the other as our Second Vice-President.

I hope someone following me, if that meets with your approval, will nominate Mr. Minor, but I arise now formally to nominate Colonel James S. Barron as the First Vice-President of this Convention.

President Goolrick: The Chair suggests if the gentleman desires to do it the Chair will be very glad if the gentleman will nominate both Mr. Barron and Mr. Minor.

Mr. Stearnes: Then I also nominate the Hon. John B. Minor, that worthy son of an illustrious sire, as Second Vice-President of this Convention.

President Goolrick: Does any other delegate desire to address the Chair? The Chair takes great pleasure in placing before this Convention—somewhat late, but that was perhaps not the fault of the gentleman from Salem—the nomination of Mr. James S. Barron as First Vice-President of the Convention and Mr. Jno. B. Minor as Second Vice-President.

All those in favor will say Aye, contrary No. The Ayes have it and I declare Mr. Barron elected First Vice-President and Mr. Minor Second Vice-President of the Virginia Constitutional Convention. (Applause.)

The Chair recognizes the gentleman from Fairfax—Mr. Pickett.

Mr. Pickett: Mr. President, there is one thing that has not been said today that I hoped would be said and in view of the fact it has not been said I ask the indulgence of the time of the Convention.

I find, Mr. President, that the Eighteenth Amendment to the Constitution of the United States was submitted to the several States by the Congress of the United States on December 17, 1917; that the General Assembly of Virginia convened on January 9,

1918, and ratified that Amendment—it was signed on January 14 and I believe ratified on January 11; in other words, after a deliberation of two days and after the matter has been before the people of Virginia less than a month that Amendment was adopted, and I think, Mr. President, it should be said in this place that that Amendment to the Constitution never represented the will of the people of Virginia. (Applause.)

In contrast to the action taken by Virginia in adopting the Eighteenth Amendment we, who have been regarded as radical wets in this State, have conducted an orderly election under the act approved in August of this year, an election held in October of this year, and that we have registered the deliberate and well-considered opinion for the first time of the people of this Commonwealth.

I further want to sav, Mr. President, that representing as I do the county in which is located the homes of George Mason and George Washington, and my adjoining county embracing the home of Robert E. Lee, and my other adjoining county in which are situated the battlefields of Manassas—I say this Convention for the first time declares the will of the people of Virginia, that they are a sovereign State and are fit and able to govern themselves, free from the interference of the people of the other States or of the people of the United States. (Applause.)

Upon motion of Mr. Whittle, the Virginia Constitutional Convention of 1933 adjourned *sine die.*

The foregoing is a true and complete Journal of the proceedings of the Convention held this the 25th day of October, 1933, in pursuance of act approved August 28, 1933.

C. O'Conor Goolrick
President of the Convention

Jno. W. Williams
Secretary of the Convention

WASHINGTON*

PROCEEDINGS

OF THE

WASHINGTON REPEAL CONVENTION

HELD UNDER THE PROVISIONS OF

An Act Relating to and Providing for the calling and holding of a convention to act upon and ratify or reject proposed amendments or repeals of amendments or other parts of the constitution of the United States

APPROVED MARCH 20, 1933
IN FORCE MARCH 20, 1933

HELD IN THE CITY OF OLYMPIA, OCTOBER 3, 1933
AT 2:00 P.M.

IN
THE CHAMBERS OF THE

HOUSE OF REPRESENTATIVES

IN THE STATE CAPITOL

OFFICERS OF THE CONVENTION

Convening Chairman
ERNEST N. HUTCHINSON
Secretary of State

President
EDWIN M. CONNOR
South Bend

Secretary
AUGUSTA W. TRIMBLE
Seattle

Chief Clerk	J. C. Herbsman, Seattle
Official Stenographer	Nema Hofstede, Seattle
Reading Clerk	Robert Waldron, Spokane
Minute Clerk and Reporter	A. C. Baker, Olympia
Sergeant-at-Arms	Joe Mehan, Almira
Assistant Sergeant-at-Arms	S. R. Holcomb, Olympia

* Printed.

Assistant Sergeant-at-Arms	Pat Hooper, Elma
Assistant Sergeant-at-Arms	E. J. Thompson, Olympia
Assistant Sergeant-at-Arms	Geo. Ryan, Seattle
Assistant Sergeant-at-Arms	Morton Gregory, Tacoma
Page	Tiny Maxwell, Olympia
Page	Filson Marshall, Olympia
Page	Richard Yantis, Olympia
Chaplain	Rt. Rev. Bishop Arthur S. Huston, Seattle
Elevator	Ed Walsh, Seattle
Elevator	J. Blanchette, Olympia
Cloakroom	Ben Sawyer, Jr., Olympia
Cloakroom	C. Van Dyke, Olympia
Janitor	J. Towey, Olympia

MINUTES OF THE CONSTITUTIONAL CONVENTION

FOR

REJECTION OR ADOPTION OF THE TWENTY-FIRST AMENDMENT TO THE CONSTITUTION OF THE UNITED STATES

CHAMBER OF THE HOUSE OF REPRESENTATIVES
STATE CAPITOL

TUESDAY, OCTOBER 3, 1933
2:00 o'clock P.M.

Pursuant to an Act of the Legislature of the State of Washington entitled: "AN ACT relating to and providing for the calling and holding of a convention to act upon and ratify or reject proposed amendment or repeals or amendments or other parts of the Constitution of the United States; providing for the election of delegates to such convention; providing for the defraying of the expenses of such election and convention; and making appropriation and declaring an emergency," approved March 20, 1933; the delegates elected to the convention were called to order by the Honorable Ernest N. Hutchinson, the Secretary of State, in the House of Representatives in the State Capitol Building in the city of Olympia, at the hour of two o'clock P.M. on October third, 1933.

CHAIRMAN HUTCHINSON: "Men and women, these delegates of this convention, the hour of the clock prescribed by law has ticked for the opening of this convention. The delegates will take their seats. Representative Robert Waldron, Reading Clerk of the temporary organization, will read the proclamation under which this body has, by its authority, gathered."

Representative Robert Waldron read as follows:

STATE OF WASHINGTON

EXECUTIVE OFFICE

Olympia

A PROCLAMATION BY THE GOVERNOR

WHEREAS, The Congress of the United States, by joint resolution, proposed the following article as an amendment to the Constitution of the United States, which shall be valid to all intents and purposes as part of the Constitution when ratified by conventions in three-fourths of the several states.

Said proposed amendment reads as follows:

ARTICLE ____

Section 1. The eighteenth article of amendment to the Constitution of the United States is hereby repealed.

Section 2. The transportation or importation into any State, Territory or possession of the United States for delivery or use therein of intoxicating liquors, in violation of the laws therefor, is hereby prohibited.

Section 3. This article shall be inoperative unless it shall have been ratified as an amendment to the Constitution by conventions in the several states, as provided in the Constitution, within seven years from the date of the submission hereof to the States by the Congress.

WHEREAS, The Legislature of the State of Washington at the 1933 Session passed a law entitled:

"AN ACT relating to and providing for the calling and holding of a convention to act upon and ratify or reject proposed amendment or repeals of amendments or other parts of the Constitution of the United States, providing for the election of delegates to such conventions; providing for defraying of the expenses of such election and convention; and making an appropriation and declaring an emergency," said act being Chapter 181 of the Session Laws of 1933 of the State of Washington.

NOW, THEREFORE, In compliance with the provisions of said law, I, Clarence D. Martin, Governor of the State of Washington, do hereby call the election, as in said law provided and give notice that the same will be held on Tuesday, August 29, A.D. 1933, for the purpose of electing delegates to meet in convention, to be held in the Chambers of the House of Representatives in the State Capitol on Tuesday, October 3, 1933, at 2 o'clock P.M. of said day for the purpose of ratifying or rejecting said proposed amendment, the delegates to said convention to be elected and said convention to be held in all respects in compliance with law.

In witness whereof, I have hereunto set my hand and caused the Seal of the State of Washington to be affixed at Olympia, this 23rd day of March, A.D. 1933.

(*Signed*) CLARENCE D. MARTIN
Governor of Washington

By the Governor:
ERNEST N. HUTCHINSON
Secretary of State

CHAIRMAN HUTCHINSON: Men and women delegates of this convention, the first people that came to this new world from the old world came with the avowed purpose of finding a place where they could worship God in freedom of their own conscience and, ever since that time, there has been no event of any moment in the history of this State, whether in Congress or in conventions assembled or in the Nation that the blessings of God are not invoked upon such proceedings.

We may not comprehend God, but without God, we can comprehend nothing else.

I am going to ask the Right Reverend Bishop Arthur S. Huston to invoke the presence of the Divine Spirit to aid you that you may comprehend the significance of your being called together.

The Right Reverend Bishop Arthur S. Huston then read the following prayer:

"Almighty God our heavenly Father, 'who are always more ready to hear than we to pray, and art wont to give more than we desire or deserve,' we come before Thee in an humble sense of our own unworthiness, but mindful of Thy great mercy and conscious of Thy loving kindness.

"Thou who has taught us that Thou hast 'made of one blood all nations of men to dwell on the face of the whole earth' and didst preach 'peace to them that are far off as well as to them that are nigh,' we commend the peoples of the earth to Thy merciful guidance and protection; guard them against the threat of tumult and of war, bestow upon them 'that concord among men and nations without which there can be neither happiness nor true friendship nor any wholesome fruit of toil or thought in the world,' and 'to this end we pray Thee that Thou forgive us our sins, our ignorance of Thy holy will, our wilfulness and many errors, and lead us in the paths of obedience to places of vision and to thoughts and counsels that purge and make wise.'

"Thou God of our fathers, 'Who has raised up this nation for a glorious mission' and has given us this good land for our heritage, 'make us to be truly thankful for this Thy great mercy and benefit and help us to share our strength with the weak, our liberties with the oppressed, our bounty with all them that are in need. Pour out Thy blessing upon the President of these United States, upon the Governor of this State and upon all who are in positions of authority.' Grant unto them 'the wisdom to know what things they ought to do, and give them the grace and the power faithfully to fulfill the same.'

" 'Incline our hearts and the hearts of all our citizens' to cultivate a spirit of subordination and obedience to government, and that we may entertain for one another a spirit of brotherly love and affection.

"Bless the homes in which our people dwell. Uplift those who are cast down. Cheer with hope all discouraged and unhappy people and suffer them not to lose confidence in the eternal verities, nor hope in Thy overruling providence. Bless all those who labor in works of mercy and in schools of sound learning and grant that by Thy holy inspiration our moral growth may come to match our scientific achievements.

"For all the manifold blessings which Thou has given us, for our creation, preservation and for our redemption, give us a deeper sense of gratitude and a hearty determination to use our blessings to help our nation to achieve its mission among the nations of the earth.

"Be present with us in the deliberations of this hour, and when we shall have finished the work which has been given us to do, let it not be that we depart with a feeling that we have solved a problem but rather that we have created a new one, in the solution of which we shall need Thy constant guidance and direction.

"Grant us therefore a 'right judgment in all things' and a pure intention that we may ever acquit ourselves as worthy of Thy help and of the respect and commendation of our fellow men.

"Lord, hear our prayer and let our cry come unto Thee, who are with the Son and the Holy Spirit, one God, world without end. Amen."

CHAIRMAN HUTCHINSON: Assistant Secretary of State, Rudolph Naccarato, will now call the roll of all delegates to whom certificates of election were sent. You will all answer as your names are called because that answer will be your warrant for that ten dollars that you paid for the privilege of being here.

Assistant Secretary of State Rudolph Naccarato then read as follows:

OLYMPIA, WASHINGTON, October 3, 1933

STATE OF WASHINGTON }
COUNTY OF THURSTON } ss.

The following is a true and correct list of all persons elected at an election held on August 29th, 1933, as delegates to a convention to be held in the City of Olympia on October 3rd, 1933, which convention was called for the purpose of ratifying or refusing to ratify a proposed amendment to the Federal Constitution, which proposed amendment is as follows:

JOINT RESOLUTION
Proposing an amendment to the Constitution
of the United States

Resolved, by the Senate and House of Representatives of the United States of America in Congress assembled (two-thirds of each House concurring therein), that the following article is hereby proposed as an amendment to the Constitution of the United States, which shall be valid to all intents and purposes as part of the Constitution when ratified by conventions in three-fourths of the several states:

ARTICLE ___

Section 1. The Eighteenth Article of Amendment to the Constitution of the United States is hereby repealed.

Section 2. The transportation or importation into any State, Territory or possession of the United States for delivery or use therein of intoxicating liquor, in violation of the laws thereof, is hereby prohibited.

Section 3. This article shall be inoperative unless it shall have been ratified as an amendment to the Constitution by conventions in the several states, as provided in the Constitution, within seven years from the date of the submission thereof to the states by the Congress.

The said election and convention were called pursuant to the provisions of an Act passed by the Twenty-third Regular Legislative Session and approved by the Governor on March 20, 1933.

DELEGATES TO CONSTITUTIONAL CONVENTION

Charles C. Rumbolz
B. Fitzgerald
Harry C. Meyers
D. A. Newland
N. S. Dressler
Geo. E. Van Hersett
Joseph F. Hunt
W. A. Monroe
Andrew J. Gage
Oscar E. Johnson
Howard J. Burnham
Sam Davis
Paul M. Elwell
Fred W. Crystal
R. B. Jones
Edwin M. Connor
G. E. Crosby
J. M. Ponder
Chester A. Riddell
W. J. Bogart
Paul W. Houser
Wm. D. Kenney
John J. O'Donovan
Harry D. Austin
John N. Wilson
J. R. Binyon
James E. Kelly
Augusta W. Trimble
Frank C. Dean
Ben M. Paris
Joseph McCarthy
Richard S. Munter
Vincent Donahue

A. P. Mitchell
P. Faldborg
J. P. Keller
Lew Brown
Edward F. Gaines
Charles M. Baldwin
J. G. Carrick
F. M. Lowden, Jr.
Henry H. Vincent
Earl I. Babcock
J. D. Bonar
Andrew Hunter
Austin Mires
Frederick Mercy
Joseph C. Cheney
Harrison A. Miller
E. F. Blaine
Charles S. Bilger
Geo. F. Christenson
Dr. F. H. Collins
Stephen A. Girard
Ven Gregg
Ralph E. Peasley
Frank G. Blakeslee
K. L. Partlow
R. W. Condon
Martin P. Halleran
William M. Beach
Marya Gibbs
Cromwell Stacey
Harvey W. Dodd
C. Garrett
Robert Alexander
A. O. Burmeister
Harold F. Broomell
Michael Green
R. P. Fulkerson
V. H. Leonard
Edward Burke
Ralph Burt
Sidney Boucher
Edw. L. Cochrane
Tom Dobson
Victor Zednick
Tom Drummey
Warren G. Magnuson
George A. Gue
Katharine Le Beau
E. D. McGill
Chas. C. Bannwarth
Marie Bock
L. F. Clark
I. B. Hall
George Hammer
H. A. Cassils
C. E. Fitzgerald
Don W. Clarke
J. N. Donovan
James R. Brewster
W. W. Conner
William S. Dixon
Ralph B. Randall
W. H. Medaris
M. D. Pence
Benj. E. Boone
Wm. Brown

I, Ernest N. Hutchinson, Secretary of State of the State of Washington, do hereby certify that the above is a true and correct list of delegates elected as stated above, and as shown by the abstracts of votes from the various county clerks of this state, the originals of which are now on file in my office.

(*Signed*) Ernest N. Hutchinson
Secretary of State

All delegates answered "present" with the exception of Fred W. Crystal of Cathlamet, Washington.

Assistant Secretary of State Rudolph Naccarato: Mr. Chairman, only one reports absent, ninety-eight present, Fred W. Crystal reporting absent.

Chairman Hutchinson: Men and women delegates, elected as delegates here, I think you are due a high degree of commendation that you have followed up and are here as you should be. Does anyone know if Mr. Crystal is in the city or not? Mr. R. B. Jones of the same Legislative district, being present, can you tell me if Mr. Crystal is here?

Delegate R. B. Jones: No, I cannot. He expected to be.

Chairman Hutchinson: If anyone here tells me that he is in the city I will send out and get him. If he appears later after the oath is administered to you he is not entitled to a declaration of principle or intent. It having appeared that there is more than the required sixty-six for a quorum, after the oath of office is administered this body becomes a body legally qualified for the transaction of such business as I may bring before it preparatory to its being organized as a deliberative body. Judge Walter B. Beals will now administer the oath to you. The delegates will please rise and take the oath, holding up your right hand.

Justice Walter B. Beals administered the oath of office as follows:

"You and each of you do solemnly swear that you will support the Constitution of the United States and the Constitution and laws of the State of Washington and that you will in all respects faithfully perform your duties as delegates to this convention, so help you God."

To which all the delegates responded "I do."

JUSTICE BEALS: Mr. Chairman, the delegates to the convention have been sworn according to law.

CHAIRMAN HUTCHINSON: Thank you.

CHAIRMAN HUTCHINSON: Men and women, it becomes my duty, before proceeding with the receipt of nominations, to give you a short address.

In the rolling stream of events constituting the course and record of our progress as a State, that part, written in since a year ago has shown a consistency of purpose to run side by side with National policies of the Democratic party.

On August 29th, Washington stood in the very middle of this National stream and definitely turned it towards the old Democratic doctrine of States Rights and the new Democratic doctrine of Repeal of Prohibition!

This convention simply affords you delegates the privilege of carrying out the instructions born on that overwhelming inundation of November last, and in the great majority of August 29th.

You are the chosen ones to do a specific popular act.

There rests upon you another, an ethical responsibility, to remember that Washington is a Temperance State. Her demand to be rid of the narrow restrictions of Prohibition is only one phase of her determination to re-establish the broad teachings of temperance and restore that companion of education, discipline, that makes teaching effective.

That old fashioned discipline of the railroads, the factories and shops, department stores and banks, which said:

> " 'No Drinker Need Apply!'
> "And we can just add to it, that
> " 'No Drinker May Drive!' "

This is that form of discipline that carries within itself the germ of its own acceptance and its own enforcement. (Applause.)

The time has now come, the most critical of all probably, in this convention. The convention will now be opened for nominations for permanent president of the convention. Inasmuch as you have not all had time to become acquainted with each other, I would ask that each one making a nomination would announce his name and his district so that the rest may know you and it has been requested of me that it is the wish of some, although it is governed by your own individual wishes, it has been asked that we ask you to confine the preliminary nomination to a talk of not much more than five minutes and the seconding nominations should be even less. Nomination for president is now open.

Delegate Vincent Donahue placed in nomination the name of W. W. Conner for president of the convention and stated as follows:

Mr. Chairman, I would like to ask and I consider it a pleasure to present the name of W. W. Conner as president of this convention. I never thought a few years ago that I would be able to see a delegation like this when the prohibition amendment would be repealed but I think after all the work Mr. Conner has put in and the loyalty he has given to the cause and the work that he has done places him in a position where he should be elected president of this convention and, as I say, I respectfully present the name of Mr. W. W. Conner for nomination for president of this convention.

CHAIRMAN HUTCHINSON: Mr. W. W. Conner is nominated.

DELEGATE A. O. BURMEISTER: Mr. Chairman, we are assembled here today under this inspiring dome in answer to the edict enacted in these sacred halls for a solemn and dignified purpose. We know no State or the boundaries of any State. The voice of the people came from Pend O'Reille to Wahkiakum to say that the wrong must be righted. We have a unique situation here. Never before in the history of this State, or may I say, in the history of any other State, have delegates assembled such as we, fresh from the people to deal with a Federal Constitutional problem and it is indeed an honor—I deem it an honor to sit here in this convention to deliberate, a body of ladies and men, upon this momentous proposition and this will go down as a monument, in my opinion, in the annals of the history of this State as a great achievement and as a monument to those who made this achievement possible.

We now come to the proposition, as Your Honor has said, of approaching the great question before us today and that is the nomination of a president who will take the gavel when you, Mr. Secretary of State have yielded it. I wish to say to you, Mr. Chairman, that I am going to present the name of one whose escutcheon is unsullied, whose name has been the by-word in every household of this State, who has protected this country and this State in time of peace and in peril, a man who led the youth of this land into Cuba under Shafter and Theodore Roosevelt, Senior. This nominee heard the call of our lamented and honored and approved Ex-president Wilson when the call to arms came. This man who I am going to place before you, this body, for consideration as president, heard that call. He led the youth of this land into Flanders Field, from Chateau Thierry to the Argonne. He was known as the spearhead of the Argonne; he led his 77th Division through shell and fire of the German army. He is the man that rescued that immortal Major Whittlesey. In time of war he was a savior. He is retired now and he is resting in a peaceful quiet place with his family, doing what he can for civic enterprises and civic causes. It is an honor to us, not an honor to him, to elect him as president of this convention. He knows no north, no south, nor east nor west; he knows no state but his dear Washington. I take pleasure in presenting to you the name of General Robert Alexander. (Applause.)

CHAIRMAN HUTCHINSON: General Robert Alexander is nominated.

DELEGATE HOWARD J. BURNHAM: In a letter which I recently received from one of the delegates to this convention, there appeared the following quotation: "It's of small moment who's elected President of the convention." If we measure the importance of such selection merely as it affects the action of the State of Washington on the ratification of the Twenty-first amendment, the statement is correct. But if we make our selection as an honor conferred in recognition of indefatigable efforts and unswerving service toward the accomplishment of repeal, then our choice is of great moment and should be made thoughtfully, without prejudice, partisanship or log-rolling.

For we must take a fearless and dignified stand against bigotry and corruption, the handmaidens of prohibition. The present picture is not a pleasant one. The vast majority of us here assembled realize that and so do the great mass of voters who sent us here—but, for the benefit of the ninth and tenth representative districts, in the southeastern corner of the State, I beg leave to sketchily paint a few of the brush-strokes that make that picture.

This can best be done, I think, by taking as a base for our set-up that delightful pageant presented some time since in my community by the ladies of the Women's

Christian Temperance Union, "The Patriotic Wedding"—for such was its George M. Cohanesque title—charmingly depicted the wedding of Miss Eighteenth Amendment to Mr. Patriotic Citizen. The bride's parents, Mr. Anti-Saloon League and Mrs. W. C. T. U., were on hand to guard the exits until the fateful knot was tied. Not that marriage isn't a fine thing—no family should be without it.

The flaw in this beautiful extravaganza—if a flaw were possible—was that the dramatist labored under the common delusion that wedding bells end the story and that "they lived happily ever after."

For the acquisition and dissemination of scientific knowledge, let us pursue the bridal pair after the front porch has been cleared of rice and the honeymoon has set. Marriage bonds, in common with all other bonds, have a weaker trend during times of depression—and, as we watch the connubial career of the Patriotic Citizen family, the question keeps recurring to us: "How permanent is a shotgun wedding, anyway?"

For Mrs. Citizen is consorting indiscriminately with speakeasy proprietors, federal agents, bootleggers, coast guardsmen and gangsters. The bride may have been pure as snow but, like snow, she drifted.

To make matters worse right after the ceremony mama and papa moved in to live with the newlyweds and sponge on their son-in-law. As if getting him married wasn't bad enough, the old folks even tried to make him stop smoking cigarettes!

"Marry in haste and repent at leisure." At times Mr. Patriotic Citizen even regretted having been a slacker during the World War, because it was while the worthwhile fellows of his age were in the service of their country that he was inveigled in the "Patriotic Wedding."

* * * * *

Among those who served their Nation in those trying times, none stands out more brilliantly than our own Robert Alexander. General Alexander was in command of the gallant 77th Division and the laurels which they so justly earned were due in no small part to their leader—soon to be ours, too, I hope.

He was Commanding General of the famed Lost Battalion, which braved the fusillade of shell-fire, the deadly gas attacks and savage hand-to-hand struggles in the Argonne, against heavy odds,—to return triumphant.

And so General Alexander was singularly fitted to lead another "Lost Cause" to victory. For Repeal was exactly that. We have the word of Morris Sheppard, father of the Eighteenth Amendment, to verify it. Said he, "There's as much chance of repealing the Eighteenth Amendment as there is for a humming bird to fly to Mars with the Washington Monument tied to its tail." Morris Sheppard, however, reckoned without considering such leaders as our General, and, when the votes are counted in Virginia this evening, the hummingbird—and the Washington Monument—will be eight-ninths of the way to Mars!

In times that try the hearts of men, a farseeing Providence always sends a leader to guide his people out of the morass. You will, I am sure, agree with my statement if I but mention the name Franklin D. Roosevelt. And, as we turn back a few pages in history we find that our Nation has been builded, state by stage, by a people laboring under the spell of a great leader. From those pages stand out the personalities of such as that other Roosevelt, "The Rough Rider"; the martyred Lincoln; Thomas Jefferson; and the Father of his Country for whom this State was named.

And thus it has been throughout the world for all time that a few have directed the destiny of empires and of all mankind.

Consider the greatest Leader of them all, the Galilean, Jesus Christ. Did you ever pause to ponder how He would handle the liquor traffic? "Be temperate in all things" is a foundation stone of Christianity. The Nazarene bade His disciples to carry to the masses the tenets of the Christian faith, and, by instruction and example, to guide them in the right path. Christ did not appeal to the police courts of that day for mandatory enforcement of His precepts.

Many leaders there are who, unsung, mould the opinion of their associates in smaller fields—local, county and state. General Alexander has done his part, in his sphere, dauntlessly and courageously. By his sincerity and unswerving purpose he has been instrumental in drawing the elaborately embroidered cloak of Hypocrisy from the sordid facts of Prohibition, and in bringing to the people of our great State a realization of the iniquity and futility of the Eighteenth Amendment. At long last they have seen the light and have voiced the awakened thought and conscience of this Commonwealth, as evidenced on August 29th last.

And so, in recognition of his signal service to the State of Washington in awakening an understanding concept of the underlying principles which gave our Nation birth, I take pride and pleasure in seconding the nomination, for President of this convention, of General Robert Alexander.

Delegate Victor Zednick seconded the nomination of W. W. Conner for president of the convention as follows:

MR. ZEDNICK: Mr. Chairman and delegates, my name is Victor Zednick, 36th District, Seattle. I think it is most appropriate in view of the State-wide acquaintance of former State Senator W. W. Conner and the fact that he is beloved and admired throughout the length and breadth of this State from Okanogan and Spokane on the east side to the Pacific on the west side, I think that the delegates from the east side should join with the delegates from the west side in putting forward the name of Senator Conner of Seattle for president of this convention. I am pleased and I deem it a privilege and an honor to second his nomination, especially for two reasons:

First, from the very beginning and for years and years as a member of the State Senate and a member of the State House of Representatives he has been opposed to the 18th Amendment but in favor of temperance and liberty. He toured this State in behalf of the measure last fall to repeal the Bone-Dry law in this State and he assisted that excellent organization, the women's organization for National prohibition reform headed by Miss Augusta Trimble, in going up and down the State in support of delegates who are now seated in this convention. My first reason for seconding his nomination is that from the standpoint of a supporter of the cause for which we are now assembled here, all of us but four, he has been a foremost and consistent fighter for that cause and the cause of true temperance.

My second oustanding reason for seconding his nomination is his ability as a presiding officer and I believe that he should be recognized in this deliberative body. It was my privilege to serve with Mr. Conner in the House of Representatives in 1911, 1913 and 1915. In 1915 he was Speaker of the House. At that time he earned the reputation for being capable, an excellent Parliamentarian and absolutely fair in his ruling. I think it is no exaggeration to say, as Secretary of the House and Senate of this State, that Senator Conner was the best presiding officer this State ever had and I have personally observed them, as Secretary of the House and the Senate, for the last twenty-five years.

I deem it a pleasure for those two outstanding reasons to second his nomination, and to say that as a citizen and as a patriot, he is one of the finest men in the State of Washington and I second the nomination of Senator W. W. Conner.

CHAIRMAN HUTCHINSON: I recognize Mr. Harry D. Austin, 33rd District.

DELEGATE HARRY D. AUSTIN: Mr. Chairman, ladies and gentlemen, I, too, want to submit to you the name of a warrior. I want to submit the name of a man who resides at South Bend, Washington, a newspaper editor running a newspaper for years in the same town as the editor of another newspaper run by Mr. Hazeltine, a dry, formerly prohibition administrator. The man that I will name to you has been fighting the battle for repeal ever since the State went dry. It takes a lot of nerve to publish a newspaper in a dry community headed by the dry editor of that newspaper as my candidate has done. He is an outstanding citizen known to most men of the State.

I therefore submit for nomination the name of Ed Connor of South Bend, Washington.

CHAIRMAN HUTCHINSON: Edwin M. Connor has been nominated.

DELEGATE J. R. BINYON: Mr. Chairman, I would like to put before you the name of a man to preside over this gathering. This man has served and will serve in a judicious manner, a man that will decide all questions fairly. I believe by placing Mr. Frank C. Dean's name before you, you will have a man who is fair and a good presiding officer.

CHAIRMAN HUTCHINSON: The name of Frank C. Dean is presented.

DELEGATE BEN PARIS: Mr. Chairman, I feel that I would not have done my duty in this convention if I hadn't got up and seconded the nomination of a man who has been oustanding in the State of Washington as one of our leaders; a man who for seventeen years has fought the eighteenth amendment; a man who has not been afraid to stand on his feet and say that he was opposed to the eighteenth amendment, the effect of which has been brought about in the State of Washington. We know what it has done for our country; we know what it has been and we know we have one man who has stood for the repeal of the eighteenth amendment ever since its inauguration and I say to you today—we have a man who has been presented to you that I think is an outstanding citizen, a man who has fought for what is right, decent and honest and at this time, Mr. Chairman, I wish to second the nomination of the man who has had the courage and the ability to stand up and fight for the repeal of the eighteenth amendment, fight for temperance, fight for the best interests of this country and a man whom I would like to see elected as chairman of this convention, W. W. Conner.

DELEGATE RALPH B. RANDALL: Mr. Chairman, my name is Ralph B. Randall of the 44th District. I would like to second the nomination of Frank C. Dean. Mr. Frank C. Dean has, like many of us, taken the position that the return of liquor was not the prime factor in the repealing of the eighteenth amendment.

Mr. Dean stood for personal liberty and Mr. Dean is a temperance man. Mr. Dean, in everything that he has said and done in connection with the eighteenth amendment, has always been consistent with temperance and I would like to read you a letter received by Mr. Dean from Arthur C. Bannon, the author of Initiative Measure No. 61. [Mr. Randall read the letter.]

As an outstanding candidate for the position of president of your august body, I desire to recommend him for consideration for the following reasons: When I first started out in my campaign to make this State wet Mr. Dean was one of the very few men to offer aid and encouragement. He was one of the few men who gave his time and money and his efforts and, to my mind, he is one of the very few—and I say this advisedly—outstanding wets.

Had it not been for Mr. Dean and a very few more like him it is my earnest opinion that Initiative 61 would never have gained the impetus to go through to a successful conclusion. It is my earnest conviction that the extremely high honor of being elected president of this convention is none too great for such a man as Frank C. Dean and I take pleasure in seconding his nomination.

Delegate Richard S. Munter: Mr. Chairman, my name is Richard S. Munter, 6th District, Spokane. It has always been my observation that, in these assemblies held in the State of Washington, when you boys of the west side get into your friendly conflicts, eventually you have to look to the east side to settle your little difficulties. Several of us from the eastern part of the State wish to present the name of Mr. Joseph McCarthy, my team-mate here at this convention. He is a member of the State Bar Association and has been one of the oustanding Democrats of this State for a number of years and has taken a very sensible attitude toward this law and, in the parlance of sport, when you boys from the west side get through rowing around we ask that you come around and vote for Mr. McCarthy as president of this convention.

Chairman Hutchinson: The name of Joseph McCarthy has been presented.

Delegate Edward L. Cochrane: Mr. Chairman, I move that the nominations be closed.

Chairman Hutchinson: It is moved and seconded that the nominations be closed.

Delegate Joseph C. Cheney (interrupting): After having heard all of the eulogies of various individuals I would like to bring before the men and women of this convention an individual who has not been campaigning over the State for that job——

Delegate Cochrane (interrupting): I rise to a point of order. A motion has been put.

Chairman Hutchinson: The motion has not been put. The gentleman is in order.

Delegate Cochrane: There is a motion and it was seconded.

Delegate Cheney: The motion hasn't been stated.

Chairman Hutchinson: The Chairman did not recognize the motion. Mr. Cheney was recognized before the motion was recognized and the Chair will rule Mr. Cheney is in order.

Delegate Joseph C. Cheney: I have heard how they have attempted to create the best interests of this convention. I have heard Spokane come in with a very courteous offer to settle all the problems and I have heard, also, all about the troubles of prohibition and along with the record of General Alexander, I have heard about how the war was won. Those things, to me, seem wholly immaterial. The fact still remains that the position of chairman of this convention is purely an honorary position.

It is a position purely honorary and I want to simply make a gesture of respect to a man from the irrigated valley of the Yakima River and I might call your attention to the fact that we have an expert authority on the question of irrigation. We have, today a man to be presented at this convention, a man who has, for more than thirty years last past, been an authority in the State of Washington. He has been and is given the credit for being the father of irrigation in the State of Washington and a man who has served the State for years and years and who has never yet, insofar as my knowledge goes, been a candidate for personal advertisement. Even now he is not well advised as to whether or not his name is going to be presented but I take pleasure, as a delegate from Yakima County, in presenting to you the name of the grand old man of irrigation, Mr. E. F. Blaine.

CHAIRMAN HUTCHINSON: The name of E. F. Blaine has been presented.

DELEGATE EDWARD L. COCHRANE: Mr. Chairman, I again move the nominations be closed.

CHAIRMAN HUTCHINSON: It is moved and seconded that the nominations be closed. Are you ready for the question? All those in favor signify by saying "Aye"; those opposed "No."

CHAIRMAN HUTCHINSON: The motion prevails.

CHAIRMAN HUTCHINSON: Gentlemen, you are now ready for the voting. It has been called to my attention that I should call to your attention and emphasize the fact that we have the honored name of Conner represented by two very agreeable gentlemen, Mr. Edwin M. Connor and Mr. W. W. Conner. In responding to the call of your name it is necessary that you designate which of these very elegant men you wish to express a preference for.

It is necessary that the representative respond as his name is called.

Reading Clerk Robert Waldron called the roll of all the delegates present.

The result of the voting was 44 for W. W. Conner, 33 for Robert Alexander, 7 for Edwin M. Connor, 7 for Frank C. Dean, 1 for Joseph McCarthy and 5 for E. F. Blaine.

Delegate Wm. N. Beach voted for Augusta W. Trimble, said vote, by order of the Chairman, not being counted.

CHAIRMAN HUTCHINSON: Out of 97 votes cast, W. W. Conner received 44, General Alexander 33, Edwin M. Connor 7, Mr. Dean 7, Mr. McCarthy 1, Mr. Blaine 5, 97 votes cast.

That makes necessary for a choice 49. There was one not voting. I am holding there was only one not voting. It requires fifty for a choice. It will be necessary for the clerk to call the roll once more. You may be at ease for another three minutes and maybe you will come to a conclusion in that time.

(Short intermission.)

CHAIRMAN HUTCHINSON: The delegates will all please take their seats now promptly.

DELEGATE J. M. PONDER: May I suggest that the Clerk repeat the name of each vote as it has been cast.

CHAIRMAN HUTCHINSON: He has been so instructed. Now, gentlemen and ladies, it has been suggested by other delegates who have approached the Chair during this interim that some of these candidates who have received the honor of mention and nomination might wish to withdraw. I will give you a moment or two for such deliberation. The clerk will call the roll of the nominations as made. I would like again to emphasize the necessity of mentioning Edwin M. Connor or Ed Connor so that we may distinguish him from the other bearer of that honorable name and be a little louder in your replies and it will lessen the work of the clerk.

Reading Clerk Robert Waldron again called the roll.

The voting resulted in, out of 98 votes cast, 45 for W. W. Conner, 32 for Robert Alexander, 7 for Frank S. Dean, 1 for Joseph McCarthy, 4 for E. F. Blaine and 9 for Edwin M. Connor.

CHAIRMAN HUTCHINSON: Ninety-eight votes were cast. Necessary for a choice, 50. There not being any decisive vote, the clerk will call the roll again. I will give you a few moments for deliberation. I will give you five minutes this time.

(Short intermission.)

CHAIRMAN HUTCHINSON: Gentlemen and ladies, you will all be seated. The delegates will be seated, please. The clerk will again call the roll for the election for president with the same nominees as have prevailed in the two previous votes.

Reading Clerk Robert Waldron again called the roll.

Out of 98 votes cast: W. W. Conner received 43, Robert Alexander 33, Edwin M. Connor 9, Frank S. Dean 7, Joseph McCarthy 1 and E. F. Blaine 5.

CHAIRMAN HUTCHINSON: No one having received the necessary number, the clerk will again call the roll. There will be no recess until there is a nomination. You may be at ease for ten minutes.

CHAIRMAN HUTCHINSON: I will recognize General Alexander. If he were not as great a man as he is I would not recognize anyone until after the roll call but I will recognize General Alexander and ask him to wait until all are in their seats.

DELEGATE ROBERT ALEXANDER: Anticipatory to this roll call I wish to withdraw my candidacy for president of this assembly in favor of my warm friend, Mr. Edwin M. Connor.

DELEGATE FRANK S. DEAN: Mr. Chairman, I wish to withdraw my candidacy in favor of Edwin M. Connor.

DELEGATE JOSEPH MCCARTHY: Mr. Chairman, while I sought to elect a good candidate, I believe there are certain reasons that I didn't vote for myself, knowing there were two good men for the office of the president and, seeing that there is a deadlock, I wish to withdraw my candidacy in favor of Edwin M. Connor.

DELEGATE JOSEPH C. CHENEY: Mr. Chairman, Candidate Blaine withdraws his candidacy in favor of Edwin M. Connor.

DELEGATE W. W. CONNER: Mr. Chairman so that there may be a saving of time and a unanimity of thought and to bring victory to the name Connor and to elect Connor president of this convention, I therefore withdraw my candidacy in favor of Edwin M. Connor.

DELEGATE WARREN G. MAGNUSON: Mr. Chairman, I would like, at this time, to suggest to this body if it is not proper to make a motion, I think we can interrupt the proceedings long enough for this purpose and I suggest the names of W. W. Conner and General Robert Alexander as Honorary Vice Chairman of this convention.

DELEGATE W. W. CONNER: Mr. Chairman, I rise to a point of order.

CHAIRMAN HUTCHINSON: That is an admirable motion, but it happens it is out of order.

DELEGATE W. W. CONNER: Mr. Chairman, I move that the Secretary be instructed to cast the unanimous vote of this convention for Edwin M. Connor and that the record show the roll was called and all delegates present voted for Edwin M. Connor.

CHAIRMAN HUTCHINSON: It has been moved and seconded that the Secretary cast the unanimous vote of this convention for Edwin M. Connor. All in favor of the motion will signify by saying aye, opposed no.

A viva voce vote was taken.

CHAIRMAN HUTCHINSON: The motion is carried unanimously. Mr. Edwin M. Connor is now declared the permanent president of this convention and I will appoint Mrs. Marya Gibbs, W. W. Conner and General Robert Alexander to conduct the president, Edwin M. Connor, to the Chair while I turn over this emblem of authority to him.

President Edwin M. Connor was conducted to the Chair by the committee.

DELEGATE MARYA GIBBS: Mr. Chairman, I am very happy to present Mr. Edwin M. Connor as president of this convention.

CHAIRMAN HUTCHINSON: Mr. Edwin M. Connor, I am happy to turn this emblem of authority over to you and I turn it over to you most graciously because I never had one in my hand before.

PRESIDENT EDWIN M. CONNOR: Mr. Chairman and fellow delegates, this is indeed a great honor and a great responsibility.

As you know, I was not an active candidate for this high honor. I came to the convention pledged and as a man of honor I fulfilled my pledge until such time as I was released. It is indeed a great honor. Little did I dream, when I filed as a candidate that I would be your president at the present time.

I have fought the battle for a great many years for just such a situation and epochal occasion as we are now enjoying. I am not going to make you a long talk. I know the delegates want to get away. I don't know what the order of business is because this was a surprise honor and I appreciate it.

DELEGATE W. W. CONNER: Mr. President and members of this convention, something over forty years ago in a little building which, I am sorry to say, was not preserved for posterity, there assembled in this State the original Constitutional Convention in 1889. We have a member of that convention, one of the three living signers of the Constitution of the State of Washington. We feel that we are really doing something here but, when we consider the comparatively small task that we have compared with that performed by the members of the Constitutional Convention of this State, I believe you will agree with me that the member of that original Constitutional Convention, who is now a member of this convention, should be honored by us and I, therefore, Mr. President, move you that as Honorary President of this convention, we elect our good friend and one of the signers of the State Constitution, Judge Austin Mires of Ellensburg.

PRESIDENT CONNOR: It has been moved and seconded that the Honorable Austin Mires be named the honorary president of this convention. Are you ready for the question? All in favor of the motion will say aye, opposed no.

Viva voce vote was taken.

PRESIDENT CONNOR: The motion is carried unanimously.

DELEGATE WALTER G. MAGNUSON: Mr. President, again I would like to renew my motion so that when you conduct Mr. Mires to the rostrum you will take along with him W. W. Conner and General Alexander as honorary presidents of this convention.

PRESIDENT CONNOR: It has been moved and seconded that the Honorable W. W. Conner and General Robert Alexander be named as honorary vice-presidents of this convention. All in favor will say aye, opposed no.

Viva voce vote was taken.

PRESIDENT CONNOR: The ayes have it and the gentlemen are elected.

DELEGATE VICTOR ZEDNICK: Mr. President, I think it is necessary that a secretary of this convention be elected and I should like to nominate Miss Augusta W. Trimble as that secretary.

PRESIDENT CONNOR: It is moved and seconded that Miss Trimble be elected secretary of this convention. All in favor of the motion will say aye, opposed no.

A viva voce vote was taken.

PRESIDENT CONNOR: The motion is carried unanimously.

DELEGATE JOSEPH C. CHENEY: Mr. President, I think we should make Mr. Fred Mercy honorary sergeant-at-arms of this convention and I so move.

PRESIDENT CONNOR: I don't hear any second to the motion and it is lost for want of a second.

I would like to have a motion made to endorse the list of employees that carry the names and salaries which are necessary for the Secretary of State to appoint in order to organize this convention. I would like to receive a motion.

DELEGATE PAUL W. HOUSER: Mr. President, I make a motion that the employees employed by the Secretary of State be paid at the rate set by him.

PRESIDENT CONNOR: It is moved and seconded that the Secretary of State be authorized to pay the employees whom he authorized as officers of the convention. All in favor of the motion will signify by saying aye, opposed no.

A viva voce vote was taken.

PRESIDENT CONNOR: Motion carried unanimously.

DELEGATE W. W. CONNER: Mr. President and members of this convention, most of us would be happy and desire to recall many times in the later years of our lives if we had the honor of presenting the resolution which this convention will act upon to ratify the twenty-first amendment.

Therefore, so there will be no jealousies or anything else, I move you, Mr. President, that it is the sense of this convention that those five lovely women who are members here be requested to introduce their resolution ratifying the twenty-first amendment.

PRESIDENT CONNOR: The reading clerk will read the resolution.

Reading Clerk Robert Waldron then read the following resolution:

WHEREAS, The Congress of the United States on February 20, 1933, passed the following:

JOINT RESOLUTION

Proposing an amendment to the Constitution of the United States

Resolved, by the Senate and House of Representatives of the United States of America in Congress assembled (two-thirds of each House concurring therein), that the following article is hereby proposed as an amendment to the Constitution of the United States, which shall be valid to all intents and purposes as part of the Constitution when ratified by conventions in three-fourths of the several states:

Section 1. The Eighteenth Article of Amendment to the Constitution of the United States is hereby repealed.

Section 2. The transportation or importation into any state, territory or possession of the United States for delivery or use therein of intoxicating liquors, in violation of the laws thereof, is hereby prohibited.

Section 3. This article shall be inoperative unless it shall have been ratified as an amendment to the Constitution by conventions in the several states, as provided in

the Constitution, within seven years from the date of the submission hereof to the states by the Congress.

Now, therefore, be it resolved, That the convention duly elected by the electors of the State of Washington and held in the City of Olympia in said state to act upon that proposal of amendment to the Constitution of the United States which is set forth in the aforesaid joint resolution, now ratifies and approves said proposed article, as set forth in said joint resolution, as an amendment to the Constitution of the United States.

Adopted in convention assembled, this third day of October in the year of our Lord one thousand nine hundred and thirty-three.

In witness whereof, we have hereunto subscribed our names, For or Against, as we answered the roll call.

DELEGATE MRS. HALL: Mr. President, I move the adoption of the resolution, and that each delegate after voting viva voce do proceed to the secretary's desk and attach his personal signature to the resolution.

PRESIDENT CONNOR: It is necessary that the roll be called and the delegates answer to their names when the clerk calls the roll. The clerk will call the roll.

DELEGATE W. W. CONNER: Mr. President, the ladies have suggested that, as the roll is called, the delegate when answering the roll, shall advance to the secretary's desk and subscribe his name to the resolution.

PRESIDENT CONNOR: Now, ladies and gentlemen, there will be more business to come after the roll call. The convention is not adjourned, so do not leave.

DELEGATE W. W. CONNER: In seconding the motion of the lady from Skagit County here, let me say to you that, at the time of the signing of the Constitution of this State as adopted, one member of the Constitutional Convention had to leave and was not able to sign the Constitution as submitted. That man is still with us over in the city of Spokane. But, so that he could sign that Constitution it was necessary for the Legislature of this State to pass a special act authorizing the Secretary of State to allow that member of the Constitutional Convention to present himself at the State Capitol and sign that constitution.

Now, this may take us five or ten minutes but I certainly hope that the motion will carry and that we will subscribe all of our names to that resolution. I hope the motion will prevail.

PRESIDENT CONNOR: It has been moved and seconded that the resolution be now adopted and that, as your names are called, the delegates will vote, of course, where you are at your desk and you will then advance to the secretary's desk to sign the Resolution. You will answer your vote by yea or nay. The clerk will call the roll.

DELEGATE W. W. CONNER: Mr. President, there is a motion before the house.

PRESIDENT CONNOR: Yes. You have heard the motion. All in favor of the motion will say aye, those opposed, no.

A viva voce vote was taken.

PRESIDENT CONNOR: Motion carried. The clerk will call the roll.

DELEGATE PAUL W. HOUSER: Mr. President, permit me to call your attention to the fact that the legislature authorizing this convention provides that the roll shall be called and the ayes and the nays shall be entered in the journal and, for that reason, in order for us to act legally and effectively on the thing we are trying to do, it will be necessary for the roll to be called and the members answer aye or nay and that vote must be entered in the journal.

PRESIDENT CONNOR: That is what we are doing now.

The Reading Clerk, Robert Waldron, proceeded to call the roll and the following delegates voted in the affirmative:

Charles C. Rumbolz
B. Fitzgerald
Harry C. Meyers
D. W. Newland
N. S. Dressler
Geo. E. Van Hersett
Joseph F. Hunt
W. A. Monroe
Andrew J. Gage
Paul M. Elwell
R. R. Jones
Edwin M. Connor
G. E. Crosby
J. M. Ponder
Chester A. Riddell
W. J. Bogart
Stephen A. Girard
Vean Gregg
John J. O'Donovan
Harry D. Austin
John N. Wilson
J. R. Binyon
James E. Kelly
Augusta W. Trimble
Frank C. Dean
Ben M. Paris
Victor Zednick
Oscar E. Johnson
Joseph McCarthy
Richard S. Munter
Vincent Donahue
A. P. Mitchell
P. Faldborg
J. P. Keller
F. M. Lowden, Jr.
Henry H. Vincent
Earl I. Babcock
J. D. Bonar
Andrew Hunter
Austin Mires
Frederick Mercy
Joseph C. Cheney
Harrison A. Miller
E. F. Blaine
Charles S. Bilger
Geo. F. Christenson
Dr. F. H. Collins
Howard J. Burnham
Sam Davis
Ralph E. Peasley
Frank G. Blakeslee
K. L. Partlow
R. W. Condon
Martin P. Halleran
William M. Beach
Marya Gibbs
Cromwell Stacey
Harvey W. Dodd
C. Garrett
Robert Alexander
A. O. Burmeister
Harold F. Broomell
R. P. Fulkerson
Michael Green
V. H. Leonard
Edward Burke
Ralph Burt
Sidney Boucher
Edw. L. Cochrane
Tom Dobson
Paul W. Houser
Wm. D. Kenney
Tom Drummey
Warren G. Magnuson
George A. Gue
Katherine Le Beau
E. B. McGill
Chas. C. Bannworth
Marie Bock
L. F. Clark
I. B. Hall
George Hammer
H. A. Cassils
C. E. Fitzgerald
Don W. Clarke
J. N. Donovan
James R. Brewster
W. W. Conner
William S. Dixon
Ralph B. Randall
W. H. Medaris
M. D. Pence
Benj. E. Boone
Wm. Brown

Those voting in the negative were:

Lew Brown
Edward F. Gaines
Charles M. Baldwin
J. G. Carrick

PRESIDENT CONNOR: There is a total of 98 votes cast, of which 94 vote aye and 4 vote nay, one absent. Now, we can entertain no business until this roll has been signed, after which I will again ask you to take your seats and be as quiet as possible. (interruption). In keeping with the occasion and honoring the high office which he occupies, I will recognize General Alexander for a motion.

DELEGATE ROBERT ALEXANDER: Mr. President, I move that you appoint a committee to call on the Governor of this State and invite the presence of the Chief Executive of the State at this gathering.

PRESIDENT CONNOR: A committee of how many?

DELEGATE ALEXANDER: A committee of three.

PRESIDENT CONNOR: You have heard the motion. All in favor of the motion will signify by saying aye, opposed no.

A viva voce vote was taken.

PRESIDENT CONNOR: Motion is carried unanimously. I will appoint on that committee Mrs. Bock, Judge Mires and General Alexander. The delegates will please be seated and the convention will come to order. The roll has been signed and, as president of this convention, I now declare the eighteenth amendment to the Constitution repealed and the twenty-first amendment to the Constitution adopted in the State of Washington.

(Applause.)

Now, if the committee to escort the Governor here will leave and bring him over, he will be here in time and will give us a short address. The officers of the convention will now authenticate this document.

Delegates, in turn, sign their names to the resolution.

DELEGATE WILLIAM S. DIXON: Mr. President, I have a resolution to present as follows:

Be it resolved, That the president of this convention appoint a committee of nine delegates to serve as a committee to examine and transmit, with the president and secretary, to the Secretary of State of Washington the executed resolution and certificate ratifying the proposed amendment to the Constitution of the United States repealing the eighteenth amendment.

I move the adoption of the resolution.

PRESIDENT CONNOR: You have heard the reading of the resolution and it has been moved and seconded that the resolution be adopted. Are you ready for the question? All those in favor signify by saying aye, those opposed, no.

A viva voce vote was taken.

PRESIDENT CONNOR: The motion is carried and the resolution adopted.

DELEGATE VICTOR ZEDNICK: Mr. President, I desire to present the following resolution:

WHEREAS, The people of the State of Washington on August 29th, 1933, recorded by an overwhelming vote their opposition to national prohibition as a means of regulating the liquor traffic.

WHEREAS, Thirty-one states have already expressed themselves in accord with the opinion of the people of this state, giving indication that within a few months the regulation of the liquor traffic will be a local issue to be controlled by the separate states.

WHEREAS, It becomes incumbent upon the people of this state upon the repeal of the eighteenth amendment and the adoption of the twenty-first amendment as a part of the Federal Constitution of the United States, whether by special or regular session of our State Legislature or by initiative to the people to regulate the liquor traffic within the borders of the State of Washington.

WHEREAS, The historical record of this state shows that its citizens believe in temperance and regulation.

WHEREAS, The delegates of this convention elected under oath to repeal the eighteenth amendment and ratify the twenty-first amendment to the Federal Constitution.

WHEREAS, We, as delegates representing our separate constituency, are convinced that they desire from us, in addition, a declaration of our opinion regarding regulation of the liquor traffic and that such declaration by this convention will aid materially in the framing of future legislation.

WHEREAS, Governor Clarence D. Martin has appointed a commission to make a survey and a complete report to serve as a guide for future legislation.

Therefore, be it resolved, That the delegates of this convention go on record as favoring regulation of the liquor traffic for the benefit of the general welfare of the people of the State of Washington, and

Be it further resolved, That our president appoint a committee of five to whom all resolutions prepared by individual delegates in this convention pertaining to the future regulation of the liquor traffic be referred and that said committee shall have power to make any independent investigation or survey as they may see fit and that such committee shall represent the delegates in this convention to work in harmony and cooperate with the commission appointed by our Governor.

I move the adoption of this resolution.

PRESIDENT CONNOR: It has been moved and seconded that the resolution just read be adopted. Are you ready for the question?

DELEGATE HARRY D. AUSTIN: While I heartily agree with Mr. Zednick on the resolution almost in its entirety, I feel that, by reason of the fact that our Governor has appointed a committee to investigate and regulate liquor in this state, this group, as a body, should not appoint a committee of nine to work with them. If he had wanted more men and women on that committee he would have appointed them.

I, therefore, offer as a substitute motion that any and all resolutions that are presented here pertaining to the regulation of liquor, that those regulations be passed to the Governor's Committee for their perusal and inspection.

DELEGATE HARRY AUSTIN: Mr. President, I offer as a substitute motion that the Chair appoint a committee of seven to act as a resolutions committee and that all resolutions introduced in this convention be submitted to those seven.

PRESIDENT CONNOR: The committee to report back, I presume.

DELEGATE AUSTIN: At that time, Mr. President, I will ask for a recess of fifteen or twenty minutes and the committee to report back to the convention.

PRESIDENT CONNOR: That would have to be ruled out of order because it is the same spirit as the original motion.

DELEGATE EDWARD L. COCHRANE: Mr. President, I don't think Mr. Zednick's original motion is clear here. Every delegate here might have some suggestion as to how to handle the liquor traffic in this State. He is perfectly welcome to send his recommendation in to the committee of nine and this committee of nine will present that material to the commission appointed by the Governor.

There isn't a single person in this convention that can't send his resolution to that committee. He has a perfect right to send his suggestions in to this committee as originally mentioned, you to have the power to appoint nine men and all resolutions be sent in to those nine men and they will put it up to the commission.

DELEGATE W. A. MONROE: Mr. President, I move, as a substitute, the appointment of seven instead of the nine, and then, while not working in cooperation with the Governor's Committee, let this committee initiate. I had quite an experience last Fall in Eastern Washington with the Initiative Measure doing away with the dry law and I can tell you frankly there is a great desire in Eastern Washington and, I have no doubt, in Western Washington, that there should be an Initiative.

I believe that of more effect and that more practical liquor enforcement can be brought about by Initiative. I strongly favor the Initiative.

PRESIDENT CONNOR: I understand you make that as a substitute?

President Connor: There are several resolutions on the desk here now and if we are going to consider all of them we will be here until next Saturday and I don't want to stay here that long.

Delegate Austin: May I amplify my statement, Mr. President?

President Connor: Yes.

Delegate Austin: I asked that a committee of seven be appointed by the Chair to which all these resolutions will be submitted and it was my intention to ask for a recess for a few minutes. That committee will meet. We can't get together, that is a cinch.

I have seen these meetings of fifty and ten and twelve and they can't agree and we will then report back that we cannot agree and will ask that the resolutions be submitted to the Governor's commission and that is what the Governor's commission wants, all the resolutions they can get, all the ideas they can get.

I don't see why the Chairman cannot appoint a commission to take this up at this time.

Delegate Cochrane: Mr. President, I rise to a point of order.

President Connor: Whatever this committee did would be simply a recommendation to the Governor's commission or the Legislature.

Delegate Cochrane: Mr. President, I don't think we have a right to consider any resolution.

President Connor: Mr. Austin's substitute motion has been seconded by Mr. Fulkerson. You will have to vote on it and get rid of it.

I understand Mr. Austin wants a committee of seven appointed now, then take a recess for about fifteen minutes and refer all resolutions to them and then refer it back to the convention. Is that your motion?

Delegate Cochrane: Mr. President, I move we adjourn.

Delegate W. W. Conner: Just a moment, Mr. President. Before a motion for adjournment is made, we have important work to do yet.

Delegate Cochrane: A motion to adjourn takes precedence over everything.

President Connor: All in favor of the substitute motion will say aye, opposed no.

Delegate Victor Zednick: Mr. President, I thought there would be no opposition to this resolution or I would have asked leave to close the debate on the subject. This resolution specifically provides that they shall work in harmony with and cooperate with the Commission appointed by our Governor.

There is no intention on my part to set up a body that will be in conflict with or superior to those appointed by the Governor but I felt that, with the delegates having been elected from our various districts and who were selected for the reason that they had taken an interest in this subject for many, many years and had some ideas on the subject, I thought if a Committee was appointed from this body to cooperate with the Committee of the Governor it would be satisfactory.

There will be no conflict whatever under the terms of this resolution.

President Connor: Is there a second to Mr. Austin's substitute motion?

The motion was duly seconded.

President Connor: Will you restate your substitute motion, Mr. Austin?

Delegate Austin: My motion was to substitute for any and all resolutions in this Convention concerning the regulation of the liquor traffic in this State, that these resolutions be passed on to the Governor's recently appointed investigating committee.

PRESIDENT CONNOR: You have heard the restatement of the substitute motion. Are you ready for the question?

DELEGATE HARVEY W. DODD: Mr. President, I offer a motion as an amendment to that motion just made that all resolutions be submitted to the Legislature of the State of Washington in whom rests the power for liquor regulations.

A DELEGATE: Mr. President, I think this convention should have something to say about the regulation of the liquor traffic. I, therefore, Mr. President, second the resolution of Mr. Zednick. I think that this organization should have something to say with reference to the regulation of the liquor traffic and his recommendation was that we appoint a committee of nine to work with this commission. We are not going to try to tell the Governor what to do or tell this commission what to do. We want a committee of nine to which all resolutions will be left and they will take it up with the commission, but I would like to see the original motion prevail and see the motion carry.

DELEGATE W. A. MONROE: We will have to get the substitute motion out of the way first.

When the gentleman said the Legislature is the originator of all liquor laws, that is hardly true. The people have initiated and can initiate and they have not been deprived of that power and I would like to see the substitute motion defeated.

PRESIDENT CONNOR: Gentlemen and ladies, we will now vote on the substitute motion.

DELEGATE EDWARD L. COCHRANE: Mr. Chairman, I move that the substitute motion be laid on the table.

PRESIDENT CONNOR: Is there a second to that motion?

DELEGATE ZEDNICK: Just a moment. Do you move that the substitute be laid on the table without taking the original with it?

DELEGATE COCHRANE: No, I move that the substitute be laid on the table, taking the original with it.

PRESIDENT CONNOR: It is moved and seconded that a vote be taken on the tabling of the resolution. Are you ready for the question? All in favor say aye, opposed no.

A viva voce vote was taken.

PRESIDENT CONNOR: The motion is lost.

DELEGATE VICTOR ZEDNICK: Mr. President, I renew my motion for the adoption of the resolution that I read.

PRESIDENT CONNOR: It has been moved and seconded that the resolution proposed by Mr. Zednick be adopted——

DELEGATE ROBERT ALEXANDER (interrupting): Mr. President, I wish to announce that His Excellency, the Governor of the State of Washington, is present.

PRESIDENT CONNOR: You will escort the Governor and his wife to the rostrum.

The committee then escorted Governor Martin and Mrs. Martin to the rostrum.

A viva voce vote was taken.

PRESIDENT CONNOR: The substitute is lost, so far as I can determine. The question is on the original motion now. All in favor of Mr. Zednick's motion to appoint a committee of nine to which all of these resolutions shall be referred please answer by saying aye, contrary, no.

A viva voce vote was taken.

PRESIDENT CONNOR: The ayes have it and the motion is carried.

Delegate W. W. Conner: Mr. President and members, I move you, Mr. President that a committee of three be appointed to act with the President and Secretary of this convention and that they be given power to approve the minutes of this convention after they are prepared. In substantiation of that I may say that our records must be checked and they must be approved to be entirely legal and all of that. And without such a committee, or if we adjourn without approving our records, our action here would be void. I move that we adopt that motion.

President Connor: It has been moved and seconded that a committee of three be appointed to act with the President and Secretary of this convention and that they be given power to approve the minutes of this convention after they are prepared. All in favor of the motion will say aye, opposed, no.

A viva voce vote was taken.

President Connor: The motion is carried unanimously and I will appoint that committee very soon.

Delegate Andrew J. Gage: Mr. President, I now renew my motion that we now hear from Governor Martin.

President Connor: I now take great pleasure in introducing the Chief Executive of our State who has taken a large part in this memorable occasion here, the preliminary part. Before I introduce the Governor, I want to introduce his charming wife, Mrs. Martin.

Mrs. Martin presented to the convention.

(Applause.)

President Connor: Gentlemen and ladies, I take pleasure in presenting our good Governor, the Honorable Clarence D. Martin, who will now speak to you.

Governor Martin: Mr. Connor and Mr. President and my fellow citizens, members of the convention: A speech would be much out of place this afternoon. I judge you have had a lot of speech making here, in fact I have heard of it downstairs. I want to say in the very beginning that you members of this convention remind me much of the scenes of the Legislature of last winter and perhaps you are just as smart and bright as the members of the Legislature last winter.

Now, you gentlemen and you ladies, members of this convention, have honored me by asking me to come up here. I am intensely interested in your deliberations. In the first place, I want to congratulate you on giving your time and your means in an effort to carry out the spirit of this convention. I know that some of you men have given long study to this problem. You have made sacrifices in order to be here this day. I appreciate that. The State of Washington appreciates it. You are rendering a real service for the people of this State. It is a question that must be settled and must be taken care of and you people, in coming here this day, have rendered a distinct service to the people of the State of Washington.

Now, I hear much concern over the resolutions that were proposed to be adopted here this afternoon. I want you to know that every resolution you adopt will be of much value to the commission that has been selected to find out and make such recommendation. This fact-finding commission that I selected a day or two ago can utilize to their advantage and to the advantage of the people of this State in connection with this problem any resolutions that you may propose and I know they will accept them in the spirit in which they are given and don't be afraid that you will submit resolutions to that commission. And then, when you have adjourned and have completed your work here, feel free to cooperate in every way, both by letter and in person and by resolutions with this commission that may continue for the next few weeks, leading up to a definite proposal as to how the liquor business of the State should be handled. I know they will welcome any suggestions that you may give.

Now, I am not going to speak longer. This isn't a political meeting. This is a meeting of our citizens of this State and I know that you people are better informed on this question than I am. I just want, in conclusion, to thank you again for the honor of being invited to come here and meet you. I want you to know that every effort we will make, both through the commission and through the Legislature, when it assembles, and through the administration of this government, will be to try and solve this problem as far as possible to the end that all the people of the State are measurably well satisfied with the repeal of the eighteenth amendment.

Now, Mr. Connor, I think I have talked long enough. I know that it was a pleasure on my part to come here and look the people in the face and have the people get a glimpse of me, those that haven't seen me. I appreciate the honor and my office is at your command in any way at any time on any question that we can be helpful, one to another. I thank you so much.

(Applause.)

PRESIDENT CONNOR: I know that the delegates to this convention feel honored in having the Governor and his good wife with us and we appreciate his presence here. He is a very busy man as we all know and we appreciate his presence and his little talk and I will ask the same committee to escort them back as far as the door.

The committee escorts Governor Martin and Mrs. Martin to the door of the House Chamber.

DELEGATE PAUL W. HOUSER: Mr. President, I have a resolution I would like to submit and I will read it.

PRESIDENT CONNOR: I think if the clerk reads it we can hear better.

DELEGATE HOUSER: I would like to read it. May I read it, Mr. President?

PRESIDENT CONNOR: Yes.

DELEGATE HOUSER:

WHEREAS, The American people have demanded the repeal of the eighteenth amendment to the Constitution of the United States, and whereas it is necessary to adopt some reasonable system of regulation for the manufacture, control and sale of intoxicating liquors——(interruption).

DELEGATE W. W. CONNER: Mr. President, a point of order. Mr. President, this convention has just adopted a resolution declaring that all resolutions be referred to a committee and therefore I contend that the resolution offered by the gentleman from King County is out of order.

PRESIDENT CONNOR: I think your point of order is well taken.

DELEGATE HOUSER: Mr. President, may I be permitted to be heard on that motion, may I be permitted to be heard on the question of the point of order?

PRESIDENT CONNOR: Yes, you are entitled to that.

DELEGATE HOUSER: In answer to this courteous gentleman from King County, I want to advise him that if he will permit me to read the balance of this resolution he will find it a memorial to Congress, that is all. It doesn't pertain to the regulation of liquor in this State at all but it is asking Congress to take such steps at the special session in December as is recommended by this convention and I want to tell you, Mr. President, in support of my resolution, that this is entirely proper on the question of parliamentary procedure and the distinguished gentleman from King County knows it.

PRESIDENT CONNOR: I think the gentleman is right because it is a totally different subject matter than the one that Mr. Zednick offered and I think the gentleman should be allowed and the Chair will rule that he be allowed to read his memorial to Congress if it does not pertain to anything else.

Delegate Houser continues reading:

Resolved, That this Convention favors a uniform system for the sale of liquor in the various states of the Union to provide that liquors of high alcoholic content may be sold only in government or state liquor stores in sealed packages, and

Be it further resolved, That this resolution be submitted to the Congress of the United States as the official recommendation of this Convention.

Be it further resolved, That the Government of the United States shall fix the retail price of whiskey at not to exceed $1.25 per quart, and other hard liquors in proportion thereto, and

I move the adoption of this resolution.

DELEGATE W. W. CONNER: The resolution speaks about money, a dollar and a quarter. We don't know what it will be in six months from now. I move that the resolution be laid on the table.

The motion was duly seconded.

DELEGATE HOUSER: It is easy enough for you gentlemen to vote this motion down if you don't care to adopt it, but I would like to talk with this——

DELEGATE W. W. CONNER (interrupting): A point of order, Mr. President. A motion to lay on the table is not debatable.

PRESIDENT CONNOR: No, it is not debatable. You have heard the motion by Mr. Conner. Are you ready for the question? All in favor of the motion say aye, contrary no.

A viva voce vote was taken.

PRESIDENT CONNOR: The ayes have it.

DELEGATE SIDNEY BOUCHER: I have a resolution, gentlemen of the convention, I have a resolution here I want to submit to you.

Resolved, That the Secretary of the Convention be and is hereby authorized to have a photostatic copy of the resolution repealing the eighteenth amendment, containing the signatures of the delegates made and to have printed and bound fifteen hundred copies of the Journal of the Proceedings of this Convention and that one copy be mailed to each delegate of the Convention, one copy to each member of the Legislature and such other persons as make request for the same, and be it further

Resolved, That twenty-five copies be furnished to the State Library, twenty-five copies to the State Law Library, two hundred and fifty copies to the Secretary of State to supply any request made, one copy to each of the state officers and department and fifteen copies to the Clerk of the Supreme Court for the use of the Court.

I move the adoption of the resolution.

The motion was duly seconded.

PRESIDENT CONNOR: It has been moved and seconded that the resolution just read be adopted. Are you ready for the question? All in favor of the motion will say aye, contrary no.

A viva voce vote was taken.

PRESIDENT CONNOR: The motion is carried.

DELEGATE FRANK C. DEAN: Mr. Chairman and fellow delegates, I think it would be very inopportune if we adjourn without giving a rising vote of thanks to the women of the United States and the Women's Organization for National Prohibition Reform and Miss Trimble as representing that organization in this State. And I ask for a rising vote of thanks.

PRESIDENT CONNOR: All in favor of the motion will please rise.

All delegates stood.

DELEGATE HARRY D. AUSTIN: Mr. President, I would like to offer resolution as follows:

WHEREAS, The Honorable Ernest N. Hutchinson, Secretary of State, under the act providing for the assembling of this Convention was charged with the responsibility of preparing the House of Representatives for the holding of this convention, therefore, be it

Resolved, That this Convention assembled express to the Honorable Ernest N. Hutchinson, Secretary of State, its deep appreciation and thanks for the expeditious manner in which he arranged and prepared this chamber for the meeting of this Convention and to his assistants and to the other State Officials for the courtesies extended to the delegates of this Convention.

I move the adoption of the resolution.

PRESIDENT CONNOR: You have heard the reading of the resolution and the motion for its adoption. Are you ready for the question? All in favor of the motion say aye, contrary no.

A viva voce vote was taken.

PRESIDENT CONNOR: The motion is carried.

DELEGATE JOSEPH MCCARTHY: Mr. President, I move to reconsider the resolution submitted by the Mayor of Kent referring to the sending out of fifteen hundred copies. This will entail a large expense and I don't think it is justified under present conditions.

DELEGATE ROBERT ALEXANDER: I second the motion.

PRESIDENT CONNOR: It has been moved and seconded that the resolution submitted by the Mayor of Kent, Mr. Boucher, be reconsidered. Are you ready for the question?

DELEGATE W. W. CONNER: Mr. President, may I be permitted to say this regarding that resolution? I have obtained and have here the proceedings of practically every State in the Union that has held a convention regarding the eighteenth amendment. Some of them are mimeographed, some printed on cheap newspaper and one State, Illinois, got out a bound volume. This resolution doesn't say what printing or what paper shall be used; it is entirely up to the Secretary of State and I think that he should have this record available for the Supreme Court and available for the Governor's office and other officers of the State. It won't cost much to get these out. I think it can be done for a very nominal sum and I trust that my good friend from Spokane will withdraw his motion for reconsideration. It is entirely up to that saving soul in the Secretary of State's office and he can do the whole job for ten or fifteen dollars by mimeographing it if he wishes it done that way.

DELEGATE JOSEPH MCCARTHY: Well, Mr. President, if it could be done with anything like the economy that Mr. Conner suggests I would withdraw my motion with the consent of my second.

DELEGATE ALEXANDER: If Mr. Conner assures us this will be mimeographed at the cost stated by him, I will second the withdrawal.

DELEGATE WARREN G. MAGNUSON: Mr. President, three thousand dollars was appropriated for the purposes of this convention. I don't know whether that three thousand dollars has been spent but, if it has been spent, the Secretary of State has no money. If it hasn't been spent the resolution is in order but I think you should add to this resolution "if the money is available." I don't know if the Secretary of State has any money on hand. If he has he can do it.

DELEGATE W. W. CONNER: That is all there is to it, then.

PRESIDENT CONNOR: If there isn't any money then, of course, it won't be printed.

DELEGATE HARRY D. AUSTIN: There are a lot of you boys and girls that came down here that probably were never to the State House before in your lives. We are proud of the fact that you came down here with no salary or expenses. I am a member of the Legislature along with Mr. Magnuson and we appropriated three thousand dollars for the purposes of this convention. Now, let's assume that it has all been spent. I think the thing we have done to put this State wet will bring us a lot of money in taxes and I think the State could well afford to print a little booklet and mail it to all of us so we can show it to our grandchildren.

PRESIDENT CONNOR: I would like to ask General Alexander if you agree to withdraw your second.

DELEGATE ALEXANDER: With the permission of the Chair it is withdrawn.

PRESIDENT CONNOR: Then the original motion stands.

DELEGATE L. F. CLARK: There was a motion before the house, Mr. President, authorizing you to appoint a committee of three. That committee has not been appointed yet.

PRESIDENT CONNOR: I think I will let the convention be at ease for five minutes until I can name that committee and the other committee as well.

DELEGATE L. F. CLARK: I move you, Mr. President, that you appoint W. W. Conner as one member of that committee.

PRESIDENT CONNOR: Well, I think you are out of order. I will appoint the committee. The convention may be at ease for ten or fifteen minutes. I shall retire to one of the anterooms and shall ask Vice-president W. W. Conner to assume the chair during my absence.

(Short intermission.)

(Returned to the Chamber and President Connor assumed the chair.)

PRESIDENT CONNOR: I will now appoint a committee of nine as provided in the Zednick resolution. They will be

Joseph McCarthy, Spokane, 5th District,
Tom Drummey, Seattle, 1st District,
R. B. Fulkerson, Tacoma, 6th District,
E. F. Blaine, Longview, 4th District,
Don W. Clarke, Bellingham, 42nd District,
Frank G. Blakeslee, Olympia, 22nd District,
Marie Bock, Monroe, 39th District,
Ralph E. Peasley, Aberdeen, 21st District,
Lew Brown, Colfax, 9th District.

DELEGATE PAUL HOUSER: Mr. President, I move that the committee so appointed be approved by the convention.

PRESIDENT CONNOR: You have heard the motion that the committee appointed be approved. Are you ready for the question? All in favor of the motion say aye, opposed no.

A viva voce vote was taken.

PRESIDENT CONNOR: The motion is carried. Is there any other business to come before the convention?

DELEGATE W. W. CONNER: Mr. President, you have not yet appointed the committee of three for the purpose of approving the minutes.

PRESIDENT CONNOR: I will appoint on that committee W. W. Conner of King, Vincent Donahue of Spokane and Katherine Le Beau.

That is the committee to work with the president and the secretary in looking over the minutes of the convention.

DELEGATE ROBERT ALEXANDER: Mr. President, I now move you that this convention adjourn *sine die*.

DELEGATE W. W. CONNER: Mr. President I would like to make a substitute for that motion and, if I may be permitted, explain the motion.

A great many of the States of the Union holding conventions, instead of adjourning *sine die*, have adjourned without day and that fixes it so if there is anything that might happen or that might be incorrect in our records, the chairman could call us back into session, therefore, I move you as a substitute, that this convention do now adjourn without day. The only difference is when we adjourn *sine die* we absolutely cannot come back and the other is if we adjourn without day and we find anything wrong with our record the president can again call us into session.

DELEGATE ALEXANDER: I withdraw my motion in favor of the substitute.

PRESIDENT CONNOR: You have heard the motion that we do now adjourn without day. Are you ready for the question? All in favor say aye, opposed no.

A viva voce vote was taken.

PRESIDENT CONNOR: The motion is carried unanimously.

At 6:45 P.M. the convention adjourned without day.

ATTEST

We, the undersigned, Edwin M. Connor, President and Miss Augusta W. Trimble, Secretary of the Convention, do hereby certify that we have examined the above and foregoing record and minutes of the proceedings of said convention and we and each of us certify that the said record and minutes are a true and correct report of the proceedings of said convention.

EDWIN M. CONNOR
President
AUGUSTA W. TRIMBLE
Secretary

W. W. CONNER
L. VINCENT DONAHUE
KATHARINE LEBEAU
Committee

WEST VIRGINIA*

PROCEEDINGS

OF THE

CONSTITUTIONAL CONVENTION

PROVIDING FOR THE REPEAL

OF THE

EIGHTEENTH ARTICLE OF AMENDMENT TO THE CONSTITUTION

OF THE

UNITED STATES OF AMERICA

Proceedings of the Constitutional Convention providing for the repeal of the Eighteenth Article of Amendment to the Constitution of the United States of America, as set forth in Senate Bill 174, passed by the Legislature of West Virginia, on March 10, 1933, as amended by House Bill 7, passed by the Legislature of West Virginia, on the 12th day of April, 1933, assembled at the Capitol of said State, in the Chamber of the House of Delegates, in the City of Charleston, Kanawha County, West Virginia, on the 25th day of July, 1933, at 12 o'clock, noon, as provided by law.

The Convention was called to order at 1 o'clock P.M., by Delegate Joseph Holt Gaines.

MR. GAINES: Ladies and Gentlemen of the Constitutional Convention of West Virginia, the Act of the Legislature of March 10, 1933, providing for this convention, contains the direction that it shall be called to order by the oldest delegate chosen at the election. Occupying that position of statutory prominence, but doubtful desirability, I now declare the Convention in session. (Applause.)

Following the precedent of former constitutional conventions in this state and in Virginia; and, in fact, the precedent of almost all deliberative bodies in organizing, I declare it to be the first duty of the convention to select a temporary president. But before that is done, since we have not yet received official notice of our election, I shall ask the Governor of the State, whose proclamation will legally and officially certify our rights to be delegates to this convention, to present his proclamation.

Since the Governor is not present, and we have to select a temporary secretary of the Convention, the Chair will now receive nominations to that effect.

DELEGATE ANDREW EDMISTION, JR.: I nominate for the position of temporary secretary of this convention, Mrs. Frances Evans, of Logan County.

DELEGATE W. H. SAWYERS: I second the nomination of Mrs. Frances Evans for temporary secretary.

THE CHAIRMAN: Are there any further nominations?

There being no further nominations, the motion was put by the Chairman, and unanimously carried.

* From a typewritten copy. The vote for delegates by counties is omitted here.

CHAIRMAN GAINES: I therefore declare Mrs. Frances Evans unanimously elected temporary secretary of this convention. Mrs. Evans, will you be good enough to take this chair?

Whereupon Mrs. Frances Evans assumed the position of temporary secretary. (Applause.)

CHAIRMAN GAINES: We will await the Governor's proclamation.

DELEGATE CLARENCE E. MARTIN: Mr. Chairman, I move that a Committee of three be appointed by the Chair to wait upon the Governor and request his presence in the convention.

Which motion was duly seconded by Delegate C. E. (Ned) Smith, put by the Chair, and unanimously carried.

CHAIRMAN GAINES: I will appoint upon that Committee Delegates Clarence E. Martin, Wells Goodykoontz and Carl O. Schmidt.

DELEGATE WELLS GOODYKOONTZ: Mr. Chairman, in pursuance to the motion, your committee desires to present the Governor of the State of West Virginia.

CHAIRMAN GAINES: Governor Kump, will you come to the stand? Ladies and Gentlemen, I present to you one who needs no introduction—Governor H. G. Kump, of the State of West Virginia. (Applause.)

GOVERNOR H. G. KUMP: Mr. Chairman, Ladies and Gentlemen of the Convention, you are very gracious, and I am truly appreciative.

You have been called here to perform a duty under the mandate of the citizens of the State of West Virginia. I greet you and assure you that the state officials will render you every assistance in their power to facilitate the discharge of your duty, and to make you comfortable and happy while you are here. The personnel of the delegates to this convention is sufficient guarantee that your work will be faithfully performed.

This assemblage of distinguished citizens of our State will expect me to speak of the great and devoted effort of His Excellency, President Roosevelt, to stabilize industry, reduce unemployment, and to restore comfort and prosperity among our people. The earnest and dramatic radio appeal made by the President last night must have stirred every patriotic American, and called for new recognition of our duty to one another and for our rebaptism in the faith of our fathers.

In the administration of the National Recovery Act, the Executive Department of West Virginia consecrates itself to the duty of co-operation with the President and those about him, with a singleness of purpose and loyalty that knows neither halt nor hesitation.

To withhold co-operation in these humane measures is reprehensible. To seek to subvert them to selfish ambition, either personal or political, is diabolical. For myself, I serve today without thought of tomorrow.

I appeal to all patriotic citizens, and all those who love their country and their fellowman, to support the National Recovery Administration to the fullest extent, and give of themselves and their substance, without stint, in the campaign for the recovery of things which we hold dear, and for the restoration of social and business tranquillity among us.

I urge all employers of labor and all employees, to promptly and cheerfully accept the spirit and letter of the blanket agreement proposed by the President, and to diligently keep faith therewith.

"We do our part." (Applause.)

I have been told that it is my duty to proclaim you the duly elected delegates to this convention. I may say that I have not had the opportunity to read the Act of the Legislature that provided for this convention which called you into existence through the election that was held on the 27th day of June, 1933, and I therefore read to you my proclamation, as follows:

STATE OF WEST VIRGINIA

EXECUTIVE DEPARTMENT

A PROCLAMATION

By the Governor

The Governor having this day, as required by law, tabulated the vote cast in all the counties in the State at the special election held on the twenty-seventh day of June, one thousand nine hundred thirty-three, for the purpose of choosing delegates to a convention to pass on the proposed amendment to the Constitution of the United States providing for the repeal of the eighteenth article of amendment to the Constitution, as set forth in Senate Bill 174, passed by the Legislature of West Virginia on the tenth day of March, one thousand nine hundred thirty-three, as amended by House Bill 7, passed by the Legislature of West Virginia on the twelfth day of April, one thousand nine hundred thirty-three, and it appearing from the certificates returned to the Governor by the Boards of canvassers of the several counties of West Virginia that the vote for said delegates was as follows:

[Vote for delegates omitted.]

NOW, THEREFORE, I, H. G. KUMP, Governor, hereby proclaim the result of said special election and declare the said J. Patrick Beacom, Edith W. Breckinridge, Mary S. Brewster, Nat C. Burdette, Paul J. Carr, L. H. Clark, Andrew Edmiston, Jr., Mrs. Frances Evans, Joseph Holt Gaines, Wells Goodykoontz, Howard H. Holt, Sam T. Mallison, Clarence E. Martin, Hetzel S. Pownall, David C. Reay, William H. Sawyers, Carl O. Schmidt, C. E. (Ned) Smith, Mrs. Kenner B. Stephenson and Natalie Sutherland Walker, duly chosen the delegates to the aforesaid convention for the State of West Virginia.

In witness whereof, I have hereunto set my hand and caused the Great Seal of the State to be affixed. Done at the Capitol in the City of Charleston, this twenty-fifth day of July, in the year of our Lord one thousand nine hundred and thirty-three, and of the State the seventy-first.

SEAL

H. G. KUMP

By the Governor:

WM. S. O'BRIEN
Secretary of State

STATE OF WEST VIRGINIA

OFFICE OF SECRETARY OF STATE

I, WM. S. O'BRIEN, Secretary of State of the State of West Virginia, having carefully and impartially examined the returns and certificates now on file in the office of the Secretary of State, to-wit: the returns of the Boards of Canvassers of the several counties composing the State of West Virginia, showing the number of votes cast for the following candidates at the election held on June 27, 1933:

FOR RATIFICATION		AGAINST RATIFICATION	
J. Patrick Beacom	218296	D. L. Auvil	136552
Edith W. Breckinridge	218236	George W. Bright	136529
Mary S. Brewster	218234	Charles E. Carrigan	136526
Nat C. Burdette	218233	Thomas J. Davis	136523
Paul J. Carr	218234	Raymond V. Humphreys	136522
L. H. Clark	218235	Dr. Dan P. Kessler	136522
Andrew Edmiston, Jr.	218227	Will R. Keyser	136522
Mrs. Frances Evans	218233	William McDonald	130529
Joseph Holt Gaines	218235	Dr. C. H. Maxwell	136528
Wells Goodykoontz	218233	Mrs. F. L. Miller	136526
Howard H. Holt	218235	Harry W. Miller	136522
Sam T. Mallison	218236	O. J. Morrison	136524
Clarence E. Martin	218234	Harry W. Paull	136525
Hetzel S. Pownall	218236	John Raine	136526
David C. Reay	218235	E. R. Reed	136524
William H. Sawyers	218236	E. Bunker Reynolds	136516
Carl O. Schmidt	218240	John T. Simms	136516
C. E. (Ned) Smith	218236	Geo. S. Strader	136514
Mrs. Kenner B. Stephenson	218637	Albert B. White	136515
Natalie Sutherland Walker	218638	Geo. N. Yoho	136512

SEAL

In testimony whereof, I have hereunto set my hand and attached the Less Seal of the State of West Virginia, at the Capitol in the City of Charleston this 24th day of July, 1933.

WM. S. O'BRIEN
Secretary of State

CHAIRMAN GAINES: I am sure I voice the unanimous judgment of the delegates to this Convention when I express our thanks to the Governor for his personal appearance before us.

DELEGATE CLARENCE E. MARTIN: I move you, Mr. Chairman, that the proclamation of the Governor of West Virginia be made a part of the record of this convention.

DELEGATE WILLIAM H. SAWYERS: I second that motion.

The motion was then put by the Chair, and unanimously carried.

DELEGATE C. E. (NED) SMITH: I move that the Chair appoint a committee on Privileges and Elections.

DELEGATE CLARENCE E. MARTIN: I second that motion.

CHAIRMAN GAINES: I think the convention should first elect a temporary president before that motion is put. I am simply calling the convention to order, as provided by the statute.

DELEGATE C. E. (NED) SMITH: Doesn't the statute require you to be the temporary president?

CHAIRMAN GAINES: It does not; I only occupy the distinction of being the oldest member or delegate elected, and am acting under the statute. I will now say, subject to correction by the convention, that the next order of business is the selection of a temporary president.

DELEGATE HOWARD H. HOLT: I take the same view, Mr. Chairman, and I therefore nominate Hon. Joseph Holt Gaines as temporary president of this convention.

Which motion being seconded by Delegate Paul J. Carr, was put by Delegate Clarence E. Martin, and unanimously carried.

PRESIDENT GAINES: Ladies and Gentlemen, I thank you for this expression of confidence, and shall not attempt to take your time by making a speech. I intentionally hastened beyond my right, perhaps, in the selection of a temporary secretary, so that Mrs. Evans might be in position to record the proceedings of the convention. Now, if there is no objection, the Chair will again declare her the choice of the convention for temporary secretary.

The next business before the convention is the selection of a committee on Privileges and Election. If that meets with the approval of the convention, the Chair will await a motion to that effect.

DELEGATE WILLIAM H. SAWYERS: I make a motion to the effect that the Chair appoint a Committee of three on Privileges and Elections, to report to the convention.

Which motion being duly seconded, put by the Chair and carried, the Chair appointed as such committee Delegates William H. Sawyers, Edith W. Breckinridge and Sam T. Mallison.

Whereupon, later, Delegate William H. Sawyers, of said Committee, reported as follows:

Mr. Chairman, we find that the following are elected delegates to this convention:

J. Patrick Beacom
Edith W. Breckinridge
Mary S. Brewster
Nat C. Burdette
Paul J. Carr
L. H. Clark
Andrew Edmiston, Jr.
Mrs. Frances Evans
Joseph Holt Gaines
Wells Goodykoontz
Howard H. Holt
Sam T. Mallison
Clarence E. Martin
Hetzel S. Pownall
David C. Reay
William H. Sawyers
Carl O. Schmidt
C. E. (Ned) Smith
Mrs. Kenner B. Stephenson
Natalie Sutherland Walker

We are informed also that there is a vacancy caused by the resignation of Dr. L. H Clark and Mrs. Natalie Sutherland Walker.

PRESIDENT GAINES: Those vacancies, the Chair takes it, subject to a better opinion, will be filled by the delegates who are officially determined to be elected.

DELEGATE WILLIAM H. SAWYERS: Your Committee on Privileges and Elections reports 18 delegates present and two absent.

PRESIDENT GAINES: The statute requires that we shall not proceed until we shall have taken the oath of office. Of course, we must organize, and find out who is entitled to take that oath.

DELEGATE WILLIAM H. SAWYERS: I move the adoption of the report of the committee on Privileges and Elections.

Which motion was duly seconded, put by the Chair and carried, and the Chair declared the report adopted.

PRESIDENT GAINES: The Chair takes it that the next order of business, in compliance with the terms of the Statute creating this convention, that the members of the convention, whose election has now been officially determined, before they take the oath, shall perform no business until we take the oath of office, and the Chair is of opinion that oath should now be administered, and will ask the Honorable A. P. Hudson, Judge of the Circuit Court of Kanawha County, to administer the oath. The Chair would also suggest unless there be a difference of opinion, that there is no reason why all of the delegates should not take the oath at the same time.

Judge Hudson, will you please come by the Chairman at this place to administer the oath to the delegates.

JUDGE A. P. HUDSON: The delegates will please rise and each hold up your right hand.

"You, and each of you, do solemnly swear that you were, on the 27th day of June, 1933, duly elected as a delegate to the convention to pass upon the amendment to the constitution of the United States providing for the repeal of the eighteenth article of amendment to the constitution; and that you will support the constitution of the United States and the constitution of the State of West Virginia, and that you will faithfully discharge the duties of your said office to the best of your skill and judgment, So help you God."

THE DELEGATES (severally): "I do."

DELEGATE HOWARD H. HOLT: I take it the next step would be the filling of these two vacancies, and to administer the oath to those delegates selected.

PRESIDENT GAINES: The Chair will ask whether that should be done now, or after the permanent organization has been effected?

DELEGATE HOWARD H. HOLT: I think it is appropriate to do it now. We are now officially in session, and I think the first step is to fill the vacancies.

PRESIDENT GAINES: The Chair therefore announces that there are two vacancies, due to the resignation of Dr. L. H. Clark, of McDowell County, who is too ill to attend this meeting of the convention; and because of the absence and resignation of Mrs. Natalie Sutherland Walker, due, as the Chair is informed, to her being out of the State because of serious illness in her family. What is the pleasure of the convention with reference to these two vacancies?

DELEGATE CLARENCE E. MARTIN: I move that we proceed to fill the vacancies, and that nominations be asked for.

DELEGATE HOWARD H. HOLT: I second that motion.

Which motion was then put by the Chair, and unanimously carried.

DELEGATE SAM T. MALLISON: I nominate Hon. J. J. O'Brien, of Ohio County, to fill the vacancy made by the resignation of Dr. L. H. Clark.

DELEGATE ANDREW EDMISTON, JR.: I second the nomination of Judge J. J. O'Brien.

PRESIDENT GAINES: There being no further nominations, and the question being on the substitution and election as a member of this convention of the Honorable J. J. O'Brien, in the place of Dr. L. H. Clark, resigned, what is your pleasure?

DELEGATE HOWARD H. HOLT: There is a question of regularity. Should not these nominees be asked to declare their political affiliation and their position upon the question of repeal?

PRESIDENT GAINES: The statute does not so require. The statute only requires that the group in which the vacancy occurs may fill it. I take it we have all thoroughly satisfied ourselves as to both politics and position on the question of abrogation of the Eighteenth Amendment.

DELEGATE HOWARD H. HOLT: That is true, but the qualifications for nominees requires the filing of a certificate with the declaration therein.

PRESIDENT GAINES: The Chair will call the attention of the delegates to the fact that while that requirement was made for nominees, it is not made for the filling of vacancies.

DELEGATE HOWARD H. HOLT: It should be a matter of record, I think.

PRESIDENT GAINES: The question is with the convention. If the convention thinks that is necessary, the Chair will, of course, obey the will of the convention.

DELEGATE CARL O. SCHMIDT: I move that the candidate be interrogated as to whether or not he is in favor of the repeal, or revision of the Twenty-first amendment.

PRESIDENT GAINES: Shall the Chair make that interrogation?

The motion was duly seconded, put by the Chair and carried.

PRESIDENT GAINES: Mr. O'Brien, will you kindly state to the convention what political party you belong to, and whether you are in favor of the repeal or abrogation of the Eighteenth Article of Amendment to the constitution of the United States?

MR. J. J. O'BRIEN: I am a democrat, and I favor the repeal of the amendment. (Applause.)

PRESIDENT GAINES: The question, therefore, is upon the election of Mr. J. J. O'Brien as a delegate to this convention.

The question was then put by the Chair, unanimously carried, and the President declared J. J. O'Brien, of Ohio County, duly elected a delegate to the convention.

PRESIDENT GAINES: The next order of business before the convention is the election of a delegate in the place of Mrs. Natalie Sutherland Walker, resigned.

DELEGATE HOWARD H. HOLT: I desire to place in nomination the name of Benjamin Rosenbloom, of Ohio County, as a delegate to this convention.

Which nomination was seconded by Delegate Andrew Edmiston, Jr., and there was no further nomination.

PRESIDENT GAINES: Is it the pleasure of the convention that the Chair shall put to Mr. Rosenbloom the questions which were put to Delegate O'Brien?

DELEGATE DAVID C. REAY: I think it is not necessary.

PRESIDENT: Mr. Rosenbloom, will you state to the convention what political party you belong to, and whether you are in favor of the repeal and abrogation of the Eighteenth Amendment to the Federal Constitution?

MR. BENJAMIN ROSENBLOOM: I am a Republican, and I certainly am in favor of the repeal and abrogation of the Eighteenth Amendment.

The question being upon the election of Benjamin Rosenbloom, was put by the Chair and unanimously carried.

PRESIDENT GAINES: Mr. Benjamin Rosenbloom is unanimously chosen, and the Chair declares him duly elected a delegate to this convention. (Applause.)

DELEGATE WILLIAM H. SAWYERS: Have Mr. Rosenbloom and Mr. O'Brien taken the oath of office?

PRESIDENT GAINES: They have not; and the Chair will ask Judge Hudson, again, to administer the oath to the newly elected delegates to this convention.

JUDGE A. P. HUDSON: Please hold up your right hands.

"You, and each of you, do solemnly swear that you were, on the 27th day of June, 1933, duly elected as a delegate to the convention to pass on the amendment to the constitution of the United States providing for the repeal of the eighteenth article of amendment to the constitution of the United States, in the convention which is duly assembled, to fill the vacancies made by the resignations of Dr. L. H. Clark and Mrs. Natalie Sutherland Walker, and that you will support the constitution of the United States, the constitution of the State of West Virginia, and that you will faithfully discharge the duties of your said office to the best of your skill and judgment. So help you God."

Mr. J. J. O'Brien and Mr. Benjamin Rosenbloom each answered to said oath, "I do."

DELEGATE CLARENCE E. MARTIN: I move that the oaths taken and subscribed to by all the members of this convention be made a part of the records and proceedings of this convention.

DELEGATE WILLIAM H. SAWYERS: I second that motion.

The motion was then put by the Chair, and unanimously carried.

PRESIDENT GAINES: The Chair declares that the next order of business before the convention is the election of a Permanent President of the convention.

DELEGATE WELLS GOODYKOONTZ: Mr. President, it affords me great pleasure to place in nomination Mr. Clarence E. Martin of Martinsburg; and about all I need to say about him—that is, to say in his favor—is that fact that he is the President of the National Bar Association, and comes to us with a certificate to that effect. I therefore place Mr. Martin in nomination.

DELEGATE DAVID C. REAY: I second the nomination.

DELEGATE BENJAMIN ROSENBLOOM: Mr. President, I move that the nominations close.

DELEGATE HOWARD H. HOLT: I second that motion.

Which motion was put by the President, and unanimously carried.

PRESIDENT GAINES: Now, the question is on the election of Mr. Clarence E. Martin as Permanent President of the convention. As many as are in favor of the motion will signify the same by saying "Aye"; and those opposed, "Nay."

The motion was then put by the Chair, and it was ascertained by the Secretary that all of the delegates elected to the convention voted "Aye."

PRESIDENT GAINES: The Chair therefore declares that Mr. Clarence E. Martin has been unanimously elected Permanent President of this convention, and declares him to be that Permanent President. Mr. Martin, will you kindly come forward?

Whereupon, Delegate Clarence E. Martin assumed the Chair. (Applause.)

PRESIDENT MARTIN: Mr. Chairman, Ladies and Gentlemen of the Convention, the time is fairly late. May I say to you, in as few words as it is possible for me to command, how much I appreciate the honor and confidence that you have reposed in me on this occasion.

I will say to you, gathered as we are, from the four corners of the State, we are here merely to carry out the mandate of the people of this State as expressed in the recent election. We are here merely for the purpose of restoring to this State the old constitutional government that we once had, and to rectify the mistake that was made some years ago, when we granted to the National Government the power that should never have been given to it, and by reason of that fact, we are here for the purpose of registering the will of the people of West Virginia—they desire to recall that grant that has been made to the National Government, and again look after and carry out the powers of local government in West Virginia. (Applause.)

The next order of business is the election of a permanent Secretary for the convention. Whom will you have?

DELEGATE J. PATRICK BEACOM: Mr. President, it affords me great pleasure at this time to place in nomination, as permanent secretary of this convention, the name of a woman who, in my belief, has done more toward the repeal of the prohibition amendment in this state than any other woman in West Virginia. I place in nomination for that position the name of Mrs. Mary S. Brewster. (Applause.)

PRESIDENT MARTIN: Are there any further nominations?

DELEGATE HOWARD H. HOLT: I desire to second the nomination of one who has served as a real prohibition repealist and its objects for twenty-five years. I endorse, with commendation, the nomination of Mrs. Mary S. Brewster, by Mr. Beacom, and urge her immediate election.

DELEGATE WILLIAM H. SAWYERS: Mr. President, I move that the nominations be closed, and that Mrs. Mary S. Brewster be elected Secretary of this convention by acclamation.

DELEGATE JOSEPH HOLT GAINES: I second that motion and nomination.

Which motion being put by the Chair, and unanimously carried, the President declared Mrs. Mary S. Brewster duly elected Permanent Secretary of the convention.

PRESIDENT MARTIN: In the absence of a committee on Rules, and under the statute calling this convention, the Chair now rules that the convention is open for business. What is the pleasure of the Convention?

DELEGATE PATRICK BEACOM: Mr. Chairman, I have before me a resolution which I would like to present to the Chair, and have the Secretary read to the members of this convention to be acted upon.

PRESIDENT MARTIN: The Secretary will read the resolution.

Whereupon the Secretary read the following:

RESOLUTION

Ratifying the Proposed amendment to the Constitution of the United States

WHEREAS, The Congress of the United States has submitted to Convention, to be held in the several states, the following proposed amendment to the Constitution of the United States:

Section 1. The eighteenth article of amendment to the Constitution of the United States is hereby repealed.

Section 2. The transportation or importation into any State, Territory, or possession of the United States for delivery or use therein of intoxicating liquors, in violation of the laws thereof, is hereby prohibited.

Section 3. This article shall be inoperative unless it shall have been ratified as an amendment to the Constitution by conventions in the several States, as provided in the

Constitution, within seven years from the date of the submission thereof to the States by the Congress; and

WHEREAS, The delegates to this convention were elected in the election, held throughout the State of West Virginia on Tuesday, June 27, 1933, to act upon the ratification of the foregoing proposed amendment to the Constitution of the United States: therefore, be it

Resolved, That this Convention hereby ratifies the foregoing proposed amendment to the Constitution of the United States; and

Resolved further, That the President and Secretary of this convention be and they are hereby authorized, empowered and instructed to certify the adoption of the foregoing preamble and resolution to the proper authorities, so as to evidence the action of this convention.

DELEGATE J. PATRICK BEACOM: Mr. President, I move the adoption of the resolution as read.

DELEGATE J. J. O'BRIEN: I second that motion.

DELEGATE WELLS GOODYKOONTZ: Upon that motion, I call for an Aye and Nay vote, and move that the roll be called.

Which motion was seconded by Delegate Howard H. Holt, put by the Chair and carried, and the demand being sustained, the Secretary proceeded to call the roll, and the Ayes were:

J. Patrick Beacom,
Edith W. Breckinridge,
Mary S. Brewster,
Nat C. Burdette,
Paul J. Carr,
J. J. O'Brien,
Andrew Edmiston, Jr.,
Mrs. Frances Evans,
Joseph Holt Gaines,
Wells Goodykoontz,
Howard H. Holt,
Sam T. Mallison,
Hetzell S. Pownall,
David C. Reay,
William H. Sawyers,
Carl O. Schmidt,
C. E. (Ned) Smith,
Mrs. Kenner B. Stephenson,
Benjamin Rosenbloom, and the President,
Clarence E. Martin.

The Nayes were:
None.

PRESIDENT MARTIN: The roll of the convention having been called, and all of the delegates elected to the convention have voted in the affirmative, and no one in the negative, I declare the preamble and resolution offered by Mr. Beacom, adopted as and for the action of this convention.

Is there any further business before the convention?

DELEGATE CARL O. SCHMIDT: Mr. President, while I appreciate that I have perhaps already taken too much time of the convention, yet, our privilege of being here today is not due to any effort perhaps of our own, but has been due to two men particularly. I refer to Mr. Patrick D. Koontz, Chairman of the United Repeal Council, and to Mr. E. W. Knight. Mr. Koontz not only directed the campaign with the very able assistance and guidance of Mr. Knight, but Mr. Koontz has been responsible for the program that has been carried out here today. He had charge of the arrangements for this convention, and I think it only fitting, before we adjourn the convention, to extend to those two gentlemen a vote of thanks for their efforts.

Before that motion is put, however, the thought has occurred to me that the United

Repeal Council of West Virginia, having been successful at the recent election, its work is not fully completed, and I offer as a suggestion that the Council, together with those who have been privileged to be delegates here today, form themselves into a Law Observance Council, and really offer that suggestion for your thought after the convention is over.

I now move formally that a vote of thanks be extended to Mr. Patrick D. Koontz, and that beloved gentleman, Mr. E. W. Knight.

DELEGATE MRS. FRANCES EVANS: I second that motion.

The question was then put by the President, and unanimously carried.

PRESIDENT MARTIN: The thanks of this convention will be extended to the persons suggested, by Mr. Schmidt.

Is there any further business before the convention?

DELEGATE WELLS GOODYKOONTZ: Mr. President, I move that the convention adjourn.

DELEGATE JOSEPH HOLT GAINES: Mr. Chairman, wouldn't it be well to take a recess of five minutes, in order that we may determine whether there is any matter of detail we may have neglected.

PRESIDENT MARTIN: I don't think we have overlooked anything, Mr. Gaines, but before we adjourn, probably an enabling resolution or motion might be put, and then there will not be any question.

DELEGATE J. PATRICK BEACOM: Mr. President, I wondered if the convention had overlooked the fact that the statute provided that we report our mileage before adjournment.

PRESIDENT MARTIN: The statute provides that the convention shall keep a journal of its proceedings, and the recorded vote of each delegate. On final adjournment, the journal having been duly verified by the President and Secretary of the convention, shall be filed with the Secretary of State. If the convention shall agree by the vote of a majority of the total number of delegates for ratification of the proposed amendment, a certificate to that effect shall be executed by the President and Secretary of the convention, and transmitted to the Secretary of State of the State of West Virginia, who shall transmit the certificate, under the Great Seal of the State, to the Secretary of State of the United States. All of the details of the matter seem to have been fixed by statute.

I have no objection, of course, and I will entertain a motion, so there will be no question, if desired, that the journal, after being duly verified by the President and Secretary of the convention, shall be filed with the Secretary of State.

DELEGATE J. PATRICK BEACOM: Then, Mr. President, I move that the journal of this convention, after being duly verified by the President and Secretary of the convention, be filed with the Secretary of State.

Which motion being duly seconded, was put by the President and unanimously carried.

DELEGATE WILLIAM H. SAWYERS: Mr. President, I want to bring a matter before the convention. One of the most earnest workers for the repeal of the eighteenth amendment is unable to be present with us. He has worked in season and out of season. I refer to none other than my old friend and co-worker, J. Lewis Bumgardner, of Beckley. I think it would be fitting and right for this convention to pass a resolution recognizing his excellent work for the repeal of the eighteenth amendment, and expressing to him our extreme sorrow that he cannot be with us on the present occasion. I offer that as a resolution to the convention, and move its adoption.

DELEGATE C. E. (NED) SMITH: I second that motion.

The question was then put by the President, unanimously carried, and the resolution was adopted.

PRESIDENT MARTIN: The next business before the convention is the question of mileage and compensation of the delegates. The Statute provides for a compensation of $10 each day, and in addition, mileage at the rate allowed members of the Legislature. May I ask each of you to certify to the Secretary of the convention the number of miles that you have traveled to and from this convention, so that the Secretary and President may be able to certify the same to the State Treasurer.

DELEGATE WILLIAM H. SAWYERS: I suggest that the Secretary call the roll, that the same may be ascertained.

PRESIDENT: Gentlemen of the convention, the Sergeant-at-Arms of the House of Delegates advises me that he has the mileage of the members of the House in his office, and if it is satisfactory to this convention, may we not certify the same amount of mileage that would be certified by the various delegates, as ascertained by him, so there will not be any question about it.

DELEGATE NAT C. BURDETTE: I move that suggestion be adopted.

Which motion was seconded by Delegate Wells Goodykoontz, put by the President and carried.

Whereupon, on motion of Wells Goodykoontz, duly seconded, put by the President and carried, the convention adjourned *sine die.*

STATE OF WEST VIRGINIA,

COUNTY OF KANAWHA, to-wit:

I, Madison L. Davis, do hereby certify that the foregoing is a full, true and complete transcript and journal of the proceedings of the convention held, as stated in the caption hereof, as reported by me in shorthand.

Given under my hand this 25th day of July, 1933.

MADISON L. DAVIS (S)
Shorthand reporter

The foregoing is a true and correct journal of the proceedings of the convention.

CLARENCE E. MARTIN (S)
President

Attest:
MARY S. BREWSTER (S)
Secretary

WISCONSIN*

MINUTES

OF THE

STATE CONSTITUTIONAL CONVENTION

OF WISCONSIN

RELATIVE TO RATIFICATION OF REPEAL

OF THE

EIGHTEENTH AMENDMENT

HELD IN THE STATE CAPITOL

AT MADISON, WISCONSIN,

APRIL 25, 1933

Pursuant to the notice of the Honorable Theodore Dammann, Secretary of State of the State of Wisconsin, the fifteen delegates elected to the State Constitutional Convention of Wisconsin relative to ratification of repeal of the Eighteenth Amendment met in the Hearing Room of the Public Service Commission in the State Capitol at Madison, Wisconsin, April twenty-fifth, nineteen hundred and thirty-three.

Thereupon Charles Broughton of Sheboygan was nominated as president by William Mauthe of Fond du Lac. There being no further nominations, Mr. Charles Broughton was unanimously elected president.

Harry Sauthoff of Madison was nominated for the office of secretary. There being no further nominations, Mr. Harry Sauthoff was unanimously elected secretary.

Thereupon the roll was called from the certified list of delegates duly elected as certified to by the Honorable Theodore Dammann, Secretary of State, a copy of which certified list is hereto attached and made a part of these minutes.

UNITED STATES OF AMERICA

THE STATE OF WISCONSIN

DEPARTMENT OF STATE

To all to whom these presents shall come:

Certified List

of

Delegates

I, THEODORE DAMMANN, Secretary of State of the State of Wisconsin, do hereby certify that the following is a true and correct list of persons duly elected as DELEGATES to the State Constitutional Convention, to be held at the Capitol, in the City of Madi-

* From a typewritten copy.

son, on the 25th day of April, 1933, pursuant to Chapter 23 of the Laws of 1933, for the purpose of ratifying or rejecting the Federal Constitutional Amendment repealing the Eighteenth Amendment to the United States Constitution; To wit:

Louis A. Arnold,
2145 No. 44th S., Milwaukee
Gertrude Bowler,
512 St. Clair Ave., Sheboygan
A. J. Branstad,
414 Marston Ave., Eau Claire
Lawrence J. Brody,
2123 Grandview Place, La Crosse
Charles E. Broughton,
315 Erie Ave., Sheboygan
Wm. George Bruce,
1137 So. 3rd St., Milwaukee
Peter B. Cadigan,
1701 - 24th St., Superior
John A. Frey,
Eau Claire Blvd., Wausau

H. L. Hoard,
604 So. Main St., Ft. Atkinson
William Mauthe,
108 W. Division St., Fon du Lac
Victor I. Minahan,
823 North Broadway, De Pere
Harry Sauthoff,
926 Spaight St., Madison
Robert C. Thackeray,
912 Monroe St., Racine
George Vits,
610 No. Sixth St., Manitowoc
Chauncey Yockey,
710 E. Mason Street, Milwaukee

All of which appears from the certificate of the Board of State Canvassers now on file and of record in this office.

SEAL

In testimony whereof, I have hereunto set my hand and affixed my official seal, at the Capitol, in the City of Madison, this 25th day of April, A.D. One Thousand, Nine Hundred and Thirty-three.

THEODORE DAMMANN
Secretary of State

As the roll was called the following answered present:

Louis A. Arnold
Gertrude Bowler
A. J. Branstad
Lawrence J. Brody
Charles E. Broughton
William George Bruce
Peter B. Cadigan
John A. Frey
H. L. Hoard
William Mauthe
Victor I. Minahan
Harry Sauthoff
Robert C. Thackeray
Chauncey Yockey

The following were absent:

George Vits.

The president appointed Chauncey Yockey of Milwaukee as Sergeant-at-Arms.

Victor Minahan moved that the president appoint a committee of three on credentials of delegates. Upon being seconded, the motion was carried unanimously. The president appointed as a committee on credentials of delegates Victor Minahan, Louis Arnold and H. J. Branstad.

Louis Arnold moved that the rules of the Assembly of the Wisconsin Legislature be adopted as rules of this convention. Upon being seconded the motion was unanimously carried.

William George Bruce moved that the president appoint five members as a committee on resolutions. Upon being seconded the motion was unanimously carried. The president thereupon appointed as a committee on resolutions the following: William

George Bruce, William Mauthe, Gertrude Bowler, Robert C. Thackeray and George Vits.

William Mauthe moved that the president appoint a committee of three to wait on the Honorable A. G. Schmedeman, Governor of the State of Wisconsin, to invite him to address the convention. Upon being seconded the motion was unanimously carried. The president appointed as such committee Chauncey Yockey, John A. Frey and Lawrence Brody.

Victor Minahan moved that a committee of two be appointed to wait upon Chief Justice Rosenberry of the Supreme Court of the State of Wisconsin, to invite him to administer the oath of office to the members of the convention. Upon being seconded, the motion was unanimously carried. The president thereupon appointed Chauncey Yockey and Robert C. Thackeray as such a committee.

The committee of credentials was now ready to report and its chairman, Victor Minahan, reported that the following had been properly elected, qualified and certified as members of this State Convention:

Louis A. Arnold,
2145 No. 44th Street, Milwaukee
Gertrude Bowler,
512 St. Clair Avenue, Sheboygan
A. J. Branstad,
414 Marston Avenue, Eau Claire
Lawrence Brody,
2123 Grandview Place, La Crosse
Charles E. Broughton,
315 Erie Avenue, Sheboygan
William George Bruce,
1137 So. 3rd Street, Milwaukee
Peter B. Cadigan,
1701 - 24th Street, Superior
John A. Frey,
Eau Claire Blvd., Wausau
H. L. Hoard,
604 South Main Street, Ft. Atkinson
William Mauthe,
108 W. Division Street, Fond du Lac
Victor I. Minahan,
823 North Broadway, De Pere
Harry Sauthoff
926 Spaight Street, Madison
Robert C. Thackeray,
912 Monroe Street, Racine
George Vits,
601 No. Sixth Street, Manitowoc
Chauncey Yockey,
710 Mason Street, E., Milwaukee

Gertrude Bowler moved that the report of the credentials committee be adopted. Upon being seconded the motion was carried unanimously by roll call; Mr. George Vits being absent, all the rest of the members voting in the affirmative. Thereupon the president declared the report of the credentials committee adopted.

It was moved by William Mauthe that the vacancy of George Vits be filled by the election of J. J. Seelman of Milwaukee as delegate to the convention. The motion being seconded, the president called for a vote by roll call of the delegates. All present voted in the affirmative, and the president thereupon declared J. J. Seelman of Milwaukee as duly elected to serve as a delegate in the State Constitutional Convention in the place of George Vits, absent.

Thereupon the oath of office was administered by Chief Justice Rosenberry of the Supreme Court of the State of Wisconsin, and each delegate signed his name to the oath of office which is hereto attached and made a part of these minutes.

Oath of Delegates to the Convention to pass upon the question of whether or not the proposed amendment to the Constitution of the United States shall be ratified.

STATE OF WISCONSIN }
COUNTY OF DANE } ss

We the undersigned, who have been elected as delegates to the Convention to pass upon the question of whether or not the proposed amendment to the Constitution of the United States shall be ratified, but who have not yet entered upon the duties thereof, swear that we will support the Constitution of the United States and the Constitution of the State of Wisconsin, and will faithfully discharge our duties as delegates to the best of our ability.

Gertrude Bowler of Sheboygan
Wm. Mauthe of Fond du Lac
Lawrence J. Brody of La Crosse
Halbert L. Hoard of Fort Atkinson, Wis.
Louis A. Arnold of Milwaukee
Harry Sauthoff of Madison, Wis.
J. J. Seelman of Milwaukee, Wis.
Peter B. Cadigan of Superior, Wis.
John A. Frey of Wausau, Wis.
Robert C. Thackeray of Racine, Wis.
C. E. Broughton of Sheboygan, Wis.
A. J. Branstad of Eau Claire, Wis.
Wm. Geo. Bruce of 1137 So. 3rd St., Milwaukee
Victor I. Minahan of De Pere, Wis.
Chauncey Yockey of Milwaukee, Wis.

Subscribed and sworn to before me this 25th day of April 1933.

MARVIN B. ROSENBERRY
Chief Justice

It was thereupon moved by Chauncey Yockey that the temporary organization be made permanent. Upon being seconded, the motion was carried unanimously by roll call.

An announcement was made that the Assembly Chamber of the Wisconsin Legislature tendered an invitation to the convention to adjourn to said chamber and continue its deliberations in the presence of said body. Thereupon Louis Arnold moved that the convention take a recess for ten minutes and when it again convened, it convened in the Assembly Chamber of the Legislature of the State of Wisconsin in the State Capitol at Madison, Wisconsin. Being seconded the motion was unanimously carried.

Ten minutes later the president, Charles Broughton, called the convention to order in the Assembly Chamber where Chief Justice Rosenberry again administered the oath of office orally to the delegates.

The committee appointed to wait upon the Governor thereupon announced that the Governor was in attendance and Sergeant-at-Arms Chauncey Yockey welcomed the Governor and escorted him to the chair. The president, Charles Broughton, in a befitting manner introduced the Honorable A. G. Schmedeman, Governor of the State of Wisconsin, and invited him to address the convention. Thereupon Governor Schmedeman addressed the convention in the following terms:

ADDRESS OF WELCOME OF GOVERNOR SCHMEDEMAN TO DELEGATES TO CONSTITUTIONAL CONVENTION

Madison, Wisconsin, Tuesday, April 25, 1933, 10:00 A.M.
Hearing Room, State Capitol
LADIES AND GENTLEMEN:

I need not tell you that it is a pleasure for me to greet and welcome you here today. The occasion is at once a happy and important one. Happy, since the citizens of Wisconsin have expressed in unmistakable terms the longing in their hearts and see in this gathering the partial fulfilment of their desires.

You, delegates, in the fullest sense of the phrase, are the people's chosen representatives. Therefore, you should rejoice in the opportunity each one of you has to carry out the will of the voters. You all are especially honored in the overwhelming manner your principles were approved by the electors on April fourth.

Your convention is important, politically, morally and historically. It is important politically, that is, from the standpoint of the body politic. The subject matter of your deliberations involves matters of grave consequence not only to this state, but also to the United States. It goes to the very root and fiber of our entire government. It calls for a consideration of the very fundamentals upon which the several states are grounded. In you is vested perhaps the most sovereign power the state possesses. In a word, it is for you to say whether a radical change shall be made in the "greatest document ever struck off by the hand of man," the Constitution of the United States.

Morally, your actions here are important because of the effect it will have upon the citizens and representatives of our sister states. What you do here today will be eagerly watched throughout the land. Moreover, you will determine to a very large extent what the future disposition of the liquor question will be, by your course of conduct in this convention. Upon you rests the responsibility of doing what right reason and the dictates of your conscience demand.

This body is the first of its kind ever to be assembled in Wisconsin to perform the function of passing upon a proposed amendment to the Constitution of the United States. Because of the great public interest and the vital concern to the nation, your assemblage in Madison naturally partakes of a truly great and historical event. Your names will be indelibly inscribed upon the pages of Wisconsin's glorious history.

I leave you with the confidence that you will bring to your labors a deep appreciation of the people's choice, a clear understanding of the importance of your duties and a high resolve to carry them out. May your association prove a pleasant one and may your endeavors be guided by the best interest and welfare of the people of Wisconsin, in whose name I wish you Godspeed.

At the conclusion of the Governor's remarks it was moved by William Mauthe and seconded that the address of the Governor be spread upon the record of the convention. Carried Unanimously.

William George Bruce as chairman of the resolutions committee reported that the Committee on resolutions was ready with its report and the president requested that the report of the resolutions committee be read. Thereupon William George Bruce read the following report of the resolutions committee and moved its adoption:

RESOLUTION

Ratifying the proposed amendment to the Constitution of the United States.

WHEREAS, The Congress of the United States has submitted to conventions, to be held in the several states, the following proposed amendment to the Constitution of the United States:

Section 1. The eighteenth article of amendment to the Constitution of the United States is hereby repealed.

Section 2. The transportation or importation into any State, Territory, or possession of the United States for delivery or use therein of intoxicating liquors, in violation of the laws thereof, is hereby prohibited.

Section 3. This article shall be inoperative unless it shall have been ratified as an amendment to the Constitution by conventions in the several States, as provided in

the Constitution, within seven years from the date of the submission hereof to the States by the Congress; and

WHEREAS, The delegates to this convention were elected in the election held throughout the State of Wisconsin on Tuesday, April 4, 1933, to act upon the ratification of the foregoing proposed amendment to the Constitution of the United States; therefore, be it

Resolved, That this convention hereby ratifies as an amendment to the Constitution of the United States the foregoing proposed amendment.

WM. GEO. BRUCE, *Chairman*
GERTRUDE BOWLER
WM. MAUTHE
J. J. SEELMAN
R. C. THACKERAY

Being properly seconded, the president put the motion and the roll was called of all the delegates, each of whom voted in the affirmative, and the president thereupon declared the report of the resolutions committee unanimously adopted.

The certificate of the president and secretary of the State Constitutional Convention relative to the ratification of repeal of the Eighteenth Amendment held April 25, 1933, and containing the resolution and the vote of the delegates is hereto attached and made a part of these minutes.

It was moved by Harry Sauthoff that the secretary convey the condolences of the convention to Mr. George Vits because of a death in the family, which was unanimously carried.

It was also moved by the secretary that a letter of thanks be addressed to the Assembly Chamber for the courtesy extended to the convention by said body. Unanimously carried.

Thereupon it was moved and seconded that this State Convention do adjourn. Unanimously carried and the president thereupon declared the State Convention adjourned.

C. E. BROUGHTON
President
HARRY SAUTHOFF
Secretary

WYOMING*

PROCEEDINGS AND MINUTES

OF

THE CONSTITUTIONAL CONVENTION

FOR THE

STATE OF WYOMING

HELD AT

CASPER, WYOMING

MAY 25th, 1933

Pursuant to the statutes of the State of Wyoming providing for the calling of state conventions; prescribing the method and manner in which such conventions shall be called and held in the State of Wyoming to consider and vote on the question of repealing, amending or altering the Constitution of the United States of America; providing for the payment of the expenses thereof; prescribing the duties of the Governor, the Secretary of State, the Chairman or other member of the Board of County Commissioners and the officers of the several counties; and appropriating money to defray the expenses incurred thereby; and a public proclamation by Honorable Leslie A. Miller, Governor of the State of Wyoming, which proclamation reads as follows:

PUBLIC PROCLAMATION

Under and by virtue of the power vested in me by reason of the Laws of the State of Wyoming, I, LESLIE A. MILLER, Governor of the State of Wyoming, do hereby order and proclaim that on the 25th day of May, A.D. 1933, at ten o'clock A.M. at the City Hall in the City of Casper, in the State of Wyoming, there shall be held a state convention to which state convention there shall be submitted the following "Joint Resolution proposing an amendment to the Constitution of the United States" for such action as may be had thereon:

SEVENTY-SECOND CONGRESS OF THE UNITED STATES OF AMERICA

AT THE SECOND SESSION

Begun and held at the City of Washington on Monday, the fifth day of December, one thousand nine hundred and thirty-two.

JOINT RESOLUTION

Proposing an amendment to the Constitution
of the United States

Resolved by the Senate and House of Representatives of the United States of America in Congress assembled (two-thirds of each house concurring therein), That the following article is hereby proposed as an amendment to the Constitution of the

* From a mimeographed copy.

United States, which shall be valid to all intents and purposes as part of the Constitution when ratified by conventions in three-fourths of the several states:

ARTICLE ___

Section 1. The eighteenth article of Amendment to the Constitution of the United States is hereby repealed.

Section 2. The transportation or importation into any State, Territory, or possession of the United States for delivery or use therein of intoxicating liquors, in violation of the laws thereof, is hereby prohibited.

Section 3. This article shall be inoperative unless it shall have been ratified as an amendment to the Constitution by conventions in the several States, as provided in the Constitution, within seven years from the date of the submission hereof to the States by the Congress.

JNO. N. GARNER
Speaker of the House of Representatives
CHARLES CURTIS
Vice-President of the United States and President of the Senate.

The number of delegates (who shall be qualified electors) of which said convention shall consist, and the method and manner by and in which delegates to such state convention shall be elected, shall be in all respects in conformity with the provisions of Enrolled Act No. 53, Senate, Twenty-second Legislature of the State of Wyoming, and as herein ordered.

IT IS FURTHER ORDERED AND PROCLAIMED that on the 15th day of May, A.D. 1933, at ten o'clock A.M., in each of the election precincts in each of the counties of this state there shall be held a meeting of the qualified electors of such precinct, at which meeting there shall be held a precinct election at which election there shall be elected one delegate from each of such precincts and one additional delegate for each six hundred, or major portion thereof, of the inhabitants of such precinct to a convention of such delegates to be held at the county seat of such county. Such precinct meetings shall be held at the established polling place in each of the election precincts as the same are now or as may be hereafter constituted and shall be presided over by any qualified elector of such precinct. The presiding officer of each of such precinct meetings shall forthwith certify to the county convention, under oath, the names of the delegates to such county convention chosen by such precinct meetings.

IT IS FURTHER ORDERED AND PROCLAIMED that on the 18th day of May, A.D. 1933, at ten o'clock A.M., there shall be held a county convention in each of the counties of this state and the delegates thereto shall assemble and elect one delegate for each county and one delegate for each five thousand, or major fraction thereof, of the inhabitants of such county as delegates to the state convention hereinbefore mentioned. The meeting place shall be in the court room of the court house, if there be one in such county; and if not, in the court room in said county whereat the business of the District Court is usually transacted. It shall be the duty of the Chairman of the Board of County Commissioners, or some other member of such Board in each county, to convene such county convention and to preside over the same until the delegates chosen thereto shall select a chairman of such convention; and the delegates shall thereafter select a secretary of such convention. It shall be the duty of the chairman and secretary of such county convention to certify to the Secretary of State of the State of Wyoming and to said State convention, hereby called, under oath, the names of the delegates to such state convention chosen by such county convention.

The rules of practice, procedure and conduct of the business of the several county conventions shall be those prescribed by Roberts' Rules of Parliamentary Procedure and Order.

The vote on the selection of delegates to either of the conventions herein mentioned shall be by written or printed ballot.

In the apportionment of representation in the several conventions herein mentioned, the last census enumeration, taken and made by the United States Government, shall be the basis upon which the right to representation in such conventions shall be determined.

The Secretary of State of the State of Wyoming shall convene such state convention at the time and place herein designated and shall preside over the same until the delegates chosen thereto shall select a chairman of such state convention, and the delegates shall thereafter select a secretary of such state convention. It shall be the duty of the officers of such state convention to certify to the Secretary of State of the State of Wyoming, under oath, the result of the vote cast at such state convention upon the question hereby submitted to such state convention.

In witness whereof, I, Leslie A. Miller, Governor of the State of Wyoming, have hereunto set my hand and caused the Great Seal of the State of Wyoming to be affixed.

Done at the Capitol in the City of Cheyenne, this *14th* day of *March,* A.D. 1933, and in the year of the Independence of the United States, the One Hundred Fifty-seventh.

Leslie A. Miller
Governor

By the Governor
A. M. Clark
Secretary of State

SEAL

The State convention provided for by said proclamation was convened by Honorable A. M. Clark, Secretary of State of and for the State of Wyoming, on the 25th day of May, A.D. 1933, at ten o'clock A.M. at the City Hall in the City of Casper, Natrona County, Wyoming, as follows:

Secretary of State Clark: I notice that we are short the official certificates for four counties, and I am going to call those four counties' names and if the chairman of your delegation has your certificate, will he please bring it to the desk so that we can complete our list of official delegates. Campbell County, Converse County, Lincoln County and Weston County.

At this time the delegates from the four counties mentioned presented to Mr. Clark their credentials.

SECRETARY OF STATE CLARK: Members of this convention, we now have the credentials, seemingly, from all counties and the certificates necessary to entitle the delegates to sit at this convention. I have appointed Mr. J. R. French as temporary secretary of this convention, and I am inclined to do my little part as quickly as possible, and in as short a manner as possible. If I remember correctly in the list of delegates to this convention there is one lady. (Applause.) I don't know how many drys there are because, you know, it looks as though we drys are all wet. I am going to dispense with the reading of the proclamation of the Governor, as copies have been distributed among you, as have also copies of the law providing for this convention, and a little later we will try to furnish each one of you with one of our official directories, which will give your names as well as those of other state officers.

Before we go further I will ask the temporary secretary, who is taking a report of the convention, to call the roll of delegates and alternates.

The secretary then proceeded with the roll call of the delegates by counties, as follows:

There were present and answering to roll call at said convention the following named delegates (or alternates), from the following named counties for whom certificates had been filed, showing that they were entitled to vote at said convention, to-wit:

Albany County	N. A. Swenson, alternate for T. L. Johnson J. R. Sullivan Oscar Hammond
Big Horn	J. P. Wheeler, alternate for T. K. Bishop J. R. French, alternate for H. B. Richardson
Campbell County	Guy Garrett W. D. McGrew
Carbon	Victor H. Scepansky, alternate for H. J. Cashman Gus Larson C. D. Williamson
Converse	Waldo Bolln Joe Garst
Crook	Chas. Louis, alternate for James T. McGuckin G. W. Earle, alternate for Jay Durfee
Fremont	Mrs. Sam Payne Walter Oswald R. S. Price (Also alternates Charles Moore and A. O. Heyer)
Goshen	L. G. Flannery J. M. Roushar Erle H. Reid (Also alternate Wm. Bosse)
Hot Springs	Henry Cottle John McCullum
Johnson	Frank O. Horton Jean Van Dyke (Also alternates Berton Hill and Richie Young)
Laramie	A. D. Homan Fred W. Roedel Wilfrid O'Leary Abe Goldstein Perry Williams Fred Hofmann (Also alternates W. Q. Phelan and T. Joe Cahill)
Lincoln County	Dr. C. D. Stafford Glen E. Sorensen Oluf Jefson

Natrona County	Robert N. Ogden
	J. E. Jones, alternate for John Nance
	T. F. Speckbacker
	T. C. Spears
	E. J. Sullivan
	J. F. Cowan
	(Also alternate L. B. Townsend)
Niobrara County	Albert P. Bruch
	C. W. Erwin
Park County	Alex Linton
	B. C. Rumsey
	M. L. Simpson
	(Also alternate Eugene Phelps)
Platte County	Hans Christiansen
	B. L. Dixon
Sheridan County	Malcolm Moncreiffe
	Peter Kooi
	R. A. Keenan
	Roy Bedford
Sublette County	Albert Larsen
	(Also E. D. Key, his alternate)
Sweetwater County	William Evers
	Dr. R. H. Sanders
	Glen A. Knox
	P. C. Bunning
	Joe Bertagnolli
Teton County	R. C. Lundy, Sr.
	O. A. Pendergraft
Uinta County	Matthew Morrow
	S. S. Kastor
	J. H. Holland
Washakie County	Dr. W. O. Gray
	R. C. Shultz
	(Also L. L. Dorman, alternate)
Weston County	A. F. Leslie, Alternate for E. C. Raymond
	M. M. Falk
	(Also A. S. Boatsman, alternate)

SECRETARY OF STATE CLARK: If there are any reporters in the room who want room at the table there is plenty of room up here, and you are welcome to use it. What is the next pleasure of this convention?

SENATOR FRANK O. HORTON: Mr. Chairman, I presume the next order of business is the selection of a permanent chairman, but before going into that I would like the privilege of the floor. There undoubtedly are a great many men here entitled to that honor, irrespective of their party affiliations. Perhaps it would be well if we could select a democrat, because they have been honest in their stand, and due largely to that stand are they in power in this state today, and I am not talking politics, I am just giving credit where credit belongs. Mr. Chairman, there is some one person who is entitled to be Chairman of this Convention because his work and labor has been more outstanding than that of any one else. It is almost impossible at an open convention of this kind to find that one man, therefore I have this suggestion to make, that the temporary Chairman appoint as a nominating committee the Chairman of each of the county delegations, let this committee of one delegate from each county retire and thresh the entire field and find that one man and come back here and tell us about it. This would, of course, not proclude other nominations. I give you that in the form of a motion.

SECRETARY OF STATE CLARK: Do I hear a second?

(Motion seconded from the floor.)

SECRETARY OF STATE CLARK: It has been moved and seconded that the chair appoint the chairman of each county delegation as a committee to retire for a short time and submit the name of some person for Chairman of this convention. Are there any more remarks? All in favor of the motion say "Aye," contrary minded, "No." The motion has prevailed. The committee on nominations will retire, for I hereby appoint the Chairman of each county delegation as a nominating committee, and I believe they will select a good man.

FROM THE FLOOR: Mr. Chairman, while the committee is out may we not have a short recess?

SECRETARY OF STATE CLARK: I had that in mind, if no objection we will stand in recess subject to the call of the chair.

(During this recess Governor Miller was brought in and introduced to the convention, and made a very fine talk regarding the matter for which this convention was called.)

SECRETARY OF STATE CLARK: Is the committee on nominations ready to report?

SENATOR HORTON: Your committee is ready to report. I would like to say that there were one hundred and six men whose names were considered, and every one of them were outstanding, and we thought each one should be the choice for permanent chairman of this convention, but we had to narrow it down, and we have decided upon a man who has the ability to preside and whose work has been outstanding over all the rest. I have the pleasure of presenting to you the name of Mr. Erle H. Reid for permanent Chairman, and move the adoption of the report.

(The motion was seconded from the floor.)

SECRETARY OF STATE CLARK: You have heard the report and motion, and its second. Are there any remarks? All in favor of the motion say "Aye," contrary minded "No." The motion has carried unanimously, and it is so ordered.

FROM THE FLOOR: Mr. Secretary, I move the temporary secretary be instructed to cast the unanimous vote of this convention for Mr. Reid, for permanent Chairman of this convention.

(Motion seconded from the floor.)

SECRETARY OF STATE CLARK: It has been regularly moved and seconded that the secretary be instructed to cast the unanimous vote of this convention for Mr. Erle H. Reid as Chairman of this convention. Are there any remarks? (Question called for.) All in favor of the motion as stated say "Aye," contrary "No." The motion has carried. Mr. Secretary cast the vote of this convention for Mr. Reid, as Chairman.

TEMPORARY SECRETARY FRENCH: I hereby cast the unanimous vote of this convention for Mr. Erle H. Reid, for permanent Chairman of this convention.

SECRETARY OF STATE CLARK: I declare Mr. Erle H. Reid elected. Mr. Reid, will you come forward? Members of this convention, I wish to introduce to you your permanent Chairman of this convention, Mr. Erle H. Reid, of Torrington. Mr. Reid, you will now take the chair. (Applause.)

CHAIRMAN REID: Thank you, Governor. Madam Delegate and gentlemen, you have done me a great honor this morning, and I want to assure you I appreciate it very much. I am here, interested as you are, in the accomplishment of a great thing for the State of Wyoming and this United States of ours. A movement toward better government in our State and Country, and I speak your co-operation to that end, and I hope the work of this convention will be speedily taken care of so we may return home. I presume the next work of this convention is the selection of a credentials committee. May I suggest, that while I am acquainted with a great many here, there are also a number here whom I have not met and it might expedite business if you give your name and county when addressing the Chair.

MR. VAN DYKE, of Buffalo: Mr. Chairman, I move you the chair appoint a credentials committee of three.

MR. MORROW, of Uinta County: I second the motion.

MR. HORTON, of Johnson County: I suggest the gentleman from Buffalo withhold that motion for a moment, as I wonder if the next order of business would not be the selection of a permanent secretary.

CHAIRMAN REID: I think that is right.

MR. ROUSHAR, of Goshen County: I move you, Mr. Chairman, that the temporary secretary be made the permanent secretary of this convention.

(Motion seconded from the floor.)

MR. GARST, of Converse County: Mr. Chairman, does the Secretary have to be from the delegates?

CHAIRMAN REID: I think that the secretary need not be, however, the present secretary is one of the delegates. Are there any remarks? So many as are in favor of the temporary secretary for the office of permanent secretary will please rise. The Motion is carried unanimously. Mr. French, you are elected permanent Secretary of this meeting. We will now return to the other order of business, and I will take up the motion as made by Mr. Van Dyke and seconded by Mr. Morrow, for the appointment of a credentials committee. Are there any remarks? All in favor of the motion as stated signify by saying "Aye," contrary "No." The motion is carried, and I will appoint on that committee: Mr. Ogden, of Natrona, Mr. Glen Knox, of Sweetwater; and Mr. Wilfrid O'Leary, of Laramie County.

SECRETARY OF STATE CLARK: Mr. Chairman, I would like to meet with that committee at once, I have the credentials sent in for the delegates and believe I can assist them materially.

MR. HORTON, Johnson County: Mr. Chairman, I move you we stand in recess, while this committee is out, and subject to the call of the Chair.

(Motion seconded from the floor.)

CHAIRMAN REID: You have heard the motion and its second, are there any remarks? All in favor of the motion as stated signify by saying "Aye," contrary "No." The motion is carried, the convention will stand in recess subject to the call of the chair.

(At this time a recess of fifteen minutes was taken.)

CHAIRMAN REID: The convention will be in order, is the Credentials Committee ready to report?

MR. OGDEN, of Casper: Yes, Mr. Chairman. Your committee finds that the respective delegates and alternates answering the roll call are all properly accredited. In Uinta County three delegates were elected, and the Honorable Secretary of State informs us two is all that were entitled to, we therefore find that the delegates from Uinta County are entitled to only two-thirds vote each in this convention. We find that the following delegates are entitled to seats and to vote in this convention:

Albany County	N. A. Swenson, J. R. Sullivan, and Oscar Hammond
Big Horn County	J. P. Wheeler and J. R. French
Campbell County	Guy Garrett and W. D. McGrew
Carbon County	Victor H. Scepansky, Gus Larson and C. D. Williamson
Converse County	Waldo Bolln and Joe Garst
Crook County	Charles Louis and G. W. Earle
Fremont County	Mrs. Sam Payne, Walter Osward, and R. S. Price
Goshen County	J. G. Flannery, J. M. Roushar, and Erle H. Reid
Hot Springs County	Henry Cottle and John McCullum
Johnson County	Frank O. Horton and Jean Van Dyke
Laramie County	A. D. Homan, Fred W. Roedel, Wilfrid O'Leary, Abe Goldstein, Perry Williams and Fred Hofmann
Lincoln County	Dr. C. D. Stafford, Glen E. Sorensen, and Oluf Jefsen
Natrona County	Robert N. Ogden, J. E. Jones, T. F. Speckbacker, T. C. Spears, E. J. Sullivan and J. F. Cowan
Niobrara County	Albert P. Bruch and C. W. Erwin
Park County	Alex Linton, B. C. Rumsey and M. L. Simpson
Platte County	Hans Christiansen and B. L. Dixon
Sheridan County	Malcolm Moncreiffe, Peter Kooi, R. A. Keenan and Roy Bedford
Sublette County	Albert Larsen
Sweetwater County	William Evers, Dr. R. H. Sanders, Glen A. Knox, P. C. Bunning and Joe Bertagnolli
Teton County	R. C. Lundy, Sr., and O. A. Pendergraft
Uinta County	Matthew Morrow, S. S. Kastor, and J. H. Holland
Washakie County	Dr. W. O. Gray and R. C. Shultz
Weston County	A. F. Leslie and M. M. Falk

I move you the adoption of the report, Mr. Chairman, and that the committee be discharged.

MR. KNOX, of Sweetwater County: I second the motion.

CHAIRMAN REID: You have heard the motion and second that the report of the credentials committee be accepted and the committee be discharged, are there any remarks? All in favor of the motion signify by saying "Aye," contrary "No," the motion has prevailed, the report of the Credentials Committee is accepted and the committee discharged with the thanks of the Chair.

I think at this time the Chair will entertain a motion to dispense with reading the proclamation of the Governor calling this convention, you all have copies of the proclamation, and a copy will be spread in the minutes by the Secretary, and I see no purpose that will be served by reading it at this time.

MR. GARST, Converse County: Mr. Chairman, I move you we dispense with reading the proclamation of the Governor.

MR. HOFMANN, Laramie County: I second the motion.

CHAIRMAN REID: You have heard the motion and the second, are there any remarks? If not, all in favor of the motion signify by saying "Aye," opposed "No," the motion is carried. We are met here this morning as a result of three distinct actions that have been taken; in the first place, The Congress of the United States has submitted to the several states, for ratification or rejection, a proposed amendment to the Constitution of the United States. Second, the legislature of this state has passed a law providing for this convention, or similar convention which may be called in the future. And third, The Governor of this State has called this convention, who are now assembled, by proclamation. You have passed on the names of those who will constitute your convention. I take it there is but one thing before this convention at this time, and that is "Shall this convention ratify or reject the proposed amendment to the Constitution?" I will ask at this time that the Secretary read the joint resolution of the Seventy-second Congress of the United States submitting this amendment.

(Whereupon, the Secretary read the amendment, as follows:)

Section 1. The Eighteenth Article of amendment to the Constitution of the United States is hereby repealed.

Section 2. The transportation or importation into any State, Territory, or possession of the United States for delivery or use therein of intoxicating liquors, in violation of the laws thereof, is hereby prohibited.

Section 3. This article shall be inoperative unless it shall have been ratified as an amendment to the Constitution by conventions in the several States, as provided in the Constitution, within seven years from the date of the submission hereof to the States by the Congress.

CHAIRMAN REID: The question before us is, shall the proposed 21st Amendment be ratified or rejected, the Secretary will call the roll by counties.

MR. SIMPSON, of Park County: Mr. Chairman, before that roll call is taken may I say, I am a bit fearful of the outcome of this vote, and I understand from other sources, as well as from the Governor, that there is some money left in the fund created to cover the expenses of this convention. Inasmuch as Natrona County and the City of Casper don't seem to be going to take care of us, I suggest we spend this money for a few bottles of beer for the delegates to this convention.

CHAIRMAN REID: The motion is carried. The Secretary will call the roll and the Chairman will respond for his county, giving the number of votes and whether for or against the adoption of the proposed amendment.

FROM THE FLOOR: In order that the question might be perfectly clear, should it be specified how the vote should be given, that is for the adoption of the 21st Amendment?

CHAIRMAN REID: I take it the vote should be, for instance, three votes for ratification or three votes against ratification, however knowing the sentiment of the convention I take it there will be none against ratification.

MR. GARST, of Converse County: Mr. Chairman, I don't like to do too much talking, but there is a question in my mind whether there should not be a motion on the minutes of this meeting so we can vote whether to ratify or not ratify, I think that is a matter of procedure.

MR. FLANNERY, Goshen County: Mr. Chairman, we are here to bury Caesar, and the quicker the better, I move you this convention ratify this proposed Twenty-first Amendment to the Constitution of the United States.

(Motion seconded from the floor.)

MR. ERLE, Crook County: Are we to vote individually or by acclamation?

CHAIRMAN REID: I think we should have a roll call and vote by counties.

MR. SULLIVAN, Natrona County: I admit we are here to bury Caesar, but when he is buried let him be wholly interred. The danger in this convention is in not having a minority, we might do things in an irregular way, the question is known over the state as; "Will we repeal the Eighteenth Amendment," but the question here is will the State of Wyoming ratify the action of the Congress of the United States in submitting the Twenty-first Amendment to the Constitution of the United States, and if there is no objection I would like to present that language in place of that in the motion.

MR. GARST, of Converse County: My motion was to ratify the resolution as read by the Secretary, I thing that would be proper.

MR. SULLIVAN, Natrona County: I withdraw my suggestion.

SECRETARY OF STATE MR. CLARK: Mr. Chairman, I am in a rather peculiar situation here, while I must work with the convention yet I am not a delegate, so if you will pardon this intrusion; while it is the office of the officers of this convention to make such report as they see fit to the Secretary of State, we need to keep in mind that the Secretary of State is required to report to the United States. In the suggested outline which I presented your Secretary, for his minutes, it has been our purpose to see that every vote be recorded individually and by counties, however there is no necessity for this convention following that order. If there should be a question raised, as there might be for thirteen States can prevent the ratification of the Twenty-first Amendment, as to the sufficiency of our action, it is a good thing to have a complete record, that is the reason I have asked the reporter to sit here and take the minutes. In making this outline it has been our idea that even though there be but one in the minority that he be allowed to record his vote in the minutes of this meeting.

CHAIRMAN REID: I take it you think we should call the roll by delegates and not by counties.

SECRETARY OF STATE MR. CLARK: You can call it by both county and delegate, as they are all shown on the list there.

CHAIRMAN REID: I think you have the right idea, and if there is no objection we will have the Secretary call the roll on the question; "That the State of Wyoming, by this Convention, do ratify the proposed twenty-first amendment to the Constitution of the United States of America," as read by the Secretary and to be transcribed in the minutes.

(No objection being made the Secretary proceeded to call the roll by delegates and counties, as follows:)

Albany County, three votes:	N. A. Swenson	Aye
	J. R. Sullivan	Aye
	Oscar Hammond	Aye
Big Horn County, three votes: (one vote absent)	J. P. Wheeler	Aye
	J. R. French	Aye
Campbell County, two votes:	Guy Garrett	Aye
	W. D. McGrew	Aye
Carbon County, three votes:	Gus Larson	Aye
	Victor H. Scepansky	Aye
	C. D. Williamson	Aye
Converse County, two votes:	Waldo Bolln	Aye
	Joe Garst	Aye
Crook County, two votes:	Charles Louis	Aye
	G. W. Earle	Aye
Fremont County, three votes:	Mrs. Sam Payne	Aye
	Walter Oswald	Aye
	R. S. Price	Aye
Goshen County, three votes:	L. G. Flannery	Aye
	J. M. Roushar	Aye
	Erle H. Reid	Aye

Hot Springs County, two votes:	Henry Cottle	Aye
	John McCullum	Aye
Johnson County, two votes:	Frank O. Horton	Aye
	Jean Van Dyke	Aye
Laramie County, six votes:	A. D. Homan	Aye
	Fred W. Roedel	Aye
	Wilfrid O'Leary	Aye
	Abe Goldstein	Aye
	Perry Williams	Aye
	Fred Hofmann	Aye
Lincoln County, three votes:	Dr. C. D. Stafford	Aye
	Glen E. Sorensen	Aye
	Oluf Jefsen	Aye
Natrona County, six votes:	Robert N. Ogden	Aye
	J. E. Jones	Aye
	T. F. Speckbacker	Aye
	T. C. Spears	Aye
	E. J. Sullivan	Aye
	J. F. Cowan	Aye
Niobrara County, two votes:	Albert P. Bruch	Aye
	C. W. Erwin	Aye
Park County, three votes:	Alex Linton	Aye
	B. C. Rumsey	Aye
	M. L. Simpson	Aye
Platte County, three votes: (one delegate being absent)	Hans Christiansen	Aye
	B. L. Dixon	Aye
Sheridan County, four votes:	Malcolm Moncreiffe	Aye
	Peter Kooi	Aye
	R. A. Keenan	Aye
	Roy Bedford	Aye
Sublette County, one vote:	Albert Larsen	Aye
Sweetwater County, five votes:	William Evers	Aye
	Dr. R. H. Sanders	Aye
	Glen A. Knox	Aye
	P. C. Dunning	Aye
	Joe Bertagnolli	Aye
Teton County, two votes:	R. C. Lundy	Aye
	O. A. Pendergraft	Aye
Uinta County, two votes: (two-thirds vote for each delegate)	Matthew Morrow	Aye
	S. S. Kastor	Aye
	J. H. Holland	Aye
Washakie County, two votes:	Dr. W. O. Gray	Aye
	R. C. Shultz	Aye
Weston County, two votes:	A. F. Leslie	Aye
	M. M. Falk	Aye

Whereupon it was found that sixty-five delegates had cast sixty-four votes "aye" and were in favor of the ratification of said Article and no delegates had voted nay.

CHAIRMAN REID: Ladies and Gentlemen, you have cast unanimous vote for the ratification, and the Twenty-first Article to the Constitution of the United States has been ratified by this Convention. I suggest that this finishes the official business of this convention.

MR. ROUSHAR, of Goshen County: Mr. Chairman, this is an unusual procedure, the first time such a practice has been submitted to the people, heretofore it has been done for the people by the legislature of their state, and in view of the fact that there is an unexpended fund in the hands of the State Treasurer, set aside for the purpose of bearing the expense of this convention, I feel we ought to go on record as having these minutes published and each delegate and alternate be furnished a copy thereof. Mr. Chairman, I move you we go on record as requesting the Secretary to print these minutes and a copy thereof be furnished by mail to each delegate and alternate to this meeting.

CHAIRMAN REID: The Chair suggests that the expenditure of this fund is not in the hands of the convention, and your motion should be as a request to the Governor.

MR. ROUSHAR: I amend the motion to the form stated by the Chair.

SECRETARY OF STATE CLARK: While the money is technically in the hands of the Secretary of State, I think we would have to take that up with the Governor.

MR. SIMPSON, Park County: I rise to a point of order, what became of my motion?

CHAIRMAN REID: It was carried unanimously. I see no objection, Mr. Roushar, to your motion as amended, was there a second to the motion?

(Motion seconded from the floor.)

CHAIRMAN REID: You have heard the motion and second, that we go on record as requesting the Governor to have the minutes of this meeting published and a copy furnished each delegate and alternate to this convention. Are there any remarks? Those in favor signify by saying "Aye," contrary "No," the motion is carried.

MR. GOLDSTEIN, of Laramie County: Mr. Chairman, I would like to present a resolution at this time. Be it RESOLVED that the Wyoming State Convention, assembled in Casper, Wyoming, May 25, 1933, do hereby immediately telegraph the following message to Franklin Delano Roosevelt, President of the United States of America: "Wyoming at its state convention held in Casper May 25, 1933, on that day by action of delegates assembled from the several counties of the commonwealth, has voted unanimously for repeal of the Eighteenth Amendment to the Constitution of the United States."

FROM THE FLOOR: I believe the message should be corrected to say "has ratified the Twenty-first Amendment to the Constitution of the United States."

CHAIRMAN REID: Will you permit the correction, Mr. Goldstein?

MR. GOLDSTEIN: Yes.

CHAIRMAN REID: Do I hear a motion for the adoption of the resolution?

(Motion made from the floor, and seconded, that the resolution, as amended, be adopted.)

CHAIRMAN REID: You have heard the motion for the adoption of the resolution as amended, are there any remarks? All in favor of the motion will signify by saying "Aye," contrary "No." The motion is carried. The Secretary will see that the message is forwarded.

MR. SULLIVAN, of Natrona County: Mr. Chairman, there is one more matter, there is no method provided by law for the recalling of this convention or calling another one, we have taken the action we think necessary for the ratification of the 21st Amendment, and I am sure before we adjourn a motion will be placed before this convention that the Secretary and Chairman will certify the minutes of this meeting to the Secretary of State. We hope that will be done, but being mindful of the uncertainty of human life, and if between adjournment of this convention and the time the minutes are prepared the Chairman might become disqualified, having that in view I wonder if it will be agreeable to the convention to provide for the office of Vice-Chairman, he to act only in the event of the disqualification of or disability of the Chairman. Having that in mind I move you we create the office of Vice-Chairman of this convention.

(Motion seconded from the floor.)

CHAIRMAN REID: We have heard the motion that we create the office of Vice-Chairman, he to act only in the event of the disqualification or disability of the Chairman to act; are there any remarks? (Question called for.) All in favor of the motion as stated say "Aye," opposed "No." The motion is carried unanimously.

MR. ROUSHAR, of Goshen County: I would like to move the nomination of Mr. E. J. Sullivan as Vice-Chairman.

MR. SULLIVAN: With thanks to the mover of the motion, it came in a very friendly way, but there were three men who were mentioned in the committee on nominations for the honorable office of Chairman. We might take recognition of the fact that one of the men was a man who has done a great deal, in addition to what our Chairman has done, for the worthy cause, and who is more worthy of this honor than I am. Will you remember that I am neither wet or dry. That I am one of the many who stand in the middle road seeking for temperance, and I would like permission to substitute the name of Richard A. Keenan, of Sheridan.

(Motion seconded from the floor.)

MR. BEDFORD, of Sheridan County: Mr. Chairman, I move you the nominations be closed and the Secretary instructed to cast the unanimous vote of this convention for Mr. R. A. Keenan, as vice-chairman of this convention.

MR. SIMPSON, of Park County: I second the motion.

CHAIRMAN REID: You have heard the motion and second, are there any remarks? Those in favor say "Aye," opposed "No," the motion is carried. Mr. Secretary, you will cast the unanimous vote of this convention for Mr. R. A. Keenan, of Sheridan, for Vice-Chairman. (Secretary cast the unanimous vote of the convention for Mr. Keenan.) I declare Mr. R. A. Keenan elected as Vice-Chairman of this convention.

MR. KEENAN, of Sheridan: I wish to thank you very much for the honor conferred upon me, and I can assure you I consider it a very great honor.

MR. LARSON, of Carbon County: Would it also be well for us to take the same action as to the Secretary?

MR. SULLIVAN, of Natrona County: The certificate is by the Chairman, attested by a Secretary, and should the young man French go to heaven, the Chairman can appoint another secretary.

CHAIRMAN REID: While the law provides that the Chairman and Secretary certify the record of our proceedings, I presume it will be well to have a motion.

MR. BEDFORD, of Sheridan County: I move you, Mr. Chairman, that the Chairman of this Convention and the Secretary, and in the absence or inability of the Chairman the Vice-Chairman, make the proper certification of our proceedings to the Secretary of State.

(Motion seconded from the floor.)

CHAIRMAN REID: You have heard the motion and the second, are there any remarks? Those in favor signify by saying "Aye," opposed "No," the motion is carried.

MR. HOFMANN, of Laramie County: Mr. Chairman and fellow delegates, we have had a wonderful meeting and carried our point in the State of Wyoming, and we are all proud of it. For my part I have been a wet since the day Prohibition went into effect, and as I stand on the floor here I want to say to you, our duty is not finished, we must not let the business we condemned in 1919 get into the same rut, we want to see it carried on in a clean and honorable manner, and you will never be able to do this if you have the Government, the States or the Cities mixing whiskey with beer. Whiskey should be divorced from beer, take it home to your family and teach your children its use in a proper way, and that is not standing against a bar drinking all day and having your wife waiting supper. It was the women of this country who voted it dry and it will be the women who vote it wet again, they have found out their mistake, but it wouldn't have taken near as long to get the country wet again if it had not been for the efforts of our politicians.

CHAIRMAN REID: Unless there is some other business the Chair will entertain a motion to adjourn.

(Motion from the floor, that we adjourn. Seconded from the floor.)

CHAIRMAN REID: It has been regularly moved and seconded we adjourn. Those in favor say "Aye," opposed "No." The motion is carried, we will stand adjourned.

Dated at Casper, Wyoming this 25th day of May, A.D. 1933.

ERLE H. REID
Chairman

Attest:

J. R. FRENCH
Secretary

THE STATE OF WYOMING
COUNTY OF NATRONA } ss.

ERLE H. REID and J. R. FRENCH, each being separately duly sworn on oath, each for himself, does hereby certify and depose as follows: That the said ERLE H. REID is the duly selected Chairman of the State Convention held at Casper, Wyoming, on May 25, A.D. 1933, and the said J. R. FRENCH is the duly selected Secretary of the State Convention held at Casper, Natrona County, Wyoming, on May 25, A.D. 1933; that at said convention there were present and entitled to vote therein sixty-five delegates; that on the question of ratification of the following Article:

ARTICLE ___ ___

Section 1. The eighteenth article of Amendment to the Constitution of the United States is hereby repealed.

Section 2. The transportation or importation into any State, Territory, or possession of the United States for delivery or use therein of intoxicating liquors, in violation of the laws thereof, is hereby prohibited.

Section 3. This article shall be inoperative unless it shall have been ratified as an amendment to the Constitution by conventions in the several states, as provided in the Constitution, within seven years from the date of the submission hereof to the States by the Congress. The sixty-five delegates, who were entitled to sixty-four votes, cast their unanimous vote in favor of ratification of said Article, and that no delegates present and entitled to vote voted against ratification of said Article, and that all votes cast were in favor of ratification of said Article and said Article was by said convention ratified and that annexed hereto and made a part hereof is a full, true and complete record of the proceedings had and taken and all things done by said convention held at the City Hall in the City of Casper, in The State of Wyoming on May 25, A.D. 1933, and which fully and in detail shows the result of the vote taken and had at said convention on the questions submitted.

ERLE H. REID
Chairman
J. R. FRENCH
Secretary

Subscribed in my presence and sworn to before me at Torrington, Wyoming, by Erle H. Reid, this 3rd day of June, A.D. 1933.

NELLE ARMITAGE
Notary Public

My commission expires 20th day of January, A.D. 1934.

(Notarial Seal)

Subscribed in my presence and sworn to before me at Basin, Wyoming, by J. R. French this 31st day of May, A.D. 1933.

F. H. SCHUYLER
Clerk of the District Court,
Big Horn County, Wyoming

My term expires January 2nd, 1935.
(Official Seal)

II. STATE LAWS PROVIDING FOR THE CONVENTIONS

INTRODUCTION[1]

ON February 21, 1933, Secretary of State Henry L. Stimson sent letters to the governors of the forty-eight states, enclosing a copy of the joint resolution of Congress proposing the Twenty-first Amendment, and requesting that the resolution be submitted to a state convention and that a certified copy of the action taken be communicated to the Secretary of State. Forty-three states (all except Georgia, Kansas, Louisiana, Mississippi, and North Dakota) passed laws providing for action on the proposed amendment.

In January, 1933, the legislature of California had petitioned Congress to submit a repeal amendment to state conventions and in doing so had asked Congress to provide by general law for these conventions. The California suggestions included the election of delegates at large in the several states on the basis of whether they favored or opposed the proposed amendment; a uniform date of election throughout the United States; and provision by Congress of ways and means of nominating delegates, of conducting the elections, of assembling the conventions, and of providing for the cost incurred.[2]

Although a number of bills were introduced in Congress to provide a uniform method of ratifying the proposed amendment, none was adopted, and the details were left to the states. However, there was some doubt on this point among the members of state legislatures, even after the proposed amendment had been submitted to them for ratification. In their laws providing for the conventions no less than twenty-one states included a section stating that, if Congress should prescribe the manner in which the conventions should be constituted, the provisions of the state act should be inoperative and officers of the state were authorized and directed to act in obedience to the act of Congress with the same force and effect as if acting under a state statute. The states so providing were Arizona, California, Connecticut, Delaware, Florida, Idaho, Indiana, Iowa, Maryland, Montana, Nevada, Ohio, Pennsylvania, Rhode Island, South Dakota, Tennessee, Texas, Utah, Vermont, Washington, and Wyoming.

On the other hand, New Mexico championed the cause of state rights in a declaration that any attempt on the part of Congress to prescribe the details governing the convention "shall be null and void in the state of New Mexico, and all officers of the state, or any subdivision thereof, are hereby authorized and required to resist to the utmost any attempt to execute any and all such congressional dictation and usurpation."[3]

Of the states which passed laws providing for ratifying conventions, sixteen—Arizona, Delaware, Florida, Idaho, Indiana, Iowa, Missouri, Montana, New Mexico, Ohio, South Dakota, Texas, Utah, Vermont, Washington, and Wyoming—made pro-

---

[1] This introduction is, in part, reprinted from my article entitled "The Ratification of the Twenty-first Amendment," which appeared in the *American Political Science Review,* XXIX (December, 1935), 1005-1017. I am indebted to Professor F. A. Ogg, Managing Editor of the *Review,* for giving me permission to reprint this material. See also *Ratification of the Twenty-first Amendment to the Constitution of the United States,* Publication No. 573, Department of State (1934).

[2] *Statutes of California,* 1933, Chapter 23, pp. 2939-2940; *Congressional Record,* 72d Congress, 2d Session, p. 4559 (Feb. 21, 1933).

[3] *Laws of New Mexico,* 1933, Chapter 163, section 16 (p. 404).

vision by general laws for any amendment which might be proposed in the future. The laws of the remaining twenty-seven states—Alabama, Arkansas, California, Colorado, Connecticut, Illinois, Kentucky, Maine, Maryland, Massachusetts, Michigan, Minnesota, Nebraska, Nevada, New Hampshire, New Jersey, New York, North Carolina, Oklahoma, Oregon, Pennsylvania, Rhode Island, South Carolina, Tennessee, Virginia, West Virginia, and Wisconsin—were of a special nature and related only to the amendment at hand.

There was considerable difference of opinion as to whether the delegates to the conventions should be elected by the voters of the states at large, or by districts, or by a combination of the two methods. In Maine the question was submitted to the justices of the supreme judicial court for an advisory opinion. In their reply the justices reviewed the subject historically and found that in all previous constitutional conventions delegates had been chosen by localities within the state. They declared that this method met the requirement that the members of the constitutional convention should fairly represent the people whom they served, and they consequently held that they did "not deem it advisable for the state, under the terms of Article V of the federal Constitution, to organize a convention wherein the delegates entitled to participate are all elected at large." [4]

Despite this adverse opinion of the Maine justices, twenty-five of the states—Arizona, California, Colorado, Delaware, Florida, Idaho, Illinois, Iowa, Kentucky, Minnesota, Missouri, New Hampshire, New Mexico, New York, Ohio, Oklahoma, Pennsylvania, Rhode Island, South Carolina, Tennessee, Utah, Vermont, Virginia, West Virginia, and Wisconsin—voted at large for their delegates. Fourteen states—Arkansas, Indiana, Maine, Massachusetts, Michigan, Montana, Nebraska, Nevada, North Carolina, Oregon, South Dakota, Texas, Washington, and Wyoming—chose them by districts, and four—Alabama, Connecticut, Maryland, and New Jersey—combined the methods.

The number of delegates in the ratifying conventions ranged from 329 in Indiana to three in New Mexico. However, in only six conventions did the number of delegates total 100 or more—Alabama, 116; Indiana, 329; Michigan, 100; New Jersey, 226; New York, 150; and Oregon, 116. In the other states, the numbers were: Arizona, 14; Arkansas, 75; California, 22; Colorado, 15; Connecticut, 50; Delaware, 17; Florida, 67; Idaho, 21; Illinois, 50; Iowa, 99; Kentucky, 19; Maine, 80; Maryland, 24; Massachusetts, 45; Minnesota, 21; Missouri, 68; Nevada, 40; New Hampshire, 10; Ohio, 52; Pennsylvania, 15; Rhode Island, 31; Tennessee, 63; Texas, 31; Utah, 21; Vermont, 14; Virginia, 30; Washington, 99; West Virginia, 20; Wisconsin, 15; Wyoming, 66.

The methods of nominating delegates to the conventions also showed wide variations. In twenty-five states—Alabama, Arizona, Arkansas, California, Connecticut, Delaware, Florida, Idaho, Illinois, Indiana, Kentucky, Maine, Minnesota, Montana, New Jersey, New Mexico, New York, North Carolina, Ohio, Pennsylvania, Rhode Island, South Dakota, Tennessee, Utah, and Wisconsin—the nominations were made by petitions. In the remaining eighteen almost every conceivable method was employed, including nomination by the governor, as in Colorado; by mass conventions of qualified electors, as in Iowa, Missouri, Nevada, Texas, and Wyoming; by nominating committees, boards, and caucuses of various kinds, as in Maryland, Massachusetts, Michigan, New Hampshire, South Carolina, Vermont, Virginia, and West Virginia;

[4] *Maine Legislative Record,* 1933 (Senate, March 27), p. 804.

by primary election, as in Nebraska; by personal action of the individual, as in Oregon and Washington; and by the Democratic and Republican state executive committees, as in West Virginia. Nor was there uniformity within these classifications. In Nevada and Wyoming, for example, mass conventions, held in each voting precinct, selected delegates to county conventions, which in turn elected delegates to the state convention. In Maryland the legislature selected a nominating committee of twenty-nine, composed of one member from each county and legislative district. This committee then nominated pledged and unpledged persons from each congressional district and others from the state at large. In Massachusetts the nominating agency was a caucus, composed of the governor, lieutenant-governor, councillors, state secretary, state treasurer, attorney-general, and state auditor. New Hampshire and Vermont employed a plan somewhat similar to that of Massachusetts. In Michigan boards consisting of probate judges, county clerks, and prosecuting attorneys made the nominations. In Virginia the nominating committee was composed of the governor, lieutenant-governor, the speaker of the house of delegates, and two persons selected by the governor.

In twenty-eight states the date of the proposed convention was specified in the law. Fourteen states authorized the governor to proclaim the date, while one, California, empowered the secretary of state to do so. Similarly, the date of the election of delegates to the convention was specified in the laws of twenty-seven states. It was proclaimed by the governor in fifteen states, and by the governor and council in Massachusetts.

Fourteen states made no provision by law for compensating the delegates to the convention. Some provided mileage alone; others gave mileage and necessary expenses. Where pay was given, it ranged from a flat rate of five dollars in Maine to twenty-five in Nebraska, and from four dollars a day in Utah to five in South Dakota. In some instances both pay and mileage were provided. New Mexico stipulated that delegates should receive the same compensation as presidential electors; Illinois left the matter to the convention itself.

So far as convention procedure was concerned, some of the state laws provided merely that the convention should elect its own officers and keep a journal recording the votes of the delegates. In other states further items of procedure were prescribed. Illinois authorized the governor to call the opening session to order. Massachusetts did likewise, and also named the state secretary as temporary clerk until permanent officers were elected. In Michigan the lieutenant-governor was named as president, the clerk of the house as clerk, and the sergeant-at-arms, committee clerks, and stenographers of the house were appointed to the same positions in the convention. The Michigan law further stipulated that the delegates should elect one of their own number president *pro tempore* and that the sessions should be public. New Mexico provided that the convention should be organized "as by law providing for organization of presidential electors," which meant, primarily, that the delegates should choose their own presiding officer and secretary.[5] The North Carolina law required that the convention should be called to order by a member of the supreme court. In Pennsylvania the lieutenant-governor was named as chairman, the secretary of the senate as secretary, the chief clerks of the senate and house as tellers, while the secretary of the commonwealth was to present the election returns when the convention was called to order. Rhode Island authorized the governor to call the convention to order and the secretary of state to call the temporary roll of delegates, after which a permanent president was to be elected. The laws of South Carolina and Wyoming prescribed no procedure at all. Vermont

[5] *New Mexico Statutes Annotated, 1929,* Section 41-702 (p. 777).

made the secretary of state the *ex officio* secretary of the convention. Virginia provided that the clerk of the house of delegates should act as temporary chairman and, after permanent organization, should become secretary and administer the oath of office. Procedure in the Washington convention was to be under the state senate rules so far as practicable. It was made the duty of the secretary of state to call the convention to order and to act as temporary chairman. Oaths were to be administered by the chief justice of the supreme court, after which permanent officers were to be elected. Virginia and Washington were unique in requiring more than a majority of delegates to constitute a quorum. Virginia set the number at twenty, which was two-thirds of the total, whereas Washington provided that two-thirds of the elected members should constitute a quorum. In both these states, however, a majority of those elected was sufficient to adopt or reject proposed amendments.

In nearly all the state laws provision was made for separate lists of delegates known to be in favor of or opposed to the ratification of the proposed amendment. This was true in the case of the states passing general laws to cover any proposal in the future as well as in the case of those states providing only for action on the proposed repeal of the Eighteenth Amendment. Delaware, Florida, Illinois, Maryland, New York, Ohio, Tennessee, and West Virginia provided for the selection of unpledged delegates also. The Wyoming statute made no mention of the preferences of the delegates, apparently leaving the delegates free to debate and vote as a truly deliberative body. The separate listing of nominees for the office of delegate to the convention indicates that in most of the states it was the intention to confine the activities of the delegates principally to casting votes in conformity with the expressed will of the people. However, although this was what actually happened, few of the laws specifically bound the delegates to vote in accordance with the result of the ballot. A few of them did. Alabama required of each candidate for membership in the convention a sworn statement in which he pledged himself to abide by the result of the referendum in the state, and it stipulated further that each candidate should be required to support in the convention the position declared by a majority of those casting ballots in the election. Similarly, candidates in Arkansas were required to make sworn statements as to their position for or against repeal, and the law stipulated that the convention should cast its vote in accordance with the result of a state-wide referendum on the question. Oregon likewise provided that at the same election at which delegates were elected the question of ratifying or rejecting the proposed amendment should be placed before the electors in the form of a popular referendum. Electors filing candidacy for election to the convention were required to file a pledge that in casting their votes in the constitutional convention they would vote in accordance with the will of the majority of the voters of the county from which they were candidates, as shown by the popular vote on the question. In West Virginia nominees were required to sign a written pledge in triplicate to vote in the convention for or against ratification in accordance with their statement as candidates. Unpledged candidates for the office of delegate in West Virginia could be nominated by petition and not otherwise. But it was left to Arizona to cap the climax in this respect by providing that "delegates elected upon a platform or nomination petition statement as for or against ratification must vote at such convention in accordance with such platform or nomination petition statement, and upon failure to do so will be guilty of a misdemeanor, his vote not considered, and his office deemed vacant."

The act providing for the calling of the convention was given immediate effect in twenty-nine states: California, Colorado, Florida, Idaho, Illinois, Indiana, Iowa,

Kentucky, Massachusetts, Michigan, Minnesota, Montana, Nevada, New Hampshire, New Jersey, New Mexico, New York, North Carolina, Oregon, Pennsylvania, Rhode Island, South Carolina, Tennessee, Texas, Utah, Virginia, Washington, Wisconsin, and Wyoming. The law of ten states—Alabama, Connecticut, Delaware, Missouri, Nebraska, Ohio, Oklahoma, South Dakota, Vermont, and West Virginia—contained no provision covering this subject. In Maryland it was provided that the act approved April 5, 1933, should take effect June 1 of that year. In Arizona a referendum was filed against the law. The Maine law included a provision that in case of a referendum, a special election was to be held to expedite action. In Arkansas it was enacted that the law was not subject to referendum, and the secretary of state was ordered not to receive or file any petition for a referendum. Furthermore, no court in the state was to have any authority to enjoin or otherwise interfere with the holding of the election and convention.

A survey of the laws hereinafter published illustrates the wide variety of state action possible under our federal system of government. At the same time, the texts of these laws also supply the data necessary for the drafting of a model uniform law, if the convention method of ratifying amendments is used again and such a model law is deemed desirable. From both the historical point of view and that of practical politics the publication of these laws in easily accessible form is amply justified.

ALABAMA*

AN ACT

To provide for holding a convention to pass upon the question of ratification or rejection of the proposed 21st amendment to the Constitution of the United States; to provide the date on which the members thereof shall be elected and the number thereof; the date on which the convention shall assemble; to provide for the holding of the election for delegates, the mode and manner thereof, and that each candidate shall pledge himself to abide by the results of the election in the State, and to provide that each voter shall cast his ballot for or against repeal of the 18th amendment and for or against ratification of the proposed 21st amendment.

Be It Enacted by the Legislature of Alabama:

Section 1. That a convention is hereby called to convene in the Hall of the House of Representatives at the Capitol of this State, at noon, three weeks after the first Tuesday after the expiration of three months after the final adjournment of this session of the Legislature, for the purpose of ratifying or rejecting the proposed 21st amendment to the Constitution of the United States.

Section 2. That the convention herein provided for shall be composed of 116 delegates, who shall be elected from the following area and in the following manner: There shall be as many delegates from each county in the State as such county is now entitled to members of the House of Representatives of the Legislature of Alabama, to be elected by the qualified electors in such county in the manner hereinafter provided. There shall also be elected ten delegates from the State at large who shall be bound in like manner and to the same extent as delegates from the several counties of the State are bound by a majority vote of the people of the entire State.

Section 3. That on the first Tuesday after the expiration of three months from the final adjournment of this session of the Legislature an election shall be held in the several counties of the State for the purpose of electing delegates to such convention, which election, in all respects, shall be conducted in the same manner, returns made, canvassed and results declared as elections for members of the House of Representatives of the Legislature are now conducted.

Section 4. The ballots shall be prepared and printed in all respects as are ballots prepared and printed for general elections in the counties of this State, and shall be paid for in like manner as ballots for such general elections are now paid. The candidates for membership in the convention shall be listed on such ballots in alphabetical order in each county. At the top of the ticket containing a list of candidates for membership in the convention, there shall appear, properly arranged, for the voter to indicate his choice, the words, "For repeal of 18th amendment and for ratification of proposed 21st amendment to the Constitution of the United States," which shall mean in favor of ratification of the proposed 21st amendment and underneath that, the words "Against repeal of 18th amendment and against ratification of proposed 21st amendment to the Constitution of the United States," which shall mean in favor of rejection of the proposed 21st amendment. It shall be necessary for the voter to indicate his choice,

* *Alabama General and Local Acts, Extra Session, 1933,* No. 81, pp. 77-80.

that is, whether he desires repeal, or no repeal, of the 18th amendment to the United States Constitution by the ratification or rejection of the proposed 21st amendment. Unless such voter shall indicate his choice on this question, his ballot for delegates to the convention whether from the State at large or from the counties shall not be counted, but shall be null and void. The candidates receiving the highest number of votes in the county in which they are candidates for the convention shall be declared elected, and the results of the election shall be canvassed and declared by the same officers and in the same manner as now provided by law for canvassing votes and declaring results thereof for general elections in this State. The ten candidates from the State at large receiving the highest number of votes in the State shall be declared elected as delegates from the State at large.

Section 5. Officers for holding such election in each county shall be designated in the manner provided by law for the conduct of general elections, and the compensation to such election officers shall be the same and paid in like manner as now provided by general law.

Section 6. Any person desiring to become a candidate for membership in the convention from any county in the State shall file the following statement, under oath, with the Judge of Probate in the county in which he is a candidate: "I, ..., do hereby solemnly pledge myself, in the event of my election to a convention to be held in Montgomery for the purpose of considering the ratification or rejection of the proposed 21st amendment to the Constitution of the United States, to abide by the result of the referendum in the State on the question of the ratification or rejection of the proposed 21st amendment to the Constitution of the United States; and should a majority of the votes cast in said election be for ratification, then I pledge myself to vote for the ratification of the proposed 21st amendment in the convention, but should a majority of the votes cast in said election be for rejection of the proposed 21st amendment, then I pledge myself to vote for the rejection of the proposed 21st amendment, to the United States constitution. I further promise and pledge to comply with all laws governing general elections in the State of Alabama in the conduct of the campaign in which I shall seek election." .... "Sworn to and subscribed before me this the .... day of ...., 1933." In the case of candidates for delegates from the State at large to such convention, the foregoing oath shall be taken and subscribed by each of them and filed in the office of the Secretary of State but it shall not be necessary for such candidates for delegates from the State at large to file such oath with the Judges of Probate of the several counties of this State. The Judge of Probate shall keep said affidavits as a permanent file in his office, and the Secretary of State shall keep as a permanent file in his office the affidavits filed by candidates for delegates from the State at large. The candidates elected from each county, as well as the ten candidates elected from the State at large, shall be required to support in the convention the position declared by a majority of those casting ballots in the election herein ordered in the State and if a majority of such ballots be cast for ratification, then the elected delegates whether from the State at large or from the counties, will be required to support and vote for the ratification of the proposed 21st amendment, but if a majority be in favor of rejection, the elected delegates shall support and vote for the rejection of the proposed 21st amendment.

Section 7. All delegates elected to the convention shall take the oath of office prescribed by law for officers of the State of Alabama. The convention shall determine its own rules, shall keep such journal as it may determine, and shall record its vote by yea and nay.

Section 8. Immediately after the adjournment of said convention, the proper officers shall certify, under their official signatures, the action of said convention relative to the ratification or rejection of said amendment to the Secretary of State of Alabama, who shall, in turn, certify the same to the Secretary of State of the United States of America.

Section 9. All laws and parts of laws in conflict with this act are hereby repealed; and if any section or provision of this act is held invalid because unconstitutional, the same shall not affect the other portions of this act.

Passed over the Governor's Veto March 28, 1933.

ARIZONA*

AN ACT

To provide for conventions to pass on amendments to the Constitution of the United States proposed by the Congress of the United States for ratification by conventions in the several states.

Be It Enacted by the Legislature of the State of Arizona:

Section 1. Whenever the Congress of the United States shall propose an amendment to the Constitution of the United States, and shall propose that it be ratified by conventions in the several states, the governor shall fix by proclamation the date of an election for the purpose of electing the delegates to such convention in this state. Such election may either be at a special election or may be held at the same time as a general election, but shall be held at least as soon as the next special or general election occurring more than three months after the amendment has been proposed by the Congress.

Section 2. At such election all electors who have registered may vote. Should a special election be called, registration of voters shall be re-opened by the county recorder on the third Monday preceding such special election, and shall be closed at five o'clock P.M. on the Saturday following next thereafter. All electors who were registered at the last general election, or who are registered during the period registration is re-opened for such special election may vote at such special election.

Section 3. Except as in this act otherwise provided, such election shall be conducted and the results thereof ascertained and certified in the same manner as in the case of the election of state officers in this state, and all provisions of the laws of this state relative to elections except so far as inconsistent with this act are hereby made applicable to such election.

Section 4. The number of delegates to be chosen at such convention shall be eleven to be elected from the state at large.

Section 5. Candidates for the office of delegate to the convention shall be qualified electors of this state. Nominations shall be by petition signed by not less than one thousand qualified electors, and not otherwise. Nominations shall be without party or political designation, but the nominating petitions shall contain a statement by the nominee to the effect that he favors ratification, or that he opposes ratification, and no nominating petition shall be accepted unless such statement is contained therein. No nomination shall be effective except those of the eleven nominees in favor of the ratification and the eleven nominees against ratification whose nominating petitions were first filed with the secretary of state. Within ten days after the petitions are filed, the secretary of state shall certify the candidates of each group to the board of supervisors of the respective counties of this state. All petitions shall be filed with the secretary of state not less than twenty days before the proclaimed date of the election.

Section 6. The election shall be by ballot, separate from any ballot to be used at the same election, which shall be prepared as follows: It shall first state the substance of the proposed amendment. This shall be followed by appropriate instructions to the voters. It shall then contain perpendicular columns of equal width, headed respectively

* *Laws of Arizona, 1933,* Chapter 94, pp. 403-409.

in plain type, "For Ratification," and "Against Ratification." In the column headed "For Ratification" shall be placed the names of the nominees nominated as in favor of ratification. In the column headed "Against Ratification" shall be placed the names of the nominees nominated as against ratification. The voter shall indicate his choice by making one or more cross marks in the appropriate spaces provided on the ballot. No ballot shall be held void because any such cross mark is irregular in character. The ballot shall be so arranged that the voter may, by making a single cross mark, vote for the entire group of the nominees whose names are comprised in any column. The ballot shall be in substantially the following form:

PROPOSED AMENDMENT TO THE CONSTITUTION OF THE UNITED STATES

The Congress has proposed an amendment to the Constitution of the United States which provides (insert here the substance of the proposed amendment).

The Congress has also proposed that the said amendment shall be ratified by conventions in the states.

INSTRUCTIONS TO VOTERS

Do not vote for more than eleven (11) candidates.

To vote for all candidates in favor of ratification, or for all candidates against ratification, make a cross-mark in the CIRCLE at the head of the list of candidates for whom you wish to vote. If you do this, make no other mark.

To vote for an individual candidate make a cross-mark in the SQUARE at the left of the name.

For Ratification	Against Ratification
○	○
☐ John Doe	☐ Charles Coe
☐ Richard Roe	☐ Michael Moe
☐	☐

Sec. 7. The eleven nominees who shall receive the highest number of votes shall be the delegates at the convention. If there shall be a vacancy in the convention caused by the death or disability of any delegate, or any other cause, the same shall be filled by appointment by the majority vote of the delegates comprising the group from which such delegate was elected and if the Convention contains no other delegate of that group, shall be filled by the governor. Delegates elected upon a platform or nomination petition statement as for or against ratification must vote at such convention in

accordance with such platform or nomination petition statement, and upon failure to do so will be guilty of a misdemeanor, his vote not considered, and his office will be deemed vacant to be filled as herein provided for filling vacancies.

Sec. 8. The delegates to the convention shall meet at the capitol on the twenty-eighth day after their election at 10:00 o'clock A.M. and shall thereupon constitute a Convention to pass upon the question of whether or not the proposed amendment shall be ratified.

Sec. 9. The convention shall be the judge of the election and qualification of its members; and shall have power to elect its president, secretary and other officers, and to adopt its own rules.

Sec. 10. The convention shall keep a journal of its proceedings in which shall be recorded the vote of each delegate on the question of ratification of the proposel amendment. Upon final adjournment the journal shall be filed with the secretary of state.

Sec. 11. If the convention shall agree, by vote of a majority of the total number of delegates, to the ratification of the proposed amendment, a certificate to that effect shall be executed by the president and secretary of the convention and transmitted to the secretary of state of this state, who shall transmit the certificate under the great seal of the state to the secretary of state of the United States.

Sec. 12. Delegates shall receive ten dollars, and shall also receive mileage one way by the shortest practical route at the rate of twenty cents per mile.

Sec. 13. If at or about the time of submitting any such amendment, Congress shall either in the resolution submitting the same or by statute, prescribe the manner in which the conventions shall be constituted, and shall not except from the provisions of such statute or resolution such states as may theretofore have provided for constituting such conventions, the preceding provisions of this act shall be inoperative, the convention shall be constituted and shall operate as the said resolution or act of Congress shall direct, and all officers of the state who may by the said resolution or statute be authorized or directed to take any action to constitute such a convention for this state are hereby authorized and directed to act thereunder and in obedience thereto with the same force and effect as if acting under a statute of this state.

Approved March 18, 1933.

Referendum Filed Against This Act, June 1, 1933.

ARKANSAS*

AN ACT Providing for a Convention to Ratify or Reject the Proposed Twenty-First Amendment to the Constitution of the United States, Same Being an Amendment to Repeal the Eighteenth Amendment, and to Provide for the Election of Delegates to Such Convention.

Be It Enacted by the General Assembly of the State of Arkansas:

Section 1. A Convention is hereby called to meet in the Hall of the House of Representatives in the State Capitol in Little Rock on the First day of August, 1933, at ten o'clock in the forenoon, to reject or ratify the proposed Twenty-first Amendment to the Constitution of the United States, same being an amendment to repeal the Eighteenth or Prohibition Amendment to said constitution. Said Convention shall be composed of one delegate from each county, a total of Seventy-five (75) delegates.

Section 2. An election is hereby called to be held on the 18th day of July, 1933, for the purpose of electing delegates to said Convention. Said election shall be held as provided under the general election laws and shall be paid for by the counties as is provided for general elections.

Section 3. Any qualified elector may become a candidate for delegate to the State Convention, upon filing with the County Clerk a petition signed by at least one hundred qualified electors of the county, which petition must be accompanied by a statement in writing, subscribed and sworn to by the candidate as to whether or not said individual is "For repeal of the 18th Amendment" or "Against the Repeal of the 18th Amendment"; said petition, when filed with the County Clerk, shall entitle said candidate to have his name placed on the ticket in the election. The County Board of Election Commissioners in the several counties of the State of Arkansas shall also place upon the ticket to be voted on at the election held for the election of delegates, the following:

"FOR REPEAL OF THE 18TH AMENDMENT"

"AGAINST THE REPEAL OF THE 18TH AMENDMENT"

and said Commissioners shall canvass said vote and declare the same as they do other returns.

The County Boards of Election Commissioners shall cause said election to be held by the Judges and Clerks who held the last General Election, any vacancies to be filled by said Board as now provided by law. The results of said election shall be canvassed by the County Board of Election Commissioners and Certified to the Secretary of State within five days after said election. Persons so certified as receiving the highest number of votes shall be entitled to sit as members of said Convention. The County Boards of Election Commissioners shall also certify the results of the election on the question of "For Repeal" and "Against Repeal" in the different counties, to the Secretary of State, who shall tabulate and declare the results, and shall immediately, upon the meeting of the Meeting of the Convention, certify to the Chairman of the Convention, the total number of votes cast in the entire state for the "Repeal of the 18th Amendment" and the total number of votes cast in the State "Against the Repeal of the 18th Amend-

* *Arkansas Acts of the 49th General Assembly, 1933,* No. 151, pp. 457-470.

ment." Upon the receipt of said certificate of the Secretary of State, said Convention shall thereupon cast the vote of the Convention for whichever side of the question a majority of the total number of votes cast in the entire state was cast. Said Convention shall thereupon immediately adjourn.

The Convention shall elect one of its members as Chairman and one as Secretary, and it shall be the duty of the Secretary of said Convention to certify the result of the election to the proper authorities.

Section 4. The General Assembly in calling this Convention and this election for delegates thereto is acting under powers derived from and conferred upon it by the Constitution of the United States and actions of the Congress of the United States, and its actions herein are Federal functions and are not subject to any limitations imposed by the Constitution of the State, as has been held by the United States Supreme Court in the case of *Hawks* v. *Smith,* 253 U. S. 221, 64 L. ed. 871, and *Leser* vs. *Garnett,* 258 I. S. 130, 66 L. ed. 505. It is therefore ascertained and declared that this Act is not subject to the referendum, and the Secretary of State is hereby ordered and directed not to receive or file any petitions for a referendum, and no Court of this State shall have any authority to enjoin or otherwise interfere with the holding of the election and convention herein provided for.

Section 5. The Sections of this Act are declared to be severable and if any section is declared unconstitutional such fact shall not affect the validity of any other section.

Approved March 24, 1933.

CALIFORNIA*

AN ACT to provide for a convention in the State of California to pass on the amendment to the Constitution of the United States for the repeal of the Eighteenth Amendment thereof and for the prohibition of the transportation and importation of intoxicating liquor into the States and territories in violation of the laws thereof, proposed by the Congress for ratification by conventions in the several States, and to call a special election for the purpose of filling the offices of delegates to such convention in this State, and to provide that this act shall take effect immediately.

[Approved by the Governor April 21, 1933. In effect immediately.]

The people of the State of California do enact as follows:

Section 1. The Congress of the United States having proposed a certain amendment to the Constitution of the United States, an amendment providing for the repeal of the Eighteenth Amendment to said Constitution and prohibiting the transportation and importation of intoxicating liquor into the States and territories in violation of the laws thereof, and the Congress having proposed that said proposed amendment be ratified by conventions in the several States, a special election for the purpose of filling the offices of delegates to such convention in this State is hereby called, to be held throughout the State of California in the year 1934, on the same day as the "August primary election" in said year is held, unless prior to said date there is called and held a special election throughout the State for the submission to the electors of amendments to the State Constitution proposed by the Legislature, in which latter event said special election for the purpose of filling the offices of delegates to such convention is hereby called to be held throughout the State on the same day as such election for submission of said amendments to the State Constitution.

Section 2. At such election for the filling of the offices of delegates to such convention, all persons qualified to vote for members of the State Legislature shall be entitled to vote.

Section 3. Except as in this act otherwise provided, such election shall be called, conducted and the results thereof canvassed and certified in the same manner as in the case of election in this State of electors of President and Vice President of the United States, and all provisions of the laws of this State relevant to the election of such electors of President and Vice President of the United States except in so far as inconsistent with this act are hereby made applicable to the election of delegates to such convention.

Section 4. The number of delegates to be chosen to such convention shall be twenty-two and each candidate for the office of delegate to the convention shall be voted on throughout the entire State.

Section 5. Each candidate for the office of delegate to the convention shall be a qualified elector of the State, and each candidate nominated from a congressional district shall be a qualified elector of that district. Nomination for the office of delegate shall be by petition and not otherwise, and no candidate shall be nominated by a petition of less than one hundred qualified electors of the State. Each person signing a nominating petition shall be a qualified elector of this State, and each person signing a nomi-

* *Statutes of California, 1933,* Chapter 149, pp. 598-602.

nating petition of a candidate to be nominated from a congressional district shall be a qualified elector of such congressional district.

Nominations shall be without party or political designation but the nominating petition shall contain a statement as to each nominee to the effect that such candidate favors ratification of the proposed amendment to the Constitution of the United States or that such candidate opposes the ratification thereof, and no single nominating petition shall contain the name of any nominee whose position as to favoring or opposing such ratification as stated in said petition is different from that of any other nominee as stated therein. All such nominating petitions shall be certified in the same manner as initiative petitions and shall be filed with the Secretary of State at least thirty-five days before the date of such election. The number of candidates stated to favor ratification shall be twenty-two and the number of candidates stated to oppose ratification shall be twenty-two.

One candidate who favors ratification and one candidate who opposes ratification shall be nominated from each congressional district of the State; and two candidates who favor ratification and two candidates who oppose ratification shall be nominated from the State at large.

The candidate stated to favor ratification to be nominated from each congressional district shall be the one whose nominating petition or petitions is or are signed by the largest number of electors of such congressional district signing the petition or petitions of any candidate stated to favor ratification; and the candidate stated to oppose ratification to be nominated from each congressional district shall be the one whose nominating petition or petitions is or are signed by the largest number of electors of such congressional district signing the petition or petitions of any candidate stated to oppose ratification. The candidates stated to favor ratification to be nominated from the State at large shall be those whose nomination petitions are signed by the largest number of electors of the State signing petitions for candidates at large stated to favor ratification, and the candidates stated to oppose ratification to be nominated from the State at large shall be those whose nominating petitions are signed by the largest number of electors of the State signing petitions for candidates at large stated to oppose ratification.

In the event that the petitions of two or more candidates are signed by the same number of electors, the Secretary of State shall decide between such candidates by lot. Within four days after the last date for the filing of such nominating petitions the Secretary of State shall determine the candidates nominated in accordance with the foregoing and shall certify the names of such candidates to the county clerk or registrar of voters of every county or city and county in the State.

Section 6. The election of delegates to such convention shall be by ballot separate from any ballot to be used at the same election and which shall be prepared as follows: The ballot shall first state the substance of the proposed amendment, and this shall be followed by appropriate instructions to the voter. The ballot shall then contain two perpendicular columns of equal width, headed respectively in plain type "For ratification and for repeal" and "Against ratification and against repeal." In the column headed "For ratification and for repeal" shall be placed the names of the nominees nominated as in favor of ratification. In the column headed "Against ratification and against repeal" shall be placed the names of the nominees nominated as against ratification. The voter shall indicate his choice by making one or more cross marks in appropriate spaces provided on the ballot. The ballot shall be so arranged that the voter may by making a single cross vote for the entire group of nominees whose names are comprised in any one of said two columns. The ballot used shall be in substantially the following form:

PROPOSED AMENDMENT TO THE CONSTITUTION OF THE UNITED STATES,

FOR THE REPEAL OF THE EIGHTEENTH AMENDMENT.

Delegates to the Convention to Ratify the Proposed Amendment.

The Congress has proposed an amendment to the Constitution of the United States repealing the Eighteenth Amendment to said Constitution and prohibiting the transportation or importation into any State or Territory of the United States for delivery or use therein of intoxicating liquor, in violation of the laws thereof.

The Congress has also proposed that said amendment shall be ratified by conventions in the States.

Instructions to Voters.

Do not vote for more than 22 candidates.

To vote for all candidates in favor of ratification and in favor of repeal, or for all candidates against ratification and against repeal, make a cross-mark in the CIRCLE at the head of the list of candidates for whom you wish to vote. If you do this, make no other mark.

To vote for an individual candidate make a cross-mark in the SQUARE at the right of the name.

For Ratification and for Repeal	Against Ratification and Against Repeal
○	○
John Doe ☐	Charles Coe ☐
Richard Roe ☐	Michael Moe ☐

Section 7. Candidates to the number of twenty-two who shall receive the highest number of votes cast at such election shall be delegates to the convention. On the fortieth day after the date of said election or as soon as the returns have been received from all counties in the State (if received within that time) the Secretary of State shall compare and estimate the vote and file in his office a statement thereof and make out and deliver or transmit by mail to each person elected a certificate of election. On the same date as the delivery or transmission by mail of such certificates of election the Secretary of State shall deliver or transmit by mail to each person elected a delegate a notice of the time when such convention shall meet which time shall be on a date selected by the Secretary of State and shall be not less than five days nor more than ten days after the delivery or transmission of such notice.

Section 8. The delegates to the convention shall meet at the Senate Chambers at the State Capitol at Sacramento at the time specified in such notice and shall thereupon constitute a convention to pass upon the question of whether or not the proposed amendment shall be ratified.

Section 9. The convention shall be the judge of the election and qualification of its members, and shall have power to elect its president, secretary and other officers and to adopt its own rules. If there shall be a vacancy in the convention caused by the death or disability of any delegate or by any other cause, such vacancy shall be filled by appointment by the majority vote of the remaining delegates whose names appeared in the same column of the ballot as did that of the member whose office as delegate shall have been so vacated; provided that if the convention contains no other delegate or delegates to fill such vacancy in the manner aforesaid such vacancy shall be filled immediately by the Governor.

Section 10. The convention shall keep a journal of its proceedings in which shall be recorded the vote of each delegate on the question of ratification of the proposed amendment. Upon final adjournment such journal shall be filed with the Secretary of State.

Section 11. If the convention shall agree by vote of a majority of the total number of delegates to the ratification of the proposed amendment a certificate to that effect shall be executed by the president and secretary of the convention and transmitted to the Governor and the Secretary of State of this State who thereupon shall transmit to the Secretary of State of the United States a certificate under the great seal of the State of California certifying to the ratification of the proposed amendment.

Section 12. If, prior to the date fixed in section 1 hereof for the holding of the election hereby called, the Congress of the United States prescribes the manner in which such convention shall be constituted and shall not except such States as theretofore may have provided for constituting such convention, then the preceding provisions of this act shall be inoperative and the convention shall be constituted and shall operate and proceed as the Congress shall direct, and all officers of the State who may by the Congress be authorized or directed to take any action to constitute such a convention for this State are hereby authorized and directed to act thereunder and in obedience thereto with the same force and effect as if acting under a statute of this State.

Section 13. Inasmuch as this act provides for the calling of an election, it shall, under the provisions of section 1 of Article IV of the Constitution, take effect immediately.

AN ACT to call a special election to be held on Tuesday, the twenty-seventh day of June, 1933, for the purpose of submitting to the qualified electors of this State certain amendments to the Constitution of this State proposed by the Legislature at its fiftieth regular session and for the purpose of electing delegates to a convention to consider and pass upon a proposed amendment to the Constitution of the United States and to provide that this act shall take effect immediately.*

[Approved by the Governor May 11, 1933. In effect immediately.]

The people of the State of California do enact as follows:

Section 1. A special election is hereby called to be held throughout the State of California on Tuesday, the twenty-seventh day of June, 1933. At said special election there shall be submitted to the qualified electors of the State the following:

Senate Constitutional Amendment No. 30—A resolution to propose to the people of the State of California, an amendment to the Constitution of the State by adding a new section to be numbered 34a to Article IV, by amending section 12 of Article XI,

* *Statutes of California,* 1933, Chapter 279, pp. 841-843.

by adding a new section to be numbered 20 to Article XI, by amending sections 14, 15 and 16 by adding three new sections to be numbered 14½, 15½ and 16½, and by repealing sections 12½ and 18 of Article XIII, relating to taxation;

Senate Constitutional Amendment No. 16—A resolution to propose to the people of the State of California an amendment to the Constitution of said State repealing sections 4 and 9 of Article XI thereof, and amending section 5 of said article, relating to county government;

Assembly Constitutional Amendment No. 101—A resolution to propose to the people of the State of California an amendment to the Constitution of said State by adding to Article XIII thereof a new section, to be numbered 8a, relating to taxation;

Assembly Constitutional Amendment No. 16—A resolution to propose to the people of the State of California an amendment to the Constitution of said State, by adding to Article XVI thereof a new section to be numbered 9, authorizing the Legislature to provide for assistance by the State in the refinancing of irrigation and reclamation districts, and approving and ratifying the District Finance Act of 1933;

Assembly Constitutional Amendment No. 108—A resolution to propose to the people of the State of California an amendment to Article IV of the Constitution of said State by adding to said article a new section, to be numbered section 1a, relating to the time of taking effect of acts passed at the fiftieth regular session of the Legislature;

Senate Constitutional Amendment No. 41—A resolution to propose to the people of the State of California an amendment to the Constitution of said State by adding to Article XVI thereof a new section to be numbered 9, relating to loans to counties and municipalities for unemployment relief;

Assembly Constitutional Amendment No. 119—A resolution to propose to the people of the State of California, an amendment to the Constitution of said State by adding to Article IV thereof a new section to be numbered 25a, relating to the regulation and licensing of horse racing, horse race meetings, and the wagering on the results thereof;

Assembly Constitutional Amendment No. 47—A resolution to propose to the people of the State of California an amendment to the Constitution of said State by amending section 1a of Article XIII thereof, relating to exemption of private nonprofit educational institutions from taxation; also, any other constitutional amendment or proposition that the Legislature shall lawfully submit at such election.

Each of the foregoing are amendments to the Constitution of the State of California proposed to the electors of the State of California by the Legislature thereof at its fiftieth regular session in accordance with the provisions of section 1 of Article XVIII of said Constitution.

Section 2. Said special election and the special election called by an act adopted by the Legislature of the State of California at its fiftieth regular session and entitled "An act to provide for a convention in the State of California to pass on the amendment to the Constitution of the United States for the repeal of the Eighteenth Amendment thereof and for the prohibition of the transportation and importation of intoxicating liquor into the States and Territories in violation of the laws thereof, proposed by the Congress for ratification by conventions in the several States, and to call a special election for the purpose of filling the offices of delegates to such convention in this State, and to provide that this act shall take effect immediately," approved April 21, 1933, are hereby consolidated; and such special elections so hereby consolidated shall be conducted as one election and as provided in section 3 of this act.

Section 3. The special election provided for in this act shall be proclaimed, held, conducted, and the ballots shall be prepared, marked, voted, counted, canvassed, and the results shall be ascertained and the returns thereof made in all respects in accordance with the provisions of the Constitution applicable thereto and the law governing general elections in so far as provisions thereof are applicable to the election provided for by this act; provided, however, that the governing boards or bodies charged with the conduct of elections in the counties or cities and counties may consolidate the precincts of the counties and cities and counties for the purposes of this election and shall also appoint as officers of this election one inspector, one judge, and one clerk, who shall receive as compensation for their services a sum not to exceed three dollars each, which sum shall be paid out of the treasuries of the counties or cities and counties by which such persons are employed.

Section 4. The presiding officer of the house in which each proposed constitutional amendment originates shall immediately appoint the author or one of the authors of such proposed amendment to the Constitution of this State and one member of the same house who voted in favor thereof to draft an argument giving the reasons for the adoption thereof, and he shall also appoint a member of the same house who voted against such proposed constitutional amendment to draft an argument against the adoption thereof. If no member of the same house voted against such proposed amendment, he shall appoint a qualified person to draft such argument. Each argument shall consist of not more than five hundred words in length and shall be submitted by the author or authors to the Secretary of State within five days after this act takes effect.

Section 5. It shall be the duty of the Attorney General to prepare and deliver to the Secretary of State ballot titles prescribed by section 1197 of the Political Code within five days after this act takes effect. Written objections to the titles prepared by the Attorney General shall be filed with the Secretary of State within five days from such delivery and the Secretary of State shall forthwith file a copy of the constitutional amendment, together with the title thereof so prepared by the Attorney General and the said objections thereto, with the Board of Title Commissioners as provided by section 1197 of the Political Code. Said Title Commissioners shall determine the validity of such objections within three days after the objections are filed. The determination by said board shall be final and conclusive.

Section 6. Inasmuch as this act provides for the calling of an election, it shall, under the provisions of section 1 of Article IV of the Constitution, take effect immediately.

COLORADO*

(Senate Bill No. 4. By Senator Knous, and Representatives Keating, Hoefnagels, Dunn, Hallen, Hirschfeld, Hoag and Morris.)

AN ACT

To provide for a convention to act upon the amendment to the Constitution of the United States, providing for the repeal of the eighteenth amendment.

Be It Enacted by the General Assembly of the State of Colorado:

Section 1. A convention, the delegates to which shall be elected in the manner as herein provided, shall be held in the Senate Chamber at the Capitol, in the City and County of Denver, Colorado, on Tuesday, September 26, 1933, at the hour of ten o'clock A.M., to consider and act upon the ratification of the following amendment to the Constitution of the United States, proposed by the Congress of the United States to the several states:

"Section 1. The eighteenth article of amendment to the Constitution of the United States is hereby repealed.

"Section 2. The transportation or importation into any state, territory or possession of the United States for delivery or use therein of intoxicating liquors, in violation of the laws thereof, is hereby prohibited.

"Section 3. This article shall be inoperative unless it shall have been ratified as an amendment to the Constitution by conventions in the several states, as provided in the Constitution, within seven years from the date of the submission hereof to the states by the Congress."

Section 2. The number of delegates to be elected at such convention shall be fifteen in number, to be elected from the state at large. The election of said delegates shall be held on the second Tuesday in September, 1933. At such election, all persons qualified to vote for members of the General Assembly shall be entitled to vote.

Section 3. Except as otherwise provided herein, all provisions of the statutes relating to registration of voters, and the conduct of General or Special elections shall, so far as applicable, and not inconsistent herewith, apply to the election of such delegates. Publication of the notice of registration and election shall be made once at least five (5) days before the first registration day and stating the date and place of the registration and of the election. Such notice shall appear in two (2) newspapers in each county; such newspapers to be selected by the Board of County Commissioners. If there be only one newspaper in any county, publication in that newspaper shall be sufficient, while if there is no newspaper in a county, posting of the notice of the election shall be sufficient, provided such posting be made at each polling place at least five (5) days before the day of registration. The total cost of such publication in any one newspaper shall not exceed the sum of Two Dollars ($2.00), notwithstanding any law relating to the cost of publications now effective in this State. The State Board of Canvassers shall canvass the returns for delegates to said convention not later than September 25, 1933, and shall, immediately thereafter, issue certificates of election to the delegates elected.

---

* *Colorado Session Laws, Extraordinary Session, 1933,* Chapter 7, pp. 51-59.

Section 4. There shall be no primary election for the nomination of delegates to the said convention. Not less than five days after the approval of this act, the Governor shall nominate and forthwith announce the names of thirty candidates for delegates, such candidates being, in his opinion, representative citizens of Colorado. Such nominations shall be without party or political designation. Fifteen of these candidates shall be persons who assent to the placing of their names on the ballot as "For ratification of repeal of the Eighteenth Amendment" and fifteen shall be persons who assent to the placing of their names on the ballot as "Against ratification of repeal of the Eighteenth Amendment." On accepting such designation by the Governor, each candidate shall file his acceptance with the Secretary of State as follows: "I do hereby accept this nomination as candidate for delegate to the Convention to be held on the 26th day of September, 1933, and assent to the placing of my name on the ballot as for ratification of repeal of the Eighteenth Amendment (or against ratification of repeal of the Eighteenth Amendment).

Signed................................

Section 5. All persons who would on the 12th day of September, 1933, be entitled to vote at a general election under the laws of the State of Colorado, shall be entitled to vote at the election herein provided for. Electors shall be registered as now provided by law. In towns or cities or precincts where electors are registered by the County Clerk and Recorder or by an Election Commission, registration may be made until and including September 9, 1933. In all precincts where registration is now made by registration Committees or by Judges of Election sitting as a Board of Registration, such Committee and Judges of Election shall meet for such purpose between the hours of 8 A.M. and 7 P.M., September 5, 1933. Registration of electors shall be in accordance with the provisions relative to the first day of registration as now provided for by statute.

Section 6. Polling places at such election shall be established by the Board of County Commissioners of each county, and by the Election Commission in the City and County of Denver, not later than August 29, 1933, in each election precinct, but only such polling places shall be selected as shall be agreed to be furnished free. In the event a free polling place cannot be obtained in any election precinct, the nearest convenient public school building or other public building within the precinct shall be designated as the polling place for such election precinct, and the Boards of Education in all public school districts are directed to make school buildings available as polling places and to declare a school holiday on the election day if necessary. If no free polling place can be secured within a precinct and no school building or other public building exists within a precinct, the county commissioners may hire a polling place and pay not more than $3.00 for the use of said polling place.

Section 7. Such election shall be conducted by the precinct judges of election, except that there shall be no counting judges in any precinct and in precincts where there now are both receiving and counting judges, the receiving judges shall constitute the election board. Necessary clerks shall be appointed as provided by law. All judges of election and clerks shall be paid not more than $1.00 for services performed on the day of such election and members of registration committee shall be paid at the rate of $1.00 per day. All costs and expenses incurred in carrying out the provisions of this Act in each county, shall be borne and paid by the county in which such costs and expenses are incurred.

Section 8. The election shall be by ballot separate from any ballot to be used at the same election, which shall be prepared as follows: It shall first state the substance of the proposed amendment. This shall be followed by appropriate instructions to the voter. It shall then contain perpendicular columns of equal width, headed respectively, in plain type, "For Ratification of Repeal of the Eighteenth Amendment," and "Against Ratification of Repeal of the Eighteenth Amendment." The words, "For," "Against" and "Repeal" in the headings to such columns shall be printed on separate lines in type at least twice as large as the other words in said headings. In the column headed "For Ratification of Repeal of the Eighteenth Amendment," shall be placed the names of the several nominees nominated as in favor of ratification. In the column headed "Against Ratification of Repeal of the Eighteenth Amendment," shall be placed the names of the nominees nominated as against ratification. The voter shall indicate his choice by making one or more cross marks in appropriate spaces provided on the ballot. No ballot shall be held void because any such cross mark is irregular in character. The ballot shall be so arranged that the voter may, by making a single cross mark, vote for the entire group of nominees whose names are comprised in any column. If the voter shall indicate his choice by making a cross mark in the circle for or against repeal, such mark shall be counted as made, regardless of any other cross mark, or other marks, made on said ballot, and each nominee, in the column where such cross mark appears, shall receive one vote as a result of such ballot. If any voter shall make no cross mark in the circle provided to vote for or against repeal and shall vote for more than fifteen nominees, such ballot shall be counted only as a vote for the nominees in the column containing the greater number of marks made by such voter, and as a vote for such nominees in the other column, which, added to the first number, will make a total of fifteen nominees. In such case, those nominees voted for in the column having the lesser number of marks shall be included, according to the order of their appearance on the ballot. The ballot shall be in substantially the following form:

PROPOSED AMENDMENT TO THE CONSTITUTION

OF THE UNITED STATES

Delegates to the Convention to Ratify the Proposed Amendment

The Congress has proposed an amendment to the Constitution of the United States which provides in substance that the Eighteenth Article of Amendment to the Constitution of the United States, relating to the manufacture, transportation and sale of intoxicating liquors for beverage purposes, shall be repealed, and prohibiting shipment of intoxicating liquors into any state or territory in violation of the laws of such state or territory.

Congress has proposed that said amendment shall be ratified by conventions in the several states.

INSTRUCTIONS TO VOTERS

Do not vote for more than fifteen candidates.

To vote for all candidates in favor of ratification of repeal of the Eighteenth Amendment, or for all candidates against ratification of repeal of the Eighteenth Amendment, make a cross in the circle at the head of the list of candidates for whom you wish to vote. If you do this, make no other mark. To vote for an individual candidate, make a cross in the square ☐ at the right of the name of the candidate for whom you wish to vote.

FOR Ratification of the Amendment to REPEAL The Eighteenth Amendment ○	AGAINST Ratification of the Amendment to REPEAL The Eighteenth Amendment ○
Joe Doe .... ☐	Charles Coe .... ☐
Richard Doe .... ☐	Michael Moe .... ☐

Section 9. The fifteen nominees who shall receive the highest number of votes cast at said election shall be the delegates to the Convention. If there shall be a vacancy in the Convention caused by the death or disability of any delegate, or any other cause, the same shall be filled by appointment by the majority vote of the delegates comprising the group from which such delegate was elected, but such delegate so appointed shall file his acceptance in the form prescribed in Section 4. If the Convention contains no other delegate of that group, the vacancy shall be filled by appointment by the Governor, and such appointee shall file his acceptance as prescribed in Section 4.

Section 10. The delegates to the convention shall meet at the time and place as herein provided and shall thereupon constitute a Convention to pass upon the question of whether or not the proposed amendment shall be ratified. Delegates to said Convention shall receive no compensation for their services, nor any allowance for their expenses.

Section 11. The Convention shall be the judge of the election and qualification of its members, and shall have power to elect its president, secretary, and other officers, and to adopt its own rules.

Section 12. The Convention shall keep a journal of its proceedings, in which shall be recorded the vote of each delegate on the question of ratification of the proposed amendment. Upon final adjournment, the journal shall be filed by the secretary of the Convention in the office of the Secretary of State.

Section 13. If the Convention shall agree by a majority of the total number of delegates to the ratification of the proposed amendment, a certificate to that effect shall be executed by the president and secretary of the Convention, and transmitted to the Secretary of State of this State, who shall transmit the certificate under the Great Seal of the State of Colorado to the Secretary of State of the United States, in the manner in which amendments to the Constitution of the United States submitted to the Legislature for ratification are certified.

Section 14. There is hereby appropriated from any moneys in the State Treasury not otherwise appropriated, the sum of $1,000.00 or as much thereof as shall be necessary for the use of the Secretary of the State for the expenses incident to the election herein provided for.

Section 15. The General Assembly hereby finds, determines and declares this Act to be necessary for the immediate preservation of the public peace, health and safety.

Section 16. In the opinion of the General Assembly an emergency exists; therefore, this Act shall take effect and be in force from and after its passage.

Approved August 10, 1933.

CONNECTICUT*

AN ACT providing for a convention to consider the question of the adoption or rejection of an amendment repealing the eighteenth amendment submitted to this state by the Congress of the United States.

Be it enacted by the Senate and House of Representatives in General Assembly convened:

WHEREAS, The congress of the United States has proposed an amendment to the constitution of the United States to be valid when ratified by conventions in three-fourths of the states, which proposed amendment is as follows:

Section 1. The eighteenth article of amendment to the Constitution of the United States is hereby repealed.

Section 2. The transportation or importation into any State, Territory, or possession of the United States for delivery or use therein of intoxicating liquors, in violation of the laws thereof, is hereby prohibited.

Section 3. This article shall be inoperative unless it shall have been ratified as an amendment to the Constitution by conventions in the several States, as provided in the Constitution, within seven years from the date of the submission hereof to the States by the Congress.

NOW THEREFORE, To provide for the constitution of such convention in this state, the time and place of holding the same and the manner of election of delegates thereto, Be it enacted by the Senate and House of Representatives in General Assembly convened:

Section 1. A convention for the sole purpose of ratifying or rejecting the proposed amendment to the constitution of the United States recited in the preamble shall be held in the Hall of the House of Representatives in the State Capitol at Hartford on such date as shall be fixed by the governor by proclamation.

Section 2. Said convention shall be composed of fifty delegates, one to be elected from each senatorial district, and fifteen to be elected at large, in the manner hereinafter provided.

Section 3. The governor shall, by proclamation, fix a date for the election of such delegates, which date shall be not less than ten days nor more than sixty days after the final adjournment of the present session of the general assembly. Said proclamation shall be issued at least six weeks before such date and shall set forth the manner of and time for nominating such delegates as hereinafter provided.

Section 4. At said election all persons qualified to vote for members of the general assembly, and who were registered on the revised registry list then last completed according to law, shall be entitled to vote.

Section 5. Except as in this act otherwise provided, said election shall be conducted and the results thereof ascertained and certified in the same manner as in the case of the election of presidential electors in this state, and all provisions of the statutes of this state relative to elections, except so far as inconsistent with this act, are made applicable to said election.

Section 6. Each delegate to said convention shall be an elector and resident of the

* *Connecticut Special Laws, 1933,* Vol. XXI, part 2, No. 137, pp. 835-838.

state, and each district delegate shall be a resident of the senatorial district by which he is to be elected. Nominations shall be by petition and not otherwise. Nominating petitions shall be filed with the secretary of the state at least four weeks prior to the proclaimed date of the election. Each petition nominating a candidate for a district delegate shall be signed by not less than one hundred electors resident within the district, and each petition for delegates at large shall be signed by not less than five hundred electors resident within the state. Such petitions shall contain the name, street and town address of each signer, and shall be submitted to the town clerks of the towns in which such signers reside at least one week prior to the filing thereof, and such town clerks shall certify thereon the electors signing such petitions whose names appear on the voting list last completed in their respective towns. Each petition nominating a district delegate shall state that the nominee is in favor of the proposed amendment, or that he is opposed to the proposed amendment, as the case may be; and each petition nominating delegates at large shall contain the names of fifteen candidates, and shall state that all of them are in favor of, or that all of them are opposed to, the proposed amendment, as the case may be. Any person circulating a nominating petition for signature shall leave in the town clerk's office in the town where he is circulating such petition a copy thereof, including the names of the candidates named in such petition, and such petition may be then signed by qualified electors. If more than one petition nominating different candidates for a district delegate in favor of said proposed amendment, or more than one petition nominating different candidates opposed to such proposed amendment, shall be received by the secretary of the state, or more than one petition nominating delegates at large in favor of, or more than one petition nominating delegates at large opposed to, said proposed amendment, shall be received by the secretary of the state, he shall act on the petition containing the largest number of certified signatures, or, in case of a tie, shall select by lot the petition to be acted upon, and shall disregard the other petitions. If no proper petition be filed nominating candidates favoring ratification or opposing ratification within the time herein provided, the governor shall nominate such candidates and the candidates so nominated shall be placed upon the ballots or voting machines in the same manner as if regularly nominated by petition.

Section 7. The secretary of the state shall then cause to be printed for each senatorial district a sufficient number of ballots. Said ballots shall contain a statement of the proposed amendment to the constitution of the United States, followed by a clear statement of the way in which the voter is to mark the ballot. They shall be arranged in perpendicular columns of equal width, headed, respectively, in plain type, "For Ratification" and "Against Ratification." In the column headed "For Ratification" shall be placed the names of the candidates for delegates at large nominated as in favor of ratification, followed by the name of the candidate for district delegate nominated as in favor of ratification. In the column headed "Against Ratification" shall be placed the names of the candidates for delegates at large nominated as opposed to ratification, followed by the name of the candidate for district delegate nominated as opposed to ratification. At the left of each name shall be a printed square. At the head of each column shall be a circle. To vote for all the candidates in favor of ratification, or to vote for all the candidates opposed to ratification, the voter may make a cross-mark in the circle at the head of the list of candidates. Any voter may, if he shall so prefer, make no mark in either circle, and vote for the individual candidates whom he shall prefer, not exceeding sixteen, making a cross-mark in the square at the left of the name of the candidate.

Section 8. For use in towns or voting precincts in which the voting machine is used in general elections, the secretary of the state shall cause to be printed a sufficient supply of instructions to voters, giving the text of the proposed amendment, clear instructions to voters and the names of the candidates arranged in horizontal rows, one row bearing the names of all the candidates in favor of ratification and the other row bearing the names of all the candidates against ratification. The names shall be arranged on the voting machine in the same manner; and the voter may vote for the entire list of candidates for or against ratification, or he may vote for the individual candidates whom he shall prefer, not exceeding sixteen. The secretary of the state shall determine by lot which list of candidates shall have the upper position on the voting machine or the left hand position on the ballot.

Section 9. The candidate for district delegate who shall receive the highest vote in each senatorial district shall be a delegate to the convention and the fifteen candidates for delegates at large who shall receive the highest number of votes shall also be delegates. If in any district there shall be a tie, there shall be no delegate from that district, and the total membership of the convention shall be correspondingly reduced. If there shall be a failure to choose fifteen delegates at large because of a tie, only the delegates who have a plurality of votes shall be elected, and the total number of delegates shall be correspondingly reduced.

Section 10. The secretary of the state shall canvass the returns of the election, and shall cause the list of delegates elected to be published as soon as the result shall be ascertained.

Section 11. The convention shall be the judge of the election and qualifications of its members; and shall have power to elect its president, secretary and other officers, and adopt its own rules. It shall keep a journal of its proceedings in which shall be recorded the vote of each delegate on the question of ratification of the proposed amendment. Upon final adjournment, the journal of the convention shall be filed with the secretary of the state.

Section 12. A majority of the elected delegates shall be required to ratify the proposed amendment. A certificate stating whether the convention has ratified or failed to ratify the proposed amendment shall be executed by the president and secretary of the convention and transmitted to the secretary of the state, who shall transmit such certificate under the great seal of the state to the secretary of state of the United States.

Section 13. The delegates shall receive no compensation; but each delegate shall receive an allowance for his travel from his home to the capitol and return, at the same rate as is allowed for members of the general assembly. The comptroller is instructed to draw his order on the treasurer payable to each delegate who shall attend the convention, for his expenses so determined. The board of finance and control shall determine the expense of preparing the ballots and other expenses incurred by the secretary of the state in carrying out the provisions of this act, and such expenses, together with any expenses of the convention other than for the travel of delegates, shall be paid to the persons designated by the board of finance and control, by the treasurer, upon order of the comptroller. The expenses of the election for the choice of delegates in each town shall be borne by such town.

Section 14. If congress shall hereafter prescribe by statute the manner in which the convention shall be constituted and shall not except from the provisions of such statute such states as may theretofore have provided for constituting such conventions, the preceding provisions of this act shall be inoperative, and the convention of the state of Connecticut shall be constituted and held as such act of congress shall direct. All officers of the state who may, by such act of congress, be authorized or directed to take any action to constitute such a convention for this state, are authorized to act thereunder and in obedience thereto, in the same manner as if they were so authorized and directed by a statute of this state.

Approved April 10, 1933.

AN ACT amending an act providing for a convention to consider the question of the adoption or rejection of an amendment repealing the eighteenth amendment submitted to this state by the Congress of the United States.*

Be it enacted by the Senate and House of Representatives in General Assembly convened:

Section ten of number 137 of the special acts of 1933 is amended to read as follows: the secretary of the state shall canvass the returns of the election on the first Wednesday of the month following the month in which the election is held, and shall cause the list of delegates elected to be published as soon as the result shall be ascertained.

Approved May 5, 1933.

AN ACT providing for challengers at the election to be held for the choice of delegates to the convention to consider the question of the adoption or rejection of an amendment repealing the Eighteenth Amendment.†

Be it enacted by the Senate and House of Representatives in General Assembly convened:

Any registrar of voters of any town within the senatorial district from which any candidate is finally nominated for district delegate to the convention to be held under the provisions of number 137 of the special acts of 1933, as amended by number 247 of said special acts, shall, upon written request preferred by such candidate, not less that ten days prior to the date fixed for the election of delegates to such convention, appoint, for each of the polling places in such town, an elector thereof designated by such candidate, to serve as a challenger during such election.

Approved May 24, 1933.

* *Connecticut Special Laws, 1933,* No. 247, p. 913.

† *Ibid.*, No. 315, p. 984.

DELAWARE*

AN ACT to provide for Conventions in the State of Delaware to take action upon Amendments to the Constitution of the United States which may be proposed by the Congress for Ratification by Conventions in the Several States.

WHEREAS, Article V of the Constitution of the United States provided as follows:

The Congress, whenever two-thirds of both Houses shall deem it necessary, shall propose Amendments to this Constitution, or, on the Application of the Legislatures of two-thirds of the several States, shall call a Convention for proposing Amendments, which, in either Case, shall be valid to all Intents and Purposes, as part of this Constitution, when ratified by the Legislatures of three-fourths of the several States, or by Conventions in three-fourths thereof, as the one or the other Mode of Ratification may be proposed by the Congress; Provided that no Amendment which may be made prior to the Year One Thousand Eight Hundred and Eight shall in any Manner affect the first and fourth Clauses in the Ninth Section of the first Article; and that no State, without its Consent, shall be deprived of its equal Suffrage in the Senate.
and

WHEREAS, There are no provisions in either the Constitution or the Laws of the State of Delaware for conventions in the State of Delaware to take action upon Amendments to the Constitution of the United States which may be proposed by the Congress for ratification by conventions in the several States;
and

WHEREAS, It is apparent that action by such conventions should truly reflect the true state of public opinion throughout the State of Delaware;

Therefore, Be it enacted by the Senate and House of Representatives of the State of Delaware, in General Assembly met:

Section 1. Whenever the Congress of the United States shall propose an Amendment to the Constitution of the United States and shall propose that the same shall be valid when ratified by conventions in three-fourths of the several States, the Governor of this State shall fix by proclamation the date of an election for the purpose of electing delegates to such convention of this State. Such election may be either at a special election or may be held at the same time as a general election, or special, but shall be held at least as soon as the next general election occurring more than three months after the Amendment has been proposed by the Congress.

Section 2. If such election be held at the same time as a general election, all persons qualified to vote at such general election for representatives to the General Assembly of this State, shall be entitled to vote.

If such election be held at a time other than at the same time as a general election, all persons qualified to vote for representatives to the General Assembly of this State at the last general election next preceding said special election, shall be entitled to vote. There shall be one or more registration days prior to such special election, as the Governor in his proclamation, fixing the date for the special election, may determine.

* *Delaware Laws, 1933,* Chapter 5, pp. 33-43.

The Governor shall also, in said proclamation, fix the date or dates of such registration day or days, provided that no registration shall be held within ten days next prior to such special election. On said registration day or days persons whose names are not on the list of registered voters established by law for said last general election, may apply for registration, and on said registration day or days applications may be made to strike from the said registration list names of persons on said list who are not eligible to vote at such election.

Section 3. Except as in this Act otherwise provided, such election shall be conducted and the results thereof ascertained and certified in the same manner as in the case of the election of Electors of President and Vice-President in this State and the Governor shall, without delay, examine the certificates and ascertain the delegates to such Convention chosen and make known the same by proclamation, and cause notice to be given to each delegate so elected of his election as a delegate. All provisions of the laws of this State relative to elections, except so far as inconsistent with the provisions of this Act, are hereby made applicable to such election.

Section 4. The number of delegates to be chosen to such convention shall be seventeen, to be elected from the State at large. Seven of such delegates shall be residents of New Castle County, five of such delegates shall be residents of Kent County, and five of such delegates shall be residents of Sussex County.

Section 5. Candidates for the office of delegate to the convention shall be citizens and qualified voters of this State. Nominations shall be by petition and not otherwise. A single petition may nominate any number of candidates not exceeding the total number of delegates to be elected from each county, and all candidates on any such petition shall be residents of the same County and shall reside in the County which said candidates propose to represent at such convention and every such petition shall be signed by not less than one hundred (100) persons who are qualified voters of the County wherein such candidate or candidates reside. Nominating petitions shall be filed with the Clerk of the Peace of the County which said candidates propose to represent. Nominations shall be without party or political designation, but the nominating petitions shall contain a statement as to each nominee to the effect that he favors ratification, or that he opposes ratification, or that he remains uncommitted to either ratification or rejection of the proposed amendment to the Constitution of the United States, and no nominating petition shall contain the name of any nominee whose position as stated therein is inconsistent with that of the position of any other nominee as stated therein.

Section 6. The sixteenth day before the day fixed for the holding of such election shall be the last day for the filing of nominating petitions with the respective Clerks of the Peace, or if said sixteenth day falls upon a Sunday or a legal holiday, the day following shall be the last day for the filing of said nominating petitions, and thereafter nominations for the office of delegate to such convention shall be closed. After the closing of such nominations, the respective Clerks of the Peace shall forthwith count and determine the number of signatures which each candidate for nomination as delegate to such convention, has obtained upon his or their respective nominating petition or petitions. In making such count and determination, the respective Clerks of the Peace shall only count the signatures of those persons who are qualified voters of the County which the candidates propose to represent at such convention. A signature to such nominating petition shall be prima facie evidence that the person purporting to sign the same did actually sign the same and that such person is a qualified voter of the same county as the county of residence of the Candidate or Candidates whose names appear in said nominating petition, and all signatures to such nominating petitions shall be counted by the respective Clerks of the Peace, unless within five days after the closing of nominations as aforesaid, evidence satisfactory to the Clerk of the Peace, shall have been produced before him that a person whose name purports to have been signed to a nominating petition is either a fictitious person or not a qualified voter of the County of residence of the candidate or candidates whose nominating petition he purports to have signed. After the closing of nominations all nominating petitions shall be open to the inspection of any qualified voter of the County in which such petitions have been filed.

Section 7. No nominations shall be effective except those of the seven candidates from New Castle County in favor of ratification, the seven candidates from New Castle County against ratification and the seven candidates from New Castle County not committed to either ratification or rejection of the proposed Amendment, the five candidates from Kent County in favor of ratification, the five candidates from Kent County against ratification and the five candidates from Kent County not committed to either ratification or rejection of the proposed Amendment, the five candidates from Sussex County in favor of ratification, the five candidates from Sussex County against ratification and the five candidates from Sussex County not committed to either ratification of rejection of the proposed Amendment, whose nominating petitions have respectively been signed by the largest number of qualified persons, ties to be decided by lot drawn by the respective Clerks of the Peace.

Section 8. After the nominees for delegates to such Convention shall have been determined by the Clerks of the Peace as aforesaid, it shall be the duty of each Clerk of the Peace to certify to the other Clerks of the Peace in this State the names of the nominees from their respective Counties to such convention and to further certify which nominees from their respective Counties were nominated as in favor of ratification, which nominees from their respective Counties were nominated as opposed to ratification and which nominees from their respective Counties were nominated as uncommitted either to ratification or rejection of the proposed Amendment.

Section 9. Candidates for nomination not nominated as aforesaid, shall be deemed to be alternates to the nominees in their respective groups in the order of the number of signatures which they have respectively received upon their nominating petitions, and in the event of the death, resignation or removal of any nominee, the first alternate shall take his place as nominee, and so on, ties to be decided by lot drawn by the respective Clerks of the Peace. In the event of such death, resignation or removal, it shall be the duty of the Clerk of the Peace of the County from which said nominee was nominated, to forthwith certify to the other Clerks of the Peace the fact of such death, resignation or removal, together with the name of the new nominee. In the event of the death, resignation or removal of any nominee after the printing of the ballots for such election, it shall be the duty of the Clerks of the Peace to provide the election officers of each election district with a number of pasters containing only the name of such nominee, at least equal to the number of ballots provided for each election district and it shall be the duty of the Clerks of election to put one of such pasters in a careful and proper manner in the proper place on each ballot before they shall deliver the same to voters.

Section 10. It shall be the duty of the Clerk of the Peace of each County to cause to be printed and distributed the ballots for said election in the quantity and in the manner provided by law for general elections; provided that such ballots as are required under the election laws to be delivered to the chairmen of the various political parties shall, in lieu thereof, be distributed to the various nominees as equally as possible, and provided further that the Clerk of the Peace in each County, in addition to the above mentioned ballots, shall cause to be printed such further number of ballots as shall be directed by any nominee in any County; provided, however, that the said Clerk of the Peace shall not have printed any ballots upon the order or request of any nominee, unless the said request shall have been made to him in writing at least ten days prior to the holding of the election at which the said ballots are to be used, nor unless a deposit sufficient to cover the cost of the ballots be made at the time they are ordered. The ballots so ordered by the said nominees shall be delivered to the said nominees or to their agents upon their request or order at least five days before the election at which the said ballots are to be used.

Section 11. The election shall be by ballot, separate from any ballot to be used at the same election. Such ballot, if used at a general election, shall be enclosed in the same envelope as the ballot for use at such general election, otherwise each ballot cast shall be enclosed in a separate envelope. Said ballot shall first state the substance of the proposed Amendment. This shall be followed by appropriate instructions to the voter. It shall then contain perpendicular columns of equal width headed respectively in plain type "For Ratification" "Against Ratification" and "Uncommitted." In the column headed "For Ratification" shall be placed the names of the nominees nominated from the entire State as in favor of ratification, in alphabetical order. In the column headed "Against Ratification" shall be placed the names of the nominees nominated from the entire State as against ratification, in alphabetical order. In the column headed "Uncommitted" shall be placed the names of the nominees nominated from the entire State, as uncommitted to either ratification or rejection in alphabetical order. The voter shall indicate his choice by making one or more cross marks in the appropriate spaces provided on the ballot. No ballot shall be held void because any such cross mark is irregular in character. The ballot shall be so arranged that the voter may by making a single cross mark, vote for the entire group of nominees whose names are comprised in any column. The ballot shall be as like as possible to the form of the official ballot now used in this State and substantially in the following form:

OFFICIAL BALLOT

PROPOSED AMENDMENT TO THE

CONSTITUTION OF

UNITED STATES

Delegates to the Convention to Ratify the Proposed Amendment.

The Congress has proposed an amendment to the Constitution of the United States which provides (insert here the substance of the proposed amendment).

The Congress has also proposed that the said amendment shall be ratified by Conventions in the States.

INSTRUCTIONS TO VOTERS

Do not vote for more than 17 candidates

To vote for all candidates in favor of Ratification of the proposed amendment, or for all candidates against Ratification of the proposed amendment, or for all candidates who intend to remain uncommitted to either Ratification or rejection of the proposed amendment, make a cross-mark in the Block at the head of the list of candidates for whom you wish to vote. If you do this, make no other mark.

To vote for an individual candidate make a cross-mark in the Block at the left of the name.

FOR RATIFICATION		AGAINST RATIFICATION		UNCOMMITTED	
	For Delegates to the Convention.		For Delegates to the Convention.		For Delegates to the Convention.
	JOHN DOE		JOHN DOE		JOHN DOE
	JOHN DOE		JOHN DOE		JOHN DOE
	JOHN DOE		JOHN DOE		JOHN DOE
	JOHN DOE		JOHN DOE		JOHN DOE

All ballots used at elections for ratifying conventions shall be printed as outlined in the paragraph immediately above. However, if the Governor, in his proclamation, calling for election of Delegates to a ratifying convention, deems it expedient to further print on the ballots information that will be more informative to the electorate on the subject, which is being voted upon, this act will give the Governor the power to do so.

Section 12. The seventeen nominees who shall receive the highest number of votes shall be the Delegates to the Convention. If there shall be a vacancy in the Convention caused by the death or disability of any delegate or any other cause, the same shall be filled by appointment by the majority vote of the delegates comprising the group from which such delegates were elected and if the Convention contains no other delegate of that group, shall be filled by the Governor.

Section 13. The Delegates to the Convention shall meet in the Senate Chamber at the State House in Dover on the twenty-eighth day after their election at twelve o'clock noon, and shall thereupon constitute a Convention to pass upon the question of whether or not the proposed Amendment shall be ratified.

Section 14. The Convention shall have power to elect its president, secretary and other officers, and to adopt its own rules.

Section 15. The Convention shall keep a journal of its proceedings in which shall be recorded the vote of each Delegate on the question of ratification of the proposed Amendment.

Section 16. After the sense of the majority of the total number of Delegates composing the Convention is taken upon the question of the ratification of the proposed amendment to the Constitution of the United States, the Convention shall certify a resolution of its vote over the hand of the President, attested by the Secretary and signed by all of the members of the Convention. Such resolution shall be so certified in duplicate originals. The duplicate originals shall then be delivered by the Convention to the Secretary of State together with the Journal and any other records of the Convention.

If it appears from the resolutions so certified to the Secretary of State that the proposed amendment to the Constitution of the United States has been ratified by the Convention, it shall be the duty of the Secretary of State to send to the Secretary of State of the United States one of the duplicate originals certified under his hand and the seal of the State of Delaware. The remaining duplicate original shall be proclaimed by publication and shall be deposited together with the journal and any other records of the Convention in the State Archives. If it appears from the resolutions so certified to the Secretary of State that the proposed amendment to the Constitution of the United States has not been ratified, the resolution shall be proclaimed by publication and the duplicate originals of the resolution together with the journal and any other record of the Convention shall be deposited in the State Archives.

Section 17. Every delegate to such convention shall receive Ten Dollars ($10.00) for every day he is in attendance at such convention, not exceeding three, and in addition thereto, ten cents (10c) for each mile necessarily travelled by him in making one round trip from the place of his residence to Dover. The president, secretary and other officers shall receive such compensation as may be fixed by the convention not in excess of Twenty-five Dollars ($25.00) for any such officer, in addition to his compensation as such delegate. Disbursements for the foregoing purposes and for other necessary expenses of the convention, when approved by the convention and signed by the President, shall be paid by the State Treasurer out of any monies not otherwise appropriated. The expenses of holding a special election shall be borne as now provided by law for the holding of a general election.

Section 18. If at or about the time of submitting any such Amendment, Congress shall either in the resolution submitting the same or by a statute, prescribe the manner in which the conventions shall be constituted, and shall not except from the provisions of such statute or resolution such states as may theretofore have provided for constituting such conventions, the preceding provisions of this Act shall be inoperative, the convention shall be constituted and shall operate as the said resolution or Act of Congress shall direct, and all officers of the State who may by the said resolution or statute be authorized or directed to take any action to constitute such a convention for this State are hereby authorized and directed to act thereunder and in obedience thereto with the same force and effect as if acting under a statute of this State.

Approved April 11, 1933.

FLORIDA*

AN ACT to Provide for the Holding of State Conventions for the Purpose of Ratifying or Rejecting Proposed Amendments to the Constitution of the United States.

Be It Enacted by the Legislature of the State of Florida:

Section 1. *Conventions—How Constituted.* Whenever the Congress of the United States shall propose, to conventions in the several states, an amendment to the Constitution of the United States, for ratification or rejection, and shall not have provided the manner in which such conventions shall be constituted, the conventions in this state shall be chosen and constituted in the manner herein prescribed and shall function in accordance with this Act.

Section 2. *Number and Qualifications of Delegates.* Such conventions shall consist of sixty-seven delegates from the State at large. Each delegate shall possess the qualifications of a member of the House of Representatives of the Legislature of this state; and each shall hold office from the date of his election and until the convention shall have discharged the duties for which it was selected.

Section 3. *Special Elections—Qualifications of Voters.* The delegates composing such convention shall be elected at a special election which shall be held in each county of this state on a date to be fixed by the Governor, not less than five (5) months and not more than ten (10) months after the date of the proposal by the Congress. The Governor shall issue his call for such election at least forty-five (45) days prior to the date thereof, which, as soon as issued, shall be published by the Secretary of State at least one time, in a newspaper of general circulation in each county. Such election shall be conducted, except as herein specified, in all respects in the manner and form prescribed by the laws of this state for holding general elections.

All electors who were duly qualified to vote in the last preceding general election shall be qualified to vote in such special election without further registration or further payment of poll taxes. The registration books in each county shall be opened ten (10) days after the Governor shall issue his call and shall remain open, in each county, until and including the tenth day before the election, during which time all persons who have not been registered, though entitled to be or who shall have become entitled to registration since the last general election, shall be permitted to register. During the time in which the registration books are required to be kept open by this section, any registered voter shall be permitted to qualify to vote in such election.

PROVIDED: That if any general election be held in this state within one (1) year after the date of the proposal by the Congress, such delegates shall be chosen at such general election and all electors qualified to vote in such general election shall be qualified to vote for such delegates, unless the Governor, by his proclamation, shall require such delegates to be chosen at a special election, in which event they shall be elected as herein provided.

Section 4. *Candidates—How Qualified—Petitions.* Any person desiring to become a candidate for election as a delegate to said convention shall file a sworn application with the Secretary of State on such form as that official shall prescribe, not less than twenty (20) days before the date of election, in which shall be stated his name in full,

* *Laws of Florida, 1933,* Vol. I, Chapter 16180 (No. 323), pp. 740-744.

his residence, his age, his color and his occupation. Such application shall also state, under oath, that the applicant is a citizen of the United States and of the State of Florida and that he is a qualified elector of the county in which he resides. The applicant may also state whether or not he favors the ratification of the proposed amendment or opposes it and whether or not he desires his name to appear upon the ballot as favoring or opposing such amendment or as unpledged.

If the applicant shall request that his name appear on the ballot as favoring or as opposing the amendment, his application shall be accompanied by a qualification fee of Twenty-five Dollars ($25.00) and by one or more petitions, requesting that his name be placed upon the official ballot, and signed by not fewer than five hundred qualified electors. It shall be permissible for any number of qualified voters to join in one or more petitions requesting the placing on the official ballot of the names of more than one candidate but not exceeding the total number to be elected. Any applicant may withdraw his name at any time before the ballots are actually printed.

Section 5. *Ballots—Preparation and Form of.* The ballots shall be prepared by the Secretary of State and distributed by him to the County Commissioners in the several counties at least ten (10) days prior to such election. They shall contain the substance of the proposed amendment and in alphabetical order (a) the names of all candidates who shall have declared in favor of the ratification of such amendment; and (b) the names of all candidates who shall have declared against the ratification of such amendment; and (c) the names of all candidates who shall have qualified without pledging themselves either for or against the amendment. When delegates are elected at general elections as provided in Section 3, such matters shall be printed on the general election ballots. In either event, in addition to the names of unpledged candidates printed on said ballots and whether there be any such names on said ballots or not, there shall be provided, under the caption "(c)" blank lines in equal number to the number of persons who may be elected as such delegates.

Section 6. *Clerk and Inspectors.* The Board of County Commissioners of each county shall appoint clerks and inspectors of election for such special election in accordance with the general election laws, except that such appointments may be made at any time more than five (5) days prior to the election; whereupon they shall publish the names of such inspectors and clerks in a newspaper printed in the county. The clerks and inspectors of election shall receive compensation at the rate of Five Dollars ($5.00) per diem for each day actually and necessarily served in performing their duties as such. Such compensation, together with other lawful expenses incurred by the several Boards of County Commissioners, shall be paid as provided in Section 11, after the several Boards of County Commissioners shall have certified the same to the Board of State Canvassers and such accounts shall have been approved by such Board of State Canvassers.

Section 7. *Canvass of Returns.* Within three (3) days after the date of such special elections the County Commissioners shall meet and canvass the returns thereof in their respective counties and transmit the same to the Secretary of State. Within fourteen (14) days after the date of such special elections the Board of State Canvassers shall meet and canvass such returns. Such Board shall thereupon declare the sixty-seven candidates who receive the greatest number of votes in the State at Large, to have been elected as delegates to such convention; and shall immediately issue a certificate of election to each of such persons. In case of a tie the Board of State Canvassers shall select the delegates from those receiving the tie votes.

Section 8. *Convention—Time and Place of Meeting.* The delegates to the convention shall meet in such place as shall be provided for that purpose by the Secretary of State, at the State Capitol at Tallahassee on the second Tuesday in the month following their election, at twelve o'clock noon. They shall thereupon constitute a convention to ratify or reject the proposed amendment to the Constitution of the United States.

Section 9. *Convention—Quorum—Officers—Powers—Expenses.* The convention shall have power to ratify or reject the proposed amendment to the Constitution of the United States for which it shall have been selected; to choose a President and a Secretary and all other necessary officers, clerks and attaches; to fill vacancies in its membership; and to make rules governing its procedure. It shall be the sole judge of the election and qualifications of its members. A majority of the total number of delegates elected to the convention shall constitute a quorum.

The delegates to such convention shall serve without compensation or expenses; but the Secretary and other officers, clerks and attaches shall receive such compensation as may be fixed by the convention.

The convention shall have no other power than that hereby expressly conferred or is necessarily incident to the purpose of its creation; any other action attempted to be taken by it shall be utterly null, void and of non effect.

Section 10. *Convention—Record of Action.* When the convention shall have agreed, by "yea" and "nay" vote of a majority of the total number of delegates elected, to the ratification or rejection of the proposed amendment to the Constitution of the United States, a certificate to that effect shall be executed by its President and Secretary and filed with the Secretary of State of Florida. A copy of the minutes of its proceedings, likewise signed by such officials, shall also be filed with the Secretary of State. It shall be the duty of the Secretary of State of Florida, after the filing of such certificate, to transmit a copy thereof, certified under the Great Seal of Florida, to the Secretary of State of the United States.

Section 11. *Appropriation.* For the purpose of defraying the expenses of preparing for, conducting, holding and declaring the result of the election provided for by this Act, and also for the purpose of defraying the expenses allowed by this Act for the holding of sessions of the convention as herein provided, to be audited by the Comptroller, there is hereby appropriated out of the general revenue fund of the State of Florida a sufficient sum of money for the payment of all amounts necessary to be expended under the terms of this Act, which sums of money shall be disbursed by the State of Florida and pursuant to warrants drawn by the Comptroller upon the Treasurer for the payment of same.

Section 12. *Effective Date.* This Act shall take effect upon its becoming a law.

Approved June 7th, 1933.

IDAHO*

AN ACT

To provide for conventions to pass on amendments to the Constitution of the United States which are now or may hereafter be proposed by the Congress of the United States for ratification by conventions in the several states: providing that this act may be inoperative if Congress shall prescribe the manner in which constitutional conventions shall be constituted; providing that if any part of the act is adjudged unconstitutional or invalid, such adjudication shall not affect the validity of the remaining portions which can be given effect; providing that this act may be referred to as the "Constitutional Convention Act," and declaring an emergency.

Be It Enacted by the Legislature of the State of Idaho:

Section 1. Whenever the Congress of the United States has proposed, or shall hereafter propose, an amendment to the Constitution of the United States, and proposes that it be ratified by conventions in the several states, the Governor shall fix by proclamation the date of an election for the purpose of electing delegates to such convention in the State of Idaho. The proclamation for such election shall be issued by the Governor under his hand and the Great Seal of the State of Idaho at least ninety days before such election and copies thereof shall be transmitted to the Board of County Commissioners of the counties in which such elections are to be held. Such election may either be at a special election or may be held at the same time as a general election, but shall be held at least as soon as the next general election occurring more than three months after the amendment has been proposed by the Congress of the United States.

Section 2. At such election all persons qualified to vote for presidential electors shall be entitled to vote.

Section 3. Except as in this Act otherwise provided, such election shall be conducted and the results thereof ascertained and certified in the same manner as in the case of the election of presidential electors in this state, and all the provisions of the laws of this state relative to general elections, except in so far as inconsistent with this Act, are hereby made applicable to such election.

Section 4. The number of delegates to be chosen to such Convention shall be twenty-one (21), to be elected from the state at large.

Section 5. Candidates for the office of delegate to the Convention shall be qualified electors of the State of Idaho. Nominations shall be by petition and not otherwise. A single petition shall nominate but one candidate, who may have one or more separate petitions. Nominations shall be without party or political designation, but the nominating petitions shall each contain a declaration of the candidate that he is a candidate for election to the office of delegate to the Constitutional Convention, and a statement to the effect that he favors ratification of, or that he is against ratification of the proposed Constitutional amendment to be acted upon by the Constitutional Convention, and the total number of voters joining in the nomination of a candidate shall not be less than one hundred.

---

* *Idaho General Laws of the 22nd Session, 1933,* Chapter 179, pp. 328-334.

The candidate's declaration in the nominating petition shall be in substantially the following form, to-wit:

"I, the undersigned, being a qualified elector of....................precinct, ...County, State of Idaho, hereby declare myself to be a candidate for the office of delegate to the Constitutional Convention, to be voted for at the election to be held on the ...... day of ...., 19...., and that I

....

(Insert one only of the following: 'favor ratification of'

....,

or 'am against ratification of')

the proposed Constitutional Amendment to be acted upon by the Constitutional Convention, and certify that I possess the legal qualifications to fill said office, and that my postoffice address is ....

"I further certify and declare that if nominated I hereby accept said office.

"(Signed) ...."

All blank spaces shall be properly filled in with the necessary information and the declaration of candidacy shall be subscribed and sworn to before an officer authorized to administer oaths, and the signatures of the voters joining in such petitions, each of which signatures shall be followed by the signer's residence address and date, shall be prefaced by a declaration in substantially the following form to-wit:

"I, the undersigned, being a qualified elector of the State of Idaho, do hereby declare that I am in accord with the statement and declaration of ...., a candidate for the office of delegate to the Constitutional Convention, to be voted for at the election to be held on the ...... day of ...., 19...., and do hereby join in this petition for his nomination for such office.

Name of Petitioner	*Post office*	*Date of Signing*
....	....	.................."

Each nominating petition shall, at the time of filing in the office of the Secretary of State, bear an affidavit in substantially the following form, executed and verified by a citizen and resident of the State of Idaho:—

"State of Idaho
County of .... } ss.

"I do solemnly swear (or affirm) that I am a citizen and resident of the State of Idaho; that each of the petitioners whose name is affixed to the above paper signed the same personally, together with his postoffice address and date of signing, and that each signed the same with full knowledge of its contents; that to the best of my knowledge each is a qualified elector of the State of Idaho.

"(Signed) ....

"Subscribed and sworn to before me this ...... day of ...., 19....

....

"Notary Public for the State of Idaho; residence ...."

No voter shall sign more than twenty-one nominating petitions nor more than one petition for the same candidate, and if he does either, his signatures shall not be counted on any nominating petition.

All acceptances and petitions shall be filed with the Secretary of State not less than forty-five days before the date fixed for the election. No nomination shall be effective except those of the twenty-one (21) candidates in favor of ratification and the twenty-one (21) candidates against ratification whose nominating petitions have respectively been signed by the largest number of voters, ties, if any, to be decided by lot drawn by the Secretary of State; PROVIDED, HOWEVER, that if there be less than twenty-one (21) candidates in favor of ratification, all such candidates shall be considered as nominated, or if there be less than twenty-one (21) candidates against ratification all such candidates shall be considered as nominated.

Within ten days after the petitions are filed with him, the Secretary of State shall certify to each county auditor within the state, a certified list of the candidates of each group entitled to be voted for at such election, as appears from the acceptances and nominating petitions filed in the office of the Secretary of State.

Section 6. The election shall be by ballot, separate from any ballot to be used at the same election, which ballot shall be prepared as follows: It shall first state the substance of the proposed Constitutional Amendment. This shall be followed by appropriate instructions to the voter. It shall then contain perpendicular columns of equal width headed respectively, in plain type, "For Ratification" and "Against Ratification." In the column headed "For Ratification" shall be placed the names of the candidates nominated in favor of ratification. In the column headed "Against Ratification" shall be placed the names of the candidates nominated as against ratification. The voter shall indicate his choice by making one or more cross-marks in the appropriate spaces provided on the ballot. No ballot shall be held void because any such cross-mark is irregular in character. The ballot shall be so arranged that the voter may, by making a single cross-mark, vote for the entire group of candidates whose names are comprised in any column.

The ballot shall be in substantially the following form:

PROPOSED AMENDMENT TO THE CONSTITUTION

OF THE UNITED STATES

Delegates to the Convention to Ratify the Proposed Amendment.

The Congress has proposed an amendment to the Constitution of the United States which provides (insert here the substance of the proposed amendment).

The Congress has also proposed that the said amendment shall be ratified by Conventions in the several states.

INSTRUCTIONS TO VOTERS

Do not vote for more than 21 candidates altogether.

To vote for all candidates in favor of Ratification, or for all candidates against Ratification, make a cross-mark in the CIRCLE at the head of the list of candidates for whom you wish to vote. If you do this, make no other mark.

To vote for an individual candidate make a cross-mark in the SQUARE at the left of the name.

FOR RATIFICATION	AGAINST RATIFICATION
◯	◯
☐ John Doe	☐ Charles Coe
☐ Richard Roe	☐ Michael Moe
☐	☐

All circular spaces in said ballot shall be one-half inch in diameter.

All square spaces in said ballot shall be one-half inch square.

Except as herein otherwise provided, ballots and supplies for said election shall be prepared and furnished as provided by Chapter 8 of Title 33, Idaho Code Annotated, and acts amendatory thereof.

Section 7. The twenty-one candidates who shall receive respectively the highest numbers of the total number of votes cast at said election shall be the delegates to the Convention. If there shall be a vacancy in the Convention caused by the death or disability of any delegate or any other cause, the same shall be filled by appointment by the majority vote of the delegates comprising the group from which such delegate was elected and if the Convention contains no other delegate of that group, shall be filled by the Governor.

Section 8. The delegates to the Convention shall meet and assemble in the House of Representatives in the Capitol at Boise, Idaho, on the twenty-eighth day after their election, at twelve o'clock noon, and shall thereupon organize as, be and constitute a Convention to pass upon the question of whether or not the proposed Amendment shall be ratified.

Section 9. The Convention shall be the judge of the election and qualification of its members; and shall have the power to elect its president, secretary and other officers and/or employees and to adopt its own rules.

Section 10. The Convention shall keep a journal of its proceedings in which shall be recorded the vote of each delegate on the question of ratification of the proposed Amendment. Upon final adjournment the Journal shall be certified to by the president and secretary of the Convention and be filed with the Secretary of State.

Section 11. If the Convention shall agree, by a vote of a majority of the total number of delegates, to the ratification of the proposed amendment, a certificate to that effect shall be executed by the president and secretary of the Convention and transmitted to the Secretary of State of this state, who shall transmit the certificate under the Great Seal of the state to the Secretary of State of the United States.

Section 12. No delegate to a constitutional convention shall receive any compensation except that such delegate shall be paid his actual, necessary and reasonable expenses in traveling to and from and attendance at said Convention.

Section 13. All the expenses of the Constitutional Convention and the expenses allowed delegates thereto shall be allowed and paid by the State of Idaho in the same manner as other claims against the state are allowed and paid, and from such appropriations as are, or may be, available therefor.

Section 14. If at or about the time of submitting any such Amendment, Congress shall either in the resolution submitting the same or by statute, prescribe the manner in which the conventions shall be constituted, and shall not except from the provisions of such statute or resolution such states as may theretofore have provided for constituting such conventions, the preceding provisions of this Act shall be inoperative, the convention shall be constituted and shall operate as the said resolution or Act of Congress shall direct, and all officers of the state who may by the said resolution or statute be authorized or directed to take any action to constitute such a convention for this state are hereby authorized and directed to act thereunder and in obedience thereto with the same force and effect as if acting under a statute of this state.

Section 15. If any part or parts of this Act shall be adjudged by the courts to be unconstitutional or invalid, the same shall not affect the validity of any part or parts thereof which can be given effect without the part or parts adjudged to be unconstitutional or invalid. The Legislature hereby declares that it would have passed the remaining parts of this Act if it had been known that such other part or parts thereof would be declared to be unconstitutional or invalid.

Section 16. This Act may be cited as the "Constitutional Convention Act."

Section 17. An emergency existing therefor, which emergency is hereby declared to exist, this Act shall be in force and effect from and after its passage and approval.

Approved March 11, 1933.

ILLINOIS*

CONVENTION TO CONSIDER PROPOSED AMENDMENTS TO THE CONSTITUTION OF THE UNITED STATES

(House Bill No. 441. Approved April 28, 1933.)

AN ACT *to assemble a convention to ratify or refuse to ratify a proposed amendment to the Constitution of the United States.*

Whereas: The Congress of the United States has adopted Senate Joint Resolution No. 211 which is as follows:

JOINT RESOLUTION

Proposing an amendment to the Constitution of the United States.

Resolved by the Senate and House of Representatives of the United States of America in Congress Assembled (Two-thirds of Each House Concurring Therein), That the following article is hereby proposed as an amendment to the Constitution of the United States, which shall be valid to all intents and purposes as part of the Constitution when ratified by conventions in three-fourths of the several states:

ARTICLE ___

Section 1. The Eighteenth article of Amendment to the Constitution of the United States is hereby repealed.

Section 2. The transportation or importation into any State, Territory or possession of the United States for delivery or use therein of intoxicating liquor, in violation of the laws thereof, is hereby prohibited.

Section 3. This article shall be inoperative unless it shall have been ratified as an amendment to the Constitution by conventions in the several states, as provided in the Constitution, within seven years from the date of the submission thereof to the States by the Congress.

Now, therefore,

Be it enacted by the People of the State of Illinois, represented in the General Assembly:

* *Laws of Illinois, 58th General Assembly, 1933,* pp. 12-18.

Section 1. At the hour of 12 o'clock noon, on the 10th day of July, 1933, a convention to ratify or refuse to ratify the proposed amendment to the Constitution of the United States as stated in the preamble to this Act, shall meet in the hall of Representatives of the General Assembly in the Capitol Building in the city of Springfield. The Secretary of State shall take such steps as may be necessary to prepare the hall of Representatives for the meeting of the convention.

Section 2. The convention shall consist of fifty delegates who shall be elected at large by the electors of the State of Illinois, on Monday, June 5, 1933. No person shall be elected a delegate who shall not have attained the age of twenty-five years nor who is not a citizen of the United States nor who shall not have been a resident of this State for five years next preceding his election.

Section 3. Nomination of candidates for delegate shall be by petition. Petitions for nomination shall specify:

1. The name and residence of the candidate;

2. That he is a candidate for delegate; and may specify that he is "for ratification" or "against ratification."

The names of any number of candidates not exceeding fifty may be included in one petition, but all candidates included in the same petition must be for ratification or all must be against ratification, or all must express no preference for or against ratification.

Attached to such petition shall be a statement or statements of candidacy for each of the candidates named therein signed and sworn to by each such candidate before some officer authorized to take acknowledgements in this State, such statement to be substantially in the following form:

STATE OF ILLINOIS }
County of........ } ss.

I, ..., being first duly sworn, say that I reside at .... street, in the city (or village) of .... in the county of........................., State of Illinois; and that I am a qualified voter therein; that I am a candidate for election to the office of delegate to the convention to meet July 10, 1933, to ratify or refuse to ratify a proposed amendment to the Constitution of the United States to be voted upon at the election to be held on the fifth day of June, A.D. 1933; that I am legally qualified to hold such office; and (if the candidate desires to express whether he favors ratification or not) that I favor (or do not favor) the ratification of the proposed amendment to the Constitution of the United States repealing the Eighteenth Amendment to said Constitution; and I hereby request that my name be printed upon the official ballot for election to such office.

Signed ....

Subscribed and sworn to (or affirmed) before me by........................ who is to me personally known, this .... day of ...., A.D. 19.........

Signed..................................

(Official Character)

Section 4. Such petitions shall be prepared and signed in the same manner and by the same number of qualified voters as is required for the nomination of independent candidates for an office to be filled by the voters of the State at large in accordance with the provisions of sections 5 and 5½ of "An Act to provide for the printing and distribution of ballots at public expense, and for the nomination of candidates for public offices, to regulate the manner of holding elections, and to enforce the secrecy of the ballot," approved June 22, 1891, as amended, and all of the provisions of these sections of the Act referred to shall, so far as applicable, govern and control the petitions for nomination of delegates.

Such petitions shall be presented not less than twenty-five days before such election to the Governor, the Auditor of Public Accounts and the Secretary of State. The Governor, the Auditor of Public Accounts and the Secretary of State shall each endorse on the petitions, his signature and the date and hour of presentment to him and the petitions so endorsed shall then be deposited in the office of the Secretary of State for preservation.

Any person whose name has been presented as a candidate may cause his name to be withdrawn in the manner provided in section 8 of the Act above referred to, for independent candidates for offices to be filled by the voters of the State at large. Objections to petitions may be made not later than three days after the last day for filing such petitions. The State Officers Electoral Board created by section 10b of the Act referred to shall hear and pass upon such objections within three days after the filing of the objection. Except as herein provided, objections to petitions, hearing of such objections, certification of nominations shall all be in accordance with the provisions of the Act above referred to for independent candidates for offices to be filled by the voters of the State at large. Names of candidates shall be certified by the Governor, the Auditor of Public Accounts and the Secretary of State to the several county clerks not later than fifteen days before said election in the order in which they have been filed and in the case of a petition containing the names of two or more candidates, the names of candidates in such petition shall be certified in the order they appear upon the petition.

The county clerks shall forthwith certify to the board of election commissioners, if any, in the particular county, the names of such candidates in the order certified to them.

Section 5. The names of all candidates for delegate shall be printed on a separate ballot. The names of all candidates in favor of ratification shall be placed in one column under the designation:

FOR RATIFICATION

(For Repeal of 18th Amendment)

and the names of all candidates opposing ratification shall be placed in another column under the designation:

AGAINST RATIFICATION

(Against Repeal of 18th Amendment)

and the names of all candidates who have not specified in favor of ratification or against ratification, shall be placed in another column under the designation:

"NO PREFERENCE EXPRESSED"

The names of candidates in each column shall be placed in the order in which they were certified to the several county clerks. At the left of each name shall be placed a square. If fifty or less candidates are nominated who are in favor of ratification, and fifty or less candidates are nominated who are against ratification, and fifty or less candidates are nominated who have not declared for ratification or against ratification, there shall be placed in each column on the ballot a circle immediately above the names of candidates and a cross mark in any circle shall be counted as a vote for each of the candidates in the column in which is the circle in which such cross is placed. If the names of more than fifty candidates are placed upon the ballot in either the column headed "for ratification" or "against ratification" or in the column, if any, headed "no preference expressed" no such circle shall be placed upon the ballot.

The ballot shall be in substantially the following form:

BALLOT

For Delegates to the State Convention to Consider the Following Proposed Amendment to the Constitution of the United States

JOINT RESOLUTION

Proposing an Amendment to the Constitution of the United States.

Resolved by the Senate and House of Representatives of the United States of America in Congress assembled (two-thirds of each House concurring therein), That the following article is hereby proposed as an amendment to the Constitution of the United States, which shall be valid to all intents and purposes as part of the Constitution when ratified by conventions in three-fourths of the several states:

ARTICLE ___ ___

Section 1. The Eighteenth article of Amendment to the Constitution of the United States is hereby repealed.

Section 2. The transportation or importation into any State, Territory or possession of the United States for delivery or use therein of intoxicating liquor, in violation of the laws thereof, is hereby prohibited.

Section 3. This article shall be inoperative unless it shall have been ratified as an amendment to the Constitution by conventions in the several States, as provided in the Constitution, within seven years from the date of the submission thereof to the States by the Congress.

INSTRUCTION TO VOTERS

*A cross in any circle will count a vote for each candidate in the column under the circle.

A cross in any circle will not count a vote for any candidate in the column under the circle if any candidate is voted for in another column.*

A cross in the square at the left of the name of any candidate will count one vote for such candidate.

For ratification (For repeal of 18th Amendment	Against ratification (Against repeal of 18th Amendment	No Preference Expressed
○	○	○
☐ William E. White	☐ Benjamin Black	☐ John Brown
☐ Edward Smith	☐ Henry Z. Jones	☐ Arthur Robinson

* Instruction between asterisks to be omitted if there are no circles.

In all other respects such ballot shall conform as nearly as may be to the provisions of the laws regulating the form of ballots for general elections.

Section 6. A blank space shall be left on the ballot both under the column headed "For ratification," the column headed "Against ratification" and the column headed "No preference expressed" and any voter may write in such blank space the name or names of the candidates of his choice for one or more but not more than fifty, for the office of delegate. In voting for a candidate whose name was not printed upon the ballot, the voter after writing in the name of such candidate, shall indicate his choice of such candidate by placing to the left of and opposite the name thus written, a square and placing in the square a cross (X).

Section 7. The election to be held Monday, June 5, 1933, for delegates to the convention shall in all respects be conducted in conformity with the laws of this State relating to the conduct of elections to the extent that such laws are applicable.

All votes cast in the election for delegates shall be tabulated, returned and canvassed in the manner then provided by law for the tabulation, return and canvass of votes cast in elections for United States Senators and Representatives in Congress.

All other provisions of law relating to elections, unless otherwise provided by this Act, shall, so far as applicable, control and govern the election of delegates.

The fifty candidates who receive the highest number of votes shall be declared duly elected delegates to the convention herein provided for. Ties shall be decided in the manner provided by law in the case of United States Senators and Representatives in Congress.

The official or officials, charged with the duty of issuing certificates of election to persons elected to the United States Senate and the House of Representatives in Congress shall issue certificates of election to all persons duly elected as delegates.

Election contests for membership in the convention shall be heard and determined by the convention.

Section 8. Each delegate before entering upon his duties as a member of the convention, shall take an oath to support the Constitution of the United States and of the State of Illinois, and to discharge faithfully his duties as a member of the convention. In going to and returning from the convention and during the sessions thereof the delegates shall, in all cases, except treason, felony or breach of the peace, be privileged from arrest; and they shall not be questioned in any other place for any speech or debate in the convention.

The delegates shall receive no compensation for their services nor reimbursement for their expenses.

Section 9. The convention shall determine the rules of its procedure, shall be the judge of the election, returns, and qualifications of its members and shall keep a journal of its proceedings.

The Governor shall call the convention to order at its opening session and shall preside over it until a temporary or permanent presiding officer shall have been chosen by the delegates.

The delegates shall elect one of their own number as president of the convention, and they shall have power to appoint a secretary and such employes as may be deemed necessary. The employes of the convention shall receive such compensation as shall be determined upon by the convention.

Section 10. If the convention shall agree, by vote of a majority of the total number of delegates to the ratification of the proposed amendment a certificate to that effect shall be executed by the president and secretary of the convention and transmitted to the Secretary of State of this State, who shall transmit the certificate under the Great Seal of the State to the Secretary of State of the United States.

Section 11. The sum of two thousand five hundred dollars ($2,500.00), or so much thereof as may be necessary, is hereby appropriated for the expenses properly incident to the convention. The Auditor of Public Accounts is hereby authorized and directed to draw warrants on the State treasury for the foregoing amount or any part thereof upon the presentation of itemized vouchers certified to as correct by the president of the convention.

Section 12. In as much as it is necessary to provide for a convention to consider the amendment proposed to the United States Constitution and in order not to incur unnecessary expense, it is deemed desirable to provide for the election of delegates to such convention at some regular election without undue delay and an election will be held in all the voting precincts of the State on June 5, 1933, therefore, an emergency is declared to exist and this Act shall take effect upon its passage.

Approved April 28, 1933.

INDIANA*

AN ACT to provide for conventions to pass on amendments or an amendment to the constitution of the United States which has or have been or may hereafter be proposed by the congress for ratification by conventions in the several states and declaring an emergency.

(H. 526. Approved March 8, 1933.)

Federal Constitutional Amendment—Election of Delegates—Time—General Election—Constitutional Convention—Election Commissioners—Election Boards—Pay of Boards

Section 1. *Be it enacted by the general assembly of the State of Indiana,* That whenever the Congress of the United States shall propose an amendment to the Constitution of the United States, and shall propose that it be ratified by conventions in the several states, the governor shall fix, by proclamation, the date of an election for the purpose of electing the delegates to such convention in this state. Such elections shall be held within sixty days from the date of the proclamation of the governor and within four months of the date of the receipt by the proper official of the proposed amendment from the secretary of state of the United States. If a general election occur within such period the said special election shall be held at the same time and by the same election officials who conduct such general election.

Such delegates when elected, assembled and organized as hereinafter provided shall constitute a convention for the purpose of the ratification or rejection of such proposed amendments.

The county election commissioners of the last preceding general election shall constitute the county election commissioners at the elections provided for herein. The precinct election officials shall consist of one inspector and two clerks to be appointed by the county election commissioners at least ten days before the election and shall have the same powers and duties as other election officers, and receive the sum of two dollars for each twenty-four hours employed in such election.

Legal Voters

Section 2. At such election all legal voters of the state shall be qualified to vote.

Conduct of Election

Section 3. Except as in this act otherwise provided, such election shall be conducted and the results thereof ascertained, canvassed and certified in the same manner as in the case of election of governor in this state, and all provisions of the laws of this state relative to general elections, except so far as inconsistent with this act, are hereby made applicable to such election.

Apportionment of Delegates

Section 4. Each county shall elect one delegate, and each county having a population exceeding ten thousand according to the last preceding United States census, shall

---

* *Indiana Acts of the 78th Session, 1933,* Chapter 163, pp. 851-858.

elect one additional delegate for each additional ten thousand of the population of such county, or major fraction thereof, according to the last preceding United States census. The number of delegates to which each county is entitled under the provisions of this section, shall be determined by the governor and contained in his proclamation.

Delegates—Qualifications—Petition—Declaration—Petition May Nominate Full Delegation—Inconsistency—Ties—Filing Certification of Nominees—Written Objections—Certification of Election

Section 5. Candidates for the office of delegate to the convention shall be citizens and residents of the county, and shall be at least twenty-one years of age. Nomination shall be by petition and not otherwise. Every candidate for the office of delegate to such convention shall, before his name is placed on any petition herein provided for, file in the office of the clerk of the circuit court of the county in which he resides, a declaration stating his or her name, and his or her residence, with the street and number, if any, and also stating whether if elected as a delegate, he or she will vote for the ratification or for the rejection of such amendment to be considered by such convention. No petition containing the name of any candidate who shall have failed to file such declaration as herein provided, shall be valid, and the same shall not be received by the clerk of the circuit court for filing. A single petition may nominate any number of candidates not exceeding the total number of delegates to be elected from such county, and shall be signed by not less than five hundred voters for each delegate to be named. Nomination shall be without party or political designation, but the nominating petitions shall contain a statement as to each nominee, to the effect that he favors ratification, or that he opposes ratification, and no nominating petition shall contain the name of any nominee whose position as stated therein is inconsistent with that of any other nominee as stated therein. No person shall sign a petition for the nomination of a candidate or candidates who are in favor of ratification and a petition for the nomination of a candidate or candidates who are opposed to ratification. No nomination shall be effective except those of the nominees in favor of ratification, and of the nominees against ratification, whose nominating petitions have respectively been signed by the largest number of voters, ties to be decided by lot drawn by the governor. The petitions shall contain the names of the candidates, his or her place of residence, with the street and number thereof, if any, and a declaration and pledge that the said candidate will, if elected, vote for or against ratification at the convention provided for herein. Within fifteen days after the petitions have been filed with the respective clerks of the respective circuit court the said clerks shall certify the names of the successful nominees to the governor. All petitions and acceptances thereof shall be filed with the clerk of the circuit court within the county not less than thirty days before the proclaimed date of the election.

When filed, with the clerk of the circuit court, the petitions shall be preserved and be opened under proper regulations to public inspection; and if written objection is not made within ten days to the said clerk after the filing thereof, the decision of the clerk shall be final. If such objection be made, then such objection, together with the petition shall be immediately certified by the said clerk to the governor who shall consider the same and his decision thereon shall be final. Within ten days after any such election the clerk of the circuit court shall certify the election of each delegate to the secretary of state. The clerk of the circuit court shall deliver a certificate of election to each successful delegate.

Election—Ballot—Form of Ballot

Section 6. The election shall be by ballot, separate from any ballot to be used at the same election, which shall be prepared as follows: It shall first state the substance of the proposed amendments. This shall be followed by appropriate instructions to the voter. It shall then contain three perpendicular columns of equal width, headed respectively in plain type, "For Ratification," and "Against Ratification," and one column containing nothing more than blank lines. In the column headed "For Ratification," shall be placed the names of the nominees nominated as in favor of ratification. In the column headed "Against Ratification" shall be placed the names of the nominees nominated as against ratification. The voter shall indicate his choice by making one or more cross-marks in the appropriate spaces provided on the ballot. No ballot shall be held void because any such cross-mark is irregular in character. The ballot shall be so arranged that the voter may, by making a single cross-mark, vote for the entire group of nominees whose names are comprised in any column as hereinafter set out; *Provided,* That each elector shall have the right to inscribe as many named "for ratification" or "against ratification" as the county shall be allowed delegates by the governor's proclamation in the additional column provided on said ballot.

The ballots shall be prepared in series, equal to the total number of delegates to be elected, as in this section provided by the county election commissioners. The names of the candidates shall be arranged in alphabetical order in the first series of ballots printed. The first name shall be placed last on the next series printed, and the process shall be repeated in the same manner until each name shall have been first. These ballots shall then be combined in tablets with no two of the same order of names together, except where there is but one candidate in each column and when impracticable to do so. The ballot shall be in substantially the following form:

PROPOSED AMENDMENT TO THE CONSTITUTION OF THE UNITED STATES

Delegates to the convention to ratify the proposed amendment.

The congress has proposed an amendment to the Constitution of the United States which provides (insert here the substance of the proposed amendment).

The congress has also proposed that the said amendment shall be ratified by conventions in the states.

INSTRUCTIONS TO VOTERS

Do not vote for more than   candidates.

To vote for all candidates in favor of ratification, or for all candidates against ratification, make a cross-mark in the CIRCLE at the head of the list of candidates for whom you wish to vote. If you do this, make no other mark.

To vote for an individual candidate make a cross-mark in the SQUARE at the left of the name.

To vote for a person not named in either column write the names of the individual or individuals you desire to vote for in the blank column and by writing under each name "For ratification" or "Against ratification."

For Ratification	Against Ratification	Write names in here
○	○	○
☐ John Doe	☐ Charles Coe	☐
☐ Richard Doe	☐ Michael Moe	☐
☐	☐	☐
☐	☐	☐

Election of Delegates—Vacancy

Section 7. The nominees not exceeding the total number to be chosen, who shall receive the highest number of votes, shall be the delegates to the convention. If there shall be a vacancy in the convention caused by the death or disability of any delegate or any other cause, the same shall be filled by appointment by the majority vote of the delegates from any county comprising the group wherein such vacancy exists and if the convention contains no other delegate of that group, shall be filled by the governor.

Meeting of Delegates—Time—Place—Quorum

Section 8. The delegates to the convention shall meet at the capitol in the chamber of the House of Representatives on the third Monday following their election at two o'clock P.M., central standard time, and shall thereupon constitute a convention to pass upon the question of whether or not the proposed amendment shall be ratified. A majority of the delegates elected to such convention shall constitute a quorum.

Organization of Convention

Section 9. The convention shall be the judge of the election and qualifications of its members; and shall have power to elect its president, secretary and other officers, and to adopt its own rules after being called to order by the lieutenant-governor and oath administered by a judge of the supreme court.

Journal of Proceedings Filed

Section 10. The convention shall keep a journal of its proceedings and debates in which shall be recorded the vote of each delegate on the question of ratification of the proposed amendment. Upon final adjournment the journal shall be filed with the secretary of state.

Ratification Procedure

Section 11. If the convention shall agree, by vote of a majority of the total number of delegates, to the ratification of the proposed amendment, a certificate to that effect shall be executed by the president and secretary of the convention and transmitted to the secretary of state of this state, who shall transmit the certificate under the great seal of the state to the secretary of state of the United States.

Federal Legislation—Conflict—Effect—Procedure

Section 12. If at or about the time of submitting any such amendment, congress shall, either in the resolution submitting the same, or by statute, prescribe the manner in which the conventions shall be constituted, and shall not except from the provisions of such statute or resolution such states as may theretofore have provided for constituting such conventions, the preceding provisions of this act shall be inoperative, the convention shall be constituted and shall operate as the said resolution or act of congress shall direct, and all officers of the state who may by the said resolution or statute be authorized or directed to take any action to constitute such a convention for this state are hereby authorized and directed to act thereunder and in obedience thereto with the same force and effect as if acting under a statute of this state.

Appropriation—Elections

Section 13. The expenses of the elections herein provided for shall be allowed and paid by the county commissioners without the necessity of an appropriation therefor.

Appropriation—Convention

Section 14. There is hereby appropriated the sum of five thousand dollars for each such convention as provided in this act, to defray the expense thereof.

Emergency

Section 15. Whereas an emergency exists for the immediate taking effect of this act, it shall be in full force and effect from and after its passage.

IOWA*

AN ACT to provide for a state convention to determine whether an amendment or amendments to the constitution of the United States, as proposed and submitted by the congress of the United States, shall be ratified, and for the calling of a special election to elect delegates-at-large to such convention, and making appropriations therefor.

Be it enacted by the General Assembly of the State of Iowa:

Section 1. Within sixty days from the date on which the governor of Iowa shall receive notice of an amendment to the constitution of the United States proposed by the congress of the United States for ratification by convention in the several states, it shall be the duty of the governor of Iowa, by proclamation to call such convention, to be held at the seat of government in Des Moines, Iowa, not later than three months from the date of issuance of such proclamation.

Section 2. The proclamation to be issued by the governor, as provided in section one (1), shall fix the date and time for the holding of such convention and the date of the holding of a special election for the election of delegates to such convention.

Section 3. The date of the special election provided to be stated in the said proclamation shall not be more than thirty (30) days before the date fixed for the holding of such convention.

Section 4. Subject to the provisions of this act, each county in the state of Iowa shall be entitled to nominate two persons from among the qualified voters in each county, respectively, to be candidates for the office of delegate-at-large to the state convention, provided, however, that one of such candidates shall be nominated by those favoring the ratification of such amendment, and one nominated by those opposed to the ratification of such amendment. Said delegates shall be nominated as hereinafter provided.

Section 5. The nominations for delegates to such convention from each county shall be made at mass conventions of the qualified electors of such county in the manner provided for in this act.

Section 6. Upon the issuance of a proclamation by the governor of the state of Iowa calling such convention, the qualified voters in each county in the state shall organize themselves into two groups, one of which groups shall consist of those persons favoring the ratification of the amendment proposed by the congress of the United States, and the other to consist of persons opposed thereto.

Section 7. At eleven o'clock A.M., on the fourth Monday following the date of issuance of such proclamation by the governor of the state of Iowa, the group of qualified voters in each county favoring the ratification of such proposed amendment, and the group opposed thereto, shall convene in separate county conventions at the seat of government of such county, at such places as the county auditor of such county shall designate, and such auditor shall publish such designation of places by one (1) publication in two (2) newspapers if there be such two (2) newspapers of general circula-

* *Iowa Acts Regular Session, 45th General Assembly, 1933,* Chapter 1, pp. 1-5.

tion in said county, at least three (3) days prior to said convention, and shall nominate one delegate as a candidate to the convention hereinafter provided for.

Section 8. No person shall be nominated at any county convention held under the provisions of this act until he has executed and delivered to the chairman of such county convention a statement signed by him or her and attested by the chairman and secretary of the convention in the following form:

DELEGATE'S STATEMENT

I, ..., hereby certify that I am a qualified elector of the state of Iowa; that for more than............(years) (months) last past I have resided in the........................; that I am favorable to (or opposed to) the ratification of the amendment to the constitution of the United States of America, proposed by the congress of the United States on the..............day of....................., 19.....

Dated this..........................day of...................., 19.....

....

For ratification

..................................Against ratification

Chairman, county convention

For ratification

..................................Against ratification

Secretary, county convention

Section 9. It shall be the duty of the chairman and secretary of each of such county conventions before adjournment thereof to certify the name of the person nominated as delegate to the convention by their respective county conventions to the secretary of state of the state of Iowa, which certification and the written statement of the person so nominated shall be delivered to the secretary of state not later than nine o'clock in the forenoon of the third day following the day during which the county convention was held.

Section 10. It shall be the duty of the secretary of state, as the certificates of nomination of candidates for election to the office of delegate-at-large to the state convention are filed in his office, as in this act provided, to list the same alphabetically in two (2) groups, one (1) group to consist of the names of the nominees favoring the ratification of the proposed constitutional amendment, and the other to consist of the names of the nominees opposed thereto.

Section 11. The chairman and secretary of each county convention shall select from among the membership of its group in such county one person to act as judge of election, and two persons to act as clerks of election, in each of the several voting precincts in such county; the persons so selected to perform such services without compensation, and the said chairman and secretary of each of such county conventions shall certify to the county auditor the names and addresses of the persons so selected, which certification shall be made not later than nine o'clock in the forenoon of the second day following the date on which such county convention was held. In the event that the judge and clerk or clerks of election, as above provided, shall fail or refuse to act, the chairman and secretary of the respective county conventions are authorized to fill the vacancy thus caused, and if practicable shall certify the names appointed to fill such vacancy to the county auditor. If vacancies occur in the office of the judge or clerk of election, and they are not filled as herein provided, then and in that event, the acting judges and clerks shall fill such vacancies, and the failure of any judge or clerk of election named, as in this act provided, to act at the election, shall in no wise invalidate the election.

Section 12. The ballot to be voted at such special election shall be in substantially the following form:

BALLOT FOR VOTING FOR DELEGATES-AT-LARGE TO A STATE CONVENTION

(THE PROPOSED AMENDMENT TO THE CONSTITUTION OF THE UNITED STATES)

(Here set out proposed amendment)

INSTRUCTIONS TO VOTERS

CANDIDATES FOR DELEGATES-AT-LARGE TO THE STATE CONVENTION

Group of Candidates Favoring Ratification	Group of Candidates Opposing Ratification	Group of Unofficial Candidates* Names to be Written in by Voter if He so Desires
○	○	○
....	....	....
....	....	....
....	....	....
....	....	....

The use of voting machines at such special election is hereby prohibited.

Section 13. At the special election to be held for the purpose of electing delegates to the state convention, as in this act provided, each of the groups of candidates officially nominated shall be voted upon as a unit by placing a cross in the circle at the head of such group; provided, however, if any qualified voter shall so choose to do, he may disregard each of the groups of candidates officially nominated as in this act provided, and cast his ballot for any other qualified elector of the state of Iowa. If any such voter shall so determine to disregard the groups of candidates officially nominated and desire to vote for some other elector or electors as candidates, he shall write such elector's name or names, in number not to exceed ninety-nine (99), on the blank lines provided therefor appearing on the ballot in the right hand column designated "Group of unofficial candidates—names to be written in by voter if he so desires"; and shall vote for such candidates whose names are so written in by him as a unit by placing a cross in the circle appearing at the head of such group. The candidates in the group receiving the largest number of votes shall be the delegates to said convention.

Section 14. The convention shall be the judge of the election and qualification of its members and shall have power to elect its president, secretary, and other officers and to adopt its own rules.

Section 15. The convention shall keep a journal of its proceedings in which shall be recorded the vote of each delegate on the question of ratification of the proposed amendment. Upon final adjournment the journal shall be filed with the secretary of state of the state of Iowa.

Section 16. If the convention shall agree, by vote of the majority of the total number of delegates present, to the ratification of the proposed amendment, a certificate to that effect shall be executed by the president and secretary of the convention and transmitted to the secretary of state of the state of Iowa, who shall transmit the certificate under the great seal of the state of Iowa, to the secretary of state of the United States.

Section 17. All the statutes relating to the manner of conducting elections for state and county officers, so far as applicable, shall govern the election of delegates, except the canvass of the vote and certification thereof shall be made in accordance with section 885 of the code of Iowa, 1931.

Section 18. The expense of holding such election shall be paid by the state treasurer of the state of Iowa, out of funds in his hands not otherwise appropriated. All bills of necessary and proper expense incurred according to law, shall be submitted to the county auditors in the several counties by claimants with itemized, verified statements of account, which shall be filed with said county auditors within ten (10) days after the holding of such election, and the several county auditors shall thereupon duly itemize and certify such claims for expense to the auditor of state of the state of Iowa, who shall draw warrants therefor to the persons entitled thereto in the amount found to be due. All the ballots for such special election shall be furnished by the secretary of state of the state of Iowa and delivered by him to the several county auditors in the state for distribution to each election precinct in their respective counties at least three (3) days prior to the date of such special election.

Section 19. No delegate shall receive any compensation, directly or indirectly, for his services as such delegate.

Section 20. If at or about the time of submitting any such amendment, congress shall either in the resolution submitting the same or by statute prescribe the manner in which the conventions shall be constituted and shall not except from the provisions of such statute or resolution such states as may theretofore have provided for constituting such conventions, the preceding provisions of this act shall be inoperative; the convention shall be constituted and shall operate as the said resolution or act of congress shall direct; and all officers of the state who may, by the said resolution or statute, be authorized or directed to take any action to constitute such a convention for this state, are hereby authorized and directed to act thereunder and in obedience thereto, with the same force and effect as if acting under a statute of this state.

Section 21. This act being deemed of immediate importance shall be in full force and effect after its passage and publication in two (2) newspapers of the state as provided by law.

Senate File No. 477. Approved April 10, 1933.

I hereby certify that the foregoing act was published in the *Sioux City Tribune* April 13, 1933, and the *Burlington Gazette* April 13, 1933.

MRS. ALEX MILLER, *Secretary of State.*

Note: *Sioux City Tribune* and *Burlington Gazette* selected in accordance with section fifty-five (55), code, 1931.

KENTUCKY*

AN ACT to provide for a convention to act upon the amendment to the Constitution of the United States providing for the repeal of the Eighteenth Amendment; and to appropriate funds for certain expenses.

Be it enacted by the General Assembly of the Commonwealth of Kentucky:

Section 1. A convention, the delegates to which shall be elected in the manner as herein provided, shall be held at Frankfort, Kentucky, in the room of the House of the General Assembly in the State Capitol Building on Monday, November 27, 1933, at 10 o'clock A.M., to consider and act upon the ratification of the following amendment to the Constitution of the United States, proposed by the Congress of the United States to the several states:

"Section 1. The eighteenth article of amendment to the Constitution of the United States hereby repealed.

"Section 2. The transportation or importation into any State, territory or possession of the United States for delivery or use therein of intoxicating liquors in violation of the laws thereof, is hereby prohibited.

"Section 3. This article shall be inoperative unless it shall have been ratified as an amendment to the Constitution by conventions in the several States, as provided in the Constitution, within seven years from the date of the submission hereof to the States by the Congress."

Section 2. The number of delegates to be elected to such convention shall be nineteen in number, to be elected from the State at Large. The election of said delegates shall be held on the first Tuesday after the first Monday in November, 1933 (November 7, 1933). At such election all persons qualified to vote for members of the General Assembly of the Commonwealth of Kentucky shall be entitled to vote.

Section 3. Except as otherwise provided herein, all provisions of the Statutes of this Commonwealth relating to nomination papers, the furnishing and distribution of election supplies, the preparation, printing, distribution, voting, counting, recounting, returning and canvassing of ballots for general elections and all other election laws of the State shall, as far as applicable, and not inconsistent herewith, apply to the election of such delegates. The votes cast in such election for said delegate shall be canvassed and certified in the manner now required by law for general elections. The State Board of Election Commissioners shall canvass the returns for delegates to the convention herein provided for and shall issue certificates of election to each of the delegates elected in the same manner as is required by law to be done in a general election for State officers.

Section 4. Each group of delegates shall be nominated by a petition signed by not less than one thousand (1000) qualified voters of this state who shall indicate his or her residence. Each petition shall state the name and residence of each of the proposed candidates for delegates to said convention, and shall be headed in plain type "For ratification of repeal of the Eighteenth Amendment" or "Against ratification of repeal of

* *Kentucky Acts of General Assembly, Extra Session, 1933,* Chapter 6, pp. 22-29.

the Eighteenth Amendment." It shall further contain a statement that each candidate subscribing his or her name thereto is in favor of or against repeal of the Eighteenth Amendment, as the heading may indicate. All petitions shall be filed with the Secretary of State not less than forty-five (45) days before November 7, 1933. No nomination shall be effective except those of the nineteen nominees in favor of ratification, and the nineteen nominees against ratification whose nominating petitions have been signed by the largest number of voters, such designation and determination to be made by the Secretary of State. The Secretary of State shall certify the candidates of each group to the respective county clerks of the various counties of the State as is required by law. All candidates or delegates to the convention shall be citizens and residents of this State and be at least twenty-four years of age.

Section 5. The election shall be by ballot, by the use of the same official ballots as are used in the General Election to be held November 7, 1933. It shall first state the substance of the proposed amendment, and this shall be followed by appropriate instructions to the voter. It shall then contain parallel columns of equal width, headed respectively in plain type, "For Ratification of Repeal of the Eighteenth Amendment," "Against Ratification of Repeal of the Eighteenth Amendment." The words FOR, AGAINST and REPEAL in the headings of such columns shall be printed on separate lines in type at least twice as large as the other words in said headings.

In the column headed "For Ratification of Repeal of the Eighteenth Amendment," shall be placed the names of the several nominees nominated as in favor of ratification. In the column headed "Against Ratification of Repeal of the Eighteenth Amendment," shall be placed the names of the nominees nominated as against ratification. Underneath the name of each candidate there shall be left a blank space large enough to contain a written name. The voter shall indicate his or her choice by making one or more marks with the stencil in appropriate spaces provided on the ballot. The ballot shall be so arranged that the voter may, by making a single mark with the stencil, vote for the entire group of nominees whose names are in either of said columns. The ballot shall be in substantially the following form:

"Proposed Amendment to the Constitution of the United States.

"Delegates to the Convention to Ratify the Proposed Amendment.

"The Congress has proposed an amendment to the Constitution of the United States which provides in substance that the Eighteenth Article of Amendment to the Constitution of the United States relating to the manufacture, transportation and sale of intoxicating liquors for beverage purposes shall be repealed, and prohibiting shipment of intoxicating liquors into any State or Territory in violation of the laws of such State or Territory.

"Congress has proposed that said amendment shall be ratified by conventions in the several States."

"Instructions to Voters:

"Do not vote for more than nineteen candidates.

"To vote for all candidates in favor of ratification of repeal of the Eighteenth Amendment, or for all candidates against ratification of repeal of the Eighteenth Amendment, make a cross with the stencil in the circle at the head of the list of candidates for whom you wish to vote. If you do this, make no other mark. To vote for an individual candidate, make a cross with the stencil in the square opposite the name of the candidate for whom you wish to vote, or you may write in the name and vote therefor in the same manner.

FOR Ratification of the Amendment to REPEAL the Eighteenth Amendment ◯	AGAINST Ratification of the Amendment to REPEAL the Eighteenth Amendment ◯
John Doe.................... ☐	Charles Mick................. ☐
.... ☐	.... ☐
Richard Doe.................. ☐	William Mick................. ☐
.... ☐	.... ☐

Section 6. The nineteen nominees who shall receive the highest number of votes cast at said election shall be the delegates to the convention. If there shall be a vacancy in the convention caused by the death or disability of any delegate or any other cause, the same shall be filled by appointment by a majority vote of the delegates comprising the group from which such delegate was elected, and if the convention contains no other delegate of that group, shall be filled by appointment by the Governor.

Section 7. The delegates to said convention shall meet at the time and place herein provided, and shall thereupon constitute a convention to pass upon the question of whether or not the proposed amendment shall be ratified.

Delegates to such convention shall receive no compensation for their services, but shall be paid their actual and necessary expenses.

There is hereby appropriated from the State Treasury a sum sufficient to pay the actual and necessary expenses of the delegates to said convention. Such sum to be out of the funds of the State not otherwise appropriated.

The Auditor of Public Accounts is hereby authorized and directed to issue a warrant upon the State Treasury, payable to each of said delegates to said convention, for their actual and necessary expenses when such claim of each delegate is certified to the Auditor by the Secretary of said convention, countersigned by the President of said convention, and after same has been audited by said Auditor as is required by law as to other claims upon the Treasury. There shall be filed with such claims receipts, showing the expenditures made, as is now required by law.

Section 8. The convention shall be the judge of the election and qualifications of its members; and shall have power to elect its President, Secretary and other officers, and to adopt its own rules.

Section 9. The convention shall keep a journal of its proceedings, in which shall be recorded the vote of each delegate on the question of ratification of the proposed amendment. Upon final adjournment, the said journal shall be filed by the Secretary of the convention in the office of the Secretary of State.

Section 10. If the convention shall agree by a majority of the total number of delegates to the ratification of the proposed amendment, a certificate to that effect shall be executed by the President and Secretary of the convention, and delivered to the Secretary of State of Kentucky, who shall transmit such certificate under the great seal of the Commonwealth of Kentucky to the Secretary of State of the United States in the manner in which amendments to the Constitution of the United States submitted to the legislature for ratification are certified.

Section 11. It being necessary to nominate candidates for delegates to the convention herein provided for by petition, and it requiring considerable time to accomplish such end, and it being necessary that said delegates be elected at the General Election to be held on November 7, 1933, and the time intervening between now and said General Election being short for such purposes and all things connected therewith, an emergency is declared to exist and this Act shall be and become effective from and after its passage and approval by the Governor.

FRANK LEBUS
Speaker of the House of Representatives
A. B. CHANDLER
President of the Senate

9/7/33
Approved:

RUBY LAFFOON, *Governor of Kentucky*

MAINE*

AN ACT To Provide for a Constitutional Convention to Pass on the Proposed Twenty-first Amendment to the Constitution of the United States.

Be it enacted by the People of the State of Maine, as follows:

Section 1. *Constitutional convention to be convened.* A constitutional convention shall be convened in the hall of the house of representatives at the capitol on the first Wednesday in December, 1933, to act on the question of the ratification or rejection of the 21st amendment to the constitution of the United States.

Section 2. *Delegates to convention.* Said convention shall be composed of 80 delegates who shall be elected from the counties as follows:
2 each from the counties of Lincoln, Sagadahoc, Piscataquis, Franklin and Waldo,
3 each from the counties of Hancock and Knox,
4 each from the counties of Washington, Somerset, and Oxford,
7 each from the counties of Kennebec, Androscoggin and York,
9 each from the counties of Aroostook and Penobscot, and
13 from the county of Cumberland.

Section 3. *Election of delegates.* The delegates to said convention shall be elected at a general election to be held on the 2nd Monday in September, 1933, the ballots for which shall be prepared and distributed by the secretary of state as in the case of general elections and notifications of which shall be prepared and posted as required by law for such general elections.

Section 4. *Qualifications of delegates.* The qualifications for delegates to said convention shall be the same as the qualifications for members of the house of representatives in the state legislature. Only persons qualified to vote for governor shall be entitled to vote for delegates to said convention.

Section 5. *Nomination of delegates; nomination petitions.* Candidates for election as delegates shall be nominated by petition and shall be residents of the electoral district in which they are candidates. Nomination petitions shall be prepared and distributed by the secretary of state and shall specify as to each candidate, his name, his residence, the electoral district or division in which he is a candidate. The total number of signatures for the nomination of each candidate or delegate must amount in the aggregate to at least two per cent and not more than four per cent of the total vote cast for governor in the election held on the 2nd Monday of September, 1932, in the electoral district or division within which such candidate is to be voted for, provided, however, that each petition must be signed by at least 150 qualified voters. There shall not be in any nomination petition the name of more than one candidate proposed for nomination. Only persons qualified to vote for delegates shall sign a nomination petition and each signer shall make his signature in person, to which shall be added his place of residence. Each signer shall subscribe his name to only such number of petitions as there are delegates to be elected in the electoral district or division in which such nomination is proposed. One of the signers of each separate petition or the person circulating the peti-

* *Maine Acts and Resolves of 1933,* Chapter 83, pp. 840-843.

tion shall make oath thereto that he believes the signatures are genuine and that the persons signing the same are qualified voters within the electoral district or division for which the nomination is proposed. Nomination petitions shall not be signed prior to the date of the taking effect of this act. All petitions shall be filed with the secretary of state on or before the 11th day of August, 1933.

Section 6. *Contents of ballot.* The ballots shall contain the names and residences of all candidates duly nominated in the county in which such candidates are to be voted upon, the names to be arranged in alphabetical order.

Appropriate instructions at the head of the ballot shall instruct the voter as to the number of candidates to be voted for.

The ballot shall contain in addition to the names and the instructions, a statement in appropriate language setting forth the purpose of the convention and the language of the proposed amendment to the constitution of the United States. The persons to the number to be elected in the county in which the said persons are candidates who shall receive the highest number of votes shall be declared to be elected. In case of a tie between two or more persons the person or persons elected shall be determined in the manner provided by law in the case of a tie in a primary election.

Section 7. *Canvass of returns.* The result of the election shall be canvassed by the governor and council in accordance with the provisions of law governing the canvassing of the returns in general elections; the delegates-elect shall be notified of their election and the roll of convention shall be prepared by the secretary of state as in the case of election to the legislature.

Section 8. *Certified roll of delegates to be furnished to secretary of senate.* The secretary of state shall on or before the day preceding the meeting of the convention furnish to the secretary of the senate a certified roll under the seal of the state with the names and residences of the delegates-elect according to the report of the governor and council and shall report the vacancies if any exist.

Section 9. *Convening of convention.* The secretary of the senate at 10 o'clock in the forenoon on the day appointed for the meeting of the convention as provided in section 1 shall call the delegates-elect present to order and from the certified roll furnished him as aforesaid shall call their names and if a quorum respond, he shall preside until they are qualified and a president of the convention is elected and if no quorum appear, he shall preside and the delegates present shall adjourn from day to day until a quorum appear and are qualified and a president is elected. In case of a vacancy in the office of the secretary of the senate, the clerk of the house shall act in his stead.

Section 10. *Administration of oath.* The governor shall administer the oath to the delegates-elect as the same is administered to members of the legislature.

Section 11. *Organization of convention.* The convention shall be the judge of the qualification and election of its own members and shall organize by the election of a president and a secretary with such subordinate officers as may be in the opinion of the convention necessary for the transaction of its business.

Section 12. *Compensation.* Delegates to the convention shall draw the same mileage as members of the legislature and shall receive as compensation for their services $5 each.

Section 13. *Journal of the convention.* The convention shall keep a journal of its proceedings in which shall be recorded the vote of each delegate on the question of ratification of the proposed amendment. Upon final adjournment the journal shall be filed with the secretary of state.

Section 14. *Certification of ratification.* If the convention shall agree, by vote of a majority of the total number of delegates, to the ratification of the proposed amendment, a certificate to that effect shall be executed by the president and secretary of the convention and transmitted to the secretary of state of this state, who shall transmit a copy thereof under the great seal of the state to the secretary of state of the United States.

Section 15. *Report of candidates' expenditure.* Every candidate for nomination as a delegate shall report to the secretary of state all expenditures made and all liabilities incurred by him in behalf of his election; and every person, firm, association, committee, organization or corporation making any expenditure or incurring any liability in aid of the election of any candidate shall report to the secretary of state all expenditures made and all liabilities incurred to the amount of $5 or more in behalf of such candidate. Such reports shall be in the form prescribed in chapter 263 of the laws of 1931 for the return of expenditures in a primary election. One report shall be made 10 days prior to the date of said election and a second report shall be made so as to reach the office of the secretary of state not later than 10 o'clock in the forenoon of the 7th day preceding said election which said reports shall be published by the secretary of state in all the daily newspapers published in the state not later than the 5th day next preceding said election. A final report shall be filed with the secretary of state not later than 15 days next following said election. Any statement in any of said reports which is wilfully false shall be deemed to be perjury and shall be punished accordingly.

Section 16. *Provisions in case of a referendum.* In the event that this act shall be referred to the people under the provisions of article XXXI of the Constitution and its operation suspended so that the election cannot be held on the second Monday in September as provided in section 3 a special election shall be held on a date to be fixed by the governor by proclamation not more than 3 months after this act becomes effective if it becomes effective by vote of the people at referendum election. In such event all of the provisions of this act shall apply to the election date so fixed by proclamation of the governor the nominations to be filed not less than 20 days before the date of the election. The nominating petitions to be available for signature at least 30 days before said date and the convention to be held 28 days after the date of such election.

Approved March 31, 1933.

MARYLAND*

AN ACT to provide for a Convention in the State of Maryland, for the ratification or rejection of the proposed amendment to the Constitution of the United States, repealing the Eighteenth Article of Amendment to said Constitution, and prohibiting the transportation or importation in any State, Territory or Possession of the United States for delivery or use therein of intoxicating liquors in violation of the laws thereof, which said amendment has been proposed by the Congress of the United States in accordance with Article V of the Constitution of the United States.

WHEREAS, The Congress of the United States on the 20th day of February, 1933, by a Resolution duly passed in accordance with Article V of the Constitution of the United States proposed the following amendment to the Constitution of the United States:

JOINT RESOLUTION

PROPOSING AN AMENDMENT TO THE CONSTITUTION OF THE UNITED STATES

Resolved, by the Senate and House of Representatives of the United States of America in Congress assembled (two-thirds of each House concurring therein), That the following Article is hereby proposed as an amendment to the Constitution of the United States, which shall be valid to all intents and purposes as part of the Constitution when ratified by Conventions in three-fourths of the several States:

ARTICLE ___

"Section 1. The Eighteenth Article of Amendment to the Constitution of the United States is hereby repealed.

"Section 2. The transportation or importation into any State, Territory, or Possession of the United States for delivery or use therein of intoxicating liquors, in violation of the laws thereof, is hereby prohibited.

"Section 3. This Article shall be inoperative unless it shall have been ratified as an amendment to the Constitution by Conventions in the several States, as provided in the Constitution, within seven years from the date of the submission hereof to the States by the Congress." And

WHEREAS, It is deemed to be the duty of the State of Maryland, acting through the General Assembly, the duly constituted law-making body for said State, to provide for the calling of a Convention to ratify or reject the aforesaid proposed amendment to the Constitution of the United States, with reasonable promptness and without unnecessary delay, therefore,

Section 1. *Be it enacted by the General Assembly of Maryland,* That on the 12th day of September, 1933, there shall be a special election in the State of Maryland at which there shall be elected by the legally qualified voters in each Congressional District, three delegates, and in the State at large six delegates, (making a total of twenty-four Delegates) to the Convention provided for by this Act.

* *Maryland Laws, 1933,* Chapter 253, pp. 447-454.

Section 2. *And be it further enacted,* That at the said special election all persons who are entered upon the registry books as qualified voters shall be entitled to vote and in addition thereto all persons who are entitled to be registered as legally qualified voters of this State shall be permitted to register and vote on said day of election.

Section 3. *And be it further enacted,* That except as otherwise provided in this Act, said special election shall be conducted and the results thereof ascertained and certified in accordance with the Constitution and laws of this State relating to elections for the Senate and House of Delegates of Maryland.

Section 4. *And be it further enacted,* That no person shall be eligible as a Delegate to said Convention who, at the time of the election, is not a citizen of the State of Maryland, and who has not resided therein for at least three years next preceding the date of the election and the last year thereof, in the case of Delegates from the Congressional Districts, in the Congressional District which he or she may be chosen to represent; nor shall any person be eligible as a Delegate who has not attained the age of twenty-five years and no person holding any office or employment under the United States, the State of Maryland, or any County, City, town or political sub-division thereof, shall be eligible as a Delegate to said Convention.

Section 5. *And be it further enacted,* That there shall be no primary election for the nomination of Delegates to said Convention. The candidates for election to said Convention shall be nominated in the following manner:

(A) There shall be a nominating Committee consisting of twenty-nine members, one from each county and legislative district as follows:

Baltimore City	Name	Address
1st Legis. Dist.	William F. Jacobs	120 S. Washington St.
2nd Legis. Dist.	William L. Rawls	Maryland Trust Bldg.
3rd Legis. Dist.	Harry G. Talbot	604 Venable Avenue
4th Legis. Dist.	Louis N. Frank	1007 W. North Ave.
5th Legis. Dist.	James T. Verney	3121 Presbury St.
6th Legis. Dist.	Gilbert A. Dailey	129 E. Redwood St.

County	Name	Address
Allegany	Thomas B. Finan	Cumberland
Anne Arundel	George T. Cromwell	Ferndale
Baltimore	Harrison Rider	Towson
Calvert	H. Clare Briscoe	Ireland Creek
Caroline	Charles B. Harrison	Preston
Carroll	James M. Shriver	Westminster
Cecil	James F. Evans	Elkton
Charles	Thomas P. McDonagh	LaPlata
Dorchester	Samuel L. Byrn	Cambridge
Frederick	James H. Cramer	Frederick
Garrett	Asa T. Matthews	Oakland
Harford	Robert H. Archer	Belair
Howard	Joshua N. Warfield	Florence
Kent	Marion deK. Smith, Jr.	Chestertown

Montgomery	J. Bond Smith	Tacoma Park
Pr. George's	George N. Palmer	Seat Pleasant
Queen Anne's	Dr. C. H. Metcalfe	Sudlersville
St. Mary's	Dr. Francis F. Greenwell	Leonardtown
Somerset	Edgar A. Jones	Princess Anne
Talbot	T. Hughlett Henry	Easton
Washington	J. Vincent Jamison, Jr.	Hagerstown
Wicomico	Paul E. Watson	Salisbury
Worcester	Horace Davis	Berlin

(B) Promptly after the taking effect of this Act, the Governor shall call a meeting of the above named Committee at such time and place as he may designate, and at said meeting the said Committee shall organize by the election of a Chairman and Secretary, and adopt such rules as it may deem proper for the selection of candidates as hereinafter provided.

(C) The said Committee shall nominate from each of the Congressional Districts, three candidates, and from the State at large, six candidates, who shall have declared an intention to vote for the ratification of the proposed amendment to the Constitution of the United States; in like manner the said Committee shall nominate from each Congressional District, three candidates, and from the State at large, six candidates, who shall have declared an intention to vote against the ratification of said proposed amendment; and in like manner the said Committee shall nominate from each Congressional District, three candidates, and from the State at large six candidates, who are unpledged with respect to the ratification of said proposed amendment.

(D) That on or before the first day of August, 1933, the said Committee shall make its selection of candidates as above provided, and the selections so made shall be filed with the Secretary of State on or before said date under the signature of the Chairman and Secretary of said Committee. The nominations shall be without party designation, but each certificate shall plainly indicate which of said candidates have indicated an intention to vote for the ratification of the proposed amendment which have indicated an intention to vote against the ratification of said proposed amendment and which are unpledged with respect to the ratification of said proposed amendment.

Section 6. *And be it further enacted,* That in addition to the candidates nominated by the Committee as above provided, other candidates may be nominated at any time after August 1st, 1933, in the manner provided by Section 51 of Article 33 of the Code of Public General Laws, provided the petition of nomination be filed with the Secretary of State not later than twenty days before the day of election. Each such petition shall plainly state whether the candidate nominated thereby has expressed an intention to vote for the ratification of the proposed amendment to the Constitution or against the ratification of said proposed amendment.

Section 7. *And be it further enacted,* That not less than eighteen days before the day of election, the Secretary of State shall certify to the Boards of Supervisors of Elections for each County and for Baltimore City, all of the candidates for Delegates at large who have been nominated as above provided, and to the respective Boards of Supervisors of the several counties and of Baltimore City, all of said candidates for whom the voters of said respective counties or city, will be entitled to vote.

Section 8. *And be it further enacted,* That said election shall be by ballot which shall be in the following form:

"OFFICIAL BALLOT

"The Congress of the United States has proposed an amendment to the Constitution of the United States to read as follows:

"Section 1. The Eighteenth Article of Amendment to the Constitution of the United States is hereby repealed.

"Section 2. The transportation or importation into any State, Territory, or Possession of the United States for delivery or use therein of intoxicating liquors in violation of the law thereof is hereby prohibited.

"Section 3. This Article shall be inoperative unless it shall have been ratified as an amendment to the Constitution by Conventions in the several States, as provided in the Constitution within seven years from the date of the submission hereof to the States by the Congress."

The Legislature of Maryland has provided for the holding of this special election for the selection of delegates to assemble in Convention for the purpose of ratifying or rejecting the aforesaid amendment.

The following candidates for delegate at large have indicated an intention to vote for the ratification of the above mentioned amendment.	The following candidates for delegate at large have indicated an intention to vote against the ratification of the above mentioned amendment.	The following candidates for delegate at large are unpledged with respect to the ratification of the above mentioned amendment.
	Vote for six	
(Here insert the names of the candidates in alphabetical order who have been nominated and have indicated an intention to vote for the ratification of the amendment, with the customary separate box arrangement)	(Here insert the names of the candidates in alphabetical order who have been nominated and have indicated an intention to vote against the ratification of the amendment, with the customary box arrangement)	(Here insert the names of the candidates in alphabetical order who have been nominated and are unpledged with respect to the ratification or rejection of the amendment, with the customary box arrangement)
The following candidates have indicated an intention to vote for the ratification of the above mentioned amendment.	The following candidates have indicated an intention to vote against the ratification of the above mentioned amendment.	The following candidates are unpledged with respect to the ratification of the above mentioned amendment.
	Vote for Three	
(Here insert the name of the candidates in alphabetical order who have indicated an intention to vote for the ratification of the amendment, with the customary separate box arrangement)	(Here insert the name of the candidates in alphabetical order who have indicated an intention to vote against the ratification of the amendment, with the customary separate box arrangement)	(Here insert the name of the candidates in alphabetical order who are unpledged with respect to the ratification or rejection of the amendment, with the customary box arrangement)

On the back and outside of all ballots shall be printed the words "Official Ballot For," followed by the designation of the city or county for which it is prepared, the date of the election and a facsimile of the signature of the President and the Board of Supervisors of Elections by whom the ballots have been prepared.

Section 9. *And be it further enacted,* That the six candidates at large and the three candidates in each of the several Congressional Districts, receiving the highest number of votes, shall be the Delegates to the Convention.

Section 10. *And be it further enacted,* That the Delegates elected as aforesaid, shall meet at the State House at Annapolis on the 18th day of October, 1933, at noon, and shall thereupon constitute a Convention to pass upon the question of whether the proposed amendment to the Constitution of the United States shall be ratified or rejected. If there shall be a vacancy in the Convention caused by death, absence, disability or any other cause, the same shall be filled by appointment by the remaining Delegates to said Convention, provided that any person selected to fill a vacancy shall be a resident of the same District in which the deceased, disqualified, or absent Delegate had his residence, and shall before his appointment declare his intention to vote in accordance with the expressed intention of the duly elected Delegate whose place in the Convention he is selected to fill.

Section 11. *And be it further enacted,* That the Convention shall be the judge of election and qualification of its members and shall have the power to elect its President, Secretary and such other officers as it may deem necessary. The said Convention shall also have power to adopt rules for the transaction of the business of said Convention.

Section 12. *And be it further enacted,* That the Convention shall keep a Journal of its proceedings in which shall be recorded the vote of each Delegate on the question of the ratification of the proposed amendment, which said Journal shall be filed with and remain in the office of the Secretary of State at Annapolis

Section 13. *And be it further enacted,* That if a majority of the total number of Delegates to said Convention shall vote for the ratification of the proposed amendment, a certificate to that effect shall be executed by the President and Secretary of the Convention and transmitted to the Secretary of State of this State who shall transmit the said certificate under the Great Seal of the State of Maryland to the Secretary of State of the United States.

Section 14. *And be it further enacted,* That no Delegate to said Convention shall receive any compensation or reimbursement for expenses incurred in connection with his election or attendance at said Convention.

Section 15. *And be it further enacted,* That the Judges and Clerks of Election who shall act at the special election provided for by this Act, shall be entitled to receive as compensation for their services in connection with said election, one-third of the compensation paid to such officials at the Presidential Election of 1932. The respective Boards of Supervisors of Elections shall have full power and authority to fill any vacancy that may exist in the office of any Judge or Clerk, and vacancies occurring on the day of election may be filled in the manner now provided by law.

Section 16. *And be it further enacted,* That it shall be the duty of the respective Boards of Supervisors of Elections to make all necessary arrangements for the holding of said elections, including the selection of suitable polling places in the respective voting precincts throughout the State, at a rental not to exceed $5.00 in any one precinct.

Section 17. *And be it further enacted,* That if the Congress of the United States shall, by statute, prescribe a different manner in which the Convention of this State, to consider the ratification of the proposed amendment to the Constitution of the United States, shall be constituted, and shall not except from the provisions of such statute, such State statutes as may theretofore have provided for constituting such Conventions, the preceding provisions of this Act shall be inoperative, and the Convention shall be constituted and shall operate as the said Act of Congress shall direct, and all officers of the State who may by said statute be authorized or directed to take any action to constitute such Convention for this State are hereby authorized and directed to act thereunder and in obedience thereto, with the same force and effect as if acting under a statute of this State.

Section 18. *And be it further enacted,* That this Act shall take effect on June 1st, 1933.

Approved April 5, 1933.

MASSACHUSETTS*

AN ACT providing for a convention to act upon a proposed amendment to the Constitution of the United States relative to the repeal of the Eighteenth Amendment.

WHEREAS, In order that immediate action may be taken hereunder, if deemed urgent by the governor and council, this act is hereby declared to be an emergency law, necessary for the immediate preservation of the public convenience.

Be it enacted, etc., as follows:

Section 1. For the purpose of acting upon an amendment to the constitution of the United States proposed by a joint resolution of congress, whereof a certified copy has been transmitted by the department of state under date of February twenty-first, nineteen hundred and thirty-three, to his excellency the governor of the commonwealth, with the request that the same be submitted to a convention for such action as may be had, there shall meet in the state house in Boston a convention of delegates, elected as hereinafter provided. The convention shall be held at such time following the election of such delegates as the governor may determine.

Section 2. The number of delegates to the convention shall be forty-five, and each district established under section one of chapter fifty-seven of the General Laws, as appearing in the Tercentenary Edition thereof, for the purpose of electing representatives in the congress of the United States, shall elect three delegates, all of whom shall be residents of the district. Voters participating in such election shall have the qualifications prescribed by law of voters for state officers. The election of such delegates in the several districts shall occur at the biennial state election in the year nineteen hundred and thirty-four, or at a special state election, as the governor and council may order; and full power and authority are hereby vested in the governor and council to order such special election and to appoint the time for holding the same. A special election hereunder shall be held wholly or partly by wards, precincts or towns, as the election commissioners in Boston and the aldermen in other cities and selectmen in towns may designate, and they shall give notice of their determination to the state secretary on or before the sixth Tuesday preceding the day set for the election. In wards or towns where voting at elections is commonly by precincts, the election commissioners and city and town clerks shall designate which of the election officers shall serve, in case such election is held in larger units.

Section 3. As soon as may be after the date of the election of delegates hereunder has been determined as provided in section two, the governor, lieutenant governor, councillors, state secretary, state treasurer, attorney general and state auditor shall, on the call of the governor, meet in caucus in the state house for the purpose of nominating candidates to be voted for in the several districts at such election. The caucus may adopt rules for its procedure and may adjourn from time to time. The governor and state secretary shall respectively serve as its president and clerk. The caucus shall nominate by a majority vote a group of three candidates from each district favoring ratification of the proposed amendment and a group of three candidates from each district opposing such ratification, as evidenced by signed statements of their respective

* *Massachusetts Acts and Resolves, 1933,* Chapter 132, pp. 161-163.

positions on the question of ratification filed with the clerk of the caucus. A return of the proceedings of the caucus and of its nominees, grouped in accordance with their position in relation to the ratification of the proposed amendment, shall be filed in the office of the state secretary, certified by the president and clerk of the caucus, not later than the fifth Tuesday preceding the day of the election. In case of any vacancy occurring in the list of nominees in any district, the remaining nominees from the same district and in the same group shall, if the time is sufficient therefor, fill the same.

Section 4. The provisions of law relative to ballots used in the election of state officers shall apply, so far as applicable, and except as otherwise provided herein, to ballots used in the election of delegates under this act. The names of the persons nominated for each district under section three shall appear on the ballots to be used therein, arranged alphabetically by their surnames in groups as nominated, one group under the designation:—"Delegates Favoring Ratification (For Repeal)" and the other group under the designation:—"Delegates Opposed to Ratification (Against Repeal)." To the name of each candidate shall be added the name of the street, with street number, if any, and the name of the city or town, where he resides. The relative positions of the two groups on the ballot shall be determined by the state secretary by lot. Directly preceding the aforesaid designations shall appear the following general heading:—"Election of Delegates to a Constitutional Convention called to Ratify or Reject the Following Amendment to the Constitution of the United States, proposed by Joint Resolution of Congress." Then shall follow the text of the proposed amendment. No designation, save as aforesaid, shall appear in connection with any name appearing on the ballot. No name of any candidate, except of nominees under section three, shall be printed on the ballot, but three blank spaces shall be left in which the voter may insert the name of any legal voter of the district not printed on the ballot for whom he desires to vote.

Section 5. All laws governing the election of state officers, including the canvassing, recount and return of votes therefor and the determination of the results of the voting, shall, so far as applicable and except as otherwise provided in this act, apply to the election of delegates under this act. No ballots cast at the election of delegates under this act shall be counted until the close of the polls. The time within which copies of records of votes cast under this act shall be transmitted to the state secretary, as provided in section one hundred and twelve of chapter fifty-four of the General Laws, shall be seven days.

Section 6. The state secretary shall, as soon as the results of the election have been finally determined, notify the successful candidates of their election and shall summon them to meet in convention in the state house at such time as shall have been designated for the convening thereof. The governor shall call the convention to order and shall preside thereover until a president is chosen. The state secretary shall call the roll of the delegates and act as clerk of the convention until a clerk is chosen. The delegates shall be judges of the returns and elections of the members of the convention. The convention shall proceed to organize by the choice of a president, clerk and such other officers as it may determine, and by establishing rules for its procedure. Twenty-three delegates shall constitute a quorum. Upon the completion of its organization, the convention shall take into consideration the advisability and propriety of ratifying or rejecting the amendment to the constitution submitted as aforesaid and shall vote to ratify or reject the same. The convention shall be provided by the superintendent of buildings, at the expense of the commonwealth, with suitable quarters and facilities for exercising its functions. The members shall receive no compensation for their services, but shall each be entitled to receive the sum of ten cents for every mile of ordinary traveling distance from his place of abode to the place of sitting of the convention. The convention shall, subject to the approval of the governor and council, provide for such other necessary expenses of its session as it shall deem expedient. The governor, with the advice and consent of the council, is hereby authorized to draw his warrant on the treasury for any of the foregoing expenses.

Section 7. If the convention ratifies such proposed amendment to the constitution of the United States by a majority of its members present and voting, the president of the convention shall thereupon transmit to the governor duly authenticated certificates of the action of the convention, in triplicate, and thereupon the governor shall transmit to the secretary of state of the United States one of said triplicates, duly authenticated by the state secretary under the great seal of the commonwealth. Another of said triplicates, authenticated in like manner, shall be deposited by the state secretary in the state archives.

Approved April 20, 1933.

MICHIGAN*

AN ACT to provide for a convention for the purpose of ratifying or rejecting the twenty-first amendment to the Constitution of the United States of America.

The People of the State of Michigan enact:

Delegates to convention to consider twenty-first amendment; election.

Section 1. At the biennial spring election to be held on the first Monday of April, nineteen hundred thirty-three, delegates shall be elected to meet in convention for the purpose of ratifying or rejecting the twenty-first amendment to the constitution of the United States of America proposed by joint resolution of the Congress of the United States of America.

Same; number, qualified electors.

Section 2. The number of delegates to such convention shall be one hundred consisting of one delegate from each representative district in this state now existing: *Provided,* That in districts having more than one representative, they shall elect the same number of delegates as they have representatives in the house of representatives. Each person entitled by law to vote for members of the legislature shall be entitled to vote in the election provided for in section one of this bill for as many delegates to the convention hereinafter provided for as there are representatives in the house of representatives from the district in which such elector resides. The person or persons to a number equal to the number of representatives in the house of representatives from such district receiving the highest number of votes for delegates to said convention in each representative district shall be elected delegate.

Same; nomination.

Section 3. Delegates from each representative district to said convention shall be nominated by a board consisting of the respective judges of probate, county clerks, and prosecuting attorneys of the county or counties in which such representative district lies, who shall meet at least fifteen days before said election and select two candidates for delegates to such convention by such methods as they may desire, one of whom shall pledge himself to vote for ratification of the said twenty-first amendment to the constitution of the United States of America, and one of whom shall pledge himself to vote for rejection of said twenty-first amendment to the constitution of the United States of America before accepting such nomination. In districts comprising more than one county, the county clerk of the county having the largest population as determined by the United States census of nineteen hundred thirty, shall call a meeting, naming the time and place, of the judges of probate, county clerks, and prosecuting attorneys of the several counties in the district for the purpose of nominating candidates as provided herein.

Same; qualification, vacancies.

Section 4. Such candidates shall be citizens of this state, above the age of twenty-one years, and a resident of the districts in which they are candidates. In case a vacancy occurs at any time by reason of death, resignation, or failure to nominate and

* *Michigan Public Acts, 1933,* No. 28, pp. 24-26.

elect under the provisions of this act, or otherwise, the governor may appoint some duly qualified resident of such district, pledged as aforesaid, to fill such vacancy, and the person so appointed shall, by virtue of such appointment, be a member of such convention and in all respects have the same rights as if he had been originally elected delegate.

Same; certification of candidates.

Section 5. The nominating board provided for in section three shall forthwith prepare and certify to the secretary of the state who shall immediately certify to the election commissioners of each county the names of the candidates for delegates so selected. The various county clerks and boards of county election commissioners shall then proceed in accordance with the general election laws of this state.

Same; canvass and declaration of election.

Section 6. The returns of such election of delegates shall be canvassed and the results declared in the same manner and by the same officers as is provided for in the general election laws for canvassing all returns and declaring the results in general elections.

Same; ballots.

Section 7. The board of election commissioners in each county shall cause the names of the candidates for delegates to such convention to be printed on one ballot, separate from any other ballot, which ballot shall be in the following form:

"Delegates to the convention called for the purpose of ratifying or rejecting the following proposed amendment to the constitution of the United States of America":

"Section 1. The Eighteenth Article of Amendment to the Constitution of the United States is hereby repealed."

"Section 2. The transportation or importation into any state, territory or possession of the United States for delivery or use therein of intoxicating liquors, in violation of the laws thereof, is hereby prohibited."

"Delegation for the repeal of the Eighteenth Amendment and ratification of the Twenty-first Amendment."

☐ John Doe

"Delegation against the repeal of the Eighteenth Amendment and ratification of the Twenty-first Amendment."

☐ Richard Roe

Convention; time, place and organization.

Section 8. The delegates so chosen shall meet in convention in the hall of the house of representatives in the Capitol in the City of Lansing on the tenth day of April, nineteen hundred thirty-three, at ten o'clock in the forenoon. A majority of the delegates elected shall constitute a quorum for the transaction of business, but a small number will have the power to adjourn from day to day and compel the attendance of absent members. The lieutenant governor shall be president of said convention and said convention shall elect one of their own number as president pro tem. The clerk of the house of representatives shall be the secretary of the convention, and the sergeant-at-arms, committee clerks and stenographers of the house of representatives shall be the sergeant-at-arms, committee clerks and stenographers of the convention. They shall adopt their own rules of order, shall be the absolute judges of the election, qualification and return of their own members and may punish for contempt by fine or imprisonment in their discretion, but no term of imprisonment shall continue beyond the date of the final adjournment of the convention. The convention shall have the power to fix the duties and compensation of its officers and employees. The delegates shall receive no compensation, but shall receive ten cents per mile for each mile traveled by the nearest practical route for going to and coming from the place of holding the convention. The compensation of the officers and employees of the convention, and expenses of the delegates and all incidental expenses of the convention shall be paid in the same manner as provided by law for the payment of similar claims in the legislature. The secretary of state shall certify to said convention at the opening thereof the names of the delegates and the district they represent according to the returns on file in his office. The lieutenant governor shall attend the said convention at the opening thereof and call the convention to order. He shall then direct the secretary to read the communication from the secretary of state certifying the names of the delegates and the districts they represent. The secretary of the convention shall arrange the names in alphabetical order, and the roll shall be called in that order. The delegates shall then take and subscribe the constitutional oath of office, which shall be administered by the president of the convention. The delegates shall be assigned to seats now occupied by the member of the legislature from their respective districts. The president of the convention shall preside at all meetings of the convention, but shall have no vote therein. All votes shall be taken by yea and nay and entered upon the journal.

Same; journal and debates, open sessions, privileges of delegates.

Section 9. A journal of the proceedings of such convention shall be kept, and the journal and debates of the convention shall be published in such form and style as may be determined by the convention, and when so published they shall be deemed the official records of the convention. The doors of the convention shall be kept open to the public during all of its sessions. Every delegate to the convention shall in all cases except treason, felony or breach of the peace, be privileged from arrest. They shall not be subject to any civil proceedings during the session of the convention or for fifteen days next before the convention and after the final adjournment of the same. For any speech or debate in the convention, the members shall not be questioned in any other place.

Same; certification of action.

Section 10. After the convention shall have ratified or rejected the proposed Twenty-first Amendment to the constitution of the United States of America, the lieutenant governor shall certify to the secretary of state and the secretary of state shall certify, as to the action taken, and forward such certificate to the secretary of state of the United States of America.

Nomination and election of delegates.

Section 11. Such candidates shall be nominated, certified and elected as hereinbefore provided, any provisions in the general election laws to the contrary notwithstanding.

This act is ordered to take immediate effect.

Approved March 11, 1933.

MINNESOTA*

AN ACT to provide for a convention to pass on the proposed amendment to the Constitution of the United States which has been proposed by the Congress of the United States for ratification by conventions in the several states.

Be it enacted by the Legislature of the State of Minnesota:

Section 1. *Constitutional convention to be held September 12, 1933.*—The Congress of the United States, having proposed an amendment to the Constitution of the United States, and having proposed that it be ratified by conventions in several states, an election shall be held for the purpose of electing delegates to such a convention in this state. Such election shall be a special election, for that purpose only, to be held on September 12, 1933.

Section 2. *Persons entitled to vote.*—At such election all persons qualified to vote for members of the Legislature shall be entitled to vote.

Section 3. *Conduct of election.*—Except as in this Act otherwise provided such election shall be conducted and the results thereof ascertained and certified in the same manner as in the case of the election of Presidential Electors in this State, and all provisions of the Laws of this State relative to elections except so far as inconsistent with this Act are hereby made applicable to such election.

Section 4. *Delegates.*—The number of Delegates to be chosen to such Convention shall be 21, to be elected from the State at large.

Section 5. *Candidates for delegate.*—Candidates for the office of Delegate to the Convention shall be citizens and residents of the State and of age. Nomination shall be by petition and not otherwise and shall be filed with the Secretary of State. A single petition may nominate any number of candidates not exceeding the total number of Delegates to be elected, and shall be signed by not less than 100 voters. Nomination shall be without party or political designation, but the nominating petitions shall contain a statement as to each nominee, to the effect that he favors ratification, or that he opposes ratification, and no nominating petition shall contain the name of any nominee whose petition as stated therein is inconsistent with that of any other nominee as stated therein. Each nominee shall file a statement of acceptance or declination with the Secretary of State, stating he will or will not accept the nomination. No nomination shall be effective except those of the 21 nominees in favor of ratification, and the 21 nominees against ratification, whose nominating petitions have respectively been signed by the largest number of voters, ties to be decided by lot drawn by the Secretary of State. At least 60 days before the election the Secretary of State shall certify the candidates of each group to the county auditor of each county, and shall transmit at that time all petitions and acceptances and a sufficient number of suitable blank forms for lists, registers and affidavits, and such other blanks as are required in preparation for and conduct of such election; also copies of this act, or so much thereof as pertains to the duties of election officers. The auditor shall forthwith deliver to the clerk of each city, town and village in his county the necessary copies of each of such blanks, and one copy of the law for each judge.

* *Minnesota Laws, 1933,* Chapter 214, pp. 272-276.

Section 6. *Election by ballot.*—The election shall be by ballot, separate from any ballot to be used at the same election which shall be prepared as follows: It shall first state the substance of the proposed Amendment.

PROPOSED AMENDMENT

Section 1. The Eighteenth Article of Amendment to the Constitution of the United States is hereby repealed.

Section 2. The transportation or importation into any state, territory or possession of the United States for delivery or use therein of intoxicating liquors in violation of the laws thereof, is hereby prohibited.

Section 3. This article shall be inoperative unless ratified by constitutional conventions in the several states within seven years from date of submission hereof to the states by Congress.

This shall be followed by appropriate instructions to the voter. The ballots to be used in voting for delegates shall be constructed as is now by law required, but said ballots shall have spaces four-eighths of an inch wide and three-eighths of an inch high in which the voter may designate his choice on the right edge of the ballot, same being formed as described in Mason's Minnesota Statutes of 1927, Section 537-5.

Section 7. *Ballots.*—Nominees' names shall be grouped and printed together, the names of each group to be arranged in the order in which they were filed. The Secretary of State shall cause the names of the nominees of each group to be printed in capital letters, set in six point type, the names to be arranged in two columns. Each group shall be designated "For Repeal" and/or "Against Repeal," as the case may be. The designation shall appear but once for each group, said designation following a scroll or bracket on the right, and immediately following this, in the center, shall be printed in bold type "For Repeal" and/or "Against Repeal." To the right of, and on a line such surnames, near the margin, shall be placed a square in which the voter may indicate his choice by a mark (X), and one such mark opposite a group of nominees shall be counted as a vote for each nominee in such group, the form of each group to be substantially as follows:

John Doe Richard Roe }	For Repeal	☐
Frank Smith John Smith }	Against Repeal	☐

The relative positions of each group shall be determined by the rules applicable to other state officers. The groups of nominees shall be separated by a blank space one quarter of an inch in width and no blank lines shall be printed therein as in the case of other candidates or groups. Above the names of the nominees shall be printed in bold type, "VOTE ONCE OPPOSITE EITHER GROUP."

Section 8. *General election laws to govern.*—The qualification of voters, the preparation of ballots and the returns thereof, the canvassing, the certifications, and laws governing elections not stated in this act shall be in the manner provided by law with reference to the election of state officers.

Section 9. *Vacancies.*—The 21 nominees who shall receive the highest number of votes shall be the Delegates to the Convention. If there shall be a vacancy in the Convention caused by the death or disability of any delegate or any other cause, the same shall be filled by appointment by the majority vote of the delegates comprising the group from which such delegate was elected and if the Convention contains no other delegate of that group, shall be filled by the Governor.

Section 10. *Constitutional convention.*—The Delegates to the Convention shall meet at the Capitol on the twenty-eighth day after their election at 12 o'clock noon and shall thereupon constitute a Convention to pass upon the question of whether or not the proposed Amendment shall be ratified.

Section 11. *Convention to be judge of election of delegates.*—The Convention shall be the judge of the election and qualification of its members; and shall have power to elect its president, secretary and other officers, and to adopt its own rules.

Section 12. *Convention to keep record of proceedings.*—The Convention shall keep a journal of its proceedings in which shall be recorded the vote of each Delegate on the question of ratification of the proposed Amendment. Upon final adjournment the Journal shall be filed with the Secretary of State.

Section 13. *Shall certify results to Secretary of State of the United States.*—If the Convention shall agree, by vote of a majority of the total number of Delegates, to the ratification of the proposed amendment, a certificate to that effect shall be executed by the President and Secretary of the Convention and transmitted to the Secretary of State of this State, who shall transmit the certificate under the Great Seal of the State to the Secretary of State of the United States.

Section 14. *Compensation of delegates.*—The compensation for services performed under this act shall be as follows:

1. To delegates, $5.00 for each day's attendance at the Capitol and 5c for each mile necessarily travelled in going to and returning from St. Paul.

Section 15. This Act shall be in force and effect from and after its passage and approval.

Approved April 13, 1933.

MISSOURI*

AN ACT authorizing the Governor, by proclamation to call an election for the election of delegates to a state convention, to be held for the purpose of voting upon the ratification of any amendment to the Constitution of the United States of America, proposed by the Congress thereof, and submitted to the several states for ratification by the convention method; providing for the nomination of candidates for delegates to such conventions, and the manner of their election; and making the election laws of this state, insofar as such laws will apply, applicable to the election of such delegates.

Be it enacted by the General Assembly of the State of Missouri, as follows:

Section 1. *Special election to be called by governor—when.*—Whenever the Congress of the United States of America shall propose an amendment to the Constitution thereof and submit such amendment to the several States for ratification by Conventions, such Delegates shall be elected at a special election to be called and held on the date fixed by the Governor and his Official Proclamation calling said election, within six months next following the submission of the Amendment to the Constitution of the United States of America upon which the Delegates to be elected shall vote.

Section 2. *Date of election—judges and clerks—duties.*—For the purpose of electing delegates to any convention to vote upon the ratification of any proposed amendment to the Constitution of the United States, the Governor is hereby authorized by proclamation to call a special election and fix the date of holding thereof, which shall not be held within ninety days of the date of any primary or any general election in this state. For each such special election there shall be appointed by the county court two judges and two clerks who are in favor of the proposed amendment and two judges and two clerks who are opposed to the proposed amendment, who shall be qualified electors within their respective precinct. In all other respects, such special election in each precinct in this state shall be conducted under the provisions of the election laws of this state, insofar as such laws shall apply and the judges and clerks of each such election shall be paid in the manner provided by law of paying the costs of special elections, and shall perform the duties required and be subject to the

* *Missouri Laws, 1933,* [H.B. 514], pp. 233-237.

penalties imposed upon judges and clerks of elections under the election laws of this state.

Section 3. *Number of delegates from each senatorial district—how elected.*—The state convention held under the provisions of this act shall be composed of two delegates elected from each senatorial district of this state, who shall be nominated in the manner hereinafter provided, and elected at large by the majority vote of the qualified electors of this state voting at the election for such delegates.

Section 4. *Governor to fix mass convention date—where held—manner and order of business.*—In his proclamation calling a State Convention under the authority of this act, the Governor shall fix the date and hour upon which the qualified electors of each precinct or voting district, of all counties and cities in the State having less than three hundred and fifty thousand inhabitants, shall meet in mass convention. Said mass conventions shall meet at places in such precinct or voting districts as shall be designated by the county court or board of election commissioners of such counties or cities, and elect 4 delegates, qualified electors of such precinct or voting district, to attend a county convention to be held at the county seat of such county on the date and hour fixed by the Governor in such proclamation; the qualified electors attending each precinct or voting district convention shall divide into two groups, one favoring and one opposing the proposed amendment, and each group shall elect 2 delegates to said county convention. The delegates so selected shall assemble in such county convention, and divide into two groups, one favoring and one opposing the proposed amendment, and each group shall elect 4 delegates to the senatorial district convention to be held on the date and hour and at the place in the senatorial district fixed by the Governor in such proclamation. In such proclamation, the Governor shall also fix the date and hour upon which the qualified electors of each precinct or voting district, of all counties and cities in the state having three hundred and fifty thousand inhabitants or more shall meet in mass convention at places in such precinct or voting district to be designated by the board or boards of election commissioners of such counties and cities, and elect 2 delegates, qualified electors of such precinct or voting district, to attend a senatorial district convention to be held on the date and hour and at the place in the senatorial district fixed by the Governor in such proclamation; the qualified electors attending each such precinct, or voting district convention shall divide into two groups, one favoring and one opposing the proposed amendment, and each group shall elect 1 delegate to said senatorial district convention.

Section 5. *Senatorial convention—favorable and opposing groups.*—The delegates so elected to Senatorial District Convention held under the authority of this act shall divide into two groups, one favoring and one opposing the proposed amendment, and each group shall nominate two candidates from such senatorial district to be voted upon at large by the qualified electors of their state as delegates to the State Convention, to be held at the State Capitol at the date and at the hour fixed by the Governor in such proclamation, to vote upon the ratification of the proposed amendment.

Section 6. *Governor to name delegates to state convention—when.*—If any county or senatorial district shall fail to meet for the election of delegates as in this act authorized, such failure shall in no manner affect the validity of any convention called and held under the provisions of this act, provided if any county or senatorial district shall fail to elect delegates as in this act authorized, the Governor shall, by proclamation, name from such district two candidates who are in favor of the proposed amendment and two candidates who are opposed to such amendment, and certify their names to the Secretary of State, at least twenty days before the date of the special election to be held for the election of delegates to such state convention.

Section 7. *Compensation of delegates to mass conventions.*—No per diem, mileage fees or other compensation whatsoever, shall be allowed by, or charged against the state or any county of this state for attendance at any mass meeting or district convention held under authority of this act.

Section 8. *Proposed amendment ballot.*—The names of any candidates for delegates to any convention held under the provisions of this act shall not be printed on the ballot, but the proposed amendment shall be printed on the ballot, followed by:

(1) For the delegates favoring the pending amendment to the Constitution of the United States.

(2) For the delegates opposing the pending amendment to the Constitution of the United States.

(To vote for the delegates favoring the pending amendment to the Constitution of the United States draw a line through clause 2.)

(To vote for the delegates opposing the pending amendment to the Constitution of the United States draw a line through clause 1.)

Section 9. *Persons receiving majority of votes shall be delegates.*—The persons whose names are filed with the Secretary of State as candidates for delegates to any convention held under the authority of this act, who shall receive a majority of the votes of the qualified electors of this State voting at any election held hereunder, whether for or against the pending amendment, shall constitute the delegates to such convention.

Section 10. *Delegates to meet at capitol twenty days after election.*—The delegates elected to any such state convention in the manner in this act provided shall meet at the State Capitol within twenty days after their election, on the date and hour fixed by proclamation of the Governor, and proceed to organize by the election of a chairman and a secretary, and when so organized shall immediately vote upon the proposed amendment and certify the result of such vote to the Secretary of State of the United States and the Secretary of State of the State of Missouri, who shall transmit said certificate under the great seal of the State of Missouri immediately to the Secretary of State of the United States of America. The certificate of said convention filed with the Secretary of State of the United States and the Secretary of State of the State of Missouri shall be signed by the chairman whose signature shall be attested by the Secretary of said convention.

Section 11. *Compensation of state delegates.*—As their sole and only compensation as delegates to any state convention held under the provisions of this act, such delegates shall be entitled to receive the sum of Ten Dollars ($10.00) if in actual attendance at said state convention, to be paid by appropriation out of State Revenue to be made by the General Assembly provided that the chairman and secretary of said convention shall certify the names of the delegates thereto, and the amount respectively due such delegates, to the state auditor, who shall issue his warrant upon the state treasury to the delegates to said convention for the respective amounts shown by such certificate as due such delegates.

Section 12. *Defining "proposed amendment."*—The phrase "the proposed amendment" shall be construed to refer to mean the pending amendment to the constitution of the United States of America, submitted to the several states of the union for ratification by conventions of the several states.

Section 13. *Shall publish notice of elections.*—Notice of the proposed amendment and the time and place of electing delegates to any convention called under the provisions of this act to vote upon the ratification thereof, shall be published by the authority and in the manner provided by law for the publications of notices of amendments to the Constitution of the State of Missouri.

Section 14. *Qualifications of delegates—powers of convention.*—No person shall be eligible to membership in any convention held under authority of this act, who is not a qualified elector of this State, and no such convention shall have power to take any action except to vote to ratify or reject the pending amendment to the Constitution of the United States proposed by the Congress thereof, and to certify to the Secretary of State of the United States and to the Secretary of State of the State of Missouri the result of such vote.

Approved April 13, 1933.

MONTANA*

AN ACT to Provide for Conventions to Ratify Proposed Amendments to the Constitution of the United States.

Be it enacted by the Legislative Assembly of the State of Montana:

Section 1. Whenever the Congress shall propose an amendment to the Constitution of the United States and shall propose that the same be ratified by convention in the states, a convention shall be held, as provided herein, for the purpose of ratifying such amendment.

Section 2. The number of delegates to be chosen to such convention shall be not less than one-half of the number of the members of the Legislative Assembly of Montana, and each county shall have one-half of the number of delegates as it is then entitled to elect members of the Legislative Assembly of Montana, provided, that when the number is an odd number, each county shall be entitled to one-half of the next even number. The delegates shall be elected at the next general election or primary nominating election held throughout the state, after the Congress has proposed the amendment, or at a special election to be called by the Governor, at his discretion, by proclamation at any time after the Congress has proposed the amendment, and except as otherwise provided herein, the election, in all respects, from the nomination of candidates to and including the certificate of election, shall be in accordance as nearly as may be with the laws of the state relating to the election of members of the Legislative Assembly of the state.

Section 3. Nomination of a candidate for the office of delegate shall be by petition, which shall be signed by not less than one hundred voters of the county. Nominations shall be without party or political designation, but shall be as "in favor of" or "opposed to" ratification of the proposed amendment. All petitions and the acceptances thereof shall be filed not less than thirty days prior to the election.

Section 4. The results of the election shall be determined as follows: The total number of votes cast for each candidate "in favor of" ratification, and the total number of votes cast for all candidates "in favor of " ratification and the total number of votes cast for each candidate "opposed to" ratification and the total number of votes cast for all candidates "opposed to" ratification shall be ascertained, and the candidates equal to the number to be elected receiving the highest number of votes from the side that casts the greater number of votes in favor of or opposed to ratification, as the case may be, shall be deemed elected.

Section 5. On the official ballot there shall be printed the proposed amendment, the names of candidates for delegates to the convention, and appropriate instructions to the voters, all in substantially the following form:

PROPOSED AMENDMENT TO THE CONSTITUTION OF THE UNITED STATES

Delegates to the Convention to Ratify the Proposed Amendment.

The Congress has proposed an amendment to the Constitution of the United States which provides, (insert here the substance of the proposed amendment).

* *Montana Laws, 1933,* Chapter 188, pp. 458-461.

The Congress has also proposed that the said amendment shall be ratified by conventions in the states.

In favor of	Opposed to
ratification of the proposed amendment.	ratification of the proposed amendment.
Vote for	Vote for ....
....	....
candidates only.	candidates only.
Names of candidates.	Names of candidates.

Section 6. The delegates to the convention shall meet at the State Capitol on the first Monday in the month following the election, at 10:00 o'clock A.M., and shall constitute a convention to act upon the proposed amendment to the Constitution of the United States

Section 7. A majority of the total number of delegates to the convention shall constitute a quorum. The convention shall have power to choose a President and Secretary, and all other necessary officers, and to make rules governing the procedure of the convention. It shall be the judge of the qualifications and election of its own members.

Section 8. Each delegate shall receive mileage and per diem as provided by law for members of the Legislative Assembly. The Secretary and other officers shall receive such compensation as may be fixed by the convention.

Section 9. When the convention shall have agreed by a majority of the vote of the total number of delegates in attendance at such convention, a certificate to that effect shall be executed by the President and Secretary of the convention, and transmitted to the Secretary of State of the United States.

Section 10. Those entitled to petition for the nomination of candidates and to vote at such election shall be determined as now provided by the registration laws of Montana.

Section 11. If the Congress shall either in the resolution submitting the proposed amendment, or by statute, prescribe the manner in which the convention shall be constituted, the preceding provisions of this Act shall be inoperative, and the convention shall be constituted and held as the said resolution or Act of Congress shall direct, and all officers of the State of Montana who may by said resolution or statute be authorized to direct, or be directed to take any action to constitute such a convention for this state, are hereby authorized and directed to act thereunder, and in obedience thereto, with the same force and effect as if acting under a statute of this state.

Section 12. This Act shall be in full force and effect from and after its passage and approval.

Approved March 17, 1933.

NEBRASKA*

Providing for a state convention to ratify or reject a proposed amendment repealing the Eighteenth (Prohibition) Amendment.

House Roll No. 602

Introduced by Representative Geo. W. O'Malley of Greeley by the specific message from Governor Charles W. Bryan.

AN ACT to provide for a convention to be called and held, in accordance with Article V. of the Constitution of the United States, to ratify or reject an amendment to said Constitution, relating to the Eighteenth Article of the Amendments thereto, proposed by the Congress of the United States; for the nomination, election and compensation of delegates to such convention, and for the payment of expenses incident thereto.

WHEREAS, The Governor of the State of Nebraska has been officially notified of the adoption by the Congress of the United States of a joint resolution, as follows:

Resolved by the Senate and House of Representatives of the United States of America in Congress assembled (two-thirds of each House concurring therein), That the following article is hereby proposed as an amendment to the Constitution of the United States, which shall be valid to all intents and purposes as part of the Constitution when ratified by conventions in three-fourths of the several States:

ARTICLE ___

"Section 1. The Eighteenth Article of Amendment to the Constitution of the United States is hereby repealed.

"Section 2. The transportation or importation into any state, territory, or possession of the United States for delivery or use therein of intoxicating liquors, in violation of the laws thereof, is hereby prohibited.

"Section 3. This article shall be inoperative unless it shall have been ratified as an amendment to the Constitution by conventions in the several states, as provided in the Constitution, within seven years from the date of the submission hereof to the states by the Congress."

Be it Enacted by the People of the State of Nebraska:

Section 1. A convention for the purpose of ratifying or rejecting the amendment to the Constitution of the United States proposed by the Congress thereof, relating to the Eighteenth Article of the Amendments to said Constitution, shall be held in the City of Lincoln on the first Tuesday in December in the year 1934. The said conventions shall be composed of 100 delegates to be nominated and elected, as hereinafter provided, by the electors of the respective representative districts described and set forth in Section 5-105, Compiled Statutes of Nebraska, 1929, the electors of each said district to be entitled to elect and to be represented in said convention by one delegate.

* *Laws of Nebraska, 1933,* Chapter 153, pp. 581-586.

Section 2. Candidates for delegates to said convention shall be nominated at the primary election to be held on the date provided by law in the year 1934 for the nomination of candidates for public offices to be voted for at the general election in November of that year. At such primary election an official ballot, separate and distinct from other ballots used thereat, shall be furnished to each qualified elector, which said ballots shall have printed thereon, at or near the top, the words: "Candidates for Delegate to Convention to Ratify or Reject proposed Amendment to Constitution of United States repealing Eighteenth (Prohibition) Amendment. Vote for one only." Underneath said heading, after a suitable space, shall be printed the following: "For Repeal," under which shall be printed, each on a separate line, the names of all candidates so pledged, who shall have made their filings as hereinafter provided. Following the names of such candidates, after a suitable space, there shall be printed on said ballot the following: "Against Repeal," under which shall be printed, each on a separate line, the names of all candidates so pledged, who shall have made their filings as hereinafter provided. If no candidate should file under one or the other of said headings, then the same shall not be printed on said primary ballots. At the left of each candidate's name appearing on said ballot shall be printed a square within which the elector voting said ballot may mark a cross indicating his choice among the candidates whose names appear under one or the other of said headings, but no ballot marked with a cross opposite the name of more than one candidate, or marked for a candidate under more than one of said headings, shall be counted. The names of candidates to be printed under each of the above mentioned headings, if more than one, shall be rotated on the ballots used in each election precinct or district, in the manner provided in Section 32-1140, Compiled Statutes of Nebraska, 1929. There shall also be printed on each ballot a blank line on which the voter may write in the name of any person for whom he may desire to vote for delegate. The county clerks of the respective counties shall certify to the secretary of state the results of the said primary election with respect to candidates for delegate to said convention. Except as in this Act otherwise expressly provided, the provisions of the general primary election laws of this state shall be applicable to the nomination of candidates for delegate to said convention.

Section 3. Any candidate desiring to have his name appear upon the primary ballot referred to in the next preceding section, shall, at least thirty days prior to the date of holding said primary election in the year 1934, file in the office of the secretary of state a statement signed and sworn to by the candidate, in substantially the following form: "Petition and Affidavit. Candidate for Delegate to Convention to Ratify or Reject proposed Amendment to Repeal Eighteenth Amendment to United States Constitution. State of Nebraska, ... County, ss. I, ... being first duly sworn, say that I reside at ...., in the city of ...., in the county of ...., in the State of Nebraska, and am a qualified elector thereof; that I am a candidate for nomination for delegate to the Convention above referred to, at the primary election to be held on the ...... day of ...., 1934, and I hereby request that my name be printed upon the official primary ballot for nomination as such delegate at said primary election, as a candidate pledged to vote, if elected, for the ratification (or rejection, as the case may be) of the proposed amendment repealing the Eighteenth Amendment to the Constitution of the United States, and I hereby so pledge myself. (Signed) .... Subscribed in my presence and sworn to before me this ...... day of ...., 1934." Accompanying said statement, there shall also be filed therewith a receipt for the sum of Ten Dollars signed by the County Treasurer of the county in which such candidate resides, said amount to be used to help defray the expense of said primary election. Secretary of State to certify names to County Clerks.

Section 4. A separate official ballot shall be prepared and used for the general election in November 1934, in substantially the same general form as hereinbefore specified for the primary election, except that under the heading: "For Repeal" shall be printed the name of the candidate receiving the highest number of votes at the primary election under that heading, if more than one shall have been voted for thereunder; under the heading: "Against Repeal" the name of the candidate receiving the highest number of votes at the primary election under that heading, if more than one shall have been voted for thereunder. In case only one candidate shall have been voted for at the primary election under either of said headings, his name shall be printed under such heading upon the official ballot at the general election. There shall be printed on each ballot a blank line on which the voter may write in the name of any person for whom he may desire to vote for delegate. The county clerks of the respective counties shall certify to the secretary of state the results of the general election with respect to delegates to said convention. Except as in this Act otherwise expressly provided, the general election laws of this state shall be applicable to the election of delegates to said convention.

Section 5. Should a vacancy or vacancies arise, for any cause, after the primary election and before the general election, the Governor shall designate the person or persons whose name or names shall be printed upon the general election ballots to fill such vacancy or vacancies in the district in which the same may occur, having regard to the attitude of the person or persons so designated as to whether he or they be pledged to ratification or rejection on said subject, in order that the vacancy, if any, among those nominated at the primary election under either of said headings shall be filled on the general election ballot by the designation of a qualified elector of the district wherein any such vacancy may occur. Should a vacancy or vacancies arise among the delegates elected at the general election, the Governor shall designate the person or persons to fill the same, having regard to the attitude of the person or persons so designated as hereinbefore stated, so that the person designated to fill the vacancy shall represent the same attitude as that expressed on the ballot by the elected delegate whose place he is to fill.

Section 6. The delegates elected to the Convention shall assemble in the hall of the House of Representatives in the City of Lincoln on the first Tuesday in December in the year 1934, and shall be called to order by the Secretary of State. The Convention shall have power to determine and adopt its own rules and procedure, to elect such officers as it may deem necessary and to prescribe their powers and duties. The debates and proceedings of the Convention shall be made a matter of record. The result of its deliberations as to the ratification or rejection of the proposed amendment to the Constitution of the United States shall be certified by the presiding officer and secretary of the Convention to the Governor and to the Secretary of State, who, in turn, shall certify the same, under the Great Seal of the State of Nebraska, to the Secretary of State of the United States.

Section 7. The compensation of each delegate to said Convention shall be the sum of twenty-five dollars and mileage from his place of residence to the City of Lincoln and return at the rate of five cents per mile. The officers and employees of the Convention, other than delegates, shall receive such compensation as shall be fixed by the Convention, not exceeding in all the sum of $1,000.00, including the record of the proceedings thereof. Compensation of delegates and other expenditures hereinbefore authorized shall be paid by warrants upon the state treasurer, payable out of the general fund, vouchers therefor being duly certified by the presiding officer and secretary of the Convention.

Approved May 1, 1933.

NEVADA*

An Act to provide for the calling and holding of a state convention to consider the joint resolution of Congress proposing an amendment to the constitution of the United States to repeal the 18th amendment; and other matters relating thereto.

WHEREAS, The secretary of state of the United States has transmitted to the governor of the State of Nevada a certified copy of a resolution of Congress entitled "Joint Resolution Proposing an Amendment to the Constitution of the United States," passed during the second session of the seventy-second Congress of the United States, "begun and held at the city of Washington on Monday, the fifth day of December, one thousand nine hundred and thirty-two"; and

WHEREAS, The said secretary of state of the United States requested that the governor of the State of Nevada cause said joint resolution to be submitted to a convention in this state for such action as may be had, and that a certified copy of any action taken be communicated to the said secretary of state of the United States, as required by section 160, title 5, United States Code; now, therefore,

The People of the State of Nevada, represented in Senate and Assembly, do enact as follows:

Section 1. For the purpose of considering the ratification or rejection of the joint resolution of the Congress of the United States entitled "Joint Resolution Proposing an Amendment to the Constitution of the United States," passed during the second session of the seventy-second Congress of the United States, begun on the 5th day of December, 1932, and reading as follows:

SEVENTY-SECOND CONGRESS OF THE UNITED STATES OF AMERICA
AT THE SECOND SESSION

Begun and held at the City of Washington on Monday, the fifth day of December, one thousand nine hundred and thirty-two.

JOINT RESOLUTION

Proposing an amendment to the Constitution of the United States.

Resolved by the Senate and House of Representatives of the United States of America in Congress assembled (two-thirds of each House concurring therein), That the following article is hereby proposed as an amendment to the Constitution of the United States, which shall be valid to all intents and purposes as part of the Constitution when ratified by conventions in three-fourths of the several States:

ARTICLE ——

Section 1. The eighteenth article of amendment to the Constitution of the United States is hereby repealed.

Section 2. The transportation or importation into any State, Territory, or posses-

* *Nevada Statutes, 1933,* Chapter 179, pp. 252-258.

sion of the United States for delivery or use therein of intoxicating liquors, in violation of the laws thereof, is hereby prohibited.

Section 3. This article shall be inoperative unless it shall have been ratified as an amendment to the Constitution by conventions in the several States, as provided in the Constitution, within seven years from the date of the submission hereof to the States by the Congress.

JNO. N. GARNER
Speaker of the House of Representatives
CHARLES CURTIS
Vice President of the United States and President of the Senate

The governor of the State of Nevada is hereby authorized and directed to call a convention to convene in the assembly chamber of the state capitol at Carson City, Nevada, on the 5th day of September, 1933, at 11 o'clock A.M. of said day, for the purpose of considering the ratification or rejection of a joint resolution of the second session of the seventy-second Congress, begun on the 5th day of December, 1932. The governor shall, on or before the 1st day of May, 1933, call said convention by the issuance of a proclamation, and giving notice thereof by publication in one newspaper of each county of the state wherein a newspaper is published, and by posting in each voting precinct of each county wherein no newspaper is published, said notice and call for said convention, to be in substantially the following form:

PROCLAMATION OF A STATE CONVENTION CALLED TO CONSIDER THE RATIFICATION OR REJECTION OF THE JOINT RESOLUTION OF CONGRESS SUBMITTING TO CONVENTIONS OF THE STATES THE REPEAL OF THE 18TH AMENDMENT TO THE CONSTITUTION OF THE UNITED STATES.

It is hereby proclaimed that a state convention in the State of Nevada is to be held in the assembly chamber of the state capitol of the State of Nevada at Carson City, Nevada, on the 5th day of September, 1933, at the hour of 11 o'clock A.M. of said day, for the purpose of considering the ratification or rejection of the following joint resolution of Congress:

SEVENTY-SECOND CONGRESS OF THE UNITED STATES OF AMERICA

AT THE SECOND SESSION

Begun and held at the City of Washington on Monday, the fifth day of December, one thousand nine hundred and thirty-two.

JOINT RESOLUTION

Proposing an amendment to the Constitution of the United States.

Resolved by the Senate and House of Representatives of the United States of America in Congress assembled (two-thirds of each House concurring therein), That the following article is hereby proposed as an amendment to the Constitution of the United States, which shall be valid to all intents and purposes as part of the Constitution when ratified by conventions in three-fourths of the several States:

ARTICLE ___ ___

Section 1. The eighteenth article of amendment to the Constitution of the United States is hereby repealed.

Section 2. The transportation or importation into any State, Territory, or possession of the United States for delivery or use therein of intoxicating liquors, in violation of the laws thereof, is hereby prohibited.

Section 3. This article shall be inoperative unless it shall have been ratified as an amendment to the Constitution by conventions in the several States, as provided in the Constitution, within seven years from the date of the submission hereof to the States by the Congress.

JNO. N. GARNER
Speaker of the House of Representatives
CHARLES CURTIS
Vice President of the United States and President of the Senate

Forty delegates are to be elected to attend said convention, and each county shall be entitled to one delegate for each member of the assembly to which said county was entitled in the assembly in the thirty-sixth session of the Nevada state legislature, said delegates to be elected as provided by law.

Dated: ....day of ...., 1933.
[GREAT SEAL] ....
Attest: .... Governor.

Secretary of State.

Section 2. On the second Saturday in June, 1933, a county convention shall be held at the county seat of each county in the state for the purpose of electing delegates to the state convention provided for in this act. The boards of county commissioners of the several counties shall on or before the 15th day of May, 1933, cause notice of the holding of such county convention to be published in at least one newspaper, if any is published in such county, which notice shall be in substantially the following form:

NOTICE OF COUNTY CONVENTION

Notice is hereby given that a county convention for .... County is hereby called to be held in the county courthouse at .... in said county at 11 o'clock A.M. on the 10th day of June, 1933; that at said county convention delegates to the state convention to be held at Carson City, Nevada, on the 5th day of September, 1933, for the purpose of considering the ratification or rejection of the joint resolution of Congress repealing the 18th amendment to the constitution of the United States, will be elected; that delegates to such county convention shall be chosen at mass meetings to be held in each voting precinct in the county on the 27th day of May, 1933, and that each of such voting precincts is entitled to the number of delegates to such county convention, who shall be qualified electors therein, specified below after the name or number of such precinct as follows:

Name of precinct Number of delegates
.... to ....

By order of the board of county commissioners of .... County.
[SEAL] By ....
County Clerk.

The number of delegates from each voting precinct in each county to the county convention for such county shall be in proportion to the number of votes cast within such precinct for congressman for all candidates for such office in the general election held in November, 1932, as follows:

Counties casting under 400 votes. In counties in which the total vote cast at such preceding November election for congressman shall not have exceeded four hundred, each precinct shall have one delegate for each ten votes, or major fraction thereof so cast within such precinct;

Counties casting 400–600 votes. In counties in which such total vote so cast shall have exceeded four hundred and shall not have exceeded six hundred, each precinct shall have one delegate for each sixteen votes, or major fraction thereof, so cast within such precinct;

Counties casting 600–800 votes. In counties in which such total vote so cast shall have exceeded six hundred but shall not have exceeded eight hundred, each precinct shall have one delegate for each twenty votes, or major fraction thereof, so cast within such precinct;

Counties casting 800–1,400 votes. In counties in which such total vote so cast shall have exceeded eight hundred but shall not have exceeded fourteen hundred, each precinct shall have one delegate for each thirty votes, or major fraction thereof, so cast within such precinct;

Counties casting 1,400–2,000 votes. In counties in which such total vote so cast shall have exceeded fourteen hundred but shall not have exceeded two thousand, each precinct therein shall have one delegate for each forty votes, or major fraction thereof, so cast within such precinct;

Counties casting 2,000–3,000 votes. In counties in which such total vote so cast shall have exceeded two thousand but shall not have exceeded three thousand, each precinct therein shall have one delegate for each sixty votes, or major fraction thereof, so cast within such precinct;

Counties casting 3,000–4,000 votes. In counties in which such total vote so cast shall have exceeded three thousand but shall not have exceeded four thousand, each precinct therein shall have one delegate for each seventy votes, or major fraction thereof, so cast within such precinct;

Counties casting over 4,000 votes. In counties in which such total vote so cast shall have exceeded four thousand, each precinct therein shall have one delegate for each one hundred votes, or major fraction thereof, so cast within such precinct.

Provided, that in all counties every precinct shall be entitled to at least one delegate to each county convention.

The county clerk in each county shall cause a mass meeting of the qualified electors residing in each voting precinct entitled to delegates in the county convention, to be called and held in such precinct on or before the 27th day of May, 1933; and shall cause notice of the time and place of the holding of such meeting to be posted in at least three public places in each precinct at least five days prior to the day of such meeting. Said notice shall specify the number of delegates to the county convention to be chosen at such meeting.

At the time and place appointed therefor, such mass meeting shall be convened and organized in each precinct, and at such meeting the delegates to which such precinct shall be entitled in the county convention shall be elected by ballot, and the result of such election shall be certified to the county convention by the chairman and the secretary of said meeting.

At 11 o'clock A.M. on the 10th day of June, 1933, the delegates so elected to each county convention shall convene at the county courthouse in the county seat, and there organize and elect the delegates to the state convention, and take such other action, consistent with the provisions of this act, as they may deem proper. The chairman and secretary of each county convention shall certify to the state convention the result of the election by the county convention of delegates to the state convention.

The number of delegates to the state convention shall be forty, and each county convention shall elect one delegate for each member of the assembly to which said county was entitled in the assembly in the thirty-sixth session of the Nevada state legislature. Every delegate to the state or any county convention shall, at the time of his election, be a qualified elector of the State of Nevada, and may publicly declare whether he favors ratification or rejection of the proposed amendment.

Section 3. At 11 o'clock A.M. on the 5th day of September, 1933, the delegates elected to the state convention by the several county conventions shall convene in the assembly chamber of the state capitol in Carson City, Nevada, and there organize by electing a chairman, secretary and such other officers as they may desire, but before proceeding with the business of the convention each of said delegates shall present his credentials and, upon approval thereof, the accredited delegates shall take the constitutional oath of office as provided for state officers, which oaths shall be taken before the chief justice or any justice of the supreme court of the State of Nevada. Only such delegates duly elected and whose credentials are approved by the convention shall be entitled to vote, and no proxies shall be allowed to vote at such convention.

Section 4. When such state convention shall have been organized and is ready for business, the governor of Nevada shall transmit to said convention the certified copy of the aforesaid joint resolution.

Section 5. The said joint resolution of Congress shall upon its receipt by the convention be submitted thereto for its ratification or rejection, and a majority vote of the duly elected and accredited delegates shall be sufficient to either ratify or reject said joint resolution. The vote upon ratification or rejection of said joint resolution shall be taken upon a roll call of said delegates, and the vote thereon shall be duly recorded by the secretary of said convention, and thereupon the chairman and secretary of said convention shall cause a certified copy of the action taken by said convention on the question of the ratification or rejection of said joint resolution to be made, affix their signatures thereto as such officers, and the secretary of State of Nevada shall certify to the same, whereupon the governor of Nevada shall transmit such certified copy to the secretary of state of the United States, as required by section 160, title 5, United States Code.

Section 6. Each delegate elected to said state convention and participating therein shall be entitled to and be paid mileage for attendance at said convention at the rate of five cents per mile actually and necessarily traveled, and there is hereby appropriated out of any money in the state treasury not otherwise appropriated the sum of twenty-five hundred dollars to pay said mileage and such other expenses of publication of notices as may be required by this act.

The state controller is hereby authorized and directed to pay each of said delegates the amount of mileage certified by the proper officers of said state convention, and the state treasurer is hereby authorized and directed to pay the same.

Section 7. If, at or about the time of the submission of said joint resolution, Congress shall, by resolution or by statute, prescribe the manner in which such conventions shall be constituted or held, or enact any law or resolution in conflict herewith, the provisions of this act, in so far as they may be in conflict with such action of Congress, shall be inoperative, and the convention shall be constituted and shall operate in accordance with the action and direction of Congress; and all officers of this state who may by such resolution or statute be authorized or directed to take any action to constitute such a convention for this state are authorized and directed to act thereunder and in obedience thereto with the same force and effect as if acting under a law of this state.

Section 8. This act shall become effective from and after its passage and approval.

NEW HAMPSHIRE*

AN ACT providing for a convention to pass on a proposed amendment to the Constitution of the United States

Be it enacted by the Senate and House of Representatives in General Court convened:

1. *Proclamation.* The governor shall issue a call for the election on the day hereinafter named of delegates to a convention to act upon an amendment to the Constitution of the United States submitted by the Congress of the United States, as hereinafter fully set forth, and shall fix the date and hour for the holding of such convention.

2. *Delegates, Meeting.* The convention shall be composed of ten delegates elected at large by the qualified voters of New Hampshire. It shall meet in the senate chamber of the capitol at Concord. The date for the holding of such convention shall be not less than twenty nor more than forty-five days after the election of delegates.

3. *Date of Election.* The election of delegates shall take place on the third Tuesday of June 1933, and no other election or referendum shall be held by any town or ward on the same day.

4. *Nomination of Delegates.* Not less than thirty days before the date of the election of delegates, the governor, the president of the senate and the speaker of the house of representatives, or in case of incapacity of any one of them, the secretary of state in his stead, shall appoint and forthwith announce the names of twenty candidates for delegates, such candidates being in their opinion representative citizens of New Hampshire. Ten of these candidates shall be persons who assent to the placing of their names on the ballot as pledged to vote For Ratification; and ten shall be persons who assent to the placing of their names on the ballot as pledged to vote Against Ratification. One candidate for ratification and one candidate against ratification shall be appointed from each county in the state.

5. *Acceptance of Nomination.* On accepting such designation, each candidate shall file his acceptance as follows: "I do hereby accept this appointment as candidate for delegate to the convention to be held on the..........day of.........., ...; and assent to the placing of my name on the ballot as pledged to vote For Ratification (or Against Ratification).

(Signed)............................."

6. *Ballot, Form, Contents.* The form of the ballot to be used shall be as follows: DELEGATES TO CONVENTION TO VOTE UPON THE FOLLOWING PROPOSED AMENDMENT TO THE CONSTITUTION OF THE UNITED STATES:

---

* *New Hampshire Laws, 1933,* Chapter 110, pp. 153-157.

"Resolved by the Senate and House of Representatives of the United States of America in Congress assembled (two-thirds of each House concurring therein), That the following article is hereby proposed as an amendment to the Constitution of the United States, which shall be valid to all intents and purposes as part of the Constitution when ratified by conventions in three-fourths of the several States:

ARTICLE ____

"Section 1. The eighteenth article of amendment to the Constitution of the United States is hereby repealed.

"Section 2. The transportation or importation into any State, Territory, or possession of the United States for delivery or use therein of intoxicating liquors, in violation of the laws thereof, is hereby prohibited.

"Section 3. This article shall be inoperative unless it shall have been ratified as an amendment to the Constitution by conventions in the several States, as provided in the Constitution, within seven years from the date of the submission hereof to the States by the Congress."

Instructions

To vote for all the delegates who stand For Ratification, make a cross (X) in the circle at the head of the column marked FOR RATIFICATION. To vote for all the delegates who stand Against Ratification, make a cross (X) in the circle at the head of the column marked AGAINST RATIFICATION. If you do not wish to vote for every candidate in one column, make a cross (X) opposite the name of the candidates of your choice, not to exceed ten in all. If you do not wish to vote for the candidates named in the column "For Ratification" or the candidates named in the column "Against Ratification" you may write in the names of other delegates not to exceed ten in number in the spaces provided below. Ballots on which more than ten names are marked will be considered defective.

FOR RATIFICATION Candidates favoring repeal of the 18th [Prohibition] amendment. ○	AGAINST RATIFICATION Candidates against repeal of the 18th [Prohibition] amendment. ○	The space below is provided for voters who wish to vote for delegates other than those whose names appear in the two adjoining columns.

7. ——, *Verification.* Upon each ballot shall be endorsed the words "Official Ballot," followed by the name of the town or ward in which it is to be used, the date of the election, and a facsimile of the signature of the secretary of state with his official title.

8. *Check-List.* The check-list used in the last preceding general election shall apply, but may be revised as now provided by law for check-lists used at general elections. The polls for this election shall open at 10 A.M. and close at 7 P.M.

9. *Canvass of Returns.* The governor, the president of the senate and the speaker of the house of representatives, shall canvass the ballots, declaring elected the ten candidates who have received the greatest number of votes; and the secretary of state shall publish the results. The secretary of state shall upon the completion of the canvass mail or deliver in person to each delegate so elected a notice of his election and of the date of the Convention, and such delegates so elected shall be members of the convention.

10. *Application of Election Laws.* Expenses of such election shall be paid by the state or town, as in the case of general elections. The names of candidates on all ballots shall be arranged alphabetically in each column. All other statutory provisions as to holding general elections, furnishing ballots, instructions, and forms, appointment and payment of election officers, filling of vacancies, solicitation of voters at the polls, challenging of voters, manner of conducting elections, counting, inspecting and preserving the ballots and making returns thereof, and all other kindred subjects shall apply to such elections so far as they are consistent with this act, it being the intent of this act to place such elections under the regulation and protection of the laws relating to general elections.

11. *Construction of Act.* The provisions of this act shall be liberally construed, so that the real will of the voters shall not be defeated, and so that the voters shall not be deprived of their right because of informality or failure to comply with provisions of law as to notice or conduct of the election, or of certifying the results thereof.

12. *Organization, Duties.* A majority of the delegates shall constitute a quorum to do business, when convened according to the provisions of this act. The convention shall be the judge of the election and qualification of its members and shall have the power to adopt such rules as may be necessary for the conduct of its business. The convention shall keep a journal of its proceedings in which shall be recorded the vote of each delegate on the question of ratification of the proposed amendment. Upon final adjournment the journal shall be filed with the secretary of state. The secretary of state shall be *ex officio* secretary of the convention, and he, with the chairman of the convention, shall certify the vote of the convention to the secretary of state of the United States under the seal of this state.

13. *Compensation.* Delegates to the convention shall not be entitled to compensation but shall receive mileage for travel as now provided for members of the legislature.

14. *Appropriation.* A sum not exceeding three thousand dollars is hereby appropriated for paying the expenses of said election and of said convention, and the governor is authorized to draw his warrant for so much of said sum as may be necessary for said expenses.

15. *Takes Effect.* This act shall take effect upon its passage.

[Approved May 6, 1933.]

NEW JERSEY*

AN ACT providing for the election of delegates to a convention and providing for the holding of a convention to consider the article of amendment, proposed by the Congress, to the Constitution of the United States designed to repeal the eighteenth article of amendment.

WHEREAS, The Senate and House of Representatives of the United States of America in Congress assembled (two-thirds of each House concurring therein) did resolve that the following article is hereby proposed as an amendment to the Constitution of the United States, which shall be valid to all intents and purposes as a part of the Constitution when ratified by conventions in three-fourths of the several States; and

WHEREAS, The said proposed amendment reads as follows:

Section 1. The eighteenth article of amendment to the Constitution of the United States is hereby repealed.

Section 2. The transportation or importation into any State, territory, or possession of the United States for delivery or use therein of intoxicating liquors, in violation of the laws thereof is hereby prohibited.

Section 3. This article shall be inoperative unless it shall have been ratified as an amendment to the Constitution by conventions in the several States, as provided in the Constitution, within seven years from the date of submission hereof to the States by the Congress; therefore,

BE IT ENACTED *by the Senate and General Assembly of the State of New Jersey:*

1. For the purpose of considering the article of amendment to the Constitution of the United States proposed by the Congress, as recited in the preamble of this act, there shall be held in this State a convention of delegates. Such convention shall consist of two hundred and twenty-six delegates as follows:

Sixty-four delegates shall be elected from the State at large, and one hundred and sixty-two county delegates hereinafter called district delegates shall be elected in the several counties of this State; each county being entitled to delegate representation on the basis of twice as many delegates to represent such county as the said county is entitled to elect members of the Senate and the House of Assembly of this State.

2. Any person having the qualifications which would entitle him to a seat in the House of Assembly may be elected as a delegate-at-large or district delegate to said convention.

3. The election for delegates shall be held on the third Tuesday in May, one thousand nine hundred and thirty-three, coincident with and upon the same day with the holding of the primary election for the general election, and shall in all respects, except as herein otherwise provided, be conducted in accord with the provisions of an act entitled "An act to regulate elections" (Revision 1930), approved April eighteenth, one thousand nine hundred and thirty, and the acts amendatory and supplemental thereto. A separate ballot printed on bluish tint paper and a separate ballot box shall be provided for the ballots for convention delegates. The form of the ballot shall be

* *New Jersey Laws, 1933,* Chapter 73, pp. 143-148.

uniform in all the counties of the State and the form thereof shall be prescribed by the Secretary of State. The officials now obligated under such "An act to regulate elections" to furnish ballots, tally sheets, ballot boxes and other equipment necessary for the conduct of an election are hereby directed to furnish similar supplies for the election herein directed to be held. The district boards of election that shall conduct the primary election are hereby required to conduct the election for convention delegates and without additional compensation. The powers of all other officials given to or directed to be employed by such "An act to regulate elections" are hereby given to such officials.

4. Any person desiring to be a delegate-at-large to said convention shall prior to twenty days before the fixed date for holding such election file a petition with the Secretary of State. Any person desiring to be a candidate for district delegate to said convention shall prior to twenty days before the date fixed for holding such election file his petition with the clerk of the county in which he is a resident. The form of the petition in either case shall be prescribed by the Secretary of State.

5. Any person desiring to be a candidate for delegate-at-large shall file with the Secretary of State a petition, which petition must be signed by at least twenty-five thousand voters who were legally registered for the last general election. Any person desiring to be a candidate for district delegate from a county in which he resides shall file with the clerk of the county a petition, which petition shall be signed by such registered voters of the county equal to at least one-tenth of the vote cast in the preceding general election for members of the Assembly in such county; *provided,* that not more than ten thousand signatures shall be required for any district delegate petition.

6. Candidates for the position of either delegate-at-large or district delegate may join in a petition to have his or her name bracketed with that of any other candidate or candidates for such position. Delegates-at-large who desire to be bracketed may file one petition or one series of petitions aggregating twenty-five thousand signatures of such registered voters, which petition shall be sufficient. District delegates who desire to be bracketed may file one petition or one series of petitions aggregating the number of such registered voters as hereinbefore indicated, which shall be sufficient. A single petitioner may state opposite his name, or bracketed petitioners may state outside of the bracket whether he or they will vote in the convention for or against ratification of the amendment, and so as not to confuse the voter the candidates so pledging themselves shall state the question on the ballot as follows:

For Repeal
of
18th Amendment.
or
Against Repeal
of
18th Amendment.

7. All citizens of the State who are qualified to vote for members of the General Assembly and who are qualified to vote at the primary election shall be qualified to vote in the election in this act authorized and shall be permitted to vote in the election district in which he is legally entitled to vote.

8. Delegates-at-large who have petitioned to be bracketed may, in writing, signed by such delegates and addressed to the Secretary of State, petition to be bracketed together, and district delegates who have petitioned to be bracketed together may, in writing, signed by such delegates and addressed to the county clerk, petition to be

bracketed together. Where the delegates are so bracketed together a box or a square shall be placed above the name of the first delegate in the bracket and opposite such bracket or square to the right thereof, shall be printed in the following words: "To vote for all of the delegates in the bracket make a cross X or plus + mark in the square to the left." If a cross or plus mark shall be made in the said square it shall be counted as a vote for all of the delegates who are bracketed together, both as to the delegates-at-large and the district delegates.

The sixty-four (64) candidates for delegates-at-large receiving the highest number of votes shall be declared elected delegates-at-large, and the number of candidates for district delegates apportioned to each county who receive the highest number of votes in such county shall be declared elected as such district delegates for such county. The elected delegates shall be entitled to be seated in such convention. Certificates of election of delegates-at-large shall be issued by the Secretary of State and certificates of election of district delegates shall be issued by the clerk of the county for which such delegates are elected.

9. Each candidate or each group of bracketed candidates for delegates-at-large or district delegates to the convention as provided in this act shall be allowed to appoint one challenger in each election district who shall have such powers as are given to challengers under "An act to regulate elections," approved April eighteenth, one thousand nine hundred and thirty, together with any supplements thereto or amendments thereof.

10. The board of county canvassers of each county shall meet on Monday next, after such election, at twelve o'clock noon, at the courthouse of such county, for the purpose of checking the statements of the district boards filed in the office of the county clerk.

11. The county clerk of each county shall certify to the Secretary of State on the form provided by the Secretary of State the number of votes cast for each delegate-at-large and each district delegate not later than the second Thursday following the election.

12. The Board of State Canvassers shall meet at Trenton on the second Tuesday next after the day of election, for the purpose of canvassing and estimating the votes cast for each person for whom any votes shall have been cast for delegates-at-large, and of determining and declaring the persons who shall have been duly elected as such delegates-at-large. The said board shall meet in the chamber of the Senate or some other convenient place at Trenton at the hour of two o'clock in the afternoon.

13. Within twenty days after the holding of the said election, the Governor of this State, by proclamation, shall convene the said convention. The convention shall meet in the city of Trenton and shall organize by the selection of a chairman and secretary, and such other officers as may be necessary, and shall adopt rules governing the deliberations thereof. The convention shall proceed to consider the proposed article of amendment and shall by a vote thereon either approve or reject the same, and the action of the said convention thereon shall be valid to all intents and purposes as representing the people of the State of New Jersey. The chairman and the secretary of the convention shall certify the results of the votes of the delegates to the Secretary of State, who shall certify the result of the vote to the Secretary of State of the United States and to the Senate and House of Representatives of the United States.

14. This act shall take effect immediately.

Approved March 23, 1933.

A SUPPLEMENT to an act entitled "An act providing for the election of delegates to a convention and providing for the holding of a convention to consider the article of amendment, proposed by the Congress, to the Constitution of the United States designed to repeal the eighteenth article of amendment," approved March twenty-third, one thousand nine hundred and thirty-three.*

BE IT ENACTED *by the Senate and General Assembly of the State of New Jersey:*

1. The ballots to be printed pursuant to the provisions of the act to which this act is supplementary shall be printed by the county clerks of the several counties under the direction of the Secretary of State. No sample ballots shall be required to be mailed to electors. The Secretary of State shall furnish to the several county clersk for distribution poll books, in order that the names of the voters voting at the election to be held pursuant to the act to which this act is supplementary, may be recorded. The cost of the printing of the ballots shall be borne by the State. The county clerks shall contract for the printing of the ballots with the approval of the Secretary of State, and all bills for services rendered in printing such ballots shall be forwarded to the Secretary of State and, if found correct, shall be approved by such officer and paid out of the treasury of this State as other bills are now paid.

2. This act shall take effect immediately.

Approved April 11, 1933.

AN ACT to amend an act entitled "An act providing for the election of delegates to a convention and providing for the holding of a convention to consider the article of amendment, proposed by the Congress, to the Constitution of the United States designed to repeal the eighteenth article of amendment," approved March twenty-third, one thousand nine hundred and thirty-three.†

BE IT ENACTED *by the Senate and General Assembly of the State of New Jersey:*

1. Section twelve of the act of which this act is amendatory be and the same is hereby amended to read as follows:

12. The Board of State Canvassers shall meet at Trenton on the twenty-ninth day of May next after the day of election, for the purpose of canvassing and estimating the votes cast for each person for whom any votes shall have been cast for delegates-at-large, and of determining and declaring the persons who shall have been duly elected as such delegates-at-large. The said board shall meet in the chamber of the Senate or some other convenient place at Trenton at the hour of two o'clock in the afternoon.

2. This act shall take effect immediately.

Approved May 24, 1933.

---

* *New Jersey Laws, 1933,* Chapter 111, pp. 226-227.

† *Ibid.,* Chapter 171, p. 371.

NEW MEXICO*

AN ACT to prescribe the date, manner and form delegates to a convention to ratify or reject a proposed amendment to the Constitution of the United States shall be chosen in the state of New Mexico; prescribing the manner and form of organizing and holding such convention; the method of voting and manner of certifying the result of the vote at such convention and providing for the compensation of the delegates to such convention.

Be It Enacted by the Legislature of the State of New Mexico:

Section 1. Whenever, within the limits imposed upon their actions by Art. V of the Constitution of the United States, the Congress shall propose to conventions in the several states an amendment to the Constitution of the United States, then, in that event, within ten days subsequent to receipt of official notice of such proposal, or within ten days subsequent to the passage and approval of this Act, the Governor, by virtue of the authority hereby vested in him, shall by public proclamation call a convention for the purpose of ratifying or rejecting such proposed amendment.

Section 2. Said proclamation by the Governor shall set forth, as provided in this Act; the purpose of, the time and place of meeting of such convention, and the manner, times and places of choosing delegates to such convention, all in accordance with the provisions of this Act and not otherwise.

Section 3. The Governor shall transmit a copy of such proclamation to the Secretary of the State of New Mexico who shall cause same to be published once within the next following ten days, in such newspapers as published official notices of the election next preceding.

Section 4. Ten days after such call there may be circulated petitions of nominations for the office of delegate to the convention and all completed nomination petitions shall be filed with the Secretary of State at his office in Santa Fe not later than noon of the tenth day next preceding the first regular day for registration of voters next succeeding, as provided by the election laws of the State. In the event a special election is to be held for the purpose of electing delegates to such convention, all completed nomination petitions shall be filed with the Secretary of State at his office in Santa Fe not later than noon of the 60th day next preceding such election.

Section 5. No petition for nomination for delegate to the convention shall be circulated in behalf of any person until such person shall have filed with the Secretary of State at his office in Santa Fe an instrument in writing signed by the prospective candidate, setting forth his full name and place of residence, the length of time during which he has resided within the State, and a definite pledge as to how he will vote in convention on the pending amendment as proposed by Congress, in the event that he shall have been elected as a delegate to the convention. The Secretary of State shall thereupon issue to such prospective candidate a certificate of filing, setting forth the full text of the instrument so filed, and a copy of such certificate shall appear at the top of each nominating petition.

---

* *New Mexico Laws, 1933,* Chapter 163, pp. 400-405.

Section 6. All nominations for the office of delegate to the convention shall be by petition in the manner and form, as required by the Secretary of State not inconsistent with this Act; *Provided, however,* that the number of signatures required shall be 500 irrespective of the place of residence within the state of the signers, *provided* that said signers shall be qualified electors of the State of New Mexico.

Neither the name, designation nor emblem of any political party shall appear on any petition of nomination for the office of delegate to the convention.

Section 7. The number of delegates to the convention shall be the same as the number of Presidential Electors to which the state shall at the time be entitled; and the names of those persons not in excess of such number, pledged respectively to ratify or reject the proposed amendment who shall first have filed proper nominating petitions with the Secretary of State at his office in Santa Fe, shall be placed on the ballot as candidates for the office of delegate to the convention.

Section 8. The names of candidates for delegates to the convention thus ascertained shall be placed on a paper ballot separate from and of a color easily distinguishable from any other ballot to be used at the same time, and said ballot shall be in the following form:

The ballot shall be printed in plain black type.

Across the top of the ballot shall be printed the words "BALLOT FOR CANDIDATE FOR THE OFFICE OF DELEGATE TO A CONVENTION CALLED FOR THE PURPOSE OF RATIFYING OR REJECTING AN AMENDMENT TO THE CONSTITUTION OF THE UNITED STATES PROPOSED BY THE CONGRESS IN THE FOLLOWING LANGUAGE."

Text of proposed amendment.

Below the text of the amendment shall be printed a horizontal black line across the width of the ballot, and beneath such line shall be printed to the left of the ballot the caption "Candidates for Convention Delegates Pledged to vote Yes on Ratification of the Foregoing Amendment;" immediately below such caption shall be printed a voting space in the form of a circle; and immediately below such voting space shall be printed in a vertical column the names of the candidates for the office of delegate to the convention who are pledged to ratify the proposed amendment.

In like manner to the right of the ballot, and parallel to the foregoing, there shall be printed the caption "Candidates for Convention Delegates Pledges to vote No on Ratification of the Foregoing Amendment;" and immediately below such caption shall be printed a voting space in the form of a circle; and immediately below such voting space shall be printed in a vertical column the names of those candidates for the office of delegate to the convention who are pledged to reject the proposed amendment. Such ballots shall be distributed to election officials in the manner prescribed by law for distribution of other ballots in general elections.

Section 9. A voter shall designate his choice of delegates by marking a cross with a pen or a pencil having an indelible lead, within either circle and such cross shall be counted as a vote for each and every candidate whose name appears immediately below the circle so marked.

Section 10. Identical ballots shall be used throughout the state and those candidates for delegates to the convention who shall have received the greater number of all votes cast for delegates throughout the state shall be declared elected and shall constitute the convention.

Certificates of election shall be issued as provided in the Election Laws of this state; such certificates shall also contain the pre-election pledge of each delegate.

Section 11. The convention shall meet in the Senate Chamber of the Capitol at Santa Fe, New Mexico, on the third Thursday after the official canvass of the votes, and at noon the convention shall thereupon organize as by law provided for organizing the Presidential Electors. After verifying the certificates of election of the delegates, the convention shall proceed to ratify or reject the proposed amendment in accordance with the pre-election pledges of the delegates. A majority of all the delegates elected shall constitute a quorum of the convention, and a majority of such quorum shall be required to ratify or reject the proposed amendment.

The proceedings of the convention shall be certified to in the manner and form prescribed by existing law in respect to state action on proposed amendments to the Constitution of the United States.

Section 12. Any citizen of this State, who is a qualified elector, shall be qualified to vote for delegates to the convention.

Section 13. Any citizen of the State of New Mexico qualified to hold the office of Presidential Elector shall be qualified to hold the office of delegate to the convention.

Section 14. The day on which delegates to the convention shall be elected shall be the next regular election day on which State officers are chosen, next following the proclamation of the Governor calling the convention, *Provided* such proclamation shall be made thirty days prior to the first regular day of registration of voters next following.

In the event that the proclamation of the Governor calling the convention shall have been issued at a time less than thirty days prior to the next succeeding regular day for the registration of voters, the day on which delegates to the convention shall be elected shall be the regular day on which State officers are chosen next following. *Provided, however,* that delegates to a convention for the purpose of adopting or rejecting the proposed Twenty-first amendment to the Constitution of the United States, relating to the repeal of the Eighteenth Amendment to the Constitution of the United States, shall be elected at a special election to be held on the 19th day of September, 1933 for such purpose and for other purposes.

Section 15. In all other particulars the procedure prescribed by the Election Laws of the state in respect of Presidential Electors shall be followed in the election of delegates to a convention, and the provisions of the General Election Laws of the state concerning the casting of votes, the counting of ballots, the making and canvassing of the returns thereof, the certificate of election, and the punishment of any and all violations of the Election Laws, as well as all other applicable provisions of said Election Laws not inconsistent with the terms of this Act, shall apply to the election of the delegates to such state conventions herein provided.

Section 16. Any attempt on the part of Congress in any manner to prescribe how and when the delegates to the convention may be nominated or elected, the date on which said convention shall be held in the several states, the number of delegates required to make a quorum, and the number of affirmative votes necessary to ratify the amendment submitted to such conventions, or any other requirements, shall be null and void in the State of New Mexico, and all officers of the state, or any subdivision thereof, are hereby authorized and required to resist to the utmost any attempt to execute any and all such congressional dictation and usurpation.

Section 17. Delegates to the convention shall receive as compensation for their services an amount equal to the compensation to which the Presidential Electors are entitled. Delegates shall also receive a traveling allowance of ten (10) cents per mile to and from their place of residence and place of meeting of the convention.

Section 18. That it is necessary for the preservation of the public peace, health and safety of the inhabitants of State of New Mexico that this Act shall become effective at the earliest possible time, and therefore an emergency is hereby declared to exist, and this Act shall take effect and be in full force and effect from and after its passage and approval.

NEW YORK*

AN ACT to provide for a convention to consider and act upon the ratification of the amendment to the United States constitution providing for the repeal of the eighteenth amendment

Became a law April 6, 1933, with the approval of the Governor. Passed, three-fifths being present

The People of the State of New York, represented in Senate and Assembly, do enact as follows:

Section 1. *Convention.* A state convention, the delegates to which shall be elected in the manner herein provided, shall be held in the assembly chamber, at the capitol, in the city of Albany, in the state of New York, on Tuesday, June twenty-seventh, nineteen hundred thirty-three, at the hour of eleven antemeridian, to consider and act upon the ratification of the following amendment to the constitution of the United States proposed by the congress of the United States to the several states:

ARTICLE ___ ___

Section 1. The eighteenth article of amendment to the constitution of the United States is hereby repealed.

Section 2. The transportation or importation into any state, territory, or possession of the United States for delivery or use therein of intoxicating liquors, in violation of the laws thereof, is hereby prohibited.

Section 3. This article shall be inoperative unless it shall have been ratified as an amendment to the constitution by conventions in the several states, as provided in the constitution, within seven years from the date of the submission hereof to the states by the congress.

The convention provided for by this act is hereby made and declared to be an official convention in the state of New York for the above purposes, and to be a convention authorized by the fifth article of the United States constitution and contemplated by section three of such proposal.

Section 2. *Election of delegates; qualifications and registration of voters.* The number of delegates to be elected to such convention shall be one hundred and fifty, to be elected from the state at large, each of whom shall be a citizen and inhabitant of the state. The election of said delegates shall be held on Tuesday, May twenty-third, nineteen hundred thirty-three, between the hours of twelve o'clock noon and ten postmeridian. A person qualified at the time of such election to vote in his or her election district for a member of assembly had such election been a special election called by the governor for the election of member of assembly shall be qualified to vote thereat for delegates to such convention. Statutes disqualifying a person for public office because he then holds another public office shall not apply to delegates to such convention, nor shall the election of any such person to such convention work a forfeiture of any other public office. The provisions of the election law relative to registers and registrations of voters which apply to a special election called by the governor shall apply to the special elec-

* *New York Laws of the 156th Session, 1933,* Chapter 143, pp. 525-535.

tion herein appointed to be held. The notice of election shall be published in the newspapers specified or referred to in section eighty-one of the election law, once in each of the two weeks only which precedes such election.

Section 3. *Nominations of candidates.* There shall be no primary election for the nomination of delegates to said convention. Nomination shall be by petition and not otherwise. Any number of candidates may be placed in nomination by such petitions, but only one hundred and fifty each for repeal, against repeal, and uninstructed, shall be nominated, as hereinafter provided. Each petition shall be signed by not less than twelve thousand qualified electors of this state. Nomination shall be without party or political designation. A single petition may nominate any number of candidates not exceeding the total number of delegates to be elected. The said petitions shall be substantially in the following form:

This petition is for candidates for repeal (or against repeal or uninstructed), as the case may be.

I, the undersigned, do hereby state that I am a duly qualified voter of the state of New York; that my place of residence is truly stated opposite my signature hereto, and that I intend to support at the ensuing election of delegates to the convention to consider and act upon the ratification of the amendment to the United States constitution providing for the repeal of the eighteenth amendment, and I do hereby nominate, the following named person (or persons) as a candidate (or as candidates) for nomination for delegate (or delegates) to said convention, to be voted for at the election to be held on May twenty-third, nineteen hundred thirty-three, for ratification (or against ratification, or uninstructed, as the case may be.)

Name of Candidate.	Place of Residence.	Place of Business.

I do hereby appoint (here insert the names and addresses of at least three persons, all of whom shall be voters) as a committee to fill vacancies and to select an emblem.

IN WITNESS WHEREOF, I have hereunto set my hand the day and year placed opposite my signature.

Date	Name of Signer	Residence	County, Assembly and Election Districts, Town or Ward

The petition shall be verified by the signers or authenticated by witness, as provided in the election law in respect of a designating petition.

The members of all committees to fill vacancies for candidates nominated as hereinafter provided for each of the three groups shall choose an emblem for their group. The emblem so chosen shall not be the emblem of any political party, and shall conform to the provisions of section twenty of the election law. The secretary of state shall decide any disputed question as to any emblem, and shall select an emblem for any group, if its committee or committees fail to file a certificate, designating an emblem at least twenty days before such election. All nominating petitions shall be filed with the secretary of state not less than twenty days before such election. No nomination of a candidate shall be effective except for the one hundred and fifty nominees in favor of ratification, the one hundred and fifty nominees against ratification, and the one hundred and fifty nominees who are uninstructed, whose petitions have been signed by the largest number of qualified electors. The secretary of state shall determine any question as to which candidates placed in nomination in each group have been so nominated; and, in case of any tie, the same shall be decided by lot drawn by him. The secretary of state shall determine any question arising and make such order as justice may require, with respect to the nomination of any candidate or his election to the office of delegate to said convention and his decision shall be final and conclusive. Any and all petitions not delivered to or received by the secretary of state before midnight of the last day for filing petitions shall not be accepted or considered by him but shall be disregarded. Within three days after the last day for filing said petitions the secretary of state shall certify the candidates of each group to the appropriate election authorities.

Section 4. *Election; ballots.* The election shall be by paper ballots; they shall be numbered consecutively from one upwards by election districts and shall also contain the county and the number of the assembly and election district for which they are printed. These numbers shall be printed on the stubs of said ballots as now provided for in the election law.

On the stubs of the ballots shall be printed in heavy black type the following instructions:

1. Mark only with a pencil having black lead.
2. Do not vote for more than one hundred and fifty candidates.
3. To vote for all the delegates of one group, make a cross (X) mark within the circle above that group's column.
4. To vote for some, but not all, of the delegates of one or more groups, make a cross (X) mark in the square at the left of the name of every candidate printed on the ballot for whom you desire to vote.
5. To vote for any person whose name is not printed on the ballot, write his or her name in the blank space provided therefor.
6. If you tear, or deface, or wrongly mark the ballot, return it and obtain another.

Also any additional instructions which the secretary of state may prepare for the information of voters.

There shall be printed upon said ballots the proposed amendment, or the substance thereof. The ballot shall contain four perpendicular columns of equal width, the first three of which shall be headed with the respective emblems, followed by, in plain type, the following column headings:

For Repeal. Against Repeal. Uninstructed.

The words for repeal, against repeal and uninstructed in each case in the headings to such columns shall be printed on separate lines in type at least twice as large as the other words in said headings. In the column headed for repeal shall be placed the names of the candidates nominated as for ratification. In the column headed against repeal shall be placed the names of the candidates nominated as against ratification. In the column headed uninstructed shall be placed the names of the candidates, if any, so nominated.

If no petition is filed for any group of delegates, or if a petition be filed but the same be defective or for any reason the names of delegates therein named are not entitled to appear upon the ballot, then the ballot shall not contain such a column.

In each column there shall be a blank circle three-quarters of an inch in diameter; below this the heading of the group; below this the names of the candidates, arranged in the alphabetical order of the surnames; above the name of the first delegate shall be printed the words "Delegates to Convention." The names of the delegates shall be printed in spaces one-quarter of an inch in depth. The spaces shall be divided from each other by light horizontal lines. At the left of the name of each delegate shall be printed a voting space one-quarter of an inch square.

The circle in each column shall be surrounded by the following instructions plainly printed: "For a straight ticket, mark within this circle."

In addition to said three columns there shall be a blank column with lines for writing in which voters may write the names of candidates for delegates to said convention not on the ballot, and which shall be sufficient to contain as many names as there are delegates to be chosen. It shall be designated as the blank column and shall contain no voting spaces.

In the blank column the space occupied by the emblem and voting circle in the other columns shall be occupied by the following instructions plainly printed: "In the column below the voter may write the name or names of any person or persons not exceeding one hundred and fifty, for whom he desires to vote, whose name or names are not printed on the ballot." Below the line dividing the heading from the blank spaces shall be printed, as in the other columns, the words: "Delegates to Convention."

The ballot shall be in substantially the following form:

Stub

Below the stub shall be printed:

The Congress has proposed an amendment to the Constitution of the United States reading as follows:

"RESOLVED, By the Senate and House of Representatives of the United States of America in Congress assembled (two-thirds of each House concurring therein), That the following article is hereby proposed as an amendment to the Constitution of the United States, which shall be valid to all intents and purposes as part of the Constitution when ratified by conventions in three-fourths of the several States:

"ARTICLE ____

"Section 1. The eighteenth article of amendment to the Constitution of the United States is hereby repealed.

"Section 2. The transportation or importation into any State, Territory, or possession of the United States for delivery or use therein of intoxicating liquors, in violation of the laws thereof, is hereby prohibited.

"Section 3. This article shall be inoperative unless it shall have been ratified as an amendment to the Constitution by conventions in the several States, as provided in the Constitution, within seven years from the date of the submission hereof to the States by the Congress."

<table>
<tr>
<td colspan="2">EMBLEM
FOR REPEAL
For a Straight Ticket
Mark Within This Circle
○
Delegates to Convention
FOR REPEAL</td>
<td colspan="2">EMBLEM
AGAINST REPEAL
For a Straight Ticket
Mark Within This Circle
○
Delegates to Convention
AGAINST REPEAL</td>
<td colspan="2">EMBLEM
UNINSTRUCTED
For a Straight Ticket
Mark Within This Circle
○
Delegates to Convention
UNINSTRUCTED</td>
<td>BLANK COLUMN
IN THE COLUMN BELOW, THE VOTER MAY WRITE THE NAME OR NAMES OF ANY PERSON OR PERSONS NOT EXCEEDING 150, FOR WHOM HE DESIRES TO VOTE, WHOSE NAME OR NAMES ARE NOT PRINTED ON THE BALLOT.</td>
</tr>
<tr><td></td><td>Delegates to Convention</td><td></td><td>Delegates to Convention</td><td></td><td>Delegates to Convention</td><td>Delegates to Convention</td></tr>
<tr><td></td><td></td><td></td><td></td><td></td><td></td><td></td></tr>
<tr><td></td><td></td><td></td><td></td><td></td><td></td><td></td></tr>
</table>

Section 5. *Canvass and certification of results; preservation of boxes.* Outside as well as within the city of New York the board of elections instead of the board of supervisors shall be the board of county canvassers to canvass the results of the votes cast at such election in the several election districts, as returned by the inspectors of election of said election districts, and each shall have the powers and duties of such a canvassing board prescribed by the election law. Each board of elections shall complete its said canvass and make a certified return thereof to the secretary of state within ten days after the election. The secretary of state may require delayed returns to be made and insufficient returns supplemented forthwith as in the case of a general election to fill a state office.

The one hundred and fifty persons who shall receive the highest number of votes cast at said election shall be the delegates to the convention. A vote cast for any or all of the candidates whose names appear in the column headed for repeal shall be held to be a vote for the delegates voted for who favor ratification of the amendment to repeal the Eighteenth Amendment. A vote cast for any or all of the candidates whose names appear in the column headed against repeal shall be held to be a vote in favor of the delegates voted for who are opposed to ratification of the amendment to repeal the Eighteenth Amendment. A vote cast for any or all of the candidates whose names appear in the column headed uninstructed shall be held to be a vote for the delegates voted for who are to be uninstructed. A vote shall be counted for each person whose name is written by the voter upon the ballot in the proper space provided therefor and which name is not printed on the ballot. No ballot shall be held void because any cross (x) mark is irregular in character. The votes on such a ballot shall be counted in accordance with rules seven and eight of section two hundred and nineteen of the election law, relating to ballots for presidential electors. The secretary of state immediately after the receipt of said returns shall prepare a list of the elected delegates, cause the same to be filed in the department of state, and mail to each delegate a certificate of his election, and notice of the time and place that the convention will open. The ballot boxes to be used at said election, and containing voted ballots, and the stubs thereof shall be preserved inviolate for thirty days after the said election, but may be opened thereafter and the contents removed therefrom, so that use may be made of the same at the fall primary election occurring in September, nineteen hundred thirty-three.

Section 6. *Expenses of the election; how paid.* In the first instance, each county, city and town shall pay or incur the necessary expenses of and connected with the holding of such election, chargeable to it under the election law, as if it were a special election of a state senator, including the expense of revising registers and of special registration, but each shall be reimbursed therefor by the state. Each board of elections, after ascertaining its own expenses, paid or incurred, chargeable to its county, or the city of New York, and the expenses so paid or incurred by the cities and towns within the board's jurisdiction, shall present an account thereof, including interest, if any, on money borrowed, if any, to meet such expenses, to the secretary of state; and the amount thereof, as approved or revised by the secretary of state, shall be included in the next annual estimate submitted to the governor, pursuant to the constitution, of appropriations to meet the financial needs of the department of state. The legislature shall appropriate the amount needed to make the reimbursements herein provided. The moneys so appropriated shall be paid to the several boards of elections, for the counties of their jurisdiction and cities and towns therein, on the vouchers of such boards, approved by the secretary of state, and on the audit and warrant of the comptroller. Moneys so paid to any board of elections shall be paid over forthwith by it to the county treasurer, or in the case of New York City to its chief fiscal officer. The amount received by the latter shall belong to the general fund of such city. The amount received by a county treasurer shall be apportioned and retained by or paid over to the county and several cities and towns in a manner that will provide for such reimbursement to each. Moneys so paid to a county, city or town shall be applied by it first to the repayment of moneys borrowed by it, if any, including interest, for such expenses, and the remainder only shall be applicable to its general fund.

Section 7. Except as otherwise herein provided, all the provisions of the election law shall govern the said election, and all matters and proceedings prior and subsequent thereto, in so far as the same may be applicable.

Section 8. *Greater New York charter and other laws not to control.* The provisions of section four hundred and nineteen of the Greater New York charter, providing for competitive bidding after ten days advertising, shall not apply to the election provided for in this act and the board of elections in the city of New York is hereby authorized to obtain the necessary official and sample ballots and other election equipment, supplies and paraphernalia, without advertisement and public bidding. Ballots, ballot boxes, labels and other printed matter and all supplies, equipment and paraphernalia required for carrying out the provisions of this act may be obtained by the state, county, city or town, and may be obtained without advertisement, estimate, proposal or competitive or other bidding, notwithstanding any general, special or local law to the contrary.

Section 9. *Filling vacancies.* If there shall be a vacancy in the convention caused by death, resignation or disability of any delegate, or any other cause, the same shall be filled by appointment by a majority of the delegates comprising the group from which said delegate was elected, and if the convention contains no other delegate of that group, shall be filled by appointment by the governor.

Section 10. *Convention; no compensation of delegates; quorum.* The delegates to the convention shall meet at the time and place as herein provided, and shall thereupon constitute a convention to pass upon the question of whether or not the proposed amendment shall be ratified. They shall be called to order by the governor, or, in his absence, by the lieutenant governor, who shall act as temporary president and designate a temporary secretary. Delegates to said convention shall receive no compensation for their services. Each delegate shall take the constitutional oath of office before acting as such delegate. The said convention shall continue its sessions until the business of the convention shall have been completed, and a final vote taken on the said amendment to the constitution of the United States. A majority of the convention shall constitute a quorum for the transaction of business, and a majority of such quorum shall be sufficient to determine any and all questions, except the question of ratification of the amendment, which must be decided by a majority vote of all the delegates elected to such convention. The "yeas" and "nays" shall be entered on the journal to be kept by it.

Section 11. *Rules and powers of convention.* The convention shall be the judge of the election and qualification of its members, and shall have power to adopt its own rules, elect its president, secretary and other officers, appoint stenographers and other employees and fix the compensation of such stenographers and employees. The convention may adjourn from day to day. It shall keep a journal of its proceedings, in which shall be recorded the vote of each delegate on the question of ratification of the proposed amendment. Upon final adjournment the journal shall be filed by the secretary of the convention in the office of the secretary of state. For any speech or debate in the convention, the delegates shall not be questioned in any other place. The compensation of stenographers and other employees and other necessary expenses incurred in holding the convention shall be paid from moneys appropriated on the certificate of the president or vice-president of the convention and the audit and warrant of the comptroller.

Section 12. *Ratification; how certified.* If the convention shall agree by the vote of a majority of the total number of delegates to the ratification of the proposed amendment, a certificate to that effect shall be made in triplicate by the president and secretary of the convention, and there shall be attached to each a true copy, certified by such officers, of the record of the vote taken, showing the yeas and nays. Such certificates and certified copies of such record shall be deposited with the secretary of state, and he shall transmit one, under the great seal of the state of New York, to the secretary of state of the United States, one to the presiding officer of the senate of the United States, and one to the speaker of the house of representatives of the United States in the manner in which amendments to the constitution of the United States, submitted to the legislature for ratification are certified, accompanied with his own certificate that the persons signing the certificates so transmitted were the duly constituted president and secretary of such convention and that their signatures are genuine. Before transmitting the certificates and copies of records so deposited with him, he shall make a copy of one of them and certify it as such, and record it as a permanent record of the department of state. The president, the secretary and any other officer of the convention and the delegates and secretary of state, or any or either of them, are hereby authorized to comply with any act or resolution of congress requiring other or further confirmation of such ratification or rejection of said proposed amendment.

Section 13. *Immediate distribution of copies of this act.* As soon as practicable after the act takes effect, the secretary of state shall transmit a copy thereof to the board of elections of each county of the state and to the board of elections in the city of New York.

Section 14. *Time of taking effect.* This act shall take effect immediately.

NORTH CAROLINA*

AN ACT to provide for the calling of a convention of the people of North Carolina for the purpose of considering the proposed amendment to the Constitution of the United States repealing the Eighteenth Amendment.

WHEREAS, The seventy-second Congress of the United States of America, at the second session thereof, begun and held at the City of Washington on Monday, the fifth day of December, one thousand nine hundred thirty-two, adopted a joint resolution proposing an amendment to the Constitution of the United States, which said joint resolution is as follows:

"Resolved by the Senate and House of Representatives of the United States of America in Congress assembled (two-thirds of each House concurring therein), That the following article is hereby proposed as an amendment to the Constitution of the United States, which shall be valid to all intents and purposes as part of the Constitution when ratified by conventions in three-fourths of the several States.

ARTICLE ___ ___

"Section 1. The eighteenth article of amendment to the Constitution of the United States is hereby repealed.

"Section 2. The transportation or importation into any State, Territory, or possession of the United States for delivery or use therein of intoxicating liquors, in violation of the laws thereof, is hereby prohibited.

"Section 3. This article shall be inoperative unless it shall have been ratified as an amendment to the Constitution by conventions in the several States, as provided in the Constitution, within seven years from the date of the submission hereof to the States by the Congress."

And WHEREAS, The people of this State should have the opportunity to pass upon and determine whether a convention shall be called for the purpose of considering said proposed amendment: *Now, therefore,*

The General Assembly of North Carolina do enact (two-thirds of all the Members of each House Concurring):

Section 1. At a general election to be held in the State of North Carolina on Tuesday after the first Monday in November, one thousand nine hundred thirty-three, the proposition of "Convention" or "No Convention" shall be submitted to the qualified voters of the whole State, and an election held thereon, and the result thereof ascertained and determined in the manner as set out in this act. The said election shall be for the sole and exclusive purpose of passing on the proposition of "Convention" or "No Convention," and the election of delegates thereto, as provided for in this act, and it shall not be competent or lawful to elect any officers of the State or local governments, or to vote or pass on any other proposition at said election.

Section 2. If a majority of the votes cast at the said election on said proposition shall be for "Convention," as ascertained and determined under the provisions of this act, the said convention shall consist of one hundred twenty delegates, and each county

* *North Carolina Public Laws, 1933,* Chapter 403, pp. 600-607.

shall be entitled to the same number of delegates to the said convention as such county has members in the House of Representatives of the General Assembly of One Thousand nine hundred thirty-three. Each delegate to said convention shall be a qualified elector of the State and shall reside in the county from which he is chosen for one year preceding his election. Laws disqualifying a person for public office because he then holds another public office under the State or National Government shall not apply to delegates to such Convention. All qualified electors shall have the right to participate in said election in their several precincts as now provided by law. The registration books shall be open in the several precincts on the second Saturday before said election for the purpose of registration of persons entitled thereto in such precincts.

Section 3. It shall be the duty of the State Board of Elections to prescribe, provide, and print the official convention ballots to be voted on at said election. No ballot shall be used or counted except such official ballots. Upon said ballots there shall appear the words "Convention" and "No Convention," and opposite and to the left of each voting square, in either of which the elector may make a cross mark (x) indicating that he thereby votes "Convention" or "No Convention." The ballots shall be headed "Official Convention Ballot." Below said title appropriate instructions shall be printed as follows:

1. To vote for "Convention," make a cross mark (x) in the square to the left of the word "Convention."

2. To vote "No Convention," make a cross mark (x) in the square to the left of the words "No Convention."

3. Mark only with a pencil or pen and ink.

4. If you tear or deface or wrongly mark this ballot, return it and get another. At the bottom, on the face of said ballot shall be printed the following endorsement, the blanks being properly filled in:

"OFFICIAL CONVENTION BALLOT

"STATE OF NORTH CAROLINA,.............................(Date of election)

....

"(Facsimile of signature of Chaiman
of State Board of Elections.)"

Section 4. At said election it shall be the duty of each county board of elections to provide for each voting precinct in said county a ballot box to contain said official convention ballots, in which all qualified electors shall have the right to vote on the proposition of "Convention" or "No Convention."

Section 5. Except as otherwise provided in this act, the said election shall be held and conducted under the same laws, rules and regulations as now prescribed for the holding and conduct of elections of members of the General Assembly. The several county boards of elections shall meet in their respective counties, not later than the tenth day of September, in the year one thousand nine hundred thirty-three, and arrange for the holding of said election. The registrars appointed to act at the last general election in the year One thousand nine hundred thirty-two shall act as registrars for the election herein provided for. The several county boards of elections shall appoint two judges of election for each election precinct in their county, whose duties and powers shall be in all respects as provided in the general election laws of the State. In making appointment of the judges of election, the county boards of elections shall appoint for each election precinct one competent person generally known to be in favor of the proposition submitted by this act, and one competent person generally known to be opposed to the proposition submitted in this act. The several county boards of elections shall make publication of the names of the registrars and judges of election, and serve notice upon them as required by the general election laws of the State.

Section 6. The registrar and judges of election of the several voting precincts in each county shall count the ballots and make return thereof to the County Board of Elections on forms prepared and furnished by the State Board of Elections. Upon the receipt of the returns of said election, and not later than the sixth day thereafter, the county boards of elections shall tabulate the returns from said election and declare the results thereof in their several counties. The returns from the several counties on the proposition of "Convention" or "No Convention" shall, by the chairman of the County Board of Elections, be certified to the State Board of Elections, who shall, not later than the twentieth day after the election, tabulate and officially declare the result of said election on said proposition "Convention" or "No Convention."

Section 7. That at the said general election to be held on Tuesday after the first Monday of November, One thousand nine hundred thirty-three, as provided for in this act, there shall be voted for in the several counties of the State, in a separate box to be provided by the several county boards of elections, a delegate or delegates, in accordance with the number as is prescribed in section two of this act. Party nominations for delegates to said convention shall not be made. Any person desiring to become a candidate for delegate from his county to said Convention shall, thirty days before the date of said election, file notice of his candidacy for delegate to said Convention with the county board of elections, containing declaration that he is "For Repeal of the Eighteenth Amendment," or "Against Repeal of the Eighteenth Amendment," and supported by a written petition signed by qualified voters of the county equal in number to two per cent of the total vote cast for Governor in said county in the gubernatorial election of one thousand nine hundred thirty-two. If such notice of candidacy with such declaration and so supported shall be filed in a county by candidates on the one side or the other of such question, more in number than such county is entitled to delegates in said Convention, the county board of elections shall put on the official ballot the names of such candidates "For Repeal of the Eighteenth Amendment" and "Against Repeal of the Eighteenth Amendment," equal respectively to the number of delegates to which such county is entitled in said convention, as have the largest number of such signers to his or their petition. The county board of elections shall place on the ballot a candidate or candidates for such delegates from said county, both "For Repeal of the Eighteenth Amendment" and "Against Repeal of the Eighteenth Amendment," in accordance with the terms of this act, if a candidate or candidates have complied with its terms. The ballot shall be made up showing on the face and at the top thereof that the candidates are "For Repeal of the Eighteenth Amendment" and "Against Repeal of the Eighteenth Amendment." Any person seeking a place on said ballot may appeal from the decision of the county board of elections to the State Board of Elections for a determination of the question as to whether he is entitled to a place thereon, and said appeal shall be heard promptly by said State Board of Elections, whose decision thereon shall be final.

Section 8. It shall be the duty of the county board of elections of each county to provide printed ballots to be voted in said county for the election of delegates to the Convention. Only official ballots shall be used and counted. On such official ballots shall be printed the names of all candidates for delegates to such Convention from said county, nominated as herein prescribed and permitted. The names of said delegates shall be printed in columns separated by black lines as now provided for by law for the printing of ballots in general elections. At the head of said ballot shall be printed "Official Ballot for Delegates to Convention to Pass Upon the Proposed Amendment to the Constitution of the United States for the Repeal of the Eighteenth Amendment." At the head of one column shall be printed the words "Delegate or Delegates for Repeal of the Eighteenth Amendment," and at the head of the other column, "Delegate or Delegates Against Repeal of the Eighteenth Amendment."

Section 9. Upon said official ballots, arranged in the usual way, the appropriate instructions shall be printed as follows:

(1). To vote for any candidate whose name appears in the column below, mark a cross (x) in the square at the left of the name of the candidate.

(2). Vote only for the number of delegates indicated below.

(3). Mark only with a pencil or pen and ink.

(4). If you tear or deface or wrongly mark this ballot, get another. At the bottom, on the face of the ballot, shall be printed the following endorsement, the blanks being properly filled in:

"OFFICIAL BALLOT FOR DELEGATES TO CONVENTION TO PASS UPON PROPOSED AMENDMENT REPEALING THE EIGHTEENTH AMENDMENT

County of ....

....(Date of election)

....

Facsimile of signature of Chairman of
County Board of Elections"

Section 10. No markers or assistants shall be allowed in said election. No vote shall be cast or counted except such votes as are cast by electors who present themselves in person and cast their ballots at the polling place, in the precinct of which they are electors. Any person who is physically unable to enter a voting booth, or to mark his ballot, may be assisted in entering such booth and in marking his ballot, by the election official upon whom he may call for assistance.

Section 11. Except as otherwise provided in this act, the said elections for the election of delegate or delegates to the said Convention shall be held and conducted under the same laws, rules and regulations as now prescribed for the holding and conduct of elections of members of the General Assembly. The registrar and judges of election of the several voting precincts in each county shall count the ballots and make return thereof to the County Board of Elections on forms prepared and furnished by the State Board of Elections. Upon the receipt of the returns of said election, and not later than the sixth day thereafter, the County Boards of Elections shall tabulate the returns from said election and declare the results thereof in their several counties.

Section 12. It shall be the duty of the chairman of the county board of elections to issue certificates of election to the delegate or delegates ascertained and declared to be elected from his county. And it shall be the duty of the State Board of Elections, upon ascertaining and declaring the result of the election on the proposition "Convention" or "No Convention," to make certificate thereof, certifying the same to the

Governor. If the majority of votes cast shall be "No Convention," then said Convention shall not be held and no duties and powers shall devolve upon, or be exercised by, any person elected as delegate to said Convention, as a consequence of his said election.

Section 13. If, upon the canvass of the election upon the question "Convention" or "No Convention," as hereinbefore prescribed, it shall be ascertained that a majority of the votes cast in said election are in favor of "Convention," then the delegates so declared to have been elected shall convene in the hall of the House of Representatives at Raleigh on Wednesday after the first Monday of December, one thousand nine hundred thirty-three, at twelve o'clock noon, when and where the said delegates shall be called to order by the Chief Justice or one of the Associate Justices of the Supreme Court, who, if there be not a majority present, shall adjourn then to the same place, and from day to day, until a majority appear, and on the appearance of a majority, he shall administer to each of them the following oath:

"You, A. B., do solemnly swear (or affirm, as the delegate-elect shall choose) that you will bear true allegiance to the government of the United States and the State of North Carolina, and will faithfully maintain and support the Constitution of the United States, and the State of North Carolina: that you will faithfully, conscientiously, and without fear or favor, perform the duties required of you as a delegate to this convention, and that you will neither directly nor indirectly evade or disregard the duties enjoined, or the restrictions imposed upon the convention by the act of the General Assembly authorizing your election, and that you will in your capacity as a delegate to this convention serve the people of this State to the best of your skill, knowledge and ability: so help you, God."

No delegate shall be permitted to sit or be entitled to a seat in the said convention or to act as a member thereof until he or she shall have taken and subscribed the said oath or affirmation as above set out.

Section 14. As soon as a majority of the delegates-elect shall have thus appeared and taken the oath or affirmation as prescribed, they shall proceed to elect a president, who shall serve as presiding officer of the convention, and shall choose such other officers, clerks, stenographers, and servants as they shall find necessary.

Section 15. The delegates to such Convention shall receive as compensation for their services the sum of ten ($10.00) dollars and they shall also be entitled to receive five cents per mile both while coming to Raleigh and while going home, the said distance to be computed by the nearest line and route of public travel. The compensation of the President, or presiding officer, shall be twelve ($12.00) dollars and mileage.

Section 16. A majority of the total number of delegates to the Convention shall constitute a quorum. The Convention shall be judge of the election and qualifications of its members. For any speech or debate in the Convention, the delegate shall not be questioned in any other place.

Section 17. It shall be the duty of the Governor of the State to transmit to the Convention, upon its convening, the resolution of the Congress of the United States submitting the proposed amendment for the repeal of the eighteenth amendment. It shall thereupon be the sole and only duty of the said Convention to consider, debate, and act upon said proposed amendment to the Constitution of the United States, the said action to be determined by a vote of the majority of the delegates to the Convention present and voting thereon. And the action of the Convention, as called under the provisions of this act, shall be limited and restricted to debating and acting upon the said proposed amendment to the Constitution of the United States, and when said action is completed, whether the result be ratification or rejection thereof, the powers and duties of the Convention and its delegates shall cease and the Convention shall thereupon adjourn *sine die*.

Section 18. If and when the said proposed amendment to the Constitution of the United States shall have been ratified by said Convention in the manner as hereinbefore set out, a certificate of that fact shall be made in quadruplicate by the President and Secretary of such Convention, and there shall be attached to each a true copy of the record of the vote so taken, showing the yeas and nays. Such certificate and certified copies of such record shall be deposited with the Governor, and he shall thereupon transmit one of such certificates and certified copies to the Secretary of State of the United States at Washington, one to the presiding officer of the United States Senate, one to the Speaker of the House of Representatives, accompanied with his own certificate that the persons signing the certificates so transmitted were the duly constituted officers of such Convention, and that their signatures are genuine. One of such certificates and copies of records shall be filed as a permanent record in the office of the Secretary of State of North Carolina. The President, the Secretary, and any other officers of the Convention, the delegates, and the Governor, and any of them, are hereby authorized to comply with any act of Congress requiring any further act of confirmation or rejection of such ratification.

Section 19. Upon the ratification of this act, it shall be the duty of the Secretary of State to print such reasonable number of copies thereof as may be approved by the Governor and Council of State.

Section 20. The expense of holding said Convention shall be certified by the President and Secretary thereof to the State Auditor, who shall audit and pass upon the accounts so made and rendered to him, and said expenses, when so audited and approved, shall be paid by the State Treasurer out of any funds not otherwise appropriated.

Section 21. This act shall be in full force and effect from and after its ratification.

Ratified this the 9th day of May, A.D. 1933.

OHIO*

AN ACT

To provide for a convention to pass on amendments to the constitution of the United States which may hereafter be proposed by the congress for ratification by conventions in the several states.

Be it enacted by the General Assembly of the State of Ohio:

Sec. 4785-235. Amendment to the constitution of United States, how ratified; election.

Section 1. Whenever the congress of the United States shall propose an amendment to the constitution of the United States, and shall propose that it be ratified by conventions in the several states, the governor shall fix by proclamation the date of an election for the purpose of electing the delegates to such convention in this state. Such election may either be at a special election or may be held at the same time as a general election, but shall be held at least as soon as the next general election occurring more than three months after the amendment has been proposed by the congress.

Sec. 4785-236. Qualification of voters.

Section 2. At such election all persons qualified to vote for members of the general assembly shall be entitled to vote.

Sec. 4785-237. Conduct of election.

Section 3. Except as in this article otherwise provided, such election shall be conducted and the results thereof ascertained and certified in the same manner as in the case of the election of presidential electors in this state, and all provisions of the laws of this state relative to elections except so far as inconsistent with this act are hereby made applicable to such election.

Sec. 4785-238. Number of delegates.

Section 4. The number of delegates to be chosen to such convention shall be fifty-two (52), to be elected from the state at large.

Sec. 4785-239. Qualifications of delegates; nomination, when effective.

Section 5. Candidates for the office of delegate to the convention shall be citizens and residents of the state, and of age. Nomination of candidates for the office of delegate shall be by petition and not otherwise. A single petition may nominate any number of candidates not exceeding the total number of delegates to be elected, and shall be signed by not less than five thousand voters. Nomination shall be without party or political designation, but the nominating petitions shall contain a statement as to each nominee, to the effect that he favors ratification, or that he opposes ratification, or that he will remain unpledged, and no nominating petition shall contain the name of any nominee whose position as stated therein is inconsistent with that of any other nominee as stated therein. No nomination shall be effective except those of the fifty-two (52) nominees in favor of ratification, and the fifty-two (52) nominees against ratifica-

* *Ohio Laws, 1933* [Amended Senate Bill No. 204], pp. 74-77.

tion, and the fifty-two (52) nominees to remain unpledged, whose nominating petitions have respectively been signed by the largest number of voters, ties to be decided by lot drawn by the secretary of state. Within ten days after the petitions are filed, the secretary of state shall certify the candidates of each group to the appropriate local election authorities. All petitions and acceptances thereof shall be filed with the secretary of state not less than thirty days before the proclaimed date of the election.

Sec. 4785-240. Form of ballot.

Section 6. The election shall be by ballot, separate from any ballot to be used at the same election, which shall be prepared as follows: It shall first state the substance of the proposed amendment. This shall be followed by appropriate instructions to the voter. It shall then contain perpendicular columns of equal width, headed respectively in plain type, "for ratification," "against ratification" and "unpledged." In the column headed "for ratification" shall be placed the names of the nominees nominated as in favor of ratification. In the column headed "against ratification" shall be placed the names of the nominees nominated as against ratification. In the column headed "unpledged" shall be placed the names of the nominees nominated as unpledged. The voter shall indicate his choice by making one or more cross-marks in the appropriate spaces provided on the ballot. No ballot shall be held void because any such cross-mark is irregular in character. The ballot shall be so arranged that the voter may, by making a single cross-mark, vote for the entire group of nominees whose names are comprised in any column. The ballot shall be in substantially the following form:

PROPOSED AMENDMENT TO THE CONSTITUTION OF THE UNITED STATES

Delegates to the convention to ratify the proposed amendment.

The congress has proposed an amendment to the constitution of the United States which provides (insert here the substance of the proposed amendment).

The congress has also proposed that the said amendment shall be ratified by conventions in the states.

INSTRUCTIONS TO VOTERS

Do not vote for more than fifty-two candidates.

To vote for all candidates in favor of ratification, or for all candidates against ratification, or for all candidates who intend to remain unpledged, make a cross-mark in the CIRCLE. If you do this, make no other mark. To vote for an individual candidate make a cross-mark in the SQUARE at the left of the name.

For Ratification	Against Ratification	Unpledged
○	○	○
☐ John Doe	☐ Charles Coe	☐ Daniel De Foe
☐ Richard Doe	☐ Michael Moe	☐ Louis St Loe

All rights on the part of lists of candidates to name challengers and witnesses in the polling places shall be the same as those under the general election laws.

Sec. 4785-241. Vacancy, how filled.

Section 7. The fifty-two (52) nominees who shall receive the highest number of votes shall be the delegates to the convention. If there shall be a vacancy in the convention caused by the death or disability of any delegate or any other cause, the same shall be filled by appointment by the majority vote of the delegates comprising the group from which such delegate was elected and if the convention contains no other delegate of that group, shall be filled by the governor.

Sec. 4785-242. Meeting, when held.

Section 8. The delegates to the convention shall meet at the capitol on the twenty-eighth day after their election at one o'clock after noon, and shall thereupon constitute a convention to pass upon the question of whether or not the proposed amendment shall be ratified.

Sec. 4785-243. Powers of the convention.

Section 9. The convention shall be the judge of the election and qualification of its members; and shall have power to elect its president, secretary and other officers, and to adopt its own rules.

Sec. 4785-244. Journal.

Section 10. The convention shall keep a journal of its proceedings in which shall be recorded the vote of each delegate on the question of ratification of the proposed amendment. Upon final adjournment the journal shall be filed with the secretary of state.

Sec. 4785-245. Certification in case of ratification.

Section 11. If the convention shall agree, by vote of a majority of the total number of delegates, to the ratification of the proposed amendment, a certificate to that effect shall be executed by the president and secretary of the convention and transmitted to the secretary of state of this state who shall transmit the certificate under the great seal of the state to the secretary of state of the United States.

Sec. 4785-246. Mileage.

Section 12. Each delegate to the convention shall receive the legal rate of railroad transportation each way for mileage from and to his place of residence by the most direct route of public travel to and from the city of Columbus, Ohio.

Sec. 4785-247. Provisions of act inoperative, when.

Section 13. If at or about the time of submitting any such amendment, congress shall either in the resolution submitting the same or by statute, prescribe the manner in which the convention shall be constituted, and shall not except from the provisions of such statute or resolution such states as may theretofore have provided for constituting such conventions, the preceding provisions of this act shall be inoperative, the convention shall be constituted and shall operate as the said resolution or act of congress shall direct, and all officers of the state who may by the said resolution or statute be authorized or directed to take any action to constitute such a convention for this state are hereby authorized and directed to act thereunder and in obedience thereto with the same force and effect as if acting under a statute of this state.

FRANK CAVE
Speaker of the House of Representatives
CHARLES SAWYER
President of the Senate

Passed March 20, 1933.
Approved March 23, 1933.

GEORGE WHITE
Governor

OKLAHOMA*

A JOINT RESOLUTION providing for the method and manner of nominating Delegates to a State Convention to ratify or reject the proposed Twenty-First Article of Amendment to the Constitution of the United States; providing for the call of County Conventions and prescribing qualifications of Delegates to County Conventions; providing for the time, place and manner of holding same; providing for the holding of Congressional District Conventions and prescribing qualifications of Delegates and manner, time and place of holding same; providing for the manner in which Delegates shall be elected and manner in which Convention of Delegates shall meet; providing for payments of expenses; providing manner of certifying results of the Election and result of the Ballot of Delegates.

Be it resolved by the House of Representatives and the Senate of the extraordinary session of the fourteenth legislature of the State of Oklahoma:

State Election Board—Electors—Governor—Convention.

Section 1. The State Election Board of the State of Oklahoma on the first Tuesday following the 105th day after the adjournment of the Extraordinary Session of the Fourteenth Legislature shall certify to the Governor of the State of Oklahoma the names of two qualified electors in each of the several counties of the State, said electors being residents of the counties for which they are selected and who shall have been residents of such county for more than two years next preceding the time of their selection, to call County Conventions in each of the several counties of the State to be held at a time to be designated by the Governor of the State of Oklahoma not more than twenty (20) days after the date of their selection and certification. That upon the certification of the names to the Governor of the State of Oklahoma and when it shall appear to him that the persons selected are qualified within the meaning of this Resolution, the Governor shall issue commissions to such persons designating the time of holding the Convention hereinafter provided for and designating the said persons to be Chairmen of the County Conventions. One of said qualified electors so appointed in each county shall favor adoption by the State of Oklahoma of the proposed Twenty-first Article of Amendment to the Constitution of the United States and the other of said qualified electors in each county shall favor rejection of said Twenty-first Article of Amendment. Each person so selected and commissioned in each of the several counties of the State of Oklahoma who shall favor adoption of said Amendment shall be designated as "Temporary Chairmen of County Convention Favoring Repeal," and the other of said persons so selected and commissioned in the several counties of the State of Oklahoma shall be designated as "Temporary Chairmen of County Convention Against Repeal."

Chairman of County Conventions—Place of Holding Conventions.

Section 2. When the several Chairmen of the several County Conventions shall have been commissioned as above provided and notified of the date for the County Conventions, it shall be the duty of each of said Chairmen to secure some suitable place for the holding of the particular Convention over which such Temporary Chairman

* *Oklahoma Session Laws, 1933,* Chapter 212, pp. 499-503.

is to preside. Such Conventions for the several counties of the State shall be held in the County Seat and shall be held at the time designated in the commission and each of said Conventions shall be held at 2:30 P.M., on the day designated. Any elector who is duly registered as an elector may participate in the County Convention in the county in which he is registered, but cannot participate in any convention outside of the county of his residence or in which he holds certificate of registration, and such electors may participate in either of said conventions but cannot participate in more than one, and it shall be sufficient credentials for any such elector to show to the convention of his or her choice that he or she is a duly registered citizen of that county and will support the principles of the particular convention at the election hereafter provided for. The temporary chairman above provided for shall call the respective conventions to order and preside until such a time as there shall have been elected, first, a secretary of such convention, and second, a permanent chairman. Such temporary chairmen, permanent chairmen, other officers or participants in such county convention shall receive no compensation for such services. The temporary chairmen shall certify to the Secretary of the State Election Board the names of the permanent chairmen and the secretary.

At each of said county conventions there shall be elected delegates to Congressional District Conventions to be held as hereinafter provided. The several conventions shall elect one delegate to the Congressional District Convention for each five hundred electors or major fraction thereof voting for presidential electors at the preceding presidential election. The chairman of the respective conventions electing said delegates shall certify their election to the chairman of the Congressional District Conventions as hereafter provided, and the secretary of said convention shall attest the same.

That any delegate from any convention in the State shall be an elector duly registered as such in the county he is chosen to represent as a delegate to the Congressional District Convention.

Congressional Districts—Chairmen—Place for Holding Conventions.

Section 3. The State Election Board of the State of Oklahoma shall on the same date chosen for selection of County Chairmen likewise select two qualified electors in each of the several Congressional Districts of the State. Said persons so selected to be commissioned by the Governor in the same manner as provided in Section 2 hereof and such Congressional Chairmen shall have the same qualifications as said County Chairmen. In the commissions to the said Congressional Chairmen the Governor of the State of Oklahoma shall designate a time for the holding of Congressional Conventions at a time two (2) weeks after the date of the County Conventions, and one of said Congressional Chairmen in each said district shall favor adoption of the 21st Article of Amendment to the Constitution of the United States of America and the other of whom shall oppose the adoption of the 21st Article of Amendment to the Constitution of the United States of America. One of such persons so designated and appointed in each of the several Congressional Districts of the State of Oklahoma shall be known and designated as "Temporary Chairman of Congressional District Convention Favoring Repeal" and the other person so designated and appointed in each of the several Congressional Districts shall be known and designated as "Temporary Chairman of Congressional District Convention Against Repeal." Each Congressional District Chairman so commissioned by the Governor shall select some suitable place in the County Seat of one of the counties of his district as a place for holding such Congressional District Convention and it shall be the duty of such Temporary Chairman of the District Convention to give public notice of the place of holding such convention and such district convention shall be called to order by said Temporary Chairman of the District Conventions at 2:30 P.M., on the day designated by the Governor of the State of Oklahoma as set forth in Section 2 above. The Temporary Chairmen of the said district conventions shall call the conventions of said Congressional Districts to order and preside until a permanent chairman has been elected by the delegates from the several counties of said Congressional District. The several delegates from the several counties of such Congressional Districts shall be entitled to vote the full quota of their particular county as a unit and no delegate shall be entitled to vote by proxy for any absent delegate.

The Temporary Chairmen of the Congressional District Convention, the Permanent Chairmen, or other officer or delegate, shall not be entitled to receive any compensation for participation in such Congressional District Convention. At said district convention, there shall be nominated two candidates from each of said district conventions, which said candidates shall have the same qualifications as candidates for Congress of the United States, and no person who is holding any office of trust or emolument in the State of Oklahoma shall be eligible to be a candidate for delegate to such State Convention, and the names of such two candidates from each of the district conventions in favor of the adoption of the 21st Article of Amendment to the Constitution of the United States shall be placed upon the ballot hereafter provided for and shall be designated on said ballot "For Repeal of the 18th Amendment" and the two candidates from each of said district conventions against the adoption of the 21st Article of Amendment to the Constitution of the United States shall be placed upon the ballot hereafter provided for and shall be designated on said ballot "Against Repeal of the 18th Amendment."

The Temporary Chairmen of the Congressional District Conventions shall certify to the Secretary of the State Election Board the names of the secretary and permanent chairmen of the several district conventions. The permanent chairmen and secretaries shall certify to the Secretary of the State Election Board the names of the delegates to the State Convention so nominated at the several Congressional District Conventions. In the event of the vacancy in either temporary County Chairman or temporary Congressional Chairman, the Governor of the State of Oklahoma shall have the authority and is hereby vested with the power to fill any vacancy by appointment of a person having the same qualifications and views as originally provided herein.

In the event any person selected as a candidate for Congressional Delegate shall die, leave the State, or otherwise become disqualified, the vacancy so created shall be filled by a majority of the permanent County Chairmen of the Congressional District, provided that no County Chairman favoring repeal shall participate in the selection of a delegate to fill the vacancy against repeal, and no County Chairman against repeal shall participate in selecting a delegate to fill a vacancy for repeal.

Ballots—Form—For Repeal—Against Repeal—Record of Proceedings.

Section 4. The State Election Board shall prepare and furnish ballots which shall contain the sixteen names of the delegates from the several Congressional District Conventions which shall favor adoption of the 21st Article of Amendment to the Constitution of the United States of America and in lieu of party emblem at the top of such ballot shall cause to be printed the words "For Repeal," and on said ballots of the State Election Board shall have placed the sixteen names of the delegates from the several Congressional District Conventions which favor rejection of the 21st Article of Amendment to the Constitution of the United States and in lieu of party emblem at the top of such ballot shall cause to be printed the words "Against Repeal." Such candidates shall be voted upon by the electors of the entire State at large and at such election the general election laws of the State of Oklahoma shall govern, and such election shall be held at the first statewide election in the State of Oklahoma held after the date of the said Congressional District Conventions or at any special election which may be called by the Governor. That after the election of such delegates the State Election Board shall certify to the delegates' election in the same manner as certifying to the election of a Representative to the State Legislature. That within twenty days after the issuance of such certificate of election the Governor of the State of Oklahoma shall by proclamation call a State Convention of the delegates so elected. The delegates provided for herein shall receive as compensation for their services, the sum of Six Dollars per day not to exceed a period of one day, and five cents per mile for each mile necessarily traveled by the nearest route to and from the residence of such delegate to Oklahoma City. In the event there shall be a vacancy, by reason of the death, removal or disqualification of any of the delegates, the remaining delegates at the convention, hereinafter provided for, shall select a successor for such deceased, removed or disqualified delegate, provided, however, such successor shall be from the same Congressional District as his predecessor, and shall be of the same belief with reference to repeal or against repeal as the belief of the man whom the delegate is selected to succeed. At the time designated by the Governor of the State of Oklahoma, said convention shall assemble in the Assembly Room of the House of Representatives at the State Capitol Building in Oklahoma City, Oklahoma, and shall be composed of the delegates duly elected and they shall proceed by electing a presiding officer and clerk and thereafter shall ballot upon the question presented to the State of Oklahoma by the United States Senate Joint Resolution 211 passed by the Second Session of the 72nd Congress of the United States and received by the Governor of the State of Oklahoma on the 23rd day of February, 1933, proposing an amendment to the Constitution of the United States to be known as the 21st Article of Amendment thereto. The Question shall be:

"Shall this Convention, representing the entire people of the State of Oklahoma, adopt the proposed amendment to the Constitution of the United States of America to be known as the 21st Article of Amendment thereto?"

A record shall be kept of the proceedings of said Convention. The general record of the voting of the ayes and nays and result thereof shall be forthwith transmitted to the Secretary of State and said Convention shall thereafter transact no further business.

Approved July 18, 1933.

OREGON*

AN ACT

To provide for the election of delegates to a convention to determine whether the state of Oregon shall ratify or reject proposal to repeal the 18th Article of Amendment to the constitution of the United States of America, to ratify or reject the amendment to said constitution covering such repeal submitted under the provisions of the resolution of the congress of the United States designated as "senate joint resolution 211," and to provide for the holding of said convention and other matters incidental and relating thereto, and declaring an emergency.

Be It Enacted by the People of the State of Oregon:

Section 1. Unless otherwise provided by the congress of the United States, delegates to a state convention to determine whether the state of Oregon shall ratify or reject the proposal to repeal the 18th Article of Amendment to the constitution of the United States to ratify or reject the amendment to said constitution covering such repeal submitted under the provisions of the resolution of the congress of the United States designated as "senate joint resolution 211," shall be elected at the next general or special state election held not less than 70 days from receipt of official notice that the congress of the United States has submitted to the various states the question of repealing said 18th Article of Amendment; provided, that nothing herein contained shall be construed to permit the calling of a special election for the sole purpose of electing such delegates. If at or about the time of submitting any such amendment, congress shall by statute, prescribe the manner in which the conventions shall be constituted, and shall not except from the provisions of such statute such states as may have provided for constituting such conventions, the provisions of this act, in so far as the same may conflict with such act of congress, shall be inoperative, and the convention shall be constituted and shall operate as the said act of congress shall direct, and all officers of the state who may by the said statute be authorized or directed to take any action to constitute such convention for the states are hereby authorized and directed to act thereunder and in obedience thereto with the same force and effect as if acting under a statute of this state, but such delegate to such convention shall be elected and shall act in accordance with the provisions of this act in so far as the same shall not be inconsistent with the said act of congress.

Section 2. Within 30 days subsequent to said election and at a time named by the governor, the delegates so selected shall meet at the statehouse in Salem, Oregon, and after taking their oaths of office shall elect a president and a chief clerk of said convention, and shall thereafter and thereupon proceed to vote upon the question as to whether the state of Oregon shall ratify or reject the said proposed article of amendment to the constitution of the United States.

Section 3. Any elector who has been a resident of the county for at least one year may be a candidate for election to said convention by filing his declaration of candidacy with, and paying a filing fee of $5 to the secretary of state, and by filing with such fee and declaration his pledge and statement as follows: "In casting my

* *Oregon Laws, 1933,* Chapter 447, pp. 845-848.

vote in the constitutional convention called for the purpose of ratifying or rejecting the proposal to repeal the 18th Article of Amendment to the constitution of the United States of America and to ratify or reject the amendment to the said constitution covering such repeal submitted under the provisions of the resolution of the congress of the United States, designated as 'senate joint resolution 211,' I pledge myself to vote in accordance with the will of the majority of the voters of the county from which I am a candidate as shown by their vote on the proposition of ratifying or rejecting such proposal." Such candidates shall also sign one of the following statements: "I personally favor the adoption of the proposed article of amendment," or, "I personally oppose the adoption of the proposed article of amendment." The statement so signed by such candidate shall be placed upon the ballot following his name. Said declaration, fee, pledge and statement shall be filed with the secretary of state at least 40 days prior to the date of such election. The secretary of state shall, thereafter, forthwith certify to the respective county clerks, in the manner provided by section 36-1207, Oregon Code 1930, as far as said selection can be given effect, the names of all candidates at said election and said county clerks shall cause ballots to be printed and furnished as now provided for general elections.

Section 4. A majority of the elected and qualified members to said convention shall constitute a quorum to do business and a majority of those present and voting shall be sufficient to adopt any proposition or motion coming before said convention.

Section 5. The said convention shall, upon organizing, adopt rules of procedure and when it has finally voted upon the question for which it was called, the action of said convention shall be enrolled, signed by its president and chief clerk and filed with the secretary of state of the state of Oregon, and it shall thereupon be the duty of the secretary of state of the state of Oregon to notify the secretary of state of the United States of the action taken by the state of Oregon upon said question, by properly certifying the same.

Section 6. The delegates elected to said convention shall receive no compensation whatsoever for their services in attending said convention and shall not be entitled to any mileage for attending the same.

Section 7. In each county of the state having not more than 10,000 population, as shown by the last federal census, one delegate shall be elected; in each county having more than 10,000 population and not more than 20,000 population, as shown by the last federal census, two delegates to said convention shall be elected; in each county having more than 20,000 population and not more than 30,000 population, as shown by the last federal census, three delegates shall be elected; in each county having more than 30,000 population and not more than 40,000 population, as shown by the last federal census, four delegates shall be elected; in each county having more than 40,000 population and not more than 50,000 population, as shown by the last federal census, five delegates shall be elected; in each county having more than 50,000 population and not more than 60,000 population, as shown by the last federal census, six delegates shall be elected; in each county having more than 60,000 population and not more than 70,000, as shown by the last federal census, seven delegates shall be elected; in each county having more than 70,000 and less than 330,000 population, as shown by the last federal census, one delegate for each 10,000 of such population shall be elected; in each county having more than 330,000 population and not more than 350,000 population, as shown by the last federal census, 34 delegates shall be elected. In such election the candidate, or, in case more than one delegate is to be elected, the candidates receiving the highest number of votes as shown by the abstract of votes returned by the several county clerks to the secretary of state as is required by law with respect to a regular election, shall be elected and their election shall be certified and proclaimed in the manner provided for the certification and proclamation of the election of candidates for state offices. Any elector who has been a resident of the county for one year, whether holding an office of profit or otherwise, shall be entitled to sit as a delegate in such convention and to become a nominee therefor. If there shall be a vacancy in the convention caused by the death or disability of any delegate, or by any other cause, and the same shall appear to the satisfaction of the secretary of the state of Oregon, the candidate, or candidates, receiving the next highest number of votes shall fill such vacancy and the secretary of state is authorized and directed to issue to such candidates a certificate of his or their election; provided, that no candidate filling any such vacancy shall qualify until he has again signed the same pledge as the pledge signed by the delegate whose position he is appointed to fill.

Section 8. There shall likewise be submitted to the legal electors of the state of Oregon at such election the question of ratifying or rejecting the proposed amendment. Said question shall be certified to the several county clerks and submitted to the electors, in so far as consistent with the provisions of this act, in the manner provided by law for certifying proposed amendments to the constitution of the state, and said question shall be printed upon the ballot in the following form:

AN AMENDMENT

To the constitution of the United States of America

Vote Yes or No

Purpose: To instruct the delegates to the constitutional convention as to whether the electors of the respective counties of the state of Oregon desire the amendment of the constitution of the United States by the adoption of the proposed article of amendment:

ARTICLE ___ ___

Section 1. The eighteenth article of amendment to the constitution of the United States hereby is repealed.

Section 2. The transportation or importation into any state, territory, or possession of the United States for delivery or use therein of intoxicating liquors, in violation of the laws thereof, hereby is prohibited.

Section 3. This article shall be inoperative unless it shall have been ratified as an amendment to the constitution by conventions in the several states, as provided in the constitution, within seven years from the date of the submission hereof to the states by the congress.

300 Yes. I vote for the proposed amendment.

301 No. I vote against the proposed amendment.

Section 9. If any clause, sentence, paragraph or part of this act shall for any reason be adjudged by any court of competent jurisdiction to be invalid, such judgment shall not affect, impair of invalidate the remainder of this act but shall be confined in its operation to the clause, sentence, paragraph or part thereof directly involved in the controversy in which such judgment shall have been rendered.

Section 10. It hereby is adjudged and declared that existing conditions are such that this act is necessary for the immediate preservation of the public peace, health and safety; and an emergency hereby is declared to exist, and this act shall take effect and be in full force and effect from and after its passage.

Approved by the governor March 15, 1933.
Filed in the office of the secretary of state March 15, 1933.

PENNSYLVANIA*

AN ACT

To provide for a convention to ratify or reject an amendment to the Constitution of the United States, proposed by both Houses of Congress, for the repeal of the eighteenth amendment to the said Constitution, and for the prohibition of the transportation, importation, delivery, or use of intoxicating liquors in violation of the laws of States, territories, or possessions of the United States; and to provide for the election of delegates to such convention.

WHEREAS, The Congress of the United States has proposed an amendment to the Constitution of the United States, in the following language:—

"JOINT RESOLUTION

"Proposing an amendment to the Constitution of the United States.

"Resolved by the Senate and House of Representatives of the United States of America in Congress assembled (two-thirds of each House concurring therein), That the following article is hereby proposed as an amendment to the Constitution of the United States, which shall be valid to all intents and purposes as part of the Constitution when ratified by conventions in three-fourths of the several States:

ARTICLE ___ ___

"Section 1. The eighteenth article of amendment to the Constitution of the United States is hereby repealed.

"Section 2. The transportation or importation into any State, territory, or possession of the United States, for delivery or use therein, of intoxicating liquors in violation of the laws thereof is hereby prohibited.

"Section 3. This article shall be inoperative unless it shall have been ratified as an amendment to the Constitution by conventions in the several States, as provided in the Constitution, within seven years from the date of the submission hereof to the States by the Congress."

Section 1. Be it enacted, &c., That a convention shall be held in this State for the purpose of ratifying or rejecting the proposed amendment to the Constitution of the United States recited in the preamble hereof. An election shall be held, at the same time as the municipal election, in the year one thousand nine hundred and thirty-three for the election of delegates to such convention.

Section 2. At such election, all persons qualified as electors shall be entitled to vote.

Section 3. Except as in this act otherwise provided, such election shall be conducted, and the results thereof ascertained and certified, in the same manner as in the case of the election of Representatives in Congress of the United States at large at general elections; and all provisions of the laws of this State relative to elections, except so far as inconsistent with this act, are hereby made applicable to such election. The expenses incident to such election of delegates to the said convention shall be paid by the respective counties.

---

* *Pennsylvania Laws, 1933,* No. 81, pp. 233-237.

Section 4. The number of delegates to be elected at such convention shall be fifteen, all of whom shall be elected from the State at large.

Section 5. Candidates for the office of delegate to the convention shall be qualified electors of the State. Nominations shall be by petition and not otherwise. A single petition may place in nomination any number of candidates for delegate, not exceeding the total number of such delegates to be elected, and nomination petitions shall be signed by at least two thousand resident voters in each of at least ten congressional districts in the State, as apportioned by the act of June twenty-seventh, one thousand nine hundred and thirty-one (Pamphlet Laws, one thousand four hundred sixteen), entitled "An act to apportion the State into congressional districts." Nomination shall be without party or official designation, but the nominating petitions shall contain a statement by each nominee to the effect that he favors ratification or that he opposes ratification of the proposed amendment. No nominating petition for delegate shall contain the name of any nominee whose position as stated therein is different from that of any other nominee as stated therein. Nominating petitions shall be prepared and furnished by the Secretary of the Commonwealth, and, except as above provided, shall be substantially in the form provided by the election laws for nomination petitions for candidates at primaries for the office of Representative in Congress of the United States at large. Any number of petitions may be circulated for a candidate or group of candidates, and, when filed, shall be considered as one petition for that candidate or group of candidates. Signatures shall not be obtained on any petitions prior to one hundred and twenty days before the date of the election.

All nomination petitions shall be filed with the Secretary of the Commonwealth not less than sixty (60) days before the date of the election. After the last day for filing petitions, the Secretary of the Commonwealth shall proceed to ascertain the nominees by selecting two groups of nominees.

The two groups of nominees shall be the fifteen having the largest number of signers to their petitions among those favoring ratification, and the fifteen having the largest number of signers to their petitions among those opposing ratification.

Ties shall be decided by lot drawn by the Secretary of the Commonwealth.

Within thirty days after the last day for filing petitions, the Secretary of the Commonwealth shall certify the nominees to the county commissioners of the respective counties.

Section 6. The election shall be by ballot, separate from any ballot to be used at the same election, which shall be prepared by the Secretary of the Commonwealth in substantially the following form, and shall be furnished to the various election districts by the county commissioners of the respective counties:

CONSTITUTIONAL CONVENTION BALLOT

(Copy of Amendment)

Instructions to Voters. A cross mark (X) in the square at the head of any one of the two columns on this ballot votes for all candidates for delegates named in that column. Do not mark a cross mark in more than one square at the head of a column.

If you do not desire to vote for the group of nominees in any one column, mark a cross mark (X) after the name or names of the candidates of your choice to the number indicated on the ballot.

Delegates Favor Ratification (Repeal) ☐ Vote for 15	
John Doe	
Richard Roe	
John Smith	
(Etc.)	

Delegates Oppose Ratification (Against Repeal) ☐ Vote for 15	
John Doe	
Richard Roe	
John Smith	
(Etc.)	

Each elector may vote for fifteen candidates for delegate. A cross mark (X) in the square at the head of any one of the two columns on the ballot shall count as a vote for each of the candidates for delegate appearing in that column. If an elector does not desire to vote by a cross mark (X) in the square at the head of a column, then he may indicate the fifteen candidates for delegates of his choice by marking a cross mark (X) in the square opposite their respective names, or he may insert the name of any candidate or candidates for whom he desires to vote in the appropriate blank spaces provided on the ballot.

When an elector votes in the square at the head of a column, his power to vote is exhausted, and, if he thereafter inserts any cross mark (X) in any other square at the head of another column, or after the name of a candidate in any column other than the one at the head of which he has placed his cross mark (X), his ballot shall be void.

Section 7. The fifteen candidates receiving the highest number of votes in the entire State at said election shall be the delegates to said convention. Any vacancy in the membership of the convention, caused by the death or disability of any delegate, or for any other cause, shall be filled by appointment of a person by the majority vote of the group of delegates favoring ratification or opposing ratification, as the case may be, to which the absent delegate belonged.

Section 8. The delegates to the convention shall serve without compensation, and shall meet at the Capitol on the twenty-eighth day after their election, at twelve o'clock noon, in the hall of the Senate, and shall thereupon constitute a convention to pass upon the question of whether or not the proposed amendment shall be ratified.

Section 9. The convention shall be the judge of the election and qualification of its members. The convention shall be called to order by the Lieutenant Governor, who shall be the chairman thereof, but who shall not have any vote unless elected as a delegate. The secretary of the Senate shall be the secretary of the convention, and the chief clerk of the Senate and the chief clerk of the House of Representatives shall be the tellers of the convention. The secretary of the Senate shall provide a reporter or reporters for the convention, a sergeant-at-arms, and one page, whose compensation shall be paid out of the appropriation made by this act, upon the approval of the Lieutenant Governor and secretary of the Senate. In case of the inability of any of the persons herein named to be present, the convention shall name some one in his stead.

The Secretary of the Commonwealth shall, as soon as the convention is called to order, present the election returns of delegates, which shall be opened and read, after which the roll of names of those elected, as shown by the returns, shall be called, and if any elected delegate is absent, the vacancy shall then be filled as in this act provided.

Before proceeding with the business of the convention, the delegates shall take the constitutional oath of office, which shall be administered by a judge of the court of common pleas.

Section 10. The convention shall keep a journal of its proceedings, in which shall be recorded the vote of each delegate on the question of ratification of the proposed amendment, and the debates thereon. Upon final adjournment, the journal shall be filed with the Secretary of the Commonwealth.

Section 11. If the convention shall agree by vote of a majority of the total number of delegates to the ratification of the proposed amendment, a certificate to that effect shall be executed by the president and secretary of the convention and transmitted to the Secretary of the Commonwealth of this State, who shall transmit the certificate, under the great seal of the Commonwealth, to the Secretary of State of the United States.

Section 12. If, at or about the time of submitting any such amendment, Congress shall, by statute, prescribe the manner in which the conventions shall be constituted, and shall not except from the provisions of such statute such States as may theretofore have provided for constituting such conventions, the preceding provisions of this act shall be inoperative and the convention shall be constituted and shall operate as the said act of Congress shall direct, and all officers of the State who may, by the said statute, be authorized or directed to take any action to constitute such a convention for this State are hereby authorized and directed to act thereunder and in obedience thereto with the same force and effect as if acting under a statute of this State.

Section 13. The sum of one thousand dollars ($1,000), or so much thereof as may be necessary, is hereby specifically appropriated to the secretary of the Senate for the payment of the compensation of the reporter or reporters, sergeant-at-arms, and page, and for the payment of all other incidental and necessary expenses in connection with said convention.

Section 14. This act shall become effective immediately upon final enactment.

APPROVED—The 3d day of May, A.D. 1933.

GIFFORD PINCHOT

RHODE ISLAND*

AN ACT to provide for a convention to pass on a proposal of amendment to the Constitution of the United States made on February 20, 1933, at the Second Session of the Seventy-second Congress.

It is enacted by the General Assembly as follows:

Section 1. The congress of the United States on February 20, 1933, (at the second session of the seventy-second congress) having passed the following:

"JOINT RESOLUTION

Proposing an amendment to the Constitution of the United States.

Resolved, By the senate and house of representatives of the United States of America in congress assembled (two-thirds of each house concurring therein)

THAT, the following article is hereby proposed as an amendment to the constitution of the United States, which shall be valid to all intents and purposes as part of the constitution when ratified by conventions in three-fourths of the several states:

ARTICLE ___ ___

"Section 1. The eighteenth article of amendment to the constitution of the United States is hereby repealed.

"Section 2. The transportation or importation into any state, territory, or possession of the United States for delivery or use therein of intoxicating liquors, in violation of the law thereof, is hereby prohibited.

"Section 3. This article shall be inoperative unless it shall have been ratified as an amendment to the constitution by conventions in the several states, as provided in the constitution, within seven years from the date of the submission hereof to the states by the Congress";

a convention shall be held in 1933 in the State of Rhode Island and Providence Plantations to act upon said proposal of amendment. Preceding said convention there shall be a special election in this state to elect delegates to said convention. The governor is hereby authorized and directed by his proclamation or proclamations to fix the dates of said convention and of said special election, which said special election may be held on a date on which no other special election is being held or on the same date with any other legally authorized special election.

Section 2. There shall be thirty-one (31) delegates to said convention. Only qualified electors resident within the state at the time of nomination shall be eligible to be delegates; but no person holding any office of trust or profit under the United States shall be eligible to the office of delegate.

Section 3. Qualified electors desiring to be candidates for the office of delegate shall not less than fourteen (14) days before the proclaimed date of said election file with the secretary of state a written declaration to the effect that he is such candidate and that he is in favor of repealing the said 18th amendment or that he is against repealing said 18th amendment or that he stands unpledged with respect to such repeal,

* *Rhode Island Acts and Resolves, 1933,* Chapter 2014, pp. 74-87.

provided that candidates whose names shall be written on the official ballot to fill vacancies as hereinafter provided shall be eligible without the filing of such declaration. Said declaration may be in substantially the following form:

To *Honorable Louis W. Cappelli, Secretary of State of the State of Rhode Island*

I, ... of ....
(Name of candidate as on official voting list.) (Residence of candidate street and number as on official voting list.)

.... hereby declare: (1) that I am and now offer
(Town or City.)
myself as a candidate for nomination as a delegate to the convention to be held on
.... 1933;
(Date of convention as per Governor's proclamation)

and (2) that I favor
oppose
stand unpledged as to } the repeal of the 18th amendment to the constitution of the United States

(Signature of candidate
as per official voting list) ....
(Address of candidate as per official voting list)

Section 4. Except as is above provided only electors who within the time aforesaid shall have filed such a declaration shall be eligible to be nominated as candidates for the office of delegate to said convention. Nominations shall be by nomination papers and not otherwise. Such nomination papers shall be filed in the office herein provided on or before the fourteenth day preceding the date of the election. Nomination papers shall indicate as to each nominee consistently with the statement filed or to be filed as above provided that he is in favor of the repeal of the said 18th amendment or that he is opposed to the repeal thereof or that he stands unpledged with respect to such repeal. Petitions in support of nominations shall be circulated and signed in such manner that the names of electors, signing the same in support of the nomination or nominations, residing in a town or city, shall appear only with the names of other electors residing in the same town or city so that the petitions may be filed with the board of canvassers and registration or with the board, body or official exercising the functions of such a board that they may be checked in the office where filed, and each such board, body or official between the fourteenth and tenth days preceding the date of the election shall certify to the secretary of state the names and addresses of all candidates in whose support petitions shall have been filed with them together with the number of qualified electors who have signed petitions in support of such nominations. The secretary of state shall tabulate the total number of names so certified for each candidate in the three classes in favor of, opposed to, and unpledged with respect to the repeal of said 18th amendment, and the 31 electors receiving the highest number of signatures as ascertained by the secretary of state shall be the candidates of that class; that is to say, candidates in favor of such repeal, opposed to such repeal and unpledged with respect thereto.

No nomination paper shall contain the name of any nominee whose position as stated therein is inconsistent with that of any other nominee as stated therein. Only signatures and addresses corresponding with the names and addresses as they appear on the official voting list of the board, body or official with whom filed shall be counted. Each qualified elector shall be entitled to sign nomination papers for 31 candidates; and the signing by an elector of a paper containing the names of more than one candidate shall be considered as the signing for each such candidate. The papers containing the names of such signers shall be filed marked with the date, hour and minute of filing and in case an elector signs for more than 31 candidates, he shall be counted only for the 31 candidates for whom his name is first filed. The declarations of intentions and signatures may be filed from time to time until the time for filing the same expires. No person shall be disqualified from participating in any party caucus under the provisions of the General Laws as amended by reason of having signed any nomination papers authorized by this act.

Section 5. Nomination papers shall be in substantially the following form:

STATE OF RHODE ISLAND AND PROVIDENCE PLANTATIONS

To *Louis W. Cappelli, Secretary of State of the State of Rhode Island*

The qualified elector (s) named below being (a) candidate (s) for the office (s) of delegate (s) to the convention called to act on the proposal of amendment to the constitution of the United States submitted by the second session of the seventy-second congress (which proposal is in effect for the repeal of the 18th amendment to the constitution of the United States)

(t) he (y) being	In favor of	
	Opposed to	Such Repeal
	Unpledged as to	

Namely:

....
....
....

[Here follow twenty-seven similar dotted lines in double columns.]

(Names and addresses of proposed delegate (s) supported by signers hereof.)

The undersigned qualified electors of the City Town of hereby petition for the nomination as delegates to said convention of the person (s) named above as candidate (s).

Nominating Signatures	Addresses
....	....
....	....
....	....

Section 6. In case of vacancy by death or otherwise of any candidate in any class, that is, in favor of, opposed to, or unpledged with respect to such repeal, the electors may write in on the official ballot the name and address of a candidate or candidates to fill such vacancy or vacancies. In order to fill vacancies electors may write in the names of candidates who have not filed the declaration required by section 3 of this act.

Section 7. The secretary of state shall in number equal to that required for the general election of 1932 prepare, have printed, and distributed within the times required for general elections the ballots to be used at the election herein provided for in each election district, printing at the head thereof said proposal of amendment which may be followed by such brief instructions to the voters as the secretary of state deems appropriate concluding with three perpendicular columns at the head of the first of which shall be printed: "In favor of the repeal of the 18 amendment." At the head of the second shall be printed: "Against the repeal of the 18th amendment"; and at the head of the third shall be printed: "Unpledged."

At the head of each column under the words above quoted, there shall be placed a circle below which shall appear the names and addresses of the candidates nominated as provided in section 4 of this act. To the right of the name of each candidate and of each blank line hereinafter provided for shall appear a small box; and below the names and addresses so printed shall be a sufficient number of blank lines to permit voters to write in names and addresses of candidates for the purpose of filling vacancies in the official ballot existing on election day. Names so written in and voted for shall with or without the printed name or names, as the case may be, be counted in the same manner as other names. No vote shall be rejected if it is reasonably possible to determine the voter's intention. Merely technical rules shall be disregarded.

Electors may vote for the 31 candidates in any column by making a cross in the circle at the top of the column or by making a cross or crosses in the boxes at the right of names printed or written below the circle, and the making of a cross in a circle and at the right of names in that column shall not invalidate the ballot. Each voter may vote for 31 candidates. In case a voter votes for more than 31 candidates in any column, his vote shall be counted for the 31 candidates at the top of column counting downward. If a voter shall place a cross in more than one circle or if he votes in more than one column and for more than 31 candidates, his ballot shall not be counted. Ballots shall be in substantially the following form:

STATE OF RHODE ISLAND AND PROVIDENCE PLANTATIONS

Special election on 1933, to elect delegates to the convention to act on the proposal of amendment to the constitution of the United States made on February 20, 1933, at the second session of the seventy-second congress.

(Copy joint resolution in Sec. 1 hereof) (Instructions)

In Favor of Repeal of 18th Amendment	Opposed to Repeal of 18th Amendment	Unpledged as to Repeal of 18th Amendment
....	....	....
....	....	....

Section 8. Upon the making of the governor's proclamation fixing the date of the special election hereby provided for, the boards of canvassers and registration or the boards, bodies, or official having the functions of such boards throughout the state shall be and they hereby are authorized and directed to issue their warrants or notices by them to be issued previous to said special election for the purpose of warning the town, ward, or district meetings for said election on the day so fixed by the governor in his proclamation relating thereto, and shall insert in said warrants and notices a copy of the governor's proclamation; the town, ward, and district meetings to be held in pursuance of said warrants and notices shall be warned and the lists of voters shall be canvassed and made out and the said town, ward, and district meetings shall be conducted in the same manner as is now provided by law for the town, ward and district meetings for the election of general officers for the state, provided, that the polls in cities as distinguished from towns shall be open on said election day at seven o'clock A.M.

and shall be closed at seven o'clock P.M.; and in towns as distinguished from cities the polls shall be open and closed as provided by law for general elections and the moderators and town clerks or the wardens or moderators and district clerks shall proceed in open town, ward and district meetings to count said ballots and declare the result of the same and forthwith certify the said result to the board, body or official exercising in such town or city the functions of a board of canvassers and registration.

Section 9. Said ballots shall be retained by said board, body or official for sixty (60) days after said election and shall be disposed of as the convention may direct. Said ballots shall be destroyed by said board, body or official after the expiration of said sixty days unless the convention shall otherwise direct. The results so declared shall in every case be final unless a candidate shall call in question by petition for a recount or by a petition containing some allegations of irregularity the result in any town or city. No such petitions shall be considered unless filed with the board, body or official to which the ballots shall have been returned within forty-eight hours after the close of the polls in that town or city. Each body or official shall (except in case of petition for a recount or on allegations of irregularity) forthwith upon the expiration of said period of forty-eight hours certify the result to the secretary of state, stating in their certificate the names and addresses of the candidates and the number of votes received by each. In case of the filing of a petition for a recount or of petition containing allegations of irregularity, the board, body or official with whom such petition shall be filed shall proceed to hear and determine the same within the same time in the same manner and with the same powers in all respects as they or he is required to proceed in like matters following general elections under the general laws as amended of this state. Upon the conclusion of such proceedings, said board, body or official shall forthwith certify to the secretary of state the result of the same, certifying the names and addresses of the candidates concerned with the number of votes received by each. The secretary of state shall tabulate the results and shall ascertain the 31 candidates who have received the highest number of votes as shown by such certificates, and he shall declare such 31 persons elected as delegates and shall issue certificates of election to them; said certificates shall entitle the holders thereof to seats in said convention. All ties as to nominees or candidates shall be determined by lot to be drawn by the secretary of state.

Section 10. The secretary of state shall make up a list of the names and addresses of the elected delegates. Said list shall form the temporary roll of the convention and shall be open to correction if the same does not conform with the certificates of election to be presented to said convention by the delegates elected thereto.

Section 11. If there be a vacancy in the membership of the convention caused by the death or disability of any delegate or delegates, or from any other cause, the same shall be filled by election by a majority vote of the remaining delegates of the class in which the vacancy occurs and if there be no remaining delegate of that class, the governor shall name a delegate or delegates to fill the vacancy or vacancies declaring the same views as were declared or held by the delegate or delegates whose office or offices are vacant.

Section 12. All questions of law arising with respect to the interpretation of this act and to the nomination and election of delegates to said convention in pursuance hereof shall be heard and determined summarily by the supreme court upon appropriate original petition, *provided* that the power hereby given the supreme court shall not be taken to limit or in any way lessen the power of the convention to determine the election and qualifications of its own members.

Section 13. The convention shall be the judge of the qualifications and elections of its own members.

Section 14. The secretary of state shall be ex officio the secretary of the convention. The convention shall meet at one o'clock P.M. on the day named in the proclamation of the governor with respect thereto in the chamber of the house of representatives of the state of Rhode Island in the state house at Providence. The governor shall at one o'clock P.M. of the proclaimed date of the convention call the delegates to the convention to order and the secretary of state shall call the temporary roll of the delegates. If it be found that sixteen (16) delegates be present (the same being hereby declared to be a quorum of the convention) the convention shall proceed to establish its permanent roll of members and shall then proceed by ballot to the election of a president of the convention from among the delegates. The ballots shall be counted by the governor and the secretary of state and the governor shall declare the result and the balloting shall continue until some person shall receive a majority of all the votes cast and the person receiving such majority shall be the president of said convention; *provided* that if after five ballots no delegate shall have been elected president of the convention, the governor shall forthwith designate one of the delegates to be the president of the convention. The governor while presiding shall not, except as is above provided, receive, entertain nor put to vote any motion or question whatever or point of order while acting as presiding officer. The president of the convention upon being elected or selected as aforesaid shall immediately take over the duties of his office.

Section 15. The convention shall adopt rules governing debate and such other rules as it may deem advisable. It shall keep a journal of its proceedings in which shall be recorded the vote of each delegate on the question of the ratification of the proposal of amendment to the constitution of the United States, referred to in the first section hereof, which journal upon final adjournment shall be filed in the office of the secretary of state.

Section 16. If the convention by vote of the majority of the delegates present thereat shall favor the ratification of the proposed amendment, a certificate that the convention held in the state of Rhode Island and Providence Plantations to act upon the said proposal of amendment to the constitution of the United States has ratified said proposal of amendment shall be executed by the president and the secretary of the convention and filed in the office of the secretary of state of this state. The governor and secretary of state shall append thereto a certificate that the certificate of the said president and secretary is in all respects true and the secretary of state shall affix thereto the great seal of the state and shall transmit said certificate to the secretary of state of the United States, or to such other body or official as is authorized under the laws of the United States to receive the same.

Section 17. The convention shall transact no business except the business in this act expressly provided for it to transact or business strictly germane to such business, and upon the completion of such business the convention shall adjourn *sine die*.

Section 18. If before the holding of the convention provided for by this act, the congress of the United States shall prescribe the manner in which the convention in this state shall be called, held or constituted to act on the proposal of amendment to the constitution of the United States, mentioned in section 1 of this act, then the provisions of this act shall be suspended and the convention shall be called, held and constituted in accordance with the act of congress, provided that if any such act of congress shall provide for the conventions to be held in accordance with the laws of the state where held, then the provisions of this act shall not be suspended.

Section 19. The members of said convention shall serve without pay.

Section 20. This act shall take effect upon its passage; and the operation of all acts inconsistent herewith is hereby suspended so as to permit the full and complete operation hereof and the doing of every act herein contemplated; but no act is repealed hereby.

SOUTH CAROLINA*

AN ACT to Provide for a Convention for the Purpose of Considering and Acting Upon the Proposed Amendment to the Constitution of the United States to Repeal the 18th Amendment; to Provide for the Number and Qualification of the Members of the Convention; to Provide for the Date and Manner of the Election and to Fix the Time and Place for the Holding of Said Convention and to Appropriate a Sum of Money to Cover the Cost of Said Election and Convention.

WHEREAS, On the 20th of February, 1933, Congress of the United States did pass the following Resolution:

"*Resolved*, by the Senate and House of Representatives of the United States of America in Congress assembled (two-thirds of each house concurring therein:)

"That, the following article is hereby proposed as an amendment to the Constitution of the United States, which shall be valid to all intents and purposes as part of the Constitution when ratified by conventions in three-fourths of the several states:

ARTICLE ___ ___

"Section 1. The Eighteenth Article of amendment to the Constitution of the United States is hereby repealed.

Section 2. The transportation or importation into any state, territory or possession of the United States for delivery or use therein of intoxicating liquors, in violation of the laws thereof, is hereby prohibited."

WHEREAS, It is the desire of the General Assembly of the State of South Carolina to elect delegates who represent the wishes of a majority of the qualified voters of the State of South Carolina on the question of ratification or rejection of the said proposed 21st Amendment of the Constitution of the United States, which amendment would repeal the 18th Amendment to the Constitution of the United States, and

WHEREAS, The choosing of a large convention would be unnecessary and expensive; now, therefore,

Section 1. *Convention to Vote on Proposed 21st Amendment to U. S. Constitution—Time—Place.*—Be it enacted by the General Assembly of the State of South Carolina: There shall be held in the City of Columbia, South Carolina at twelve o'clock noon on Monday, December 4, 1933, a convention to ratify or reject the proposed 21st Amendment to the Constitution of the United States.

Section 2. *Election of Delegates.*—The Convention shall be comprised of forty-six delegates to be elected by the State at large and in the manner hereinafter provided, which special election, for the purpose of electing delegates, shall be held on the first Tuesday in November, 1933. Said special election shall be held at the regular voting precincts in the several counties in the manner as is now provided by law for the holding of general elections in this State: *Provided,* that the provisions of the Australian Ballot law, now applicable to primary elections in this State, shall be enforced at all precincts in this election; and the time and purpose for the holding of said election shall be advertised as is now provided by law for general elections. The State Commissioners of Election in the several counties shall provide for the conducting of this election in the

* *South Carolina Acts, 1933,* No. 625, pp. 1180-1184.

manner now provided by law for the conducting of general elections, save as is herein specified to the contrary, and shall appoint managers for the several precincts who shall be paid the sum of One Dollar each for their services.

Section 2-A. *Candidates for Delegates—Nomination.*—The delegation from each County to the General Assembly, or a majority thereof, shall nominate one elector a resident of the county who has signified to the delegation his intentions to vote for the rejection of the proposed amendment; and shall also nominate one elector a resident of the county who has signified to the delegation his intention to vote for the adoption of the proposed amendment. The delegation, or a majority thereof, shall certify said nominations to the Secretary of State to be placed on the ballot as candidates to said Convention. *Provided,* that no member of the General Assembly shall be named as a candidate for delegate to the Convention.

Section 3. *Returns.*—The said State Commissioners of Election in the several counties shall meet on the Thursday following this election and shall proceed to canvass the votes, and within five days thereafter shall forward to the Governor and the Secretary of State, by a messenger, the returns of the election, the poll list and all other papers appertaining to the election. Said messenger shall be paid his actual expenses, upon a certificate to be furnished him by the Secretary of State, out of funds herein provided for the expenses of this election and Convention.

Section 4. *Ballots.*—The ballot to be used in this election shall be provided by the State Commissioners of Election, and the cost of same shall be borne out of the sum hereinafter appropriated, and shall be as follows:

"PROPOSED AMENDMENT TO THE CONSTITUTION OF THE UNITED STATES.

"Delegates to the Convention to ratify the proposed amendment.

"The Congress has proposed an amendment to the Constitution of the United States which provides in substance that the Eighteenth Article of Amendment to the Constitution of the United States relating to the manufacture, transportation and sale of intoxicating liquors for beverage purposes shall be repealed, and prohibiting shipment of intoxicating liquors into any state or territory in violation of the laws of such state or territory.

"Congress has proposed that said amendment shall be ratified by conventions in the several states.

CANDIDATES FOR Ratification of the Amendment to REPEAL the Eighteenth Amendment	CANDIDATES AGAINST Ratification of the Amendment to REPEAL the Eighteenth Amendment
John Doe	Charles Coe
Richard Doe	Michael Moe

INSTRUCTIONS TO VOTERS

"Strike in pen or pencil the names you do not desire to vote for, leaving untouched the names of persons for whom you desire to vote. If you do not desire to vote for any of the above you may substitute the names of other qualified electors."

Section 5. *Vote for Only Forty-six Persons.*—There shall be a space left at the bottom of the ballot in which the voter shall insert the name of any other person for whom he desires to vote: *Provided,* that no ballot shall be valid on which there has been voted for more or less than forty-six persons.

Section 6. *Delegates.*—The forty-six persons who shall receive the highest number of votes cast at said election shall be the delegates to the Convention.

Section 7. *Qualification to Vote.*—Every person qualified to vote in a general election under the laws of the State of South Carolina, or who may qualify according to the Constitution and laws of this State not later than thirty days prior to the first Tuesday in November, 1933, shall be entitled to vote in this election.

Section 8. *Registration Books—Time Open.*—In addition to the time now required by law for the registration books to be open, the Board of Registration of each county shall cause the books of registration to be opened on the first Monday in September, 1933, and shall cause the same to be held open for fifteen consecutive calendar days therefrom, except Sundays, during the hours now provided for by law.

Section 9. *Declaration of Result—Commission Delegates.*—The Secretary of State shall call a meeting of the State Board of Canvassers to be held at his office, or some other convenient place, within six days next after receipt of the county returns for the purpose of canvassing the votes thereof. When the Board of Canvassers shall have canvassed the results of the said election and declared the same, the Secretary of State shall thereupon issue to each person elected a certificate of his election, under his official seal and he shall, upon presentation thereof, be entitled to a seat in the Convention.

Section 10. *Convention—Organization—Vote on Question—Publish Result.*—The Convention shall determine the manner and form of its organization and the manner in which it shall act upon the proposed amendment, and upon determination of said question shall submit the result thereof to the Secretary of State and to the Secretary of State of the United States and such other officer as may be designated by the Congress of the United States.

Section 11. *Appropriation.*—That the sum of Ten Thousand Dollars, if so much be necessary, be and the same is hereby appropriated to defray the expenses of the election of the delegates and of the Convention.

Section 12. *Pay Expenses of Delegates.*—The delegates shall be paid actual expenses incident to attending this Convention, to be furnished them by the Secretary of State out of funds herein appropriated.

Section 13. *Interpretation.*—Any question arising in regard to the regulations herein provided for the election ordered by this Resolution, shall be interpreted, in the light of the purpose of the General Assembly as is declared in the preambles hereto.

Section 14. All Acts or parts of Acts inconsistent herewith are hereby repealed to the extent of such inconsistency.

Section 15. This Act shall take effect upon its approval by the Governor.

Approved the 9th day of May, 1933.

SOUTH DAKOTA*

AN ACT Entitled, An Act to Authorize and Provide for a State Convention to Ratify Proposed Amendments to the Constitution of the United States if and When Submitted by Action of the Congress of the United States, and Providing the Mode of Nominating and Electing Delegates to Such Convention, and Providing for the Time, Place and Manner of Holding Such Convention, and the Method of Ratifying Such Proposed Amendments and Making the Same Effective.

Be It Enacted by the Legislature of the State of South Dakota:

Section 1. Whenever the Congress of the United States of America shall propose an amendment to the Constitution of the United States and shall propose that the same be ratified by conventions in the respective states, a Convention shall be held as provided for herein, for the purpose of ratifying such amendment.

Section 2. The number of Delegates to be chosen to such convention shall be equal to the number of legislative representatives in the state of South Dakota, and each representative district in the state shall constitute a Delegate District and be represented in said Convention by the same number of delegates as it is now or may hereafter be entitled to elect legislative representatives. The delegates shall be elected at the next general election succeeding the proposal of any amendment to the constitution of the United States by the Congress of the United States, and except as otherwise herein provided the nomination and election of such delegates shall in all respects be the same as is now by law provided for the nomination and election of representatives of the Legislature of South Dakota, except as herein otherwise provided.

Section 3. Nomination of candidates for the office of Delegate shall be by petition signed by not less than two nor more than five per cent of the duly qualified electors of the district respectively in which the candidate or candidates reside, as shown by the total vote cast for the successful candidate for the office of Governor at the last general election within said legislative district. Such nomination shall be without party or political designation but shall indicate thereon whether the candidate named in said petition is "in favor of," or "opposed to," the ratification of the proposed amendment, and said petitions shall be filed at the time and in the manner provided for filing nominating petitions for legislative representatives for the primary election, as now provided for.

Section 4. It shall be the duty of the Secretary of State, as soon as the time for filing nominating petitions in his office has expired, to immediately certify to the several county auditors of the state the names of the persons in whose behalf nominating petitions have been filed as a candidate for delegate in districts comprising more than one county, and the county auditor shall thereafter immediately prepare and have printed official primary election ballots for all delegates, nominated upon a separate ballot, without party or political designation, in substance as follows:

"PROPOSED AMENDMENT TO THE CONSTITUTION OF THE UNITED STATES

"Delegates to the Convention to Ratify the Proposed Amendment

---

* *South Dakota Session Laws of 1933,* Chapter 107, pp. 100-103.

"The Congress has proposed an amendment to the Constitution of the United States which provides (insert here the substance of the proposed amendment).

"The Congress has also proposed that the said amendment shall be ratified by Conventions in the States.

The Following Candidates for Delegates to the State Convention are In Favor of the ratification of the proposed amendment.	The Following Candidates for Delegates to the State Convention are Opposed to the ratification of the proposed amendment.
To vote for any candidate whose name appears in the column below mark an X or cross in the square at the left of the name of the candidate. Do not vote for more candidates than are to be elected to said office.	To vote for any candidate whose name appears in the column below mark an X or cross in the square at the left of the name of the candidate. Do not vote for more candidates than are to be elected to said office.
Vote for (insert number of delegates to be nominated).	Vote for (insert number of delegates to be nominated).
DELEGATES TO CONVENTION	DELEGATES TO CONVENTION
( ) John Doe	( ) Henry Coe
( ) Richard Roe	( ) Samuel Moe

And said official ballots and sample ballots shall be provided in the same manner as the official primary election ballots are supplied, pursuant to Section 13, Chapter 118, South Dakota Session Laws 1929; and said separate ballots shall be delivered to all electors of whatever party or designation at the biennial primary election to be held as now provided, and the manner of voting, conduct of election, canvass and certification of votes upon said ballots shall be conducted in the same manner as the primary election now provides for the election of Representatives of the Legislature."

Section 5. That the Secretary of State in the preparation of the ballots for the succeeding general election shall certify to the county auditors of said legislative districts respectively the names of the successful candidates, designating those who are in favor of the ratification of the amendment and those opposed to the ratification of the amendment, and the county auditor of each county in the state at the time of the preparation for the general election, shall prepare separate official ballots upon which shall be printed the substance of the proposed amendment, the names of the candidates for delegates to the convention as theretofore nominated as candidates in favor of and the candidates opposed to the ratification of the amendment, provided that the electors may vote for all of the candidates either in favor of or those opposed to the ratification of said amendment, by putting a cross or X in the circle at the head of the names in the column under the designation "In Favor of," the ratification, or in the circle at the head of the names in the column under the designation "Opposed to" the ratification, and a ballot so marked in said circle shall be counted as a vote, by the Judges and Canvassers, for each of the delegates respectively, whose name or names appear in the column under the circle so marked, and proper instructions to the voters in substantially the following form, to-wit:

PROPOSED AMENDMENT TO THE CONSTITUTION OF THE UNITED STATES

Delegates to the Convention to Ratify the Proposed Amendment

The Congress has proposed an amendment to the Constitution of the United States which provides (insert here the substance of the proposed amendment).

The Congress has also proposed that the said amendment shall be ratified by Conventions in the States.

To vote for the Delegates In Favor of Ratification of the proposed amendment place a cross or X in the circle below. ( ) DELEGATES TO CONVENTION John Doe Richard Roe	To vote for the Delegates Opposed to Ratification of the proposed amendment place a cross or X in the circle below. ( ) DELEGATES TO CONVENTION Henry Coe Samuel Moe

Section 6. That said ballot shall be submitted to the electors of the state of South Dakota in the same manner and at the same time as the official ballots for the general election are now submitted; and the same shall be canvassed and certified by the Judges of election and the County Canvassing Board, or by the State Canvassing Board where the Delegate District comprises more than one county, in the same manner and at the same time as the official ballots for the general election are canvassed, and a certificate of election, and except as otherwise provided herein such election shall be conducted and the results thereof ascertained and certified in the same manner as now provided by the laws of this state pertaining to the general election, except in so far as the same may be inconsistent herewith.

Section 7. The delegates so elected shall meet at the Capitol Building in the City of Pierre, on the third Tuesday in the month of January following their election, at two o'clock P.M., in the afternoon of said day, and shall constitute a convention to ratify or reject the proposed amendment to the constitution of the United States.

Section 8. A majority of the total number of delegates to the convention shall constitute a quorum. The convention shall have power to choose a President and Secretary and all other necessary officers, and to make rules governing the procedure of the convention; such convention shall be the judge of the qualification and of the election of its own members and each delegate shall receive Five Dollars per day for the first five days he is in attendance at said convention, and ten cents per mile for each mile necessarily traveled in going to and returning from said Convention. The Secretary and other officers shall receive such compensation as may be fixed by the convention. Disbursements for the foregoing purposes and for other necessary expenses of the convention, when approved by the convention and signed by the president and secretary, shall be made by the State Treasurer out of any appropriation available therefor.

When the convention shall have agreed by a vote of a majority of the total number of delegates present and voting to the ratification or rejection of the proposed amendment, a certificate to that effect shall be executed by the President and Secretary of the convention and filed in the office of the Secretary of State of South Dakota, and the said Secretary of State shall forthwith transmit to the Secretary of State of the United States of America, a certified copy thereof.

Section 9. If at or about the time of submitting any such amendment, Congress shall either in the resolution submitting the same or by statute, prescribe the manner in which the conventions shall be constituted, and shall not except from the provisions of such statute or resolution such states as may theretofore have provided for constituting such conventions, the preceding provisions of this Act shall be inoperative, the convention shall be constituted and shall operate as the said resolution or Act of Congress shall direct, and all officers of the state who may by the said resolution or statute be authorized or directed to take any action to constitute such a convention for this State are hereby authorized and directed to act thereunder and in obedience thereto with the same force and effect as if acting under a statute of this state.

Section 10. All Acts or parts of Acts in conflict with this Act are hereby repealed.

Approved March 8, 1933.

TENNESSEE*

AN ACT to provide for a convention to pass on an amendment to the Constitution of the United States, relating to the repeal of the Eighteenth Article of amendment to said Constitution, which has heretofore been proposed by the Congress for ratification by conventions in the several States.

Section 1. *Be it enacted by the General Assembly of the State of Tennessee,* That an election for the purpose of electing Delegates to a Convention in this State to pass on an amendment to the Constitution of the United States, relating to the repeal of the Eighteenth Article of Amendment to said Constitution, shall be held on the Third Thursday in July, 1933.

Section 2. *Be it further enacted,* That, for the purposes of conveniences, the last preceding election of presidential electors, to-wit, the one held on the eighth day of November, 1932, is hereinafter referred to as "the 1932 presidential election" and wherever such phrase appears in this Act it shall mean and be construed to mean "the last preceding election of presidential electors in this State, to-wit, the one held on the eighth day of November, 1932."

That at such election, any citizen of Tennessee, who was qualified to vote at the 1932 Presidential Election, shall be entitled to vote in the precinct or Civil District in which he or she was then entitled to vote. In addition thereto, any citizen of Tennessee becoming twenty-one years of age after the 1932 presidential election shall be entitled to vote at such election of delegates, in the precinct or civil district in which he or she resides at the time of the 1932 presidential election; *provided,* any such citizen prior to voting, shall make and file with the judges of election in his or her particular precinct or civil district an affidavit to the effect that he or she has become twenty-one years of age since the 1932 presidential election, such affidavit to be in such form as the State Board of Elections shall prescribe and have furnished. Also, in addition thereto, any citizen of Tennessee, who would have been entitled to vote in the 1932 presidential election but for the fact he or she had not theretofore paid the required poll tax, shall be entitled to vote at such election for delegates in the precinct or civil district in which he or she resides at the time of the 1932 presidential election; *provided,* any such citizen, at least sixty days prior to the date of the election of delegates, shall have paid his or her 1931 poll tax and, at such election, shall furnish evidence of payment thereof in the same manner required by law of voters in general elections.

Anything in this Section of this Act to the contrary notwithstanding, the law relating to absentees voting in elections in this State, to-wit, Chapter 8 of the Acts of the General Assembly of the State of Tennessee for the year 1917, as codified and reenacted in Sections 2228-2250, inclusive, of the Code of 1932, and/or as same may be amended or changed at any time prior to such election of delegates, shall be applicable to the election of delegates, except that written notice or application of any such absentee voter to vote shall be given not less than five days nor more than fifteen days prior to the date of the election of delegates and the ballot of such absentee voter shall be cast and counted in the precinct or civil district in which he or she resides at the time

* *Tennessee Public Acts, 1933,* Chapter No. 38, pp. 53-64.

of 1933 Presidential election and the election official or officials of such precinct or civil district, or those having jurisdiction over the question of absentees voting in such precinct or civil district, shall perform the same duties under the aforesaid absentee voting law as if, at the time of such election of delegates, such absentee voter resides in the same civil district or precinct as he or she did at the time of the 1932 presidential election. There shall be held a supplemental registration as required by law for all regular elections held for other purposes.

Section 3. *Be it further enacted,* That except as in this Act otherwise provided, such election shall be conducted and the results thereof ascertained and certificated in the same manner as in case of the 1932 presidential election and all provisions of the laws of this State, relative to election for presidential electors, in force at the time of the election of delegates except in so far as same are inconsistent with this Act, are hereby made applicable to such election, that all laws, penalties, rules and regulations applicable to general elections, as well as the rules of contest, shall apply, and the respective sets of nominees for delegates to said convention nominated in each congressional district shall have the right to suggest, and the County Boards of Election Commissioners in each congressional district, upon the written request of each set of nominees, shall give each of said respective sets of nominees at least one judge in each voting precinct or district on the day of election. *Provided, however,* any voter may pay his or her poll tax for the year 1931, up to within ten days of said election.

Section 4. *Be it further enacted,* That the number of delegates shall be sixty-three; candidates for the offices of delegates shall be nominated as hereinafter provided, but they shall be elected from the State at large and any citizen of the State, entitled to vote in the election of delegates, may vote for the said sixty-three, or whole number of, delegates to be elected.

Section 5. *Be it further enacted,* That candidates for the office of delegates to the convention shall be citizens and residents of this State, entitled to vote at the election of delegates and who shall be of an age not less than twenty-one years. Nomination shall be by petition or petitions, signed by residents, entitled to vote in the election, of the particular congressional district in which the delegates to be elected must reside. A single petition, which may be in one or more counterparts, substantially identical in form except as to verifications of the parties circulating the counterparts and signatures, may nominate any number of candidates not exceeding seven, and shall be signed by not less than fifteen persons, residing in the same congressional district in which said candidates reside, who, under the provisions of Section 2 hereof, would be entitled to vote in the election of delegates. Said nominating petitions shall be substantially in such form as the State Board of Elections, or a majority of said Board, shall prescribe and the said State Board of Elections, or a majority thereof, shall, within ten days after the passage of this Act prescribe such form. Nomination shall be without party or political designation, but each nominating petition shall contain a statement, signed by each nominee named therein, to the effect that he or she favors ratification of the proposed amendment, or that he or she opposes ratification of the proposed amendment, or that he or she expresses no opinion, and no nominating petition shall contain the name of any nominee whose position, as stated therein, is inconsistent with that of any other nominee in the same petition; and each such petition or counterpart thereof shall contain a written signed statement of the party circulating said petition, verified by him or her before a notary public, that each person whose name appears as a signer of said petition or counterpart signed same in his or her presence. Each such petition shall recite in substance, in the forepart thereof, that each party signing same, by the act of such signing, represents and certifies that he or she is a citizen and resident of the particular congressional district entitled to vote in said election of delegates. Each person signing any such petition or counterpart thereof shall place opposite his or her name the date on which he or she signs such petition or counterpart; and if any such person so signing any such petition or counterpart thereof later signs the petition of any other nominee whose position is inconsistent with that of the nominee or nominees named in the petition or counterpart theretofore signed by such person, the name of any such person so signing shall be stricken by the State Board of Elections from any such petition or counterpart thereof that is later signed by any such person. No nomination shall be effective except those of not exceeding seven nominees, resident in each congressional district, in favor of ratification, and not exceeding seven nominees, resident in each congressional district, against ratification, and not exceeding seven nominees, if any there be, resident in each congressional district and expressing no opinion, whose nominating petitions have been respectively signed by the largest number of voters in each congressional district, ties to be decided by lot promptly drawn by the President of the State Board of Elections. Said nominating petitions shall be filed with the Secretary of the State Board of Elections not later than thirty days prior to the election of delegates and the State Board of Elections shall immediately convene and canvass the nominating petitions so filed and, not later than twenty days before the date of election, shall certify the names of the candidates or nominees to the Secretary of State; *provided,* that in such canvassing and certification, the State Board of Elections, or a majority thereof, shall only consider petitions signed and filed in conformity with this Act. Such canvassing and certification by the State Board of Elections, or a majority thereof, shall be final and conclusive as to the candidates entitled to be voted for at the election of delegates.

Section 6. *Be it further enacted,* That prior to the date of election, the said State Board of Elections shall have prepared poll books, tally sheets, ballots, blank affidavits for young voters to execute as provided in Section 2 hereof, etc., and furnish same to the respective County Boards of Commissioners of Elections and the number of ballots printed for use in such election and distributed to the several County Boards of Commissioners of Elections shall be twice or double the number of ballots cast in the respective counties at the 1932 presidential election. The number of poll books, tally sheets, blank affidavits, etc., furnished to the several County Boards of Commissioners of Elections shall be in such number as shall be sufficient to meet the needs of the respective counties. Such ballots, so furnished to the several County Boards of Commissioners of Elections, shall be identified on the back thereof by having the name of the county in which they are to be used printed thereon and they shall also have on said back the facsimile signatures of the members of the State Board of Elections. All such ballots, poll books, tally sheets, blank affidavits, etc., shall be furnished to the respective County Boards of Commissioners of Elections not less than ten days prior to the date of such election and shall be promptly distributed by them among the several voting precincts or districts of each county, as provided by law in case of an election for presidential electors.

Section 7. *Be it further enacted,* That said ballots shall be prepared as follows: It shall first state the substance of the proposed amendment. This shall be followed by appropriate instructions to the voter. It shall then contain perpendicular columns of equal width, headed respectively in plain type, "For Ratification," "Against Ratification," and "No Opinion Expressed." In the column headed "For Ratification," shall be placed the names of the nominees nominated as in favor of ratification. In the column headed "Against Ratification" shall be placed the names of the nominees nominated as against ratification. In the column headed "No Opinion Expressed" shall be placed the names of the nominees nominated as expressing no opinion. In each column, the names of the candidates shall be arranged alphabetically according to the initials of their surnames. The voter shall indicate his choice by making one or more cross-marks in the appropriate spaces provided on the ballot. No ballot shall be held void because any such cross-mark is irregular in character. The ballot shall be so arranged that the voter may, by making a single cross-mark, vote for the entire group of nominees whose names are comprised in any column. The ballot shall be in substantially the following form:

PROPOSED AMENDMENT TO THE CONSTITUTION OF THE UNITED STATES

Delegates to the convention to ratify the proposed amendment

The Congress has proposed an amendment to the Constitution of the United States which provides, in substance, that the Eighteenth Article of Amendment to the Constitution of the United States is hereby repealed and the transportation into any State, territory or possession of the United States for delivery or use therein of intoxicating liquors, in violation of the laws thereof, is hereby prohibited; and this Article shall be inoperative unless it shall have been ratified as an amendment to the Constitution by conventions in the several states, within seven years from the date of the submission thereof to the States by the Congress.

The Congress has also proposed that the said amendment shall be ratified by Convention in the States.

INSTRUCTIONS TO VOTERS

Do not vote for more than sixty-three candidates.

It is recommended by the so-called wets or those who favor the repeal of the Eighteenth Amendment, that all voters favoring the repeal of the Eighteenth Amendment should vote for the sixty-three candidates whose names appear under the heading "For Ratification." It is recommended by the so-called drys or those who do not favor the repeal of the Eighteenth Amendment that all voters who do not favor the repeal of the Eighteenth Amendment should vote for the sixty-three candidates whose names appear under the heading "Against Ratification."

To vote for all candidates in favor of Ratification, or for all candidates against Ratification, or for all candidates who express no opinion, make a cross-mark in the *Circle* at the head of the list of candidates for whom you wish to vote. If you do this, make no other mark.

To vote for an individual candidate make a cross-mark in the *Square* at the right of the name.

For Ratification	Against Ratification	No Opinion Expressed
○	○	○
John Coe .... [ ]	Charles Coe .... [ ]	Daniel Foe .... [ ]
Richard Doe .... [ ]	Michael Moe .... [ ]	Louis Loe .... [ ]

The above instructions to voters shall be printed on said ballot in not less than twelve point type.

Section 8. *Be it further enacted,* That the Governor and Secretary of State shall furnish to the sixty-three nominees, receiving the highest number of votes, certificates of their election as is provided by law in case of presidential electors. The said sixty-three nominees, so furnished the said certificates of election, shall be the delegates to, and shall constitute, the convention, which convention, as thus constituted, shall be the sole judge of the election and qualification of its members and, in case of any contest, shall be the sole, exclusive and final judge and trier thereof. *However,* if there shall be a vacancy in the convention caused by a tie or by the death or disability or unseating of any delegate, the same shall be filled by a majority vote of the remaining delegates, as and when the convention convenes, which remaining delegates shall then constitute the convention until any such vacancy is filled, and same shall be filled by the selection of a person qualified to vote in the election of the delegates and who shall reside in the same congressional district where the delegate resides, whose office is or becomes vacant.

Section 9. *Be it further enacted,* That the delegates to the convention shall meet in the Chamber of the House of Representatives at the Capitol at Nashville, Tennessee, at ten o'clock A.M., on the eleventh day of August, 1933, and shall thereupon constitute a convention to pass upon the question of whether or not the proposed Amendment shall be ratified. If no quorum be present at such time, a majority of the delegates then present may adjourn the convention from day to day until a majority of the delegates are present.

Section 10. *Be it further enacted,* That the convention shall have the power to elect its president, secretary and other officers, and to adopt its own rules.

Section 11. *Be it further enacted,* That the convention shall keep a journal of its proceedings in which shall be recorded the vote of each delegate on the question of ratification of the proposed Amendment. Upon final adjournment, the Journal shall be filed with the Secretary of State of Tennessee.

Section 12. *Be it further enacted,* That if the convention shall agree, by vote of majority of the total number of delegates, to the ratification of the proposed Amendment, a certificate to that effect shall be executed forthwith by the President and Secretary of the convention and transmitted to the Secretary of State of this State, who shall promptly transmit the certificate under the Great Seal of the State to the Secretary of State of the United States.

Section 13. *Be it further enacted,* That no delegate nor employee of said convention shall receive any compensation for his attendance upon, service to, or traveling to or from the said convention or for any other expense in connection therewith.

Section 14. *Be it further enacted,* That there is hereby appropriated from the General Fund of the State a sufficient amount for the payment of the expenses of preparing for and holding said election, payable out of moneys in said fund not otherwise appropriated. Warrants therefor shall be issued by the Comptroller and same shall be honored and paid by the Treasurer. Warrants for the expenses incurred by the State Board of Elections for the printing of poll books, tally sheets, ballots, blank affidavits for young voters to execute as provided in Section 2 hereof, etc., shall be issued and paid to the parties shown by the certificate of the State Board of Elections to be entitled thereto, such certificate to be promptly filed with the Comptroller by said Board. The respective County Boards of Commissioners of Elections shall promptly, after said election is held, certify to the Comptroller the expenses of holding the election in their respective counties, which certificate shall show the names of the parties entitled to payment and the respective amounts for which they are entitled to receive payment and the character of service rendered. Each said certificate shall be filed with the Comptroller and a duplicate thereof shall be filed with the County Judge or Chairman of the County Court of each County. The Comptroller shall thereupon issue his warrants to the Trustees of the several counties of the State, the County Judge or Chairman of the County Court of each county shall thereupon issue county warrants to the parties entitled to receive payment in the several counties, which warrants shall be honored by the respective County Trustees from the funds realized upon the warrants of the Comptroller issued to said Trustees, and said warrants so issued by the Comptroller to said Trustee shall be promptly paid by the Treasurer. No County Trustee shall receive any compensation for moneys so received or disbursed.

Section 15. *Be it further enacted,* That if after the passage of this Act and before the holding of any such election, the Congress shall by statute prescribe the manner in which the State Conventions to pass on the aforesaid amendment shall be constituted, and shall not except from the provisions of such statute or resolution such States as may theretofore have provided for constituting such conventions, the preceding provisions of this Act shall be inoperative, the convention shall be constituted and shall operate as the said resolution or Act of Congress shall direct, and all officers of the State who may by the said resolution or statute be authorized or directed to take any action to constitute such a convention for this State are hereby authorized and directed to act thereunder and in obedience thereto with the same force and effect as if acting under a Statute of this State.

Section 16. *Be it further enacted,* That this Act shall take effect from and after its passage, the public welfare requiring it.

Passed March 29, 1933.

Frank W. Moore
Speaker of the House of Representatives

A. F. Officer
Speaker of the Senate

Approved March 31, 1933.

Hill McAlister
Governor

TEXAS*

AN ACT to provide for conventions to pass on amendments to the Constitution of the United States which may be now or may be hereafter proposed by the Congress of the United States for ratification by conventions in the several States; setting the time of said elections; prescribing the method of nominating delegates and alternates; prescribing the manner and method in which delegates and alternates shall be elected to attend such convention; providing the form of the ballot to be used at such election; prescribing certain duties of the public officials of this State with reference to the conduct of such election; and declaring an emergency.

Be it enacted by the Legislature of the State of Texas:

Section 1. Whenever the Congress of the United States shall submit to the respective States a proposed Amendment to the Constitution of the United States and shall propose that it be ratified by conventions in the several States, an election shall be held on the fourth (4th) Saturday in August of the year in which any such amendment is submitted by the Congress of the United States, at which election thirty-one (31) delegates and thirty-one (31) alternates each, such total number of delegates and such total number of alternates to be composed of one (1) delegate and one (1) alternate from each of the several thirty-one (31) Senatorial Districts of the State, shall be elected, provided that the same is submitted to this State within the time necessary to comply with the provisions hereof, otherwise at the succeeding General Election.

Section 2. On the sixtieth (60th) day preceding the day of the election those persons, groups and organizations in favor of the ratification of the Amendment, and those persons, groups and organizations against the ratification of the Amendment shall hold separate Conventions in the City of Austin. Any qualified voter of this State shall be entitled to participate and vote in either of said Conventions, but not in both. Ten (10) days prior to the meeting of such Conventions it shall be the duty of the Governor of this State to designate a qualified voter of this State known by him personally to be in favor of the ratification of such Amendment, and it shall be the duty of the person so appointed to select and designate the place in the City of Austin at which the Convention of those persons, groups and organizations favoring the ratification of the Amendment shall convene and hold its meeting and the person so appointed shall preside as president pro tem until the permanent officers of the Convention are elected. The Governor shall likewise appoint a qualified voter of this State, known to him to oppose the ratification of the proposed Amendment, and the person so appointed shall select and designate the place in the City of Austin where the Convention of those persons, groups and organizations opposing the ratification of the proposed Amendment shall convene and hold their meeting, and the person so appointed shall preside and act as president pro tem until the permanent officers of the Convention of those persons opposing the ratification of the Amendment are elected.

Section 3. After each such Convention has been organized and its permanent officers elected the same shall proceed to nominate thirty-one (31) delegates and thirty-one (31) alternates each, such total number of delegates and such total number of alternates to

* *Texas General Laws, 43rd Legislature, Regular Session, 1933,* Chapter 139, pp. 358-364.

be composed of one (1) delegate and one (1) alternate from each of the several thirty-one (31) Senatorial Districts of the State. Candidates for the offices of delegates and alternates to the Convention to pass on the proposed amendment shall be citizens and residents of this State and duly qualified voters in the Senatorial District from which they offer their candidacy for election, and their names shall be certified by the Chairman and Secretary of the respective Conventions to the Secretary of State within five (5) days after the day of holding the respective Convention. No person shall be eligible as a delegate or alternate of the Convention of those persons opposing the ratification of the Amendment unless he shall make affidavit before some officer authorized to administer oaths that he is opposed to the ratification of the Amendment, and will so cast his vote in Convention, and no person shall be eligible as a delegate or alternate of the Convention favoring the ratification of the proposed Amendment unless he shall make affidavit in writing before some officer authorized to administer oaths that he favors the ratification of the Amendment, and will so cast his vote in Convention, and each such delegate and alternate shall file his affidavit with the Chairman of the Convention of which he is the nominee, or with the Secretary of State, which affidavit shall be filed within fifteen (15) days after the date of the filing of the list of delegates and alternates with the Secretary of State by the respective Chairmen of the Conventions. No nominee of either Convention shall be either a State, District or County office holder. The Chairman of each convention shall file the affidavit of the respective nominees of each Convention with the Secretary of State, together with the certified list of nominees for said Convention.

Section 4. Each such Convention shall be required to keep a journal of its proceedings and set forth among the minutes thereof the respective names of each delegate and alternate nominated at such Convention, together with the number of votes received by each such nominee, together with all other proceedings that may be had in said Convention. It shall be the duty of the Chairman of each such Convention, upon the adjournment thereof, to deposit each such journal with the Secretary of State where the same shall remain as a permanent public record.

Section 5. It shall be the duty of the Secretary of State to certify to the County Clerk of each county in this State the names of the persons selected as the nominees of each Convention and to show in his certificate those delegates and alternates in favor of the ratification of the Amendment and those delegates and alternates against the ratification of such Amendment.

Section 6. All laws pertaining to conducting and holding General Elections and the qualifications of voters shall apply to the holding of the election ordered by the Governor except in so far as they are inconsistent with the provisions of this Act.

Section 7. The election shall be by ballot, separate from any ballot to be used at the same election, and shall be prepared as follows: It shall first state the substance of the proposed Amendment. This shall be followed by appropriate instructions to the voter. It shall then contain perpendicular columns of equal width headed respectively, in plain type "For Ratification of the above Amendment," and "Against Ratification of the above Amendment." In the column headed "For Ratification of the above Amendment" shall be placed the names of the nominees or delegates and alternates nominated as in favor of the ratification; in the column headed "Against Ratification of the above Amendment" shall be placed the names of the nominees or delegates and alternates nominated as opposed to the ratification. The voter shall be entitled to vote for any number of candidates whose names appear on such ballot, not to exceed thirty-one (31) delegates and thirty-one (31) alternates. Such voter shall indicate his choice by drawing a line through or striking out all the names of such candidates other than the ones for whom he desires to cast his vote.

The ballot shall be substantially in the following form:

PROPOSED AMENDMENT TO THE CONSTITUTION
OF THE UNITED STATES

The Congress has proposed an amendment to the Constitution of the United States which reads as follows:

(Here insert the proposed amendment)

INSTRUCTIONS TO THE VOTER

For the ratification of the above amendment. (Insert names of delegates and then alternates in alphabetical order favoring the ratification of the amendment)	Against the ratification of the above amendment. (Insert names of delegates and then alternates in alphabetical order against the ratification of the amendment)

Section 7-a. Provided, however, that if such proposed amendment, is one which repeals another amendment to the Constitution of the United States then it shall not be necessary to state the substance of the proposed amendment; and in lieu of the words "for ratification of the above amendment," and "against ratification of the above amendment" at the top of the two perpendicular columns, there shall be inserted the words "For repeal of the ———— amendment," and the words "Against repeal of the ———— amendment," respectively; the number of such amendment which it is proposed to repeal to be inserted in the blank space above, as e.g. "For repeal of the Eighteenth (18th) Amendment," and "Against repeal of the Eighteenth (18th) Amendment." In such instances the ballot shall be substantially in the following form:

INSTRUCTIONS TO THE VOTER

For the repeal of the ——— amendment. (Inserting in the blank the number of the amendment proposed to be repealed) (Insert names of delegates and then alternates in alphabetical order favoring the repeal of the amendment)	Against the repeal of the ——— amendment. (Inserting in blank the number of the amendment proposed to be repealed) (Insert names of delegates and then alternates in alphabetical order against the repeal of the amendment)

Section 7-b. The voter shall be entitled to vote for not more than thirty-one (31) delegates (candidates) and thirty-one (31) alternates (candidates) and shall indicate his choice by drawing a line through or marking out all the names of such delegates (candidates) and alternates (candidates) other than the ones for whom he desires to cast his vote.

Section 8. Returns shall be made of the election in the same manner and by the same officers as is provided by law for the making of returns of elections for Railroad Commissioners. On the thirtieth (30th) day following the day of the election and not before, the Secretary of State, in the presence of the Governor and the Attorney General, or either of them, shall open and canvass the returns of the election.

Section 9. The thirty-one (31) delegates and the thirty-one (31) alternates receiving the highest number of votes shall be declared elected and the Governor shall issue to each of those persons a certificate of election which shall be signed by the Governor and attested by the Secretary of State.

Section 10. On the ninetieth (90th) day following the day of the election the thirty-one (31) delegates and thirty-one (31) alternates elected at the said election and commissioned by the Governor shall convene in the City of Austin at 10 o'clock A.M., and shall thereupon constitute a convention to pass upon the question of whether or not the proposed amendment to the Constitution shall be ratified.

Section 11. A majority of the delegates so elected shall constitute a quorum at such convention for the purpose of transacting business. A majority of the quorum present and voting may act for the convention. In the event any delegate to such conventions, after he has been duly elected, shall die, resign, become incapacitated or fail to attend such convention, then and in any such event the alternate of such delegate shall act in the stead of said delegate with the full and complete powers of said delegate.

Section 12. The convention shall keep a journal of its proceedings in which shall be recorded the vote of each delegate on the question of the ratification of the proposed Amendment, and upon final adjournment the journal reflecting the vote of the delegates, together with the minutes of the convention, shall be filed with the Secretary of State of the State of Texas where it shall remain on file as a public record.

Section 13. If the convention shall agree to the ratification of the proposed Amendment, a certificate to that effect shall be executed by the President and Secretary of the Convention and transmitted to the Secretary of State of this State and to the Secretary of State of the United States. The Secretary of State shall in turn transmit such certificate under the great Seal of the Sovereign State of Texas to the Secretary of State of the United States.

Section 14. The expenses necessary to conduct such election shall be paid for by the respective counties of this State in the same manner as is now provided by law with reference to any other general or special State-wide election and the duties of all public officials with reference to providing for such election shall be the same as is now prescribed by law with reference to other elections except as herein provided.

Section 15. The permanent chairman of each Convention provided for in Section 2 hereof is hereby empowered to appoint a chairman and vice-chairman for each county. The chairman in each county (or the vice-chairman in event of failure or inability of the chairman) is hereby empowered to appoint one assistant election judge and one clerk for each voting precinct for the purpose of assisting in holding the election provided for by this Act. Should a chairman or vice-chairman fail to make such appointments, then the presiding judge of each precinct is hereby empowered to appoint such assistants, in the manner now provided by statute, the appointees, however, shall be selected to equally represent both sides of the question; otherwise the said election, manner of conducting the same and the returns, thereof, shall be in all things held as is now provided by statute for the holding of general elections. None of the expenses arising or accruing because of the appointment of or the services rendered by the officials provided for in this Section shall be borne by the State or any county thereof; provided, however, any other usual, customary election expenses for officials to hold said election and for other election expenses shall be paid as is now provided by law for general elections.

Section 16. The delegates elected to such Convention shall defray their own expenses incurred in connection therewith.

Section 17. If Congress should, at any time, either by Resolution or by Statute, prescribe the method and manner in which the Convention shall be constituted, and shall not except from the provisions of such Statute or Resolution such States as may have theretofore provided for constituting such conventions, the provisions of this Act shall be inoperative in so far as the same shall operate as to conflict with such Resolution or Act of Congress.

Section 18. The fact that Congress has recently submitted to the several States for ratification or rejection, an Amendment to the Constitution of the United States, to be acted upon in convention in the respective States, and in such Resolution did not provide the manner and method in which such convention shall be constituted, and due to the further fact that there are no adequate laws at this time in this State for constituting such convention, create an emergency and an imperative public necessity that the Constitutional Rule requiring bills to be read on three several days in each House be suspended, and said Rule is hereby suspended, and this Act shall take effect and be in force from and after its passage, and it is so enacted.

[NOTE.—H. B. No. 807 passed the House March 17, 1933, by a vote of 120 yeas, 5 nays; House refused to concur in Senate amendments April 14, 1933, and Conference Committee was appointed; House adopted Conference Committee Report May 4, 1933, by a vote of 119 yeas, 9 nays; passed the Senate, with amendments, April 13, 1933, by a vote of 31 yeas, 0 nays; Senate adopted Conference Committee Report May 4, 1933, by a vote of 31 yeas, 0 nays.]

Approved May 16, 1933.

Effective May 16, 1933.

UTAH*

AN ACT to Provide for Conventions to Pass on Amendments to the Constitution of the United States Which Have or May Hereafter Be Proposed by Congress for Ratification by Conventions in the Several States.

Be it enacted by the Legislature of the State of Utah:

Section 1. Election of Delegates to Convention.

Whenever the congress of the United States proposes an amendment to the constitution of the United States, and proposes that it be ratified by conventions in the several states, the governor shall fix by proclamation the date of an election for the purpose of electing the delegates to such convention in this state. Such election may either be at a special election or may be held at the same time as a general election, but shall be held at least as soon as the next such general election occurring more than three months after the amendment has been proposed by the congress.

Section 2. Id. Qualification of Voters.

At such election all persons qualified to vote at a general election in this state shall be entitled to vote.

Section 3. Id. General Election Laws Applicable.

Except as in this act otherwise provided such election shall be conducted and the results thereof ascertained and certified in the same manner as in the case of the election of presidential electors in this state, and all provisions of the laws of this state relative to elections except so far as inconsistent with this act are hereby made applicable to such election.

Section 4. Number of Delegates.

The number of delegates to be chosen to such convention shall be twenty-one, to be elected from the state at large.

Section 5. Qualification of Delegates—Nomination.

Candidates for the office of delegate to the convention shall be citizens and residents of the state, and of the age of at least 21 years. Nominations shall be by petition and not otherwise. A single petition may nominate any number of candidates not exceeding the total number of delegates to be elected, and shall be signed and acknowledged in the manner required for certificates of nomination by section 25-4-4 Revised Statutes of Utah, 1933, by not less than 100 voters. Nomination shall be without party or political designation, but the nominating petitions shall contain a written statement signed by each nominee, to the effect either that he will vote for ratification of the proposed amendment or that he will vote against such ratification, and no nominating petition shall contain the name of any nominee whose position as stated therein is inconsistent with that of any other nominee as stated therein. No nomination shall be effective except those of the twenty-one nominees in favor of ratification, and the twenty-one nominees against ratification, whose nominating petitions have respectively been signed by the largest number of voters, ties to be decided by lot drawn by the secretary of state. All petitions shall be filed with the secretary of state not less than 40 days before the proclaimed date of the election and within 10 days after the last day for

* *Utah Laws, 1933,* Chapter 22, pp. 36-38.

filing such petitions the secretary of state shall canvass said petitions and certify the nominated candidates of each group to the county clerk of each county within the state.

Section 6. Ballot—Form of—Manner of Marking and Voting—Watchers.

The election shall be by ballot, separate from any ballot to be used at the same election, which shall be prepared as follows: It shall first state the substance of the proposed amendment. This shall be followed by appropriate instructions to the voter. It shall then contain perpendicular columns of equal width, headed respectively in plain type "For Ratification of Proposed Change in Constitution of the United States," "Against Ratification of proposed change in Constitution of the United States" and a third column without heading or names. In the column headed "For Ratification of proposed change in constitution of the United States," shall be placed the names of the nominees nominated as in favor of ratification. In the column headed "Against Ratification of proposed change in Constitution of the United States" shall be placed the names of the nominees nominated as against ratification. In the column without heading shall be printed spaces permitting the writing in of other names desired by the voter. The voter shall indicate his choice by making one or more cross-marks in the appropriate spaces provided on the ballot. No ballot shall be held void because any such cross-mark is irregular in character. The ballot shall be so arranged that the voter may, by making a single cross-mark, vote for the entire group of nominees whose names are comprised in any column. The ballot shall be in substantially the following form:

OFFICIAL BALLOT

for delegates to convention to ratify or reject proposed amendment to the constitution of the United States.

The congress has proposed an amendment to the constitution of the United States which provides, (insert here the substance of the proposed amendment).

The congress has also proposed that the said amendment shall be ratified by conventions in the states.

INSTRUCTIONS TO VOTERS

Do not vote for more than 21.

To vote for all candidates in favor of ratification, or for all candidates against ratification, make a cross-mark in the CIRCLE at the head of the list of candidates for whom you wish to vote. If you do this, make no other mark.

To vote for an individual candidate make a cross-mark in the SQUARE at the right of the name.

To vote for a person other than candidates listed on the ballot, write in name in blank column.

For ratification of proposed change in constitution of the United States.

◯

(Name of Candidate) .... ☐

Against ratification of proposed change in constitution of the United States.

◯

(Name of Candidate) .... ☐

◯

(.......................) .... ☐

If the election of delegates to such a convention be held at the same time as a general election, the ballots used for the purpose of voting for such delegates shall be of a color to distinguish them from the general ballot but the numbering on the stubs of both ballots shall be the same. In such cases there shall be handed to each voter by an election judge, at the same time that the general ballot is handed to him, one and only one ballot for use in voting for such delegates and the number on its stub shall be the same as the number on the stub of the general ballot used by such voter and when marked by the voter, both of such ballots shall be deposited in the ballot box in the manner prescribed by law. If any voter declines to use the special ballot herein provided for, such unused ballot shall thereupon be immediately marked "void" by the election judges and shall be safely kept and returned by them to the county clerk.

Upon recommendation of one or more of the candidates listed upon the official ballot under the heading "For Ratification of proposed change in Constitution of the United States" the county commissioners shall designate a person so recommended to act as watcher to represent such group at each polling place within the county. Upon like recommendation of one or more candidates listed on the official ballot as being "against ratification of proposed change in Constitution of the United States" the county commissioners shall designate a person so recommended to act as watcher to represent such group of candidates at each polling place.

Section 7. Highest Number of Votes Elects—Vacancies, How Filled.

The twenty-one nominees who shall receive the highest number of votes shall be the delegates to the convention. If there shall be a vacancy in the convention caused by the death or disability of any delegate or any other cause, the same shall be filled by appointment by the majority vote of the delegates comprising the group from which such delegate was elected and if the convention contains no other delegate of that group, shall be filled by the governor.

Section 8. Convention, Time and Place of Holding.

The delegates to the convention shall meet at the capitol on the twenty-eighth day after their election at 12 o'clock noon, and shall thereupon constitute a convention to pass upon the question of whether or not the proposed amendment shall be ratified.

Section 9. Id. Organization.

The convention shall have power to elect its president, secretary and other officers, and adopt its own rules.

Section 10. Id. To Keep a Journal.

The convention shall keep a journal of its proceedings in which shall be recorded the vote of each delegate on the question of ratification of the proposed amendment. Upon final adjournment the journal shall be filed with the secretary of state.

Section 11. Certificate of Ratification.

If the convention shall agree, by vote of a majority of the total number of delegates, to the ratification of the proposed amendment, a certificate to that effect shall be executed by the president and secretary of the convention and transmitted to the secretary of this state, who shall transmit the certificate under the great seal of the state to the secretary of state of the United States.

Section 12. Compensation of Delegates—Expenses of Convention, How Paid.

Delegates to the convention shall receive a per diem of $4 per day while the convention is in session and mileage at the rate of ten cents per mile for the distance necessarily traveled in going to and returning from the place of meeting by the most usual route and they shall receive no other pay or perquisite. Such per diem and mileage, together with the necessary expenses of such convention for printing and stenographic services shall be paid out of the state treasury.

Section 13. Acts of Congress Prescribing Manners of Constituting Conventions Accepted.

If at or about the time of submitting any such amendment, congress shall either in the resolution submitting the same or by statute, prescribe the manner in which the conventions shall be constituted, and shall not except from the provisions of such statute or resolution such states as may theretofore have provided for constituting such conventions, the preceding provisions of this act shall be inoperative, the convention shall be constituted and shall operate as the said resolution or act of congress shall direct, and all officers of the state who may by the said resolution or statute be authorized or directed to take any action to constitute such a convention in this state are hereby authorized and directed to act thereunder and in obedience thereto with the same force and effect as if acting under a statute of this state.

Section 14.

This act shall take effect upon approval.

Approved March 21, 1933.

VERMONT*

CONVENTIONS TO AMEND UNITED STATES CONSTITUTION

Section 294. *Governor to call.* Whenever the Congress of the United States shall submit to the several states an amendment to the constitution of the United States, and pursuant to Article V of such constitution shall provide that such amendment be acted upon by conventions in the several states: the governor shall, within sixty days after such amendment has been officially transmitted from the United States to this state, issue a call for the election of delegates to a convention to act upon such amendment; and shall set the date for the election of delegates; and the date and hour for the holding of such convention.

Section 295. *Convention; how constituted; date; place of meeting.* The convention shall be composed of fourteen delegates elected at large by the qualified voters of Vermont. It shall meet in the senate chamber of the capitol at Montpelier. The date for the holding of such convention shall be not less than twenty nor more than thirty days after the election of delegates.

Section 296. *Delegates; date of election.* The election of delegates shall take place not less than three nor more than twelve months after the call; but in no case shall it occur within forty days of the date fixed by law for a general or primary election.

Section 297. *Delegates; number; qualification.* Not less than thirty days before the date of the election of delegates, the governor, the lieutenant governor, and the speaker of the house of representatives, or in case of incapacity of any one of them, the secretary of state in his stead, shall appoint and forthwith announce the names of twenty-eight candidates for delegates, such candidates being in their opinion representative citizens of Vermont. Fourteen of these candidates shall be persons who assent to the placing of their names on the ballot as "For Ratification;" and fourteen shall be persons who assent to the placing of their names on the ballot as "Against Ratification." One candidate for ratification, and one candidate against ratification shall be appointed from each county in the state.

Section 298. *Delegates; acceptance of office.* On accepting such designation, each candidate shall file his acceptance as follows:

"I do hereby accept this appointment as candidate for delegate to the convention to be held on the........day of................; and assent to the placing of my name on the ballot as For Ratification or Against Ratification.

Signed..............................."

Section 299. *Form of ballot.* The form of the ballot to be used shall be as follows:

DELEGATES TO CONVENTION TO VOTE UPON THE FOLLOWING PROPOSED AMENDMENT

TO THE CONSTITUTION OF THE UNITED STATES:

(Here shall follow the text of the proposed amendment.)

---

* *Vermont Public Laws, 1933,* Chapter 18, pp. 118-120.

Instructions

To vote for all the delegates who stand For Ratification, make an (X) in the square at the head of the column marked NAMES FOR RATIFICATION. To vote for all the delegates who stand Against Ratification, make a cross (X) in the square at the head of the column marked NAMES AGAINST RATIFICATION. If you do not wish to vote for every candidate in one column, make a cross (X) opposite the names of the candidates of your choice, not to exceed fourteen in all. If you do not wish to vote for the candidates named in the column "For Ratification" or the candidates named in the column "Against Ratification" you may write in the names of other delegates not to exceed fourteen in number in the spaces provided below. Ballots on which more than fourteen names are marked will be considered defective.

NAMES FOR RATIFICATION	NAMES AGAINST RATIFICATION	The space below is provided for voters who wish to vote for delegates other than those whose names appear in the two adjoining columns
☐	☐	

Section 300. *Secretary of state; endorsement of ballot.* Upon each ballot shall be endorsed the words "official ballot," followed by the name of the town in which it is to be used, the date of the election, and a facsimile of the signature of the secretary of state with his official title.

Section 301. *Check list used.* The check list used in the last preceding general election shall apply, but may be revised as now provided by law for check lists used at general elections. The polls for this election shall open at 10 A.M. and close at 8 P.M.

Section 302. *Canvassing board.* The lieutenant governor, the speaker of the house of representatives, and the secretary of state shall canvass the ballots, declaring elected the fourteen candidates who have received the greatest number of votes; and the secretary of state shall publish the results. The secretary of state, upon the completion of the canvass, shall mail or deliver in person to each delegate so elected a notice thereof and such delegates so elected shall be members of the convention.

Section 303. *Expense of election; election laws to govern.* Expenses of such election shall be paid by the state or town, as in the case of general elections. The statutory provisions as to holding general elections, furnishing ballots, instructions and forms, appointment and payment of election officers, filling of vacancies, solicitation of voters at the polls, challenging of voters, manner of conducting elections, counting and preserving the ballots and making returns thereof, and all other kindred subjects shall apply to such elections in so far as they are consistent with this chapter, it being the intent of this chapter to place such elections under the regulation and protection of the laws relating to general elections.

Section 304. *Construction of chapter.* The provisions of this chapter shall be liberally construed, so that the real will of the voters shall not be defeated, and so that the voters shall not be deprived of their right because of informality or failure to comply with provisions of law as to notice or conduct of the election, or of certifying the results thereof.

Section 305. *Vacancies, how filled.* In case of vacancies caused by death, disability, or resignation, the governor shall fill the vacancies by appointment.

Section 306. *Quorum; secretary.* A majority of the delegates shall constitute a quorum to do business, when convened according to the provisions of this chapter. The secretary of state shall be ex officio secretary of the convention, and he, with the chairman of the convention, shall certify the vote of the convention to the secretary of state of the United States.

Section 307. *Compensation.* The compensation of each delegate shall be ten dollars and actual expenses.

Section 308. *Manner.* Provided however, that if, at, about, or prior to the time of submitting any such amendment, Congress shall, in the resolution submitting the same, or by statute, prescribe the manner in which the conventions shall be constituted, the preceding provisions of this chapter shall be inoperative; the conventions shall be constituted and shall operate as the resolution or act of Congress shall direct, and all officers of the state who may by the resolution or statute be authorized or directed to take any action to constitute such a convention for this state are hereby authorized and directed to act thereunder and in obedience thereto, with the same force and effect as if acting under a statute of this state.

VIRGINIA*

AN ACT to provide for a convention to ratify or reject an amendment to the Constitution of the United States, proposed by the Congress of the United States, for repeal of the eighteenth article of amendment to the said Constitution, and for the prohibition of the transportation or importation into any state, territory or possession of the United States for delivery or use therein of intoxicating liquors in violation of the laws thereof; to provide for the nomination and election of delegates to such convention; and to make an appropriation therefor.

Approved August 28, 1933

WHEREAS, The Congress of the United States has proposed an amendment to the Constitution of the United States in the following language:

"JOINT RESOLUTION

"Proposing an amendment to the Constitution of the United States.

"Resolved by the Senate and House of Representatives of the United States of America in Congress assembled (two-thirds of each House concurring therein), That the following article is hereby proposed as an amendment to the Constitution of the United States, which shall be valid to all intents and purposes as part of the Constitution when ratified by conventions in three-fourths of the several states;

ARTICLE ___ ___

"Section 1. The eighteenth article of amendment to the Constitution of the United States is hereby repealed.

"Section 2. The transportation or importation into any state, territory, or possession of the United States for delivery or use therein of intoxicating liquors, in violation of the laws thereof, is hereby prohibited.

"Section 3. This article shall be inoperative unless it shall have been ratified as an amendment to the Constitution by conventions in the several states, as provided in the Constitution, within seven years from the date of the submission hereof to the states by the Congress"; now, therefore,

1. Be it enacted by the General Assembly of Virginia, as follows:

Section 1. A special election for the purpose of electing delegates to a convention in this State, for the purpose of ratifying or rejecting the proposed amendment to the Constitution of the United States, recited in the preamble of this act, is hereby called, to be held in all of the counties and cities of the State on Tuesday, the third day of October, nineteen hundred and thirty-three.

The said election shall be held and conducted by the regular election officers, except that the services of the regular clerks of election shall be dispensed with and one of the judges of election at each voting precinct shall perform the duties of clerk. The judges and commissioners of election shall receive as compensation for their services the sum of three dollars each for each day's service rendered and such mileage as is now provided by general law.

---

* *Virginia Acts, Extra Session, 1933,* Chapter 2, pp. 3-8.

Section 2. The persons entitled to vote in the said election shall be electors qualified to vote for members of the General Assembly at the regular election to be held on the Tuesday after the first Monday in November, nineteen hundred and thirty-three.

Section 3. Except as in this act otherwise provided, the said election shall be conducted, and the results thereof canvassed and certified in the same manner as in the case of the election in this State of electors for President and Vice-President of the United States, and all provisions of the laws of this State relevant to the election of electors for President and Vice-President of the United States, except in so far as inconsistent with this act, are hereby made applicable to the election of delegates to the convention provided for herein.

Section 4. The number of delegates to be chosen to such convention shall be thirty, all of whom shall be elected from the State at large.

Section 5. Each candidate for the office of delegate to the said convention shall be qualified to vote in the election herein provided for.

Each person desiring to be nominated as a candidate for the office of delegate to the said convention shall, on or before the second day of September nineteen hundred and thirty-three, make, sign and file with the Secretary of the Commonwealth a written declaration of candidacy for such nomination, which shall be in substantially the following form:

"I, ..., of the county (or the city) of ...., declare myself to be a candidate for nomination as candidate for the office of delegate to the convention called by the General Assembly to ratify or reject an amendment to the Constitution of the United States, proposed by the Congress of the United States for the repeal of the Eighteenth Amendment to the said Constitution, and for the prohibition of the transportation or importation into any state territory or possession of the United States for delivery or use therein of intoxicating liquors in violation of the laws thereof.

"Given under my hand this ...... day of ...., 1933.

"(Signed) ...."

The said declaration shall also contain a statement as to whether the person signing the same favors the ratification or opposes the ratification of the said amendment.

The said declaration shall be acknowledged before some officer who has the authority to take acknowledgments to deeds, or attested by two persons who can write, signing as witnesses.

As soon as may be after the second day of September, nineteen hundred and thirty-three, and on or before the ninth day of the said month, the Governor, the Lieutenant Governor, the Speaker of the House of Delegates and two persons (one of whom shall be a member of that political party which at the last presidential election in this State cast the highest number of votes, and the other of whom shall be a member of that political party which at the same election cast the next highest number of votes) selected by the Governor, shall, on the call of the Governor, meet in the capitol at Richmond for the purpose of nominating candidates to be voted for in the election provided for herein. Any three of the persons named shall, for such purposes, constitute a quorum. They may adopt rules for their procedure and may adjourn from time to time. To them the Secretary of the Commonwealth shall certify the names and addresses of all persons who shall have filed declarations of candidacy for nomination with him in accordance with the provisions of this act, listing separately those favoring the ratification and those opposing the ratification of the proposed amendment herein referred to. From the names so certified the Governor, the Lieutenant Governor, the Speaker of the House of Delegates and the two persons selected by the Governor, or any three or more of them as shall be present, shall, by a majority vote, nominate from those favoring the ratification of the said amendment a group of thirty candidates, and from those opposing the ratification of the said amendment a group of thirty candidates. The names of the thirty candidates so nominated favoring the ratification of the said amendment and of the thirty candidates so nominated opposing the ratification of the said amendment shall be certified by the Governor to the Secretary of the Commonwealth, who shall immediately thereafter certify their names to the electoral boards of the counties and of the cities of the State, listing the names of the candidates in their respective groups. The said boards shall immediately thereafter cause to be printed and distributed the necessary ballots for the said election.

Section 6. The election shall be by ballot separate from any ballot to be used at the same election.

The names of the candidates nominated in accordance with the provisions of the preceding section shall appear on the ballots in groups as nominated, the group favoring the ratification of the proposed amendment under the designation "For Ratification (For Repeal)," and the group opposing the ratification of the proposed amendment under the designation "Against Ratification (Against Repeal)," the two groups being placed on the ballot in the order herein named. Directly preceding the aforesaid designations and names of candidates shall appear the following general heading: "Election of delegates to a Constitutional Convention called to ratify or reject the following amendment to the Constitution of the United States, proposed by Joint Resolution of Congress"; then shall follow the text of the proposed amendment and the words "(Vote for thirty delegates)." No name shall be printed on the ballots except the names of the candidates selected as provided in section five of this act, but three blank spaces shall be left following the names in each group in which the voter may insert the name of any person qualified to vote in the said election and not printed on the ballot for whom he desires to vote.

Each elector may vote for thirty candidates. In order to vote, each elector shall draw a line through the name of each candidate for whom he does not wish to vote, leaving the names of the candidates for whom he wishes to vote unscratched; or he may vote for the thirty candidates who favor ratification by drawing a line through the words "Against Ratification" and leaving the words "For Ratification" unscratched, or for the thirty candidates who oppose ratification by drawing a line through the words "For Ratification" and leaving the words "Against Ratification" unscratched, in which event the ballot shall be counted as if each of the names in the group under the words through which the line is drawn, had been drawn through or scratched. If any line is drawn two-thirds of the way through the words "For Ratification," or "Against Ratification," or the name of any candidate, such words or such name or names shall be counted as having been drawn through or scratched.

Section 7. The thirty candidates receiving the highest number of votes at said election shall be the delegates to the said convention.

For the purpose of canvassing the results of the said election, the Board of State

Canvassers shall meet at the office of the Secretary of the Commonwealth on Tuesday, the tenth day of October, next after the said election, when they shall, upon the certified abstracts on file in the office of the Secretary of the Commonwealth, proceed to examine and make a statement of the whole number of votes given at such election for delegates to the said convention. If said abstracts, or any of them, shall not be received at the time of such meetings, the board may adjourn from time to time until the abstracts shall be received and their labors are completed. The statement herein provided for shall show the names of persons for whom such votes have been given and the whole number given to each, distinguishing the several cities and counties in which they were given; the Board of State Canvassers shall certify such statements to be correct and subscribe their names thereto, and they shall thereupon determine what persons have been by the greatest number of votes duly elected delegates to the said convention, and shall endorse and subscribe on such statement a certificate of such determination and deliver it to the Secretary of the Commonwealth. The Secretary of the Commonwealth shall record in a suitable book to be kept in his office for that purpose such certified statement and determination as made by the Board of State Canvassers, and shall without delay make out and transmit to each of the persons thereby declared to be elected a certificate of his election, certified by him under the seal of his office. He shall thereupon transmit to the clerk of the House of Delegates a list of the delegates elected. He shall also lay before the convention herein provided for immediately upon its meeting, a list of the delegates elected thereto.

Section 8. The delegates to the convention shall meet in the hall of the House of Delegates, in the State Capitol, in Richmond, or in such other suitable place as may be provided by the Director of the Division of Grounds and Buildings, at noon on Wednesday, the twenty-fifth day of October, nineteen hundred and thirty-three. The clerk of the House of Delegates shall act as temporary chairman in the organization of the convention, shall administer the oath of office to the delegates, and, after permanent organization of the convention shall have been perfected, shall act as secretary of the said convention, without additional compensation. The delegates, after taking the oath of office required by the Constitution, shall thereupon constitute a convention to pass upon the question of whether or not the proposed amendment shall be ratified. Twenty members shall constitute a quorum.

If because of sickness or for any other reason the clerk of the House of Delegates cannot perform the duties herein imposed upon him, the Governor shall designate some other person who shall exercise all the powers and perform all the duties vested in and imposed upon the said clerk of the House of Delegates by this act.

Section 9. The convention shall be the judge of the election and qualification of its members, and shall have power to elect its president and other officers and to adopt its own rules. If there shall be a vacancy in the convention caused by the death or disability of any delegate, or by any other cause, such vacancy shall be filled by appointment by a majority vote of the remaining delegates whose names appeared in the same group on the ballot as did that of the member whose office as delegate shall have been so vacated; if the convention contains no other delegate or delegates to fill such vacancy in the manner aforesaid such vacancy shall be filled immediately by the Governor.

Section 10. The convention shall keep a journal of its proceedings in which shall be recorded the vote of each delegate on the question of ratification of the proposed amendment. Upon final adjournment such journal shall be filed with the Secretary of the Commonwealth.

Section 11. If the convention shall agree by vote of a majority of the total number of delegates to the ratification of the proposed amendment, a certificate, in duplicate, to that effect shall be executed by the president and secretary of the convention and transmitted to the Governor, who thereupon shall transmit to the Secretary of State of the United States one of the said certificates duly authenticated under the great seal of the Commonwealth.

Section 12. The delegates to the convention shall receive no compensation; each delegate shall receive, however, mileage at the rate of five cents per mile for every mile of necessary travel to and from the place of meeting to be computed according to the nearest mail route.

For the purpose of defraying such mileage and the actual expenses of the convention, a sum not exceeding fifteen hundred dollars, or so much thereof as may be necessary, is hereby appropriated out of any monies in the treasury not otherwise appropriated, the same to be paid by the Treasurer on the warrant of the Comptroller, upon the proper voucher or vouchers required by the Comptroller, signed by the secretary of the convention.

2. An emergency existing, this act shall be in force from its passage.

WASHINGTON*

AN ACT relating to and providing for the calling and holding of a convention to act upon and ratify or reject proposed amendment or repeals of amendments or other parts of the constitution of the United States; providing for the election of delegates to such conventions; providing for defraying of the expenses of such election and convention; and making an appropriation and declaring an emergency.

Be it enacted by the Legislature of the State of Washington:

Section 1. Whenever the congress of the United States shall submit to the several states for ratification or rejection by convention a proposed amendment to the constitution of the United States, it shall be the duty of the governor within thirty days after the date of receipt of official notice of such congressional action to issue a proclamation fixing a time for holding the convention to vote upon and ratify or reject such proposed amendment and fix a time for holding an election to elect delegates to such convention. The convention shall be held in the chambers of the house of representatives in the state capitol or in some other suitable place in the state capitol selected by the governor. The date for holding the convention shall not be less than five nor more than eight months from the date of the first publication of the proclamation as hereinafter provided and the convention shall be held not less than one month nor more than six weeks from the date of the election. The proclamation shall be published once each week for two successive weeks in one newspaper published and of general circulation in each of the congressional districts of the state. The first publication of the proclamation shall be within thirty days of the receipt of official notice by the state of the submission to it of the amendment.

Section 2. Each state representative district shall be entitled to as many delegates in the convention as it has members in the house of representatives of the state legislature. No person shall be qualified to act as a delegate in said convention who does not possess the same qualifications required of representatives in the state legislature from the same district.

Section 3. Anyone desiring to file as a candidate for election as a delegate to said convention shall, not less than thirty nor more than sixty days prior to the date fixed for holding the election, file his declaration of candidacy with the secretary of state. Filings shall be made on a form to be prescribed by the secretary of state and shall include a sworn statement of the candidate that he is either for or against, as the case may be, the amendment which will be submitted to a vote of the convention and that he will, if elected as a delegate, vote in accordance with his declaration. The form shall be so worded that the candidate must give a plain unequivocal statement of his views as either for or against the proposal upon which he will, if elected, be called upon to vote. No candidate shall in any such filing make any statement or declaration as to his party politics or political faith or beliefs. The fee for filing as a candidate shall be ten dollars ($10.00) and shall be transmitted to the secretary of state with the filing papers and be by the secretary of state transmitted to the state treasurer for the use of the general fund.

---

* *Washington Laws, 1933*, Chapter 181, pp. 697-702.

Section 4. The election herein provided for shall as far as practicable be called, held and conducted except as herein otherwise provided, in the same manner as a general election under the election laws of this state. The ballots shall follow the form prescribed by general law except as herein otherwise provided. The ballot shall be headed "Delegate to Convention for Ratification or Rejection of Proposed Amendment to the United States Constitution, Relating .... (stating briefly the substance of amendment proposed for adoption or rejection)." The names of all candidates who have filed for a district shall be printed on the ballots for that district in two separate groups. In one group under the heading, "For the Amendment" shall be printed in alphabetical order of their surnames, the names of all candidates, who in their filed declaration of candidacy have declared themselves to be in favor of the amendment; and in the other group under the heading, "Against the Amendment" shall be printed in alphabetical order of their surnames, the names of all candidates, who in their filed declaration of candidacy have declared themselves to be against the amendment. The wording of the headings for the two groups may be varied from that prescribed above if the nature of the proposal submitted by congress requires a different heading in order to clearly and briefly express the attitude of the candidates as disclosed in their declarations of candidacy. One of said groups shall occupy the left, and the other the right, column on said ballot. At the top of the ballot preceding the list of names shall be the statement, "Vote For" then the word, "two" of [or] a spelled number designating the number of delegates to which the district is entitled, and "To vote for a person, make a cross (X) in the square at the right of the name of each person for whom you desire to vote."

Section 5. Every person possessing the qualifications entitling him to vote at an election for state representatives, if held on the same date as an election herein provided for, shall be entitled to vote at said election.

Section 6. The election officials shall count and determine the number of votes cast for each individual; and shall also count and determine the aggregate number of votes cast for all candidates whose names appear under each of the respective headings. Where more than the required number have been voted for, the ballot shall be rejected. The figures determined by the various counts shall be entered in the poll books of the respective precincts. The vote shall be canvassed in each county by the county canvassing board and certificate of results shall within twelve days after the election be transmitted to the secretary of state. Upon receiving such certificate, the secretary of state shall have power to require returns or poll books from any county precinct to be forwarded for his examination.

Where a district embraces precincts of more than one county, the secretary of state shall combine the votes from all the precincts included in each district. The delegates elected in each district shall be the number of candidates, corresponding to the number of state representatives from the district, who receive the highest number of votes in the group (either "For" or "Against"), which received an aggregate number of votes for all candidates in the group greater than the aggregate number of votes for all the candidates in the other group, and the secretary of state shall issue certificates of election to the delegates so elected.

Section 7. The convention shall meet at the time and place fixed in the governor's proclamation. It shall be called to order by the secretary of state, who shall then call the roll of the delegates and preside over the convention until its president is elected.

The oath of office shall then be administered to the delegates by the chief justice of the supreme court. As far as practicable, the convention shall proceed under the rules adopted by the last preceding session of the state senate. The convention shall elect a president and a secretary and shall thereafter and thereupon proceed to vote viva voce upon the proposition submitted by the congress of the United States. The vote of each member shall be recorded in the journal of the convention, which journal shall be preserved by the secretary of state as a public document.

Section 8. Two-thirds of the elected members of said convention shall constitute a quorum to do business, and a majority of those elected shall be sufficient to adopt or reject any proposition coming before the convention. If such majority vote in favor of the ratification of the amendment submitted to the convention, the said amendment shall be deemed ratified by the State of Washington; and if a majority shall vote in favor of rejecting or not ratifying the amendment, the same shall be deemed rejected by the State of Washington. The action of said convention shall be enrolled, signed by its president and secretary and filed with the secretary of state, and it shall be the duty of the secretary of state to properly certify the action of the convention to the congress of the United States as provided by general law.

Section 9. If a general state election is to be held within not more than six months nor less than three months of the date when the state is officially notified of the submission to it of the proposed amendment to the United States constitution, the election herein provided for shall be held on the date and as a part of general election and the proclamation of the governor herein provided for shall fix as the date of the election herein provided for the date fixed by the law for holding of such general election.

Section 10. The delegates attending the convention shall be paid the amount of their filing fee, upon vouchers approved by the president and secretary of the convention and state warrants issued thereon and payable from the general fund of the state treasurer. The delegates shall receive no other compensation or mileage. All other necessary expenses of the convention shall be payable from the general fund of the state upon vouchers approved by the president and secretary of the convention.

Section 11. If a congressional measure, which submits to the several states an amendment to the constitution of the United States for ratification or rejection, provides for or requires a different method of calling and holding conventions to ratify or reject said amendment, the requirements of said congressional measure shall be followed so far as they conflict with the provisions of this act.

Section 12. There is hereby appropriated from the general fund the sum of three thousand dollars ($3,000.00) or so much thereof as may be necessary for the purpose of paying the expenses of the conventions provided for in this act.

Section 13. This act is necessary for the immediate preservation of the public peace, health and safety and shall take effect immediately.

Passed the Senate February 27, 1933.
Passed the House March 6, 1933.

Approved by the Governor March 20, 1933.

WEST VIRGINIA*

AN ACT to provide for a convention to pass on the amendment to the constitution of the United States providing for the repeal of the Eighteenth article of Amendment to the constitution and the prohibition of the transportation or importation into any state, territory or possession of the United States for delivery or use therein of intoxicating liquors in violation of the laws thereof proposed by the congress for ratification by conventions in the several states.

[Passed March 10, 1933; in effect from passage. Became a law without the approval of the Governor.]

Be it enacted by the Legislature of West Virginia:

Section 1. The congress of the United States having proposed an amendment to the constitution of the United States providing for the repeal of the eighteenth article of amendment to the constitution and the prohibition of the transportation or importation into any state, territory or possession of the United States for delivery or use therein of intoxicating liquors in violation of the laws thereof to be ratified by conventions in the several states, a special election for the purpose of electing delegates to such convention in this state is hereby called and shall be held on Tuesday the twenty-seventh day of June, one thousand nine hundred thirty-three.

Section 2. At such election all persons qualified to vote for members of the legislature shall be entitled to vote.

Section 3. Except as in this act otherwise provided such election shall be conducted and the results thereof ascertained and certified in the same manner as in the case of the election of presidential electors in this state, and all provisions of the laws of this state relative to elections except so far as inconsistent with this act are hereby made applicable to such election. The county court of each county shall appoint for each precinct in such county three commissioners of election, and no more and

* *West Virginia Acts, 1933,* Chapter 22, pp. 78-84.

no poll clerks, for the special election hereby called, and at least one commissioner shall be known to the court to be for ratification and one shall be so known to be against ratification. The commissioners shall designate two of their number, one known to be for ratification and one known to be against ratification, as poll clerks, who shall perform all duties of poll clerks as well as commissioners at such election. Each commissioner of election shall receive one dollar for each day actually employed instead of the compensation provided by statute, which compensation shall be allowed and paid by the county court upon application within ten days after the day of election by the person entitled thereto, attested by the commissioners of election, and not otherwise. The registrars for the performance of their duties under section ten of article two of chapter three of the code in connection with such special election shall receive one dollar per day instead of the compensation provided by statute, and the clerk of each county court shall furnish to the election commissioners of the respective voting precincts one of the registration books filed with him instead of a certified list of voters.

Section 4. The number of delegates to be chosen to such convention shall be twenty, who shall be citizens and residents of the state, and shall be elected by the vote of the state at large.

Section 5. Nominations of candidates for the office of delegate to the convention shall be made as follows:

The Democratic state executive committee and the Republican state executive committee shall each nominate ten persons who shall have signed a written pledge in triplicate to vote in such convention for ratification of the amendment and filed one counterpart thereof with the secretary of state of West Virginia and two with the secretary of such committee, and ten persons who shall have signed a written pledge in triplicate to vote in such convention against ratification of the amendment, and filed one counterpart thereof with the secretary of state of West Virginia and two with the secretary of such committee. In each group of ten each congressional district of the state shall be represented by at least one and not more than two residents thereof. No person shall be nominated by either committee who shall not have filed counterparts of a written pledge as aforesaid on or before the fifteenth day of April, one thousand nine hundred thirty-three, and nominations shall be made by said committees, respectively, and a certificate thereof, showing under separate and distinguishing headings the list of the ten nominees pledged to vote for ratification and the ten nominees pledged to vote against ratification, forwarded to the secretary of state of West Virginia, with one counterpart of the pledge of each person so nominated, on or before the first day of May, one thousand nine hundred thirty-three. The twenty persons so nominated, ten by each of said committees, pledged to vote for ratification, shall be the candidates favoring ratification of the amendment, and the twenty persons so nominated, ten by each of said committees, pledged to vote against ratification of the amendment, shall be the candidates opposing ratification. If a vacancy shall occur in any nomination so made, from death, withdrawal or other cause, the vacancy shall be filled and the name of the candidate certified by the state executive committee which made the original nomination, or the chairman thereof, as the case may be, according to the provisions of chapter three, article four, section twenty-three of the West Virginia code of one thousand nine hundred thirty-one, and the nominee to fill such vacancy shall be chosen from among persons who shall have filed with such committee a pledge similar to the pledge filed by the original nominee.

If either committee shall fail to make and file nominations as hereinbefore provided on or before the first day of May, one thousand nine hundred thirty-three, the secretary of state shall on or before the tenth day of May, one thousand nine hundred thirty-three, make up the lists, which such committee should have made, of ten nominees pledged to vote for ratification and ten pledged to vote against ratification, according to the counterpart pledges filed with the secretary of such committee and the secretary of state, drawing names by lot in any case where there shall be more than one person eligible for either list resident in any congressional district, and if when a nomination for either list shall have been made from each congressional district there shall remain more than four persons eligible for such list. And the lists so made up by the secretary of state shall be held and serve the same purposes as if made up by such committee failing to do its duty hereunder. If a vacancy shall occur in any nomination so made by the secretary of state, he shall fill the vacancy, drawing the name by lot if there remain more than one person eligible for the list in which the vacancy shall have occurred who shall have filed counterparts of a written pledge as aforesaid.

Unpledged candidates for the office of delegate to the convention may be nominated by petition and not otherwise. A single petition may nominate any number of nominees, not exceeding the total number of delegates to be elected, shall be signed by not less than two hundred voters, shall show the residence of each signer thereof and shall have attached the promise in writing of each nominee therein named that he will remain unpledged. The twenty nominees, whose nominating petitions have respectively been signed by the largest number of voters, ties to be decided by lot drawn by the secretary of state, shall be the unpledged candidates. If a vacancy shall occur in any nomination so made it shall be filled by the designation by the secretary of state of the remaining nominee whose nominating petitions filed with the secretary of state as aforesaid shall have been signed by the largest number of voters, a tie to be decided by lot drawn as aforesaid.

Section 6. The election shall be by ballot which shall first state the substance of the proposed amendment, followed by appropriate instructions to the voter and containing perpendicular columns of equal width, headed respectively in plain type. "For Ratification," "Against Ratification" and "Unpledged." In the column headed "For Ratification" shall be placed the names of the candidates nominated as in favor of ratification. In the column headed "Against Ratification" shall be placed the names of the candidates nominated as against ratification. In the column headed "Unpledged" shall be placed the names of the candidates nominated as unpledged. The voter shall indicate his choice by making one or more cross-marks in the appropriate spaces provided on the ballot. No ballot shall be held void because any such cross-mark is irregular in character. The ballot shall be so arranged that the voter may, by making a single cross-mark, vote for the entire group of nominees whose names are comprised in any column, and shall be in substantially the following form:

PROPOSED AMENDMENT TO THE CONSTITUTION

OF THE UNITED STATES

Delegates to the Convention to Ratify the Proposed Amendment.

The congress has proposed an amendment to the constitution of the United States which provides:

"Section 1. The eighteenth article of amendment to the constitution of the United States is hereby repealed."

"Section 2. The transportation or importation into any state, territory, or possession of the United States for delivery or use therein of intoxicating liquors, in violation of the laws thereof, is hereby prohibited."

The congress has also proposed that the said amendment shall be ratified by convention in the states.

INSTRUCTIONS TO VOTERS

Do not vote for more than twenty (20) candidates.

To vote for all candidates in favor of Ratification or for all candidates against Ratification, or for all candidates Unpledged, make a cross-mark in the CIRCLE at the head of the list of candidates for whom you wish to vote. If you do this, make no other mark.

To vote for an individual candidate make a cross-mark in the SQUARE at the left of the name.

For Ratification	Against Ratification	Unpledged
○	○	○
☐ John Doe	☐ Charles Coe	☐ Peter Roe
☐ Richard Poe	☐ Thomas Moe	☐ James Defoe

Section 7. The twenty nominees who shall receive the highest number of votes shall be the delegates to the convention. If there shall be a vacancy in the convention caused by the death or disability of any delegate or any other cause, the same shall be filled by appointment by the majority vote of the delegates comprising the group in which such delegate was included and if the membership of the convention contains no other delegate of that group, shall be filled by the governor. If any nominee shall die before such special election without a nomination having been made to fill the vacancy thus created as hereinbefore provided, and if the remaining members of the group of candidates in which such decedent was included shall be elected, such death shall create a vacancy in the convention within the meaning of this act and no other candidate shall be held as elected at such election in the place of such decedent.

Section 8. The delegates to the convention shall meet at the Capitol on the twenty-eighth day after their election at twelve o'clock noon, and shall thereupon constitute a convention to pass upon the question of whether or not the proposed amendment shall be ratified. It shall be called to order by the oldest delegate present.

Section 9. The convention shall be the judge of the election and qualification of its members; and shall have power to elect its president, secretary and other officers, and to adopt its own rules.

Section 10. The convention shall keep a journal of its proceedings, in which shall be recorded the vote of each delegate on the question of ratification of the proposed amendment. Upon final adjournment the journal, having been duly verified by the president and secretary of the convention, shall be filed with the secretary of state.

Section 11. If the convention shall agree, by vote of a majority of the total number of delegates, to the ratification of the proposed amendment, a certificate to that effect shall be executed by the president and secretary of the convention and transmitted to the secretary of state of the state of West Virginia, who shall transmit the certificate under the great seal of the state to the secretary of state of the United States.

Section 12. Each delegate to the convention shall receive ten dollars for his compensation and in addition mileage at the same rate as members of the legislature receive. And for the expenses of the convention the sum of one thousand dollars, or so much thereof as is necessary, shall be appropriated payable out of the state treasury from moneys not otherwise appropriated.

Section 13. If congress shall take action effective before the date of such convention prescribing the manner in which conventions to vote upon the ratification of said amendment shall be constituted, and shall not except from the provisions of such statute or resolution such states as may theretofore have provided for constituting such conventions, this act shall be inoperative, and no expense, or no further expense, as the case may be, shall be incurred pursuant hereto, but such expense, if any, as shall have been lawfully incurred pursuant hereto shall be paid according to law.

WISCONSIN*

AN ACT to provide for a convention to act upon the amendment to the Constitution of the United States, providing for the repeal of the Eighteenth Amendment.

The people of the state of Wisconsin, represented in senate and assembly, do enact as follows:

Section 1. A convention, the delegates to which shall be elected in the manner as herein provided, shall be held in the hearing room at the capitol in the city of Madison, Dane county, Wisconsin, on Tuesday, April 25, 1933, at the hour of ten o'clock A.M., to consider and act upon the ratification of the following amendment to the Constitution of the United States, proposed by the Congress of the United States to the several states:

"Section 1. The Eighteenth Article of Amendment to the Constitution of the United States is hereby repealed.

"Section 2. The transportation or importation into any State, Territory, or possession of the United States for delivery or use therein of intoxicating liquors, in violation of the laws thereof, is hereby prohibited.

"Section 3. This article shall be inoperative unless it shall have been ratified as an amendment to the Constitution by conventions in the several States, as provided in the Constitution, within seven years from the date of the submission hereof to the States by the Congress."

Section 2. The number of delegates to be elected at such convention shall be fifteen in number, to be elected from the state at large. The election of said delegates shall be held on the first Tuesday in April, 1933. At such election, all persons qualified to vote for members of the legislature shall be entitled to vote.

Section 3. Except as otherwise provided herein, all provisions of the statutes relating to nomination papers and the preparation, printing, distribution, voting, counting, recounting, returning and canvassing of ballots for judicial election shall, as far as applicable, and not inconsistent herewith, apply to the election of such delegates. The State Board of Canvassers shall canvass the returns for delegates to the convention herein provided for, not later than April 21, 1933, and shall immediately thereafter issue certificates of election to the delegates elected.

Section 4. There shall be no primary election for the nomination of delegates to said convention. Nomination shall be by petition and not otherwise. Each petition shall be signed by not less than one thousand qualified electors of this state. Nomination shall be without party or political designation, but the nominating petition shall contain a statement as to each nominee, to the effect that he favors ratification or that he opposes ratification. All petitions shall be filed with the secretary of state not less than twenty days before such election. No nomination shall be effective except those of the fifteen nominees in favor of ratification, and the fifteen nominees against ratification, whose nominating petitions have been signed by the largest number of voters, such designation and determination to be made by the secretary of state. In the event

* *Wisconsin Laws, 1933,* Chapter 23, pp. 180-184.

of ties, the same shall be decided by lot drawn by the secretary of state. Within seven days after the last date for the filing of said petitions, the secretary of state shall certify the candidates of each group to the appropriate election authorities.

Section 5. The election shall be by ballot, separate from any ballot to be used at the same election, which shall be prepared as follows: It shall first state the substance of the proposed amendment. This shall be followed by appropriate instructions to the voter. It shall then contain perpendicular columns of equal width, headed respectively, in plain type, "For Ratification of Repeal of the Eighteenth Amendment," "Against Ratification of Repeal of the Eighteenth Amendment." The words, 'For', 'Against', and 'Repeal' in the headings to such columns shall be printed on separate lines in type at least twice as large as the other words in said headings. In the column headed "For Ratification of Repeal of the Eighteenth Amendment," shall be placed the names of the several nominees nominated as in favor of ratification. In the column headed "Against Ratification of Repeal of the Eighteenth Amendment," shall be placed the names of the nominees nominated as against ratification. The voter shall indicate his choice by making one or more cross marks in appropriate spaces provided on the ballot. No ballot shall be held void because any such cross mark is irregular in character. The ballot shall be so arranged that the voter may, by making a single cross mark, vote for the entire group of nominees whose names are comprised in any column. The ballot shall be in substantially the following form:

PROPOSED AMENDMENT TO THE CONSTITUTION OF THE UNITED STATES

Delegates to the Convention to Ratify the Proposed Amendment

The Congress has proposed an amendment to the Constitution of the United States which provides in substance that the Eighteenth Article of Amendment to the Constitution of the United States relating to the manufacture, transportation and sale of intoxicating liquors for beverage purposes shall be repealed, and prohibiting shipment of intoxicating liquors into any state or territory in violation of the laws of such state or territory.

Congress has proposed that said amendment shall be ratified by conventions in the several states.

INSTRUCTIONS TO VOTERS

Do not vote for more than fifteen candidates.

To vote for all candidates in favor of ratification of repeal of the Eighteenth Amendment, or for all candidates against ratification of repeal of the Eighteenth Amendment make a cross in the *circle* ◯ at the head of the list of candidates for whom you wish to vote. If you do this make no other mark. To vote for an individual candidate make a cross in the *square* ☐ at the left of the name of the candidate for whom you wish to vote.

FOR	AGAINST
Ratification of the Amendment to	Ratification of the Amendment to
REPEAL	REPEAL
the Eighteenth Amendment	the Eighteenth Amendment
○	○
☐ John Doe	☐ Charles Coe
☐ Richard Doe	☐ Michael Moe

Section 6. The fifteen nominees who shall receive the highest number of votes cast at said election shall be the delegates to the convention. If there shall be a vacancy in the convention caused by the death or disability of any delegate or any other cause, the same shall be filled by appointment by the majority vote of the delegates comprising the group from which such delegate was elected, and if the convention contains no other delegate of that group, shall be filled by appointment by the Governor.

Section 7. The delegates to the convention shall meet at the time and place as herein provided, and shall thereupon constitute a convention to pass upon the question of whether or not the proposed amendment shall be ratified. Delegates to said convention shall receive no compensation for their services, but shall be reimbursed their actual and necessary expenses.

Section 8. The convention shall be the judge of the election and qualification of its members; and shall have power to elect its president, secretary and other officers, and to adopt its own rules.

Section 9. The convention shall keep a journal of its proceedings, in which shall be recorded the vote of each delegate on the question of ratification of the proposed amendment. Upon final adjournment, the journal shall be filed by the secretary of the convention in the office of the secretary of state.

Section 10. If the convention shall agree by a majority of the total number of delegates to the ratification of the proposed amendment, a certificate to that effect shall be executed by the president and secretary of the convention, and transmitted to the secretary of state of this state, who shall transmit the certificate under the great seal of the state of Wisconsin to the secretary of state of the United States, in the manner in which amendments to the Constitution of the United States submitted to the legislature for ratification are certified.

Section 11. This act shall take effect upon passage and publication.

Approved March 6, 1933.

WYOMING*

AN ACT providing for the calling of state conventions; prescribing the method and manner in which such conventions shall be called and held in the State of Wyoming to consider and vote on the question of repealing, amending or altering the Constitution of the United States of America; providing for the payment of the expense thereof; prescribing the duties of the Governor, the Secretary of State, the Chairman or other member of the Board of County Commissioners and the officers of the several Counties; and appropriating money to defray the expenses incurred thereby.

Be It Enacted by the Legislature of the State of Wyoming:

State Convention—Place—Time.

Section 1. Whenever the Congress of the United States of America shall enact any law requiring any question of repealing, amending or altering the Constitution of the United States of America, or any part thereof, to be submitted to a convention of delegates chosen by the qualified electors of such state and does not prescribe the manner and method of calling, holding and conducting such convention and of canvassing the returns of the votes of the delegates thereto and determining, declaring and publishing the result of the vote of the delegates to such convention on any question voted upon, for which such convention is called, held and conducted, it shall be the duty of the Governor to make a public proclamation calling such state convention, and calling for the election of delegates to such state convention, in which proclamation he shall specify the place where and the time when said state convention shall be held, the number of delegates (who shall be qualified electors) of which said convention shall consist, and the method and manner by and in which delegates to such convention shall be elected.

Delegates.

Section 2. In each of the election precincts in each of the counties of this State there shall be held a meeting of the qualified electors of such precinct at the time fixed by said proclamation, at which meeting there shall be held a precinct election, at which election there shall be elected not less than one delegate from each of such precincts and one additional delegate for each six hundred or major portion thereof of the inhabitants of such precinct to a convention of such delegates to be held at the county seat of such county. Such precinct meetings shall be held in each of the election precincts as the same are now or as may be hereafter constituted, and shall be presided over by any qualified elector of such precinct. Upon the day fixed by such Governor for the holding of such county convention the delegates thereto shall assemble and elect one delegate for each county, and one delegate for each five thousand or major fraction thereof of the inhabitants of such county, as delegates to the state convention hereinbefore mentioned.

Certify to the Secretary of State.

Section 3. It shall be the duty of the Chairman of the Board of County Commis-

* *Wyoming Session Laws, 1933,* Chapter 93, pp. 111-113.

sioners or some other member of such Board in each County to convene such county convention and preside over the same until the delegates chosen thereto shall select a chairman of such convention. It shall be the duty of the chairman and secretary of such convention to certify to the Secretary of State and to said State convention, under oath, the names of the delegates to such State convention chosen by such county convention.

Rules.

Section 4. The rules of practice, procedure and conduct of the business of the several county conventions mentioned herein shall be those prescribed by "Roberts' Rules of Parliamentary Procedure and Order."

Written or Printed Ballot.

Section 5. The vote on the selection of delegates to either of the conventions herein mentioned shall be by written or printed ballot.

Apportionment of Representation.

Section 6. In the apportionment of representation in the several conventions herein mentioned, the last census enumeration taken and made by the U. S. Government shall be the basis upon which the right to representation in such conventions shall be determined.

Board of County Commissioners—Duties.

Section 7. For the purpose of providing the necessary facilities and conveniences for carrying on and conducting each and all of the meetings and conventions provided for by this act, the Board of County Commissioners of the several counties of this state shall be and they hereby are constituted and appointed election commissioners of their respective counties and it shall be their duty to do all things necessary and proper to facilitate the qualified electors of their respective counties in expressing their will upon any question so as aforesaid submitted to them by the Congress of the United States of America.

Costs and Expenses.

Section 8. That all costs and expenses incurred in carrying out the provisions of this act in each county shall be borne and paid by the county in which such cost and expenses accrued.

Secretary of State—Duties.

Section 9. That it shall be the duty of the Secretary of State to convene such state convention and make all necessary arrangements for the convenient holding of such state convention if and when the Governor of this state shall by proclamation call the same, and the costs and expenses incidental to the holding of such convention shall be borne and paid by the State. It shall be the duty of the officers of such state convention to certify to the Secretary of State, under oath, the result of the vote cast at such convention on such question or questions submitted thereto, and upon the result of the vote of the delegates to such state convention being certified to said Secretary of State, it shall be his duty to certify the same to the President and Secretary of State of the United States, and to the President of the Senate and the Speaker of the House of Representatives of the then existing Congress of the United States.

Appropriation.

Section 10. There is hereby appropriated out of the funds in the treasury of the State not otherwise appropriated the sum of $2,000.00, or so much thereof as may be necessary, to defray the expenses incidental to the holding of the state convention hereinbefore mentioned.

Congressional Action.

Section 11. Provided, however, that if at or about the time of the submission of any such question, Congress shall either in the resolution submitting the same or by statute, prescribe the manner in which such conventions shall be constituted, the preceding provisions of this act shall be inoperative, and the convention shall be constituted and shall operate as the said resolution or act of Congress shall direct, and all officers of the State who may by the said resolution or statute be authorized or directed to take any action to constitute such a convention for this State are hereby authorized and directed to act thereunder and in obedience thereto with the same force and effect as if acting under a statute of this State.

Section 12. All acts or parts of acts in conflict herewith are hereby repealed.

Section 13. This act shall take effect and be in force from and after its passage.

Approved February 18, 1933.

INDEX

INDEX

(References to pages before 513 have to do with state conventions; those to pages after 513, with state laws.)

www.ingramcontent.com/pod-product-compliance
Lightning Source LLC
LaVergne TN
LVHW091521200926
848483LV00002B/268

* 9 7 8 1 5 8 4 7 7 2 7 8 1 *